Index of American Periodical Verse: 1990

Rafael Catalá
and
James D. Anderson

assisted by

Sarah Park Anderson
and
Martha Park Sollberger

The Scarecrow Press, Inc.
Metuchen, N.J., & London
1992

Library of Congress Catalog Card No. 73-3060
ISBN 0-8108-2587-2
Copyright © 1992 by Rafael Catalá and James D. Anderson
Manufactured in the United States of America
Printed on acid-free paper

Contents

Dedication   v

Introduction   vii

Abbreviations   xi

Periodicals Added   xii

Periodicals Deleted   xiv

Periodicals Indexed, Arranged by Acronym   1

Alphabetical List of Journals Indexed   21

The Author Index   27

The Title Index   515

Introduction

Scope

The *Index of American Periodical Verse* indexes poems published in a broad cross-section of poetry, literary, scholarly, popular, general, and "little" magazines, journals and reviews published in the United States, Canada, and the Caribbean. The periodicals included are listed in the "Periodicals Indexed" section, together with name of editor(s), address, issues indexed in this volume, and subscription information. Selection of periodicals to index is the responsibility of the editors, based on recommendations of poets, librarians, literary scholars and publishers. Publishers participate by supplying copies of all issues to the editors. Criteria for inclusion include the quality of poems and their presentation and the status or reputation of poets. Within these very broad and subjective guidelines, the editors attempt to include a cross-section of periodicals by type of publisher and/or publication, place of publication, language, and type of poetry. Periodicals published outside of North America are included only if they have North American editors.

Compilation

Citation data are compiled using the WordStar word-processing program, version 4, on a 286 MS/DOS computer. "Shorthand" macro programs are used to repeat author headings for multiple poems by the same poet, create translator entries from author entries for translated poems, and transform complex author names into cross-reference entries. Sorting is done by "IOTA Big Sort," a fast program for sorting very large files written by Fred A. Rowley. Title entries were extracted from the original author entries and sorted, and formatted author and title entries were transferred to a Macintosh computer with laser printer for typesetting and page formatting using MacWrite and PageMaker programs.

Persons interested in the precise details of compilation, including the computer programs used for error checking, sorting and formatting, should write to the editors at P.O. Box 38, New Brunswick, NJ 08903-0038. The *Indexes* for 1982 through 1990 are available from the editors on micro-computer disks.

Names and Cross References

Because many poets have compound surnames and surnames containing various prefixes, we recognize the need for systematic provision of cross references from alternative forms of surname to the form chosen for entry in the *Index*. We have included cross references whenever the form used for entry does not fall under the last part or element of the name. In addition, many poets publish under different forms of the same name, for example, with or without a middle initial. When poets are known to use different forms of the same name, alternative forms may be indicated using the format authorized by the *Anglo-American Cataloguing Rules*, Second Edition. For example:

> WHEATLEY, Pat (Patience)

This heading indicates that this poet has poems published under two forms of name: Pat Wheatley and Patience Wheatley.

When two or more different names refer to the same poet, one name will be chosen, with "see" references to the chosen name from other names. When it is not possible to determine with assurance whether a single poet is using variant forms of name or different poets have similar names, both names will be used. In such cases, "see also" references may be added to headings to remind users to check the variant name forms which might possibly refer to the same poet.

Format and Arrangement of Entries

The basic format and style of the *Index* remain unchanged. Poets are arranged alphabetically by surname and forenames. In creating this alphabetical sequence, we have adopted principles of the filing rules issued in 1980 by the American Library Association and the Library of Congress. Names are arranged on the basis of their spelling, rather than their pronunciation, so that, for example, names beginning with "Mac" and "Mc" are no longer interfiled. Similarly, the space consistently counts as a filing element, so that similar compound and prefixed surnames are often separated by some distance, as illustrated in the following examples. Note that "De BOLT" precedes "DeBEVOISE" by a considerable number of entries.

De ANGELIS	Van BRUNT
De BOLT	Van DUYN
De GRAVELLES	Van HALTEREN
De LOACH	Van TOORN
De PALCHI	Van TROYER
De RONSARD	Van WERT
De VAUL	Van WINCKEL
DEAL	VANCE
DeBEVOISE	Vander DOES
DeFOE	VANDERBEEK
DEGUY	VanDEVENTER
Del VECCHIO	
DeLISLE	
DeMOTT	
DENNISON	
Der HOVANESSIAN	
DESY	
DeYOUNG	

Abbreviations are also arranged on the basis of spelling, rather than pronunciation, so that "ST. JOHN" is *not* filed as "SAINT JOHN", but as "S+T+space+JOHN". Punctuation, signs and symbols other than alphabetic letters and numerals are not considered; a hyphen is filed as if it were a space and apostrophes and accents are ignored for purposes of filing. In title entries, initial articles are also ignored. Numerals are arranged in numerical order preceding alphabetical letters rather than as if they were spelled out.

Under each poet's name, poems are arranged alphabetically by title or, if there is no title, by first line. Poems with only "Untitled" printed as if it were the title are entered as "Untitled" plus the first line of the poem under the name of the poet. In the title index, two entries are provided, one under "Untitled" plus the first line, and one directly under the first line. Numbered poems are handled in the same way. Under poets, initial numbers are treated as the first part of titles, and they are so entered. In the title index, they are entered both under their initial numbers and under the part following the number, if any.

Poem titles and first lines are placed within quotation marks. All significant words of titles are capitalized, but in first lines, only the first word and proper nouns are capitalized. Incomplete excerpts from larger works are followed by the note "Excerpt" or "Excerpts", or, if they are presented as complete sections, by "Selection" or "Selections". The title, first line or number of excerpts or selections may follow if given in the publication. For example:

WALCOTT, Derek
    "Midsummer" (Selections: XXXIV-XXXVI). [Agni] (18) 83, p. 5-7.

WEBB, Phyllis
    "The Vision Tree" (Selection: "I Daniel"). [PoetryCR] (5:2) Wint 83-84, p. 11.

WAINWRIGHT, Jeffrey
    "Heart's Desire" (Excerpt: "Some Propositions and Part of a Narrative"). [Agni] (18) 83, p. 37.

WATTEN, Barret
    "One Half" (Excerpts). [ParisR] (24:86) Wint 82, p. 112-113.

If an excerpt is treated as a complete "sub-work", it receives an independent entry, with reference to the larger work in a note. For example:

ANDERSON, Jack
    "Magnets" (from "The Clouds of That Country"). [PoNow] (7:2, #38) 83, p. 23.

Notes about dedications, joint authors, translators, and sources follow the title, enclosed in parentheses. A poem with more than one author is entered under each author. Likewise, a translated poem is entered under each translator, as well as its author(s). Each entry includes the names of all authors and all translators. Multiple authors or translators are indicated by the abbreviation "w.", standing for "with". Translators are indicated by the abbreviation "tr. by", standing for "translated by", and original authors are indicated by the abbreviation "tr. of", standing for "translation of". For example:

AGGESTAM, Rolf
"Old Basho" (tr. by Erland Anderson and Lars Nordström).
[NewRena] (16) Spr 83, p. 25.

ANDERSON, Erland
"Old Basho" (tr. of Rolf Aggestam, w. Lars Nordström).
[NewRena] (16) Spr 83, p. 25.

NORDSTRÖM, Lars
"Old Basho" (tr. of Rolf Aggestam, w. Erland Anderson).
[NewRena] (16) Spr 83, p. 25.

The periodical citation includes an abbreviation standing for the periodical title, followed by volume and issue numbers, date, and pages. The periodical abbreviation is enclosed in square brackets. An alphabetical list of these periodical abbreviations is included at the front of the volume, followed by the full periodical title, name of editor(s), address, the numbers of the issues indexed for this volume of the *Index*, and subscription information. A separate list of indexed periodicals is arranged by full periodical title, with a reference to the abbreviated title. Volume and issue numbers are included within parentheses, e.g., (16:5) stands for volume 16, number 5; (21) refers to issue 21 for a periodical which does not use volume numbers. Dates are given using abbreviations for months and seasons. Year of publication is indicated by the last two digits of the year, e.g., 90. Please see the separate list of abbreviations at the front of the volume.

Compiling this year's *Index* has been an adventure into the wealth and variety of poetry published in U. S., Caribbean and Canadian periodicals as well as the intricacies of bringing this richness together and organizing it into a consistent index. The world of poetry publication is a dynamic one, with new periodicals appearing, older periodicals declining, dying, reviving and thriving. This year saw the loss of 9 periodicals and the addition of 29 new ones, with a net gain of 20 periodicals. Both deleted and newly added periodicals are listed at the front of the volume. Keeping up with these changes is a big job, and we solicit our readers' suggestions as to periodicals which should be included in future volumes of the *Index*, and also, periodicals which could be dropped. Editors who would like their periodicals considered for inclusion in future volumes should send sample issues to:

Rafael Catalá, Editor
Index of American Periodical Verse
P.O. Box 38
New Brunswick, NJ 08903-0038

Although indexing is indispensable for the organization of any literature so that particular works can be found when needed and scholarship and research facilitated, it is a tedious business. I know that we have made mistakes. We solicit your corrections and suggestions, which you may send to me at the above address.

James D. Anderson
Co-Editor

Abbreviations

dir., dirs.	director, directors
ed., eds.	editor, editors
(for.)	price for foreign countries
(ind.)	price for individuals
(inst.)	price for institutions
(lib.)	price for libraries
NS	new series
p.	page, pages
po. ed.	poetry editor
pub.	publisher
(stud.)	price for students
tr. by	translated by
tr. of	translation of
U.	University
w.	with

Months

Ja	January	Jl	July
F	February	Ag	August
Mr	March	S	September
Ap	April	O	October
My	May	N	November
Je	June	D	December

Seasons

Aut	Autumn	Spr	Spring
Wint	Winter	Sum	Summer

Years

86	1986	88	1988
87	1987	89	1989
90	1990	91	1991

Periodicals Added

Periodical acronyms are followed by titles. Full information may be found in the list of periodicals indexed.

Arc: ARC

Asylum: ASYLUM

Avec: AVEC

BlackBR: BLACK BEAR REVIEW

ChironR: CHIRON REVIEW

CityLR: CITY LIGHTS REVIEW

CoalC: COAL CITY REVIEW

ContextS: CONTEXT SOUTH

Crucible: CRUCIBLE

DogRR: DOG RIVER REVIEW

DustyD: DUSTY DOG

GreenMR: GREEN MOUNTAINS REVIEW

Gypsy: GYPSY LITERARY MAGAZINE

Hellas: HELLAS

Imagine: IMAGINE

LullwaterR: LULLWATER REVIEW

NewDeltaR: NEW DELTA REVIEW

NewMyths: NEW MYTHS

NewYorkQ: THE NEW YORK QUARTERLY

NorthStoneR: THE NORTH STONE REVIEW

OnTheBus: ONTHEBUS

Parting: PARTING GIFTS

Pearl: PEARL

PoetryC: POETRY CANADA

PoetryUSA: POETRY USA

ShadowP: SHADOW PLAY

Shiny: SHINY

SycamoreR: SYCAMORE REVIEW

WillowR: WILLOW REVIEW

Periodicals Deleted

Bound: BOUNDARY 2, William V. Spanos, ed., Dept. of English, State U. of New York, Binghamton, NY 13901. "As of the 1990 volume, no longer publishes poetry."

DeKalbLAJ: THE DEKALB LITERARY ARTS JOURNAL, Charleise T. Young, ed., DeKalb College, 555 N. Indian Creek Dr., Clarkston, GA 30021. Vol. 22, nos. 1/4, indexed in the 1989 volume, was the "final issue."

LetFem: LETRAS FEMENINAS, Asociación de Literatura Femenina Hispánica, Adelaida López de Martínez, ed., Dept. of Modern Languages, U. of Nebraska-Lincoln, Lincoln, NE 68588-0315. No 1989 or 1990 issues received. Letters not answered.

Lips: LIPS, Laura Boss, ed., P.O. Box 1345, Montclair, NJ 07042. No 1989 or 1990 issues received. Letters not answered.

LittleBR: THE LITTLE BALKANS REVIEW: A Southeast Kansas Literary and Graphics Quarterly, Gene DeGruson, ed., 601 Grandview Heights Terrace, Pittsburg, KS 66762. No 1989 or 1990 issues received. Letters not answered.

Mairena: MAIRENA: Revista de Crítica y Poesía, Manuel de la Puebla, director, Himalaya 257, Urbanización Monterrey, Río Piedras, PR 00926. No 1990 issues received; letters returned.

Margin: MARGIN: A Quarterly Magazine for Imaginative Writing and Ideas, Orion Ross, USA ed., 1430 Massachusetts Ave., #306-17, Cambridge, MA 02138-3810. No 1990 issues received; letters returned.

Sink: SINK, Spencer Selby, ed., P.O. Box 590095, San Francisco, CA 94159. No 1989 or 1990 issues received. Letters not answered.

StoneC: STONE COUNTRY, Judith Neeld, ed., The Nathan Mayhew Seminars of Martha's Vineyard, P.O. Box 132, Menemsha, MA 02552. Volume 17, numbers 1 & 2 (1989) was "Final Issue".

Periodicals Indexed

Arranged by acronym, with names of editors, addresses, issues indexed, and subscription information. New titles added to the *Index* in 1990 are marked with an asterisk (*).

Abraxas: ABRAXAS, Ingrid Swanberg, ed., 2518 Gregory St., Madison, WI 53711. Issues indexed: (38/39). Subscriptions: $12/4 issues; Single issues: $3; Double issues: $6.

Acts: ACTS: A Journal of New Writing, David Levi Strauss, ed. & pub., 514 Guerrero St., San Francisco, CA 94110. Issues indexed: No 1990 issues received. Subscriptions: $12/yr. (2 issues, ind.), $16/yr. (2 issues, inst. & for.); $20/2 yrs. (4 issues, ind.), $28/2 yrs. (4 issues, inst. & for.); Single issues: $10.

Aerial: AERIAL, Rod Smith, ed., P.O. Box 25642, Washington, DC 20007. Issues indexed: No 1990 issues received. Subscriptions: $15/3 issues; Single issues: $7.50.

Agni: AGNI, Askold Melnyczuk, ed., Creative Writing Program, Boston U., 236 Bay State Rd., Boston, MA 02115. Issues indexed: (29/30, 31/32). Subscriptions: $12/yr., $23/2 yrs.; $24/yr., $48/2 yrs. (inst.); plus $5/yr. (for.); Single issues: $6; Double issues: $12.

AlphaBS: ALPHA BEAT SOUP, Dave Christy, ed., 68 Winter Ave., Scarborough, Ont. M1K 4M3 Canada. Issues indexed: No 1990 issues received. Subscriptions: $5/yr. (2 issues); Single issues: $3.

Amelia: AMELIA, Frederick A. Raborg, Jr., ed., 329 "E" St., Bakersfield, CA 93304. Issues indexed: (6:1-2, #16-17); #15 not received; 6:1 #16 labeled "Vol IV, No. 1" in error. Subscriptions: $20/yr. (4 issues), $38/2 yrs., $56/3 yrs.; $22/yr., $42/2 yrs., $62/3 yrs. (Canada, Mexico); $36/yr., $70/2 yrs., $104/3 yrs. (for. air mail); Single issues: $6.50, $7 (Canada & Mexico), $10 (for. air mail).

Americas: THE AMERICAS REVIEW, A Review of Hispanic Literature and Art of the USA, Julián Olivares, ed., U. of Houston, Houston, TX 77204-2090. Issues indexed: (18:1-3/4). Subscriptions: $15/yr. (ind.), $20/yr. (inst.); Single issues: $5; Double issues. $10.

AmerPoR: THE AMERICAN POETRY REVIEW, David Bonanno, Stephen Berg, Arthur Vogelsang, eds., 1721 Walnut St., Philadelphia, PA 19103. Issues indexed: (19:1-6). Subscriptions: $12/yr., $21/2 yrs., $29/3 yrs.; $15/yr., $27/2 yrs., $38/3 yrs. (for.); classroom rate $6/yr. per student; Single issues: $2.50.

AmerS: THE AMERICAN SCHOLAR, Joseph Epstein, ed., The Phi Beta Kappa Society, 1811 Q St. NW, Washington, DC 20009. Issues indexed: (59:1-4). Subscriptions: $21/yr., $38/2 yrs.; $25/yr., $48/2 yrs. (inst.); plus $3/yr. (for.); Single issues: $5.75; $7 (inst.).

AmerV: THE AMERICAN VOICE, Sallie Bingham, Frederick Smock, eds., The Kentucky Foundation for Women, Inc., 332 West Broadway, Suite 1215, Louisville, KY 40202. Issues indexed: (18-21). Subscriptions: $12/yr. Single issues: $4.

AnotherCM: ANOTHER CHICAGO MAGAZINE, Lee Webster, Barry Silesky, eds. & pubs., Box 11223, Chicago, IL 60611. Issues indexed: (21-22). Subscriptions: $15/yr., $60/5 yrs., $199.95/lifetime; Single issues: $8.

Antaeus: ANTAEUS, Daniel Halpern, ed., The Ecco Press, 26 W. 17th St., New York, NY 10011. Issues indexed: (64/65). Subscriptions: $30/4 issues; Single issues: $10; Double issues: $15.

2

Periodicals Indexed

AnthNEW: THE ANTHOLOGY OF NEW ENGLAND WRITERS, Frank Anthony, ed., New England Writers (Vermont Poets Association), 151 Main St., Windsor, VT 05089. Issues indexed: (2).

AntigR: THE ANTIGONISH REVIEW, George Sanderson, ed., St. Francis Xavier U., Antigonish, Nova Scotia B2G 1C0 Canada. Issues indexed: (80, 81/82, 83). Subscriptions: $18/4 issues; Single issues: $5.

AntR: THE ANTIOCH REVIEW, Robert S. Fogarty, ed., David St. John, po. ed., P.O. Box 148, Yellow Springs, OH 45387. Issues indexed: (48:1-4). Subscriptions: $20/yr. (4 issues), $38/2 yrs., $54/3 yrs. (ind.); $30/yr., $58/2 yrs., $86/3 yrs. (inst.); plus $5/yr. (for.); Single issues: $5. Subscription address: P.O. Box 862, Farmingdale, NY 11737-0862.

ApalQ: APALACHEE QUARTERLY, Barbara Hamby, Pam Ball, Bruce Boehrer, Claudia Johnson, Paul McCall, eds., P.O. Box 20106, Tallahassee, FL 32316. Issues indexed: (33/34). Subscriptions: $12/yr. (2 issues, ind.), $15/yr. (inst.), $20/yr. (for.); Single issues: $5; Double issues: $7./50.

*Arc: ARC, John Barton, Nadine McInnis, eds., P.O. Box 7368, Ottawa, Ont. K1L 8E4 Canada. Issues indexed: (24-25). Subscriptions: $14/4 issues (2 years); Single issues: $4.

Areíto: AREITO, Andrés Gómez, Director, P.O. Box 44-1803, Miami, FL 33144. Issues indexed: Segunda Epoca (2:7-8). Subscriptions: $12/yr. (ind.), $20/yr. (inst.), $18/yr. (for. ind.), $30/yr. (for. inst.).

ArtfulD: ARTFUL DODGE, Daniel Bourne, Karen Kovacik, eds., Dept. of English, College of Wooster, Wooster, OH 44691. Issues indexed: (18/19). Subscriptions: $10/4 issues (ind.), $16/4 issues (inst.); Single issues: $5.

Ascent: ASCENT, Audrey Curley, Mark Costello, Paul Friedman, Rocco Fumento, Philip Graham, Jerry Mirskin, Nancy Roberts, George Scouffas, Jean Thompson, Michael Van Walleghen, Kirsten Wasson, eds., P.O. Box 967, Urbana, IL 61801. Issues indexed: (15:1). Subscriptions: $3/yr. (3 issues), $4.50/yr. (for.); Single issues: $1 (bookstore), $1.50 (mail).

*Asylum: ASYLUM, Greg Boyd, ed., P.O. Box 6203, Santa Maria, CA 93456. Issues indexed: (5:4, 6:1-2). Subscriptions: $10/yr. (ind.), $15/yr. (inst.), plus $2/yr. (for.); Single issues: $3.

Atlantic: THE ATLANTIC, William Whitworth, ed., Peter Davison, po. ed., 745 Boylston St., 7th fl., Boston, MA 02116-2603. Issues indexed: (265:1-6, 266:1-6). Subscriptions: $14.95/yr., $27.95/2 yrs., $39.95/3 yrs., plus $4/yr. (Canada), $6/yr. (for.); Single issues: $2.50, $2.95 (Canada). Subscription address: Atlantic Subscription Processing Center, Box 52661, Boulder, CO 80322.

*Avec: AVEC: A Journal of Writing, Cydney Chadwick, ed., P.O. Box 1059, Penngrove, CA 94951. Issues indexed: (3:1). Subscriptions: $12/2 issues; $15/issue (inst.); Single issue: $7.50.

BallSUF: BALL STATE UNIVERSITY FORUM, Bruce W. Hozeski, ed., Darlene Mathis-Eddy, po. ed., Ball State U., Muncie, IN 47306. Issues indexed: No 1990 issues received. Subscriptions: $20/yr. (4 issues), Single issues: $6.

BambooR: BAMBOO RIDGE: The Hawaii Writers' Quarterly, Eric Chock, Darrell H. Y Lum, eds., P.O. Box 61781, Honolulu, HI 96839-1781. Issues indexed: (47, 48/49). Subscriptions: $12/yr. (4 issues), $16/yr. (inst.).; Single issues, $4; Double issues: $8.

BellArk: BELLOWING ARK, Robert R. Ward, ed., P.O. Box 45637, Seattle, WA 98145. Issues indexed: (6:1-6). Subscriptions: $12/yr. (6 issues), $20/2 yrs.; Single issues: $2.

BellR: THE BELLINGHAM REVIEW, Susan E. Hilton, ed., 1007 Queen St., Bellingham, WA 98226. Issues indexed: (13:1-2, #27-28). Subscriptions: $5/yr. (2 issues), $9.50/2 yrs., $12.50/3 yrs.; through agencies, $6/yr.; Single issues: $2.50.

3

BelPoJ: THE BELOIT POETRY JOURNAL, Marion K. Stocking, ed., RFD 2, Box 154, Ellsworth, ME 04605. Issues indexed: (40:3-4, 41:1-2). Subscriptions: $8/yr. (4 issues, ind.), $22/3 yrs.; $12/yr., $33/3 yrs. (inst.); plus $2.96/yr. (Canada), $3.20/yr. (for.); Single issues: $2.

BilingR: THE BILINGUAL REVIEW / LA REVISTA BILINGÜE, Gary D. Keller, ed., Hispanic Research Center, Arizona State U., Tempe, AZ 85287-2702. Issues indexed: (13:3, 14:1/2-3) 1986-1988, c1990-1991. Subscriptions: $16/yr., $30/2 yrs., $42/3 yrs. (ind.); $26/yr. (inst.).

BlackALF: BLACK AMERICAN LITERATURE FORUM, Division on Black American Literature and Culture, Modern Language Association, Joe Weixlmann, ed., Thadious Davis, Pinkie Gordon Lane, Sterling Plumpp, po. eds., Dept. of English, Indiana State U., Terre Haute, IN 47809. Issues indexed: (24:1-4). Subscriptions: $19/yr. (ind.), $30/yr. (inst.), $24/yr. (for.), $35/yr. (for. inst.). Single issues: $8.

*BlackBR: BLACK BEAR REVIEW, Ave Jeanne, po. ed., 1916 Lincoln St., Croydon, PA 19021. Issues indexed: (11-12). Subscriptions: $8/yr. (2 issues); Single issues: $4.

BlackWR: BLACK WARRIOR REVIEW, Alicia Griswold, ed., Glenn Mott, po. ed., U. of Alabama, P.O. Box 2936, Tuscaloosa, AL 35487-2936. Issues indexed: (16:2, 17:1). Subscriptions: $9/yr. (ind.), $14/yr. (inst.); Single issues: $5.

BlueBldgs: BLUE BUILDINGS: An International Magazine of Poetry, Translations and Art, Guillaume Williams, ed., Dept. of English, Drake U., Des Moines, IA 50311. Issues indexed: (12). Subscriptions: $20/2 issyus; $12/1 issue; Back issues: $4.

Blueline: BLUELINE, Anthony Tyler, ed., Jonathan Dallas, Stephanie Coyne DeGhett, Richard Londraville, Alan Steinberg, Warren Wigutow, po. eds., English Dept., Potsdam College, SUNY, Potsdam, NY 13676. Issues indexed: (11:1/2). Single issues: $6.

Bogg: BOGG, John Elsberg, ed., 422 N. Cleveland St., Arlington, VA 22201. Issues indexed: (62-63). Subscriptions: $10/3 issues; Single issues: $4.

Bomb: BOMB MAGAZINE, Betsy Sussler, ed. & pub., Roland Legiardi-Laura, po. ed., New Art Publications, P.O. Box 2003, Canal Station, New York, NY 10013. Issues indexed: (31, 33); No. 32 not received. Subscriptions: $16/yr., $30/2 yrs.; $26/yr. (for.); Single issues: $4.

BostonR: BOSTON REVIEW, Margaret Ann Roth, ed., 33 Harrison Ave., Boston, MA 02111. Issues indexed: (15:1-6). Subscriptions: $15/yr., $25/2 yrs. (ind.); $18/yr., $31/2 yrs. (inst.); plus $6/yr. (for.); Single issues: $4.

Boulevard: BOULEVARD, Richard Burgin, ed., 2400 Chestnut St., No. 3301, Philadelphia, PA 19103. Issues indexed: (4:3/5:1, 5:2, #12/13-14). Subscriptions: $12/3 issues, $20/6 issues, $25/9 issues; Single issues: $5.

BrooklynR: BROOKLYN REVIEW, Ronna Z. Levy, David Trinidad, eds., Dept. of English, Brooklyn College, Brooklyn, NY 11210. Issues indexed: (7); Note: Issues 5 and 6 were indexed in the 1989 volume, but not so listed. Subscriptions: $5/issue.

Caliban: CALIBAN, Lawrence R. Smith, ed., P.O. Box 4321, Ann Arbor, MI 48106. Issues indexed: (8-9). Subscriptions: $10/yr. (2 issues), $18/2 yrs. (ind.); $17/yr. (inst.); plus $2/yr. (for.); Single issues: $6.

Callaloo: CALLALOO: A Journal of Afro-American and African Arts and Letters, Charles H. Rowell, ed., Dept. of English, Wilson Hall, U. of Virginia, Charlottesville, VA 22903. Issues indexed: (13:1-4). Subscriptions: $20.50/yr. (ind.), $43/yr. (inst.); plus $7 (Canada, Mexico); plus $14 (outside North America, airfreight); Subscription address: The Johns Hopkins University Press, Journals Publishing Division, 701 W. 40th St., Suite 275, Baltimore, MD 21211.

CalQ: CALIFORNIA QUARTERLY, Elliot L. Gilbert, ed., Brian Knave, Ari Sherman, po. eds., 100 Sproul Hall, U. of California, Davis, CA 95616. Issues indexed: (34); Nos. 31-33 not received. Subscriptions: $14/yr. (4 issues); Single issues: $4.

Periodicals Indexed

Calyx: CALYX: A Journal of Art and Literature by Women, Margarita Donnelly, Managing ed., Catherine Holdorf, Beverly McFarland, Linda Varsell Smith, eds, P.O. Box B, Corvallis, OR 97339-0539. Issues indexed: (12:3, 13:1). Subscriptions: $18/yr. (3 issues), $32/2 yrs., $42/3 yrs., plus $4/yr. (for.), $9/yr. (for. airmail); $22.50/yr. (inst.); $15/yr. (low income individual); Single issues: $8, Double issues: $16, plus $1 postage.

CanLit: CANADIAN LITERATURE, W. H. New, ed., U. of British Columbia, 2029 West Mall, Vancouver, B.C. V6T 1W5 Canada. Issues indexed: (124/125, 126-127). Subscriptions: $25/yr. (ind.), $35/yr. (inst.) plus $5/yr. outside Canada; Single issues: $10.

CapeR: THE CAPE ROCK, Harvey Hecht, ed., Southeast Missouri State U., Cape Girardeau, MO 63701. Issues indexed: (25:1-2). Subscriptions: $5/yr. (2 issues); Single issues: $3.

CapilR: THE CAPILANO REVIEW, Pierre Coupey, ed., Capilano College, 2055 Purcell Way, North Vancouver, B.C. V7J 3H5 Canada. Issues indexed: (Series 2:2-4). Subscriptions: $16/yr. (3 issues), $36/3 yrs.; $25/yr. (inst.); same rates in U.S. funds (U.S.A.); plus $3/yr. (for.); Single issues: $8.

CarolQ: CAROLINA QUARTERLY, David Kellogg, ed., Barnsley Brown, po. ed., Greenlaw Hall CB#3520, U. of North Carolina, Chapel Hill, NC 27599-3520. Issues indexed: (42:2-3, 43:1). Subscriptions: $10/yr. (ind.), $12/yr. (3 issues) (inst.), $11/yr. (for.); Single issues: $5.

CentR: THE CENTENNIAL REVIEW, R. K. Meiners, ed., College of Arts and Letters, 312 Linton Hall, Michigan State U., East Lansing, MI 48824-1044. Issues indexed: (34:1-4). Subscriptions: $10/yr., $15/2 yrs., plus $3/yr. (for.); Single issues: $3.

CentralP: CENTRAL PARK, Stephen-Paul Martin, Eve Ensler, Richard Royal, eds., Box 1446, New York, NY 10023. Issues indexed: (17/18). Subscriptions: $15/yr., 2 issues (ind.), $16/yr. (inst.); Single issues: $7.50 (ind), $8 (inst).

ChamLR: CHAMINADE LITERARY REVIEW, Loretta Petrie, ed., Jim Kraus, po. ed., Chaminade U. of Honolulu, 3140 Waialae Ave., Honolulu, HI 96816. Issues indexed: (3:2, 4:1; #6-7). Subscriptions: $10/yr. (2 issues); $18/2 yrs.; plus $2 (for.).; Single issues: $5.

ChangingM: CHANGING MEN: Issues in Gender, Sex and Politics, Michael Biernbaum, Rick Cote, managing eds., 306 N. Brooks St., Madison, WI 53715, Daniel Garrett, po. ed. (105-63 135th St., Queens, NY 11419). Issues indexed: (21). Subscriptions: $16/4 issues, $30/4 issues (inst.); $12/4 issues (limited income); $18/4 issues (Canada & Mexico); $27/4 issues (for., air mail); Single issues: $4.50.

CharR: THE CHARITON REVIEW, Jim Barnes, ed., Northeast Missouri State U., Kirksville, MO 63501. Issues indexed: (16:1-2). Subscriptions: $9/4 issues; Single issues: $2.50.

ChatR: THE CHATTAHOOCHEE REVIEW, Lamar York, ed., DeKalb College, 2101 Womack Road, Dunwoody, GA 30338-4497. Issues indexed: (10:2-4, 11:1). Subscriptions: $15/yr. (4 issues), $25/2 yrs.; Single issues: $3.50.

Chelsea: CHELSEA, Sonia Raiziss, ed., P.O. Box 5880, Grand Central Station, New York, NY 10163. Issues indexed: (49). Subscriptions: $11/2 issues or 1 double issue, $13 (for.); Single issues: $6, $7 (for.).

ChiR: CHICAGO REVIEW, Andy Winston, ed., Anne Myles, po. eds., 5801 South Kenwood, Chicago, IL 60637. Issues indexed: (37:1). Subscriptions: $20/ yr. (ind.), $40/2 yrs., $60/3 yrs., plus $6/yr. (for.); $25/yr. (inst.); Single issues: $5.

*ChironR: CHIRON REVIEW, Michael Hathaway, ed., 1514 Stone, Great Bend, KS 67530. Issues indexed: (9:1-4). Subscriptions: $8/yr. (4 issues); $16/yr. (for.); $20/yr. (inst.); Single issues: $2; $4. (for.).

ChrC: THE CHRISTIAN CENTURY, James M. Wall, ed., 407 S. Dearborn St., Chicago, IL 60605. Issues indexed: (107:1-37). Subscriptions: $30/yr.; Single issues: $1.50. Christian Century Subscription Service, 5615 W. Cermak, Cicero, IL 60650.

5

Periodicals Indexed

CimR: CIMARRON REVIEW, Gordon Weaver, ed., Jack Myers, Randy Phillis, Sally Shigley, po. eds., 205 Morrill Hall, Oklahoma State U., Stillwater, OK 74078-0135. Issues indexed: (90-93). Subscriptions: $12/yr., $15 (Canada); $30/3 yrs., $40 (Canada); plus $2.50/yr. (for.); Single issues: $3.

CinPR: CINCINNATI POETRY REVIEW, Dallas Wiebe, ed., Dept. of English, ML 069, U. of Cincinnati, Cincinnati, OH 45221. Issues indexed: No 1990 issues received. Subscriptions: $9/4 issues; Single issues: $3.

*CityLR: CITY LIGHTS REVIEW, Nancy J. Peters, Lawrence Ferlinghetti, eds., City Lights Bookstore, 261 Columbus Ave., San Francisco, CA 94133. Issues indexed: (4). Single issues: $10.95.

ClockR: CLOCKWATCH REVIEW: A Journal of the Arts, James Plath, ed., Dept. of English, Illinois Wesleyan Univ., Bloomington, IL 61702. Issues indexed: (6:1-2). Subscriptions: $8/yr. (2 issues); Single issues: $4.

*CoalC: COAL CITY REVIEW, Brian Daldorph, Sandra Tompson, eds., U. of Kansas, English Dept., Lawrence, KS 66045. Issues indexed: (1-2). Subscriptions: $6/2 issues; Single issues: $4.

ColEng: COLLEGE ENGLISH, National Council of Teachers of English, James C. Raymond, ed., Dara Wier, po. ed., P.O. Drawer AL, Tuscaloosa, AL 35487. Issues indexed: (52:1-8). Subscriptions: $35/yr. (ind.), $40/yr. (inst.), plus $4/yr. (for.); Single issues: $5.; NCTE, 1111 Kenyon Rd., Urbana, IL 61801.

ColR: COLORADO REVIEW, Bill Tremblay, ed., Dept. of English, Colorado State U., 360 Eddy Bldg., Fort Collins, CO 80523. Issues indexed: (NS 17:1). Subscriptions: $9/yr. (2 issues), $17.50/2 yrs.; Single issues: $5.

Colum: COLUMBIA: A Magazine of Poetry & Prose, Elizabeth Osborne, ed., Cynthia Atkins, po. ed., 404 Dodge Hall, Columbia Univ., New York, NY 10027. Issues indexed: No 1990 issues received. Subscriptions: $4.50/yr. (1 issue).

Comm: COMMONWEAL, Margaret O'Brien Steinfels, ed., Rosemary Deen, po. ed., 15 Dutch St., New York, NY 10038. Issues indexed: (117:1-22). Subscriptions: $32/yr., $34/yr. (Canada), $37/yr. (for.); $57/2 yrs., $61/2 yrs. (Canada), $67/2 yrs. (for.), ; Single issues: $2.

Cond: CONDITIONS: A Feminist Magazine of Writing by Women with an Emphasis on Writing by Lesbians, Cheryl Clarke, Melinda Goodman, Paula Martinac, Mariana Romo-Carmona, P. Mikie Sugino, eds., P.O. Box 159046, Van Brunt Station, Brooklyn, NY 11215-9046. Issues indexed: (17). "This is the last issue . . . in journal form; Conditions will appear from now on as an anthology, . . . and will be published less frequently" -- Introduction.

Confr: CONFRONTATION, Martin Tucker, ed., Katherine Hill-Miller, po. ed., English Dept., C. W. Post Campus of Long Island U., Brookville, NY 11548. Issues indexed: (42/43-44/45). Subscriptions: $10/yr., $20/2 yrs., $30/3 yrs.; Single issues: $6-7.

Conjunc: CONJUNCTIONS: Bi-Annual Volumes of New Writing, Bard College, Bradford Morrow, ed., 33 W. 9th St., New York, NY 10011. Issues indexed: (15). Subscriptions: P.O. Box 115, Bard College, Annandale-on-Hudson, NY 12504; $18/yr. (2 issues), $32/2 yrs.; $25/yr., $45/2 yrs. (inst., for.); $45/yr., $85/ 2 yrs. (cloth binding); Single issues: $9.95.

ConnPR: THE CONNECTICUT POETRY REVIEW, J. Clair White, James Wm. Chichetto, eds., P.O. Box 3783, Amity Station, New Haven, CT 06525. Issues indexed: (9:1). Single issues: $3 (including postage).

Contact: CONTACT II: A Poetry Review, Maurice Kenny, J. G. Gosciak, eds., P.O. Box 451, Bowling Green, New York, NY 10004. Issues indexed: (9:56/57/58). Subscriptions: $10/yr. (ind.); $16/yr. (inst.); Single issues: $6.

Periodicals Indexed

*ContextS: CONTEXT SOUTH, David Breeden, po. ed., pub., Box 2244, State University, AR 72467. Issues indexed: (1:1). Subscriptions: $10/yr.

CrabCR: CRAB CREEK REVIEW, Linda Clifton, ed., 4462 Whitman Ave. N., Seattle WA 98103. Issues indexed: (6:3, 7:1). Subscriptions: $8/yr. (3 issues), $15/2 yrs.; Single issues: $3.

Crazy: CRAZYHORSE, K. Z. Derounian-Stodola, managing ed., Dept. of English, U. of Arkansas, 2801 S. University, Little Rock, AR 72204. Send poetry to: Lynda Hull, David Wojahn, Dean Young, po. eds., Dept. of English, Ballantine Hall, Indiana Univ., Bloomington, IN 47405. Issues indexed: (38-39). Subscriptions: $10/yr. (2 issues), $18/2 yrs., $27/3 yrs. Single issues: $5.

CreamCR: CREAM CITY REVIEW, Valerie Ross, ed., Marilyn Taylor, Robert Brown, po. eds., English Dept., U. of Wisconsin, P.O. Box 413, Milwaukee, WI 53201. Issues indexed: (14:1). Subscriptions: $10/yr. (2 issues), $14/2 yrs.; Single issues: $6; Sample & back issues: $4.50.

CrossC: CROSS-CANADA WRITERS' MAGAZINE, Ted Plantos, ed., George Swede, po. ed., 137 Birmingham St., Stratford, Ontario N5A 2T1 Canada. Issues indexed: (12:1) 1990; last issue; convered to "Paragraph: The Fiction Magazine."

CrossCur: CROSSCURRENTS, Linda Brown Michelson, ed., 2200 Glastonbury Road, Westlake Village, CA 91361. Issues indexed: (9:1-3). Subscriptions: $18/yr. (4 issues), $25/2 yrs.; Single issues: $6.

*Crucible: CRUCIBLE, Terrence L. Grimes, ed., Barton College, College Station, Wilson, NC 27893. Issues indexed: (26). Subscriptions: $4/yr. (1 issue), $8/2 yrs; Back issues: $3.

CuadP: CUADERNOS DE POÉTICA, Diógenes Céspedes, Director, Apartado Postal 1736, Santo Domingo, República Dominicana; US Editors: Kate Nickel, 1111 Oldfather Hall, U. of Nebraska, Lincoln, NE 68588-0315, Rafael Catalá, P.O. Box 450, Corrales, NM 87048. Issues indexed: (7:20). Subscriptions: America & Europe, $25/yr. (ind.), $30/yr. (inst.); Africa, Asia & Oceania, $30/yr. (ind.), $40/yr. (inst.)

CumbPR: CUMBERLAND POETRY REVIEW, Ingram Bloch, Bob Darrell, Malcolm Glass, Jeanne Gore, Thomas Heine, Laurence Lerner, Anthony Lombardy, Alison Reed, Eva Touster, eds., Poetics, Inc., P.O. Box 120128, Acklen Station, Nashville, TN 37212. Issues indexed: (9:2, 10:1). Subscriptions: $12/yr, $22/2 yrs. (ind.); $15/yr., $27/2 yrs. (inst.); $21/yr., $33/2 yrs. (for.); Single issue: $6.

CutB: CUTBANK, David Curran, ed., Henry Gerfen, po. ed., Dept. of English, U. of Montana, Missoula, MT 59812. Issues indexed: (33-34). Subscriptions: $12/yr.; Single issues: $8.95.

Dandel: DANDELION, John McDowell, managing ed., Christopher Wiseman, Nancy Holmes, po eds., Alexandra Centre, 922 - 9th Ave., S.E., Calgary, Alberta T2G 0S4 Canada. Issues indexed: (17:1-2). Subscriptions: $10/yr. (2 issues), $18/2 yrs.; $15/yr. (inst.); Single issues: $6.

DenQ: DENVER QUARTERLY, Donald Revell, ed., U. of Denver, Denver, CO 80208. Issues indexed: (24:3-4, 25:1-2). Subscriptions: $15/yr., $18/yr. (inst.); $28/2 yrs.; plus $1/yr. (for.); Single issues: $5.

Descant: DESCANT, Karen Mulhallen, ed., P.O. Box 314, Station P, Toronto M5S 2S8, Ontario, Canada. Issues indexed: (21:1-3, 21:4/22:1, #68-70, 71/72). Subscriptions: $22.47/yr., $40.66/2 yrs., $58.85/3 yrs. (ind.); $31.03/yr., $62.06/2 yrs., $88.81/3 yrs. (inst.); plus $6/yr. (for.); Single/double issues: $10.95-$14.95.

*DogRR: DOG RIVER REVIEW, Laurence F. Hawkins, Jr., ed., Trout Creek Press, 5976 Billings Road, Parkdale, OR 97041. Issues indexed: (9:1-2, #17-18). Subscriptions: $6/yr.; Single issues: $3; Sample copy: $2.

*DustyD: DUSTY DOG, John Pierce, ed., P.O. Box 1103, Zuni, NM 87327. Issues indexed: (1:2). Subscriptions: $7/yr. (3 issues, U.S.A.), $8/yr. (Canada); Single issues: $4.

EmeraldCR: EMERALD COAST REVIEW: A Collection of Works of West Florida Writers, Ronald B. Cannon, ed., West Florida Literary Federation, P.O. Box 1644, Pensacola, FL 32597-1644. Issues indexed: (1990, c1989). Single issues: $12.

EngJ: ENGLISH JOURNAL, National Council of Teachers of English, Ben F. Nelms, ed., 200 Norman Hall, U. of Florida, Gainesville, FL 32611; Paul Janeczko, po. ed., P.O. Box 1079, Gray, ME 04039. Issues indexed: (79:1-8). Subscriptions: $40/yr. (inst.), $35/yr. (ind.), plus $4/yr. (for.); Single issues: $5; Subscription address: 1111 Kenyon Rd., Urbana, IL 61801.

Epoch: EPOCH, Michael Koch, ed., 251 Goldwin Smith Hall, Cornell U., Ithaca, NY 14853-3201. Issues indexed: (39:1//2-3). Subscriptions: $11/yr.; Single issues: $4.

Event: EVENT: The Douglas College Review, Dale Zieroth, ed., Douglas College, P.O. Box 2503, New Westminster, B.C. V3L 5B2 Canada. Issues indexed: (19:1-3). Subscriptions: $12/yr., $20/2 yrs.; Single issue: $5.

EvergreenC: THE EVERGREEN CHRONICLES: A Journal of Gay and Lesbian Writers, Randy Beard, Jim Berg, Michael Bonacci, Sima Rabinowitz, Betsy Rivers, eds., P.O. Box 8939, Minneapolis, MN 55408. Issues indexed: (5:2, 6:1). Subscriptions: $15/yr. (2 issues); Single issues: $4.

Farm: FARMER'S MARKET, Jean C. Lee, John E. Hughes, Lisa Ress, eds., Midwest Farmer's Market, Inc., P.O. Box 1272, Galesburg, IL 61402. Issues indexed: (7:1-2). Subscriptions: $8/yr. (2 issues); Single issues: $4.50.

Field: FIELD: Contemporary Poetry and Poetics, Stuart Friebert, David Young, eds., Rice Hall, Oberlin College, Oberlin, OH 44074. Issues indexed: (42-43). Subscriptions: $10/yr., $16/2 yrs.; Single issues: $5.; Back issues: $10.

FiveFR: FIVE FINGERS REVIEW, Aleka Chase, Elizabeth Claman, Marsha Drummond, J. Malcolm Garcia, John High, eds., 553 - 25th Ave., San Francisco, CA 94121. Issues indexed: No 1990 issues received. Subscriptions: $23/4 issues, $12/2 issues, plus $5 (for.); $24/4 issues, $13/2 issues (inst.); Single issues: $7; Sample issues: $5.

FloridaR: THE FLORIDA REVIEW, Russ Kesler, ed., Dept. of English, U. of Central Florida, Orlando, FL 32816. Issues indexed: (17:1-2). Subscriptions: $7/yr., $11/2 yrs.; Single issues: $4.50.

Footwork: FOOTWORK: The Paterson Literary Review, A Literary Collection of Contemporary Poetry, Short Fiction, and Art, Maria Mazziotti Gillan, ed., Passaic County Community College, College Boulevard, Paterson, NJ 07509. Issues indexed: (1990). Subscriptions: $5/issue + $1 for postage and handling.

FourQ: FOUR QUARTERS, John J. Keenan, ed., La Salle U., Philadelphia, PA 19141. Issues indexed: Second Series (4:1). Subscriptions: $8/yr. (2 issues), $13/2 yrs.; Single issues: $4.

FreeL: FREE LUNCH: A Poetry Journal, Free Lunch Arts Alliance, Ron Offen, ed., P.O. Box 7647, Laguna Niguel, CA 92607-7647. Issues indexed: (4-6). Subscriptions: $10/3 issues; $13/3 issues (for.); Single issues: $4, $5 (for.).

Gargoyle: GARGOYLE MAGAZINE, Richard Peabody, Peggy Pfeiffer, eds., Paycock Press, P.O. Box 30906, Bethesda, MD 20814. Issues indexed: (37/38) "last issue" -- label on issue wrapper; "reported deceased, has merely changed editors" to Toby Barlow, 4953 Desmond, Oakland, CA -- Black Bear (12) p. 57.

GeoR: GEORGIA REVIEW, Stanley W. Lindberg, ed., U. of Georgia, Athens, GA 30602. Issues indexed: (44:1/2-4). Subscriptions: $12/ yr., $20/2 yrs., plus $3/yr. (for.); Single issues: $9; Back issues: $5.

GettyR: GETTYSBURG REVIEW, Peter Stitt, ed., Gettysburg College, Gettysburg, PA 17325-1491. Issues indexed: (3:1-4). Subscriptions: $12/yr., $22/2 yrs., $30/3 yrs., plus $4 (for.); Single issues: $5.

8

Periodicals Indexed

GrahamHR: GRAHAM HOUSE REVIEW, Peter Balakian & Bruce Smith, eds., Colgate U. Press, Box 5000, Colgate U., Hamilton, NY 13346; Issues indexed: (12). Subscriptions: $15/2 yrs. (2 issues); Single issues: $7.50.

Grain: GRAIN, Saskatchewan Writers Guild, Geoffrey Ursell, ed., Lorna Crozier, po. ed., Box 1154, Regina, Saskatchewan S4P 3B4 Canada. Issues indexed: (18:1-4). Subscriptions: $15/yr., $28/2 yrs. (ind.); $20/yr., $40 2 yrs. (inst.); Single issues: $4.

GrandS: GRAND STREET, Jean Stein, ed. & pub., 135 Central Park West, New York, NY 10023. Issues indexed: (9:2-4). Subscriptions: $24/yr. (4 issues), $34/yr. (for.); Single issues: $8.50; Subscription address: 305 Main St., Westport, CT 06880.

*GreenMR: GREEN MOUNTAINS REVIEW, Neil Shepard, po. ed., Box A58, Johnson State College, Johnson, VT 05656. Issues indexed: (NS 3:2, 4:1). Single issues: $4.

GreensboroR: THE GREENSBORO REVIEW, Jim Clark, ed., Claudia Emerson Andrews, Kathleen Mason Driskell, po. eds., Dept. of English, U. of North Carolina, Greensboro, NC 27412. Issues indexed: (48-49). Subscriptions: $8/yr. (2 issues), $20/3 yrs.; Single issues: $4.

*Gypsy: GYPSY LITERARY MAGAZINE, Belinda Subraman, S. Ramnath, eds, 10708 Gay Brewer Dr., El Paso, TX 79935. Issues indexed: (15). Subscriptions: $10/2 issues (ind.); $14/2 issues (inst.); Single issues: $7.

HampSPR: THE HAMPDEN-SYDNEY POETRY REVIEW, Tom O'Grady, ed., P.O. Box 126, Hampden-Sydney, VA 23943. Issues indexed: Anthology 1975-1990. Subscriptions: $5/yr. (single issue); Anthology, $12.95.

HangL: HANGING LOOSE, Robert Hershon, Dick Lourie, Mark Pawlak, Ron Schreiber, eds., 231 Wyckoff St., Brooklyn, NY 11217. Issues indexed: (56-57). Subscriptions: $12.50/3 issues, $24/6 issues, $35/9 issues (ind.); $15/3 issues, $30/6 issues, $45/9 issues (inst.); $22/3 issues, $42/6 issues, $62/9 issues (for.); Sample issues: $5 plus $1.50 postage and handling.

Harp: HARPER'S MAGAZINE, Lewis H. Lapham, ed., 666 Broadway, New York, NY 10012. Issues indexed: (280:1676-1681, 281:1682-1687). Subscriptions: $18/yr., plus $2/yr. (USA possessions, Canada), plus $20/yr. (for.); Single issues: $2; Subscription address: P.O. Box 1937, Marion, OH 43305.

HarvardA: THE HARVARD ADVOCATE, Greer Hersch, Managing ed., Kenji Yoshino, po. ed., 21 South St., Cambridge, MA 02138. Issues indexed: (124:2-4, 125:1-2); Nov. 90 [125:2] is unnumbered. Subscriptions: $15/yr. (ind.), $17/yr. (inst.), $20/yr. (for.); Single issues: $4.

HawaiiR: HAWAI'I REVIEW, Galatea Maman, ed., David Ming Gravatt, po. ed., Dept. of English, U. of Hawai'i, 1733 Donaghho Rd., Honolulu, HI 96822. Issues indexed: (14:1-3, 15:1, #28-31). Subscriptions: $12/yr. (3 issues), $20/2 yrs.; Single issue: $5.

HayF: HAYDEN'S FERRY REVIEW, Salima Keegan, Managing ed., Mary Gannon, Elizabeth McNeil, po. eds., Matthews Center, Arizona State U., Tempe, AZ 85287-1502. Issues indexed: (6-7). Subscriptions: $10/yr. (2 issues), $18/2 yrs.; $13/yr., $26/2 yrs. (inst.); Single issues: $5 plus $1 postage.

HeavenB: HEAVEN BONE, Steven Hirsch, ed., pub., P.O. Box 486, Chester, NY 10918. Issues indexed: (8). Subscriptions: $14.95/2 yrs. (4 issues); Single issue: $5.

HeliconN: HELICON NINE: The Journal of Women's Arts & Letters, Gloria Vando Hickok, ed., P.O. Box 22412, Kansas City, MO 64113. Issues indexed: No 1990 issues received. Subscriptions: $18/yr. (3 issues), $33/2 yrs., $22/yr. (inst.), plus $1/issue (for.); Single issues: $8-12.

*Hellas: HELLAS: A Journal of Poetry and the Humanities, Gerald Harnett, ed., 304 S. Tyson Ave., Glenside, PA 19038. Subscriptions: $12/yr. (2 issues), $22/2 yrs.; plus $4/yr. (for.); Single issues: $5.50.

Periodicals Indexed

HighP: HIGH PLAINS LITERARY REVIEW, Robert O. Greer, Jr., ed., Michael J. Rosen, po. ed., 180 Adams St., Suite 250, Denver, CO 80206. Issues indexed: (5:1-3). Subscriptions: $20/yr. (3 issues), $38/2 yrs., plus $5/yr. (for.); Single issues: $7.

HiramPoR: HIRAM POETRY REVIEW, English Dept., Hiram College, Hale Chatfield & Carol Donley, eds., P.O. Box 162, Hiram, OH 44234. Issues indexed: (47-48/49) plus supplement #11. Subscriptions: $4/yr. (2 issues); Single issues: $2; Supplements, $4.

HolCrit: THE HOLLINS CRITIC, John Rees Moore, ed., Hollins College, VA 24020. Issues indexed: (27:1-5). Subscriptions: $6/yr., $10/2 yrs., $14/3 yrs.; $7.50/yr., $11.50/2 yrs., $15.50/3 yrs. (for.).

Hudson: THE HUDSON REVIEW, Paula Deitz, Frederick Morgan, eds., 684 Park Ave., New York, NY 10021. Issues indexed: (42:4, 43:1-3). Subscriptions: $20/yr., $38/2 yrs., $56/3 yrs., plus $4/yr. (for.); Single issues: $6.

*Imagine: IMAGINE: International Chicano Poetry Journal, Tino Villanueva, ed., 89 Mass. Ave., Suite 270, Boston, MA 02115. Issues indexed: (2:2, 3:1/2). Subscriptions: $8/yr. (2 issues), $14/2 yrs. (ind.); $12/yr., $18/2 yrs. (inst.); plus $1/yr. (for.); Single issues: $6.50-8.00.

IndR: INDIANA REVIEW, Renée Manfredi, ed., Bret Flournoy, Peggy Hardesty, J. D. Scrimgeour, po. eds., 316 N. Jordan Ave., Bloomington, IN 47405. Issues indexed: (13:2-3, 14:1). Subscriptions: $12/3 issues, $15/3 issues (inst.); $22/6 issues (ind.), $25/6 issues (inst.); plus $5/3 issues (for.). Single issues: $5.

Interim: INTERIM, A. Wilber Stevens, ed., Dept. of English, U. of Nevada, 4505 Maryland Parkway, Las Vegas, NV 89154-5011. Issues indexed: (9:1-2). Subscriptions: $5/yr. (2 issues), $8/2 yrs., $10/3 yrs. (ind.); $8/yr. (lib.), $10/yr. (for.); Single issues: $3, $5 (for.).

InterPR: INTERNATIONAL POETRY REVIEW, Evalyn P. Gill, ed., Box 2047, Greensboro, NC 27402. Issues indexed: (16:1-2). Subscriptions: $8/yr. (2 issues); Single issues: $4.

Inti: INTI, Revista de Literatura Hispánica, Roger B. Carmosino, ed., Dept. of Modern Languages, Providence College, Providence, RI 02918. Issues indexed: (31-32). Subscriptions: $25/yr. (2 issues, ind.), $40/yr. (inst.); Single issues: $20, $30 (double issues).

Iowa: IOWA REVIEW, David Hamilton, ed., 308 EPB, U. of Iowa, Iowa City, IA 52242. Issues indexed: (20:1-3). Subscriptions: $15/yr. (3 issues, ind.), $20/yr. (inst.), plus $3/yr. (for.); Single issues: $6.95.

Jacaranda: THE JACARANDA REVIEW, Bruce Kijewski, ed., Dept. of English, U. of California, Los Angeles, CA 90024. Issues indexed: No 1990 issues received. Subscriptions: $8/yr. (2 issues, ind.), $12/yr. (inst.).

JamesWR: THE JAMES WHITE REVIEW, A Gay Men's Literary Journal, Greg Baysans, ed., P.O. Box 3356, Traffic Station, Minneapolis, MN 55403. Issues indexed: (7:2-4, 8:1). Subscriptions: $12/yr., $20/2 yrs.; $14/yr. (Canada); $17/yr. (other for.); Single issues: $3; Back issues: $2.

JINJPo: THE JOURNAL OF NEW JERSEY POETS, Sander Zulauf, ed., English Dept., Division of Humanities, County College of Morris, Route 10 & Center Grove Rd., Randolph, NJ 07869. Issues indexed: (12:1-2). Subscriptions: $5/yr. (2 issues); Single issues: $4.

Journal: THE JOURNAL: The Literary Magazine of The Ohio State University, David Citino, ed., The Ohio State U., Dept. of English, 164 W. 17th Ave., Columbus, OH 43210. Issues indexed: (13:2). Subscriptions: $5/yr. (2 issues), $10/2 yrs., $15/3 yrs.; Single issues: $3.

Kaleid: KALEIDOSCOPE, International Magazine of Literature, Fine Arts, and Disability, Darshan Perusek, ed., Chris Hewitt (500 West End Ave., Apt. 5D, New York, NY 10024), po. ed., United Cerebral Palsy and Services for the Handicapped, 326 Locust St.,

10

Periodicals Indexed

Akron, OH 44302. Issues indexed: (20-21). Subscriptions: $9/yr. (2 issues, ind.), $12/yr. (inst.), plus $5/yr. (for.); Single issues: $4.50, $7 (for.); Sample issue: $2.

Kalliope: KALLIOPE: A Journal of Women's Art, Mary Sue Koeppel, ed., Florida Community College at Jacksonville, 3939 Roosevelt Blvd., Jacksonville, FL 32205. Issues indexed: (12:1-3). Subscriptions: $10.50/1 yr. (3 issues), $20/2 yrs.; $18/yr. (inst.); plus $6/yr. (for.); free to women in prison; Single issues: $7; Back issues: $4-8.

KanQ: KANSAS QUARTERLY, Harold Schneider, Ben Nyberg, W. R. Moses, John Rees, eds., Dept. of English, Denison Hall, Kansas State U., Manhattan, KS 66506-0703. Issues indexed: (22:1/2-4). Subscriptions: $20/yr., $35/2 yrs. (USA, Canada, Latin America); $21/yr., $37/2 yrs. (other countries); Single issues: $6; Double issues: $8.

KenR: KENYON REVIEW, Marilyn Hacker, ed., David Baker, po. ed., Kenyon College, Gambier, OH 43022. Issues indexed: (NS 12:1-4). Subscriptions: Kenyon Review, P.O. Box 837, Farmingdale, NY 11735; $20/yr., $35/2 yrs., $45/3 yrs. (ind.); $23/yr. (inst.); plus $5 (for.); Single issues: $7; Back issues: $10.

KeyWR: KEY WEST REVIEW, William J. Schlicht, Jr., ed., 9 Ave. G, Key West, FL 33040. Issues indexed: No 1990 issues received. "Publication . . . temporarily suspended." Subscriptions: P.O. Box 2082, Key West, FL 33045-2082, $17/yr. (4 issues); Single issues: $5, double issues: $10.

Lactuca: LACTUCA, Mike Selender, ed., P.O. Box 621, Suffern, NY 10901. Issues indexed: No 1990 issues published. Subscriptions: $10/yr. (3 issues), $13/yr. (for.); Single issues: $3.50, plus $1 (for.).

LakeSR: THE LAKE STREET REVIEW, Kevin FitzPatrick, ed., Box 7188, Minneapolis, MN 55407. Issues indexed: (24); No. 23 was indexed in the 1989 volume, not No. 22 as stated; No. 22 was indexed in the 1988 volume. Subscriptions: $4/2 yrs. (2 issues); Single issues: $2.

LaurelR: LAUREL REVIEW, Craig Goad, David Slater, William Trowbridge, eds., Green Tower Press, Dept. of English, Northwest Missouri State U., Maryville, MO 64468. Issues indexed: (24:1-2). Subscriptions: $8/yr. (2 issues), $14/2 yrs.; Single issues: $5; Back issues: $4.50.

LightY: LIGHT YEAR: The Biennial of Light Verse & Witty Poems, Robert Wallace, ed., Bits Press, Dept. of English, Case Western Reserve U., Cleveland, OH 44106. Issues indexed: No issues received since 1988/89. Subscriptions: '87, $13.95; '88/9, $15.95.

LindLM: LINDEN LANE MAGAZINE, Belkis Cuzá Malé, ed., P.O. Box 2384, Princeton, NJ 08543-2384. Issues indexed: (9:1/2-4). Subscriptions: $12/yr. (ind.), $18/yr. (inst.), $22/yr. (Latin America, Europe); Single issues: $2-5.

LitR: THE LITERARY REVIEW, Walter Cummins, ed., Fairleigh Dickinson U., 285 Madison Ave., Madison, NJ 07940. Issues indexed: (33:2-4, 34:1). Subscriptions: $18/yr., $21/yr. (for.); $30/2 yrs., $36/2 yrs. (for.); Single issues: $5, $6 (for.).

*LullwaterR: LULLWATER REVIEW, Robert T. Webb, ed., Box 22036, Emory Univ., Atlanta, GA 30322. Issues indexed: (1:1, 2:1). Subscriptions: $10/yr. (2 issues), plus $3 (for.); Single issues: $5.

Lyra: LYRA, Lourdes Gil, Iraida Iturralde, eds., P.O. Box 3188, Guttenberg, NJ 07093. Issues indexed: No 1990 issues received. Subscriptions: $15/yr. (4 issues, ind.), $20/yr. (inst.), plus $5/yr. (for.); Single issues: $4, $6 (for.).

MalR: THE MALAHAT REVIEW, Constance Rooke, ed., P.O. Box 3045, Victoria, B. C., Canada V8W 3P4. Issues indexed: (90-93). Subscriptions: $15 plus $1.05 GST/yr. (4 issues), $40 plus $2.80/3 yrs., (ind., USA, Canada); $25 plus $1.75 GST/yr. (inst., USA, Canada); $20/yr., $50/3 yrs. (other countries); $10/yr. (stud., USA, Canada); Single issues: $7 (USA, Canada), $8 (other countries).

ManhatPR: MANHATTAN POETRY REVIEW, Elaine Reiman-Fenton, ed., P.O. Box 8207, New York, NY 10150. Issues indexed: (11-12). Subscriptions: $12/yr. (2 issues); Single issues: $7; plus $5 per item (for.).

ManhatR: THE MANHATTAN REVIEW, Philip Fried, ed., 440 Riverside Dr., #45, New York, NY 10027. (5:1-2). Subscriptions: $8/2 issues (ind.), $12/2 issues (inst.), plus $2.50/2 issues (outside USA & Canada); Back issues: $4 (ind.), $6 (inst); include 6" x 9" envelope and $1.25 for postage.

Manoa: MANOA: A Pacific Journal of International Writing, Robert Shapard, ed., English Dept., U. of Hawaii, Honolulu, HI 96822. Issues indexed: (2:1-2). Subscriptions: $12/yr. (2 issues), $21.60/2 yrs., $28.80/3 yrs. (ind.); $18/yr., $32.40/2 yrs., $43.20/3 yrs. (inst.); plus $12/yr. for airmail; $15/yr. (for. ind.); $22/yr. (for. inst.).

MassR: THE MASSACHUSETTS REVIEW, Jules Chametzky, Mary Heath, Paul Jenkins, eds., Anne Halley, Paul Jenkins, po. eds., Memorial Hall, U. of Massachusetts, Amherst, MA 01003. Issues indexed: (31:1/2-4). Subscriptions: $14/yr. (4 issues, ind.), $17/yr. (lib.), $20/yr. (for.); Single issues: $5.

MemphisSR: MEMPHIS STATE REVIEW: name changed to RiverC: RIVER CITY.

Mester: MESTER, Kristine Ibsen, ed., Dept. of Spanish and Portuguese, U. of California, Los Angeles, CA 90024-1532. Issues indexed: (18:1-2); no poetry. Subscriptions: $12/yr. (2 issues, ind.), $20/yr. (inst.), $8/yr. (stud.), plus $4/yr. outside U.S., Canada, Mexico.

MichQR: MICHIGAN QUARTERLY REVIEW, Laurence Goldstein, ed., 3032 Rackham Bldg., U. of Michigan, Ann Arbor, MI 48109. Issues indexed: (29:1-4). Subscriptions: $13/yr., $24/2 yrs. (ind.), $15/yr. (inst.); Single issues: $3.50; Back issues: $2.

MidAR: MID-AMERICAN REVIEW, Ken Letko, ed., John Bradley, po. ed., 106 Hanna Hall, Dept. of English, Bowling Green State U., Bowling Green, OH 43403. Issues indexed: (10:1-2). Subscriptions: $6/yr. (2 issues), $10/2 yrs., $14/3 yrs.

MidwQ: THE MIDWEST QUARTERLY: A Journal of Contemporary Thought, James B. M. Schick, ed., Stephen E. Meats, po. ed., Pittsburg State U., Pittsburg, KS 66762-5889. Issues indexed: (31:2-4, 32:1). Subscriptions: $10/yr. plus $3 (for.); Single issues: $3.

Mildred: MILDRED, Ellen Biss, Kathryn Poppino, eds., 961 Birchwood Lane, Schenectady, NY 12309. Issues indexed: (4:1). Subscriptions: $12/yr. (2 issues), $20/2 yrs., $28/3 yrs.; $14/yr., $24/2 yrs., $30/3 yrs. (inst.); Single issues: $6.

MinnR: THE MINNESOTA REVIEW, Michael Sprinker, Susan Squier, Helen Cooper, eds, Cornelius Eady, William J. Harris, po. eds., Dept. of English, State U. of New York, Stony Brook, NY 11794-5350. Issues Indexed: (NS 34/35). Subscriptions: $8/yr. (2 issues), $14/2 yrs. (ind.); $16/yr., $28/2 yrs. (inst. & for.); Single issues: $4.50.

MissouriR: THE MISSOURI REVIEW, Speer Morgan, ed., 1507 Hillcrest Hall, U. of Missouri, Columbia, MO 65211. Issues indexed: (13:1-2). Subscriptions: $12/yr. (3 issues), $21/2 yrs.; Single issues: $5.

MissR: MISSISSIPPI REVIEW, Frederick Barthelme, ed., The Center for Writers, U. of Southern Mississippi, Southern Station, Box 5144, Hattiesburg, MS 39406-5144. Issues indexed: (18:2/3, 19:1/2, #53/54, 55/56). Subscriptions: $15/yr. (2 issues), $28/2 yrs., $40/3 yrs., plus $2/yr. (for.); Single issues: usually $8.

MoodySI: MOODY STREET IRREGULARS, Joy Walsh, ed., P.O. Box 157, Clarence Center, NY 14032. Issues indexed: (22/23). Subscriptions: $10/4 single, 2 double issues (ind.), $15/4 single, 2 double issues (lib.); Single issues: $3, double issues: $5.

MSS: MSS, L. M. Rosenberg, ed., State U. of NY at Binghamton. Issues indexed: (7:1); last issue: superseded by New Myths, Robert Mooney, ed., State U. of New York, P.O. Box 6000, Binghamton, NY 13902-6000.

Nat: THE NATION, Victor Navasky, ed., Grace Schulman, po. ed., 72 Fifth Ave., New York, NY 10011. Issues indexed: (250:1-25, 251:1-23). Subscriptions: $44/yr., $75/2 yrs., plus $14/yr. (for.); Single issues: $1.75; Back issues: $3, $4 (for.). Send subscription correspondence to: P.O. Box 10763, Des Moines, IA 50340-0763.

NegC: NEGATIVE CAPABILITY, Sue Walker, ed., 62 Ridgelawn Dr. East, Mobile, AL 36608. Issues indexed: (9:3, 10:1-2/3). Subscriptions: $12/yr. (3 issues, ind.), $16/yr. (inst., for.); Single issues: $5.

NewAW: NEW AMERICAN WRITING, Paul Hoover, Maxine Chernoff, eds., OINK! Press, 2920 West Pratt, Chicago, IL 60645. Issues indexed: (6). Subscriptions: $12/yr. (2 issues); $16/yr. (for., lib.).; Single issues: $6.

*NewDeltaR: NEW DELTA REVIEW, Kathleen Fitzpatrick, ed., David Starkey, po. ed., English Dept., Louisiana State U., Baton Rouge, LA 70803. Issues indexed: (7:1-2). Subscriptions: $7/yr. (2 issues); Single issues: $4.

NewEngR: NEW ENGLAND REVIEW, Middlebury Series, T. R. Hummer, ed, Middlebury College, Middlebury, VT 05753. Issues indexed: (12:3-4, 13:1-2). Subscriptions: $18/yr. (4 issues), $33/2 yrs., $50/3 yrs. (ind.); $30/yr., $55/2 yrs., $83/3 yrs. (lib., inst.); plus $6/yr. (for. surface) or $15/yr. (for. airmail); Single issues: $6, $7 (for. surface), $9.50 (for. airmail); subscription address: University Press of New England, 17 1/2 Lebanon St., Hanover, NH 03755.

NewL: NEW LETTERS, James McKinley, ed., U. of Missouri-Kansas City, 5100 Rockhill Rd., Kansas City, MO 64110. Issues indexed: (56:4, 57:1-2). Subscriptions: $17/yr. (4 issues), $28/2 yrs., $55/5 yrs. (ind.); $20/yr., $34/2 yrs., $65/5 yrs. (lib.); Single issues: $5.

*NewMyths: NEW MYTHS, Robert Mooney, ed., State U. of New York, P.O. Box 6000, Binghamton, NY 13902-6000. Issues indexed: (1:1). Subscriptions: $8.50/yr. (2 issues), $15/2 yrs. (ind.); $13/yr., $23/2 yrs. (libs.); Single issues: $5.

NewOR: NEW ORLEANS REVIEW, John Biguenet, John Mosier, eds., Box 195, Loyola U., New Orleans, LA 70118. Issues indexed: (17:1-4). Subscriptions: $25/yr. (ind.), $30/yr. (inst.), $35/yr. (for.); Single issues: $9.

NewRena: THE NEW RENAISSANCE, Louise T. Reynolds, ed., James E. A. Woodbury, po. ed., 9 Heath Road, Arlington, MA 02174. Issues indexed: (8:1, #24). Subscriptions: $12.50/3 issues, $23.50/6 issues; $14.50/3 issues, $27/6 issues (Canada, Mexico, Europe); $15.50/3 issues, $28.50/6 issues (elsewhere); Single issues: $6.

NewRep: THE NEW REPUBLIC, Martin Peretz, ed., Richard Howard, po. ed., 1220 19th St. NW, Washington, DC 20036. Issues indexed: (202:1-26, 203:1-27). Subscriptions: $9.97/yr., $84.97/yr. (Canada), $99.97/yr. (elsewhere). Back issues: $3.50. Single issues: $2.95. Subscription Service Dept., The New Republic, P.O. Box 56515, Boulder, CO 80322.

NewYorker: THE NEW YORKER, 25 W. 43rd St., New York, NY 10036. Issues indexed: (65:46-52, 65:1-46). Subscriptions: $32/yr., $52/2 yrs.; $50/yr. (Canada); $56/yr. (other for.); Single issues: $1.75; Subscription correspondence to: Box 56447, Boulder, CO 80322.

*NewYorkQ: THE NEW YORK QUARTERLY, William Packard, ed., P.O. Box 693, Old Chelsea Station, New York, NY 10113. Issues indexed: (41-43). Subscriptions: $15/yr., $30/2 yrs., $45/3 yrs.; $25/yr. (lib.); plus $5/yr. (for.); Single issues: $6; subscription address: 302 Neville Hall, U. of Maine, Orono, ME 04469.

NewYRB: THE NEW YORK REVIEW OF BOOKS, Robert B. Silvers, Barbara Epstein, eds., 250 W. 57th St., New York, NY 10107. Issues indexed: (36:21/22, 37:1-20). Subscriptions: $39/yr.; Single issues: $2.50; NY Review of Books, Subscription Service Dept., P.O. Box 2094, Knoxville, IA 50197-2094.

Nimrod: NIMROD, Francine Ringold, ed., Manly Johnson, po. ed., Arts and Humanities Council of Tulsa, 2210 S. Main St., Tulsa, OK 74114. Issues indexed: (33:2, 34:1). Subscriptions: $10/yr. (2 issues), $18/2 yrs., $26/3 yrs.; $13/yr. (for.); Single issues: $6.95.

Periodicals Indexed

NoAmR: THE NORTH AMERICAN REVIEW, Robley Wilson, Jr., ed., Peter Cooley, po. ed., U. of Northern Iowa, Cedar Falls, IA 50614. Issues indexed: (275:1-4). Subscriptions: $14/yr., $17/yr. (Canada, Latin America), $18/yr. (elsewhere); Single issues: $4, $5 (Canada).

NoDaQ: NORTH DAKOTA QUARTERLY, Robert W. Lewis, ed., Jay Meek, po. ed., Box 8237, U. of North Dakota, Grand Forks, ND 58202-8237. Issues indexed: (58:1-4). Subscriptions: $15/yr., $20/yr. (inst.); $23/yr. (for. ind.), $28/yr. (for. inst.); Single issues: $5 (ind.), $7 (for.).

Northeast: NORTHEAST, John Judson, ed., Juniper Press, 1310 Shorewood Dr., La Crosse, WI 54601. Issues indexed: (Ser. 5:2-3). Subscriptions: $33 (2 issues, ind.), $38 (inst.), includes "books and gifts of the press" in addition to NORTHEAST; Single issues: $4.

*NorthStoneR: THE NORTH STONE REVIEW, James Naiden, ed., D Station, Box 14098, Minneapolis, MN 55414. Issues indexed: (9). Subscriptions: $15/yr. (2 issues); Single issues: $6.

Notus: NOTUS, New Writing, Pat Smith, ed., 2420 Walter Dr., Ann Arbor, MI 48103. Issues indexed: (5:1). Subscriptions: $10/yr. (2 issues, U.S. & Canada, ind.), $14/yr. (elsewhere), $20/yr. (inst.).

NowestR: NORTHWEST REVIEW, John Witte, ed. & po. ed., 369 PLC, U. of Oregon, Eugene, OR 97403. Issues indexed: (28:1-2, 28:3/29:1). Subscriptions: $14/yr. (3 issues), $26/2 yrs., $35/3 yrs.; $12/yr., $22/2 yrs. (stud.); plus $2/yr. (for.); Single issues: $5.

Obs: OBSIDIAN II: Black Literature in Review, Gerald Barrax, ed., Dept. of English, Box 8105, North Carolina State U., Raleigh, NC 27695-8105. Issues indexed: (5:1-3). Subscriptions: $12/yr. (3 issues), $20/2 yrs.; $13/yr. (Canada), $15/yr. (other for.); Single issues: $5; Double issues: $10.

OhioR: THE OHIO REVIEW, Wayne Dodd, ed., Ellis Hall, Ohio U., Athens, OH 45701-2979. Issues indexed: (45). Subscriptions: $12/yr. (3 issues), $30/3 yrs.; Single issues: $4.25.

Ometeca: OMETECA: Ciencia y Literatura, Science & Literature, Ciência e literatura, Rafael Catala, ed., P.O. Box 450, Corrales, NM 87048. Issues Indexed: (1:2/2:1). Subscriptions: $20/yr. (2 issues) (ind.), $30/yr. (inst.) (USA, Canada, Mexico); $33/yr. (elsewhere).

*OnTheBus: ONTHEBUS: A New Literary Magazine, Jack Grapes, ed., Bombshelter Press, 6421-1/2 Orange St., Los Angeles, CA 90048. Issues indexed: (5, 6/7). Subscriptions: $24/3 issues (ind.), $27/3 issues (inst.); Single issues: $9, plus $1 postage.

OntR: ONTARIO REVIEW, Raymond J. Smith, ed., 9 Honey Brook Dr., Princeton, NJ 08540. Issues indexed: (32-33). Subscriptions: $10/yr. (2 issues), $18/2 yrs., $24/3 yrs., plus $2/yr. (for.); Single issues: $4.95.

Os: OSIRIS, Andrea Moorhead, ed., Box 297, Deerfield, MA 01342. Issues indexed: (30-31). Subscriptions: $8/2 issues, $10/2 issues (inst.). Single issues: $4.

Outbr: OUTERBRIDGE, Charlotte Alexander, ed., English Dept. (A323), College of Staten Island, 715 Ocean Terrace, Staten Island, NY 10301. Issues indexed: (21). Subscriptions: $5/yr. (1 issue).

OxfordM: OXFORD MAGAZINE, Constance Pierce, editorial advisor, Bachelor Hall, Miami U., Oxford, OH 45056. Issues indexed: (6:1). Single issues: $4.

PacificR: THE PACIFIC REVIEW: A Magazine of Poetry and Prose, James Brown, faculty ed., Dept. of English, California State U., 5500 University Parkway, San Bernardino, CA 92407-2397. Issues indexed: (8). Single issues: $4; $6.50 (inst.). Published annually.

Periodicals Indexed

Paint: PAINTBRUSH: A Journal of Poetry, Translations, and Letters, Ben Bennani, ed., Northeast Missouri State U., Kirksville, MO 63501. Issues indexed: (17:33/34). Subscriptions: $9/yr. (2 issues, ind.), $12/yr. (inst.); Single & back issues: $7.

PaintedB: PAINTED BRIDE QUARTERLY, Louis Camp, Joanna DiPaolo, eds., Painted Bride Arts Center, 230 Vine St., Philadelphia, PA 19106. Issues indexed: (40/41). Subscriptions: $16/yr. (4 issues), $28/2 yrs., $20/yr. (lib, inst.); Single issues: $5. Distributed free to inmates.

PaperAir: PAPER AIR, Gil Ott, ed. and pub., Singing Horse Press, P.O. Box 40034, Philadelphia, PA 19106. Issues indexed: (4:3), "final issue".

ParisR: THE PARIS REVIEW, George A. Plimpton, Peter Matthiessen, Donald Hall, Robert B. Silvers, Blair Fuller, Maxine Groffsky, eds., Patricia Storace, po. ed., 541 East 72nd St., New York, NY 10021. Issues indexed: (32:114-117). Subscriptions: $20/4 issues, $40/8 issues, $60/12 issues, $1000/life, plus $6/4 issues (for.); Single issues: $6; Subscription address: 45-39 171st Place, Flushing, NY 11358.

*Parting: PARTING GIFTS, Borbert Bixby, ed., 3006 Stonecutter Ter., Greensboro, NC 27405. Issues indexed: (3:1-2). Subscriptions: $5/yr. (2 issues), $9/2 yrs., $13/3 yrs.; Single issues: $3.

PartR: PARTISAN REVIEW, William Phillips, ed., Boston U., 236 Bay State Rd., Boston, MA 02215. Issues indexed: (57:1-4). Subscriptions: $18/yr. (4 issues), $33/2 yrs., $47/3 yrs.; $21/yr., $36/2 yrs. (for.); $28/yr. (inst.); Single issues: $5 plus $1 per issue postage and handling.

PassN: PASSAGES NORTH, Ben Mitchell, ed., Mark Cox, po. ed., Kalamazoo College, 1200 Academy St., Kalamazoo, MI 49007. Issues indexed: (11:1-2). Subscriptions: $5/yr., $8/2 yrs; Single issues: $3.

*Pearl: PEARL, Joan Jobe Smith, Marilyn Johnson, Barbara Hauk, eds., 3030 E. 2nd St., Long Beach, CA 90803. Issues indexed: (10-12). Subscriptions: $10/yr. (ind.); $15/yr. (lib.); $25/yr. (patrons); Single issues: $5.

Pembroke: PEMBROKE MAGAZINE, Shelby Stephenson, ed., Box 60, Pembroke State U., Pembroke, NC 28372. Issues indexed: (22). Subscriptions: $5/issue (USA, Canada, Mexico), $5.50/issue (for.).

PennR: THE PENNSYLVANIA REVIEW, Ed Ochester, executive ed., Deborah Pursifull, ed., Jan Beatty, po. ed., 526 Cathedral of Learning, U. of Pittsburgh, Pittsburgh, PA 15260. Issues indexed: (4:2). Subscriptions: $10/yr. (2 issues), $18/2 yrs.; Single issues: $5.

Pequod: PEQUOD, Mark Rudman, ed., Dept. of English, Room 200, New York U., 19 University Place, New York, NY 10003. Issues indexed: (31). Subscriptions: $10/yr. (2 issues), $18/2 yrs. (ind.); $17/yr., $30/2 yrs. (inst.); plus $3/yr. (for.); Single issues: $7.50.

Pig: PIG IRON, Jim Villani, Naton Leslie, eds., Pig Iron Press, P.O. Box 237, Youngstown, OH 44501. Issues indexed: (16). Single issues: $9.95.

PikeF: THE PIKESTAFF FORUM, Robert D. Sutherland, James R. Scrimgeour, eds./pubs., P.O. Box 127, Normal, IL 61761. Issues indexed: No 1990 issues published. Subscriptions: $10/6 issues; Single issues: $2.

Plain: PLAINSONGS, Dwight Marsh, ed., Dept. of English, Hastings College, Hastings, NE 68902. Issues indexed: (10:2-3, 11:1). Subscriptions: $9/yr. (3 issues).

Ploughs: PLOUGHSHARES, DeWitt Henry, executive director, Joyce Peseroff, po. ed., Division of Writing, Publishing and Literature, Emerson College, 100 Beacon St., Boston, MA 02116. Issues indexed: (16:1, 2/3, 4). Subscriptions: $15/yr. (ind.), $19/yr. (for. ind.); $18/yr. (inst.), $22/yr. (for. inst.). Single issues: $7.95.

Poem: POEM, Huntsville Literary Association, Nancy Frey Dillard, ed., c/o English Dept., U. of Alabama, Huntsville, AL 35899. Issues indexed: (63-64). Subscriptions: $10/yr.; Back issues: $5; subscription address: Huntsville Literary Association, P.O. Box 919,, Huntsville, AL 35804.

PoetC: POET AND CRITIC, Neal Bowers, ed., 203 Ross Hall, Iowa State U., Ames, IA 50011. Issues indexed: (21:2-4, 22:1); 21:4 is a special issue: "Five Years of Iowa Literary Awards." Subscriptions: Iowa State U. Press, South State St., Ames, IA 50010, $16/yr. (3 issues), plus $3/yr. (for.); Single issues: $6.

PoetL: POET LORE, Philip K. Jason, Roland Flint, Barbara Goldberg, executive eds., The Writer's Center, 7815 Old Georgetown Rd., Bethesda, MD 20814. Issues Indexed: (85:1-4). Subscriptions: $8/yr. (Writer's Center members); $12/yr. (ind.); $20/yr. (inst.), plus $5/yr. (for.); Single issues: $4.50; Samples: $4.

Poetry: POETRY, Joseph Parisi, ed., 60 W. Walton St., Chicago, IL 60610. Issues indexed: (155:4-6, 156:1-6, 157:1-3). Subscriptions: $25/yr. (ind.); $31/yr. (for.); $27/yr. (inst.); $33/yr. (for. inst.); Single issues: $2.50 plus $1 postage; Back issues: $3 plus $1 postage.

*PoetryC: POETRY CANADA, Barry Dempster, po. ed., P.O. Box 1061, Kingston, Ont. K7L 4Y5 Canada. Issues indexed: (11:1-4). Subscriptions: $16.05/4 issues (ind.); $32.10/4 issues (inst.); Back issues: $5; Single issues: $3.95.

PoetryE: POETRY EAST, Richard Jones, ed., Dept. of English, 802 W. Belden Ave., DePaul Univ., Chicago, IL 60614. Issues indexed: (29-30). Subscriptions: $10/yr.; Single issues: $7-$8.

PoetryNW: POETRY NORTHWEST, David Wagoner, ed., U. of Washington, 4045 Brooklyn Ave., NE, Seattle, WA 98105. Issues indexed: (31:1-4); Note: 31:1 has "XXX, number 4" on cover, in error. Subscriptions: $10/yr., $12/yr. (for.); Single issues: $3, $3.50 (for.).

*PoetryUSA: POETRY USA, National Poetry Association, Jack Foley, ed., 2569 Maxwell Ave., Oakland, CA 94601. Issues indexed: (5:1-3) plus Winter 90 (unnumbered). Subscriptions: $7.50/yr.; subscription address: Fort Mason Center, Bldg. D, San Francisco, CA 94123.

PottPort: THE POTTERSFIELD PORTFOLIO: New Writing From Atlantic Canada, Peggy Amirault, Barbara Cottrell, Donalee Moulton-Barrett, eds., 19 Oakhill Dr, Halifax, Nova Scotia B3M 2V3 Canada. Issues indexed: (11-12). Subscriptions: $12/3 yrs. (3 issues, ind.), $15/3 yrs. (inst.); $15/3 yrs. (USA, for. ind.); $18/3 yrs. (USA, for. inst.); Single issues: $4.50.

PraF: PRAIRIE FIRE: A Canadian Magazine of New Writing, Andris Taskans, managing ed., Di Brandt, po. ed., 423-100 Arthur Street, Winnipeg, Manitoba R3B 1H3 Canada. Issues indexed: (11:1-4, #50-53). Subscriptions: $22/yr., $40/2 yrs. (ind.); $28/yr. (inst.), plus $4 (USA), plus $8 (for.); Single issues: $6.95-11.95.

PraS: PRAIRIE SCHOONER, Hilda Raz, ed., 201 Andrews Hall, U. of Nebraska, Lincoln, NE 68588-0334. Issues indexed: (64:1-4). Subscriptions: $15/yr., $28/2 yrs., $39/3 yrs. (ind.); $19/yr. (lib.); Single issues: $4.

Prima: PRIMAVERA, Lisa Grayson, Elizabeth Harter, Ruth Young, eds., 700 E. 61st St, Box 37-7547, Chicago, IL 60637. Issues indexed: No 1990 issues published; vol. 14/15 published in 1991. Single issues: $6-7; Back issues: $5-6.

Quarry: QUARRY, Steven Heighton, ed., P.O. Box 1061, Kingston, Ontario K7L 4Y5 Canada. Issues indexed: (39:1-4). Subscriptions: $18/yr. (4 issues), $32/2 yrs. (8 issues); Single issues: $5.

QRL: QUARTERLY REVIEW OF LITERATURE, T. & R. Weiss, 26 Haslet Ave., Princeton, NJ 08540. Issues indexed: No 1990 issues published. Subscriptions: $20/2 volumes (paper), $20/volume (cloth, inst.).

Periodicals Indexed

QW: QUARTERLY WEST, C. F. Pinkerton, Tom Schmid, eds., 317 Olpin Union, U. of Utah, Salt Lake City, UT 84112. Issues indexed: (30-31). Subscriptions: $8.50/yr. (2 issues), $16/2 yrs.; $12.50/yr., $24/2 yrs. (for.); Single issues: $4.50.

RagMag: RAG MAG, Beverly Voldseth, ed. & pub., Black Hat Press, Box 12, Goodhue, MN 55027. Issues indexed: (7:2, 8:1-2). Subscriptions: $8/yr. (2 issues), $12/yr. (inst.); Single issues: $4.50.

Rampike: RAMPIKE, Karl Jirgens, Jim Francis, James Gray, eds., 95 Rivercrest Road, Toronto, Ontario M6S 4H7 Canada. Issues indexed: No 1990 issues received. Subscriptions: $14/yr. (2 issues); Single issues: $7.

Raritan: RARITAN: A Quarterly Review, Richard Poirier, ed., Rutgers U., 165 College Ave., New Brunswick, NJ 08903. Issues indexed: (9:3-4, 10:1-2). Subscriptions: $16/yr., $26/2 yrs. (ind.); $20/yr., $30/2 yrs. (inst.); plus $4/yr (for.); Single issues: $5; Back issues: $6.

RedBass: RED BASS, Jay Murphy, ed., 2425 Burgundy St., New Orleans, LA 70117. Issues indexed: No 1990 issues received. Subscriptions: $10/2 issues (ind.), $15 (inst., for.); Single issues: $5.

RiverC: RIVER CITY (formerly MEMPHIS STATE REVIEW), Sharon Bryan, ed., Dept. of English, Memphis State U., Memphis, TN 38152. Issues indexed: (10:2, 11:1). Subscriptions: $6/yr. (ind., 2 issues), $7/yr. (inst).; Single issues: $4.

RiverS: RIVER STYX, Jennifer Atkinson, ed., 14 South Euclid, St. Louis, MO 63108. Issues indexed: (31-32). Subscriptions: $20/yr. (3 issues, ind.); $38/yr. (inst.); Single issues: $7.

Rohwedder: ROHWEDDER, Nancy Antell, Robert Dassanowsky-Harris, Hans Jürgen Schacht, eds., P.O. Box 29490, Los Angeles, CA 90029. Issues indexed: (5). Subscriptions: $12/4 issues (USA, Canada, Mexico, ind.); $18/4 issues (inst.); $16/4 issues (other for., surface mail, plus $1/copy airmail); Single issues: $4.

Salm: SALMAGUNDI, Robert Boyers, ed., Skidmore College, Saratoga Springs, NY 12866. Issues indexed: (85/86, 87, 88/89). Subscriptions: $12/yr., $18/2 yrs. (ind.); $16/yr., $25/2 yrs. (inst.); Plus $2/yr. (for.); Sample issues: $4; Single issues: $5; Dougle issues: $8.

Screens: SCREENS AND TASTED PARALLELS, Terrel Hale, ed. & pub., 3032 Emerson St., Palo Alto, CA 94306. Issues indexed: (1). Subscriptions: $10/2 issues (ind.); $15 (inst.); Single issues: $6.

SenR: SENECA REVIEW, Deborah Tall, ed., Hobart & William Smith Colleges, Geneva, NY 14456. Issues indexed: (20:1-2). Subscriptions: $8/yr. (2 issues), $15/2 yrs.; Single issues: $5.

Sequoia: SEQUOIA: The Stanford Literary Journal, Annie Finch, po. ed., Storke Publications Building, Stanford U., Stanford, CA 94305. Issues indexed: (33:2). Subscriptions: $10/yr. (2 issues), $11/yr. (for.), $15/yr. (inst.); Single issues: $5.

SewanR: THE SEWANEE REVIEW, George Core, ed., U. of the South, Sewanee, TN 37375. Issues indexed: (98:1-2). Subscriptions: $15/yr., $27/2 yrs., $38/3 yrs. (ind.); $20/yr., $37/2 yrs., $54/3 yrs. (inst.); plus $4/yr. (for.); Single issues: $5; Back issues: $7-10.

*ShadowP: SHADOW PLAY, Jan Bender and Joe Zanoni, eds., Landside Press, Grand Isle, VT 05458. Issues indexed: (1). Single issues: $3.

Shen: SHENANDOAH, Dabney Stuart, ed., Washington and Lee U., Box 722, Lexington, VA 24450. Issues indexed: (40:1-4). Subscriptions: $11/yr., $18/2 yrs., $25/3 yrs.; $14/yr., $24/2 yrs., $33/3 yrs. (for.); Single issues: $3.50; Back issues: $6.

*Shiny: SHINY: The Magazine of the Future, Michael Friedman, ed. & pub., 39 E. 12th St., Suite 603, New York, NY 10003. Issues indexed: (5). Subscriptions: $12/4 issues; Single issues: $3.50.

17

Periodicals Indexed

SilverFR: SILVERFISH REVIEW, Rodger Moody, ed., P.O. Box 3541, Eugene, OR 97403. Issues indexed: (19). Subscriptions: $9/3 issues (ind.), $12/3 issues (inst.), Single issues: $4.

SingHM: SING HEAVENLY MUSE!: Women's Poetry and Prose, Ruth Berman, Bonnie Fisher, Joline Gitis, Carol Masters, Sue Ann Martinson, Kathleen Todd, Diane Rubright, Rafael Tilton, Linda Webster, eds, P.O. Box 13320, Minneapolis, MN 55414. Issues indexed: (17-18). Subscriptions: $14/2 issues, $19/3 issues, $36/6 issues (ind.), $21/3 issues, $40/6 issues (inst.); $16/3 issues (low income); Single issues: $7.

SinW: SINISTER WISDOM: A Journal for the Lesbian Imagination in the Arts and Politics, Elana Dykewomon, ed. & pub., P.O. Box 3252, Berkeley, CA 94703. Issues indexed: (40-42). Subscriptions: $17/yr. (4 issues), $30/2 yrs. (ind.); $30/yr. (inst.); $22/yr. (for.); $6-10/yr. (hardship); Free on request to women in prisons and mental institutions; Single issues: $5.

SlipS: SLIPSTREAM, Robert Borgatti, Livio Farallo, Dan Sicoli, eds., Box 2071, New Market Station, Niagara Falls, NY 14301. Issues indexed: (10). Subscriptions: $7.50/2 issues; Single issues: $4.

SmPd: THE SMALL POND MAGAZINE OF LITERATURE, Napoleon St. Cyr, ed., pub., P.O. Box 664, Stratford, CT 06497. Issues indexed: (27:1-3, #78-80). Subscriptions: $7/yr. (3 issues), $13/2 yrs., $19/3 yrs.; Single issues: $3.

Sonora: SONORA REVIEW, Martha Ostheimer, Laurie Schorr, eds, Debra Gregerman, po. ed., Dept. of English, U. of Arizona, Tucson, AZ 85721. Issues indexed: (18-19). Subscriptions: $8/yr. (2 issues); Single issues: $5.

SoCaR: SOUTH CAROLINA REVIEW, Richard J. Calhoun, executive ed., Dept. of English, Clemson U., Clemson, SC 29634-1503. Issues indexed: (22:2, 23:1). Subscriptions: $7/yr., $13/2 yrs. (USA, Canada, Mexico); $8/yr., $15/2 yrs. (inst.); plus $.50/yr. (other for.); Back issues: $5.

SoCoast: SOUTH COAST POETRY JOURNAL, John J. Brugaletta, ed., English Dept., California State U., Fullerton, CA 92634. Issues indexed: (8-9). Subscriptions: $9/yr. (2 issues), $17/2 yrs. (ind.); $10/yr. (inst.); Single issues: $5.

SoDakR: SOUTH DAKOTA REVIEW, John R. Milton, ed., Dept. of English, U. of South Dakota, Box 111, U. Exchange, Vermillion, SD 57069. Issues indexed: (28:1-4). Subscriptions: $15/yr., $25/2 yrs. (USA, Canada); plus $1/yr. elsewhere; Single issues: $5.

SouthernHR: SOUTHERN HUMANITIES REVIEW, Dan R. Latimer, Thomas L. Wright, eds., R. T. Smith, po. ed., 9088 Haley Center, Auburn U., AL 36849. Issues indexed: (24:1-4). Subscriptions: $12/yr.; Single issues: $4.

SouthernPR: SOUTHERN POETRY REVIEW, Robert Grey, ed., English Dept., U. of North Carolina, Charlotte, NC 28223. Issues indexed: (30:1-2). Subscriptions: $6 yr.; Single issues: $3.50.

SouthernR: SOUTHERN REVIEW, James Olney, Dave Smith, eds., Louisiana State U., 43 Allen Hall, Baton Rouge, LA 70803. Issues indexed: (26:1-4). Subscriptions: $15/yr., $27/2 yrs., $38/3 yrs.; $30/yr., $52/2 yrs., $75/3 yrs. (inst.); Single issues: $5, $10 (inst.).

SouthwR: SOUTHWEST REVIEW, Willard Spiegelman, ed., Southern Methodist U., 6410 Airline Rd., Dallas, TX 75275. Issues indexed: (75:1-4). Subscriptions: $20/yr., $40/2 yrs., $50/3 yrs. (ind.); $25/yr. (inst.); Single issues: $5.

Sparrow: SPARROW POVERTY PAMPHLETS, Felix Stefanile, ed./pub., Sparrow Press, 103 Waldron St., West Lafayette, IN 47906. Issues indexed: (57). Subscriptions: $7.50/3 issues; Single issues: $3.

Periodicals Indexed

Spirit: THE SPIRIT THAT MOVES US, Morty Sklar, ed., pub., P.O. Box 820, Jackson Heights, NY 11372. Issues indexed: (10:1-2). Also published as monographs, "Speak to Me: Swedish-language Women Poets" (10:1, 1989, $8.75 paper, $14.75 cloth); "Free Parking" (10:2, 1990, $7).

SpiritSH: SPIRIT, David Rogers, ed., Seton Hall U., South Orange, NJ 07079. Issues indexed: No 1990 issues received; vol. 56 dated Spr-Sum 91. Subscriptions: $4/yr.; Single issues: $2.

SpoonRQ: THE SPOON RIVER QUARTERLY, Lucia Cordell Getsi, ed., English Dept., Illinois State U., Normal, IL 61761. Issues indexed: (15:1-4). Subscriptions: $12/yr.; $15/yr. (inst.); Single issues: $3; Anthology: $5.

Stand: STAND, Jessie Emerson, U.S.A. ed., P.O. Box 5923, Huntsville, AL 35814; Howard Fink, Canadian ed., 4054 Melrose Ave., Montreal, Quebec H4A 2S4 Canada. Issues indexed: (31:1-4). Subscriptions: $22/yr., $40/2 yrs.; $18/yr. (students, unwaged); Single issues: $6.50; U.S.A. distributor: Anton J. Mikovsky, 57 West 84th St., #1-C, New York, NY 10024.

Sulfur: SULFUR: A Literary Bi-Annual of the Whole Art, Clayton Eshleman, ed., English Dept., Eastern Michigan U., Ypsilanti, MI 48197. Issues indexed: (10:1-2, #26-27). Subscriptions: $12/2 issues (ind.), $17/2 issues (inst.), plus $3 (for.) or $8 for airmail postage; Single issues: $7.

SwampR: SWAMP ROOT, Al Masarik, ed., Route 2, Box 1098, Hiwassee One, Jacksboro, TN 37757. Issues indexed: (5-6). Subscriptions: $12/3 issues; $15/3 issues (inst.); Single issues: $5.

*SycamoreR: SYCAMORE REVIEW, Michael Kiser, ed., Helene Barker, po. ed., Dept. of English, Purdue U., West Lafayette, IN 47907. Issues indexed: (2:1-2). Subscriptions: $8/yr., $14/2 yrs.; Single issues: $4.

Talisman: TALISMAN: A Journal of Contemporary Poetry and Poetics, Edward Foster, ed., Box 1117, Hoboken, NJ 07030. Issues indexed: (4-5). Subscriptions: $9/yr. (2 issues); $13/yr. (inst.); plus $2/yr. (for.); Single issues: $5.

TampaR: TAMPA REVIEW: Literary Journal of the University of Tampa, Richard Mathews, ed., Donald Morrill, Kathryn Van Spanckeren, po. eds., Box 19F, U. of Tampa, 401 W. Kennedy Blvd., Tampa, FL 33606-1490. Issues indexed: (3). Subscriptions: $7.50/yr. (1 issue); plus $2.50/yr. (for.); Single issues: $7.95 plus $1 postage.

TarRP: TAR RIVER POETRY, Luke Whisnant, ed., Dept. of English, General Classroom Bldg., East Carolina U., Greenville, NC 27858-4353. Issues indexed: (29:2, 230:1). Subscriptions: $6/yr (2 issues), $10/2 yrs.; Single issues: $3.

Temblor: TEMBLOR, Contemporary Poets, Leland Hickman, ed., 4624 Cahuenga Blvd., #307, North Hollywood, CA 91602. Issues indexed: No 1990 issues received. Subscriptions: $16/2 issues, $30/4 issues (ind.); $20/2 issues, $40/4 issues (inst.); plus $2.50/issue (for.); Single issues: $8.50 (ind.), $10 (inst.).; Back issues: $12.50; plus $2.50 (for.).

TexasR: TEXAS REVIEW, Paul Ruffin, ed., English Dept., Sam Houston State U., Huntsville, TX 77341. Issues indexed: (11:3/4); vol. 11, nos. 1-2 received to late for indexing & will be included in the 1991 volume.. Subscriptions: $10/yr., $10.50/yr. (Canada), $11/yr. (for.); Single issues: $5.

ThRiPo: THREE RIVERS POETRY JOURNAL, Gerald Costanzo, ed., Three Rivers Press, P.O. Box 21, Carnegie-Mellon U., Pittsburgh, PA 15213. Issues indexed: (35/36). Subscriptions: $10/4 issues; Single issues: $2.50; Double issues: $5.

Thrpny: THE THREEPENNY REVIEW, Wendy Lesser, ed., pub., P.O. Box 9131, Berkeley, CA 94709. Issues indexed: (40-43). Subscriptions: $10/yr., $16/2 yrs., $18/yr. (surface for.), $24/yr. (airmail for.); Single issues: $3.

19

Timbuktu: TIMBUKTU, Molly Turner, ed., pub., RR 1, Box 758, Scottsville, VA 24590. Issues indexed: No 1990 issues received. Subscriptions: $6/yr. (2 issues); $10/yr. (lib.); Single issues: $5.

Trans: TRANSLATION, The Journal of Literary Translation, Frank MacShane, Lane Dunlop, Julio Marzan, eds., The Translation Center, 412 Dodge Hall, Columbia U., New York, NY 10027. Issues indexed: (23-24). Subscriptions: $17/yr. (2 issues), $30/2 yrs.; Single issues: $9.

Tribe: TRIBE: An American Gay Journal, Bernard Rabb, ed., Columbia Publishing Co., 234 E. 25th St., Baltimore, MD 21218. Issues indexed: No 1990 issues received. Subscriptions: $22/yr. (4 issues), $40/2 yrs., $58/3 yrs.; $26/yr., $48/2 yrs., $70/3 yrs. (for.); Single issues: $6 plus $1.50 postage and handling, $2.50 (for.).

TriQ: TRIQUARTERLY, Reginald Gibbons, ed., Northwestern U., 2020 Ridge Ave., Evanston, IL 60208. Issues indexed: (78-80). Subscriptions: $18/yr. (3 issues), $32/2 yrs., $250/life (ind.); $26/yr., $44/2 yrs., $300/life (inst.), plus $4/yr. (for.); Single issues: cost varies; Sample copies: $4.

Turnstile: TURNSTILE, Jill Benz, Lindsey Crittenden, Ann Biester Deane, Twisne Fan, Sara Gordonson, John Paul Jones, Philip Metcalf, Mitchell Nauffts, Paolo Pepe, Jonah Winter, George Witte, eds., 175 Fifth Avenue, Suite 2348, New York, NY 10010. Issues indexed: (2:1-2). Subscriptions: $12/2 issues, $22/4 issues; Single issues: $6.50.

US1: US 1 WORKSHEETS, Sondra Gash, ed., Jean Hollander, Frederick Tibbetts, po eds., US 1 Poets' Cooperative, P.O. Box 1, Ringoes, NJ 08551. Issues indexed: None published in 1990; nos. 24/25 published in 1991. Subscriptions: $8/2 double issues; Single issues: $5.

Verse: VERSE, Henry Hart, U. S. ed., Dept. of English, College of William and Mary, Williamsburg, VA 23185. Issues indexed: (7:1-3). Subscriptions: $12/yr. (3 issues); Single issues: $4.

VirQR: THE VIRGINIA QUARTERLY REVIEW: A National Journal of Literature and Discussion, Staige D. Blackford, ed., Gregory Orr, po. consultant, One West Range, Charlottesville, VA 22903. Issues indexed: (66:1-4). Subscriptions: $15/yr., $22/2 yrs., $30/3 yrs. (ind.); $22/yr., $30/2 yrs., $50/3 yrs. (inst.); plus $3/yr. (for.); Single issues: $5.

Vis: VISIONS INTERNATIONAL, Bradley R. Strahan, po. ed., pub., Black Buzzard Press, 1110 Seaton Lane, Falls Church, VA 22046. Issues indexed: (32-34). Subscriptions: $14/yr., $27/2 yrs. (ind.); $42/3 yrs. (lib.).; Single issues: $5.

WashR: WASHINGTON REVIEW, Clarissa K. Wittenberg, ed., P.O. Box 50132, Washington, DC 20091. Issues indexed: (15:5-6. 16:1-4). Subscriptions: $12/yr. (6 issues), $20/2 yrs.; Single issues: $3.

WeberS: WEBER STUDIES: An Interdisciplinary Humanities Journal, Neila Seshachari, ed., Weber State College, Ogden, UT 84408-1214. Issues indexed: (7:1-2). Subscriptions: $5/yr. (2 issues), $10/yr. (inst.); plus actual postage extra per year (for.); Back issues: $5; Single issues: $2.75.

WebR: WEBSTER REVIEW, Nancy Schapiro, ed., Pamela White Hadas, Jerred Metz, po. eds., Webster U., 470 E. Lockwood, Webster Groves, MO 63119. Issues indexed: (14:2). Subscriptions: $5/yr. (2 issues); Single issues: $2.50.

WestB: WEST BRANCH, Karl Patten, Robert Taylor, eds., Bucknell Hall, Bucknell U., Lewisburg, PA 17837. Issues indexed: (26-27). Subscriptions: $7/yr. (2 issues), $11/2 yrs.; Single issues: $4.

WestCL: WEST COAST LINE: A Journal of Contemporary Writing and Criticism (formerly West Coast Review), Roy Miki, ed., English Dept., Simon Fraser U., Burnaby, B.C. V5A 1S6 Canada. Issues indexed: (24:1-3). Subscriptions: $18/yr. (ind., 3 issues), $24/yr. (inst.); Single issues: $8.

Periodicals Indexed

WestHR: WESTERN HUMANITIES REVIEW, Barry Weller, eds., Richard Howard, po. ed., U. of Utah, Salt Lake City, UT 84112. Issues indexed: (44:1-4). Subscriptions: $18/yr. (4 issues, ind.), $24/yr. (inst.); Single issues: $5.

WilliamMR: THE WILLIAM AND MARY REVIEW, Christopher Vitiello, ed., Paula Hopping, po. ed., College of William and Mary, Williamsburg, VA 23185. Issues indexed: (28). Subscriptions: $4.50/single issue, plus $1.50 (for.); Single issues: $5.

*WillowR: WILLOW REVIEW, Paulette Roeske, ed., College of Lake County, 19351 w. Washington St., Grayslake, IL 60030-1198. Issues indexed: 1990.

WillowS: WILLOW SPRINGS, Nance Van Winckel, ed., Scott Starbuck, po. ed., Eastern Washington U., MS-1, Cheney, WA 99004-2496. Issues Indexed: (25-26). Subscriptions: $7/yr. (2 issues), $13/2 yrs.; Single issues: $4.

Wind: WIND, Quentin R. Howard, ed., RFD Route 1, Box 809K, Pikeville, KY 41501. Issues indexed: (20:66-67). Subscriptions: $7/3 issues (ind.), $8/3 issues (inst.), $12/3 issues (for.); Single issues: $2.50; $5 (for.).

WindO: THE WINDLESS ORCHARD, Robert Novak, ed., English Dept., Indiana-Purdue U., Fort Wayne, IN 46805. Issues indexed: (53). Subscriptions: $8/yr. (4 issues), $20/3 yrs.; Single issues: $3.

Witness: WITNESS, Peter Stine, ed., 31000 Northwestern Highway, Suite 200, Farmington Hills, MI 48018. Issues indexed: (4:1); vol. 3, no. 4 not received, "no poetry"; publication suspended after vol. 4, no. 1, but will resume in 1991. Subscriptions: $15/yr. (4 issues), $28/2 yrs.; $20/yr., $38/2 yrs. (inst.); plus $4/yr. (for.); Single copies: $6.

WorldO: WORLD ORDER, Firuz Kazemzadeh, Betty J. Fisher, Howard Garey, Robert H. Stockman, James D. Stokes, eds., National Spiritual Assembly of the Bahá'ís of the United States, 415 Linden Ave., Wilmette, IL 60091. Issues indexed: (22:3/4, 23:1/2-3/4). Subscriptions: $10/yr., $18/2 yrs. (USA, Canada, Mexico); $15/yr., $28/2 yrs. (elsewhere); $20/yr., $38/2 yrs. (for. airmail); Single issues: $3.

WormR: THE WORMWOOD REVIEW, Marvin Malone, ed., P.O. Box 4698, Stockton, CA 95204-0698. Issues indexed: (30:1, 2/3, 4; #117, 118/119, 120). Subscriptions: $8/4 issues (ind.), $10/4 issues (inst.); Single issues: $4.

Writ: WRIT, Roger Greenwald, ed., Innis College, U. of Toronto, 2 Sussex Ave., Toronto, Canada M5S 1J5. Issues indexed: (21-22). Subscriptions: $15/2 issues (ind.), $18/2 issues (inst.); same amount in U.S. funds outside Canada; Back issues: $7.50-15.

Writer: THE WRITER, Sylvia K. Burack, ed., pub., 120 Boylston St., Boston, MA 02116. Issues indexed: (103:1-12). Subscriptions: $24.75/yr., $48/2 yrs., $71.50/3 yrs.; plus $8/yr. (for.); $10/6 issues for new subscribers; Single issues: $2.

WritersF: WRITERS' FORUM, Alexander Blackburn, Victoria McCabe, Craig Lesley, Bret Lott, eds., P.O. Box 7150, U. of Colorado, Colorado Springs, CO 80933-7150. Issues indexed: (16). Subscriptions: $8.95/yr. plus $1.05 postage and handling; Back issue sample: $5.95 plus $1.05 postage and handling..

YaleR: THE YALE REVIEW, Penelope Laurans, ed., J. D. McClatchy, po. ed., Yale U., 1902A Yale Station, New Haven, CT 06520. Issues indexed: (79:2-4); publication discontinued following vol. 79, no. 4.

YellowS: YELLOW SILK, Journal of Erotic Arts, Lily Pond, ed., pub., P.O. Box 6374, Albany, CA 94706. Issues indexed: (33-35). Subscriptions: $24/yr. (ind.), $30/yr. (lib., inst.), plus $6/yr. (for. surface) or $20/yr. (for. air). Single issues: $6.

Zyzzyva: ZYZZYVA: The Last Word, West Coast Writers & Artists, Howard Junker, ed, 41 Sutter St., Suite 1400, San Francisco, CA 94104. Issues indexed: (6:1-4, #17-20). Subscriptions: $20/yr. (4 issues), $32/2 yrs. (ind.); $28/yr. (inst.); $30/yr. (for.); Single copies: $8 post paid.

Alphabetical List of Journals Indexed, with Acronyms

Abraxas : Abraxas
Acts: A Journal of New Writing : Acts
Aerial : Aerial
Agni : Agni
Alpha Beat Soup : AlphaBS
Amelia : Amelia
The American Poetry Review : AmerPoR
The American Scholar : AmerS
The American Voice : AmerV
The Americas Review : Americas
Another Chicago Magazine : AnotherCM
Antaeus : Antaeus
The Anthology of New England Writers : AnthNEW
The Antigonish Review : AntigR
The Antioch Review : AntR
Apalachee Quarterly : ApalQ
Arc : Arc
Areſto : Areſto
Artful Dodge : ArtfulD
Ascent : Ascent
Asylum : Asylum
The Atlantic : Atlantic
Avec : Avec

Ball State University Forum : BallSUF
Bamboo Ridge : BambooR
The Bellingham Review : BellR
Bellowing Ark : BellArk
The Beloit Poetry Journal : BelPoJ
The Bilingual Review/La Revista Bilingüe : BilingR
Black American Literature Forum : BlackALF
Black Bear Review : BlackBR
Black Warrior Review : BlackWR
Blue Buildings : BlueBldgs
Blueline : Blueline
Bogg : Bogg
Bomb Magazine : Bomb
Boston Review : BostonR
Boulevard : Boulevard
Brooklyn Review : BrooklynR

Caliban : Caliban
California Quarterly : CalQ
Callaloo : Callaloo
Calyx : Calyx
Canadian Literature : CanLit
The Cape Rock : CapeR
The Capilano Review : CapilR
Carolina Quarterly : CarolQ
The Centennial Review : CentR
Central Park : CentralP
Chaminade Literary Review : ChamLR
Changing Men : ChangingM
The Chariton Review : CharR
The Chattahoochee Review : ChatR
Chelsea : Chelsea

Alphabetical List of Journals

Chicago Review : ChiR
Chiron Review : ChironR
The Christian Century : ChrC
Cimarron Review : CimR
Cincinnati Poetry Review : CinPR
City Lights Review : CityLR
Clockwatch Review : ClockR
Coal City Review : CoalC
College English : ColEng
Colorado Review : ColR
Columbia : Colum
Commonweal : Comm
Conditions : Cond
Confrontation : Confr
Conjunctions : Conjunc
The Connecticut Poetry Review : ConnPR
Contact II : Contact
Context South : ContextS
Crab Creek Review : CrabCR
Crazyhorse : Crazy
Cream City Review : CreamCR
Cross-Canada Writers' Quarterly : CrossC
Crosscurrents : CrossCur
Crucible : Crucible
Cuadernos de Poética : CuadP
Cumberland Poetry Review : CumbPR
Cutbank : CutB

Dandelion : Dandel
Denver Quarterly : DenQ
Descant : Descant
Dog River Review : DogRR
Dusty Dog : DustyD

Emerald Coast Review : EmeraldCR
English Journal : EngJ
Epoch : Epoch
Event: The Douglas College Review : Event
The Evergreen Chronicles : EvergreenC

Farmer's Market : Farm
Field: Contemporary Poetry and Poetics : Field
Five Fingers Riview : FiveFR
The Florida Review : FloridaR
Footwork : Footwork
Four Quarters : FourQ
Free Lunch : FreeL

Gargoyle Magazine : Gargoyle
Georgia Review : GeoR
Gettysburg Review : GettyR
Graham House Review : GrahamHR
Grain : Grain
Grand Street : GrandS
Green Mountains Review : GreenMR
The Greensboro Review : GreensboroR
Gypsy Literary Magazine : Gypsy

The Hampden-Sydney Poetry Reivew : HampSPR
Hanging Loose : HangL
Harper's Magazine : Harp
The Harvard Advocate : HarvardA
Hawaii Review : HawaiiR
Hayden's Ferry Review : HayF
Heaven Bone : HeavenB

Helicon Nine : HeliconN
Hellas : Hellas
High Plains Literary Review : HighP
Hiram Poetry Review : HiramPoR
The Hollins Critic : HolCrit
The Hudson Review : Hudson

Imagine : Imagine
Indiana Review : IndR
Interim : Interim
International Poetry Review : InterPR
Inti : Inti
Iowa Review : Iowa

The Jacaranda Review : Jacaranda
The James White Review : JamesWR
The Journal : Journal
The Journal of New Jersey Poets : JINJPo

Kaleidoscope : Kaleid
Kalliope : Kalliope
Kansas Quarterly : KanQ
Kenyon Review : KenR
Key West Review : KeyWR

Lactuca : Lactuca
The Lake Street Review : LakeSR
Laurel Review : LaurelR
Light Year : LightY
Linden Lane Magazine : LindLM
The Literary Review : LitR
Lullwater Review : LullwaterR
Lyra : Lyra

The Malahat Review : MalR
Manhattan Poetry Review : ManhatPR
The Manhattan Review : ManhatR
Manoa : Manoa
The Massachusetts Review : MassR
Memphis State Review : *Name changed to* River City : RiverC
Mester : Mester
Michigan Quarterly Review : MichQR
Mid-American Review : MidAR
The Midwest Quarterly : MidwQ
Mildred : Mildred
The Minnesota Review : MinnR
Mississippi Review : MissR
The Missouri Review : MissouriR
Moody Street Irregulars : MoodySI
Mss : MSS

The Nation : Nat
Negative Capability : NegC
New American Writing : NewAW
New Delta Review : NewDeltaR
New England Review : NewEngR
New Letters : NewL
New Myths : NewMyths
New Orleans Review : NewOR
The New Renaissance : NewRena
The New Republic : NewRep
The New York Quarterly : NewYorkQ
The New York Review of Books : NewYRB
The New Yorker : NewYorker
Nimrod : Nimrod

Alphabetical List of Journals

The North American Review : NoAmR
North Dakota Quarterly : NoDaQ
The North Stone Review : NorthStoneR
Northeast : Northeast
Northwest Review : NowestR
Notus : Notus

Obsidian II : Obs
The Ohio Reivew : OhioR
Ometeca : Ometeca
Ontario Review : OntR
OnTheBus : OnTheBus
Osiris : Os
Outerbridge : Outbr
Oxford Magazine : OxfordM

Pacific Review : PacificR
Paintbrush : Paint
Painted Bride Quarterly : PaintedB
Paper Air : PaperAir
The Paris Review : ParisR
Parting Gifts : Parting
Partisan Review : PartR
Passages North : PassN
Pearl : Pearl
Pembroke Magazine : Pembroke
The Pennsylvania Review : PennR
Pequod : Pequod
Pig Iron : Pig
The Pikestaff Forum : PikeF
Plainsongs : Plain
Ploughshares : Ploughs
Poem : Poem
Poet And Critic : PoetC
Poet Lore : PoetL
Poetry : Poetry
Poetry Canada : PoetryC
Poetry East : PoetryE
Poetry Northwest : PoetryNW
Poetry USA : PoetryUSA
The Pottersfield Portfolio : PottPort
Prairie Fire : PraF
Prairie Schooner : PraS
Primavera : Prima

Quarry : Quarry
Quarterly Review of Literature : QRL
Quarterly West : QW

Rag Mag : RagMag
Rampike : Rampike
Raritan: A Quarterly Review : Raritan
Red Bass : RedBass
River City : RiverC
River Styx : RiverS
Rohwedder : Rohwedder

Salmagundi : Salm
Screens and Tasted Parallels : Screens
Seneca Review : SenR
Sequoia : Sequoia
The Sewanee Review : SewanR
Shadow Play : ShadowP
Shenandoah : Shen
Shiny : Shiny

Silverfish Review : SilverFR
Sing Heavenly Muse! : SingHM
Sinister Wisdom : SinW
Slipstream : SlipS
The Small Pond Magazine of Literature : SmPd
Sonora Review : Sonora
South Carolina Review : SoCaR
South Coast Poetry Journal : SoCoast
South Dakota Review : SoDakR
Southern Humanities Review : SouthernHR
Southern Poetry Review : SouthernPR
Southern Review : SouthernR
Southwest Review : SouthwR
Sparrow Poverty Pamphlets : Sparrow
Spirit : SpiritSH
The Spirit That Moves Us : Spirit
The Spoon River Quarterly : SpoonRQ
Stand : Stand
Sulfur : Sulfur
Swamp Root : SwampR
Sycamore Review : SycamoreR

Talisman : Talisman
Tampa Review : TampaR
Tar River Poetry : TarRP
Temblor : Temblor
Texas Review : TexasR
Three Rivers Poetry Journal : ThRiPo
The Threepenny Review : Thrpny
Timbuktu : Timbuktu
Translation : Translation
Tribe : Tribe
Triquarterly : TriQ
Turnstile : Turnstile

US 1 Worksheets : US1

Verse : Verse
The Virginia Quarterly Review : VirQR
Visions International : Vis

Washington Review : Wash
Weber Studies : WeberS
Webster Review : WebR
West Branch : WestB
West Coast Line (*formerly* West Coast Review) : WestCL
Western Humanities Review : WestHR
The William and Mary Review : WilliamMR
Willow Review : WillowR
Willow Springs : WillowS
Wind : Wind
The Windless Orchard : WindO
Witness : Witness
World Order : WorldO
The Wormwood Review : WormR
Writ : Writ
The Writer : Writer
Writers' Forum : WritersF

The Yale Review : YaleR
Yellow Silk : YellowS

Zyzzyva : Zyzzyva

The Author Index

1. AAFJES, Bertus
   "Master Frans" (Painting: Regents of the Old Men's Home by Frans Hals, tr. by Johanna H. Prins and Johanna W. Prins). [Trans] (24) Fall 90, p. 59-61.
2. AAL, Katharyn Machan
   "The Animals." [ChamLR] (3:2, #6) Spr 90, p. 109.
   "Beauty." [ChamLR] (4:1, #7) Fall 90, p. 116.
   "Dying." [ChamLR] (4:1, #7) Fall 90, p. 117.
   "Every Night She Dreams" (From "A Slow Bottle of Wine"). [Nimrod] (34:1) Fall-Wint 90, p. 42.
   "Helen." [Nimrod] (34:1) Fall-Wint 90, p. 43.
   "How to Eat in the House of Death." [ArtfulD] (18/19) 90, p. 58-59.
   "John Moody, 1888." [DogRR] (9:1, #17) Spr 90, p. 57.
   "Merville Findley, 1988." [DogRR] (9:1, #17) Spr 90, p. 56.
   "Midlife." [ChamLR] (3:2, #6) Spr 90, p. 110.
   "On the Eve of Hallow's Eve." [SenR] (20:2) Fall 90, p. 73.
   "St. Valentine's Day." [ChironR] (9:2) Sum 90, p. 20.
   "The Woman in the Brown Coat." [SwampR] (6) Sum-Fall 90, p. 41-43.
3. AALFS, Janet (Janet E.)
   "Leaf Machines." [EvergreenC] (6:1) Wint 90-Spr 91, p. 37.
   "Separation Ritual." [EvergreenC] (6:1) Wint 90-Spr 91, p. 52-53.
4. AARNES, William
   "Now That It's June." [PoetC] (22:1) Fall 90, p. 23.
   "Trespass." [PoetC] (22:1) Fall 90, p. 24.
5. AARON, Jonathan
   "The Last of the Medici." [NewRep] (202:21) 21 My 90, p. 36.
   "The Voice from Paxos." [NewYRB] (37:13) 16 Ag 90, p. 28.
6. ABBOT, Jesse
   "God's Torment" (Selections, tr. of Alain Bosquet). [Trans] (24) Fall 90, p. 213-217.
7. ABBOTT, Anthony (Anthony S.)
   "The Beginning." [SouthernPR] (30:1) Spr 90, p. 43-44.
   "Ely Cathedral: Toward Evensong." [Crucible] (26) Fall 90, p. 53-54.
   "The Muse Is Angry." [LullwaterR] (1:1) Spr 90, p. 36.
   "The Muse Is Gone." [LullwaterR] (1:1) Spr 90, p. 39.
   "The Muse Is Silent." [LullwaterR] (1:1) Spr 90, p. 38.
   "The Muse Is Sullen." [LullwaterR] (1:1) Spr 90, p. 37.
   "The Poet, the Lovers and the Nuns" (Sam Ragan Prize). [Crucible] (26) Fall 90, p. 51-52.
8. ABBOTT, Darleen B.
   "In Her Image." [EmeraldCR] (1990) c89, p. 66.
   "Pendulum." [EmeraldCR] (1990) c89, p. 66.
9. ABBOTT, Dickson
   "Heatwave." [Bogg] (62) 90, p. 41.
10. ABBOTT, Keith
   "Today at the Start." [OnTheBus] (2:1, #5) Spr 90, p. 11.
   "Today the Poetry Reading Review." [OnTheBus] (2:1, #5) Spr 90, p. 11.
11. ABE, Tamiko
   "Having come far on my journey" (tr. by Janet Lewis). [SouthernR] (26:1) Ja 90, p. 205.
12. ABEL, Ben
   "Nightmare Comfort." [CanLit] (124/125) Spr-Sum 90, p. 112.
13. ABELL, Steven
   "Pull Over." [Plain] (11:1) Fall 90, p. 24-25.
14. ABELLO, Montserrat
   "VI Variations" (from "L'infant i la Mort," 1989, tr. of Margarita Ballester). [PoetryC] (11:4) Wint 90, p. 21.
   "And Inside Me a Voice Tells Me" (tr. by the author, from "Foc a les mans," 1990). [PoetryC] (11:4) Wint 90, p. 20.
   "The Day of the Dead" (from "La pluja sobre els Palaus," 1990, tr. of Olga Xirinacs).

ABELLO
[PoetryC] (11:4) Wint 90, p. 23.
"Homage to Frida Kahlo" (from "Llengua Abolida," 1989, tr. of Maria Mercè Marçal).
[PoetryC] (11:4) Wint 90, p. 22.
"I Am Sure There Are Red Women" (from "Versos a Anais," 1989, tr. of Maria
Oleart). [PoetryC] (11:4) Wint 90, p. 23.
"I Will Tell You About" (from "Versos a Anais," 1989, tr. of Maria Oleart). [PoetryC]
(11:4) Wint 90, p. 23.
"If You Are Not There Anymore" (from "La pluja sobre els Palaus," 1990, tr. of Olga
Xirinacs). [PoetryC] (11:4) Wint 90, p. 23.
"It Seems That Everything" (tr. by the author, from "El blat del Temps," 1986).
[PoetryC] (11:4) Wint 90, p. 20.
"Moon Born from the Moon" (from "Versos a Anais," 1989, tr. of Maria Oleart).
[PoetryC] (11:4) Wint 90, p. 23.
"My Love without a Home" (from "Llengua Abolida," 1989, tr. of Maria Mercè
Marçal). [PoetryC] (11:4) Wint 90, p. 22.
"Secret" (from "La pluja sobre els Palaus," 1990, tr. of Olga Xirinacs). [PoetryC]
(11:4) Wint 90, p. 23.
"A Truce in January" (from "Kyparissia," 1980, tr. of Maria Angels Anglada).
[PoetryC] (11:4) Wint 90, p. 21.
"We Walk" (from "Estelles," 1978, tr. of Rosa Fabregat). [PoetryC] (11:4) Wint 90, p.
22.
"Who Knows What There Is Under This Mask" (tr. of Rosa Fabregat). [PoetryC]
(11:4) Wint 90, p. 22.
15. ABERNETHY, Hugh, Jr. (Hugh C., Jr.)
"Anxious About the Streak." [Confr] (44/45) Fall 90-Wint 91, p. 180-181.
"Finger-Stories in the Blue Room." [Confr] (44/45) Fall 90-Wint 91, p. 182.
"Lime Harbor." [KanQ] (22:3) Sum 90, p. 115.
16. ABOUZEID, Chris
"Joseph" (for Tania). [SouthernR] (26:3) Jl 90, p. 693-696.
17. ABRAMS, David
"Tracks." [ChrC] (107:8) 7 Mr 90, p. 246.
18. ABSE, Dannie
"Anti-Clockwise 1." [BelPoJ] (40:4) Sum 90, p. 9.
"Anti-Clockwise 2." [BelPoJ] (40:4) Sum 90, p. 9-10.
"Musical Moments." [Poetry] (156:5) Ag 90, p. 278-280.
19. ABU NUWAS
"Poem in Archaic Meter (Manhukah)" (tr. by Eric Ormsby). [Chelsea] (49) 90, p.
117-120.
"To His Mistress" (tr. by Ben Bennani). [Os] (30) Spr 90, p. 2.
20. ACHEBE, Chinua
"Agostinho Neto." [Callaloo] (13:1) Wint 90, p. 73.
"Butterfly." [Callaloo] (13:1) Wint 90, p. 81.
"Flying." [Callaloo] (13:1) Wint 90, p. 74-75.
"Knowing Robs Us." [Callaloo] (13:1) Wint 90, p. 78.
"A Mother in a Refugee Camp." [Callaloo] (13:1) Wint 90, p. 76.
"The Old Chief and the Census." [Callaloo] (13:1) Wint 90, p. 79-80.
"Pine Tree in Spring" (for Leon Damas). [Callaloo] (13:1) Wint 90, p. 77.
21. ACHTENBERG, Anya
"Shoes." [AmerPoR] (19:4) Jl-Ag 90, p. 14.
"The Street of the Lost Child." [AmerPoR] (19:4) Jl-Ag 90, p. 14.
"Tirza in the Land of Numbers." [AmerPoR] (19:4) Jl-Ag 90, p. 13.
22. ACHTERBERG, Gerrit
"Calamity" (tr. by Kees Snoek). [Vis] (34) 90, p. 33.
"Dream Judgment" (tr. by Kees Snoek). [Vis] (34) 90, p. 31.
"In Profundis" (tr. by Kees Snoek). [Vis] (33) 90, p. 47.
"Somnambule" (tr. by Kees Snoek). [Vis] (34) 90, p. 31.
"Thebe" (tr. by Kees Snoek). [Vis] (34) 90, p. 32.
23. ACKER, Kathy
"Ode to a Drunk Fly" (in the tradition of landscape poetry). [Gargoyle] (37/38) 90, p.
25.
"Poem in the Tradition of the Poet Maudit." [Gargoyle] (37/38) 90, p. 25.
24. ACKERMAN, Diane
"Antarctica Considers Her Explorers." [MichQR] (29:2) Spr 90, p. 209-210.
"Painter." [HampSPR] (Anthology 1975-1990) 90, p. 59.
"When Handling *Desolata*." [MichQR] (29:2) Spr 90, p. 210-212.
25. ACOSTA, Oscar
"Grandfathers" (tr. by Ann Neelon). [PoetryE] (30) Fall 90, p. 29.

26. ADAMS, Anna
"Ballad of Captain Jack Macfadden." [NewYorkQ] (42) Sum 90, p. 67.
"E-li, E-li, La-ma Sa-bach-tha-ni?" [NewYorkQ] (43) Fall 90, p. 43.
"Metamorphosis." [NewYorkQ] (41) Spr 90, p. 85.
27. ADAMS, B. B.
"Sour Wine." [Gypsy] (15) 90, p. 40.
"Trusted Remedies." [Confr] (44/45) Fall 90-Wint 91, p. 198-199.
28. ADAMS, Barbara
"Rag Time." [AntigR] (81/82) Spr-Sum 90, p. 118.
"Rag Time." [AntigR] (83) Aut 90, p. 35.
29. ADAMS, Coralie
"Echoes." [Bogg] (62) 90, p. 34.
30. ADAMS, David (David J.)
"A View of Advent from High Street: Hollowell, ME." [Wind] (20:67) 90, p. 1.
"January: A Woman Chases Her Horse." [HiramPoR] (47) Wint 90, p. 9.
31. ADAMS, Erika B.
"The Ancestor Tree." [BellArk] (6:3) My-Je 90, p. 5.
"The Calling Woods." [BellArk] (6:2) Mr-Ap 90, p. 18.
"Heart Lake August." [BellArk] (6:1) Ja-F 90, p. 22.
32. ADAMS, Gladys M.
"Morning." [EmeraldCR] (1990) c89, p. 17.
33. ADAMS, Keith
"Thoughts." [LitR] (33:4) Sum 90, p. 469-473.
34. ADAMS, Mary
"Tryst." [AntR] (48:4) Fall 90, p. 490-491.
35. ADAMS, Michael E.
"Pawnee Buttes." [MidwQ] (31:2) Wint 90, p. 225-226.
36. ADAMS, Paul E.
"Lemon Doorknob in the Rain." [Pearl] (10) Spr 90, p. 26.
37. ADAMSON, Gil
"Dogs Could Forgive Me." [Caliban] (8) 90, p. 150.
"The Neon Cross." [Caliban] (8) 90, p. 149.
"Untitled: A gas station explodes." [Caliban] (8) 90, p. 147-148.
"Untitled: Sad black mole on hip." [Caliban] (8) 90, p. 148.
38. ADCOCK, Betty
"Owed to Betty Hodges." [Pembroke] (22) 90, p. 142-143.
39. ADDINGTON, Rosa Lee
"Transference." [ChatR] (11:1) Fall 90, p. 21.
40. ADELMAN, Miriam
"Michoacan." [ManhatPR] (12) [90?], p. 7.
41. ADLER, Frances Payne
"Riding the Eye." [Calyx] (13:1) Wint 90-91, p. 33.
"Simply." [Calyx] (13:1) Wint 90-91, p. 32.
42. ADLER, Jocelyn
"World Class Vixen." [PoetryUSA] (5:3) Fall 90, p. 8.
43. ADNAN, Etel
"Description of a Friend: His Peace, Made of Terror." [Zyzzyva] (6:2, #22) Sum 90, p.
81-85.
"Narration d'Equilibre 5-America Domino" (Selections: 12 poems, P.O.L., Paris,
1987, tr. of Jean Daive). [Avec] (3:1) 90, p. 82-84.
ADORNO, Pedro López
See LOPEZ ADORNO, Pedro
44. ADRES, Ben
"Landlocked." [BambooR] (47) Sum 90, p. 42.
"Return Visit." [BambooR] (47) Sum 90, p. 43.
45. ADRIAN, Loretta
"Woman in the Well." [SingHM] (17) 90, p. 8.
46. AESCHYLUS
"Prometheos Auomenos" (Fragments, tr. by John Taggart). [Conjunc] (15) 90, p.
359-360.
47. AFONSO, Otavio
"Dead City" (Excerpts, tr. by Tom Page, from "Cidade Morta"). [MinnR] (NS 34/35)
Spr-Fall 90, p. 10-12.
48. AGARD, John
"Limbo Dancer & the Press." [LitR] (34:1) Fall 90, p. 49.
"Limbo Dancer's Reading Habits." [LitR] (34:1) Fall 90, p. 48.

"Palm Tree King." [LitR] (34:1) Fall 90, p. 45-48.
"Rhyme-time Crime-time But who Care." [LitR] (34:1) Fall 90, p. 50-51.
AGHA SHAHID ALI
   See ALI, Agha Shahid
49. AGOSIN, Marjorie
   "Burial and Blaze of Pablo Neruda" (tr. by Cola Franzen). [Agni] (29/30) 90, p.
      206-207.
   "La Patria." [Americas] (18:3/4) Fall-Wint 90, p. 114.
   "Retornos." [Americas] (18:3/4) Fall-Wint 90, p. 115-116.
   "Semejanzas." [ContextS] (1:1) 89, p. 46.
   "Similarities" (tr. by Sara Heikoff Woehrlen). [ContextS] (1:1) 89, p. 47.
   "Untitled: It was in the plains" (tr. by Elizabeth Horan). [Agni] (29/30) 90, p. 209-211.
50. AGOSTINO, Paul
   "Hais and Lows" (Senryu). [Northeast] (5:2) Spr 90, p. 37.
   "The Legitimate Smart-Ass." [ChironR] (9:3) Aut 90, p. 15.
   "Reincarnation and the Holy Commonwealth." [ChironR] (9:3) Aut 90, p. 15.
   "To the Protestors Who Violated St. Patrick's Cathedral for the Love of A.I.D.S.
      Victims." [ChironR] (9:3) Aut 90, p. 15.
   "What Do You Say at a Communist Funeral? (Everyone Gets Buried Sometime, Mr.
      Krushchev)." [ChironR] (9:4) Wint 90, p. 14.
51. AGÜEROS, Jack
   "Psalm #1." [Agni] (31/32) 90, p. 114.
   "Sonnet: News from the World, Tompkins Square Park & the Metropolitan
      Transportation Authority." [Agni] (31/32) 90, p. 115.
52. AGUIAR, Fernando
   "Con Text." [WestCL] (24:2) Fall 90, p. 96.
   "Hommage to Adriano Spatola in the Shape of a Sonnet." [WestCL] (24:2) Fall 90, p.
      95.
   "Structural Texture." [WestCL] (24:2) Fall 90, p. 98.
AGUIAR, Fred d'
   See D'AGUIAR, Fred
53. AGUILAR-CARIÑO, Maria Luisa B.
   "Arcanum." [BlackWR] (17:1) Fall-Wint 90, p. 90.
   "At Hann's Cliff" (23 February 1904, Camp One, Kennon Road). [BlackWR] (17:1)
      Fall-Wint 90, p. 86-87.
   "Curse." [BlackWR] (17:1) Fall-Wint 90, p. 96.
   "Death Anniversary." [BlackWR] (17:1) Fall-Wint 90, p. 93.
   "Dissections." [BlackWR] (17:1) Fall-Wint 90, p. 94-95.
   "Encounter." [BlackWR] (17:1) Fall-Wint 90, p. 97.
   "From the Diary of D. Burnam" (December 1904). [BlackWR] (17:1) Fall-Wint 90, p.
      88-89.
   "Legend." [BlackWR] (17:1) Fall-Wint 90, p. 98-99.
   "The Secret Language." [BlackWR] (17:1) Fall-Wint 90, p. 91-92.
54. AGUILERA DIAZ, Gaspar
   "Finally After So Many Years Hernan Cortez Declares" (to Eduardo Langagne, tr. by
      John Oliver Simon). [Caliban] (9) 90, p. 144-145.
55. AHO, Margaret
   "For My Sister Elizabeth, Bookkeeper and Mother of Four." [Calyx] (13:1) Wint
      90-91, p. 44.
   "Handless Maiden and Child." [WillowS] (25) Wint 90, p. 13.
   "In the Middle." [Calyx] (13:1) Wint 90-91, p. 43.
   "Seeing Eye to Eye with My Father." [WillowS] (25) Wint 90, p. 12.
56. AI
   "Archangel" (for Chet Baker). [OnTheBus] (2:2/3:1, #6/7) Sum-Fall 90 Wint-Spr 91,
      p. 13-14.
   "Eve's Story." [Pequod] (31) 90, p. 122-124.
   "Evidence: From a Reporter's Notebook." [Pequod] (31) 90, p. 125-129.
   "Fate." [Manoa] (2:2) Fall 90, p. 38-40.
   "Last Seen" (for Alfred Hitchcock). [Pequod] (31) 90, p. 118-121.
   "Lesson, Lesson." [CimR] (93) O 90, p. 79.
   "Twenty-One." [GrahamHR] (13) Spr 90, p. 21-22.
57. AI, Qing
   "The Pearl Oyster" (tr. by Li Xijian and Gordon Osing). [Paint] (17:33/34) Spr-Aut 90,
      p. 31.
58. AICHINGER, Ilse
   "Through and Through" (tr. by Allen H. Chappel). [NewOR] (17:1) Spr 90, p. 32.

59. AIELLO, Kate
    "Mt. Tajumulco Climb." [Bogg] (63) 90, p. 23.
60. AIKEN, William
    "Our Hands Our Coffee Cups." [HampSPR] (Anthology 1975-1990) 90, p. 212.
61. AIKINS, Suezan
    "Spring Wind." [PottPort] (11) 89, p. 32.
62. AINSWORTH, Alan
    "Rather Than Stories." [Nimrod] (34:1) Fall-Wint 90, p. 79-82.
63. AISENBERG, Nadya
    "Natural History." [PartR] (57:3) Sum 90, p. 438.
    "The Self Talks to the Self." [PartR] (57:1) Wint 90, p. 109-110.
64. AJAY, Stephen
    "Goa Lawah, Bali." [Ploughs] (16:1) Spr-Sum 90, p. 101-102.
65. AKERS, Deborah
    "Sunset at Ocean Beach." [WritersF] (16) Fall 90, p. 16-17.
66. AKHMADULINA, Bella
    "Biographical Information" (tr. by Albert C. Todd). [Nimrod] (33:2) Spr-Sum 90, p.
        51-52.
    "Going Up on Stage" (tr. by Albert C. Todd). [Nimrod] (33:2) Spr-Sum 90, p. 88.
    "Now About Those" (tr. by Albert C. Todd). [Nimrod] (33:2) Spr-Sum 90, p. 47-48.
    "Remembrances of Yalta" (tr. by Albert C. Todd). [Nimrod] (33:2) Spr-Sum 90, p. 45.
    "Snowfall" (tr. by Albert C. Todd). [Nimrod] (33:2) Spr-Sum 90, p. 46.
    "St. Bartholomew's Night" (tr. by Albert C. Todd). [Nimrod] (33:2) Spr-Sum 90, p.
        49-50.
67. AKHMATOVA, Anna
    "125. Oh, it was a cold day" (tr. by Judith Hemschemeyer). [Agni] (29/30) 90, p. 194.
    "208. To wake at dawn" (tr. by Judith Hemschemeyer). [Agni] (29/30) 90, p. 195.
    "212. And now you are depressed and despondent" (tr. by Judith Hemschemeyer).
        [Agni] (29/30) 90, p. 193.
    "289. Betrayal" (tr. by Judith Hemschemeyer). [Agni] (29/30) 90, p. 196.
    "541. This is how I am. I wish you another" (tr. by Judith Hemschemeyer). [Agni]
        (29/30) 90, p. 197-198.
    "The First Long-Range Artillery Fire on Leningrad" (tr. by Daniela Gioseffi, w. Sophia
        Buzevska). [PoetryE] (30) Fall 90, p. 23.
AKIRA, Fukuda
    See FUKUDA, Akira
AKITAKA, Uchimura
    See UCHIMURA, Akitaka
68. AKMAKJIAN, Alan P.
    "2 Victims." [BlackBR] (12) Fall-Wint 90, p. 5.
    "Apple Blossoms." [BlackBR] (12) Fall-Wint 90, p. 10-11.
    "The Pilgrim" (from "Walking," for Elsa). [Wind] (20:66) 90, p. 15.
69. Al-AS'AD, Muhammad
    "The Earth Also Dies" (Excerpt, tr. by May Jayyusi and Jack Collom). [Screens] (2)
        90, p. 26.
    "Personal Account" (tr. by May Jayyusi and Jack Collom). [Screens] (2) 90, p. 25-26.
70. Al-YAHUDI, Qazmuna Bint Isma'il (Granada, 12th c.)
    "Seeing Herself Beautiful and Nubile" (tr. by Christopher Middleton and Leticia Garza
        Falcón). [Trans] (23) Spr 90, p. 192.
Al-ZAQQAQ, Ben
    See BEN AL-ZAQQAQ
71. ALABAU, Magali (Magaly)
    "Liebe / Querida." [Inti] (31) Primavera 90, p. 172-174.
    "Panteon." [LindLM] (9:4) O-D 90, p. 13.
    "Rezar en Roma." [Inti] (31) Primavera 90, p. 175-176.
72. ALARCON, Francisco X.
    "Against Unruly Ants" (compilation of original Nahuatl spell, Mexico 1629, tr. of
        Hernando Ruiz de Alarcón). [PoetryUSA] (5:3) Fall 90, p. 14.
    "Midnight Water Song." [PoetryUSA] (5:3) Fall 90, p. 16.
ALARCON, Hernando Ruiz de
    See RUIZ DE ALARCON, Hernando
73. ALBA, Alicia Gaspar de
    "Beggar on the Córdoba Bridge" (40 poems). [BilingR] (14:1/2) 87-88, c89, p. 1-50.
    "Karmic Revolution." [BostonR] (15:4) Ag 90, p. 4.
    "The Philosophy of Frijoles." [HangL] (57) 90, p. 26.

74. ALBAN, Laureano
"Close-Up of Death" (tr. by Frederick H. Fornoff). [NewOR] (17:3) Fall 90, p. 82-83.
"The Creation of Birds" (tr. by Frederick H. Fornoff). [NewOR] (17:3) Fall 90, p. 48-49.
75. ALBERTI, Rafael
"Blue" (tr. by Carolyn Tipton). [HawaiiR] (14:3, #30) Fall 90, p. 109-112.
"Yellow" (tr. by Carolyn Tipton). [HawaiiR] (14:2, #29) Spr 90, p. 63-66.
76. ALBIACH, Anne-Marie
"Vertical Efforts in White" ("Travail vertical et blanc," Spectres Familliers, 1989, tr. by Joseph Simas). [Avec] (3:1) 90, p. 56-58.
77. ALBRECHT, Laura
(Anonymous poem). [FreeL] (4) 90.
"Collector." [CoalC] (2) D 90, p. 5.
"Memory XXIII." [CoalC] (2) D 90, p. 5.
78. ALBRECHT, Michael
"De Lacu Aliciae" (ad Richardum Eberhart). [NewYorkQ] (41) Spr 90, p. 72.
"Lake Alice" (to Richard Eberhart, tr. by John Siman). [NewYorkQ] (41) Spr 90, p. 72.
79. ALCALAY, Ammiel
"For the Old Gang." [LitR] (33:4) Sum 90, p. 460-462.
"Magnificat" (tr. of Jose Kozer). [LitR] (33:4) Sum 90, p. 446-447.
80. ALCOSSER, Sandra
"Azaleas." [AmerPoR] (19:6) N-D 90, p. 44.
81. ALDAN, Daisy
"Instinct" (tr. of Edith Södergran, w. Leif Sjöberg). [PoetryE] (30) Fall 90, p. 97.
82. ALDRICH, Jeff
"The Day of the Big Wind." [BambooR] (47) Sum 90, p. 44.
83. ALDRICH, Marcia
"Beauties" (from the 1855 woodcut by Toyokuni 3rd). [RiverC] (11:1) Fall 90, p. 60-62.
84. ALECKOVIC, Mira
"All the Stars" (tr. by Jacqueline and Quentin Vest). [HampSPR] (Anthology 1975-1990) 90, p. 260.
"Roll On, River, Weighed Down by the Breath of the Dead" (tr. by Jacqueline and Quentin Vest). [HampSPR] (Anthology 1975-1990) 90, p. 260.
"Sutjeska" (tr. by Jacqueline and Quentin Vest). [HampSPR] (Anthology 1975-1990) 90, p. 261.
"Trackless Quest" (tr. by Jacqueline and Quentin Vest). [HampSPR] (Anthology 1975-1990) 90, p. 262.
"Wooden Shoes" (tr. by Jacqueline and Quentin Vest). [HampSPR] (Anthology 1975-1990) 90, p. 261.
85. ALEJANDRO, Ann
"Nothing Is Ever Mutual." [SouthernPR] (30:2) Fall 90, p. 42.
86. ALEMAN, Michael P.
"Running in the Sun." [WindO] (53) Fall 90, p. 28.
87. ALENIER, Karren L.
"Tante Lottie Suffers Concussion." [PoetL] (85:4) Wint 90-91, p. 20.
88. ALESHIRE, Joan
"Addiction." [Crazy] (39) Wint 90, p. 42-43.
"Memory." [Crazy] (39) Wint 90, p. 40-41.
89. ALEXANDER, Charlotte
"My Lord's Little Volta." [Outbr] (21) 90, p. 74-75.
"On Professing Henry James to an Empty Seat." [Outbr] (21) 90, p. 76-77.
90. ALEXANDER, Elizabeth
"Compass." [Chelsea] (49) 90, p. 99-100.
"The Texas Prophet" (found poem). [Chelsea] (49) 90, p. 101.
91. ALEXANDER, Francis
"Old crumbling wall." [BlackBR] (11) Spr-Sum 90, p. 32.
92. ALEXANDER, Meena
"Blood Line" (For Svati Mariam, one year old). [Cond] (17) 90, p. 11.
"Deer Park at Sarnath" (For Anita Desai). [LitR] (33:4) Sum 90, p. 474.
"Indian Sandstone." [Nimrod] (34:1) Fall-Wint 90, p. 84-85.
"Kitchen Work." [Arc] (25) Aut 90, p. 43.
"Landscape with Door." [LitR] (33:4) Sum 90, p. 475.
"Looking Glass." [Arc] (25) Aut 90, p. 45.
"Lost Language." [Nimrod] (34:1) Fall-Wint 90, p. 83-84.

"No Man's Land." [NewL] (57:1) Fall 90, p. 79.
"Revelation." [DenQ] (25:2) Fall 90, p. 5.
"Room Without Walls." [Arc] (25) Aut 90, p. 44.
"Toxic Petals." [Cond] (17) 90, p. 12.
93. ALEXANDER, Pamela
"Three Poems about Audubon" (selected from "Commonwealth of Wings," a sequence
of persona poems based on the life of John James Audubon). [MichQR] (29:2)
Spr 90, p. 204-208.
94. ALEXANDER, Ronald
"I Sent Roses to My Mother." [OnTheBus] (2:2/3:1, #6/7) Sum-Fall 90 Wint-Spr 91,
p. 15-16.
95. ALEXANDER, Will
"Albania & the Death of Enver Hoxha" (from "Impulse & Nothingness). [Screens] (2)
90, p. 185-188.
96. ALEXIE, Sherman
"13/16." [Caliban] (8) 90, p. 12-13.
"The Business of Fancydancing." [BelPoJ] (41:1) Fall 90, p. 14-15.
"Crazy Horse Speaks." [Caliban] (8) 90, p. 14-17.
"Distances." [HangL] (56) 90, p. 5-6.
"House Fires." [BlackBR] (11) Spr-Sum 90, p. 27.
"Learning to Drown." [BelPoJ] (41:1) Fall 90, p. 11-13.
"Road Signs" (for John & Alex). [BlackBR] (12) Fall-Wint 90, p. 26-27.
"Translated from the American." [AnotherCM] (21) 90, p. 5.
97. ALEXIS
"Wrote after Reading Some Poems Composed by Phillis Wheatley, an African Girl."
[BlackALF] (24:3) Fall 90, p. 566.
98. ALEXIS, Austin
"Ballet Studio at Noon." [Hellas] (1:1) Spr 90, p. 42.
ALI, Aga Shahid
    See ALI, Agha Shahid
99. ALI, Agha Shahid
"At the Museum." [Poetry] (156:1) Ap 90, p. 34.
"Bangladesh-II" (tr. of Faiz Ahmed Faiz). [GrahamHR] (13) Spr 90, p. 96-97.
"Beyond the Ash Rains." [AntR] (48:4) Fall 90, p. 487.
"Death Row." [Arc] (25) Aut 90, p. 49.
"Desire" (tr. of Faiz Ahmed Faiz). [GrahamHR] (13) Spr 90, p. 91.
"Electric Chair." [NewMyths] (1:1) 90, p. 136.
"Eurydice." [Arc] (25) Aut 90, p. 47-48.
"Exit to Calcutta." [Field] (43) Fall 90, p. 83-84.
"Fragrant Hands" (For the anonymous woman who sent me a bouquet of flowers in
prison, tr. of Faiz Ahmed Faiz). [GrahamHR] (13) Spr 90, p. 89-90.
"Ghazal" (tr. of Faiz Ahmed Faiz). [GrandS] (9:2) Wint 90, p. 139.
"I Dream I Return to Tucson in the Monsoons." [NewMyths] (1:1) 90, p. 135.
"It Is Spring Again" (tr. of Faiz Ahmed Faiz). [GrahamHR] (13) Spr 90, p. 94.
"Let Me Think" (for Andrei Voznesensky, tr. of Faiz Ahmed Faiz). [GrahamHR] (13)
Spr 90, p. 92-93.
"No." [Arc] (25) Aut 90, p. 50.
"No Trace of Blood" (tr. of Faiz Ahmed Faiz). [GrandS] (9:2) Wint 90, p. 141.
"On My Return from Dhaka (Bangladesh-III)" (Revisited after the massacre, tr. of
Faiz Ahmed Faiz). [GrahamHR] (13) Spr 90, p. 98.
"Stay Away from Me (Bangladesh-I)" (tr. of Faiz Ahmed Faiz). [GrahamHR] (13)
Spr 90, p. 95.
"Wash the Blood Off Your Feet" (tr. of Faiz Ahmed Faiz). [GrandS] (9:2) Wint 90, p.
140.
100. ALIEVA, Fazu G.
"Morning" (Originally written in Avari, tr. from the Russian by Birgitta Ingemanson
and Manly Johnson). [Nimrod] (33:2) Spr-Sum 90, p. 44.
"The Thirst for Beauty" (Originally written in Avari, tr. from the Russian by Birgitta
Ingemanson and Manly Johnson). [Nimrod] (33:2) Spr-Sum 90, p. 43-44.
101. ALKALAY-GUT, Karen
"A Visitor." [MassR] (31:3) Aut 90, p. 340.
"We Did What Was Expected of Us" (tr. of Yehuda Amichai). [PartR] (57:3) Sum 90,
p. 429-430.
102. ALLAN, A. T.
"Rose Window." [ChamLR] (3:2, #6) Spr 90, p. 125-126.

103. ALLEN, Annette
"The Dance." [Boulevard] (5:2, #14) Fall 90, p. 85.
"Travel Back in Time Not So Far Out" (New York Times). [HeavenB] (8) Wint
90-91, p. 2.
104. ALLEN, Barbara
"The Beheading." [NewEngR] (13:2) Wint 90, p. 173.
105. ALLEN, Cheryl
"Loneliness." [PottPort] (11) 89, p. 51.
106. ALLEN, Dick
"The Adventure into Someone Else's Life." [HampSPR] (Anthology 1975-1990) 90,
p. 33-34.
"Doing Mazes." [HampSPR] (Anthology 1975-1990) 90, p. 36-37.
"Letter from a Connecticut Country House." [Hudson] (42:4) Wint 90, p. 589-591.
"Meditation." [HampSPR] (Anthology 1975-1990) 90, p. 34-35.
"Mime." [HampSPR] (Anthology 1975-1990) 90, p. 37.
"On the New Haven Line." [Hudson] (42:4) Wint 90, p. 592-593.
"A Refusal, Like Hers." [HampSPR] (Anthology 1975-1990) 90, p. 35-36.
"The Report." [Atlantic] (265:1) Ja 90, p. 82.
"Talking with Poets." [Hudson] (42:4) Wint 90, p. 591-592.
107. ALLEN, Edward
"Coming Home in a Window Seat." [PraS] (64:1) Spr 90, p. 67-68.
"Gloomy Sunday with Orange Quangaroos." [BlackWR] (16:2) Spr-Sum 90, p.
106-107.
"Love Song in the Humidity." [PraS] (64:1) Spr 90, p. 68-69.
108. ALLEN, Gilbert
"Gardenias." [AmerS] (59:3) Sum 90, p. 426.
"Her Mother Explains." [ChatR] (10:2) Wint 90, p. 33.
"Reading the Landscape Again." [Poem] (64) N 90, p. 64.
"Spirits in the Suburbs." [Poem] (64) N 90, p. 65.
109. ALLEN, Jed
"Trees and Mirrors." [HayF] (7) Fall-Wint 90, p. 103.
110. ALLEN, Jeffery R. (Jeffery Renard, Jeffrey Renard)
"Ancient Songs." [Obs] (5:1) Spr 90, p. 45-47.
"Backstreets." [HawaiiR] (14:2, #29) Spr 90, p. 67-70.
"Beginnings." [BlackALF] (24:3) Fall 90, p. 556-557.
"Even the Blues." [ChrC] (107:27) 3 O 90, p. 876.
"Home" (two for Sterling Plumpp). [Obs] (5:2) Sum 90, p. 73-76.
"Juba." [Obs] (5:2) Sum 90, p. 72-73.
"Love Songs for My People." [Obs] (5:1) Spr 90, p. 47-48.
"Mens" (for Tonia). [Obs] (5:2) Sum 90, p. 76-78.
"Osun." [Obs] (5:2) Sum 90, p. 78-79.
"Preview of America." [WashR] (16:3) O-N 90, p. 18.
"Saturday Blues." [HangL] (56) 90, p. 9-11.
"The Story Told: Blues Had a Baby" (for Sterling Plumpp). [Obs] (5:1) Spr 90, p.
48-49.
"Touched" (for Tonia). [HangL] (56) 90, p. 7-9.
"Untitled: Scrape memory from my brain" (For Michael Griffith, Murdered Dec. 21,
1986, Howard Beach, N.Y.). [BlueBldgs] (12) 90, p. 32.
111. ALLEN, Laura
"We Plan Our Days." [SmPd] (27:1, #78) Wint 90, p. 26.
112. ALLEN, Paul
"Dear Friend." [Iowa] (20:2) Spr-Sum 90, p. 127-128.
"Sabbatical." [Iowa] (20:2) Spr-Sum 90, p. 124-126.
113. ALLEN, William
"Memorizing Chaucer." [IndR] (14:1) Wint 90, p. 12-13.
"Montagne des Singes." [DenQ] (25:2) Fall 90, p. 6-7.
"Where Little Pond Meets the Ocean" (to V. F. W. Allen). [IndR] (14:1) Wint 90, p.
14-15.
ALLESANDRO, Sam d'
See D'ALLESANDRO, Sam
114. ALLIN, Louise
"Our Neighbour." [OxfordM] (6:1) Spr-Sum 90, p. 35.
115. ALLISON, Dorothy
"Writing the Novel." [CityLR] (4) 90, p. 101-102.
116. ALLISON, Margaret-Ann
"Television." [EmeraldCR] (1990) c89, p. 37-38.

35

117. ALMEDER, Melanie
"From the Front Door to the Mailbox and Back." [GeoR] (44:1/2) Spr-Sum 90, p. 217-218.
118. ALMQUIST, Norma
"Selifke." [CrossCur] (9:2) Je 90, p. 49.
"Waltz." [CrossCur] (9:2) Je 90, p. 50.
119. ALTIMONT, Alan
"For a Stranger" (Barbara Jones). [NorthStoneR] (9) 90, p. 50.
120. ALTIZER, Nell
"1832, Kona Wind, Honolulu." [MassR] (31:4) Wint 90, p. 498.
"1845, Parnelly Pierce Draws the Night-Blooming Cereus." [MassR] (31:4) Wint 90, p. 495-497.
"The Daughter's Runes for the Stepmother." [Shen] (40:2) Sum 90, p. 39.
121. ALTMAN, Heidi M.
"For My Father on the Occasion of Carrie's Wedding." [ApalQ] (33/34) 90, p. 52-53.
122. ALVAREZ, Julia
"Beginning Love." [GreenMR] (NS 3:2) Fall-Wint 89-90, p. 100-101.
"Bookmaking." [GreenMR] (NS 3:2) Fall-Wint 89-90, p. 103-104.
"Mami and Gauguin." [KenR] (NS 12:3) Sum 90, p. 35-36.
123. ALVAREZ BRAVO, Armando
"Poema para Nicolas Perez Diez-Arguelles, Largo Nombre de Tan Buen Hombre, Que No Lo Necesita . . ." [LindLM] (9:4) O-D 90, p. 9.
124. ALVAREZ-SOSA, Arturo
"NarcisoLASER." [Ometeca] (1:2/2:1) 89-90, p. 26.
"El Péndulo de Foucault." [Ometeca] (1:2/2:1) 89-90, p. 27.
"Los Quarks Saben Contar." [Ometeca] (1:2/2:1) 89-90, p. 28.
125. ALVER, Betti
"Nerves of Steel, or The Poet's Prayer" (tr. by William Pitt Root). [PoetryE] (30) Fall 90, p. 12.
126. AMABILE, George
"Adultery." [PoetryC] (11:4) Wint 90, p. 13.
"Basilico." [Descant] (21:4/22:1, #71/72) Wint-Spr 90-91, p. 18-20.
"Grief." [PoetryC] (11:4) Wint 90, p. 13.
"Landscape with Snow." [CanLit] (126) Aut 90, p. 114.
"Owls." [Descant] (21:4/22:1, #71/72) Wint-Spr 90-91, p. 15.
"Peanuts." [Descant] (21:4/22:1, #71/72) Wint-Spr 90-91, p. 14.
"Picking Over the Bones." [Descant] (21:4/22:1, #71/72) Wint-Spr 90-91, p. 16-17.
"*Sotto Voce* Over a Shopping Cart." [Descant] (21:4/22:1, #71/72) Wint-Spr 90-91, p. 13.
127. AMICHAI, Yehuda
"We Did What Was Expected of Us" (tr. by Karen Alkalay-Gut). [PartR] (57:3) Sum 90, p. 429-430.
128. AMICO, Santa Helena
"A Mother's Tale." [Footwork] 90, p. 113.
129. AMICOST, Chele
"Horse-and-Buggy Heart." [EmeraldCR] (1990) c89, p. 109.
130. AMIDON, Richard
"The New Math." [RagMag] (8:2) 90, p. 46-47.
131. AMIRTHANAYAGAM, Indran
"The Beat of the Wind." [HangL] (57) 90, p. 24-25.
"The Commissioner of Salt." [HangL] (57) 90, p. 21.
"The Empire of Meat." [Bomb] (33) Fall 90, p. 85.
"First Words." [LitR] (33:4) Sum 90, p. 495.
"For My Autistic Brother, Chutta." [HangL] (57) 90, p. 22-23.
"Pagan Love Song." [Bomb] (33) Fall 90, p. 84.
"Sirens." [MassR] (31:4) Wint 90, p. 534-536.
"Wuot Woth (Mad Po(e)t." [HangL] (57) 90, p. 23.
132. AMMONS, A. R.
"Antithesis." [HampSPR] (Anthology 1975-1990) 90, p. 153.
"Cracking a Few Hundred Million Years." [ManhatR] (5:1) Spr 90, p. 24.
"Range." [HampSPR] (Anthology 1975-1990) 90, p. 153-154.
"Sweetened Change." [HampSPR] (Anthology 1975-1990) 90, p. 154.
133. AMNASAN, Michael
"Joe Liar" (Excerpt). [Screens] (2) 90, p. 193-194.
134. AMPRIMOZ, Alexandre L.
"The Clarity of Programs." [PraF] (11:3) Aut 90, p. 12.

"The Language of Trains." [PraF] (11:3) Aut 90, p. 13.
"Solitaire." [PraF] (11:3) Aut 90, p. 13.
135. AMSBERRY, Jan
"Turnips." [Amelia] (6:2, #17) 90, p. 133.
136. ANANIA, Michael
"Seven Pieces for Unaccompanied Voice" (for Charles Simic). [ApalQ] (33/34) 90, p. 38-40.
137. ANAPORTE-EASTON, Jean
"Sources." [Mildred] (4:1) 90, p. 16-17.
138. ANDERS, Stefan
"The Sadness Within Us All" (for Beauford White & the Ray family). [SlipS] (10) 90, p. 31.
139. ANDERSEN, Benny
"The Face about the Face" (tr. by Cynthia La Touche Andersen). [CimR] (92) Jl 90, p. 11-12.
140. ANDERSEN, Cynthia La Touche
"The Face about the Face" (tr. of Benny Andersen). [CimR] (92) Jl 90, p. 11-12.
141. ANDERSEN, Steen
"Disorderly Images" (from "The Light's Prism, Attika, 1988, tr. by the author). [CimR] (92) Jl 90, p. 13.
142. ANDERSON, Doug
"Ambush." [RiverC] (11:1) Fall 90, p. 64.
"Bamboo Bridge." [RiverC] (11:1) Fall 90, p. 63.
"Infantry Assault." [MassR] (31:3) Aut 90, p. 407.
"The Wall" (For Maya Lin). [MassR] (31:3) Aut 90, p. 408.
"We Sweat." [RiverC] (11:1) Fall 90, p. 65.
143. ANDERSON, Jack
"The Daily Life of the Poem." [AnotherCM] (21) 90, p. 6.
144. ANDERSON, Jeanne
"Some Note I Can Not Hold." [Comm] (117:11) 1 Je 90, p. 352.
145. ANDERSON, Ken
"Picture This Cove." [LullwaterR] (2:1) Wint 90, p. 11-13.
146. ANDERSON, Linda
"Motion." [Crucible] (26) Fall 90, p. 86.
147. ANDERSON, Maggie
"Gifts." [Ploughs] (16:4) Wint 90-91, p. 191-192.
"Heart Labor" (for Tanya Anagnostopoulou." [PennR] (4:2) 90, p. 1.
148. ANDERSON, Mark
"Easter Eggs." [Poetry] (156:1) Ap 90, p. 35.
"Hearing through Light." [Hudson] (43:1) Spr 90, p. 75.
"Homecoming." [CumbPR] (10:1) Fall 90, p. 1.
"Out There." [PoetryNW] (31:4) Wint 90-91, p. 31.
"The Promise." [GreenMR] (NS 4:1) Spr-Sum 90, p. 121.
"The Thaw on Slack's Pond." [Hudson] (43:1) Spr 90, p. 76.
"What Is There to Say." [PoetryNW] (31:4) Wint 90-91, p. 30-31.
149. ANDERSON, Murray
"When You're Away" (To my daughter in a group home. Reprinted from #18, 1989). [Kaleid] (20) Wint-Spr 90, p. 27.
150. ANDERSON, Robert
"Convict." [CreamCR] (14:1) Spr 90, p. 152-153.
151. ANDERSON, Robert R.
"Big Sister." [RiverC] (11:1) Fall 90, p. 58-59.
"Orion." [MichQR] (29:1) Wint 90, p. 109-110.
152. ANDERSON, Sascha
"Jewish Jetset" (Selection: "Exhale, End, A," tr. by Karen Margolis). [Screens] (2) 90, p. 80.
153. ANDERSON, Teresa
"Poem to Be Sung to No One." [ChironR] (9:4) Wint 90, p. 15.
154. ANDERSON, Vicky
"Substantial." [PoetC] (21:2) Wint 90, p. 9-10.
155. ANDERSON, Virginia
"A Calendar of Women." [OnTheBus] (2:1, #5) Spr 90, p. 17-18.
"Hands." [OnTheBus] (2:1, #5) Spr 90, p. 14-15.
"Orange Juice." [OnTheBus] (2:1, #5) Spr 90, p. 12-13.
156. ANDERSON-DARGATZ, Gail
"Here I am again letting my thoughts." [PraF] (11:4) Wint 90-91, p. 20.

"My Foot Is On My Tongue." [PraF] (11:4) Wint 90-91, p. 21.
157. ANDINA, Peter T.
    "Abandoned Sailboat." [Wind] (20:67) 90, p. 2.
158. ANDRADE, Eugenio de
    "Another Example: Visconti" (tr. by Alexis Levitin). [OnTheBus] (2:2/3:1, #6/7)
        Sum-Fall 90 Wint-Spr 91, p. 240.
    "Between the First and Last Twilight" (tr. by Alexis Levitin). [ApalQ] (33/34) 90, p.
        76.
    "The Body Does Not Always Seem" (tr. by Alexis Levitin). [PoetryE] (30) Fall 90, p.
        68.
    "Borges and the Tigers" (tr. by Alexis Levitin). [MidAR] (10:1) 90, p. 111.
    "Boulevard Delessert" (tr. by Alexis Levitin). [HampSPR] (Anthology 1975-1990)
        90, p. 273.
    "Endless" (tr. by Alexis Levitin). [Asylum] (6:2) S 90, p. 16.
    "Estou Sentado Nos Primeiros Anos de Minha Vida." [NegC] (10:2/3) 90, p. 146.
    "House in the Sun" (tr. by Alexis Levitin). [ApalQ] (33/34) 90, p. 78.
    "I am faithful to the heat" (tr. by Alexis Levitin). [Trans] (24) Fall 90, p. 229.
    "I Am Seated in the First Years of My Life" (tr. by Alexis Levitin). [NegC] (10:2/3)
        90, p. 147.
    "I know of a stone where I can sit" (tr. by Alexis Levitin). [Trans] (24) Fall 90, p.
        230.
    "I saw them in ruins, those houses" (tr. by Alexis Levitin). [Trans] (24) Fall 90, p.
        229.
    "Last Example: Carlos de Oliveira" (tr. by Alexis Levitin). [OnTheBus] (2:2/3:1, #6/7)
        Sum-Fall 90 Wint-Spr 91, p. 241.
    "Materia Solar" (Selections: 8-9, 12-13, 19, 32-33). [InterPR] (16:2) Fall 90, p. 62,
        64.
    "Melusine" (tr. by Alexis Levitin). [OnTheBus] (2:2/3:1, #6/7) Sum-Fall 90 Wint-Spr
        91, p. 240-241.
    "Morandi: An Example" (tr. by Alexis Levitin). [OnTheBus] (2:2/3:1, #6/7) Sum-Fall
        90 Wint-Spr 91, p. 240.
    "A Name for Earth" (tr. by Alexis Levitin). [SenR] (20:2) Fall 90, p. 42.
    "Other Days" (tr. by Alexis Levitin). [NowestR] (28:1) 90, p. 99.
    "Praca da Alegria" (tr. by Alexis Levitin). [HampSPR] (Anthology 1975-1990) 90, p.
        273.
    "The Seagulls" (tr. by Alexis Levitin). [SenR] (20:2) Fall 90, p. 41.
    "Solar Matter" (Selection: #27, tr. by Alexis Levitin). [PoetryE] (30) Fall 90, p. 69.
    "Solar Matter" (Selections: 8-9, 12-13, 19, 32-33, tr. by Alexis Levitin). [InterPR]
        (16:2) Fall 90, p. 63, 65.
    "Sovereignty" (tr. by Alexis Levitin). [ApalQ] (33/34) 90, p. 77.
    "Stones" (tr. by Alexis Levitin). [OnTheBus] (2:2/3:1, #6/7) Sum-Fall 90 Wint-Spr
        91, p. 239.
    "Terreiro de S. Vicente" (tr. by Alexis Levitin). [OnTheBus] (2:2/3:1, #6/7) Sum-Fall
        90 Wint-Spr 91, p. 239.
    "That's What Poetry Is Like" (tr. by Alexis Levitin). [ApalQ] (33/34) 90, p. 79.
    "Two Solar Matters" (tr. by Alexis Levitin). [Confr] (44/45) Fall 90-Wint 91, p. 178.
    "Two Time Matters" (tr. by Alexis Levitin). [Confr] (44/45) Fall 90-Wint 91, p. 179.
    "With the Eyes" (tr. by Alexis Levitin). [Asylum] (6:2) S 90, p. 17.
159. ANDREA, Marianne
    "Chekhov's Visit." [Kalliope] (12:1) 90, c89, p. 32-33.
160. ANDRESEN, Sophia de Mello Breyner
    "Women by the Seashore" (tr. by Lisa Sapinkopf). [HampSPR] (Anthology
        1975-1990) 90, p. 270.
161. ANDREUS, Hans
    "After All" (tr. by Arie Staal). [Vis] (34) 90, p. 43.
    "Lying Nights" (tr. by Kees Snoek). [Vis] (34) 90, p. 42.
    "My Son" (tr. by Arie Staal). [Vis] (34) 90, p. 42.
162. ANDREWS, Bruce
    "Dear World, *fuck off* advice ingredients, empty swing." [Conjunc] (15) 90, p. 283.
    "Definition" (Selections: U-Z). [WestCL] (24:3) Wint 90, p. 148-149.
    "Facts Are Stupid Things." [Verse] (7:1) Spr 90, p. 58-60.
    "Half-willed absence. Neckband, cosmetology, it's o.k." [Conjunc] (15) 90, p.
        287-288.
    "Let me try to explain this rather cryptic statement." [Conjunc] (15) 90, p. 285.
    "Looked like a flip visor, a 'technical mother lode,' one loser called it." [Conjunc]
        (15) 90, p. 286-287.

"Mavericks do not become great leaders." [Conjunc] (15) 90, p. 283-284.
"War: trading real estate for men." [Conjunc] (15) 90, p. 288.
"With a tact, with a tact that renders them almost subliminal." [Conjunc] (15) 90, p. 284-285.

163. ANDREWS, Claudia Emerson
"As the Crow Flies." [VirQR] (66:3) Sum 90, p. 455.
"Brothers and Bootleggers." [HolCrit] (27:2) Ap 90, p. 17.
"Maintenance." [GeoR] (44:4) Wint 90, p. 670.
"Tractor Accident." [GreensboroR] (48) Sum 90, p. 117-118.
"Wanda." [Poetry] (156:2) My 90, p. 76.

164. ANDREWS, Jessica
"Love, Itself." [PoetryUSA] (5:2) Sum 90, p. 7.
"Thee." [PoetryUSA] (5:2) Sum 90, p. 7.
"The Watcher" (from a painting by Magritte). [PoetryUSA] (5:2) Sum 90, p. 7.

165. ANDREWS, Linda
"The Escape of the Birdwomen." [PoetryNW] (31:4) Wint 90-91, p. 34-35.
"For the Long Distance Rider." [Nimrod] (34:1) Fall-Wint 90, p. 88.
"In the Museum of Man" (Balboa Park, San Diego." [SwampR] (5) Wint-Spr 90, p. 93-94.
"Mill of the Fates." [Nimrod] (34:1) Fall-Wint 90, p. 86-87.
"Sanctuary of the Newborn" (for Judith). [BellR] (13:1, #27) Spr 90, p. 35.

166. ANDREWS, Michael
"Democracy in the Corporate States of America." [OnTheBus] (2:2/3:1, #6/7) Sum-Fall 90 Wint-Spr 91, inside back cover.
"Fat Chance." [OnTheBus] (2:2/3:1, #6/7) Sum-Fall 90 Wint-Spr 91, p. 31-32.
"Most Men." [DogRR] (9:1, #17) Spr 90, p. 51.
"A Short Timer's Bed" (San Jose, Costa Rica). [OnTheBus] (2:2/3:1, #6/7) Sum-Fall 90 Wint-Spr 91, p. 28-30.
"A Small God" (Kamarpukur, India). [DogRR] (9:1, #17) Spr 90, p. 51.
"Things That Break." [OnTheBus] (2:2/3:1, #6/7) Sum-Fall 90 Wint-Spr 91, p. 33-34.

167. ANDREWS, Nin
"The Dream." [MichQR] (29:4) Fall 90, p. 499-500.
"Morning Bath." [Plain] (10:2) Wint 90, p. 6.

168. ANDREWS, Shari
"Broken." [PottPort] (11) 89, p. 46.
"One Whose Child Dies at Birth." [PottPort] (11) 89, p. 46.
"The Voyeur." [Grain] (18:2) Sum 90, p. 50.

169. ANDREWS, Tom
"Three Purgatory Poems." [KenR] (NS 12:4) Fall 90, p. 40-41.

170. ANDREYEVA, Victoria
"Dream of the Firmament" (tr. by Richard McKane). [LitR] (33:4) Sum 90, p. 513.
"Farewell Gentlemen We Are Setting Off" (tr. by Richard McKane). [LitR] (33:4) Sum 90, p. 514.
"Having Lived an Alien Life" (tr. by Richard McKane). [LitR] (33:4) Sum 90, p. 513-514.
"Oh, Is It Irretrievable or Not?" (tr. by Richard McKane). [LitR] (33:4) Sum 90, p. 514.

171. ANDROLA, Ron
"The Coming Disaster" (for Kurt Nimmo). [Bogg] (63) 90, p. 16.
"Farting with James Joyce." [Bogg] (62) 90, p. 36.
"It's These Bodies." [Gargoyle] (37/38) 90, p. 53.
"Z Particles & Summer Morning Rain." [Gargoyle] (37/38) 90, p. 53.

172. ANGEL, George
"Ballista and Bassoon in March." [Caliban] (8) 90, p. 72.
"The Dark." [NewOR] (17:3) Fall 90, p. 50-51.

173. ANGEL, Ralph
"Among Fields of Shocked Corn." [PassN] (11:1) Sum 90, p. 15.
"At the Seams." [Pearl] (11) Sum 90, p. 60.
"Breaking Rhythm." [AntR] (48:3) Sum 90, p. 334-335.
"Getting Honest." [AntR] (48:3) Sum 90, p. 339.
"Inside a World the World Fits Into." [AntR] (48:3) Sum 90, p. 333.
"It Could Have Been More." [AntR] (48:3) Sum 90, p. 336.
"Planets, Cars, Observers, Living Under Siege, Reading Schuyler's *Selected*." [DenQ] (24:4) Spr 90, p. 24.
"A Rat in the Room." [CimR] (90) Ja 90, p. 55-56.

39

ANGEL

"The River Has No Hair to Hold Onto." [CimR] (90) Ja 90, p. 59-60.
"Try and Run." [CimR] (90) Ja 90, p. 57-58.
"Untitled: Surely everyone is born unfinished." [AntR] (48:3) Sum 90, p. 337.
"Where All the Streets Lead to the Sea." [AntR] (48:3) Sum 90, p. 338.
174. ANGELERI, Lucy
"June Night, 1953." [SlipS] (10) 90, p. 39.
175. ANGELINE, Mary
"A Crown for Fox Point at Ives & William." [CentralP] (17/18) Spr-Fall 90, p. 115-117.
"Vision & Providence" (Excerpts). [Talisman] (4) Spr 90, p. 82-83.
"Vital." [Notus] (5:1) Spr 90, p. 71-77.
ANGELIS, Milo de
See De ANGELIS, Milo
176. ANGELL, Roger
"Greetings, Friends." [NewYorker] (66:45) 24 D 90, p. 33.
ANGELO, Gregory de
See DeANGELO, Gregory
177. ANGKUW, Rietje Marie
"First Impression." [Amelia] (6:1, #16) 90, p. 59.
178. ANGLADA, Maria Angels
"A Truce in January" (from "Kyparissia," 1980, tr. by Montserrat Abelló). [PoetryC] (11:4) Wint 90, p. 21.
179. ANGLESEY, Zoë
"6:00 a.m. in Tegucigalpa." [Rohwedder] (5) Spr 90, p. 26.
"After the Eyes Have It." [OnTheBus] (2:1, #5) Spr 90, p. 19.
"The Ones Who Died in April" (tr. of José Luis Quesada). [OnTheBus] (2:1, #5) Spr 90, p. 193-194.
"Satisfaction" (tr. of Otto René Castillo). [OnTheBus] (2:1, #5) Spr 90, p. 184.
"Take a Listen." [OnTheBus] (2:1, #5) Spr 90, p. 19-20.
180. ANKIEWICZ, Kristen
"Letter from a Mermaid" (pencil drawing and poem, with Nora McCauley). [HarvardA] (125:1) S 90, p. 26.
181. ANNENSKY, Innokenty
"The Bronze Poet" (from "Trefoil in the Park," #2, tr. by Nancy Tittler and Devon Miller-Duggan). [Gargoyle] (37/38) 90, p. 87.
"Second Tormenting Sonnet" (tr. by Nancy Tittler and Devon Miller-Duggan). [Gargoyle] (37/38) 90, p. 87.
182. ANNHARTE
"The Art of Talking Indian Art Shows" (for Richard Danay-Glazer). [Cond] (17) 90, p. 104.
"Upbraid." [Cond] (17) 90, p. 105.
183. ANNINO, Cristina
"The Double" (tr. by Pasquale Verdicchio). [Screens] (2) 90, p. 111.
184. ANONYMOUS (See also following anonymous entries by date)
"Another Mexico." [FreeL] (4) 90, p. 29.
"Aubade." [FreeL] (4) 90, p. 11.
"Barlaban: a Mandinka Epic" (Excerpt, tr. by Kandioura Dramé). [Callaloo] (13:3) Sum 90, p. 435-466.
"Candlemas." [FreeL] (4) 90, p. 8.
"Ceremonies for Boys and Girls" (Found Poem, From "Tairu: Commemorating the Independence of Papua New Guinea," pub. by Sogeri National High School). [Manoa] (2:1) Spr 90, p. 54.
"Circumstances Told by a German" (tr. out of the Croato-Serbian by William McLaughlin). [HampSPR] (Anthology 1975-1990) 90, p. 191.
"Clock Mania." [FreeL] (4) 90, p. 11.
"Cloisters." [FreeL] (4) 90, p. 36.
"Dead." [FreeL] (4) 90, p. 13-17.
"The Detective's Valentine." [FreeL] (4) 90, p. 10.
"Disbelieving Anti-Veal Propaganda, White Boy Gets in Calf Costume." [FreeL] (4) 90, p. 34.
"Don't! Stop!" [FreeL] (4) 90, p. 23.
"Down by the Foam-Washed Shore" (Macedonian folksong, tr. by David Conrad). [AntigR] (80) Wint 90, p. 135.
"Eche Rori Ile" (Udu song). [WashR] (16:2) Ag-S 90, p. 25.
"Every Night in Our Sleeping." [FreeL] (4) 90, p. 12.
"For My Daughter." [FreeL] (4) 90, p. 26-27.

40

ANONYMOUS

"Forestation." [FreeL] (4) 90, p. 34.
"Gathas" (9 poems from the "Gatha-Saptasati," tr. by David Ray). [PoetryE] (30) Fall 90, p. 74-76.
"Hearts and Flowers." [FreeL] (4) 90, p. 6-7.
"I see high old trees" (Poem written in English by high school students from the Ukraine, collected by Maureen Hurley). [PoetryUSA] (5:1) Spr 90, p. 18.
"In L.A. You Don't Walk." [FreeL] (4) 90, p. 30.
"In the Mind of God" (tr. out of the Croato-Serbian by William McLaughlin). [HampSPR] (Anthology 1975-1990) 90, p. 190-191.
"Isheja" (Ujevwe song). [WashR] (16:2) Ag-S 90, p. 25.
"Isheja" (Ujevwe song, tr. by Tanure Ojaide). [WashR] (16:2) Ag-S 90, p. 25.
"Lament for a Stranger, Alone Among Savages." [DogRR] (9:2, #18) Aut 90, p. 54.
"Lies About Magnolias." [FreeL] (4) 90, p. 21.
"Lucretius Addresses the Academic Senate." [FreeL] (4) 90, p. 32-33.
"Mental Health." [FreeL] (4) 90, p. 28.
"Meridians." [FreeL] (4) 90, p. 31.
"Misfit." [FreeL] (4) 90, p. 25.
"Never go to bed" (Found on a wall in midtown Sacramento, painted over approximately Sept. 1990). [PoetryUSA] ([5:4?]) Wint 90, p. 24.
"Northwesterly." [FreeL] (4) 90, p. 24.
"Rough House" (tr. from the Irish by Richard O'Connell). [HampSPR] (Anthology 1975-1990) 90, p. 246.
"Seeing Their Shoes." [FreeL] (4) 90, p. 18-19.
"Shot Through the Head by Zeno's Arrow." [FreeL] (4) 90, p. 22.
"Slamming the Score Shut." [FreeL] (4) 90, p. 20.
"Stoma 1903." [FreeL] (4) 90, p. 9.
"Taking the Blame." [FreeL] (4) 90, p. 35.
"Thaw." [FreeL] (4) 90, p. 5.
"Things and Their Absence." [FreeL] (4) 90, p. 9.
"Three Riddles" (adapted by Christopher Merrill). [PoetryE] (30) Fall 90, p. 67.
"To Have and Have Not." [FreeL] (4) 90, p. 19.
"Upsy Daisy" (tr. by Graeme Wilson). [LitR] (33:2) Wint 90, p. 194.
"Walking on Water." [FreeL] (4) 90, p. 37.
"Whenever Songs Are to Be Composed" (Udu song, tr. by Tanure Ojaide). [WashR] (16:2) Ag-S 90, p. 25.
"Yedi Koule" (Sephardic folksong, tr. by David Conrad). [AntigR] (80) Wint 90, p. 134.

185. ANONYMOUS (Seventh century)
"Sunbear Rapids" (tr. by Graeme Wilson). [LitR] (33:2) Wint 90, p. 193.
186. ANONYMOUS (Late seventh century)
"Loneliness" (tr. by Graeme Wilson). [LitR] (33:2) Wint 90, p. 193.
187. ANONYMOUS (Eighth century)
"Modesty" (tr. by Graeme Wilson). [LitR] (33:2) Wint 90, p. 192.
"Valley of the Hatsuse" (tr. by Graeme Wilson). [LitR] (33:2) Wint 90, p. 193.
188. ANONYMOUS (14th century)
"Saint Erkenwald" (Middle-English, tr. by Casey Finch). [HawaiiR] (14:3, #30) Fall 90, p. 60-68.
189. ANOS, Joanna
"Attractive Possibility." [TriQ] (80) Wint 90-91, p. 53.
"The Barn." [TriQ] (80) Wint 90-91, p. 55-56.
"Green Street." [TriQ] (80) Wint 90-91, p. 52.
"Maple Tree and Bench." [GreensboroR] (48) Sum 90, p. 17.
"Prayer-Box on the Road from Delphi." [GreensboroR] (48) Sum 90, p. 16.
"Questions of Love." [TriQ] (80) Wint 90-91, p. 54.
190. ANSTETT, Aaron
"Ballast." [WormR] (30:1, #117) 90, p. 1.
"I've Tried So Many Times." [WormR] (30:1, #117) 90, p. 2.
191. ANTHONY, Frank
"Happy Hunting Ground" (In memory of Robert Penn Warren). [AnthNEW] 90, p. 7.
192. ANTHONY, Pat
"After Reading That Joanna Burden Has Grown Too Old." [KanQ] (22:3) Sum 90, p. 36.
193. ANTLER
"All the Breaths." [CityLR] (4) 90, p. 55.
"American Literature in Context." [NewYorkQ] (41) Spr 90, p. 60-61.

"Bubble Hubbub." [KenR] (NS 12:2) Spr 90, p. 15-16.
"I Beg to Disagree." [NewYorkQ] (43) Fall 90, p. 40-41.
"Laboring the Obvious." [AnotherCM] (22) 90, p. 5-7.
"Meadow in a Can." [CityLR] (4) 90, p. 55.
"Milky Way Exposé from Gogebic Peak." [NewYorkQ] (42) Sum 90, p. 65-66.
"Sweet-Talk." [HeavenB] (8) Wint 90-91, p. 42-43.
"Unbrainwash Work-Ethic." [Pig] (16) 90, p. 126-127.
"A Whole Lake to Yourself." [HeavenB] (8) Wint 90-91, p. 41.
194. AONGHUS NA N-AOR
"At Finn's" (tr. by Richard O'Connell). [HampSPR] (Anthology 1975-1990) 90, p. 245.
"Consolation" (tr. by Richard O'Connell). [HampSPR] (Anthology 1975-1990) 90, p. 245.
"Poets Anonymous" (tr. by Richard O'Connell). [HampSPR] (Anthology 1975-1990) 90, p. 245.
195. APOLLINAIRE, Guillaume
"Annie" (in French). [SycamoreR] (2:2) Sum 90, p. 52.
"Annie" (tr. by Diane Lunde). [SycamoreR] (2:2) Sum 90, p. 53.
"I Had the Courage" (tr. by Diane Lunde). [SycamoreR] (2:2) Sum 90, p. 51.
"J'Ai Eu le Courage." [SycamoreR] (2:2) Sum 90, p. 50.
196. APOLLONI, Ignazio
"The Shadow" (from the Sicilian Antigruppo, tr. by Nat Scammacca). [Footwork] 90, p. 104.
197. APONICK, Kathleen
"Your Words." [TarRP] (29:2) Spr 90, p. 33.
198. APPEL, Cathy
"Pieta." [NewL] (57:1) Fall 90, p. 107.
199. APPEL, Dori
"The Face of Madness" (From a series of 19th Century photographs of female mental patients). [ChamLR] (4:1, #7) Fall 90, p. 114-115.
"First Love." [ChamLR] (4:1, #7) Fall 90, p. 113.
200. APPLEBAUM, Mika
"Notes from a Greek Mother." [Footwork] 90, p. 65.
201. APPLEBY, Frank W.
"Morning Surprise." [Wind] (20:67) 90, p. 30.
202. APPLEMAN, Philip
"Eve." [Confr] (44/45) Fall 90-Wint 91, p. 175.
"Life on the Mississippi Queen." [Nat] (250:12) 26 Mr 90, p. 426.
"Under a Crown of Thorns, Some Questions Arise about Genesis I:27." [PartR] (57:2) Spr 90, p. 274-275.
203. APPLEWHITE, James
"Accident of Inheritance." [OhioR] (45) 90, p. 88-89.
"Crossing Over" (Somerset, by the Bristol channel). [HampSPR] (Anthology 1975-1990) 90, p. 92-93.
"Evening in Bath." [HampSPR] (Anthology 1975-1990) 90, p. 94.
"A Father and Son." [PoetC] (22:1) Fall 90, p. 17-18.
"A Place in the Past." [SouthernR] (26:2) Ap 90, p. 313-314.
"Remembering William Blackburn in a Leaf." [SouthernR] (26:2) Ap 90, p. 312-313.
204. APRIL, Susan
"What I Do for a Living." [SingHM] (18) 90, p. 16.
205. Ar-RUSAFI (Valencia, 1141/2?-1177)
"On the Death of a Friend by Drowning" (tr. by Christopher Middleton and Leticia Garza Falcón). [Trans] (23) Spr 90, p. 193.
206. ARA, Agneta
"Aldrig Trodde Jag." [Spirit] (10:1) 89, p. 58.
"De Enda Krig." [Spirit] (10:1) 89, p. 54.
"Dusk Comes All the Time Now" (tr. by Lennart Bruce and Sonja Bruce). [Spirit] (10:1) 89, p. 67.
"Emellanåt Går Vi Upp." [Spirit] (10:1) 89, p. 56.
"Flickan." [Spirit] (10:1) 89, p. 60.
"The Girl" (tr. by Lennart Bruce and Sonja Bruce). [Spirit] (10:1) 89, p. 61.
"I Never Believed" (tr. by Lennart Bruce and Sonja Bruce). [Spirit] (10:1) 89, p. 59.
"I Watch the People" (tr. by Lennart Bruce and Sonja Bruce). [Spirit] (10:1) 89, p. 63.
"Jag Betraktar Människorna." [Spirit] (10:1) 89, p. 62.
"Längtan Är Sveket Mot Dig Själv." [Spirit] (10:1) 89, p. 64.

"Longing Is Betrayal of Oneself" (tr. by Lennart Bruce and Sonja Bruce). [Spirit]
(10:1) 89, p. 65.
"November" (in Swedish). [Spirit] (10:1) 89, p. 62.
"November" (tr. by Lennart Bruce and Sonja Bruce). [Spirit] (10:1) 89, p. 63.
"Now and Then We Get Up" (tr. by Lennart Bruce and Sonja Bruce). [Spirit] (10:1)
89, p. 57.
"The Only Wars" (tr. by Lennart Bruce and Sonja Bruce). [Spirit] (10:1) 89, p. 55.
"Skymningen Kommer Varje Gång Nu." [Spirit] (10:1) 89, p. 66.
"Speak to Me" (tr. by Lennart Bruce and Sonja Bruce). [Spirit] (10:1) 89, p. 69.
"Tala till Mig." [Spirit] (10:1) 89, p. 68.
"Vi Hade Alla Möjligheter i Hela Världen." [Spirit] (10:1) 89, p. 52.
"We Had All the Possibilities in the World" (tr. by Lennart Bruce and Sonja Bruce).
[Spirit] (10:1) 89, p. 53.
207. ARAGON, Louis
"Free Zone" (tr. by Tom Mandel. Translation dedicated to the memory of Thaddeus
Poeller). [WashR] (16:2) Ag-S 90, p. 18.
"Zone Libre." [WashR] (16:2) Ag-S 90, p. 18.
208. ARAIDI, Naim
"Back to the Village" (tr. by Daniel Weissbort and Orna Raz). [Trans] (23) Spr 90, p.
228-229.
"If Only" (tr. by Daniel Weissbort and Orna Raz). [Trans] (23) Spr 90, p. 230.
ARANDA, Carlos García
See GARCIA-ARANDA, Carlos
209. ARANGO, Guillermo
"Mi Poema." [LindLM] (9:4) O-D 90, p. 28.
ARAUJO MESQUITA, Henrique de
See MESQUITA, Henrique de Araujo
210. ARCHER, Myrtle
"Two Simple Words." [ChangingM] (21) Wint-Spr 90, p. 12.
211. ARENAS, Amelia
"Junk Shop" (tr. of Enrique Santos Discépolo, w. Stuart Klawans). [Thrpny] (43)
Fall 90, p. 19.
"Spinning, Spinning" (tr. of Enrique Santos Discépolo, w. Stuart Klawans). [Thrpny]
(43) Fall 90, p. 18-19.
"Tonight I'm Going to Get Drunk" (tr. of Enrique Santos Discépolo, w. Stuart
Klawans). [Thrpny] (43) Fall 90, p. 18.
ARENAS, Cecilia Ubilla
See UBILLA-ARENAS, Cecilia
212. ARENAS, Marion
"Crossing the River." [BelPoR] (40:3) Spr 90, p. 27.
"The Mezzo-Soprano." [WestB] (27) 90, p. 15.
213. ARENAS, Rosa María
"Dream in the Hospital." [Americas] (18:2) Sum 90, p. 55.
"La Rosa Mordida" (For My Mother María Berta Arenas, Feb. 25, 1912-Feb. 7,
1984). [Americas] (18:2) Sum 90, p. 54.
214. ARGÜELLES, Ivan
(Anonymous poem). [FreeL] (4) 90.
"Astarte" (for Sarah). [YellowS] (34) Sum 90, p. 17.
"Celebration Oberman." [Manoa] (2:2) Fall 90, p. 134-135.
"Embraced by Stalin." [Abraxas] (38/39) 90, p. 116-117.
"Footnotes to the Soul in Anticipation" (for Sarah). [Abraxas] (38/39) 90, p. 119-121.
"Hyrcania." [SlipS] (10) 90, p. 48-49.
"Like a Fourteenth Century Love Poem" (for Sarah). [YellowS] (35) Wint 90-91, p.
36.
"Lyra Graeca" (for Sarah). [Abraxas] (38/39) 90, p. 122-123.
"Madonna." [Gargoyle] (37/38) 90, p. 95.
"Pantograph" (Selection: "Proemium"). [PoetryUSA] (5:3) Fall 90, p. 7.
"Pornographer X Musing on Hiroshima." [OnTheBus] (2:1, #5) Spr 90, p. 21-23.
"Rip Tide." [YellowS] (35) Wint 90-91, p. 40.
"Sweet Paradise" (for Sarah Cahill). [BlueBldgs] (12) 90, p. 28.
"Tube Alley / Survival" (with Andrew Joron). [Caliban] (8) 90, p. 62-69.
"Urtext" (from "Pantograph"). [PoetryUSA] ([5:4?]) Wint 90, p. 4-5.
"Die Vergangenheit" (in English, for Sarah Cahill). [Abraxas] (38/39) 90, p. 114-115.
"When I Think of You" (for Sarah). [Abraxas] (38/39) 90, p. 118-119.
215. ARGUETA, Jorge
"Caballo de Palo." [PoetryUSA] (5:3) Fall 90, p. 16.

43

"Me Reclutaron a Mi Hijo." [PoetryUSA] (5:3) Fall 90, p. 16.
"San Salvador" (tr. by Beatriz Johnston Hernandez). [CityLR] (4) 90, p. 208-209.
"Stick Horse" (tr. by Beatriz Johnston-Hernández and Barbara Jamison).
    [PoetryUSA] (5:3) Fall 90, p. 16.
"They Drafted My Son" (tr. by Beatriz Johnston-Hernández and Barbara Jamison).
    [PoetryUSA] (5:3) Fall 90, p. 16.
"To Those Who Ask" (tr. by Beatriz Johnston Hernandez). [CityLR] (4) 90, p.
    206-208.
216. ARGYROS, Alex
    "Cant." [Wind] (20:67) 90, p. 3.
    "The Mandelbrot Set." [Poem] (63) My 90, p. 71.
    "My Father's Promise." [Poem] (63) My 90, p. 73-75.
    "The Public Well in Mathraki." [Poem] (63) My 90, p. 72.
    "Terra Cotta" (For Jimmy). [Poem] (63) My 90, p. 70.
    "The Visible World." [Wind] (20:67) 90, p. 3.
217. ARISTEGUIETA, Jean
    "The Indians" (tr. by Mark Smith-Soto). [InterPR] (16:1) Spr 90, p. 105, 107.
    "Los Indios." [InterPR] (16:1) Spr 90, p. 104, 106.
218. ARIZA, Rene
    "Llego en Sueños." [LindLM] (9:4) O-D 90, p. 57.
219. ARMANTROUT, Rae
    "Covers." [Conjunc] (15) 90, p. 318-319.
    "Making It Up." [Verse] (7:1) Spr 90, p. 37.
    "Retraction." [Verse] (7:1) Spr 90, p. 38.
220. ARMENGOL, Alejandro A.
    "Los Rios." [LindLM] (9:4) O-D 90, p. 13.
221. ARMSTONG, Glen
    "Long Cool Silhouette." [ChironR] (9:4) Wint 90, p. 18.
222. ARMSTRONG, Cherryl
    "Listening to Advice." [CapeR] (25:1) Spr 90, p. 18.
223. ARMSTRONG, Gene
    "February Arroyo." [BellArk] (6:5) S-O 90, p. 23.
    "On the Far Bank." [BellArk] (6:1) Ja-F 90, p. 9.
    "On the Importance of Prickles." [BellArk] (6:1) Ja-F 90, p. 1.
    "Palm Tropic." [BellArk] (6:3) My-Je 90, p. 6.
    "Pumpkins." [BellArk] (6:5) S-O 90, p. 1.
    "Resistance." [BellArk] (6:2) Mr-Ap 90, p. 1.
224. ARMSTRONG, Glen
    "John Keats, King of Bohemia" (a midwestern corn field). [ChironR] (9:2) Sum 90,
        p. 15.
    "The Jukebox War of '67" (for Jim Gustafson). [HangL] (57) 90, p. 20.
225. ARMSTRONG, Jeannette (Jeannette C.)
    "Indian Woman." [CrossC] (12:1) 90, p. 7.
226. ARNESON, Susan
    "Lesbian Poem, Age 15." [FreeL] (6) Aut 90, p. 18.
    "One Summer." [FreeL] (6) Aut 90, p. 18.
227. ARNOLD, Bob
    "Barred Owl" (for Janine Pommy Vega). [HeavenB] (8) Wint 90-91, p. 2 7.
    "Morning Beside the Sea." [HeavenB] (8) Wint 90-91, p. 27.
228. ARONOWITZ, E. D.
    "Amelia Earhart." [Kalliope] (12:2) 90, p. 51.
    "The Ragman." [Kalliope] (12:2) 90, p. 51.
    "Rainy Day." [Kalliope] (12:2) 90, p. 50.
ARPINO, Tony d'
    See D'ARPINO, Ton
229. ARROWSMITH, William
    "The Euphrates" (tr. of Eugenio Montale). [Trans] (23) Spr 90, p. 225.
    "Floodwaters" (tr. of Eugenio Montale). [Antaeus] (64/65) Spr-Aut 90, p. 96-97.
    "In Silence" (tr. of Eugenio Montale). [Antaeus] (64/65) Spr-Aut 90, p. 98.
    "The Negative" (tr. of Eugenio Montale). [Trans] (23) Spr 90, p. 226.
    "On the Beach" (tr. of Eugenio Montale). [Trans] (23) Spr 90, p. 226.
    "The Triumph of Trash" (tr. of Eugenio Montale). [Trans] (23) Spr 90, p. 227.
230. ARROYO, Rane
    "Blonde As a Bat." [Americas] (18:1) Spr 90, p. 54-56.
    "Columbus's Children." [Americas] (18:1) Spr 90, p. 57-58.
    "My Heart." [Americas] (18:1) Spr 90, p. 59-61.

231. ARROYO, Raymond
    "Kisses of Blake." [WindO] (53) Fall 90, p. 15.
ARSDALE, Sarah van
    See Van ARSDALE, Sarah
232. ARTHUR, Jenny
    "The Air." [ColEng] (52:3) Mr 90, p. 280.
    "All That You Can Be." [ColEng] (52:3) Mr 90, p. 282.
    "Aplomb." [ColEng] (52:3) Mr 90, p. 280.
    "Cultural Literacy." [ColEng] (52:3) Mr 90, p. 281.
    "The Greatest Western of All Time." [IndR] (13:3) Fall 90, p. 99-100.
AS'AD, Muhammad al-
    See Al-AS'AD, Muhammad
233. ASAPH, Philip (R. Philip)
    "After the Funeral" (for Nancy). [GreensboroR] (48) Sum 90, p. 55.
    "Facts." [NegC] (10:2/3) 90, p. 102.
    "For the Fans." [WestB] (27) 90, p. 88.
    "Hecksher Park." [HighP] (5:1) Spr 90, p. 93-94.
    "Mr. Softee." [WestB] (27) 90, p. 87.
    "Once Upon a Suburb." [ChatR] (10:4) Sum 90, p. 31-32.
    "Permanent Disability." [MissR] (19:1/2, #55/56) 90, p. 232-234.
234. ASEKOFF, L. S.
    "Clocks of the Sea." [SouthwR] (75:4) Aut 90, p. 554.
    "Day Lilies." [Poetry] (155:4) Ja 90, p. 266.
    "Delta." [AmerPoR] (19:3) My-Je 90, p. 32.
    "Glass Opera." [AmerPoR] (19:3) My-Je 90, p. 32.
    "In the House of the Deafman." [Poetry] (157:3) D 90, p. 136.
    "Kafka's Angels." [Poetry] (157:3) D 90, p. 135.
    "Trace." [Poetry] (155:4) Ja 90, p. 267-268.
    "The White Loft." [Poetry] (155:4) Ja 90, p. 266-267.
    "Will." [NewYorker] (66:29) 3 S 90, p. 44-45.
    "Winter Roses." [Poetry] (155:4) Ja 90, p. 268-270.
235. ASH, John
    "The Burnt Pages." [Conjunc] (15) 90, p. 210-215.
    "Misconception of Richness." [NewYorker] (65:48) 15 Ja 90, p. 90.
    "Revising the Atlas." [NewYorker] (66:44) 17 D 90, p. 40.
    "Scenes From Schumann." [ParisR] (32:114) Spr 90, p. 84-85.
    "Three Scenes." [Conjunc] (15) 90, p. 207-209.
236. ASHBERY, John
    "Avant de Quitter Ces Lieux." [DenQ] (25:1) Sum 90, p. 5-7.
    "The Beer Drinkers." [GrandS] (9:4, #36) 90, p. 68-69.
    "Brute Image." [NewYorker] (66:12) 7 My 90, p. 76.
    "Film Noir." [NewYorker] (66:22) 16 Jl 90, p. 38-39.
    "Haunted Landscape." [ContextS] (1:1) 89, p. 60.
    "Hotel Lautréamont." [NewYorker] (66:33) 1 O 90, p. 44-45.
    "Just Wednesday." [Antaeus] (64/65) Spr-Aut 90, p. 11-12.
    "Korean Soap Opera." [ParisR] (32:116) Fall 90, p. 29-31.
    "Livelong Days." [SouthwR] (75:3) Sum 90, p. 320-321.
    "Minor Traveler." [NewAW] (6) Spr 90, p. 1-2.
    "Mixed Feelings." [GrandS] (9:2) Wint 90, p. 103-104.
    "Of Dreams and Dreaming." [GrandS] (9:4, #36) 90, p. 65-67.
    "Of Linnets and Dull Time." [ParisR] (32:116) Fall 90, p. 32.
    "On the Empress's Mind." [NewYRB] (37:8) 17 My 90, p. 17.
    "That You Tell." [Boulevard] (4:3/5:1, #12/13) Spr 90, p. 21-22.
    "Way of Life." [Conjunc] (15) 90, p. 140-143.
237. ASHFORTH, Nancy
    "Growing Old in Arizona." [OnTheBus] (2:1, #5) Spr 90, p. 24.
    "The Way We Travel." [OnTheBus] (2:1, #5) Spr 90, p. 24.
238. ASHLEY, Renée A.
    "Salt." [KenR] (NS 12:3) Sum 90, p. 54-58.
239. ASHTON, Jennifer
    "The Genius of Sleep." [NewRep] (203:7) 13 Ag 90, p. 41.
240. ASNIEN, Florence
    "I gave them life." [Writer] (103:12) D 90, p. 26.
241. ASPENBERG, Gary
    "Coda." [Vis] (33) 90, p. 34.

242. ASTRA
    "Femininity." [Pearl] (12) Fall-Wint 90, p. 30.
243. ASVAT, Farouk
    "Advice for a Mother Looking for her Child after a Day of Unrest." [Descant] (21:2, #69) Sum 90, p. 7.
    "Autumn." [Screens] (2) 90, p. 11.
    "Images Through a Cracked Mirror." [Descant] (21:2, #69) Sum 90, p. 35-36.
    "Tales from Daddima." [Screens] (2) 90, p. 8-11.
244. ATBASHIAN, Oleg
    "About Myself and Time." [PoetryUSA] (5:3) Fall 90, p. 18.
    "The air's full of fumes" (tr. of Andrei Lubenski, w. Maureen Hurley). [PoetryUSA] (5:2) Sum 90, p. 13.
    "And from the suffering you gave me" (tr. of Liudmila Taranenko, w. Maureen Hurley). [PoetryUSA] (5:2) Sum 90, p. 13.
    "The Answering Machine" (tr. of Yulia Pivovarova, w. Maureen Hurley). [PoetryUSA] (5:2) Sum 90, p. 14.
    "An Attempt at Statistics (Standing in Line for Vodka)" (tr. of Tatiana Milova, w. Maureen Hurley). [PoetryUSA] (5:2) Sum 90, p. 14.
    "Bad" (tr. of Alexander Chak, w. Maureen Hurley). [PoetryUSA] (5:2) Sum 90, p. 13.
    "The Chain" (tr. of Vicktoria Martsinkevich, w. Maureen Hurley). [PoetryUSA] (5:3) Fall 90, p. 18.
    "A Day in the Life" (tr. of Mukhammad Solikh, w. Maureen Hurley). [PoetryUSA] (5:2) Sum 90, p. 15.
    "December 14, 1988" (the day of the Armenian earthquake, tr. of Vladimir Sokolov, w. Maureen Hurley). [PoetryUSA] (5:2) Sum 90, p. 14.
    "Green on a Black and White Planet." [PoetryUSA] (5:3) Fall 90, p. 21-22.
    "If I were grass" (tr. of Liudmila Taranenko, w. Maureen Hurley). [PoetryUSA] (5:2) Sum 90, p. 13.
    "Knife knife knife knife knife sapper shovel" (tr. of Tatyana Sherbina, w. Maureen Hurley). [PoetryUSA] (5:2) Sum 90, p. 14.
    "Leaves fall down and down, making circles" (tr. of Liudmila Taranenko, w. Maureen Hurley). [PoetryUSA] (5:2) Sum 90, p. 13.
    "Leaving" (tr. of Ian Martsinkevich, w. Maureen Hurley). [PoetryUSA] (5:3) Fall 90, p. 19.
    "Life As It Is" (tr. of Ian Martsinkevich, w. Maureen Hurley). [PoetryUSA] (5:3) Fall 90, p. 18.
    "Lik Tvoj" (tr. of Andrei Lubenski, w. Maureen Hurley). [PoetryUSA] (5:2) Sum 90, p. 13.
    "The shopping I'll do will be simple and cheap" (tr. of Yelena Kryukova, w. Maureen Hurley). [PoetryUSA] (5:2) Sum 90, p. 15.
    "A single word -- and I'll know what to do" (tr. of Vallentina Kuzmenko, w. Maureen Hurley). [PoetryUSA] (5:2) Sum 90, p. 15.
    "Something Has Happened in This World" (Selection: "Oleg," tr. of Yelena Buyevich, w. Maureen Hurley). [PoetryUSA] (5:2) Sum 90, p. 13.
    "Spring Waters" (tr. of Mark Veitsman, w. Maureen Hurley). [PoetryUSA] (5:2) Sum 90, p. 13.
    "Sterilitism" (tr. of Dmitri Filimonov, w. Maureen Hurley). [PoetryUSA] (5:2) Sum 90, p. 15.
    "Talking to the Mirror" (tr. of Andrei Lubenski, w. Maureen Hurley). [PoetryUSA] (5:2) Sum 90, p. 13.
    "Waiting for flaming life" (tr. of Viacheslav Kupriyanov, w. Maureen Hurley). [PoetryUSA] (5:2) Sum 90, p. 15.
    "Why is the snow so blue?" (tr. of Irina Ratushinskaya, w. Maureen Hurley). [PoetryUSA] (5:2) Sum 90, p. 15.
245. ATHANASES, Steven
    "About Fathers" (Today Ernie). [EngJ] (79:7) N 90, p. 90.
    "After the Canoe Trip: How We Leave the Boundary Waters." [EngJ] (79:5) S 90, p. 102.
246. ATHANS, Philip
    "Lost Little Lost." [SlipS] (10) 90, p. 19.
247. ATKINS, Cynthia
    "Wivestales." [CumbPR] (10:1) Fall 90, p. 2-4.
248. ATKINS, Kathleen
    "Salt of the Earth." [GeoR] (44:1/2) Spr-Sum 90, p. 254-255.
    "You Conjure a Mother and Father." [Poetry] (157:1) O 90, p. 24.

249. ATKINSON, Alan
   "At Donkey Butte." [Wind] (20:66) 90, p. 1.
250. ATKINSON, Charles
   "Trouble in Summer." [Nimrod] (34:1) Fall-Wint 90, p. 44-47.
251. ATKINSON, Michael
   "Sunlight." [PoetL] (85:2) Sum 90, p. 5-6.
252. ATLIN, Gary
   "Birthday Song." [MalR] (93) D 90, p. 35.
   "The Danger of Shelter." [AntigR] (83) Aut 90, p. 127.
   "Geese." [MalR] (93) D 90, p. 36.
   "Huancayo, February 1984." [AntigR] (83) Aut 90, p. 128.
   "In the Careful Night." [AntigR] (83) Aut 90, p. 127.
   "Reply to Robert Bly." [PoetC] (21:3) Spr 90, p. 12.
   "Site Visits." [PoetC] (21:3) Spr 90, p. 11.
   "Tilapia." [PoetC] (21:3) Spr 90, p. 10.
253. ATWOOD, Margaret
   "Frogless." [ParisR] (32:117) Wint 90, p. 67-68.
   "The Loneliness of the Military Historian." [Harp] (281:1687) D 90, p. 17-18.
254. ATWOOD, Richard
   "In Love." [Plain] (10:2) Wint 90, p. 28.
255. AUBERT, Alvin
   "In a Beijing Studio." [Callaloo] (13:3) Sum 90, p. 394.
256. AUBERT, Jimmy R.
   "Closer to the Warning of Age." [KanQ] (22:3) Sum 90, p. 21.
   "Relics" (1990 Seaton Honorable Mention Poem). [KanQ] (22:3) Sum 90, p. 21.
257. AUER, Benedict
   "The Feast of St. Lawrence." [Interim] (9:2) Fall-Wint 90-91, p. 19.
258. AUGUSTINE, Jane
   "Contexts" (December 1986). [ManhatPR] (11) [89?], p. 48-51.
259. AUGUSTINE, Laura M.
   "Poem for the Fall Equinox." [HiramPoR] (47) Wint 90, p. 10.
   "What Becomes Clear." [CapeR] (25:2) Fall 90, p. 2.
260. AUSTIN, Don
   "The Arm." [Grain] (18:4) Wint 90, p. 75.
261. AUSTIN, Jerry
   "Bronko Nagurski." [BellArk] (6:5) S-O 90, p. 12.
   "Poplar." [BellArk] (6:1) Ja-F 90, p. 22.
   "Visit to Bainbridge Island." [BellArk] (6:6) N-D 90, p. 7.
   "Watching the Gibbons" (with my father, circa 1969). [BellArk] (6:1) Ja-F 90, p. 1.
262. AUSTIN, Kristyne
   "Mad People." [PoetryUSA] (5:2) Sum 90, p. 7.
263. AUSTIN, Penelope
   "Another Autumn." [QW] (31) Fall 90, p. 90.
   "On Woodward." [QW] (31) Fall 90, p. 91-92.
264. AUXEMERY, Jean-Paul
   "Allegory" (tr. by Richard Sieburth). [Sulfur] (10:2, #27) Fall 90, p. 70.
   "Futile Ode to Nobody" (in the manner of Alvaro de Campos, tr. by Richard
      Sieburth). [Sulfur] (10:2, #27) Fall 90, p. 68.
   "In San Francisco Segalen" (tr. by Richard Sieburth). [Sulfur] (10:2, #27) Fall 90, p.
      69-70.
   "Nommo" (tr. by Richard Sieburth). [Sulfur] (10:2, #27) Fall 90, p. 69.
   "Stelae" (tr. by Richard Sieburth). [Sulfur] (10:2, #27) Fall 90, p. 70-73.
265. AVDOIAN, Nancy
   "Chop Suey." [WormR] (30:1, #117) 90, p. 35.
   "A Mother's Day." [WormR] (30:1, #117) 90, p. 34-35.
266. AVENA, Thomas
   "The Apartment" (Exceprts: 4, 6). [EvergreenC] (6:1) Wint 90-Spr 91, p. 56-58.
   "Plums (1989)." [WormR] (30:1, #117) 90, p. 33.
   "Sans 11 (The Whitney Museum)." [WormR] (30:1, #117) 90, p. 33-34.
267. AVERILL, Diane
   "Bad for You." [ThRiPo] (35/36) 90, p. 18.
   "Ella's Son Brings Her Gifts from Riverview Cemetery" (from "The Ella Featherstone
      Poems). [MidwQ] (31:3) Spr 90, p. 343.
   "Firefly" (from "The Ella Featherstone Poems). [MidwQ] (31:3) Spr 90, p. 344.
   "Heron, Muskrat, Hobo, Spider." [TarRP] (30:1) Fall 90, p. 37.
   "Renewal." [ThRiPo] (35/36) 90, p. 19-20.

"When Mother Receives Gentlemen Visitors" (from "The Ella Featherstone Poems).
[MidwQ] (31:3) Spr 90, p. 346.
"When the Wild Geese Move Past the Mercantile in a Long Body, Dancing" (from
"The Ella Featherstone Poems). [MidwQ] (31:3) Spr 90, p. 345.
268. AVERILL, Kelly
"A Gatherer's Love." [MidwQ] (31:2) Wint 90, p. 234-235.
"The Popol Vuh." [MidwQ] (31:2) Wint 90, p. 193-194.
269. AVIGNONE, June
"Traveling Small Distances." [Footwork] 90, p. 54-57.
270. AWAD, Joseph
"Airports." [Paint] (17:33/34) Spr-Aut 90, p. 21-22.
271. AXELROD, David (David B.)
"Another for My Father." [Confr] (44/45) Fall 90-Wint 91, p. 277.
"Close-UP" (tr. of Jozo T. Boskovski). [Footwork] 90, p. 60.
"Court Documents: Infidelity." [Footwork] 90, p. 52.
"The Enlightened Person" (tr. of Jozo T. Boskovski, w. Cynthia Keesan).
[Footwork] 90, p. 61.
"Etymology of Love." [Footwork] 90, p. 52.
"The Gift of a Wallet." [PoetryNW] (31:4) Wint 90-91, p. 15-17.
"Loneliness" (tr. of Jozo T. Boskovski). [Footwork] 90, p. 61.
"Masks" (tr. of Jozo T. Boskovski, w. Anna Esapora). [Footwork] 90, p. 60.
"My Daughters." [Footwork] 90, p. 52.
"The Territory." [Footwork] 90, p. 52.
"Untitled: At a time when I was without love" (tr. of Jozo T. Boskovski). [Footwork]
90, p. 61.
"The Upstairs Tenant." [Footwork] 90, p. 52.
272. AXINN, Donald Everett
"Pilot's Dream." [Blueline] (11:1/2) 90, p. 34.
"Vignettes: The Senator Visits Georgia Out-Counties" (For Wyche Fowler, Jr.,
philosopher and friend). [Outbr] (21) 90, p. 59-60.
273. AYARZA DE HERRERA, Emilia
"Cage of Mirrors, or Man's Conscience" (tr. by Mark Smith-Soto). [InterPR] (16:1)
Spr 90, p. 21-29.
"Jaula de Espejos o la Conciencia del Hombre." [InterPR] (16:1) Spr 90, p. 20-28.
274. AYLSWORTH, Peggy
"Collage with Paint" (For H. B. Mistakenly attributed to Peggy Ashworth in No. 10).
[BlueBldgs] (12) 90, p. 30-31.
275. AZAD, Shamim (Shamin)
"A Different Disposition" (tr. by Rabiul Hasan). [Rohwedder] (5) Spr 90, p. 38.
"First Love" (tr. by Rabiul Hasan). [Amelia] (6:1, #16) 90, p. 48.
276. AZPADU, Dodici
"Omertà." [SinW] (41) Sum-Fall 90, p. 71.
277. AZUL, Piaf
"The secret of life." [PoetryUSA] (5:3) Fall 90, p. 27.
278. AZZOUNI, Jody
"Wings Come in Pairs." [HolCrit] (27:3) Je 90, p. 19.
BAASTAD, Erling Friis
See FRIIS-BAASTAD, Erling
279. BAATZ, Ronald
"When She Steps Out." [YellowS] (33) Spr 90, p. 35.
280. BABB, Sanora
"Night in a Greek Village." [SouthernR] (26:3) Jl 90, p. 679-680.
281. BABCOX, Emilie
"Dead Classmates." [FourQ] (4:1) Spr 90, p. 55.
282. BABKA, Nancy
"Downtown L.A." [OnTheBus] (2:2/3:1, #6/7) Sum-Fall 90 Wint-Spr 91, p. 37-38.
283. BACH, Peggy
"Silent Orator." [ChatR] (10:4) Sum 90, p. 80.
284. BACHMANN, Ingeborg
"After Many Years" (tr. by James Reidel). [PaintedB] (40/41) 90, p. 19.
"Anrufung des Grossen Bären." [PaintedB] (40/41) 90, p. 14.
"Autumn Maneuver" (tr. by James Reidel). [PaintedB] (40/41) 90, p. 13.
"Behind the Wall" (tr. by James Reidel). [PaintedB] (40/41) 90, p. 9.
"Entfremdung." [PaintedB] (40/41) 90, p. 10.
"Estrangement" (tr. by James Reidel). [PaintedB] (40/41) 90, p. 11.
"Die Grosse Fracht." [PaintedB] (40/41) 90, p. 16.

BACHMANN

"The Heavy Freight" (tr. by James Reidel). [PaintedB] (40/41) 90, p. 17.
"Herbstmanöver." [PaintedB] (40/41) 90, p. 12.
"Hinter der Wand." [PaintedB] (40/41) 90, p. 8.
"Invocation to the Great Bear" (tr. by James Reidel). [PaintedB] (40/41) 90, p. 15.
"Message" (tr. by Peter Filkins). [PoetryE] (30) Fall 90, p. 31.
"Nach Vielen Jahren." [PaintedB] (40/41) 90, p. 18.
285. BACHNER, Jane
"Adaptation." [Amelia] (6:2, #17) 90, p. 116.
286. BACK, Rachel Tzvia
"Litany (1)." [Sulfur] (10:2, #27) Fall 90, p. 5-8.
"Litany (II)." [Sulfur] (10:2, #27) Fall 90, p. 8-12.
287. BACKER, Marijn
"Love Poems" (tr. by Claus Bock). [Trans] (24) Fall 90, p. 126.
288. BACON, Crystal V.
"Letters I Did Not Get." [Footwork] 90, p. 114.
289. BACONSKY, A. E.
"Prophetic Anatomy" (tr. by Thomas C. Carlson and Vasile Poenaru). [ManhatR]
        (5:1) Spr 90, p. 11.
290. BAER, William
"Before She Sleeps." [Hellas] (1:1) Spr 90, p. 70.
"Boca do Inferno." [SouthernR] (26:3) Jl 90, p. 682.
"Christening in Coimbra." [SouthernR] (26:3) Jl 90, p. 682-683.
291. BAGGETT, Rebecca
"Lorna Sue Cantrell, Singing in the Choir." [NewEngR] (13:1) Fall 90, p. 37-38.
292. BAGRYANA, Elizaveta
"The Old Fortress" (tr. by Jascha Kessler and Alexander Shurbanov). [Screens] (2)
        90, p. 59.
293. BAILEY, Don
"Sunset on My Son." [Grain] (18:1) Spr 90, p. 37.
294. BAILEY, Michael
"Seated Alone." [ChatR] (10:3) Spr 90, p. 46.
295. BAILEY-WOFFORD, Jan
"Fire Dance." [Amelia] (6:2, #17) 90, p. 99.
296. BAKAITIS, Vyt
"Blue for You." [LitR] (33:4) Sum 90, p. 512.
"From Nowhere" (tr. of Jonas Mekas). [LitR] (33:4) Sum 90, p. 448-449.
297. BAKER, Brian
"Changing Order." [AntigR] (80) Wint 90, p. 141.
"Dreaming of Madrid." [AntigR] (80) Wint 90, p. 142.
298. BAKER, David
"Bad Blood Blues." [IndR] (14:1) Wint 90, p. 17.
"Contract." [NewRep] (203:11/12) 10-17 S 90, p. 46.
"The Death of God" (for Sherod Santos). [SenR] (20:2) Fall 90, p. 28-30.
"Demolition Night at the Speedway" (no cover charge). [CharR] (16:1) Spr 90, p. 73.
"Faith." [NewYorker] (66:13) 14 My 90, p. 42.
"Herbs: Our Catalog." [IndR] (14:1) Wint 90, p. 18-19.
"The Marriage." [AntR] (48:4) Fall 90, p. 492.
"Narrative." [TampaR] (3) 90, p. 56.
"The Odyssey: An Epic for Minimalists." [KanQ] (22:3) Sum 90, p. 105.
"Patriotics." [Shen] (40:1) Spr 90, p. 61-62.
"Sentences for a New Year." [SenR] (20:2) Fall 90, p. 31-33.
"To Cross Barbed Wire" (for David Citino). [LaurelR] (24:1) Wint 90, p. 12-13.
"Trees in the Night." [Nat] (251:8) 17 S 90, p. 286.
"Witness." [IndR] (14:1) Wint 90, p. 16.
299. BAKER, Dean
"Insurance Policy." [OnTheBus] (2:2/3:1, #6/7) Sum-Fall 90 Wint-Spr 91, p. 39.
300. BAKER, Donald W.
"Indiana." [LaurelR] (24:1) Wint 90, p. 41.
"West Palm Beach." [LaurelR] (24:1) Wint 90, p. 40.
301. BAKER, Houston A., Jr.
"A Birthday in the Dust" (for Mandela in his Seventies). [Callaloo] (13:3) Sum 90, p.
        428.
"Why LeRoi Wanted Himself As Dance." [Callaloo] (13:3) Sum 90, p. 429-430.
302. BAKER, John
"Your Frame, or Mine?" [Amelia] (6:1, #16) 90, p. 74.

49

303. BAKER, Susan
    "Zelda." [Bogg] (63) 90, p. 45.
304. BAKER, Tony
    "From Far Away" (with Harry Gilonis). [WestCL] (24:3) Wint 90, p. 44-54.
    "Small." [Screens] (2) 90, p. 136.
    "Three Variations on an Absent Theme." [Screens] (2) 90, p. 136.
    "Two (Separate) Extracts from a Collaborative Renga (1989) Odd-Numbered Stanzas:
        Harry Gilonis, Even-Numbered Stanzas: Tony Baker." [Screens] (2) 90, p.
        137-138.
305. BAKER, Winona
    "Documentary." [PoetryUSA] (5:1) Spr 90, p. 7.
    "Lion's Bay: Death by Drowning." [PoetryUSA] (5:1) Spr 90, p. 4.
    "Moss-hung trees." [CrossC] (12:1) 90, p. 20.
    "Pub Crawl." [PoetryUSA] (5:2) Sum 90, p. 4.
    "The Reading." [Bogg] (62) 90, p. 13.
306. BAKKEN, Dick
    "Going Into Moonlight." [Ploughs] (16:1) Spr-Sum 90, p. 67-68.
    "The Huge High Engines Unheard." [WillowS] (25) Wint 90, p. 55.
    "Learning to Drive." [Ploughs] (16:1) Spr-Sum 90, p. 64-66.
    "Learning to Drive." [PoetryUSA] (5:3) Fall 90, p. 15.
    "Tamarack." [PoetryUSA] (5:3) Fall 90, p. 16.
307. BAKOWSKI, Peter
    "48 Hours with a Loaded Gun That Never Went Off in My Hands." [Bogg] (63) 90,
        p. 13.
    "Sorting Out the Garbage" (Self-portrait, London, March 1989). [Gypsy] (15) 90, p.
        13.
308. BALABAN, John
    "For the Missing in Action." [WashR] (15:5) F-Mr 90, p. 3.
309. BALAKIAN, Peter
    "East and West." [Agni] (31/32) 90, p. 102-106.
    "Mandelstam in Armenia, 1930." [PartR] (57:2) Spr 90, p. 276-277.
310. BALASHOVA, Elena
    "Xenia" (Excerpt, tr. of Arkadii Dragomoschenko, w. Lyn Hejinian). [PoetryUSA]
        (5:3) Fall 90, p. 19.
    "Xenia" (Excerpt, tr. of Arkadii Dragomoshchenko, w. Lyn Hejinian). [Screens] (2)
        90, p. 5-7.
311. BALAZ, Joseph P.
    "Da History of Pigeon." [ChamLR] (4:1, #7) Fall 90, p. 164.
    "Eh, You Like Poetry or Wat?" [ChamLR] (3:2, #6) Spr 90, p. 32-34.
    "Ku'u Momi Makamae." [ChamLR] (4:1, #7) Fall 90, p. 162.
    "My Precious Pearl" (for Eunice K. Balaz). [ChamLR] (4:1, #7) Fall 90, p. 163.
312. BALAZS, Mary
    "Comma." [KanQ] (22:3) Sum 90, p. 190.
    "Fatigue, This Afternoon, Weariness: A Conceit." [KanQ] (22:3) Sum 90, p.
        190-191.
    "First Swim." [Wind] (20:66) 90, p. 2.
    "In the Botanical Park." [Crucible] (26) Fall 90, p. 74.
    "Widow." [Wind] (20:66) 90, p. 2-3.
313. BALBO, Ned
    "Children Threatened by a Nightingale" (After Max Ernst, oil on wood with wood
        construction). [CarolQ] (42:2) Wint 90, p. 21.
    "Whose Son, Whose Daughter." [CapeR] (25:1) Spr 90, p. 32.
314. BALDERSTON, Jean
    "Manissean Burial Ground" (Block Island, Rhode Island). [SingHM] (17) 90, p. 1.
    "Oh Bawd." [NewYorkQ] (43) Fall 90, p. 64.
315. BALDRIDGE, Wilson
    "Manufacture" (tr. of Michel Deguy, w. Jacques Servin and the author). [NewDeltaR]
        (7:1) 90, p. 12.
316. BALDWIN, Joseph
    "Certain Assumptions Concerning the Curriculum Vitae." [Northeast] (5:2) Spr 90, p.
        12.
    "Elms and Tudor Cottages." [KanQ] (22:1/2) Wint-Spr 90, p. 124.
317. BALDWIN, Tama
    "Woman, Waking." [AntR] (48:1) Wint 90, p. 90.
318. BALESTRIERI, Elizabeth
    "Grouping Fowl" (tr. of Shûji Miya, w. Machiko Okuda). [PoetryC] (11:2) Sum 90,

50

p. 20.
"Letter" (tr. of Min Zheng, w. Yafeng Bao). [PoetryC] (11:1) Spr 90, p. 22.
"The Thin Country." [PoetryC] (11:1) Spr 90, p. 27.
319. BALL, Angela
"Baptism." [PraS] (64:3) Fall 90, p. 95-96.
"Drive." [PraS] (64:3) Fall 90, p. 94-95.
"Hobo." [Ploughs] (16:1) Spr-Sum 90, p. 124-125.
"Jamaica." [PartR] (57:3) Sum 90, p. 442-443.
"Materials." [VirQR] (66:4) Aut 90, p. 669-670.
"A Moon at Maximum Eclipse." [VirQR] (66:4) Aut 90, p. 670-671.
320. BALL, David
"Les Ravagés" (Selections: 10, 16, 27, tr. of Henri Michaux). [Notus] (5:1) Spr 90,
p. 65-67.
321. BALL, Joseph H.
"All Giving Is Not Kindness." [SoDakR] (28:2) Sum 90, p. 161.
"Short Note." [Wind] (20:67) 90, p. 10.
"Skipping Stones." [EngJ] (79:5) S 90, p. 103.
"A Summer Poem" (for Margaret). [CapeR] (25:2) Fall 90, p. 30.
"To Have and Have Not." [ClockR] (6:1) 90, p. 75-76.
"The Woman Who Sits in the Sun." [SoDakR] (28:2) Sum 90, p. 162.
322. BALL, Sally
"31 October." [MissR] (19:1/2, #55/56) 90, p. 235.
323. BALLARD, Charles G.
"Farmers." [EngJ] (79:6) O 90, p. 95.
324. BALLERINI, Luigi
"(At)tendere" (For Glauco, tr. by Stephen Sartarelli). [LitR] (33:4) Sum 90, p. 466.
325. BALLESTER, Margarita
"VI Variations" (from "L'infant i la Mort," 1989, tr. by Montserrat Abelló). [PoetryC]
(11:4) Wint 90, p. 21.
326. BALTENSPERGER, Peter
"Butterflies on Ice." [Grain] (18:2) Sum 90, p. 28.
"Connectives in the Night." [PottPort] (11) 89, p. 19.
"Counting By Rote." [PottPort] (11) 89, p. 18.
"Ice Patches on Parquet." [PottPort] (12) 90, p. 51.
"Seeing Through Dark Eyes." [PottPort] (12) 90, p. 51.
327. BANAI, Peretz-Dror
"Orange Street, Kefar Sava" (tr. by Linda Pastan). [PoetL] (85:4) Wint 90-91, p. 23.
328. BANANI, Sheila
"Intone." [OnTheBus] (2:2/3:1, #6/7) Sum-Fall 90 Wint-Spr 91, p. 40.
"My Daddy Wrote Rock 'n' Roll." [OnTheBus] (2:1, #5) Spr 90, p. 26-27.
"On a Painting by David Hockney." [OnTheBus] (2:2/3:1, #6/7) Sum-Fall 90
Wint-Spr 91, p. 41.
"Taking Chances: Windward in a Time of Butterflies." [OnTheBus] (2:1, #5) Spr 90,
p. 25.
"Waterfall" (for Joe Goode). [OnTheBus] (2:2/3:1, #6/7) Sum-Fall 90 Wint-Spr 91,
p. 40.
"Wild Greek Chickens." [OnTheBus] (2:1, #5) Spr 90, p. 25-26.
329. BANERJEE, Paramita
"Amnesiac River" (tr. of Devarati Mitra, w. Carolyne Wright). [HawaiiR] (14:1, #28)
Wint 89-90, p. 70.
"Flowers Born Blind" (tr. of Devarati Mitra, w. Carolyne Wright). [HawaiiR] (14:1,
#28) Wint 89-90, p. 69.
"The Green Stigma" (tr. of Devarati Mitra, w. Carolyne Wright). [HawaiiR] (14:1,
#28) Wint 89-90, p. 72.
"No, No, and No" (tr. of Devarati Mitra, w. Carolyne Wright). [HawaiiR] (14:1,
#28) Wint 89-90, p. 71.
330. BANG, Mary Jo
"Beckett Remembered." [Kalliope] (12:1) 90, c89, p. 58.
BANGJUN, Huang
See HUANG, Bangjun
331. BANKS, Lorna
"Heritage." [PottPort] (11) 89, p. 9.
332. BANKS, Stanley E.
"Stella." [NewL] (57:1) Fall 90, p. 73.
333. BANUS, Maria
"The Abandoned Pharmacy" (tr. by Mary Mattfield). [PoetryE] (30) Fall 90, p. 18.

"The New Notebook" (tr. by Mary Mattfield). [WebR] (14:2) Spr 90, p. 102.
"On a Glass Icon" (tr. by Mary Mattfield). [PoetryE] (30) Fall 90, p. 16.
"Die Reichs-Kanzlei" (tr. by Mary Mattfield). [PoetryE] (30) Fall 90, p. 17.
"Your Name" (tr. by Mary Mattfield). [WebR] (14:2) Spr 90, p. 100-101.
334. BAO, Yafeng
"Letter" (tr. of Min Zheng, w. Elizabeth Balestrieri). [PoetryC] (11:1) Spr 90, p. 22.
335. BAPST, Don
"The Pink Bathroom." [BrooklynR] (7) 90, p. 37.
336. BAQUERO, Gaston
"Manuela Saenz Baila con Giuseppe Garibaldi el Rigodon Final de la Existencia" (Para
Carlos Contramaestre y Salvador Garmendia). [LindLM] (9:4) O-D 90, p. 20.
337. BARAKA, Amiri
"The Customer." [NewYorkQ] (42) Sum 90, p. 58-61.
"Jarman Said, 'Our Whole Universe Is Generated by a Rhythm'." [NewYorkQ] (41)
Spr 90, p. 62.
338. BARANCZAK, Stanislaw
"Garden Party" (tr. by Aleksandra and Michael Parker). [Verse] (7:2) Sum 90, p. 13.
"It Would Have Taken So Little." [OnTheBus] (2:2/3:1, #6/7) Sum-Fall 90 Wint-Spr
91, p. 244-245.
"Photograph of a Writer." [OnTheBus] (2:2/3:1, #6/7) Sum-Fall 90 Wint-Spr 91, p.
243-244.
"Resume" (tr. by Aleksandra and Michael Parker). [Verse] (7:2) Sum 90, p. 12.
"September" (tr. by Aleksandra and Michael Parker). [Verse] (7:2) Sum 90, p. 12.
"Taking Along the Dust." [OnTheBus] (2:2/3:1, #6/7) Sum-Fall 90 Wint-Spr 91, p.
245.
"Temporary Limitations." [OnTheBus] (2:2/3:1, #6/7) Sum-Fall 90 Wint-Spr 91, p.
243.
"Whole Life in Suitcases." [OnTheBus] (2:2/3:1, #6/7) Sum-Fall 90 Wint-Spr 91, p.
242-243.
339. BARASCH, Robert
"Reconstituting." [AnthNEW] 90, p. 16.
340. BARATTA, Edward
"Dead Boys." [Confr] (44/45) Fall 90-Wint 91, p. 327.
"Lullaby." [MassR] (31:3) Aut 90, p. 468.
BARBARA EVE
See EVE, Barbara
341. BARBARESE, J. T.
"Bad Conscience." [SouthernR] (26:3) Jl 90, p. 684-685.
"The Fallen Thing." [SouthernR] (26:3) Jl 90, p. 685.
"Fog Covering the Pier." [SouthernR] (26:3) Jl 90, p. 685-686.
"Solstice." [SouthernR] (26:3) Jl 90, p. 684.
342. BARDENS, Ann
"Taking Apart the Porch" (for R. J.). [Plain] (10:2) Wint 90, p. 35.
343. BARDON, Jim
"Myths Before Breakfast." [Crucible] (26) Fall 90, p. 72.
344. BARDWELL, Leland
"Snow Love." [Quarry] (39:1) Wint 90, p. 58.
"The Wells" (tr. of Nicole de Pontcharra). [Trans] (23) Spr 90, p. 142.
345. BARGEN, Walter
"Awards." [SpoonRQ] (15:1) Wint 90, p. 19.
"A Brief Note on Principles." [CharR] (16:1) Spr 90, p. 64-65.
"The Collectors" (for Rod Santos). [CharR] (16:1) Spr 90, p. 62-63.
"Dialects." [LaurelR] (24:2) Sum 90, p. 44-45.
"Godspeed." [CapeR] (25:2) Fall 90, p. 40.
"Heavenly Host." [Farm] (7:1) Spr 90, p. 40.
"Relativity." [CharR] (16:1) Spr 90, p. 63-64.
"Stardom." [SpoonRQ] (15:1) Wint 90, p. 18.
"Syndrome." [CapeR] (25:2) Fall 90, p. 41.
"White Out." [PoetryNW] (31:2) Sum 90, p. 25.
346. BARGHOUTHI, Mureed
"The Guards" (tr. by Lena Jayyusi and W. S. Merwin). [PaperAir] (4:3) 90, p. 67.
"Refuge" (tr. by Lena Jayyusi and W. S. Merwin). [PaperAir] (4:3) 90, p. 68.
"The Tribes" (tr. by Lena Jayyusi and W. S. Merwin). [PaperAir] (4:3) 90, p. 68.
347. BARKA, Wasyl
"The Mad Woman" (tr. by Stash). [Agni] (31/32) 90, p. 243.

52

BARKAN

348. BARKAN, Stanley H.
"An Ancient Diary" (from the Sicilian Antigruppo, tr. of Ignazio Navarra, w. Nat
Scammacca). [Footwork] 90, p. 104.
"December." [Footwork] 90, p. 84.
"Encounter." [Footwork] 90, p. 85.
"June." [Footwork] 90, p. 84.
"May." [Footwork] 90, p. 84.
"Ruler." [Footwork] 90, p. 84.
"Seeds." [Footwork] 90, p. 85.
349. BARKER, Sebastian
"Bluebells." [Quarry] (39:1) Wint 90, p. 11-13.
350. BARKER, Wendy
"Father's Fish." [Nimrod] (34:1) Fall-Wint 90, p. 89-90.
"From the Attic at Thornfield." [Poetry] (156:2) My 90, p. 82-83.
"Heat, Letting Go" (for Larry). [SouthernPR] (30:1) Spr 90, p. 46-47.
351. BARKS, Coleman
"Small Talk" (for Mike Nicholson). [KenR] (NS 12:3) Sum 90, p. 125-138.
352. BARLOW, John
"Feeling Defensive?" [PraF] (11:4) Wint 90-91, p. 29.
353. BARNES, Dick
"Goodbye Big Ed." [SoCoast] (9) Fall 90, p. 52.
"A Pantoum for Anselm Kiefer." [OnTheBus] (2:1, #5) Spr 90, p. 28.
354. BARNES, Jim
"At a Crossing, Somewhere in Ulster." [Hellas] (1:2) Fall 90, p. 224.
"For Roland, Presumed Taken." [Hellas] (1:2) Fall 90, p. 225-226.
"Learning Balance." [Amelia] (6:2, #17) 90, p. 46.
"On Hearing the News That Hitler Was Dead." [TriQ] (79) Fall 90, p. 109-110.
"The Ranch, Wild Horse Canyon, 1943." [NewEngR] (13:2) Wint 90, p. 157-158.
"Today for Breakfast We Had" (tr. of William Cliff). [ArtfulD] (18/19) 90, p. 97.
"Under the Tent." [Paint] (17:33/34) Spr-Aut 90, p. 8.
355. BARNES, Kate
"Where the Deer Were." [NewYorker] (66:18) 18 Je 90, p. 78.
356. BARNES, R. G.
"Buenos Aires, 1899" (tr. of Jorge Luis Borges, w. Robert Mezey). [SoCoast] (8)
Spr 90, p. 13.
"Emerson" (tr. of Jorge Luis Borges, w. Robert Mezey). [SoCoast] (8) Spr 90, p. 17.
"Unrecognized Street" (tr. of Jorge Luis Borges, w. Robert Mezey). [SoCoast] (8)
Spr 90, p. 11.
"Written in a Copy of the Geste of Beowulf" (tr. of Jorge Luis Borges, w. Robert
Mezey). [SoCoast] (8) Spr 90, p. 15.
357. BARNETT, S. L.
"Haiku Collection." [ChamLR] (4:1, #7) Fall 90, p. 80-81.
358. BARNIDGE, Mary Shen
"The Elegy Writer's Blues." [WillowR] Spr 90, p. 10-11.
359. BARNIE, John
"My Cousin Told Me This." [AmerPoR] (19:4) Jl-Ag 90, p. 47.
360. BARNSTONE, Tony
"Night: Theme and Variations" (tr. of Bei Dao, w. Liu Xuemin). [CityLR] (4) 90, p.
154.
361. BARNSTONE, Willis
"Gospel of Eve with Adam." [TarRP] (30:1) Fall 90, p. 6.
"Gospel of the Moon." [TarRP] (30:1) Fall 90, p. 6.
"Only white walls know the horror" (tr. of Bronislava Volková, w. the author).
[PoetryE] (30) Fall 90, p. 66.
362. BAROFFIO, David
"Empty Space." [OnTheBus] (2:2/3:1, #6/7) Sum-Fall 90 Wint-Spr 91, p. 42.
"It Happened Again." [OnTheBus] (2:2/3:1, #6/7) Sum-Fall 90 Wint-Spr 91, p. 42.
363. BARON, Mary
"Dead Butterfly." [HampSPR] (Anthology 1975-1990) 90, p. 27.
"Love Letter." [HampSPR] (Anthology 1975-1990) 90, p. 27.
"Pythia." [HampSPR] (Anthology 1975-1990) 90, p. 27.
364. BARON, Todd
"Bartelby." [Talisman] (4) Spr 90, p. 49-50.
365. BAROQUE, Ben
"Shanty-Town Shankton Lee." [EmeraldCR] (1990) c89, p. 7.

366. BARQUET, Jesús J.
  "Optica." [Ometeca] (1:2/2:1) 89-90, p. 33.
367. BARR, John
  "Deer Xing." [Confr] (42/43) Spr-Sum 90, p. 151.
  "Sign Shop, Sing Sing." [Confr] (42/43) Spr-Sum 90, p. 152.
  "The Water Bed." [Amelia] (6:2, #17) 90, p. 28-31.
368. BARR, Tina
  "Antique Shop." [SwampR] (6) Sum-Fall 90, p. 18.
  "Borderline." [SwampR] (5) Wint-Spr 90, p. 78.
  "A Boy Dives from a Rock." [Confr] (42/43) Spr-Sum 90, p. 238.
  "Buttonwood." [SwampR] (6) Sum-Fall 90, p. 22-23.
  "Cutaway." [SwampR] (6) Sum-Fall 90, p. 28-29.
  "Dissembler." [SwampR] (6) Sum-Fall 90, p. 17.
  "Green Moths." [SwampR] (6) Sum-Fall 90, p. 26-27.
  "Guardian." [SwampR] (6) Sum-Fall 90, p. 31.
  "Music Box." [SwampR] (6) Sum-Fall 90, p. 24-25.
  "Snake." [SwampR] (6) Sum-Fall 90, p. 21.
  "Two Journeys Across the Lake." [SwampR] (6) Sum-Fall 90, p. 19-20.
  "Underwater." [SwampR] (6) Sum-Fall 90, p. 30.
369. BARRAL, Jacqueline
  "The Immigrant" (tr. by Jane Brierley). [PraF] (11:1) Spr 90, p. 157.
  "L'Immigrant/e." [PraF] (11:1) Spr 90, p. 156.
370. BARRATT, Robin Rhein
  "Collect for Women." [Pearl] (12) Fall-Wint 90, p. 44.
371. BARRERA VALVERDE, Alfonso
  "Aristocracy" (tr. by Maria Herrera Sobek). [OnTheBus] (2:2/3:1, #6/7) Sum-Fall 90
      Wint-Spr 91, p. 250.
  "Existence" (tr. by Maria Herrera Sobek). [OnTheBus] (2:2/3:1, #6/7) Sum-Fall 90
      Wint-Spr 91, p. 250.
  "Resolutions" (tr. by Maria Herrera Sobek). [OnTheBus] (2:2/3:1, #6/7) Sum-Fall 90
      Wint-Spr 91, p. 250.
  "Stone Cross" (To my brother Wilfrido, tr. by Maria Herrera Sobek). [OnTheBus]
      (2:2/3:1, #6/7) Sum-Fall 90 Wint-Spr 91, p. 251.
372. BARRESI, Dorothy
  "Cinderella and Lazarus, Part II." [DenQ] (25:2) Fall 90, p. 8-9.
  "Straw into Gold." [Crazy] (38) Spr 90, p. 20-22.
  "Van Gogh Among the Poor on the Subject of His Art (Deferred)." [MinnR] (NS
      34/35) Spr-Fall 90, p. 32-33.
  "Venice Beach: Brief Song." [Crazy] (38) Spr 90, p. 23-24.
373. BARRETT, Herb
  "City Fog." [Amelia] (6:1, #16) 90, p. 69.
374. BARRETT, Joseph
  "Critique at a Local Show." [Bogg] (62) 90, p. 23.
  "Nocturne in an Oriental Garden." [Bogg] (62) 90, p. 42-43.
375. BARRIENTOS, Raúl
  "All That Jazz" (tr. by Ben A. Heller). [MassR] (31:4) Wint 90, p. 549-554.
376. BARRINGTON, Judith
  "The Age of the Sea" (tr. of Cristina Peri Rossi). [Trans] (23) Spr 90, p. 187.
  "Infancy" (tr. of Cristina Peri Rossi). [Trans] (23) Spr 90, p. 188.
  "Meditation (I)" (tr. of Cristina Peri Rossi). [Trans] (23) Spr 90, p. 189.
  "Meditation (II)" (tr. of Cristina Peri Rossi). [Trans] (23) Spr 90, p. 189.
  "Quotation from a Poet" (tr. of Cristina Peri Rossi). [Trans] (23) Spr 90, p. 188.
377. BARRIOS, Jarrett
  "Lara in It" (Honorable Mention). [HarvardA] (124:3) Mr 90, p. 17.
378. BARRY, Christopher
  "Election Mutter." [BrooklynR] (7) 90, p. 42.
379. BARRY, Coyla
  "Rain Crow." [SouthernPR] (30:1) Spr 90, p. 59-60.
380. BARRY, Sebastian
  "Harbour House." [Quarry] (39:1) Wint 90, p. 59.
381. BARSAMIAN, Anahid
  "Fractions" (tr. by Diana Der-Hovanessian). [Nimrod] (33:2) Spr-Sum 90, p. 37.
382. BARST, Fran
  "An Edward Hopper Painting." [SwampR] (6) Sum-Fall 90, p. 77-78.
  "On Route to Nong Khai." [SlipS] (10) 90, p. 54.
  "Psyche's First Task." [SlipS] (10) 90, p. 53-54.

"Surgery." [SwampR] (6) Sum-Fall 90, p. 75-76.
383. BARTEK, Maggy Coopersmith
"Angel." [SmPd] (27:1, #78) Wint 90, p. 27.
"Changes in My Father." [SmPd] (27:1, #78) Wint 90, p. 28.
384. BARTH, R. L.
"To a Man Who Said He Would Live Forever." [Hellas] (1:2) Fall 90, p. 232.
"What Kind of Mistress He Wants." [Hellas] (1:2) Fall 90, p. 228.
385. BARTHELME, Steve
"No." [NewAW] (6) Spr 90, p. 102.
386. BARTLEBY, Bee
"Our Men." [Pearl] (10) Spr 90, p. 23.
387. BARTLETT, Brian
"Bear Bell." [MalR] (90) Spr 90, p. 42-43.
"If I Knew the Names of Everything." [MalR] (90) Spr 90, p. 44-45.
"Kissing in the Carwash." [AntigR] (81/82) Spr-Sum 90, p. 119-120.
"Prèmiere Pédicurie" (New Orleans, 1873). [MalR] (90) Spr 90, p. 46-48.
388. BARTLETT, Elizabeth
"Housewife." [Gypsy] (15) 90, p. 16.
389. BARTLEY, Jackie
"The Gift." [WestB] (27) 90, p. 30.
390. BARTON, John
"Patterns." [Dandel] (17:1) Spr-Sum 90, p. 6-7.
391. BARTOW, Stuart
"Bull Thistle." [Mildred] (4:1) 90, p. 86.
"The Flight of Frogs." [Mildred] (4:1) 90, p. 84-85.
"The Spiders Are But Sirens." [Mildred] (4:1) 90, p. 85.
392. BARWIN, Gary
"Ayme walkynge on aire." [WestCL] (24:3) Wint 90, p. 76.
"Heere i aym." [WestCL] (24:3) Wint 90, p. 74.
"One legge on th'grounde." [WestCL] (24:3) Wint 90, p. 75.
"The stars are a pale pox on the sky's dark chicken." [WestCL] (24:3) Wint 90, p. 70-72.
"Yes, overre theire." [WestCL] (24:3) Wint 90, p. 73.
393. BARYLANKA, Jola
"Dance" (for Maria Kuncewiczowa, tr. by Reuel K. Wilson). [Trans] (24) Fall 90, p. 189.
"Music" (tr. by Reuel K. Wilson). [Trans] (24) Fall 90, p. 188.
394. BARZA, Steven
"The Moon and the Tides Are Not in Simple Relation." [CapeR] (25:2) Fall 90, p. 23.
"Shadow Optics." [Ascent] (15:1) 90, p. 62.
395. BASINSKI, Michael
"Homage to Senator J. Helms." [PoetryUSA] ([5:4?]) Wint 90, p. 14.
"Odin Marz." [PoetryUSA] ([5:4?]) Wint 90, p. 14.
396. BASS, Ellen
"Courage, 1983." [SingHM] (17) 90, p. 4.
397. BATEMAN, Claire
"Convert." [SingHM] (17) 90, p. 5.
"The Frog Princess." [SoCaR] (23:1) Fall 90, p. 35.
398. BATES, Tamara
"Indifference." [RagMag] (7:2) Spr 90, p. 8.
"Stubborn Woman" (for Teresa). [RagMag] (7:2) Spr 90, p. 8.
399. BATHURST, Kirsten
"This is just to say." [PoetryUSA] (5:2) Sum 90, p. 7.
"Waterbed Dreams." [PoetryUSA] (5:2) Sum 90, p. 7.
400. BATISTA, Victor
"I. Humanismo." [LindLM] (9:4) O-D 90, p. 53.
"II. Justicia Social." [LindLM] (9:4) O-D 90, p. 53.
"III. Metanoia." [LindLM] (9:4) O-D 90, p. 53.
"IV. Credo." [LindLM] (9:4) O-D 90, p. 53.
401. BATTIN, Wendy
"The News from Mars." [NewEngR] (13:2) Wint 90, p. 109-110.
"One." [NewEngR] (13:2) Wint 90, p. 111.
402. BATTRAM, Michael R.
"Be Brave." [WormR] (30:1, #117) 90, p. 5.
"Earl Reconsiders His Views on Israel." [WormR] (30:1, #117) 90, p. 4-5.
"A Guy I Know." [WormR] (30:1, #117) 90, p. 3.

"His Name Was Steve." [WormR] (30:1, #117) 90, p. 3.
"The Kid Believes in Management." [WormR] (30:1, #117) 90, p. 4.
"The Writer at Home." [WormR] (30:1, #117) 90, p. 4.
403. BAUCHAU, Henry
"The Dazzled One" (tr. by Daniel de Bruycker). [Vis] (32) 90, p. 33.
404. BAUDELAIRE, Charles
"Parisian Dream" (for W. T. Bandy, tr. by Walter Martin). [SouthernR] (26:2) Ap 90, p. 319-323.
"Rêve Parisien" (A Constantin Guys). [SouthernR] (26:2) Ap 90, p. 318-322.
405. BAUER, Carlos
"Ode to Salvador Dali" (tr. of Federico García Lorca). [AnotherCM] (21) 90, p. 111-114.
406. BAUER, Grace
"Dear Absence." [Shen] (40:2) Sum 90, p. 85.
"Eve Recollecting the Garden." [Poetry] (156:1) Ap 90, p. 11.
"Frida Digresses on Red." [Poetry] (156:1) Ap 90, p. 9-10.
"Her Great Escape." [SoDakR] (28:1) Spr 90, p. 28.
"How I'm Doing. What It's Like." [SwampR] (5) Wint-Spr 90, p. 70-72.
"Keeping in Touch." [SwampR] (6) Sum-Fall 90, p. 11-12.
"My Grandmother Started Dying." [SouthernPR] (30:2) Fall 90, p. 47-48.
"Passengers." [SwampR] (6) Sum-Fall 90, p. 10.
"Second Lining at My Own Jazz Funeral" (for Rette & Nancy). [Shen] (40:2) Sum 90, p. 84.
"The Visiting Paleontologist Feels Her Thigh." [SoDakR] (28:1) Spr 90, p. 26-27.
"When in Doubt." [SwampR] (5) Wint-Spr 90, p. 73.
407. BAUMEL, Judith
"And to See the City Again" (tr. of Patrizia Cavalli). [NewYorker] (66:43) 10 D 90, p. 96.
"Far from Kingdoms" (tr. of Patrizia Cavalli). [NewYorker] (66:33) 1 O 90, p. 78.
"World Without End." [NewYorker] (66:18) 18 Je 90, p. 32.
408. BAUMGAERTNER, Jill P.
"We Cannot Keep It." [ChrC] (107:28) 10 O 90, p. 903.
409. BAUSCH, Victor H.
"The Dioxin Blues." [SlipS] (10) 90, p. 63.
410. BAWER, Bruce
"Devotions." [Verse] (7:3) Wint 90, p. 45-46.
"Ferry" (for Chip). [Verse] (7:3) Wint 90, p. 44-45.
"Jeremy." [Agni] (31/32) 90, p. 153-156.
411. BAXTER, Charles
"This Stranger." [Notus] (5:1) Spr 90, p. 39.
412. BAYDUN, Abbas
"The Girl Servant" (tr. by May Jayyusi and John Heath-Stubbs). [Screens] (2) 90, p. 16-18.
"Suicide" (tr. by May Jayyusi and John Heath-Stubbs). [Screens] (2) 90, p. 13-15.
413. BAYER, Deanne
"Before Goodbye." [DustyD] (1:2) O 90, p. 13.
"Grant Wood's People." [DustyD] (1:2) O 90, p. 13.
"Holding Patterns." [DustyD] (1:2) O 90, p. 13.
"Hologram." [DustyD] (1:2) O 90, p. 12.
414. BAYRON-BRUNET, Vilma
"Que no se nos enquiste el absurdo." [Ometeca] (1:2/2:1) 89-90, p. 30.
"Trapo, trapos." [Ometeca] (1:2/2:1) 89-90, p. 29.
415. BAYSANS, Greg
"Burning." [JamesWR] (7:3) Spr 90, p. 10.
416. BBB
"Animals -- Especially a Squirrel on Grandfather's Far Hill." [Wind] (20:67) 90, p. 4-5.
417. BEACH, Jack
"Aftermath" (Amsterdam, December 1988). [EmeraldCR] (1990) c89, p. 87-88.
"Anne Frank Huis." [EmeraldCR] (1990) c89, p. 88-89.
418. BEAKE, Fred
"Through a Window." [Stand] (31:1) Wint 89-90, p. 35.
"The Whaler." [Stand] (31:1) Wint 89-90, p. 34-35.
BEAR, Shirley
See MINGWON, Mingwôn (Shirley Bear)

56

BEASLEY

419. BEASLEY, Bruce
  "After an Adoration." [Poetry] (157:3) D 90, p. 127-128.
  "Black Wednesday with Ashes." [Hudson] (43:1) Spr 90, p. 72-74.
  "The Cursing of the Fig Tree." [Amelia] (6:1, #16) 90, p. 80.
  "Eurydice in Hades." [YaleR] (79:4) Sum 90 c1991, p. 688-689.
  "January Thaw" (elegy for my mother). [Hudson] (43:1) Spr 90, p. 70-72.
420. BEATTY, Jan
  "Fog." [Nimrod] (34:1) Fall-Wint 90, p. 5.
  "Love Poem." [Nimrod] (34:1) Fall-Wint 90, p. 3.
  "Not Thinking About Gardenias." [Nimrod] (34:1) Fall-Wint 90, p. 1.
  "Visiting My Father a Few Days Before His Operation." [Nimrod] (34:1) Fall-Wint
      90, p. 4.
  "What We Can Count On." [Nimrod] (34:1) Fall-Wint 90, p. 2.
421. BEATTY, Paul
  "EP." [PoetryUSA] (5:3) Fall 90, p. 13.
422. BEAUCHAMP, Steven
  "Reporter Covering an Auto Wreck." [ChatR] (11:1) Fall 90, p. 22.
423. BEAUMONT, Jeanne
  "Healing Thyself." [NoDaQ] (58:2) Spr 90, p. 107.
  "Honeymoon Cottage." [GettyR] (3:4) Aut 90, p. 628.
  "Ivy." [CreamCR] (14:1) Spr 90, p. 118.
  "Metro Forecast I." [Caliban] (9) 90, p. 116.
  "Passive Today." [PoetryNW] (31:3) Aut 90, p. 33-34.
  "Still." [GettyR] (3:4) Aut 90, p. 629.
  "The Topless Lunch." [Kalliope] (12:2) 90, p. 13.
  "Vernal Tea." [CreamCR] (14:1) Spr 90, p. 119.
424. BECK, Barbara
  "Chinatown (Paris, 18th Arrondissement)" (tr. of Yves Di Manno). [Trans] (23) Spr
      90, p. 158-159.
425. BECK, Glenn
  "A Sort of Love Poem from a Bathtub in Winter." [SycamoreR] (2:1) Wint 90, p.
      38-39.
426. BECKER, Carol
  "The Big Move." [SmPd] (27:3, #80) Fall 90, p. 32.
  "Society." [SmPd] (27:3, #80) Fall 90, p. 33-34.
427. BECKERMAN, H. N.
  "Adjustments." [Kaleid] (20) Wint-Spr 90, p. 15.
428. BECKETT, Samuel
  "Long After Chamfort" (Eight Maxims, tr. of Nicolas-Sébastien de Chamfort).
      [Trans] (23) Spr 90, p. 76-77.
  "What Is the Word" (for Joe Chaikin). [GrandS] (9:2) Wint 90, p. 17-18.
429. BECKETT, Tom
  "Moisture." [Talisman] (4) Spr 90, p. 45-48.
430. BEEKMAN, E. M.
  "Homage to Mondrian" (tr. by the author). [Trans] (24) Fall 90, p. 62-64.
431. BEGGS-UEMA, Marck (Marck L.)
  "A Border." [MissouriR] (13:2) 90, p. 75.
  "Grave." [WillowS] (26) Spr 90, p. 78-79.
  "Kilty Sue." [ManhatPR] (12) [90?], p. 40.
  "A Vision of Love." [HawaiiR] (15:1, #31) Wint 90, p. 29-30.
  "Wood-Split." [ManhatPR] (12) [90?], p. 39.
432. BEHAN, Marie
  "The Spiral of Archimedes." [NegC] (10:1) 90, p. 33-35.
433. BEHN, Robin
  "Aubade." [MissouriR] (13:2) 90, p. 48-49.
  "The God Hole." [Ploughs] (16:4) Wint 90-91, p. 142-143.
  "Husbandry." [Iowa] (20:3) Fall 90, p. 33-36.
  "Midwestern Villanelle." [Iowa] (20:3) Fall 90, p. 37.
  "The Name of God." [Agni] (31/32) 90, p. 182-183.
  "The Oboist" (Winner, 10th Annual New England Review Narrative Poetry
      Competition). [NewEngR] (13:1) Fall 90, p. 86-87.
  "Ten Years After Your Deliberate Drowning." [IndR] (14:1) Wint 90, p. 22-23.
  "Vision Near Ice" (For D.). [IndR] (14:1) Wint 90, p. 20-21.
434. BEHRENDT, Stephen C.
  "Before the Autumn Equinox." [Plain] (10:3) Spr 90, p. 23.
  "The Cemetery at Bark River." [SpoonRQ] (15:2) Spr 90, p. 16-18.

"Easter Flood." [Plain] (10:3) Spr 90, p. 17.
"Ice Fishing at Night." [KanQ] (22:1/2) Wint-Spr 90, p. 123.
435. BEI, Dao
"The Answer" (tr. by Bonnie S. McDougall). [ManhatR] (5:2) Fall 90, p. 46-47.
"April" (tr. by Bonnie S. McDougall and Chen Maiping). [ManhatR] (5:2) Fall 90, p. 11.
"A Bach Concert" (tr. by Bonnie S. McDougall and Chen Maiping). [ManhatR] (5:2) Fall 90, p. 8.
"Blanks" (tr. by Bonnie S. McDougall). [ManhatR] (5:2) Fall 90, p. 48-49.
"The Collection" (tr. by Bonnie S. McDougall and Chen Maiping). [ManhatR] (5:2) Fall 90, p. 6.
"Coming Home at Night" (tr. by Bonnie S. McDougall and Chen Maiping). [ManhatR] (5:2) Fall 90, p. 11.
"Declaration" (for Yu Luoke, tr. by Bonnie S. McDougall). [PoetryUSA] ([5:4?]) Wint 90, p. 22.
"Declaration" (to Yu Luoke, martyr, in Chinese and English, tr. by Wu Keming). [PaintedB] (40/41) 90, p. 50-51.
"Discovery" (tr. by Bonnie S. McDougall and Chen Maiping). [ManhatR] (5:2) Fall 90, p. 12.
"The East's Imagination" (tr. by Bonnie S. McDougall and Chen Maiping). [ManhatR] (5:2) Fall 90, p. 7.
"An End or a Beginning" (for Yu Luoke, tr. by Bonnie S. McDougall). [PoetryUSA] ([5:4?]) Wint 90, p. 22.
"Expectation" (tr. by Bonnie S. McDougall). [PoetryUSA] ([5:4?]) Wint 90, p. 21.
"Expectation" (tr. by Dong Jiping). [Footwork] 90, p. 43.
"Following Thoughts" (tr. by James A. Wilson). [CityLR] (4) 90, p. 151-152.
"For Only a Second" (tr. by Bonnie S. McDougall and Chen Maiping). [ManhatR] (5:2) Fall 90, p. 5.
"A Formal Declaration" (tr. by James A. Wilson). [CityLR] (4) 90, p. 153.
"Gains" (tr. by Bonnie S. McDougall and Chen Maiping). [ManhatR] (5:2) Fall 90, p. 10.
"Getting an Electric Shock" (tr. by Dong Jiping). [Footwork] 90, p. 43.
"Let's Go" (tr. by Sam Hamill). [PoetryE] (30) Fall 90, p. 101.
"Love Story" (tr. by Bonnie S. McDougall). [PoetryUSA] ([5:4?]) Wint 90, p. 22.
"The Morning's Story" (tr. by Bonnie S. McDougall and Chen Maiping). [ManhatR] (5:2) Fall 90, p. 4.
"Night: Theme and Variations" (tr. by Tony Barnstone and Liu Xuemin). [CityLR] (4) 90, p. 154.
"Nightmare" (tr. by James A. Wilson). [CityLR] (4) 90, p. 152.
"Notes on Reading" (tr. by Bonnie S. McDougall and Chen Maiping). [ManhatR] (5:2) Fall 90, p. 9.
"Portrait of a Young Poet" (tr. by Bonnie S. McDougall). [ManhatR] (5:2) Fall 90, p. 50-51.
"Résumé" (tr. by Bonnie S. McDougall). [PoetryUSA] ([5:4?]) Wint 90, p. 21.
"Song of Migrating Birds" (tr. by Bonnie S. McDougall). [PoetryUSA] ([5:4?]) Wint 90, p. 22.
"Untitled: As if hinted by distant mountains" (tr. by Dong Jiping). [Footwork] 90, p. 43.
"Untitled: Forever like this" (tr. by Dong Jiping). [Footwork] 90, p. 43.
"Untitled: I cannot see" (in Chinese and English, tr. by Bonnie S. McDougall). [GrandS] (9:4, #36) 90, p. 174-175.
"Untitled: More unfamiliar than an accident" (in Chinese and English, tr. by Bonnie S. McDougall). [GrandS] (9:4, #36) 90, p. 172-173.
"The Window on the Cliff" (tr. by Dong Jiping). [Footwork] 90, p. 43.
"You're Waiting for Me in the Rain" (in Chinese and English, tr. by Wu Keming). [PaintedB] (40/41) 90, p. 52-53.
436. BEI, Ling
"I Stroke You with All My Years" (in Chinese and English, tr. by Jin Zhong and William Slaughter). [Gargoyle] (37/38) 90, p. 8-9.
437. BEINING, Guy R.
(Anonymous poem). [FreeL] (4) 90.
"Demonic Metamorphoses." [PoetryC] (11:2) Sum 90, p. 14.
"No Subject But a Matter 1." [Caliban] (9) 90, p. 158.
"No Subject But a Matter 2." [Caliban] (9) 90, p. 159.
"Sounds of Gurgling Water." [PoetryC] (11:2) Sum 90, p. 14.
"A Spiritual Note to NEA Flock Within Context of Stoma." [Caliban] (8) 90, p. 165.

58

BEINING

"Stoma 1932." [Caliban] (9) 90, p. 154.
"Stoma 1934." [Caliban] (9) 90, p. 155.
"Stoma 1935." [Caliban] (9) 90, p. 156.
"Stoma 1936." [Caliban] (9) 90, p. 157.
438. BELANCE, Rene
"Gulf Stream" (tr. by Dennis Egan and Jean-Clarence Lambert, w. Bradley R.
Strahan). [Vis] (32) 90, p. 24.
439. BELCHETZ, Ruth
"Larchmont, Winter 1986." [SlipS] (10) 90, p. 58.
440. BELDING, Patricia W.
"Depot of Dreams." [CapeR] (25:1) Spr 90, p. 44.
"Taking Chances." [CapeR] (25:1) Spr 90, p. 42-43.
441. BELEV, Georgi
"Childhood Bolted" (tr. by Lisa Sapinkopf and the author). [Trans] (23) Spr 90, p.
249.
"Sealed Garden" (tr. by the author and Lisa Sapinkopf). [AnotherCM] (22) 90, p. 8.
"Spaces" (tr. by the author and Lisa Sapinkopf). [AnotherCM] (22) 90, p. 9.
"Woman" (tr. by Lisa Sapinkopf and the author). [Trans] (23) Spr 90, p. 250.
442. BELIECH, Mamie Alexander
"The Empty Fireplace." [EmeraldCR] (1990) c89, p. 73-74.
443. BELITT, Ben
"The Bathers: A Triptych." [Salm] (87) Sum 90, p. 169-172.
"Battle-Piece" (Uccello's "Battaglia di San Romano"). [Salm] (87) Sum 90, p. 96-99.
"Block Island: After The Tempest." [Salm] (87) Sum 90, p. 182-190.
"Esmiss Esmoor" (Homage to E. M. Forster). [Salm] (87) Sum 90, p. 206-207.
"Graffiti." [Salm] (87) Sum 90, p. 214-215.
"The Hornet's House." [Salm] (87) Sum 90, p. 159.
"Lily Briscoe: A Failed Painting." [Salm] (88/89) Fall 90-Wint 91, p. 149-150.
"On Quaking Bog" (for Tom and Jean Brockway). [Salm] (87) Sum 90, p. 135-136.
"Possessions" (for Nick Mayer). [Salm] (87) Sum 90, p. 65-67.
"The Repellant" (for Melissa Hayden). [Salm] (87) Sum 90, p. 78-79.
"Sumac." [Salm] (87) Sum 90, p. 123-126.
"Swan Lake." [Salm] (87) Sum 90, p. 111.
"This Scribe, My Hand" (for Joan Hutton Landis). [Salm] (87) Sum 90, p. 8-11.
"Thoreau on Paran Creek." [Salm] (87) Sum 90, p. 147.
"Xerox." [Salm] (87) Sum 90, p. 58.
444. BELL, Carolyn Light
"The Cow and Her Uterus" (for Liz). [SingHM] (17) 90, p. 25.
445. BELL, Marvin
"The Bow." [RiverC] (11:1) Fall 90, p. 51.
"By the Iowa." [NoAmR] (275:2) Je 90, p. 42.
"Ending with a Line from Lear." [Atlantic] (266:5) N 90, p. 124.
"Gone." [BostonR] (15:1) F 90, p. 3.
"He Had a Good Year." [Antaeus] (64/65) Spr-Aut 90, p. 13.
"Heat at the Center." [Ploughs] (16:4) Wint 90-91, p. 127.
"How to Everything." [Poetry] (155:6) Mr 90, p. 391-393.
"I Will Not Be Claimed." [VirQR] (66:3) Sum 90, p. 450-451.
"Icarus Thought." [VirQR] (66:3) Sum 90, p. 451-452.
"Initial Conditions." [KenR] (NS 12:4) Fall 90, p. 62-70.
"Just a Moment -- I Am Busy Being a Man." [VirQR] (66:3) Sum 90, p. 450.
"Language Without Miracles." [VirQR] (66:3) Sum 90, p. 449.
"A Man May Change." [AntR] (48:3) Sum 90, p. 353.
"Nature." [AmerPoR] (19:2) Mr-Ap 90, p. 8.
"Not Joining the Wars." [AntR] (48:3) Sum 90, p. 355.
"O'Keeffe Left to Herself." [GettyR] (3:2) Spr 90, p. 329-332.
"Sevens (Version 3): In the Closed Iris of Creation." [AmerPoR] (19:2) Mr-Ap 90, p.
7.
"Spot Six Differences." [Zyzzyva] (6:2, #22) Sum 90, p. 57.
"Tie-Down of A Bonsai." [NoAmR] (275:2) Je 90, p. 43.
446. BELLEN, Martine
"Absolutely." [Conjunc] (15) 90, p. 262-266.
"Camisado." [Conjunc] (15) 90, p. 261.
"Sky Frames." [CentralP] (17/18) Spr-Fall 90, p. 156.
"The Still-Bound." [Conjunc] (15) 90, p. 262.
447. BELLI, Gioconda
"Dressed in Dynamite" (tr. by Steven F. White). [Calyx] (12:3) Sum 90, p. 55.

59

448. BELLIN, Steve
"Instructions to Friends Who Have Lost Touch." [RagMag] (7:2) Spr 90, p. 10.
"Kind of Blue." [RagMag] (7:2) Spr 90, p. 9.
"Running the Film Backwards" (J.G. 1947-85). [RagMag] (7:2) Spr 90, p. 11.
"What I Meant to Say." [RagMag] (7:2) Spr 90, p. 10.
449. BELLINGER, Daniel
"The River." [Pig] (16) 90, p. 61.
450. BELLOWS, Timothy P.
"A Boy to His Girl (Just Inside Her Front Door)." [Interim] (9:2) Fall-Wint 90-91, p. 17.
"Desert Town." [Interim] (9:2) Fall-Wint 90-91, p. 16.
451. BEN AL-ZAQQAQ (Valencia, c. 1095-1133/5)
"Drunken Beauty" (tr. by Christopher Middleton and Leticia Garza Falcón). [Trans] (23) Spr 90, p. 195.
452. BEN CHARUF (Cordova, ?-1220)
"The Young Tailor" (tr. by Christopher Middleton and Leticia Garza Falcón). [Trans] (23) Spr 90, p. 194.
453. BEN-DOR, Dan
"Amidst Stones" (June 18, 1944, tr. by LiLi Cahlon). [Vis] (33) 90, p. 20.
454. BEN SHAUL, Moshe
"Wind in the Hills" (tr. by Jean Nordhaus). [PoetL] (85:4) Wint 90-91, p. 21.
455. BENDALL, Molly
"Conversation with Isadora Duncan." [GeoR] (44:1/2) Spr-Sum 90, p. 50.
"A Painter of Destinies." [DenQ] (25:1) Sum 90, p. 8-9.
"Pavlova: Elements of Evening." [WestHR] (44:2) Sum 90, p. 174-178.
456. BENDER, Norman
"Dressing the Stage." [Amelia] (6:2, #17) 90, p. 81.
457. BENDON, Chris
"An Attempted Portrait of the North in Short Trousers." [Stand] (31:4) Aut 90, p. 64.
"Chateau Cliche." [Verse] (7:2) Sum 90, p. 88.
"Peace Day (1919)." [Stand] (31:4) Aut 90, p. 63.
"A Poem with Two Endings." [Verse] (7:2) Sum 90, p. 87.
"Ten Approaches to Her." [PoetryC] (11:1) Spr 90, p. 22.
458. BENEDETTO, Judith
"Autumn Fog." [Crucible] (26) Fall 90, p. 65.
459. BENEDICT, Fr., O.S.B.
"Renoir's Last Painting." [WindO] (53) Fall 90, p. 25.
"The Victoria and Albert Museum on a Rainy Morning." [WindO] (53) Fall 90, p. 26.
460. BENEDICT, Michael
"To Peggy Gabson in Boston from New York City, the 22nd of December." [HampSPR] (Anthology 1975-1990) 90, p. 170-171.
461. BÉNÉZET, Mariana
"Closed letter" (tr. by Tom Mandel). [WashR] (16:2) Ag-S 90, p. 18.
"The crêpe of still water's core" (tr. by Tom Mandel). [WashR] (16:2) Ag-S 90, p. 18.
"Le crépuscule d'eau où le ciel blanc s'éclaircit encore." [WashR] (16:2) Ag-S 90, p. 18.
"Lettre close." [WashR] (16:2) Ag-S 90, p. 18.
462. BENIS, Allison
"1:25 a.m." (for Leslie). [OnTheBus] (2:2/3:1, #6/7) Sum-Fall 90 Wint-Spr 91, p. 44-45.
"All for My Baby." [OnTheBus] (2:2/3:1, #6/7) Sum-Fall 90 Wint-Spr 91, p. 43-44.
463. BENN, Gottfried
"Chopin" (tr. by Lauren Hahn). [WebR] (14:2) Spr 90, p. 107-108.
"I Have Met Persons Who" (tr. by Francis Golffing). [AmerPoR] (19:3) My-Je 90, p. 20.
"No Mourning" (tr. by Teresa Iverson). [Agni] (29/30) 90, p. 9.
464. BENNANI, Ben
"A Certain Song to Palestine" (tr. of Mahmud Darwish). [Os] (30) Spr 90, p. 22.
"On the Sabbath." [CharR] (16:1) Spr 90, p. 60.
"Psalm Four" (from Psalms for Palestine, tr. of Mahmud Darwish). [Os] (30) Spr 90, p. 23.
"To His Mistress" (tr. of Abu Nuwas). [Os] (30) Spr 90, p. 2.
"The Truth." [CharR] (16:1) Spr 90, p. 60-61.
465. BENNETT, Bruce
"Adolescence." [HiramPoR] (47) Wint 90, p. 11.

"Attention Miniature Lovers" (-- headline in *The Cricket*, February 1990). [SenR]
    (20:2) Fall 90, p. 79-80.
"Escape." [LaurelR] (24:2) Sum 90, p. 26.
"Joyce." [ClockR] (6:1) 90, p. 57.
"The Reviewer." [TarRP] (29:2) Spr 90, p. 7-8.
"The Set-Up." [TarRP] (29:2) Spr 90, p. 6.
466. BENNETT, John
    "Sex Dies." [OnTheBus] (2:2/3:1, #6/7) Sum-Fall 90 Wint-Spr 91, p. 46.
467. BENNETT, John M.
    (Anonymous poem). [FreeL] (4) 90.
    "Abundant Paradigm." [Contact] (9:56/57/58) Spr 90, p. 31.
    "Blurting." [Bogg] (62) 90, p. 44.
    "Closet." [Asylum] (5:4) 90, p. 38.
    "Declension." [Caliban] (8) 90, p. 168.
    "Diamond Transform." [Contact] (9:56/57/58) Spr 90, p. 31.
    "From the Worm's Eye." [Caliban] (9) 90, p. 186.
468. BENNETT, Maria
    "Canto Llano (Plain Song)" (Selection: XXIII, tr. of Cintio Vitier). [CrabCR] (6:3)
        Spr 90, p. 17.
    "Elegy" (tr. of Cintio Vitier). [CrabCR] (6:3) Spr 90, p. 17-18.
    "Light from the Cay" (tr. of Cintio Vitier). [CrabCR] (6:3) Spr 90, p. 18.
    "Ofumeyi" (sign given in a divination ceremony among the Yoruba, tr. of Cintio
        Vitier). [CrabCR] (7:1) Wint 90, p. 4-7.
    "The Rope Held Fast" (tr. of Nancy Morejon). [CrabCR] (7:1) Wint 90, p. 3.
    "Unexpected" (tr. of Nancy Morejon). [CrabCR] (7:1) Wint 90, p. 3.
469. BENSE, Robert
    "Celadon." [PaintedB] (40/41) 90, p. 162.
470. BENSON, Steve
    "The Medium" (for Norman Fischer and Andrew Levy). [Zyzzyva] (6:2, #22) Sum
        90, p. 124-125.
471. BENTLEY, Nelson
    "The Dungeness Spit Apocalypses." [BellArk] (6:3) My-Je 90, p. 7-9.
    "La Push Apocalypse." [BellArk] (6:1) Ja-F 90, p. 6-7.
    "Moolack Apocalypse." [BellArk] (6:5) S-O 90, p. 5.
472. BENTLEY, Roy
    "Death Speaks of a Man Who Started the Day Reading Rubber Trees" (In memoriam
        Francisco Mendes Filho, Brazilian environmentalist, 1944-1988). [MidAR]
        (10:1) 90, p. 18-19.
    "The Gift of Fury." [Journal] (13:2) Fall-Wint 89-90, p. 26-27.
    "A Place to Come Back To." [ArtfulD] (18/19) 90, p. 131.
473. BENTLEY, Sean
    "The Big Things." [WritersF] (16) Fall 90, p. 128-129.
    "This Rain." [BellR] (13:1, #27) Spr 90, p. 36.
474. BENTTINEN, Ted
    "Droplets of Milk." [YellowS] (34) Sum 90, p. 5.
    "If Your Hair." [YellowS] (34) Sum 90, p. 5.
475. BENVENISTE, Rachelle
    "Looking at Family Slides with His Children." [SingHM] (17) 90, p. 6-7.
476. BERG, Stephen
    "Like a knifeblade the moon will be full then less" (tr. of Ikkyu Sojun). [Hudson]
        (43:2) Sum 90, p. 340.
    "Listen whose face is it a piece" (tr. of Ikkyu Sojun). [Hudson] (43:2) Sum 90, p.
        340.
    "Oblivion" (2 selections). [Ploughs] (16:4) Wint 90-91, p. 104-107.
    "Oblivion" (Selection). [PassN] (11:2) Wint 90, p. 15.
    "Rubber Rats." [Ploughs] (16:4) Wint 90-91, p. 103.
    "Those old koans meaningless just ways of faking virtue" (tr. of Ikkyu Sojun).
        [Hudson] (43:2) Sum 90, p. 340.
    "The Unkown Pain: Matos." [MissouriR] (13:2) 90, p. 132.
    "What Never Comes Back: Huidobro." [MissouriR] (13:2) 90, p. 130-131.
477. BERG, Viola Jacobson
    "The Fleet's In." [NewRena] (8:1, #24) Spr 90, p. 129-130.
478. BERGAMINO, Gina
    "Conversation with a Zuni Indian." [BlackBR] (12) Fall-Wint 90, p. 42-43.
    "In Harrisonville Missouri." [NewYorkQ] (43) Fall 90, p. 65.
    "In Missouri." [ChrC] (107:19) 13-20 Je 90, p. 588.

"In Siberia." [BlackBR] (11) Spr-Sum 90, p. 7.
"Like a Dead Man's Life." [ChrC] (107:32) 7 N 90, p. 1033.
"October Chill." [HeavenB] (8) Wint 90-91, p. 46.
"Our Last Night in Italy." [Footwork] 90, p. 95.
"Our New Apartment." [NewYorkQ] (43) Fall 90, p. 65.
"Schizophrenic Baby." [BlackBR] (11) Spr-Sum 90, p. 6.
479. BERGAN, Brooke
"Pastorals" (tr. of Guillevic). [Trans] (23) Spr 90, p. 124-125.
480. BERGER, Andrés
"Carta a un Compatriota" (Para mi colega, el Dr. Francisco Gómez). [Americas]
(18:2) Sum 90, p. 49.
"El Día Que Yo Muera." [Americas] (18:2) Sum 90, p. 48.
"Olé, Manuel Báez 'Litri', Olé!" [Americas] (18:2) Sum 90, p. 50-53.
481. BERGIE, Sigrid
"Bus Ride." [NorthStoneR] (9) 90, p. 74-75.
"Cataclysmic Nippers" (with James Naiden and Michael Tjepkes). [NorthStoneR] (9)
90, p. 80-81.
"Home Movie." [NorthStoneR] (9) 90, p. 76.
482. BERGMAN, Denise
"Smelling Necco on Essex Street." [Pig] (16) 90, p. 33.
483. BERGMAN, Susan
"My Life, I Lose You." [Chelsea] (49) 90, p. 88-92.
484. BERGSTEDT, Lowell
"After March" (tr. of Giuseppe Conte, w. Anna Stortoni). [MidwQ] (32:1) Aut 90, p.
94.
"Tezcatlipoca: The Song of a Human Sacrifice" (tr. of Giuseppe Conte, w. Laura
Stortoni). [MidwQ] (31:2) Wint 90, p. 195-196.
485. BERKE, Judith
"Cries and Shispers" (for Peggotty and for Lois). [KenR] (NS 12:4) Fall 90, p.
166-167.
"Dancer in an All Day, All Night Festival for the Revolution, Paris 1794." [DenQ]
(25:1) Sum 90, p. 11.
"Mata Hari in Saint-Lazare Prison, 1917." [MassR] (31:4) Wint 90, p. 511-512.
"Old Eight-by-Ten Glossy." [KenR] (NS 12:4) Fall 90, p. 167.
"The Returner." [AmerPoR] (19:5) S-O 90, p. 32.
"The Silent Movie Director" (for Fred Fischbach, 1895-1925). [DenQ] (25:1) Sum
90, p. 10.
"The Three Faces of Eve." [Poetry] (156:1) Ap 90, p. 7.
"The Walk, Paris, 1960." [TampaR] (3) 90, p. 80.
486. BERKE, Nancy
"In Ellipsis." [Rohwedder] (5) Spr 90, p. 34-37.
"She's Thinking About." [SlipS] (10) 90, p. 66.
"Violence." [SlipS] (10) 90, p. 65-66.
487. BERKELEY, Sara
"December 1st." [Quarry] (39:1) Wint 90, p. 60-61.
488. BERKMAN, Linda
"Warning: War Toys" (Toys R US Action, Brooklyn, December 1989). [CentralP]
(17/18) Spr-Fall 90, p. 243-244.
489. BERKSON, Bill
"Baby's Awake Now." [Zyzzyva] (6:3 #23) Fall 90, p. 120.
"Don't Knock It" (for Lynn). [Zyzzyva] (6:3 #23) Fall 90, p. 119.
"Serenade." [PoetryUSA] (5:1) Spr 90, p. 10.
490. BERLANDT, Herman
"3 Odes to Crones." [PoetryUSA] (5:3) Fall 90, p. 5.
"Acid Trip." [PoetryUSA] ([5:4?]) Wint 90, p. 15.
"Art Reflecting Life?" [PoetryUSA] (5:1) Spr 90, p. 4.
"Hangover." [PoetryUSA] ([5:4?]) Wint 90, p. 15.
"Inheritance." [PoetryUSA] (5:1) Spr 90, p. 4.
"Lady on the Bus." [PoetryUSA] (5:3) Fall 90, p. 5.
"Old Ladies Banking." [PoetryUSA] (5:3) Fall 90, p. 5.
"On the Beach." [PoetryUSA] (5:1) Spr 90, p. 11.
"Post-Operative Video Therapy" (written an hour after his superpubicprostatectomy).
[PoetryUSA] (5:3) Fall 90, p. 3.
"Prayer for Simplicity." [PoetryUSA] (5:3) Fall 90, p. 13.
"Tripping Out As Narcissus." [PoetryUSA] (5:2) Sum 90, p. 9.

491. BERLIND, Bruce
"Defend It" (tr. of Agnes Nemes Nagy). [PoetryE] (29) Spr 90, p. 62.
"For Life" (tr. of János Pilinszky, w. Mária Körösy). [PoetryE] (29) Spr 90, p. 59.
"For Quite Some Time" (tr. of Imre Oravecz, w. Mária Körösy). [ManhatR] (5:1) Spr 90, p. 13.
"I No Longer Walk" (tr. of Imre Oravecz, w. Mária Körösy). [Abraxas] (38/39) 90, p. 85.
"I Want Only" (tr. of Imre Oravecz, w. Mária Körösy). [NewEngR] (13:1) Fall 90, p. 41.
"I'd Like to Talk to You Now" (tr. of Imre Oravecz, w. Mária Körösy). [Abraxas] (38/39) 90, p. 81.
"In the Roman Forum" (from the Hungarian of Istvan Vas). [Confr] (42/43) Spr-Sum 90, p. 202.
"It May Have Begun This Way" (tr. of Imre Oravecz, w. Mária Körösy). [NewEngR] (13:1) Fall 90, p. 40.
"The Last Home" (tr. of Gyula Illyés, w. Mária Körösy). [Os] (30) Spr 90, p. 9.
"Lorca's New York" (tr. of Ottó Orbán, w. Mária Körösy). [PoetryE] (29) Spr 90, p. 57.
"My Time's Running Out" (tr. of Imre Oravecz, w. Mária Körösy). [ManhatR] (5:1) Spr 90, p. 12.
"On a Private Golgotha" (tr. of Gyula Illyés, w. Mária Körösy). [Os] (30) Spr 90, p. 7.
"One Sentence on Tyranny" (tr. of Gyula Illyés, w. Mária Körösy). [PoetryE] (29) Spr 90, p. 42-49.
"Procession in the Fog" (tr. of Gyula Illyés, w. Mária Körösy). [Os] (30) Spr 90, p. 5.
"Stephen Spender in Mount Vernon" (tr. of Ottó Orbán, w. Mária Körösy). [PoetryE] (29) Spr 90, p. 58.
"This Is the City" (tr. of Imre Oravecz, w. Mária Körösy). [Abraxas] (38/39) 90, p. 83.
"To Be Rich" (tr. of Ottó Orbán, w. Mária Körösy). [PoetryE] (29) Spr 90, p. 56.
"To Freedom" (tr. of Agnes Nemes Nagy). [PoetryE] (29) Spr 90, p. 63-64.
"Trees" (tr. of Agnes Nemes Nagy). [PoetryE] (29) Spr 90, p. 61.
"Veil" (tr. of János Pilinszky, w. Mária Körösy). [PoetryE] (29) Spr 90, p. 60.
"When It Was Over" (tr. of Imre Oravecz, w. Mária Körösy). [NewEngR] (13:1) Fall 90, p. 41-42.
"You Had Dressed by Then" (tr. of Imre Oravecz, w. Mária Körösy). [Abraxas] (38/39) 90, p. 87.
492. BERMAN, David
"California." [Caliban] (8) 90, p. 24.
"James A. Garfield and All the Shot People." [Caliban] (8) 90, p. 27.
"O." [Caliban] (8) 90, p. 25.
"Texas." [Caliban] (8) 90, p. 26.
"Untitled: I don't think I'll ever make it home." [Caliban] (8) 90, p. 28.
"Untitled: If it's not bugs, it's the weather." [Caliban] (8) 90, p. 29.
493. BERMAN, Ruth
"Get Rid of Unsightly." [KanQ] (22:3) Sum 90, p. 123.
"Season Drink." [KanQ] (22:3) Sum 90, p. 123.
494. BERNAL LABRADA, Emilio
"The Fog Casts Its Spell" (tr. by the author). [WashR] (16:2) Ag-S 90, p. 15.
"Mujer." [WashR] (16:2) Ag-S 90, p. 15.
"Niebla Encantada." [WashR] (16:2) Ag-S 90, p. 15.
"Woman" (tr. by the author). [WashR] (16:2) Ag-S 90, p. 15.
495. BERNARD, April
"Psalm of the Canal-Dweller." [Sulfur] (10:2, #27) Fall 90, p. 191-192.
"Psalm of the City-Dweller Gone Home." [Sulfur] (10:2, #27) Fall 90, p. 190-191.
"Psalm of the Spit-Dweller." [Sulfur] (10:2, #27) Fall 90, p. 192-193.
"Psalm of the Surprised." [Sulfur] (10:2, #27) Fall 90, p. 193.
496. BERNARD, Kenneth
"History." [Asylum] (6:2) S 90, p. 18.
"Impasse." [Asylum] (6:2) S 90, p. 19.
497. BERNARDIN, Libby
"Serpent." [NegC] (10:1) 90, p. 36.
498. BERNHARD, Jim
"Record Album Eulogy." [BellArk] (6:5) S-O 90, p. 9.
"Sasha at Three and a Half." [BellArk] (6:4) Jl-Ag 90, p. 19.

499. BERNLEF, J.
    "Before It Begins" (tr. by Scott Rollins). [Writ] (22) 90 c1991, p. 5.
    "An Encounter with Pieter Saenredam" (Painting: St. Bavo Church by Pieter
        Saenredam, tr. by Scott Rollins). [Trans] (24) Fall 90, p. 40-41.
    "Francis Bacon" (tr. by Scott Rollins). [Writ] (22) 90 c1991, p. 10.
    "Grammars" (tr. by Scott Rollins). [Writ] (22) 90 c1991, p. 8.
    "On Systems" (tr. by Scott Rollins). [Writ] (22) 90 c1991, p. 7.
    "Spirit Grounds" (tr. by Scott Rollins). [Writ] (22) 90 c1991, p. 9.
    "Tulle, reed, paper, taffeta" (tr. by Scott Rollins). [Writ] (22) 90 c1991, p. 11.
    "Winter Routes" (tr. by Scott Rollins). [Writ] (22) 90 c1991, p. 6.
500. BERNSTEIN, Carole
    "Alligator." [HawaiiR] (14:2, #29) Spr 90, p. 9-11.
    "And Then, Her Mother's Dresses Torn Out of the Closet." [HawaiiR] (14:2, #29)
        Spr 90, p. 12-13.
    "The Carpet." [Shen] (40:1) Spr 90, p. 82-83.
    "Caught." [HawaiiR] (14:3, #30) Fall 90, p. 33.
    "The Fire." [HawaiiR] (14:3, #30) Fall 90, p. 31-32.
    "Fretwork" (For E.B.). [Confr] (42/43) Spr-Sum 90, p. 127.
    "Symbolon." [Shen] (40:1) Spr 90, p. 81.
501. BERNSTEIN, Charles
    "Beginning with Lines Torn from Irby." [NewAW] (6) Spr 90, p. 29.
    "Cumulative Erasure." [NewAW] (6) Spr 90, p. 30.
    "Damage Control." [Talisman] (4) Spr 90, p. 57.
    "Debris of Shock/Shock of Debris." [Verse] (7:1) Spr 90, p. 69-73.
    "Poem: Reason and felicity dissolves" (w. Ray DiPalma). [Screens] (2) 90, p. 196.
    "Red, Green & Black" (Excerpts, tr. of Olivier Cadiot, w. the author). [WashR]
        (16:2) Ag-S 90, p. 4-6.
    "Reveal Codes." [Sulfur] (10:2, #27) Fall 90, p. 194-201.
    "Virtual Reality" (for Susan). [Conjunc] (15) 90, p. 258-260.
502. BERNSTEIN, Lisa
    "Purgatory." [Ploughs] (16:1) Spr-Sum 90, p. 122-123.
503. BERNSTEIN, Ori
    "Memory" (tr. by Daniel Weissbort and Orna Raz). [Trans] (24) Fall 90, p. 231.
    "Procession" (tr. by Daniel Weissbort and Orna Raz). [Trans] (24) Fall 90, p. 232.
    "What Can You Tell Me?" (tr. by Daniel Weissbort and Orna Raz). [Trans] (24) Fall
        90, p. 232.
504. BERRIS, Sandra
    "Revelation." [WillowR] Spr 90, p. 21.
505. BERROA, Rei
    "Seis Poemas" (Del *Libro de los fragmentos*: I, III, IX, X, XVIII, "El Son del
        Desgraciado"). [CuadP] (7:20) Enero-Abril 90, p. 73-82.
506. BERRY, D. C.
    "Shadow." [FloridaR] (17:2) Fall-Wint 90, p. 35.
    "Sidewalk." [FloridaR] (17:2) Fall-Wint 90, p. 34.
507. BERRY, David
    "How to Beat Dr. Feel Good." [SouthernHR] (24:4) Fall 90, p. 365.
    "Pulitzer Prize Action Photo 1989" (photographer Ron Olshwanger). [RiverC] (10:2)
        Spr 90, p. 78.
    "Sparrow." [Shen] (40:2) Sum 90, p. 23-24.
508. BERRY, Jake
    "Ab:Prophetics" (#10-16). [PoetryUSA] ([5:4?]) Wint 90, p. 9.
    "Ab:Prophetics #9." [PoetryUSA] (5:3) Fall 90, p. 1.
509. BERRY, Wendell
    "Let Us Pledge." [Harp] (281:1686) N 90, p. 42.
510. BERSSENBRUGGE, Mei-mei
    "Ideal." [Conjunc] (15) 90, p. 137-139.
511. BERTA, Renee
    "At My Garage Sale." [CentR] (34:3) Sum 90, p. 399.
    "Blood Sisters." [CentR] (34:3) Sum 90, p. 399-400.
512. BERTHELOT, Dolly Adams
    "The (W)Hole." [EmeraldCR] (1990) c89, p. 48-50.
513. BERTOLINO, James
    "Lines to Restore Van Gogh's Ear." [Gargoyle] (37/38) 90, p. 74.
514. BERTOLUCCI, Attilio
    "Eliot at Twelve Years" (from a photograph, tr. by Charles Tomlinson). [ParisR]
        (32:116) Fall 90, p. 103.

64

BERTOLUCCI

"The Months" (tr. by Charles Tomlinson). [ParisR] (32:116) Fall 90, p. 98.
"Near Shrine B on an August Day" (tr. by Charles Tomlinson). [ParisR] (32:116) Fall
90, p. 99-102.
515. BERTONE, Gary
"Coming Down." [PoetryUSA] (5:2) Sum 90, p. 4.
"Little Saint Anthony and the Supreme Temptation." [PoetryUSA] (5:2) Sum 90, p. 3.
516. BESSER, Ya'akov
"A Field Stoned" (tr. by Henry Taylor). [PoetL] (85:4) Wint 90-91, p. 24.
517. BESSETTE, Hélène
"MaternA" (Excerpts, Editions Gallimard, Paris, 1954, tr. by Keith Waldrop). [Avec]
(3:1) 90, p. 67-70.
518. BETT, Stephen
"L.K. XXV : S.B. I (Lucy Strikes Back)." [PraF] (11:4) Wint 90-91, p. 23-24.
"Lucy Kent XXIV (Poem for the Sucks)." [PraF] (11:4) Wint 90-91, p. 22-23.
"Self-Portraits." [PoetryC] (11:2) Sum 90, p. 26.
519. BETTARINI, Mariella
"You Find the Poets Among the Men." [Footwork] 90, p. 105.
520. BETTENCOURT, Michael
"Road." [ManhatPR] (11) [89?], p. 26.
521. BEVERIDGE, Robert P.
"How to Write Poetry." [ChironR] (9:3) Aut 90, p. 40.
522. BEYER, William
"Emily Dickinson: In Retrospect." [Wind] (20:67) 90, p. 6.
523. BEZNER, Kevin
"Farm." [AntigR] (81/82) Spr-Sum 90, p. 174.
"Playing Ball." [Gargoyle] (37/38) 90, p. 84.
"The Tools of Ignorance." [OnTheBus] (2:1, #5) Spr 90, p. 29-36.
524. BHUYAN, Janet J.
"Lucille." [NegC] (10:1) 90, p. 37.
525. BIALOSKY, Jill
"Ruined Secret." [Agni] (31/32) 90, p. 263-265.
526. BIALOSZEWSKI, Miron
"Study of a Key" (tr. by Daniel Weissbort and Grzegorz Musial). [PoetryE] (29) Spr
90, p. 23.
527. BIBLE. O.T. SONG OF SONGS
"The Song of Songs" (An adaptation-translation by Diane Wolkstein). [Confr] (42/43)
Spr-Sum 90, p. 74-85.
528. BIDART, Frank
"Now in Your Hand." [Agni] (29/30) 90, p. 56-57.
"Poem in the Stanza of the 'Rubaiyat'." [Agni] (29/30) 90, p. 59.
"You Remain." [Agni] (29/30) 90, p. 58.
529. BIERDS, Linda
"And the Ship Sails On" (Federico Fellini, Cinécittá). [Field] (42) Spr 90, p. 50-51.
"April." [NewEngR] (13:2) Wint 90, p. 91-92.
"Bird in Space: First Study." [NewYorker] (65:48) 15 Ja 90, p. 38.
"From the Danube, 1829." [IndR] (14:1) Wint 90, p. 24-25.
"White Bears: Tolstoy at Astapovo." [NewYorker] (66:38) 5 N 90, p. 54.
"The Wind Tunnel" (Wilbur Wright, 1887-1912). [Field] (42) Spr 90, p. 52-53.
"Yellow Chambers." [NewEngR] (13:2) Wint 90, p. 92-93.
530. BIESPIEL, David
"The Autumn of the Body." [PoetryNW] (31:3) Aut 90, p. 19-20.
531. BIGEAGLE, Duane
"Love Song." [Zyzzyva] (6:1 #21) Spr 90, p. 104.
532. BIGGINS, Michael
"The Deer" (tr. of Tomaz Salamun). [Ploughs] (16:4) Wint 90-91, p. 76.
"Distant Voices in My Heart" (Selections: 1, 3, tr. of Ales Debeljak). [Screens] (2) 90,
p. 71.
"For David" (tr. of Tomaz Salamun). [DenQ] (25:1) Sum 90, p. 33.
"The Forms of Love" (Selection: 2, tr. of Ales Debeljak). [Screens] (2) 90, p. 70.
"Functions" (tr. of Tomaz Salamun). [Ploughs] (16:4) Wint 90-91, p. 77-79.
"Happiness Is Hot, Splattered Brains" (tr. of Tomaz Salamun). [Ploughs] (16:4) Wint
90-91, p. 81.
"My Tribe" (tr. of Tomaz Salamun). [DenQ] (25:1) Sum 90, p. 34-35.
"Nihil Est in Intellectu" (tr. of Tomaz Salamun). [Ploughs] (16:4) Wint 90-91, p. 80.
"One, My Arm" (tr. of Tomaz Salamun). [DenQ] (25:1) Sum 90, p. 32.
"Outline of History 7" (tr. of Ales Debeljak). [ManhatR] (5:2) Fall 90, p. 36.

65

"To the Deaf Ones" (tr. of Tomaz Salamun). [DenQ] (25:1) Sum 90, p. 36-37.
"Without Anaesthetic" (tr. of Ales Debeljak). [ManhatR] (5:2) Fall 90, p. 36.
533. BIGGS, Margaret Key
"Beneath a Full Summer Moon." [YellowS] (34) Sum 90, p. 7.
534. BIGHAM, Ken
"For Christ's Sake." [SmPd] (27:3, #80) Fall 90, p. 16.
"Perspective." [SmPd] (27:1, #78) Wint 90, p. 26.
535. BILGERE, George
"Convalescents." [TarRP] (29:2) Spr 90, p. 16.
"The Dealer." [PraS] (64:1) Spr 90, p. 38.
"Dime Western." [PraS] (64:1) Spr 90, p. 39-40.
"Edison Films an Execution." [TarRP] (29:2) Spr 90, p. 14-15.
"Family Album." [TarRP] (29:2) Spr 90, p. 15.
536. BILOTSERKIVETS', Natalka
"Untitled: Scents, colors, lines and hues fade" (tr. by Vera L. Kaczmarskyj). [Agni] (31/32) 90, p. 119-120.
537. BIRCHARD, Guy
"Armagnac." [Sćreens] (2) 90, p. 184.
"Sketch: Young Woman, Luxembourg Gardens." [Screens] (2) 90, p. 184.
538. BIRD, Gloria
"The Unfaithful." [Calyx] (12:3) Sum 90, p. 54.
"The Women Fell Like Beautiful Horses" (Excerpt from a series of poems in progress on Chief Joseph and the Nez Perce wars). [Calyx] (12:3) Sum 90, p. 52-53.
539. BIRNBAUM, Adam
"Spill and Scape" (ink, pastel, papier mâché and poem, with Deborah Fass). [HarvardA] (125:1) S 90, p. 6.
540. BISHOP, Bonnie
"All the Walls in Gubbio Will One Day Converge." [CumbPR] (9:2) Spr 90, p. 1.
"The Perfect Woman." [Grain] (18:2) Sum 90, inside back cover.
541. BISHOP, Elizabeth
"One Art." [NewEngR] (13:2) Wint 90, p. 122-123.
542. BISHOP, Judith
"Ancestors." [Mildred] (4:1) 90, p. 77-78.
"In the Company of Hawks." [Mildred] (4:1) 90, p. 79.
"The Old Ones -- a Journey." [Mildred] (4:1) 90, p. 80.
543. BISHOP, Michael
"The Memory of Water" (Excerpts, tr. of Hélène Cadou). [Trans] (23) Spr 90, p. 14-16.
544. BISHOP, Neil B.
"Le Sourire des Chefs" (Selections: 15-17, tr. of Michel Savard). [AntigR] (80) Wint 90, p. 96-101.
545. BISHOP, Suzette
"House-Sitting." [AntR] (48:1) Wint 90, p. 91.
546. BISHOP, Wendy
"Colorless Green Ideas Sleep Furiously." [HighP] (5:2) Fall 90, p. 100-101.
"In Summer." [GreenMR] (NS 4:1) Spr-Sum 90, p. 65.
"Journey" (after Peter Fruchin's Book of the Eskimo). [EngJ] (79:5) S 90, p. 102.
"On the Chihuahua-Pacifico Railway." [RiverC] (10:2) Spr 90, p. 84.
"Sandhill Crane." [HighP] (5:2) Fall 90, p. 102-103.
"Tait." [RiverS] (32) [90?], p. 37.
547. BISS, Ellen
"Day Lily." [Spirit] (10:2) 90, p. 14.
"First Snow." [Blueline] (11:1/2) 90, p. 72.
"First Snow." [Spirit] (10:2) 90, p. 14.
548. BISSETT, Bill
"Is for the use of th peopul." [PoetryUSA] (5:1) Spr 90, p. 15.
549. BISSONETTE, David
"A Young Newspaperboy Mistaken for the Messiah." [Amelia] (6:1, #16) 90, p. 52.
550. BITNEY, Katharine
"Because in Space." [Dandel] (17:1) Spr-Sum 90, p. 28.
"Minton." [Dandel] (17:1) Spr-Sum 90, p. 27.
551. BITZ, Gregory W.
"Autumn." [LakeSR] (24) 90, p. 21.
552. BIVONA, Francesco
"When I Die." [RagMag] (8:2) 90, p. 56.

553. BIXBY, Robert
   "Is the Title a Headstone or the Manifest on a Bus?" [ContextS] (1:1) 89, p. 34.
554. BJØRNIVIG, Thorkild
   "Hebride Bay" (tr. by Monique M. Kennedy). [CimR] (92) Jl 90, p. 14.
   "A Mauve Fragrance in the Dark" (tr. by Monique M. Kennedy). [CimR] (92) Jl 90,
      p. 14.
555. BLACK, David
   "The Quitter." [DogRR] (9:2, #18) Aut 90, p. 25.
556. BLACK, Patricia
   "Save for Their Likeness." [EmeraldCR] (1990) c89, p. 106-107.
557. BLACK, Sophie Cabot
   "The Misunderstanding of Nature." [PartR] (57:2) Spr 90, p. 272-273.
558. BLACKFORD, Tom
   "Foreign." [ArtfulD] (18/19) 90, p. 144.
559. BLACKMAN, Roy
   "Ouroboros." [Stand] (31:1) Wint 89-90, p. 26-27.
   "The Voluntry Red Cross Stroke-Patient Rehabilitation Scheme." [Stand] (31:1) Wint
      89-90, p. 25.
560. BLACKSTONE, Alice
   "Reverie for a Seventy-Seventh Birthday." [Plain] (10:2) Wint 90, p. 34.
561. BLACKWELL, Charles Curtis
   "Shortly after the Death of Huey Newton." [BlackALF] (24:3) Fall 90, p. 540-541.
562. BLAGG, Max
   "Licking the Fun Up." [Bomb] (31) Spr 90, p. 58-61.
563. BLAKER, Margaret
   "The Buffalo Soldier's Wife." [AnthNEW] 90, p. 13.
BLANCO, Rocío Escobar
   See ESCOBAR-BLANCO, Rocío
564. BLAND, Celia
   "The Map of the Heart." [WashR] (15:5) F-Mr 90, p. 14.
   "Misconceptions of Childhood." [WashR] (15:5) F-Mr 90, p. 14.
   "My Grandmother's Heart." [WashR] (15:5) F-Mr 90, p. 14.
   "She Attempts to Create." [WashR] (15:5) F-Mr 90, p. 14.
   "She Becomes the Body." [WashR] (15:5) F-Mr 90, p. 14.
   "She Conquers the Heart." [WashR] (15:5) F-Mr 90, p. 14.
   "She Looks Outside." [WashR] (15:5) F-Mr 90, p. 14.
565. BLANDIANA, Ana
   "So Cold" (tr. by Thomas C. Carlson and Vasile Poenaru). [ManhatR] (5:1) Spr 90,
      p. 10.
   "The Soul" (tr. by Thomas C. Carlson and Vasile Poenaru). [ManhatR] (5:1) Spr 90,
      p. 10.
566. BLASER, Robin
   "Even on Sunday." [CapilR] (2:4) Wint 90, p. 119-123.
   "Giving the Glitter to Some Body Else and Not Wanting It Back." [CapilR] (2:4) Wint
      90, p. 124-125.
   "Of the Land of Culture." [CapilR] (2:4) Wint 90, p. 126-127.
567. BLASING, Randy
   "Burial Grounds." [Poetry] (155:4) Ja 90, p. 262-263.
   "Lifelines." [Poetry] (156:5) Ag 90, p. 261-262.
   "Permanent Ink." [Poetry] (156:5) Ag 90, p. 261.
   "Personal History." [SouthernR] (26:3) Jl 90, p. 671-672.
   "The Sky As the Limit." [MichQR] (29:3) Sum 90, p. 413-414.
   "Sunset Beach." [SouthernR] (26:3) Jl 90, p. 671.
568. BLASKI, Steven
   "The Tale of the Man Who Loves Too Much." [ChangingM] (21) Wint-Spr 90, p. 16.
569. BLATNER, Barbara Ann
   "Deckertown Falls" (for Arthur). [PoetryNW] (31:2) Sum 90, p. 27-29.
570. BLAUNER, Laurie
   "Lightning's Attraction to Solitary Objects." [PoetryNW] (31:3) Aut 90, p. 27-28.
   "The Man Who Discovered Entropy While on Vacation." [PoetryNW] (31:3) Aut 90,
      p. 26-27.
   "What Your Body Holds Against You." [Nat] (251:14) 29 O 90, p. 503.
571. BLAXILL, Peter
   "To Her Gigolo." [NewYorkQ] (41) Spr 90, p. 86.
572. BLEI, Norbert
   "Midwest Haiku." [KenR] (NS 12:2) Spr 90, p. 31.

573. BLEVINS, Richard
"Letters form Kansas" (for Sherman Paul). [Notus] (5:1) Spr 90, p. 42-48.
574. BLEWETT, Peter
"The Poem." [CreamCR] (14:1) Spr 90, p. 143.
"Surgery" (for David Dunn, a Plainsongs Award Poem). [Plain] (10:3) Spr 90, p. 16.
575. BLISS, S. W.
"Harvest." [WindO] (53) Fall 90, p. 21.
576. BLITCH, Lynn
"Flies, Bumblebees, and God." [SoCoast] (8) Spr 90, p. 55.
577. BLIZNETSOVA, Ina
"Words Resound in My Ears to This Day" (tr. by the author and Marc Nasdor). [LitR]
(33:4) Sum 90, p. 485.
578. BLIZZARD, Gloria
"The Caribs." [PoetryC] (11:1) Spr 90, p. 17.
"The Chocolate Lambs." [PoetryC] (11:1) Spr 90, p. 17.
579. BLOCH, Chana
"Afterlife." [Poetry] (156:1) Ap 90, p. 17.
"At an Unknown Altitude." [PoetryNW] (31:2) Sum 90, p. 13-15.
"Blue-Black." [Poetry] (157:2) N 90, p. 88.
"Chez Pierre, 1961." [Poetry] (156:4) Jl 90, p. 213.
"In the Land of the Body." [Field] (43) Fall 90, p. 55.
"Little Love Poem." [Field] (43) Fall 90, p. 57.
"Looking at the X-Rays." [Field] (43) Fall 90, p. 56.
"Rising to Meet It." [Poetry] (156:1) Ap 90, p. 16.
"Signals" (For Benjamin). [Poetry] (156:4) Jl 90, p. 214.
"White Petticoats" (For Ariel). [Poetry] (156:1) Ap 90, p. 18.
580. BLONSTEIN, Anne
"When Meret Oppenheim Was Thirty-Six." [AntigR] (81/82) Spr-Sum 90, p.
157-158.
581. BLOOD, Drew
"Tenement Night." [JamesWR] (8:1) Fall 90, p. 7.
582. BLOODGOOD, Forest
"Hairbrain" (for A.). [Caliban] (9) 90, p. 19-20.
583. BLOSSOM, Laurel
"Evolution, an Unfinished Sestina." [NewYorkQ] (43) Fall 90, p. 63-64.
"Florida." [NewYorkQ] (41) Spr 90, p. 84.
584. BLUE, Jane
"Drifting" (for Peter). [Vis] (33) 90, p. 20-21.
585. BLUESTONE, Stephen
"The Unveiling." [Poetry] (157:3) D 90, p. 140-141.
586. BLUGER, Marianne
"The End of the Absolute." [PoetryC] (11:4) Wint 90, p. 7.
"The Salmon." [PoetryC] (11:4) Wint 90, p. 7.
587. BLUMBERG, Michele
"The Love of Small Cold Towns." [CapeR] (25:2) Fall 90, p. 28.
588. BLUMENTHAL, Jay (Jay A.)
"An Academic Reading." [TarRP] (30:1) Fall 90, p. 2.
"Atlantic City." [NowestR] (28:3/29:1) 90-91, p. 190.
"Before Poetry There Is Truth." [AmerS] (59:4) Aut 90, p. 575.
"Bread Loaf." [Wind] (20:67) 90, p. 7.
"Capitalism on the Moon." [LitR] (33:3) Spr 90, p. 378.
"The Complete Angler." [Pembroke] (22) 90, p. 56.
"Death Is Not for Duffers." [WestB] (26) 90, p. 127.
"Deconstructions." [ChamLR] (3:2, #6) Spr 90, p. 118-119.
"Deconstructions." [HawaiiR] (14:2, #29) Spr 90, p. 111-112.
"Dream and Ambition." [ChamLR] (3:2, #6) Spr 90, p. 116-117.
"The Dust Jacket at Waldenbooks." [Comm] (117:19) 9 N 90, p. 651.
"Genesis." [HawaiiR] (14:3, #30) Fall 90, p. 118-119.
"Holding Pattern." [BrooklynR] (7) 90, p. 54.
"Holding Pattern." [HawaiiR] (14:2, #29) Spr 90, p. 110.
"The Homecoming." [GrahamHR] (13) Spr 90, p. 85-86.
"I'll Be Home for Christmas." [HiramPoR] (48/49) 90-91, p. 11.
"A Mad Poet's Estate." [SoCaR] (23:1) Fall 90, p. 92.
"The Midnight Shark." [NowestR] (28:3/29:1) 90-91, p. 189.
"Nemesis." [HawaiiR] (14:3, #30) Fall 90, p. 117.
"On Contemplating My Wife's Bed." [HawaiiR] (14:2, #29) Spr 90, p. 109.

"Parallel Universe." [NewDeltaR] (7:1) 90, p. 38.
"A Portrait of a Marriage: 'The Red Roofs' of Camille Pissarro." [ChamLR] (3:2, #6) Spr 90, p. 120-121.
"A Portrait of Marriage: 'The Red Roofs' of Camille Pissarro." [CumbPR] (9:2) Spr 90, p. 4.
"The Sequel as Prelude to an Emotion." [GrahamHR] (13) Spr 90, p. 87.
"The Snowman." [Pembroke] (22) 90, p. 57.
"Sound Stage." [ChamLR] (3:2, #6) Spr 90, p. 115.
589. BLUMENTHAL, Michael
"Poem for My Father at 85 After Cross-Country Skiing with My Nephew, Marlon, Age 7." [Nat] (251:15) 5 N 90, p. 539.
"Yin and Yang." [Nat] (250:22) 4 Je 90, p. 798.
590. BLY, David
"Beauty Is Nothing But the Beginning of Terror" (-- Rilke). [RagMag] (8:2) 90, p. 53.
"The Coming of the King." [RagMag] (8:2) 90, p. 54.
"Racing with the Hare." [RagMag] (8:1) 90, p. 72.
"The Surrender of the Senses." [RagMag] (8:2) 90, p. 52.
591. BLY, Robert
"The Clouds" (tr. of Mirabai). [HampSPR] (Anthology 1975-1990) 90, p. 264.
"Let's Count the Bodies Over Again." [Quarry] (39:4) Fall 1990, p. 74.
"The Trees" (tr. of Aleksandr Tkachenko, w. Valentina Sinkevich). [PaintedB] (40/41) 90, p. 27.
"Why Mira Can't Go Back to Her Old House" (tr. of Mirabai). [HampSPR] (Anthology 1975-1990) 90, p. 264.
592. BLYSTONE, Sandra
"Afterlife." [Calyx] (12:3) Sum 90, p. 5.
"Under August." [HiramPoR] (48/49) 90-91, p. 12.
593. BLYTHE, Randy
"Altar of the Visible." [HiramPoR] (48/49) 90-91, p. 13.
594. BOBIC, Bogdana Gagrica
"Fear" (Excerpt, tr. of Dusan Vukajlovic). [Screens] (2) 90, p. 66.
595. BOBRICK, James
"Bank." [Pig] (16) 90, p. 59.
"Jury Duty." [LaurelR] (24:1) Wint 90, p. 21.
"Throwbacks." [SoCoast] (9) Fall 90, p. 3.
596. BOBROWSKI, Johannes
"Lake Shore" (tr. by Paul Morris). [BlueBldgs] (12) 90, p. 13.
"Seeufer." [BlueBldgs] (12) 90, p. 12.
597. BOBYSHEV, Dmitry
"Any Excuse" (Venus in a Puddle, tr. by H. W. Tjalsma). [Nimrod] (33:2) Spr-Sum 90, p. 75.
"An Inland Indian Sea" (tr. by Joseph Langland, w. the author). [Nimrod] (33:2) Spr-Sum 90, p. 74.
"The Other World" (for O.S. --B., tr. by Michael Van Walleghen). [TriQ] (79) Fall 90, p. 106-107.
598. BOCK, Claus
"Love Poems" (tr. of Marijn Backer). [Trans] (24) Fall 90, p. 126.
599. BOCK, David
"Albright." [Pearl] (11) Sum 90, p. 35.
"Torino." [Pearl] (11) Sum 90, p. 35.
600. BOCKES, Zan
"My Father Teaches Me to Fly." [CutB] (33) 90, back cover.
601. BODA, Tom
"Her Face." [CapeR] (25:2) Fall 90, p. 26.
602. BODENHAMER, Heather James
"For Xen, Because You Asked Me and Because I Wanted to Tell You." [PaintedB] (40/41) 90, p. 130.
603. BODIEN, Richard
"Our first *haiku, koans,* and other nonsense." [PoetryUSA] (5:2) Sum 90, p. 12.
604. BOE, Marilyn J.
"Grandma Came to America" (March 21, 1883). [SingHM] (18) 90, p. 66-67.
605. BOEHRER, Bruce Thomas
"Sestina for Tea." [HiramPoR] (47) Wint 90, p. 12-13.
606. BOES, Don
"Motivational Tape Pantoum." [CutB] (34) Sum-Fall 90, p. 40.

"Three Fish Stories." [ArtfulD] (18/19) 90, p. 66.
607. BOETHIUS, Anicius Manlius Severinus
"Eala!" (poems from "On the Consolation of Philosophy": I-III, VI-VII, in Latin).
[WashR] (16:2) Ag-S 90, p. 10-11.
"Eala!" (poems from "On the Consolation of Philosophy": I-III, VI-VII, tr. by Peter
Glassgold). [WashR] (16:2) Ag-S 90, p. 10-11.
608. BOGAN, Louise
"Henceforth, from the mind." [ChiR] (37:1) Wint 90, p. 33-34.
609. BOGDANOVIC, Simha Levi
"The Invitations" (tr. of Predrag Bogdanovic Ci). [Screens] (2) 90, p. 65.
"The Palimpsest" (tr. of Predrag Bogdanovic Ci). [Screens] (2) 90, p. 65.
BOGDANOVIC CI, Predrag
See CI, Predrag Bogdanovic
610. BOGEN, Don
"A Luddite Lullaby." [Poetry] (155:6) Mr 90, p. 383.
"Slum Corner." [NewRep] (202:15) 9 Ap 90, p. 35.
"Tableau." [Poetry] (155:6) Mr 90, p. 382.
611. BOGEN, Laurel Ann
"Also Frankenstein." [ChironR] (9:2) Sum 90, p. 3.
"Listen." [ChironR] (9:2) Sum 90, p. 3.
612. BOGGS, W. (William O.)
"Eddy Johnson's American Dream" (35 poems, To J. M. and F. L.). [HiramPoR]
(Supplement No. 11) 90, 43 p.
"Hood and Leathers." [Pig] (16) 90, p. 44.
613. BOGUS, SDiane A.
"Woman Statement." [PoetryUSA] (5:3) Fall 90, p. 5.
614. BOHL, Florence
"Light Years." [Pearl] (12) Fall-Wint 90, p. 43.
615. BOISSEAU, Michelle
"Kindly Stopped." [IndR] (14:1) Wint 90, p. 27.
"More and More." [PoetL] (85:3) Fall 90, p. 22.
"Sleeplessness." [IndR] (14:1) Wint 90, p. 26.
"Timbre." [PoetL] (85:3) Fall 90, p. 23.
616. BOLAND, Eavan
"The Achill Woman." [AmerPoR] (19:2) Mr-Ap 90, p. 27.
"The Black Lace Fan My Mother Gave Me." [Quarry] (39:1) Wint 90, p. 62.
"Daphne Heard with Horror the Addresses of the God." [AmerPoR] (19:2) Mr-Ap 90,
p. 29.
"Distances." [NewYorker] (66:1) 19 F 90, p. 44.
"A False Spring." [AmerPoR] (19:2) Mr-Ap 90, p. 27.
"In Exile." [AmerPoR] (19:2) Mr-Ap 90, p. 30.
"The Latin Lesson." [Atlantic] (266:3) S 90, p. 66.
"The Making of an Irish Goddess." [AmerPoR] (19:2) Mr-Ap 90, p. 28.
"An Old Steel Engraving." [AmerPoR] (19:2) Mr-Ap 90, p. 30.
"On the Gift of The Birds of America by John James Audubon." [Antaeus] (64/65)
Spr-Aut 90, p. 14-15.
"Outside History." [AmerPoR] (19:2) Mr-Ap 90, p. 31.
"The Photograph on My Father's Desk." [AmerPoR] (19:2) Mr-Ap 90, p. 29.
"We Are Always Too Late." [AmerPoR] (19:2) Mr-Ap 90, p. 30.
"We Are Human History. We Are Not Natural History." [AmerPoR] (19:2) Mr-Ap
90, p. 29.
"What We Lost." [AmerPoR] (19:2) Mr-Ap 90, p. 31.
"White Hawthorn in the West of Ireland." [AmerPoR] (19:2) Mr-Ap 90, p. 28.
617. BOLLING, Madelon
"A Letter to Those Who Stayed." [BellArk] (6:2) Mr-Ap 90, p. 5.
"Migration." [BellArk] (6:2) Mr-Ap 90, p. 3-5.
618. BOLSTRIDGE, Alice
"First Ladies' Room" (at the L.B.J. Library). [SingHM] (18) 90, p. 12-13.
619. BOLTON, Joe
"Aubade." [Agni] (31/32) 90, p. 188-189.
"Flamingos" (after Rilke). [Thrpny] (41) Spr 90, p. 16.
"Sardis Reservoir, Mississippi." [HighP] (5:1) Spr 90, p. 52-53.
"Tropical Watercolor: Sarasota" (after Vallejo). [TampaR] (3) 90, p. 11.
620. BOLZ, Jody
"Late at Night, the Lightning." [RiverS] (32) [90?], p. 65.

621. BOMBA, Bernard
"The Ethical Hunter." [WebR] (14:2) Spr 90, p. 63.
"To My Daughter at Her Window." [WebR] (14:2) Spr 90, p. 64.
622. BOND, Adrienne
"Time Was, She Declares" (for Stephen W. Hawking). [GeoR] (44:1/2) Spr-Sum 90,
    p. 110-111.
623. BOND, Bruce
"Alban Berg." [NewRep] (203:16) 15 O 90, p. 46.
"Augustus Purchases His New Teeth." [HawaiiR] (15:1, #31) Wint 90, p. 17-18.
"Bach's Idiot Son." [NewRep] (202:19) 7 My 90, p. 37.
"Disappearances." [CreamCR] (14:1) Spr 90, p. 133.
"The Fall." [Wind] (20:66) 90, p. 4.
"Golden Dragon." [HawaiiR] (15:1, #31) Wint 90, p. 19.
"Lady in a Wood" (after Rousseau). [CreamCR] (14:1) Spr 90, p. 132.
"Motet." [CarolQ] (43:1) Fall 90, p. 42-43.
"A Narcoleptic in Los Angeles." [Gargoyle] (37/38) 90, p. 36.
"Paradise Carnival." [DenQ] (25:2) Fall 90, p. 10-11.
"Piano." [NewRep] (203:4) 23 Jl 90, p. 36.
"Planetarium." [Poetry] (156:3) Je 90, p. 152.
"Prayer." [MissouriR] (13:1) 90, p. 156-157.
"Processionals." [Paint] (17:33/34) Spr-Aut 90, p. 24.
"The Radio." [WestHR] (44:3) Aut 90, p. 323.
"Tattoo." [PraS] (64:2) Sum 90, p. 95-96.
"Whistler: The White Girl." [NewRep] (203:27) 31 D 90, p. 41.
"The White Birch." [Wind] (20:66) 90, p. 4.
624. BOND, Harold
"The Game" (reprinted from #8, 1984). [Kaleid] (20) Wint-Spr 90, p. 27.
625. BONENBERGER, Sheila Dietz
"In Granada." [SpoonRQ] (15:3) Sum 90, p. 62-63.
626. BONFANTI, Philip
"Carnival '89." [ArtfulD] (18/19) 90, p. 106-107.
627. BONIFAY, Kurt E.
"Chains, My Own." [EmeraldCR] (1990) c89, p. 58-59.
628. BONNEFOY, Yves
"Art de la Poesie." [NegC] (10:2/3) 90, p. 156.
"The Art of Poetry" (tr. by James Sallis). [NegC] (10:2/3) 90, p. 157.
"The Art of Poetry" (tr. by Lisa Sapinkopf). [HampSPR] (Anthology 1975-1990) 90,
    p. 271.
"Country of the Tree-tops" (tr. by Lisa Sapinkopf). [PassN] (11:2) Wint 90, p. 15.
"The Memory" (tr. by Lisa Sapinkopf). [PassN] (11:2) Wint 90, p. 16-17.
"The Snow" (tr. by John Naughton). [GrahamHR] (13) Spr 90, p. 106.
"The Swiftness of the Clouds" (tr. by John Naughton). [GrahamHR] (13) Spr 90, p.
    107.
"The Well, the Brambles" (tr. by John Naughton). [GrahamHR] (13) Spr 90, p. 105.
BONTÉ, Karen la
    See LaBONTÉ, Karen
629. BONVENTRE, Enzo
"Do Not Call Me Queen, Odysseus" (tr. by Nat Scammacca). [Footwork] 90, p. 63.
"Non Chiamarmi Regina Ulisse." [Footwork] 90, p. 63.
630. BONZA, Elise J.
"The Composer's Daughter." [ArtfulD] (18/19) 90, p. 145.
631. BOOKER, Stephen Todd
"The Wrong Boy." [SouthernR] (26:4) O 90, p. 885-890.
632. BOOTH, Philip
"A Few Riffs for Hayden, Sitting in With His Horn." [SenR] (20:1, 20th-Anniversary
    Special Edition) 90, p. 14-15.
"Hey, Bro." [BelPoJ] (40:4) Sum 90, p. 11.
"Saying It." [SenR] (20:2) Fall 90, p. 12-13.
633. BORAN, Pat
"Strangers Buried Him." [Quarry] (39:1) Wint 90, p. 63-64.
634. BORCHARDT, Rudolf
"Underworld North of Lugano" (tr. by John Peck). [Salm] (88/89) Fall 90-Wint 91,
    p. 229-233.
635. BORCHERS, Elisabeth
"Let's Stop Talking" (tr. by Anneliese Wagner). [PoetryE] (30) Fall 90, p. 22.

71

636. BORDAO, Rafael
"Senda de Agua" (a mi padre). [LindLM] (9:4) O-D 90, p. 42.
637. BORDEN, Jonathan
"Some Tuesday at Two O'Clock" (For William Harren, 1955-1989). [LakeSR] (24) 90, p. 25.
638. BORDEN, William
"Standing Up." [SlipS] (10) 90, p. 47.
639. BORGE, Tomás
"Algún Día." [Areíto] (2:7) My 90, p. 25.
"Mi Venganza Personal." [Areíto] (2:7) My 90, inside front cover.
"Mi vida?" [Areíto] (2:7) My 90, inside back cover.
640. BORGES, Jorge Luis
"Ars Poetica" (tr. by Jim Powell). [Agni] (29/30) 90, p. 54-55.
"Buenos Aires, 1899" (in Spanish). [SoCoast] (8) Spr 90, p. 12.
"Buenos Aires, 1899" (tr. by Robert Mezey and R. G. Barnes). [SoCoast] (8) Spr 90, p. 13.
"Calle Desconocida." [SoCoast] (8) Spr 90, p. 10.
"Composición Escrita en un Ejemplar de la Gesta de Beowulf." [SoCoast] (8) Spr 90, p. 14.
"Emerson" (in Spanish). [SoCoast] (8) Spr 90, p. 16.
"Emerson" (tr. by Robert Mezey and R. G. Barnes). [SoCoast] (8) Spr 90, p. 17.
"Unrecognized Street" (tr. by Robert Mezey and R. G. Barnes). [SoCoast] (8) Spr 90, p. 11.
"Written in a Copy of the Geste of Beowulf" (tr. by Robert Mezey and R. G. Barnes). [SoCoast] (8) Spr 90, p. 15.
641. BORGES, Millicent C.
"The Chameleon." [ChironR] (9:1) Spr 90, p. 5.
"The Chattel Element." [ChironR] (9:1) Spr 90, p. 5.
"Transit Confessional." [ChironR] (9:1) Spr 90, p. 5.
"An Uninvited Guest's Description of a Parisian Cafe." [ChironR] (9:1) Spr 90, p. 5.
642. BORINSKY, Alicia
"Carreras." [RiverS] (32) [90?], p. 58.
"Lo Que Le Dijo la Mamá." [RiverS] (32) [90?], p. 56.
"Races" (tr. by Cola Franzen). [RiverS] (32) [90?], p. 59.
"What Her Mother Told Her" (tr. by Cola Franzen). [RiverS] (32) [90?], p. 57.
643. BORKHUIS, Charles
"Continental Drift." [OnTheBus] (2:2/3:1, #6/7) Sum-Fall 90 Wint-Spr 91, p. 47.
BORKOWSKI, Miriam Halliday
See HALLIDAY-BORKOWSKI, Miriam
644. BORN, Anne
"Heavenly Geometry" (tr. of Pia Tafdrup). [Verse] (7:2) Sum 90, p. 11.
"Years Like Leaves" (Selections: 4 poems, tr. of Bo Carpelan). [Verse] (7:2) Sum 90, p. 10-11.
645. BORN, Heidi von
"Ålderdomshem." [Spirit] (10:1) 89, p. 114.
"The Drowning" (Antonin Artaud, also called Nanaqui, in Smyrna, tr. by Lennart Bruce and Sonja Bruce). [Spirit] (10:1) 89, p. 113.
"Drunkningen" (Antonin Artaud, även kallad Nanaqui i Smyrna). [Spirit] (10:1) 89, p. 112.
"Old Folks Home" (tr. by Lennart Bruce and Sonja Bruce). [Spirit] (10:1) 89, p. 115.
"Snappsaras Olycka." [Spirit] (10:1) 89, p. 116.
"The Tragedy of Snappen-Sara" (tr. by Lennart Bruce and Sonja Bruce). [Spirit] (10:1) 89, p. 117.
646. BORN, Nicolas
"Three Wishes" (tr. by Ken Fontenot). [NewOR] (17:1) Spr 90, p. 48.
647. BORNHOLDT, Jenny
"Waiting Shelter." [Verse] (7:2) Sum 90, p. 51-52.
648. BOROWSKI, Tadeusz
"Dream Pictures" (tr. by Addison Bross). [NewL] (57:1) Fall 90, p. 6-8.
"Untitled: I'm thinking of you" (tr. by Addison Bross). [NewL] (57:1) Fall 90, p. 8.
649. BORSON, Roo
"Drought." [MalR] (91) Je 90, p. 42.
"Eyes." [MalR] (91) Je 90, p. 43.
"Home." [MalR] (91) Je 90, p. 41.
"It's Raining." [MalR] (91) Je 90, p. 45.
"Love." [MalR] (91) Je 90, p. 44.

"Starting the Tape" (for David McFadden). [MalR] (91) Je 90, p. 46-47.
650. BORUCH, Marianne
"Dr. Williams' Desk." [PraS] (64:3) Fall 90, p. 50.
"For Emily Dickinson." [Field] (43) Fall 90, p. 66-67.
"In April." [Field] (43) Fall 90, p. 68.
"The Junked Cars." [Crazy] (39) Wint 90, p. 34-35.
"Painting Ferms a Mile from the Stadium." [PraS] (64:3) Fall 90, p. 48.
"Rare Old Violins." [Poetry] (156:5) Ag 90, p. 276-277.
"The Surveying Class." [GettyR] (3:2) Spr 90, p. 387.
"To All Those Poets One Reads in Childhood." [PraS] (64:3) Fall 90, p. 49-50.
"Work." [Crazy] (39) Wint 90, p. 32-33.
651. BORUN-JAGODZINSKA, Katarzyna
"Aida" (tr. by the author and Lia Purpura). [PoetryE] (29) Spr 90, p. 16.
"At Dusk" (tr. by the author and Lia Purpura). [PoetryE] (29) Spr 90, p. 17.
"From the Book of Job" (tr. by the author and Lia Purpura). [PoetryE] (29) Spr 90, p. 18.
"Last Photograph of Teresa Martin" (tr. by the author and Lia Purpura). [PoetryE] (29) Spr 90, p. 19.
"A Very Bourgeois Lyric" (tr. by the author and Lia Purpura). [PoetryE] (29) Spr 90, p. 20.
652. BOSCH, Daniel
"I bowl to avoid silence." [Amelia] (6:1, #16) 90, p. 18.
"Mackerel." [Turnstile] (2:2) 90, p. 26-27.
653. BOSKOVSKI, Jozo T.
"Close-UP" (tr. by David B. Axelrod). [Footwork] 90, p. 60.
"The Enlightened Person" (tr. by Cynthia Keesan and David B. Axelrod). [Footwork] 90, p. 61.
"Jackals" (tr. by Anna Esapora). [Footwork] 90, p. 60.
"Loneliness" (tr. by David B. Axelrod). [Footwork] 90, p. 61.
"Masks" (tr. by Anna Esapora and David B. Axelrod). [Footwork] 90, p. 60.
"Untitled: At a time when I was without love" (tr. by David B. Axelrod). [Footwork] 90, p. 61.
"Untitled: Long ago we were swiftly flowing water" (tr. by Svetlana Dimic). [Footwork] 90, p. 61.
654. BOSLEY, John
"Tops Off." [Bogg] (62) 90, p. 14.
655. BOSLEY, Keith
"The Final Incantation" (tr. of Fernando Pessoa). [Stand] (31:2) Spr 90, p. 35-36.
"The Keeper of Flocks" (Excerpt, tr. of Fernando Pessoa). [Stand] (31:2) Spr 90, p. 36.
"Martial Ode" (tr. of Fernando Pessoa). [Stand] (31:2) Spr 90, p. 33-34.
656. BOSQUET, Alain
"God's Torment" (Selections, tr. by Jesse Abbot). [Trans] (24) Fall 90, p. 213-217.
657. BOSS, Laura
"Proofreading with My Mother." [Footwork] 90, p. 31.
658. BOSWORTH, David
"Pathetic Fallacy: A Field Guide for the Biologist." [NewEngR] (12:4) Sum 90, p. 351-357.
"The Reformation of Rhetoric on the Occasion of the Dead." [CrossCur] (9:2) Je 90, p. 138-146.
659. BOTTA, Tim
"Silver Disc." [HiramPoR] (48/49) 90-91, p. 14.
"Sunday Afternoon." [HiramPoR] (48/49) 90-91, p. 14.
660. BOTTOMS, David
"American Mystic." [ParisR] (32:116) Fall 90, p. 127.
"Cemetery Wings." [Poetry] (156:4) Jl 90, p. 208.
"Chinese Dragons." [Poetry] (156:3) Je 90, p. 134.
"Paper Route, Northwest Montana" (for Rick Bass). [ParisR] (32:116) Fall 90, p. 128.
"Sierra Bear." [ParisR] (32:116) Fall 90, p. 129.
661. BOUCHER, Patricia
"Moral Fabric." [EmeraldCR] (1990) c89, p. 35-36.
BOUCHET, André du
See Du BOUCHET, André
662. BOUCHT, Birgitta
"It" (Excerpt, tr. by Stina Katchadourian). [Screens] (2) 90, p. 87-90.

663. BOUDREAU, Jean
"A Simpler Version of Sound." [BellArk] (6:3) My-Je 90, p. 6.
664. BOURASSA, Alan
"Chasing a Black Dog." [Event] (19:3) Fall 90, p. 53.
665. BOURLAND, Eryc
"Hunt of Color." [Gypsy] (15) 90, p. 3.
666. BOURNE, Daniel
"Alarm" (tr. of Tomasz Jastrun). [PoetryE] (29) Spr 90, p. 29.
"Children" (tr. of Krystyna Lars). [LitR] (33:3) Spr 90, p. 294-295.
"Coming To" (tr. of Tomasz Jastrun). [MidAR] (10:2) 90, p. 167.
"Continuing Education." [BelPoJ] (41:2) Wint 90-91, p. 20-21.
"A Country Gentleman Stands at the Window, September 24, 1863" (tr. of Krystyna
      Lars). [LitR] (33:3) Spr 90, p. 295.
"Courage" (tr. of Tomasz Jastrun). [MidAR] (10:2) 90, p. 169.
"Covenant." [Field] (42) Spr 90, p. 33.
"Defeat" (tr. of Tomasz Jastrun). [MidAR] (10:2) 90, p. 166.
"Elegy for the Woman across the Street." [NoDaQ] (58:1) Wint 90, p. 31.
"Emilia Plater" (tr. of Krystyna Lars). [LitR] (33:3) Spr 90, p. 296.
"Evening, the Krakow train station, three gypsy" (tr. of Bronislaw Maj). [ManhatR]
      (5:1) Spr 90, p. 6.
"Hands" (tr. of Tomasz Jastrun). [PoetryE] (29) Spr 90, p. 28.
"Hiding the Knives." [BelPoJ] (41:2) Wint 90-91, p. 22.
"An Illegal Photograph in American Poetry Review." [BelPoJ] (41:2) Wint 90-91, p.
      21.
"In Mourning (1983)" (tr. of Tomasz Jastrun). [MidAR] (10:2) 90, p. 168.
"In the Exercise Yard" (tr. of Tomasz Jastrun). [MidAR] (10:2) 90, p. 165.
"Iowa Cow." [Field] (42) Spr 90, p. 34.
"Life swells to twice, three times its normal size" (tr. of Bronislaw Maj). [ManhatR]
      (5:1) Spr 90, p. 5.
"Manifesto." [KanQ] (22:1/2) Wint-Spr 90, p. 170.
"The Military Governor Contemplates the Statue of Adam M." (tr. of Krystyna Lars).
      [LitR] (33:3) Spr 90, p. 298.
"The most acute of all" (tr. of Mira Kus). [HawaiiR] (14:3, #30) Fall 90, p. 92.
"On her way out this morning, she left" (tr. of Bronislaw Maj). [ManhatR] (5:1) Spr
      90, p. 4.
"One of the last leaves to break loose from the maple" (tr. of Bronislaw Maj).
      [ManhatR] (5:1) Spr 90, p. 5.
"Planet" (tr. of Tomasz Jastrun). [PoetryE] (29) Spr 90, p. 27.
"Rat" (tr. of Tomasz Jastrun). [PoetryE] (29) Spr 90, p. 26.
"Rejtan" (tr. of Krystyna Lars). [LitR] (33:3) Spr 90, p. 296.
"A September afternoon, I inhale" (tr. of Bronislaw Maj). [ManhatR] (5:1) Spr 90, p.
      4.
"Small Grains" (tr. of Tomasz Jastrun). [PoetryE] (30) Fall 90, p. 95.
"Soiree at the Czar's Plenipotentiary" (tr. of Krystyna Lars). [LitR] (33:3) Spr 90, p.
      297.
"This Is Not Death Yet" (tr. of Otto Tolnai, w. Nicholas Kolumban and Karen
      Kovacik). [ArtfulD] (18/19) 90, p. 35.
"Transition." [OxfordM] (6:1) Spr-Sum 90, p. 87.
"Travelogue." [KanQ] (22:1/2) Wint-Spr 90, p. 170-171.
"Where No One Spoke the Language." [BelPoJ] (41:2) Wint 90-91, p. 20.
"While the Ground Is Still Warm." [WillowS] (26) Spr 90, p. 58.
"Will There Be Enough Light Years" (tr. of Mira Kus). [CrossCur] (9:2) Je 90, p.
      157.
667. BOURNE, Lesley-Anne
"The Story of Pears." [Event] (19:3) Fall 90, p. 46.
668. BOURNE, Louis
"Between the Fascinating and the Frightening" (To the artist, José Hernández, tr. of
      Claudio Rodríguez). [Stand] (31:3) Sum 90, p. 70-71.
669. BOUVARD, Marguerite
"Of Light and Silence." [MidwQ] (31:2) Wint 90, p. 197.
"The Old Portraits of the Indians." [MidwQ] (31:2) Wint 90, p. 229.
670. BOWDEN, Karen
"Cat." [HayF] (7) Fall-Wint 90, p. 96.
"David." [Wind] (20:66) 90, p. 5-6.
"Romance." [PoetL] (85:3) Fall 90, p. 6.
"A Thin Moon." [PoetL] (85:3) Fall 90, p. 7.

671. BOWEN, Janene
     "Row 23." [ColEng] (52:1) Ja 90, p. 38-39.
672. BOWERING, George
     "Creeley In." [WestCL] (24:3) Wint 90, p. 12-13.
673. BOWERS, Andrea L.
     "Narcissus." [GrahamHR] (13) Spr 90, p. 37-38.
BOWERS, Cathy Smith
     See SMITH-BOWERS, Cathy
674. BOWERS, Edgar
     "Clothes" (Bavaria, 1946). [YaleR] (79:3) Spr 90, p. 383-384.
675. BOWERS, Neal
     (Anonymous poem). [FreeL] (4) 90.
     "Ciphering." [NewL] (57:1) Fall 90, p. 74.
     "The Dare." [SouthernR] (26:4) O 90, p. 875-876.
     "Finale." [SouthernR] (26:4) O 90, p. 875.
     "Integrations." [Hudson] (43:1) Spr 90, p. 100-101.
     "Laws of Nature" (For Nancy). [Poetry] (157:2) N 90, p. 78.
     "The Loaner." [FreeL] (5) Sum 90, p. 22.
     "The Noonan Variations." [SewanR] (98:1) Wint 90, p. 1-3.
     "Old Man at the Municipal Pool." [SouthernPR] (30:2) Fall 90, p. 46.
     "RSVP." [Poetry] (156:6) S 90, p. 336-337.
     "Tenth-Year Elegy." [Poetry] (156:6) S 90, p. 337.
     "Thaw" (For Nancy). [Poetry] (156:1) Ap 90, p. 6.
     "Trouble in a Minnesota Town." [AmerS] (59:4) Aut 90, p. 568.
676. BOWERS, Star
     "Frank." [Spirit] (10:2) 90, p. 32-33.
677. BOWIE, Robert
     "Erosion Factor" (for A.R. Ammons). [SouthwR] (75:4) Aut 90, p. 552.
678. BOWLES, Ka
     "Different Shoes." [CapeR] (25:2) Fall 90, p. 11.
     "Nos Dar." [Poem] (64) N 90, p. 32.
     "Winter in the House." [LullwaterR] (2:1) Wint 90, p. 71.
679. BOWLES, Paul
     "The Host" (tr. of Rodrigo Rey Rosa). [Screens] (2) 90, p. 130-131.
680. BOWLING, Tim
     "After Leafing Through a Book of Classical Sculpture." [Bogg] (63) 90, p. 8.
681. BOWMAN, Catherine
     "Can You Tell Us Something About Him?" [ParisR] (32:116) Fall 90, p. 170.
     "LBJ Ranch Barbecue." [ParisR] (32:116) Fall 90, p. 171.
682. BOWMAN, William R., Sr.
     "Salute." [EmeraldCR] (1990) c89, p. 90.
683. BOYCE, Pleuke
     "Letters From My Father." [AntigR] (80) Wint 90, p. 94-95.
684. BOYCE, Robert (Robert C.)
     "Beethoven." [Bogg] (63) 90, p. 27.
     "Wouldn't You Know It!" [Bogg] (62) 90, p. 54.
685. BOYE, Karin
     "De Gangna Dagarna." [WashR] (16:2) Ag-S 90, p. 34.
     "Den Vägen Ar Smal." [WashR] (16:2) Ag-S 90, p. 34.
     "Havet." [WashR] (16:2) Ag-S 90, p. 34.
     "The Sea" (tr. by Charles Wadsworth). [WashR] (16:2) Ag-S 90, p. 34.
     "That Path" (tr. by Charles Wadsworth). [WashR] (16:2) Ag-S 90, p. 34.
     "Those Past Days" (tr. by Charles Wadsworth). [WashR] (16:2) Ag-S 90, p. 34.
686. BOYER, Gloria (Gloria F.)
     "Bad Animals." [PoetryNW] (31:3) Aut 90, p. 22-23.
     "Jake's Garden." [PennR] (4:2) 90, p. 47.
     "Letter to My Twin." [PoetryNW] (31:1) Spr 90, p. 20.
     "A Life: Exploded View." [PennR] (4:2) 90, p. 48.
     "Red Sweater." [PoetryNW] (31:3) Aut 90, p. 22.
     "The Romance of the Bees." [PoetryNW] (31:1) Spr 90, p. 21.
687. BOYER, Maggi Ruth P.
     "Three Mile Island." [SlipS] (10) 90, p. 68-69.
688. BOYLE, Kevin
     "Getting Clean." [AntR] (48:4) Fall 90, p. 494.
689. BOYMAN, Bonnie Grady
     "Playing the Lounge." [Amelia] (6:2, #17) 90, p. 97.

75

BOZANIC

690. BOZANIC, Nick
"Hunting Ducks at Dawn." [Manoa] (2:1) Spr 90, p. 126.
691. BRACKENRIDGE, Valery
"An Answer for My Mother." [Footwork] 90, p. 87.
"Coloring the Tree of Night." [Footwork] 90, p. 87.
"My Howl." [Footwork] 90, p. 87.
"October 1989." [Footwork] 90, p. 87.
"To My Lover." [Footwork] 90, p. 87.
692. BRACKETT, Cori
"Wedding Portrait of My Father" (after Rilke). [MissR] (19:1/2, #55/56) 90, p. 236.
693. BRADEN, David
"Laura." [CutB] (33) 90, p. 75.
694. BRADFORD, Jay
"Walt Whitman Was Always Out There" (Excerpt). [PoetryUSA] (5:3) Fall 90, p. 10.
695. BRADFORD-WHITE, Glenn
"Old Enough to Know." [AnthNEW] 90, p. 19.
696. BRADLEY, Ardyth
"Key." [Poetry] (156:4) Jl 90, p. 196.
697. BRADLEY, George
"A Georgic for Doug Crase." [WestHR] (44:4) Wint 90, p. 353-365.
"Great Stone Face." [PartR] (57:3) Sum 90, p. 441.
"Notes for an Epigram." [NewRep] (202:1) 1 Ja 90, p. 39.
698. BRADLEY, John
"Goat's Horn with Red." [YellowS] (34) Sum 90, p. 19.
"The Phenomenology of Roundness." [Caliban] (9) 90, p. 130-133.
BRADLEY, Martha Carlson
See CARLSON-BRADLEY, Martha
699. BRADLEY, Robert
"Harrowed Minds." [FreeL] (6) Aut 90, p. 25.
"Sunday Morning." [FreeL] (6) Aut 90, p. 24.
700. BRADT, David
"Letter Home to Ann." [PoetryUSA] (5:1) Spr 90, p. 6.
701. BRADY, Philip
"Mother Superior's Deathbed." [NewMyths] (1:1) 90, p. 110-112.
702. BRAEFF, Ann
"I Guess I'm Too Dumb to Give Up." [OnTheBus] (2:2/3:1, #6/7) Sum-Fall 90
Wint-Spr 91, p. 48.
"The Patriarchs." [OnTheBus] (2:1, #5) Spr 90, p. 37-38.
703. BRAGADO, Reinaldo
"Casablanca." [LindLM] (9:4) O-D 90, p. 35.
704. BRAGGS, Earl S.
"The Birth of Tally's Blues." [Ploughs] (16:1) Spr-Sum 90, p. 53-54.
705. BRAGI, Einar
"At Evening" (tr. by Greg Richter). [CharR] (16:1) Spr 90, p. 49.
"Before Sunset" (tr. by Greg Richter). [CharR] (16:1) Spr 90, p. 49.
"Wilderness Landscape" (tr. by Greg Richter). [CharR] (16:1) Spr 90, p. 48.
706. BRAID, Kate
"The Little Poem." [MalR] (93) D 90, p. 42-43.
"Summer Rites." [MalR] (93) D 90, p. 38.
"Think Like a Weightlifter, Think Like a Woman." [MalR] (93) D 90, p. 39-41.
707. BRAME, Gloria Glickstein
"Not Death." [Boulevard] (4:3/5:1, #12/13) Spr 90, p. 181.
"Then the Sickness." [Sequoia] (33:2) Wint 90, p. 103.
"Watermill." [Boulevard] (4:3/5:1, #12/13) Spr 90, p. 182-183.
"The Whole World of History and You." [Confr] (44/45) Fall 90-Wint 91, p. 297.
708. BRAMHALL, Mark
"Elegy for the Girls of Jiangxi Province." [MalR] (92) S 90, p. 77-81.
709. BRAND, Alice G.
"Twos." [NewL] (57:1) Fall 90, p. 104.
710. BRANDEL, Christine
"The Day I Became Golden." [Caliban] (8) 90, p. 70.
"The Gift." [Caliban] (8) 90, p. 70.
"My Hair Talks." [Caliban] (8) 90, p. 71.
711. BRANDER, John
(Anonymous poem). [FreeL] (4) 90.
"Green Haloes." [OnTheBus] (2:2/3:1, #6/7) Sum-Fall 90 Wint-Spr 91, p. 49-50.

"Hermosillo." [Amelia] (6:1, #16) 90, p. 66.
"While Women Were Washing Corpses" (The Africa Poems). [Rohwedder] (5) Spr 90, p. 31.
712. BRANDON, Kevin
"Carl Among the Heathen." [OnTheBus] (2:1, #5) Spr 90, p. 39-40.
"Inventing the Universe." [OnTheBus] (2:1, #5) Spr 90, p. 40.
713. BRANDON, Sherry
"The Marilyn Moment." [BellArk] (6:6) N-D 90, p. 24.
"Ruins of Sabratha." [BellArk] (6:5) S-O 90, p. 24.
714. BRANDT, Di
"Nonresistance or, Love Mennonite Style" (for L. & the others). [PraF] (11:2) Sum 90, p. 180.
"Scapegoat." [PraF] (11:2) Sum 90, p. 182.
"Why My Father Beat Us (When We Were Little)." [PraF] (11:2) Sum 90, p. 181.
715. BRANDT, Jørgen Gustava
"It Is the Bird in the Tree" (tr. by Alexander Taylor and the author). [CimR] (92) Jl 90, p. 15-16.
716. BRASFIELD, James
"The Entrepreneur." [BlackWR] (16:2) Spr-Sum 90, p. 56-57.
"Moonlight Marine." [BlueBldgs] (12) 90, p. 8-9.
717. BRASS, Deborah
"The Empty Set of Instructions." [Ploughs] (16:4) Wint 90-91, p. 66-69.
718. BRASS, Perry
"Footprints of Whales." [Mildred] (4:1) 90, p. 88-89.
719. BRAUN, Jenifer
"End in Sight." [HangL] (56) 90, p. 62.
"Great Grandmother's Bridesmaid." [HangL] (56) 90, p. 61.
"Momma Mia." [Footwork] 90, p. 88.
"Paterson." [HangL] (56) 90, p. 63.
"Reed." [HangL] (56) 90, p. 64.
"Vanessa." [Footwork] 90, p. 89.
720. BRAUN, Volker
"The Noises of My Country" (tr. by Ulrike Weber and Richard Jones). [PoetryE] (29) Spr 90, p. 76.
"The Oysters" (for Alain Lance, tr. by Ulrike Weber and Richard Jones). [PoetryE] (29) Spr 90, p. 80.
"Pleasure-Garden, Prussia" (tr. by Ulrike Weber and Richard Jones). [PoetryE] (29) Spr 90, p. 78.
"Praise for the Masses" (tr. by Ulrike Weber and Richard Jones). [PoetryE] (29) Spr 90, p. 77.
"Zentrum" (tr. by Ulrike Weber and Richard Jones). [PoetryE] (29) Spr 90, p. 79.
721. BRAVERMAN, Kate
"Prophecy in July." [OnTheBus] (2:1, #5) Spr 90, p. 42-43.
"Prophecy in May." [OnTheBus] (2:1, #5) Spr 90, p. 41-42.
"Words in July." [OnTheBus] (2:2/3:1, #6/7) Sum-Fall 90 Wint-Spr 91, p. 51-52.
"Words in July (2)." [OnTheBus] (2:1, #5) Spr 90, p. 42.
BRAVO, Armando Alvarez
See ALVAREZ BRAVO, Armando
722. BRAXTON, Jason
"Old Woman." [PoetryUSA] (5:1) Spr 90, p. 17.
723. BREBNER, Diana
"Astounded Souls." [Arc] (25) Aut 90, p. 4.
"Meditations on the Serene Blue Shirt" (Selections: 2 poems). [Descant] (21:1 #68) Spr 90, p. 31-32.
"The Perfect Garden" (for Blaine). [MalR] (92) S 90, p. 101.
"Sensors." [Arc] (25) Aut 90, p. 5.
"The Sparrow Drawer." [Arc] (25) Aut 90, p. 6-9.
"Thrall." [MalR] (92) S 90, p. 99.
"The Walls." [MalR] (92) S 90, p. 100.
724. BRECHT, Bertolt
"Erinnerung an die Marie A." [NewEngR] (13:2) Wint 90, p. 147-148.
"Fahrend in einem Bequemen Wagen." [InterPR] (16:2) Fall 90, p. 20.
"Fragen eines Lesenden Arbeiters." [InterPR] (16:2) Fall 90, p. 18.
"Memories of Marie" (tr. by Richard Moore). [NewEngR] (13:2) Wint 90, p. 148.
"Questions of a Literate Worker" (tr. by Brent Duffin). [InterPR] (16:2) Fall 90, p. 19.

"Traveling in a Comfortable Car" (tr. by Michael Landolt and Brent Duffin). [InterPR] (16:2) Fall 90, p. 21.
725. BREEN, Nancy
"And another one is gone." [Amelia] (6:1, #16) 90, p. 28.
"Sarasota Vespers." [SoCoast] (8) Spr 90, p. 56.
726. BREEZE, Jean Binta
"Get Flat." [LitR] (34:1) Fall 90, p. 88-89.
"Ordinary Mawning." [LitR] (34:1) Fall 90, p. 89-90.
727. BREHM, John
"The Fence." [PoetryNW] (31:1) Spr 90, p. 30-32.
"Now and Then." [SoDakR] (28:2) Sum 90, p. 166-167.
"Thinking About the Weather." [SoDakR] (28:2) Sum 90, p. 164-165.
728. BREIDENBACH, Tom
"The Red Scare." [MissR] (19:1/2, #55/56) 90, p. 237.
"Sera, Sera." [DenQ] (25:1) Sum 90, p. 12.
729. BRENNAN, Mathew
"Sky Lights." [Mildred] (4:1) 90, p. 109.
730. BRENNAN, Scott
"Camping Near Teton Mountain." [Paint] (17:33/34) Spr-Aut 90, p. 20.
"Shadows at Yellowstone." [Paint] (17:33/34) Spr-Aut 90, p. 19.
731. BRENNAN, Sherry
"Points." [NewAW] (6) Spr 90, p. 87-88.
732. BRENT, Frances Padorr
"After the Flood." [TriQ] (80) Wint 90-91, p. 29-30.
"Des Éclairs de Chaleur." [TriQ] (80) Wint 90-91, p. 31.
"Underwater House." [TriQ] (80) Wint 90-91, p. 33.
"The Whale." [TriQ] (80) Wint 90-91, p. 32.
733. BRESLIN, Paul
"A Visit (1959)." [Agni] (29/30) 90, p. 98-100.
734. BREWER, Gay
"Archeology." [Wind] (20:66) 90, p. 7-8.
"Honey, Would You Kill for Me?" [LullwaterR] (2:1) Wint 90, p. 38.
"Lost Library of Bucharest." [Bogg] (63) 90, p. 68.
"Melville's Old Men." [Wind] (20:66) 90, p. 7.
"Mountains." [NewDeltaR] (7:2) Spr-Sum 90, p. 71.
"Reviewing Options." [ChamLR] (4:1, #7) Fall 90, p. 171.
"The Sea." [LullwaterR] (1:1) Spr 90, p. 50.
"Then She Says." [DogRR] (9:2, #18) Aut 90, p. 40.
"To a Satanic Friend." [LullwaterR] (2:1) Wint 90, p. 69.
735. BREWER, Jack
"Sands Poured." [Pearl] (10) Spr 90, p. 56.
736. BREWER, Kenneth W.
"Astronomy" (for my son). [WritersF] (16) Fall 90, p. 141.
737. BREWSTER, Elizabeth
"Meditation on the *Meditations*." [Grain] (18:3) Fall 90, p. 28-30.
BREYNER, Sophia de Mello
See ANDRESEN, Sophia de Mello Breyner
BREYNER ANDRESEN, Sophia de Mello
See ANDRESEN, Sophia de Mello Breyner
738. BRICKWOOD, Sarah
"Television" (tr. of Jacques Rancourt). [Vis] (32) 90, p. 49.
"This Evening" (tr. of Jacques Rancourt). [Vis] (32) 90, p. 48.
739. BRIDGER, Howard
"Duet with My Five Year Old Son." [Grain] (18:1) Spr 90, p. 36.
740. BRIDGES, Constance Quarterman
"Under the Locust Tree." [Footwork] 90, p. 86.
741. BRIDGES, Lawrence
"Art Is Doing: A Bowl." [ManhatPR] (12) [90?], p. 8.
742. BRIDGES, Pat
"Along the Common Road One Cattail." [MissouriR] (13:1) 90, p. 153.
743. BRIDGES, William
"The Shipyard." [PassN] (11:2) Wint 90, p. 26.
744. BRIDGFORD, Kim
"Angel." [GeoR] (44:1/2) Spr-Sum 90, p. 192-193.
"The Difference the Sky Makes." [NoDaQ] (58:3) Sum 90, p. 1-2.
"Roses, You Say, Roses." [WestB] (26) 90, p. 90-91.

745. BRIDSON, Mary
"Locked in the Stone." [PottPort] (11) 89, p. 25.
746. BRIEFS, Elinor
"Pathetique" (tr. of Anna, Comtess de Noailles). [Vis] (32) 90, p. 36.
747. BRIEGER, Randy
"Baby Blue." [JamesWR] (7:3) Spr 90, p. 15.
"Civil Defense." [EvergreenC] (5:2) Wint 90, p. 20.
"Doug & Marilyn." [JamesWR] (8:1) Fall 90, p. 7.
"Neighbors" (for my father). [WestB] (26) 90, p. 28.
"Phorkyads." [JamesWR] (7:3) Spr 90, p. 15.
"The Pool Player" (for a Playwright). [JamesWR] (7:3) Spr 90, p. 15.
"The Two Who Jumped." [HawaiiR] (14:3, #30) Fall 90, p. 96.
748. BRIERLEY, Jane
"Airplane" (tr. of François-Xavier Eygun). [PraF] (11:1) Spr 90, p. 99.
"And we'll head for the horror of loveless beds" (tr. of Louis-Philippe Corbeil).
[PraF] (11:1) Spr 90, p. 91, 93.
"Daybreak" (tr. of François-Xavier Eygun). [PraF] (11:1) Spr 90, p. 97.
"For the Survivors" (tr. of Charles Leblanc). [PraF] (11:1) Spr 90, p. 49, 51.
"I have played in the optics of human perspectives" (tr. of Louis-Philippe Corbeil).
[PraF] (11:1) Spr 90, p. 89.
"The Immigrant" (tr. of Jacqueline Barral). [PraF] (11:1) Spr 90, p. 157.
"Migrations" (tr. of François-Xavier Eygun). [PraF] (11:1) Spr 90, p. 97.
"Pale dawn melts over the sleeping thing" (tr. of Louis-Philippe Corbeil). [PraF]
(11:1) Spr 90, p. 87.
"Paris" (tr. of Gilles Cop). [PraF] (11:1) Spr 90, p. 153.
"Plains" (tr. of François-Xavier Eygun). [PraF] (11:1) Spr 90, p. 95.
"Snowdrifts" (tr. of François-Xavier Eygun). [PraF] (11:1) Spr 90, p. 99.
"Tonight I saw a rose" (tr. of Gilles Cop). [PraF] (11:1) Spr 90, p. 155.
"Uncalm Meditation" (tr. of Charles Leblanc). [PraF] (11:1) Spr 90, p. 47, 49.
"Vexation" (tr. of Charles Leblanc). [PraF] (11:1) Spr 90, p. 53.
749. BRIGGS, Elizabeth
"The Tunnel Men." [Pig] (16) 90, p. 16.
750. BRIGGS, John D.
"Rain Stanzas." [EmeraldCR] (1990) c89, p. 62-63.
751. BRIGHT, Susan
"Our Lady of Guadalupe." [BilingR] (13:3) S-D 86 c90, p. 67-70.
752. BRINES, Francisco
"Song of Sleeplessness" (tr. by Don Share). [PartR] (57:2) Spr 90, p. 270.
753. BRINT, Armand
"A Short Note to Marilyn Monroe Twenty-Six Years After Her Death." [Pearl] (12)
Fall-Wint 90, p. 55.
754. BRINTON, Ruth
"I See You, Standing at a Sticky Table." [PoetryUSA] (5:2) Sum 90, p. 12.
755. BRIXIUS, Liz
"The Latest from a Little World Gently Abuzz with Itself." [BlackWR] (16:2)
Spr-Sum 90, p. 26.
"A Little Tent History." [MissR] (19:1/2, #55/56) 90, p. 238.
756. BROADHURST, Nicole
"Jalousies." [PraS] (64:2) Sum 90, p. 23-24.
"Time Flies at 22." [PraS] (64:2) Sum 90, p. 27.
"To My Mother, Remembering How We Bought Candles." [PraS] (64:2) Sum 90, p.
25-26.
757. BROCK, James
"The Buried Son, 1907." [MidwQ] (31:2) Wint 90, p. 221-222.
"Voices on the Air." [SycamoreR] (2:1) Wint 90, p. 48-49.
758. BROCK, Randall
"I Am." [Wind] (20:67) 90, p. 27.
"Inside." [Wind] (20:67) 90, p. 27.
759. BROCKENBROUGH, Anne
"Self Portrait in Water." [Shen] (40:2) Sum 90, p. 53.
760. BROCKI, A. C.
"Love Poem." [Bogg] (63) 90, p. 12.
761. BROCKWAY, James
"Johnson Brothers Ltd." (tr. of Rutger Kopland). [Stand] (31:1) Wint 89-90, p. 24.
"Miss A" (tr. of Rutger Kopland). [Stand] (31:1) Wint 89-90, p. 24.

"The Power of Evangelism" (tr. of Rutger Kopland). [Stand] (31:1) Wint 89-90, p. 23-24.
762. BROCKWELL, Stephen
"Tobogganing." [CanLit] (126) Aut 90, p. 103.
763. BRODERICK, Frank
"Signature." [Chelsea] (49) 90, p. 32-33.
764. BRODERICK, Richard
"At Forty." [LakeSR] (24) 90, p. 24.
"The Fire Next Time." [BellR] (13:2, #28) Fall 90, p. 5.
765. BRODERSON, Lucille
"At Eighty-Five." [Poetry] (157:1) O 90, p. 11-12.
766. BRODEY, Jim
"Low Planes" (w. Elio Schneeman). [Shiny] (5) 90, p. 24.
767. BRODKEY, Harold
"April Fools' Day, New York State." [NewYorker] (66:7) 2 Ap 90, p. 44.
"To a Child." [NewYorker] (66:28) 27 Ag 90, p. 54.
768. BRODSKY, Joseph
"In Memory of My Father: Australia" (tr. by the author). [NewYorker] (66:3) 5 Mr 90, p. 40.
769. BRODY, Harry
"The Graves in October." [WritersF] (16) Fall 90, p. 53.
"How Creation Occurs on Old 61." [RagMag] (8:2) 90, p. 64.
"In Her Heaven of Sorts." [WashR] (16:1) Je-Jl 90, p. 15.
"Mark Bowden." [WritersF] (16) Fall 90, p. 52.
"On Learning I'm to Be a Father Again." [RagMag] (8:2) 90, p. 65.
"Tonight, He Is Travelling in the Past." [CarolQ] (42:3) Spr 90, p. 39.
"Two Nights in 1956." [Spirit] (10:2) 90, p. 15.
770. BRODY, Polly
"Under the Mountain." [MidwQ] (31:3) Spr 90, p. 347.
BROEK, Gonny van den
See Van den BROEK, Gonny
771. BROMIGE, David
"Romantic Traces." [Verse] (7:1) Spr 90, p. 50-51.
772. BROMLEY, Anne C.
"Blue Marriage." [SouthernPR] (30:1) Spr 90, p. 49-50.
"The Night of His Life." [ColR] (NS 17:1) Spr-Sum 90, p. 31.
773. BROMSTEDT, Jackie
"Ebbtide." [QW] (30) Spr 90, p. 119.
774. BRONDY, Michele
"Crepuscule" (tr. by the author). [Vis] (32) 90, p. 38.
"Travel" (tr. by the author). [Vis] (32) 90, p. 37.
775. BROOKHOUSE, Christopher
"Tonight." [Asylum] (5:4) 90, p. 7.
776. BROOKS, Eunice
"For Their Wellbeing." [CanLit] (126) Aut 90, p. 19.
777. BROOKS, Gwendolyn
"The Artists' and Models' Ball." [BlackALF] (24:3) Fall 90, p. 572.
"A Black Wedding Song" (from "To Disembark," Chicago: Third World Press, 1981). [PoetryUSA] (5:3) Fall 90, p. 11.
"The Egg Boiler." [BlackALF] (24:3) Fall 90, p. 571.
"Jane Addams" (September 6, 1860-May 21, 1935). [BelPoJ] (40:4) Sum 90, p. 12-13.
"The Mother." [CimR] (93) O 90, p. 78.
"Paul Robeson" (from "To Disembark," Chicago: Third World Press, 1981). [PoetryUSA] (5:3) Fall 90, p. 13.
"Primer for Blacks." [CimR] (93) O 90, p. 78.
778. BROSMAN, Catharine Savage
"Journeying from Canyon de Chelly." [SouthernR] (26:1) Ja 90, p. 194-195.
779. BROSS, Addison
"Dream Pictures" (tr. of Tadeusz Borowski). [NewL] (57:1) Fall 90, p. 6-8.
"Untitled: I'm thinking of you" (tr. of Tadeusz Borowski). [NewL] (57:1) Fall 90, p. 8.
780. BROSSA, Joan
"Choral" (tr. by Susan Schreibman). [PaintedB] (40/41) 90, p. 25.
"Coral." [PaintedB] (40/41) 90, p. 24.

781. BROSSARD, Nicole
"La Matière Harmonieuse Manoeuvre encore." [MassR] (31:1/2) Spr-Sum 90, p. 87-95.
"Matter Harmonious Still Maneuvering" (tr. by Lise Weil). [MassR] (31:1/2) Spr-Sum 90, p. 86-94.
782. BROUGHTON, James
"Calling All Bards." [PoetryUSA] ([5:4?]) Wint 90, p. 14.
"The Last Sermon of Gnarley Never." [NewYorkQ] (41) Spr 90, p. 51-54.
"Laughing Matter." [NewYorkQ] (43) Fall 90, p. 48.
783. BROUGHTON, T. Alan
"Archeology Professor, Emeritus." [Confr] (42/43) Spr-Sum 90, p. 166.
"Banished." [Confr] (42/43) Spr-Sum 90, p. 167.
"Blues for a Dancer." [SouthernR] (26:3) Jl 90, p. 670.
"The Generous Past." [ThRiPo] (35/36) 90, p. 14.
"Mappemonde." [ThRiPo] (35/36) 90, p. 12-13.
"An Old Riddle." [Poetry] (156:1) Ap 90, p. 19.
"Outside In." [CharR] (16:2) Fall 90, p. 66-67.
"Screen for the Still Hours of Memory." [SouthernR] (26:3) Jl 90, p. 668-669.
"Serenade for Winds." [VirQR] (66:2) Spr 90, p. 271-272.
"Serious Thinking." [LitR] (33:3) Spr 90, p. 335.
"Toward Light." [Poetry] (156:1) Ap 90, p. 20.
784. BROUSSARD, Yves
"Enclosed Field" (tr. by William Jay Smith). [Trans] (23) Spr 90, p. 149-151.
785. BROWDER, Clifford
"Scratch." [SoCoast] (9) Fall 90, p. 8.
786. BROWN, Allan
"Aubade." [PoetryC] (11:4) Wint 90, p. 26.
"City Without Walls" (after Calvino). [AntigR] (81/82) Spr-Sum 90, p. 52.
"L'Envoy" (for Robert Lowell). [PoetryC] (11:4) Wint 90, p. 26.
"Forgetting." [PoetryC] (11:4) Wint 90, p. 26.
"Nocturne." [PoetryC] (11:4) Wint 90, p. 26.
"Unmoving." [PoetryC] (11:4) Wint 90, p. 26.
787. BROWN, Amy Benson
"My Last Executive." [LullwaterR] (2:1) Wint 90, p. 47.
788. BROWN, Beth Philips
"Ladies' Night at the Disco." [PaintedB] (40/41) 90, p. 142-143.
789. BROWN, Betsy
"Landlords, We Don't Just Disappear into Those Homes." [CimR] (92) Jl 90, p. 116-117.
790. BROWN, Christopher
"James Dickey." [NewYorkQ] (41) Spr 90, p. 87.
"Rahsaan Roland Kirk." [BlackALF] (24:3) Fall 90, p. 564.
791. BROWN, Christopher, I
"Child Eyes." [PoetryUSA] (5:1) Spr 90, p. 16.
"Cries." [PoetryUSA] (5:1) Spr 90, p. 15.
"Love Relics." [PoetryUSA] ([5:4?]) Wint 90, p. 25.
"Sparks Flying." [PoetryUSA] (5:3) Fall 90, p. 23.
792. BROWN, Cory
"Dear Nominalist." [NowestR] (28:2) 90, p. 22-23.
"Decisioning Sky." [Farm] (7:1) Spr 90, p. 46-47.
"Late Evening." [WestB] (27) 90, p. 83.
793. BROWN, Craig S.
"The Story of This Place." [Outbr] (21) 90, p. 44.
"We Sing a Bit Less Often." [Outbr] (21) 90, p. 45.
794. BROWN, David
"Bluegill Silhouette." [Poem] (64) N 90, p. 28.
"Coup de Grâce." [CapeR] (25:2) Fall 90, p. 34.
"On the First Day of Class." [Poem] (64) N 90, p. 27.
795. BROWN, Frank A.
"Ecclesiastes." [EmeraldCR] (1990) c89, p. 61.
796. BROWN, Harry
"Cock of the August Berm, or, Rise and Fall." [Poem] (64) N 90, p. 60.
"Everything Is Its Opposite." [Poem] (64) N 90, p. 59.
797. BROWN, Lee Ann
"Chain Reaction." [Shiny] (5) 90, p. 16.
"White Slippers." [Shiny] (5) 90, p. 16.

798. BROWN, Lloyd W.
"Gonaives." [Obs] (5:3) Wint 90, p. 120-122.
"Marley's Ghost." [Obs] (5:3) Wint 90, p. 118-120.
"The Return of the Native." [Obs] (5:3) Wint 90, p. 115-118.
799. BROWN, Marc W.
"Santa Claus Memorial." [EmeraldCR] (1990) c89, p. 9.
800. BROWN, Robert
"Cascade of Genitives" (tr. of Jean Tardieu). [Vis] (33) 90, p. 23.
"Dust Settling Before Sleep." [Plain] (10:2) Wint 90, p. 22.
"In the Foggy Mirror, Beneath Ockham's Razor." [CharR] (16:1) Spr 90, p. 69.
"Nocturne, Late Spring." [BlueBldgs] (12) 90, p. 24.
"When She Hears the Wolves." [KanQ] (22:3) Sum 90, p. 179.
801. BROWN, Stacey
"The Mandarin House." [LullwaterR] (2:1) Wint 90, p. 88.
802. BROWN, Stephanie
"Interview with an Alchemist in the New Age." [AmerPoR] (19:3) My-Je 90, p. 52.
803. BROWN, Steven Ford
"December" (tr. of Angel Gonzalez). [ConnPR] (9:1) 90, p. 7-8.
"Rain Upon the Snow in the Spring" (tr. of Angel Gonzalez). [ConnPR] (9:1) 90, p.
13.
"Song to Sing a Song" (tr. of Angel Gonzalez). [ConnPR] (9:1) 90, p. 10.
"That's Enough for Me" (tr. of Angel Gonzalez). [ConnPR] (9:1) 90, p. 11-12.
"They Are the Seagulls, My Love" (tr. of Angel Gonzalez). [ConnPR] (9:1) 90, p. 9.
804. BROWNE, Colin
"Lunatick Bawling." [WestCL] (24:1) Spr 90, p. 26-29.
"Salt? Scrape." [WestCL] (24:1) Spr 90, p. 133-134.
805. BROWNE, Michael Dennis
"The House without Us." [PraS] (64:1) Spr 90, p. 72-73.
"Wedding Figures." [PraS] (64:1) Spr 90, p. 71-72.
806. BROWNING, Barbara
"We Were All Hungry." [YaleR] (79:2) Wint 90, p. 222.
807. BROX, Jane
"6 A.M." [Hudson] (43:3) Aut 90, p. 450-451.
"March Hill Road." [Hudson] (43:3) Aut 90, p. 451.
"November." [Hudson] (43:3) Aut 90, p. 450.
"Waiting Tables." [VirQR] (66:4) Aut 90, p. 663-664.
808. BROXSON, Gary
"Good Night, Sleep Tight." [EmeraldCR] (1990) c89, p. 81-82.
809. BROXSON, Perry
"Psych Ward Queen." [EmeraldCR] (1990) c89, p. 13-14.
"San Carlos Speaks." [EmeraldCR] (1990) c89, p. 15-16.
810. BRUBAKER, Ron
"I have saw something" (reprinted from #2, 1980). [Kaleid] (20) Wint-Spr 90, p. 41.
811. BRUCE, Debra
"In the Twilight Lounge." [PennR] (4:2) 90, p. 6.
"I've Decided to Tell You Anyway." [PraS] (64:3) Fall 90, p. 97.
"The Usual Time." [PraS] (64:3) Fall 90, p. 98.
812. BRUCE, Jean
"Rain, I Recon." [NewRena] (8:1, #24) Spr 90, p. 69-70.
813. BRUCE, Lennart
"The Adopted Child" (tr. of Madeleine Gustafsson, w. Sonja Bruce). [Spirit] (10:1)
89, p. 139.
"Angel Movie" (tr. of Agneta Pleijel, w. Sonja Bruce). [Spirit] (10:1) 89, p. 83-89.
"At an Outdoor Cafe" (tr. of Margareta Renberg, w. Sonja Bruce). [Spirit] (10:1) 89,
p. 127.
"Autumn, I Wrote" (tr. of Gurli Lindén, w. Sonja Bruce). [Spirit] (10:1) 89, p. 105.
"But Do You Remember August" (tr. of Tua Forsström, w. Sonja Bruce). [Spirit]
(10:1) 89, p. 189.
"But Incessantly" (tr. of Tua Forsström, w. Sonja Bruce). [Spirit] (10:1) 89, p. 177.
"Children" (tr. of Elsa Grave, w. Sonja Bruce). [Spirit] (10:1) 89, p. 29.
"The City Was Emptied" (tr. of Gurli Lindén, w. Sonja Bruce). [Spirit] (10:1) 89, p.
109.
"Clarity" (tr. of Ingela Strandberg, w. Sonja Bruce). [Spirit] (10:1) 89, p. 163.
"Come Inside" (tr. of Ingela Strandberg, w. Sonja Bruce). [Spirit] (10:1) 89, p. 153.
"Damned" (tr. of Elsa Grave, w. Sonja Bruce). [Spirit] (10:1) 89, p. 25.
"Dark Wind" (tr. of Eva Runefelt, w. Sonja Bruce). [Spirit] (10:1) 89, p. 215.

82

"Declaration" (tr. of Margareta Renberg, w. Sonja Bruce). [Spirit] (10:1) 89, p. 135.
"Did You See the Graves" (tr. of Gurli Lindén, w. Sonja Bruce). [Spirit] (10:1) 89, p. 107.
"Do You Remember" (tr. of Gurli Lindén, w. Sonja Bruce). [Spirit] (10:1) 89, p. 103.
"The Dolls" (tr. of Solveig von Schoultz, w. Sonja Bruce). [Spirit] (10:1) 89, p. 39.
"Don't Distrust Me" (tr. of Tua Forsström, w. Sonja Bruce). [Spirit] (10:1) 89, p. 179.
"Drawing" (tr. of Margareta Renberg, w. Sonja Bruce). [Spirit] (10:1) 89, p. 123.
"Dream" (tr. of Solveig von Schoultz, w. Sonja Bruce). [Spirit] (10:1) 89, p. 35.
"The Drops" (tr. of Tua Forsström, w. Sonja Bruce). [Spirit] (10:1) 89, p. 193.
"The Drowning" (Antonin Artaud, also called Nanaqui, in Smyrna, tr. of Heidi von Born, w. Sonja Bruce). [Spirit] (10:1) 89, p. 113.
"Dusk Comes All the Time Now" (tr. of Agneta Ara, w. Sonja Bruce). [Spirit] (10:1) 89, p. 67.
"The Farewell Letter" (tr. of Margareta Renberg, w. Sonja Bruce). [Spirit] (10:1) 89, p. 125.
"Flimsy Kitchen Light" (tr. of Eva Runefelt, w. Sonja Bruce). [Spirit] (10:1) 89, p. 209.
"Forgetting Is Remembering Intensely" (tr. of Tua Forsström, w. Sonja Bruce). [Spirit] (10:1) 89, p. 183.
"From Home" (tr. of Margareta Renberg, w. Sonja Bruce). [Spirit] (10:1) 89, p. 121.
"Gallup" (tr. of Tua Forsström, w. Sonja Bruce). [Spirit] (10:1) 89, p. 197.
"The Girl" (tr. of Agneta Ara, w. Sonja Bruce). [Spirit] (10:1) 89, p. 61.
"Grass in August" (tr. of Eva Runefelt, w. Sonja Bruce). [Spirit] (10:1) 89, p. 203, 205.
"The Guide" (tr. of Madeleine Gustafsson, w. Sonja Bruce). [Spirit] (10:1) 89, p. 149.
"Heart" (tr. of Solveig von Schoultz, w. Sonja Bruce). [Spirit] (10:1) 89, p. 47.
"Here, I've Peeled an Orange" (tr. of Tua Forsström, w. Sonja Bruce). [Spirit] (10:1) 89, p. 187.
"I Believe in Fresh Starts" (tr. of Ingela Strandberg, w. Sonja Bruce). [Spirit] (10:1) 89, p. 171.
"I Built Small Nests / under Your Heart" (tr. of Gurli Lindén, w. Sonja Bruce). [Spirit] (10:1) 89, p. 99.
"I Never Believed" (tr. of Agneta Ara, w. Sonja Bruce). [Spirit] (10:1) 89, p. 59.
"I Put My Skis" (tr. of Ingela Strandberg, w. Sonja Bruce). [Spirit] (10:1) 89, p. 161.
"I Really Want to Make Love" (tr. of Gurli Lindén, w. Sonja Bruce). [Spirit] (10:1) 89, p. 101.
"I Too Am Alone Again" (tr. of Madeleine Gustafsson, w. Sonja Bruce). [Spirit] (10:1) 89, p. 143.
"I Watch the People" (tr. of Agneta Ara, w. Sonja Bruce). [Spirit] (10:1) 89, p. 63.
"In an Unfamiliar Apartment" (tr. of Agneta Pleijel, w. Sonja Bruce). [Spirit] (10:1) 89, p. 79.
"In the Grass" (tr. of Ingela Strandberg, w. Sonja Bruce). [Spirit] (10:1) 89, p. 157, 159.
"Incisions" (tr. of Eva Runefelt, w. Sonja Bruce). [Spirit] (10:1) 89, p. 211.
"The Instant" (tr. of Solveig von Schoultz, w. Sonja Bruce). [Spirit] (10:1) 89, p. 45.
"Isaac Newton's Second Awakening" (tr. of Margareta Renberg, w. Sonja Bruce). [Spirit] (10:1) 89, p. 133.
"It Takes a Long Time" (tr. of Gurli Lindén, w. Sonja Bruce). [Spirit] (10:1) 89, p. 95-97.
"It's May and the Apple Trees Bloom" (tr. of Ingela Strandberg, w. Sonja Bruce). [Spirit] (10:1) 89, p. 165, 167.
"Lake Hörende, August" (tr. of Madeleine Gustafsson, w. Sonja Bruce). [Spirit] (10:1) 89, p. 147.
"A Long Farewell" (tr. of Tua Forsström, w. Sonja Bruce). [Spirit] (10:1) 89, p. 195.
"Longing Is Betrayal of Oneself" (tr. of Agneta Ara, w. Sonja Bruce). [Spirit] (10:1) 89, p. 65.
"Look How She Walks!" (tr. of Solveig von Schoultz, w. Sonja Bruce). [Spirit] (10:1) 89, p. 45.
"Lullaby for My Unborn Child" (tr. of Elsa Grave, w. Sonja Bruce). [Spirit] (10:1) 89, p. 27.
"March, Early Spring" (tr. of Eva Runefelt, w. Sonja Bruce). [Spirit] (10:1) 89, p. 201.
"Morning" (tr. of Eva Runefelt, w. Sonja Bruce). [Spirit] (10:1) 89, p. 207.

83

"Morning in Suburbia" (tr. of Eva Runefelt, w. Sonja Bruce). [Spirit] (10:1) 89, p. 213.

"Movies" (tr. of Margareta Renberg, w. Sonja Bruce). [Spirit] (10:1) 89, p. 129.

"My Grandmother" (tr. of Agneta Pleijel, w. Sonja Bruce). [Spirit] (10:1) 89, p. 73.

"New" (tr. of Eva Runefelt, w. Sonja Bruce). [Spirit] (10:1) 89, p. 221, 223.

"No, It Has to Fit Tightly" (tr. of Tua Forsström, w. Sonja Bruce). [Spirit] (10:1) 89, p. 185.

"November" (tr. of Agneta Ara, w. Sonja Bruce). [Spirit] (10:1) 89, p. 63.

"November Sea" (tr. of Solveig von Schoultz, w. Sonja Bruce). [Spirit] (10:1) 89, p. 41.

"Now and Then We Get Up" (tr. of Agneta Ara, w. Sonja Bruce). [Spirit] (10:1) 89, p. 57.

"Oh Dear" (tr. of Tua Forsström, w. Sonja Bruce). [Spirit] (10:1) 89, p. 191.

"Old Folks Home" (tr. of Heidi von Born, w. Sonja Bruce). [Spirit] (10:1) 89, p. 115.

"The Only Wars" (tr. of Agneta Ara, w. Sonja Bruce). [Spirit] (10:1) 89, p. 55.

"Poetry Is Dangerous" (tr. of Elsa Grave, w. Sonja Bruce). [Spirit] (10:1) 89, p. 17-21.

"Quiet Now, by My Round Table" (tr. of Agneta Pleijel, w. Sonja Bruce). [Spirit] (10:1) 89, p. 91.

"Raspberry Portrait" (tr. of Solveig von Schoultz, w. Sonja Bruce). [Spirit] (10:1) 89, p. 43.

"The Room" (tr. of Solveig von Schoultz, w. Sonja Bruce). [Spirit] (10:1) 89, p. 33.

"Room for the Night" (tr. of Ingela Strandberg, w. Sonja Bruce). [Spirit] (10:1) 89, p. 169.

"Run Away?" (tr. of Madeleine Gustafsson, w. Sonja Bruce). [Spirit] (10:1) 89, p. 141.

"Sequence" (tr. of Ingela Strandberg, w. Sonja Bruce). [Spirit] (10:1) 89, p. 173.

"The Slaughterhouse" (tr. of Eva Runefelt, w. Sonja Bruce). [Spirit] (10:1) 89, p. 217, 219.

"Sometimes I Dream" (tr. of Ingela Strandberg, w. Sonja Bruce). [Spirit] (10:1) 89, p. 155.

"Speak to Me" (tr. of Agneta Ara, w. Sonja Bruce). [Spirit] (10:1) 89, p. 69.

"Still It Returns" (tr. of Tua Forsström, w. Sonja Bruce). [Spirit] (10:1) 89, p. 181.

"Summer Grave" (tr. of Solveig von Schoultz, w. Sonja Bruce). [Spirit] (10:1) 89, p. 49.

"There Are Deeper Waters" (tr. of Agneta Pleijel, w. Sonja Bruce). [Spirit] (10:1) 89, p. 81.

"Things You Can't Talk About" (tr. of Margareta Renberg, w. Sonja Bruce). [Spirit] (10:1) 89, p. 131.

"This Is a Transformation" (tr. of Gurli Lindén, w. Sonja Bruce). [Spirit] (10:1) 89, p. 105.

"The Tragedy of Snappen-Sara" (tr. of Heidi von Born, w. Sonja Bruce). [Spirit] (10:1) 89, p. 117.

"Unmanned Telephone Receivers" (tr. of Elsa Grave, w. Sonja Bruce). [Spirit] (10:1) 89, p. 23.

"We Had All the Possibilities in the World" (tr. of Agneta Ara, w. Sonja Bruce). [Spirit] (10:1) 89, p. 53.

"When I Was a Child / the Ladies" (tr. of Agneta Pleijel, w. Sonja Bruce). [Spirit] (10:1) 89, p. 73.

"When I Was a Child I Walked the Meadow" (tr. of Agneta Pleijel, w. Sonja Bruce). [Spirit] (10:1) 89, p. 75.

"When I Was a Child My Grandfather" (tr. of Agneta Pleijel, w. Sonja Bruce). [Spirit] (10:1) 89, p. 77.

"Whitsun, Thirty Years Later" (tr. of Madeleine Gustafsson, w. Sonja Bruce). [Spirit] (10:1) 89, p. 145.

"Winter Shore" (tr. of Solveig von Schoultz, w. Sonja Bruce). [Spirit] (10:1) 89, p. 37.

814. BRUCE, Sonja

"The Adopted Child" (tr. of Madeleine Gustafsson, w. Lennart Bruce). [Spirit] (10:1) 89, p. 139.

"Angel Movie" (tr. of Agneta Pleijel, w. Lennart Bruce). [Spirit] (10:1) 89, p. 83-89.

"At an Outdoor Cafe" (tr. of Margareta Renberg, w. Lennart Bruce). [Spirit] (10:1) 89, p. 127.

"Autumn, I Wrote" (tr. of Gurli Lindén, w. Lennart Bruce). [Spirit] (10:1) 89, p. 105.

BRUCE

"But Do You Remember August" (tr. of Tua Forsström, w. Lennart Bruce). [Spirit] (10:1) 89, p. 189.
"But Incessantly" (tr. of Tua Forsström, w. Lennart Bruce). [Spirit] (10:1) 89, p. 177.
"Children" (tr. of Elsa Grave, w. Lennart Bruce). [Spirit] (10:1) 89, p. 29.
"The City Was Emptied" (tr. of Gurli Lindén, w. Lennart Bruce). [Spirit] (10:1) 89, p. 109.
"Clarity" (tr. of Ingela Strandberg, w. Lennart Bruce). [Spirit] (10:1) 89, p. 163.
"Come Inside" (tr. of Ingela Strandberg, w. Lennart Bruce). [Spirit] (10:1) 89, p. 153.
"Damned" (tr. of Elsa Grave, w. Lennart Bruce). [Spirit] (10:1) 89, p. 25.
"Dark Wind" (tr. of Eva Runefelt, w. Lennart Bruce). [Spirit] (10:1) 89, p. 215.
"Declaration" (tr. of Margareta Renberg, w. Lennart Bruce). [Spirit] (10:1) 89, p. 135.
"Did You See the Graves" (tr. of Gurli Lindén, w. Lennart Bruce). [Spirit] (10:1) 89, p. 107.
"Do You Remember" (tr. of Gurli Lindén, w. Lennart Bruce). [Spirit] (10:1) 89, p. 103.
"The Dolls" (tr. of Solveig von Schoultz, w. Lennart Bruce). [Spirit] (10:1) 89, p. 39.
"Don't Distrust Me" (tr. of Tua Forsström, w. Lennart Bruce). [Spirit] (10:1) 89, p. 179.
"Drawing" (tr. of Margareta Renberg, w. Lennart Bruce). [Spirit] (10:1) 89, p. 123.
"Dream" (tr. of Solveig von Schoultz, w. Lennart Bruce). [Spirit] (10:1) 89, p. 35.
"The Drops" (tr. of Tua Forsström, w. Lennart Bruce). [Spirit] (10:1) 89, p. 193.
"The Drowning" (Antonin Artaud, also called Nanaqui, in Smyrna, tr. of Heidi von Born, w. Lennart Bruce). [Spirit] (10:1) 89, p. 113.
"Dusk Comes All the Time Now" (tr. of Agneta Ara, w. Lennart Bruce). [Spirit] (10:1) 89, p. 67.
"The Farewell Letter" (tr. of Margareta Renberg, w. Lennart Bruce). [Spirit] (10:1) 89, p. 125.
"Flimsy Kitchen Light" (tr. of Eva Runefelt, w. Lennart Bruce). [Spirit] (10:1) 89, p. 209.
"Forgetting Is Remembering Intensely" (tr. of Tua Forsström, w. Lennart Bruce). [Spirit] (10:1) 89, p. 183.
"From Home" (tr. of Margareta Renberg, w. Lennart Bruce). [Spirit] (10:1) 89, p. 121.
"Gallup" (tr. of Tua Forsström, w. Lennart Bruce). [Spirit] (10:1) 89, p. 197.
"The Girl" (tr. of Agneta Ara, w. Lennart Bruce). [Spirit] (10:1) 89, p. 61.
"Grass in August" (tr. of Eva Runefelt, w. Lennart Bruce). [Spirit] (10:1) 89, p. 203, 205.
"The Guide" (tr. of Madeleine Gustafsson, w. Lennart Bruce). [Spirit] (10:1) 89, p. 149.
"Heart" (tr. of Solveig von Schoultz, w. Lennart Bruce). [Spirit] (10:1) 89, p. 47.
"Here, I've Peeled an Orange" (tr. of Tua Forsström, w. Lennart Bruce). [Spirit] (10:1) 89, p. 187.
"I Believe in Fresh Starts" (tr. of Ingela Strandberg, w. Lennart Bruce). [Spirit] (10:1) 89, p. 171.
"I Built Small Nests / under Your Heart" (tr. of Gurli Lindén, w. Lennart Bruce). [Spirit] (10:1) 89, p. 99.
"I Never Believed" (tr. of Agneta Ara, w. Lennart Bruce). [Spirit] (10:1) 89, p. 59.
"I Put My Skis" (tr. of Ingela Strandberg, w. Lennart Bruce). [Spirit] (10:1) 89, p. 161.
"I Really Want to Make Love" (tr. of Gurli Lindén, w. Lennart Bruce). [Spirit] (10:1) 89, p. 101.
"I Too Am Alone Again" (tr. of Madeleine Gustafsson, w. Lennart Bruce). [Spirit] (10:1) 89, p. 143.
"I Watch the People" (tr. of Agneta Ara, w. Lennart Bruce). [Spirit] (10:1) 89, p. 63.
"In an Unfamiliar Apartment" (tr. of Agneta Pleijel, w. Lennart Bruce). [Spirit] (10:1) 89, p. 79.
"In the Grass" (tr. of Ingela Strandberg, w. Lennart Bruce). [Spirit] (10:1) 89, p. 157, 159.
"Incisions" (tr. of Eva Runefelt, w. Lennart Bruce). [Spirit] (10:1) 89, p. 211.
"The Instant" (tr. of Solveig von Schoultz, w. Lennart Bruce). [Spirit] (10:1) 89, p. 45.
"Isaac Newton's Second Awakening" (tr. of Margareta Renberg, w. Lennart Bruce). [Spirit] (10:1) 89, p. 133.

"It Takes a Long Time" (tr. of Gurli Lindén, w. Lennart Bruce). [Spirit] (10:1) 89, p. 95-97.

"It's May and the Apple Trees Bloom" (tr. of Ingela Strandberg, w. Lennart Bruce). [Spirit] (10:1) 89, p. 165, 167.

"Lake Hörende, August" (tr. of Madeleine Gustafsson, w. Lennart Bruce). [Spirit] (10:1) 89, p. 147.

"A Long Farewell" (tr. of Tua Forsström, w. Lennart Bruce). [Spirit] (10:1) 89, p. 195.

"Longing Is Betrayal of Oneself" (tr. of Agneta Ara, w. Lennart Bruce). [Spirit] (10:1) 89, p. 65.

"Look How She Walks!" (tr. of Solveig von Schoultz, w. Lennart Bruce). [Spirit] (10:1) 89, p. 45.

"Lullaby for My Unborn Child" (tr. of Elsa Grave, w. Lennart Bruce). [Spirit] (10:1) 89, p. 27.

"March, Early Spring" (tr. of Eva Runefelt, w. Lennart Bruce). [Spirit] (10:1) 89, p. 201.

"Morning" (tr. of Eva Runefelt, w. Lennart Bruce). [Spirit] (10:1) 89, p. 207.

"Morning in Suburbia" (tr. of Eva Runefelt, w. Lennart Bruce). [Spirit] (10:1) 89, p. 213.

"Movies" (tr. of Margareta Renberg, w. Lennart Bruce). [Spirit] (10:1) 89, p. 129.

"My Grandmother" (tr. of Agneta Pleijel, w. Lennart Bruce). [Spirit] (10:1) 89, p. 73.

"New" (tr. of Eva Runefelt, w. Lennart Bruce). [Spirit] (10:1) 89, p. 221, 223.

"No, It Has to Fit Tightly" (tr. of Tua Forsström, w. Lennart Bruce). [Spirit] (10:1) 89, p. 185.

"November" (tr. of Agneta Ara, w. Lennart Bruce). [Spirit] (10:1) 89, p. 63.

"November Sea" (tr. of Solveig von Schoultz, w. Lennart Bruce). [Spirit] (10:1) 89, p. 41.

"Now and Then We Get Up" (tr. of Agneta Ara, w. Lennart Bruce). [Spirit] (10:1) 89, p. 57.

"Oh Dear" (tr. of Tua Forsström, w. Lennart Bruce). [Spirit] (10:1) 89, p. 191.

"Old Folks Home" (tr. of Heidi von Born, w. Lennart Bruce). [Spirit] (10:1) 89, p. 115.

"The Only Wars" (tr. of Agneta Ara, w. Lennart Bruce). [Spirit] (10:1) 89, p. 55.

"Poetry Is Dangerous" (tr. of Elsa Grave, w. Lennart Bruce). [Spirit] (10:1) 89, p. 17-21.

"Quiet Now, by My Round Table" (tr. of Agneta Pleijel, w. Lennart Bruce). [Spirit] (10:1) 89, p. 91.

"Raspberry Portrait" (tr. of Solveig von Schoultz, w. Lennart Bruce). [Spirit] (10:1) 89, p. 43.

"The Room" (tr. of Solveig von Schoultz, w. Lennart Bruce). [Spirit] (10:1) 89, p. 33.

"Room for the Night" (tr. of Ingela Strandberg, w. Lennart Bruce). [Spirit] (10:1) 89, p. 169.

"Run Away?" (tr. of Madeleine Gustafsson, w. Lennart Bruce). [Spirit] (10:1) 89, p. 141.

"Sequence" (tr. of Ingela Strandberg, w. Lennart Bruce). [Spirit] (10:1) 89, p. 173.

"The Slaughterhouse" (tr. of Eva Runefelt, w. Lennart Bruce). [Spirit] (10:1) 89, p. 217, 219.

"Sometimes I Dream" (tr. of Ingela Strandberg, w. Lennart Bruce). [Spirit] (10:1) 89, p. 155.

"Speak to Me" (tr. of Agneta Ara, w. Lennart Bruce). [Spirit] (10:1) 89, p. 69.

"Still It Returns" (tr. of Tua Forsström, w. Lennart Bruce). [Spirit] (10:1) 89, p. 181.

"Summer Grave" (tr. of Solveig von Schoultz, w. Lennart Bruce). [Spirit] (10:1) 89, p. 49.

"There Are Deeper Waters" (tr. of Agneta Pleijel, w. Lennart Bruce). [Spirit] (10:1) 89, p. 81.

"Things You Can't Talk About" (tr. of Margareta Renberg, w. Lennart Bruce). [Spirit] (10:1) 89, p. 131.

"This Is a Transformation" (tr. of Gurli Lindén, w. Lennart Bruce). [Spirit] (10:1) 89, p. 105.

"The Tragedy of Snappen-Sara" (tr. of Heidi von Born, w. Lennart Bruce). [Spirit] (10:1) 89, p. 117.

"Unmanned Telephone Receivers" (tr. of Elsa Grave, w. Lennart Bruce). [Spirit] (10:1) 89, p. 23.

"We Had All the Possibilities in the World" (tr. of Agneta Ara, w. Lennart Bruce). [Spirit] (10:1) 89, p. 53.

BRUCE

"When I Was a Child / the Ladies" (tr. of Agneta Pleijel, w. Lennart Bruce). [Spirit] (10:1) 89, p. 73.
"When I Was a Child I Walked the Meadow" (tr. of Agneta Pleijel, w. Lennart Bruce). [Spirit] (10:1) 89, p. 75.
"When I Was a Child My Grandfather" (tr. of Agneta Pleijel, w. Lennart Bruce). [Spirit] (10:1) 89, p. 77.
"Whitsun, Thirty Years Later" (tr. of Madeleine Gustafsson, w. Lennart Bruce). [Spirit] (10:1) 89, p. 145.
"Winter Shore" (tr. of Solveig von Schoultz, w. Lennart Bruce). [Spirit] (10:1) 89, p. 37.

815. BRUCHAC, Joseph
"Blue Coyote." [HampSPR] (Anthology 1975-1990) 90, p. 197.
"In the Sweat Lodge the Women Are Singing." [PoetryC] (11:1) Spr 90, p. 9.
"A Song at Season's End." [PoetryC] (11:1) Spr 90, p. 9.
"Song of the Potato." [HampSPR] (Anthology 1975-1990) 90, p. 197-198.

816. BRUCK, Julie
"Who We Are Now." [NewYorker] (66:20) 2 Jl 90, p. 46.

817. BRUINING, Anne Mi Ok
"Stones in Somerville" (For Jeanne). [SinW] (40) Spr 90, p. 91-93.

BRUNET, Vilma Bayron
See BAYRON-BRUNET, Vilma

818. BRUNGARDT, Carl
"Wet Fire Dream." [PacificR] (8) 90, p. 62.

819. BRUNK, Juanita
"Mrs. Richards Plays a Starlight Waltz." [PassN] (11:2) Wint 90, p. 3.

BRUNO, Michael La
See LaBRUNO, Michael

820. BRUNSVOLD, Emily
"The Beach." [PoetryUSA] ([5:4?]) Wint 90, p. 27.
"Hair." [PoetryUSA] ([5:4?]) Wint 90, p. 27.
"My Mom." [PoetryUSA] ([5:4?]) Wint 90, p. 27.

BRUNT, H. L. van
See Van BRUNT, Lloyd

BRUNT, Lloyd van
See Van BRUNT, Lloyd

821. BRUSH, Thomas
"Point Defiance" (for my brother). [PoetryNW] (31:4) Wint 90-91, p. 19-20.

822. BRUYCKER, Daniel de
"The Dazzled One" (tr. of Henry Bauchau). [Vis] (32) 90, p. 33.
"The 'L's'" (Selections, tr. of Philippe Remy). [Vis] (32) 90, p. 31.
"The Outrage" (Excerpt, tr. of Marc Quaghebeur). [Vis] (32) 90, p. 34.
"Poem: The long day's journey" (tr. by the author). [Vis] (32) 90, p. 34.
"Voices, Garments, Plunders" (Excerpts, tr. of Jacques Izoard). [Vis] (32) 90, p. 32-33.

823. BRUYN, Guido de
"A Glass Falls" (tr. by David Siefkin and Catharina Kochuyt). [Vis] (34) 90, p. 15.

824. BRYAN, Sharon
"Away." [GeoR] (44:4) Wint 90, p. 668-669.
"Beholden." [GeoR] (44:3) Fall 90, p. 411.
"Imitations of Mortality." [HayF] (6) Sum 90, p. 87.

825. BRYANT, Jane
"Somewhere on Route 15." [AnthNEW] 90, p. 14.

826. BRYANT, Valerie
"The Game." [Amelia] (6:2, #17) 90, p. 148.

827. BRYN MAWR TRANSLATION SEMINAR
"Ninel" (tr. of Evgenii Rein, under the supervision of George L. Kline). [Nimrod] (33:2) Spr-Sum 90, p. 40-42.

828. BRYNER, Jeanne
"August Moonlight." [HiramPoR] (48/49) 90-91, p. 15-17.
"Kick the Can." [Poem] (64) N 90, p. 52-53.

829. BUCHANAN, Carl
"Anywhere." [PoetL] (85:3) Fall 90, p. 8.
"Gatsby." [SoDakR] (28:1) Spr 90, p. 77.
"Hamlet Exits the Castle." [KanQ] (22:3) Sum 90, p. 84.

830. BUCK, Paul
"Recollection & Misunderstanding" (Selections: 2 poems). [Screens] (2) 90, p. 133.

831. BUCK, Paula Closson
   "Little Spanish Poems." [Shen] (40:4) Wint 90, p. 94-95.
832. BUCKAWAY, C. M.
   "The Crisis." [Grain] (18:3) Fall 90, p. 37.
833. BUCKLEY, Christopher
   "Dark Matter." [Iowa] (20:2) Spr-Sum 90, p. 50-51, plus 2 unnumbered pages.
   "Midlife." [Poetry] (157:2) N 90, p. 91-93.
   "Note to Tomaz Salamun While Flying Through a Thunderstorm en Route to a
      Writers' Conference." [DenQ] (25:1) Sum 90, p. 13-14.
   "Serenade in Blue." [Iowa] (20:2) Spr-Sum 90, p. 46-47.
   "Sun Spots." [Iowa] (20:2) Spr-Sum 90, p. 48-49.
   "Tabula Rasa." [MissouriR] (13:2) 90, p. 50-53.
   "Trying Not to Think of Politics, May Day, Belgrade 1989." [Crazy] (39) Wint 90, p.
      24-26.
834. BUDDINGA, C.
   "Birdcage" (tr. from the Dutch). [Vis] (34) 90, p. 43.
835. BUDREWICZ, Leszek
   "In Lieu Of" (tr. by Reuel K. Wilson). [Trans] (24) Fall 90, p. 190.
836. BUDY, Andrea Hollander
   "Asleep in the Forest" (after "Hansel & Grettel," a painting by Monique Felix). [IndR]
      (13:2) Spr 90, p. 58-59.
   "Fairy Tale." [ContextS] (1:1) 89, p. 9.
   "Fire." [HighP] (5:1) Spr 90, p. 48.
   "Firmly Married." [Poetry] (156:3) Je 90, p. 132.
   "Moon in Cancer." [ContextS] (1:1) 89, p. 11.
   "No One Wants to Be the Witch." [IndR] (13:2) Spr 90, p. 60-61.
   "Permission." [SouthernPR] (30:2) Fall 90, p. 42-43.
   "Red." [LaurelR] (24:1) Wint 90, p. 87.
   "This Is an Answer." [HighP] (5:1) Spr 90, p. 49.
   "This Will Be My Only." [LaurelR] (24:1) Wint 90, p. 86.
   "When She Named Fire." [GeoR] (44:1/2) Spr-Sum 90, p. 11-12.
   "Why She Will Not Sleep." [ContextS] (1:1) 89, p. 10.
837. BUFFONI, Franco
   "Adidas." [Os] (30) Spr 90, p. 29.
   "The Baptistry" (in English and Italian). [Os] (30) Spr 90, p. 28.
   "L'Odore di Resina e C'era." [Os] (30) Spr 90, p. 27.
838. BUFIS, Paul
   "My Father Steps Clear Into the Future." [SouthernPR] (30:1) Spr 90, p. 32-34.
839. BUGEJA, Michael J.
   "Amnesty Orange" (for Brooks). [CharR] (16:1) Spr 90, p. 53-54.
   "Anthem: Love and the Antipodes." [CharR] (16:1) Spr 90, p. 54.
   "The Club House" (for you, Dad). [PoetC] (22:1) Fall 90, p. 20-21.
   "Locution, Locomotive Case." [PoetL] (85:2) Sum 90, p. 11-12.
   "Love, Hate: The Life We Learn." [HawaiiR] (14:3, #30) Fall 90, p. 6-7.
   "Mein Holocaust -- Gedicht." [CharR] (16:1) Spr 90, p. 52-53.
   "Thaw." [HawaiiR] (14:3, #30) Fall 90, p. 8-9.
   "When I Feel Your Soul, I Reach for You with These Arms." [HawaiiR] (14:2, #29)
      Spr 90, p. 113.
840. BUHROW, Bonnie
   "Nothing to Eat." [MinnR] (NS 34/35) Spr-Fall 90, p. 7.
841. BUKOWSKI, Charles
   "2 Henry Miller Paintings and Etc." [Gargoyle] (37/38) 90, p. 62.
   "Accepted." [AnotherCM] (22) 90, p. 10-11.
   "Birthday Poem at 67." [NewYorkQ] (42) Sum 90, p. 57.
   "Credo." [BelPoJ] (40:4) Sum 90, p. 14-15.
   "The Darlings." [WormR] (30:4, #120) 90, p. 139.
   "Don't Call Me, I'll Call You." [CharR] (16:2) Fall 90, p. 73-75.
   "Flat Tire." [AnotherCM] (22) 90, p. 12-14.
   "For Marilyn M." [Pearl] (12) Fall-Wint 90, p. 65.
   "Freedom" (reprinted from *The Earth Rose*, 1966). [Pearl] (10) Spr 90, p. 46.
   "Getting Old." [SycamoreR] (2:1) Wint 90, p. 45-47.
   "The GIGANTIC Thirst." [OnTheBus] (2:2/3:1, #6/7) Sum-Fall 90 Wint-Spr 91, p.
      53.
   "Going Out." [NewYorkQ] (41) Spr 90, p. 49.
   "The Gravel of Sunlight." [CharR] (16:2) Fall 90, p. 72-73.
   "Henry Miller and Burroughs." [ChironR] (9:1) Spr 90, p. 4.

"I Am Chastised." [WormR] (30:1, #117) 90, p. 46.
"I Might Get Traded." [WormR] (30:1, #117) 90, p. 46.
"Liszts." [AnotherCM] (22) 90, p. 15.
"Mugged." [ChironR] (9:3) Aut 90, p. 4.
"My Father." [Gargoyle] (37/38) 90, p. 63.
"My Turn." [ChironR] (9:1) Spr 90, p. 4.
"The National Endowment for the Farts." [NewYorkQ] (43) Fall 90, p. 36-38.
"Now." [NewYorkQ] (42) Sum 90, p. 56.
"Old Man Dead in a Room" (from "It Catches My Heart in Its Hands"). [OnTheBus]
    (2:2/3:1, #6/7) Sum-Fall 90 Wint-Spr 91, p. 288-290.
"The Only Life." [BelPoJ] (40:4) Sum 90, p. 16-17.
"An Overheard Conversation." [NewYorkQ] (41) Spr 90, p. 45.
"Poetry Contest." [NewYorkQ] (43) Fall 90, p. 35.
"She Said." [WormR] (30:1, #117) 90, p. 45-46.
"Slicing Hell." [WormR] (30:4, #120) 90, p. 138-139.
"The Spill." [CharR] (16:2) Fall 90, p. 75-77.
"Such Luck." [NewYorkQ] (41) Spr 90, p. 47.
"The Valet." [ChironR] (9:3) Aut 90, p. 4.
"The Waitress at the Yogurt Shop." [CharR] (16:2) Fall 90, p. 77-78.
"What a Girl." [NewYorkQ] (41) Spr 90, p. 48.
"Who's the Worst?" [NewYorkQ] (41) Spr 90, p. 46.
842. BULL, Tom
    "The Indoors Is Infinite" (tr. of Tomas Tranströmer, w. Jim Wine). [WashR] (16:2)
        Ag-S 90, p. 33.
843. BULLOCK, Donald R.
    "On Driving Into Town." [EmeraldCR] (1990) c89, p. 105.
844. BULLOCK, Marnie
    "Weedy Lullaby" (For Anna and Lanier). [TarRP] (30:1) Fall 90, p. 30.
845. BULMER, April
    "Wishbone." [MalR] (90) Spr 90, p. 93-97.
846. BUNCH, Richard Alan
    "Essays in Divinity." [HawaiiR] (14:3, #30) Fall 90, p. 58-59.
847. BUNTING, Basil
    "Dear be still! Time's start of us lengthens slowly." [ChiR] (37:1) Wint 90, p. 22.
    "Nothing substance utters." [ChiR] (37:1) Wint 90, p. 19-20.
848. BURCH, Wendy Jeanne
    "Fog" (An excerpt from "Water Dreams," a novella). [RiverS] (31) [90?], p. 71.
    "Three Song Bird" (An excerpt from "Water Dreams," a novella). [RiverS] (31) [90?],
        p. 72-73.
849. BURDEN, Jean
    "News of a Death." [GeoR] (44:1/2) Spr-Sum 90, p. 148-149.
850. BURFORD, Ted
    "Museum of the Moving Image." [SoCoast] (9) Fall 90, p. 20-21.
851. BURGALES, Pero Garcia
    "Song for a Troubadour Who Dies and Dies" (tr. by Richard Zenith). [LitR] (33:2)
        Wint 90, p. 188.
852. BURGESS, Stephen
    "Lucerne." [Farm] (7:2) Fall 90, p. 120.
853. BURGGRAF, Linda P. (Linda Parsons)
    "The House Grants Favor." [ApalQ] (33/34) 90, p. 62.
    "Losing a Breast: Prayer Before Surgery" (for Libba). [Iowa] (20:3) Fall 90, p. 125.
854. BURGIN, Diana L.
    "Day" (tr. of Ksenia Nekrasova). [Boulevard] (4:3/5:1, #12/13) Spr 90, p. 110-111.
    "The February Snow Lies at My Feet" (tr. of Ksenia Nekrasova). [Boulevard]
        (4:3/5:1, #12/13) Spr 90, p. 107.
    "From Childhood" (tr. of Ksenia Nekrasova). [Boulevard] (4:3/5:1, #12/13) Spr 90,
        p. 105.
    "How Am I to Write My Poems?" (tr. of Ksenia Nekrasova). [Boulevard] (4:3/5:1,
        #12/13) Spr 90, p. 106.
    "I Know" (tr. of Ksenia Nekrasova). [Boulevard] (4:3/5:1, #12/13) Spr 90, p. 109.
    "My Room" (tr. of Ksenia Nekrasova). [Boulevard] (4:3/5:1, #12/13) Spr 90, p. 108.
855. BURGO, Henry
    "Sister." [PoetryUSA] (5:2) Sum 90, p. 8.
856. BURHANNA, K. J.
    "A Broken Egg at Breakfast." [HolCrit] (27:3) Je 90, p. 16.

857. BURIANOVA, Svetlana
"I Want" (tr. by Richard Katrovas and Dominika Winterová). [PoetryE] (29) Spr 90,
p. 114.
858. BURK, Ronnie
"The Children of Paradise." [Caliban] (8) 90, p. 23.
"Mad Sonnet" (stream of events poem for Valery Oisteanu). [Caliban] (9) 90, p. 36.
859. BURKARD, Michael
"But Beautiful." [ParisR] (32:116) Fall 90, p. 39-41.
"House by the Sea." [WillowS] (25) Wint 90, p. 18-20.
"A Kind of Ink against the Twilight." [WillowS] (25) Wint 90, p. 21-22.
860. BURKE, Anne
"The Home Family." [PraF] (11:4) Wint 90-91, p. 30-37.
"Metamorphosis." [Pig] (16) 90, p. 99.
861. BURKE, Brian
"In Search of a Foremother." [AntigR] (81/82) Spr-Sum 90, p. 159-160.
"Spying on My Father as Gardener" (First place CCW Editors' Prize). [CrossC]
(12:1) 90, p. 13.
862. BURKE, Helen
"Mellow Yellow." [Bogg] (63) 90, p. 40.
863. BURKE, Kenneth
"Adam's Song, and Mine" (*The Sansculotte*, April, 1917). [JINJPo] (12:2) Aut 90, p.
1.
"Case History" (*The Nation*, July, 1956). [JINJPo] (12:2) Aut 90, p. 2.
"In Retrospective Prospect." [JINJPo] (12:2) Aut 90, p. 3.
864. BURKE, Linda Joy
"Artificial Light." [Obs] (5:3) Wint 90, p. 109-111.
"Le Pointe D'Appui IV." [Obs] (5:3) Wint 90, p. 111.
865. BURKE, Marianne
"Hands." [NewYorker] (66:36) 22 O 90, p. 88.
866. BURKE, Rebecca Ann
"The Wandering Linguist." [YellowS] (34) Sum 90, p. 16.
867. BURKETT, Thomas D.
"In the Crazy Mountains." [SoDakR] (28:3) Aut 90, p. 135-136.
868. BURKHAMMER, Vic
"The Butcher." [HampSPR] (Anthology 1975-1990) 90, p. 309.
"Thistlebloom." [HampSPR] (Anthology 1975-1990) 90, p. 308.
869. BURKHART, Kathe
"Williamsburg." [BrooklynR] (7) 90, p. 31.
870. BURNETT, Maud Gwynn
"Camera Obscura." [Descant] (21:4/22:1, #71/72) Wint-Spr 90-91, p. 60.
"Choosing a Pomegranate." [Descant] (21:4/22:1, #71/72) Wint-Spr 90-91, p. 58-59.
871. BURNHAM, Deborah
"Abishag the Shunammite." [WestB] (27) 90, p. 63.
"Bad Habits." [WestB] (26) 90, p. 110.
"Bonnard." [LitR] (33:3) Spr 90, p. 348.
"Bread." [WestB] (27) 90, p. 62.
872. BURNS, Gerald
"Autumn Garden." [AnotherCM] (21) 90, p. 17-18.
"In Her *Selected Poems*." [AnotherCM] (21) 90, p. 20-21.
"Pas de Valéry" (for Henry, gone, tr. of Paul Valéry's "Ebouche d'un serpent").
[WashR] (16:2) Ag-S 90, p. 9.
"Saint Femina's Liquefaction." [AnotherCM] (21) 90, p. 19.
"To Paul of Saint Victor." [Screens] (2) 90, p. 204.
873. BURNS, Heather
"Staying Up." [Nimrod] (34:1) Fall-Wint 90, p. 48.
874. BURNS, Jim
"In Praise of the Urban." [Bogg] (63) 90, p. 6.
875. BURNS, Joanne
"The First Few Lines: A Synopsis." [Screens] (2) 90, p. 96.
"Hegemonies" (Excerpts). [Screens] (2) 90, p. 97.
876. BURNS, Michael
"A Friend Gets Divorced." [GeoR] (44:3) Fall 90, p. 508.
"Venom, Thorn." [CharR] (16:2) Fall 90, p. 89.
877. BURNS, Ralph
"Memory." [GettyR] (3:4) Aut 90, p. 726-727.
"Son, When I Hold You Tightly." [GettyR] (3:4) Aut 90, p. 724-725.

878. BURNS, Richard
"Commandments" (tr. of Ivana Milankova, w. Darinka Petkovic). [Screens] (2) 90, p. 68.
"Visions" (tr. of Ivana Milankova, w. Darinka Petkovic). [Screens] (2) 90, p. 69.
"White Angels, As They Crucified Me" (tr. of Ivana Milankova, w. Darinka Petkovic). [Screens] (2) 90, p. 67.
879. BURR, David Stanford
"An Abidance." [Poetry] (157:3) D 90, p. 147.
"Dowsing for the Mole at Age Eight." [Poetry] (157:3) D 90, p. 148.
880. BURR, Gray
"After-Lives." [Hellas] (1:2) Fall 90, p. 237-238.
"Reflections." [Hellas] (1:2) Fall 90, p. 236.
"A Warm Spell in November." [Hellas] (1:2) Fall 90, p. 235-236.
"Winter and Summer." [Hellas] (1:2) Fall 90, p. 238-239.
881. BURR, Lonnie
"EECummings." [Pearl] (10) Spr 90, p. 19.
"Festive Isolation." [Pearl] (10) Spr 90, p. 19.
882. BURRELL, Clarice A.
"To Emerson -- and Jeanette." [EmeraldCR] (1990) c89, p. 92.
883. BURRELL, Todd
"V. We have loved each other" (tr. of Marta Palchevich). [CrabCR] (6:3) Spr 90, p. 22.
"VIII. I could ask him if it's the sun he wants" (tr. of Marta Palchevich). [CrabCR] (6:3) Spr 90, p. 22.
"XV. We are they that search for bees in the fold of a curtain" (tr. of Marta Palchevich). [CrabCR] (6:3) Spr 90, p. 22.
"The Tall Grass on the Hill" (tr. of Anabel Torres). [CrabCR] (6:3) Spr 90, p. 23.
"That Second-Rate Film" (tr. of Anabel Torres). [CrabCR] (6:3) Spr 90, p. 22.
884. BURRIS, Sidney
"Love Letter." [Verse] (7:3) Wint 90, p. 46.
885. BURROWS, E. G.
"Cobra." [Ascent] (15:1) 90, p. 10.
"Fred." [CrabCR] (6:3) Spr 90, p. 29.
"Horseshoe Canyon." [SwampR] (5) Wint-Spr 90, p. 90.
"Low Tide." [SwampR] (5) Wint-Spr 90, p. 89.
"Ode to a Vermilion Flycatcher Seen in February in Redmond, Washington." [Ascent] (15:1) 90, p. 11.
"Oresteia." [WillowS] (25) Wint 90, p. 39.
"A Tent Pitched Among White Birches." [Ascent] (15:1) 90, p. 9.
886. BURSK, Chris
"Chief Never Wearying." [MinnR] (NS 34/35) Spr-Fall 90, p. 34-42.
887. BURSK, Christopher
"The Dandelion." [ManhatR] (5:1) Spr 90, p. 32-33.
"Let This Cup Pass From Me." [ManhatR] (5:1) Spr 90, p. 31.
"Santa Lucia." [ManhatR] (5:1) Spr 90, p. 28-30.
888. BURSKY, Rick
"The Elephants." [OnTheBus] (2:2/3:1, #6/7) Sum-Fall 90 Wint-Spr 91, p. 54-55.
889. BURT, Brian
"What Is It Makes My Eyes So Weary." [HiramPoR] (48/49) 90-91, p. 18-19.
890. BURT, John
"The Match." [GreensboroR] (49) Wint 90-91, p. 73.
891. BURT, Kathryn
"At the Ruins of the Aztec Goddess Ix-Chel." [Kalliope] (12:2) 90, p. 58-59.
"Day of Atonements." [Kalliope] (12:2) 90, p. 60.
892. BURT, Stephen
"A Postcard from Kanawha City." [HarvardA] (125:2) N 90, p. 14.
893. BUSAILAH, R. (Reja-e)
"The Bard, or Hanging the Moon" (for Mahmoud Darwish). [ContextS] (1:1) 89, p. 27.
"In the Shadow of the Holy Heights" (for Hanlya Suleiman Zarawneh, killed by the Israelis, at the age of 25, near Jerusalem, January 4, 1988). [SlipS] (10) 90, p. 61-62.
"Nostalgia." [ContextS] (1:1) 89, p. 29.
"A Palestinian Dream." [ContextS] (1:1) 89, p. 30.
"Shiver." [ContextS] (1:1) 89, p. 28.

894. BUSCH, Trent
"The Lost." [ManhatPR] (12) [90?], p. 14.
"Mona Richards, R.F.D." [OxfordM] (6:1) Spr-Sum 90, p. 53-54.
"Soap." [SpoonRQ] (15:1) Wint 90, p. 58-59.
"Uncle Ace." [WritersF] (16) Fall 90, p. 98-99.
895. BUSCHEK, John
"Rain." [Arc] (24) Spr 90, p. 13.
"Woodchucks." [Arc] (24) Spr 90, p. 12.
896. BUSH, Debbie
"Christmas (Portland, Oregon, 1969)." [EngJ] (79:7) N 90, p. 29.
897. BUSH, K. K.
"A Fruit Fell Down." [FourQ] (4:1) Spr 90, p. 62.
898. BUSH, Stacy
"Human Abstract." [AmerPoR] (19:6) N-D 90, p. 20.
"When It Was Good." [AmerPoR] (19:6) N-D 90, p. 20.
899. BUSTAMANTE, Cecilia
"Aquí Es la Tierra" (Selections). [InterPR] (16:1) Spr 90, p. 76, 78.
"Here Is the Earth" (Selections, tr. by Mark Smith-Soto). [InterPR] (16:1) Spr 90, p.
77, 79.
BUSTILLO, Camilio Pérez
See PÉREZ, Camilo
900. BUTCHER, Grace
"Hummingbird." [WebR] (14:2) Spr 90, p. 68.
"Star." [WebR] (14:2) Spr 90, p. 67.
"Tag." [VirQR] (66:3) Sum 90, p. 454-455.
"Waiting for the Word." [WebR] (14:2) Spr 90, p. 68.
901. BUTLER, Geoffrey R.
"November Salmon Run." [AnthNEW] 90, p. 21.
902. BUTLER, Jack
"Graduation Present." [Hellas] (1:1) Spr 90, p. 64.
"Woodwork." [Hellas] (1:1) Spr 90, p. 65.
"The Year Began in Crystalline." [ChatR] (11:1) Fall 90, p. 20.
903. BUTLER, Lynne B.
"Brother Bat." [SoCoast] (9) Fall 90, p. 38.
"For My Son Gone to College." [PraS] (64:1) Spr 90, p. 85.
"Learning to Tango." [PraS] (64:1) Spr 90, p. 86.
"Magic Stones." [PraS] (64:1) Spr 90, p. 84.
904. BUTSON, Barry
"Out of Darkness He Comes." [Dandel] (17:2) Fall-Wint 90, p. 15-16.
905. BUTSON, Denver S.
"Lying Awake, I Hear the Wind and Think About James Wright." [QW] (30) Spr 90,
p. 112.
906. BUTTACI, Sal M.
"Ziu Piu." [Footwork] 90, p. 86.
907. BUTTON, Greg
"Cardiac." [AntigR] (81/82) Spr-Sum 90, p. 171.
908. BUTTRESS, Derrick
"The Ministry of G." [Bogg] (63) 90, p. 63.
"Music at Dawn." [Bogg] (62) 90, p. 19.
909. BUYEVICH, Yelena
"Something Has Happened in This World" (Selection: "Oleg," tr. by Oleg Atbashian
and Maureen Hurley). [PoetryUSA] (5:2) Sum 90, p. 13.
910. BUYS, Anneke
"Canterbury Cathedral." [WorldO] (23:3/4) Spr-Sum 89 c1991, p. 32.
"Flashes." [WorldO] (23:3/4) Spr-Sum 89 c1991, p. 32.
911. BUZEVSKA, Sophia
"The First Long-Range Artillery Fire on Leningrad" (tr. of Anna Akhmatova, w.
Daniela Gioseffi). [PoetryE] (30) Fall 90, p. 23.
912. BYER, Kathryn Stripling
"Circuit Rider." [GeoR] (44:1/2) Spr-Sum 90, p. 96.
913. BYRD, Stephanie
"The Homesick River." [AmerV] (20) Fall 90, p. 19.
"Libido." [Cond] (17) 90, p. 75.
"Sweet Potato Pie." [Cond] (17) 90, p. 74.
914. BYRON, Sharon
"Be-." [RiverS] (32) [90?], p. 36.

915. CABACUNGAN, Darryl Keola
"Anahola Store." [ChamLR] (3:2, #6) Spr 90, p. 40.
"The Quilt." [ChamLR] (4:1, #7) Fall 90, p. 69-75.
916. CABLE, Gerald
"Egg Lake." [CarolQ] (42:2) Wint 90, p. 64-65.
"One Morning." [ConnPR] (9:1) 90, p. 33.
"Pioneers." [ConnPR] (9:1) 90, p. 34-35.
"To a Small Lizard." [CarolQ] (42:2) Wint 90, p. 66.
917. CADDY, David
"Sanctuary." [Amelia] (6:2, #17) 90, p. 51.
918. CADDY, John
"Ceremony for Morning" (for Lin). [NorthStoneR] (9) 90, p. 112.
"City Winterscape." [NorthStoneR] (9) 90, p. 110.
"Encounter with a Cooper's Hawk" (a ritual for seeing). [NorthStoneR] (9) 90, p. 109.
"Ishmael in the White Again." [NorthStoneR] (9) 90, p. 108.
"The Length of These Generations." [NorthStoneR] (9) 90, p. 113.
"A Love Triangle: Howard and Pearl and John." [NorthStoneR] (9) 90, p. 114.
"Making Art." [NorthStoneR] (9) 90, p. 115.
"Questions for the Kingfisher." [NorthStoneR] (9) 90, p. 105-107.
"Ritual for Hairwashing" (Manitou River, Lake Superior). [NorthStoneR] (9) 90, p. 111-112.
"That Humans Could Be Numb." [NorthStoneR] (9) 90, p. 116.
"Waking Vision for Franklin Brainard." [NorthStoneR] (9) 90, p. 117.
919. CADELL, Marsha
"November Snow, Bristol, Virginia." [KanQ] (22:1/2) Wint-Spr 90, p. 74-75.
920. CADIOT, Olivier
"Red, Green & Black" (Excerpts, tr. by Charles Bernstein and the author). [WashR] (16:2) Ag-S 90, p. 4-6.
"Rouge, Vert & Noir" (Excerpts). [WashR] (16:2) Ag-S 90, p. 4-6.
921. CADNUM, Michael
"The Beasts of the Field." [Comm] (117:7) 7 Ap 90, p. 224.
"Catfish." [PoetryNW] (31:2) Sum 90, p. 31.
"Clearing the Table." [Comm] (117:4) 23 F 90, p. 115.
"Dreams." [GeoR] (44:3) Fall 90, p. 503-504.
"A Drought Is a Kind of Winter." [ManhatPR] (12) [90?], p. 10.
"The Fisherman and His Wife." [FloridaR] (17:1) Spr-Sum 90, p. 30-31.
"The Gingerbread Man." [FloridaR] (17:1) Spr-Sum 90, p. 28-29.
"A Guest in a Strange House." [Poem] (63) My 90, p. 34-35.
"Independence Day." [SouthernPR] (30:2) Fall 90, p. 35-36.
"Inheriting the Farm." [Poem] (63) My 90, p. 33.
"The Martian Landscape." [Comm] (117:7) 7 Ap 90, p. 216.
"Poem Written from Memory." [PoetryNW] (31:2) Sum 90, p. 32.
"Taking Pictures." [PoetryNW] (31:2) Sum 90, p. 32-33.
"We Return at Last to the Place We Dreamed of." [HolCrit] (27:4) O 90, p. 19.
"X-Ray of Vermeer's 'Woman in Blue Reading a Letter'." [PoetryNW] (31:2) Sum 90, p. 30.
922. CADOU, Hélène
"The Memory of Water" (Excerpts, tr. by Michael Bishop). [Trans] (23) Spr 90, p. 14-16.
CAEIRO, Alberto
See PESSOA, Fernando
923. CAFAGNA, Marcus
"It's All Over Now But the Drinking." [MinnR] (NS 34/35) Spr-Fall 90, p. 16-17.
"Mama's Boy" (for my daughter Noelle). [MinnR] (NS 34/35) Spr-Fall 90, p. 15-16.
"Mammography." [NegC] (10:1) 90, p. 38-39.
"Teachers." [TarRP] (29:2) Spr 90, p. 27.
924. CAGNONE, Nanni
"And now that moved it cannot" (tr. by Pasquale Verdicchio). [Screens] (2) 90, p. 109.
"But dreams that do not lend figures" (tr. by Pasquale Verdicchio). [Screens] (2) 90, p. 110.
"Envied emptiness" (tr. by Pasquale Verdicchio). [Screens] (2) 90, p. 110.
"It does not become fond of only one" (tr. by Pasquale Verdicchio). [Screens] (2) 90, p. 110.
"Not one's own difficult hollowed" (tr. by Pasquale Verdicchio). [Screens] (2) 90, p.

109.
"Similar Sphynx, which you are not" (tr. by Pasquale Verdicchio). [Screens] (2) 90, p. 109.
925. CAHAN, Alfred
"Hart Crane" (townsman). [HiramPoR] (48/49) 90-91, p. 20.
926. CAHLON, LiLi
"Amidst Stones" (June 18, 1944, tr. of Dan Ben-Dor). [Vis] (33) 90, p. 20.
927. CAIRNS, Scott
"The Sheriff's Last Pronouncement." [ColR] (NS 17:1) Spr-Sum 90, p. 37.
928. CALABRESE, John M.
"Letter to Peter" (for Peter Kapaln, 1957-1977). [Footwork] 90, p. 92.
"Mama's Shadow." [Footwork] 90, p. 93.
"Portrait for My Mother." [JamesWR] (8:1) Fall 90, p. 15.
"Sprouting Legs" (for Amy). [Footwork] 90, p. 92.
929. CALBERT, Cathleen
"Chapel of Forgiveness." [SouthernPR] (30:1) Spr 90, p. 21-22.
"Flour Angels." [NegC] (10:1) 90, p. 40-41.
930. CALDER, Alison
"Lately She Can't Stand." [Grain] (18:3) Fall 90, p. 89.
"When You Left." [AntigR] (81/82) Spr-Sum 90, p. 198.
931. CALDICOTT, Edric
"Gravitation" (tr. of Jacques Rancourt). [Trans] (23) Spr 90, p. 138.
"With a Clear Head" (tr. of Jacques Rancourt). [Trans] (23) Spr 90, p. 137.
932. CALDIERO, A. F.
"The gorilla dressed as a bellhop." [Screens] (2) 90, p. 117.
"It was taken from us." [Screens] (2) 90, p. 116.
"Spiders." [Screens] (2) 90, p. 116.
933. CALDWELL, Polly
"I Dare to Be True to Myself." [EmeraldCR] (1990) c89, p. 99-100.
934. CALHOUN, Frank
"Lost in the Lens." [EmeraldCR] (1990) c89, p. 36-37.
935. CALHOUN, Harry
"Take the Kid Out." [ChironR] (9:2) Sum 90, p. 15.
"What the Minstrel Thinks." [ChironR] (9:1) Spr 90, p. 23.
936. CALIFIA, Pat
"Gender Fuck Gender." [Cond] (17) 90, p. 1-3.
"I Love Butches." [Cond] (17) 90, p. 4-6.
937. CALLANAN, Deirdre
"The Curve of Forgetting." [BelPoJ] (41:1) Fall 90, p. 24-27.
"Opals Receive Their Coloration." [BelPoJ] (41:1) Fall 90, p. 28-30.
938. CALVERT, R. A.
"The Day Joy Discomeboomulated, Disappeared." [HawaiiR] (15:1, #31) Wint 90, p. 31.
939. CALVI, Lisa
"Cycle." [PottPort] (12) 90, p. 49.
CAMARA, Mary Philip de
See De CAMARA, Mary Philip
940. CAMERON, Mary
"Cactus." [Quarry] (39:4) Fall 1990, p. 67.
"A Cloud No Bigger than a Man's Hand." [Quarry] (39:4) Fall 1990, p. 66.
"Coming Through Winter." [PraF] (11:3) Aut 90, p. 53.
"Is This Snow." [PraF] (11:3) Aut 90, p. 52.
941. CAMILLO, Victor
"I Remember Peter." [Footwork] 90, p. 59.
"Peter Calls Again." [Footwork] 90, p. 59.
"A True Story." [Footwork] 90, p. 59.
942. CAMPANILE, Ben
"I'm Shrinking." [PoetryUSA] (5:2) Sum 90, p. 8.
943. CAMPBELL, Carolyn E. (Carolyn Evans)
"Another Gift From the Sea." [PoetryUSA] (5:3) Fall 90, p. 9.
"Hop-A-Long Hunter." [PoetryUSA] (5:1) Spr 90, p. 6.
"Hop-Along Hunter." [SycamoreR] (2:2) Sum 90, p. 8-9.
"In Search of Mom's Cafe." [Bogg] (62) 90, p. 39.
"Lucy in the Sky" (a pantoum). [PoetryUSA] ([5:4?]) Wint 90, p. 18.
"Three Finger Bones." [PoetryUSA] (5:2) Sum 90, p. 5.
"Too Soon." [PoetryUSA] (5:1) Spr 90, p. 3.

"What Kind of Love Was That?" [PoetryUSA] (5:1) Spr 90, p. 7.
"Whores." [Bogg] (63) 90, p. 48-49.
"The Woman Tribe." [PoetryUSA] (5:3) Fall 90, p. 5.
944. CAMPBELL, Jill
"The Analysis of Beauty." [WestHR] (44:3) Aut 90, p. 308.
945. CAMPBELL, John
"Forgiveness." [ThRiPo] (35/36) 90, p. 54.
"Geese." [ThRiPo] (35/36) 90, p. 55.
946. CAMPBELL, Katie
"America." [Descant] (21:4/22:1, #71/72) Wint-Spr 90-91, p. 73-74.
"Only Connect." [Grain] (18:2) Sum 90, p. 30.
"Shirley's Place." [Descant] (21:4/22:1, #71/72) Wint-Spr 90-91, p. 75.
947. CAMPBELL, Mary B.
"U.S. Out of El Salvador, or, Amy & Bill 4-Ever." [MassR] (31:1/2) Spr-Sum 90, p.
306-307.
948. CAMPBELL, Nicholas
"The Visit." [Asylum] (6:2) S 90, p. 13.
949. CAMPBELL, P. Michael
"Fourteen Constituents of Happiness." [YellowS] (35) Wint 90-91, p. 6.
"No Word for Now -- Dreamscape." [YellowS] (35) Wint 90-91, p. 6.
"Poem of the Beginning." [YellowS] (35) Wint 90-91, p. 4.
950. CAMPBELL, Rick
"The Geography of Desire." [TarRP] (30:1) Fall 90, p. 23.
951. CAMPBELL, Siobhan
"Grandmother." [Quarry] (39:1) Wint 90, p. 65.
CAMPOS, Alvaro de
See PESSOA, Fernando
952. CANAN, Janine
"Father Chant." [PoetryUSA] (5:3) Fall 90, p. 4.
953. CANASSATEGO, Chief
"Chief Canassatego Reflects on American Education, 1744" (adapted by Stephen
Meats). [MidwQ] (31:2) Wint 90, p. 198-199.
954. CANDELARIA, Cordelia
"An Ancient Alphabet." [Agni] (31/32) 90, p. 202.
"Mamá." [Agni] (31/32) 90, p. 203-204.
"Sold Girl." [Agni] (31/32) 90, p. 201.
955. CANNON, Melissa
"Still Life" (for Ruth Canuto, d. March 8, 1983 e.v., 1st Prize, 4th Annual Contest).
[SoCoast] (8) Spr 90, p. 51.
956. CANON, Virginia Adams
"A Tribute to the 'Unknown Hero'" (Of the Flight 90 plane crash in the Potomac
River, January 13, 1982). [EmeraldCR] (1990) c89, p. 102.
957. CANTRELL, Charles
"Ball-peen." [LaurelR] (24:2) Sum 90, p. 21.
"Kafka's Janitor." [SouthernPR] (30:1) Spr 90, p. 72.
958. CANTRELL, Mary
"Higher Ground." [Farm] (7:1) Spr 90, p. 22-24.
959. CANTWELL, Kevin
"End of Summer, Below the Fall-line, Central Georgia." [MissR] (19:1/2, #55/56)
90, p. 239-240.
"Learning to Read." [SouthwR] (75:2) Spr 90, p. 211.
960. CAO, Juan Manuel
"Decision." [LindLM] (9:4) O-D 90, p. 16.
961. CAPECELATRO, Guy, III
"Fireflies." [HawaiiR] (14:1, #28) Wint 89-90, p. 55.
"Heaven." [HawaiiR] (14:1, #28) Wint 89-90, p. 55.
"The Man, the Woman and the Other Man." [HawaiiR] (14:1, #28) Wint 89-90, p.
54.
"Movie." [HawaiiR] (14:1, #28) Wint 89-90, p. 55.
962. CAPONE, Janet
"In Answer to Their Questions." [SinW] (41) Sum-Fall 90, p. 122-127.
963. CAPPELLO, Mary
"Wishes for My Niece." [Pearl] (11) Sum 90, p. 55.
964. CAPPELUTI, Jo-Anne
"Man." [SoCoast] (8) Spr 90, p. 57.
"Tuck." [SoCoast] (8) Spr 90, p. 57.

965. CARANO, Antonio
"Mi avvicino alla pagina in ombra." [Os] (31) 90, p. 31.
CARBEAU, Mitchell Les
See LesCARBEAU, Mitchell
966. CARDENAL, Ernesto
"Canto Cuántico." [Ometeca] (1:2/2:1) 89-90, p. 13-22.
"Journey to New York" (tr. by Steve Kowit and Cecilia Ubilla-Arenas). [OnTheBus]
(2:1, #5) Spr 90, p. 178-183.
967. CARDONA TORRICO, Alcira
"Carcajada de Estaño." [InterPR] (16:1) Spr 90, p. 12, 14.
"Tin Laughter" (tr. by Mark Smith-Soto). [InterPR] (16:1) Spr 90, p. 13, 15.
968. CARE, Ross
"Rain at Midnight -- Insomnia I." [Writer] (103:12) D 90, p. 25.
969. CAREY, Barbara
"Changing States." [Quarry] (39:4) Fall 1990, p. 68-69.
"Why Is It the Road." [Quarry] (39:4) Fall 1990, p. 69.
970. CAREY, Macdonald
"The Art of Seeing." [NewYorkQ] (41) Spr 90, p. 67-68.
"At Paramount in 1945 They Used to Send Out My Picture with Wendell Corey's
Name Under It and Wendell's Picture With My Name Under It." [NewYorkQ]
(43) Fall 90, p. 39.
"A Catholic Shredding in Beverly Hills." [NewYorkQ] (42) Sum 90, p. 62.
971. CAREY, Michael
"Birdbrain" (for Max Garland). [Iowa] (20:1) Wint 90, p. 48-49.
"Dry Winter" (for Sue and Tom Reiber). [LaurelR] (24:1) Wint 90, p. 19.
"The Extravagance of Dirt and the Comparable Merits of Root Systems." [LaurelR]
(24:1) Wint 90, p. 18.
"Frozen Harvest." [Iowa] (20:1) Wint 90, p. 49-50.
"Learning to Dance." [Iowa] (20:1) Wint 90, p. 50-51.
"The Reason for Poetry." [Iowa] (20:1) Wint 90, p. 51-52.
"The Story of Our Lives" (for Arlen and Fran Gangwish). [Iowa] (20:1) Wint 90, p.
51.
972. CAREY, Tom
"Swallow It." [BrooklynR] (7) 90, p. 39-41.
CARIÑO, Maria Luisa B. Aguilar
See AGUILAR-CARIÑO, Maria Luisa B.
973. CARLE, John C.
"Children in Autumn Memory." [Nimrod] (34:1) Fall-Wint 90, p. 91.
"Stones." [Nimrod] (34:1) Fall-Wint 90, p. 92.
"Thunderhead." [Nimrod] (34:1) Fall-Wint 90, p. 92.
974. CARLILE, Henry
"Divorce." [AmerPoR] (19:2) Mr-Ap 90, p. 40.
"Graveyard Shift." [Shen] (40:1) Spr 90, p. 65.
"Metamorphosis and Marriage." [Shen] (40:1) Spr 90, p. 64.
"The Triangle." [AmerPoR] (19:2) Mr-Ap 90, p. 40.
975. CARLIN, Lisa
"The Significance of Stones." [SinW] (42) Wint 90-91, p. 47-48.
976. CARLISLE, Thomas John
"For Martin Luther King's Birthday." [ChrC] (107:1) 3-10 Ja 90, p. 4.
977. CARLSEN, Ioanna
"Do Flies Sleep?" [Chelsea] (49) 90, p. 142-143.
"Morning Sea" (tr. of Constantine Cavafy). [CumbPR] (9:2) Spr 90, p. 2-3.
978. CARLSEN, Susan
"Womb Envy." [BlackWR] (17:1) Fall-Wint 90, p. 154.
979. CARLSON, Donald
"Manifesto" (for J.L.B. III). [Poem] (64) N 90, p. 33.
"The Paradox of Chinese Pots on Exhibition." [Poem] (64) N 90, p. 34.
980. CARLSON, Thomas C.
"Georgic III" (tr. of Mircea Cartarescu, w. Vasile Poenaru). [ManhatR] (5:1) Spr 90,
p. 8.
"Harvest" (tr. of Gu Cheng, w. Li Xijian). [AntigR] (81/82) Spr-Sum 90, p. 69.
"Outside Our Door" (tr. of Gu Cheng, w. Li Xijian). [AntigR] (81/82) Spr-Sum 90,
p. 68.
"Prophetic Anatomy" (tr. of A. E. Baconsky, w. Vasile Poenaru). [ManhatR] (5:1)
Spr 90, p. 11.
"So Cold" (tr. of Ana Blandiana, w. Vasile Poenaru). [ManhatR] (5:1) Spr 90, p. 10.

"The Soul" (tr. of Ana Blandiana, w. Vasile Poenaru). [ManhatR] (5:1) Spr 90, p. 10.
"Time" (tr. of Marius Robescu, w. Vasile Poenaru). [ManhatR] (5:1) Spr 90, p. 9.
981. CARLSON-BRADLEY, Martha
"The Man Who Disappeared." [CarolQ] (43:1) Fall 90, p. 82.
CARMEN, Aisha Eshe
See ESHE, Aisha
CARMEN, Marilyn Elain
See ESHE, Aisha
CARMONA, Mariana Romo
See ROMO-CARMONA, Mariana
982. CAROUTCH, Yvonne
"When we become like two drunken suns" (tr. by Annabelle Honza). [PoetryE] (30)
Fall 90, p. 72.
983. CARPELAN, Bo
"Years Like Leaves" (Selections: 4 poems, tr. by Anne Born). [Verse] (7:2) Sum 90,
p. 10-11.
984. CARPENTER, Bogdana
"Elegy for the Departure of Pen, Ink and Lamp" (tr. of Zbigniew Herbert, w. John
Carpenter). [Antaeus] (64/65) Spr-Aut 90, p. 52-56.
985. CARPENTER, J. D.
"Lakeview." [CanLit] (126) Aut 90, p. 49.
986. CARPENTER, John
"Elegy for the Departure of Pen, Ink and Lamp" (tr. of Zbigniew Herbert, w.
Bogdana Carpenter). [Antaeus] (64/65) Spr-Aut 90, p. 52-56.
987. CARPENTER, Lucas
"At the Moon-Lit Drive-In" (for T.J. Worthington). [ChatR] (10:3) Spr 90, p. 47.
988. CARPENTER, Sandra
"Fourteen Lines a Sonnet Makes." [WindO] (53) Fall 90, p. 10.
"Witchcraft Made with Marmalade." [Writer] (103:9) S 90, p. 22.
989. CARPER, Thomas
"A Corner of the Garden with Dahlias." [Boulevard] (5:2, #14) Fall 90, p. 67.
"A Couple in the Café de la Gare." [Boulevard] (5:2, #14) Fall 90, p. 69.
"A Display of Birds." [FreeL] (6) Aut 90, p. 19.
"A Guardian Tanya." [Poetry] (156:4) Jl 90, p. 192.
"Her Diamond Ring." [Poetry] (156:3) Je 90, p. 133.
"Like the Spaniards." [Poetry] (157:3) D 90, p. 137.
"Maluku in Cornish." [FreeL] (6) Aut 90, p. 19.
"Titian Makes Preliminary Studies for a Picture of Saint Sebastian." [Boulevard] (5:2,
#14) Fall 90, p. 68.
"Versions of Corot." [AmerS] (59:1) Wint 90, p. 38.
990. CARR, Robin
"June." [Shiny] (5) 90, p. 8.
"Murder at the Library." [BrooklynR] (7) 90, p. 13-14.
991. CARR, Sharon
"Cages." [LullwaterR] (1:1) Spr 90, p. 10.
"The Subterranean Battle." [LullwaterR] (1:1) Spr 90, p. 90.
992. CARRIGAN, Andrew G.
"Coast to Coast." [Notus] (5:1) Spr 90, p. 49.
993. CARRILLO, Albino
"Green Religions." [Caliban] (8) 90, p. 111.
"We Walk." [Caliban] (8) 90, p. 110.
994. CARRINO, Michael
"Across the Bay the Saxony Is Burning." [Hudson] (43:3) Aut 90, p. 452.
"This Thing We All Have to Get Through." [Hudson] (43:3) Aut 90, p. 453.
"What Hurt So Much." [Hudson] (43:3) Aut 90, p. 454.
995. CARROL, Mary
"Woman with a Red Wall." [BlackBR] (12) Fall-Wint 90, p. 13.
996. CARROLL, Kenneth
"New Season" (in memory of Fannie Lou Hamer). [BlackALF] (24:3) Fall 90, p.
544-546.
997. CARROLL, Mary
"Woman of the Sand." [DogRR] (9:2, #18) Aut 90, p. 20.
998. CARROLL, Rhoda
"Feeling the Trees' Breath." [LaurelR] (24:1) Wint 90, p. 85.
"The Trouble We've Always Had with April." [LaurelR] (24:1) Wint 90, p. 84.

999. CARRUTH, Hayden
"Aeolian." [Hudson] (43:1) Spr 90, p. 67-68.
"Emergency Haying." [SenR] (20:1, 20th-Anniversary Special Edition) 90, p.
   50-52.
"Gods." [Hudson] (43:1) Spr 90, p. 68.
"Opusthirteen." [Hudson] (43:1) Spr 90, p. 69.
"Pray You Young Woman." [BelPoJ] (40:4) Sum 90, p. 18.
"Silence." [Atlantic] (266:6) D 90, p. 78.
"Sonnets" (Selections: 1, 5, 11, 16-17, 22, 29-30, 37, 39, 46, 51, 55). [SenR]
   (20:1, 20th-Anniversary Special Edition) 90, p. 7-13.
"Waking." [Boulevard] (5:2, #14) Fall 90, p. 86.
"The Way of the Conventicle of the Trees." [Ploughs] (16:4) Wint 90-91, p.
   189-190.
1000. CARSON, Anne
"Now What?" [GrandS] (9:3) Spr 90, p. 43-45.
1001. CARSON, Meredith
"Ancient Hawaiian Village." [ChamLR] (4:1, #7) Fall 90, p. 160.
"Schooling Fish." [ChamLR] (4:1, #7) Fall 90, p. 161.
1002. CARSON, Mike
"Irish Monk, Near the Year 1000." [SpoonRQ] (15:2) Spr 90, p. 20.
"What an O'Brien Is." [SpoonRQ] (15:2) Spr 90, p. 19.
1003. CARTARESCU, Mircea
"Georgic III" (tr. by Thomas C. Carlson and Vasile Poenaru). [ManhatR] (5:1) Spr
   90, p. 8.
1004. CARTER, Ann
"It's March. We're Out on the Porch with Cabernet Sauvignon." [SoCoast] (9) Fall
   90, p. 9.
1005. CARTER, Anne Babson
"Sheep Sacrifice." [Nat] (250:20) 21 My 90, p. 714.
1006. CARTER, Jared
"Chert Quarry" (for Terry Wooten). [MidwQ] (31:2) Wint 90, p. 214-215.
"For an Old Flame." [Poetry] (156:2) My 90, p. 69.
"Head of the God of the Number Zero." [MidwQ] (31:2) Wint 90, p. 233.
"Journey." [MidwQ] (31:4) Sum 90, p. 486-487.
"Madstone" (for Fred Whitehead). [NoDaQ] (58:4) Fall 90, p. 37-39.
"Mounds." [SoDakR] (28:2) Sum 90, p. 163.
"Scoring." [Stand] (31:1) Wint 89-90, p. 20-21.
"Seed Storm." [KenR] (NS 12:3) Sum 90, p. 119.
1007. CARTER, John
"Circe." [PoetryUSA] (5:3) Fall 90, p. 10.
1008. CARTER, Kim
"The Child of Chess." [Dandel] (17:1) Spr-Sum 90, p. 22.
CARTER, Roberta Rennert
   See RENNERT-CARTER, Roberta
CARTERET, Mark de
   See DeCARTERET, Mark
1009. CARTLEDGE-HAYES, Mary
"Brother's Keeper." [ChrC] (107:26) 19-26 S 90, p. 823.
1010. CASAS, Luis Angel
"Sintonizando el Cosmos." [Ometeca] (1:2/2:1) 89-90, p. 34.
1011. CASAS, Walter de las
"Cuervos." [LindLM] (9:4) O-D 90, p. 4.
1012. CASE, David
"Calculating the Evening." [NewDeltaR] (7:2) Spr-Sum 90, p. 70.
1013. CASEY, Deb
"(Justification)" (DROP-OFF/PICK-UP PANIC In Those No Baby-Room Days,
      For MOTHERS WORKING Outside-the-Home, a Familiar Story). [Calyx]
      (12:3) Sum 90, p. 33-34.
1014. CASEY, Philip
"A Page Falls Open." [Quarry] (39:1) Wint 90, p. 66.
1015. CASEY, Susan M.
"Lesson." [EmeraldCR] (1990) c89, p. 8.
1016. CASSELLS, Cyrus
"At My Loom." [Agni] (31/32) 90, p. 109-110.
"The Desert as My Cradle." [Ploughs] (16:1) Spr-Sum 90, p. 35-36.
"Muscle and Prayer." [Agni] (31/32) 90, p. 107-108.

"Woodwind and Thunderbird." [Ploughs] (16:1) Spr-Sum 90, p. 32-34.
1017. CASSELMAN, Barry
"In a Hurry." [NoDaQ] (58:1) Wint 90, p. 66.
"Net Words." [LakeSR] (24) 90, p. 22-23.
1018. CASSIAN, Nina
"Ballad of the Jack of Diamonds" (tr. by Richard Wilbur). [NewYorker] (65:46) 1 Ja
    90, p. 30.
"The Couple" (tr. by Christopher Hewitt). [AmerPoR] (19:1) Ja-F 90, p. 25.
"Dead Still" (tr. by William Jay Smith). [NewYorker] (65:46) 1 Ja 90, p. 30.
"Extraordinary Performance" (tr. by William Jay Smith). [AmerPoR] (19:1) Ja-F 90,
    p. 25.
"Game Mistress" (tr. by the author). [AmerPoR] (19:1) Ja-F 90, p. 26.
"Greed" (tr. by Stanley Kunitz). [NewYorker] (65:46) 1 Ja 90, p. 30.
"Joyful Sacrifice" (tr. by Barbara Howes and Kim Cushman). [AmerPoR] (19:1)
    Ja-F 90, p. 25.
"A Man" (tr. by Daniela Gioseffi, w. the author). [PoetryE] (29) Spr 90, p. 124.
"On a Japanese Beach" (Hiroshima Memento, tr. by Daniela Gioseffi, w. the
    author). [PoetryE] (29) Spr 90, p. 125.
"Orchestra" (tr. by Dana Gioia). [NewYorker] (65:46) 1 Ja 90, p. 30.
"Ready for Goodbye" (tr. by William Jay Smith). [AmerPoR] (19:1) Ja-F 90, p. 26.
"Sacrilege" (tr. by Petre Solomon and William Jay Smith). [AmerPoR] (19:1) Ja-F
    90, p. 26.
"Self-Portrait" (tr. by William Jay Smith). [AmerPoR] (19:1) Ja-F 90, p. 25.
"Tirade for the Next-to-Last Act" (tr. by Carolyn Kizer). [AmerPoR] (19:1) Ja-F 90,
    p. 26.
"World War" (tr. by Daniela Gioseffi, w. the author). [PoetryE] (29) Spr 90, p. 126.
1019. CASSITY, Turner
"By the Time You Get to Phoenix It May All Be Over." [LullwaterR] (2:1) Wint 90,
    p. 32.
"He Whom Ye Seek." [SouthernR] (26:4) O 90, p. 880-881.
"Lucky Pierre." [LullwaterR] (1:1) Spr 90, p. 40.
"Quasimodo of the Singing Tower." [LullwaterR] (1:1) Spr 90, p. 76.
1020. CASSUTT, Glenda
"Hsan the Monk." [Kalliope] (12:2) 90, p. 71.
"Voice of the Bodhi Tree" (The Tree Under Which Buddha Became Enlightened).
    [Kalliope] (12:2) 90, p. 70-71.
1021. CASTELLANOS, Gilberto
"Yacimientos del Verano." [Inti] (31) Primavera 90, p. 162-164.
1022. CASTILLO, Otto René
"Apolitical Intellectuals" (tr. by Margaret Randall). [Quarry] (39:4) Fall 1990, p.
    76-78.
"Satisfaction" (tr. by Zoë Anglesey). [OnTheBus] (2:1, #5) Spr 90, p. 184.
1023. CASTILLO, Sandra M.
"Dreams, or, On the Occasion of My Sister's Wedding." [ApalQ] (33/34) 90, p.
    50-51.
"Red Letters" (for Mark, my American friend studying at the Seminary." [ApalQ]
    (33/34) 90, p. 48-49.
1024. CASTLEBURY, John
"Long Island Sounds" (Selections: 1). [AntigR] (81/82) Spr-Sum 90, p. 36-44.
1025. CASTLEMAN, D.
"Echoes Blossom with Remembered Prayer." [DustyD] (1:2) O 90, p. 2.
"Nocturne." [DustyD] (1:2) O 90, p. 11.
"Why Does Reality Pretend Itself Alive?" [DustyD] (1:2) O 90, p. 2.
CASTRO, Tania Diaz
    See DIAZ CASTRO, Tania
1026. CATACALOS, Rosemary
"The Lesson in 'A Waltz for Debby'" (in memory of Bill Evans). [CimR] (91) Ap
    90, p. 63-64.
"With the Conchero Dancers, Mission Espada, July." [SouthwR] (75:4) Aut 90, p.
    568.
1027. CATALA, Rafael
"Epitaph for the Twentieth Century" (tr. by Suzanne Sausville). [Footwork] 90, p.
    90-91.
1028. CATAÑO, Jose Carlos
"Cangrejos de la Playa de Ma'Bwá." [Inti] (32/33) Otoño 90-Primavera 91, p.
    227-228.

"El Consul del Mar del Norte" (Selections: 3 poems). [Inti] (32/33) Otoño
90-Primavera 91, p. 228-229.
"El Hombre de Montevideo." [Inti] (32/33) Otoño 90-Primavera 91, p. 226.
"No Sostener Nada Jamás." [Inti] (32/33) Otoño 90-Primavera 91, p. 227.
"Noli Me Tangere." [Inti] (32/33) Otoño 90-Primavera 91, p. 227.
"Prólogo a la Lengua." [Inti] (32/33) Otoño 90-Primavera 91, p. 226.
1029. CATCHES, J. Stephen
"Beneath a City-light." [EmeraldCR] (1990) c89, p. 96.
1030. CATLIN, Alan
"Bus Stop." [Pearl] (12) Fall-Wint 90, p. 50.
"The Day We Bombed Utah." [SlipS] (10) 90, p. 78-79.
"Detainee Cuban Refugee Camp." [SlipS] (10) 90, p. 79.
"Guards National Stadium, Santiago, Chile 1973." [SlipS] (10) 90, p. 80.
"A Last Will and Testament Poem." [Asylum] (5:4) 90, p. 40-41.
"She Asked." [Bogg] (62) 90, p. 40.
1031. CATTAFI, Bartolo
"Chimera" (tr. by Ruth Feldman and Brian Swann). [HampSPR] (Anthology
1975-1990) 90, p. 248.
"E Qui Che Dio." [InterPR] (16:2) Fall 90, p. 48.
"Folate di Primavera." [InterPR] (16:2) Fall 90, p. 48.
"Gusts of Spring Air." (tr. by Rina Ferrarelli). [InterPR] (16:2) Fall 90, p. 49.
"Here" (tr. by Rina Ferrarelli). [InterPR] (16:2) Fall 90, p. 51.
"Il Tuo Rilievo." [InterPR] (16:2) Fall 90, p. 50.
"Into Its Cold" (tr. by Rina Ferrarelli). [InterPR] (16:2) Fall 90, p. 51.
"It's Here That God" (tr. by Rina Ferrarelli). [InterPR] (16:2) Fall 90, p. 49.
"Key Word" (tr. by Ruth Feldman and Brian Swann). [HampSPR] (Anthology
1975-1990) 90, p. 249.
"Nel Suo Gelo." [InterPR] (16:2) Fall 90, p. 50.
"Pyracantha." [InterPR] (16:2) Fall 90, p. 48.
"Pyracantha" (in English, tr. by Rina Ferrarelli). [InterPR] (16:2) Fall 90, p. 49.
"Qui." [InterPR] (16:2) Fall 90, p. 50.
"Your Relief" (tr. by Rina Ferrarelli). [InterPR] (16:2) Fall 90, p. 51.
1032. CATULLUS (CATULLUS, Gaius Valerius)
"A Broken Contract: 110" (to Aufilena, tr. by Geoffrey Cook). [PoetryUSA] ([5:4?])
Wint 90, p. 18.
"The evil shadows of Orcius" (tr. by Geoffrey Cook). [PoetryUSA] (5:1) Spr 90, p.
4.
"If any ever deserved such underarm goatodor" (tr. by Charles Martin). [Hudson]
(43:2) Sum 90, p. 342.
"Lesbia, let us live only for loving" (tr. by Charles Martin). [Hudson] (43:2) Sum
90, p. 343.
"Quintius: 82" (tr. by Geoffrey Cook). [PoetryUSA] ([5:4?]) Wint 90, p. 18.
"Securer a bo? no sacred armpits lair hops as that he-goat's" (tr. by Louis
Zukofshy). [Hudson] (43:2) Sum 90, p. 342.
"Siquoi iure bono sacer alarum obstitit hircus." [Hudson] (43:2) Sum 90, p. 342.
"Two personal problems: under-arm goat" (tr. by Frederic Raphael and Kenneth
McLeish). [Hudson] (43:2) Sum 90, p. 342.
1033. CAUDRON, Cordell
"Atomic Sun" (tr. of Robert Sabatier, w. Elisabeth Lapeyre). [InterPR] (16:2) Fall
90, p. 47.
"The Child Within the Man" (tr. of Robert Sabatier, w. Elisabeth Lapeyre). [InterPR]
(16:2) Fall 90, p. 39.
"Communication" (tr. of Robert Sabatier, w. Elisabeth Lapeyre). [InterPR] (16:2)
Fall 90, p. 45.
"The Journey of a Tree" (tr. of Robert Sabatier, w. Elisabeth Lapeyre). [InterPR]
(16:2) Fall 90, p. 43.
"Summer Earth" (tr. of Robert Sabatier, w. Elisabeth Lapeyre). [InterPR] (16:2) Fall
90, p. 41.
1034. CAULFIELD, Carlota
"Carta de Una Aclla a Su Amante." [Inti] (32/33) Otoño 90-Primavera 91, p. 212.
"Castidad Maya." [Inti] (32/33) Otoño 90-Primavera 91, p. 212.
"Il Faut Faire la Fête" (A Albert, quien me salvó de morir en el siglo XV). [Inti]
(32/33) Otoño 90-Primavera 91, p. 211.
"Stolen Kisses Are the Sweetest, Louveciennes, 1932." [Inti] (32/33) Otoño
90-Primavera 91, p. 210.
"War Ich Wie Du. Warst Du Wie Ich (Si Yo Fuera Como Tu, Si Tu Feueras Como

Yo)." [Inti] (32/33) Otoño 90-Primavera 91, p. 213.
"Zoccoli, Esos Zapatos Tan Altos, Tan Altos." [Inti] (32/33) Otoño 90-Primavera
    91, p. 211.
1035. CAVAFY, Constantine (Constantine P.)
"As Long as You Can" (tr. by Theoharis C. Theoharis). [Agni] (31/32) 90, p. 121.
"Morning Sea" (in Greek and English, tr. by Ioanna Carlsen). [CumbPR] (9:2) Spr
    90, p. 2-3.
"Waiting for the Barbarians" (tr. by Theoharis C. Theoharis). [Agni] (31/32) 90, p.
    122-123.
1036. CAVALIERI, Grace
"Meeting the Man on the Road." [WashR] (16:4) D 90-Ja 91, p. 10.
"Trenton High." [JINJPo] (12:2) Aut 90, p. 40-41.
"What She Is." [WashR] (16:4) D 90-Ja 91, p. 10.
1037. CAVALLI, Patrizia
"And to See the City Again" (tr. by Judith Baumel). [NewYorker] (66:43) 10 D 90,
    p. 96.
"Far from Kingdoms" (tr. by Judith Baumel). [NewYorker] (66:33) 1 O 90, p. 78.
1038. CAWLEY, Kevin
"The Walk." [RiverC] (11:1) Fall 90, p. 66.
1039. CAWOOD, Jenny Lind
"Writing Alone." [Wind] (20:66) 90, p. 34.
1040. CAY, Marilyn
"A Crow, the First One We've Seen This Spring." [Grain] (18:4) Wint 90, p. 36.
"In the Storm." [Grain] (18:4) Wint 90, p. 36.
1041. CECCHETTI, Giovanni
"The Lot of Great Waves" (tr. by Graziella Sidoli). [Screens] (2) 90, p. 118.
1042. CECIL, Richard
"Les Belles Dames Sans Merci." [Crazy] (38) Spr 90, p. 71-72.
"Fifteen Years Ago." [NewEngR] (12:3) Spr 90, p. 296-297.
"Junk Calls." [SycamoreR] (2:2) Sum 90, p. 5-7.
"Memorial." [Crazy] (38) Spr 90, p. 73-75.
1043. CELAN, Paul
"Death Fugue" (tr. by Thomas Dorsett). [InterPR] (16:2) Fall 90, p. 25, 27.
"Es War Erde in Ihnen, Und Sie Gruben." [Sequoia] (33:2) Wint 90, p. 32.
"Homecoming" (tr. by Robert Pinsky). [ParisR] (32:116) Fall 90, p. 185.
"Love Crown" (tr. by Robert Pinsky). [ParisR] (32:116) Fall 90, p. 185.
"Mit Wechselndem Schlüssel." [InterPR] (16:2) Fall 90, p. 22.
"There Was Earth Inside Them" (tr. by John Felstiner). [AmerPoR] (19:4) Jl-Ag 90,
    p. 31.
"There Was Earth Inside Them, and They Dug" (tr. by John Felstiner). [Sequoia]
    (33:2) Wint 90, p. 33.
"Todesfuge." [InterPR] (16:2) Fall 90, p. 24, 26.
"With a Changing Key" (tr. by Thomas Dorsett). [InterPR] (16:2) Fall 90, p. 23.
1044. CELLI, Roberto
"Hospital." [CharR] (16:2) Fall 90, p. 95.
"Tiger Grease." [CharR] (16:2) Fall 90, p. 94.
1045. CENDRARS, Blaise
"Easter in New York" (To Agnès, tr. by Ron Padgett). [Shiny] (5) 90, p. 25-32.
"Panama, or the Adventures of My Seven Uncles" (tr. by Ron Padgett). [ParisR]
    (32:117) Wint 90, p. 43-61.
1046. CENI, Alessandro
"The Captivity of the Lesser" (tr. by Pasquale Verdicchio). [Screens] (2) 90, p. 107.
"The Hearts of Eagles" (tr. by Pasquale Verdicchio). [Screens] (2) 90, p. 108.
1047. CENTOLELLA, Thomas
"Easter." [AmerPoR] (19:2) Mr-Ap 90, p. 18.
"Fog Light" (for PYJ). [AmerPoR] (19:2) Mr-Ap 90, p. 18.
"Magic Hour." [OnTheBus] (2:1, #5) Spr 90, p. 49-50.
"Misterioso." [AmerPoR] (19:2) Mr-Ap 90, p. 16-17.
"Plumosa." [OnTheBus] (2:2/3:1, #6/7) Sum-Fall 90 Wint-Spr 91, p. 56.
"Prologue to the Happy Poem You Asked For." [AmerPoR] (19:2) Mr-Ap 90, p. 17.
1048. CERULLI, Francette
"The Black Skirt" (For Celia). [NegC] (10:1) 90, p. 22.
"The Borrower." [NegC] (10:1) 90, p. 23-24.
"Dissection at Nine Years." [NegC] (10:1) 90, p. 25-26.
1049. CERVANTES, Lorna Dee
"On the Fear of Going Down." [MidAR] (10:1) 90, p. 139-141.

101

CETRANO

1050. CETRANO, Sal
"Convection." [CalQ] (34) 90, p. 21.
"Hunters." [KanQ] (22:1/2) Wint-Spr 90, p. 33.
1051. CHABEREK, Ed
"Reflections." [Plain] (11:1) Fall 90, p. 23.
1052. CHACE, Joel
"Relic." [Wind] (20:67) 90, p. 8.
1053. CHADWICK, Cydney
"Houdini." [Sequoia] (33:2) Wint 90, p. 48.
1054. CHAK, Alexander
"Bad" (tr. by Oleg Atbashian and Maureen Hurley). [PoetryUSA] (5:2) Sum 90, p.
13.
CHALLANDER, Craig
See CHALLENDER, Craig
1055. CHALLENDER, Craig
"Bloodwork." [SouthernPR] (30:2) Fall 90, p. 48-49.
"Breath Poem" (For My Father). [SycamoreR] (2:1) Wint 90, p. 51-52.
"Halfway Home" (for our daughters). [Northeast] (NS 5:3) Wint 90-91, p. 6.
"Pot of Gold." [HampSPR] (Anthology 1975-1990) 90, p. 222.
1056. CHALMER, Judith
"Lead Letters." [GreenMR] (NS 3:2) Fall-Wint 89-90, p. 92-93.
"Something Harder." [AnthNEW] 90, p. 8.
1057. CHALONER, David
"Marking the Blue." [Talisman] (5) Fall 90, p. 19-22.
1058. CHAMBERLAIN, Cara
"Along the Route of the Donner Party." [CentR] (34:3) Sum 90, p. 395-396.
"An Approach to the Sea -- Illumination." [HiramPoR] (47) Wint 90, p. 14.
"A Dinner in Plano, Texas." [Sequoia] (33:2) Wint 90, p. 76.
"Indian Agent." [HighP] (5:1) Spr 90, p. 95-97.
"John Xantus: The Tidal Station at Cabo San Lucas." [SycamoreR] (2:2) Sum 90, p.
28-29.
"Near Folsom, New Mexico." [Wind] (20:66) 90, p. 26.
"Sequence of Thought." [HiramPoR] (47) Wint 90, p. 15.
"Within Doves Within." [Sequoia] (33:2) Wint 90, p. 75.
1059. CHAMFORT, Nicolas-Sébastien de
"Long After Chamfort" (Eight Maxims, tr. by Samuel Beckett). [Trans] (23) Spr 90,
p. 76-77.
1060. CHANDLER, Tom
"A Planetary Directory." [MidwQ] (31:3) Spr 90, p. 348-349.
"Puukohola." [SoCoast] (8) Spr 90, p. 28-29.
"Smuttynose Island" (12 miles off Maine). [HiramPoR] (48/49) 90-91, p. 21.
"Zippy Mitchell." [SoCoast] (9) Fall 90, p. 12.
1061. CHANDONNET, Ann (Ann Fox)
"Plumeria, Sunset (Kauai)." [SingHM] (17) 90, p. 2-3.
"The Poet as the Letter P: Stevens Requests More Prunes." [KanQ] (22:4) Fall 90, p.
74-76.
1062. CHANDRA, G. S. Sharat
"Bangladesh Poems." [NewL] (57:1) Fall 90, p. 12-16.
"Moths." [CharR] (16:2) Fall 90, p. 90-93.
"Stillness." [WeberS] (7:1) Spr 90, p. 66.
"Waking at Fifty." [WeberS] (7:1) Spr 90, p. 65.
1063. CHANEY, Joseph
"Going." [HiramPoR] (48/49) 90-91, p. 22.
1064. CHANG, Lisa
"Burning Flower." [NewAW] (6) Spr 90, p. 92.
1065. CHANG, Lisbeth
"Flower Street West." [HarvardA] (124:4) My 90, p. 10.
"On Learning of the Suspension of the Caboose." [HarvardA] (125:2) N 90, p. 16.
CHANG, Soo Ko
See KO, Chang Soo
1066. CHAO, I
"This Poem" (tr. by Graeme Wilson). [LitR] (33:2) Wint 90, p. 195.
1067. CHAPMAN, Jane Autenrieth
"A surgeon from far Indonesia." [Amelia] (6:2, #17) 90, p. 34.
1068. CHAPMAN, Michael (Michael J.)
"Exits." [OnTheBus] (2:1, #5) Spr 90, p. 52-53.

"Gorgon Song for Patient Zero." [JamesWR] (7:4) Sum 90, p. 9.
"The Quiet of Night." [OnTheBus] (2:2/3:1, #6/7) Sum-Fall 90 Wint-Spr 91, p. 57-58.
"Snapshots." [OnTheBus] (2:1, #5) Spr 90, p. 51-52.
1069. CHAPMAN, R. S.
"The Unitarian Minister in Oak Ridge, Tennessee" (for Arthur Graham). [SouthernR] (26:2) Ap 90, p. 325.
"Wish for the New Year." [SouthernR] (26:2) Ap 90, p. 324.
"Zeno's Paradox" (for Bill Hunter). [Northeast] (NS 5:3) Wint 90-91, p. 12.
1070. CHAPPEL, Allen H.
"Through and Through" (tr. of Ilse Aichinger). [NewOR] (17:1) Spr 90, p. 32.
1071. CHAR, Rene
"At the Gateways of Aerea" (tr. by Gustaf Sobin). [Sulfur] (10:1, #26) Spr 90, p. 76-77.
"Celebrating Giacometti" (tr. by Gustaf Sobin). [Sulfur] (10:1, #26) Spr 90, p. 78-79.
"Cherishing Thouzon" (tr. by Gustaf Sobin). [Sulfur] (10:1, #26) Spr 90, p. 75.
"Convergence of Multiples" (tr. by Gustaf Sobin). [Sulfur] (10:1, #26) Spr 90, p. 78.
"Lied of the Fig Tree" (tr. by Gustaf Sobin). [Sulfur] (10:1, #26) Spr 90, p. 80.
"The Merciful Thirst" (tr. by Gustaf Sobin). [Sulfur] (10:1, #26) Spr 90, p. 78.
"Mirage of the Needles" (tr. by Gustaf Sobin). [Sulfur] (10:1, #26) Spr 90, p. 76.
"October's Judgment" (tr. by Gustaf Sobin). [Sulfur] (10:1, #26) Spr 90, p. 80.
"Septentrion" (tr. by Gustaf Sobin). [Sulfur] (10:1, #26) Spr 90, p. 79.
"Servant" (tr. by Gustaf Sobin). [Sulfur] (10:1, #26) Spr 90, p. 81.
"Slowness of the Future" (tr. by Gustaf Sobin). [Sulfur] (10:1, #26) Spr 90, p. 81.
"The Vicinities of Alsace" (tr. by Gustaf Sobin). [Sulfur] (10:1, #26) Spr 90, p. 77.
1072. CHARACH, Ron
"A Brief Secular History." [Descant] (21:4/22:1, #71/72) Wint-Spr 90-91, p. 79-82.
"Distances across the Sink." [Descant] (21:4/22:1, #71/72) Wint-Spr 90-91, p. 78.
"Doing Well in the Restaurant." [Descant] (21:4/22:1, #71/72) Wint-Spr 90-91, p. 77.
"Eating Houses." [Descant] (21:4/22:1, #71/72) Wint-Spr 90-91, p. 83-89.
"Everything's Funny (Till the Tiny Seed Surrenders)." [Descant] (21:4/22:1, #71/72) Wint-Spr 90-91, p. 76.
CHARITY, Ralph la
See LaCHARITY, Ralph
1073. CHARLES, Christophe
"Le Cycle de la Parole" (Excerpt, tr. by Jean-Clarence Lambert and Bradley R. Strahan). [Vis] (32) 90, p. 24.
1074. CHARLTON, Elizabeth
"Dream of Grand Teton." [MidwQ] (31:3) Spr 90, p. 350.
1075. CHARLTON, George
"Monsters of the Deep." [Verse] (7:3) Wint 90, p. 101.
1076. CHARNEY, Lena L.
"Finger Reading." [Wind] (20:67) 90, p. 6.
1077. CHASE, Jill O.
"Kaikoura." [Abraxas] (38/39) 90, p. 131.
1078. CHASE, Karen
"The Beach." [Shen] (40:1) Spr 90, p. 63.
"The Girl from Morbisch." [HawaiiR] (14:3, #30) Fall 90, p. 12.
"Gouldsboro." [Shen] (40:1) Spr 90, p. 62.
"I'm Scared of Shampoo." [HawaiiR] (14:3, #30) Fall 90, p. 10.
"Jimmy Keenan." [HawaiiR] (14:3, #30) Fall 90, p. 11.
1079. CHASE, Naomi Feigelson
"Dissatisfaction." [CreamCR] (14:1) Spr 90, p. 108.
"The Life of Desire." [CreamCR] (14:1) Spr 90, p. 107.
1080. CHAVEZ, Lisa D.
"At the Sorbonne, 1925." [ChironR] (9:2) Sum 90, p. 5.
"Fetish." [Mildred] (4:1) 90, p. 90.
"In a Letter Unsent." [ChironR] (9:2) Sum 90, p. 5.
"The Unveiling of the Paris Collections, 1926." [ChironR] (9:2) Sum 90, p. 5.
"Wild Horses." [Calyx] (12:3) Sum 90, p. 50-51.
1081. CHEDID, Andrée
"Life Voyage" (tr. by William Jay Smith). [Trans] (23) Spr 90, p. 46.
"Man Still Stands" (tr. by William Jay Smith). [Trans] (23) Spr 90, p. 47.

1082. CHEN, Dongdong
    "Backgrounds" (tr. by Dong Jiping). [Footwork] 90, p. 39.
    "Talking of the Flying Rollers with Gary Snyder" (tr. by Dong Jiping). [Footwork] 90, p. 40.
    "World" (tr. by Dong Jiping). [Footwork] 90, p. 39.
1083. CHEN, Irwin
    "Embers" (for William Faulkner). [CumbPR] (10:1) Fall 90, p. 5.
1084. CHEN, Jingrong
    "The Forest Is Growing" (tr. by Emily Yau). [PoetryUSA] ([5:4?]) Wint 90, p. 22.
    "If You Come" (tr. by Emily Yau). [PoetryUSA] ([5:4?]) Wint 90, p. 22.
    "The Modern Prometheus" (tr. by Emily Yau). [PoetryUSA] ([5:4?]) Wint 90, p. 21.
CHEN, Joshua Gero
    See GERO-CHEN, Joshua
1085. CHEN, Maiping
    "April" (tr. of Bei Dao, w. Bonnie S. McDougall). [ManhatR] (5:2) Fall 90, p. 11.
    "A Bach Concert" (tr. of Bei Dao, w. Bonnie S. McDougall). [ManhatR] (5:2) Fall 90, p. 8.
    "The Collection" (tr. of Bei Dao, w. Bonnie S. McDougall). [ManhatR] (5:2) Fall 90, p. 6.
    "Coming Home at Night" (tr. of Bei Dao, w. Bonnie S. McDougall). [ManhatR] (5:2) Fall 90, p. 11.
    "Discovery" (tr. of Bei Dao, w. Bonnie S. McDougall). [ManhatR] (5:2) Fall 90, p. 12.
    "The East's Imagination" (tr. of Bei Dao, w. Bonnie S. McDougall). [ManhatR] (5:2) Fall 90, p. 7.
    "For Only a Second" (tr. of Bei Dao, w. Bonnie S. McDougall). [ManhatR] (5:2) Fall 90, p. 5.
    "Gains" (tr. of Bei Dao, w. Bonnie S. McDougall). [ManhatR] (5:2) Fall 90, p. 10.
    "The Morning's Story" (tr. of Bei Dao, w. Bonnie S. McDougall). [ManhatR] (5:2) Fall 90, p. 4.
    "Notes on Reading" (tr. of Bei Dao, w. Bonnie S. McDougall). [ManhatR] (5:2) Fall 90, p. 9.
1086. CHEN, Willi
    "Give Me Only Silence" (To the Memory of My Father -- John Chen). [Writer] (103:6) Je 90, p. 24.
    "Night-Fall in Cachipe." [Callaloo] (13:2) Spr 90, p. 303-304.
CHENG, Gu
    See GU, Cheng
1087. CHENOWETH, Okey
    "Autumn Sunrise." [Footwork] 90, p. 109.
    "A Fumbling Poem." [Footwork] 90, p. 109.
    "Losses." [Footwork] 90, p. 110.
    "Men on Motorcycles." [Footwork] 90, p. 110.
    "When It Rains Bubble Gum." [Footwork] 90, p. 109.
    "Wild Places Such As Eyes." [Footwork] 90, p. 110.
1088. CHERKOVKI, Neeli
    "Knowledge." [OnTheBus] (2:2/3:1, #6/7) Sum-Fall 90 Wint-Spr 91, p. 59.
1089. CHERNOFF, Maxine
    "Measuring." [ParisR] (32:116) Fall 90, p. 174-175.
    "The New Money." [Caliban] (8) 90, p. 8.
    "Notes for a Mural." [Caliban] (8) 90, p. 9.
    "The Painter Discusses 'Apples'." [ParisR] (32:116) Fall 90, p. 176.
1090. CHERRY, Kelly
    "Bat Mother." [Sequoia] (33:2) Wint 90, p. 18.
    "Berlin: An Epithalamion." [NewL] (57:1) Fall 90, p. 4-5.
    "Grace." [Atlantic] (265:5) My 90, p. 54.
    "Green That Inspires Longings for Joy." [GettyR] (3:2) Spr 90, p. 359.
    "History." [AmerS] (59:3) Sum 90, p. 371.
    "In the Field." [Agni] (31/32) 90, p. 214.
    "The Name." [Shen] (40:2) Sum 90, p. 51.
    "On Looking at a Yellow Wagon." [GettyR] (3:2) Spr 90, p. 360.
    "The Promise." [Shen] (40:2) Sum 90, p. 52.
    "Why It Is Necessary to Love." [Sequoia] (33:2) Wint 90, p. 19.
1091. CHESS, Richard
    "Baby Boomer" (for Salomon Hugo Lieben). [AmerV] (18) Spr 90, p. 17.
    "The Week." [AmerV] (20) Fall 90, p. 47.

1092. CHESTER, Bruce
"Eagles Caught Salmon." [CanLit] (124/125) Spr-Sum 90, p. 182.
"The Wet." [CanLit] (124/125) Spr-Sum 90, p. 181.
"Working on Titles." [CanLit] (124/125) Spr-Sum 90, p. 181-182.
1093. CHETWYND, Richard
"Cavafy's Motif" (tr. of Grzegorz Musial, w. the author). [PoetryE] (29) Spr 90, p. 22.
"The Exile" (tr. of Grzegorz Musial, w. the author). [PoetryE] (29) Spr 90, p. 21.
"Poem for Allen Ginsberg" (tr. of Grzegorz Musial). [ArtfulD] (18/19) 90, p. 98-99.
1094. CHI, Emily E.
"Copenhagen Interpretation." [Crucible] (26) Fall 90, p. 82.
CHIAO, Meng
See MENG, Chiao
1095. CHIDESTER, E. Leon
"How Long?" (tr. of Pablo Neruda). [InterPR] (16:2) Fall 90, p. 67, 69.
"Miracles." [Wind] (20:67) 90, p. 9-10.
1096. CH'IEN, Evelyn
"Largesse" (poem and monotype, with Andrew Osborn). [HarvardA] (125:1) S 90, p. 4.
"Seven-Minute Storm Song" (poem and monotype, with Andrew Osborn). [HarvardA] (125:1) S 90, p. 3.
"Staghorn Sumac" (poem and monotype, with Andrew Osborn). [HarvardA] (125:1) S 90, p. 5.
CHIHA, Kim
See KIM, Chiha
1097. CHILD, Abigail
"Narrative" (with Hannah Weiner). [Avec] (3:1) 90, p. 121-122.
1098. CHILDERS, Joanne
"On the Ferry to Waterford." [PoetC] (22:1) Fall 90, p. 13.
1099. CHILDISH, Billy
"Day Up London." [WormR] (30:4, #120) 90, p. 108.
"The Roadsweeper of Rochester High Street." [WormR] (30:4, #120) 90, p. 107.
"The Trap." [WormR] (30:4, #120) 90, p. 108.
"Women." [WormR] (30:4, #120) 90, p. 107.
1100. CHIN, David
"A Seven Day Diary" (first line from Alan Dugan). [MissR] (19:1/2, #55/56) 90, p. 241-247.
1101. CHIN, Marilyn
"Autumn Leaves." [AmerV] (18) Spr 90, p. 3.
"The Barbarians Are Coming." [Ploughs] (16:1) Spr-Sum 90, p. 104.
"Clear White Stream." [Iowa] (20:2) Spr-Sum 90, p. 89-90.
"Exile's Letter: After the Failed Revolution." [AmerV] (21) Wint 90, p. 23.
"The Floral Apron" (for the Chinese Democratic Movement). [Ploughs] (16:1) Spr-Sum 90, p. 103.
"How I Got That Name" (An essay on assimilation -- or: Deng Xiao Ping, are we not your children?, for Gwendolyn Brooks). [Iowa] (20:2) Spr-Sum 90, p. 86-88.
"Ode to Prized Koi and Baby Finches." [SenR] (20:2) Fall 90, p. 49-50.
"Where Is the Moralizer, Your Mother?" [QW] (30) Spr 90, p. 113-114.
1102. CHINELLY, Cynthia
"For an Anniversary." [NorthStoneR] (9) 90, p. 53.
"Later." [NorthStoneR] (9) 90, p. 52.
1103. CHINN, Daryl
"On a Gray Street." [OnTheBus] (2:2/3:1, #6/7) Sum-Fall 90 Wint-Spr 91, p. 60-62.
"The Open-Ended Bill for Sacrifice." [OnTheBus] (2:1, #5) Spr 90, p. 54-55.
1104. CHIPASULA, Frank M.
"Meditation on My Son's Sixth Birthday." [ArtfulD] (18/19) 90, p. 132.
1105. CHITWOOD, Michael
"Appetite." [Thrpny] (42) Sum 90, p. 20.
"Goats." [HampSPR] (Anthology 1975-1990) 90, p. 209.
"Hauling Manure, Late October." [Crucible] (26) Fall 90, p. 87.
"In the Weave Room." [Thrpny] (40) Wint 90, p. 4.
"Martyrdom of the Onions." [RiverC] (11:1) Fall 90, p. 71.
"Real Jazz." [AntR] (48:4) Fall 90, p. 488.
1106. CHMIELARZ, Sharon
"In a Russian Garden." [LakeSR] (24) 90, p. 14.

105

"Meeting Gogol's Akaky Akakiyevich on Kalinkin Bridge." [LakeSR] (24) 90, p. 15.
"Tea." [ArtfulD] (18/19) 90, p. 56.
1107. CHOE, Sungho
"I Breathe" (tr. by Kim Uchang). [Manoa] (2:2) Fall 90, p. 150.
"Snow Falling into a White Night" (tr. by Kim Uchang). [Manoa] (2:2) Fall 90, p. 151.
1108. CHOE, Wolhee
"Covering the Earth: I, an Ant" (tr. of Chong Hyon-jong, w. Constantine Contogenis). [PoetryE] (30) Fall 90, p. 9.
"Everything You Do" (tr. of Songi, w. Constantine Contogenis). [PoetryE] (30) Fall 90, p. 84.
"Old Mountain" (tr. of Hwang Jini, w. Constantine Contogenis). [PoetryE] (30) Fall 90, p. 88.
"Pink Flowers" (tr. of Kim Tong-ni, w. Constantine Contogenis). [PoetryE] (30) Fall 90, p. 103.
"When Butterfly Sees Flower" (tr. of Songi, w. Constantine Contogenis). [PoetryE] (30) Fall 90, p. 84.
"Wild Geese Sang" (tr. of Kumhong, w. Constantine Contogenis). [PoetryE] (30) Fall 90, p. 104.
1109. CHOI, Janet
"In the Flowers of Your Leaving." [HarvardA] (124:4) My 90, p. 5.
"Small Graces." [HarvardA] (125:2) N 90, p. 8.
"What I'm Wild For." [HarvardA] (125:2) N 90, p. 29.
"While Dancing with Fred Astaire, She Reflects." [HarvardA] (124:4) My 90, p. 35.
1110. CHOI, Kathleen T.
"English Class." [BambooR] (47) Sum 90, p. 45.
1111. CHONAIRE, Flaithri O Maoil
"Bardic" (tr. by Richard O'Connell). [HampSPR] (Anthology 1975-1990) 90, p. 245.
1112. CHONG, Hyon-jong
"Covering the Earth: I, an Ant" (tr. by Constantine Contogenis and Wolhee Choe). [PoetryE] (30) Fall 90, p. 9.
"Song in Praise of Thunder." [PoetryUSA] (5:3) Fall 90, p. 20.
1113. CHORLTON, David
"Arahova." [ChamLR] (4:1, #7) Fall 90, p. 24.
"The Bats' Rebellion." [HawaiiR] (14:3, #30) Fall 90, p. 80.
"A Conquistador's Testament." [ChamLR] (4:1, #7) Fall 90, p. 23.
"Crossings." [ContextS] (1:1) 89, p. 24.
"Dancing on the Glacier." [OxfordM] (6:1) Spr-Sum 90, p. 34.
"The Document." [ChamLR] (4:1, #7) Fall 90, p. 25-26.
"Doubles." [SlipS] (10) 90, p. 46-47.
"Earth Is Their Memorial." [SlipS] (10) 90, p. 46.
"The Emperor, Kao Tsung." [CumbPR] (9:2) Spr 90, p. 6.
"The Emperor, Shun." [InterPR] (16:2) Fall 90, p. 133.
"Encounter." [CumbPR] (9:2) Spr 90, p. 5.
"Estéban in Cibola." [InterPR] (16:2) Fall 90, p. 131.
"Ever closer to the Milky Way" (tr. of Christine Lavant). [Rohwedder] (5) Spr 90, p. 20.
"Family Reunion." [PoetL] (85:2) Sum 90, p. 15-16.
"In a green hollow a horse was grazing" (tr. of Christine Lavant). [Rohwedder] (5) Spr 90, p. 20.
"In Leningrad." [FreeL] (5) Sum 90, p. 21.
"Moskva Hotel." [FreeL] (5) Sum 90, p. 20.
"On the eleventh step of the fir" (tr. of Christine Lavant). [Rohwedder] (5) Spr 90, p. 21.
"Spring Night in Montenegro." [ContextS] (1:1) 89, p. 25.
"Studies" (For Donald Locke). [HawaiiR] (14:2, #29) Spr 90, p. 85-87.
"Tarascon." [InterPR] (16:2) Fall 90, p. 132.
"Twist the spindle in my heart further" (tr. of Christine Lavant). [Rohwedder] (5) Spr 90, p. 20.
"Vignettes." [ChamLR] (3:2, #6) Spr 90, p. 59-60.
1114. CHORON, Rose
"Sugar and Spice." [Pearl] (12) Fall-Wint 90, p. 64.
1115. CHOW, John
"Sunshine, Lift Your Foot and Let My Shadow Go" (tr. of Yan Li). [LitR] (33:4)

Sum 90, p. 492.
1116. CHOWN, Bill
"The Guys." [WormR] (30:1, #117) 90, p. 6.
"Williams." [WormR] (30:1, #117) 90, p. 6.
1117. CHOYCE, Lesley
"Seaforth Remembered." [PottPort] (12) 90, p. 35.
1118. CHRISTAKOS, Margaret
"Natural Disaster." [WestCL] (24:3) Wint 90, p. 90-91.
1119. CHRISTENSEN, Inger
"The Scene" (from "It," tr. by Birgit and Gregory Stephenson). [CimR] (92) Jl 90,
p. 17.
1120. CHRISTINA-MARIE
"Dust." [HiramPoR] (48/49) 90-91, p. 23.
"The Rite of Passage." [Caliban] (9) 90, p. 125.
1121. CHRISTOPHER, Nicholas
"Approaching Antarctica." [GrandS] (9:3) Spr 90, p. 151-153.
"The Black Bells from Gina's House." [WestHR] (44:2) Sum 90, p. 221-222.
"Outside Perpignan in Heavy Rain." [NewYorker] (66:19) 25 Je 90, p. 58.
"Rooftop." [PartR] (57:3) Sum 90, p. 435-436.
"Scarlet Lake." [NewRep] (202:2/3) 8-15 Ja 90, p. 36.
CHUAN, Xi
See XI, Chuan
CHUILLEANAIN, Eileán Ní
See Ní CHUILLEANAIN, Eileán
1122. CHURA, David
"Easter Season: Turtle Pond." [EngJ] (79:3) Mr 90, p. 90.
1123. CHUTE, Robert M.
"All Is Not Lost at Sea." [LitR] (33:3) Spr 90, p. 379.
"Epiphany on the Crooked River." [LitR] (33:2) Wint 90, p. 230.
"From a Photograph" (of Amelia Earhart). [CapeR] (25:1) Spr 90, p. 25.
"I Love a Broad Margin to My Life." [KanQ] (22:1/2) Wint-Spr 90, p. 169.
"Perfect Pitch." [NoDaQ] (58:1) Wint 90, p. 67-68.
"Unsliced Bread." [KanQ] (22:1/2) Wint-Spr 90, p. 169.
1124. CI, Predrag Bogdanovic
"The Invitations" (tr. by Simha Levi Bogdanovic). [Screens] (2) 90, p. 65.
"The Palimpsest" (tr. by Simha Levi Bogdanovic). [Screens] (2) 90, p. 65.
1125. CIECKO, Anne T.
"The Black Swan." [LullwaterR] (2:1) Wint 90, p. 70.
1126. CIRINO, Leonard
"The Pond." [Plain] (10:2) Wint 90, p. 25.
"Sweeney: A Man for All Seasons." [ChironR] (9:3) Aut 90, p. 25.
"Sweeney Descends the Stairs." [ChironR] (9:3) Aut 90, p. 23.
1127. CISNEROS, Antonio
"Entonces en las Aguas de Conchán." [Abraxas] (38/39) 90, p. 70, 72.
"In the Waters of Conchan" (tr. by John Oliver Simon). [Abraxas] (38/39) 90, p. 71,
73.
1128. CITINO, David
"Dear Robert: I Dreamed Last Night That You Were Dead." [SenR] (20:2) Fall 90, p.
43-44.
"Hiding the Skeleton." [SouthernR] (26:1) Ja 90, p. 219.
"Journey to Calabria." [Salm] (85/86) Wint-Spr 90, p. 129-135.
"Letter from the Shaman: The Contrary Tribe." [LitR] (33:3) Spr 90, p. 264-265.
"The Line." [LaurelR] (24:1) Wint 90, p. 90-91.
"The Man Who Found a Poem in Everything." [SouthernHR] (24:2) Spr 90, p.
164-165.
"Meditation on Gödel's Second Incompleteness Theorem." [WestB] (27) 90, p.
24-25.
"Three Versions Culminating in the Minimal." [KanQ] (22:3) Sum 90, p. 37.
"The Train into the Mountainside, the Miracle of the Bus." [PraS] (64:3) Fall 90, p.
118-120.
CLAIR, Linda Le
See LeCLAIR, Linda
1129. CLAIRE, Thomas
"Castle in Spain." [DustyD] (1:2) O 90, p. 10.
"The Nomad." [DustyD] (1:2) O 90, p. 8.
"The Poker Bar (Sitges)." [DustyD] (1:2) O 90, p. 8.

107

CLAIRMAN

1130. CLAIRMAN, Gary Phillip
"For Lynn MacGillivray." [Dandel] (17:1) Spr-Sum 90, p. 41.
1131. CLAMAN, Elizabeth
"Love Song" (for my mother). [NegC] (10:1) 90, p. 17-19.
1132. CLAMPITT, Amy
"At Muker, Upper Swaledale." [NewYorker] (66:45) 24 D 90, p. 45.
"Fireweed." [WilliamMR] (28) 90, p. 34.
"Having Lunch at Brasenose." [MichQR] (29:1) Wint 90, p. 27-28.
"A Hedge of Rubber Trees." [MichQR] (29:1) Wint 90, p. 24-26.
"The Prairie." [NewYorker] (65:50) 29 Ja 90, p. 30-31.
"A Whippoorwill in the Woods." [Boulevard] (4:3/5:1, #12/13) Spr 90, p. 23-24.
1133. CLANCY, Thomas Owen
"Signatures." [Stand] (31:4) Aut 90, p. 74.
1134. CLARK, Evelyn
"Not by Bread Alone." [TarRP] (30:1) Fall 90, p. 26.
1135. CLARK, G. O.
"Distracted by Sirens." [ManhatPR] (12) [90?], p. 28.
1136. CLARK, J. Wesley
"D. W. Griffith's Dreamgirl." [Bogg] (63) 90, p. 17.
1137. CLARK, Jason
"No Need to Rush Into Print" (a collage poem). [PoetryUSA] (5:3) Fall 90, p. 27.
1138. CLARK, Jeanne
"A Day for Fishing." [WillowS] (26) Spr 90, p. 68.
"The House Next Door." [WillowS] (26) Spr 90, p. 69.
1139. CLARK, Jim
"Handiwork." [PraS] (64:2) Sum 90, p. 60-61.
"You." [PraS] (64:2) Sum 90, p. 62.
1140. CLARK, Leslie
"Road Work Ahead." [Bogg] (63) 90, p. 50.
1141. CLARK, Mary
"Love Caught." [BlackWR] (16:2) Spr-Sum 90, p. 110.
1142. CLARK, Naomi
"After Emergency Surgery." [PraS] (64:2) Sum 90, p. 65.
"At Mendenhall Glacier." [GreenMR] (NS 4:1) Spr-Sum 90, p. 46.
"Aubade: Cardboard Fan from a Baptist Church." [NoDaQ] (58:2) Spr 90, p.
121-122.
"Brands." [SoDakR] (28:3) Aut 90, p. 103.
"The Children Help Me Die." [PoetryNW] (31:1) Spr 90, p. 8-9.
"Cutting a Firebreak." [NoDaQ] (58:4) Fall 90, p. 3.
"Flute on the Mountain." [NoDaQ] (58:4) Fall 90, p. 4.
"God's One-eyed Horse." [PraS] (64:2) Sum 90, p. 67.
"Hannah at the Creek." [SoDakR] (28:3) Aut 90, p. 102.
"Journey of the Fat Man and His Barren Wife." [LaurelR] (24:2) Sum 90, p. 50-52.
"The Muses." [BellR] (13:2, #28) Fall 90, p. 35.
"One on the Shore." [PoetryNW] (31:1) Spr 90, p. 10-11.
"The Poinsettia." [NoDaQ] (58:2) Spr 90, p. 122-123.
"Sailing." [HawaiiR] (14:3, #30) Fall 90, p. 104-105.
"Scavenger." [PraS] (64:2) Sum 90, p. 64.
"The Sow." [PraS] (64:2) Sum 90, p. 65-66.
"Yes." [ClockR] (6:1) 90, p. 58.
1143. CLARK, Ron
"Art Catalogue #4." [Grain] (18:3) Fall 90, p. 98.
"Crypto Erotica #3." [Grain] (18:3) Fall 90, p. 97.
"Extinction Ode: For Pansies." [Grain] (18:3) Fall 90, p. 98.
"Four Poems From a Sequence" (#9, #12, #17, #21). [Dandel] (17:2) Fall-Wint 90,
p. 34-35.
"The Lovely Chthonic Roots." [Grain] (18:1) Spr 90, p. 13.
"Novena for Grace Kelly." [Grain] (18:3) Fall 90, p. 99.
"Poem Lost in Mind Tibet." [Grain] (18:3) Fall 90, p. 99.
"Terrors from Beyond the Grave." [Grain] (18:1) Spr 90, p. 13.
1144. CLARKE, Catherine
"Caffe Lena, November 25, 1989" (for Lena Spencer). [Chelsea] (49) 90, p. 82.
"For Sterling Brown." [Chelsea] (49) 90, p. 81.
"Poem After Fixing the Fence." [Chelsea] (49) 90, p. 83.
CLARKE, George Elliot
See CLARKE, George Elliott

1145. CLARKE, George Elliott
"The Apocrypha of Liana." [PottPort] (12) 90, p. 42.
"The Argument." [Grain] (18:1) Spr 90, p. 49.
"The Argument." [PottPort] (12) 90, p. 43.
"The Ballad of Othello Clemence." [Grain] (18:1) Spr 90, p. 48.
"The First Day of Desire." [PottPort] (11) 89, p. 35.
"The History of Death." [Grain] (18:1) Spr 90, p. 47.
"How Long Can Love Go Wrong?" [Grain] (18:1) Spr 90, p. 46.
"The Ladies Auxiliary." [AntigR] (80) Wint 90, p. 37.
"May 19___." [Callaloo] (13:2) Spr 90, p. 200.
"Revolutionary Epoch." [Callaloo] (13:2) Spr 90, p. 199.
"Sixhiboux Motors." [Grain] (18:1) Spr 90, p. 47.
"Unnatural Disaster." [Callaloo] (13:2) Spr 90, p. 198.
"Whylah Falls" (Selections). [Quarry] (39:2) Spr 90, p. 15-19.
"Whylah Falls" (Selections: "Preface" and 7 poems). [Descant] (21:1 #68) Spr 90, p. 33-43.
1146. CLARKE, John
"The Antithetical Movement of Post-Production." [Notus] (5:1) Spr 90, p. 11.
"Aquarius Pouring It On" (for Artie Shaw). [Notus] (5:1) Spr 90, p. 14.
"Christmas 1988, Each Breath a Tennis Court Oath." [Notus] (5:1) Spr 90, p. 15.
"Dopplering Central Deeming Melanogensis" (for Peter Middleton). [Notus] (5:1) Spr 90, p. 17.
"Heap Yourself Free." [Notus] (5:1) Spr 90, p. 13.
"The Ichor of Chthonios." [Notus] (5:1) Spr 90, p. 16.
"Sometimes at Night." [Notus] (5:1) Spr 90, p. 12.
1147. CLARVOE, Jennifer
"Vanity." [Agni] (29/30) 90, p. 130-131.
1148. CLARY, Killarney
"Blindly. Because you, my two real friends, are strangers to me tonight." [AmerPoR] (19:4) Jl-Ag 90, p. 20.
"Deep under water where every bit of my surface is pressed." [AmerPoR] (19:4) Jl-Ag 90, p. 20.
"In the morning, smoke from the garbage of Soller caught in the blinds." [AmerPoR] (19:4) Jl-Ag 90, p. 20.
"My telling is numb, the listeners are people I've invented." [AmerPoR] (19:4) Jl-Ag 90, p. 20.
"Stretched out, I'm a carrier, open and empty." [AmerPoR] (19:4) Jl-Ag 90, p. 20.
1149. CLAUS, Hugo
"Flight into Egypt" (Painting: The Massacre of the Innocents by Pieter Breughel, tr. by Paul Vincent). [Trans] (24) Fall 90, p. 45.
"In the Chicago Museum" (Painting: Saint Jerome by Joachim Patinir, tr. by Paul Vincent). [Trans] (24) Fall 90, p. 44.
"Visio Tondalis" (Painting by Hieronymus Bosch, tr. by Paul Vincent). [Trans] (24) Fall 90, p. 42-43.
1150. CLAUSEN, Christopher
"Birds and the Reader." [Hellas] (1:1) Spr 90, p. 57.
1151. CLAUSER, Grant
"America Farts at Commercials." [BlackBR] (12) Fall-Wint 90, p. 20.
1152. CLAVIJO, Uva A.
"Sin Otra Pretension." [LindLM] (9:4) O-D 90, p. 44.
1153. CLAYTON, Deborah
"Tulips." [OnTheBus] (2:2/3:1, #6/7) Sum-Fall 90 Wint-Spr 91, p. 63.
1154. CLEARY, Brendan
"Sealink." [Stand] (31:4) Aut 90, p. 4-5.
"Slouch." [Stand] (31:4) Aut 90, p. 5.
1155. CLEARY, Suzanne
"Ivory Bracelets." [PraS] (64:3) Fall 90, p. 92-94.
"Learning a New Language" (for Riva Fishbeyn). [NewMyths] (1:1) 90, p. 31.
"Nettle." [NewMyths] (1:1) 90, p. 30.
"Preliminary Sketch" (after John Singer Sargent). [LitR] (33:2) Wint 90, p. 244.
"There Are People Who Cannot Cross Bridges Without Wanting to Jump." [SouthernR] (26:3) Jl 90, p. 660-661.
"Unborn." [NewMyths] (1:1) 90, p. 28-29.
"Yasmin" (after the film "Son of the Sheik"). [GeoR] (44:1/2) Spr-Sum 90, p. 60-61.

109

1156. CLEGHORN, James
"One-Night Stand." [CapeR] (25:2) Fall 90, p. 48.
1157. CLEMENT, Jennifer
"Cemetery of Acatitlan." [AmerPoR] (19:3) My-Je 90, p. 34.
"Travelers" (for Captain George N. Sibley). [AmerPoR] (19:3) My-Je 90, p. 34.
1158. CLEMENTE, Vince
"Garibaldi Leaves Rome." [Confr] (42/43) Spr-Sum 90, p. 203.
1159. CLEMENTS, Arthur L.
"List Poem for the Birds in My Backyard." [Footwork] 90, p. 96.
"Naples, Florida, March 5, 1990." [Footwork] 90, p. 96.
"Of a Sudden." [Footwork] 90, p. 96.
1160. CLEMENTS, Brian
"Spelunking." [NewMyths] (1:1) 90, p. 130-131.
1161. CLEMENTS, Susan Hauptfleisch
"Annie's Doll." [Footwork] 90, p. 14.
"Bitter Resins." [NewMyths] (1:1) 90, p. 57-58.
"Blessing." [Footwork] 90, p. 13.
"Court of the Lions, Alhambra." [Footwork] 90, p. 13.
"Swans of Sligo." [NewMyths] (1:1) 90, p. 56.
"Woman in Yellow Bathrobe, Montmartre." [Footwork] 90, p. 14.
"Woman Who Walks." [Footwork] 90, p. 15.
1162. CLEVER, Bertolt
"And a Thousand Miles Behind." [FourQ] (4:1) Spr 90, p. 57.
"Distinction." [CapeR] (25:1) Spr 90, p. 27.
"Gloom." [FourQ] (4:1) Spr 90, p. 56.
1163. CLEWELL, David
"Lost in the Fire." [KenR] (NS 12:2) Spr 90, p. 36-51.
"Sitting Out the Sadness." [Boulevard] (5:2, #14) Fall 90, p. 143-147.
1164. CLIFF, William
"Today for Breakfast We Had" (tr. by Jim Barnes). [ArtfulD] (18/19) 90, p. 97.
1165. CLIFT, Elayne
"Putting It in Perspective." [Pearl] (10) Spr 90, p. 50.
1166. CLIFTON, Harry
"Winter in Glenmacnass." [Quarry] (39:1) Wint 90, p. 68.
1167. CLIFTON, Lucille
"February 11, 1990" (for Nelson Mandela and Winnie." [Chelsea] (49) 90, p. 78.
"Poem Beginning in No and Ending in Yes" (for Hector Peterson, aged 13, first child killed in Soweto riot 1976). [Chelsea] (49) 90, p. 78.
"Poem in Praise of Menstruation." [RiverS] (32) [90?], p. 64.
"Shooting Star" (for Huey P. Newton, r.i.p.). [RiverS] (32) [90?], p. 63.
"To My Friend Jerina." [Chelsea] (49) 90, p. 79.
"White Lady" (a street name for cocaine). [Chelsea] (49) 90, p. 80.
1168. CLIMENHAGA, Joel
"A Greeting to All Who Still Care." [Pig] (16) 90, p. 55.
1169. CLINTON, DeWitt
"Art & Imagination in the New World." [OxfordM] (6:1) Spr-Sum 90, p. 88.
"Europe in 1914." [KenR] (NS 12:2) Spr 90, p. 52-54.
1170. CLINTON, Michelle T.
"Dating the Dick Heads." [Gargoyle] (37/38) 90, p. 34.
1171. CLOUGH, Sheryl
"Morning of the Bears." [BellArk] (6:5) S-O 90, p. 18.
1172. CLOUSTON, Judy
"Uncolicited." [Amelia] (6:1, #16) 90, p. 106.
1173. CLOVER, Joshua
"Dancer, PS 122, 10/14/89." [MissR] (19:1/2, #55/56) 90, p. 238.
1174. CLUETT, Donna Samuelson
"Crimson Quest." [WorldO] (23:3/4) Spr-Sum 89 c1991, p. 31.
1175. COAKLEY, William Leo
"Concrete Poem." [YellowS] (34) Sum 90, p. 40.
"Still Life." [YellowS] (34) Sum 90, p. 40.
1176. COBB, Faye Alderman
"I Wonder Who." [EmeraldCR] (1990) c89, p. 98-99.
1177. COCHRANE, Guy R.
"Human." [WormR] (30:1, #117) 90, p. 16.
"Lineage." [WormR] (30:1, #117) 90, p. 16.
"Lover's Leap." [WormR] (30:1, #117) 90, p. 16.

110

"Road Kill." [WormR] (30:1, #117) 90, p. 16.
"Systematic." [WormR] (30:1, #117) 90, p. 16.
1178. COCHRANE, Mark
"If You Are Suicidal, Marry a Writer." [Quarry] (39:4) Fall 1990, p. 36-37.
"Medea." [Quarry] (39:4) Fall 1990, p. 35.
1179. COCKRELL, Andrea Cook
"Communion Meditation." [ChrC] (107:35) 5 D 90, p. 1134.
1180. COCKRELL, Melanie
"Persephone: A Letter Home." [Iowa] (20:3) Fall 90, p. 126.
1181. COCTEAU, Jean
"At Lipp's" (tr. by Charles Guenther). [InterPR] (16:2) Fall 90, p. 35.
"Le Bourreau Chinois." [InterPR] (16:2) Fall 90, p. 34.
"Chez Lipp" (from "Poèmes," 1948). [InterPR] (16:2) Fall 90, p. 34.
"The Chinese Executioner" (tr. by Charles Guenther). [InterPR] (16:2) Fall 90, p. 35.
"Homage to Kleist" (tr. by Charles Guenther). [InterPR] (16:2) Fall 90, p. 37.
"Hommage a Kleist" (from "Clair-Obscur: Poèmes," 1954). [InterPR] (16:2) Fall 90, p. 36.
1182. COESTER, Danah
"Design for a Menu" (from the etchings, engravings and lithographs of Odilon Redon). [CreamCR] (14:1) Spr 90, p. 136-137.
"Santiago and the Insane Asylum in Juarez." [Nimrod] (34:1) Fall-Wint 90, p. 93.
"To the Photographer of the Egg Woman in Juarez." [CreamCR] (14:1) Spr 90, p. 134-135.
1183. COFER, Judith Ortiz
"Blood" (In memory of C.H.C.). [LullwaterR] (2:1) Wint 90, p. 90.
"The Dream of Birth." [SouthernPR] (30:1) Spr 90, p. 43-44.
"Juana: An Old Story." [Americas] (18:2) Sum 90, p. 37.
"La Nada." [Americas] (18:2) Sum 90, p. 34-35.
"Saint Rose of Lima (Isabel de Flores)." [Americas] (18:2) Sum 90, p. 38.
"That Old Tune" (indexed from table of content -- page blank in indexed copy). [Americas] (18:2) Sum 90, p. 36.
"They Never Grew Old." [KenR] (NS 12:3) Sum 90, p. 69-70.
"Women Who Love Angels." [SingHM] (17) 90, p. 98.
1184. COFER, Matt
"The Voice of One Raging in the Suburbs." [PacificR] (8) 90, p. 61.
1185. COFFMAN, Lisa
"Brother Ass." [WestB] (26) 90, p. 23-24.
"The Small Town." [WestB] (26) 90, p. 22-23.
1186. COGSWELL, Fred
"Envoi." [CanLit] (126) Aut 90, p. 48.
1187. COHEN, A. S.
"'N' Street Mobile." [NewRena] (8:1, #24) Spr 90, p. 80.
1188. COHEN, Andrea
"The Cartographer's Vacation." [HighP] (5:3) Wint 90-91, p. 60-61.
"Gogol's Madman." [Crazy] (38) Spr 90, p. 57.
"Mild Instructions for Travel." [PoetryNW] (31:1) Spr 90, p. 36-37.
1189. COHEN, Bernard
"Inflation" (7 selections). [Screens] (2) 90, p. 93-95.
1190. COHEN, Bruce
"1990." [PassN] (11:2) Wint 90, p. 24.
"Walking in Traffic." [PassN] (11:2) Wint 90, p. 24.
1191. COHEN, Carole
"Hired." [CapeR] (25:2) Fall 90, p. 20.
1192. COHEN, Elizabeth
"Ashtrays." [RiverS] (32) [90?], p. 18.
"Light Years." [PoetL] (85:3) Fall 90, p. 9-10.
"Twisting." [RiverS] (32) [90?], p. 17.
1193. COHEN, Mitch
"Between Haste and Deceit" (tr. of Stefan Doring, w. Roderick Iverson). [Sulfur] (10:2, #27) Fall 90, p. 101-102.
"Silence the Rest, Awakening" (tr. of Stefan Doring, w. Roderick Iverson). [Sulfur] (10:2, #27) Fall 90, p. 102-103.
1194. COHEN, Sascha Benjamin
"I Dreamt One Night in Autumn." [BellArk] (6:3) My-Je 90, p. 11.
"King Joey." [BellArk] (6:3) My-Je 90, p. 12.

1195. COKE, Sandra
"Families." [Plain] (10:2) Wint 90, p. 27.
1196. COKINOS, Christopher
"The Earth Movers." [PoetC] (22:1) Fall 90, p. 42-44.
"Vision of the World Instantly White." [Witness] (4:1) 90, p. 52-54.
1197. COLANDER, Valerie Nieman
"Persephone in Suburbia." [Poetry] (156:6) S 90, p. 332-333.
1198. COLE, E. R.
"Eine Kleine Light Music" (A Sequence). [Amelia] (6:2, #17) 90, p. 27.
"Flypaper Poem." [Vis] (33) 90, p. 40.
1199. COLE, Henri
"The Bird Show at Aubagne." [YaleR] (79:3) Spr 90, p. 482-483.
"Christmas in Carthage" (for Jerl Surratt and Paul Young). [YaleR] (79:3) Spr 90, p.
484-485.
1200. COLE, James
"All the Odors." [GreensboroR] (49) Wint 90-91, p. 32-33.
"The Car." [NoDaQ] (58:4) Fall 90, p. 156.
"The Dandelion." [RiverC] (10:2) Spr 90, p. 86.
"The Five-and-Ten." [BellR] (13:2, #28) Fall 90, p. 37.
"The Painters." [NewMyths] (1:1) 90, p. 137.
"Walking the Schnauzer." [RiverC] (10:2) Spr 90, p. 87.
1201. COLE, Lyllian D.
"Ivy bears yellow blossoms." [Amelia] (6:1, #16) 90, p. 33.
1202. COLE, Norma
"Aurora" (Excerpt). [Avec] (3:1) 90, p. 22-23.
"My Bird Book" (Selections: 7 poems). [Conjunc] (15) 90, p. 110-116.
"Notebooks 1956-78" (Selections: "Notes," published in 1983 by Editions
Seghers/Laffont as "Cahiers 1956-1978," tr. of Danielle Collobert). [Avec]
(3:1) 90, p. 85-86.
"The of of explanation." [Talisman] (4) Spr 90, p. 43.
"The Picture" (Excerpts, in "Epoques pour la guerre," Flammarion, France, 1984, tr.
of Edith Dahan). [Avec] (3:1) 90, p. 60-62.
1203. COLE, Peter
"I'm in Uniform" (from "Lowell," tr. of Harold Schimmel). [PartR] (57:3) Sum 90,
p. 437.
"The Land" (Selection: VIII, tr. of Harold Schimmel). [Screens] (2) 90, p. 27-36.
"One to Bet: A Jerusalem Pamphlet." [Conjunc] (15) 90, p. 324-354.
1204. COLE, Richard
"My Wife Believes in Reincarnation." [Poetry] (155:5) F 90, p. 331-332.
1205. COLE, Robert
"Emergency." [Gargoyle] (37/38) 90, p. 93.
"Emergency." [Interim] (9:1) Spr-Sum 90, p. 10-11.
"Great Aunt Laura." [Interim] (9:1) Spr-Sum 90, p. 13.
"Party Pieces." [Interim] (9:1) Spr-Sum 90, p. 9.
"Resort." [Interim] (9:1) Spr-Sum 90, p. 11.
"Unlucky for Some" (i.m. Bert Cole). [Interim] (9:1) Spr-Sum 90, p. 12.
1206. COLE, Williams Rossa
"Belly of the Flames." [Confr] (44/45) Fall 90-Wint 91, p. 196.
1207. COLEMAN, Arthur
"Dead Sea Nursery Rimes." [Confr] (44/45) Fall 90-Wint 91, p. 197.
1208. COLEMAN, Mary Ann
"The Burning" (for Guy Owen). [LullwaterR] (2:1) Wint 90, p. 65-66.
"Mexican Vacation." [EngJ] (79:8) D 90, p. 89.
1209. COLEMAN, Wanda
"Dancer in the Window." [Caliban] (8) 90, p. 113.
"For Me When I Am Myself." [Caliban] (9) 90, p. 88-95.
"Mr. Lopez." [OnTheBus] (2:2/3:1, #6/7) Sum-Fall 90 Wint-Spr 91, p. 64.
"Reflections on a Yardbird." [Caliban] (8) 90, p. 112.
1210. COLES, Don
"Night Game." [MalR] (91) Je 90, p. 70-72.
1211. COLES, Katharine
"Love Poem for the Nuclear Age: Utah, 1950-[   ]." [ColEng] (52:5) S 90, p.
528-531.
1212. COLLIER, Michael
"The Barber." [NewYorker] (66:31) 17 S 90, p. 40.
"Encanto Park, 1961." [Agni] (29/30) 90, p. 144-145.

"Robert Wilson." [Atlantic] (266:2) Ag 90, p. 42.
"Spider Tumor" (for John Murphy). [Agni] (29/30) 90, p. 142-143.
1213. COLLINS, Billy
"The Afterlife." [Poetry] (156:5) Ag 90, p. 267-268.
"Boredom." [FreeL] (6) Aut 90, p. 4.
"The Death of Allegory." [Poetry] (155:4) Ja 90, p. 276-277.
"February Twenty-Second." [FreeL] (6) Aut 90, p. 4.
"Forgetfulness." [Poetry] (155:4) Ja 90, p. 277.
"Going Out for Cigarettes." [ParisR] (32:116) Fall 90, p. 110.
"Illustration." [FreeL] (6) Aut 90, p. 3.
"Mappamundi." [Poetry] (156:5) Ag 90, p. 268-269.
"Part of Speech." [FreeL] (6) Aut 90, p. 5.
"Reading Myself to Sleep." [Boulevard] (5:2, #14) Fall 90, p. 172-173.
1214. COLLINS, Byron
"Coke." [Writer] (103:3) Mr 90, p. 24.
"The Hoe Makes a Hushed Sound." [Writer] (103:6) Je 90, p. 23.
1215. COLLINS, Jeffrey
"At the Astronomy Lecture." [GreensboroR] (49) Wint 90-91, p. 3.
1216. COLLINS, Loretta
"Saturday Story." [PoetL] (85:2) Sum 90, p. 13-14.
1217. COLLINS, M. N.
"Foolscap." [Hellas] (1:1) Spr 90, p. 48.
1218. COLLINS, Martha
"After Ontario." [CarolQ] (42:2) Wint 90, p. 45-48.
"Background/Information." [Field] (42) Spr 90, p. 43-44.
"Coast." [Field] (42) Spr 90, p. 48-49.
"Findings." [WestB] (27) 90, p. 48-50.
"Good Friday." [Confr] (44/45) Fall 90-Wint 91, p. 193.
"In Black and White." [Field] (42) Spr 90, p. 45.
"Sleep, Baby, Sleep!" [Field] (42) Spr 90, p. 46-47.
1219. COLLINS, Richard
"Fitful Sleep." [YellowS] (34) Sum 90, p. 41.
1220. COLLINS, Robert
"Stanley's Confectionery." [ChatR] (11:1) Fall 90, p. 43-44.
1221. COLLINS, Terry
"Anniversary Poem" (for Joanne). [AntigR] (80) Wint 90, p. 7.
"Where the Poetry Comes From." [AntigR] (80) Wint 90, p. 8.
1222. COLLINSWORTH, Damon
"Danger in the Ocean." [PoetryUSA] (5:2) Sum 90, p. 8.
1223. COLLOBERT, Danielle
"Notebooks 1956-78" (Selections: "Notes," published in 1983 by Editions
        Seghers/Laffont as "Cahiers 1956-1978," tr. by Norma Cole). [Avec] (3:1) 90,
        p. 85-86.
1224. COLLOM, Jack
"The Earth Also Dies" (Excerpt, tr. of Muhammad al-As'ad, w. May Jayyusi).
        [Screens] (2) 90, p. 26.
"Personal Account" (tr. of Muhammad al-As'ad, w. May Jayyusi). [Screens] (2) 90,
        p. 25-26.
"Quintana Roo Beach, 6 A.M." (Agosto '88). [HeavenB] (8) Wint 90-91, p. 4-6.
1225. COLONNESE, Michael
"Because of Local Flooding." [PoetL] (85:3) Fall 90, p. 14.
1226. COLONOMOS, Jean
"Definition." [ContextS] (1:1) 89, p. 52.
1227. COLVIN, Norma Thomas
"Cowboy-Boot Sale." [Kaleid] (20) Wint-Spr 90, p. 16.
"On Forgetting to Cry." [Kaleid] (20) Wint-Spr 90, p. 16.
1228. COLWELL, Anne A.
"The Centaur Comes Down Main Street in March." [MidwQ] (31:4) Sum 90, p.
        475-476.
"Troop 603." [MidwQ] (31:4) Sum 90, p. 473.
1229. COMANN, Brad
"The Months: Twelve Vignettes." [WindO] (53) Fall 90, p. 44-45.
"On the Death of Francis Bacon, 1626." [WindO] (53) Fall 90, p. 46.
1230. COMBELLICK, Henry
"Fulton Valley Washout." [NoDaQ] (58:2) Spr 90, p. 48.
"Near Arivaca, Arizona." [NoDaQ] (58:2) Spr 90, p. 47.

1231. COMER, Suzanne
"Fragility Is My Goal." [SouthwR] (75:3) Sum 90, p. 290.
COMPTE, Kendall Le
See LeCOMPTE, Kendall
1232. CONELLY, William
"In the Ninth Month." [Hellas] (1:2) Fall 90, p. 216.
1233. CONGDON, Kirby
"For Sara M. at Twelve" (On Being Given a Book of John Donne's "Poems").
[Contact] (9:56/57/58) Spr 90, p. 26.
"Pool-Boy." [Contact] (9:56/57/58) Spr 90, p. 26-27.
1234. CONIBEAR, Frank
"Artifacts." [CanLit] (124/125) Spr-Sum 90, p. 9.
1235. CONLEY, Glenn
"I came home late." [Bogg] (63) 90, p. 45.
1236. CONLON, Christopher
"For Wilfred Owen" (Kalahari Desert, Southern Africa). [NegC] (10:2/3) 90, p.
114-115.
"Kalahari" (from "The Africa Poems"). [Wind] (20:66) 90, p. 12.
1237. CONN, Christopher
"The clanking." [Amelia] (6:1, #16) 90, p. 91.
1238. CONN, Jan
"Against the Impenetrable Blue Light." [Arc] (24) Spr 90, p. 20.
"The Biggest Species of Hylid Frog in the World Joins Us for Dinner." [PraF]
(11:3) Aut 90, p. 34.
"Electrophorus Electricus." [PraF] (11:3) Aut 90, p. 35.
"Exposure." [MalR] (91) Je 90, p. 50-51.
"Fire and Water." [MalR] (91) Je 90, p. 48-49.
"Into the Gathering Dark." [Arc] (24) Spr 90, p. 20-21.
"Predictions." [Arc] (24) Spr 90, p. 19.
1239. CONNELLAN, Leo
"An Image from Howard Coughlin." [NewYorkQ] (43) Fall 90, p. 34.
1240. CONNELLY, Karen
"Amaya." [Grain] (18:1) Spr 90, p. 18-21.
"The Autopsy." [Grain] (18:1) Spr 90, p. 22.
"Living Nowhere." [Dandel] (17:2) Fall-Wint 90, p. 5-6.
"The Ocean from the Cliffs at Sopelana." [Grain] (18:1) Spr 90, inside front cover.
1241. CONNELLY, Michele
"Functional Poetry." [SwampR] (6) Sum-Fall 90, p. 83-84.
"Peacekeeper." [SlipS] (10) 90, p. 76-77.
1242. CONNOLLY, Geraldine
"Black Landscape." [LaurelR] (24:1) Wint 90, p. 9.
"The Entropy of Pleasure." [Poetry] (155:5) F 90, p. 330.
"Lydia." [GeoR] (44:3) Fall 90, p. 506-507.
1243. CONNOLLY, Kevin
"Alexander the Conqueror." [Arc] (24) Spr 90, p. 30.
"Asphalt Cigar." [WestCL] (24:3) Wint 90, p. 96.
"Junk Male." [WestCL] (24:3) Wint 90, p. 94.
"Spray Nozzle." [WestCL] (24:3) Wint 90, p. 95.
"They Remain Hatless." [WestCL] (24:3) Wint 90, p. 93.
"Twelve Arrests, No Convictions." [WestCL] (24:3) Wint 90, p. 92-93.
1244. CONOLEY, Gillian
"The Farmer's Daughter and the Travelling Salesman." [Poetry] (156:2) My 90, p.
74-75.
"I Have Forgotten the Word I Wanted to Say." [ColEng] (52:3) Mr 90, p. 274.
"I'd Like a Little Love in the Wine-Red Afternoon." [ColEng] (52:3) Mr 90, p. 272.
"Native Grace." [MissouriR] (13:2) 90, p. 80.
"Overtime." [Zyzzyva] (6:1 #21) Spr 90, p. 125-127.
"Unchained Melody." [DenQ] (25:1) Sum 90, p. 15-16.
"The Woman on the Homecoming Float." [ColEng] (52:3) Mr 90, p. 273.
1245. CONOVER, Carl
"Naming the Snow." [KanQ] (22:1/2) Wint-Spr 90, p. 238.
1246. CONRAD, David
"Archilochos." [AntigR] (80) Wint 90, p. 133.
"Down by the Foam-Washed Shore" (tr. of anonymous Macedonian folksong).
[AntigR] (80) Wint 90, p. 135.
"Yedi Koule" (tr. of anonymous Sephardic folksong). [AntigR] (80) Wint 90, p.

134.
1247. CONRAD, Robert
"The Lion." [PottPort] (12) 90, p. 25.
1248. CONROY, Carol
"The Deer Man." [Agni] (31/32) 90, p. 225-226.
"The Woman Who Held Waterfalls." [Agni] (31/32) 90, p. 223-224.
1249. CONSTANTINE, David
"A Blind Elephant Man in the Underground." [Quarry] (39:1) Wint 90, p. 14.
1250. CONTE, Giuseppe
"After March" (tr. by Anna Stortoni and Lowell Bergstedt). [MidwQ] (32:1) Aut 90,
p. 94.
"Tezcatlipoca: The Song of a Human Sacrifice" (tr. by Lowell Bergstedt and Laura
Stortoni). [MidwQ] (31:2) Wint 90, p. 195-196.
1251. CONTENT, Rob
"Tank Hill." [MissR] (19:1/2, #55/56) 90, p. 249-250.
1252. CONTOGENIS, Constantine
"Covering the Earth: I, an Ant" (tr. of Chong Hyon-jong, w. Wolhee Choe).
[PoetryE] (30) Fall 90, p. 9.
"Everything You Do" (tr. of Songi, w. Wolhee Choe). [PoetryE] (30) Fall 90, p. 84.
"Old Mountain" (tr. of Hwang Jini, w. Wolhee Choe). [PoetryE] (30) Fall 90, p. 88.
"Pink Flowers" (tr. of Kim Tong-ni, w. Wolhee Choe). [PoetryE] (30) Fall 90, p.
103.
"When Butterfly Sees Flower" (tr. of Songi, w. Wolhee Choe). [PoetryE] (30) Fall
90, p. 84.
"Wild Geese Sang" (tr. of Kumhong, w. Wolhee Choe). [PoetryE] (30) Fall 90, p.
104.
1253. CONWAY, Jeffery
"HIV." [BrooklynR] (7) 90, p. 25.
1254. CONYER, James A.
"Metamorphosis" (1. 525-539, tr. of Ovid). [Hellas] (1:1) Spr 90, p. 41.
1255. COOK, Geoffrey
"A Broken Contract: 110" (to Aufilena, tr. of Gaius Valerius Catullus). [PoetryUSA]
([5:4?]) Wint 90, p. 18.
"The evil shadows of Orcius" (tr. of Gaius Valerius Catullus). [PoetryUSA] (5:1)
Spr 90, p. 4.
"Quintius: 82" (tr. of Gaius Valerius Catullus). [PoetryUSA] ([5:4?]) Wint 90, p.
18.
1256. COOK, R. L.
"Rising Before Dawn on a Winter Morning to Make Coffee" (After the Chinese).
[LitR] (33:3) Spr 90, p. 377.
"Treefishing." [DogRR] (9:1, #17) Spr 90, p. 3.
1257. COOKSHAW, Marlene
"Pollen." [PraF] (11:3) Aut 90, p. 24.
"Trestle." [PraF] (11:3) Aut 90, p. 25.
1258. COOLEY, Peter
"All Souls' Day." [ThRiPo] (35/36) 90, p. 37.
"Aubade." [Crazy] (38) Spr 90, p. 44.
"Carousel." [IndR] (14:1) Wint 90, p. 28.
"Child at Play." [PraS] (64:4) Wint 90, p. 10-11.
"Countdown." [Nat] (250:10) 12 Mr 90, p. 358.
"Father and Children." [GreenMR] (NS 4:1) Spr-Sum 90, p. 39.
"Gravity." [SouthernR] (26:2) Ap 90, p. 337.
"Husband and Wife." [PraS] (64:4) Wint 90, p. 10.
"In My Best Recurrent Dream." [Ploughs] (16:1) Spr-Sum 90, p. 179-180.
"The Joshua Tree." [Crazy] (38) Spr 90, p. 43.
"Matins." [Shen] (40:2) Sum 90, p. 87.
"Mother and Son." [PraS] (64:4) Wint 90, p. 12.
"Soul Making." [ThRiPo] (35/36) 90, p. 38.
"Stepping In." [SouthernR] (26:2) Ap 90, p. 336.
"Texas Skyline." [Shen] (40:2) Sum 90, p. 86-87.
"Your Own Hour." [GreenMR] (NS 4:1) Spr-Sum 90, p. 38.
1259. COOLIDGE, Clark
"In Dream" (Excerpt). [Sulfur] (10:1, #26) Spr 90, p. 170-179.
"Loplop Twines." [PaintedB] (40/41) 90, p. 156-158.
"Red White Blue." [Avec] (3:1) 90, p. 7-12.
"Shied Witnesses." [Talisman] (4) Spr 90, p. 88.

115

COOLIDGE

"Two" (Exceprt, "from the long prose"). [Talisman] (4) Spr 90, p. 92-106.
"Two" (Excerpt, "from the long prose," continued from Talisman #4). [Talisman]
(5) Fall 90, p. 137-143.
1260. COONEY, Ellen
"The Approach of Winter." [Parting] (3:2) Wint 90-91, p. 27.
1261. COOP, Mahlon
"Suburban Drought." [KanQ] (22:1/2) Wint-Spr 90, p. 48-49.
1262. COOPER, Charles
"Starlings" (for Lewis Chesser). [KanQ] (22:3) Sum 90, p. 226.
1263. COOPER, Dennis
"Hustlers." [OnTheBus] (2:1, #5) Spr 90, p. 206.
1264. COOPER, Jane
"Bloodroot." [Antaeus] (64/65) Spr-Aut 90, p. 16.
"Hotel de Dream" (for Muriel Rukeyser and James Wright, died February/March
1980). [AmerV] (19) Sum 90, p. 3-4.
"Long, Disconsolate Lines" (in memory of Shirley Eliason Haupt). [Iowa] (20:2)
Spr-Sum 90, p. 42.
1265. COOPER, Karen Coody
"Beware of Accidents in the Home." [ManhatPR] (12) [90?], p. 18.
"Circles, Always Circles." [ManhatPR] (12) [90?], p. 20.
"Cowboys." [ManhatPR] (12) [90?], p. 19-20.
"The Naked Spiral" (to Lani). [ManhatPR] (12) [90?], p. 18-19.
1266. COOPER, Lisa
"Columnar." [Caliban] (9) 90, p. 146-147.
"Fulcrum." [Caliban] (9) 90, p. 148-149.
"Gold Rail." [AmerPoR] (19:3) My-Je 90, p. 11.
"A History Through Dreams." [BlueBldgs] (12) 90, p. 21-23.
"Hunger." [SycamoreR] (2:1) Wint 90, p. 50.
"More Bones and Some Thank You's for Porridge and Soup." [NewAW] (6) Spr
90, p. 97-98.
"Purge." [NewAW] (6) Spr 90, p. 96.
"Wheel." [Caliban] (9) 90, p. 150.
1267. COOPER, M. Truman
"The Coastal Access Stairway" (for Dr. Marti Glenn). [PoetryNW] (31:4) Wint
90-91, p. 35-36.
"The Fiftieth Element Makes Soft Soldiers." [RiverS] (32) [90?], p. 20.
"Ironing after Midnight." [RiverS] (32) [90?], p. 19.
"Making Sandbags." [TarRP] (29:2) Spr 90, p. 31.
"Stillness." [Blueline] (11:1/2) 90, p. 59.
"The Whelping Box." [NewL] (57:1) Fall 90, p. 87.
1268. COOPERMAN, Matthew
"Barbeque Sauce." [CumbPR] (10:1) Fall 90, p. 6-7.
"Say It." [Plain] (10:3) Spr 90, p. 6-7.
1269. COOPERMAN, Robert
"Agnes Smedley with Mao Zedong in China, 1934." [LitR] (33:3) Spr 90, p. 336.
"Andre Chenier Writes His Last Poem, 1794." [DustyD] (1:2) O 90, p. 16.
"Because They're Happy." [InterPR] (16:2) Fall 90, p. 130.
"The Bird of Life." [SwampR] (6) Sum-Fall 90, p. 95.
"Eliza Westbrook, After the Suicide of Her Sister, Harriet Westbrook Shelley,
1816." [Poem] (64) N 90, p. 66-67.
"Explanations." [AntigR] (81/82) Spr-Sum 90, p. 60.
"Going the Distance" (for Bob Lietz). [SwampR] (5) Wint-Spr 90, p. 35.
"Hero and Leander." [Event] (19:1) Spr 90, p. 46-47.
"I Swear." [HiramPoR] (47) Wint 90, p. 16-17.
"If You Think It's Hot Now." [AntigR] (81/82) Spr-Sum 90, p. 59.
"Lady Caroline Lamb Remembers Lord Byron." [GrahamHR] (13) Spr 90, p.
67-68.
"Lady Shelley Replies to Her Son's Accusations of Adultery." [SoCoast] (8) Spr 90,
p. 6.
"A Madam at the Funeral of One of Her Girls, Galveston, Texas, 1891." [CoalC] (2)
D 90, p. 15.
"The Malaysian Students Play Badminton." [RiverC] (11:1) Fall 90, p. 70.
"Marrianne Reynolds Writes to Keats About Her Ex-Suitor, Benjamin Bailey."
[FreeL] (6) Aut 90, p. 6-7.
"Mary Shelley Receives Her Dead Husband's Heart from Captain Trelawny."
[SoCoast] (9) Fall 90, p. 24-25.

"Mixed Marriages, Broken Homes." [NoDaQ] (58:2) Spr 90, p. 106.
"Nostalgia." [ApalQ] (33/34) 90, p. 65-66.
"Orchids" (for Hugh Ruppersburg). [HampSPR] (Anthology 1975-1990) 90, p. 227.
"Ovid in Exile." [Poem] (64) N 90, p. 70.
"Percy Bysshe Shelley aboard the *Don Juan*." [Hellas] (1:2) Fall 90, p. 244-245.
"Percy Bysshe Shelley Is Shown, by Lord Byron, the Fifth Canto of Don Juan, Ravenna, 1821." [SoCoast] (9) Fall 90, p. 26.
"The Poodle in Offit's Bayou: Galveston, Texas, 1964." [HolCrit] (27:2) Ap 90, p. 18.
"The Puritan Commander of the Firing Squad During the English Civil War." [Interim] (9:2) Fall-Wint 90-91, p. 21.
"The Rev. Jocelyn Walker, Fellow of New College, Oxford, Explains the Expulsion of Percy Bysshe Shelley." [Hellas] (1:2) Fall 90, p. 245-246.
"The Reverend George Whitefield, on His Orphanage, Savannah, Ga., 1735." [NewYorkQ] (43) Fall 90, p. 71.
"Self-Taught." [FreeL] (6) Aut 90, p. 7.
"Shelley Sees Spirits, Casa Magni, Bay of Spezia, June, 1822." [Poem] (64) N 90, p. 68-69.
"Sophia Starling Attends the Episcopal Church in Denver, 1874." [AntigR] (81/82) Spr-Sum 90, p. 61.
"Sophia Starling Considers the Sinclairs, Colorado Territory, 1873." [AntigR] (81/82) Spr-Sum 90, p. 62-63.
"Sophia Starling Writes to Her Sister in England: Denver, September, 1873." [InterPR] (16:2) Fall 90, p. 128-129.
"Spitting Like the Treed Lynx." [Gypsy] (15) 90, p. 39.
"Summer in Beirut." [ChatR] (10:3) Spr 90, p. 45.
"Tapestries of Song." [ChamLR] (4:1, #7) Fall 90, p. 31.
"This Far From Town." [DogRR] (9:2, #18) Aut 90, p. 8.
"While There's Still Time." [SwampR] (6) Sum-Fall 90, p. 93-94.
"Whittling." [HampSPR] (Anthology 1975-1990) 90, p. 226.
"Wilbur Wright Remembers His First Landing." [SpoonRQ] (15:2) Spr 90, p. 64.

1270. COP, Gilles
"Ce soir j'ai vu une rose." [PraF] (11:1) Spr 90, p. 154.
"Paris" (in French). [PraF] (11:1) Spr 90, p. 152.
"Paris" (tr. by Jane Brierley). [PraF] (11:1) Spr 90, p. 153.
"Tonight I saw a rose" (tr. by Jane Brierley). [PraF] (11:1) Spr 90, p. 155.

1271. COPE, Steven R.
"Standing in November." [Outbr] (21) 90, p. 11.
"Tokens." [InterPR] (16:1) Spr 90, p. 116-117.
"Withdrawal." [InterPR] (16:1) Spr 90, p. 117.

1272. COPE, Wendy
"Valentine." [Quarry] (39:1) Wint 90, p. 15.

1273. COPELAND, Helen
"The Whistle in the Field." [NewRena] (8:1, #24) Spr 90, p. 92.

1274. COPITHORNE, Judith
"Disordering." [WestCL] (24:2) Fall 90, p. 29-30.
"Pantoun for the New Year, New Year's Eve 1989." [WestCL] (24:2) Fall 90, p. 25.
"She has 2 minds." [WestCL] (24:2) Fall 90, p. 27.
"We can't afford to write or not to." [WestCL] (24:2) Fall 90, p. 32.

1275. CORBEIL, Louis-Philippe
"And we'll head for the horror of loveless beds" (tr. by Jane Brierley). [PraF] (11:1) Spr 90, p. 91, 93.
"L'Aurore blonde fond sur la chose endormie." [PraF] (11:1) Spr 90, p. 86.
"Et nous irons vers l'horreur des lits sans amour." [PraF] (11:1) Spr 90, p. 90, 92.
"I have played in the optics of human perspectives" (tr. by Jane Brierley). [PraF] (11:1) Spr 90, p. 89.
"J'ai joué dans l'optique des perspectives humaines." [PraF] (11:1) Spr 90, p. 88.
"Pale dawn melts over the sleeping thing" (tr. by Jane Brierley). [PraF] (11:1) Spr 90, p. 87.

1276. CORBETT, William
"One Day." [NewAW] (6) Spr 90, p. 26.
"Roast hot red pepper." [Talisman] (5) Fall 90, p. 106.
"Twined Dream." [NewAW] (6) Spr 90, p. 25.

117

CORBETT-FIACCO

1277. CORBETT-FIACCO, Christopher
"True Stories." [ChironR] (9:1) Spr 90, p. 26.
1278. CORCORAN, Kelvin
"Lyric Lyric" (Selections: 2 poems). [Screens] (2) 90, p. 168.
1279. CORDING, Robert
"All Souls' Morning." [Nat] (250:25) 25 Je 90, p. 904.
"Goat." [Poetry] (157:3) D 90, p. 153-154.
"Hurricane." [IndR] (14:1) Wint 90, p. 35-38.
"Starlings." [NewEngR] (13:2) Wint 90, p. 153.
1280. CORE, Elizabeth
"Recycling a Memory." [CarolQ] (43:1) Fall 90, p. 83.
1281. COREY, Anne
"Plain Geometry." [SinW] (40) Spr 90, p. 99-100.
1282. COREY, Stephen
"Making the Mouth." [KenR] (NS 12:3) Sum 90, p. 37-38.
1283. CORKERY, Christopher Jane
"Patio." [Atlantic] (266:5) N 90, p. 84.
1284. CORLESS-SMITH, Martin
"Directing a LOVE STORY." [CimR] (93) O 90, p. 54.
"The Meal." [CimR] (93) O 90, p. 53.
1285. CORLEY, Wm. J.
"Chocolate Ice Cream." [PoetryUSA] (5:3) Fall 90, p. 23.
CORMACK, Karen Mac
See Mac CORMACK, Karen
1286. CORMAN, Cid
"1/ There Are No Others." [BelPoJ] (40:4) Sum 90, p. 21.
"2/ The Four-Letter Word." [BelPoJ] (40:4) Sum 90, p. 21.
"3/ The Shuffle." [BelPoJ] (40:4) Sum 90, p. 21.
"All Yours or Nothing Doing" (for Jan, 45 poems). [ShadowP] (1) Spr 90, p. 1-56.
"The Baptism." [ShadowP] (1) Spr 90, p. 71.
"Dans la Chaleur Vacante (In the Vacant Heat)" (Selections: 4 poems, Published by
Mercure de France, 1961, tr. of André Du Bouchet). [Avec] (3:1) 90, p.
78-81.
"The Hospitality." [ShadowP] (1) Spr 90, p. 72-73.
"The Offerings." [ShadowP] (1) Spr 90, p. 74.
"The Puzzle." [ShadowP] (1) Spr 90, p. 73-74.
CORMIER-SHEKERJIAN, Regina de
See DeCORMIER-SHEKERJIAN, Regina
1287. CORN, Alfred
"Cannot Be a Tourist." [NewRep] (202:23) 4 Je 90, p. 28.
"Contemporary Culture and the Letter 'K'." [GrandS] (9:2) Wint 90, p. 94-95.
"Infernal Regions and the Invisible Girl." [Poetry] (156:5) Ag 90, p. 287-291.
"The Jaunt." [Salm] (88/89) Fall 90-Wint 91, p. 154-155.
"My Neighbor, the Distinguished Count." [NewRep] (203:20) 12 N 90, p. 38.
"Resolutions." [Nat] (250:24) 18 Je 90, p. 870.
1288. CORNFORD, Adam
"R.E.M." (for my unborn child). [CityLR] (4) 90, p. 159-160.
1289. CORNIERE, François de
"After the Storm" (tr. by Judith Cowan). [Trans] (23) Spr 90, p. 37-38.
"Token" (tr. by Judith Cowan). [Trans] (23) Spr 90, p. 38.
1290. CORNISH, Sam
"A Garvey Man." [Agni] (31/32) 90, p. 157-158.
1291. CORSE, Elizabeth
"The Edible Woman." [Grain] (18:4) Wint 90, p. 45.
"I Have Trouble with the Endings." [Grain] (18:4) Wint 90, p. 46.
"No Love in This Poem." [Grain] (18:4) Wint 90, p. 44.
1292. CORTEZ, Carlos
"Chickens on the Top." [Pig] (16) 90, p. 55.
1293. CORTEZ, Jayne
"Atmospheric Burn" (For the Print Making Workshop). [Confr] (42/43) Spr-Sum
90, p. 34.
"Global Inequalities." [Confr] (42/43) Spr-Sum 90, p. 35.
"New York's Bullfighter Gums." [Confr] (42/43) Spr-Sum 90, p. 36.
1294. CORY, Cynthia Jay
"Everything About Winter." [AmerPoR] (19:6) N-D 90, p. 18.
"Moon / Mirror." [AmerPoR] (19:6) N-D 90, p. 18.

"The Plum Tree: Self-Portrait." [AmerPoR] (19:6) N-D 90, p. 18.
"The Terminology of Winter (How the Past Exists)." [AmerPoR] (19:6) N-D 90, p. 17.
"What Is America?" [AmerPoR] (19:6) N-D 90, p. 18.
1295. CORY, Jim
"A Name." [JamesWR] (7:3) Spr 90, p. 14.
"Straight." [Pearl] (11) Sum 90, p. 38.
"To Cross." [JamesWR] (7:3) Spr 90, p. 14.
1296. COSBY, Nancy
"American Scene." [Writer] (103:9) S 90, p. 21.
1297. COSEM, Michel
"Je t'appelle du fond de l'hiver." [Os] (31) 90, p. 19.
"Quel oiseau étonné." [Os] (31) 90, p. 18.
1298. COSENS, Susan
"At Dusk." [SingHM] (18) 90, p. 39.
1299. COSIER, Tony
"Below the Dam Site: The Caribou." [Amelia] (6:1, #16) 90, p. 110.
1300. COSMA, Flavia
"Anniversary" (tr. by Roger Greenwald and the author). [Writ] (21) 89 c1990, p. 9.
"As If in Child's Play" (tr. by Roger Greenwald). [PoetryE] (29) Spr 90, p. 135.
"Autumn Jumps" (tr. by Roger Greenwald and the author). [Writ] (21) 89 c1990, p. 8.
"Eagles Are Whirling" (tr. by Roger Greenwald and the author). [Writ] (21) 89 c1990, p. 13.
"New Year's Eve" (tr. by Roger Greenwald and the author). [Writ] (21) 89 c1990, p. 11.
"No Bird" (tr. by Roger Greenwald). [PoetryE] (29) Spr 90, p. 137.
"Now I Know" (tr. by Roger Greenwald). [PoetryE] (29) Spr 90, p. 136.
"The Other Window" (tr. by Roger Greenwald and the author). [Writ] (21) 89 c1990, p. 12.
"Questions" (tr. by Roger Greenwald). [PoetryE] (29) Spr 90, p. 134.
"Ready to Set Out" (tr. by Roger Greenwald and the author). [Writ] (21) 89 c1990, p. 7.
"Reconciliation" (tr. by Roger Greenwald). [PoetryE] (29) Spr 90, p. 138.
"Switching Shadows" (tr. by Roger Greenwald and the author). [Writ] (21) 89 c1990, p. 10.
"You, Who Have Left" (tr. by Roger Greenwald). [PoetryE] (29) Spr 90, p. 139.
1301. COSTA, Chad
"Summer Nights." [PoetryUSA] (5:2) Sum 90, p. 7.
1302. COSTA, Tina
"The Summer of the Yellow Bikini" (In memory of Laura Jacomelli perished in a bombing while attempting to reach a church shelter, Italy 1944). [Vis] (33) 90, p. 27.
1303. COSTOPOULOS, Olga
"Pilgrimage '88." [Dandel] (17:2) Fall-Wint 90, p. 38.
1304. COTTER, Craig
"Anna's Hummingbird." [NegC] (10:1) 90, p. 44.
"At the Bar" (for William Carlos Williams). [PoetryUSA] ([5:4?]) Wint 90, p. 18.
"Beside the arroyo." [NegC] (10:1) 90, p. 46.
"Fifteen." [NegC] (10:1) 90, p. 45.
"For Leonora." [NegC] (10:1) 90, p. 42.
"I've Got to Write." [PoetryUSA] ([5:4?]) Wint 90, p. 18.
"To Leonora." [NegC] (10:1) 90, p. 43.
"You remember." [PoetryUSA] ([5:4?]) Wint 90, p. 18.
1305. COTTER, Patrick
"The Voyeuress of Mintrop Strasse" (for D.D.). [Quarry] (39:1) Wint 90, p. 69.
1306. COUCH, Larry
"Biography" (tr. of Joyce Mansour). [Vis] (32) 90, p. 43.
"I Planted a Hand" (tr. of Joyce Mansour). [Vis] (32) 90, p. 43.
1307. COULEHAN, Jack
"All Souls' Day." [SoCoast] (8) Spr 90, p. 50.
"A Blessing for Midgets and Dwarves." [GreenMR] (NS 4:1) Spr-Sum 90, p. 107-108.
"Buried Tooth." [HiramPoR] (47) Wint 90, p. 20-21.
"The Dynamizer and the Oscilloclast" (for Albert Abrams, an American quack). [ManhatPR] (11) [89?], p. 22.

"The Garden of Paradise." [Parting] (3:1) Sum 90, p. 16.
"Good News." [OxfordM] (6:1) Spr-Sum 90, p. 52.
"Horses Drinking" (for Al Clah). [HiramPoR] (47) Wint 90, p. 18-19.
"My Poetry Teacher Sells Used Cars" (for Rosaly). [Wind] (20:67) 90, p. 11.
"Mysterious Shoes." [WebR] (14:2) Spr 90, p. 22-23.
"Rock of Ages." [Wind] (20:67) 90, p. 12-13.
"Skinwalkers." [ManhatPR] (11) [89?], p. 23.
"The Sorrow of the World." [WebR] (14:2) Spr 90, p. 21-22.
1308. COULETTE, Henri
    "The Art of Translation." [Raritan] (10:2) Fall 90, p. 18.
    "At the Grave of the Fourth Man" (for Jean Maloney). [Raritan] (10:2) Fall 90, p.
        21.
    "Coming to Terms." [NewYorker] (66:37) 29 O 90, p. 42.
    "Correspondence." [Poetry] (156:3) Je 90, p. 136.
    "Horace, IV, 1." [Raritan] (10:2) Fall 90, p. 19-20.
    "Lines for a Blue Lady." [Raritan] (10:2) Fall 90, p. 25.
    "Memoir." [Raritan] (10:2) Fall 90, p. 24.
    "Period Piece." [Raritan] (10:2) Fall 90, p. 20.
    "Postscript." [Raritan] (10:2) Fall 90, p. 23.
    "The Renaissance in England." [Raritan] (10:2) Fall 90, p. 22.
1309. COULSON, Joseph
    "After the Rain." [OnTheBus] (2:1, #5) Spr 90, p. 56.
COURCY, Lynne H. de
    See DeCOURCY, Lynne H.
1310. COURTS, Patrick L.
    "Still Life." [HawaiiR] (15:1, #31) Wint 90, p. 20-21.
1311. COUSINEAU, Phil
    "Tarantula." [PoetryUSA] ([5:4?]) Wint 90, p. 17.
1312. COUTO, Nancy Vieira
    "Magalhães' Last Testament." [Epoch] (39:1/2) 90, p. 54.
    "Tea Party." [Epoch] (39:1/2) 90, p. 53.
1313. COVEY, Patricia
    "Ghost Story." [WillowS] (25) Wint 90, p. 35-36.
1314. COWAN, Judith
    "After the Storm" (tr. of François de Cornière). [Trans] (23) Spr 90, p. 37-38.
    "Token" (tr. of François de Cornière). [Trans] (23) Spr 90, p. 38.
1315. COWAN, Thomas Dale
    "True Places." [ChangingM] (21) Wint-Spr 90, p. 29.
1316. COWING, Sue
    "In Time, for Margaret Mee." [ChamLR] (4:1, #7) Fall 90, p. 119.
1317. COWSER, Robert
    "Now." [LakeSR] (24) 90, p. 23.
    "Winter Beacon." [EngJ] (79:6) O 90, p. 95.
1318. COX, Larry
    "Louie." [Plain] (10:3) Spr 90, p. 24.
1319. COX, Wayne
    "After All" (tr. of Miquel Martí i Pol, w. Lourdes Manyé i Martí). [Poetry] (155:6)
        Mr 90, p. 400.
    "If I Talk About Death" (tr. of Miquel Martí i Pol, w. Lourdes Manyé i Martí).
        [Poetry] (155:6) Mr 90, p. 401.
    "Rooms" (tr. of Miquel Martí i Pol, w. Lourdes Manyé i Martí). [Poetry] (155:6) Mr
        90, p. 399.
1320. COYLE, Charles
    "Dover." [LullwaterR] (2:1) Wint 90, p. 30.
    "For John Berryman." [HayF] (7) Fall-Wint 90, p. 63.
1321. COYNE, Peter
    "The Winter Drowse." [Vis] (33) 90, p. 33.
CRABBE, Chris Wallace
    See WALLACE-CRABBE, Chris
1322. CRABTREE, David
    "A Secret: Four Images." [Stand] (31:4) Aut 90, p. 66-69.
1323. CRAMER, Steven
    "The Accident." [Atlantic] (266:6) D 90, p. 112.
    "Devotion Street." [Crazy] (38) Spr 90, p. 25-26.
    "From the Corner of His Eye" (Genesis 22). [TarRP] (30:1) Fall 90, p. 39-40.
    "The Parade, 1968." [TarRP] (30:1) Fall 90, p. 40-41.

1324. CRATE, Joan
"The Blizzard Moans My Name." [CanLit] (124/125) Spr-Sum 90, p. 18.
"Negative of You." [CanLit] (124/125) Spr-Sum 90, p. 16.
"Shawnandithit (Last of the Beothuks)." [CanLit] (124/125) Spr-Sum 90, p. 17.
1325. CRAVES, Peter
"The Legal Killing of Elephants." [OnTheBus] (2:2/3:1, #6/7) Sum-Fall 90 Wint-Spr
91, p. 65-66.
"The Mystified Staring Babies." [OnTheBus] (2:2/3:1, #6/7) Sum-Fall 90 Wint-Spr
91, p. 66.
1326. CRAWFORD, C. Slade
"Triumph of the Holy Cross" (Thoughts on Jacob's Ladder). [EmeraldCR] (1990)
c89, p. 84-86.
1327. CREASY-FONTAINE, Paula
"Untitled: Being a little kid and trying to masturbate is rough." [ChironR] (9:4) Wint
90, p. 16.
"Untitled: French Tickler he says proudly." [ChironR] (9:4) Wint 90, p. 16.
"Writing As Cunt or Eat Me Just You Try It." [ChironR] (9:4) Wint 90, p. 16.
1328. CREBOLDER, Emma
"Four Swim Sonnets" (tr. by Claire Nicolas White). [Trans] (24) Fall 90, p.
127-130.
1329. CREEDE, Gerald
"Resumé." [WestCL] (24:1) Spr 90, p. 61-69.
1330. CREEGAN, Catherine M.
"Trying to Get Across the Line." [Bogg] (63) 90, p. 37.
1331. CREEL, Melanie Paige
"Contrived." [EmeraldCR] (1990) c89, p. 53-54.
1332. CREELEY, Robert
"Abstract." [WestCL] (24:3) Wint 90, p. 28.
"Body." [MichQR] (29:4) Fall 90, p. 681-682.
"Chain." [BelPoJ] (40:4) Sum 90, p. 19.
"The Farm." [WestCL] (24:3) Wint 90, p. 16.
"Figure of Fun." [WestCL] (24:3) Wint 90, p. 29.
"Have a Heart." [WestCL] (24:3) Wint 90, p. 29.
"Old." [WestCL] (24:3) Wint 90, p. 28.
"The Old Days." [WestCL] (24:3) Wint 90, p. 26-27.
"Old Mister Moonlight." [Notus] (5:1) Spr 90, p. 19.
"Old Words." [Notus] (5:1) Spr 90, p. 18.
"Shadow." [BelPoJ] (40:4) Sum 90, p. 19.
"Skin." [BelPoJ] (40:4) Sum 90, p. 20.
"Waldoboro Eve." [WestCL] (24:3) Wint 90, p. 29.
1333. CREIGHTON, Jane
"Walk softly & carry a wept stream." [WestCL] (24:3) Wint 90, p. 83-86.
1334. CREMONA, Antonio
"Moonglow" (Agrigento). [Footwork] 90, p. 105.
1335. CRESWELL, Marc A.
"11:42 p.m., May 07, 1989." [EmeraldCR] (1990) c89, p. 57-58.
1336. CREW, Louie
"Calling All Epic Seers" (No Closet Lyricists Need Apply). [Spirit] (10:2) 90, p.
148-150.
"For a Spell." [NegC] (10:2/3) 90, p. 62-63.
"Terminal." [Amelia] (6:2, #17) 90, p. 13.
1337. CREWS, Judson
"The Cambrian Dusk Should Evoke Some." [Pembroke] (22) 90, p. 49.
"Haunted, As If. Haunted with a Fear." [ChironR] (9:3) Aut 90, p. 23.
"How Can It Be That My Sexual Imagery." [Pembroke] (22) 90, p. 49.
"Is There a Hiss of Love As Snakes Get Together?" [NewYorkQ] (41) Spr 90, p.
68.
"A Long Line." [HampSPR] (Anthology 1975-1990) 90, p. 42.
"The residue or fall-out flaking my." [WritersF] (16) Fall 90, p. 54.
"She Laid a Lot of Eggs, Blew Them." [Pembroke] (22) 90, p. 50.
"So, Rexroth." [HampSPR] (Anthology 1975-1990) 90, p. 41-42.
"That Diet Cock, Lite, That Never Cums Off." [AnotherCM] (21) 90, p. 22.
"An Unaccountable Meshing of Gears." [Pembroke] (22) 90, p. 50.
"What Is Her Vulva Really Like -- a Tiger." [NewYorkQ] (43) Fall 90, p. 44.
1338. CREWS, Mary
"For Alison, My Niece, Recovering from a Gunshot Wound to the Head." [Crucible]

(26) Fall 90, p. 63-64.
1339. CRICHTON, Juliet
"The Angry Poem." [HayF] (7) Fall-Wint 90, p. 90-91.
1340. CRISICK, Maureen Micus
"Linear Arrangement." [CumbPR] (9:2) Spr 90, p. 10.
1341. CRIST, Robert
"The Lizards of Ios" (Ios, 7-7-89, for Michael & Robin Waters). [PraS] (64:3) Fall
90, p. 51-52.
1342. CROHN, Frank T.
"Throwaway." [NewYorkQ] (43) Fall 90, p. 65.
1343. CROLL, Su
"Consider the House." [AntigR] (80) Wint 90, p. 131.
"A Few Days Left." [PoetryC] (11:1) Spr 90, p. 27.
"Going to the Butcher's with Daddy." [Grain] (18:4) Wint 90, p. 72-73.
"Here Is the House That Has Folded." [AntigR] (80) Wint 90, p. 129.
"Last Days." [Grain] (18:1) Spr 90, p. 58.
"Only Forest." [AntigR] (80) Wint 90, p. 130.
1344. CROMER, J. J.
"The Mourning Dove." [Plain] (10:2) Wint 90, p. 13.
1345. CRONSHEY, R.
"The End of Undressing Is the End of Flesh." [Caliban] (8) 90, p. 34-35.
"The Necessity of an Inner Nativity." [Caliban] (8) 90, p. 36-37.
1346. CROOKER, Barbara
"All Soul's Day." [WestB] (26) 90, p. 48.
"The Iris Work in the Year's Rhythm." [WestB] (26) 90, p. 131.
"Learning to Speak Neurosurgery" (Published in *Poets on*, 1986 and in *Muse*,
September/October 1989). [Kaleid] (21) Sum-Fall 90, p. 44.
"Looking for Loons." [WestB] (26) 90, p. 47.
"Meditations on Grass" (for Anne Zellars). [WestB] (26) 90, p. 46.
1347. CROSBIE, Lynn
"Miss Pamela's Mercy" (for Pamela Des Barres). [WestCL] (24:3) Wint 90, p.
77-79.
1348. CROSS, Elsa
"Bacchantes" (Selections: I, VII, XV, tr. by John Olver Simon). [OnTheBus] (2:1,
#5) Spr 90, p. 185-187.
1349. CROSSLAND, Richard I., Jr.
"Eternal Lights" (for Penelope, 1949-1987). [BellR] (13:1, #27) Spr 90, p. 40.
1350. CROW, Mary
"Afternoon" (tr. of Jorge Teillier). [CrabCR] (6:3) Spr 90, p. 19.
"Cityscape." [RiverS] (32) [90?], p. 75.
"Far Away, From My Hill" (tr. of Olga Orozco). [AmerPoR] (19:1) Ja-F 90, p. 6.
"Hard Things." [HampSPR] (Anthology 1975-1990) 90, p. 206.
"In the Secret House of Night" (tr. of Jorge Teillier). [CrabCR] (6:3) Spr 90, p. 19.
"It Arrives in Every Storm" (tr. of Olga Orozco). [AmerPoR] (19:1) Ja-F 90, p. 6.
"Pearl Divers." [MidwQ] (32:1) Aut 90, p. 81-82.
"The White Lily." [HampSPR] (Anthology 1975-1990) 90, p. 205.
1351. CROWELL, Doug
"Under Late Capitalism." [SlipS] (10) 90, p. 75.
1352. CROZIER, Lorna
"Angel of Bees." [Event] (19:1) Spr 90, p. 66.
"Angel of Mercy." [Event] (19:1) Spr 90, p. 62.
"The Baker." [Descant] (21:4/22:1, #71/72) Wint-Spr 90-91, p. 91.
"Canada Day Parade." [Grain] (18:3) Fall 90, p. 10-11.
"The Gardens Wtihin Us." [Descant] (21:4/22:1, #71/72) Wint-Spr 90-91, p. 92.
"The Motionless Angel." [Event] (19:1) Spr 90, p. 63.
"News Flash from the Fashion Magazines." [Grain] (18:3) Fall 90, p. 12-13.
"Plato's Angel." [Event] (19:1) Spr 90, p. 65.
"Small Resurrections." [Grain] (18:3) Fall 90, p. 14.
"The Unknown Angel." [Event] (19:1) Spr 90, p. 64-65.
"Waiting for the Test Results." [Descant] (21:4/22:1, #71/72) Wint-Spr 90-91, p.
90.
1353. CRUMMEY, Michael
"Kingston, Friday Afternoon." [AntigR] (83) Aut 90, p. 107-108.
"The Weather" (for Oscar Romero). [AntigR] (83) Aut 90, p. 109-110.
1354. CRUMP, Charles H.
"Perspective." [BellArk] (6:5) S-O 90, p. 9.

1355. CRUMP, Galbraith M.
"Houses in a Landscape, Saint George's Cove, Forillon, Quebec." [SewanR] (98:1)
Wint 90, p. 23.
"Shadow and Light." [SewanR] (98:1) Wint 90, p. 23.
1356. CRUNK, T.
"Christmas Morning." [LaurelR] (24:1) Wint 90, p. 70.
"Until the Parodist Arrives, We'll Have to Settle for These Prophets" (for Jonah).
[Wind] (20:67) 90, p. 14.
1357. CRUNK, T. L.
"Post-Metaphysical Man at Home." [HampSPR] (Anthology 1975-1990) 90, p. 218.
"Winter." [HampSPR] (Anthology 1975-1990) 90, p. 218.
1358. CRUZ, Juana Inés de la, Sor
"145. Este, que ves, engaño colorido." [WashR] (16:2) Ag-S 90, p. 20.
"147. Rosa divina que en gentil cultura." [WashR] (16:2) Ag-S 90, p. 20.
"156. Portia, what passion, what blind pain" (tr. by Susan Smith Nash). [WashR]
(16:2) Ag-S 90, p. 21.
"156. Que pasión, Porcia, qué dolor tan ciego." [WashR] (16:2) Ag-S 90, p. 21.
"164. This evening, my dear, when I was speaking to you" (tr. by Susan Smith
Nash). [WashR] (16:2) Ag-S 90, p. 21.
"Divine rose, you exist in a genteel culture" (tr. by Susan Smith Nash). [WashR]
(16:2) Ag-S 90, p. 20.
"Esta tarde, mi bien, cuando te hablaba." [WashR] (16:2) Ag-S 90, p. 21.
"What you see is a painted fraud" (tr. by Susan Smith Nash). [WashR] (16:2) Ag-S
90, p. 20.
CRUZ, Luis Gonzalez
See GONZALEZ-CRUZ, Luis
1359. CRUZ, Victor Hernandez
"Good Waters." [PoetryUSA] (5:3) Fall 90, p. 12.
"Tradición." [PoetryUSA] (5:3) Fall 90, p. 12.
1360. CRUZKATZ, Ida
"The Noise." [ManhatPR] (12) [90?], p. 15.
1361. CSABANE, Szabó
"There Are Some Countries" (tr. of Sándor Kányádi, w. Len Roberts). [MidAR]
(10:1) 90, p. 59.
1362. CSAMER, M. E. (Mary Ellen)
"Daughter." [Dandel] (17:1) Spr-Sum 90, p. 15.
"Learning the Words." [Quarry] (39:4) Fall 1990, p. 52-57.
"Shadow Man." [Event] (19:2) Sum 90, p. 78.
1363. CSOORI, Sándor
"Ague" (tr. by Len Roberts). [PoetryE] (30) Fall 90, p. 15.
"Barbarous Prayer" (tr. by Len Roberts and László Vértes). [AmerPoR] (19:5) S-O
90, p. 26.
"Because There Was a Time" (tr. by Len Roberts and Claudia Zimmerman).
[CrabCR] (6:3) Spr 90, p. 10.
"Because There Was a Time" (tr. by Len Roberts and Claudia Zimmerman).
[ArtfulD] (18/19) 90, p. 23.
"Day by Day" (tr. by Len Roberts and Miklós Horváth). [ArtfulD] (18/19) 90, p. 24.
"Day by Day" (tr. by Len Roberts and Miklós Horváth). [Chelsea] (49) 90, p. 122.
"Dozing on the Train" (tr. by Len Roberts and László Vértes). [MidAR] (10:1) 90, p.
73, 75.
"Éjszakai Utazás Némethonban." [MidAR] (10:1) 90, p. 86, 88.
"Everyday History" (tr. by Len Roberts). [MidAR] (10:1) 90, p. 81.
"Green Twig in My Hand" (Kezemben Zöld ág, tr. by Len Roberts and Claudia
Zimmerman). [Plain] (10:3) Spr 90, p. 29.
"A Harmadik Nap Esni Kezdett a Hó." [MidAR] (10:1) 90, p. 82, 84.
"I'd Rather Stay at Home" (tr. by Len Roberts). [CrabCR] (6:3) Spr 90, p. 9-10.
"Let the Timbrel Rattle" (Szóljon a csörgódob, tr. by Len Roberts). [Plain] (10:2)
Wint 90, p. 32.
"Memories of November" (tr. by Len Roberts). [CrabCR] (6:3) Spr 90, p. 9.
"Message" (tr. by Len Roberts, Miklós Telbisz and Gábor Töró). [NowestR] (28:1)
90, p. 101.
"Mindennapi Történelem." [MidAR] (10:1) 90, p. 80.
"A Night Journey in Germany" (tr. by Len Roberts and Tibor Tengerdi). [MidAR]
(10:1) 90, p. 87, 89.
"On the Third Day the Snow Began to Fall" (tr. by Len Roberts, Miklós Telbisz, and
László Vértes). [MidAR] (10:1) 90, p. 83, 85.

"On the Third Day the Snow Began to Fall" (tr. by Len Roberts, Miklos Telbisz, and László Vértes). [Chelsea] (49) 90, p. 123.
"People, Boughs" (tr. by Len Roberts and László Vértes). [AmerPoR] (19:5) S-O 90, p. 25.
"Postponed Nightmare" (tr. by Len Roberts and László Vertes). [LitR] (33:3) Spr 90, p. 293.
"Prophesying About Your Time" (tr. by Len Roberts and Judit Vértes). [AmerPoR] (19:5) S-O 90, p. 25-26.
"Sea Gull-Line" (tr. by Len Roberts and László Vértes). [Chelsea] (49) 90, p. 124.
"Szendergés Vonaton." [MidAR] (10:1) 90, p. 72, 74.
"A Thin, Black Band" (tr. by Len Roberts and Tibor Tengerdi). [MidAR] (10:1) 90, p. 77, 79.
"Vékony, Fekete Csík." [MidAR] (10:1) 90, p. 76, 78.
"The Wind with Its Nerves" (tr. by Len Roberts). [Vis] (33) 90, p. 25-26.
"The Wind with Its Nerves" (tr. by Len Roberts). [Verse] (7:3) Wint 90, p. 100.
"You're Rising and Vanishing" (tr. by Len Roberts and László Vértes). [AmerPoR] (19:5) S-O 90, p. 26.

1364. CUADRA, Pablo Antonio
"The Ceiba" (tr. by W. S. Merwin). [Trans] (24) Fall 90, p. 196-198.

1365. CUCULLU, Lois
"The Hongch'on River" (tr. of Shin Kyung-rim, w. Sym Myoung-ho). [PoetL] (85:2) Sum 90, p. 37-38.

1366. CULBERSON, Steven
"Climbing to Ngorongoro." [Field] (42) Spr 90, p. 29-30.
"The Killing of the Cobra." [Field] (42) Spr 90, p. 31-32.

1367. CULHANE, Brian
"Caelian." [SenR] (20:2) Fall 90, p. 37.
"Capitoline." [SenR] (20:2) Fall 90, p. 36.
"Palatine." [SenR] (20:2) Fall 90, p. 38.

1368. CULLA, Daniel de
"Luz I." [LindLM] (9:3) Jl-S 90, p. 27.
"Luz II." [LindLM] (9:3) Jl-S 90, p. 27.
"Luz III." [LindLM] (9:3) Jl-S 90, p. 27.

1369. CULLEN, Michael
"Breath." [OnTheBus] (2:2/3:1, #6/7) Sum-Fall 90 Wint-Spr 91, p. 67-68.
"Other Worlds." [OnTheBus] (2:1, #5) Spr 90, p. 57-58.
"Pumpkin Seeds." [OnTheBus] (2:1, #5) Spr 90, p. 58.
"Shadows." [OnTheBus] (2:2/3:1, #6/7) Sum-Fall 90 Wint-Spr 91, p. 67.

1370. CULLEY, Peter
"Der Hirt Auf Dem Felsen (The Shepherd on the Rock) after F. Schubert" (for Susan Lord and Lisa Goldberg). [WestCL] (24:1) Spr 90, p. 51-53.

1371. CULLY, Barbara
"Because Everything Is Passed On." [RiverS] (32) [90?], p. 77.
"Field Tone." [Sonora] (19) Spr-Sum 90, p. 3-4.
"Hatfield Apts." [WillowS] (25) Wint 90, p. 16-17.
"In Their City, the Desert." [RiverS] (32) [90?], p. 76.
"Once You've Collected Your Selves Like Books About You." [WillowS] (25) Wint 90, p. 14-15.
"Straw on Canvas" (Anselm Kiefer, MOMA, 1989). [Sonora] (19) Spr-Sum 90, p. 1-2.

1372. CULROSS, Michael
"The President." [Spirit] (10:2) 90, p. 47-48.

1373. CUMBERLAND, Sharon
"Piney Point." [PoetL] (85:1) Spr 90, p. 42.

1374. CUMMINGS, Tim
"The Collector." [Bogg] (62) 90, p. 20.

1375. CUMPIANO, Ina
"In Vitro." [SenR] (20:2) Fall 90, p. 61-62.
"To Jimmy, Found in His Room at 28." [SenR] (20:2) Fall 90, p. 63-64.

1376. CUNEO, Pablo
"On the Bars." [PoetryUSA] (5:1) Spr 90, p. 17.

1377. CUNNINGHAM, Mark
"All Through March." [MidwQ] (32:1) Aut 90, p. 83.
"All Through Winter." [LitR] (33:3) Spr 90, p. 318.
"Between the Shadow and Its Object." [SpoonRQ] (15:1) Wint 90, p. 24.

124

CUNNINGHAM

1378. CUNNINGHAM, Michael
"Here Comes Debbie." [Bogg] (63) 90, p. 36.
1379. CUOMO, Chris
"The Wax Problem." [SinW] (41) Sum-Fall 90, p. 114-115.
1380. CURBELO, Silvia
"Because Nothing Stands Still." [LindLM] (9:3) Jl-S 90, p. 5.
"Bedtime Stories" (after Chagall). [Caliban] (9) 90, p. 79-81.
"Listening to a White Man Play the Blues." [WillowS] (26) Spr 90, p. 17.
"Photograph from Berlin." [LindLM] (9:3) Jl-S 90, p. 5.
"Some Nights You Crank Up the Car Radio and Just Drive." [WillowS] (26) Spr 90,
        p. 15-16.
"Summer Storm." [LindLM] (9:3) Jl-S 90, p. 5.
1381. CURL, John
"I'm Still Alive!" [PoetryUSA] ([5:4?]) Wint 90, p. 11.
1382. CURLEY, Daniel
"Going Ahead." [Ascent] (15:1) 90, p. 82.
1383. CURRY, Kita Shantiris
"Three Chairs in Creel, Mexico." [OnTheBus] (2:1, #5) Spr 90, p. 59.
1384. CURTIS, Craig
"Narcissus." [KanQ] (22:1/2) Wint-Spr 90, p. 160-161.
"Now." [KanQ] (22:1/2) Wint-Spr 90, p. 161.
1385. CURTIS, David
"Creative Process." [FourQ] (4:1) Spr 90, p. 27.
"Mater Diminuendo." [FourQ] (4:1) Spr 90, p. 28.
1386. CURTIS, Mary Louise
"Cat and Flowers." [EmeraldCR] (1990) c89, p. 12.
1387. CURTIS, Rex
"Puzzle of Foreclosure." [JamesWR] (7:2) Wint 90, p. 13.
1388. CUSAC, Anne-Marie
"Joanie: Moncton, 1946." [TriQ] (80) Wint 90-91, p. 36-37.
"Mama's Dream." [TriQ] (80) Wint 90-91, p. 34-35.
"Poem for Jade." [TriQ] (80) Wint 90-91, p. 38.
1389. CUSHING, James
"If I Were a Bell." [GreenMR] (NS 4:1) Spr-Sum 90, p. 86.
"Misty." [Asylum] (5:4) 90, p. 26.
"Misty." [MassR] (31:3) Aut 90, p. 356.
"Some Enchanted Evening." [GreenMR] (NS 4:1) Spr-Sum 90, p. 85.
"Some Enchanted Evening." [MassR] (31:3) Aut 90, p. 355.
1390. CUSHMAN, Kim
"Joyful Sacrifice" (tr. of Nina Cassian, w. Barbara Howes). [AmerPoR] (19:1) Ja-F
        90, p. 25.
1391. CUSTER, Chris
"Theme: The Freudian Eve-&-Adam." [Sulfur] (10:1, #26) Spr 90, p. 65-66.
"Three Poems on Larrieu's Le Lit Défait (The Bed Unmade)" (for John Taggart).
        [NowestR] (28:3/29:1) 90-91, p. 179-184.
1392. CUSTIS, Keith
"Whitewater Camp at Black Rock." [PoetL] (85:2) Sum 90, p. 29-30.
1393. CUTLER, Bruce
"Afterlife." [PoetryNW] (31:2) Sum 90, p. 18-20.
"Angel." [SpoonRQ] (15:3) Sum 90, p. 17.
"Elevens." [Shen] (40:1) Spr 90, p. 38.
"News from the North." [SpoonRQ] (15:3) Sum 90, p. 20.
"School, by the Nose." [SpoonRQ] (15:3) Sum 90, p. 18.
"Segesta." [MidwQ] (31:3) Spr 90, p. 351.
"This Magazine Is Full of Poems." [SpoonRQ] (15:3) Sum 90, p. 19-20.
"Unanswered Letters." [MidwQ] (31:3) Spr 90, p. 352.
1394. CUZA MALE, Belkis
"La Canción de Silvia Plath." [LindLM] (9:4) O-D 90, p. 55.
CVETAN, Verda Nobel
        See NOBEL-CVETAN, Verda
1395. CVETIC, Jim
"The Wall." [PennR] (4:2) 90, p. 82-85.
1396. CZARNECKI, Michael
"Healing Powers." [Mildred] (4:1) 90, p. 146.
1397. CZAYKOWSKI, Bogdan
"A Confession" (tr. of Jan Twardowski, w. Iain Higgins). [PoetryE] (29) Spr 90, p.

10-11.
"How many devout books are written" (tr. of Jan Twardowski, w. Iain Higgins).
[PoetryE] (29) Spr 90, p. 9.
"Intimates and Strangers" (tr. of Jan Twardowski, w. Iain Higgins). [PoetryE] (29)
Spr 90, p. 12.
"Justice" (tr. of Jan Twardowski, w. Iain Higgins). [PoetryE] (29) Spr 90, p. 8.
1398. CZECHOWSKI, Heinz
"Niobe" (tr. by Ulrike Weber and Richard Jones). [PoetryE] (29) Spr 90, p. 75.
"We Need Language" (tr. by Ulrike Weber and Richard Jones). [PoetryE] (29) Spr
90, p. 74.
1399. CZURY, Craig
"Paint Island Nursery." [Footwork] 90, p. 78-79.
1400. DABYDEEN, David
"The Servants' Song" (in dialect with English translation). [LitR] (34:1) Fall 90, p.
39-41.
1401. DACEY, Philip
"The Accident." [RiverC] (11:1) Fall 90, p. 55.
"At the Club." [CoalC] (2) D 90, p. 19.
"The Blizzard." [HampSPR] (Anthology 1975-1990) 90, p. 122-123.
"Chiaroscuro." [PoetryNW] (31:3) Aut 90, p. 14-15.
"For the God Poseidon." [FloridaR] (17:2) Fall-Wint 90, p. 31.
"Four Men in a Car." [PoetryNW] (31:3) Aut 90, p. 13.
"Letter to His Daughter." [FreeL] (6) Aut 90, p. 22.
"The Loose Garment" (for a friend who says he wants to wear his life like a loose
garment). [FreeL] (6) Aut 90, p. 20-21.
"Miners' Heaven" (i. m. William Dacey, 1869-1908). [MidwQ] (32:1) Aut 90, p.
84.
"Pilgrimage to Medugorje." [PraS] (64:3) Fall 90, p. 99-101.
"Troy." [CoalC] (2) D 90, p. 2.
"Vigil Strange." [DenQ] (25:2) Fall 90, p. 12-13.
1402. DAEN, Daniel
"Icy" (tr. by Rod Jellema). [Vis] (34) 90, p. 28.
1403. D'AGUIAR, Fred
"Colour Codes." [Quarry] (39:1) Wint 90, p. 16-17.
1404. DAHAN, Edith
"The Picture" (Excerpts, in "Epoques pour la guerre," Flammarion, France, 1984, tr.
by Norma Cole). [Avec] (3:1) 90, p. 60-62.
1405. DAHBOUR, Ahmad
"Our Country" (tr. by Lena Jayyusi and Jeremy Reed). [PaperAir] (4:3) 90, p. 63.
1406. DAHLEN, Beverly
"Hearings (the Effects of Light)." [Sequoia] (33:2) Wint 90, p. 78-93.
DAI, Fang
See FANG, Dai
1407. DAIGON, Ruth
(Anonymous poem). [FreeL] (4) 90.
"It Is Enough." [Footwork] 90, p. 80.
1408. DAIVE, Jean
"Narration d'Equilibre 5-America Domino" (Selections: 12 poems, P.O.L., Paris,
1987, tr. by Etel Adnan). [Avec] (3:1) 90, p. 82-84.
1409. DAKEYO, Paul
"I Belong to the High Day" (tr. by Dennis Egan and Jean-Clarence Lambert, w.
Bradley R. Strahan). [Vis] (32) 90, p. 9.
1410. DALACHINSKY, Steve
"Blues for Lowell." [MoodySI] (22/23) Wint 89-90, p. 27.
DALAIGH, Gofraidh Fionn O
See O DALAIGH, Gofraidh Fionn
1411. DALDORPH, Brian
(Anonymous poem). [FreeL] (4) 90.
"Casualty." [DustyD] (1:2) O 90, p. 8.
"Itch." [Bogg] (62) 90, p. 24.
1412. DALE, Karen
"Corsage." [GreensboroR] (49) Wint 90-91, p. 52.
1413. DALE, Peter
"Portents." [Quarry] (39:1) Wint 90, p. 18.
1414. DALES, Jennifer
"Is a Small Red Bird Like a Heart." [Arc] (24) Spr 90, p. 28-29.

126

1415. DALEY, Michael
"The Gatekeeper." [Hudson] (43:1) Spr 90, p. 104-105.
"In the Water That Comes Before Dawn" (Ios, 7-7-89, for Michael & Robin
Waters). [PraS] (64:3) Fall 90, p. 24-25.
"Joey Nee." [PraS] (64:3) Fall 90, p. 25-26.
"Recognizing a Salvadoran in Safeway, Yakima, 1984." [Spirit] (10:2) 90, p. 98.
1416. DALLAS, Mark
"Prana Yama." [HeavenB] (8) Wint 90-91, p. 15.
1417. D'ALLESANDRO, Sam
"After Being Wanted." [PoetryUSA] (5:1) Spr 90, p. 13.
"Red Cats." [PoetryUSA] (5:2) Sum 90, p. 16.
1418. DALTON, Anne B.
"Eidetic Images." [SinW] (42) Wint 90-91, p. 85.
1419. DALTON, Roque
"I Wanted" (tr. by Alan West). [Agni] (29/30) 90, p. 7-8.
"On Headaches" (tr. by Margaret Randall). [Quarry] (39:4) Fall 1990, p. 95-96.
1420. DALY, Chris
"God's Precis." [ChironR] (9:3) Aut 90, p. 14.
"Industry Leader." [ChironR] (9:3) Aut 90, p. 14.
"Mister Moonlight." [ChironR] (9:3) Aut 90, p. 14.
1421. DALY, Daniel
"Kalawao, Molokai." [ChamLR] (4:1, #7) Fall 90, p. 132.
1422. DAMACION, Kenneth Zamora
"Black Humor." [MissouriR] (13:1) 90, p. 194-195.
"Murder." [HiramPoR] (48/49) 90-91, p. 24-25.
1423. DAMBROFF, Susan
"For Kimi." [SinW] (40) Spr 90, p. 89-90.
1424. DAMERON, Chip
"Hook and Bloodline." [HayF] (7) Fall-Wint 90, p. 55-56.
1425. DANA, Robert
"Aquamarine." [Shen] (40:4) Wint 90, p. 42-43.
"Summer in a Very Small Town" (For Mary). [HampSPR] (Anthology 1975-1990)
90, p. 166-167.
"Testament." [HampSPR] (Anthology 1975-1990) 90, p. 167.
1426. DANIEL, Hal J., III
"C-Squared Vision." [ChironR] (9:2) Sum 90, p. 2.
"My Mother's Drippings." [ChironR] (9:2) Sum 90, p. 2.
"The Red Poppy." [SlipS] (10) 90, p. 36.
"Suzuki Lullaby." [ContextS] (1:1) 89, p. 38.
"Why I Like My Father." [ChironR] (9:2) Sum 90, p. 2.
1427. DANIEL, John
"Dependence Day." [Poetry] (157:2) N 90, p. 84.
"The Echoing Lake" (For John Stacey). [Poetry] (157:2) N 90, p. 83.
"For Our Fifth Anniversary, Seven Days Late." [Poetry] (156:3) Je 90, p. 129.
"Here." [SouthernR] (26:2) Ap 90, p. 358.
"In Sky Lakes Wilderness." [Poetry] (157:2) N 90, p. 82.
"In Thanks for Feeling Happier." [SouthernR] (26:2) Ap 90, p. 359.
"Mushrooms." [NorthStoneR] (9) 90, p. 43-44.
"Opal Creek" (The largest stand of old-growth forest remaining in the Oregon
Cascades, scheduled for logging by the U.S. Forest Service). [SouthernR]
(26:2) Ap 90, p. 360-361.
"The Pelicans of San Felipe." [SouthernR] (26:2) Ap 90, p. 359.
"The Rising Wind." [Poetry] (156:3) Je 90, p. 129-130.
"Video." [NorthStoneR] (9) 90, p. 41.-42.
1428. DANIEL, Yuli
"Romance About My Motherland" (tr. by B. Z. Niditch). [CrabCR] (6:3) Spr 90, p.
4.
1429. DANIELS, Jim
"Anita, a New Hire on the Line" (from "Places / Everyone"). [SwampR] (6)
Sum-Fall 90, p. 33.
"Called Back." [Pig] (16) 90, p. 24.
"The Costs." [Pig] (16) 90, p. 25.
"Exploring." [WormR] (30:4, #120) 90, p. 106.
"In Black Gloves." [Journal] (13:2) Fall-Wint 89-90, p. 31.
"M-80s." [MichQR] (29:3) Sum 90, p. 332-334.
"A Matter of Pride." [WormR] (30:4, #120) 90, p. 105.

"Night Janitor, McMahon Oil" (for J.P.). [CarolQ] (42:3) Spr 90, p. 25-27.
"Odie's Story." [WormR] (30:4, #120) 90, p. 105.
"One of Those Things, Detroit." [WestB] (26) 90, p. 108-109.
"Places Everyone" (from "Places / Everyone"). [SwampR] (6) Sum-Fall 90, p. 32.
"Quality / Control." [Pig] (16) 90, p. 24.
"Raw October." [Journal] (13:2) Fall-Wint 89-90, p. 32.
"A Real Comedian: The True Genius of Bob Hope" (December, 1988). [IndR]
      (13:2) Spr 90, p. 19-20.
"Rip." [WillowS] (26) Spr 90, p. 18.
"Running." [SwampR] (5) Wint-Spr 90, p. 36.
1430. DANIELS, Kate
"Evening News in February." [CimR] (93) O 90, p. 32-33.
"The Women's Room in Pennsylvania Station." [CimR] (93) O 90, p. 31-32.
1431. DANKLEFF, Richard
"February." [VirQR] (66:1) Wint 90, p. 88-89.
"In the Islands." [VirQR] (66:1) Wint 90, p. 89-90.
"Off Watch." [NowestR] (28:2) 90, p. 54-55.
"Submarine." [NowestR] (28:2) 90, p. 56.
DAO, Bei
      See BEI, Dao
1432. DARCHINOVA, Lena
"The first that I have seen" (Poem written in English by high school students from
      the Ukraine, collected by Maureen Hurley). [PoetryUSA] (5:1) Spr 90, p. 18.
DARGATZ, Gail Anderson
      See ANDERSON-DARGATZ, Gail
1433. DARLING, Charles
"Growing Old with Frank and Joe." [Amelia] (6:2, #17) 90, p. 93.
1434. DARLING, Robert
"Teaching." [Hellas] (1:2) Fall 90, p. 227-228.
1435. DARLINGTON, Andrew
"This Is Not an American Planet" (Eating Chromosomes). [Bogg] (63) 90, p. 52-54.
1436. DARNELL, Bernadette
"The Accident." [SpoonRQ] (15:1) Wint 90, p. 17.
"Family Album" (for A. L.). [SpoonRQ] (15:1) Wint 90, p. 14-16.
1437. D'ARPINO, Tony
"Document." [OnTheBus] (2:2/3:1, #6/7) Sum-Fall 90 Wint-Spr 91, p. 69-70.
"Dovetail of the Day." [Parting] (3:2) Wint 90-91, p. 21.
"Inscription for a Sundial." [Parting] (3:2) Wint 90-91, p. 21.
"Phoenicia." [Spirit] (10:2) 90, p. 113-114.
"Relativity, Babycakes." [OnTheBus] (2:2/3:1, #6/7) Sum-Fall 90 Wint-Spr 91, p.
      69.
1438. DARR, Ann
"The Curious Night Before Elizabeth." [HampSPR] (Anthology 1975-1990) 90, p.
      43.
"Filling in the Blanks." [HampSPR] (Anthology 1975-1990) 90, p. 44-46.
1439. DARRAGH, Tina
"Bunch-Ups." [Verse] (7:1) Spr 90, p. 46-47.
1440. DARUWALLA, Keki
"History." [Arc] (25) Aut 90, p. 39-40.
"Invoking the Goddess." [Arc] (25) Aut 90, p. 41-42.
1441. DARWISH, Mahmud
"A Certain Song to Palestine" (tr. by Ben Bennani). [Os] (30) Spr 90, p. 22.
"Psalm Four" (from Psalms for Palestine, tr. by Ben Bennani). [Os] (30) Spr 90, p.
      23.
1442. DASSANOWSKY-HARRIS, Robert
"And Over It Was." [BellR] (13:2, #28) Fall 90, p. 8.
"Fibel." [Os] (30) Spr 90, p. 35.
"Knowing the Time Is Nothing." [Asylum] (5:4) 90, p. 33.
"Three Letters Not Written, 1926." [ManhatR] (5:1) Spr 90, p. 34-36.
1443. DATTA, Jyotirmoy
"The Hunt" (tr. of Anuradha Mahapatra, w. Carolyne Wright). [IndR] (13:2) Spr 90,
      p. 73.
"Mother of the Bud" (tr. of Anuradha Mahapatra, w. Carolyne Wright). [IndR]
      (13:2) Spr 90, p. 72.
"To the Mountaintop" (tr. of Anuradha Mahapatra, w. Carolyne Wright). [IndR]
      (13:2) Spr 90, p. 74.

"The Year 1984" (tr. of Anuradha Mahapatra, w. Carolyne Wright). [IndR] (13:2)
Spr 90, p. 75.
1444. DAUNT, Jon
"The Night the V-2's Hit London" (for my parents). [Wind] (20:66) 90, p. 9.
1445. DAVENPORT, Guy
"Fragments" (Selections: 97-102, tr. of Herakleitos). [Zyzzyva] (6:2, #22) Sum 90,
p. 134-135.
1446. DAVENPORT, William L.
"Did You Tell It Like It Is, Robert Frost?" [LullwaterR] (1:1) Spr 90, p. 29.
1447. DAVEY, Frank
"Walking Canlit in India." [CanLit] (127) Wint 90, p. 109-113.
1448. DAVIDSON, Cynthia
"Precision." [WillowR] Spr 90, p. 25.
1449. DAVIDSON, Daniel
"Collected Works" (Excerpt). [CentralP] (17/18) Spr-Fall 90, p. 209-211.
1450. DAVIDSON, Emily
"Am." [BlackBR] (11) Spr-Sum 90, p. 4.
1451. DAVIDSON, Margie
"Loreen." [OnTheBus] (2:1, #5) Spr 90, p. 60.
"Twenty-One." [OnTheBus] (2:2/3:1, #6/7) Sum-Fall 90 Wint-Spr 91, p. 71.
1452. DAVIDSON, Phebe
"Bulbs." [JINJPo] (12:1) Spr 90, p. 8-9.
"First Son." [JINJPo] (12:1) Spr 90, p. 11.
"Ice." [Amelia] (6:2, #17) 90, p. 45.
"October Snow." [JINJPo] (12:1) Spr 90, p. 9-10.
"Pollywog." [JINJPo] (12:1) Spr 90, p. 12-13.
1453. DAVIDUKE, Michael S.
"Letter Home from the Tropic of Cancer." [ClockR] (6:1) 90, p. 44.
"Synapse." [ClockR] (6:1) 90, p. 42-43.
1454. DAVIES, Alan
"By Inference." [Verse] (7:1) Spr 90, p. 14.
"Literature, so boyish." [Verse] (7:1) Spr 90, p. 14.
"The New Sentience." [Verse] (7:1) Spr 90, p. 13.
"This leaf is death." [Verse] (7:1) Spr 90, p. 14.
1455. DAVIES, Hilary
"Heine in Paris." [Quarry] (39:1) Wint 90, p. 19.
1456. DAVIGNON, Richard
"30 Day Evaluation." [DogRR] (9:1, #17) Spr 90, p. 26.
"Crazy Ralphie's." [CoalC] (2) D 90, p. 17.
"Devil Captured, See Page 3" (Tabloid headline). [CoalC] (2) D 90, p. 17.
"Each November." [Plain] (11:1) Fall 90, p. 16.
"Elvis Is Dead, Bubba." [DogRR] (9:1, #17) Spr 90, p. 26.
"Witch Children of Samhain." [RagMag] (8:1) 90, p. 61.
1457. DAVIS, Carol V.
"Los Angeles: 12th and Olive." [Parting] (3:2) Wint 90-91, p. 14.
"Driving Through Kansas." [Parting] (3:2) Wint 90-91, p. 23-24.
"Going to My Child." [BlueBldgs] (12) 90, p. 26.
"In the Garden After the Rain." [Parting] (3:2) Wint 90-91, p. 22.
"Letter to Jon." [Parting] (3:2) Wint 90-91, p. 15.
1458. DAVIS, Christopher
"Aborted Fetus." [Ploughs] (16:4) Wint 90-91, p. 88.
"Asking to Be Useful Somewhere Near the End." [IndR] (14:1) Wint 90, p. 39.
"Atlas and Mary, If Thy Son Lives, Where?" [IndR] (14:1) Wint 90, p. 40.
"Debt Is Survival's Ringing Phone." [AntR] (48:1) Wint 90, p. 83.
"Endlessly Rocking." [BlackWR] (17:1) Fall-Wint 90, p. 36-37.
"A Fallen Candle at the Center of Our Picnic." [Caliban] (9) 90, p. 23.
"Genesis." [Ploughs] (16:4) Wint 90-91, p. 90.
"Good Friday." [BlackWR] (17:1) Fall-Wint 90, p. 38.
"The Patriot." [Ploughs] (16:4) Wint 90-91, p. 89.
"Rapture." [HayF] (6) Sum 90, p. 78.
"Trying Not to Tease Him." [Iowa] (20:3) Fall 90, p. 70-71.
"Trying to Flee a Dark Bedroom." [Iowa] (20:3) Fall 90, p. 70.
"Two Dead Marriages." [BlackWR] (17:1) Fall-Wint 90, p. 35.
"Voice Against Christ from Inside a Clock Mask" (cruising a rest area, high).
[BlackWR] (17:1) Fall-Wint 90, p. 34.

1459. DAVIS, Cortney
"Duet." [PoetC] (21:2) Wint 90, p. 5-6.
"The Woman Who Lost Her Breast to Cancer and Said She Didn't Mind." [PoetC]
(21:2) Wint 90, p. 3-4.
1460. DAVIS, Dick
"Anthony (1946-1966)." [YaleR] (79:3) Spr 90, p. 486-487.
"Two Poems on Exile" (for the Iranians in America). [YaleR] (79:3) Spr 90, p.
485-486.
1461. DAVIS, Jodi
"One Who Is Praised." [PoetryUSA] (5:3) Fall 90, p. 27.
1462. DAVIS, Marilyn
"Departure" (reprinted from #12, 1986). [Kaleid] (20) Wint-Spr 90, p. 110.
"The Departure" (reprinted from #12, 1986). [Kaleid] (20) Wint-Spr 90, p. 110.
1463. DAVIS, Nedine
"I Am Mama Bear." [Kaleid] (20) Wint-Spr 90, p. 15.
1464. DAVIS, Tim
"16 Dolomite appletree icons people the hill." [Notus] (5:1) Spr 90, p. 87-88.
"Blue." [YellowS] (33) Spr 90, p. 20.
"Love Poem #3." [YellowS] (33) Spr 90, p. 28.
"Love Poem #4." [YellowS] (33) Spr 90, p. 32.
"Taurus Glares Down the Giant Hunter." [Notus] (5:1) Spr 90, p. 89.
1465. DAVIS, William Virgil
"Bog Man." [Bogg] (62) 90, p. 7.
"The Bones Die and Go on Living." [HampSPR] (Anthology 1975-1990) 90, p.
104.
"Prologue to an Explanation." [HampSPR] (Anthology 1975-1990) 90, p. 104-105.
"The Resurrection of the Bones." [HampSPR] (Anthology 1975-1990) 90, p. 103.
"Scandanavia." [WestB] (27) 90, p. 29.
"Seasonal Changes." [NoDaQ] (58:2) Spr 90, p. 44.
"Variation on a Theme from Stevens." [NoDaQ] (58:2) Spr 90, p. 44.
"Winterset." [NoDaQ] (58:2) Spr 90, p. 45-46.
1466. DAVISON, Neil (Neil R.)
"Glenn's Bird." [SmPd] (27:3, #80) Fall 90, p. 10.
"The Split of Wood" (For My Father). [FreeL] (6) Aut 90, p. 10-11.
1467. DAVISON, Peter
"Autobiographer." [Hudson] (43:2) Sum 90, p. 182.
1468. DAVTIAN, Vahakn
"First Snow" (tr. by Diana Der-Hovanessian). [Nimrod] (33:2) Spr-Sum 90, p. 37.
1469. DAWE, Gerald
"The *de facto* Territory" (For Dennis O'Driscoll). [Quarry] (39:1) Wint 90, p. 70.
1470. DAWSON, Hester
"A Drinking Song." [JINJPo] (12:1) Spr 90, p. 17.
"Saturday Morning." [JINJPo] (12:1) Spr 90, p. 18.
1471. DAY, Jean
"Dialogue." [Screens] (2) 90, p. 191-192.
"More With Than On." [Zyzzyva] (6:1 #21) Spr 90, p. 71-72.
1472. DAY-ROBERTS, Cynthia
"Those Who Cannot Be Together." [CrabCR] (7:1) Wint 90, p. 15.
De . . .
See also names beginning with "De" without the following space, filed below in their
alphabetical positions, e.g., DeFOE.
De ALARCON, Hernando Ruiz
See RUIZ DE ALARCON, Hernando
De ALBA, Alicia Gaspar
See ALBA, Alicia Gaspar de
De ANDRADE, Eugenio
See ANDRADE, Eugenio de
1473. De ANGELIS, Milo
"Annual Doorway" (tr. by Pasquale Verdicchio). [Screens] (2) 90, p. 112.
"The Assassins" (tr. by Lawrence Venuti). [WashR] (16:2) Ag-S 90, p. 31.
"Chronology" (tr. by Lawrence Venuti). [PaintedB] (40/41) 90, p. 63.
"Continuous Time" (tr. by Lawrence Venuti). [PaintedB] (40/41) 90, p. 64.
"Cronología" (from "Terra del viso," 1985). [PaintedB] (40/41) 90, p. 62.
"Double Justice" (for Nadia Campana, tr. by Pasquale Verdicchio). [Screens] (2) 90,
p. 113.
"The Drop Ready for the Globe" (tr. by Lawrence Venuti). [PaintedB] (40/41) 90, p.

69.
"Elegy" (tr. by Pasquale Verdicchio). [Screens] (2) 90, p. 112.
"For You Who" (tr. by Lawrence Venuti). [WashR] (16:2) Ag-S 90, p. 31.
"Form" (tr. by Lawrence Venuti). [PoetryE] (30) Fall 90, p. 86.
"La Goccia Pronta per il Mappamondo" (from "Millimetri," 1983). [PaintedB]
    (40/41) 90, p. 68.
"I Recover a Syntax" (tr. by Lawrence Venuti). [WashR] (16:2) Ag-S 90, p. 31.
"I Sicari." [WashR] (16:2) Ag-S 90, p. 31.
"In History" (tr. by Lawrence Venuti). [WashR] (16:2) Ag-S 90, p. 30.
"The Incident" (tr. by Lawrence Venuti). [PaintedB] (40/41) 90, p. 65.
"L'Incidente" (from "Somiglianze"). [PaintedB] (40/41) 90, p. 65.
"The Legend of Monferrato" (tr. by Lawrence Venuti). [WashR] (16:2) Ag-S 90, p.
    31.
"Leggenda del Monferrato." [WashR] (16:2) Ag-S 90, p. 31.
"Nella Storia." [WashR] (16:2) Ag-S 90, p. 30.
"Per Voi Che." [WashR] (16:2) Ag-S 90, p. 31.
"Ritrovo una Sintassi." [WashR] (16:2) Ag-S 90, p. 31.
"The Selection" (tr. by Lawrence Venuti). [PaintedB] (40/41) 90, p. 67.
"La Selezione" (from "Somiglianze," 1976). [PaintedB] (40/41) 90, p. 66.
"Le Sentinelle." [WashR] (16:2) Ag-S 90, p. 31.
"The Sentries" (tr. by Lawrence Venuti). [WashR] (16:2) Ag-S 90, p. 31.
"Tempo Continuato" (from "Distante un padre," 1989). [PaintedB] (40/41) 90, p.
    64.
De ARAUJO MESQUITA, Henrique
    See MESQUITA, Henrique de Araujo
De BRUYCKER, Daniel
    See BRUYCKER, Daniel de
De BRUYN, Guido
    See BRUYN, Guido de
1474. De CAMARA, Mary Philip
    "Yellow-Starred." [Amelia] (6:2, #17) 90, p. 73.
De CAMPOS, Alvaro
    See PESSOA, Fernando
De CHAMFORT, Nicolas-Sébastien
    See CHAMFORT, Nicolas-Sébastien de
De CORNIERE, François
    See CORNIERE, François de
De CULLA, Daniel
    See CULLA, Daniel de
De GUILHADE, Joam Garcia
    See GUILHADE, Joam Garcia de
De HARO, José Elgarresta Ramirez
    See ELGARRESTA, José
De HELL, Xavier Hommaire
    See HELL, Xavier Hommaire de
De HERRERA, Emilia Ayarza
    See AYARZA DE HERRERA, Emilia
De HOYOS, Angela
    See HOYOS, Angela de
De IBAÑES, Sara
    See IBAÑES, Sara de
1475. De JOUX, Alicia
    "Quiet Time." [Vis] (33) 90, p. 29.
De la CRUZ, Juana Inés, Sor
    See CRUZ, Juana Inés de la, Sor
De las CASAS, Walter
    See CASAS, Walter de las
1476. De Leithauser, Brad
    "Glow." [AmerS] (59:4) Aut 90, p. 528-530.
De los SANTOS, Marisa
    See SANTOS, Marisa de los
1477. De MARIS, Ron
    "Sometimes the Sun." [KanQ] (22:1/2) Wint-Spr 90, p. 188.
    "Sometimes the Sun." [LitR] (33:2) Wint 90, p. 222.
    "Timidity." [KanQ] (22:1/2) Wint-Spr 90, p. 189.
    "Voyeur." [NewOR] (17:3) Fall 90, p. 10-11.

"Wind From the Sea" (after Wyeth). [Ploughs] (16:4) Wint 90-91, p. 260.
De MONTELLANO, Ana Ortiz
   See ORTIZ de MONTELLANO, Ana
1478. De NICOLA, Deborah
   "The Physicist's Wife." [CimR] (93) O 90, p. 44-45.
De OLIVEIRA GOMES, Aila
   See GOMES, Aila de Oliveira
De PEREZ, Matilde Espinosa
   See ESPINOSA DE PEREZ, Matilde
De PONTCHARRA, Nicole
   See PONTCHARRA, Nicole de
1479. De QUESADA, Isa
   "I Need a Hearing Aid." [OnTheBus] (2:1, #5) Spr 90, p. 64.
   "Strawberries." [OnTheBus] (2:2/3:1, #6/7) Sum-Fall 90 Wint-Spr 91, p. 73.
De RIBELA, Roi Paes
   See RIBELA, Roi Paes de
De SENA, Jorge
   See SENA, Jorge de
1480. De STEFANO, John
   "On Reading an X-ray." [SenR] (20:2) Fall 90, p. 65.
   "Remembering the Waves on the Rocks." [Wind] (20:67) 90, p. 15.
   "Two Poems / Matins." [SouthwR] (75:2) Spr 90, p. 281.
1481. De VITO, E. B.
   "However I Miss You." [AmerS] (59:2) Spr 90, p. 198.
   "Tithes." [Comm] (117:11) 1 Je 90, p. 349.
1482. De VRIES, Carrow
   "Haiku." [WindO] (53) Fall 90, p. 56.
   "Poem: Cowboy I fell for." [WindO] (53) Fall 90, p. 56.
1483. DEAN, Debi Kang
   "Hawaiian Time." [CutB] (34) Sum-Fall 90, p. 37.
   "No Pilikia, or, Piece of Cake" (for Uncle Jimmy). [CutB] (34) Sum-Fall 90, p. 38.
   "Proteus." [LaurelR] (24:2) Sum 90, p. 24-25.
1484. DEAN, Gerald L.
   "Faith." [ChironR] (9:2) Sum 90, p. 7.
1485. DEAN, Larry O.
   "The Holy Trinity." [ChironR] (9:3) Aut 90, p. 23.
1486. DEANE (?)
   "Does the government have the power to take our lives?" (Found Poem).
      [PoetryUSA] (5:2) Sum 90, p. 17.
1487. DEANE, John F.
   "On a Dark Night." [Quarry] (39:1) Wint 90, p. 71.
1488. DEANE, Seamus
   "Aisling." [Quarry] (39:1) Wint 90, p. 72.
1489. DeANGELO, Gregory
   "The Roadwraithes." [EmeraldCR] (1990) c89, p. 62.
1490. DEANOVICH, Connie
   "African Jack Benny." [PaintedB] (40/41) 90, p. 160.
   "Thinks the Peeping Toms." [BrooklynR] (7) 90, p. 44-45.
1491. DEBELJAK, Ales
   "Distant Voices in My Heart" (Selections: 1, 3, tr. by Michael Biggins). [Screens]
      (2) 90, p. 71.
   "The Forms of Love" (Selection: 2, tr. by Michael Biggins). [Screens] (2) 90, p. 70.
   "Outline of History 7" (tr. by Michael Biggins). [ManhatR] (5:2) Fall 90, p. 36.
   "Without Anaesthetic" (tr. by Michael Biggins). [ManhatR] (5:2) Fall 90, p. 36.
1492. DECARNIN, C. M.
   "Ten of St. Helens." [SingHM] (18) 90, p. 50-53.
1493. DeCARTERET, Mark
   "She Still Loves My After-Shave." [Turnstile] (2:2) 90, p. 24-25.
1494. DECEMBER, John
   "Harvest Letter." [CutB] (33) 90, p. 32.
1495. DeCORMIER-SHEKERJIAN, Regina
   "Christina, Queen of the Swedes" (1989 John Williams Andrews Prize Winner).
      [PoetL] (85:1) Spr 90, p. 5-15.
   "Mrs. Bach." [Salm] (88/89) Fall 90-Wint 91, p. 82-88.
1496. DeCOURCY, Lynne H.
   "Manhattan." [PassN] (11:1) Sum 90, p. 14.

"Truce." [TarRP] (29:2) Spr 90, p. 24.
1497. DEELEY, Patrick
 "1969." [Quarry] (39:1) Wint 90, p. 73-74.
1498. DeFOE, Mark
 "Hell." [Comm] (117:16) 28 S 90, p. 543.
 "His Hands." [OxfordM] (6:1) Spr-Sum 90, p. 37-38.
 "Teenagers at the Mall." [AntigR] (81/82) Spr-Sum 90, p. 204.
1499. DeFREES, Madeline
 "Stages of Family Life." [PoetryUSA] (5:2) Sum 90, p. 11.
1500. DEGENHARDT, Elizabeth
 "Menthol Eucalyptus Cough Drops." [OnTheBus] (2:2/3:1, #6/7) Sum-Fall 90
 Wint-Spr 91, p. 72.
 "Red Red Wine." [OnTheBus] (2:1, #5) Spr 90, p. 61-62.
1501. DeGRAZIA, Emilio
 "Rainbow Man." [LaurelR] (24:1) Wint 90, p. 74-75.
1502. DEGRIO, Missi
 "So many social laws -- why?" [PoetryUSA] ([5:4?]) Wint 90, p. 27.
1503. DEGUY, Michel
 "Manufacture" (tr. by Jacques Servin and Wilson Baldridge, w. the author).
 [NewDeltaR] (7:1) 90, p. 12.
1504. Del GUERCIO, Margaret
 "Galleries of Angels." [JINJPo] (12:1) Spr 90, p. 25-26.
 "Just a Junkyard Dog." [JINJPo] (12:1) Spr 90, p. 21.
 "Sestina for the Dancing Smile." [JINJPo] (12:1) Spr 90, p. 23.
 "This Ain't Plutonic, Baby, or, She Knows She Has the Divine Gift." [JINJPo]
 (12:1) Spr 90, p. 24-25.
 "To the Lord or to Me." [JINJPo] (12:1) Spr 90, p. 22.
1505. DELANO, Page Dougherty
 "Floorscrapers" (Paris 1871, after a painting by Gustave Caillebotte). [WestHR]
 (44:4) Wint 90, p. 407-408.
 "Reba Talks of the August Strike." [WestB] (27) 90, p. 12-14.
1506. DELANTY, Greg
 "Deora Dé" (to Louis). [Quarry] (39:1) Wint 90, p. 75.
1507. DELANY, Carol
 "Twinkle Little Star." [OnTheBus] (2:1, #5) Spr 90, p. 63.
1508. DeLAURENTIS, Louise Budde
 "Grandma Budde." [Plain] (10:2) Wint 90, p. 23.
1509. DELEHANT, Jane E.
 "Pillow Mints." [Wind] (20:67) 90, p. 23.
1510. DELGADO, Juan
 "The Pink Letters of Grade School." [MissouriR] (13:1) 90, p. 196.
1511. DELIGIORGIS, Stavros (Stravros)
 "Dearest Thrushes" (tr. of Silvino Poesini). [Iowa] (20:1) Wint 90, p. 23-24.
 "The Flower of No Smell Is Speaking" (tr. of Silvino Poesini). [Iowa] (20:1) Wint
 90, p. 24-25.
 "From the Earth: Joys and Sorrows" (tr. of Silvino Poesini). [Iowa] (20:1) Wint 90,
 p. 25.
 "Gully" (tr. of Marin Sorescu). [HampSPR] (Anthology 1975-1990) 90, p. 263.
 "I Call Them the Giants" (tr. of Silvino Poesini). [Iowa] (20:1) Wint 90, p. 22-23.
1512. DELJON, Renée
 "On the Arm of Gravity." [CreamCR] (14:1) Spr 90, p. 145.
1513. DELLABOUGH, Robin
 "1966." [Mildred] (4:1) 90, p. 117.
 "Exchange Student." [Mildred] (4:1) 90, p. 118.
1514. DELP, Michael
 "The Abandonment of Poetry." [PoetryNW] (31:2) Sum 90, p. 39-40.
1515. DeMARS, Douglas
 "Last Days of Jerry Bill Smith." [ThRiPo] (35/36) 90, p. 21-22.
1516. DEMETRE, Sheila
 "Persephone at the Festival." [PoetryNW] (31:2) Sum 90, p. 12-13.
 "Yellow Jacket." [PoetryNW] (31:2) Sum 90, p. 11-12.
1517. DEMETRICK, Mary Russo
 "Madeline." [SinW] (41) Sum-Fall 90, p. 22.
1518. DEMPSTER, Barry
 "Envy." [Bogg] (63) 90, p. 61.
 "Envy 5." [AntigR] (81/82) Spr-Sum 90, p. 30.

133

"Learning How to Sing." [AntigR] (81/82) Spr-Sum 90, p. 29-30.
1519. DeNIORD, Chard
    "Barber." [Chelsea] (49) 90, p. 146.
    "Fire Road." [MidAR] (10:1) 90, p. 135.
    "Harold Bloom." [Ploughs] (16:4) Wint 90-91, p. 261.
    "Operation." [GrahamHR] (13) Spr 90, p. 66.
1520. DENISOFF, Dennis
    "Country Is Photos." [WestCL] (24:1) Spr 90, p. 120-121.
    "Hallelujah Pancake Syrup." [WestCL] (24:1) Spr 90, p. 118-119.
1521. DENNIS, Carl
    "The Anthropic Cosmological Principle." [Salm] (88/89) Fall 90-Wint 91, p.
        156-157.
    "At the Lake." [MissouriR] (13:2) 90, p. 73.
    "Defining Time." [Poetry] (157:2) N 90, p. 80-81.
    "Infidel." [Agni] (31/32) 90, p. 186-187.
    "Oedipus the King." [NewRep] (202:14) 2 Ap 90, p. 30.
    "Our Guardians." [VirQR] (66:1) Wint 90, p. 80-81.
    "Persuasion." [VirQR] (66:1) Wint 90, p. 79-80.
    "The Window." [Poetry] (157:2) N 90, p. 79-80.
1522. DENNISON, Michael
    "Sea Full." [NewDeltaR] (7:1) 90, p. 40.
DeNORD, Chard
    See DeNIORD, Chard
1523. DEPESTRE, Rene
    "For Haiti" (tr. by Dennis Egan). [Vis] (32) 90, p. 22.
1524. DEPPE, Theodore
    "West Branch." [BlueBldgs] (12) 90, p. 19.
1525. DEPTA, Victor M.
    "But Marriage, God." [NewDeltaR] (7:2) Spr-Sum 90, p. 69.
    "Hunter's Moon" (Martin, Tennessee 1989). [VirQR] (66:4) Aut 90, p. 672-673.
    "Old and Young." [ChatR] (10:2) Wint 90, p. 25.
    "Telephone Call." [VirQR] (66:4) Aut 90, p. 671- 672.
    "Winter Sparrow." [WindO] (53) Fall 90, p. 41.
    "You Are of More Value." [Amelia] (6:1, #16) 90, p. 49.
1526. DER-HOVANESSIAN, Diana
    "Altitude" (tr. of Maro Markarian). [PoetryE] (30) Fall 90, p. 99.
    "The Baker's Apprentice." [GrahamHR] (13) Spr 90, p. 48-49.
    "California Forest." [GrahamHR] (13) Spr 90, p. 45.
    "Come Back Safely" (tr. of Sylvia Gaboudikian). [Agni] (31/32) 90, p. 242.
    "Crane" (tr. of Loudvig Dourian). [Nimrod] (33:2) Spr-Sum 90, p. 38.
    "Etchmiadzin" (tr. of Zahrad). [Trans] (23) Spr 90, p. 251.
    "First Snow" (tr. of Vahakn Davtian). [Nimrod] (33:2) Spr-Sum 90, p. 37.
    "Florence" (tr. of Zahrad). [Trans] (23) Spr 90, p. 252.
    "Four and Five." [Agni] (31/32) 90, p. 238-239.
    "Fractions" (tr. of Anahid Barsamian). [Nimrod] (33:2) Spr-Sum 90, p. 37.
    "Goddess of Hunting." [Agni] (31/32) 90, p. 240.
    "How to Fall Asleep." [GrahamHR] (13) Spr 90, p. 46-47.
    "If I Don't Love You" (tr. of Sylvia Gaboudikian). [Agni] (31/32) 90, p. 241.
    "If You Are a Poet" (tr. of Gevorg Emin). [PoetryE] (30) Fall 90, p. 8.
    "It Is Said" (tr. of Maro Markarian). [PoetryE] (30) Fall 90, p. 98.
    "Mykonos" (tr. of Zahrad). [Trans] (23) Spr 90, p. 252.
    "Shiraz" (tr. of Zahrad). [Trans] (23) Spr 90, p. 253.
    "With Grief and Regret" (tr. of Maro Markarian). [PoetryE] (30) Fall 90, p. 100.
1527. DERBY, Cheryl
    "Deaf and Blind." [Footwork] 90, p. 82.
    "Drifter." [Footwork] 90, p. 82.
    "Syracuse to Albany" (from my mother's house). [Footwork] 90, p. 82.
1528. DERBY, Edward (Edward K.)
    "Cape Cod Evening." [PraS] (64:2) Sum 90, p. 89.
    "Citrus Workers" (from a family album). [Field] (42) Spr 90, p. 39.
    "The Elephants." [PraS] (64:2) Sum 90, p. 90-91.
1529. DERKSEN, Jeff
    "Mister" (From "Redress"). [Verse] (7:1) Spr 90, p. 39-40.
    "Solace." [WestCL] (24:1) Spr 90, p. 85-98.
1530. DeROSE, John Richard
    "The Doorgunner." [Writer] (103:9) S 90, p. 21.

1531. DERRICOTTE, Toi
"Fearful Flyers, Inc." [Footwork] 90, p. 20.
"Whitman, Come Again to the Cities." [Footwork] 90, p. 21.
1532. DERRY, Alice
"Daughter, My Daughter." [WillowS] (26) Spr 90, p. 81-82.
"If She Could Talk, You Couldn't Explain." [PassN] (11:2) Wint 90, p. 23.
1533. DERVIN, Dan
"Not the Dance." [Hellas] (1:1) Spr 90, p. 115-116.
"Sunfall and Waterrise." [Hellas] (1:2) Fall 90, p. 277.
1534. DESMARAIS, Michele
"Of You and the Scotch." [PraF] (11:4) Wint 90-91, p. 38.
"Virgin in a Rainstorm." [PraF] (11:4) Wint 90-91, p. 39.
1535. DESMOND, Walter
"Dance the Night Away" (Wind River Reservation, Wyoming). [BlueBldgs] (12) 90,
    p. 27.
1536. DESNOS, Robert
"Announcement" (tr. by William Kulik). [AmerPoR] (19:3) My-Je 90, p. 21.
"Ars Poetica" (tr. by Carolyn Forché). [AmerPoR] (19:3) My-Je 90, p. 25.
"At Dawn" (tr. by Carolyn Forché). [AmerPoR] (19:3) My-Je 90, p. 28.
"The Bottle in the River" (tr. by William Kulik). [AmerPoR] (19:3) My-Je 90, p. 24.
"Door to the Second Infinity" (tr. by William Kulik). [AmerPoR] (19:3) My-Je 90,
    p. 21.
"From the Marble Rose to the Iron Rose" (tr. by William Kulik). [AmerPoR] (19:3)
    My-Je 90, p. 24.
"Identity of Images" (tr. by William Kulik). [AmerPoR] (19:3) My-Je 90, p. 22.
"If, Like the Winds Drawn on the Compass Face" (tr. by Carolyn Forché).
    [AmerPoR] (19:3) My-Je 90, p. 27.
"Letter to Youki" (tr. by Carolyn Forché). [AmerPoR] (19:3) My-Je 90, p. 28.
"The Night Watchman of Pont-au-Change" (tr. by Carolyn Forché). [AmerPoR]
    (19:3) My-Je 90, p. 26-27.
"No, Love Is Not Dead" (tr. by William Kulik). [AmerPoR] (19:3) My-Je 90, p. 22.
"Once There Was a Leaf" (tr. by William Kulik). [AmerPoR] (19:3) My-Je 90, p.
    21.
"Song of Taboo" (tr. by Carolyn Forché). [AmerPoR] (19:3) My-Je 90, p. 27.
"The Sun's Despair" (tr. by William Kulik). [AmerPoR] (19:3) My-Je 90, p. 23.
"This Heart That Hated War" (tr. by Carolyn Forché). [AmerPoR] (19:3) My-Je 90,
    p. 25.
"To the Headless" (tr. by William Kulik). [AmerPoR] (19:3) My-Je 90, p. 23.
"Tour of the Tomb" (tr. by Carolyn Forché). [AmerPoR] (19:3) My-Je 90, p. 28.
"The Way a Hand at the Moment of Death" (tr. by William Kulik). [AmerPoR]
    (19:3) My-Je 90, p. 22.
1537. DesRUISSEAUX, Pierre
"Où au commencement est la cicatrice sur la pierre." [Os] (31) 90, p. 22.
"Poésie Mode d'Emploi." [Os] (31) 90, p. 24.
"Vous observez." [Os] (31) 90, p. 23.
1538. DESSOUROUX, Marguerite
"Liege" (tr. by Philippe Remy and David Siefkin). [Vis] (34) 90, p. 18.
1539. DESY, Peter
"Drought." [NewMyths] (1:1) 90, p. 54.
"First Lent." [PoetL] (85:2) Sum 90, p. 17.
"The Garden." [ManhatPR] (12) [90?], p. 11.
"The Holding." [CapeR] (25:2) Fall 90, p. 35.
"I Was Small and You Were Dying." [NewMyths] (1:1) 90, p. 55.
"Initiation." [SwampR] (6) Sum-Fall 90, p. 70.
"Paging Through an Old Anthology." [Poem] (63) My 90, p. 41.
"Painting the Statues." [Poem] (63) My 90, p. 40.
"Routine." [ChamLR] (4:1, #7) Fall 90, p. 129.
"September, 1988." [HiramPoR] (47) Wint 90, p. 23.
"Something." [HiramPoR] (47) Wint 90, p. 22.
1540. DeVALL, Sally
"News." [Amelia] (6:2, #17) 90, p. 133.
1541. DEVINE, Richard
"Kilhope." [Stand] (31:4) Aut 90, p. 73.
1542. DeVINO, Joanne
"Magazine Dream, Video Queens." [PoetryUSA] (5:2) Sum 90, p. 6.

1543. DeVITO, Allove
"My Words." [DogRR] (9:2, #18) Aut 90, p. 31.
"Secrets for the Wind" (for the Specialist). [DogRR] (9:2, #18) Aut 90, p. 30-31.
1544. DEVOY, Adriana
"Seal Island." [PoetL] (85:3) Fall 90, p. 15-16.
1545. DeVRIES, Rachel Guido
"First Desire / First Time." [YellowS] (35) Wint 90-91, p. 18.
"Full of Desire, Dreaming." [YellowS] (35) Wint 90-91, p. 21.
"Litany on the Equinox." [SinW] (41) Sum-Fall 90, p. 38-39.
"Little Fires." [YellowS] (35) Wint 90-91, p. 18.
"Wild." [YellowS] (35) Wint 90-91, p. 21.
1546. DEWDNEY, Christopher
"The Beach." [Verse] (7:1) Spr 90, p. 20.
"The Theatre Party." [Verse] (7:1) Spr 90, p. 21.
1547. DeWITT, Jim
"Ivan of a Urals Village." [CrabCR] (6:3) Spr 90, p. 14.
"Last Protrusion." [Blueline] (11:1/2) 90, p. 60.
"Menage-a-Trois Beginning." [SmPd] (27:2, #79) Spr 90, p. 24.
"Once I wanted to Real Bad." [BlackBR] (12) Fall-Wint 90, p. 33.
"Scoff Scoff." [BlackBR] (12) Fall-Wint 90, p. 32.
"The Wild Streak in My Stallion." [DogRR] (9:1, #17) Spr 90, p. 46.
DEWITT, Susan Kelly
See KELLY-DEWITT, Susan
1548. DEY, Richard Morris
"Aboard the *Friendship Rose*, Bequia Channel." [HawaiiR] (14:3, #30) Fall 90, p.
102-103.
"The Hotel Arawak." [HawaiiR] (14:3, #30) Fall 90, p. 101.
"The North Road." [HawaiiR] (14:3, #30) Fall 90, p. 101.
1549. DeYOUNG, Robert
"House Spider." [GreensboroR] (49) Wint 90-91, p. 4.
1550. DHARWADKER, Vinay
"Copper, Khetri, Rajasthan." [Arc] (25) Aut 90, p. 60-61.
"For Three Weeks in May." [Arc] (25) Aut 90, p. 59.
"Fragment" (tr. of Dhoomil). [Screens] (2) 90, p. 47.
"Frog Time" (tr. of Arun Kolatkar). [Screens] (2) 90, p. 45.
"Horse" (tr. of Arun Kolatkar). [Screens] (2) 90, p. 44.
"Lying Beside That Woman" (tr. of Dhoomil). [Screens] (2) 90, p. 46-47.
"Solitary" (tr. of Raghuvir Sahay). [Screens] (2) 90, p. 48.
"Touch" (tr. of Arun Kolatkar). [Screens] (2) 90, p. 44.
DHOMHNAILL, Nuala Ni
See Ni DHOMHNAILL, Nuala
1551. DHOOMIL
"Fragment" (tr. by Vinay Dharwadker). [Screens] (2) 90, p. 47.
"Lying Beside That Woman" (tr. by Vinay Dharwadker). [Screens] (2) 90, p. 46-47.
Di . . .
See also names beginning with "Di" without the following space, filed below in their
alphabetic positions, e.g., DiPALMA
Di MANNO, Yves
See MANNO, Yves Di
1552. Di MICHELE, Mary
"Angel of Slapstick" (for Bronwen Wallace). [Quarry] (39:2) Spr 90, p. 82-86.
1553. Di PIERO, W. S.
"The Early Part of the Day." [SouthernR] (26:3) Jl 90, p. 676-677.
"Far West." [SouthernR] (26:3) Jl 90, p. 677-678.
"Gethsemane." [TriQ] (80) Wint 90-91, p. 51.
"Karloff and the Rock" (for Injun Joe). [TriQ] (79) Fall 90, p. 111-112.
"Leopardi's *La sera del dì di festa*." [TriQ] (80) Wint 90-91, p. 48-49.
"The Mummers." [TriQ] (79) Fall 90, p. 113-114.
"Near Damascus." [TriQ] (80) Wint 90-91, p. 50.
"The Next Room." [TriQ] (80) Wint 90-91, p. 46-47.
1554. Di PRIMA, Diane
"Notes on 'The Nature of Poetry'." [PoetryUSA] ([5:4?]) Wint 90, p. 5-7.
"A Part of the Thousand Ways to Say Goodbye" (Psyche to Amor). [MichQR]
(29:4) Fall 90, p. 739-740.
Di STEFANO, John
See De STEFANO, John

1555. Di SUVERO, Victor
"With Each Other." [OnTheBus] (2:2/3:1, #6/7) Sum-Fall 90 Wint-Spr 91, p. 74.
DIAZ, Gaspar Aguilera
See AGUILERA DIAZ, Gaspar
1556. DIAZ, Michael Anthony
"Amarillo." [Writer] (103:12) D 90, p. 25.
1557. DIAZ CASTRO, Tania
"Mala Memoria" (Un poema inédito). [LindLM] (9:1/2) Ja/Mr-Ap/Je 90, p. 5.
1558. DICKENSON, Joan
"The Puffin's Song." [Amelia] (6:2, #17) 90, p. 123.
1559. DICKERSON, David
"Lazarus." [MissR] (19:1/2, #55/56) 90, p. 251.
1560. DICKEY, James
"Show Us the Sea" (an opening fragment). [PartR] (57:3) Sum 90, p. 428.
1561. DICKEY, William
"At Shag and Rosie's." [HampSPR] (Anthology 1975-1990) 90, p. 174.
"Food Stamps." [HampSPR] (Anthology 1975-1990) 90, p. 173.
"I Hear You Breathing." [HampSPR] (Anthology 1975-1990) 90, p. 174-175.
"Language Envying Geometry." [HampSPR] (Anthology 1975-1990) 90, p. 177.
"The Language of the Making." [HampSPR] (Anthology 1975-1990) 90, p.
175-176.
"Valentine." [HampSPR] (Anthology 1975-1990) 90, p. 176.
1562. DICKMAN, Susan
"Inscribing." [ThRiPo] (35/36) 90, p. 83.
"The Watermelon Season." [ThRiPo] (35/36) 90, p. 81-82.
1563. DICKSON, John
"Looking Ahead." [Poetry] (156:5) Ag 90, p. 263-264.
1564. DICKSON, Martha L.
"The Big Apple." [EmeraldCR] (1990) c89, p. 26.
"Seekers." [EmeraldCR] (1990) c89, p. 27.
1565. DICKSON, Melissa
"As Promise Is Related to Fulfillment" (A Series on the Caves). [SouthernHR]
(24:1) Wint 90, p. 48-49.
1566. DICKSON, Ray Clark
"The Big Fish of the Mind." [BelPoJ] (41:2) Wint 90-91, p. 14-15.
1567. DIDIER-KING, Jody
"The Little Grey Man." [Dandel] (17:2) Fall-Wint 90, p. 31-32.
1568. DIECIDUE, Gianni
"Sicily, the Peasant Mother" (from the Sicilian Antigruppo, tr. by Nat Scammacca).
[Footwork] 90, p. 102.
1569. DIESENDORF, Margaret
"Displaced." [Bogg] (63) 90, p. 6.
1570. DIETZ, Elizabeth
"Crazy Blue." [Ploughs] (16:4) Wint 90-91, p. 187-188.
1571. DIFALCO, Sam
"The Attitude." [AntigR] (81/82) Spr-Sum 90, p. 139-140.
"Less Pleasant Music." [AntigR] (81/82) Spr-Sum 90, p. 140-141.
1572. DIGGES, Deborah
"Hall of Souls." [Agni] (31/32) 90, p. 98-99.
"London Zoo." [Antaeus] (64/65) Spr-Aut 90, p. 19.
"My Amaryllis." [Ploughs] (16:4) Wint 90-91, p. 132.
"Tartarchos." [Agni] (31/32) 90, p. 100-101.
1573. DIGUETTE, Rick
"Visitation." [LullwaterR] (2:1) Wint 90, p. 48-49.
1574. DILLARD, Annie
"Class Notes on Painting and the Arts" (from "The Art Spirit," by Robert Henri
compiled by his student, Margery A. Ryerson -- Found Poems). [KenR] (NS
12:2) Spr 90, p. 61-64.
"Light in the Open Air" (pieced from "The Nature of Light and Colour in the Open
Air," by the 19th c. Dutch physicist M. Minnaert). [Antaeus] (64/65) Spr-Aut
90, p. 20-22.
"Observations and Experiments." [Harp] (281:1683) Ag 90, p. 34.
"Observations and Experiments in Natural History" (from the book of that title by
Alan Dale -- Found Poems). [KenR] (NS 12:2) Spr 90, p. 58-61.
1575. DILLARD, Gavin
"Untitled: The wind makes the cats crazy, blowin up their kazoos." [ChironR] (9:1)

Spr 90, p. 22.
1576. DILLES, Jim
"A Haunt of Echoes." [PoetryUSA] ([5:4?]) Wint 90, p. 9.
"Shanty." [PoetryUSA] ([5:4?]) Wint 90, p. 11.
1577. DILLON, Andrew
"At a Motel in Summer." [RiverC] (10:2) Spr 90, p. 9.
"At Night." [KanQ] (22:1/2) Wint-Spr 90, p. 198.
"At Vicksburg." [KanQ] (22:1/2) Wint-Spr 90, p. 199-200.
"The Berry House -- Route 555 in Northern Kentucky." [Poem] (63) My 90, p. 42.
"The Coming of Winter in North Dakota." [KanQ] (22:4) Fall 90, p. 14.
"A Dream of 1300" (for William Stafford). [KanQ] (22:1/2) Wint-Spr 90, p. 200.
"A Dream of Venice." [ContextS] (1:1) 89, p. 54.
"End of the Weekend." [Poem] (63) My 90, p. 43.
"The First Visit." [KanQ] (22:4) Fall 90, p. 29.
"Fishing, Wyoming." [ManhatPR] (12) [90?], p. 36.
"For I-90 -- in South Dakota." [SoDakR] (28:3) Aut 90, p. 88.
"Historic Houses in Virginia." [ApalQ] (33/34) 90, p. 61.
"In Carlyle, Illinois." [ManhatPR] (12) [90?], p. 35.
"In-House Sonnet" (for Mrs. Elizabeth Hudson). [ManhatPR] (12) [90?], p. 36.
"McPherson, Kansas." [MidwQ] (31:4) Sum 90, p. 469.
"Middle-aged." [Poem] (63) My 90, p. 44.
"Mother and Daughter." [SpoonRQ] (15:1) Wint 90, p. 52.
"Oakley, Kansas." [PoetC] (21:3) Spr 90, p. 27.
"Really Driving America." [KanQ] (22:1/2) Wint-Spr 90, p. 199.
"Small Town in the Midwest." [FloridaR] (17:2) Fall-Wint 90, p. 133.
"To Bill Stafford." [PoetC] (21:3) Spr 90, p. 28.
"The Weeping Sharks." [NegC] (10:1) 90, p. 47.
"Words." [SoDakR] (28:3) Aut 90, p. 87.
1578. DILLON, Mike
"Labor Day." [Amelia] (6:1, #16) 90, p. 92.
1579. DILSAVER, Paul
"The Fat Life." [Bogg] (62) 90, p. 19.
"Lessons in Zen Pessimism." [DogRR] (9:1, #17) Spr 90, p. 16-17.
"Sharpening the Craft." [DogRR] (9:1, #17) Spr 90, p. 14-15.
1580. DIMAGGIO, Jill
"Insanity." [BlackBR] (12) Fall-Wint 90, p. 8.
1581. DIMIC, Svetlana
"Untitled: Long ago we were swiftly flowing water" (tr. of Jozo T. Boskovski).
[Footwork] 90, p. 61.
1582. DIMITROVA, Blaga
"11. Am I forgetting that until recently" (tr. by Ludmilla Popova-Wightman).
[PoetryE] (29) Spr 90, p. 155.
"25. Blinded, they march on, the soldiers of Tsar Samuil" (tr. by Ludmilla
Popova-Wightman). [PoetryE] (29) Spr 90, p. 156-157.
"29. I become more intimate with the dead" (tr. by Ludmilla Popova-Wightman).
[PoetryE] (29) Spr 90, p. 157-158.
"33. Be prepared, be prepared!" (tr. by Ludmilla Popova-Wightman). [PoetryE] (29)
Spr 90, p. 158-159.
"42. You set out to measure the world with your step" (tr. by Ludmilla
Popova-Wightman). [PoetryE] (29) Spr 90, p. 159.
"51. A prisoner in the solitary cell of this body" (tr. by Ludmilla Popova-Wightman).
[PoetryE] (29) Spr 90, p. 160.
"Bee Lesson" (tr. by Ludmilla Popova-Wightman). [PoetryE] (30) Fall 90, p. 57.
"Circle" (tr. by Ludmilla Popova-Wightman). [PoetryE] (30) Fall 90, p. 58.
"Dimension or Crucifix" (tr. by Ludmilla Popova-Wightman). [PoetryE] (30) Fall
90, p. 55.
"Frost" (tr. by Ludmilla Popova-Wightman). [PoetryE] (29) Spr 90, p. 154.
"Transformations" (tr. by Ludmilla Popova-Wightman). [PoetryE] (30) Fall 90, p.
56.
1583. DINE, Carol
"Learning to Sail." [ColR] (NS 17:1) Spr-Sum 90, p. 95-96.
1584. DING, Dennis
"Black Marsh" (from "Black Desert," tr. of Tang Yaping, w. Edward Morin and Dai
Fang). [Screens] (2) 90, p. 42.
"Dark Night on a Southbound Train" (tr. of Wang Xiao-Ni, w. Edward Morin).
[Screens] (2) 90, p. 41.

"Random Thoughts While Skating" (tr. of Gao Fa-Lin, w. Edward Morin).
[Screens] (2) 90, p. 37.
1585. DINGS, Fred
"The Grammar of Hope." [ContextS] (1:1) 89, p. 50.
"Matthew 6:9-13." [NewRep] (203:10) 3 S 90, p. 37.
"Odysseus on the Côte d'Azur." [AntR] (48:4) Fall 90, p. 484.
"Post-Copernican." [ContextS] (1:1) 89, p. 51.
"Riva Looking Towards Sirmione." [NewRep] (202:8) 19 F 90, p. 35.
DiNIORD, Chard
See DeNIORD, Chard
1586. DINO
"Poem by Dino." [PoetryUSA] (5:3) Fall 90, p. 25.
DiNORD, Chard
See DeNIORD, Chard
1587. DIORIO, Margaret
"The Graduate." [ChironR] (9:3) Aut 90, p. 17.
1588. DiPALMA, Ray
"Mock Fandango." [Avec] (3:1) 90, p. 40-42.
"Poem: Reason and felicity dissolves" (w. Charles Bernstein). [Screens] (2) 90, p.
196.
"Rebus Brag." [Caliban] (9) 90, p. 37.
"Spyder Rockett." [NewAW] (6) Spr 90, p. 31-34.
1589. DiSANTO, Grace
"Bread Makes Stone." [Pembroke] (22) 90, p. 116-119.
"A Year After" (For My Father-in-law). [Pembroke] (22) 90, p. 120.
1590. DISCÉPOLO, Enrique Santos
"Junk Shop" (tr. by Amelia Arenas and Stuart Klawans). [Thrpny] (43) Fall 90, p.
19.
"Spinning, Spinning" (tr. by Amelia Arenas and Stuart Klawans). [Thrpny] (43) Fall
90, p. 18-19.
"Tonight I'm Going to Get Drunk" (tr. by Amelia Arenas and Stuart Klawans).
[Thrpny] (43) Fall 90, p. 18.
1591. DISCH, Thomas M.
"The Eightfold Way" (A Masque in Five Tableaux). [GrandS] (9:2) Wint 90, p.
55-73.
1592. DISCH, Tom
"A Cape Mendocino Rose." [Sequoia] (33:2) Wint 90, p. 23.
"A Centenary Observation." [Boulevard] (4:3/5:1, #12/13) Spr 90, p. 92.
"A Diatribe." [Boulevard] (4:3/5:1, #12/13) Spr 90, p. 95-96.
"Riddle." [YaleR] (79:3) Spr 90, p. 387.
"Slouches." [Boulevard] (4:3/5:1, #12/13) Spr 90, p. 93-94.
1593. DISCHELL, Stuart
"After the Glacier: Lascaux" (for Zbigniew Herbert). [SouthwR] (75:4) Aut 90, p.
553.
"Cares." [BostonR] (15:2) Ap 90, p. 23.
"Hates." [Ploughs] (16:4) Wint 90-91, p. 185-186.
"Household Gods." [NewRep] (203:13) 24 S 90, p. 38.
"Needs." [Agni] (31/32) 90, p. 266-267.
1594. DITCHOFF, Pamela (Pamela J.)
"Address." [SlipS] (10) 90, p. 67-68.
"All Things Being Equal." [NegC] (10:1) 90, p. 51-52.
"Bath Mirror." [Amelia] (6:2, #17) 90, p. 116.
"Second Sight." [NegC] (10:1) 90, p. 48-50.
1595. DITSKY, John
"Pickups." [Paint] (17:33/34) Spr-Aut 90, p. 13.
"Protocol." [Paint] (17:33/34) Spr-Aut 90, p. 14.
"The Scout." [LaurelR] (24:2) Sum 90, p. 20.
1596. DITTBERNER-JAX, Norita
"Altered States: The Lilies." [SingHM] (18) 90, p. 41.
1597. DIVAKARUNI, Chitra
"At That Very Instant." [Mildred] (4:1) 90, p. 13.
"Family Photo in Black and White." [CapeR] (25:1) Spr 90, p. 28-29.
"The Gift." [BelPoR] (40:3) Spr 90, p. 30-31.
"If You Meet a White Horse at Sunrise." [Mildred] (4:1) 90, p. 11.
"In the Backyard." [InterPR] (16:2) Fall 90, p. 127.
"Indian Movie, New Jersey." [IndR] (14:1) Wint 90, p. 41-42.

"Late One Afternoon." [Mildred] (4:1) 90, p. 12-13.
"Living Underground: Nicaragua, 1988." [InterPR] (16:2) Fall 90, p. 126.
"Mother and Child." [Calyx] (12:3) Sum 90, p. 8-9.
"My Mother Combs My Hair." [InterPR] (16:2) Fall 90, p. 125-126.
"Nargis' Toilette." [CapeR] (25:1) Spr 90, p. 30-31.
"Outside Pisa." [IndR] (14:1) Wint 90, p. 43-44.
"The Rainflies" (for Champa). [Thrpny] (42) Sum 90, p. 34.
"The Rat Trap" (after Adoor Gopalakrishnan's film "Elippathayam"). [Calyx] (12:3)
    Sum 90, p. 10-11.
1598. DIXON, K. Reynolds
    "Breaking Faith." [GreensboroR] (49) Wint 90-91, p. 13.
    "Fallow" (Honorable Mention). [GreensboroR] (49) Wint 90-91, p. 11.
    "Hiros' Rock Garden in Bloom." [InterPR] (16:2) Fall 90, p. 124.
    "The Thunder Chair." [GreensboroR] (49) Wint 90-91, p. 12.
1599. DIXON, Melvin
    "Elegy for Martin Luther King" (for jazz orchestra, tr. of Léopold Sédar Senghor).
        [Callaloo] (13:1) Wint 90, p. 22-27.
    "Elegy of Midnight" (tr. of Léopold Sédar Senghor). [Callaloo] (13:1) Wint 90, p.
        20-21.
    "Letter to a Poet" (to Aimé Césaire, tr. of Léopold Sédar Senghor). [Callaloo] (13:1)
        Wint 90, p. 14-15.
    "To New York" (for jazz orchestra and trumpet solo, tr. of Léopold Sédar Senghor).
        [Callaloo] (13:1) Wint 90, p. 18-19.
    "To the Black American Troops" (to Mercer Cook, tr. of Léopold Sédar Senghor).
        [Callaloo] (13:1) Wint 90, p. 16-17.
1600. DJANIKIAN, Gregory
    "My Aunt Gives Me a Clarinet Lesson." [AmerS] (59:2) Spr 90, p. 272-273.
1601. DJIN, Yana
    "The Day After." [WashR] (16:2) Ag-S 90, p. 7.
    "Something Spoken." [WashR] (16:2) Ag-S 90, p. 7.
    "To Chekhov and Konchalovski." [WashR] (16:2) Ag-S 90, p. 7.
1602. DLUGOS, Tim
    "G-9." [ParisR] (32:115) Sum 90, p. 244-260.
    "Powerless." [BrooklynR] (7) 90, p. 1-3.
1603. DOBBS, Kevin
    "Music from Bavaria." [WritersF] (16) Fall 90, p. 110-111.
1604. DOBLER, Patricia
    "For Mothers." [SouthernPR] (30:2) Fall 90, p. 35.
    "Juarez, 1978" (Honorable Mention Poem, 1989/1990). [KanQ] (22:1/2) Wint-Spr
        90, p. 16.
    "November Morning: Augsburg." [KanQ] (22:1/2) Wint-Spr 90, p. 16-17.
1605. DOBYNS, Stephen
    "The Belly." [AmerPoR] (19:4) Jl-Ag 90, p. 27.
    "Black Girl Vanishing: Detroit, 1970." [AmerPoR] (19:4) Jl-Ag 90, p. 28.
    "The Body's Curse." [Antaeus] (64/65) Spr-Aut 90, p. 28-29.
    "The Body's Hope." [Antaeus] (64/65) Spr-Aut 90, p. 23-24.
    "The Body's Journey." [VirQR] (66:2) Spr 90, p. 263-265.
    "The Body's Joy." [VirQR] (66:2) Spr 90, p. 267-268.
    "The Body's Repose and Discontent." [IndR] (13:3) Fall 90, p. 31-32.
    "The Body's Weight." [AmerPoR] (19:4) Jl-Ag 90, p. 21.
    "Canto Hondo." [IndR] (13:3) Fall 90, p. 37-40.
    "Careers." [AmerPoR] (19:4) Jl-Ag 90, p. 24.
    "Cézanne and the Love of Color." [GettyR] (3:2) Spr 90, p. 347.
    "Cézanne's *A Modern Olympia* -- 1872." [GettyR] (3:2) Spr 90, p. 346.
    "Desire." [Antaeus] (64/65) Spr-Aut 90, p. 25-27.
    "Expansion Slots." [AmerPoR] (19:4) Jl-Ag 90, p. 24.
    "Feet." [AmerPoR] (19:4) Jl-Ag 90, p. 26.
    "The Future." [Boulevard] (5:2, #14) Fall 90, p. 24.
    "How It Was at the End." [IndR] (13:3) Fall 90, p. 36.
    "How You Are Linked." [AmerPoR] (19:4) Jl-Ag 90, p. 23.
    "Invasions." [VirQR] (66:2) Spr 90, p. 265-266.
    "Laughter." [AmerPoR] (19:4) Jl-Ag 90, p. 26.
    "The Proof." [AmerPoR] (19:4) Jl-Ag 90, p. 27.
    "Receivers of the World's Attention." [AmerPoR] (19:4) Jl-Ag 90, p. 22.
    "Spleen." [VirQR] (66:2) Spr 90, p. 262-263.
    "Surprise." [IndR] (13:3) Fall 90, p. 34-35.

"Tongue." [IndR] (13:3) Fall 90, p. 33.
"Toting It Up." [Boulevard] (5:2, #14) Fall 90, p. 25.
"Traffic." [AmerPoR] (19:4) Jl-Ag 90, p. 25.
"Walls to Put Up, Walls to Take Down." [CutB] (34) Sum-Fall 90, p. 7-11.
1606. DODD, Elizabeth
"Aviary." [GeoR] (44:1/2) Spr-Sum 90, p. 93-95.
"Elegy" (Betty Gay Coshow Dodd, 1932-1989). [AntR] (48:2) Spr 90, p. 231.
"Investigation and Lament." [PoetC] (21:3) Spr 90, p. 21-23.
1607. DODD, Wayne
"Breakdown." [CharR] (16:1) Spr 90, p. 44-45.
"Four Poems About Poetry." [ContextS] (1:1) 89, p. 6-7.
"News." [NowestR] (28:1) 90, p. 95.
"No Not, Say the Words, As If." [MissouriR] (13:2) 90, p. 156.
"On the Page." [ContextS] (1:1) 89, p. 5.
"Primitive." [CharR] (16:1) Spr 90, p. 45.
"Seals." [AntR] (48:1) Wint 90, p. 86-87.
"Some First Line." [ContextS] (1:1) 89, p. 4.
"Song." [ContextS] (1:1) 89, p. 3.
"Subjunctive." [AntR] (48:1) Wint 90, p. 85.
"The Women." [AntR] (48:1) Wint 90, p. 84.
1608. DODGE, George Burton, Sr.
"All That Surrounds Me Here This Night." [EmeraldCR] (1990) c89, p. 79-80.
1609. DODGE, Jim
"The Cookie Jar." [PoetryUSA] (5:3) Fall 90, p. 12.
1610. DODGE, Virginia
"Country Wash." [Plain] (10:2) Wint 90, p. 18.
"Raven." [Plain] (10:3) Spr 90, p. 28.
1611. DODSON, Keith A.
"And Me in My First Suit." [ChironR] (9:1) Spr 90, p. 6.
"Bent After Dinner." [ChironR] (9:1) Spr 90, p. 6.
"A Birthday R.S.V.P., or, 2 out of 3 Women Do Not Recommend Sleeping with the
Kennedys." [Pearl] (12) Fall-Wint 90, p. 26.
"Breaking in the New Boss." [Pearl] (10) Spr 90, p. 29.
"The Chameleon Changes His Colors." [ChironR] (9:4) Wint 90, p. 14.
"The First and Last Date." [Pearl] (10) Spr 90, p. 28.
"Listening to the Radio (FM)." [SlipS] (10) 90, p. 80.
"Sitting on the Couch." [Pearl] (10) Spr 90, p. 28.
"Too Early for Questions." [ChironR] (9:1) Spr 90, p. 6.
"Would You Like That Giftwrapped?" [Pearl] (12) Fall-Wint 90, p. 36.
1612. DOERFLER, R. Eric
"Writing Poems at the Slaughterhouse." [BlackBR] (12) Fall-Wint 90, p. 21.
1613. DOERING, Steven
"Additional Evidence of the Onset of Aging." [ChironR] (9:2) Sum 90, p. 13.
"All the Good Women Have Been." [Bogg] (63) 90, p. 46.
"Brahms Pours Into." [ChironR] (9:2) Sum 90, p. 13.
"De Tocqueville Revisited." [SlipS] (10) 90, p. 13.
"Death Became a Habit." [ChironR] (9:2) Sum 90, p. 13.
"It's Not How You Look, But How They Look At You." [ChironR] (9:2) Sum 90,
p. 13.
1614. DOLGIN, Steve
"The Famous Book of Russian Poems." [CoalC] (1) Ag 90, p. 3.
"Holy Night." [CoalC] (2) D 90, p. 9.
"In the Icebox." [CoalC] (1) Ag 90, p. 44.
"Juarez." [CoalC] (2) D 90, p. 9.
"A Photograph." [CoalC] (1) Ag 90, p. 2.
"The Weight of This Night." [CoalC] (1) Ag 90, p. 4.
1615. DOLGORUKOV, Florence
"On the Beginning of Wisdom." [InterPR] (16:2) Fall 90, p. 122.
1616. DOLLINGER, Mimi
"Filled with Cheer." [Parting] (3:1) Sum 90, p. 5.
1617. DOLPHIN, W. K.
"Blackbird." [MidwQ] (31:3) Spr 90, p. 353.
1618. DOMANSKI, Don
"Dangerous Words." [Event] (19:1) Spr 90, p. 32-33.
"On a Winter's Night." [Event] (19:1) Spr 90, p. 30.
"A Perfect Forehead." [Event] (19:1) Spr 90, p. 34.

141

"Poetry." [Event] (19:1) Spr 90, p. 31.
1619. DOMINA, Lynn
"The Long Grief" (For Ann Marie Halubschock). [HawaiiR] (14:2, #29) Spr 90, p. 29.
1620. DOMINGUEZ, Delia
"Caballo en Llamaradas." [InterPR] (16:1) Spr 90, p. 44.
"Horse Aflame" (tr. by Mark Smith-Soto). [InterPR] (16:1) Spr 90, p. 45.
1621. DONAGHUE, Marie E.
"Grammie's Rescue of Me with Pillsbury Rolls." [Amelia] (6:2, #17) 90, p. 95-96.
1622. DONAGHY, Michael
"Cage." [Poetry] (156:3) Je 90, p. 126.
1623. DONAGHY, Tom
"Untitled: If we could home." [Turnstile] (2:1) 90, p. 107-108.
1624. DONAHUE, Joseph
"Alternate Island II." [LitR] (33:4) Sum 90, p. 415-417.
"Christ Enters Manhattan." [CentralP] (17/18) Spr-Fall 90, p. 104-105.
"Passagework." [Talisman] (4) Spr 90, p. 51-52.
DONG, Han
    See HAN, Dong
1625. DONG, Jiping
"After Being Toothless" (tr. of Zhai Yongming). [Footwork] 90, p. 38.
"At Night, Sleep Leading Me to Another House" (tr. of Sun Wenbo). [Footwork] 90, p. 41.
"At the End of a Street Thinking of Van Gogh" (tr. of Wang Jiaxin). [Footwork] 90, p. 34.
"At the Stern of a Ship" (tr. of Meng Lang). [Footwork] 90, p. 37.
"Autumn" (tr. of Hai Zi). [Footwork] 90, p. 42.
"Autumn" (tr. of Wang Jiaxin). [Footwork] 90, p. 34.
"Autumn Afternoon" (tr. of Xiao Jun). [Footwork] 90, p. 44.
"Backgrounds" (tr. of Chen Dongdong). [Footwork] 90, p. 39.
"Black Horse and Fish" (tr. of Zhao Jianxiong). [Footwork] 90, p. 40.
"Celestial Burial" (tr. of Wu Yuancheng). [Footwork] 90, p. 38.
"Concert" (tr. of Qi Wei). [Footwork] 90, p. 44.
"Craft" (after Marina Tzvetayeva, tr. by the author). [Footwork] 90, p. 33.
"Dante" (tr. of Xi Chuan). [Footwork] 90, p. 44.
"The Day Without Wind" (tr. of Zhao Jianxiong). [Footwork] 90, p. 40.
"Empty Seat" (tr. of Zhu Lingbo). [Footwork] 90, p. 41.
"Expectation" (tr. of Bei Dao). [Footwork] 90, p. 43.
"A Fresco" (tr. of Wu Yuancheng). [Footwork] 90, p. 38.
"Getting an Electric Shock" (tr. of Bei Dao). [Footwork] 90, p. 43.
"God" (tr. of Guo Hong). [Footwork] 90, p. 36.
"Haiku" (tr. by the author). [Footwork] 90, p. 33.
"Han Haiku" (tr. of Hai Zi). [Footwork] 90, p. 42.
"Hostages" (tr. of Ma Li). [Footwork] 90, p. 35.
"I Am Sick" (tr. of Hai Zi). [Footwork] 90, p. 42.
"In His Requiem Mozart Said" (tr. of Hai Zi). [Footwork] 90, p. 42.
"The Invisible Stone" (tr. of Mo Fei). [Footwork] 90, p. 35.
"Jorge Louis Borges: 'The Secret Miracle'" (tr. of Guo Hong). [Footwork] 90, p. 36.
"Listening to a Flute" (tr. of Li Yuansheng). [Footwork] 90, p. 40.
"Little Poem" (tr. of Li Yuansheng). [Footwork] 90, p. 40.
"Long-Winged Bird" (tr. by the author). [Footwork] 90, p. 33.
"Losing" (tr. of Meng Lang). [Footwork] 90, p. 37.
"Night Birds" (tr. of Xi Chuan). [Footwork] 90, p. 44.
"On That Side" (tr. of Ma Li). [Footwork] 90, p. 35.
"Organ" (tr. of Sun Wenbo). [Footwork] 90, p. 41.
"Premonition" (tr. of Wang Jiaxin). [Footwork] 90, p. 34.
"Premonition" (tr. of Zhai Yongming). [Footwork] 90, p. 37.
"Returning to My Valley" (tr. of Wang Jiaxin). [Footwork] 90, p. 34.
"The Sixth Floor" (tr. by the author). [Footwork] 90, p. 33.
"Soundless Is Midnight" (tr. of Ma Li). [Footwork] 90, p. 35.
"Street Scene" (tr. of Xiao Jun). [Footwork] 90, p. 44.
"Talking of the Flying Rollers with Gary Snyder" (tr. of Chen Dongdong). [Footwork] 90, p. 40.
"There Is Something Drawing Me" (tr. of Zhai Yongming). [Footwork] 90, p. 38.
"Three O'Clock in the Afternoon" (tr. of Wang Jiaxin). [Footwork] 90, p. 34.

"Untitled: As if hinted by distant mountains" (tr. of Bei Dao). [Footwork] 90, p. 43.
"Untitled: Forever like this" (tr. of Bei Dao). [Footwork] 90, p. 43.
"White Night" (tr. of Zhu Lingbo). [Footwork] 90, p. 41.
"The Window on the Cliff" (tr. of Bei Dao). [Footwork] 90, p. 43.
"Words" (tr. of Meng Lang). [Footwork] 90, p. 37.
"World" (tr. of Chen Dongdong). [Footwork] 90, p. 39.
DONGDONG, Chen
    See CHEN, Dongdong
1626. DONLAN, John
    "Footnoted." [NewAW] (6) Spr 90, p. 69.
    "If Pleasure Were Happiness." [NewAW] (6) Spr 90, p. 68.
    "Some of us would like to save the world and some of us." [Caliban] (8) 90, p. 167.
    "Thinking Like a Mountain." [MalR] (92) S 90, p. 48.
    "Tough Enough." [NewAW] (6) Spr 90, p. 67.
    "Utility." [MalR] (92) S 90, p. 49.
    "Wade." [MalR] (92) S 90, p. 50.
1627. DONNELLY, J. R.
    "Fast Is." [AntigR] (80) Wint 90, p. 128.
    "Kindly Refrain from Sneezing on the Exhibits." [SmPd] (27:1, #78) Wint 90, p.
        29.
1628. DONNELLY, Susan
    "Doctor." [GreenMR] (NS 3:2) Fall-Wint 89-90, p. 107.
    "Level 2, Room 20." [GreenMR] (NS 3:2) Fall-Wint 89-90, p. 108.
    "On Throwing Away a Bottle of Tranquilizers." [GreenMR] (NS 3:2) Fall-Wint
        89-90, p. 105-106.
    "The Widener Bird" (Harvard University). [PassN] (11:2) Wint 90, p. 6.
1629. DONOVAN, Deborah
    "A Banner." [AnthNEW] 90, p. 28.
1630. DONOVAN, Gerard Anthony
    "The Seventh." [SycamoreR] (2:1) Wint 90, p. 27.
1631. DONOVAN, Gregory
    "Rural Electrification." [KenR] (NS 12:3) Sum 90, p. 120-122.
1632. DONOVAN, Karen
    "Chemo." [WillowS] (26) Spr 90, p. 39-40.
    "Dissecting *Drosophila* with Marcie: Tucson, Arizona." [IndR] (13:3) Fall 90, p.
        26-27.
    "The Fishway at Holyoke." [IndR] (13:3) Fall 90, p. 29-30.
    "The Protective Waves of the Ordinary." [IndR] (13:3) Fall 90, p. 28.
1633. DONOVAN, Laurence
    "Eleven for Paul Klee" (English Language Poetry Prize). [LindLM] (9:3) Jl-S 90, p.
        20.
    "The Jeweler" (English Language Poetry Prize). [LindLM] (9:3) Jl-S 90, p. 20.
1634. DONOVAN, Stewart
    "Death of the Inshore." [AntigR] (83) Aut 90, p. 99.
    "Frozen Shut." [AntigR] (81/82) Spr-Sum 90, p. 142.
    "Morley Callaghan, 1903-1990." [AntigR] (83) Aut 90, p. 98.
    "Quebec North of Englishtown, Cape Breton." [AntigR] (83) Aut 90, p. 96-97.
1635. DOOLEY, David
    "Cool for April." [Hellas] (1:2) Fall 90, p. 232.
    "O'Keeffe and Stieglitz" (8 selections). [Hudson] (42:4) Wint 90, p. 577-588.
1636. DOOLEY, J.
    "Mr. Poetry." [DogRR] (9:2, #18) Aut 90, p. 11.
    "Where Did She Go?" [DogRR] (9:2, #18) Aut 90, p. 10.
1637. DOORTY, John
    "The Kiss of Death." [BellR] (13:2, #28) Fall 90, p. 9.
DOR, Dan Ben
    See BEN-DOR, Dan
1638. DOR, Moshe
    "Basic Vocabulary" (tr. by Catherine Harnett Shaw). [PoetL] (85:4) Wint 90-91, p.
        22.
    "Dawn" (tr. by Barbara Goldberg). [Confr] (44/45) Fall 90-Wint 91, p. 176.
    "New Alphabet" (tr. by Barbara Goldberg). [Confr] (44/45) Fall 90-Wint 91, p.
        177.
1639. DORESKI, William
    "All Rivers Flow South." [SwampR] (6) Sum-Fall 90, p. 8-9.
    "The Bombing of Tripoli." [DogRR] (9:1, #17) Spr 90, p. 24-25.

"The Onset of Literacy." [DogRR] (9:1, #17) Spr 90, p. 23-24.
"Plane Expressions." [SwampR] (6) Sum-Fall 90, p. 6-7.
"Pond, by Dürer." [LitR] (33:3) Spr 90, p. 334.
"Rimbaud, a Self-Elegy." [Salm] (85/86) Wint-Spr 90, p. 138-139.
"A View of the Desert." [Nimrod] (34:1) Fall-Wint 90, p. 94.
"Washing My Old Yellow Car." [KanQ] (22:3) Sum 90, p. 213-214.
"Writing on the Wall." [KanQ] (22:3) Sum 90, p. 212-213.
1640. DORF, Marilyn
"In Silence." [Plain] (11:1) Fall 90, p. 19.
"Trees Come to the River." [Plain] (10:3) Spr 90, p. 35.
1641. DORING, Stefan
"Between Haste and Deceit" (tr. by Mitch Cohen and Roderick Iverson). [Sulfur] (10:2, #27) Fall 90, p. 101-102.
"Silence the Rest, Awakening" (tr. by Mitch Cohen and Roderick Iverson). [Sulfur] (10:2, #27) Fall 90, p. 102-103.
1642. DORION, Hélène
"Poèmes" (4 poems). [Os] (31) 90, p. 4-7.
1643. DORN, Alfred
"Air Mail." [ManhatPR] (12) [90?], p. 31.
"Digging at Babylon." [ManhatPR] (12) [90?], p. 31.
"A man in the fur trade named Jeeve." [Amelia] (6:2, #17) 90, p. 23.
"Skins." [ManhatPR] (12) [90?], p. 32.
"To a Friend Who Mailed Me His Latest Epic." [Amelia] (6:2, #17) 90, p. 31.
1644. DORNIN, Christopher L.
"The Governor Powell Building." [Nimrod] (34:1) Fall-Wint 90, p. 95.
"Room at Nine." [Amelia] (6:2, #17) 90, p. 61.
"Three Masses of Light." [Amelia] (6:2, #17) 90, p. 61.
"Unknown Veteran." [Nimrod] (34:1) Fall-Wint 90, p. 96.
1645. DORO, Sue
"Bicycles and Other Machines -- 1986." [Pig] (16) 90, p. 51.
"Blue Collar Goodbyes." [Pig] (16) 90, p. 51.
1646. DORSETT, Robert
"The Violinist to His Love." [Paint] (17:33/34) Spr-Aut 90, p. 15.
1647. DORSETT, Thomas
"Death Fugue" (tr. of Paul Celan). [InterPR] (16:2) Fall 90, p. 25, 27.
"The Knee" (tr. of Christian Morgenstern). [InterPR] (16:2) Fall 90, p. 29.
"The Lovely Nasobime" (tr. of Christian Morgenstern). [InterPR] (16:2) Fall 90, p. 31.
"The Murdered Idealist." [InterPR] (16:2) Fall 90, p. 123.
"Phoenix to Photons." [Mildred] (4:1) 90, p. 108.
"The Pike" (tr. of Christian Morgenstern). [InterPR] (16:2) Fall 90, p. 31.
"Sea Gull Song" (tr. of Christian Morgenstern). [InterPR] (16:2) Fall 90, p. 29.
"With a Changing Key" (tr. of Paul Celan). [InterPR] (16:2) Fall 90, p. 23.
1648. DOTREMONT, Christian
"The Queen of Walls" (Excerpt, tr. by Jean-Clarence Lambert and Bradley R. Strahan). [Vis] (32) 90, p. 35.
1649. DOTY, Catherine
"Daddy." [NegC] (10:1) 90, p. 53.
"Landscape with Ponytrack." [NegC] (10:1) 90, p. 54.
1650. DOTY, Mark
"Chanteuse." [IndR] (13:2) Spr 90, p. 66-70.
"The Death of Antinoüs." [Poetry] (156:2) My 90, p. 98-99.
"Lament-Heaven." [Ploughs] (16:1) Spr-Sum 90, p. 188-193.
"Tiara." [Ploughs] (16:1) Spr-Sum 90, p. 186-187.
"The Ware Collection of Glass Flowers and Fruit, Harvard Museum." [Boulevard] (5:2, #14) Fall 90, p. 33-34.
"The Wings." [MissouriR] (13:1) 90, p. 19-27.
"Winter Journal." [MidAR] (10:1) 90, p. 1-6.
1651. DOUBIAGO, Sharon
"Free (Your Father)." [Pearl] (12) Fall-Wint 90, p. 63.
"Poem to the Child Never to Be Born" (The last two lines are from a song by Desirée). [PennR] (4:2) 90, p. 43-44.
"Self" (Selections from "Part I. The Journal of Albion Moonlight"). [PennR] (4:2) 90, p. 37-42.
"This Morning I Woke into the Body" (occurred May 4, 1977, Albion Ridge). [PennR] (4:2) 90, p. 45-46.

144

D'OUESSANT

D'OUESSANT, Ile
   See OUESSANT, Ile d'
DOUGALL, Alan Mac
   See Mac DOUGALL, Alan
1652. DOUGHERTY, Sean Thomas
   "The Cat's Face." [BlackBR] (12) Fall-Wint 90, p. 40.
   "In the Shoe and Garment District." [BlackBR] (12) Fall-Wint 90, p. 37.
   "Paragraph from a Letter to Suzanne." [OnTheBus] (2:2/3:1, #6/7) Sum-Fall 90
      Wint-Spr 91, p. 75.
   "Table Sugar." [OnTheBus] (2:1, #5) Spr 90, p. 65.
   "Walking Past Construction" (for GJV 1964-1983). [MoodySI] (22/23) Wint 89-90,
      p. 24.
1653. DOUGLAS, Ann
   "The Photographer." [ConnPR] (9:1) 90, p. 22-23.
1654. DOUGLAS, Bernard M.
   "The Library." [BlackBR] (11) Spr-Sum 90, p. 24.
1655. DOUGLAS, Charles
   "Nineteen Poems" (Selections: xiii-xiv, xvi-xix). [Writ] (21) 89 c1990, p. 80-85.
   "Paving Stones." [Writ] (21) 89 c1990, p. 79.
   "What the Poets Are." [Writ] (21) 89 c1990, p. 78.
1656. DOUGLASS, Karen
   "Handling the Dead." [GreenMR] (NS 3:2) Fall-Wint 89-90, p. 111.
   "The Rich Man Eats a Cracker." [GreenMR] (NS 3:2) Fall-Wint 89-90, p. 109-110.
1657. DOURIAN, Loudvig
   "Crane" (tr. by Diana Der-Hovanessian). [Nimrod] (33:2) Spr-Sum 90, p. 38.
1658. DOUSKEY, Franz
   "Old Dog." [NewYorkQ] (43) Fall 90, p. 45.
   "Winter Among the Blackfeet." [NewYorkQ] (42) Sum 90, p. 37.
1659. DOVE, Rita
   "The Musician Talks About 'Process'" (after Anthony "Spoons" Pough). [Chelsea]
      (49) 90, p. 60.
   "On Veronica." [GeoR] (44:1/2) Spr-Sum 90, p. 62.
1660. DOW, Mark
   "Late Summer Sunset, West Coast of Florida" (In Memory of Robert Penn Warren,
      1905-1989). [SouthernR] (26:4) O 90, p. 904-905.
1661. DOW, Philip
   "D'Amour et D'Eau Fraîche." [Ploughs] (16:4) Wint 90-91, p. 128.
1662. DOWNE, Lise
   "Summertime Brochure." [WestCL] (24:3) Wint 90, p. 67-69.
   "Visitation." [Screens] (2) 90, p. 181.
1663. DOWNEY, Patrick
   "Quandary." [JINJPo] (12:2) Aut 90, p. 18.
1664. DOWNIE, Glen
   "The Secret Dream of Space." [Rohwedder] (5) Spr 90, p. 23.
1665. DOWNS, Buck
   "The Sonnets" (Selections: Five Poems). [WashR] (16:4) D 90-Ja 91, p. 11.
1666. DOYLE, James
   "The Brides." [HawaiiR] (14:2, #29) Spr 90, p. 39.
   "Christ in Abeyance." [Poem] (64) N 90, p. 48.
   "The Crossing of Legs." [HawaiiR] (14:3, #30) Fall 90, p. 14.
   "The Hours." [HawaiiR] (14:3, #30) Fall 90, p. 14.
   "The Origin of the Milky Way." [SoDakR] (28:3) Aut 90, p. 74.
   "The Sculpture." [DogRR] (9:1, #17) Spr 90, p. 53.
   "The Village." [Poetry] (156:4) Jl 90, p. 200.
1667. DOYLE, Lynn
   "Best Friend." [VirQR] (66:1) Wint 90, p. 77-79.
   "The High School of O." [WestHR] (44:4) Wint 90, p. 418-420.
   "Rote of Forgetfulness." [Field] (43) Fall 90, p. 54.
1668. DOYLE, Nancy
   "Remains." [Plain] (10:2) Wint 90, p. 31.
1669. DOYLE, Sally
   "Shepherding (Transporting Sheep)" (Selections). [Avec] (3:1) 90, p. 33.
1670. DRAEGER, Amy
   "December 24th." [EvergreenC] (5:2) Wint 90, p. 18-19.
1671. DRAGNEA, Gabriela
   "Pure Conversation with a Chinese Character" (tr. of Marin Sorescu, w. Stuart

Friebert). [NewYorker] (66:15) 28 My 90, p. 36.
"Thoughts" (tr. of Marin Sorescu, w. Stuart Friebert). [PoetryE] (29) Spr 90, p. 132.
1672. DRAGOMOSHCHENKO, Arkadii
"Xenia" (Excerpt, tr. by Elena Balashova and Lyn Hejinian). [PoetryUSA] (5:3) Fall 90, p. 19.
"Xenia" (Excerpt, tr. by Lyn Hejinian and Elena Balashova). [Screens] (2) 90, p. 5-7.
1673. DRAKE, Albert
"Tansy Ragwort." [SwampR] (5) Wint-Spr 90, p. 33.
1674. DRAMÉ, Kandioura
"Barlaban: a Mandinka Epic" (Excerpt, tr. of Anonymous). [Callaloo] (13:3) Sum 90, p. 435-462.
1675. DREHER, Dorothy
"Ozy's Mandate" (with respects to Shelly). [Wind] (20:67) 90, p. 26.
DRESSAY, Anne Le
See Le DRESSAY, Anne
1676. DREW, George
"Julius II" (The Court of Angels, 20 February 1513). [Salm] (85/86) Wint-Spr 90, p. 53-54.
"Tell Me About the Soul: Leonardo at Cloux, 1916-19." [Salm] (85/86) Wint-Spr 90, p. 50-51.
"Tell Me If: Leonardo in the Belvedere, 1513-16." [Salm] (85/86) Wint-Spr 90, p. 47-49.
"Torrigiano." [Salm] (85/86) Wint-Spr 90, p. 52.
1677. DREXEL, John
"Virginia Woolf at Giggleswick." [Salm] (85/86) Wint-Spr 90, p. 140-141.
1678. DRINKARD, Tom
"Chapels at Dauchau, 1971." [NegC] (10:2/3) 90, p. 116.
1679. DRISCOLL, Jack
"Bounty Hunting for Snappers" (from "Building the Cold from Memory"). [SwampR] (6) Sum-Fall 90, p. 35.
"Look Park: Florence, Massachusetts, 1958" (for Mary Ruefle, from "Building the Cold from Memory"). [SwampR] (6) Sum-Fall 90, p. 34.
"The Outfielder" (w. Bill Meissner). [ColEng] (52:8) D 90, p. 884.
"The Trap" (with Bill Meissner). [KenR] (NS 12:2) Spr 90, p. 65.
"Voices of Ice" (with Bill Meissner). [KenR] (NS 12:2) Spr 90, p. 65.
1680. DRIZHAL, Peter
"At a Crosswalk." [BlackBR] (11) Spr-Sum 90, p. 11.
"The Lecturer." [BlackBR] (11) Spr-Sum 90, p. 10.
1681. DRUCKER, Johanna
"Future Language." [Screens] (2) 90, p. 209-210.
"Past Tension." [Screens] (2) 90, p. 206-207.
"Present Perfected." [Screens] (2) 90, p. 207-209.
1682. DRUMMEY, Jenny
"What We Did with the Bodies." [NewYorkQ] (42) Sum 90, p. 90.
1683. DRUMMOND, Robbie Newton
"Of Your Love." [CanLit] (126) Aut 90, p. 131.
"The Ride of the Pale Horse." [Quarry] (39:2) Spr 90, p. 31-33.
"With a Knowing Smile." [AntigR] (80) Wint 90, p. 132.
1684. DRURY, John
"Burning the Flags." [NewRep] (203:21) 19 N 90, p. 38.
"The Coming On." [PoetryNW] (31:3) Aut 90, p. 32-33.
"Disastrous Love." [WestHR] (44:4) Wint 90, p. 421.
"Matinee." [HighP] (5:3) Wint 90-91, p. 77.
"Suicide Bridge." [TarRP] (29:2) Spr 90, p. 29-30.
1685. D'SOUZA, Charmayne
"God's Will?" [Arc] (25) Aut 90, p. 70.
"I Would Like to Have a Movie Cowboy for a Husband." [Arc] (25) Aut 90, p. 69.
Du . . .
See also names beginning with "Du" without the following space, filed below in their alphabetic positions, e.g., DuPLESSIS.
1686. DU, Fu
"Before the Rebellion" (tr. by Graeme Wilson). [LitR] (33:2) Wint 90, p. 195.
1687. DU BOUCHET, André
"Dans la Chaleur Vacante (In the Vacant Heat)" (Selections: 4 poems, Published by

Mercure de France, 1961, tr. by Cid Corman). [Avec] (3:1) 90, p. 78-81.
1688. DUBIE, Norman
"In a Time Out of Joint" (homage to Philip K. Dick). [Manoa] (2:1) Spr 90, p.
116-117.
"A Renunciation of the Desert Primrose" (For J. Robert Oppenheimer). [NewEngR]
(12:4) Sum 90, p. 349.
"Riddle" (in memory of the painter Stephen Davis). [OnTheBus] (2:2/3:1, #6/7)
Sum-Fall 90 Wint-Spr 91, p. 78.
"Safe Conduct." [OnTheBus] (2:2/3:1, #6/7) Sum-Fall 90 Wint-Spr 91, p. 76-78.
"Two Women on the Potomac Parkway." [Manoa] (2:1) Spr 90, p. 115-116.
1689. DUBIELAK, C. A.
"The Note." [MidAR] (10:2) 90, p. 160.
1690. DUCAL, Charles
"Dawn" (tr. by David Siefkin and Catharina Kochuyt). [Vis] (34) 90, p. 9.
"East of Eden" (tr. by David Siefkin and Catharina Kochuyt). [Vis] (34) 90, p. 10.
"Eden" (tr. by David Siefkin and Catharina Kochuyt). [Vis] (34) 90, p. 9.
"The Hare" (tr. by David Siefkin and Catharina Kochuyt). [Vis] (34) 90, p. 10.
"Mother Tongue" (tr. by David Siefkin and Catharina Kochuyt). [Vis] (34) 90, p.
11.
"Odysseus" (tr. by David Siefkin and Catharina Kochuyt). [Vis] (34) 90, p. 12.
"Wife" (tr. by David Siefkin and Catharina Kochuyt). [Vis] (34) 90, p. 11.
1691. DUCHARME, Guy
"Les abeilles seules remuent." [Os] (30) Spr 90, p. 26.
"Irrésolu le matin." [Os] (30) Spr 90, p. 25.
"Quelqu'un rit." [Os] (30) Spr 90, p. 24.
1692. DUCORNET, Rikki
"Unicorn" (tr. of Federico Patán, w. the author). [DenQ] (24:3) Wint 90, p. 44.
"The Uranoscopes" (tr. of Pierre Laurendeau). [DenQ] (24:3) Wint 90, p. 45.
1693. DUDDY, Patrick
"A Dream of Permanence." [GreensboroR] (48) Sum 90, p. 120.
"Parenting." [GreensboroR] (48) Sum 90, p. 120.
1694. DUDLEY, Deborah
"Meeting You in Me." [ChangingM] (21) Wint-Spr 90, p. 29.
1695. DUEHR, Gary
"Echo." [ConnPR] (9:1) 90, p. 27.
"Green." [WestHR] (44:2) Sum 90, p. 224.
DUEHR, Gloria Mindock
See MINDOCK-DUEHR, Gloria
1696. DUER, David
"By Scottish Roads." [BlueBldgs] (12) 90, p. 25.
1697. DUFFIN, Brent
"Traveling in a Comfortable Car" (tr. of Bertolt Brecht, w. Michael Landolt).
[InterPR] (16:2) Fall 90, p. 21.
1698. DUFFIN, K. E.
"Goethe at Naples." [PartR] (57:2) Spr 90, p. 277-278.
1699. DUFFY, Carol Ann
"Foreign." [Quarry] (39:1) Wint 90, p. 20.
1700. DUFRESNE, John
"Someone My Father Knew." [MidwQ] (31:4) Sum 90, p. 485.
1701. DUGAN, Alan
"Against the Text 'Art Is Immortal'." [Agni] (29/30) 90, p. 160-161.
"Know Thyself." [Agni] (29/30) 90, p. 159.
1702. DUGAN, Irene
"Halloweening." [SenR] (20:2) Fall 90, p. 58.
"What I Think My Brother Saw." [SenR] (20:2) Fall 90, p. 59.
DUGGAN, Devon Miller
See MILLER-DUGGAN, Devon
1703. DUGGIN, Lorraine
"Blessings Sonnet." [Plain] (11:1) Fall 90, p. 30.
"Your Face" (For Bruce). [Plain] (10:3) Spr 90, p. 19.
1704. DUHAMEL, Denise
"Asthma." [OntR] (32) Spr-Sum 90, p. 94-95.
"Boy." [Confr] (44/45) Fall 90-Wint 91, p. 142.
"The Boy Who Dimmed Light Bulbs" (for Phil). [SycamoreR] (2:2) Sum 90, p.
22-24.
"How Pluperfect Our Past Lives" (for J. K.). [NoDaQ] (58:3) Sum 90, p. 4.

147

"A Lesson in What Romance Is." [CutB] (34) Sum-Fall 90, p. 39.
"Mr. Donut." [Confr] (44/45) Fall 90-Wint 91, p. 143.
"My Mother Dreams: If Her Husband Dies, Who Will Cut the Lawn?" [WestB] (27) 90, p. 27-29.
"Sleeping and Wings" (To My Grandmother). [FreeL] (5) Sum 90, p. 10-11.
"Sometimes the First Boys Don't Count." [NoDaQ] (58:3) Sum 90, p. 3-4.
"Ten Qualities As a Cosmo Girl I Really Want in My Man" (for Jean Valentine, after seeing "Bambi"). [Gargoyle] (37/38) 90, p. 29.
1705. DUMARAN, Adele
"Fieldwork, Devil's Lake, Wisconsin." [Nimrod] (34:1) Fall-Wint 90, p. 49.
1706. DUMARS, Denise
"In the Bar at the Cockatoo Inn" (w. Todd Mecklam). [Pearl] (10) Spr 90, p. 11.
"It All Started Very Early." [Pearl] (11) Sum 90, p. 46.
"Marilyn Reading Rilke" (a true story). [Pearl] (12) Fall-Wint 90, p. 34.
1707. DUMITRU, Cyra Sweet
"February Faultline." [Nimrod] (34:1) Fall-Wint 90, p. 97.
"Green Field." [Nimrod] (34:1) Fall-Wint 90, p. 98-99.
"Witnessing Wind." [Nimrod] (34:1) Fall-Wint 90, p. 100.
1708. DUNCAN, B. N.
"Expectation." [PoetryUSA] (5:3) Fall 90, p. 25.
"Will Berkeley, CA., Become Just Another Sick American City?" [PoetryUSA] (5:3) Fall 90, p. 25.
1709. DUNCAN, Graham
"At Bay." [Wind] (20:66) 90, p. 10-11.
"Cement Town." [Wind] (20:66) 90, p. 10.
"White Histories." [Blueline] (11:1/2) 90, p. 24.
DUNCAN, Malcolm Mac
See Mac DUNCAN, Malcolm
1710. DUNCAN, Peter
"The Falls Revisited." [Footwork] 90, p. 65.
1711. DUNETZ, Lora
"The Scenic Side." [Confr] (44/45) Fall 90-Wint 91, p. 205.
1712. DUNHAM, Vera
"After the War" (tr. of Yunna Moritz, w. William Jay Smith). [AmerPoR] (19:6) N-D 90, p. 42.
"And Stands Reflected in the Mirror Across the Room" (tr. of Yunna Moritz, w. William Jay Smith). [AmerPoR] (19:6) N-D 90, p. 42.
"A Bad Memory" (tr. of Aleksandr Tkachenko, w. William Jay Smith). [AmerPoR] (19:6) N-D 90, p. 43.
"In April" (tr. of Yunna Moritz, w. William Jay Smith). [AmerPoR] (19:6) N-D 90, p. 42.
"Letters" (tr. of Aleksandr Tkachenko, w. William Jay Smith). [AmerPoR] (19:6) N-D 90, p. 43.
"Three Lakes" (tr. of Aleksandr Tkachenko, w. William Jay Smith). [AmerPoR] (19:6) N-D 90, p. 43.
1713. DUNKELBERG, Kendall
"Evenings" (tr. of Paul Snoek). [Farm] (7:1) Spr 90, p. 73.
"Landscapes" (tr. of Paul Snoek). [Farm] (7:1) Spr 90, p. 75-79.
"The Scarecrow" (tr. of Paul Snoek). [Farm] (7:1) Spr 90, p. 69, 71.
1714. DUNN, Racous Robert
"St. Misbehavin'." [ChironR] (9:1) Spr 90, p. 13.
1715. DUNN, Stephen
"Beautiful Women." [Poetry] (155:5) F 90, p. 337-339.
"Elegy for My Innocence." [PoetryNW] (31:1) Spr 90, p. 40-41.
"Epithalamion" (for a second marriage). [ParisR] (32:114) Spr 90, p. 120.
"An Erotics for Browsing in a Museum" (Another Memo to Myself). [ThRiPo] (35/36) 90, p. 65-66.
"Landscape at the End of the Century." [Poetry] (155:5) F 90, p. 335-336.
"Little Essay on Communication." [Poetry] (155:5) F 90, p. 336-337.
"Long Term." [Hudson] (43:2) Sum 90, p. 274-275.
"Loves." [Poetry] (155:5) F 90, p. 339-350.
"Middle Class Poem." [CimR] (92) Jl 90, p. 134-135.
"Not the Occult." [GeoR] (44:3) Fall 90, p. 461-463.
"The Routine Things Around the House." [Hudson] (43:2) Sum 90, p. 270-272.
"A Secret Life." [Antaeus] (64/65) Spr-Aut 90, p. 30.
"The Storm." [PoetryNW] (31:1) Spr 90, p. 41-42.

"The Sudden Light and the Trees" (Syracuse, 1969). [ParisR] (32:114) Spr 90, p. 118-119.
"What They Wanted." [AmerPoR] (19:6) N-D 90, p. 56.
1716. DUNN, Susan
"If I could watch the calliopied prance of the orange-maned poinies" (reprinted from #6, 1982). [Kaleid] (20) Wint-Spr 90, p. 52.
"You wish you could bring her back from so far away" (reprinted from #6, 1982). [Kaleid] (20) Wint-Spr 90, p. 52.
1717. DUNNQUEA, Sebasijobriel
"Heirloom" (in memory of Dr. Martin Luther King). [KanQ] (22:3) Sum 90, p. 46.
1718. DUNPHY, Thomas
"No Turkeys Allowed." [PoetryUSA] (5:2) Sum 90, p. 4.
1719. DUNWOODY, Michael
"Indian Sonnets." [AntigR] (80) Wint 90, p. 26-28.
1720. DUO, Duo
"My Uncle." [PoetryUSA] (5:3) Fall 90, p. 19.
1721. DuPLESSIS, Rachel Blau
"Page." [Conjunc] (15) 90, p. 243-247.
"The Section Called O" (from "Draft X, Letters," dedicated here to Susan Howe). [Talisman] (4) Spr 90, p. 44.
1722. DUPREY, Jean Pierre
"Bedroom" (tr. by Jean-Clarence Lambert and Bradley R. Strahan). [Vis] (32) 90, p. 39.
1723. DuPRIEST, Travis
"Flying Home on Sunday Morning." [ChrC] (107:34) 21-28 N 90, p. 1098.
1724. DURBIN, Jacob
"The teacher scrawls cold calculations." [PoetryUSA] ([5:4?]) Wint 90, p. 26.
1725. DURBIN, Martina
"The Dismorphia Butterfly: Protective Mimicry in a Single Species." [InterPR] (16:2) Fall 90, p. 120.
"Sparrow Hawk Season." [InterPR] (16:2) Fall 90, p. 119.
"The Time I Was Very Quiet and Just Listened." [InterPR] (16:2) Fall 90, p. 118.
"Walking Away from Things That Are Important" (for Michael Wilds). [InterPR] (16:2) Fall 90, p. 121.
"With the Koi." [InterPR] (16:2) Fall 90, p. 116-117.
1726. DURHAM, Flora
"Anima." [SwampR] (6) Sum-Fall 90, p. 64-65.
"Body Count 1952." [SwampR] (6) Sum-Fall 90, p. 52-53.
"For As Long As We've Worn Our Bodies." [SwampR] (5) Wint-Spr 90, p. 101-102.
"The Going On." [SwampR] (6) Sum-Fall 90, p. 60-61.
"He Didn't Get Leda." [SwampR] (6) Sum-Fall 90, p. 68.
"Ikinokoru" (Selections: 4 poems). [SwampR] (6) Sum-Fall 90, p. 56-59.
"A Proper Introduction." [SwampR] (6) Sum-Fall 90, p. 62-63.
"Sheep Camp." [SwampR] (6) Sum-Fall 90, p. 50-51.
"Sometimes All at Once." [SwampR] (6) Sum-Fall 90, p. 66-67.
"Still at War." [SwampR] (6) Sum-Fall 90, p. 54-55.
"Where the Music Comes From." [SwampR] (5) Wint-Spr 90, p. 99-100.
DUSEN, Kate van
See Van DUSEN, Kate
1727. DUVAL, Quinton
"Flying." [HayF] (6) Sum 90, p. 85.
"In Vino Veritas." [GettyR] (3:1) Wint 90, p. 168.
"Testing." [HayF] (6) Sum 90, p. 86.
DUYN, Mona van
See Van DUYN, Mona
1728. DWELLER, Cliff
"Author in Search of a Sonnet." [ContextS] (1:1) 89, p. 32-33.
1729. DWYER, William
"Two Wars." [Wind] (20:67) 90, p. 15.
1730. DYCK, Marje A.
"Easy Passage." [Grain] (18:3) Fall 90, p. 59.
"A Sure Thing." [Grain] (18:3) Fall 90, p. 59.
1731. DYKEWOMON, Elana
"Some Things Chava Meyer Says." [SinW] (42) Wint 90-91, p. 29-31.

149

1732. DYMENT, Margaret
"Love, the Word." [Arc] (25) Aut 90, p. 12.
1733. EADS, Winifred E.
"Durable Rustproof Saturday Night." [SinW] (42) Wint 90-91, p. 92-93.
1734. EADY, Cornelius
"Muddy Waters & The Chicago Blues." [MinnR] (NS 34/35) Spr-Fall 90, p. 3.
"My Gratitude." [Pequod] (31) 90, p. 26-31.
"The Supremes." [MinnR] (NS 34/35) Spr-Fall 90, p. 2.
"Why Do So Few Blacks Study Creative Writing?" [MinnR] (NS 34/35) Spr-Fall
90, p. 1-2.
EAGLE, Duane Big
See BIGEAGLE, Duane
EASTON, Jean Anaporte
See ANAPORTE-EASTON, Jean
1735. EATON, Charles Edward
"Afflatus." [HawaiiR] (14:2, #29) Spr 90, p. 118.
"Blue Dancers." [HawaiiR] (14:3, #30) Fall 90, p. 107.
"The Clown in the Closet." [LullwaterR] (2:1) Wint 90, p. 89.
"Cottonmouth." [HiramPoR] (47) Wint 90, p. 24.
"The Crank." [CharR] (16:1) Spr 90, p. 79.
"Day Lilies." [Poem] (64) N 90, p. 61.
"Delta." [CharR] (16:1) Spr 90, p. 80.
"Flaws." [Confr] (42/43) Spr-Sum 90, p. 134.
"Front Porch Glider." [FloridaR] (17:2) Fall-Wint 90, p. 157.
"Home Thoughts from Abroad." [CrossCur] (9:2) Je 90, p. 91-92.
"The Javelin." [ConnPR] (9:1) 90, p. 41-42.
"La Loge." [InterPR] (16:2) Fall 90, p. 114.
"Palmy Days." [Paint] (17:33/34) Spr-Aut 90, p. 11-12.
"Pliers." [ManhatPR] (12) [90?], p. 41.
"Regrets Only." [PraS] (64:2) Sum 90, p. 21-22.
"Snow Leopard." [Poem] (64) N 90, p. 62.
"Squashes." [HiramPoR] (47) Wint 90, p. 60.
"Squeegee." [Salm] (88/89) Fall 90-Wint 91, p. 153.
"Stalactite." [Poem] (64) N 90, p. 63.
"Stylebook." [Salm] (88/89) Fall 90-Wint 91, p. 151-152.
"The Thread." [InterPR] (16:2) Fall 90, p. 115.
"Touch and Go." [CharR] (16:1) Spr 90, p. 77-78.
"The Wetback." [CalQ] (34) 90, p. 23.
1736. EBERHART, Richard
"June 22." [BelPoJ] (40:4) Sum 90, p. 22.
"Slant Angle." [AnthNEW] 90, p. 6.
1737. EBERLY, Kathryn
"This Poem Speaks for Itself." [SingHM] (18) 90, p. 73.
1738. EBERSOLE, Glenda
"Visiting Your Sister in the Psychiatric Ward." [SouthernPR] (30:2) Fall 90, p.
52-53.
'EBINYO OGBOWEI, G.
See OGBOWEI, G. 'Ebinyo
1739. ECHAVARREN, Roberto
"Clearing." [LitR] (33:4) Sum 90, p. 419.
"Footlights." [LitR] (33:4) Sum 90, p. 420.
"Just on the Thirty-first." [LitR] (33:4) Sum 90, p. 418.
1740. ECHELBERGER, M. J.
"Union Men." [HiramPoR] (48/49) 90-91, p. 26.
1741. ECHERRI, Vicente
"Yo Te Habia Visto." [LindLM] (9:4) O-D 90, p. 46.
1742. ECREVAN, Marée Dzian
"To Grandmother's Bed." [SinW] (41) Sum-Fall 90, p. 118.
1743. EDELSTEIN, Carol
"Desire." [YellowS] (33) Spr 90, p. 25.
"Marriage Song." [GreenMR] (NS 4:1) Spr-Sum 90, p. 116.
"Orchard." [Kalliope] (12:2) 90, p. 54.
"Polishing the Hardware." [GreenMR] (NS 4:1) Spr-Sum 90, p. 115.
"Sunday Night Rapids." [Kalliope] (12:2) 90, p. 55.
"Today." [GreenMR] (NS 4:1) Spr-Sum 90, p. 117.

1744. EDFELT, Johannes
"The Bed" (tr. by Robin Fulton). [OntR] (33) Fall-Wint 90-91, p. 92.
"The Dog at Bruges" (tr. by David Ignatow and Leif Sjöberg). [OntR] (33) Fall-Wint 90-91, p. 91.
"The Logjam" (tr. by Robin Fulton). [OntR] (33) Fall-Wint 90-91, p. 93.
"Senex" (tr. by David Ignatow and Leif Sjöberg). [OntR] (33) Fall-Wint 90-91, p. 92.
"The Solitary" (tr. by Robin Fulton). [OntR] (33) Fall-Wint 90-91, p. 93.
1745. EDGAR, Vernon
"High Utterance." [PoetryUSA] (5:3) Fall 90, p. 17.
1746. EDLIN, Ken
"Close Calling." [Verse] (7:2) Sum 90, p. 50.
"Ectopic Pregnancy." [Verse] (7:2) Sum 90, p. 48.
"A Little Twist of the Lips." [Verse] (7:2) Sum 90, p. 49-50.
"Nightmares." [Verse] (7:2) Sum 90, p. 49.
"This is salamander country." [Verse] (7:2) Sum 90, p. 48.
1747. EDMISTEN, Patricia Taylor
"Worth Avenue." [EmeraldCR] (1990) c89, p. 16-17.
1748. EDMOND, Lauris
"Breakdown." [CumbPR] (9:2) Spr 90, p. 7.
"Brian." [Verse] (7:2) Sum 90, p. 25.
"Dog." [Verse] (7:2) Sum 90, p. 24-25.
"Writing on the Wall." [Verse] (7:2) Sum 90, p. 24.
1749. EDMONSON, Roger A.
"The Consort to the King of Naples." [JamesWR] (7:2) Wint 90, p. 8-9.
1750. EDMUNDS, Martin
"Bella Roma." [ParisR] (32:116) Fall 90, p. 44-45.
"December 27, 1988." [Agni] (31/32) 90, p. 177-181.
1751. EDSON, Russell
"The Enchantment." [WillowS] (25) Wint 90, p. 7.
"The House Frog." [WillowS] (25) Wint 90, p. 8.
"The Position." [SycamoreR] (2:1) Wint 90, p. 15.
"Soup Song." [SycamoreR] (2:1) Wint 90, p. 14.
"The While Awaying." [WillowS] (25) Wint 90, p. 9.
1752. EDWARDS, Nancy
"His Conversion." [Amelia] (6:2, #17) 90, p. 74.
1753. EDWARDS, Robert
"Calf Creek Falls." [Spirit] (10:2) 90, p. 112.
"The Dead Poets." [DogRR] (9:2, #18) Aut 90, p. 50-51.
"Dream Poem #7." [RagMag] (8:1) 90, p. 52.
"Dream Poem #8." [DogRR] (9:2, #18) Aut 90, p. 49.
"Shaman Fable." [RagMag] (7:2) Spr 90, p. 12.
1754. EDWARDS, Thomas
"Attempt at Paradise" (tr. of Ulrich Schacht). [PoetryE] (29) Spr 90, p. 86.
"The Craftsmen Have Left" (tr. of Reiner Kunze). [PoetryE] (29) Spr 90, p. 84.
"Distant morning" (tr. of Ulrich Schacht). [PoetryE] (29) Spr 90, p. 89-90.
"How many dreams" (tr. of Ulrich Schacht). [PoetryE] (29) Spr 90, p. 88.
"Lübars" (tr. of Ulrich Schacht). [PoetryE] (29) Spr 90, p. 87.
"A man set out" (tr. of Ulrich Schacht). [PoetryE] (29) Spr 90, p. 88-89.
"Out of Sight" (tr. of Friedhelm Mäker). [PoetryE] (29) Spr 90, p. 83.
"This hardened suspicion" (tr. of Ulrich Schacht). [PoetryE] (29) Spr 90, p. 85.
"To an Actor, Who Asked That His Role Be Lengthened" (tr. of Reiner Kunze). [PoetryE] (29) Spr 90, p. 84.
1755. EFIRD, Susan
"The Faceless." [SouthernPR] (30:1) Spr 90, p. 13-14.
1756. EFTHIMIADES, Despina
"The Poems, a River, the Poet" (tr. of George Markópoulos). [GrahamHR] (13) Spr 90, p. 99.
"Vacations, 1978" (tr. of Manólis Peatikákis). [GrahamHR] (13) Spr 90, p. 100-101.
"Who Art You?" (tr. of Andónis Fostiéris). [GrahamHR] (13) Spr 90, p. 102.
1757. EGAN, Dennis
"Bush Fire" (tr. of Tichicaya U Tam'si). [Vis] (32) 90, p. 9.
"The Comrade" (tr. of Gaston Miron). [Vis] (32) 90, p. 50.
"For Haiti" (tr. of Rene Depestre). [Vis] (32) 90, p. 22.
"Gulf Stream" (tr. of Rene Belance, w. Jean-Clarence Lambert and Bradley R.

Strahan). [Vis] (32) 90, p. 24.
"I Belong to the High Day" (tr. of Paul Dakeyo, w. Jean-Clarence Lambert and
    Bradley R. Strahan). [Vis] (32) 90, p. 9.
"In Outaouais" (tr. of Gaston Miron). [Vis] (32) 90, p. 49.
"The Lovers at Teruel" (tr. of Jean-Clarence Lambert). [Vis] (32) 90, p. 45.
"Poem: What is it to be face to face?" (tr. of Bernard Noel, w. Jean-Clarence
    Lambert and Bradley R. Strahan). [Vis] (32) 90, p. 46.
"Poetry Festival" (Paris, 1987, tr. of Jean Baptiste Tiemele, w. Jean-Clarence
    Lambert and Bradley R. Strahan). [Vis] (32) 90, p. 11.
"Sorrow" (tr. of Gaston Miron). [Vis] (32) 90, p. 50.
"Still Life" (tr. of Tichicaya U Tam'si). [Vis] (32) 90, p. 10.
1758. EGAN, Desmond
    "Two Worlds" (Spoleto, Italy 1966). [NewYorkQ] (41) Spr 90, p. 80-81.
1759. EGAN, Michael
    "The Hex." [HampSPR] (Anthology 1975-1990) 90, p. 160.
    "The Keys." [HampSPR] (Anthology 1975-1990) 90, p. 161.
1760. EGAN, Moira
    "Legacy." [Pearl] (12) Fall-Wint 90, p. 37.
1761. EGEMO, Constance
    "Night Gallery" (form an exhibit at Walker Art Gallery). [SingHM] (17) 90, p.
        36-37.
1762. EGGAN, Ferd
    "Fulfill Desire." [HangL] (56) 90, p. 12-14.
1763. EHRENBURG, Ilya
    "The Invader" (tr. by William Pitt Root). [PoetryE] (30) Fall 90, p. 30.
1764. EHRHART, W. D.
    "Afraid of Myself." [ChironR] (9:1) Spr 90, p. 22.
    "America Enters the 1990's." [ConnPR] (9:1) 90, p. 28.
    "Games People Play." [ChironR] (9:2) Sum 90, p. 20.
    "Unaccustomed Mercies" (for Larry Heinemann). [AmerPoR] (19:5) S-O 90, p. 10.
1765. EHRLICH, P. S.
    "Apologia to the Back of Our Necks." [DogRR] (9:1, #17) Spr 90, p. 45.
1766. EHRLICH, Shelley
    "Lot's Wife, Amzar by Name." [ManhatPR] (12) [90?], p. 44-46.
    "A Student of Forsythia." [ManhatPR] (12) [90?], p. 44.
1767. EIGNER, Larry
    "I want to go home" (First published in Kaleidoscope Magazine). [PoetryUSA]
        ([5:4?]) Wint 90, p. 12.
1768. EIMERS, Nancy
    "Another Kimono." [PassN] (11:1) Sum 90, p. 29.
    "No Friends of the Heart." [AntR] (48:2) Spr 90, p. 222-223.
    "Punk Girl, Wedding." [PassN] (11:1) Sum 90, p. 29.
    "A Visit to Amherst." [PassN] (11:1) Sum 90, p. 30.
EINAR BRAGI
    See Bragi, Einar
1770. EINZIG, Barbara
    "After Christoph Hein's The Distant Lover." [Conjunc] (15) 90, p. 199-206.
1771. EISELE, Thomas
    "I can remember." [NewYorkQ] (43) Fall 90, p. 72.
1772. EISENBERG, Ruth F.
    "Circling." [Spirit] (10:2) 90, p. 127.
1773. EISENBERG, Susan
    "Perspective." [SingHM] (18) 90, p. 22.
1774. EKLUND, George
    "26. The only loves they've known longer." [ChironR] (9:4) Wint 90, p. 8.
    "27. For a moment she does not feel." [ChironR] (9:4) Wint 90, p. 8.
    "28. I looked in her mirror." [ChironR] (9:4) Wint 90, p. 8.
    "29. The flies had been driven mad." [ChironR] (9:4) Wint 90, p. 8.
1775. El RAMEY, Debra
    "Music in the Night." [Crucible] (26) Fall 90, p. 78.
1776. ELDER, Karl
    "Leland." [Parting] (3:1) Sum 90, p. 35.
    "Zero." [Parting] (3:1) Sum 90, p. 6.
1777. ELDER, Theresa
    "Gingko." [Parting] (3:1) Sum 90, p. 10.
    "Gingko." [Parting] (3:2) Wint 90-91, p. 30.

1778. ELDRIDGE, Kevin Joe
"Postcard from Weeping Water, Nebraska" (for Laurie Ann). [Shen] (40:3) Fall 90,
p. 40.
1779. ELENKOV, Luchezar
"Poet" (tr. by Jascha Kessler and Alexander Shurbanov). [Screens] (2) 90, p. 62.
1780. ELGARRESTA, José (Elgarresta Ramirez de Haro, José)
"The Advertising Man" (tr. by Sara Heikof Woehrlen). [Agni] (29/30) 90, p.
203-204.
"Psalm XVIII" (tr. by Sara Heikoff Woehrlen). [LitR] (33:2) Wint 90, p. 190.
"Psalm XXIV" (tr. by Sara Heikoff Woehrlen). [LitR] (33:2) Wint 90, p. 191.
1781. ELIZABETH, Martha
"Manon Senses the Presence of an Approaching Storm." [PoetL] (85:2) Sum 90, p.
19.
"Manon Wonders About Her Lover After Meeting One of His Former Lovers."
[PoetL] (85:2) Sum 90, p. 18.
"She Teaches Him to Reach Out." [DogRR] (9:2, #18) Aut 90, p. 3.
1782. ELKIND, Sue Saniel
"After the Funeral." [DustyD] (1:2) O 90, p. 10.
"History Lesson." [DustyD] (1:2) O 90, p. 9.
"Please Tell Me Lies." [DustyD] (1:2) O 90, p. 9.
"A Song of Summer." [CrossCur] (9:2) Je 90, p. 31.
"Tombstones." [Parting] (3:1) Sum 90, p. 18.
1783. ELLEDGE, Jim
"Carpe Diem." [SycamoreR] (2:1) Wint 90, p. 40.
"A Walk in the Alfama." [EngJ] (79:8) D 90, p. 89.
ELLEN, Patricia ver
See Ver ELLEN, Patricia
1784. ELLENBERG, Jordan
"Excerpt from the History of Navigation" (Honorable Mention). [HarvardA] (124:3)
Mr 90, p. 36.
1785. ELLIOT
"Like Always." [Gypsy] (15) 90, p. 54.
1786. ELLIOTT, Carmen
"From the Lady Fleur." [Crucible] (26) Fall 90, p. 79.
1787. ELLIS, Mary Lynn
"Acknowledgement." [WestB] (26) 90, p. 123-124.
1788. ELLIS, Thomas Sayers
"Hush Yo Mouf" (for Bob Kaufman). [Callaloo] (13:3) Sum 90, p. 431-432.
"On Display." [Callaloo] (13:3) Sum 90, p. 433.
1789. ELLISON, Julie
"Berate, Berattle." [TampaR] (3) 90, p. 13.
"Lucia di Lammermore, More More." [PassN] (11:2) Wint 90, p. 24.
"The Worry Prayer." [MichQR] (29:3) Sum 90, p. 410-411.
1790. ELMAN, Richard
"Post Time (Belmont Park)." [Confr] (42/43) Spr-Sum 90, p. 226.
1791. ELON, Florence
"Epitaph." [GeoR] (44:3) Fall 90, p. 447.
1792. ELROD, John
"The Bargain." [NewDeltaR] (7:1) 90, p. 15-16.
"Dream of an Indian." [MidwQ] (31:2) Wint 90, p. 227-228.
"Notes to an Epileptic." [BellArk] (6:1) Ja-F 90, p. 5.
1793. ELSBERG, John
"Fragment." [CoalC] (1) Ag 90, p. 5.
"Love Poem" (After Adrian Henri). [DogRR] (9:1, #17) Spr 90, p. 27.
1794. ELUARD, Paul
"A Marc Chagall." [CumbPR] (9:2) Spr 90, p. 38.
"Georges Braque" (in French). [CumbPR] (9:2) Spr 90, p. 40.
"Georges Braque" (tr. by Karen D. Sorenson and Malcolm Glass). [CumbPR] (9:2)
Spr 90, p. 41.
"To Marc Chagall" (tr. by Karen D. Sorenson and Malcolm Glass). [CumbPR] (9:2)
Spr 90, p. 39.
1795. EMANS, Elaine V.
"The Collecting Bug." [Wind] (20:67) 90, p. 17-18.
"For My Father, Belatedly." [Wind] (20:67) 90, p. 17.
"Letter to Cape Cod from Minnesota." [Wind] (20:67) 90, p. 18.
"Muse Away." [KanQ] (22:3) Sum 90, p. 114.

153

1796. EMANUEL, Lynn
"The Dig." [Ploughs] (16:4) Wint 90-91, p. 125-126.
"Domestic Violence." [KenR] (NS 12:3) Sum 90, p. 123.
"Outside Room Six." [Ploughs] (16:4) Wint 90-91, p. 122.
"The Past." [Ploughs] (16:4) Wint 90-91, p. 123-124.
"The Planet Krypton." [KenR] (NS 12:3) Sum 90, p. 124.
1797. EMBERTON, Kenneth C.
"Father, I Wade." [SmPd] (27:2, #79) Spr 90, p. 29.
1798. EMERY, Thomas
"In My 49th Summer." [Pembroke] (22) 90, p. 52-53.
"Making a Poem" (For Philip Levine). [Pembroke] (22) 90, p. 51.
1799. EMIN, Gevorg
"If You Are a Poet" (tr. by Diana Der Hovanessian). [PoetryE] (30) Fall 90, p. 8.
1800. EMINESCU, Mihai
"Mai Am un Singur Dor." [NegC] (10:2/3) 90, p. 152, 154.
"One Wish Left" (tr. by W. D. Snodgrass). [NegC] (10:2/3) 90, p. 153, 155.
"Rendezvous" (tr. by W. D. Snodgrass). [NegC] (10:2/3) 90, p. 149, 151.
"Revedere." [NegC] (10:2/3) 90, p. 148, 150.
1801. EMMENS, Jan
"Hard Facts" (tr. by Gonny Van den Broek). [Vis] (34) 90, p. 38.
1802. EMMONDS, David
"Guard Tower." [Quarry] (39:2) Spr 90, p. 52.
"Lajo." [Quarry] (39:2) Spr 90, p. 50-51.
1803. ENDO, Russell
"Plum Blossom" (after a painting, "A Breath of Spring," by Tsou Fu-lei). [Vis] (33) 90, p. 39.
1804. ENDREZZE, Anita
"The Map-Maker's Daughter." [YellowS] (35) Wint 90-91, p. 29.
1805. ENESDORF, Donna
"Paper Art." [Amelia] (6:2, #17) 90, p. 117.
1806. ENGLAND, Eugene
"Pilgrims." [TarRP] (29:2) Spr 90, p. 25.
1807. ENGLE, Paul
"Door." [Poetry] (156:4) Jl 90, p. 194-195.
1808. ENGLER, Robert (Robert Klein)
"Adam" (tr. of José Gorostiza). [InterPR] (16:2) Fall 90, p. 75.
"Bogotá Declaration" (tr. of José Gorostiza). [InterPR] (16:2) Fall 90, p. 87, 89.
"Chichen Itza." [InterPR] (16:2) Fall 90, p. 92.
"Chichen Itza" (in English, tr. by the author). [InterPR] (16:2) Fall 90, p. 93.
"Epilogue" (tr. of José Gorostiza). [InterPR] (16:2) Fall 90, p. 89.
"Greenland on the Map." [InterPR] (16:1) Spr 90, p. 110.
"Lessons Taught by the Eyes" (tr. of José Gorostiza). [InterPR] (16:2) Fall 90, p. 77-81.
"The Melons" (For Jeanne Inness). [WillowR] Spr 90, p. 8.
"Mirror No!" (tr. of José Gorostiza). [InterPR] (16:2) Fall 90, p. 75, 77.
"Negociando." [InterPR] (16:2) Fall 90, p. 90.
"Negotiations" (tr. by the author). [InterPR] (16:2) Fall 90, p. 91.
"Night Sail to Mallorca" (tr. by the author). [InterPR] (16:2) Fall 90, p. 91.
"La Pampa." [InterPR] (16:2) Fall 90, p. 92.
"La Pampa" (in English, tr. by the author). [InterPR] (16:2) Fall 90, p. 93.
"Pawn Shop." [Plain] (10:3) Spr 90, p. 30.
"Prelude" (tr. of José Gorostiza). [InterPR] (16:2) Fall 90, p. 71-75.
"Presence and Fugue" (tr. of José Gorostiza). [InterPR] (16:2) Fall 90, p. 83, 85.
"Santa Fe." [JamesWR] (7:4) Sum 90, p. 13.
"Seis Sacerdotes Jesuitas Estuvieron Torturado y Matado en el Salvador." [InterPR] (16:2) Fall 90, p. 94.
"Six Jesuit Priests Were Tortured and Killed in El Salvador" (tr. by the author). [InterPR] (16:2) Fall 90, p. 95.
"Summer Threnody" (for Carol Kyros Walker). [InterPR] (16:1) Spr 90, p. 110-112.
"Viaje por la Noche a Mallorca." [InterPR] (16:2) Fall 90, p. 90.
"What Are We Doing Here?" [JamesWR] (7:4) Sum 90, p. 13.
1809. ENGLISH, Thomas
"What I Have Learned." [LullwaterR] (1:1) Spr 90, p. 58-59.
1810. ENGMAN, John
"Beer." [PassN] (11:1) Sum 90, p. 10.

"Gladioli." [VirQR] (66:3) Sum 90, p. 456-457.
"The Longest Sidewalk in the Western World." [Crazy] (38) Spr 90, p. 34.
"Pastoral" (James Wright, 1927-1980). [VirQR] (66:3) Sum 90, p. 455-456.
"Rubber Roses." [NorthStoneR] (9) 90, p. 46.
"Saturday Bath." [NorthStoneR] (9) 90, p. 45.
"The Tree of Rubber Tires." [PassN] (11:1) Sum 90, p. 9.
"What I Remember of What They Told Me." [Crazy] (38) Spr 90, p. 32-33.
1811. ENNES, Marty
    "Winter Garden." [BellR] (13:2, #28) Fall 90, p. 36.
1812. ENNS, Victor Jerrett
    "My father had never eaten a banana." [PraF] (11:2) Sum 90, p. 97.
1813. ENRIGHT, D. J.
    "And." [BelPoJ] (40:4) Sum 90, p. 25.
    "Hearts." [BelPoJ] (40:4) Sum 90, p. 23.
    "Paradise Retained." [BelPoJ] (40:4) Sum 90, p. 24.
    "Primitives." [BelPoJ] (40:4) Sum 90, p. 23.
1814. ENSING, Riemke
    "The Hundred Flowers." [Descant] (21:3, #70) Fall 90, p. 30.
    "The 'K.M.' File (3)." [Verse] (7:2) Sum 90, p. 26.
    "Katherine Mansfield Contemplates a Painting of Elizabeth I (1533-1603)" (for Roy
      Strong and Julia Trevelyan and their book). [Verse] (7:2) Sum 90, p. 26.
    "The Katherine Mansfield Signature As Zen Painting" (for Antony Alpers). [Verse]
      (7:2) Sum 90, p. 27.
    "What Shall We Tell Li Po" (a sequence of poems for China). [Descant] (21:3, #70)
      Fall 90, p. 27-29.
    "What Shall We Tell Li Po" (Tiananmen Square, June 1989). [Descant] (21:3, #70)
      Fall 90, p. 31.
1815. ENSLIN, Theodore
    "Herself Com Passionate" (Selections). [Conjunc] (15) 90, p. 298-305.
    "Pater Noster." [MidAR] (10:2) 90, p. 53.
    "Veni Creator Spiritus." [MidAR] (10:2) 90, p. 52.
1816. ENTREKIN, Gail Rudd
    "Men Who Carry Women Like Lanterns." [BlueBldgs] (12) 90, p. 37-38.
1817. ENZENSBERGER, Hans Magnus
    "Finnish Tango: In Memory of Felix Pollak" (tr. by Reinhold Grimm). [Pembroke]
      (22) 90, p. 15.
    "Short History of the Bourgeoisie." [Harp] (281:1684) S 90, p. 44.
1818. EÖRSI, István
    "He and I" (tr. by Nicholas Kolumban). [WebR] (14:2) Spr 90, p. 104.
    "In a Pleading Tone of Voice" (tr. by Nicholas Kolumban). [WebR] (14:2) Spr 90,
      p. 104.
    "Utopia" (tr. by Nicholas Kolumban). [PoetryE] (30) Fall 90, p. 19.
1819. EPLING, Kathy
    "The Wanderer." [YellowS] (33) Spr 90, p. 22.
EPPLER, Vincent Sellers
    See SELLERS-EPPLER, Vincent
1820. EPSTEIN, Richard
    "Bitter Bread." [Plain] (11:1) Fall 90, p. 17.
1821. EQUI, Elaine
    "Autobiography #1." [BrooklynR] (7) 90, p. 49.
    "Common Knowledge." [BrooklynR] (7) 90, p. 51.
    "Crickets Crush Woman." [PaperAir] (4:3) 90, p. 92.
    "Destinations." [Sulfur] (10:2, #27) Fall 90, p. 188-189.
    "Dreadlocks" (for Jean-Michel Basquiat). [Sulfur] (10:2, #27) Fall 90, p. 189.
    "Folk Dance." [BrooklynR] (7) 90, p. 50.
    "Generic." [Sulfur] (10:2, #27) Fall 90, p. 187.
    "Pale Yellow." [PaperAir] (4:3) 90, p. 93.
1822. ERB, Elke
    "Text and Commentary" (tr. by Roderick Iverson). [Sulfur] (10:2, #27) Fall 90, p.
      107-112.
1823. ERB, Lisa
    "Because the Fish Did Not Seem Real." [Sonora] (18) Fall-Wint 90, p. 54.
    "Kafka Nodded, Boarding a Train." [IndR] (13:3) Fall 90, p. 85.
1824. ERNST, Myron
    "About Summer." [HiramPoR] (48/49) 90-91, p. 29.
    "Florida." [HiramPoR] (48/49) 90-91, p. 27.

"Florida -- So Sam Said." [HiramPoR] (48/49) 90-91, p. 28.
"The Ford Plant at River Rouge -- 1930" (after a painting by Charles Sheeler,
    "American Landscape"). [MidwQ] (31:3) Spr 90, p. 354.
"Gelsey Kirkland in 'The Nutcracker'." [CumbPR] (10:1) Fall 90, p. 8.
"A Little Suite for Rochester or a City Similar." [OxfordM] (6:1) Spr-Sum 90, p. 19.
"A Short Discourse on Snow." [WestB] (26) 90, p. 73.
"Those Old Faces." [LaurelR] (24:2) Sum 90, p. 46.
"Vermeer." [Wind] (20:67) 90, p. 16.
"The Wife in the Mural at Pompeii." [LaurelR] (24:2) Sum 90, p. 47.
1825. ESAPORA, Anna
    "Jackals" (tr. of Jozo T. Boskovski). [Footwork] 90, p. 60.
    "Masks" (tr. of Jozo T. Boskovski, w. David B. Axelrod). [Footwork] 90, p. 60.
1826. ESCOBAR-BLANCO, Rocío
    "The Woman." [SlipS] (10) 90, p. 42.
1827. ESHE, Aisha
    "For Those Days of Mr. and Mrs. Carmen." [Footwork] 90, p. 113.
    "In Awe of My Mother's Insanity." [BlackBR] (11) Spr-Sum 90, p. 18.
    "Momma Was Dead." [JINJPo] (12:1) Spr 90, p. 19.
1828. ESHELMAN, Martha J.
    "Do Not Come" (a prayer to the goddess). [Amelia] (6:1, #16) 90, p. 107-108.
1829. ESOLEN, Tony
    "Christmas Vacation." [ChrC] (107:36) 12 D 90, p. 1159.
1830. ESPADA, Martín
    "Clemente's Bullets" (for Clemente Soto Vélez). [BilingR] (14:3) S-D 87-88, c91, p.
        71-72.
    "Colibrí" (for Katherine, one year later). [Americas] (18:2) Sum 90, p. 30.
    "For the Landlord's Repairman, Since He Asked." [Americas] (18:2) Sum 90, p. 33.
    "Jorge the Church Janitor Finally Quits" (Cambridge, Massachusetts, 1989).
        [Ploughs] (16:1) Spr-Sum 90, p. 100.
    "The King of Books" (for Camilo Pérez-Bustillo). [Ploughs] (16:1) Spr-Sum 90, p.
        98-99.
    "Portrait of a Real Hijo de Puta" (for Michael). [Americas] (18:2) Sum 90, p. 28.
    "The Promised Land" (Selection: #18, tr. of Clemente Soto Vélez, w. Camilio
        Pérez-Bustillo). [Agni] (29/30) 90, p. 200-201.
    "Rebellion Is the Circle of a Lover's Hands (Pellín and Nina" (for the 50th
        anniversary of the Ponce Massacre). [BilingR] (14:3) S-D 87-88, c91, p.
        70-71.
    "Revolutionary Spanish Lesson." [Americas] (18:2) Sum 90, p. 29.
    "Shaking Hands with Mongo" (For Mongo Santamaría). [Americas] (18:2) Sum 90,
        p. 32.
    "La Tumba de Buenaventura Roig" (for my great-grandfather, died 1941). [Agni]
        (31/32) 90, p. 95-96.
    "The Wooden Horse" (Selection: #3, tr. of Clemente Soto Vélez, w. Camilio
        Pérez-Bustillo). [Agni] (29/30) 90, p. 199.
    "The Words of the Mute Are Like Silver Dollars" (Prince George's County,
        Maryland, 1976). [Americas] (18:2) Sum 90, p. 31.
1831. ESPAILLAT, Rhina P.
    "All of It." [Amelia] (6:1, #16) 90, p. 74.
1832. ESPINA, Eduardo
    "Mas Felices Que en Vietnam." [Inti] (32/33) Otoño 90-Primavera 91, p. 258-259.
    "La Novia de Hitler." [Inti] (32/33) Otoño 90-Primavera 91, p. 257-258.
    "Las Piedras del Momentaneo." [Inti] (32/33) Otoño 90-Primavera 91, p. 257.
1833. ESPINOSA DE PEREZ, Matilde
    "Los Hombres Penumbrosos." [InterPR] (16:1) Spr 90, p. 16, 18.
    "The Shadowy Men" (To the natives of Terradentro, tr. by Mark Smith-Soto).
        [InterPR] (16:1) Spr 90, p. 17, 19.
1834. ESPOSITO, Nancy
    "The Afternoon, the Neighborhood." [PraS] (64:2) Sum 90, p. 55-56.
    "Mêm' Rain." [PraS] (64:2) Sum 90, p. 56-59.
    "Resting Place." [PraS] (64:2) Sum 90, p. 59-60.
1835. ESSEX
    "American Hero." [CityLR] (4) 90, p. 129.
    "If We Can't Be Instructed by Grief" (for Washington D.C.). [CityLR] (4) 90, p.
        131-132.
    "Observation in a War Zone." [CityLR] (4) 90, p. 128.
    "Visiting Hours." [CityLR] (4) 90, p. 129-130.

1836. ESSEX, David
"Petros." [AmerPoR] (19:2) Mr-Ap 90, p. 41.
"Wish You Were Here." [AmerPoR] (19:2) Mr-Ap 90, p. 41.
1837. ESTABROOK, Michael
"Jimmy Told Me." [Gypsy] (15) 90, p. 62.
"She Never Expected." [RagMag] (8:2) 90, p. 49.
"An Unending Dream." [Parting] (3:1) Sum 90, p. 28.
1838. ESTES, Angie
"Aubade." [ManhatR] (5:2) Fall 90, p. 20.
"The Brain." [CharR] (16:2) Fall 90, p. 69.
"Elegy for My Corpse." [ManhatR] (5:2) Fall 90, p. 21.
"Nocturne." [ManhatR] (5:2) Fall 90, p. 20.
"Reply." [SoCoast] (9) Fall 90, p. 16-17.
1839. ESTESS, Sybil
"Pretending You Were Joseph." [NewRep] (202:20) 14 My 90, p. 36.
1840. ESTRIN, Jerry
"The Communal Pleasures of the Intermezzi" (Excerpts). [Avec] (3:1) 90, p. 12-15.
1841. ETCHECOPAR, Dolores
"Carta a" (Poética). [Inti] (32/33) Otoño 90-Primavera 91, p. 207.
"Donde Estuvieron Sentadas la Dama y Su Piedra." [Inti] (32/33) Otoño
    90-Primavera 91, p. 205-206.
"Entonces Algo Vuelve a Suceder" (a Marco). [Inti] (32/33) Otoño 90-Primavera 91,
    p. 206.
"Julio Es un Mes Oscuro." [Inti] (32/33) Otoño 90-Primavera 91, p. 206.
"Melodía Imposible para Seguir a un Caballo." [Inti] (32/33) Otoño 90-Primavera
    91, p. 208-209.
"La Orilla." [Inti] (32/33) Otoño 90-Primavera 91, p. 208.
"Poema para Paul Klee." [Inti] (32/33) Otoño 90-Primavera 91, p. 207.
1842. ETTER, Carrie
"Missing You from Illinois." [PoetL] (85:4) Wint 90-91, p. 30.
"Teachings" (for Maman). [Plain] (11:1) Fall 90, p. 22.
1843. ETTER, Dave
"Drought." [KanQ] (22:4) Fall 90, p. 133-134.
1844. EUBANK, Ilona M.
"40." [PacificR] (8) 90, p. 27.
1845. EVANOFF, Richard
"Old Photos: 2." [WormR] (30:4, #120) 90, p. 132-133.
"The Vacant Chair." [WormR] (30:4, #120) 90, p. 133-134.
1846. EVANS, Bradford
"Public Education." [SlipS] (10) 90, p. 70.
1847. EVANS, David Allan
"Hard Jaws." [NorthStoneR] (9) 90, p. 20.
"I Can See Why." [NorthStoneR] (9) 90, p. 19.
"The Man with the Chair." [NorthStoneR] (9) 90, p. 20.
"The Poem I Couldn't Write." [Shen] (40:3) Fall 90, p. 39.
"Song of Racquetball." [Shen] (40:3) Fall 90, p. 36-38.
1848. EVANS, David, Jr.
"The Compromise." [ChironR] (9:1) Spr 90, p. 21.
1849. EVANS, Deirdre
"For My Daughter, Age 8." [PoetryUSA] (5:2) Sum 90, p. 3.
1850. EVANS, George
"The Fall." [NewAW] (6) Spr 90, p. 64-65.
"Horse on a Fence." [Conjunc] (15) 90, p. 296.
"Inflation." [NewAW] (6) Spr 90, p. 55.
"Poppies Twisted to Peaks by Evening Light." [Conjunc] (15) 90, p. 297.
"What I Meant Was This." [Conjunc] (15) 90, p. 297.
1851. EVANS, J. Kelly
"The Many Nostrils of Prana." [Sequoia] (33:2) Wint 90, p. 47.
1852. EVANS, Kathy
"Parked" (for Katharine Harer." [OnTheBus] (2:1, #5) Spr 90, p. 66.
"Staying Home from Work." [OnTheBus] (2:2/3:1, #6/7) Sum-Fall 90 Wint-Spr 91,
    p. 79.
1853. EVANS, Kevin
"Children's Games." [ColEng] (52:2) F 90, p. 156.
"Fiction." [ColEng] (52:2) F 90, p. 158.
"How Name Was Invaded." [ColEng] (52:2) F 90, p. 157.

"Out of Body Travel." [ColEng] (52:2) F 90, p. 159.
1854. EVANS, Michael
"Country Singer." [Poem] (64) N 90, p. 14.
"Killdeer." [PoetL] (85:3) Fall 90, p. 20.
"Lights at One O'Clock." [Poem] (64) N 90, p. 11.
"Memento Mori." [Poem] (64) N 90, p. 12-13.
"Near the Sundial." [OnTheBus] (2:1, #5) Spr 90, p. 67.
"Soliloquy." [Poem] (64) N 90, p. 10.
"When the End Comes." [PoetL] (85:3) Fall 90, p. 21.
1855. EVANS, R. S.
"Her two brothers came." [Verse] (7:2) Sum 90, p. 7.
1856. EVARTS, Prescott, Jr.
"Inheritance." [KanQ] (22:1/2) Wint-Spr 90, p. 17.
1857. EVASCO, Marjorie M.
"Making the Broomstick Poem." [TampaR] (3) 90, p. 22.
1858. EVASON, Greg
"Beans in the Attic." [WestCL] (24:3) Wint 90, p. 65.
"I Paint Twelve Hours a Day." [WestCL] (24:3) Wint 90, p. 66.
"The." [WestCL] (24:3) Wint 90, p. 65.
"Tony." [WestCL] (24:3) Wint 90, p. 65.
"Waiting with the Rug." [WestCL] (24:3) Wint 90, p. 66.
1859. EVATT, Julia
"Noises in the House" (to DLE 1926-1986). [Confr] (42/43) Spr-Sum 90, p. 224.
"Syzygy." [Confr] (42/43) Spr-Sum 90, p. 225.
1860. EVE, Barbara
"Still Life with Orange." [FreeL] (5) Sum 90, p. 3.
1861. EVERDING, Kelly
"Men's Middles." [GeoR] (44:1/2) Spr-Sum 90, p. 194.
1862. EVERITT, Pat
"Breath in the Mouth of Sorrow." [PoetryUSA] (5:3) Fall 90, p. 9.
"Looking for the Joads." [PoetryUSA] (5:2) Sum 90, p. 9.
1863. EVETTS, Josephine
"Whatever Happened to Leda, Mother?" [Dandel] (17:2) Fall-Wint 90, p. 12.
1864. EWERS, Ruth
"Chasing Amelia." [ThRiPo] (35/36) 90, p. 52-53.
1865. EWING, Blair G.
"Farther On" (for Joseph Brodsky). [CapeR] (25:2) Fall 90, p. 46.
1866. EYBERS, Elizabeth
"I went away -- alone" (tr. of Ile d' Ouessant, w. the author). [Trans] (24) Fall 90,
    p. 14.
1867. EYGUN, François-Xavier
"Aéroplane." [PraF] (11:1) Spr 90, p. 98.
"Airplane" (tr. by Jane Brierley). [PraF] (11:1) Spr 90, p. 99.
"Aube." [PraF] (11:1) Spr 90, p. 96.
"Congères." [PraF] (11:1) Spr 90, p. 98.
"Daybreak" (tr. by Jane Brierley). [PraF] (11:1) Spr 90, p. 97.
"Migration" (in French). [PraF] (11:1) Spr 90, p. 96.
"Migrations" (tr. by Jane Brierley). [PraF] (11:1) Spr 90, p. 97.
"Plaines." [PraF] (11:1) Spr 90, p. 94.
"Plains" (tr. by Jane Brierley). [PraF] (11:1) Spr 90, p. 95.
"Snowdrifts" (tr. by Jane Brierley). [PraF] (11:1) Spr 90, p. 99.
1868. EYTAN, Eytan
"A King Held Captive in Water Troughs" (tr. by Seymour Mayne). [PoetL] (85:4)
    Wint 90-91, p. 25.
1869. EZZELL, Sun
"In my mind." [PoetryUSA] ([5:4?]) Wint 90, p. 27.
FA-LIN, Gao
    See GAO, Fa-lin
1870. FABILLI, Mary
"Surprising Event." [Talisman] (4) Spr 90, p. 86.
1871. FABREGAT, Rosa
"We Walk" (from "Estelles," 1978, tr. by Montserrat Abelló). [PoetryC] (11:4) Wint
    90, p. 22.
"Who Knows What There Is Under This Mask" (tr. by Montserrat Abelló).
    [PoetryC] (11:4) Wint 90, p. 22.

1872. FAGAN, Cary
"Little Anarchies." [Grain] (18:1) Spr 90, p. 66.
1873. FAGIN, Larry
"Stone Speech." [Shiny] (5) 90, p. 2-3.
1874. FAGLES, Robert
"The Death of Hector" (The Iliad, Book XXII, tr. of Homer). [GrandS] (9:3) Spr
90, p. 113-128.
1875. FAGONE, Robert
"The Other." [NorthStoneR] (9) 90, p. 64.
"The Shaw Memorial" (Boston Common, July 1964). [NorthStoneR] (9) 90, p. 63.
1876. FAHEY, W. A. (William A.)
"The Ears." [Confr] (44/45) Fall 90-Wint 91, p. 194.
"Lust." [Paint] (17:33/34) Spr-Aut 90, p. 25.
"Rage." [Paint] (17:33/34) Spr-Aut 90, p. 26.
1877. FAINLIGHT, Ruth
"Learning About Him." [Thrpny] (40) Wint 90, p. 9.
1878. FAIRBANKS, Lauren
"Feels Like a Real Fight (Ted and Steve)." [AnotherCM] (21) 90, p. 31-32.
"Limits." [AnotherCM] (21) 90, p. 33-34.
"Limits II." [AnotherCM] (21) 90, p. 35-36.
1879. FAIRCHILD, B. H.
"In a Cafe near Tuba City, Arizona, Beating My Head Against a Cigarette Machine."
[SouthernR] (26:3) Jl 90, p. 628-629.
"The Last Days." [SouthernR] (26:3) Jl 90, p. 630.
"Local Knowledge." [SouthernPR] (30:1) Spr 90, p. 5-10.
1880. FAIRCHILD, Laura
"Neighbors." [Bogg] (63) 90, p. 27.
1881. FAIRCHILD, Marlene
"Dancers of the Night." [AnthNEW] 90, p. 11.
"Ebb Tide." [AnthNEW] 90, p. 25.
1882. FAIRCHILD, Sarah
"Nesting." [Plain] (11:1) Fall 90, p. 16.
1883. FAIZ, Faiz Ahmed
"Bangladesh-II" (tr. by Aga Shahid Ali). [GrahamHR] (13) Spr 90, p. 96-97.
"Desire" (tr. by Aga Shahid Ali). [GrahamHR] (13) Spr 90, p. 91.
"Fragrant Hands" (For the anonymous woman who sent me a bouquet of flowers in
prison, tr. by Aga Shahid Ali). [GrahamHR] (13) Spr 90, p. 89-90.
"Ghazal" (tr. by Agha Shahid Ali). [GrandS] (9:2) Wint 90, p. 139.
"It Is Spring Again" (tr. by Aga Shahid Ali). [GrahamHR] (13) Spr 90, p. 94.
"Let Me Think" (for Andrei Voznesensky, tr. by Aga Shahid Ali). [GrahamHR] (13)
Spr 90, p. 92-93.
"No Trace of Blood" (tr. by Agha Shahid Ali). [GrandS] (9:2) Wint 90, p. 141.
"On My Return from Dhaka (Bangladesh-III)" (Revisited after the massacre, tr. by
Aga Shahid Ali). [GrahamHR] (13) Spr 90, p. 98.
"Stay Away from Me (Bangladesh-I)" (tr. by Aga Shahid Ali). [GrahamHR] (13)
Spr 90, p. 95.
"Wash the Blood Off Your Feet" (tr. by Agha Shahid Ali). [GrandS] (9:2) Wint 90,
p. 140.
1884. FALCO, Edward
"Dust." [SouthernR] (26:4) O 90, p. 906-910.
"Five Women in a Bed." [QW] (30) Spr 90, p. 115-116.
"Morning." [InterPR] (16:2) Fall 90, p. 113.
"There at the Circle." [BlackWR] (16:2) Spr-Sum 90, p. 29.
1885. FALCON, Leticia Garza
"Drunken Beauty" (tr. of Ben al-Zaqqaq, w. Christopher Middleton). [Trans] (23)
Spr 90, p. 195.
"On the Death of a Friend by Drowning" (tr. of Ar-Rusafi, w. Christopher
Middleton). [Trans] (23) Spr 90, p. 193.
"Seeing Herself Beautiful and Nubile" (tr. of Qazmuna Bint Isma'il Al-Yahudi, w.
Christopher Middleton). [Trans] (23) Spr 90, p. 192.
"The Young Tailor" (tr. of Ben Charuf, w. Christopher Middleton). [Trans] (23) Spr
90, p. 194.
1886. FALLON, Peter
"Fast." [Quarry] (39:1) Wint 90, p. 76.
1887. FALLON, Teresa
"Plainsong." [KanQ] (22:1/2) Wint-Spr 90, p. 149.

159

FALLON

"Tiger Lily." [KanQ] (22:1/2) Wint-Spr 90, p. 150.
1888. FANDEL, John
"Someone Says So." [Comm] (117:10) 18 My 90, p. 319.
1889. FANG, Dai
"Black Marsh" (from "Black Desert," tr. of Tang Yaping, w. Edward Morin and
Dennis Ding). [Screens] (2) 90, p. 42.
"A Language" (tr. of He Xiaozhu, w. Edward Morin). [Screens] (2) 90, p. 43.
"Montages in Twilight" (tr. of Shu Ting, w. Edward Morin). [Screens] (2) 90, p.
38-40.
1890. FANNING, Roger
"Duckert the Effeminate, Zephyr-Like Surgeon." [VirQR] (66:1) Wint 90, p. 81-82.
"Frog." [VirQR] (66:1) Wint 90, p. 83.
"Galapagos Islands, Guillotine Eyelids." [VirQR] (66:1) Wint 90, p. j84-85.
"Glint of Gold Tooth in a Poorly Lit Kitchen." [NewYorker] (66:39) 12 N 90, p. 48.
"Hospital Sidewalk." [VirQR] (66:1) Wint 90, p. 82-83.
"My Mother's Mouth." [VirQR] (66:1) Wint 90, p. 81.
"Skagit Valley, 1980." [NewYorker] (66:32) 24 S 90, p. 40.
"Story." [VirQR] (66:1) Wint 90, p. 83-84.
1891. FARALLO, Livio
"Bushbody." [SlipS] (10) 90, p. 109-110.
1892. FAREWELL, Patricia
"The Help She Can Get." [NewYorkQ] (41) Spr 90, p. 106.
1893. FARGAS, Laura
"Erg." [Poetry] (157:2) N 90, p. 70.
"To the Person Who Stole My Camera" (For Gayle Q. Crocker). [Poetry] (156:3) Je
90, p. 131.
FARGE, Ben La
See LaFARGE, Ben
1894. FARGNOLI, Patricia
"New Poem for a Late Spring." [GreenMR] (NS 4:1) Spr-Sum 90, p. 114.
"Passing the Outer Light." [BellR] (13:1, #27) Spr 90, p. 10.
1895. FARGUE, Léon-Paul
"The Railroad Station" (for Arthur Fontaine, tr. by Edouard Roditi). [Trans] (23) Spr
90, p. 171-173.
1896. FARLEY, Blanche
"She Pours." [SingHM] (17) 90, p. 64.
1897. FARLEY, Joseph
"House on Water." [CapeR] (25:2) Fall 90, p. 42.
"Market Day in Jiangxi." [DogRR] (9:1, #17) Spr 90, p. 28-29.
"White-Bone Demon." [DogRR] (9:2, #18) Aut 90, p. 32.
1898. FARLEY, Moonean
"Jason." [EmeraldCR] (1990) c89, p. 44.
1899. FARMER, Rod
"Scene Remembered." [DogRR] (9:2, #18) Aut 90, p. 6.
"Summer in the Saddle." [HolCrit] (27:2) Ap 90, p. 16.
1900. FARMER, Ruth
"Mistress" (from the Plantation Poems). [SinW] (42) Wint 90-91, p. 42-43.
1901. FARNETI, Millo
"Historicity." [Spirit] (10:2) 90, p. 11-13.
1902. FARNHAM, Lara
"They're waiting for me to entertain them." [PoetryUSA] ([5:4?]) Wint 90, p. 27.
1903. FARQUHAR, Dion
"Dead Set." [Asylum] (6:2) S 90, p. 4.
1904. FARRAH, David
"In Freefall Over Florida." [MissR] (19:1/2, #55/56) 90, p. 252.
1905. FARRELL, Dan
"We Were Just Tired of Their Monopoly of Power." [WestCL] (24:1) Spr 90, p.
82-84.
1906. FARRELL, Mia
"I spent the night with a man who loves me." [PoetryUSA] (5:1) Spr 90, p. 5.
1907. FARRELL, Pamela B.
"The Inheritance." [Footwork] 90, p. 69.
"To John." [Footwork] 90, p. 69.
1908. FASEL, Ida
"Clean Sweep." [ChrC] (107:18) 30 My-6 Je 90, p. 573.
"Climbers." [CapeR] (25:1) Spr 90, p. 4-5.

"Sunlight." [ChrC] (107:1) 3-10 Ja 90, p. 16.
1909. FASS, Deborah
"Before the Fault Lines" (poem, monotypes and collographs, with Rebecca Zorach).
[HarvardA] (125:1) S 90, p. 22-23.
"Spill and Scape" (ink, pastel, papier mâché and poem, with Adam Birnbaum).
[HarvardA] (125:1) S 90, p. 6.
"Under the Fourth Watch of the Night." [HarvardA] (124:4) My 90, p. 27.
1910. FASULO, Anne
"Lines for Anne Pasternak, 1957-1985" (reprinted from #19, 1989). [Kaleid] (20)
Wint-Spr 90, p. 34.
1911. FAULKNER, Pete
"Swinging London Poem." [Bogg] (62) 90, p. 10-11.
"Well Met by Moonlight." [Bogg] (63) 90, p. 41.
1912. FAVEREY, Hans
"Troublesome Gods" (Excerpt, tr. by Francis R. Jones). [Trans] (24) Fall 90, p.
143-149.
1913. FAVILLA, Candace
"Evolution." [DenQ] (25:2) Fall 90, p. 16-17.
"Poppies in Rain." [DenQ] (25:2) Fall 90, p. 14-15.
1914. FAY, Julie
"All Saints' Day" (tr. of Guy Goffette). [Trans] (23) Spr 90, p. 92.
"Christmas Card for Norman." [PraS] (64:4) Wint 90, p. 16-18.
"My Cousin's Children." [Ploughs] (16:1) Spr-Sum 90, p. 62-63.
"My Sister's Hair." [PraS] (64:4) Wint 90, p. 18-20.
"My Sister's Hair, the Sequel." [PraS] (64:4) Wint 90, p. 20-21.
"Nocturne" (tr. of Yves Di Manno). [Trans] (23) Spr 90, p. 160.
"Sarah's Story" (Selection: 4. "Metonymy"). [Calyx] (12:3) Sum 90, p. 42-43.
"Traveling." [ManhatPR] (11) [89?], p. 35.
"Winter Garden" (for Ann Elliott). [Ploughs] (16:1) Spr-Sum 90, p. 60-61.
1915. FEDERMAN, Raymond
"Statues of Kings Can Be Categorized As Follows." [Caliban] (9) 90, p. 110.
1916. FEDO, David
"Imagining the Soul." [Poem] (63) My 90, p. 48.
"Memory Forgets." [Poem] (63) My 90, p. 46-47.
"The Sex of Hamlet." [Poem] (63) My 90, p. 45.
"The State House in Columbia, South Carolina." [NoDaQ] (58:3) Sum 90, p. 95-96.
1917. FEHLER, Gene
"The Day Willie Missed the Bus." [EngJ] (79:5) S 90, p. 103.
"Pink Panties." [EngJ] (79:1) Ja 90, p. 100.
"Rhetoric Lesson." [EngJ] (79:2) F 90, p. 87.
FEI, Mo
See MO, Fei
FEI, Ye
See YE, Fei
1918. FEINDEISEN, Kurt
"Fixation" (tr. of Frances Negrón-Muntaner). [PaintedB] (40/41) 90, p. 71.
1919. FEINSTEIN, Robert N.
"Social Rising." [Bogg] (62) 90, p. 55.
1920. FEINSTEIN, Sascha
"Il Cristo Velato." [SouthernPR] (30:2) Fall 90, p. 53-54.
1921. FEITLOWITZ, Marguerite
"The Aleph & Anselm Kiefer: Pieces Toward a Parable." [CityLR] (4) 90, p. 11-12.
1922. FEKETE, Adrienne
"The Man Here" (tr. of János Pilinszky, w. Len Roberts). [AmerPoR] (19:5) S-O
90, p. 23.
"Step by Step" (tr. of János Pilinszky, w. Len Roberts). [AmerPoR] (19:5) S-O 90,
p. 23.
1923. FELDMAN, Alan
"Girls in the Museum." [Thrpny] (40) Wint 90, p. 25.
1924. FELDMAN, Irving
"WWI (Writing While Under the Influence)." [NewRep] (203:22) 26 N 90, p. 38.
1925. FELDMAN, Ruth
"Chimera" (tr. of Bartolo Cattafi, w. Brian Swann). [HampSPR] (Anthology
1975-1990) 90, p. 248.
"Decathlon Man" (tr. of Primo Levi). [NewYorker] (66:28) 27 Ag 90, p. 36.
"Economics Lesson" (tr. of Rocco Scotellaro, w. Brian Swann). [HampSPR]

(Anthology 1975-1990) 90, p. 247.
"Key Word" (tr. of Bartolo Cattafi, w. Brian Swann). [HampSPR] (Anthology
1975-1990) 90, p. 249.
"Proofreading." [SouthernR] (26:3) Jl 90, p. 662.
1926. FELL, Alison
"The Skating Lession." [TampaR] (3) 90, p. 43.
1927. FELLOWES, Peter
"Coming to Mind." [HampSPR] (Anthology 1975-1990) 90, p. 86.
"Vermin." [HampSPR] (Anthology 1975-1990) 90, p. 87.
1928. FELSTINER, John
"Floods" (tr. of Pablo Neruda). [AmerPoR] (19:4) Jl-Ag 90, p. 30.
"There Was Earth Inside Them" (tr. of Paul Celan). [AmerPoR] (19:4) Jl-Ag 90, p.
31.
"There Was Earth Inside Them, and They Dug" (tr. of Paul Celan). [Sequoia] (33:2)
Wint 90, p. 33.
1929. FELTGES, Kenneth J.
"Who Was That Masked Man." [SlipS] (10) 90, p. 86.
FEMINA, Gerry La
See La FEMINA, Gerry
1930. FENDEISEN, Kurt
"The Body Speaks" (tr. of Frances Negrón-Muntaner, w. the author). [Cond] (17)
90, p. 65, 67.
"Penelope" (tr. of Frances Negrón-Muntaner). [Cond] (17) 90, p. 63.
1931. FENG, Anita N.
"Ghost Marriage." [Ploughs] (16:1) Spr-Sum 90, p. 160.
1932. FENTON, James
"The Milkfish Gatherers" (To G.L.). [Quarry] (39:1) Wint 90, p. 21-23.
1933. FERGUSON, Deanna
"Cross Words." [WestCL] (24:1) Spr 90, p. 17-25.
1934. FERGUSON, Penny L.
"Bandages." [AntigR] (80) Wint 90, p. 106.
1935. FERNANDES, Frances C.
"A Gathering of Men." [OnTheBus] (2:2/3:1, #6/7) Sum-Fall 90 Wint-Spr 91, p.
80.
"Keeping Secrets." [OnTheBus] (2:2/3:1, #6/7) Sum-Fall 90 Wint-Spr 91, p.
80-81.
1936. FERNANDEZ, Amando
"VII Canto de la Piedra." [LindLM] (9:4) O-D 90, p. 22.
1937. FERNANDEZ, Mauricio
"Despedidas Désperdician la Sobremesa." [LindLM] (9:4) O-D 90, p. 62.
1938. FERNANDEZ, Pablo Armando
"The Cock of Pomander Walk" (tr. by Barry Silesky and Neryeda Garcia).
[AnotherCM] (21) 90, p. 37-47.
1939. FERRARELLI, Rina
"Gusts of Spring Air." (tr. of Bartolo Cattafi). [InterPR] (16:2) Fall 90, p. 49.
"Here" (tr. of Bartolo Cattafi). [InterPR] (16:2) Fall 90, p. 51.
"I Stand Up" (tr. of Leonardo Sinisgalli). [InterPR] (16:2) Fall 90, p. 53.
"Into Its Cold" (tr. of Bartolo Cattafi). [InterPR] (16:2) Fall 90, p. 51.
"It's Here That God" (tr. of Bartolo Cattafi). [InterPR] (16:2) Fall 90, p. 49.
"Passionflower" (tr. of Leonardo Sinisgalli). [InterPR] (16:2) Fall 90, p. 53.
"Pyracantha" (in English, tr. of Bartolo Cattafi). [InterPR] (16:2) Fall 90, p. 49.
"The Salmon." [DogRR] (9:2, #18) Aut 90, p. 53.
"Van Gogh's Man with a Straw Hat." [Vis] (33) 90, p. 46.
"When Autumn Returns" (tr. of Leonardo Sinisgalli). [InterPR] (16:2) Fall 90, p.
55.
"Your Relief" (tr. of Bartolo Cattafi). [InterPR] (16:2) Fall 90, p. 51.
1940. FERRARI, Julia
"Las vegas no neon red goddess cafe." [Zyzzyva] (6:3 #23) Fall 90, p. 135.
1941. FERRE, Rosario
"La Luna Ofendida." [InterPR] (16:1) Spr 90, p. 84, 86.
"Offended Moon" (tr. by Mark Smith-Soto). [InterPR] (16:1) Spr 90, p. 85, 87.
1942. FERREE, Joel
"Several Heavens." [Amelia] (6:1, #16) 90, p. 83.
1943. FERREIRA, Christine
"Mountain People" (tr. of Han Dong, w. Liu Shicong). [MichQR] (29:1) Wint 90, p.
94-95.

1944. FERRI, Gio
"5 Short Rehearsals for a Poem (Pagan Nuptials)" (tr. by Pasquale Verdicchio).
[Screens] (2) 90, p. 114-115.
1945. FERRY, David
"Herbst" (tr. of Rainer Maria Rilke). [Agni] (29/30) 90, p. 166-167.
"Horses." [Agni] (29/30) 90, p. 165.
"In the Garden." [Agni] (29/30) 90, p. 163-164.
1946. FERTIK, Ahna
"Greg." [OnTheBus] (2:2/3:1, #6/7) Sum-Fall 90 Wint-Spr 91, p. 82.
1947. FETHERLING, Douglas
"Ancient Beliefs." [CanLit] (126) Aut 90, p. 5.
FIACCO, Christopher Corbett
See CORBETT-FIACCO, Christopher
1948. FICKERT, Kurt
"Listening to the Fifth." [Wind] (20:67) 90, p. 32.
1949. FIDES, Elizabeth
"Salsa di Pomodoro." [SinW] (41) Sum-Fall 90, p. 121.
1950. FIELD, Edward
"Basketball Legs" (For Zan Knudsen). [FreeL] (5) Sum 90, p. 28.
"Dietrich." [NewRep] (203:25) 17 D 90, p. 33.
"Enconado." [ChironR] (9:4) Wint 90, p. 3.
"Garbo." [NewRep] (203:25) 17 D 90, p. 32.
"Post Masturbation." [ChironR] (9:4) Wint 90, p. 3.
"Que C'Est Drole, l'Amour Qui Marche dans les Rues." [ChironR] (9:4) Wint 90, p. 3.
1951. FIELD, Greg
"Arshile Gorky Avoids the War." [LaurelR] (24:2) Sum 90, p. 22.
"My Family Has Arshile Gorky for Dinner." [LaurelR] (24:2) Sum 90, p. 23.
1952. FIELDS, Richard J.
"James Wharton Is an Honest Man." [ChironR] (9:1) Spr 90, p. 21.
1953. FIFE, Darlene
"Childhood Sketch" (tr. of Yorges Pavlopoulos, w. Robert Head). [Bogg] (62) 90, p. 25.
"The Door" (tr. of Yórges Pavlópoulos). [OnTheBus] (2:2/3:1, #6/7) Sum-Fall 90 Wint-Spr 91, p. 248.
"The Poet and the Moon" (Salute to Jorge Luis Borges, tr. of Yórges Pavlópoulos). [OnTheBus] (2:2/3:1, #6/7) Sum-Fall 90 Wint-Spr 91, p. 249.
"The Workman" (tr. of Yórges Pavlópoulos). [OnTheBus] (2:2/3:1, #6/7) Sum-Fall 90 Wint-Spr 91, p. 249.
1954. FIFER, Ken (Kenneth)
"The Eurydice Chorus." [MissouriR] (13:2) 90, p. 127.
"No See 'Ums." [Journal] (13:2) Fall-Wint 89-90, p. 16.
"Underground at the Marmottan." [Ploughs] (16:4) Wint 90-91, p. 181-184.
1955. FILES, James
"Blossom." [WritersF] (16) Fall 90, p. 159.
1956. FILIMONOV, Dmitri
"Sterilitism" (tr. by Oleg Atbashian and Maureen Hurley). [PoetryUSA] (5:2) Sum 90, p. 15.
1957. FILIP, Raymond
"Birds Sing All the Words for Yes." [PoetryC] (11:4) Wint 90, p. 5.
"Christ of Lonely Beach" (For Mario Gross). [PoetryC] (11:4) Wint 90, p. 5.
"Sand Baby Grand" (For Andrea). [PoetryC] (11:4) Wint 90, p. 5.
1958. FILIPKOWSKI, Zoe
"Everything in This City Is Afraid." [NewOR] (17:4) Wint 90, p. 43.
1959. FILKINS, Peter
"Message" (tr. of Ingeborg Bachmann). [PoetryE] (30) Fall 90, p. 31.
1960. FILLMORE, Nicholas, Jr.
"Swimming Lesson." [SenR] (20:2) Fall 90, p. 51.
"Testimony." [SenR] (20:2) Fall 90, p. 52.
1961. FINALE, Frank
"Big Brother." [NegC] (10:2/3) 90, p. 69.
"Plane Choice." [JINJPo] (12:1) Spr 90, p. 14.
1962. FINCH, Annie
"An Anglo-Saxon Garden." [PoetryUSA] (5:1) Spr 90, p. 6.
"A Small Sound in the Dark Woods." [Hellas] (1:2) Fall 90, p. 249.

1963. FINCH, Casey
"The *Iliad*." [HawaiiR] (14:3, #30) Fall 90, p. 70-71.
"Lately I have given up on birthdays" (For Ann on her birthday). [HawaiiR] (14:2, #29) Spr 90, p. 133.
"Saint Erkenwald" (Middle-English, tr. of 14th century anonymous poem). [HawaiiR] (14:3, #30) Fall 90, p. 60-68.
"To the Reader." [HawaiiR] (14:2, #29) Spr 90, p. 134-135.
"Treatise" (For Susie on her birthday). [HawaiiR] (14:2, #29) Spr 90, p. 131-132.
1964. FINCH, Roger
"A Burst of Iris." [HiramPoR] (48/49) 90-91, p. 30.
"One Sunday in Velvet." [WillowS] (25) Wint 90, p. 43.
"Shamisen Duel." [KanQ] (22:1/2) Wint-Spr 90, p. 34.
1965. FINCH, Steven
"An American in Paris, 1984." [Amelia] (6:2, #17) 90, p. 62-63.
"Refugees." [Amelia] (6:2, #17) 90, p. 62.
1966. FINCKE, Gary
"Alien." [LitR] (33:3) Spr 90, p. 207.
"The Asthma Revenge." [WestB] (27) 90, p. 41-44.
"Calculating Pi." [NewEngR] (12:4) Sum 90, p. 350.
"The Double Negatives of the Living." [Poetry] (156:3) Je 90, p. 143-144.
"Every Reachable Feather." [PoetryNW] (31:4) Wint 90-91, p. 33-34.
"The Extrapolation Dreams." [GettyR] (3:1) Wint 90, p. 177-182.
"Faculty X." [PoetL] (85:1) Spr 90, p. 49-50.
"The Fossil Route." [PoetC] (22:1) Fall 90, p. 37-41.
"The Habits of Eating." [LaurelR] (24:1) Wint 90, p. 82-83.
"The Hell Crowds." [CapeR] (25:1) Spr 90, p. 45.
"Lying Back Like Proust." [LitR] (33:3) Spr 90, p. 306.
"May Lightning Strike Me Dead." [CharR] (16:1) Spr 90, p. 70-71.
"Nigger Island." [TarRP] (29:2) Spr 90, p. 21-22.
"Ordering." [SoCoast] (9) Fall 90, p. 41.
"Put This Gown On." [PraS] (64:1) Spr 90, p. 41-42.
"The REM Sleep of Birds." [Poetry] (156:3) Je 90, p. 144.
"Six Kinds of Music, the Wallpaper of Breasts." [BelPoJ] (41:2) Wint 90-91, p. 16-17.
"The Tentative Steps of the Obese." [PoetryNW] (31:4) Wint 90-91, p. 32-33.
"The Train Cure." [Boulevard] (5:2, #14) Fall 90, p. 107.
"The Unlikely Bluff of Sight." [PraS] (64:1) Spr 90, p. 40-41.
1967. FINK, Robert A.
"Last Words." [SouthernPR] (30:1) Spr 90, p. 34-35.
1968. FINK, Tom
"Cellar Door." [ManhatPR] (12) [90?], p. 29.
"Reading a Biography." [ManhatPR] (12) [90?], p. 29.
1969. FINKEL, Donald
"Cedar Rapids Airport" (for Paul Engle, tr. of Luis Moreno). [SenR] (20:2) Fall 90, p. 19.
"In the South" (tr. of Luis Moreno). [SenR] (20:2) Fall 90, p. 18.
"Poets and Poems" (tr. of Luis Moreno). [SenR] (20:2) Fall 90, p. 20.
"Ratio Rerum" (for José Luis y Angelines, tr. of Luis Moreno). [SenR] (20:2) Fall 90, p. 21.
"The Times and Trials of Moses Austin." [KenR] (NS 12:2) Spr 90, p. 66-75.
1970. FINKELSTEIN, Caroline
"Not Responsible." [Poetry] (157:3) D 90, p. 139.
"The Soul in the Bowl." [Poetry] (156:3) Je 90, p. 150.
1971. FINKELSTEIN, Norman
"Exile." [Salm] (85/86) Wint-Spr 90, p. 142-143.
"Four Impromptus" (Excerpt). [Talisman] (5) Fall 90, p. 62.
"From the Archives." [MissouriR] (13:2) 90, p. 147.
1972. FINLEY, Jeanne
"Aubade (Light)." [Vis] (33) 90, p. 38.
1973. FINLEY, William
"Daddy-O." [TriQ] (80) Wint 90-91, p. 39.
1974. FINN, Morgan Baylog
"Davida and I Check Out Saks." [Kalliope] (12:2) 90, p. 10-11.
"Jules Dubrin, Continuous Cat." [Mildred] (4:1) 90, p. 87.
"The Minister's Wife." [Kalliope] (12:2) 90, p. 11-12.
"Night Song." [SwampR] (5) Wint-Spr 90, p. 37.

FINN

"Viewing Sweet Peas and Their Absence Acutely." [Kalliope] (12:2) 90, p. 9-10.
1975. FINNEGAN, James
"17th Sunday in Ordinary Time." [Outbr] (21) 90, p. 34-35.
"Anyone's Life." [MinnR] (NS 34/35) Spr-Fall 90, p. 30-31.
"Beeper." [PoetL] (85:1) Spr 90, p. 37-38.
"Dead Drive-In." [HiramPoR] (48/49) 90-91, p. 31.
"The Face Given." [SouthernPR] (30:1) Spr 90, p. 12-13.
"Nature Walk." [PoetL] (85:1) Spr 90, p. 39-40.
"Self-Storage." [SouthernPR] (30:1) Spr 90, p. 11-12.
"Two Pints and a Prayer." [MinnR] (NS 34/35) Spr-Fall 90, p. 30.
1976. FINNELL, Dennis
"The Bed." [DenQ] (25:2) Fall 90, p. 18-19.
"Blue Vault." [CharR] (16:1) Spr 90, p. 67.
"The Cloud of Unknowing." [NewRep] (202:5) 29 Ja 90, p. 41.
"From Attu, 1943." [PraS] (64:1) Spr 90, p. 88-89.
"The Isle of Lepers." [CharR] (16:1) Spr 90, p. 66.
"Made in the Shade." [SouthernPR] (30:2) Fall 90, p. 56-57.
"Only Human." [DenQ] (25:2) Fall 90, p. 20-21.
"The Queen Bee under the Waterfall." [PraS] (64:1) Spr 90, p. 87.
"White Stone" (for Glenna Purcell). [NewL] (57:1) Fall 90, p. 18-19.
1977. FINNEY, Janice
"Weekdays in Wilmette." [Pig] (16) 90, p. 100.
1978. FINNEY, Nikky
"Irons at Her Feet." [Callaloo] (13:3) Sum 90, p. 467-468.
1979. FINORA, Deborah
"Summer Rain Haiku." [EmeraldCR] (1990) c89, p. 63-64.
1980. FISCHER, Aaron
"Hansel in Recovery" (for Edie Feldman). [WillowS] (25) Wint 90, p. 32-34.
1981. FISCHER, Allen C.
"Breaking Up." [PoetryNW] (31:1) Spr 90, p. 38-39.
"Charting What to Say." [PoetryNW] (31:1) Spr 90, p. 39-40.
"The Word Is Out." [PoetryNW] (31:1) Spr 90, p. 38.
1982. FISCHEROVA, Silva
"And Today in That Wine Bar on the Corner" (tr. by James Naughton). [Field] (42) Spr 90, p. 38.
"The Merriest Country on Earth" (tr. by James Naughton). [Field] (42) Spr 90, p. 36-37.
"Without Men" (tr. by James Naughton). [Field] (42) Spr 90, p. 35.
1983. FISET, Joan
"The Cinder Garden." [HayF] (7) Fall-Wint 90, p. 77-78.
1984. FISET, Louise
"Car Crazy" (tr. by S. E. Stewart). [PraF] (11:1) Spr 90, p. 109.
"I Upset Everything" (tr. by S. E. Stewart). [PraF] (11:1) Spr 90, p. 115.
"Je Dérange Tout." [PraF] (11:1) Spr 90, p. 114.
"Madrigal" (in French). [PraF] (11:1) Spr 90, p. 116.
"Madrigal" (tr. by S. E. Stewart). [PraF] (11:1) Spr 90, p. 117.
"La Mentalité d'un Char." [PraF] (11:1) Spr 90, p. 108.
"The Ol' Cowboy Saloon" (in French). [PraF] (11:1) Spr 90, p. 110, 112.
"The Ol' Cowboy Saloon" (tr. by S. E. Stewart). [PraF] (11:1) Spr 90, p. 111, 113.
1985. FISHER, David (David Lincoln)
"The Berkeley Dusk." [Interim] (9:2) Fall-Wint 90-91, p. 43.
"Homage to Kenny Poff" (Died April 14 1986 of AIDS: A Veteran). [ChamLR] (4:1, #7) Fall 90, p. 76-77.
"Inside a Painting." [Interim] (9:2) Fall-Wint 90-91, p. 42.
"Marilyn Monroe." [Pearl] (12) Fall-Wint 90, p. 49.
1986. FISHER, Joan
"Telling." [NewAW] (6) Spr 90, p. 103-104.
1987. FISHMAN, Charles
"Homo Sapiens." [ThRiPo] (35/36) 90, p. 15.
"Ice Music." [Pearl] (11) Sum 90, p. 50.
1988. FitzPATRICK, Kevin
"Unemployment Office." [Pig] (16) 90, p. 52.
1989. FIXEL, Lawrence
"The Photographers." [Talisman] (5) Fall 90, p. 24-25.
"Question of a Shovel" (Notes Toward -- and Away From -- The Writing of a Poem). [Notus] (5:1) Spr 90, p. 110-111.

"Words Out of Reach." [Talisman] (5) Fall 90, p. 23-24.
1990. FLAHERTY, Sean
"Father?" [LullwaterR] (1:1) Spr 90, p. 80.
1991. FLANDERS, Jane
"After Gethsemane." [Chelsea] (49) 90, p. 144.
"The Bat." [NewRep] (203:5/6) 30 Jl-6 Ag 90, p. 36.
"From *Best-Loved Lives of the Bards*." [WestHR] (44:3) Aut 90, p. 251.
"The King's Dwarf." [WestHR] (44:3) Aut 90, p. 252.
"Potatoes." [PraS] (64:1) Spr 90, p. 92-93.
"Reading Jeremiah to the Rats." [Chelsea] (49) 90, p. 144.
"To a Hummingbird Moth." [PraS] (64:1) Spr 90, p. 92.
1992. FLANNERY, Matthew
"Going to Hsüan-ch'eng Past Hsin-lin Beach toward Pan-ch'iao" (for MEF, tr. of
Hsieh T'iao). [CumbPR] (9:2) Spr 90, p. 8-9.
1993. FLANNERY, Robert
"When I lived in Bay City Michigan." [PoetryUSA] ([5:4?]) Wint 90, p. 20.
1994. FLECKENSTEIN, Mark
"Last Photograph of My Days as an Idealist." [CimR] (92) Jl 90, p. 115.
1995. FLEMING, L. A.
"Map." [RiverC] (10:2) Spr 90, p. 82-83.
1996. FLETCHER, Dorothy K.
"Thanh Mai's Letter." [Kalliope] (12:2) 90, p. 61.
1997. FLICK, Sherrie
"Ceres Bakery." [WestB] (27) 90, p. 9.
"John the Fisherman." [WestB] (27) 90, p. 9.
1998. FLINT, Roland
"A Spotted Cat in Indonesia." [Shen] (40:3) Fall 90, p. 90-91.
1999. FLINTOFF, Eddie
"Chevron-Titipapa" (tr. of Francisco Santos). [Verse] (7:2) Sum 90, p. 14.
2000. FLOCK, Miriam
"Live from the Met." [RiverC] (11:1) Fall 90, p. 57.
2001. FLOREA, Ted
"The Fear." [Plain] (10:2) Wint 90, p. 8.
"My Son Thinks." [Plain] (11:1) Fall 90, p. 14.
2002. FLORES, Kate
"To a Man" (tr. of Susana March). [PoetryUSA] (5:3) Fall 90, p. 9.
FLORIDO, Jorge Rodriguez
See RODRIGUEZ FLORIDO, Jorge
2003. FLORIT, Eugenio
"Las Voces II." [LindLM] (9:4) O-D 90, p. 18.
2004. FLOURNOY, Bret
"Ruminations of a Single Father." [GreensboroR] (49) Wint 90-91, p. 35.
2005. FLYNN, John
"The Correspondence." [Pig] (16) 90, p. 65.
2006. FLYNN, Patrick
"On a Given Day." [PoetryUSA] (5:1) Spr 90, p. 11.
2007. FLYNN, Richard
"The Age of Reason" (Selections: Parts I, V). [WashR] (16:1) Je-Jl 90, p. 6.
2008. FLYTHE, Starkey (Starkey, Jr.)
"Cheyne Row, Chelsea." [GeoR] (44:4) Wint 90, p. 697.
"Paying the Anesthesiologist." [SouthernPR] (30:2) Fall 90, p. 50.
FOE, Mark de
See DeFOE, Mark
2009. FOERSTER, Richard
"108 1/2°." [Boulevard] (5:2, #14) Fall 90, p. 22-23.
"Boulders." [GreenMR] (NS 3:2) Fall-Wint 89-90, p. 79.
"Kreuzberg" (in the Rhön Mountains, Bavaria). [Nat] (251:4) 30 Jl-6 Ag 90, p. 142.
"Love Affair." [Poetry] (156:5) Ag 90, p. 285.
"Maternal Grandmother" (Hamburg, 1956). [AnthNEW] 90, p. 15.
"A Mere Freak, They Said" (for Harriet). [AntigR] (81/82) Spr-Sum 90, p. 185.
"Salz." [AnthNEW] 90, p. 24.
"Some Incidental Figures." [GreenMR] (NS 3:2) Fall-Wint 89-90, p. 78.
2010. FOGEL, Aaron
"Carsick Children." [Agni] (31/32) 90, p. 149-152.
2011. FOGEL, Alice B.
"The Hoe." [Iowa] (20:3) Fall 90, p. 92.

2012. FOLEY, Jack
  "Gershwin" (Excerpt). [PoetryUSA] (5:3) Fall 90, p. 6.
  "Litanies of Satan" (--Charles Baudelaire). [PoetryUSA] ([5:4?]) Wint 90, p. 15.
2013. FOLLAIN, Jean
  "Broad Daylight" (tr. by Jacklyn Potter). [WashR] (16:2) Ag-S 90, p. 26.
  "La Guenille." [WashR] (16:2) Ag-S 90, p. 27.
  "Lamentation" (tr. by Jacklyn Potter). [WashR] (16:2) Ag-S 90, p. 26.
  "Parler Seul." [WashR] (16:2) Ag-S 90, p. 27.
  "Plainte." [WashR] (16:2) Ag-S 90, p. 26.
  "Plein Jour." [WashR] (16:2) Ag-S 90, p. 26.
  "The Rag" (tr. by Jacklyn Potter). [WashR] (16:2) Ag-S 90, p. 27.
  "Speech Alone" (tr. by Jacklyn Potter). [Vis] (32) 90, p. 39.
  "Speech Alone" (tr. by Jacklyn Potter). [WashR] (16:2) Ag-S 90, p. 27.
2014. FONDANE, Benjamin
  "Mtasipol" (tr. by Leonard Schwartz). [Harp] (281:1684) S 90, p. 45-47.
2015. FONDREN, Kervin
  "Rain and Pain." [Writer] (103:12) D 90, p. 26.
2016. FONTAINE, Diana
  "Iron Rails." [ChamLR] (4:1, #7) Fall 90, p. 124-125.
FONTAINE, Paula Creasy
  See CREASY-FONTAINE, Paula
2017. FONTENOT, Ken
  "Remembering the Wind." [GeoR] (44:4) Wint 90, p. 635.
  "Three Wishes" (tr. of Nicolas Born). [NewOR] (17:1) Spr 90, p. 48.
  "Uncommon Parents." [GeoR] (44:3) Fall 90, p. 434.
2018. FOOTE, Leonard
  "In Passing." [AnthNEW] 90, p. 28.
2019. FOPA, Alaide
  "Destierro." [InterPR] (16:1) Spr 90, p. 52.
  "Exile" (tr. by Mark Smith-Soto). [InterPR] (16:1) Spr 90, p. 53.
2020. FORAN, Charles
  "Beijing Voices." [Descant] (21:3, #70) Fall 90, p. 51-62.
2021. FORBES, John
  "Cairns" (after Ian Smith's drawings). [Verse] (7:2) Sum 90, p. 3.
  "Moondance." [Verse] (7:2) Sum 90, p. 5.
  "Popular Classics." [Verse] (7:2) Sum 90, p. 3.
  "Thin Ice" (for Ken Bolton). [Verse] (7:2) Sum 90, p. 4.
2022. FORCE, Kathy
  "A Place to Be." [LakeSR] (24) 90, p. 33.
2023. FORCHÉ, Carolyn
  "Ars Poetica" (tr. of Robert Desnos). [AmerPoR] (19:3) My-Je 90, p. 25.
  "At Dawn" (tr. of Robert Desnos). [AmerPoR] (19:3) My-Je 90, p. 28.
  "If, Like the Winds Drawn on the Compass Face" (tr. of Robert Desnos).
    [AmerPoR] (19:3) My-Je 90, p. 27.
  "Letter to Youki" (tr. of Robert Desnos). [AmerPoR] (19:3) My-Je 90, p. 28.
  "The Night Watchman of Pont-au-Change" (tr. of Robert Desnos). [AmerPoR]
    (19:3) My-Je 90, p. 26-27.
  "The Recording Angel." [Antaeus] (64/65) Spr-Aut 90, p. 31-39.
  "Song of Taboo" (tr. of Robert Desnos). [AmerPoR] (19:3) My-Je 90, p. 27.
  "This Heart That Hated War" (tr. of Robert Desnos). [AmerPoR] (19:3) My-Je 90,
    p. 25.
  "Tour of the Tomb" (tr. of Robert Desnos). [AmerPoR] (19:3) My-Je 90, p. 28.
2024. FORD, Elizabeth
  "Small Almanac for Young Widow." [GreensboroR] (48) Sum 90, p. 59.
2025. FORD, Michael C.
  "Dorothy Dandridge." [Interim] (9:2) Fall-Wint 90-91, p. 41.
  "The Dulcimer in the Basement." [OnTheBus] (2:2/3:1, #6/7) Sum-Fall 90 Wint-Spr
    91, p. 83-84.
  "From the Desert Inn / Out." [Pearl] (12) Fall-Wint 90, p. 51.
  "Poem to a Lady Movie (Falling) Star." [Pearl] (12) Fall-Wint 90, p. 60.
  "The River of No Return" (to Elaine Equi). [Pearl] (12) Fall-Wint 90, p. 34.
2026. FORD, William
  "At the Fireplace." [CrossCur] (9:2) Je 90, p. 10-11.
2027. FORHAN, Chris
  "As Columbus Would Have It, the Earth Like a Pear." [GreensboroR] (49) Wint
    90-91, p. 83.

"The Barefoot Widow." [WebR] (14:2) Spr 90, p. 65.
"The Death of a Child in Winter." [WebR] (14:2) Spr 90, p. 66.
2028. FORNOFF, Frederick H.
"Close-Up of Death" (tr. of Laureano Albán). [NewOR] (17:3) Fall 90, p. 82-83.
"The Creation of Birds" (tr. of Laureano Albán). [NewOR] (17:3) Fall 90, p. 48-49.
"General Linguistics" (For Lil, tr. of Cristina Peri Rossi). [NewOR] (17:2) Sum 90,
    p. 43-52.
2029. FORRESTER, Megan M.
"Advice Given Freely from a Dream." [BellArk] (6:3) My-Je 90, p. 10.
"Beyond." [BellArk] (6:3) My-Je 90, p. 6.
2030. FORSHAW, Cliff
"Peyote." [HeavenB] (8) Wint 90-91, p. 36.
2031. FORSSTRÖM, Tua
"But Do You Remember August" (tr. by Lennart Bruce and Sonja Bruce). [Spirit]
    (10:1) 89, p. 189.
"But Incessantly" (tr. by Lennart Bruce and Sonja Bruce). [Spirit] (10:1) 89, p. 177.
"Det Kommer Ändå Tillbaka." [Spirit] (10:1) 89, p. 180.
"Don't Distrust Me" (tr. by Lennart Bruce and Sonja Bruce). [Spirit] (10:1) 89, p.
    179.
"Dropparna." [Spirit] (10:1) 89, p. 192.
"The Drops" (tr. by Lennart Bruce and Sonja Bruce). [Spirit] (10:1) 89, p. 193.
"Ett Långt Farväl." [Spirit] (10:1) 89, p. 194.
"Forgetting Is Remembering Intensely" (tr. by Lennart Bruce and Sonja Bruce).
    [Spirit] (10:1) 89, p. 183.
"Gallup" (in Swedish). [Spirit] (10:1) 89, p. 196.
"Gallup" (tr. by Lennart Bruce and Sonja Bruce). [Spirit] (10:1) 89, p. 197.
"Glömska Är Att Minnas Häftigt." [Spirit] (10:1) 89, p. 182.
"Här, Jag Har Skalat en Apelsin." [Spirit] (10:1) 89, p. 186.
"Here, I've Peeled an Orange" (tr. by Lennart Bruce and Sonja Bruce). [Spirit]
    (10:1) 89, p. 187.
"Kära." [Spirit] (10:1) 89, p. 190.
"A Long Farewell" (tr. by Lennart Bruce and Sonja Bruce). [Spirit] (10:1) 89, p.
    195.
"Men Minns Du Angusti." [Spirit] (10:1) 89, p. 188.
"Men Oavbrutet." [Spirit] (10:1) 89, p. 176.
"Misstro Mig Inte." [Spirit] (10:1) 89, p. 178.
"Nej, Tätt Skall Det Vara." [Spirit] (10:1) 89, p. 184.
"No, It Has to Fit Tightly" (tr. by Lennart Bruce and Sonja Bruce). [Spirit] (10:1)
    89, p. 185.
"Oh Dear" (tr. by Lennart Bruce and Sonja Bruce). [Spirit] (10:1) 89, p. 191.
"Still It Returns" (tr. by Lennart Bruce and Sonja Bruce). [Spirit] (10:1) 89, p. 181.
2032. FORT, Charles
"Driving Father Down a Mountain Road in Farmington, Connecticut, 1983."
    [Crucible] (26) Fall 90, p. 89.
2033. FORTH, Steven
"/Sentencing/" (Selections). [WestCL] (24:1) Spr 90, p. 70-73.
2034. FORTNEY, Steven D.
"War" (Vietnam, 6 Feb 1968, 1 dead). [Vis] (33) 90, p. 28.
2035. FORTUNATO, Margot
"Halloween Kimonos." [LakeSR] (24) 90, p. 35.
2036. FORTUNATO, Peter
"How the Solar" (from "Bird Songs 2000"). [Nimrod] (34:1) Fall-Wint 90, p. 50.
"Swing" (from "Bird Songs 2000"). [Nimrod] (34:1) Fall-Wint 90, p. 51.
2037. FOSS, Phillip
"Geisha Mime." [Conjunc] (15) 90, p. 278-282.
"Government of Rhapsody." [Screens] (2) 90, p. 197-201.
"The Waltz." [Notus] (5:1) Spr 90, p. 40-41.
2038. FOSSUM, Cory
"The End of the Road." [PoetryUSA] (5:3) Fall 90, p. 27.
2039. FOSTER, C. S.
"Mr. and Mrs. McClusky." [PoetryUSA] (5:2) Sum 90, p. 1.
2040. FOSTER, Dot
"The Casualty." [Dandel] (17:1) Spr-Sum 90, p. 13.
2041. FOSTER, Jeanne
"Reconstruction." [Ploughs] (16:4) Wint 90-91, p. 147-151.
"Visitation." [Ploughs] (16:4) Wint 90-91, p. 144-146.

2042. FOSTER, Leslie D.
"Cousin." [Interim] (9:2) Fall-Wint 90-91, p. 40.
2043. FOSTER, Linda Nemec
"Housework." [ManhatPR] (11) [89?], p. 40.
2044. FOSTER, Sesshu
"A Little Movie." [OnTheBus] (2:2/3:1, #6/7) Sum-Fall 90 Wint-Spr 91, p. 85-86.
2045. FOSTER, Susannah
"In the Rain Today." [ChironR] (9:1) Spr 90, p. 11.
"Losing Grace" (For Isis Sari Berkholder, Maria Berkholder and Ron Berkholder,
who was shot to death five times by the L.A.P.S. . . .). [ChironR] (9:1) Spr
90, p. 11.
"Whys." [ChironR] (9:1) Spr 90, p. 11.
2046. FOSTIÉRIS, Andónis
"Who Art You?" (tr. by Despina Efthimiades). [GrahamHR] (13) Spr 90, p. 102.
2047. FOURCADE, Dominique
"Click-Rose 2" (Selections: X-XIII, XV-XIX, tr. by Keith Waldrop). [Sulfur]
(10:2, #27) Fall 90, p. 74-78.
"Xbo" (Excerpts, P.O.L., Paris, 1988, tr. by Robert Kocik). [Avec] (3:1) 90, p.
87-96.
FOUST, Michelle Mitchell
See MITCHELL-FOUST, Michelle
2048. FOWLER, Anne Carroll
"Begin in the Middle." [OxfordM] (6:1) Spr-Sum 90, p. 64-65.
"The Welcome." [Parting] (3:2) Wint 90-91, p. 16.
2049. FOX, Gail
"What We Knew." [AntigR] (80) Wint 90, p. 45-46.
2050. FOX, Hugh
(Anonymous poem). [FreeL] (4) 90.
"King of Spring." [WormR] (30:4, #120) 90, p. 131.
"Madame Butterfly, some Met travelling company." [CreamCR] (14:1) Spr 90, p.
141-142.
"Unplugging the Drain." [WormR] (30:4, #120) 90, p. 131-132.
"Unstructured Time: Wir Haben Nur Einmal, Einmal, Gewesen zu Sein / We Have
Only One Time, One Time to Be." [Gypsy] (15) 90, p. 18-19.
2051. FOX, Kate
"Fruit of Fruit." [CimR] (92) Jl 90, p. 122-123.
"The Practiced Distance." [CimR] (92) Jl 90, p. 122.
2052. FOX, Leonard
"Deer at the Red Sea" (tr. of Abraham Sutzkever). [InterPR] (16:2) Fall 90, p. 17.
"Here I Am, Then" (tr. of Abraham Sutzkever). [InterPR] (16:2) Fall 90, p. 13.
"In the Sack of the Wind" (tr. of Abraham Sutzkever). [InterPR] (16:2) Fall 90, p.
15.
"In the Village" (tr. of Abraham Sutzkever). [InterPR] (16:2) Fall 90, p. 7-11.
2053. FOX, Linda
"9 of Cups, Motherpeace Tarot." [AmerV] (18) Spr 90, p. 62.
2054. FOX, Lucia
"El Cuarto Viaje de Colón." [Inti] (31) Primavera 90, p. 165-167.
"El Mayordomo de Moctezuma." [Inti] (31) Primavera 90, p. 168-169.
2055. FOX, Margaret
"Not Satisfied." [EmeraldCR] (1990) c89, p. 76-77.
2056. FOX, Nancy
"Treadle." [FourQ] (4:1) Spr 90, p. 16.
2057. FOX, Valerie
"What Would Emma Goldman Do?" [WestB] (26) 90, p. 124-125.
2058. FOXLOW, C. J.
"In Stinsford Churchyard, Dorset" (For Thomas Hardy). [EngJ] (79:7) N 90, p. 91.
2059. FOY, John F.
"The Cape Vulture" (in the Jardin des Plantes, Paris -- in memory of Rainer Maria
Rilke). [GrahamHR] (13) Spr 90, p. 40.
"The Panther" (in the Jardin des Plantes, Paris -- in memory of Rainer Maria Rilke).
[GrahamHR] (13) Spr 90, p. 41.
"Rue des Martyrs" (25). [GrahamHR] (13) Spr 90, p. 42.
"The Watusi" (in the Jardin des Plantes, Paris -- in memory of Rainer Maria Rilke).
[GrahamHR] (13) Spr 90, p. 39.
2060. FOYE, June E.
"In Alligator Country" (Honorable Mention, 4th Annual Contest). [SoCoast] (8) Spr

90, p. 8.
2061. FRAJLICH, Anna
"Elegy on a Tile Stove" (tr. by Maya Peretz). [Screens] (2) 90, p. 49.
"Emigration" (tr. by Maya Peretz). [Screens] (2) 90, p. 49.
2062. FRANCE, J. Peter
"I Saw a Possum in the Road." [EmeraldCR] (1990) c89, p. 93-94.
"The Unnaming of the World." [EmeraldCR] (1990) c89, p. 94.
2063. FRANCIA, Luis H.
"Homeless on the Range." [LitR] (33:4) Sum 90, p. 509-510.
2064. FRANCIS, Catherine
"Reminiscences of Planet Crabby." [Asylum] (6:2) S 90, p. 20-21.
2065. FRANCIS, Scott
"Found Among Petals Dropping" (tr. of Yu Kai). [Paint] (17:33/34) Spr-Aut 90, p.
37.
"Hidden Light" (tr. of Yu Kai). [Paint] (17:33/34) Spr-Aut 90, p. 38.
2066. FRANCO, Alfredo
"House" (tr. of Vicente Huidobro). [NewOR] (17:2) Sum 90, p. 37.
2067. FRANCO, R. (Shady)
"The Umpteenth Wonder." [PoetryUSA] (5:3) Fall 90, p. 23.
2068. FRANCOIS, Rose-Marie
"Sap on the Rebound" (tr. by Christine Pagnoulle). [Vis] (32) 90, p. 28.
2069. FRANK, Bernhard
"In the Attic" (tr. of David Vogel). [WebR] (14:2) Spr 90, p. 103.
"When Night Approaches" (tr. of David Vogel). [WebR] (14:2) Spr 90, p. 103.
2070. FRANK, David
"Relic." [Wind] (20:66) 90, p. 28.
2071. FRANK, Diane
"Inseminating the Cows." [YellowS] (33) Spr 90, p. 36-37.
2072. FRANK, Lavinia
"Death." [PoetryUSA] (5:1) Spr 90, p. 17.
2073. FRANKEL, David
"Dispatch Window Dressing." [PoetryUSA] (5:2) Sum 90, p. 9.
2074. FRANKLIN, Walt
"Fireman's Auction." [Pearl] (10) Spr 90, p. 58.
"Goatsucker." [Poem] (63) My 90, p. 59.
"The Hemlock Prince." [Blueline] (11:1/2) 90, p. 86.
"Invocation." [Pearl] (11) Sum 90, p. 8.
"Raven." [Poem] (63) My 90, p. 60.
2075. FRANKS, Hazel Spaulding
"Love." [Wind] (20:66) 90, p. 25.
2076. FRANZEN, Cola
"Burial and Blaze of Pablo Neruda" (tr. of Marjorie Agosín). [Agni] (29/30) 90, p.
206-207.
"Races" (tr. of Alicia Borinsky). [RiverS] (32) [90?], p. 59.
"Snare" (tr. of Saúl Yurkievich). [NewOR] (17:2) Sum 90, p. 16.
"El Trasver" (Selections: 2 poems, tr. of Saúl Yurkievich). [Screens] (2) 90, p.
122-129.
"What Her Mother Told Her" (tr. of Alicia Borinsky). [RiverS] (32) [90?], p. 57.
2077. FRANZEN, Richard J.
"The Red Room of Happiness." [SmPd] (27:1, #78) Wint 90, p. 22.
2078. FRASER, Caroline
"Fady Frem Takes It Back." [NewYorker] (66:9) 16 Ap 90, p. 40-41.
2079. FRASER, Kathleen
"Klee at Bauhaus: Parallel Bodies" (for Hermine Ford). [Avec] (3:1) 90, p. 113-117.
"A Little Background: The Sisters." [Sulfur] (10:1, #26) Spr 90, p. 114-116.
"Trade Routes, With Silk" (for Trinh T. Minh-ha). [CentralP] (17/18) Spr-Fall 90,
p. 198-200.
2080. FRASER, Sanford
"Sunoco Kid." [NewYorkQ] (41) Spr 90, p. 88.
2081. FRASER, Wallace N.
"For Billy, at 19." [SmPd] (27:2, #79) Spr 90, p. 23.
2082. FRAZEE, James
"Cages." [SenR] (20:2) Fall 90, p. 81-84.
2083. FRAZIER, Andrea
"Assignment." [Crucible] (26) Fall 90, p. 77.

2084. FRAZIER, Hood
"At Last, at a Gas Station in Ohio." [HampSPR] (Anthology 1975-1990) 90, p. 132.
"The Centerfold." [HampSPR] (Anthology 1975-1990) 90, p. 132.
"Hunger." [HampSPR] (Anthology 1975-1990) 90, p. 131.
"To the Harpy." [HampSPR] (Anthology 1975-1990) 90, p. 131.
2085. FREDERICKSON, Todd
"Gramma Inie and the Bear." [PraS] (64:2) Sum 90, p. 91-93.
"Mille Lacs Ice." [PraS] (64:2) Sum 90, p. 93-95.
"While Canoeing the Red Lake River Near Goodridge, Minnesota, We Speak of
Direction." [CutB] (33) 90, p. 44.
2086. FREDRIKSEN, Sandra
"Cracking the Whip." [PacificR] (8) 90, p. 6.
"For Sherry." [PacificR] (8) 90, p. 7.
2087. FREEBERG, William
"Motels in the Night." [JamesWR] (7:3) Spr 90, p. 4.
2088. FREEDMAN, Robert
"Waiting for the Silkworms." [WestB] (27) 90, p. 10-11.
2089. FREEMAN, Jan
"Mother Waken." [AmerPoR] (19:3) My-Je 90, p. 37.
"Song for the Red-Haired Widow." [AmerV] (19) Sum 90, p. 33-34.
2090. FREEMAN, Jessica
"Outer Lives." [CoalC] (2) D 90, p. 6.
"This Unborn Child." [CoalC] (2) D 90, p. 16.
2091. FREEMAN, Joan
"The Party." [PottPort] (11) 89, p. 24.
2092. FREEMAN, John P.
"The Crown Conch Shell." [Poem] (63) My 90, p. 28.
2093. FREEMAN, Robbie
"The Field." [PoetryUSA] (5:3) Fall 90, p. 27.
2094. FREEMAN, Sunil
"Thirty, Feeling Like Seventeen Again." [Gargoyle] (37/38) 90, p. 136.
2095. FREEPERSON, Kathy
"Munda the Italian Witch, Rome, New York." [SinW] (41) Sum-Fall 90, p. 66.
FREES, Madeline de
See DeFREES, Madeline
2096. FREISINGER, Randall R.
"Aphasia: The Breakdown of Language." [PoetC] (22:1) Fall 90, p. 19.
"Entropy of Everyday Things." [SoCoast] (9) Fall 90, p. 28-29.
"The Place Called There." [HiramPoR] (47) Wint 90, p. 25-26.
"The Stranger." [SoCoast] (9) Fall 90, p. 33.
"Wrestling." [HiramPoR] (47) Wint 90, p. 27-28.
2097. FRENCH, Anne
"The Marine Observer's Handbook" (Selections: 11, 20). [Verse] (7:2) Sum 90, p.
43-44.
2098. FRENCH, Catherine
"Bent July Landscape." [Iowa] (20:3) Fall 90, p. 89.
"The Death of Birds." [MissR] (19:1/2, #55/56) 90, p. 253.
"Overheard." [CarolQ] (43:1) Fall 90, p. 7.
2099. FRENEAU, Philip
"Lines Written Near an Elegant and Romantic Garden Adjacent to Passaick River, in
Essex County, July, 1820." [JlNJPo] (12:1) Spr 90, p. 50-52.
2100. FREUND, Edith
"Bending the Light." [SpoonRQ] (15:1) Wint 90, p. 53.
"Questioning the Source." [SpoonRQ] (15:1) Wint 90, p. 54.
2101. FREY, Cecelia
"From One Pair of Hands." [Event] (19:1) Spr 90, p. 80-81.
"The Gingham Dog." [Descant] (21:1 #68) Spr 90, p. 44-45.
"Grandmother Was a Doctor." [Event] (19:1) Spr 90, p. 82.
"Saturday Matinee." [Descant] (21:1 #68) Spr 90, p. 46.
"Stories of Women." [Event] (19:1) Spr 90, p. 78-79.
"True Confessions." [Descant] (21:1 #68) Spr 90, p. 47.
2102. FRICK, Thomas
"Sleep" (mem. Ted Spagna). [ParisR] (32:114) Spr 90, p. 83.
2103. FRID, Marcia
"Breakfast." [Grain] (18:1) Spr 90, p. 33.

2104. FRIEBERT, Stuart
"Absurd, Idaho." [Asylum] (5:4) 90, p. 23.
"After the Creation" (tr. of Marin Sorescu, w. Adriana Varga). [PoetryE] (29) Spr
90, p. 130.
"Air Conditioning" (tr. of Karl Krölow). [Chelsea] (49) 90, p. 137.
"All the Same" (tr. of Karl Krolow). [AmerPoR] (19:5) S-O 90, p. 20.
"Alphabet" (tr. of Marin Sorescu, w. Adriana Varga). [HawaiiR] (14:1, #28) Wint
89-90, p. 41.
"At Daybreak" (tr. of Karl Krolow). [AmerPoR] (19:5) S-O 90, p. 20.
"Below the Horizon" (tr. of Marin Sorescu, w. Adriana Varga). [ArtfulD] (18/19)
90, p. 41.
"Bumblebee Duck." [OnTheBus] (2:1, #5) Spr 90, p. 68-69.
"Chalk the Rabbit." [OnTheBus] (2:1, #5) Spr 90, p. 68.
"Comet" (tr. of Judita Vaiciunaite, w. Viktoria Skrupskelis). [PoetryE] (30) Fall 90,
p. 83.
"Easter Bunny Poem." [ChamLR] (4:1, #7) Fall 90, p. 41.
"An Education." [HampSPR] (Anthology 1975-1990) 90, p. 158.
"Eurydice" (tr. of Judita Vaiciunaite, w. Viktoria Skrupskelis). [Turnstile] (2:2) 90,
p. 1.
"Family Table" (tr. of Karl Krolow). [PennR] (4:2) 90, p. 89.
"House Snake" (tr. of Marin Sorescu, w. Adriana Varga). [HawaiiR] (14:1, #28)
Wint 89-90, p. 42.
"How?" (tr. of Marin Sorescu, w. Adriana Varga). [HawaiiR] (14:1, #28) Wint
89-90, p. 40.
"In Bed, Having Just Fallen Asleep." [HampSPR] (Anthology 1975-1990) 90, p.
158.
"Knots" (tr. of Zbigniew Herbert). [Field] (43) Fall 90, p. 78.
"Last Supper." [HampSPR] (Anthology 1975-1990) 90, p. 157.
"Let Live" (tr. of Karl Krolow). [PennR] (4:2) 90, p. 86-87.
"Let's Help" (tr. of Marin Sorescu, w. Adriana Varga). [ArtfulD] (18/19) 90, p. 40.
"Little Gulls" (tr. of Judita Vaiciunaite, w. Viktoria Skrupskelis). [SenR] (20:2) Fall
90, p. 46.
"Looking for Hegel's Portrait" (tr. of Marin Sorescu, w. Adriana Varga). [PoetryE]
(29) Spr 90, p. 131.
"Mr. Cogito and Pure Thought" (tr. of Zbigniew Herbert). [Field] (43) Fall 90, p.
79-80.
"Museum Street" (tr. of Judita Vaiciunaite, w. Viktoria Skrupskelis). [Turnstile]
(2:2) 90, p. 2.
"Now That Dad Is Gone." [ArtfulD] (18/19) 90, p. 36.
"On Smoking Things Out" (tr. of Zbigniew Herbert). [Field] (43) Fall 90, p. 77.
"The Park" (tr. of Karl Krölow). [Chelsea] (49) 90, p. 136.
"Pure Conversation with a Chinese Character" (tr. of Marin Sorescu, w. Gabriela
Dragnea). [NewYorker] (66:15) 28 My 90, p. 36.
"Rift" (tr. of Marin Sorescu, w. Adriana Varga). [PoetryE] (29) Spr 90, p. 128-129.
"The Right Question." [ArtfulD] (18/19) 90, p. 37.
"Shadow Spots" (tr. of Karl Krolow). [PennR] (4:2) 90, p. 88.
"Signs" (tr. of Marin Sorescu, w. Adriana Varga). [PoetryE] (29) Spr 90, p. 133.
"Some Things" (tr. of Karl Krölow). [Chelsea] (49) 90, p. 135.
"Sometimes Mr. Cogito Receives Strange Letters Written with Irony, and an Even
Larger Dose of Compassion" (tr. of Zbigniew Herbert). [Field] (43) Fall 90, p.
81-82.
"Songs Without Names" (tr. of Karl Krolow). [AmerPoR] (19:5) S-O 90, p. 20.
"Standing Up There." [HampSPR] (Anthology 1975-1990) 90, p. 159.
"Study of Repose" (tr. of Marin Sorescu, w. Adriana Varga). [HawaiiR] (14:1, #28)
Wint 89-90, p. 43.
"Terror" (tr. of Karl Krölow). [Chelsea] (49) 90, p. 138.
"Thoughts" (tr. of Marin Sorescu, w. Gabriela Dragnea). [PoetryE] (29) Spr 90, p.
132.
"U-Turn." [ArtfulD] (18/19) 90, p. 38.
"Van Gogh's Cyclist." [ArtfulD] (18/19) 90, p. 39.
"What Mr. Cogito Thinks About Hell" (tr. of Zbigniew Herbert). [Field] (43) Fall
90, p. 76.
"Wild Raspberries" (tr. of Judita Vaiciunaite, w. Viktoria Skrupskelis). [SenR]
(20:2) Fall 90, p. 48.
"Working Yourself Sick." [LaurelR] (24:1) Wint 90, p. 31.
"Yellow Summer" (tr. of Judita Vaiciunaite, w. Viktoria Skrupskelis). [SenR] (20:2)

Fall 90, p. 45.
"Zoological Garden" (tr. of Judita Vaiciunaite, w. Viktoria Skrupskelis). [SenR]
(20:2) Fall 90, p. 47.
2105. FRIED, Elliot
"Chain Mail." [ChironR] (9:4) Wint 90, p. 7.
"Marvel Mystery Oil." [ChironR] (9:4) Wint 90, p. 7.
"Souls." [ChironR] (9:4) Wint 90, p. 7.
"Thirty-Gallon Heater." [ChironR] (9:4) Wint 90, p. 7.
2106. FRIED, Howard
"The Schizophrenia Projects." [Zyzzyva] (6:4 #24) Wint 90, p. 124.
2107. FRIED, Michael
"The Blue." [Agni] (29/30) 90, p. 65.
"The Dance." [Agni] (29/30) 90, p. 64.
"The Pool." [Agni] (29/30) 90, p. 66.
2108. FRIED, Philip
"God-the-Father Crafty in His Bathtub." [CreamCR] (14:1) Spr 90, p. 117.
2109. FRIEDLANDER, Benjamin
"The Decision." [Sulfur] (10:2, #27) Fall 90, p. 44.
"In a Previous Manner of Dunkan MkNaughton." [Sulfur] (10:2, #27) Fall 90, p.
45-46.
"It Gets That I Hate Words for Their Echoes, Dumb Repetitions in My Head."
[Sulfur] (10:2, #27) Fall 90, p. 48-49.
"Kol Nidre." [Sulfur] (10:2, #27) Fall 90, p. 47.
"The Remainder." [Sulfur] (10:2, #27) Fall 90, p. 47.
2110. FRIEDMAN, Debbie
"In a Place Where the Wood Is Rough." [BlackBR] (11) Spr-Sum 90, p. 8.
"Picking Lettuce for Magdalena" (honorable mention, Black Bear Poetry
Competition). [BlackBR] (11) Spr-Sum 90, p. 36.
"Train to Munich." [BlackBR] (11) Spr-Sum 90, p. 9.
2111. FRIEDMAN, Dorothy
"Bareback." [CrossCur] (9:2) Je 90, p. 89.
2112. FRIEDMAN, Ed
"Seeking Red As Green." [NewAW] (6) Spr 90, p. 99-100.
2113. FRIEDMAN, Jeff
"At Home." [Boulevard] (5:2, #14) Fall 90, p. 170-171.
"Portrait in 'P' of Eye and Piano." [WashR] (16:3) O-N 90, p. 17.
2114. FRIEDMAN, Michael
"The Day There Was Only Michael Friedman." [Shiny] (5) 90, p. 17-22.
"Swimming in Yugoslavia." [BrooklynR] (7) 90, p. 21.
"Vortex." [BrooklynR] (7) 90, p. 20.
2115. FRIEDMAN, Stan
"Lying with Susan." [Interim] (9:1) Spr-Sum 90, p. 44.
"Storm Belt." [Interim] (9:1) Spr-Sum 90, p. 45.
2116. FRIEDSON, A. M.
"Benina." [HawaiiR] (14:3, #30) Fall 90, p. 113-114.
"Fatal Response." [HawaiiR] (14:2, #29) Spr 90, p. 62.
"Holy Orders." [HawaiiR] (14:1, #28) Wint 89-90, p. 93-94.
2117. FRIES, Kenny
"Excavation." [AmerV] (19) Sum 90, p. 20.
2118. FRIESEN, Patrick
"Blue Shoes" (for Matilda). [PraF] (11:2) Sum 90, p. 160-161.
"A Woman from Jamaica" (for Geita Forbes). [PraF] (11:2) Sum 90, p. 162-163.
2119. FRIIS-BAASTAD, Erling
"The Inmate of This Forest." [ChironR] (9:2) Sum 90, p. 19.
2120. FRIMAN, Alice
"Archery Lesson." [BelPoR] (40:3) Spr 90, p. 34.
"Birthday in Autumn." [Poetry] (157:1) O 90, p. 26-27.
"The Blue Oranda." [BelPoR] (40:3) Spr 90, p. 33.
"In the Chronicles of Paradise." [CarolQ] (42:3) Spr 90, p. 28.
"Northwest Flight #1173." [BelPoR] (40:3) Spr 90, p. 32.
"On Perfection." [Shen] (40:2) Sum 90, p. 68.
"Recovery." [Shen] (40:2) Sum 90, p. 67.
"The Story." [WebR] (14:2) Spr 90, p. 69-70.
2121. FRITCHIE, Barbara
"Plantation Road." [NewDeltaR] (7:1) 90, p. 58.
"Trying to Stop, Trying to Keep Him." [NewDeltaR] (7:1) 90, p. 57.

173

2122. FROME, Carol
"The Kite Flyer." [Plain] (10:3) Spr 90, p. 34.
2123. FROST, Carol
"The Argument." [MassR] (31:4) Wint 90, p. 599.
"Self Portrait." [NowestR] (28:2) 90, p. 24.
2124. FROST, Celestine
"(The Eyes Do Not See Objectively)." [Epoch] (39:3) 90, p. 294.
"The Gift." [Asylum] (6:2) S 90, p. 14.
"The Kidnapping." [Asylum] (6:2) S 90, p. 13.
2125. FROST, Kenneth
"Did you ever drift like smoke." [HawaiiR] (14:1, #28) Wint 89-90, p. 90.
"A dog digs like a madman." [HawaiiR] (14:1, #28) Wint 89-90, p. 92.
"Something is stolen or disappears." [HawaiiR] (14:1, #28) Wint 89-90, p. 91.
2126. FROST, Linda A.
"We Lived in Eugene." [ContextS] (1:1) 89, p. 16.
"You Bet." [ContextS] (1:1) 89, p. 15.
2127. FROST, Richard
"The Chamber." [WestHR] (44:2) Sum 90, p. 173.
"Fifteen." [KenR] (NS 12:3) Sum 90, p. 53.
"Thebes Revisited." [WestHR] (44:2) Sum 90, p. 172.
2128. FROST, Robert
"To Earthward." [Hudson] (43:2) Sum 90, p. 265-266.
2129. FRUCHEY, Debrah
"Mental Illness Has No Manners." [PoetryUSA] (5:2) Sum 90, p. 3.
2130. FRUMKIN, Gene
"The Appointment" (For Nell Altizer). [ChamLR] (4:1, #7) Fall 90, p. 35.
"Mud." [ChamLR] (4:1, #7) Fall 90, p. 34.
2131. FRUTKIN, Mark
"Baudelaire's Letter to Ancelle." [PoetryC] (11:2) Sum 90, p. 4.
"Creation Myths." [PoetryC] (11:2) Sum 90, p. 4.
"Double." [PoetryC] (11:2) Sum 90, p. 4.
FU, Du
See DU, Fu
2132. FU, Michiko
"When the garden wood was trimmed" (tr. by Janet Lewis). [SouthernR] (26:1) Ja
90, p. 203.
FU, Tu
See DU, Fu
2133. FUCHS, Barbara
"Adapting to Land." [Grain] (18:3) Fall 90, p. 90.
"End of March." [Grain] (18:3) Fall 90, p. 90.
"Smoking." [Grain] (18:4) Wint 90, p. 76.
2134. FUCHS, Rebecca M.
"Just Right." [EngJ] (79:7) N 90, p. 91.
2135. FUJIWARA-SKROBAK, Makiko
"Before he left our village" (tr. of Shuji Terayama, w. Peter Levitt). [Zyzzyva] (6:3
#23) Fall 90, p. 105.
"Ever since my mother carried me" (tr. of Shuji Terayama, w. Peter Levitt).
[Zyzzyva] (6:3 #23) Fall 90, p. 104.
"I pressed on with the hot teeth" (tr. of Shuji Terayama, w. Peter Levitt). [Zyzzyva]
(6:3 #23) Fall 90, p. 104.
"I stroke the mountain dove" (tr. of Shuji Terayama, w. Peter Levitt). [Zyzzyva] (6:3
#23) Fall 90, p. 105.
"The rope I haven't used" (tr. of Shuji Terayama, w. Peter Levitt). [Zyzzyva] (6:3
#23) Fall 90, p. 105.
"Tonight the fingerprint" (tr. of Shuji Terayama, w. Peter Levitt). [Zyzzyva] (6:3
#23) Fall 90, p. 104.
2136. FUKUDA, Akira
"The autumn rain" (tr. by Janet Lewis). [SouthernR] (26:1) Ja 90, p. 206.
2137. FUKUDA, Tomiko
"Evening light and shade" (tr. by Janet Lewis). [SouthernR] (26:1) Ja 90, p. 204.
2138. FULKER, Tina
"Poem for Two Voices." [Bogg] (62) 90, p. 44.
2139. FULLER, Ian L.
"Civilized." [EmeraldCR] (1990) c89, p. 35.

2140. FULLER, M. T.
"Gentle Hands: An Art Preview." [DogRR] (9:2, #18) Aut 90, p. 22-23.
"Post-Feminist Ode." [DogRR] (9:2, #18) Aut 90, p. 23.
2141. FULLER, William
"Where Everyone Walked" (Excerpt). [CentralP] (17/18) Spr-Fall 90, p. 187.
2142. FULTON, Alice
"Aunt I." [KenR] (NS 12:3) Sum 90, p. 1-7.
"For in Them the Void Becomes Eloquent." [ParisR] (32:115) Sum 90, p. 265-266.
"The Fractal Lanes." [YaleR] (79:2) Wint 90, p. 227.
"Our Calling." [NewAW] (6) Spr 90, p. 70-71.
"The Pivotal Kingdom." [PartR] (57:2) Spr 90, p. 279-280.
"Silencer." [ParisR] (32:115) Sum 90, p. 263-264.
"Trophies." [NewRep] (203:15) 8 O 90, p. 36.
2143. FULTON, Graham
"Ships." [Verse] (7:2) Sum 90, p. 71.
2144. FULTON, Julie
"New Uncle." [Thrpny] (40) Wint 90, p. 27.
2145. FULTON, Robin
"The Bed" (tr. of Johannes Edfelt). [OntR] (33) Fall-Wint 90-91, p. 92.
"The Logjam" (tr. of Johannes Edfelt). [OntR] (33) Fall-Wint 90-91, p. 93.
"The Solitary" (tr. of Johannes Edfelt). [OntR] (33) Fall-Wint 90-91, p. 93.
2146. FULWYLIE, Christine B. J.
"First Shall Be, and Last Shall Be." [EmeraldCR] (1990) c89, p. 33-34.
FUMIKO, Kiyotoki
See KIYOTOKI, Fumiko
2147. FUNGE, Robert
"Apologia." [CharR] (16:1) Spr 90, p. 74.
"Dolores Street." [RiverC] (10:2) Spr 90, p. 85.
"Shelton's Moon." [CharR] (16:1) Spr 90, p. 74.
"Walls." [LitR] (33:2) Wint 90, p. 218-221.
2148. FUNK, Allison
"Backstroke." [PoetryNW] (31:4) Wint 90-91, p. 7.
"Bioluminescence." [PoetryNW] (31:4) Wint 90-91, p. 3-4.
"Night Fishing for Catfish." [PoetryNW] (31:4) Wint 90-91, p. 8.
"Ratushinskaya." [PoetryNW] (31:4) Wint 90-91, p. 4-5.
"Starburst." [PoetryNW] (31:4) Wint 90-91, p. 5-6.
2149. FUNKHOUSER, Erica
"Apology." [NewYorker] (66:10) 23 Ap 90, p. 76.
"Identification." [Poetry] (155:6) Mr 90, p. 403.
2150. FURBUSH, Matthew
"Fragments from Fort Worth, 1959." [SouthwR] (75:4) Aut 90, p. 502-504.
"Panama." [SouthwR] (75:4) Aut 90, p. 504-505.
2151. FURUICHI, Hideko
"Amid the green" (tr. by Janet Lewis). [SouthernR] (26:1) Ja 90, p. 204.
2152. FUSSELMAN, Amy
"Impotence." [NewYorkQ] (43) Fall 90, p. 76.
2153. FYMAN, Cliff
"I got big poems." [PoetryUSA] (5:2) Sum 90, p. 3.
2154. GABBARD, G. N.
"Local Aesthetic." [Hellas] (1:1) Spr 90, p. 63.
2155. GABOUDIKIAN, Sylvia
"Come Back Safely" (tr. by Diana Der-Hovanessian). [Agni] (31/32) 90, p. 242.
"If I Don't Love You" (tr. by Diana Der-Hovanessian). [Agni] (31/32) 90, p. 241.
2156. GADD, Bernard
"Blue Blood's Bard." [Bogg] (63) 90, p. 64.
2157. GAERTNER, Ken
"Brother's Keeper." [Poem] (63) My 90, p. 64-65.
"Judas." [Poem] (63) My 90, p. 62-63.
2158. GAFFNEY, Amy Runge
"Recommended Planting Depth When My Time Comes" (A Plainsongs Award
Poem). [Plain] (11:1) Fall 90, p. 4.
2159. GAGNON, Daniel
"O Rilke!" [Os] (31) 90, p. 28.
"Tu m'as ravie." [Os] (31) 90, p. 29.
2160. GAGNON, Jean Chapdelaine
"This Sudden Silence" (To the memory of Marie-Claire and Bernard Beaudin, tr. by

Andrea Moorhead). [Rohwedder] (5) Spr 90, p. 3-6.
"Ce Silence Soudain" (To the memory of Marie-Claire and Bernard Beaudin, poetic
    suite taken from Le Tant-à-coeur, Les Editions du Noroît, 1986). [Rohwedder]
    (5) Spr 90, p. 3-6.
2161. GALETA, Greg
    "The Curse." [CoalC] (2) D 90, p. 3.
2162. GALINDO, Petra
    "Morning Trilogy." [OnTheBus] (2:2/3:1, #6/7) Sum-Fall 90 Wint-Spr 91, p. 87.
2163. GALLAGHER, Diane M.
    "Sestina for the Twin" (2nd Prize, 4th Annual Contest). [SoCoast] (8) Spr 90, p.
    44-45.
2164. GALLAGHER, Tess
    "Ashtray." [PassN] (11:2) Wint 90, p. 12.
    "Blackbird." [Caliban] (8) 90, p. 30-31.
    "Corpse Cradle." [MichQR] (29:3) Sum 90, p. 331.
    "Ebony." [PoetryC] (11:3) Fall 90, p. 20.
    "Legend with Sea Breeze." [MichQR] (29:3) Sum 90, p. 328-329.
    "No Fingertips." [PoetryC] (11:3) Fall 90, p. 20.
    "Now That I Am Never Alone." [NewYorker] (66:16) 4 Je 90, p. 74.
    "Reading the Waterfall." [Atlantic] (266:5) N 90, p. 121.
    "Strange Thanksgiving." [NewYorker] (66:41) 26 N 90, p. 46.
    "Things Are Only Things." [PassN] (11:2) Wint 90, p. 12.
    "Trace, in Unison." [MichQR] (29:3) Sum 90, p. 330.
    "Why Do They Talk Sex to Me." [PassN] (11:2) Wint 90, p. 13.
    "Why Do They Talk Sex to Me." [PoetryC] (11:3) Fall 90, p. 20.
    "Widow in Red Shoes." [PoetryC] (11:3) Fall 90, p. 20.
    "Yes." [NewYorker] (65:51) 5 F 90, p. 48.
2165. GALLAHER, John
    "Cattle Shooting." [BlackWR] (17:1) Fall-Wint 90, p. 148.
    "I Thought I Was a Mailbox." [BlackWR] (17:1) Fall-Wint 90, p. 149.
2166. GALLER, David
    "Leaf Shadows on a Door." [Confr] (42/43) Spr-Sum 90, p. 101.
    "Tantalus." [Confr] (42/43) Spr-Sum 90, p. 101.
2167. GALLIANO, Alina
    "VI. Cuando la calma vuelva." [Americas] (18:3/4) Fall-Wint 90, p. 101.
    "XXII. De una isla." [Americas] (18:3/4) Fall-Wint 90, p. 102-103.
    "Residencia Plural." [Americas] (18:3/4) Fall-Wint 90, p. 104-105.
    "Ya No Me Acuerdo, No." [LindLM] (9:4) O-D 90, p. 14.
2168. GALLO, Philip
    "Articulation of a Still Life." [NorthStoneR] (9) 90, p. 47.
    "The Coin." [NorthStoneR] (9) 90, p. 48-49.
2169. GALT, Margot Kriel
    "No More Back of the Bus" (Charleston, S. C., 1957/1987). [SingHM] (17) 90, p.
    74-75.
2170. GALVIN, Brendan
    "A Carolina Wren." [TarRP] (29:2) Spr 90, p. 2-3.
    "The Day After Labor Day." [TarRP] (29:2) Spr 90, p. 3-4.
    "For a Daughter Gone Away." [Poetry] (156:6) S 90, p. 329-330.
    "If Memory Comes to the Tongue." [GeoR] (44:4) Wint 90, p. 601-602.
    "The Inishdhugan Clay" (Ireland, 6th century). [SouthernHR] (24:4) Fall 90, p.
    359-364.
    "Saints in Their Ox-Hide Boat" (Excerpt). [PoetC] (22:1) Fall 90, p. 5-12.
    "Saints in Their Ox-Hide Boat" (Excerpt). [TarRP] (29:2) Spr 90, p. 1-2.
    "Uncle Patrick Roots for the Fuzzy-Wuzzies." [TarRP] (29:2) Spr 90, p. 5.
    "The Widow at 'Roadstead's End'." [SewanR] (98:1) Wint 90, p. 24-25.
    "You Drove Out from Drogheda." [Shen] (40:1) Spr 90, p. 36-37.
2171. GALVIN, Martin
    "February Days." [Poem] (63) My 90, p. 29.
    "Grandmothers." [Poem] (63) My 90, p. 30.
    "Honey Man." [Bogg] (62) 90, p. 14.
    "Sand Girls" (after Mary Cassatt). [LullwaterR] (2:1) Wint 90, p. 8-9.
    "Thinning Peach Trees." [Poem] (63) My 90, p. 31.
2172. GALVIN, Patrick
    "My Father Spoke with Swans." [Quarry] (39:1) Wint 90, p. 77-78.
2173. GAMACHE, Laura
    "Swimming with My Children." [BellArk] (6:5) S-O 90, p. 23.

2174. GAMBOA, Manazar
"My Young People" (For Araceli). [OnTheBus] (2:2/3:1, #6/7) Sum-Fall 90
Wint-Spr 91, p. 88-91.
2175. GAMMON, Carolyn
"Packing." [Cond] (17) 90, p. 71.
"Victorian Ladies." [PottPort] (12) 90, p. 36.
2176. GANASSI, Ian
"Primary Process." [ParisR] (32:116) Fall 90, p. 42-43.
2177. GANDER, Forrest
"Eggplants and Lotus Root." [Conjunc] (15) 90, p. 289-295.
"The Man Who Won't Pay Dues." [ColEng] (52:1) Ja 90, p. 37.
"Parable in Wolves' Clothing." [ColEng] (52:1) Ja 90, p. 36.
"Unpublished Number." [ColEng] (52:1) Ja 90, p. 37.
2178. GANGEMI, Kenneth
"Calle Bolívar." [Gargoyle] (37/38) 90, p. 85.
2179. GANICK, Peter
"*856" (from "Remove a Concept"). [Talisman] (5) Fall 90, p. 82.
2180. GANSZ, David C. D.
"Per Missions" (in progress: selection: III). [Notus] (5:1) Spr 90, p. 90-91.
2181. GAO, Fa-Lin
"Random Thoughts While Skating" (tr. by Edward Morin and Dennis Ding).
[Screens] (2) 90, p. 37.
2182. GARBER, D. L.
"The Terror of Travel." [CharR] (16:1) Spr 90, p. 58-59.
"The Translation of Marangat into Morongo." [CharR] (16:1) Spr 90, p. 55-57.
"The Whole Point Is Freedom" (for D. M.). [CharR] (16:1) Spr 90, p. 57-58.
2183. GARCIA, Albert
"Canyon Venture." [Wind] (20:67) 90, p. 19.
"Late Summer Golf" (for Chris Ransick). [LaurelR] (24:2) Sum 90, p. 9-10.
"School's Ugliest Girl Dies." [LaurelR] (24:2) Sum 90, p. 10-11.
"Winter Pruning." [SouthernPR] (30:2) Fall 90, p. 59.
2184. GARCIA, Carlos Ernesto
"At the Moment of Dawn" (tr. by Elizabeth Gamble Miller). [MidAR] (10:1) 90, p.
107.
"Brief Love Poem" (tr. by Elizabeth Gamble Miller). [NewOR] (17:4) Wint 90, p.
24.
"First Kiss" (tr. by Elizabeth Gamble Miller). [NewOR] (17:4) Wint 90, p. 25.
"I Have No Home" (tr. by Elizabeth Gamble Miller). [NewOR] (17:4) Wint 90, p.
22-23.
"Love with Powder Burns" (tr. by Elizabeth Gamble Miller). [NewOR] (17:4) Wint
90, p. 28.
"Poor Company" (tr. by Elizabeth Gamble Miller). [NewOR] (17:4) Wint 90, p. 26.
"They Are Like the Dew" (tr. by Elizabeth Gamble Miller). [NewOR] (17:4) Wint
90, p. 27.
"Through the Slow Rancor of Water" (to Rigoberto Paredes, tr. by Elizabeth Gamble
Miller). [MidAR] (10:1) 90, p. 106.
"The Warrior's Rest" (tr. by Elizabeth Gamble Miller). [NewOR] (17:4) Wint 90, p.
21.
2185. GARCIA, Enildo
"Declaration of Love" (1963, October Cuban Missile Crisis, tr. of Carilda Oliver
Labra, w. Daniela Gioseffi). [PoetryE] (30) Fall 90, p. 54.
"Reportage from Viet Nam, Especially for International Woman's Day" (tr. of
Minerva Salado, w. Daniela Gioseffi). [PoetryE] (30) Fall 90, p. 27.
2186. GARCIA, Gary
"Fall." [SmPd] (27:2, #79) Spr 90, p. 17.
"Point Arena, CA." [Wind] (20:67) 90, p. 5.
2187. GARCIA, Jose
"Morning at Kamari." [Hellas] (1:1) Spr 90, p. 60.
"On Studying the Fragments of Heraclitus." [Hellas] (1:1) Spr 90, p. 61.
2188. GARCIA, Neryeda
"The Cock of Pomander Walk" (tr. of Pablo Armando Fernandez, w. Barry
Silesky). [AnotherCM] (21) 90, p. 37-47.
2189. GARCIA, Richard
"A Good Year." [OnTheBus] (2:1, #5) Spr 90, p. 70.
"Her Name Is Laughter." [YellowS] (34) Sum 90, p. 9.
"November." [OnTheBus] (2:2/3:1, #6/7) Sum-Fall 90 Wint-Spr 91, p. 92.

"One Man Band." [YellowS] (34) Sum 90, p. 8.
2190. GARCIA-ARANDA, Carlos
"Departing" (tr. of Alfonsina Storni, w. Margaret Hanzimanolis). [BelPoR] (40:3)
Spr 90, p. 23-25.
"I Am" (tr. of Alfonsina Storni, w. Margaret Hanzimanolis). [CarolQ] (43:1) Fall
90, p. 69.
"I Am Going to Sleep" (tr. of Alfonsina Storni, w. Margaret Hanzimanolis).
[CarolQ] (43:1) Fall 90, p. 70.
"I Am Useless" (tr. of Alfonsina Storni, w. Margaret Hanzimanolis). [CarolQ]
(43:1) Fall 90, p. 68.
"One More Time" (tr. of Alfonsina Storni, w. Margaret Hanzimanolis). [CarolQ]
(43:1) Fall 90, p. 67.
"Tropical" (tr. of Alfonsina Storni, w. Margaret Hanzimanolis). [BelPoR] (40:3) Spr
90, p. 25-26.
"You Want Me White" (tr. of Alfonsina Storni, w. Margaret Hanzimanolis).
[BelPoR] (40:3) Spr 90, p. 22-23.
GARCIA BURGALES, Pero
See BURGALES, Pero Garcia
GARCIA de GUILHADE, Joam
See GUILHADE, Joam Garcia de
2191. GARCIA LORCA, Federico
"Advice to the Poet" (tr. by Christopher Maurer). [NowestR] (28:3/29:1) 90-91, p.
158-159.
"Cancion del Naranjo Seco" (From "Canciones," 1921-1924). [CumbPR] (10:1) Fall
90, p. 18.
"Gacela for a Dead Child" (tr. by Pablo Medina). [ArtfulD] (18/19) 90, p. 29.
"The Guitar" (tr. by John Rosa Reyne). [ChatR] (11:1) Fall 90, p. 34.
"La Guitarra." [ChatR] (11:1) Fall 90, p. 34.
"He Died at Dawn" (tr. by Cynthia Hendershot). [CumbPR] (10:1) Fall 90, p. 17.
"Kassida of the Sleeping Woman" (tr. by Pablo Medina). [ArtfulD] (18/19) 90, p.
28.
"La Luna Asoma." [CumbPR] (10:1) Fall 90, p. 12.
"The Moon Rising" (tr. by Cynthia Hendershot). [CumbPR] (10:1) Fall 90, p. 13.
"Murió al Almancer" (From "Canciones," 1921-1924). [CumbPR] (10:1) Fall 90, p.
16.
"Ode to Salvador Dali" (tr. by Carlos Bauer). [AnotherCM] (21) 90, p. 111-114.
"Omega" (Poem for the Dead, tr. by Greg Simon and Steven F. White). [NowestR]
(28:3/29:1) 90-91, p. 178.
"A Reminder" (tr. by Joel Zeltzer). [ChironR] (9:3) Aut 90, p. 5.
"Romance of the Moon" (tr. by Joel Zeltzer). [ChironR] (9:3) Aut 90, p. 5.
"Song of the Barren Orange Tree" (tr. by Cynthia Hendershot). [CumbPR] (10:1)
Fall 90, p. 19.
"Song of the Tiny Death" (tr. by Joel Zeltzer). [ChironR] (9:3) Aut 90, p. 5.
"Suicide" (Perhaps because he didn't know geometry, tr. by Cynthia Hendershot).
[CumbPR] (10:1) Fall 90, p. 15.
"Suicidio" (Quizá fué por no saberte la geometria). [CumbPR] (10:1) Fall 90, p. 14.
"Trip to the Moon" (tr. by Greg Simon and Steven F. White). [NowestR]
(28:3/29:1) 90-91, p. 170-177.
2192. GARCIA MARRUZ, Fina
"La Demente en la Puerta de la Iglesia." [InterPR] (16:1) Spr 90, p. 36, 38.
"Un Lugar de Nombres Cariñosos." [Areíto] (2:8) N 90, p. 33-35.
"The Mad Woman at the Church Door." (tr. by Mark Smith-Soto). [InterPR] (16:1)
Spr 90, p. 37, 39.
"El Momento Que Más Amo" (Escena final de "Luces de la ciudad"). [Areíto] (2:8) N
90, inside front cover.
"La Pobre, Encantadora Melodía" (De: "Créditos de Charlot"). [Areíto] (2:8) N 90,
inside back cover.
2193. GARCIA RAMOS, Reinaldo
"London Kid." [LindLM] (9:4) O-D 90, p. 44.
"Templos Extranjeros." [LindLM] (9:1/2) Ja/Mr-Ap/Je 90, p. 8.
2194. GARDINIER, Suzanne
"Citizens." [ParisR] (32:116) Fall 90, p. 33-38.
"Dear Sam, Taken by the Adoption Agency." [ParisR] (32:114) Spr 90, p. 185.
"Two Boys." [GrandS] (9:3) Spr 90, p. 11-12.
"Usahn." [GrandS] (9:2) Wint 90, p. 32.

2195. GARDNER, Drew
"Fake Oracle." [Notus] (5:1) Spr 90, p. 92-97.
2196. GARDNER, Eric
"Ghosts." [CoalC] (1) Ag 90, p. 25.
"Studebaker." [CoalC] (1) Ag 90, p. 24.
2197. GARDNER, Geoffrey
"Docility" (tr. of Jules Supervielle). [Sequoia] (33:2) Wint 90, p. 70.
"The House Surrounded" (tr. of Jules Supervielle). [WillowS] (26) Spr 90, p. 36.
"I Dream" (tr. of Jules Supervielle). [Sequoia] (33:2) Wint 90, p. 72.
"Pines" (tr. of Jules Supervielle). [Sequoia] (33:2) Wint 90, p. 74.
"Untitled: Night inside me, night out there" (tr. of Jules Supervielle). [WillowS] (26)
    Spr 90, p. 35.
2198. GARGANO, Elizabeth
"Jonah." [SingHM] (17) 90, p. 22-23.
"Outdoor Concert." [SingHM] (17) 90, p. 20-21.
"Red Clay." [PraS] (64:3) Fall 90, p. 63-65.
"Tired Light." [SingHM] (17) 90, p. 24.
2199. GARLAND, Max
"Cappuccino at the Marconi Hotel in Venice." [Poetry] (156:4) Jl 90, p. 210.
"Fedoras." [Poetry] (156:4) Jl 90, p. 211-212.
"Homage to White Bread, Circa 1956." [Iowa] (20:1) Wint 90, p. 56-57.
"Initiation, 1965." [Iowa] (20:1) Wint 90, p. 55-56.
"Introduction to the Phenomena, Circa 1959." [Iowa] (20:1) Wint 90, p. 53-54.
"Ornament." [GeoR] (44:3) Fall 90, p. 410.
"The Postal Confessions." [Poetry] (156:4) Jl 90, p. 211.
"The Woman on the Road from Kamari." [Iowa] (20:1) Wint 90, p. 54-55.
2200. GARMON, John
"Crown Vetch." [KanQ] (22:1/2) Wint-Spr 90, p. 64.
2201. GARREN, Christine
"Flowers." [TriQ] (79) Fall 90, p. 99.
"The Fountains." [ChatR] (10:4) Sum 90, p. 63.
"The Rescue." [TriQ] (79) Fall 90, p. 98.
2202. GARRETT, Brian
"At Home." [AntigR] (83) Aut 90, p. 34.
"Heather's Vision." [AntigR] (83) Aut 90, p. 32-33.
2203. GARRETT, Daniel
"A Remembrance of Class" (for Pedro). [ChangingM] (21) Wint-Spr 90, p. 12.
2204. GARRETT, Nola
"In Vikki's Photograph." [PoetryNW] (31:3) Aut 90, p. 21.
"The Mail from Tunis." [PoetryNW] (31:3) Aut 90, p. 20-21.
"Testaments." [ChrC] (107:6) 21 F 90, p. 182.
2205. GARRIGA, Michael
"Bag Lady on My Street." [ChironR] (9:2) Sum 90, p. 17.
2206. GARRISON, David
"Goodwill." [Comm] (117:11) 1 Je 90, p. 352.
2207. GARRISON, Deborah Gottlieb
"November on Her Way." [NewYorker] (66:41) 26 N 90, p. 112.
"Saying Yes to a Drink." [NewYorker] (66:13) 14 My 90, p. 68.
"She Was Waiting to Be Told." [NewYorker] (66:29) 3 S 90, p. 38.
2208. GARRISON, Joseph
"Bombers." [HampSPR] (Anthology 1975-1990) 90, p. 98.
2209. GARTHE, Karen
"Diver." [PaintedB] (40/41) 90, p. 140-141.
GARZA FALCON, Leticia
    See FALCON, Leticia Garza
2210. GASPAR, Frank (Frank X.)
"Gall, Wormwood." [NewEngR] (13:1) Fall 90, p. 108.
"Manter Creek." [Pearl] (11) Sum 90, p. 49.
"Old Stories." [NewEngR] (13:1) Fall 90, p. 109-110.
"R and R." [WestHR] (44:2) Sum 90, p. 190.
"Where Do You Sleep?" [KenR] (NS 12:4) Fall 90, p. 155-156.
2211. GASPAR, Gail A.
"American Gothic." [SoCaR] (23:1) Fall 90, p. 149.
GASPAR DE ALBA, Alicia
    See ALBA, Alicia Gaspar de

179

2212. GASPARINI, Leonard
"Crabdance." [AntigR] (80) Wint 90, p. 143.
"Under the Ambassador Bridge." [AntigR] (80) Wint 90, p. 144.
2213. GASTON, Bill
"I Send My Birds Out." [Arc] (25) Aut 90, p. 13.
"One More Anti Ghazal Ghazal." [Arc] (25) Aut 90, p. 14-15.
2214. GATES, Bob
"Medical Center." [NewYorkQ] (42) Sum 90, p. 89.
"The Way It Is Now." [SlipS] (10) 90, p. 87-88.
2215. GATES, Edward
"V." [PottPort] (12) 90, p. 47.
2216. GATTO, Alfonso
"Anniversary" (tr. by Philip Parisi). [PartR] (57:3) Sum 90, p. 431.
"An Evening in March" (tr. by Philip Parisi). [Chelsea] (49) 90, p. 127.
"Guilt" (tr. by Philip Parisi). [ColR] (NS 17:1) Spr-Sum 90, p. 97.
"Hanno Sparato a Mezzanotte." [InterPR] (16:2) Fall 90, p. 56.
"Hear the Footstep" (tr. by Philip Parisi). [Chelsea] (49) 90, p. 126.
"Il Racconto" (from "La Storia delle Vittime"). [InterPR] (16:2) Fall 90, p. 58, 60.
"Una Madre Che Dorme." [InterPR] (16:2) Fall 90, p. 56.
"A Mother Who Sleeps" (tr. by Philip Parisi). [InterPR] (16:2) Fall 90, p. 57.
"The Tale" (tr. by Philip Parisi). [InterPR] (16:2) Fall 90, p. 59, 61.
"They Shot at Midnight" (tr. by Philip Parisi). [InterPR] (16:2) Fall 90, p. 57.
2217. GAUTHIER, Marcel G.
"Boy Travelling." [HiramPoR] (47) Wint 90, p. 29.
"The Stone" (for Kirsten, my sister). [HiramPoR] (47) Wint 90, p. 30.
2218. GAWRON, James
"Dream With a Bad Reputation." [Asylum] (5:4) 90, p. 39.
2219. GEADA, Rita
"Otra Vez Otoño en New England." [LindLM] (9:4) O-D 90, p. 46.
2220. GEIGER, Timothy
"That Past." [Poetry] (157:2) N 90, p. 94.
2221. GELETA, Greg
"Flaws." [Pearl] (10) Spr 90, p. 52.
"On Hearing of the Death of My Father." [Wind] (20:67) 90, p. 20.
2222. GELINEAU, Christine M.
"Crochet." [FloridaR] (17:2) Fall-Wint 90, p. 160.
"Raspberries." [FloridaR] (17:2) Fall-Wint 90, p. 161.
2223. GELLAND, Carolyn
"Ipiutak Burial Site, Point Hope, Alaska." [ManhatPR] (11) [89?], p. 12-13.
"Monsoon." [ManhatPR] (11) [89?], p. 11.
"Scales and Clocks." [ChamLR] (4:1, #7) Fall 90, p. 126.
"Wolsey's Death." [ManhatPR] (11) [89?], p. 10-11.
2224. GENEGA, Paul
"The Lawn." [WebR] (14:2) Spr 90, p. 90.
"Roomer." [WebR] (14:2) Spr 90, p. 91.
2225. GÉNÉREUX, M. D.
"Azimuth." [PoetryC] (11:2) Sum 90, p. 17.
"Normal Life." [PoetryC] (11:2) Sum 90, p. 17.
2226. GENNETT, Len Garretta
"Dinner at Seven." [HiramPoR] (48/49) 90-91, p. 32.
2227. GEORGE, Alice
"Remembering August in February." [Farm] (7:2) Fall 90, p. 47.
2228. GEORGE, Beth
"Bull Eating Pears." [PoetL] (85:2) Sum 90, p. 28.
"The China Cabinet." [Wind] (20:66) 90, p. 12.
2229. GEORGE, Charley
"Too Palm Tree, Too Pool." [PoetryUSA] (5:1) Spr 90, p. 3.
2230. GEORGE, Diana Hume
"The Resurrection of the Body." [SpoonRQ] (15:1) Wint 90, p. 48-50.
"While Reading Virginia Woolf at a Campsite." [SpoonRQ] (15:1) Wint 90, p. 44-47.
2231. GEORGE, Emery
"Definition" (tr. of János Pilinszky). [LitR] (33:2) Wint 90, p. 196.
"The Fans." [PartR] (57:1) Wint 90, p. 108-109.
"From the Henchman's Diary" (For Thomas Tranströmer, tr. of János Pilinszky). [LitR] (33:2) Wint 90, p. 196.

"Hölderlin" (For György Kurtág, tr. of János Pilinszky). [LitR] (33:2) Wint 90, p. 197.

"Invisible." [KanQ] (22:1/2) Wint-Spr 90, p. 72-73.

"Italian Painter" (tr. of Miklós Radnóti). [HampSPR] (Anthology 1975-1990) 90, p. 259.

"Opening" (tr. of János Pilinszky). [LitR] (33:2) Wint 90, p. 196.

"Rain" (tr. of Miklós Radnóti). [HampSPR] (Anthology 1975-1990) 90, p. 259.

"Two" (tr. of János Pilinszky). [LitR] (33:2) Wint 90, p. 197.

2232. GEORGE, Raphaële
"Bartered Nights: Three Poems" (tr. by Stephen Sartarelli). [Trans] (23) Spr 90, p. 100-101.

2233. GEORGE, Stefan
"And So I Went Forth" (tr. by Ulrike Weber and Richard Jones). [PoetryE] (30) Fall 90, p. 93.

"The Flower I Guard" (tr. by Ulrike Weber and Richard Jones). [PoetryE] (30) Fall 90, p. 91.

"I Am the One" (tr. by Ulrike Weber and Richard Jones). [PoetryE] (30) Fall 90, p. 89.

"In Purple Fire Spoke the Wrath of Heaven" (tr. by Ulrike Weber and Richard Jones). [PoetryE] (30) Fall 90, p. 90.

"My White Parrots" (tr. by Ulrike Weber and Richard Jones). [Gargoyle] (37/38) 90, p. 114.

"Was My Question" (tr. by Ulrike Weber and Richard Jones). [PoetryE] (30) Fall 90, p. 92.

2234. GERAGHTY, Thomas
"Love Poem." [Iowa] (20:2) Spr-Sum 90, p. 129.

2235. GERBER, Joanne
"Like Manna." [Grain] (18:4) Wint 90, p. 77-78.

2236. GERFEN, Henry
"Alzheimer's." [CutB] (33) 90, p. 65-66.

"Clay's Birthday." [PoetryNW] (31:2) Sum 90, p. 42.

"Communist." [CutB] (33) 90, p. 66.

2237. GERGELY, Agnes
"Mrs. Wadsworth's Letter to Emily Dickinson" (tr. by Mária Kurdi and Len Roberts). [AmerPoR] (19:5) S-O 90, p. 27.

"Rhapsody for My Birthday" (tr. by Mária Kurdi and Len Roberts). [AmerPoR] (19:5) S-O 90, p. 27.

2238. GERHARDT, Ida
"Christ As Gardener" (Painting: Christ the Gardener by Rembrandt van Rijn, tr. by Johanna H. Prins and Johanna W. Prins). [Trans] (24) Fall 90, p. 49.

"The Reviewing" (Painting: River Landscape with Ferry by Salomon van Ruysdael, tr. by Johanna H. Prins and Johanna W. Prins). [Trans] (24) Fall 90, p. 48.

2239. GERLACH, Eva
"Entropy" (tr. by Myra Scholz-Heerspink). [Trans] (24) Fall 90, p. 132.

"Letter" (tr. by Myra Scholz-Heerspink). [Trans] (24) Fall 90, p. 131.

"Season" (tr. by Myra Scholz-Heerspink). [Trans] (24) Fall 90, p. 132.

2240. GERMAN, Greg
"A Farmer's Son Gives Up and Moves to the City, or The Implications of Liquidating a Farm Operation" (1990 Seaton Honorable Mention Poem). [KanQ] (22:3) Sum 90, p. 22.

2241. GERMAN, Norman
"Catfish, Like Me." [KanQ] (22:3) Sum 90, p. 84.

"The One That Got Away." [MalR] (90) Spr 90, p. 64.

"Rising Tide." [HawaiiR] (15:1, #31) Wint 90, p. 70.

"The Space Between Stars." [MalR] (90) Spr 90, p. 63.

2242. GERO-CHEN, Joshua
"Love Made." [PoetryUSA] (5:2) Sum 90, p. 7.

2243. GERSTLER, Amy
"Overheard on the Soul Train." [BrooklynR] (7) 90, p. 6-7.

"Pronouns." [BrooklynR] (7) 90, p. 5.

2244. GERVAIS, C. H. (Marty)
"Confessions and Conclusions." [Descant] (21:1 #68) Spr 90, p. 50.

"Lies." [Descant] (21:1 #68) Spr 90, p. 48.

"Moons Dancing in Stillness." [Descant] (21:1 #68) Spr 90, p. 49.

GERVAN, Claudia van
See Van GERVEN, Claudia

GERVEN, Claudia van
    See Van GERVEN, Claudia
2245. GERY, John
    "Between." [Verse] (7:3) Wint 90, p. 48.
    "The Impropriety of Trees" (for M.D.G.). [WilliamMR] (28) 90, p. 57-58.
    "A Poem for Barbara." [Verse] (7:3) Wint 90, p. 47.
    "Speech for a Possible Ending." [Verse] (7:2) Sum 90, p. 86.
2246. GERY, Marie Vogl
    "King's Choir Cambridge: Christmas Eve 1989." [RagMag] (7:2) Spr 90, p. 13-14.
2247. GESANG, John
    "Geishas." [ChamLR] (4:1, #7) Fall 90, p. 84.
2248. GESSNER, Michael
    "Bridge at Giverny." [Poem] (64) N 90, p. 57.
    "Sunday Picnic." [Poem] (64) N 90, p. 58.
    "The Tropic Gardens of St. Gallen" (In Memory of Ezra Pound). [SycamoreR] (2:1)
        Wint 90, p. 22-23.
    "White Doors." [Poem] (64) N 90, p. 56.
2249. GETSI, Lucia Cordell
    "Geting Beyond Unity." [ClockR] (6:2) 90, p. 33.
    "Meeting the Occasion." [LaurelR] (24:2) Sum 90, p. 59.
    "You Ask How to Know a Good Man." [SouthernPR] (30:1) Spr 90, p. 70-71.
2250. GETTLER, Andrew
    "Bro." [SlipS] (10) 90, p. 35.
    "Fiscal Year." [SlipS] (10) 90, p. 35.
    "Memento - Oval Office." [SlipS] (10) 90, p. 34.
    "Mulier Cantat." [Parting] (3:2) Wint 90-91, p. 32.
    "TV Dinner." [SlipS] (10) 90, p. 36.
2251. GEWANTER, David
    "Bill." [Agni] (29/30) 90, p. 113-115.
    "The Pardon" (for Ezra Pound). [Agni] (29/30) 90, p. 111-112.
2252. GEYER, William
    "Garden Reprieve: The Paradox of Fortunate Forgetfulness." [ChrC] (107:20) 27
        Je-4 Jl 90, p. 636.
2253. GHALIB
    "For the raindrop, joy is in entering the river" (Ghazal, tr. by Jane Hirshfield).
        [ParisR] (32:115) Sum 90, p. 45.
    "In every color and circumstance, may the eyes be open for what comes" (Ghazal, tr.
        by Jane Hirshfield). [ParisR] (32:115) Sum 90, p. 45.
    "Lines" (tr. by Gregory Kozlowski). [PoetryE] (30) Fall 90, p. 73.
GHATA, Venus Khoury
    See KHOURY-GHATA, Venus
2254. GHOLSON, Christien
    "The Hint of Rain." [Bogg] (63) 90, p. 40.
    "Parables" (Excerpt). [Bogg] (62) 90, p. 41.
2255. GIBB, Robert
    "Glimpse." [PoetryNW] (31:3) Aut 90, p. 9-10.
    "Groundhog Days." [PraS] (64:3) Fall 90, p. 61-63.
    "Leaving the Valley." [PraS] (64:3) Fall 90, p. 54-61.
    "The Race." [Poetry] (156:6) S 90, p. 339-340.
    "Red Shift." [PraS] (64:3) Fall 90, p. 53.
    "Requiem." [PoetryNW] (31:3) Aut 90, p. 10-11.
    "Thawing the Vultures." [PoetryNW] (31:3) Aut 90, p. 11-12.
    "Watching for the Next Poem." [HampSPR] (Anthology 1975-1990) 90, p. 217.
2256. GIBBONS, Reginald
    "The Affect of Elms." [Atlantic] (265:6) Je 90, p. 89.
    "Before." [AmerPoR] (19:6) N-D 90, p. 39.
    "Hide from Time." [AmerPoR] (19:6) N-D 90, p. 40.
    "Order of Battle." [Chelsea] (49) 90, p. 76-77.
    "Prospect of a Village in Devon." [Boulevard] (4:3/5:1, #12/13) Spr 90, p. 171-174.
    "Stars." [AmerPoR] (19:6) N-D 90, p. 39.
GIBSON, Elisabeth Grant
    See GRANT-GIBSON, Elisabeth
2257. GIBSON, Grace Loving
    "Garden." [Pembroke] (22) 90, p. 64.
    "Self-Deception." [Pembroke] (22) 90, p. 66.
    "Wings Between the Sun and Me." [Pembroke] (22) 90, p. 65.

2258. GIBSON, Margaret
"After January 2" (in memory of D.B.C.). [NewOR] (17:2) Sum 90, p. 21.
"Countershading." [HampSPR] (Anthology 1975-1990) 90, p. 135.
"Instructions for a Somnambulist." [HampSPR] (Anthology 1975-1990) 90, p. 136.

2259. GIBSON, Mary Milam
"Sons." [EmeraldCR] (1990) c89, p. 103-104.

2260. GIBSON, Stephen
"George Segal: *Girl Putting on Scarab Necklace*." [SouthernPR] (30:1) Spr 90, p. 19.

2261. GIBSON, W. David
"Egret's Alley." [KanQ] (22:1/2) Wint-Spr 90, p. 212.

2262. GIESECKE, Lee
"Briefcase." [Bogg] (63) 90, p. 11.

GIL, Alfredo Gomez
See GOMEZ GIL, Alfredo

2263. GIL, Lourdes
"Andares del Subsuelo." [LindLM] (9:4) O-D 90, p. 6.

2264. GILBERT, Celia
"Primipara" (The medical term for a woman who has borne one child). [Poetry] (156:1) Ap 90, p. 14-15.

2265. GILBERT, Chris
"Absentee Landlord." [Ploughs] (16:1) Spr-Sum 90, p. 159.

2266. GILBERT, Gregory W.
"Enjambements." [PacificR] (8) 90, p. 28.
"Metaphors." [PacificR] (8) 90, p. 29.

2267. GILBERT, Jack
"Voices Inside and Out" (for Hayden Carruth). [Ploughs] (16:4) Wint 90-91, p. 58.
"We Are the Junction." [Ploughs] (16:4) Wint 90-91, p. 59.

2268. GILDNER, Gary
"My Father After Work." [NewL] (57:1) Fall 90, p. 24-25.
"Southpaws Are As Rare." [ThRiPo] (35/36) 90, p. 27-28.
"The Trip to Auschwitz." [ClockR] (6:1) 90, p. 25-33.
"Trying to Catch Up." [ThRiPo] (35/36) 90, p. 29.

2269. GILENS, Sharona
"Hermosa Nightmare." [OnTheBus] (2:1, #5) Spr 90, p. 71.

2270. GILES, Molly
"The Poet's Husband." [Zyzzyva] (6:3 #23) Fall 90, p. 107.

2271. GILGUN, John
"Attitude." [JamesWR] (7:2) Wint 90, p. 8.
"The Fox and the Wolf." [JamesWR] (7:2) Wint 90, p. 8.
"St. Joseph." [Pig] (16) 90, p. 61.

2272. GILL, David
"Language Drill." [Verse] (7:2) Sum 90, p. 9.

2273. GILL, Glenda
"View From My Window." [Obs] (5:3) Wint 90, p. 41-42.

2274. GILL, John
"Portraits." [HangL] (57) 90, p. 27-30.

2275. GILL, Michael J.
"I. Yeats was right: the old patterns can't hold." [Poem] (63) My 90, p. 9.
"II. The closure of an end-rhyme line stops." [Poem] (63) My 90, p. 10.
"Red Haze." [HiramPoR] (48/49) 90-91, p. 33-34.

2276. GILL-LONERGAN, Janet
"Wars I Have Known." [BellArk] (6:1) Ja-F 90, p. 12.

2277. GILLAN, Maria Mazziotti
"Connections." [SinW] (41) Sum-Fall 90, p. 32-33.
"Musings in a Hospital Room." [Ometeca] (1:2/2:1) 89-90, p. 32.
"Public School No. 18: Paterson, New Jersey." [SinW] (41) Sum-Fall 90, p. 8-9.
"When the Universe Halts Its Infinite Spinning and Light Breaks." [Ometeca] (1:2/2:1) 89-90, p. 31.

2278. GILLET, Ed
"Carol." [EmeraldCR] (1990) c89, p. 52.

2279. GILLETT, Michelle
"Beauty" (Hiroshima). [SingHM] (18) 90, p. 89.
"Earthly House" (Hiroshima). [SingHM] (18) 90, p. 94.
"O-Bon" (Buddhist festival for the dead). [SingHM] (18) 90, p. 92.
"Vision" (Hiroshima). [SingHM] (18) 90, p. 91.

"Volunteer Corps" (Hiroshima). [SingHM] (18) 90, p. 90.
"Wreckage" (Hiroshima). [SingHM] (18) 90, p. 93.
2280. GILLILAND, Gail
"Picking Raspberries." [GrahamHR] (13) Spr 90, p. 73.
2281. GILLILAND, Mary
"Ash Tuesday." [SingHM] (18) 90, p. 23.
"Sabbath." [YellowS] (33) Spr 90, p. 24.
2282. GILMORE, Christine
"August." [SouthwR] (75:2) Spr 90, p. 282.
"(Standing, Upright) Bass" (for my grandfather, who died in 1959). [GrahamHR]
    (13) Spr 90, p. 50-51.
2283. GILONIS, Harry
"Axioms" (IV, VI, from a set of 6). [Screens] (2) 90, p. 139-141.
"From Far Away" (with Tony Baker). [WestCL] (24:3) Wint 90, p. 44-54.
"Letter from Diotima" (tr. of Friedrich Hölderlin). [Stand] (31:3) Sum 90, p. 32-33.
"Two (Separate) Extracts from a Collaborative Renga (1989) Odd-Numbered
    Stanzas: Harry Gilonis, Even-Numbered Stanzas: Tony Baker." [Screens] (2)
    90, p. 137-138.
2284. GILSDORF, Ethan
"Family History: Final Examination." [NewYorkQ] (42) Sum 90, p. 74-75.
"Suffering Writer." [Pearl] (10) Spr 90, p. 20.
"Unchanged." [Pearl] (10) Spr 90, p. 20.
GINEBRA, Arminda Valdés
    See VALDÉS GINEBRA, Arminda
2285. GINGRICH-PHILBROOK, Craig
"Fireflies." [GreensboroR] (48) Sum 90, p. 41-42.
"How to Fall." [GreensboroR] (48) Sum 90, p. 43-44.
"Than I Have Ever Been" (for Chris). [GreensboroR] (48) Sum 90, p. 44-46.
2286. GINN, Robert
"James Koyle Became Paralyzed." [Plain] (10:3) Spr 90, p. 18.
2287. GINSBERG, Allen
"Personal Ad." [Harp] (280:1681) Je 90, p. 32.
"A Supermarket in California." [SouthernR] (26:3) Jl 90, p. 487-488.
2288. GIOIA, Dana
"Cleared Away." [Verse] (7:3) Wint 90, p. 49.
"Counting the Children." [Hudson] (43:2) Sum 90, p. 239-244.
"Guide to the Other Gallery." [Verse] (7:3) Wint 90, p. 49.
"I sit, in treatment, at the movies, devoted" (tr. of Valerio Magrelli). [WilliamMR]
    (28) 90, p. 8.
"If I must dial a number to call you" (tr. of Valerio Magrelli). [WilliamMR] (28) 90,
    p. 7.
"If you melt some lead" (tr. of Valerio Magrelli). [WilliamMR] (28) 90, p. 63.
"Orchestra" (tr. of Nina Cassian). [NewYorker] (65:46) 1 Ja 90, p. 30.
"Rough Country." [Verse] (7:3) Wint 90, p. 49.
"Senior" (tr. of Mario Luzi). [Sequoia] (33:2) Wint 90, p. 4.
2289. GIOSEFFI, Daniela
"Answer to 'The Suicide'." [Footwork] 90, p. 108.
"Antigone" (tr. of Ileana Malancioui, w. Ivana Spalatin). [PoetryE] (29) Spr 90, p.
    140.
"The Ballad of Deceived Flowers" (tr. of Vesna Parun). [PoetryE] (29) Spr 90, p.
    103-104.
"Declaration of Love" (1963, October Cuban Missile Crisis, tr. of Carilda Oliver
    Labra, w. Enildo García). [PoetryE] (30) Fall 90, p. 54.
"The First Long-Range Artillery Fire on Leningrad" (tr. of Anna Akhmatova, w.
    Sophia Buzevska). [PoetryE] (30) Fall 90, p. 23.
"A Man" (tr. of Nina Cassian, w. the author). [PoetryE] (29) Spr 90, p. 124.
"The Olive Branch." [JINJPo] (12:2) Aut 90, p. 19.
"On a Japanese Beach" (Hiroshima Memento, tr. of Nina Cassian, w. the author).
    [PoetryE] (29) Spr 90, p. 125.
"Reportage from Viet Nam, Especially for International Woman's Day" (tr. of
    Minerva Salado, w. Enildo García). [PoetryE] (30) Fall 90, p. 27.
"The War" (tr. of Vesna Parun). [PoetryE] (29) Spr 90, p. 105-106.
"World War" (tr. of Nina Cassian, w. the author). [PoetryE] (29) Spr 90, p. 126.
2290. GIOVANNI, Nikki
"Crutches" (reprinted from #19, 1989). [Kaleid] (20) Wint-Spr 90, p. 79.

2291. GIOVINGO, Anne M.
      "Although." [MissR] (19:1/2, #55/56) 90, p. 254.
2292. GIRARDEAU, Ronald
      "Breakout." [NewYorkQ] (42) Sum 90, p. 88.
2293. GISCOMBE, C. S.
      "(Outlying Areas)." [NewAW] (6) Spr 90, p. 15-20.
      "To James Wright 1." [AnotherCM] (22) 90, p. 42-43.
      "To James Wright 2." [AnotherCM] (22) 90, p. 44.
2294. GITLIN, Todd
      "Who Are the People." [Quarry] (39:4) Fall 1990, p. 88-89.
2295. GIUNTA, Bill
      "Assurance" (for Yvonne). [Boulevard] (5:2, #14) Fall 90, p. 133.
2296. GIZZI, Michael
      "Bad Boy" (for John Yau). [Talisman] (5) Fall 90, p. 108-109.
      "Let This Be a Lesson." [Sulfur] (10:1, #26) Spr 90, p. 194.
      "The Shell Game." [Sulfur] (10:1, #26) Spr 90, p. 193.
      "Treestains." [Sulfur] (10:1, #26) Spr 90, p. 191-192.
2297. GIZZI, Peter
      "The Creation" (from "Stage notes to the history of the world"). [Screens] (2) 90, p.
           205.
      "Mise en Scène." [Conjunc] (15) 90, p. 317.
      "Stagenotes for the History of the World" (A Voice Play: 2 selections). [Avec] (3:1)
           90, p. 123-125.
2298. GJEZEL, Bogomil
      "Silence" (tr. of Slavko Janevski, w. Herbert Kuhner and Howard Erksine Hill).
           [Footwork] 90, p. 106.
2299. GLADDING, Jody
      "But What About the Stepsisters." [GreenMR] (NS 4:1) Spr-Sum 90, p. 118.
      "Gifts." [PoetryNW] (31:4) Wint 90-91, p. 18.
      "Spell for Not Entering into the Shambles of the Gods." [PoetryNW] (31:4) Wint
           90-91, p. 17-18.
2300. GLADE, Jon Forrest
      "Card Trick." [Asylum] (5:4) 90, p. 6.
      "Ex-Roommate." [Pearl] (11) Sum 90, p. 36.
2301. GLADHART, Amalia
      "Woven Hands." [Amelia] (6:2, #17) 90, p. 94.
2302. GLADING, Jan
      "Monterey Pine Cone, Fallen from an Aged Tree" (reprinted from #13, 1986).
           [Kaleid] (20) Wint-Spr 90, p. 35.
2303. GLANCY, Diane
      "Contentment: December Twenty-Ninth." [HayF] (6) Sum 90, p. 101.
      "Homework." [HayF] (6) Sum 90, p. 100.
      "Lone Dog's Winter Count." [Journal] (13:2) Fall-Wint 89-90, p. 13-15.
      "Spiro Mounds" (Burial Mounds, Eastern Oklahoma). [ContextS] (1:1) 89, p. 26.
      "St. Louis Art Museum, a Blue Harem: Portraits of Three Women." [Pearl] (10) Spr
           90, p. 8-9.
      "Trying to Crow." [Calyx] (13:1) Wint 90-91, p. 48-53.
2304. GLANCY, Gabrielle
      "A Building We Perceive As Standing Still." [NewAW] (6) Spr 90, p. 76-77.
      "A Certain Geography." [NewAW] (6) Spr 90, p. 78-79.
2305. GLASER, Elton
      "Another One That Won't Tell." [LaurelR] (24:1) Wint 90, p. 89.
      "Blues for the Nightowl." [IndR] (13:3) Fall 90, p. 10.
      "The Faith of Forty." [NoDaQ] (58:2) Spr 90, p. 43.
      "First Earth." [LaurelR] (24:1) Wint 90, p. 88.
      "Long in the Tooth." [NoDaQ] (58:2) Spr 90, p. 42.
      "October Nocturne." [OxfordM] (6:1) Spr-Sum 90, p. 55.
      "Scars and Apologies." [IndR] (13:3) Fall 90, p. 11.
      "Spry Declensions." [IndR] (13:3) Fall 90, p. 8-9.
      "Storyville." [IndR] (14:1) Wint 90, p. 108-112.
      "Sunny Side Up." [PoetryNW] (31:2) Sum 90, p. 43.
2306. GLASS, Jesse, Jr.
      "To Johns Hopkins University." [Bogg] (63) 90, p. 32-33.
2307. GLASS, Malcolm
      (Anonymous poem). [FreeL] (4) 90.
      "At the Drive-In" (for Gerard Huber). [SwampR] (5) Wint-Spr 90, p. 26.

"Burrowing Owls" (for John Childrey). [NoDaQ] (58:4) Fall 90, p. 154-155.
"Disguised." [Poetry] (157:2) N 90, p. 89-90.
"Georges Braque" (tr. of Paul Eluard, w. Karen D. Sorenson). [CumbPR] (9:2) Spr
90, p. 41.
"Missing." [SycamoreR] (2:2) Sum 90, p. 3-4.
"One Way of Dying." [SwampR] (5) Wint-Spr 90, p. 27-28.
"Pretending." [SwampR] (5) Wint-Spr 90, p. 29.
"Second Flight." [PoetC] (21:2) Wint 90, p. 22-23.
"To Marc Chagall" (tr. of Paul Eluard, w. Karen D. Sorenson). [CumbPR] (9:2) Spr
90, p. 39.
2308. GLASS, Terrence
"Cicadas." [CentR] (34:3) Sum 90, p. 396-397.
"Month with the Word May." [CentR] (34:3) Sum 90, p. 297-398.
2309. GLASSER, Marvin
"The Rich January of the Duke of Berry." [HiramPoR] (48/49) 90-91, p. 35.
2310. GLASSER, Selma
"Burning to Return." [Writer] (103:10) O 90, p. 17.
"Improbable Proverbs." [Writer] (103:10) O 90, p. 17.
"Let's Enact the Santa 'Claus'." [Writer] (103:10) O 90, p. 17.
"Problem Thinkers." [Writer] (103:10) O 90, p. 16.
"What Goes Down Must Come Up." [Writer] (103:10) O 90, p. 17.
2311. GLASSGOLD, Peter
"Eala!" (poems from "On the Consolation of Philosophy": I-III, VI-VII, tr. of
Anicius Manlius Severinus Boethius). [WashR] (16:2) Ag-S 90, p. 10-11.
2312. GLATT, Lisa
"City." [Pearl] (10) Spr 90, p. 16.
"A Good Hag's Advice." [ChironR] (9:1) Spr 90, p. 24.
"Letting the Gowns Blow and Open." [Pearl] (11) Sum 90, p. 12-13.
"Waiting for Fillings." [Pearl] (11) Sum 90, p. 13.
2313. GLAZER, Michele
"In Concert." [PoetryNW] (31:2) Sum 90, p. 10-11.
2314. GLAZIER, Loss Pequeño
"Folded Rose" (Excerpts). [Os] (30) Spr 90, p. 18.
"Vowels and Single Vase" (Selections: 1, 2, 7, 8). [Os] (31) 90, p. 10-13.
2315. GLAZNER, Gary
"Taps." [PoetryUSA] (5:3) Fall 90, p. 15.
2316. GLAZNER, Greg
"The Metaphysician's Weekend." [SouthernPR] (30:1) Spr 90, p. 28-29.
2317. GLEASON, Marian
"Morality Play." [ChrC] (107:6) 21 F 90, p. 185.
2318. GLEN, Emile
"Same Bench, Same Bronze." [Wind] (20:66) 90, p. 13.
"Step Out." [Wind] (20:66) 90, p. 13.
2319. GLEN, Émilie
"Book to Close." [ChironR] (9:1) Spr 90, p. 23.
"Glory Pig." [NewYorkQ] (43) Fall 90, p. 82-83.
2320. GLEN-SMITH, David
"The Whales of Mare Serenitatis." [BlueBldgs] (12) 90, p. 15-17.
2321. GLENN, Laura
"If You Were You I'd Write About." [NorthStoneR] (9) 90, p. 79.
"The Living Room." [Ascent] (15:1) 90, p. 71-72.
2322. GLICK, Bert
"Captive Audience." [PoetryUSA] (5:2) Sum 90, p. 3.
"Revelation." [PoetryUSA] (5:2) Sum 90, p. 3.
GLICKSTEIN-BRAME, Gloria
See BRAME, Gloria Glickstein
2323. GLISSANT, Edouard
"Black Smoke" (tr. by Jean-Clarence Lambert and Bradley R. Strahan). [Vis] (32)
90, p. 25.
"Poetique" (tr. by Jean-Clarence Lambert and Bradley R. Strahan). [Vis] (32) 90, p.
25.
2324. GLOEGGLER, Tony
"Bath Time." [Turnstile] (2:1) 90, p. 76-78.
"Foreplay." [NewYorkQ] (41) Spr 90, p. 104-105.
"Night Shift." [BlackBR] (11) Spr-Sum 90, p. 25.
"Subway Pocket Poems." [ManhatPR] (12) [90?], p. 6-7.

2325. GLOVER, Albert
"Pastoral." [Blueline] (11:1/2) 90, p. 12.

2326. GLOVER, Toni
"The Hermit Poem." [Footwork] 90, p. 113.

2327. GLOWACKI, Richard
"'Idz Spac' Means 'Go to Bed'." [Farm] (7:2) Fall 90, p. 104.

2328. GOAD, Craig M.
"Highway Safety." [TarRP] (30:1) Fall 90, p. 1-2.

2329. GOCKER, Paula
"Lunar Eclipse." [OnTheBus] (2:2/3:1, #6/7) Sum-Fall 90 Wint-Spr 91, p. 93.
"Omens." [OnTheBus] (2:1, #5) Spr 90, p. 72.

2330. GOD (a homeless person, San Francisco) (See also WILSON, Robert (God))
"Life's Waitress." [PoetryUSA] (5:2) Sum 90, p. 19.
"Strange Bedfellows." [PoetryUSA] (5:3) Fall 90, p. 24.

2331. GODING, Cecile (Cecile Hanna)
"Chanteuse -- 1955." [HayF] (7) Fall-Wint 90, p. 75-76.
"Excavation of a Burial Mound." [PoetryNW] (31:4) Wint 90-91, p. 27-29.
"Four Speeds of an Overhead Fan." [PoetryNW] (31:4) Wint 90-91, p. 29.
"Path to the River: Bangkok." [PoetryNW] (31:2) Sum 90, p. 5.
"Snow Woman." [PoetryNW] (31:2) Sum 90, p. 6-7.
"The Witness." [PoetryNW] (31:2) Sum 90, p. 3-4.
"The Women Who Drink at the Sea." [PoetryNW] (31:2) Sum 90, p. 7-8.

2332. GOEDICKE, Patricia
"Dandelion." [WillowS] (26) Spr 90, p. 9-10.
"For Wiley, Age Six Months." [GeoR] (44:1/2) Spr-Sum 90, p. 128-129.
"Heart Land." [LaurelR] (24:2) Sum 90, p. 41-43.
"In This Flickering." [TarRP] (29:2) Spr 90, p. 23.
"Lost." [HampSPR] (Anthology 1975-1990) 90, p. 47-48.
"The Other." [KenR] (NS 12:3) Sum 90, p. 29-30.
"The Periscope of the Eye." [KenR] (NS 12:1) Wint 90, p. 125-127.
"The Trail That Turns on Itself." [HampSPR] (Anthology 1975-1990) 90, p. 48-49.
"The Verdict." [KenR] (NS 12:3) Sum 90, p. 31-32.
"What the Skin Knows." [Ploughs] (16:4) Wint 90-91, p. 43-44.
"With All That Beauty, Raving" (For Mary Chica Robinson, 1932-1976).
[HampSPR] (Anthology 1975-1990) 90, p. 49-50.

2333. GOERNER, Leslie
"The Square Root of Tyranny" (honorable mention, Black Bear Poetry Competition).
[BlackBR] (11) Spr-Sum 90, p. 43.

2334. GOETZ, Melody
"In Amsterdam." [Dandel] (17:2) Fall-Wint 90, p. 39.

2335. GOFFETTE, Guy
"All Saints' Day" (tr. by Julie Fay). [Trans] (23) Spr 90, p. 92.
"Famine" (tr. by William Jay Smith). [Trans] (23) Spr 90, p. 93.

GOH, Poh Seng
See SENG, Goh Poh

2336. GOLD, Arthur
"Poems Written During a Period of Sickness" (Selections: 6 poems). [Pequod] (31)
90, p. 18-25.

2337. GOLDBARTH, Albert
"The Children of Elmer." [SouthwR] (75:2) Spr 90, p. 207-208.
"Delft" (An Essay-Poem). [KenR] (NS 12:2) Spr 90, p. 76-96.
"Figural Study." [Journal] (13:2) Fall-Wint 89-90, p. 40-42.
"A Florid Story." [CimR] (90) Ja 90, p. 71-72.
"Forensics." [Journal] (13:2) Fall-Wint 89-90, p. 47-48.
"Gamma." [Journal] (13:2) Fall-Wint 89-90, p. 49-50.
"One Continuous Substance." [Iowa] (20:3) Fall 90, p. 93.
"The Other Eye." [Journal] (13:2) Fall-Wint 89-90, p. 39.
"Parthenogenesis." [HampSPR] (Anthology 1975-1990) 90, p. 114.
"Reality Organization." [MichQR] (29:2) Spr 90, p. 237-239.
"Sentimental." [Poetry] (156:4) Jl 90, p. 190-191.
"Some Laundry." [Journal] (13:2) Fall-Wint 89-90, p. 43.
"Spies (Spies? Spies)." [OntR] (32) Spr-Sum 90, p. 61-64.
"Los Verdados & After & Long After." [Journal] (13:2) Fall-Wint 89-90, p. 44-46.
"Waiting Thaw." [HampSPR] (Anthology 1975-1990) 90, p. 113.
"Window Zen." [TarRP] (30:1) Fall 90, p. 9.

2338. GOLDBECK, Janne
"Persephone." [BellR] (13:1, #27) Spr 90, p. 49.
2339. GOLDBERG, Barbara
"Dawn" (tr. of Moshe Dor). [Confr] (44/45) Fall 90-Wint 91, p. 176.
"Land of the Dead." [Confr] (44/45) Fall 90-Wint 91, p. 191.
"New Alphabet" (tr. of Moshe Dor). [Confr] (44/45) Fall 90-Wint 91, p. 177.
"Proximal Desire." [Salm] (85/86) Wint-Spr 90, p. 145.
"Tectonics." [Confr] (44/45) Fall 90-Wint 91, p. 191.
2340. GOLDBERG, Beckian Fritz
"Beauty Sleep." [IndR] (13:2) Spr 90, p. 56.
"The Ecstasy." [Ploughs] (16:4) Wint 90-91, p. 155-156.
"Glory." [GettyR] (3:2) Spr 90, p. 396-397.
"In the Middle of Things, Begin." [Crazy] (38) Spr 90, p. 9-10.
"The Joplin Nightingale." [PassN] (11:2) Wint 90, p. 3.
"Leda." [MichQR] (29:4) Fall 90, p. 679-680.
"Monsoon." [AmerPoR] (19:6) N-D 90, p. 16.
"Moon in Adolescence." [IndR] (13:2) Spr 90, p. 57.
"Move Me." [GettyR] (3:2) Spr 90, p. 398-399.
"The Possibilities." [Crazy] (38) Spr 90, p. 11-12.
"To a Girl Writing Her Father's Death." [Crazy] (38) Spr 90, p. 7-8.
"The Widow Map." [AmerPoR] (19:6) N-D 90, p. 16.
GOLDBERG, Caryn Mirriam
  See MIRRIAM-GOLDBERG, Caryn
2341. GOLDBERG, Janet
"Animals." [BellR] (13:1, #27) Spr 90, p. 39.
"Mural." [BellR] (13:1, #27) Spr 90, p. 38.
"Now." [Turnstile] (2:1) 90, p. 79.
2342. GOLDBERG, Josh
"Lola Somebody Dreams." [Asylum] (6:2) S 90, p. 2.
2343. GOLDBERGER, Adam
"Three Entertainments." [Asylum] (6:2) S 90, p. 3.
2344. GOLDBLATT, Mark
"No Love." [Hellas] (1:2) Fall 90, p. 215.
2345. GOLDENHAR, Edith
"After the Blues." [YellowS] (33) Spr 90, p. 21.
"Comedy with Gulkis: A Craft Interview." [HawaiiR] (14:1, #28) Wint 89-90, p. 95-96.
"Hearing a Poem the First Time." [HawaiiR] (14:1, #28) Wint 89-90, p. 97-98.
2346. GOLDENSOHN, Barry
"The Bat." [Salm] (88/89) Fall 90-Wint 91, p. 269.
"Mater Dolorosa." [Salm] (88/89) Fall 90-Wint 91, p. 268.
"Notre Dame de Paris" (for Osip Mandelstam). [Salm] (88/89) Fall 90-Wint 91, p. 264.
"Rediscovering Wonder: Santa Cruz Mts, California, 1989." [Salm] (88/89) Fall 90-Wint 91, p. 265-266.
"Rest." [Salm] (88/89) Fall 90-Wint 91, p. 267-268.
2347. GOLDHAFT, Judy
"Water Web." [CityLR] (4) 90, p. 57-59.
2348. GOLDMAN, Judy
"In Dreams I Am Always Smoking." [Shen] (40:4) Wint 90, p. 46.
"Last Night." [BlackWR] (16:2) Spr-Sum 90, p. 105.
"Wanting to Know the End." [SouthernPR] (30:1) Spr 90, p. 41-42.
2349. GOLDMAN, Kathleen Zeisler
"Meditation on Silence." [Northeast] (NS 5:3) Wint 90-91, p. 13.
2350. GOLDSMITH, Ellen
"Windows and Mirrors." [SmPd] (27:3, #80) Fall 90, p. 30.
2351. GOLDSTEIN, Judy
"Of Mere Being in Autumn." [SouthernR] (26:1) Ja 90, p. 218.
2352. GOLDSTEIN, Laurence
"Thrift Shop, Ypsilanti." [IndR] (13:3) Fall 90, p. 24-25.
2353. GOLFFING, Francis
"I Have Met Persons Who" (tr. of Gottfried Benn). [AmerPoR] (19:3) My-Je 90, p. 20.
2354. GOLLUB, David P.
"For Nelson Mandela, a Rejoicing" (from "Bull Horn"). [PoetryUSA] (5:1) Spr 90, p. 16.

2355. GOM, Leona
"Not a Boy." [Descant] (21:1 #68) Spr 90, p. 52.
"Nothing Happened." [Descant] (21:1 #68) Spr 90, p. 51.
2356. GOMES, Aila de Oliveira
"Alheias e Nossas" (Poemas 60/64, tr. of Cecilia Meireles). [Interim] (9:1) Spr-Sum
90, p. 22.
"How rapidly, rapidly, rapidly" (from "Punhalada de Poemas," tr. of Henrique de
Araujo Mesquita). [Interim] (9:1) Spr-Sum 90, p. 24.
"Miravamos a Jovem Lagartixa" (from "Metal Rosicler," tr. of Cecilia Meireles).
[Interim] (9:1) Spr-Sum 90, p. 23.
"Por Mais Que Te Celebre" (from "Mar Absoluto, 2o Motivo da Rosa," tr. of Cecilia
Meireles). [Interim] (9:1) Spr-Sum 90, p. 21.
2357. GOMEZ GIL, Alfredo
"Se Me Acaba España." [Americas] (18:3/4) Fall-Wint 90, p. 122-125.
2358. GOMEZ ROSA, Alexis
"Melodia en lo Mio." [LindLM] (9:3) Jl-S 90, p. 10.
"La Tragedia de No Llamarse Rosa Luxemburgo." [LindLM] (9:3) Jl-S 90, p. 10.
"Urbano Corazon." [LindLM] (9:3) Jl-S 90, p. 10.
2359. GÖMÖRI, György
"A Footnote on Small Nations" (tr. by Nicholas Kolumban). [PoetryE] (29) Spr 90,
p. 72.
"Yes - No" (tr. by Nicholas Kolumban). [WebR] (14:2) Spr 90, p. 105.
2360. GOMPERT, Chris
"Opening Gates." [PoetC] (22:1) Fall 90, p. 22.
"Triage" (for Skip). [PoetC] (21:2) Wint 90, p. 7-8.
2361. GONET, Jill
"Bowl of Dreams." [Ploughs] (16:4) Wint 90-91, p. 73-74.
"Dear Sinking Ship." [PoetryNW] (31:2) Sum 90, p. 16.
"Flagellation." [RiverS] (32) [90?], p. 8.
"Fortuna." [RiverS] (32) [90?], p. 5.
"A Furniture Maker." [BlackWR] (16:2) Spr-Sum 90, p. 100.
"The House of I, the House of You." [AntR] (48:2) Spr 90, p. 224-225.
"Interstate." [Calyx] (12:3) Sum 90, p. 35.
"Jokes and Their Relation to Art History." [Ploughs] (16:4) Wint 90-91, p. 75.
"Miss Sunbeam." [RiverS] (32) [90?], p. 6-7.
GONG, Gu
See GU, Gong
2362. GONG, Judyth
"L.A." [PoetryUSA] (5:2) Sum 90, p. 3.
2363. GONZALES, Jane
"Goin Home" (author's name on errata sheet). [Plain] (11:1) Fall 90, p. 18.
2364. GONZALEZ, Angel
"December" (tr. by Steven Ford Brown). [ConnPR] (9:1) 90, p. 7-8.
"Rain Upon the Snow in the Spring" (tr. by Steven Ford Brown). [ConnPR] (9:1)
90, p. 13.
"Song to Sing a Song" (tr. by Steven Ford Brown). [ConnPR] (9:1) 90, p. 10.
"That's Enough for Me" (tr. by Steven Ford Brown). [ConnPR] (9:1) 90, p. 11-12.
"They Are the Seagulls, My Love" (tr. by Steven Ford Brown). [ConnPR] (9:1) 90,
p. 9.
GONZALEZ, David Lago
See LAGO GONZALEZ, David
2365. GONZALEZ, Ray
"For the Women I Slept with Years Ago." [YellowS] (34) Sum 90, p. 37.
"Here." [YellowS] (33) Spr 90, p. 9.
"The Horse." [CharR] (16:1) Spr 90, p. 47.
"The Idea of Rexroth, the Idea of Looking Up." [CharR] (16:1) Spr 90, p. 46-47.
"The Juice." [YellowS] (34) Sum 90, p. 36.
"Making Love to a New Woman." [YellowS] (34) Sum 90, p. 37.
"Moving." [YellowS] (34) Sum 90, p. 36.
"On the 8th Anniversary of James Wright's Death, March 25th, Death by Cancer of
the Tongue." [BellR] (13:1, #27) Spr 90, p. 42.
2366. GONZALEZ-CRUZ, Luis
"Botticelli." [LindLM] (9:4) O-D 90, p. 3.
2367. GOOBIE, Beth
"The First Gods." [Grain] (18:4) Wint 90, p. 10-12.
"Time Crawls into Our Pores." [PottPort] (11) 89, p. 24.

"When Caroline Visits Her Sister Susan." [Dandel] (17:1) Spr-Sum 90, p. 29-30.
2368. GOOD, Ruth
    "Terror." [KanQ] (22:3) Sum 90, p. 114.
2369. GOODENOUGH, J. B.
    "Breakfast." [Paint] (17:33/34) Spr-Aut 90, p. 10.
    "Change of Clothes." [SmPd] (27:2, #79) Spr 90, p. 15.
    "Felling." [Paint] (17:33/34) Spr-Aut 90, p. 9.
    "Gathering Constellations." [Poetry] (157:2) N 90, p. 76.
    "Nightmare." [Poetry] (157:2) N 90, p. 77.
    "Pestilence." [FourQ] (4:1) Spr 90, p. 46.
    "Succubus." [SoCoast] (8) Spr 90, p. 18.
    "What Happened Was." [MidwQ] (31:3) Spr 90, p. 355.
    "White-Blind." [SmPd] (27:3, #80) Fall 90, p. 17.
    "The Whole Point of Apples." [Blueline] (11:1/2) 90, p. 15.
2370. GOODMAN, Dianne
    "In Consideration of Your Heart." [NegC] (10:1) 90, p. 55.
2371. GOODMAN, Melinda
    "February Ice Years." [Cond] (17) 90, p. 68-69.
2372. GOODMAN, Michael
    "An Accidental Is a Migrant." [Nat] (250:15) 16 Ap 90, p. 538.
2373. GOODMAN, Miriam
    "The Bourgeois Life." [Pig] (16) 90, p. 94-95.
    "The P.R. Person's Story: Debbie and I." [Pig] (16) 90, p. 97.
    "Warm in Winter." [DustyD] (1:2) O 90, p. 17.
2374. GOODMAN, Ryah Tumarkin
    "Sound." [Amelia] (6:2, #17) 90, p. 66.
2375. GOODREAU, William
    "Homage to Cocteau" (a variation on [La Voix Humain ." [Amelia] (6:2, #17) 90, p. 134-136.
2376. GOODRICH, Judith N.
    "Wood Nymph." [BellArk] (6:3) My-Je 90, p. 10.
2377. GOODRICH, Patricia
    "Sidelights." [JINJPo] (12:2) Aut 90, p. 8.
    "To a Friend." [Footwork] 90, p. 71.
2378. GOODWIN, Douglas
    "The Bridge." [Bogg] (62) 90, p. 21.
2379. GORBANEVSKAYA, Natalya
    "As it was before" (tr. by Daniel Weissbort). [Nimrod] (33:2) Spr-Sum 90, p. 108.
    "Do not call me this or anything" (tr. by Daniel Weissbort). [Nimrod] (33:2) Spr-Sum 90, p. 107.
    "I should like to hope that there" (In memory of E.B., tr. by Daniel Weissbort). [PoetryE] (30) Fall 90, p. 79.
    "Is this my voice, my voice -- or is it" (tr. by Daniel Weissbort). [Nimrod] (33:2) Spr-Sum 90, p. 107.
    "It's time to think" (tr. by Daniel Weissbort). [PoetryE] (30) Fall 90, p. 80.
    "On Reading Ray Bradbury's *Fahrenheit 451*" (tr. by Daniel Weissbort). [PoetryE] (30) Fall 90, p. 81-82.
    "When kings fall silent" (tr. by Daniel Weissbort). [Nimrod] (33:2) Spr-Sum 90, p. 109.
    "With our breath we'll warm the shed's cold walls" (tr. by Daniel Weissbort). [Nimrod] (33:2) Spr-Sum 90, p. 109.
2380. GORCZYNSKI, Renata
    "Anton Bruckner" (tr. of Adam Zagajewski, w. Benjamin Ivry). [NewYorker] (66:5) 19 Mr 90, p. 46.
    "At Midnight" (tr. of Adam Zagajewski, w. Benjamin Ivry). [Antaeus] (64/65) Spr-Aut 90, p. 143.
    "Daybreak" (tr. of Adam Zagajewski, w. Benjamin Ivry). [PartR] (57:1) Wint 90, p. 97.
    "Lava" (tr. of Adam Zagajewski, w. Benjamin Ivry). [PartR] (57:1) Wint 90, p. 98.
    "Presence" (tr. of Adam Zagajewski, w. Benjamin Ivry). [Antaeus] (64/65) Spr-Aut 90, p. 145.
    "R. Says" (tr. of Adam Zagajewski, w. Benjamin Ivry). [Antaeus] (64/65) Spr-Aut 90, p. 144.
    "Vacation" (tr. of Adam Zagajewski, w. Benjamin Ivry). [DenQ] (25:1) Sum 90, p. 54.

GORDER, Julia Van
    See Van GORDER, Julia
2381. GORDON, G. T.
    "Her Word." [Pearl] (12) Fall-Wint 90, p. 24.
    "Marilyn." [Pearl] (12) Fall-Wint 90, p. 29.
    "She" (after Marilyn). [Pearl] (12) Fall-Wint 90, p. 27.
2382. GORDON, Kevin
    "Bring Them All Back." [SouthernPR] (30:2) Fall 90, p. 32.
2383. GORDON, Kirpal
    "Tree, Mend Us." [HeavenB] (8) Wint 90-91, p. 13-14.
GOREK, Bert Papenfuss
    See PAPENFUSS-GOREK, Bert
2384. GORHAM, Sarah
    "The Empress's Fan." [WilliamMR] (28) 90, p. 54.
    "Imperial Gown." [WilliamMR] (28) 90, p. 53.
    "Last Request." [WilliamMR] (28) 90, p. 55.
2385. GORJUP, Branko
    "Return to the Tree of Time" (tr. of Vesna Parun). [CityLR] (4) 90, p. 196.
    "Virginity" (tr. of Vesna Parun). [CityLR] (4) 90, p. 197.
2386. GORMAN, John
    "Perry Como Sings." [Farm] (7:1) Spr 90, p. 20-21.
    "Petit Dérangement." [NewDeltaR] (7:1) 90, p. 71.
2387. GORMAN, LeRoy
    "Devotional #1." [PoetryC] (11:2) Sum 90, p. 15.
    "Lost Art." [Bogg] (62) 90, p. 25.
2388. GOROSTIZA, José
    "Adam" (tr. by Robert Klein Engler). [InterPR] (16:2) Fall 90, p. 75.
    "Adan." [InterPR] (16:2) Fall 90, p. 74.
    "Bogotá Declaration" (tr. by Robert Klein Engler). [InterPR] (16:2) Fall 90, p. 87,
        89.
    "Declaración de Bogotá." [InterPR] (16:2) Fall 90, p. 86, 88.
    "Epilogue" (tr. by Robert Klein Engler). [InterPR] (16:2) Fall 90, p. 89.
    "Epodo." [InterPR] (16:2) Fall 90, p. 88.
    "Espejo No." [InterPR] (16:2) Fall 90, p. 74, 76.
    "Lección de Ojos." [InterPR] (16:2) Fall 90, p. 75-80.
    "Lessons Taught by the Eyes" (tr. by Robert Klein Engler). [InterPR] (16:2) Fall 90,
        p. 77-81.
    "Mirror No!" (tr. by Robert Klein Engler). [InterPR] (16:2) Fall 90, p. 75, 77.
    "Prelude" (tr. by Robert Klein Engler). [InterPR] (16:2) Fall 90, p. 71-75.
    "Preludio." [InterPR] (16:2) Fall 90, p. 70-74.
    "Presence and Fugue" (tr. by Robert Klein Engler). [InterPR] (16:2) Fall 90, p. 83,
        85.
    "Presencia y Fuga." [InterPR] (16:2) Fall 90, p. 82, 84.
2389. GORRELL, Nancy
    "Blueberry Pie." [EngJ] (79:8) D 90, p. 88.
2390. GORST, Norma
    "The Color of Grief." [ChamLR] (3:2, #6) Spr 90, p. 77-78.
    "Elemental, This Roundness." [Chelsea] (49) 90, p. 139.
    "Lost Imagoes." [ChamLR] (3:2, #6) Spr 90, p. 75-76.
    "Snapshot of a German Pentecost 1917." [ChamLR] (3:2, #6) Spr 90, p. 73-74.
2391. GORYACHKO, Andy
    "We will speak when we'll feel" (Poem written in English by high school students
        from the Ukraine, collected by Maureen Hurley). [PoetryUSA] (5:1) Spr 90,
        p. 18.
2392. GOTERA, Vince
    "First Hand-Plant: Skating the Petaluma Ramp" (for Mary). [IndR] (13:2) Spr 90, p.
        17-18.
2393. GOTO, T. M.
    "God forgives volcanic eruptions" (For Nell). [HawaiiR] (14:1, #28) Wint 89-90, p.
        68.
    "Revolution" (for Dr. Cora). [HawaiiR] (15:1, #31) Wint 90, p. 52.
    "This Time." [ChamLR] (4:1, #7) Fall 90, p. 111-112.
2394. GOTT, George
    "Barabello." [Wind] (20:66) 90, p. 14.
    "Manna." [Wind] (20:66) 90, p. 14.

2395. GOTTESMAN, Carl A.
    "Bearing the Body Back to Philadelphia." [Bogg] (63) 90, p. 60-61.
    "Dilemmas of Fatherhood." [Wind] (20:67) 90, p. 21-23.
    "Ice." [BlueBldgs] (12) 90, p. 7.
    "Love Poem." [RagMag] (8:2) 90, p. 48.
    "The Mud Boat." [BlackWR] (16:2) Spr-Sum 90, p. 96-99.
    "The Poppy." [PoetL] (85:2) Sum 90, p. 21-23.
    "To Build On." [Vis] (33) 90, p. 41-42.
2396. GOULD, Janice
    "Coyotismo." [EvergreenC] (5:2) Wint 90, p. 15.
    "Questions of Healing." [EvergreenC] (5:2) Wint 90, p. 17.
2397. GOULD, M. Corbin
    "Weather Report" (For Novotny). [Cond] (17) 90, p. 112.
2398. GOULD, Martha
    "13 Ways of Looking at an Unidentified Flying Woman." [Event] (19:1) Spr 90, p.
        42-43.
    "Gorgon." [Grain] (18:3) Fall 90, p. 75.
    "My Story." [Grain] (18:3) Fall 90, p. 74.
2399. GOULD, Roberta
    "Guatemala." [SlipS] (10) 90, p. 64.
2400. GOUMAS, Yannis
    "The Farm Hand." [MalR] (90) Spr 90, p. 73.
2401. GOVE, Jim
    "1990's Fantasy, or, Song for One's Self." [ChironR] (9:1) Spr 90, p. 13.
    "Summer on the Boat." [ChironR] (9:3) Aut 90, p. 7.
    "Under the Sun." [ChironR] (9:3) Aut 90, p. 7.
    "White Pigeons." [ChironR] (9:3) Aut 90, p. 7.
2402. GOYTISOLO, José Agustín
    "At Night Alone" (tr. by Susan Schreibman). [Confr] (42/43) Spr-Sum 90, p. 48.
    "Es Como el Eco" (from "Final de un Adiós"). [PaintedB] (40/41) 90, p. 26.
    "If It's All Going to Begin Again" (tr. by Susan Schreibman). [Confr] (42/43)
        Spr-Sum 90, p. 49.
    "It's Like an Echo" (tr. by Susan Schreibman). [PaintedB] (40/41) 90, p. 26.
2403. GRACE, Susan Andrews
    "Mary Elizabeth." [Grain] (18:3) Fall 90, p. 23-24.
    "Red in Houses" (for Mary Grace). [Grain] (18:3) Fall 90, p. 24.
2404. GRAFTON, Grace
    "For the Farm." [BellArk] (6:5) S-O 90, p. 1.
    "Your Sisters' Proximity." [BellR] (13:1, #27) Spr 90, p. 5.
2405. GRAHAM, David
    "Bad Dogs" (For Art Stringer). [Poetry] (156:4) Jl 90, p. 193.
    "Notes on the Creation." [Talisman] (5) Fall 90, p. 110-111.
    "Nothing." [AmerS] (59:2) Spr 90, p. 291.
    "Self-Portrait with Wisecracks." [AmerS] (59:2) Spr 90, p. 290-291.
    "Word Hoard" (for Joe Donahue). [PoetryNW] (31:1) Spr 90, p. 17-18.
2406. GRAHAM, Jorie
    "Detail from the Creation of Man." [Antaeus] (64/65) Spr-Aut 90, p. 40-43.
    "History: But in the myth, at the beginning of our world." [AntR] (48:3) Sum 90, p.
        340-341.
    "History: So that I had to look up just now to see them." [AntR] (48:3) Sum 90, p.
        349-352.
    "Immobilism." [Thrpny] (41) Spr 90, p. 22.
    "Look Up" (After the "Canticles" of Saint Francis). [AntR] (48:3) Sum 90, p.
        345-348.
    "What Is Called Thinking: After Trakl." [AntR] (48:3) Sum 90, p. 342-344.
    "Who Watches from the Dark Porch." [ParisR] (32:117) Wint 90, p. 170-181.
2407. GRAHAM, Mally
    "Debbie Louise in Odessa TX." [BelPoR] (40:3) Spr 90, p. 14-15.
    "Farm Cornerstone." [BelPoR] (40:3) Spr 90, p. 15.
    "Miss America." [BelPoR] (40:3) Spr 90, p. 15.
    "What She Could Do." [BelPoR] (40:3) Spr 90, p. 14.
2408. GRAHAM, Neile
    "Why I Would Think I Am Leaving." [PoetL] (85:3) Fall 90, p. 5.
2409. GRAHAM, Philip
    "The Distance." [HampSPR] (Anthology 1975-1990) 90, p. 168-169.

GRAHAM, Taylor
   See TAYLOR-GRAHAM
2410. GRAHAM, Vicki
   "Classic." [Agni] (29/30) 90, p. 93.
   "Reflex." [Agni] (29/30) 90, p. 95.
   "Triptych." [Agni] (29/30) 90, p. 94.
2411. GRANATA, May
   "In the Asian Section of the Cleveland Art Museum." [HayF] (7) Fall-Wint 90, p. 54.
2412. GRANATO, Carol
   "The Artist's Lady." [MidwQ] (31:3) Spr 90, p. 356.
2413. GRANET, Roger
   "The Dutchess County Fair." [NegC] (10:2/3) 90, p. 117.
2414. GRANGER, Jamie
   "Swimming Lesson." [ApalQ] (33/34) 90, p. 74.
2415. GRANT, Grell V.
   "Island." [CanLit] (127) Wint 90, p. 92.
   "A Poem for Tourists." [Quarry] (39:4) Fall 1990, p. 23-24.
2416. GRANT, Paul
   (Anonymous poem). [FreeL] (4) 90.
   "Drinking to Forget." [LaurelR] (24:2) Sum 90, p. 19.
   "Keys" (Photo of a Family Reunion, for JR). [CapeR] (25:2) Fall 90, p. 16.
   "Photo of a Hobo Camp, 1931." [CumbPR] (9:2) Spr 90, p. 37.
2417. GRANT-GIBSON, Elisabeth
   "Visiting the Relatives." [MidwQ] (31:4) Sum 90, p. 471.
2418. GRAVE, Elsa
   "Barn." [Spirit] (10:1) 89, p. 28.
   "Children" (tr. by Lennart Bruce and Sonja Bruce). [Spirit] (10:1) 89, p. 29.
   "Damned" (tr. by Lennart Bruce and Sonja Bruce). [Spirit] (10:1) 89, p. 25.
   "Förbannad." [Spirit] (10:1) 89, p. 24.
   "Lullaby for My Unborn Child" (tr. by Lennart Bruce and Sonja Bruce). [Spirit] (10:1) 89, p. 27.
   "Obemannade Telefonlurar." [Spirit] (10:1) 89, p. 22.
   "Poesi Är Farligt." [Spirit] (10:1) 89, p. 16-20.
   "Poetry Is Dangerous" (tr. by Lennart Bruce and Sonja Bruce). [Spirit] (10:1) 89, p. 17-21.
   "Unmanned Telephone Receivers" (tr. by Lennart Bruce and Sonja Bruce). [Spirit] (10:1) 89, p. 23.
   "Vaggvisa för Mitt Ofödda Barn." [Spirit] (10:1) 89, p. 26.
2419. GRAVENITES, Diane
   "Shadow Sister." [SinW] (41) Sum-Fall 90, p. 67-70.
2420. GRAVES, Bob
   "Definition." [EmeraldCR] (1990) c89, p. 27-28.
2421. GRAVES, Michael
   "Meditations: 4." [HolCrit] (27:1) F 90, p. 17.
2422. GRAVES, Paul
   "Domitian, the last cruel and savage emperor" (tr. of Aleksandr Kushner, w. Carol Ueland). [Nimrod] (33:2) Spr-Sum 90, p. 94.
   "Folded Wings" (tr. of Aleksandr Kushner, w. Carol Ueland). [Nimrod] (33:2) Spr-Sum 90, p. 90-91.
   "O fame, you have passed us by like the rain, vanished" (tr. of Aleksandr Kushner, w. Carol Ueland). [Nimrod] (33:2) Spr-Sum 90, p. 93.
   "Our partings are more difficult, and long" (tr. of Aleksandr Kushner, w. Carol Ueland). [Nimrod] (33:2) Spr-Sum 90, p. 92.
   "This country, huge, wintry and blue" (tr. of Aleksandr Kushner, w. Carol Ueland). [Nimrod] (33:2) Spr-Sum 90, p. 91.
   "Urban Irony" (tr. of Vladimir Kostrov, w. Carol Ueland). [Nimrod] (33:2) Spr-Sum 90, p. 3.
2423. GRAVES, Steven
   "Scenes from a Suite of Rooms." [WestHR] (44:3) Aut 90, p. 320-322.
   "The Watcher." [QW] (31) Fall 90, p. 88.
2424. GRAVLEY, Ernestine
   "Photograph of You in Late Evening." [NegC] (10:1) 90, p. 56.
2425. GRAY, Allan
   "Commutation." [TriQ] (80) Wint 90-91, p. 42.
   "Dinner in the Garden District." [TriQ] (80) Wint 90-91, p. 44.

"I Do Belive Her." [TriQ] (80) Wint 90-91, p. 40.
"Ladder." [TriQ] (80) Wint 90-91, p. 43.
"The Mimic." [TriQ] (80) Wint 90-91, p. 41.
"Nocturne." [TriQ] (80) Wint 90-91, p. 45.
2426. GRAY, Darrell
"Against the Stars." [NorthStoneR] (9) 90, p. 156-157.
"An Indian Girl from Iowa." [NorthStoneR] (9) 90, p. 160.
"Little Disgestion Ode" [sic: Digestion?]. [NorthStoneR] (9) 90, p. 158.
"Oral Extracourse." [NorthStoneR] (9) 90, p. 160.
"Vita Nuova." [NorthStoneR] (9) 90, p. 159.
"Writing the Coherent Poem." [NorthStoneR] (9) 90, p. 155.
2427. GRAY, Diana Lenore
"Cheetah Is Gone." [BellArk] (6:4) Jl-Ag 90, p. 12.
2428. GRAY, Janet
"100 Flowers" (Selections: XI, XXXIX, XLI). [PaperAir] (4:3) 90, p. 83-85.
"A Hundred Flowers" (Selections: LI-XIV, LVIII, LX). [Avec] (3:1) 90, p. 109-112.
2429. GRAY, Jeffrey
"Dolphins at the Aquarium." [NewL] (57:1) Fall 90, p. 103.
"Flying West Into Light." [MidAR] (10:1) 90, p. 132-134.
"Three Years Ago." [NewL] (57:1) Fall 90, p. 102.
2430. GRAY, Pamela
"Late Irises: A Goodbye Sonnet" (for Barbara Rosenblum). [SinW] (40) Spr 90, p. 71.
2431. GRAY, Patrick Worth
"Bohemians, Bohemians." [Bomb] (33) Fall 90, p. 85.
"Canvas Eagles." [ChamLR] (4:1, #7) Fall 90, p. 11.
"Cease Fire." [ChamLR] (4:1, #7) Fall 90, p. 9.
"Dahlias." [BlackWR] (16:2) Spr-Sum 90, p. 27.
"Down to the Park." [OxfordM] (6:1) Spr-Sum 90, p. 86.
"I Was Five and She Was Eleven." [Bomb] (33) Fall 90, p. 85.
"Laager." [ChamLR] (4:1, #7) Fall 90, p. 10.
"'Uncle Billy' Goodwin." [SouthernPR] (30:1) Spr 90, p. 18-19.
"Wind." [PoetL] (85:1) Spr 90, p. 31-34.
2432. GRAY, Susan
"Revolution." [HangL] (57) 90, p. 78.
2433. GRAZIDE, Richard
"The Eyebrows of Penmanship." [Notus] (5:1) Spr 90, p. 113.
"For an Encore We Trace the Spark." [Notus] (5:1) Spr 90, p. 114.
"A Perfect Example of Luck Is Choked with No One Thing." [Notus] (5:1) Spr 90, p. 115-116.
"Rubbing Along the Chimes with 3 Brass Bells." [YellowS] (34) Sum 90, p. 38.
"Until v. Universal." [Notus] (5:1) Spr 90, p. 112.
2434. GREEAR, Mildred
"Emma's Crochet." [ChatR] (11:1) Fall 90, p. 36.
2435. GREEN, D. Rubin
"The 1929 Tuscaloosa Shout" (for my father). [Footwork] 90, p. 70.
"Names and Sorrows." [ChangingM] (21) Wint-Spr 90, p. 48.
"Names and Sorrows." [Footwork] 90, p. 77.
"Poems for Central America." [Footwork] 90, p. 70-71.
2436. GREEN, Joseph
"After Scattering My Mother's Ashes." [BellR] (13:2, #28) Fall 90, p. 15.
"Blue Cowboy Sky Behind Him" (for David H.). [BellR] (13:2, #28) Fall 90, p. 17.
"The Dream of Being Just Like Everyone Else." [BellR] (13:2, #28) Fall 90, p. 16.
"I Look Like Ogden Nash." [DustyD] (1:2) O 90, p. 8.
"In the Dream of My Father Running." [DogRR] (9:1, #17) Spr 90, p. 13.
"Marilyn's Mouth." [Pearl] (12) Fall-Wint 90, p. 43.
"Surviving Like Dummies." [WillowS] (26) Spr 90, p. 37-38.
2437. GREEN, Karen
"Sonnet to My Father: After His Stroke." [FourQ] (4:1) Spr 90, p. 45.
GREEN, Linda Stankard
See STANKARD-GREEN, Linda
2438. GREEN, Maisha
"Heart Ache." [PoetryUSA] ([5:4?]) Wint 90, p. 18.
"Never Listening." [PoetryUSA] ([5:4?]) Wint 90, p. 13.

2439. GREEN, Malcolm
"Poempoems" (12 poems, tr. of Oskar Pastior). [ParisR] (32:115) Sum 90, p. 46-50.
2440. GREEN, Melissa
"The Consolation of Boethius." [ParisR] (32:114) Spr 90, p. 86-88.
2441. GREEN, Paul
"Black Mutes." [Screens] (2) 90, p. 132.
"Iron, or Ion." [Screens] (2) 90, p. 132.
2442. GREEN, Samuel
"On Hearing Our Plans for Homesteading My Grandmother Said, 'It Will Ruin Your Hands'." [Zyzzyva] (6:1 #21) Spr 90, p. 44-45.
2443. GREEN, W. H.
"Ghost Town." [BellR] (13:1, #27) Spr 90, p. 46-47.
2444. GREENBAUM, Jessica R.
"Small Light in Big Dark House." [GettyR] (3:3) Sum 90, p. 590-591.
2445. GREENBERG, Alvin
"Almost Always." [ColR] (NS 17:1) Spr-Sum 90, p. 29.
"Going to Oklahoma." [ColR] (NS 17:1) Spr-Sum 90, p. 30.
"Holy Wars (1944)" (for Michael S. Harper). [Chelsea] (49) 90, p. 73-75.
"Midsummer Day." [BelPoR] (40:3) Spr 90, p. 5.
"Plate Tectonics." [GeoR] (44:3) Fall 90, p. 409.
2446. GREENBERG, Barbara L.
"The Nine Decades." [Salm] (85/86) Wint-Spr 90, p. 148.
2447. GREENBLATT, Ray
"At Night on the Ranch." [CoalC] (2) D 90, p. 7.
"Creeks." [CoalC] (1) Ag 90, p. 31.
"Nebraska." [CoalC] (2) D 90, p. 7.
2448. GREENE, Earl
"Winces." [HangL] (56) 90, p. 15.
"The Young Girl: Miss." [HangL] (56) 90, p. 15.
2449. GREENE, Jeffrey
"Between Heaven and Hell." [LitR] (33:3) Spr 90, p. 346-347.
2450. GREENE, Mary
"Married Under Water." [BrooklynR] (7) 90, p. 19.
2451. GREENFIELD, Robert L.
"Andy Warhol." [KanQ] (22:3) Sum 90, p. 116.
"Epistemology." [KanQ] (22:1/2) Wint-Spr 90, p. 139.
2452. GREENHUT, Deborah S.
"Last Seder: the Four Cups." [JINJPo] (12:2) Aut 90, p. 10-11.
2453. GREENLAW, Lavinia
"Anchorage." [Stand] (31:2) Spr 90, p. 62-63.
"Dried Flowers, the Chance of Fire." [Stand] (31:4) Aut 90, p. 22-23.
"North." [Stand] (31:2) Spr 90, p. 63.
2454. GREENWALD, Roger
"Anniversary" (tr. of Flavia Cosma, w. the author). [Writ] (21) 89 c1990, p. 9.
"As If in Child's Play" (tr. of Flavia Cosma). [PoetryE] (29) Spr 90, p. 135.
"Autumn Jumps" (tr. of Flavia Cosma, w. the author). [Writ] (21) 89 c1990, p. 8.
"The Beginning" (tr. of Pia Tafdrup). [Writ] (21) 89 c1990, p. 29.
"Between Forests" (tr. of Paal-Helge Haugen). [Writ] (21) 89 c1990, p. 68-69.
"Darkly Glinting" (tr. of Pia Tafdrup). [Writ] (21) 89 c1990, p. 33.
"Eagles Are Whirling" (tr. of Flavia Cosma, w. the author). [Writ] (21) 89 c1990, p. 13.
"Echo" (tr. of Pia Tafdrup). [Writ] (21) 89 c1990, p. 25-26.
"Evening Raga." [Writ] (21) 89 c1990, p. 74-77.
"The Half-life of Sorrow." [Writ] (21) 89 c1990, p. 70.
"(Lake Ohrid, Late Summer)" (tr. of Paal-Helge Haugen). [Writ] (21) 89 c1990, p. 67.
"(Lean In)" (Shostakovich, String Quartet No. 8, tr. of Paal-Helge Haugen). [Writ] (21) 89 c1990, p. 66.
"(MD)" (tr. of Paal-Helge Haugen). [Writ] (21) 89 c1990, p. 65.
"Minneapolis, for Joel O." [Writ] (21) 89 c1990, p. 73.
"New Remembered Places I" (tr. of Pia Tafdrup). [Writ] (21) 89 c1990, p. 31.
"New Remembered Places II" (tr. of Pia Tafdrup). [Writ] (21) 89 c1990, p. 32.
"New Year's Eve" (tr. of Flavia Cosma, w. the author). [Writ] (21) 89 c1990, p. 11.
"No Bird" (tr. of Flavia Cosma). [PoetryE] (29) Spr 90, p. 137.
"Now I Know" (tr. of Flavia Cosma). [PoetryE] (29) Spr 90, p. 136.

"The Other Window" (tr. of Flavia Cosma, w. the author). [Writ] (21) 89 c1990, p. 12.
"Passerby." [Writ] (21) 89 c1990, p. 72.
"Pause-beat" (tr. of Pia Tafdrup). [Writ] (21) 89 c1990, p. 28.
"Questions" (tr. of Flavia Cosma). [PoetryE] (29) Spr 90, p. 134.
"Ready to Set Out" (tr. of Flavia Cosma, w. the author). [Writ] (21) 89 c1990, p. 7.
"Reconciliation" (tr. of Flavia Cosma). [PoetryE] (29) Spr 90, p. 138.
"Setting Fire" (tr. of Pia Tafdrup). [Writ] (21) 89 c1990, p. 23.
"Sirocco Night" (tr. of Pia Tafdrup). [Writ] (21) 89 c1990, p. 27.
"The Star-Diver" (tr. of Gunnar Harding). [Writ] (21) 89 c1990, p. 86-90.
"A Stranger Takes Photos on a Boat." [Writ] (21) 89 c1990, p. 71.
"Surveyor" (tr. of Pia Tafdrup). [Writ] (21) 89 c1990, p. 24.
"Switching Shadows" (tr. of Flavia Cosma, w. the author). [Writ] (21) 89 c1990, p. 10.
"Waking Sleep" (tr. of Pia Tafdrup). [Writ] (21) 89 c1990, p. 30.
"You, Who Have Left" (tr. of Flavia Cosma). [PoetryE] (29) Spr 90, p. 139.
2455. GREENWAY, William
"I Dreamed About You Last Night." [ContextS] (1:1) 89, p. 48.
"Ohio." [Journal] (13:2) Fall-Wint 89-90, p. 28.
"Rust Belt." [Pig] (16) 90, p. 52.
"Sleep." [ContextS] (1:1) 89, p. 49.
2456. GREENWOOD, G. P.
"Some Body." [AntigR] (80) Wint 90, p. 43-44.
"Suppose." [AntigR] (80) Wint 90, p. 42.
2457. GREGER, Debora
"The Afterlife." [NewYorker] (66:4) 12 Mr 90, p. 36-37.
"The Boy Juliet." [Poetry] (156:2) My 90, p. 84-85.
"Cleopatra in the Afterworld." [Poetry] (156:2) My 90, p. 86-87.
"A Field of Rape." [GeoR] (44:1/2) Spr-Sum 90, p. 119-120.
"Like a Woman." [Nat] (250:11) 19 Mr 90, p. 392.
"Long Island Night." [Nat] (251:12) 15 O 90, p. 431.
"Notre Dame des Tourists." [Nat] (251:8) 17 S 90, p. 282.
"The Report of the Corrosion Committee." [DenQ] (25:2) Fall 90, p. 22-23.
"Vermeer." [GettyR] (3:1) Wint 90, p. 201-202.
2458. GREGERMAN, Debra
"By Word of Mouth." [AmerPoR] (19:2) Mr-Ap 90, p. 15.
"Holograph." [AmerPoR] (19:2) Mr-Ap 90, p. 15.
"Nomenclature." [AmerPoR] (19:2) Mr-Ap 90, p. 15.
2459. GREGERSON, Linda
"An Arbor." [Poetry] (157:3) D 90, p. 129-131.
"Good News." [Poetry] (157:3) D 90, p. 132-134.
"Safe" (K.M.S. 1948-1986). [Atlantic] (265:3) Mr 90, p. 84-85.
2460. GREGG, Linda
"Thirteen Shapes of Desire" (Poetry Chapbook: 13 poems). [BlackWR] (17:1) Fall-Wint 90, p. 57-71.
2461. GREGORY, M.
"White Limousine." [CrabCR] (6:3) Spr 90, p. 26.
2462. GREGORY, Robert
"That Local Knowledge." [BlackWR] (16:2) Spr-Sum 90, p. 94.
"Waiting for the Bus with the Ghost on It, in Back." [Gargoyle] (37/38) 90, p. 64.
2463. GREGSON, Ian
"Desirable Residence." [Pearl] (10) Spr 90, p. 55.
"The Wound." [Stand] (31:3) Sum 90, p. 72.
2464. GRENKEVICH, David
"Freak." [NegC] (10:2/3) 90, p. 47.
2465. GRENNAN, Eamon
"Cows." [NewYorker] (66:8) 9 Ap 90, p. 42.
"Driving North, Early Spring." [NewEngR] (13:1) Fall 90, p. 56-57.
"Driving Through Fog." [NewEngR] (13:1) Fall 90, p. 58-59.
"Liberal Learning." [Agni] (29/30) 90, p. 121-124.
"Not Standing Still." [Nat] (250:21) 28 My 90, p. 754.
"Out There." [Agni] (29/30) 90, p. 119-120.
"Passing Zone." [Quarry] (39:1) Wint 90, p. 79.
"Resident Aliens." [Nat] (250:21) 28 My 90, p. 754.
"Rights" (for the Russian poets). [Antaeus] (64/65) Spr-Aut 90, p. 44-45.
"Small Mercies." [NewYorker] (66:41) 26 N 90, p. 52.

"Station." [NewEngR] (13:1) Fall 90, p. 57-58.
"Two Photographs." [NewEngR] (13:1) Fall 90, p. 59-60.
"Walk, Night Falling, Memory of My Father." [NewYorker] (66:21) 9 Jl 90, p. 36.
"Woman Holding a Balance" (-- Vermeer). [OntR] (32) Spr-Sum 90, p. 22-23.
"Yellowthroat in October." [OntR] (32) Spr-Sum 90, p. 20-21.

2466. GREY, John
"Easily Recognized." [SlipS] (10) 90, p. 52.
"Free Verse." [FreeL] (6) Aut 90, p. 29.
"House Inside This One." [RagMag] (7:2) Spr 90, p. 15.
"Lady Chatterly's Younger Lover." [SoCoast] (9) Fall 90, p. 22.
"New Landscape." [Parting] (3:2) Wint 90-91, p. 4.
"Territory." [ChironR] (9:3) Aut 90, p. 21.
"There Is a Cheapness to the Statues." [ContextS] (1:1) 89, p. 53.
"Travelers Three." [FreeL] (6) Aut 90, p. 28.
"What the War Was About." [Wind] (20:66) 90, p. 16.
"The Woman Unchanged." [GreenMR] (NS 3:2) Fall-Wint 89-90, p. 95.

2467. GREY, Robert
"Albert." [PoetC] (21:3) Spr 90, p. 29.
"Saving the Dead." [BlackWR] (16:2) Spr-Sum 90, p. 59-60.
"Subdivision." [TarRP] (29:2) Spr 90, p. 22.

2468. GRIECO, Joseph
"Advice to the Lovelorn." [CapeR] (25:1) Spr 90, p. 50.

2469. GRIFFIN, Ransom
"Brook or Rill." [SmPd] (27:3, #80) Fall 90, p. 22.
"Revision." [SmPd] (27:3, #80) Fall 90, p. 21.

2470. GRIFFIN, Walter
"Anima." [SouthernR] (26:4) O 90, p. 912.
"Autopsy" (for Tennessee Williams." [NewRena] (8:1, #24) Spr 90, p. 27.
"Body Parts." [SouthernR] (26:4) O 90, p. 911.
"The Bones of Montgomert Clift." [Confr] (44/45) Fall 90-Wint 91, p. 185.
"Corvus." [CapeR] (25:1) Spr 90, p. 48.
"Day of the Soft Mouth." [Amelia] (6:2, #17) 90, p. 143-144.
"Dirt." [Amelia] (6:2, #17) 90, p. 144-145.
"Sliding Home." [WritersF] (16) Fall 90, p. 112.
"Stanley Smith Is Dead." [CapeR] (25:1) Spr 90, p. 47.
"Trigger Housings." [Confr] (44/45) Fall 90-Wint 91, p. 184.
"Vogelsang 5." [KanQ] (22:3) Sum 90, p. 73.
"Weight." [SouthernR] (26:4) O 90, p. 912-913.
"Wet Pavement." [Amelia] (6:2, #17) 90, p. 144.

2471. GRIFFITH, Kevin
"Autumn Ends." [CapeR] (25:1) Spr 90, p. 20.
"Chicago, 1983." [Turnstile] (2:2) 90, p. 71.
"The End of Summer." [MidwQ] (31:3) Spr 90, p. 357.
"School Bus." [Wind] (20:66) 90, p. 17.
"Soil Sampling." [BellR] (13:2, #28) Fall 90, p. 44.
"Watching My Neighbor Work on His Car, I Fall Asleep in My Lawn Chair."
    [MidAR] (10:2) 90, p. 31.
"Window Garden." [MidAR] (10:2) 90, p. 30.

2472. GRIFO, Lionello
"Stopover in Martigny" (from "La Mia Poesia," Blue-Jay, 1989). [PoetryUSA] (5:1)
    Spr 90, p. 4.

2473. GRIGG, Mary Monica Irimescu
"Not Us!" (tr. of Nicolae Labis). [PoetryE] (29) Spr 90, p. 127.

2474. GRIGG, Phoebe
"Opening" (for Fritz). [DogRR] (9:2, #18) Aut 90, p. 13.
"Trees" (from a Tai Chi exercise, for Fritz). [DogRR] (9:2, #18) Aut 90, p. 12.

2475. GRIM, Jessica
"Rodework" (Selections: 2-3, 5). [Verse] (7:1) Spr 90, p. 25-26.

2476. GRIMES, Mark
"Concurrence." [HawaiiR] (14:1, #28) Wint 89-90, p. 33.
"Quo Vadis?" [HawaiiR] (14:1, #28) Wint 89-90, p. 32.

2477. GRIMES, Susan
"The Budding of Sand." [PoetL] (85:2) Sum 90, p. 31-32.

2478. GRIMM, Reinhold
"Finnish Tango: In Memory of Felix Pollak" (tr. of Hans Magnus Enzensberger).
    [Pembroke] (22) 90, p. 15.

"The Jewish Cemetery at Berlin-Weissensee" (tr. of Guenter Kunert: translation
dedicated to Felix Pollak). [Pembroke] (22) 90, p. 18.
2479. GRIMM, Susan
"The Shape of All Things." [CapeR] (25:2) Fall 90, p. 36-37.
2480. GRINDLEY, Carl
"Composition #12." [CanLit] (127) Wint 90, p. 40.
2481. GRISWOLD, Harry
"The Lensman." [InterPR] (16:2) Fall 90, p. 134.
"That Old Garden and Etcetera." [InterPR] (16:2) Fall 90, p. 135.
2482. GRISWOLD, Jay
"Alferd Packard." [ChironR] (9:4) Wint 90, p. 15.
"Bread." [Gypsy] (15) 90, p. 31.
"Deportees." [Plain] (10:2) Wint 90, p. l5.
"Duende." [HawaiiR] (14:2, #29) Spr 90, p. 88-89.
"In Praise of Skimmerhorn." [ChironR] (9:4) Wint 90, p. 15.
"Lust." [MidwQ] (31:3) Spr 90, p. 358.
"The River" (for James Wright). [MidAR] (10:1) 90, p. 16-17.
"Thursday Night." [SouthernPR] (30:1) Spr 90, p. 16-17.
"The Unclaimed Corpse" (For Delmore Schwartz). [HawaiiR] (14:2, #29) Spr 90, p.
90.
"Willard" (A Plainsongs Award Poem). [Plain] (11:1) Fall 90, p. 20-21.
2483. GRITZ, Ona
"After the Fog Lifted" (For Sharon Kowalski). [AmerV] (21) Wint 90, p. 33-35.
2484. GROLLMES, Eugene E.
"In Western Kansas: Boswell's First Wife." [Plain] (10:2) Wint 90, p. 17.
2485. GROLMES, Sam
"When the Orange Sun Burns." [Abraxas] (38/39) 90, p. 124.
2486. GROSHOLZ, Emily
"Back Trouble." [SouthernR] (26:3) Jl 90, p. 681.
2487. GROSS, David T.
"Musical Notes." [DustyD] (1:2) O 90, p. 11.
2488. GROSS, Pam
"Pentimento." [SoCoast] (9) Fall 90, p. 48-49.
2489. GROSS, Philip
"Threads." [Quarry] (39:1) Wint 90, p. 24.
2490. GROSSMAN, Allen
"The Ether Dome (An Entertainment)." [WestHR] (44:1) Spr 90, p. 137-152.
"Mary Snorak the Cook, Skermo the Gardener, and Jack the Parts Man Provide
Dinner for a Wandering Stranger." [Agni] (29/30) 90, p. 62-63.
"Mrs. O'Leary's Cat." [Agni] (29/30) 90, p. 60-61.
"Phoenix" (Fragment: *Dichterberuf*). [Ploughs] (16:4) Wint 90-91, p. 129-131.
2491. GROSSMAN, Andrew J.
"Haiku" (5 poems). [Northeast] (5:2) Spr 90, p. 34-35.
"Tipped over." [Amelia] (6:2, #17) 90, p. 9.
2492. GROSSMAN, Florence
"Cold Springs." [PraS] (64:4) Wint 90, p. 104.
"Dead Reckoning." [PraS] (64:4) Wint 90, p. 103.
"Quarry." [Nat] (250:6) 12 F 90, p. 214.
2493. GROSSMAN, K. Margaret
"Deconstruction." [CreamCR] (14:1) Spr 90, p. 129-130.
"Erosion." [CreamCR] (14:1) Spr 90, p. 131.
"On Margins." [Pig] (16) 90, p. 98.
2494. GROTH, Lollie
"Acupuncture." [KenR] (NS 12:3) Sum 90, p. 75.
"The Dare." [KenR] (NS 12:3) Sum 90, p. 73.
"The Worry Dolls." [KenR] (NS 12:3) Sum 90, p. 74.
2495. GROW, Eric
"Hey Mister, You Want to Look at My Junk Just for the Hell of It?" [WormR] (30:4,
#120) 90, p. 109.
"The Most Hated Man in Mexico." [WormR] (30:4, #120) 90, p. 109.
2496. GRUBBS, Gerald
"Songs of the Dead." [PaintedB] (40/41) 90, p. 196-198.
2497. GRUE, Lee Meitzen
"Easter." [Ploughs] (16:4) Wint 90-91, p. 108-109.
GRUNKE, Ann Lundberg
See LUNDBERG-GRUNKE, Ann

2498. GRUWEZ, Luuk
"Arranging Space" (tr. by David Siefkin and Catharina Kochuyt, w. Bradley R.
Strahan). [Vis] (34) 90, p. 18.
"Home" (for Monique T., died 1987, at 22, in a traffic accident, tr. by David Siefkin
and Catharina Kochuyt, w. Bradley R. Strahan). [Vis] (34) 90, p. 17.
"Inhospitality" (tr. by David Siefkin and Catharina Kochuyt). [Vis] (34) 90, p. 16.
2499. GU, Cheng
"A Generation" (tr. by Sam Hamill). [PoetryE] (30) Fall 90, p. 78.
"Harvest" (tr. by Li Xijian and Thomas C. Carlson). [AntigR] (81/82) Spr-Sum 90,
p. 69.
"An Impression" (tr. by Ginny MacKenzie and Wei Guo). [PoetryE] (30) Fall 90, p.
106.
"Near and Far" (tr. by Sam Hamill). [PoetryE] (30) Fall 90, p. 77.
"Outside Our Door" (tr. by Li Xijian and Thomas C. Carlson). [AntigR] (81/82)
Spr-Sum 90, p. 68.
2500. GU, Gong
"Oh, You and Me" (tr. by Li Xijian and Gordon Osing). [Paint] (17:33/34) Spr-Aut
90, p. 34.
2501. GU, Zhen
"Seeing a Friend Off" (tr. of Li Po, w. Harry Thomas). [Agni] (29/30) 90, p. 205.
2502. GUDAS, Eric
"Down the Coastal Highway." [Crazy] (38) Spr 90, p. 29.
"Lace Huts." [Crazy] (38) Spr 90, p. 27-28.
2503. GUENTHER, Charles
"At Lipp's" (tr. of Jean Cocteau). [InterPR] (16:2) Fall 90, p. 35.
"The Chinese Executioner" (tr. of Jean Cocteau). [InterPR] (16:2) Fall 90, p. 35.
"Homage to Kleist" (tr. of Jean Cocteau). [InterPR] (16:2) Fall 90, p. 37.
GUERCIO, Margaret del
See Del GUERCIO, Margaret
2504. GUEREÑA, Jacinto-Luis
"Ces Poèmes Obscurs" (Selections: de l'ensemble en préparation). [Os] (31) 90, p.
14.
2505. GUERESCHI, Edward
"Arrested Motion." [KanQ] (22:3) Sum 90, p. 200.
2506. GUERNSEY, Bruce
"The Blind Cavefish." [AmerS] (59:4) Aut 90, p. 577-578.
"D-Day" (June 6, 1989). [NoDaQ] (58:3) Sum 90, p. 75-76.
"Flatbush Avenue." [AmerS] (59:4) Aut 90, p. 576-577.
"Grief." [IndR] (14:1) Wint 90, p. 45-46.
"Many of Our Fathers." [MichQR] (29:2) Spr 90, p. 171.
"The Search Party." [IndR] (14:1) Wint 90, p. 47-48.
2507. GUEST, Barbara
"Defensive Rapture." [Sulfur] (10:1, #26) Spr 90, p. 17-18.
"Dove." [Conjunc] (15) 90, p. 132-136.
"Elusive Presence." [Talisman] (4) Spr 90, p. 5-8.
"Paulownia." [Conjunc] (15) 90, p. 128-131.
2508. GUGLIELMI, Joseph
"Dawn" (Excerpts, from "Aube," P.O.L., Paris, 1983, tr. by Rosmarie Waldrop).
[Avec] (3:1) 90, p. 63-66.
"Dawn" (Excerpts, tr. by Rosmarie Waldrop). [Trans] (23) Spr 90, p. 129-130.
"Dawn" (Selections, tr. by Rosmarie Waldrop). [Pequod] (31) 90, p. 64-66.
GUGLIEMI, Joseph
See GUGLIELMI, Joseph
2509. GUILFORD, Chuck
"Wielder of Men." [KanQ] (22:3) Sum 90, p. 74.
2510. GUILHADE, Joam Garcia de
"Song for a Lover Who Would die" (tr. by Richard Zenith). [LitR] (33:2) Wint 90,
p. 189.
2511. GUILLEN, Jorge
"Still Life" (tr. by Carolyne Wright). [HampSPR] (Anthology 1975-1990) 90, p.
253.
2512. GUILLEVIC
"Pastorals" (tr. by Brooke Bergan). [Trans] (23) Spr 90, p. 124-125.
2513. GUILLORY, Stella Jhylih Jeng
"My Name." [BambooR] (47) Sum 90, p. 46-47.

GUIN, Ursula K. le
    See Le GUIN, Ursula K.
2514. GUITART, Jorge
    "De los Nombres." [LindLM] (9:4) O-D 90, p. 26.
2515. GULLAR, Ferreira
    "The Chicken" (tr. by Richard Zenith). [Chelsea] (49) 90, p. 131.
    "Life Pulses" (tr. by Richard Zenith). [Chelsea] (49) 90, p. 132-133.
    "Memory" (tr. by Richard Zenith). [Chelsea] (49) 90, p. 134.
    "Rooster Rooster" (tr. by Richard Zenith). [Chelsea] (49) 90, p. 129-130.
    "Sugar" (tr. by Richard Zenith). [NewOR] (17:2) Sum 90, p. 64.
2516. GULLETTE, David
    "Round Trip." [Ploughs] (16:4) Wint 90-91, p. 263.
2517. GULLI, Bruno
    "Song of the Lost Self." [PoetryUSA] ([5:4?]) Wint 90, p. 16.
2518. GUNDERSON, Keith
    "Baja Journal" (Selections). [NorthStoneR] (9) 90, p. 146-154.
2519. GUNDY, Jeff
    "Inquiries into the Technology of Hell and Certain Rumors Recently Circulating."
        [BelPoJ] (41:2) Wint 90-91, p. 5-6.
    "Inquiry into the Nurturing and Elimination of Life Forms within Marginally
        Controlled Ecosystems on the Fifteenth Anniversary of My Wedding."
        [LaurelR] (24:2) Sum 90, p. 58.
    "Inquiry on Resistance, or Snow on Martin Luther King, Jr., Day." [LaurelR] (24:2)
        Sum 90, p. 57.
    "Report on the Discovery of the City into Which the Saints Have Been Said to Go,
        Marching." [BelPoJ] (41:2) Wint 90-91, p. 7-8.
    "What To Do During the First Rain After Ten Weeks of Drought." [WindO] (53) Fall
        90, p. 13.
2520. GUNN, Thom
    "The Deeper." [Thrpny] (43) Fall 90, p. 32.
    "Memory Unsettled." [Agni] (29/30) 90, p. 53.
2521. GUO, Hong
    "God" (tr. by Dong Jiping). [Footwork] 90, p. 36.
    "Jorge Louis Borges: 'The Secret Miracle'" (tr. by Dong Jiping). [Footwork] 90, p.
        36.
2522. GUO, Wei
    "Be Patient, Be Patient" (tr. of Ya Ping Tang, w. Ginny MacKenzie). [PoetryE] (30)
        Fall 90, p. 105.
    "An Impression" (tr. of Cheng Gu, w. Ginny MacKenzie). [PoetryE] (30) Fall 90,
        p. 106.
    "Today Someone Brought You Flowers" (tr. of Han Dong, w. Ginny MacKenzie).
        [PoetryE] (30) Fall 90, p. 96.
    "Two Pieces of Birch Bark" (tr. of Lu Lu, w. Ginny MacKenzie). [PoetryE] (30)
        Fall 90, p. 11.
2523. GURNEY, Ivor
    "It Is Near Toussaints." [GrandS] (9:3) Spr 90, p. 249.
    "Looking Out." [GrandS] (9:3) Spr 90, p. 247-248.
    "Moments." [GrandS] (9:3) Spr 90, p. 246.
    "Song." [GrandS] (9:3) Spr 90, p. 245.
2524. GUSTAFSON, Jim
    "9/9/88." [HangL] (56) 90, p. 17.
    "January 21." [HangL] (56) 90, p. 16.
2525. GUSTAFSSON, Lars
    "Elegy for the Old Mexican Woman and Her Dead Child" (tr. by Yvonne L.
        Sandstroem). [NewYorker] (66:34) 8 O 90, p. 42.
2526. GUSTAFSSON, Madeleine
    "The Adopted Child" (tr. by Lennart Bruce and Sonja Bruce). [Spirit] (10:1) 89, p.
        139.
    "Adoptivbarnet." [Spirit] (10:1) 89, p. 138.
    "Ensam Igen, Jag Också." [Spirit] (10:1) 89, p. 142.
    "The Guide" (tr. by Lennart Bruce and Sonja Bruce). [Spirit] (10:1) 89, p. 149.
    "Hörendesjön, Augusti." [Spirit] (10:1) 89, p. 146.
    "I Too Am Alone Again" (tr. by Lennart Bruce and Sonja Bruce). [Spirit] (10:1) 89,
        p. 143.
    "Lake Hörende, August" (tr. by Lennart Bruce and Sonja Bruce). [Spirit] (10:1) 89,
        p. 147.

200

GUSTAFSSON

"Pingst, Trettio År Senare." [Spirit] (10:1) 89, p. 144.
"Run Away?" (tr. by Lennart Bruce and Sonja Bruce). [Spirit] (10:1) 89, p. 141.
"Springa Undan?" [Spirit] (10:1) 89, p. 140.
"Vägvisaren." [Spirit] (10:1) 89, p. 148.
"Whitsun, Thirty Years Later" (tr. by Lennart Bruce and Sonja Bruce). [Spirit]
        (10:1) 89, p. 145.
GUT, Karen Alkalay
        See ALKALAY-GUT, Karen
2527. GUTTMAN, Naomi
        "The Gift." [AntigR] (80) Wint 90, p. 122.
        "Median with Weeds." [MalR] (91) Je 90, p. 76.
        "Reasons for Winter." [MalR] (91) Je 90, p. 77.
2528. GUZLOWSKI, John
        "Mobile, January 1989." [NegC] (10:2/3) 90, p. 73.
2529. GWYNN, R. S.
        "Approaching a Significant Birthday, He Peruses The Norton Anthology of Poetry."
        [NewYorkQ] (43) Fall 90, p. 61.
        "A Song for TWU." [Verse] (7:3) Wint 90, p. 51-52.
2530. HAALAND, Tami
        "Nuclear Winter and Bicycle Dust." [Calyx] (12:3) Sum 90, p. 44-45.
2531. HAAVIKKO, Paavo
        "The Trees, All Their Green" (Excerpts, tr. by Anselm Hollo). [Writ] (21) 89 c1990,
        p. 50-54.
HABONVA, Dana
        See HABOVA, Dana
2532. HABOVA, Dana
        "1751" (tr. of Miroslav Holub, w. David Young and the author). [AmerPoR] (19:2)
        Mr-Ap 90, p. 4.
        "The Clock" (tr. of Miroslav Holub, w. David Young). [Field] (42) Spr 90, p. 7.
        "The Fall from the Green Frog" (tr. of Miroslav Holub, w. David Young). [Field]
        (42) Spr 90, p. 11.
        "Fish" (tr. of Miroslav Holub, w. David Young). [Field] (42) Spr 90, p. 8-9.
        "Glass" (tr. of Miroslav Holub, w. David Young). [Field] (42) Spr 90, p. 10.
        "Great Ancestors" (tr. of Miroslav Holub, w. David Young and the author).
        [AmerPoR] (19:2) Mr-Ap 90, p. 5.
        "Heart Transplant" (tr. of Miroslav Holub, w. David Young). [Field] (42) Spr 90, p.
        5-6.
        "Night Calamities" (tr. of Miroslav Holub, w. David Young and the author).
        [AmerPoR] (19:2) Mr-Ap 90, p. 5.
        "Parasite" (tr. of Miroslav Holub, w. David Young and the author). [AmerPoR]
        (19:2) Mr-Ap 90, p. 3.
        "Skinning" (tr. of Miroslav Holub, w. David Young and the author). [AmerPoR]
        (19:2) Mr-Ap 90, p. 4.
        "What Else" (tr. of Miroslav Holub, w. David Young and the author). [AmerPoR]
        (19:2) Mr-Ap 90, p. 3.
2533. HABRA, Hedy
        "Reflections." [NegC] (10:1) 90, p. 59-60.
        "Tea in Heliopolis." [NegC] (10:1) 90, p. 61.
        "The White Brass Bed." [NegC] (10:1) 90, p. 57-58.
2534. HACKER, Marilyn
        "For Jean Migrenne." [Ploughs] (16:1) Spr-Sum 90, p. 26-27.
        "Going Away from the River." [Ploughs] (16:1) Spr-Sum 90, p. 28.
        "Going Back to the River" (for K.J.). [Boulevard] (4:3/5:1, #12/13) Spr 90, p.
        68-70.
2535. HACKETT, Philip
        "Waiting Is Forever." [PoetryUSA] (5:2) Sum 90, p. 1.
2536. HACKETT, Ray
        "On Origins." [SouthernHR] (24:4) Fall 90, p. 370.
2537. HACKSEL, Helen
        "Thanksgiving." [Descant] (21:4/22:1, #71/72) Wint-Spr 90-91, p. 109.
2538. HACTHOUN, Augusto
        "Me aguardan celosías." [LindLM] (9:4) O-D 90, p. 24.
        "La Pera." [LindLM] (9:4) O-D 90, p. 24.
2539. HADAS, Pamela White
        "Losers, Keepers: The Opus of Wilhelmina Scrowd" (II. Wilhelmina's Opus on
        Progress). [KenR] (NS 12:2) Spr 90, p. 97-100.

2540. HADAS, Rachel
"Acts of Vanishing." [CumbPR] (9:2) Spr 90, p. 12.
"The Dream Machine" (Excerpt). [Pequod] (31) 90, p. 80-81.
"Genealogy." [Verse] (7:3) Wint 90, p. 52-53.
"In the Beginning." [CumbPR] (9:2) Spr 90, p. 11.
"In the Playground." [Boulevard] (5:2, #14) Fall 90, p. 32.
"The Mad Message." [SouthernR] (26:3) Jl 90, p. 631-632.
"Mars and Venus." [SouthwR] (75:3) Sum 90, p. 322-323.
"The Revenant." [Thrpny] (42) Sum 90, p. 14.
"Roadblock." [YaleR] (79:3) Spr 90, p. 445.
"Spring." [SouthwR] (75:3) Sum 90, p. 323-324.
2541. HADAWAY, Linnea
"She Had Been Born." [LakeSR] (24) 90, p. 34.
HAEFNER, Eberhard
See HAFNER, Eberhard
2542. HAFF, T.
"Tete-a-tete." [Amelia] (6:2, #17) 90, p. 132.
2543. HAFNER, Eberhard
"Topless Is Allowed Here" (tr. by Roderick Iverson). [Screens] (2) 90, p. 78-79.
"Topless Is Allowed Here" (tr. by Roderick Iverson). [Sulfur] (10:2, #27) Fall 90,
p. 113-114.
2544. HAFSA BINT Al-HAJJ Ar-RAKUNTYYA
17 poems (tr. by Christopher Middleton). [PartR] (57:3) Sum 90, p. 386-393.
2545. HAGEN, Cecelia
"Maneuvers." [WillowS] (25) Wint 90, p. 56-57.
"The Way Out of the Fly Bottle." [WillowS] (25) Wint 90, p. 58-59.
2546. HAGEN, Curt
"Dutch." [HawaiiR] (14:1, #28) Wint 89-90, p. 61.
2547. HAGEN, William J.
"Pan and Syrinx." [BlueBldgs] (12) 90, p. 33-36.
2548. HAGGERTON, Jeanie (Olson)
"In Lapland, Kansas." [MidwQ] (31:4) Sum 90, p. 479.
2549. HAGINO, Dave
"Roadskating." [ChamLR] (4:1, #7) Fall 90, p. 40.
2550. HAGUE, Richard
"Bound." [Wind] (20:67) 90, p. 24.
2551. HAHN, Kimiko
"The Hawaiian Shirt." [RiverS] (32) [90?], p. 43.
"The Heat." [HangL] (57) 90, p. 32-35.
"Poetry." [RiverS] (32) [90?], p. 42.
"The Room" (Selections). [Pequod] (31) 90, p. 76-78.
2552. HAHN, Lauren
"Chopin" (tr. of Gottfried Benn). [WebR] (14:2) Spr 90, p. 107-108.
2553. HAHN, Susan
"Briefcase." [NoAmR] (275:3) S 90, p. 44.
"Circumcision." [Shen] (40:3) Fall 90, p. 60-61.
2554. HAI, Zi
"Autumn" (tr. by Dong Jiping). [Footwork] 90, p. 42.
"Han Haiku" (tr. by Dong Jiping). [Footwork] 90, p. 42.
"I Am Sick" (tr. by Dong Jiping). [Footwork] 90, p. 42.
"In His Requiem Mozart Said" (tr. by Dong Jiping). [Footwork] 90, p. 42.
2555. HAI-JEW, Shalin
"Land of Mutational Artists" (Nanchang, Jiangxi Province, P.R.C. 1989). [Contact]
(9:56/57/58) Spr 90, p. 20.
2556. HAINES, Anne
"Orange Poem." [Cond] (17) 90, p. 73.
"Taking It Back." [SingHM] (18) 90, p. 68-70.
2557. HAJNAL, Anna
"Well, I Ask" (tr. by Len Roberts and Mária Kurdi). [AmerPoR] (19:5) S-O 90, p.
22.
2558. HALAS, Frantisek
"First Riddle" (tr. by Don Mager). [NewOR] (17:3) Fall 90, p. 70.
"Second Riddle" (tr. by Don Mager). [NewOR] (17:3) Fall 90, p. 70.
"Third Riddle with Its Solution" (tr. by Don Mager). [NewOR] (17:3) Fall 90, p. 70.
2559. HALBERG, Dylan
"Untitled: In this globe of numbers." [FreeL] (6) Aut 90, p. 13.

"Untitled: The door Was Left Open." [FreeL] (6) Aut 90, p. 12.
2560. HALE, Dori
"Modified Rapture." [CreamCR] (14:1) Spr 90, p. 146.
"A New Year in Vermont." [CreamCR] (14:1) Spr 90, p. 147-148.
2561. HALE, Eileen Adele
"The Shadow Behind the Watercress." [OnTheBus] (2:2/3:1, #6/7) Sum-Fall 90
Wint-Spr 91, p. 94.
2562. HALE, Terrel
"Walking Behind the Window Glass" (Excerpt). [Screens] (2) 90, p. 189-190.
2563. HALES, Corrinne
"Consummation" (for K.J.S., 1947-1988). [NewEngR] (13:2) Wint 90, p. 8-14.
"School Lunch Work Program." [Ploughs] (16:4) Wint 90-91, p. 34-37.
2564. HALEY, Vanessa
"The Entomologist's Notebooks." [GettyR] (3:3) Sum 90, p. 554-555.
2565. HALL, Bernadette
"Bacchante." [Verse] (7:2) Sum 90, p. 30.
"Cadence" (in memory of my father). [Verse] (7:2) Sum 90, p. 31-32.
"Ritual for a White Rabbit." [Verse] (7:2) Sum 90, p. 30.
2566. HALL, Daniel
"13th & Aloha." [PraS] (64:4) Wint 90, p. 105-106.
"The Beanstalk." [YaleR] (79:2) Wint 90, p. 288-289.
"Country Radio." [NewYorker] (65:46) 1 Ja 90, p. 32.
"October: November." [PraS] (64:4) Wint 90, p. 106-107.
2567. HALL, Donald
"The Coffee Cup." [Iowa] (20:1) Wint 90, p. 104-105.
"Cold Ones." [Boulevard] (5:2, #14) Fall 90, p. 66.
"Edward's Anecdote." [Harp] (281:1683) Ag 90, p. 39.
"A Grace." [SewanR] (98:2) Spr 90, p. 187.
"Maundy Thursday's Candles." [SewanR] (98:2) Spr 90, p. 187.
"Milkers Broken Up." [VirQR] (66:2) Spr 90, p. 274-275.
"Notes for Nobody." [AmerPoR] (19:3) My-Je 90, p. 12.
"Persistence of 1937." [BostonR] (15:2) Ap 90, p. 3.
"This Poem." [AmerPoR] (19:3) My-Je 90, p. 12.
"Tubes." [Boulevard] (4:3/5:1, #12/13) Spr 90, p. 18-20.
"The Valley of Morning." [Iowa] (20:1) Wint 90, p. 105-106.
2568. HALL, Earl (Earl N.)
"The Great Test." [PoetryUSA] (5:2) Sum 90, p. 17.
"Little or Nothing." [PoetryUSA] (5:2) Sum 90, p. 17.
"Shred of Dignity." [PoetryUSA] (5:3) Fall 90, p. 24.
2569. HALL, Gail A.
"Yard Work." [SouthernPR] (30:1) Spr 90, p. 65.
"Yellow Primrose." [SouthernPR] (30:1) Spr 90, p. 66.
2570. HALL, Irving C.
"Phoenix." [NewL] (57:1) Fall 90, p. 103.
2571. HALL, James Baker
"Where If I Dared I Would Put My Small Hand." [Ploughs] (16:4) Wint 90-91, p.
205-212.
2572. HALL, Judith
"Week as an Example of Years." [NewRep] (202:26) 25 Je 90, p. 34.
2573. HALL, Lisa Kahaleole Chang
"Hospital Poems" (for V.B.). [SinW] (40) Spr 90, p. 61-63.
2574. HALLA, Chris
"Compulsories." [Northeast] (NS 5:3) Wint 90-91, p. 11.
"A Lover Spurned." [Wind] (20:66) 90, p. 18-19.
"Some Things Your Mother Didn't Tell You." [Wind] (20:66) 90, p. 19.
2575. HALLAMAN, E. G.
"Unplanned Obsolescence." [Pig] (16) 90, p. 52.
2576. HALLERMAN, Victoria
"You Visit Me by the Sea." [Nat] (250:19) 14 My 90, p. 676.
2577. HALLIDAY, Mark
"Already in 1927." [KenR] (NS 12:4) Fall 90, p. 127-128.
"Another Man." [VirQR] (66:2) Spr 90, p. 268-269.
"The Elegist." [PassN] (11:1) Sum 90, p. 13.
"Failure." [SouthwR] (75:3) Sum 90, p. 379.
"Fidelity." [CimR] (92) Jl 90, p. 114.
"He Sits There and Suddenly." [CimR] (92) Jl 90, p. 113.

"The Nineties." [Crazy] (39) Wint 90, p. 44-46.
"Too Much." [Crazy] (39) Wint 90, p. 47-48.
2578. HALLIDAY-BORKOWSKI, Miriam
"Dreamboy: Laser Fantabulast." [Spirit] (10:2) 90, p. 66-68.
2579. HALLORAN, Maureen
"Another Hunger." [GreensboroR] (48) Sum 90, p. 91-92.
2580. HALMAN, Talat Sait
"A Last Lullaby." [Footwork] 90, p. 103.
"My Year of Death." [Footwork] 90, p. 103.
"Ultimate Death." [Footwork] 90, p. 103.
2581. HALME, Kathleen
"An Appalachian Town: Points of Definition." [RiverS] (32) [90?], p. 55.
2582. HALPERIN, Joan
"Iron." [SoCoast] (9) Fall 90, p. 14.
2583. HALPERIN, Mark
"For a Liar." [TarRP] (29:2) Spr 90, p. 26-27.
"Listen." [NowestR] (28:3/29:1) 90-91, p. 80.
"Not Catching Whitefish." [SwampR] (6) Sum-Fall 90, p. 13.
"On the Steps of Temple Shalom." [Poetry] (156:1) Ap 90, p. 23-24.
"Yom Kippur Again." [LaurelR] (24:2) Sum 90, p. 14.
2584. HALPERN, Daniel
"Glassworks." [HampSPR] (Anthology 1975-1990) 90, p. 117.
"You Go Out." [HampSPR] (Anthology 1975-1990) 90, p. 117.
2585. HALPERN, Sal
"A Mother's Odyssey." [CimR] (90) Ja 90, p. 77.
"Racquet Ball." [CimR] (90) Ja 90, p. 76.
2586. HALPERN, Sheryl
"An Argument Against Jumping Off a Balcony." [Quarry] (39:2) Spr 90, p. 34.
2587. HALSALL, Jalaine
"Him." [BlackWR] (17:1) Fall-Wint 90, p. 40-41.
"Lecture." [NewYorkQ] (43) Fall 90, p. 62.
2588. HALSEY, Alan
"Companion Studies." [Avec] (3:1) 90, p. 26-28.
"Eleatic Electric." [Avec] (3:1) 90, p. 28-32.
"Table Talk" (Selections: I-II, V, X, XV). [Screens] (2) 90, p. 173.
2589. HAMBURGER, Michael
"A Dream of Water." [Stand] (31:3) Sum 90, p. 50-51.
"Fragments and Commentaries" (English translations of Friedrich Hölderlin's
German translations of Pindar with commentaries). [Stand] (31:3) Sum 90, p.
36-40.
"You Firmly Built Alps!" (tr. of Friedrich Hölderlin). [Stand] (31:3) Sum 90, p.
34-35.
2590. HAMERSKI, Susan Thurston
"The Last Nun." [RagMag] (7:2) Spr 90, p. 16.
2591. HAMILL, Sam
"Blue Monody" (Blues for Thomas McGrath). [PoetryE] (29) Spr 90, p. 177-194.
"Curse" (tr. of Fei Ye). [PoetryE] (30) Fall 90, p. 32.
"A Generation" (tr. of Gu Cheng). [PoetryE] (30) Fall 90, p. 78.
"Let's Go" (tr. of Bei Dao). [PoetryE] (30) Fall 90, p. 101.
"Near and Far" (tr. of Gu Cheng). [PoetryE] (30) Fall 90, p. 77.
2592. HAMILTON, Alfred Starr
"Another Kind of a Rhinoceros." [Epoch] (39:3) 90, p. 295.
"Brethren." [Footwork] 90, p. 71.
"The Little Shop Around the Corner." [HampSPR] (Anthology 1975-1990) 90, p.
70.
"Reverse." [JINJPo] (12:2) Aut 90, p. 27.
"Sibelius." [HampSPR] (Anthology 1975-1990) 90, p. 70.
2593. HAMILTON, Bruce
"Detections have shown that the sky." [Amelia] (6:2, #17) 90, p. 78.
2594. HAMILTON, Carol
"Constellations." [CapeR] (25:1) Spr 90, p. 33-34.
"Redland IV." [GreensboroR] (49) Wint 90-91, p. 41.
"Seminole Finery." [MidwQ] (31:2) Wint 90, p. 200.
"Telescoped." [HawaiiR] (14:3, #30) Fall 90, p. 115.
2595. HAMILTON, Fritz
"Abandoned & Etc!" [SmPd] (27:2, #79) Spr 90, p. 18.

HAMILTON

204

"All God!" [Amelia] (6:2, #17) 90, p. 141-142.
"Bugged to New York City!" [Writ] (21) 89 c1990, p. 34.
"But That's What You Are." [DogRR] (9:2, #18) Aut 90, p. 14-17.
"Dog's Life -- Rejoice!" [KanQ] (22:3) Sum 90, p. 177.
"Everybody Knows!" [Kaleid] (21) Sum-Fall 90, p. 62.
"Have a Good Time" (for Jesse). [SlipS] (10) 90, p. 102.
"Minding Our Business." [MidwQ] (31:3) Spr 90, p. 359-360.
"The Newer Testament." [Writ] (21) 89 c1990, p. 39-40.
"Now Rejoice!" [SmPd] (27:1, #78) Wint 90, p. 7.
"Old Mazart!" [Writ] (21) 89 c1990, p. 41-42.
"Pigeon Amazement" (reprinted from #19, 1989). [Kaleid] (20) Wint-Spr 90, p. 51.
"Repentance." [Writ] (21) 89 c1990, p. 37.
"So What?" [HolCrit] (27:1) F 90, p. 16.
"That Little." [Kaleid] (21) Sum-Fall 90, p. 47.
"Thoughts on a Jet Flight to New York City." [Writ] (21) 89 c1990, p. 35-36.
"What's Really Going On." [Writ] (21) 89 c1990, p. 38.
2596. HAMILTON, Kitty
"In South Africa" (Seen on the MacNeil/Lehrer Newshour). [AmerPoR] (19:4) Jl-Ag 90, p. 14.
2597. HAMILTON, Marcia
"That Which Impedes." [QW] (31) Fall 90, p. 89.
2598. HAMILTON, Robin
"Blue and Green." [CutB] (34) Sum-Fall 90, p. 74.
2599. HAMILTON, Roxanne Power
"Thanksgiving." [BlackWR] (17:1) Fall-Wint 90, p. 157.
2600. HAMILTON, Saskia
"Birds" (for Sharon Olds). [Thrpny] (41) Spr 90, p. 16.
"A Mouth Full of Hair" (for Meg and Cecil). [KenR] (NS 12:3) Sum 90, p. 88-90.
2601. HAMM, Timothy
"Little Brother at Six" (for Scott). [SouthernPR] (30:2) Fall 90, p. 30-31.
"The Promise of Flight" (for those with AIDS). [SouthernPR] (30:2) Fall 90, p. 31.
2602. HAMMER, M.
"The Tragedy of Open Spaces." [CapeR] (25:1) Spr 90, p. 24.
2603. HAMMER, Margaret
"$HI (Sunday Want Ads)." [PottPort] (12) 90, p. 11.
"Red-winged Sea Gull." [PottPort] (12) 90, p. 11.
2604. HAMMER, P., Jr.
"The Colors of Saint Josephs." [JINJPo] (12:1) Spr 90, p. 32.
2605. HAMMERSCHICK, Mark
"Scent of Snow." [WillowR] Spr 90, p. 42.
2606. HAMMOND, Karla M.
"Circularity" (for Robert Creeley). [Gargoyle] (37/38) 90, p. 119.
"Hansel's Version." [Footwork] 90, p. 72.
"North Pownal: Pulling in the Moon." [Footwork] 90, p. 72.
2607. HAMMOND, Mary Stewart
"Accepting the Body." [YaleR] (79:3) Spr 90, p. 487-488.
"July." [AmerV] (19) Sum 90, p. 74-76.
"Making Breakfast." [NewYorker] (66:10) 23 Ap 90, p. 40.
"Suffrage" (for Anne). [GettyR] (3:4) Aut 90, p. 657.
2608. HAMMOND, Tionie L.
"The Interview." [HolCrit] (27:4) O 90, p. 17.
2609. HAN, Dong
"Mountain People" (tr. by Liu Shicong and Christine Ferreira). [MichQR] (29:1) Wint 90, p. 94-95.
"Today Someone Brought You Flowers" (tr. by Ginny MacKenzie and Wei Guo). [PoetryE] (30) Fall 90, p. 96.
2610. HAN, Françoise
"Darkness" (tr. by Thomas Shapcott). [Trans] (23) Spr 90, p. 167.
"The House of Childhood" (tr. by William Jay Smith). [Trans] (23) Spr 90, p. 165-166.
2611. HAN, Shan
"Da pig make kaukau from make die dead kanaka" (tr. by Suzie Wong Scollon). [BambooR] (47) Sum 90, p. 58.
"Dew drops sparkle on da maile curtains" (tr. by Suzie Wong Scollon). [BambooR] (47) Sum 90, p. 59.
"Make me laugh, dis Cold Mountain trail" (tr. by Suzie Wong Scollon). [BambooR]

(47) Sum 90, p. 57.
2612. HANCOCK, Hugh
"Beliefs from the Gulf: A Southern Upbringing." [Amelia] (6:2, #17) 90, p. 119.
2613. HANDLER, Joan Cusack
"At Thirteen: Kneeling Beside My Father." [Confr] (44/45) Fall 90-Wint 91, p. 276-277.
2614. HANDLER, Peter M.
"Dear Ann Landers." [AnotherCM] (22) 90, p. 48-50.
2615. HANDLIN, Jim
"Wellfleet." [Footwork] 90, p. 71.
2616. HANDY, Nixeon Civille
"Alexander Isaevich Solzhenitsyn." [DustyD] (1:2) O 90, p. 2.
"Iron Events." [BellArk] (6:4) Jl-Ag 90, p. 24.
2617. HANFORD, Mary
"Patrimony." [SwampR] (6) Sum-Fall 90, p. 96.
"Return Flight." [SwampR] (6) Sum-Fall 90, p. 97.
2618. HANLEY, Patricia
"Keats's House, Rome." [PraF] (11:3) Aut 90, p. 53.
2619. HANLO, Jan
"Do You Love Me Always" (tr. by Sharon Robertson). [Vis] (34) 90, p. 36.
"Not Unlike" (tr. by Sharon Robertson). [Vis] (34) 90, p. 37.
"Sonnet" (tr. by Arie Staal). [Vis] (34) 90, p. 38.
"That Is How I Think of You Too" (tr. by Sharon Robertson). [Vis] (34) 90, p. 36.
"To Winter" (tr. by Kees Snoek). [Vis] (34) 90, p. 35.
"Verse for 7 June '51" (tr. by Kees Snoek). [Vis] (34) 90, p. 38.
2620. HANLON, Patrick Henry
"The Attic." [PottPort] (12) 90, p. 39.
"Kemmel Hill." [PottPort] (12) 90, p. 19.
2621. HANNAN, Greg
"Between Friends" (Ten Oaks Farm, Nictaux, Nova Scotia, 1984). [Gargoyle] (37/38) 90, p. 132.
2622. HANNEMANN, Dee
"White Egg Shells." [Northeast] (NS 5:3) Wint 90-91, p. 7.
"Wiscasset." [Northeast] (NS 5:3) Wint 90-91, p. 8.
2623. HANNON, Michael
"Ars Poetica." [PoetryE] (29) Spr 90, p. 235.
"The Bear." [PoetryE] (29) Spr 90, p. 232.
"False Spring." [PoetryE] (29) Spr 90, p. 233.
"Mask." [PoetryE] (29) Spr 90, p. 227.
"No God But God." [PoetryE] (29) Spr 90, p. 230.
"One Day at a Time" (for Raymond Carver). [PoetryE] (29) Spr 90, p. 229.
"Oroborus." [PoetryE] (29) Spr 90, p. 234.
"Self-Knowledge." [PoetryE] (29) Spr 90, p. 231.
"The Song, Not the Singer." [PoetryE] (29) Spr 90, p. 228.
2624. HANNON, Nan
"October." [MinnR] (NS 34/35) Spr-Fall 90, p. 26-27.
"X-Rays." [MinnR] (NS 34/35) Spr-Fall 90, p. 25.
"X-Rays II." [MinnR] (NS 34/35) Spr-Fall 90, p. 26.
2625. HANOSKI, Evelyn
"Artifice." [Grain] (18:1) Spr 90, p. 40.
"Once a Week." [Grain] (18:1) Spr 90, p. 39.
"Yearly Visits." [Grain] (18:1) Spr 90, p. 40.
2626. HANSELL, Susan
"The Wolf" (reprinted from #10, 1985). [Kaleid] (20) Wint-Spr 90, p. 85.
2627. HANSEN, Dennis
"The Sale Barn." [Plain] (10:3) Spr 90, p. 35.
2628. HANSON, Julie Jordan
"Anyone's Relation." [RiverS] (31) [90?], p. 28-37.
2629. HANZIMANOLIS, Margaret
"Departing" (tr. of Alfonsina Storni, w. Carlos García-Aranda). [BelPoR] (40:3) Spr 90, p. 23-25.
"I Am" (tr. of Alfonsina Storni, w. Carlos García-Aranda). [CarolQ] (43:1) Fall 90, p. 69.
"I Am Going to Sleep" (tr. of Alfonsina Storni, w. Carlos García-Aranda). [CarolQ] (43:1) Fall 90, p. 70.
"I Am Useless" (tr. of Alfonsina Storni, w. Carlos García-Aranda). [CarolQ] (43:1)

Fall 90, p. 68.
"One More Time" (tr. of Alfonsina Storni, w. Carlos García-Aranda). [CarolQ]
(43:1) Fall 90, p. 67.
"Tropical" (tr. of Alfonsina Storni, w. Carlos Garcia-Aranda). [BelPoR] (40:3) Spr
90, p. 25-26.
"Two Holiday Meals." [ColEng] (52:4) Ap 90, p. 411-412.
"You Want Me White" (tr. of Alfonsina Storni, w. Carlos Garcia-Aranda). [BelPoR]
(40:3) Spr 90, p. 22-23.
2630. HANZLICEK, C. G.
"Mystery." [NewEngR] (13:1) Fall 90, p. 78.
2631. HARAD, Alyssa
"The Lunatic's Prayer" (Third Prize). [HarvardA] (124:3) Mr 90, p. 7.
2632. HARD, Rock
"My Parabolic Muse." [EmeraldCR] (1990) c89, p. 30-31.
2633. HARDER, Dan
"A perfect purple opening, within." [ContextS] (1:1) 89, p. 13.
2634. HARDIN, Jeff
"Staring Out a Window." [WestB] (27) 90, p. 85.
2635. HARDING, Deborah
"The Return." [PoetL] (85:4) Wint 90-91, p. 5-6.
2636. HARDING, Gunnar
"The Star-Diver" (tr. by Robert Greenwald). [Writ] (21) 89 c1990, p. 86-90.
2637. HARDING, Rachel
"Haiti Painting: Alabama Women at a Bedside." [Chelsea] (49) 90, p. 62-66.
2638. HARDING-RUSSELL, Gillian
"Full Moon This Night in January." [CapilR] (2:2) Spr 90, p. 35-37.
"Nada or the Golden Egg of Poetry." [PraF] (11:4) Wint 90-91, p. 25-27.
"Someone Tells You." [PraF] (11:4) Wint 90-91, p. 28-29.
"Turning the Breech Baby (Around)." [Dandel] (17:2) Fall-Wint 90, p. 19-20.
2639. HARDMAN, Katherine Reeves
"All the King's Men." [EmeraldCR] (1990) c89, p. 10-11.
2640. HARDMAN, Thomas
"A Short History of Sarasota." [EmeraldCR] (1990) c89, p. 105.
2641. HARDY, Jan
"Small Acts." [SinW] (40) Spr 90, p. 36-37.
2642. HARDY, Thomas
"Afterwards." [SouthernR] (26:3) Jl 90, p. 482-483.
"The End." [SouthernR] (26:3) Jl 90, p. 483-484.
2643. HARER, Katharine
"After the Chiropractor." [OnTheBus] (2:2/3:1, #6/7) Sum-Fall 90 Wint-Spr 91, p.
96.
"Circle of Chalk." [Spirit] (10:2) 90, p. 10.
"Lucky 7." [OnTheBus] (2:2/3:1, #6/7) Sum-Fall 90 Wint-Spr 91, p. 95-96.
"No One Listens to Poetry" (-- Jack Spicer). [Spirit] (10:2) 90, p. 9.
"Spring Training." [Zyzzyva] (6:1 #21) Spr 90, p. 55.
2644. HARGITAI, Peter
"Arising from the Sea." [Nimrod] (34:1) Fall-Wint 90, p. 102.
"Cats." [Nimrod] (34:1) Fall-Wint 90, p. 103.
"Mother's Visit No. 29." [Nimrod] (34:1) Fall-Wint 90, p. 101.
2645. HARINGTON, Colin
"Whitetail Omen." [Wind] (20:66) 90, p. 31.
2646. HARKNESS, Susan M.
"James River in March." [Blueline] (11:1/2) 90, p. 42.
2647. HARLEMAN, Ann
"Thirty-three Girls Are Taken to See Ninety-eight Paintings by a Dead Artist of Their
Own Sex." [ApalQ] (33/34) 90, p. 59-60.
2648. HARLOW, Robert
"Close to Home." [MidwQ] (31:3) Spr 90, p. 361-362.
"Similes for the Sun." [MidwQ] (31:3) Spr 90, p. 363-364.
2649. HARMAN, Sarah Chewning
"Valdez." [EmeraldCR] (1990) c89, p. 45-46.
2650. HARMLESS, William
"Perichoresis: Letter of Gregory of Nazianzus to Gregory of Nyssa, 362." [NewOR]
(17:1) Spr 90, p. 94-99.
"Singing the Innervoice." [ManhatPR] (11) [89?], p. 8.

2651. HARMON, William
"A Nothing Generation." [Agni] (31/32) 90, p. 163-164.
"Tahafut al-Falasifah." [Agni] (31/32) 90, p. 161-162.
2652. HARMS, James
"The Hole in the Moon." [AmerPoR] (19:2) Mr-Ap 90, p. 42.
"Safer Shadow." [MissouriR] (13:2) 90, p. 74.
"Somewhere Someone Is Saying Goodbye." [CarolQ] (42:3) Spr 90, p. 37-38.
2653. HARNACK, Curtis
"After the Fall Equinox." [Blueline] (11:1/2) 90, p. 71.
"Epithalamium." [Chelsea] (49) 90, p. 61.
"Monday Wash in Winter." [SouthwR] (75:4) Aut 90, p. 508.
"Pilgrimage." [Salm] (85/86) Wint-Spr 90, p. 146-147.
2654. HARNETT, Gerald
"Automata." [Hellas] (1:2) Fall 90, p. 213-214.
"Creation." [Hellas] (1:2) Fall 90, p. 214.
"Lauds, or, L'Allegro, or, Khan of the High Light." [Hellas] (1:1) Spr 90, p. 39-40.
"Vespers, or, Il Penseroso, or, Bualand." [Hellas] (1:1) Spr 90, p. 37-38.
HARO, José Elgarresta Ramirez de
See ELGARRESTA, José
2655. HARPER, Mary Catherine
"Deaf Enough." [NewEngR] (13:2) Wint 90, p. 181-182.
2656. HARPER, Michael (Michael S.)
"21 Feb '65, San Francisco." [Callaloo] (13:4) Fall 90, p. 764-765.
"Angola (Louisiana)" (for Ernest J. Gaines). [Callaloo] (13:4) Fall 90, p. 771-772.
"Birthday Boy." [Callaloo] (13:4) Fall 90, p. 777-778.
"Caves." [BlackALF] (24:3) Fall 90, p. 426-427.
"Dexter Leaps In." [Callaloo] (13:4) Fall 90, p. 758-759.
"Imp" (5 February 1990, for Britten Samuel Long). [Callaloo] (13:4) Fall 90, p.
773-774.
"Modulations on a Theme: For Josephus Long." [Callaloo] (13:4) Fall 90, p.
751-755.
"Motel Room" (for John and Susan). [Callaloo] (13:4) Fall 90, p. 760.
"My Father at 75." [Callaloo] (13:4) Fall 90, p. 761-762.
"Pardons (from A. Lincoln)." [Caliban] (8) 90, p. 82-83.
"Portrait of Lynn" (as Josephus would wish it). [Callaloo] (13:4) Fall 90, p.
756-757.
"Saint Dolores" (Phillips Exeter Academy). [Callaloo] (13:4) Fall 90, p. 763.
"Saint Sassy Divine." [Callaloo] (13:4) Fall 90, p. 766-768.
"The Sanctity of the Unwritten." [Callaloo] (13:4) Fall 90, p. 779.
"Teaching Institutes." [Callaloo] (13:4) Fall 90, p. 769-770.
"Thistles" (for my daughter, Rachel, 18). [Callaloo] (13:4) Fall 90, p. 775-776.
"A White Friend Flies in from the Coast." [BlackALF] (24:3) Fall 90, p. 427.
2657. HARPER, Nanette
"The Screaming Eagle Papers" (Excerpt). [EmeraldCR] (1990) c89, p. 50-51.
2658. HARPOOTIAN, Alysia K.
"Balancing." [FourQ] (4:1) Spr 90, p. 62.
"A Flower and a Stem on the Twelfth Day." [ChamLR] (4:1, #7) Fall 90, p.
120-121.
2659. HARRELL, Ken
"Enough." [SouthernPR] (30:2) Fall 90, p. 43-44.
2660. HARRELL, Sara
"The Cane of a Duck." [HayF] (6) Sum 90, p. 34-35.
2661. HARRIMAN, Eddie
"Duty." [Bogg] (62) 90, p. 50.
"Signing On." [Bogg] (63) 90, p. 44.
2662. HARRINGTON, J. R.
"Certitude." [WorldO] (23:3/4) Spr-Sum 89 c1991, p. 18.
2663. HARRIS, Beverly
"A Cloud of White Linen." [Grain] (18:1) Spr 90, p. 68.
"Reunion." [Grain] (18:1) Spr 90, p. 69.
"Summer in Full Bloom." [Grain] (18:1) Spr 90, p. 67.
2664. HARRIS, Claire
"Elegy for a Young Man Dying of AIDS." [PoetryC] (11:1) Spr 90, p. 18-19.
"Love, Do You Remember." [Dandel] (17:2) Fall-Wint 90, p. 7-9.
2665. HARRIS, Jana
"After Reading Marguerite Duras, We Celebrate Electricity" (Our Shed on First

Street, Useless Bay). [MichQR] (29:1) Wint 90, p. 55-56.
"Civic Duties: My Neighbor, Marn, Volunteer Fireman." [OnTheBus] (2:2/3:1, #6/7)
Sum-Fall 90 Wint-Spr 91, p. 97-98.
"For the First Time in Twenty-Three Years Your Family Has Dinner Together."
[BrooklynR] (7) 90, p. 55-57.
2666. HARRIS, Joseph
"The Poetry Reading." [PoetC] (21:3) Spr 90, p. 30.
"Watching Spiders." [SoDakR] (28:1) Spr 90, p. 75.
2667. HARRIS, Lynn Farmer
"Elmer Hunter Does His Time." [ChatR] (11:1) Fall 90, p. 32-33.
"Faces That We Mean to Leave Behind" (Fall 1972). [LullwaterR] (1:1) Spr 90, p.
54-55.
"Step Between." [LullwaterR] (1:1) Spr 90, p. 77-79.
"Teddy's Purples." [LullwaterR] (2:1) Wint 90, p. 25-26.
2668. HARRIS, Marie
"Physics One." [HeavenB] (8) Wint 90-91, p. 56.
2669. HARRIS, Peter
"My Father-in-Law's Contract." [HiramPoR] (47) Wint 90, p. 31-33.
"The Urge to Be Polish." [CharR] (16:1) Spr 90, p. 51.
2670. HARRIS, Phyllis
"Illinois Quakers." [CoalC] (1) Ag 90, p. 20.
2671. HARRIS, Rennick W.
"The Wonder of the Actual." [Amelia] (6:2, #17) 90, p. 122.
HARRIS, Robert Dassanowsky
See DASSANOWSKY-HARRIS, Robert
2672. HARRISON, Brady
"Holography." [PottPort] (11) 89, p. 46.
2673. HARRISON, Darrell W.
"Clear Purple, Two Stars, Moon." [Amelia] (6:2, #17) 90, p. 20.
2674. HARRISON, Devin
"Shawls." [Quarry] (39:4) Fall 1990, p. 22.
2675. HARRISON, Neil
"Fish Eagles." [Plain] (10:2) Wint 90, p. 27.
2676. HARRISON, Pamela
"Fish Story." [LaurelR] (24:2) Sum 90, p. 12-13.
"Kingdom Come." [CimR] (90) Ja 90, p. 79-80.
"October Clear." [GreenMR] (NS 4:1) Spr-Sum 90, p. 61.
2677. HARROD, Lois Marie
"And These Beds." [JINJPo] (12:1) Spr 90, p. 35.
"Common Rock." [LitR] (33:2) Wint 90, p. 255.
"Crazy Woman Creek." [OxfordM] (6:1) Spr-Sum 90, p. 20.
"Elegy for My Virginity." [JINJPo] (12:1) Spr 90, p. 33-34.
"He Enjoins Her to Be Quiet." [Pearl] (11) Sum 90, p. 7.
"He Enjoins Her to Be Quiet." [Poem] (64) N 90, p. 9.
"Honey Carcass." [Poem] (64) N 90, p. 8.
"How She Got Thin." [PoetL] (85:3) Fall 90, p. 17-18.
"Nothing Can Be Rushed." [HiramPoR] (47) Wint 90, p. 34.
"A Posteriori." [JINJPo] (12:1) Spr 90, p. 33.
"Winslow Homer's *Two Birds Shot in Flight*." [GreenMR] (NS 3:2) Fall-Wint
89-90, p. 69.
2678. HARRS, Norma
"No Expectations." [AntigR] (80) Wint 90, p. 136.
2679. HARRYMAN, Carla
"The Words" (Excerpt). [Verse] (7:1) Spr 90, p. 29.
2680. HARSHMAN, Marc
"Pilot Entries, Ohio River, Sistersville to Belpre." [Pembroke] (22) 90, p. 135-136.
"Song." [Pembroke] (22) 90, p. 131.
"Tom." [Pembroke] (22) 90, p. 132-133.
"You're In It Now." [Pembroke] (22) 90, p. 134.
2681. HART, Henry
"The Accident on Peakskill Mountain." [ConnPR] (9:1) 90, p. 20.
"Christmas Trees." [GrahamHR] (13) Spr 90, p. 35.
"The Hang-Glider." [VirQR] (66:2) Spr 90, p. 273-274.
"The Martyrs' Memorial." [GrahamHR] (13) Spr 90, p. 33-34.
2682. HART, Jack
"Body Language." [NegC] (10:2/3) 90, p. 119.

"A Cock and Fox Story." [Wind] (20:66) 90, p. 20.
"Night Hunting." [Wind] (20:66) 90, p. 20.
"Remembering Butchering." [Parting] (3:2) Wint 90-91, p. 6.
"Teaching Literature." [FourQ] (4:1) Spr 90, p. 22.
2683. HART, Joanne
"Welcome" (To Rebekah Sylvia, born in the Ituri forest, November 2, 1982 . . .).
[SingHM] (17) 90, p. 59.
2684. HART, John W.
"Artist Loft Party." [SlipS] (10) 90, p. 85.
2685. HARTER, Penny
"How Can We Not?" [SingHM] (18) 90, p. 40.
2686. HARTERY, Marion
"Bird -- Watching." [PottPort] (12) 90, p. 10.
"Intimacy." [PottPort] (12) 90, p. 10.
2687. HARTLEY, George
"Contrappunto" (for John Tritica). [CentralP] (17/18) Spr-Fall 90, p. 86-93.
2688. HARTMAN, Charles O.
"Analogue." [TriQ] (80) Wint 90-91, p. 9-10.
"Anthem." [TriQ] (80) Wint 90-91, p. 7-8.
"Extraordinary Instruments." [TriQ] (80) Wint 90-91, p. 11-15.
2689. HARTMAN, Lee
"Flight of the Gulls." [InterPR] (16:2) Fall 90, p. 112.
"A Tempest." [InterPR] (16:2) Fall 90, p. 112.
2690. HARTMAN, Yuki
"Lemonade and Lobsters" (for Sue). [HangL] (57) 90, p. 42.
"Poem: The right hand." [HangL] (57) 90, p. 44.
"To the Edge." [HangL] (57) 90, p. 45.
"What You Read." [HangL] (57) 90, p. 43.
2691. HARTNETT, Ann
"The Builder." [Kalliope] (12:2) 90, p. 26.
2692. HARTNETT, Michael
"Death of an Irishwoman." [Quarry] (39:1) Wint 90, p. 80.
2693. HARTSFIELD, Carla
"Christmas Spell." [PoetryC] (11:1) Spr 90, p. 4.
"Day and Night Baroque." [PoetryC] (11:1) Spr 90, p. 4.
"Grotesques." [PoetryC] (11:1) Spr 90, p. 4.
"Lost Souls." [PoetryC] (11:1) Spr 90, p. 4.
2694. HARTWICH, Jacqueline
"Bird's Eye, Turning From Side to Side." [BellR] (13:1, #27) Spr 90, p. 11.
"Elaboration of a Line from *The Tale of Genji*." [KanQ] (22:1/2) Wint-Spr 90, p. 34.
"The Song of a Bird on a Gravel Shore." [WillowS] (25) Wint 90, p. 42.
"Take Five." [KanQ] (22:1/2) Wint-Spr 90, p. 35.
2695. HARTZELL, Tim N.
"Untitled: I knew a man once." [ChironR] (9:3) Aut 90, p. 25.
2696. HARVEY, Andrew
"Betrothal" (tr. of Rajko Petrov Nogo, w. Svetozar Koljevic). [Screens] (2) 90, p. 63.
"Five Rumi Quatrains" (excerpted from Harvey's "recreations" of Rumi's poems in "Speaking Flame"). [PartR] (57:1) Wint 90, p. 111.
"Landscape" (tr. of Rajko Petrov Nogo, w. Svetozar Koljevic). [Screens] (2) 90, p. 63.
2697. HARVEY, Jack D.
"Too Much Exquisite Petrarch." [Vis] (33) 90, p. 37.
2698. HARVEY, Jean
"Bayou Morning." [Plain] (11:1) Fall 90, p. 32.
2699. HARVEY, Roger
"Hobos on Long Trains." [Bogg] (62) 90, p. 46.
2700. HARVEY, Suzanne (Suzanne R.)
"Case History of a Terrorist." [BlackBR] (11) Spr-Sum 90, p. 5.
"Impotence." [Amelia] (6:1, #16) 90, p. 88.
2701. HARVILCHUCK, Lucia
"Sonnet 67." [EmeraldCR] (1990) c89, p. 5.
2702. HARVOR, Elisabeth
"Afterbirth." [MalR] (93) D 90, p. 52-66.
"Love After a Long Absence (of Love)." [PoetryC] (11:3) Fall 90, p. 27.
"Night Terror." [PraF] (11:4) Wint 90-91, p. 43-44.

"The Sob of the Body." [PoetryC] (11:3) Fall 90, p. 26.
"The Teacher's Story." [PraF] (11:4) Wint 90-91, p. 40-42.
2703. HARWAY, Judith
"The Universe." [ManhatPR] (11) [89?], p. 20.
2704. HASAN, Rabiul
"A Different Disposition" (tr. of Shamim Azad). [Rohwedder] (5) Spr 90, p. 38.
"First Love" (tr. of Shamin Azad). [Amelia] (6:1, #16) 90, p. 48.
"Remaining Inward." [Wind] (20:66) 90, p. 21.
"The Sunflower." [PoetryUSA] (5:2) Sum 90, p. 4.
HASHIMOTO, Kenkichi
    See KITASONO, Katue
2705. HASHIMOTO, Sharon
"Dandelion." [Poetry] (157:1) O 90, p. 14.
"Four Weeks Unemployed: I Fail the Water Department's Lift and Carry Exam."
    [CarolQ] (43:1) Fall 90, p. 99-100.
"Midnight, Listening to the Spotted Hound Seen Wandering Through the Kobashi's
    Farm." [ConnPR] (9:1) 90, p. 19.
"The Mirror of Matsuyama." [Poetry] (157:1) O 90, p. 13.
"The Northeast Field." [Amelia] (6:1, #16) 90, p. 83.
2706. HASKINS, Lola
"Accident" (for David, 1968-1984). [RiverC] (10:2) Spr 90, p. 80.
"Accidentals." [NewYorkQ] (41) Spr 90, p. 79.
"At the Krystal." [RiverC] (10:2) Spr 90, p. 81.
"The Coup." [NewYorkQ] (43) Fall 90, p. 84.
"Florida." [NewYorkQ] (42) Sum 90, p. 87.
"For You at Five." [SouthernPR] (30:2) Fall 90, p. 34.
"Making the Choice." [BelPoR] (40:3) Spr 90, p. 1.
"Outside the Library the Woman in the Safari Dress." [TampaR] (3) 90, p. 12.
"The Pianist Who Keeps a Loaded Gun on Her Piano When She Practices."
    [BelPoJ] (41:2) Wint 90-91, p. 36.
"That House." [WestB] (27) 90, p. 61.
2707. HASS, Robert
"At Yale" (tr. of Czeslaw Milosz, w. the author). [Antaeus] (64/65) Spr-Aut 90, p.
    91-95.
"Creating the World" (tr. of Czeslaw Milosz, w. the author). [NewYorker] (66:2) 26
    F 90, p. 46.
"Gathering Apricots" (tr. of Czeslaw Milosz, w. the author). [NewYorker] (66:37)
    29 O 90, p. 34.
"Happiness." [Antaeus] (64/65) Spr-Aut 90, p. 47.
"Meaning" (tr. of Czeslaw Milosz, w. the author). [Antaeus] (64/65) Spr-Aut 90, p.
    90.
"Our Lady of the Snows." [Antaeus] (64/65) Spr-Aut 90, p. 46.
"The Return of Robinson Jeffers." [Thrpny] (43) Fall 90, p. 12.
"Spring Rain" (original version -- edited version appears in author's book "Human
    Wishes"). [PoetryUSA] ([5:4?]) Wint 90, p. 8.
2708. HASSE, Margaret
"Learning to Love By Hand" (from "In a Sheep's Eye, Darling"). [SwampR] (5)
    Wint-Spr 90, p. 38.
"Looking at Love-Making: I" (from "In a Sheep's Eye, Darling"). [SwampR] (5)
    Wint-Spr 90, p. 39.
2709. HASSELSTROM, Linda M.
"The Glacier on Crystal Lake." [SwampR] (5) Wint-Spr 90, p. 91-92.
2710. HASSLER, Donald M.
"Voyager." [Hellas] (1:1) Spr 90, p. 69.
2711. HASTINGS, Nancy Peters (See also PETERS, Nancy)
"Along the Platte." [Plain] (11:1) Fall 90, p. 9.
"Beyond Words." [Footwork] 90, p. 72.
"Left." [Poetry] (157:2) N 90, p. 68.
"To Sleep and Back." [Plain] (11:1) Fall 90, p. 9.
2712. HATHAWAY, Jeanine
"Arbor Vitae." [KanQ] (22:1/2) Wint-Spr 90, p. 177.
"Sinister." [KanQ] (22:1/2) Wint-Spr 90, p. 178.
2713. HATHAWAY, Jodi
"Alchemist." [Vis] (33) 90, p. 14.
"Day Break." [Vis] (33) 90, p. 13.

211

2714. HATHAWAY, William
"A Close Call." [FloridaR] (17:2) Fall-Wint 90, p. 32-33.
"Guillotine." [CimR] (91) Ap 90, p. 62.
"Looser Talk" (For Barry Goldensohn). [NewEngR] (13:1) Fall 90, p. 99-100.
"Messenger." [CimR] (91) Ap 90, p. 61.
"O My Soul." [SouthernR] (26:1) Ja 90, p. 209-212.
"The Red Stove." [TarRP] (29:2) Spr 90, p. 43.
"Rising Sun" (for Winnie). [PoetL] (85:2) Sum 90, p. 25-27.
"Something to Do" (for Ellen). [SouthernR] (26:1) Ja 90, p. 207-209.
2715. HAUG, James
"At Thirty." [Crazy] (39) Wint 90, p. 65-66.
"Dock of the Bay." [Crazy] (39) Wint 90, p. 67.
"Sunday." [CarolQ] (43:1) Fall 90, p. 98.
2716. HAUGEN, Paal-Helge
"Between Forests" (tr. by Roger Greenwald). [Writ] (21) 89 c1990, p. 68-69.
"(Lake Ohrid, Late Summer)" (tr. by Roger Greenwald). [Writ] (21) 89 c1990, p. 67.
"(Lean In)" (Shostakovich, String Quartet No. 8, tr. by Roger Greenwald). [Writ] (21) 89 c1990, p. 66.
"(MD)" (tr. by Roger Greenwald). [Writ] (21) 89 c1990, p. 65.
2717. HAUK, Barbara
"The Marilyn Monroe Poll." [Pearl] (12) Fall-Wint 90, p. 43.
2718. HAUPTMAN, Terry
"Gathering the Sparks" (for Marina Tsvetaeva). [SpoonRQ] (15:1) Wint 90, p. 51.
2719. HAUSEMER, Georges
"Humpen" (tr. by Karen Subach). [Vis] (34) 90, p. 21.
"Intruder" (tr. by Karen Subach). [Vis] (34) 90, p. 21.
"Nightshift" (tr. by Karen Subach). [Vis] (34) 90, p. 22.
"The Stones" (tr. by Karen Subach). [Vis] (34) 90, p. 20.
"Trees" (tr. by Karen Subach). [Vis] (34) 90, p. 21.
"Zoom" (tr. by Karen Subach). [Vis] (34) 90, p. 22.
2720. HAVEN, Stephen (Stephen Harcourt)
"Centennial." [ManhatR] (5:1) Spr 90, p. 43-44.
"The Drift of It." [GrahamHR] (13) Spr 90, p. 52.
"Light on the Sound." [ManhatR] (5:1) Spr 90, p. 42-43.
2721. HAWK, Dane T. S.
"The Four Corners of the World We Plunge Beyond" (tr. by Peter Jankovic). [Footwork] 90, p. 49.
"Untitled: If you and I were to turn the world inside out . . ." [Footwork] 90, p. 49.
HAWK, Red
   See RED HAWK
2722. HAWKINS, Judith
"The Cigarette Box." [PacificR] (8) 90, p. 49.
"No Strangers." [PacificR] (8) 90, p. 51.
"A Portrait." [PacificR] (8) 90, p. 50.
2723. HAWKINS, Tom
"Bureaucrat with Portraits." [Crucible] (26) Fall 90, p. 80-81.
2724. HAWLEY, Beatrice
"Bones." [Agni] (31/32) 90, p. 217-218.
2725. HAXTON, Brooks
"Again Consider the Wind." [TriQ] (80) Wint 90-91, p. 57-58.
"Garden." [Atlantic] (265:3) Mr 90, p. 80.
"An Orchard Oriole." [Pequod] (31) 90, p. 85-89.
2726. HAYDEN, Dolores
"Gloss." [Witness] (4:1) 90, p. 137.
"Small Business." [ManhatPR] (12) [90?], p. 12.
"Wanting a Child at Forty." [ManhatPR] (11) [89?], p. 44.
HAYES, Mary Cartledge
   See CARTLEDGE-HAYES, Mary
2727. HAYES, N.
"All Souls' Day, Blessing the Graves." [ChrC] (107:30) 24 O 90, p. 960.
2728. HAYMON, Ava Leavell
"Denmother Volunteers at the School Carnival." [Asylum] (6:2) S 90, p. 15.
"Earthworm and Narcissus: Pas de Deux." [Mildred] (4:1) 90, p. 5-7.
"Fence." [NowestR] (28:3/29:1) 90-91, p. 68-69.
"The Holy Ghost Attends Vacation Bible School." [NewDeltaR] (7:1) 90, p. 23.

"The Holy Ghost Goes Out for Little League." [Shen] (40:1) Spr 90, p. 37.
"The Holy Ghost Moves to Kilgore." [NewDeltaR] (7:1) 90, p. 25.
"In Which I Forgive My Mother Her Intentions." [GeoR] (44:1/2) Spr-Sum 90, p. 206-207.
"Sestina Written While Baking Easter Dragons." [Mildred] (4:1) 90, p. 7-8.
"You Better Enjoy This, It's Costing a Fortune" (overheard in a lift line). [Mildred] (4:1) 90, p. 8-10.
2729. HAYNES, Elizabeth
"My Uncle's Chair." [Dandel] (17:1) Spr-Sum 90, p. 8.
2730. HAYNES, William P.
"Forty." [BlackBR] (12) Fall-Wint 90, p. 39.
"The Job." [BlackBR] (12) Fall-Wint 90, p. 38.
2731. HAYS, Mary
"Freud Says My Dreams About Losing Teeth Are Sexual." [CoalC] (1) Ag 90, p. 9.
"To an Ex-Lover and D. H. Lawrence." [CoalC] (1) Ag 90, p. 18-19.
2732. HAYWARD, Camille
"Danse Macabre." [BellArk] (6:1) Ja-F 90, p. 1.
2733. HAYWARD, L. N.
"Auto Wreck." [ChironR] (9:4) Wint 90, p. 18.
2734. HAYWARD, Steve
"Grunion Run with My Imaginary Children." [RiverC] (10:2) Spr 90, p. 11.
2735. HAZEN, James
"Leaving for the Trees." [Paint] (17:33/34) Spr-Aut 90, p. 18.
"Picasso in Shorts." [HiramPoR] (48/49) 90-91, p. 36.
"The Pursuit of Daphne." [CumbPR] (10:1) Fall 90, p. 20.
"Putting Out the Fires." [Paint] (17:33/34) Spr-Aut 90, p. 17.
2736. HAZO, Samuel
"The Most You Least Expect." [TarRP] (29:2) Spr 90, p. 11-12.
"The Time It Takes to See." [AmerS] (59:4) Aut 90, p. 559-560.
"Vietnam." [TarRP] (29:2) Spr 90, p. 10.
2737. HAZZARD, Shirley
"Even If You Weren't My Father" (tr. of Camillo Sbarbaro). [NewYorker] (66:25) 6 Ag 90, p. 36.
"I Wake Alone" (tr. of Camillo Sbarbaro). [NewYorker] (66:40) 19 N 90, p. 52.
HE, Jiang
  See JIANG, He
2738. HE, Xiaozhu
"A Language" (tr. by Edward Morin and Dai Fang). [Screens] (2) 90, p. 43.
2739. HEAD, Ed W.
"Judge." [EmeraldCR] (1990) c89, p. 86.
2740. HEAD, Gwen
"The Baby Dreams." [PraS] (64:1) Spr 90, p. 47-49.
"Cinderella Rediviva." [PraS] (64:1) Spr 90, p. 50.
"Climacteric Sonnet." [PraS] (64:1) Spr 90, p. 49-50.
"La Gamme d'Amour" (after Watteau). [RiverC] (11:1) Fall 90, p. 53-54.
"Home Care" (for Richard Ronan, September 19, 1946-November 3, 1989). [AmerPoR] (19:6) N-D 90, p. 32.
"Ladies of the Farthest Province" (for Richard Ronan, September 19, 1946-November 3, 1989). [AmerPoR] (19:6) N-D 90, p. 32.
"Night Sweats" (for Richard Ronan, September 19, 1946-November 3, 1989). [AmerPoR] (19:6) N-D 90, p. 32.
"World As Will." [RiverC] (11:1) Fall 90, p. 52.
2741. HEAD, Robert
"3 Untitled: I wish you would cum back with your black hose. Bach seems to have been a rather happy man. It took a lot of courage of Xenophanes." [OnTheBus] (2:2/3:1, #6/7) Sum-Fall 90 Wint-Spr 91, p. 99.
"Childhood Sketch" (tr. of Yorges Pavlopoulos, w. Darlene Fife). [Bogg] (62) 90, p. 25.
"The pink in the morning sky." [Bogg] (63) 90, p. 19.
"Untitled: Hwen the eagle was killed" (tr. of Yórges Pavlópoulos). [OnTheBus] (2:2/3:1, #6/7) Sum-Fall 90 Wint-Spr 91, p. 248.
2742. HEALY, Eloise Klein
"Changing the Oil." [Cond] (17) 90, p. 72.
"The Concepts of Integrity and Closure in Poetry As I Believe They Relate to Sappho." [BrooklynR] (7) 90, p. 34-35.

213

2743. HEANEY, Seamus
"Glanmore Revisited." [Antaeus] (64/65) Spr-Aut 90, p. 48-51.
"Seeing Things." [Salm] (88/89) Fall 90-Wint 91, p. 78-81.
"Squarings" (6 selections). [Agni] (29/30) 90, p. 168-173.
2744. HEAP, Chad
"Ozark Halley's." [HarvardA] (124:4) My 90, p. 18.
2745. HEARLE, Kevin
"Epistle." [NewOR] (17:3) Fall 90, p. 93.
2746. HEATH, Melanie
"The Edge of Time Is Near!" (tr. of Witold Suder, w. John Nides). [PoetryUSA]
(5:1) Spr 90, p. 8.
2747. HEATH-STUBBS, John
"The Girl Servant" (tr. of Abbas Baydun, w. May Jayyusi). [Screens] (2) 90, p.
16-18.
"In the Autumn of the House" (tr. of Nouri Jarrah, w. Salwa Jabsheh). [Screens] (2)
90, p. 12.
"Mulberry Leaves for a Naked Tree" (Excerpt, tr. of Taher Riyadh, w. Lena
Jayyusi). [Screens] (2) 90, p. 24.
"The Storm" (tr. of Nouri Jarrah, w. Salwa Jabsheh). [Screens] (2) 90, p. 12.
"Suicide" (tr. of Abbas Baydun, w. May Jayyusi). [Screens] (2) 90, p. 13-15.
"To Murder Time" (Excerpt, tr. of Taher Riyadh, w. Lena Jayyusi). [Screens] (2)
90, p. 24.
2748. HÉBERT, Anne
"Il y a Certainement Quelqu'un." [WashR] (16:2) Ag-S 90, p. 27.
"The Little Towns" (tr. by Jacklyn Potter). [Vis] (32) 90, p. 50-51.
"The Little Towns" (tr. by Jacklyn Potter). [WashR] (16:2) Ag-S 90, p. 27.
"Les Petites Villes." [WashR] (16:2) Ag-S 90, p. 27.
"There Is Certainly Someone" (tr. by Jacklyn Potter). [WashR] (16:2) Ag-S 90, p.
27.
2749. HECHT, Roger
"Communicant." [OnTheBus] (2:2/3:1, #6/7) Sum-Fall 90 Wint-Spr 91, p. 100.
2750. HECHT, Susan
"Cebolla Church." [SoCoast] (8) Spr 90, p. 42.
2751. HEDIN, Robert
"Dies Illae" (tr. of Rolf Jacobsen). [PoetryE] (30) Fall 90, p. 13.
"In Lands Where Light Has Another Color" (14 poems, tr. of Rolf Jacobsen.
Translation Chapbook Series, #14). [MidAR] (10:2) 90, p. 87-117.
"Knitting Needles, Needle and Thread" (tr. of Rolf Jacobsen). [PoetryE] (30) Fall
90, p. 14.
"The Old Liberators." [CarolQ] (42:3) Spr 90, p. 68.
HEERSPINK, Myra Scholz
See SCHOLZ-HEERSPINK, Myra
2752. HEFFERNAN, Michael
"The Atonement." [GettyR] (3:1) Wint 90, p. 216.
"The Blessings of Liberty." [GettyR] (3:1) Wint 90, p. 214.
"The Light of the Living." [GettyR] (3:1) Wint 90, p. 215.
"The Monks at Large." [CharR] (16:1) Spr 90, p. 36.
"A Passerby and His Companions Visit the Widow After the Mad Avenger's
Dreadful Accident." [CharR] (16:1) Spr 90, p. 35.
"Remembering Skye." [CharR] (16:1) Spr 90, p. 35-36.
"The Undertaker's Comfort" (for Tom Lynch). [CharR] (16:1) Spr 90, p. 34.
2753. HEFFERNAN, Virginia
"I Get Sick." [Plain] (10:2) Wint 90, p. 25.
2754. HEFLIN, Jack
"The Color of Money." [PoetryNW] (31:4) Wint 90-91, p. 25.
2755. HEIE, Tom
"Aunt Esther." [RagMag] (8:1) 90, p. 31.
"I Want Silence." [RagMag] (8:1) 90, p. 29.
"Whenever I Hear a Siren." [RagMag] (8:1) 90, p. 30.
2756. HEIGHTON, Steven (Steve)
"Armistice Day, Reading Aeschylus." [Dandel] (17:1) Fall-Wint 90, p. 23.
"In Heraclitus' City." [Dandel] (17:2) Fall-Wint 90, p. 22.
"In University Gardens." [CumbPR] (10:1) Fall 90, p. 11.
"The Machine Gunner" (on targetry and the need for metaphor). [PoetryC] (11:4)
Wint 90, p. 4.
"Photographs of Mountains." [CumbPR] (10:1) Fall 90, p. 9-10.

"Unfinished Buddha, Samed Island." [LitR] (33:3) Spr 90, p. 312.
2757. HEINE, Thomas
"Inheritance." [CumbPR] (9:2) Spr 90, p. 13-14.
2758. HEINE-KOEHN, Lala
"Whom Will I Love When You Are Here?" [PraF] (11:4) Wint 90-91, p. 52.
2759. HEINER, Carson
"If you really want to see yourself" (reprinted from #4, 1981). [Kaleid] (20)
Wint-Spr 90, p. 113.
2760. HEINY, Katherine
"For My Future Biographer." [HangL] (57) 90, p. 46.
"Life After Wuthering Heights." [HangL] (57) 90, p. 48.
"Packing the Car." [HangL] (57) 90, p. 48.
"Times My Father Almost Died." [HangL] (57) 90, p. 47.
2761. HEISLER, Eva
"Margaret Fuller in the Abruzzi Mountains, June 1848." [HayF] (7) Fall-Wint 90, p.
99.
2762. HEITHAUS, Joe
"People Under Water." [NewEngR] (13:2) Wint 90, p. 183-184.
2763. HEITZMAN, Judith Page
"Dresses." [Poem] (64) N 90, p. 54.
"Sleeping in a Small Boat." [Poem] (64) N 90, p. 55.
2764. HEJINIAN, Lyn
"I carry my thoughts in an ocular bucket." [Sequoia] (33:2) Wint 90, p. 25.
"Love substantiates comedy." [Sequoia] (33:2) Wint 90, p. 26.
"Oblivion." [Verse] (7:1) Spr 90, p. 9-12.
"Oxota: A Short Russian Novel" (Selections: Chapters 42-52). [Pequod] (31) 90, p.
69-75.
"The stairs are in a certain relationship." [Sequoia] (33:2) Wint 90, p. 24.
"Xenia" (Excerpt, tr. of Arkadii Dragomoschenko, w. Elena Balashova).
[PoetryUSA] (5:3) Fall 90, p. 19.
"Xenia" (Excerpt, tr. of Arkadii Dragomoshchenko, w. Elena Balashova). [Screens]
(2) 90, p. 5-7.
2765. HEJNA, James
"Recursion." [GettyR] (3:4) Aut 90, p. 670-673.
2766. HEKKANEN, Ernest
"The Doughnut Pantry." [Descant] (21:4/22:1, #71/72) Wint-Spr 90-91, p. 141.
"Humors Off My Coast." [Descant] (21:4/22:1, #71/72) Wint-Spr 90-91, p. 139.
2767. HELGESEN, Lisa
"Poem for the Last Day of March." [Plain] (11:1) Fall 90, p. 11.
2768. HELL, Xavier Hommaire de
"A Hymn to the 21st Century." [PoetryUSA] ([5:4?]) Wint 90, p. 11.
2769. HELLER, Ben A.
"All That Jazz" (tr. of Raúl Barrientos). [MassR] (31:4) Wint 90, p. 549-554.
"Huehueteotl." [PoetryNW] (31:1) Spr 90, p. 16-17.
"Voices." [PoetryNW] (31:1) Spr 90, p. 15-16.
2770. HELLMAN, Sheila
"Ancient Eskimo Masks." [Kalliope] (12:1) 90, c89, p. 62-63.
HELM, Mark Whiteis
See WHITEIS-HELM, Mark
2771. HELMSTETLER, Elizabeth R. S.
"Bliss." [Kalliope] (12:1) 90, c89, p. 59.
2772. HELTON, Michael
"Pyro." [EmeraldCR] (1990) c89, p. 32.
2773. HELWIG, Susan Lucinda
"Freckle Remover." [Bogg] (63) 90, p. 62.
2774. HEMAN, Bob
"Capsule." [Caliban] (8) 90, p. 101.
"Emblem." [Caliban] (8) 90, p. 101.
"The prose poem the perfect incubator for the imagination." [Caliban] (8) 90, p. 166.
2775. HEMENSLEY, Kris
"Like Ulysses" (from "de Chirico"). [Talisman] (5) Fall 90, p. 102-103.
2776. HEMMINGSON, Michael
"Cocaine." [Bogg] (63) 90, p. 49.
2777. HEMPEL, Elise
"Hunting Season" (For my sister Ann). [WillowR] Spr 90, p. 41.

215

HEMSCHEMEYER

2778. HEMSCHEMEYER, Judith
"125. Oh, it was a cold day" (tr. of Anna Akhmatova). [Agni] (29/30) 90, p. 194.
"208. To wake at dawn" (tr. of Anna Akhmatova). [Agni] (29/30) 90, p. 195.
"212. And now you are depressed and despondent" (tr. of Anna Akhmatova). [Agni] (29/30) 90, p. 193.
"289. Betrayal" (tr. of Anna Akhmatova). [Agni] (29/30) 90, p. 196.
"541. This is how I am. I wish you another" (tr. of Anna Akhmatova). [Agni] (29/30) 90, p. 197-198.
"Horror and Passion" (to Anna Akhmatova). [FloridaR] (17:1) Spr-Sum 90, p. 74.
"Life Sentence." [TampaR] (3) 90, p. 62.
"On Finding Your Letter in My Notebook" (to James Wright). [FloridaR] (17:1) Spr-Sum 90, p. 72-73.
"Swiss Thoughts." [FloridaR] (17:1) Spr-Sum 90, p. 75.
2779. HENDERSHOT, Cynthia
"He Died at Dawn" (tr. of Federico García Lorca). [CumbPR] (10:1) Fall 90, p. 17.
"I Swallowed You." [Asylum] (6:2) S 90, p. 21.
"Last Night I Slept Under a Dying Tree." [DogRR] (9:2, #18) Aut 90, p. 5.
"The Moon Rising" (tr. of Federico García Lorca). [CumbPR] (10:1) Fall 90, p. 13.
"A Night of Lovers." [DogRR] (9:2, #18) Aut 90, p. 4.
"Once I Thought I Saw You." [Asylum] (6:2) S 90, p. 21.
"Song of the Barren Orange Tree" (tr. of Federico García Lorca). [CumbPR] (10:1) Fall 90, p. 19.
"Suicide" (Perhaps because he didn't know geometry, tr. of Federico García Lorca). [CumbPR] (10:1) Fall 90, p. 15.
"The Swim." [KanQ] (22:3) Sum 90, p. 137.
2780. HENDERSON, Brian
"Mother Tongue" (Selections: 10 poems). [Descant] (21:1 #68) Spr 90, p. 53-65.
2781. HENDERSON, David
"As Always." [OnTheBus] (2:2/3:1, #6/7) Sum-Fall 90 Wint-Spr 91, p. 101.
2782. HENDERSON, Donna
"Come One Step Closer." [WritersF] (16) Fall 90, p. 76.
2783. HENDERSON, Mark
"The Canadian Legion." [AntigR] (83) Aut 90, p. 105.
"Mountie Knife." [AntigR] (83) Aut 90, p. 106.
"Weir Fisherman." [AntigR] (83) Aut 90, p. 105.
2784. HENDRICKS, Brent
"The Art of Amateur Photography" (for my father). [SouthernR] (26:4) O 90, p. 914-915.
"Devotions" (Honorable Mention Poem, 1989/1990). [KanQ] (22:1/2) Wint-Spr 90, p. 19.
"The Long Haul" (for my grandfather). [TarRP] (29:2) Spr 90, p. 28.
2785. HENDRICKS, John
"Going Home." [Sonora] (18) Fall-Wint 90, p. 40.
2786. HENDRICKSON, Jared
"Echo." [Gargoyle] (37/38) 90, p. 127.
2787. HENDRICKSON, John
"At Haying Time." [WeberS] (7:1) Spr 90, p. 42.
"Penelope." [WeberS] (7:1) Spr 90, p. 41-42.
"The Sweetest Word on Sunday" (A Memory). [WeberS] (7:1) Spr 90, p. 40.
2788. HENIK, Gail
"Ironwood." [Bogg] (63) 90, p. 8.
2789. HENKE, Mark
"O.R. 1964." [HiramPoR] (48/49) 90-91, p. 37-38.
2790. HENN, Mary Ann
"To Each His Own." [CoalC] (1) Ag 90, p. 6.
"Umbilical Cord." [ChironR] (9:3) Aut 90, p. 40.
2791. HENNEDY, Hugh
"During Early Snow." [TarRP] (29:2) Spr 90, p. 20.
"Early Incense." [TarRP] (29:2) Spr 90, p. 19.
"Holloween Morning Before the Mergansers and Others." [TarRP] (29:2) Spr 90, p. 19.
"On Election Day Morning." [TarRP] (29:2) Spr 90, p. 20.
2792. HENNESSY, Eileen B.
"A Deaf Woman Describes a Concert." [ManhatPR] (11) [89?], p. 27.
2793. HENNING, Dianna
"Palm to Palm." [Pembroke] (22) 90, p. 67.

2794. HENNY, Lindy
"Suddenly You Slipped into Sleep" (tr. of Jacques Rancourt). [Vis] (32) 90, p. 48.
2795. HENRY, Lynne
"Incident on the Night Watch in the Pacific High." [PoetryNW] (31:3) Aut 90, p. 23.
2796. HENTZ, Robert R.
"Cove Neighbor." [DustyD] (1:2) O 90, p. 15.
"On the Curvature of Space." [Hellas] (1:1) Spr 90, p. 47.
"A Poem Is Not a Poem." [Hellas] (1:1) Spr 90, p. 45-46.
"Time in His Aging Overtakes All Things Alike" (Aeschylus, "The Eumenides":
286). [Hellas] (1:1) Spr 90, p. 46.
"The Uses of Philosophy." [Hellas] (1:2) Fall 90, p. 231.
2797. HERAKLEITOS
"Fragments" (Selections: 97-102, in Greek and English, tr. by Guy Davenport).
[Zyzzyva] (6:2, #22) Sum 90, p. 134-135.
2798. HERBECK, Ernst
"The Angel" (tr. by Melissa Moore). [Gargoyle] (37/38) 90, p. 27.
"The Dwarf" (tr. by Melissa Moore). [Gargoyle] (37/38) 90, p. 26.
"Der Engel." [Gargoyle] (37/38) 90, p. 27.
"I - You" (tr. by Melissa Moore). [Gargoyle] (37/38) 90, p. 26.
"Ich - Du." [Gargoyle] (37/38) 90, p. 26.
"Das Leben." [Gargoyle] (37/38) 90, p. 27.
"Life" (tr. by Melissa Moore). [Gargoyle] (37/38) 90, p. 27.
"Der Zwerg." [Gargoyle] (37/38) 90, p. 26.
2799. HERBERT, W. N.
"Location Shot." [Verse] (7:2) Sum 90, p. 69.
"Winter Prayer." [Verse] (7:3) Wint 90, p. 88.
2800. HERBERT, Zbigniew
"Elegy for the Departure of Pen, Ink and Lamp" (tr. by John and Bogdana
Carpenter). [Antaeus] (64/65) Spr-Aut 90, p. 52-56.
"Knots" (tr. by Stuart Friebert). [Field] (43) Fall 90, p. 78.
"Mr. Cogito and Pure Thought" (tr. by Stuart Friebert). [Field] (43) Fall 90, p.
79-80.
"On Smoking Things Out" (tr. by Stuart Friebert). [Field] (43) Fall 90, p. 77.
"Our Fear" (tr. by Karen Karleski). [PoetryE] (29) Spr 90, p. 15.
"Sometimes Mr. Cogito Receives Strange Letters Written with Irony, and an Even
Larger Dose of Compassion" (tr. by Stuart Friebert). [Field] (43) Fall 90, p.
81-82.
"What Mr. Cogito Thinks About Hell" (tr. by Stuart Friebert). [Field] (43) Fall 90,
p. 76.
2801. HERBST, Nikki
"Live Girls" (BC Street, Koza, Okinawa, 1971). [Cond] (17) 90, p. 113.
2802. HERLIN, John (John K.)
"Mozart." [PoetryUSA] (5:2) Sum 90, p. 16.
"Wildflowers" (for Mark). [PoetryUSA] (5:1) Spr 90, p. 13.
2803. HERMAN, Maja
"Camerography of Death" (In memoriam Danilo Kis). [Confr] (44/45) Fall 90-Wint
91, p. 186.
2804. HERMANN, Anne Elizabeth
"Listening to the Radio Late at Night." [WillowR] Spr 90, p. 57.
2805. HERNANDEZ, Beatriz Johnston
"San Salvador" (tr. of Jorge Argueta). [CityLR] (4) 90, p. 208-209.
"Stick Horse" (tr. of Jorge Argueta, w. Barbara Jamison). [PoetryUSA] (5:3) Fall
90, p. 16.
"They Drafted My Son" (tr. of Jorge Argueta, w. Barbara Jamison). [PoetryUSA]
(5:3) Fall 90, p. 16.
"To Those Who Ask" (tr. of Jorge Argueta). [CityLR] (4) 90, p. 206-208.
2806. HERNANDEZ, Miguel
"After Love" (tr. by Don Share). [Agni] (29/30) 90, p. 10-12.
"The cemetery lies near" (tr. by Don Share). [PartR] (57:2) Spr 90, p. 270.
"The Last Corner" (tr. by Don Share). [Agni] (29/30) 90, p. 13-14.
"Love rose up between us" (tr. by Don Share). [PartR] (57:2) Spr 90, p. 271.
"You were like the young" (tr. by Don Share). [PartR] (57:2) Spr 90, p. 271.
HERNANDEZ CRUZ, Victor
See CRUZ, Victor Hernandez
2807. HERNCANE, Michael Bruce
"July 4, 1989: The Tyranny of Flags." [WestB] (26) 90, p. 93-94.

HERRERA, Emilia Ayarza de
    See AYARZA DE HERRERA, Emilia
2808. HERRERA-SOBEK, María
    "Aristocracy" (tr. of Alfonso Barrera Valverde). [OnTheBus] (2:2/3:1, #6/7)
        Sum-Fall 90 Wint-Spr 91, p. 250.
    "Existence" (tr. of Alfonso Barrera Valverde). [OnTheBus] (2:2/3:1, #6/7) Sum-Fall
        90 Wint-Spr 91, p. 250.
    "Naked Moon / Luna Desnuda" (43 poems). [BilingR] (14:1/2) 87-88, c89, p.
        51-100.
    "Resolutions" (tr. of Alfonso Barrera Valverde). [OnTheBus] (2:2/3:1, #6/7)
        Sum-Fall 90 Wint-Spr 91, p. 250.
    "Stone Cross" (To my brother Wilfrido, tr. of Alfonso Barrera Valverde).
        [OnTheBus] (2:2/3:1, #6/7) Sum-Fall 90 Wint-Spr 91, p. 251.
2809. HERRICK, Steven
    "10 Years on Acid, 20 Years on King Street." [PoetryUSA] (5:1) Spr 90, p. 3.
2810. HERRON, Elizabeth
    "The Drowned Woman Waits." [NegC] (10:1) 90, p. 20-21.
2811. HERSCH, Greer
    "Says the Morning Voyeur." [HarvardA] (124:2) Ja 90, p. 10.
    "Untitled: I had wondered what color were the trees at night." [HarvardA] (124:2) Ja
        90, p. 35.
2812. HERSCHEL, John
    "Dividing by Zero." [OnTheBus] (2:2/3:1, #6/7) Sum-Fall 90 Wint-Spr 91, p. 102.
    "Poem: My mother dancing in the kitchen." [OnTheBus] (2:2/3:1, #6/7) Sum-Fall 90
        Wint-Spr 91, p. 102.
2813. HERSHEY, Christopher
    "The First Death was Seismic." [Contact] (9:56/57/58) Spr 90, p. 21-22.
    "Forgive Me If I'm Confused." [Contact] (9:56/57/58) Spr 90, p. 22.
2814. HERSHEY, Laura
    "The Prostitutes of Nairobi." [SlipS] (10) 90, p. 69-70.
2815. HERSHON, Robert
    "F Train: Beards Going to Work." [PoetryNW] (31:3) Aut 90, p. 5-7.
    "F Train: The Cloak of Respectability." [WashR] (16:1) Je-Jl 90, p. 15.
    "I'm Just." [PoetryNW] (31:3) Aut 90, p. 4.
    "Kathy I Love You Jerry 1-4-83." [PoetryNW] (31:3) Aut 90, p. 4.
    "Newsreel." [WashR] (16:1) Je-Jl 90, p. 15.
    "November, Stay Calm." [WashR] (16:1) Je-Jl 90, p. 15.
    "Same Title As Before." [PoetryNW] (31:3) Aut 90, p. 3.
2816. HERVAY, Gizella
    "Because Our Drowning Is a Sensation" (tr. by Len Roberts and Mária Kurdi).
        [MidAR] (10:1) 90, p. 53.
    "Inkstains" (tr. by Len Roberts and Kristina Lay). [AmerPoR] (19:5) S-O 90, p. 30.
    "Mert Fuldoklásunk Szenzáció." [MidAR] (10:1) 90, p. 52.
    "Stake-Fire" (tr. by Len Roberts and Kristina Lay). [AmerPoR] (19:5) S-O 90, p.
        31.
2817. HERZBERG, Judith
    "The Farmer" (On "The Fall of Icarus" by Pieter Breughel, tr. by Shirley Kaufman
        and the author). [Trans] (24) Fall 90, p. 56.
    "The Fisherman" (On "The Fall of Icarus" by Pieter Breughel, tr. by Shirley
        Kaufman and the author). [Trans] (24) Fall 90, p. 58.
    "The Sailor" (On "The Fall of Icarus" by Pieter Breughel, tr. by Shirley Kaufman
        and the author). [Trans] (24) Fall 90, p. 57.
2818. HESFORD, Wendy
    "The Father." [PoetL] (85:3) Fall 90, p. 27-28.
2819. HESS, Sonya
    "Gemini's Portrait." [HiramPoR] (47) Wint 90, p. 36.
    "Landscape with Sheep." [Caliban] (8) 90, p. 130.
    "Marguerite's Book." [HiramPoR] (47) Wint 90, p. 35.
    "Sonata for Tuba and Piccolo." [Caliban] (9) 90, p. 135.
    "Trek." [Caliban] (9) 90, p. 134.
2820. HESSE, Karen
    "Under the Stars." [AnthNEW] 90, p. 10.
2821. HESTER, Michele
    "Bees at Termes." [Poetry] (156:4) Jl 90, p. 209.
2822. HETTINGA, Tsjebbe
    "Time and Space" (tr. by Rod Jellema). [Vis] (34) 90, p. 29.

2823. HETTINGER, Gillian
"Memory." [Footwork] 90, p. 51.
"Mother." [Footwork] 90, p. 51.
2824. HETTLINGER, Graham
"During the 'Dirty Little War'." [Field] (43) Fall 90, p. 50-53.
2825. HEWITT, Bernard R.
"At Sundown." [NegC] (10:1) 90, p. 62.
2826. HEWITT, Christopher
"The Couple" (tr. of Nina Cassian). [AmerPoR] (19:1) Ja-F 90, p. 25.
"The Empty House" (reprinted from #15, 1987). [Kaleid] (20) Wint-Spr 90, p. 106.
"When I Am Old I will Be Very Nasty" (reprinted from #6, 1982). [Kaleid] (20)
Wint-Spr 90, p. 107.
"My father was an inspector of weights and measures" (Excerpt from "The
Blaspheming Moon, an Imagined Diary of Artist Achille Emperaire." Reprinted
from #7, 1983). [Kaleid] (20) Wint-Spr 90, p. 107.
2827. HEYD, Michael
"The Family." [WestB] (26) 90, p. 126-127.
2828. HEYEN, William
"Birdhouse." [GeoR] (44:4) Wint 90, p. 599-600.
"The Dead." [AmerPoR] (19:3) My-Je 90, p. 35.
"Dodo." [OntR] (33) Fall-Wint 90-91, p. 57.
"Elmwood." [OntR] (33) Fall-Wint 90-91, p. 54-55.
"The Global Economy." [Pig] (16) 90, p. 59.
"Harpoon." [OntR] (33) Fall-Wint 90-91, p. 58.
"A Jar." [OntR] (33) Fall-Wint 90-91, p. 56.
"Looking Away." [OntR] (33) Fall-Wint 90-91, p. 55.
"Night Flight from England." [PennR] (4:2) 90, p. 115.
"The Real News." [OntR] (33) Fall-Wint 90-91, p. 58.
"Trident II: 720,000 Hiroshimas." [OntR] (33) Fall-Wint 90-91, p. 52-53.
2829. HEYM, Georg
"White Butterflies of Night, So Often Near Me" (tr. by Peter Viereck). [HampSPR]
(Anthology 1975-1990) 90, p. 265.
2830. HIBBARD, T. (Tom)
"Nocturne." [NewRena] (8:1, #24) Spr 90, p. 26.
"Nocturne (No Parking)." [AnotherCM] (21) 90, p. 67.
2831. HICKOFF, Stephen
"For Groucho Marx." [Turnstile] (2:2) 90, p. 113.
"Live from the Rust Belt." [Turnstile] (2:2) 90, p. 112.
2832. HICKS, John V.
"Matisse." [Quarry] (39:4) Fall 1990, p. 32.
"Nocturne." [Quarry] (39:4) Fall 1990, p. 31.
"Prairie Interview." [CrossC] (12:1) 90, p. 22.
"Sculptor." [Quarry] (39:4) Fall 1990, p. 31.
"To a Posthumous Hyena." [Event] (19:2) Sum 90, p. 68.
2833. HICOK, Bob
"Flood." [TarRP] (30:1) Fall 90, p. 31-32.
2834. HIDDE, John
"In Defense of Allen Ginsberg." [PoetryUSA] (5:1) Spr 90, p. 2.
HIDEKO, Furuichi
See FURUICHI, Hideko
2835. HIETTER, James
"Silence = Death." [WillowS] (26) Spr 90, p. 33.
2836. HIGGINS, Anne
"Open Hearted." [FourQ] (4:1) Spr 90, p. 60-61.
2837. HIGGINS, Dick
"At Aqua Aqaba" (for Bob Peters). [Talisman] (5) Fall 90, p. 67-69.
"So." [Asylum] (6:2) S 90, p. 4.
"So Much! So Much!" [Caliban] (8) 90, p. 128-129.
2838. HIGGINS, Frank
"Blips." [NewL] (57:1) Fall 90, p. 68.
2839. HIGGINS, Iain
"A Confession" (tr. of Jan Twardowski, w. Bogdan Czaykowski). [PoetryE] (29)
Spr 90, p. 10-11.
"How many devout books are written" (tr. of Jan Twardowski, w. Bogdan
Czaykowski). [PoetryE] (29) Spr 90, p. 9.
"Intimates and Strangers" (tr. of Jan Twardowski, w. Bogdan Czaykowski).

[PoetryE] (29) Spr 90, p. 12.
"Justice" (tr. of Jan Twardowski, w. Bogdan Czaykowski). [PoetryE] (29) Spr 90, p. 8.
"Telling the Missing Days." [CanLit] (127) Wint 90, p. 30-31.
2840. HIGHTOWER, David C.
"The Fighting Cocks." [LullwaterR] (1:1) Spr 90, p. 8.
2841. HIGHWAY, Tomson
"The Lover Snake." [Descant] (21:1 #68) Spr 90, p. 66-68.
2842. HILBERRRY, Conrad
"Causation." [Shen] (40:3) Fall 90, p. 58.
"Zero." [Shen] (40:3) Fall 90, p. 55-57.
2843. HILBERT, Donna
"Mansions." [Pearl] (11) Sum 90, p. 53.
2844. HILDEBRAND, Holly
"The Marilyn Poem." [Pearl] (12) Fall-Wint 90, p. 30.
2845. HILL, Crag
"The Real Wed Pharoah" [sic]. [PoetryUSA] ([5:4?]) Wint 90, p. 14.
2846. HILL, Daniel
"For the Dirty Thirties." [Footwork] 90, p. 81.
"The Home Team." [Footwork] 90, p. 81.
"The Spirit Of." [Footwork] 90, p. 81.
2847. HILL, Gerald
"A Slow and Painful Debt: Finance and Rain." [Dandel] (17:2) Fall-Wint 90, p. 36-37.
2848. HILL, Howard Erksine
"Silence" (tr. of Slavko Janevski, w. Herbert Kuhner and Bogomil Gjezel). [Footwork] 90, p. 106.
2849. HILL, John Meredith
"Waiting." [GettyR] (3:1) Wint 90, p. 243-244.
2850. HILL, Pamela Steed
"The Gulf." [HampSPR] (Anthology 1975-1990) 90, p. 231-232.
"On Writing Poetry." [Footwork] 90, p. 73.
"Selling the Car." [ApalQ] (33/34) 90, p. 63-64.
2851. HILL, Selima
"On Being Introspective." [Quarry] (39:1) Wint 90, p. 25.
2852. HILLES, Robert
"Canto 12: Canto for a Grotesque Dance." [Event] (19:2) Sum 90, p. 73-75.
"Canto 14." [PoetryC] (11:3) Fall 90, p. 13.
"Father Remember Me." [PraF] (11:4) Wint 90-91, p. 47-48.
"God's Moustache." [Event] (19:1) Spr 90, p. 67.
"A Gust inside a God" (-- Rilke). [MalR] (90) Spr 90, p. 65.
"Jesus." [PraF] (11:4) Wint 90-91, p. 45-46.
"Married To It." [AntigR] (83) Aut 90, p. 123.
"Sometimes My Words Are Right." [AntigR] (83) Aut 90, p. 124.
2853. HILLHOUSE, Martha
"Flannelette." [Grain] (18:4) Wint 90, p. 38.
"Happy Mouth." [Grain] (18:4) Wint 90, p. 38.
2854. HILLMAN, Brenda
"Autumn Moon." [ParisR] (32:114) Spr 90, p. 38-42.
"Bedouin Tent." [Thrpny] (43) Fall 90, p. 28.
"Cosmic Pleasure." [RiverS] (32) [90?], p. 78-79.
"Dark Matter." [Antaeus] (64/65) Spr-Aut 90, p. 57-58.
"A Foghorn." [NewYorker] (65:49) 22 Ja 90, p. 44.
"His Shadow" (Steinberg Case). [Agni] (29/30) 90, p. 135-141.
"Mighty Forms." [Zyzzyva] (6:2, #22) Sum 90, p. 42-43.
"Plath's Hair" (for Patricia Hempl). [MichQR] (29:4) Fall 90, p. 649-650.
"Recycling Center." [Zyzzyva] (6:2, #22) Sum 90, p. 128-129.
"Several Errands." [RiverS] (32) [90?], p. 80-81.
"Small Spaces" (for my mother). [Ploughs] (16:4) Wint 90-91, p. 33.
"The Spell." [Ploughs] (16:4) Wint 90-91, p. 31-32.
2855. HINDLEY, Norman
"Freezing Cigarettes." [ChamLR] (3:2, #6) Spr 90, p. 58.
"Living Without John Rose." [ChamLR] (3:2, #6) Spr 90, p. 56-57.
2856. HINE, Daryl
"Bluebeard's Bungalow." [TriQ] (80) Wint 90-91, p. 25-26.
"Editio Princeps." [TriQ] (80) Wint 90-91, p. 24.

"Kimono." [TriQ] (80) Wint 90-91, p. 28.
"Tabula Rasa?" [TriQ] (80) Wint 90-91, p. 27.
"Woodcuts: Au Bois Dormant." [TriQ] (80) Wint 90-91, p. 23.
2857. HINKHOUSE, David A.
    "A Miracle." [KanQ] (22:1/2) Wint-Spr 90, p. 211.
2858. HINKLE, Charles
    "Rain." [PoetryUSA] (5:1) Spr 90, p. 13.
2859. HINMAN, Mimi Walter
    "Marilyn Lives (in Japan with James Dean)." [Pearl] (12) Fall-Wint 90, p. 42.
2860. HINRICHSEN, Dennis
    "Against Fate." [PoetryNW] (31:1) Spr 90, p. 11-12.
    "On Dante, Scorpions, Love, the Grazing Light." [Field] (43) Fall 90, p. 73-75.
    "Poem of Mercy." [Poetry] (156:2) My 90, p. 64-66.
    "Quadriplegic." [PoetryNW] (31:1) Spr 90, p. 13-15.
    "Song: Newborn." [CarolQ] (42:3) Spr 90, p. 9.
    "Testament." [Poetry] (156:2) My 90, p. 63-64.
2861. HINSHELWOOD, Nigel
    "Plain Voices." [Abraxas] (38/39) 90, p. 141-143.
2862. HINTSA, Ranney
    "The Bubble." [Grain] (18:2) Sum 90, p. 49.
2863. HINZ-PENNER, Raylene
    "Crossing Over." [KanQ] (22:4) Fall 90, p. 108.
2864. HIOTT, Judith
    "The Tandem." [HawaiiR] (14:2, #29) Spr 90, p. 30.
2865. HIPPERT, Rebecca
    "Lake Douglas, September 11, 1988" (for Max Parks). [TarRP] (29:2) Spr 90, p. 35.
2866. HIRSCH, Edward
    "4 A.M." (After Wislawa Szymborska). [NewYorker] (66:35) 15 O 90, p. 104.
    "After the Last Practice" (Grinnell, Iowa, November, 1971). [KenR] (NS 12:1) Wint 90, p. 98-101.
    "First Snowfall: Intimations." [ColR] (NS 17:1) Spr-Sum 90, p. 35-36.
    "Pilgrimage." [Ploughs] (16:4) Wint 90-91, p. 99-102.
    "Posthumous Orpheus." [Nat] (250:14) 9 Ap 90, p. 502.
    "Roman Fall: In Memoriam." [KenR] (NS 12:1) Wint 90, p. 101-103.
    "Roman Fall: In Memoriam." [PoetryC] (11:3) Fall 90, p. 21.
    "The Welcoming." [NewEngR] (13:1) Fall 90, p. 177-179.
2867. HIRSCH, Steven
    "Advocate & Enthusiast." [HeavenB] (8) Wint 90-91, p. 54.
2868. HIRSCHMAN, Jack
    "On a Line by Whitman." [OnTheBus] (2:2/3:1, #6/7) Sum-Fall 90 Wint-Spr 91, p. 103.
    "Organize the Heart." [PoetryUSA] (5:2) Sum 90, p. 17.
2869. HIRSH, Lester
    "Ground Breaking." [CoalC] (2) D 90, p. 18.
2870. HIRSHFIELD, Jane
    "At Nightfall." [Ploughs] (16:1) Spr-Sum 90, p. 155-156.
    "At the Roosevelt Baths." [ColR] (NS 17:1) Spr-Sum 90, p. 93-94.
    "For the raindrop, joy is in entering the river" (Ghazal, tr. of Ghalib). [ParisR] (32:115) Sum 90, p. 45.
    "History as the Painter Bonnard." [Nat] (251:4) 30 Jl-6 Ag 90, p. 143.
    "In every color and circumstance, may the eyes be open for what comes" (Ghazal, tr. of Ghalib). [ParisR] (32:115) Sum 90, p. 45.
    "In the Year Eight Hundred." [ColR] (NS 17:1) Spr-Sum 90, p. 92.
    "Inspiration." [AmerPoR] (19:4) Jl-Ag 90, p. 32.
    "Percolation." [YellowS] (34) Sum 90, p. 15.
    "A Plenitude." [DenQ] (25:1) Sum 90, p. 17-18.
    "The Sting." [ColR] (NS 17:1) Spr-Sum 90, p. 90-91.
    "This Love." [AmerPoR] (19:4) Jl-Ag 90, p. 32.
    "What Falls." [MissouriR] (13:2) 90, p. 178-179.
    "The World." [DenQ] (25:1) Sum 90, p. 19-20.
2871. HIRSHKOWITZ, Lois
    "Nurturer-Torturer." [JINJPo] (12:2) Aut 90, p. 36-37.
2872. HIRZEL, David
    "Building, Naming, Flying." [HampSPR] (Anthology 1975-1990) 90, p. 210-211.
    "Changing Seasons." [HampSPR] (Anthology 1975-1990) 90, p. 210.

HISAYE, Yamamoto
   See YAMAMOTO, Hisaye
HITOMARO, Kakinomoto no (681-729)
   See KAKINOMOTO no HITOMARO (681-729)
2873. HLAVSA, Virginia
   "Husbanding España." [ManhatR] (5:2) Fall 90, p. 19.
2874. HOAGLAND, Bill
   "Beaver Run." [WritersF] (16) Fall 90, p. 94-95.
   "Clepsydra." [WritersF] (16) Fall 90, p. 96.
2875. HOAGLAND, Tony
   "A Badge." [PassN] (11:2) Wint 90, p. 4.
   "Because You Are Weak You Must Be Strong." [PassN] (11:1) Sum 90, p. 19.
   "Bird That Flies." [Crazy] (39) Wint 90, p. 38-39.
   "The Delay." [PassN] (11:2) Wint 90, p. 4.
   "Fire" (for Dean Young). [Crazy] (39) Wint 90, p. 36-37.
   "How I Got to the Desert." [CimR] (90) Ja 90, p. 65-66.
   "Oceanic Kisses." [CimR] (92) Jl 90, p. 106-108.
   "Perpetual Motion." [CimR] (92) Jl 90, p. 110.
   "Second Nature." [CimR] (90) Ja 90, p. 63-64.
   "Smoke." [CimR] (92) Jl 90, p. 108-109.
   "Travellers." [PassN] (11:1) Sum 90, p. 19.
2876. HOAGLAND, William
   "Prelude on Milk River" (A Plainsongs Award Poem). [Plain] (10:2) Wint 90, p. 4.
2877. HOAGUE, Lucy
   "Mr. Fuchs." [AntigR] (83) Aut 90, p. 87.
   "Springtime." [AntigR] (83) Aut 90, p. 88.
2878. HOBBS, Vivian B.
   "At the Terminal." [SouthernHR] (24:2) Spr 90, p. 157.
   "In P'ing-Hsi." [SouthernHR] (24:1) Wint 90, p. 50.
2879. HOCHMAN, Will
   "Caller by the Constant Sea." [DustyD] (1:2) O 90, p. 14.
   "Persistance of Time." [DustyD] (1:2) O 90, p. 14.
   "Theorem." [DustyD] (1:2) O 90, p. 13.
2880. HODES, S. E.
   "I touch a woman who is not mine." [NewYorkQ] (42) Sum 90, p. 76.
2881. HODGES, Lesley
   "Bedroom Walks." [PacificR] (8) 90, p. 67.
   "The Longing." [PacificR] (8) 90, p. 68.
2882. HODGINS, Philip
   "Five Thousand Acre Paddock." [PraS] (64:2) Sum 90, p. 117.
   "Pregnant Cow." [PraS] (64:2) Sum 90, p. 116.
   "Standard Hay Bales." [PraS] (64:2) Sum 90, p. 116.
2883. HOEPPNER, Ed
   "Within Without." [ContextS] (1:1) 89, p. 36.
2884. HOEPPNER, Edward Haworth
   "Bridges We Know." [ThRiPo] (35/36) 90, p. 23.
   "Ghost Pain." [DenQ] (25:2) Fall 90, p. 24-25.
   "The Gulf." [MidAR] (10:2) 90, p. 158-159.
   "Peripheral Vision." [MidAR] (10:2) 90, p. 156-157.
2885. HOEY, Allen
   "First Winter." [Hudson] (43:3) Aut 90, p. 449.
   "Pentimento." [Hellas] (1:2) Fall 90, p. 240-241.
   "Watching Her Sleep." [NoDaQ] (58:3) Sum 90, p. 94.
2886. HOFFMAN, Daniel
   "Great Owl." [HampSPR] (Anthology 1975-1990) 90, p. 7.
   "Speech." [BelPoJ] (40:4) Sum 90, p. 26-27.
   "Ulysses' Abandoned Adventure" (tr. of István Vas, w. Miklós Vajda). [Trans] (24)
     Fall 90, p. 218-222.
   "The Voice" (tr. of István Vas, w. María Kärössy). [Trans] (24) Fall 90, p. 223.
   "Who We Are." [GrandS] (9:3) Spr 90, p. 88-89.
2887. HOFFMANN, Roald
   "The Difference Between Art and Science. II." [WebR] (14:2) Spr 90, p. 89.
   "Here's What Thistles Can Do." [BelPoJ] (41:2) Wint 90-91, p. 4.
   "Into the Stadium." [BelPoJ] (41:2) Wint 90-91, p. 2.
   "Of Scatological Interest." [HampSPR] (Anthology 1975-1990) 90, p. 225.
   "The Sensual Laboratory Assistant." [BelPoJ] (41:2) Wint 90-91, p. 3-4.

2888. HOFMANN, Michael
"Hart Crane." [Quarry] (39:1) Wint 90, p. 26.
2889. HOFMANN, Peter
"Fireworks" (Selection: 4)." [PraF] (11:4) Wint 90-91, p. 66.
2890. HOGAN, Michael
"Lección en Los Compos." [SwampR] (5) Wint-Spr 90, p. 56-57.
"Moon Over Midland." [SwampR] (6) Sum-Fall 90, p. 98-99.
"New Year's Day, 1990." [SwampR] (5) Wint-Spr 90, p. 58-59.
"Planting Trees." [SwampR] (6) Sum-Fall 90, p. 100-101.
"Pocket Knife." [SwampR] (6) Sum-Fall 90, p. 102-104.
"Say the Toughest Thing." [Spirit] (10:2) 90, p. 63-65.
"What We Saw." [SingHM] (18) 90, p. 74-75.
2891. HOGAN, Wayne
"You can't help but." [DogRR] (9:2, #18) Aut 90, p. 52.
2892. HOGGARD, James
"Sounion." [SoCoast] (9) Fall 90, p. 7.
2893. HOGUE, Cynthia
"All You Do to Call" (for Jeanne, an elegy for Michael). [HayF] (6) Sum 90, p.
    59-60.
"Dreamers Twist." [HayF] (6) Sum 90, p. 57-58.
"The Pool Shark, an American Fairytale." [HeavenB] (8) Wint 90-91, p. 44-45.
"The Pool Shark, an American Fairytale." [NegC] (10:1) 90, p. 27-28.
"Scenes From a Romance." [Ploughs] (16:1) Spr-Sum 90, p. 37-38.
2894. HOHM, J. B.
"About the 95 Minutes Spent at Studio 'C'." [Dandel] (17:1) Spr-Sum 90, p. 39.
2895. HOKANSON, Alicia
"Building the Beach Fire." [PoetryUSA] (5:2) Sum 90, p. 11.
"Riding the Conservancy Trail." [PoetryUSA] (5:2) Sum 90, p. 12.
2896. HOLAHAN, Susan
"No One Will Report You." [SlipS] (10) 90, p. 90-91.
2897. HOLBROOK, John
"Petition to Common Sense." [FloridaR] (17:2) Fall-Wint 90, p. 134-135.
2898. HOLDEN, Jonathan
"The Colors of Passion." [Poetry] (156:4) Jl 90, p. 197-198.
"Combine" (For Ruth Moritz). [Poetry] (156:4) Jl 90, p. 198-199.
2899. HOLDEN-RAMIREZ, Lillian
"White Plane in a March Sky." [PacificR] (8) 90, p. 34.
2900. HOLDERBY, Adrienne
"Dark Angels." [CapeR] (25:1) Spr 90, p. 3.
"Saint-Rémy." [CapeR] (25:1) Spr 90, p. 2.
2901. HÖLDERLIN, Friedrich
"Letter from Diotima" (tr. by Harry Gilonis). [Stand] (31:3) Sum 90, p. 32-33.
"You Firmly Built Alps!" (tr. by Michael Hamburger). [Stand] (31:3) Sum 90, p.
    34-35.
2902. HOLIHEN, J. Markham
"The Green and the Brown." [EmeraldCR] (1990) c89, p. 92-93.
2903. HOLINGER, Richard
"How I Spent My Vietnam." [AnotherCM] (21) 90, p. 68-69.
2904. HOLLADAY, Hilary
"The Fat Laugh." [HiramPoR] (48/49) 90-91, p. 39.
"Night of Repercussions." [WestB] (27) 90, p. 46.
"Running from Selinsgrove." [GrahamHR] (13) Spr 90, p. 62-63.
"Summer in Pennsylvania." [WestB] (27) 90, p. 47.
2905. HOLLAHAN, Eugene
"Healing Properties" (dedicated to Jimmy Carter and Habitat for Humanity).
    [LullwaterR] (1:1) Spr 90, p. 73.
"Leap Year." [ChatR] (10:2) Wint 90, p. 64.
"One Hopes For a Monster" (Homage à Godzilla). [LullwaterR] (1:1) Spr 90, p.
    30-31.
"Plumpes Denken." [Hellas] (1:1) Spr 90, p. 62.
2906. HOLLANDER, Jean
"The Calling of the Apostles Peter and Andrew." [PoetL] (85:2) Sum 90, p. 10.
2907. HOLLANDER, John
"Behind the Beaux-Arts." [NewYorker] (66:22) 16 Jl 90, p. 32.
"Quatrains of Doubt and Death." [Antaeus] (64/65) Spr-Aut 90, p. 59-60.
"River Remembered." [YaleR] (79:2) Wint 90, p. 247-250.

"The See-Saw." [NewRep] (203:2/3) 9-16 Jl 90, p. 35.
2908. HOLLANDER, Martha
    "In the Museum." [Poetry] (155:4) Ja 90, p. 281-282.
2909. HOLLEY, Margaret
    "Archetypes of the Collective Unconscious." [PraS] (64:1) Spr 90, p. 45-47.
    "The Blinds." [BelPoR] (40:3) Spr 90, p. 16-17.
    "Bright Wings." [Poem] (63) My 90, p. 56.
    "A Dictionary of Angels" (for Ben). [PraS] (64:1) Spr 90, p. 43-45.
    "In a Dark Age." [KanQ] (22:3) Sum 90, p. 161.
    "Morning Star." [Poem] (63) My 90, p. 53.
    "My Feathered Friend." [KanQ] (22:3) Sum 90, p. 160.
    "The Smoke Tree." [Poem] (63) My 90, p. 55.
    "Swimming in the Trees." [KanQ] (22:3) Sum 90, p. 162.
    "Trash." [MichQR] (29:4) Fall 90, p. 742-743.
    "Winter Solstice." [PraS] (64:1) Spr 90, p. 42-43.
    "Yellow." [Poem] (63) My 90, p. 54.
2910. HOLLO, Anselm
    "The Trees, All Their Green" (Excerpts, tr. of Paavo Haavikko). [Writ] (21) 89
        c1990, p. 50-54.
2911. HOLLOWAY, Glenna
    "Sunrise in St. Louis." [WebR] (14:2) Spr 90, p. 83.
    "To the Trees" (adaption of poem by Victor Hugo). [NewRena] (8:1, #24) Spr 90,
        p. 29.
2912. HOLLOWAY, John
    "Starting as Weather-Lore." [Hudson] (43:1) Spr 90, p. 103.
2913. HOLM, Sven
    "Churchyard in Umanaq" (from "Luftens Temperament," 1980, tr. by Paula
        Hostrup-Jessen). [CimR] (92) Jl 90, p. 19.
    "The Greenlanders' Problem" (from "Luftens Temperament," 1980, tr. by Paula
        Hostrup-Jessen). [CimR] (92) Jl 90, p. 20.
    "Greenland's History" (or the history of the Danes on Greenland, from "Luftens
        Temperament," 1980, tr. by Paula Hostrup-Jessen). [CimR] (92) Jl 90, p. 21.
2914. HOLMAN, Bob
    "Here's an Example." [Talisman] (4) Spr 90, p. 80.
    "Snare" (for Charlie Parker). [Talisman] (4) Spr 90, p. 80.
2915. HOLMES, Elizabeth
    "Things Past." [Poetry] (155:6) Mr 90, p. 404.
2916. HOLMES, James S
    "Heads" (tr. of Wiel Kusters). [Trans] (24) Fall 90, p. 15.
2917. HOLMGREN, Mark
    "Metamorphosis" (for my daughter, Sarah). [Grain] (18:2) Sum 90, p. 29.
    "Stum of Love." [Grain] (18:2) Sum 90, p. 29.
2918. HOLST, Adriaan Roland
    "The Prince Returned" (Painting: Portrait of William of Orange by Antonie Mor, tr.
        by Manfred Wolf). [Trans] (24) Fall 90, p. 46-47.
2919. HOLT, Beatrice G.
    "A Dot Against the Moon." [RagMag] (8:2) 90, p. 66.
    "St. Croix June." [RagMag] (8:2) 90, p. 67.
    "Still Life with Brioche 1880, Edouard Manet." [KanQ] (22:3) Sum 90, p. 140.
    "Walking July 13 Down Columbia Street in Boston Way Down." [RagMag] (8:2)
        90, p. 68.
    "The Wind Last Night." [SoCoast] (8) Spr 90, p. 40-41.
2920. HOLT, Lois
    "Secrets." [Crucible] (26) Fall 90, p. 55-56.
    "Watching a Fat Woman on the Beach." [Crucible] (26) Fall 90, p. 57.
2921. HOLT, Rochelle Lynn
    "Out of Hibernation." [ChironR] (9:3) Aut 90, p. 21.
    "The Secret Truth." [JINJPo] (12:1) Spr 90, p. 30-31.
HOLTEN, Dan von
    See Von HOLTEN, Dan
2922. HOLUB, Miroslav
    "1751" (tr. by David Young, w Dana Hábová and the author). [AmerPoR] (19:2)
        Mr-Ap 90, p. 4.
    "The Clock" (tr. by David Young and Dana Hábová). [Field] (42) Spr 90, p. 7.
    "The Fall from the Green Frog" (tr. by David Young and Dana Hábová). [Field] (42)
        Spr 90, p. 11.

"Fish" (tr. by David Young and Dana Hábová). [Field] (42) Spr 90, p. 8-9.
"Glass" (tr. by David Young and Dana Hábová). [Field] (42) Spr 90, p. 10.
"Great Ancestors" (tr. by David Young, w Dana Hábová and the author).
    [AmerPoR] (19:2) Mr-Ap 90, p. 5.
"Heart Transplant" (tr. by David Young and Dana Hábová). [Field] (42) Spr 90, p.
    5-6.
"Night Calamities" (tr. by David Young, w Dana Hábová and the author).
    [AmerPoR] (19:2) Mr-Ap 90, p. 5.
"Parasite" (tr. by David Young, w Dana Hábová and the author). [AmerPoR] (19:2)
    Mr-Ap 90, p. 3.
"Skinning" (tr. by David Young, w Dana Hábová and the author). [AmerPoR] (19:2)
    Mr-Ap 90, p. 4.
"What Else" (tr. by David Young, w Dana Hábová and the author). [AmerPoR]
    (19:2) Mr-Ap 90, p. 3.
2923. HOMER
    "The Death of Hector" (The Iliad, Book XXII, tr. by Robert Fagles). [GrandS] (9:3)
        Spr 90, p. 113-128.
2924. HOMER, Art
    "Kingbird." [NewL] (57:1) Fall 90, p. 95.
    "The Value of Art." [KanQ] (22:1/2) Wint-Spr 90, p. 138.
HOMMAIRE De HELL, Xavier
    See HELL, Xavier Hommaire de
HONG, Guo
    See GUO, Hong
2925. HONIG, Edwin
    "Grave Goods." [BelPoJ] (40:4) Sum 90, p. 28-31.
2926. HONZA, Annabelle
    "When we become like two drunken suns" (tr. of Yvonne Caroutch). [PoetryE] (30)
        Fall 90, p. 72.
2927. HOOD, Mary A.
    "Miss Johnson Poems" (5 poems). [EmeraldCR] (1990) c89, p. 41-44.
2928. HOOGESTRAAT, Jane
    "The Aesthetics of a Chicago Winter." [HighP] (5:3) Wint 90-91, p. 94-95.
    "Against the Urban Night." [HighP] (5:3) Wint 90-91, p. 92.
    "Asphodel." [Poem] (64) N 90, p. 25.
    "Dark, Small-Town Streets." [SouthernR] (26:2) Ap 90, p. 316-317.
    "The Last Class in Rhetoric." [Poem] (64) N 90, p. 26.
    "Linear Time." [HighP] (5:3) Wint 90-91, p. 91-92.
2929. HOOGLAND, Cornelia
    "Details." [PraF] (11:4) Wint 90-91, p. 50.
    "Maples Yellow as the Centre of My Cat's Eye." [Grain] (18:4) Wint 90, p. 19.
    "The One Longed For Is Never Enjoyed in the Anticipated Way." [Grain] (18:4)
        Wint 90, p. 20.
    "The Thing Which in the Waking World Comes Nearest to a Dream Is a Night Alone
        in a Big Town." [PraF] (11:4) Wint 90-91, p. 49.
    "True Religion" (for Oom Frans). [Grain] (18:4) Wint 90, p. 21.
    "Watching My Mother Dress." [Calyx] (13:1) Wint 90-91, p. 37.
    "Your Full-Cupboard Strength." [Calyx] (13:1) Wint 90-91, p. 36.
2930. HOOPER, Edward L.
    "The Visit" (for Ivan Anderson. Reprinted from #14, 1987). [Kaleid] (20) Wint-Spr
        90, p. 42.
2931. HOOPER, Patricia
    "At the Corner of the Eye." [PassN] (11:2) Wint 90, p. 6.
2932. HOOPER, Virginia
    "Drawing Room Drama." [LitR] (33:4) Sum 90, p. 463.
    "The Event." [Talisman] (5) Fall 90, p. 81.
    "Released Persona." [CentralP] (17/18) Spr-Fall 90, p. 18-19.
    "Signs." [CentralP] (17/18) Spr-Fall 90, p. 19.
    "Vacating the Premises." [LitR] (33:4) Sum 90, p. 464-465.
2933. HOOVER, Paul
    "Death." [CityLR] (4) 90, p. 156-158.
    "Lily Fiero." [CityLR] (4) 90, p. 155.
2934. HOPKINS, Gerard Manley
    "(Carrion Comfort)." [Field] (43) Fall 90, p. 34.
    "Epithalamion." [Field] (43) Fall 90, p. 39-40.
    "Felix Randal." [Field] (43) Fall 90, p. 22.

"God's Grandeur." [Field] (43) Fall 90, p. 9.
"Inversnaid." [SouthernR] (26:3) Jl 90, p. 479-480.
"Spelt from Sibyl's Leaves." [Field] (43) Fall 90, p. 30.
"Thou Art Indeed Just, Lord." [SouthernR] (26:3) Jl 90, p. 480-481.
2935. HOPPENTHALER, John
    "Gazebo." [KanQ] (22:3) Sum 90, p. 214.
2936. HOPPER, Paul
    "#3. From the half-dark hall, abruptly" (tr. of Osip Mandel'shtam). [WashR] (16:2)
        Ag-S 90, p. 14.
    "#286. We live without feeling a country beneath us" (about Stalin, tr. of Osip
        Mandel'shtam). [WashR] (16:2) Ag-S 90, p. 14.
    "#303. And this, what street is this?" (tr. of Osip Mandel'shtam). [WashR] (16:2)
        Ag-S 90, p. 14.
    "#367. Armed with the eyesight of the narrow wasps" (tr. of Osip Mandel'shtam).
        [WashR] (16:2) Ag-S 90, p. 14.
2937. HORACE
    "The Bandusian Fountain" (Odes, III, XIII, in Latin and English, tr. by Johann
        Moser). [Hellas] (1:1) Spr 90, p. 90.
2938. HORAN, Elizabeth
    "Untitled: It was in the plains" (tr. of Marjorie Agosín). [Agni] (29/30) 90, p.
        209-211.
2939. HORAN, Katy
    "The Leaf." [Amelia] (6:2, #17) 90, p. 54.
HORGAN, Chris Ward
    See WARD-HORGAN, Chris
2940. HORNE, Jennifer
    "How We Imagine the Famous, As Our Mother" (for my sister). [CarolQ] (42:2)
        Wint 90, p. 76.
2941. HORNE, Lewis
    "Exit, Pursued by a Bear." [SouthernR] (26:1) Ja 90, p. 213-214.
    "Festology." [CumbPR] (10:1) Fall 90, p. 21.
    "His Daughters." [SouthernR] (26:1) Ja 90, p. 215-216.
    "Rural Free Delivery, 1952." [CumbPR] (10:1) Fall 90, p. 22.
    "Seeing Plain." [SouthernR] (26:1) Ja 90, p. 216-217.
2942. HORNIK, Jessica
    "Instructions for the Onset of Winter." [CarolQ] (42:2) Wint 90, p. 9.
2943. HORNING, Ron
    "Just Before Sailing" (w. David Lehman). [Pequod] (31) 90, p. 145-158.
    "Second Nature." [NewYorker] (66:32) 24 S 90, p. 94.
    "The Vocalist" (Selections: 1-3, w. David Lehman). [Shiny] (5) 90, p. 13-15.
2944. HOROWITZ, Mikhail
    "Deep Listening." [HeavenB] (8) Wint 90-91, p. 15.
    "Passover." [HeavenB] (8) Wint 90-91, p. 24.
    "Real Eyes." [HeavenB] (8) Wint 90-91, p. 24.
    "What I'm Doing at This Very Moment in 12 Parallel Universes." [HeavenB] (8)
        Wint 90-91, p. 26.
2945. HOROWITZ, Rose
    "Basking in Blue." [OnTheBus] (2:2/3:1, #6/7) Sum-Fall 90 Wint-Spr 91, p.
        104-105.
    "Cactus Salad." [OnTheBus] (2:1, #5) Spr 90, p. 73.
    "Headless is Delos." [OnTheBus] (2:2/3:1, #6/7) Sum-Fall 90 Wint-Spr 91, p. 104.
2946. HORSTING, Eric
    "The Death of Harry S. Truman." [HawaiiR] (15:1, #31) Wint 90, p. 84.
    "Holland, May 1940." [Agni] (31/32) 90, p. 245.
    "Lament." [HawaiiR] (14:2, #29) Spr 90, p. 43.
    "Swimming Laps and Mozart." [MidAR] (10:2) 90, p. 28.
    "Writing Again, In Maine." [GreenMR] (NS 4:1) Spr-Sum 90, p. 113.
2947. HORSTLING, Eric
    "Assurance." [NoDaQ] (58:2) Spr 90, p. 70.
    "Mortality." [NoDaQ] (58:2) Spr 90, p. 71.
2948. HORTON, Barbara
    "Joining In." [WebR] (14:2) Spr 90, p. 92.
    "The Neighbor's Child." [WillowR] Spr 90, p. 67.
2949. HORVATH, Brooke
    "The Closet." [MissouriR] (13:2) 90, p. 148-150.
    "Consolation at Ground Zero." [TarRP] (30:1) Fall 90, p. 4-5.

"My Girl" (For my daughter, Susan Alessandra). [Poetry] (156:3) Je 90, p.
154-156.
2950. HORVATH, Elemér
"Letters to Nowhere" (Selections: VI, VIII-XI, XV, XVII, XXI, tr. by Nicholas
Kolumban). [AnotherCM] (21) 90, p. 70-73.
2951. HORVATH, Linda M.
"Inhibitions." [ChironR] (9:4) Wint 90, p. 17.
"No Grand Answers." [Bogg] (63) 90, p. 17.
"Out of Step." [Bogg] (62) 90, p. 19.
2952. HORVATH, Miklós
"Day by Day" (tr. of Sándor Csoóri, w. Len Roberts). [ArtfulD] (18/19) 90, p. 24.
"Day by Day" (tr. of Sándor Csoóri, w. Len Roberts). [Chelsea] (49) 90, p. 122.
2953. HOSPITAL, Carolina
"Alma Mater." [Americas] (18:3/4) Fall-Wint 90, p. 108.
"Finding Home." [Americas] (18:3/4) Fall-Wint 90, p. 109.
"Miami Mimesis." [Americas] (18:3/4) Fall-Wint 90, p. 106.
"The Old Order." [Americas] (18:3/4) Fall-Wint 90, p. 110.
"A Visit to West New York." [Americas] (18:3/4) Fall-Wint 90, p. 107.
2954. HOSPODAR, Riq
"Dwelling On/In." [PaintedB] (40/41) 90, p. 155.
2955. HOSTETLER, Ann
"Painting with My Daughter." [AmerS] (59:1) Wint 90, p. 66.
2956. HOSTRUP-JESSEN, Paula
"Churchyard in Umanaq" (from "Luftens Temperament," 1980, tr. of Sven Holm).
[CimR] (92) Jl 90, p. 19.
"Depression Weather" (from "Weather Days : Vejrdage," 1980, tr. of Villy
Sørensen). [CimR] (92) Jl 90, p. 43.
"Gesture" (from "Ode to an Octopus and Other Love Poems," Gyldendal, 1975, tr.
of Henrik Nordbrandt). [CimR] (92) Jl 90, p. 26.
"The Greenlanders' Problem" (from "Luftens Temperament," 1980, tr. of Sven
Holm). [CimR] (92) Jl 90, p. 20.
"Greenland's History" (or the history of the Danes on Greenland, from "Luftens
Temperament," 1980, tr. of Sven Holm). [CimR] (92) Jl 90, p. 21.
"Parikia" (from "Glas," Gyldendal, 1976, tr. of Henrik Nordbrandt). [CimR] (92) Jl
90, p. 26.
2957. HOTALING, Debra
"At 81." [SouthernR] (26:3) Jl 90, p. 675.
"Hill Estate Auction -- Stella, Missouri." [SouthernR] (26:3) Jl 90, p. 673-674.
"Letter to My Great, Great, Great Aunt Olive Strong Tenney." [SouthernR] (26:1) Ja
90, p. 198-199.
2958. HOUGEN, Judith
"Flagman, Northeast Montana." [KanQ] (22:1/2) Wint-Spr 90, p. 178-179.
2959. HOUSTMAN, Dale M.
"Beyond India." [Caliban] (8) 90, p. 118-119.
2960. HOUSTON, Beth
"Dad." [Comm] (117:19) 9 N 90, p. 634.
"Lullaby." [Comm] (117:18) 26 O 90, p. 615.
"Spell Against Love." [Kalliope] (12:1) 90, c89, p. 27.
"Woman in a Windshield." [KanQ] (22:3) Sum 90, p. 85.
HOUTEN, Lois van
See Van HOUTEN, Lois
HOVANESSIAN, Diana Der
See DER-HOVANESSIAN, Diana
2961. HOWARD, Ben
"Augustan Elegies." [PraS] (64:2) Sum 90, p. 54-55.
"Lament for the Holy Places." [Poetry] (157:2) N 90, p. 75.
"Letter." [PraS] (64:2) Sum 90, p. 53.
"The Minor Poets: An Afterlife." [Poetry] (155:4) Ja 90, p. 280.
"November." [Poetry] (157:2) N 90, p. 74.
"Ubi Caritas." [SewanR] (98:2) Spr 90, p. 188-190.
2962. HOWARD, Eugene
"Poem for Joe Beam." [PaintedB] (40/41) 90, p. 184.
"The Shadow Knows." [PaintedB] (40/41) 90, p. 185.
2963. HOWARD, Frances Minturn
"In Tiananmen Square." [Agni] (31/32) 90, p. 231.

227

2964. HOWARD, Richard
"And Tell Sad Stories" (in memoriam Donald Barthelme). [YaleR] (79:4) Sum 90
c1991, p. 745-746.
"A Beatification." [GrandS] (9:2) Wint 90, p. 38-40.
"Theory of Flight, 1908" (for Barry Weller). [KenR] (NS 12:1) Wint 90, p. 67-69.
"The Victor Vanquished" (for Tom, 1989). [Antaeus] (64/65) Spr-Aut 90, p. 61-62.
"What Word Did the Greeks Have for It?" [Thrpny] (43) Fall 90, p. 6.
2965. HOWARTH, Janet
"Love Letters." [Grain] (18:4) Wint 90, p. 79.
2966. HOWE, Fanny
"Amtrak." [NewAW] (6) Spr 90, p. 10-14.
"Our Heaven's Words." [NewYorker] (65:49) 22 Ja 90, p. 112.
2967. HOWE, Susan
"Nether John and John Harbinger" (Excerpts). [Verse] (7:1) Spr 90, p. 66-68.
"The Noncomformist's Memorial." [Conjunc] (15) 90, p. 100-109.
"To My Brother in His Casket." [LitR] (33:2) Wint 90, p. 258.
2968. HOWE, Susan Elizabeth
"Mountains Behind Her." [TarRP] (30:1) Fall 90, p. 14-15.
"Nor Am I Who I Was Then." [NewYorker] (66:43) 10 D 90, p. 58.
2969. HOWELL, Bill
"For the Time Being." [PottPort] (12) 90, p. 34-35.
"The Mist" (For Beverley). [PottPort] (12) 90, p. 33.
2970. HOWELL, Christopher
"Bird Love." [PoetryNW] (31:3) Aut 90, p. 37-38.
"The Christian Science Minotaur." [NowestR] (28:1) 90, p. 91.
"The Good Job." [MidAR] (10:2) 90, p. 29.
"The Lover Rejects Himself." [PoetryNW] (31:2) Sum 90, p. 9-10.
"Love's Fugitive on the Run." [PoetryNW] (31:3) Aut 90, p. 36-37.
"Poem Based on a Chinese Character Meaning 'A Fire to Notify Heaven'."
[WillowS] (26) Spr 90, p. 80.
"Talk with the Moon." [PoetryNW] (31:2) Sum 90, p. 8-9.
2971. HOWER, Mary
"Salt Flats." [Iowa] (20:1) Wint 90, p. 103.
2972. HOWES, Barbara
"Joyful Sacrifice" (tr. of Nina Cassian, w. Kim Cushman). [AmerPoR] (19:1) Ja-F
90, p. 25.
2973. HOYEM, Andrew
"Bluebirds." [Zyzzyva] (6:1 #21) Spr 90, p. 47.
2974. HOYOS, Angela de
"In Memoriam: William C. Velásquez." [Americas] (18:2) Sum 90, p. 41-43.
"My Mama Done Told Me." [Americas] (18:2) Sum 90, p. 47.
"The Placebo Poem" (being a toast to Samuel Beckett's 'Waiting for Godot').
[Americas] (18:2) Sum 90, p. 40.
"Ramillete para Elena Poniatowska." [Americas] (18:2) Sum 90, p. 44.
"When Conventional Methods Fail." [Americas] (18:2) Sum 90, p. 39.
"Xochitl-Poem for Paul Perry, Joseph Booker, and the Palo Alto Writer's Guild."
[Americas] (18:2) Sum 90, p. 45-46.
2975. HOYT, Don A.
"Innocent Action." [FloridaR] (17:2) Fall-Wint 90, p. 62.
2976. HSIEH, T'iao
"Going to Hsüan-ch'eng Past Hsin-lin Beach toward Pan-ch'iao" (in Chinese and
English, tr. by Matthew Flannery). [CumbPR] (9:2) Spr 90, p. 8-9.
2977. HSU, Derrick
"Razor Stubble." [Gargoyle] (37/38) 90, p. 137.
2978. HUANG, Bangjun
"A Narrow Alley" (in Chinese and English, tr. by Ji Tianxiang). [PaintedB] (40/41)
90, p. 48-49.
2979. HUDDLE, David
"Asylum." [Poetry] (156:2) My 90, p. 77-78.
"The Birds." [KenR] (NS 12:4) Fall 90, p. 106-107.
"Thinking About My Father." [KenR] (NS 12:4) Fall 90, p. 107-109.
"Tour of Duty" (4 selections). [HampSPR] (Anthology 1975-1990) 90, p. 223-224.
2980. HUDECHEK, Robin
"For My Mother (Yes, You Are Happy)." [Caliban] (8) 90, p. 157.
"Pentecost." [Caliban] (8) 90, p. 156.

2981. HUDGINS, Andrew
"Botticelli: The Cestello Annunciation." [Hudson] (43:1) Spr 90, p. 65.
"Crucifixion: Montgomery, Alabama." [NewRep] (202:13) 26 Mr 90, p. 32.
"Gauguin: The Yellow Christ." [Hudson] (43:1) Spr 90, p. 64.
"Hunting with My Brother." [Hudson] (43:1) Spr 90, p. 63.
"A Kiss in Church." [NegC] (10:2/3) 90, p. 189.
"Loose Change." [NegC] (10:2/3) 90, p. 188-189.
"My Father's Corpse." [Hudson] (43:1) Spr 90, p. 62.
"New Headstones at the Shelby Springs Confederate Cemetery." [Hudson] (43:1)
    Spr 90, p. 61-62.
"Teevee With Grandmomma." [Ploughs] (16:1) Spr-Sum 90, p. 55.
"Yellow Jackets." [Ploughs] (16:1) Spr-Sum 90, p. 56-57.
2982. HUDSON, J. Blaine
"The Illusion of Necessity" (May 25, 1969). [BlackALF] (24:3) Fall 90, p. 546.
2983. HUDSON, Marc
"Charm for an Imagined Girl." [PraS] (64:4) Wint 90, p. 40-41.
"Grace" (After Eugene Smith's photographs of the Minamata victims). [PraS] (64:4)
    Wint 90, p. 42-44.
2984. HUERTA, David
"Incurable" (Selection: Chapter I: "Simulacrum," tr. by Linda Scheer). [Caliban] (9)
    90, p. 111-115.
2985. HUEZO MIXCO, Miguel
"This Immense Oak" (tr. by Elizabeth Gamble Miller). [MidAR] (10:1) 90, p. 105.
HUFFSTICKER, Albert
    See HUFFSTICKLER, Albert
2986. HUFFSTICKLER, Albert
"Augury." [Abraxas] (38/39) 90, p. 135.
"The Certitude of Laundromats" (for Sylvia). [SwampR] (5) Wint-Spr 90, p. 68-69.
"Distraction." [Gypsy] (15) 90, p. 3.
"Monica." [Abraxas] (38/39) 90, p. 136.
"Simplicity" (From a Dream). [CoalC] (2) D 90, p. 4.
"Summation." [ChamLR] (4:1, #7) Fall 90, p. 128.
2987. HUGGINS, Peter
"Jack Talks about Politics in Lee County." [ChatR] (10:3) Spr 90, p. 18.
2988. HUGHES, Henry (Henry J.)
"Calling Down the Geese." [MalR] (91) Je 90, p. 79.
"The Fox." [BelPoR] (40:3) Spr 90, p. 4-5.
"On Audubon's *Passenger Pigeon*." [MalR] (91) Je 90, p. 78.
"Once There Were Great Birds in the World: The Auk." [CumbPR] (9:2) Spr 90, p.
    15-16.
2989. HUGHES, Ingrid
"How Do You Know." [ManhatPR] (12) [90?], p. 26.
2990. HUGHES, John
"The Jackdaw." [Quarry] (39:1) Wint 90, p. 81.
2991. HUGHES, Langston
"Motto." [EngJ] (79:4) Ap 90, p. 23.
2992. HUGHES, Peter
"Academia." [Verse] (7:3) Wint 90, p. 98.
"Election Results." [Verse] (7:3) Wint 90, p. 98.
"Giulio Agricola" (for Simon's birthday). [Verse] (7:3) Wint 90, p. 98.
2993. HUGHES, Sophie
"Oxherding." [Chelsea] (49) 90, p. 141.
2994. HUGO, Victor
"Aux Arbres." [NewRena] (8:1, #24) Spr 90, p. 28.
"To the Trees" (adapted by Glenna Holloway). [NewRena] (8:1, #24) Spr 90, p. 29.
2995. HUIDOBRO, Vicente
"House" (tr. by Alfredo Franco). [NewOR] (17:2) Sum 90, p. 37.
2996. HULL, David
"The Survivor." [MalR] (92) S 90, p. 66-67.
2997. HULL, Lonnie
"Ghosts." [RagMag] (8:1) 90, p. 70.
"Tree Cutting." [RagMag] (8:1) 90, p. 71.
2998. HULL, Lynda
"Bar Xanadu." [IndR] (13:2) Spr 90, p. 51-52.
"Studies from Life." [IndR] (13:2) Spr 90, p. 53-54.
"Vita Brevis." [NoAmR] (275:4) D 90, p. 24-25.

229

HULSE

2999. HULSE, Michael
   "Raffles Hotel" (Singapore). [Quarry] (39:1) Wint 90, p. 27-28.
3000. HUMES, Harry
   "An August White." [PoetryNW] (31:2) Sum 90, p. 23.
   "Birds in August." [Shen] (40:4) Wint 90, p. 87.
   "The Bootleg Coal Hole." [PennR] (4:2) 90, p. 51.
   "Brackish Water." [WestB] (27) 90, p. 22.
   "The Lady Oboeist Uses a Razor Blade to Make Her Reeds." [WestB] (27) 90, p.
      23.
   "Mine Settlement." [PoetryNW] (31:2) Sum 90, p. 22-23.
   "The Way They Come Ashore." [Shen] (40:4) Wint 90, p. 88.
3001. HUMES, Steve
   "Skeleton." [PoetryUSA] (5:3) Fall 90, p. 27.
3002. HUMMER, T. R.
   "Courtly Love." [Shen] (40:1) Spr 90, p. 22-23.
   "First Assembly of God." [GeoR] (44:4) Wint 90, p. 633-634.
   "Green Mountain Fever" (for my daughter). [Shen] (40:1) Spr 90, p. 24-25.
   "Worldy Beauty." [Ploughs] (16:4) Wint 90-91, p. 198-199.
3003. HUMPHRIES, Jeff
   "Cat in Window, Late Winter." [TarRP] (30:1) Fall 90, p. 10.
   "Yard Man." [TarRP] (30:1) Fall 90, p. 11.
3004. HUNT, Leigh
   "Our Secret Garden." [Amelia] (6:2, #17) 90, p. 115.
3005. HUNT, William
   "Through the Red Sea (After the Paintings of Anselm Kiefer)" (Excerpts). [TriQ]
      (80) Wint 90-91, p. 88-92.
3006. HUNTER, Donnell
   "The Broker." [HawaiiR] (14:2, #29) Spr 90, p. 81-82.
   "Catalpa." [Plain] (10:2) Wint 90, p. 15.
   "Dream People." [HawaiiR] (14:2, #29) Spr 90, p. 84.
   "Finding Your Job." [HawaiiR] (14:2, #29) Spr 90, p. 83.
   "Naming the Twins." [Poem] (64) N 90, p. 16.
   "On the Highway to the Temple of the Sun." [Poem] (64) N 90, p. 15.
   "Prayer Before Killing a Doe." [HawaiiR] (14:2, #29) Spr 90, p. 84.
   "Sycamores." [Comm] (117:22) 21 D 90, p. 749.
3007. HUNTER, Paul C.
   "At Parting." [CrabCR] (7:1) Wint 90, p. 16-18.
3008. HUNTING, Constance
   "Hawkedon." [AntigR] (83) Aut 90, p. 82-86.
   "Natural Things." [AntigR] (81/82) Spr-Sum 90, p. 216-218.
3009. HUNTINGTON, Cynthia
   "1970." [NewEngR] (12:3) Spr 90, p. 240-241.
   "At Neptune's Locker." [PassN] (11:1) Sum 90, p. 24.
   "No Flowers on Magnolia Street." [TriQ] (79) Fall 90, p. 120-122.
   "The Place of Beautiful Trees." [Agni] (31/32) 90, p. 215-216.
   "Scenes from a Western Movie." [NewEngR] (12:3) Spr 90, p. 244-247.
   "Story Heard through a Wall." [PassN] (11:1) Sum 90, p. 24.
   "Street Dance, 1959." [NewEngR] (12:3) Spr 90, p. 241-243.
   "Sybil Is Doing the Dishes." [NewEngR] (12:3) Spr 90, p. 248.
   "The Vestibule." [TriQ] (79) Fall 90, p. 119.
3010. HURDELSH, Mark
   "Early." [Wind] (20:66) 90, p. 22-23.
3011. HURLEY, Maureen
   "The air's full of fumes" (tr. of Andrei Lubenski, w. Oleg Atbashian). [PoetryUSA]
      (5:2) Sum 90, p. 13.
   "And from the suffering you gave me" (tr. of Liudmila Taranenko, w. Oleg
      Atbashian). [PoetryUSA] (5:2) Sum 90, p. 13.
   "The Answering Machine" (tr. of Yulia Pivovarova, w. Oleg Atbashian).
      [PoetryUSA] (5:2) Sum 90, p. 14.
   "L'Apres-Midi." [PoetryUSA] (5:3) Fall 90, p. 10.
   "An Attempt at Statistics (Standing in Line for Vodka)" (tr. of Tatiana Milova, w.
      Oleg Atbashian). [PoetryUSA] (5:2) Sum 90, p. 14.
   "Bad" (tr. of Alexander Chak, w. Oleg Atbashian). [PoetryUSA] (5:2) Sum 90, p.
      13.
   "Barking Up the Wrong Tree." [PoetryUSA] (5:1) Spr 90, p. 5.
   "The Chain" (tr. of Vicktoria Martsinkevich, w. Oleg Atbashian). [PoetryUSA] (5:3)

Fall 90, p. 18.
"A Day in the Life" (tr. of Mukhammad Solikh, w. Oleg Atbashian). [PoetryUSA]
(5:2) Sum 90, p. 15.
"December 14, 1988" (the day of the Armenian earthquake, tr. of Vladimir Sokolov,
w. Oleg Atbashian). [PoetryUSA] (5:2) Sum 90, p. 14.
"Eclipse Over Kiev, 8/17/89" (Written exactly two months to the day before the San
Francisco earthquake). [PoetryUSA] (5:3) Fall 90, p. 17.
"If I were grass" (tr. of Liudmila Taranenko, w. Oleg Atbashian). [PoetryUSA] (5:2)
Sum 90, p. 13.
"Knife knife knife knife knife sapper shovel" (tr. of Tatyana Sherbina, w. Oleg
Atbashian). [PoetryUSA] (5:2) Sum 90, p. 14.
"Leaves fall down and down, making circles" (tr. of Liudmila Taranenko, w. Oleg
Atbashian). [PoetryUSA] (5:2) Sum 90, p. 13.
"Leaving" (tr. of Ian Martsinkevich, w. Oleg Atbashian). [PoetryUSA] (5:3) Fall 90,
p. 19.
"Life As It Is" (tr. of Ian Martsinkevich, w. Oleg Atbashian). [PoetryUSA] (5:3) Fall
90, p. 18.
"Lik Tvoj" (tr. of Andrei Lubenski, w. Oleg Atbashian). [PoetryUSA] (5:2) Sum 90,
p. 13.
"Merwin's Inlet." [PoetryUSA] (5:1) Spr 90, p. 6.
"On the Ritual Courtship of Poets." [PoetryUSA] (5:1) Spr 90, p. 7.
"Racial Memory." [PoetryUSA] (5:3) Fall 90, p. 10.
"The shopping I'll do will be simple and cheap" (tr. of Yelena Kryukova, w. Oleg
Atbashian). [PoetryUSA] (5:2) Sum 90, p. 15.
"A single word -- and I'll know what to do" (tr. of Vallentina Kuzmenko, w. Oleg
Atbashian). [PoetryUSA] (5:2) Sum 90, p. 15.
"Something Has Happened in This World" (Selection: "Oleg," tr. of Yelena
Buyevich, w. Oleg Atbashian). [PoetryUSA] (5:2) Sum 90, p. 13.
"Spring Waters" (tr. of Mark Veitsman, w. Oleg Atbashian). [PoetryUSA] (5:2)
Sum 90, p. 13.
"Sterilitism" (tr. of Dmitri Filimonov, w. Oleg Atbashian). [PoetryUSA] (5:2) Sum
90, p. 15.
"Talking to the Mirror" (tr. of Andrei Lubenski, w. Oleg Atbashian). [PoetryUSA]
(5:2) Sum 90, p. 13.
"Waiting for flaming life" (tr. of Viacheslav Kupriyanov, w. Oleg Atbashian).
[PoetryUSA] (5:2) Sum 90, p. 15.
"Why is the snow so blue?" (tr. of Irina Ratushinskaya, w. Oleg Atbashian).
[PoetryUSA] (5:2) Sum 90, p. 15.
3012. HURLEY, Thomas
"Triumph of Measure." [Spirit] (10:2) 90, p. 43.
3013. HURLOW, Marcia L.
"The Pantheist Who Loved His Wife." [Poetry] (156:1) Ap 90, p. 8.
"Praying for Father" (For Jack C. L. Hurlow, 1924-1981). [Poetry] (156:6) S 90, p.
338.
3014. HURWITZ, Ann
"The Snow Queen." [Kalliope] (12:1) 90, c89, p. 9.
"Windshield." [Kalliope] (12:1) 90, c89, p. 8.
3015. HUTCHESON, Mark
"The Outrage" (Excerpts, tr. of Marc Quaghebeur). [Interim] (9:2) Fall-Wint 90-91,
p. 44-46.
3016. HUTCHINGS, Pat
"A Cafe in New Mexico." [NowestR] (28:2) 90, p. 21.
"Man and Woman on a Balcony in Indian Summer." [SpoonRQ] (15:2) Spr 90, p.
62-63.
3017. HUTCHISON, Joseph
"Siren." [CharR] (16:2) Fall 90, p. 62.
3018. HUTCHISON, Scott Travis
"The Green at Midnight." [Poem] (64) N 90, p. 6-7.
"Integers." [SouthernR] (26:4) O 90, p. 916-919.
"Ratting." [Poem] (64) N 90, p. 4-5.
3019. HUTH, Geof A.
"Lip." [HampSPR] (Anthology 1975-1990) 90, p. 230.
3020. HUYLER, Frank
"Host." [CarolQ] (43:1) Fall 90, p. 17.
3021. HWANG, Jini
"Old Mountain" (tr. by Constantine Contogenis and Wolhee Choe). [PoetryE] (30)

Fall 90, p. 88.
3022. HYAMS, Gina
"Animate Road." [CentralP] (17/18) Spr-Fall 90, p. 158.
"On Board Their Boat *Tigress*." [CentralP] (17/18) Spr-Fall 90, p. 157.
3023. HYATT, Ellen E.
"Wednesday's Poetry Reader." [SmPd] (27:3, #80) Fall 90, p. 30.
3024. HYATT, L. J.
"Silk Scarf." [PaintedB] (40/41) 90, p. 131.
3025. HYETT, Barbara Helfgott
"Anatomy." [Kalliope] (12:2) 90, p. 56-57.
3026. HYMAS, June Hopper
"Jaleh Talking." [SlipS] (10) 90, p. 60-61.
HYON-JONG, Chong
See CHONG, Hyon-Jong
I, Chao
See CHAO, I
I-TO, Wen
See WEN, I-to
3027. IADEROSA, Andrea
"China in the News." [OnTheBus] (2:1, #5) Spr 90, p. 74.
"My Mother Phoned Tonight." [OnTheBus] (2:2/3:1, #6/7) Sum-Fall 90 Wint-Spr
91, p. 106-107.
3028. IBAÑES, Sara de
"Las Madres" (De "Apocalipsis XX"). [InterPR] (16:1) Spr 90, p. 92, 94.
"The Mothers" (from "Apocalipsis XX," tr. by Mark Smith-Soto). [InterPR] (16:1)
Spr 90, p. 93, 95.
3029. IBUR, Jane Ellen
"Friday Nights." [RiverS] (32) [90?], p. 68.
"Sparrows." [RiverS] (32) [90?], p. 69.
3030. ICHIDA, Karl K.
"The Life We Learn With." [BambooR] (47) Sum 90, p. 48-49.
3031. IDDINGS, Kathleen
"Definitely No Marilyn Monroe." [Pearl] (12) Fall-Wint 90, p. 56.
3032. IGNATOW, David
"Adultery." [HampSPR] (Anthology 1975-1990) 90, p. 74.
"Aesthetics." [BelPoJ] (40:4) Sum 90, p. 33.
"America." [NewMyths] (1:1) 90, p. 105.
"Between Us." [Poetry] (156:3) Je 90, p. 135.
"The Bread Itself." [HampSPR] (Anthology 1975-1990) 90, p. 74.
"The Dog at Bruges" (tr. of Johannes Edfelt, w. Leif Sjöberg). [OntR] (33)
Fall-Wint 90-91, p. 91.
"Dream." [HampSPR] (Anthology 1975-1990) 90, p. 74-75.
"Every Day." [HampSPR] (Anthology 1975-1990) 90, p. 75-76.
"The fish that lives at the bottom." [PoetryE] (29) Spr 90, p. 207.
"From My Window." [HampSPR] (Anthology 1975-1990) 90, p. 76.
"I carry on a debate between the living." [PoetryE] (29) Spr 90, p. 206.
"I do not want to do the intelligent thing." [PoetryE] (29) Spr 90, p. 205.
"I Listen." [NewMyths] (1:1) 90, p. 102.
"Imagine." [BelPoJ] (40:4) Sum 90, p. 32.
"It is wonderful to die amidst the pleasures I have known." [HampSPR] (Anthology
1975-1990) 90, p. 77.
"The Manacled Youth." [BelPoJ] (40:4) Sum 90, p. 33.
"Neighborhood." [PoetryE] (29) Spr 90, p. 208.
"Now." [PoetryE] (29) Spr 90, p. 210.
"Observed." [NewMyths] (1:1) 90, p. 104.
"On Broadcastinbg." [Boulevard] (4:3/5:1, #12/13) Spr 90, p. 60.
"On Quantitative Analysis." [NewMyths] (1:1) 90, p. 101.
"A Rhyme." [HampSPR] (Anthology 1975-1990) 90, p. 75.
"Senex" (tr. of Johannes Edfelt, w. Leif Sjöberg). [OntR] (33) Fall-Wint 90-91, p.
92.
"Shadowing the Ground" (Selections: 63, 67). [Ploughs] (16:4) Wint 90-91, p.
255-256.
"Summary." [NewMyths] (1:1) 90, p. 103.
"The Wedding." [HampSPR] (Anthology 1975-1990) 90, p. 76.
"What about dying?" [PoetryE] (29) Spr 90, p. 211.
"When grandmother on my father's side died." [PoetryE] (29) Spr 90, p. 209.

IGNATOW

232

"When my hand refuses to hold the pen." [PoetryE] (29) Spr 90, p. 212.
"The World." [PoetryE] (29) Spr 90, p. 213.
3033. IKKYU, Sojun
"Like a knifeblade the moon will be full then less" (tr. by Stephen Berg). [Hudson]
(43:2) Sum 90, p. 340.
"Listen whose face is it a piece" (tr. by Stephen Berg). [Hudson] (43:2) Sum 90, p.
340.
"Those old koans meaningless just ways of faking virtue" (tr. by Stephen Berg).
[Hudson] (43:2) Sum 90, p. 340.
3034. ILLESCAS, Carlos
"If You Wish" (tr. by Victor Valle). [OnTheBus] (2:2/3:1, #6/7) Sum-Fall 90
Wint-Spr 91, p. 247.
"Invocation" (tr. by Victor Valle). [OnTheBus] (2:2/3:1, #6/7) Sum-Fall 90 Wint-Spr
91, p. 246.
"Let's Bite His Hand" (tr. by Victor Valle). [OnTheBus] (2:2/3:1, #6/7) Sum-Fall 90
Wint-Spr 91, p. 247.
3035. ILLYÉS, Gyula
"Bridges" (Budapest, 1945, tr. by Nicholas Kolumban). [PoetryE] (29) Spr 90, p.
52-53.
"Fleeing Toward Western Europe" (The year 1944, tr. by Nicholas Kolumban).
[PoetryE] (29) Spr 90, p. 50-51.
"I Came Home" (tr. by Nicholas Kolumban). [PoetryE] (29) Spr 90, p. 54-55.
"The Last Home" (tr. by Bruce Berlind, w. Mária Körösy). [Os] (30) Spr 90, p. 9.
"Magán-Golgotán." [Os] (30) Spr 90, p. 6.
"Menet a Ködben." [Os] (30) Spr 90, p. 4.
"On a Private Golgotha" (tr. by Bruce Berlind, w. Mária Körösy). [Os] (30) Spr 90,
p. 7.
"One Sentence on Tyranny" (tr. by Bruce Berlind, w. Mária Körösy). [PoetryE] (29)
Spr 90, p. 42-49.
"Procession in the Fog" (tr. by Bruce Berlind, w. Mária Körösy). [Os] (30) Spr 90,
p. 5.
"Utolsó Otthon." [Os] (30) Spr 90, p. 8.
3036. INADA, Lawson Fusao
"Clifford Brown." [Chelsea] (49) 90, p. 70-71.
"In/vocation" (for Mal Waldron). [Chelsea] (49) 90, p. 68-69.
3037. INCH, Barbara
"Remember me as you go along the street." [PoetryUSA] ([5:4?]) Wint 90, p. 26.
INÉS DE LA CRUZ, Juana, Sor
See CRUZ, Juana Inés de la, Sor
3038. INEZ, Colette
"Animal Bodies in Virginia." [Chelsea] (49) 90, p. 140.
"The Entry of James Ensor into My Memories of Brussels." [NowestR] (28:3/29:1)
90-91, p. 194-196.
"Hands." [SouthernPR] (30:2) Fall 90, p. 16-17.
"How I Was Advised by an Elderly Woman to Restrain My Sensual Heat."
[Kalliope] (12:2) 90, p. 46.
"Hybrid Song." [CrossCur] (9:2) Je 90, p. 67-68.
"I Snapped the End of My Screaming Hunger." [Kalliope] (12:2) 90, p. 45.
"Kissing the Lips of Orphanage Girls." [Kalliope] (12:2) 90, p. 39-40.
"Lines for Eastern Bluebirds." [MissouriR] (13:1) 90, p. 154.
"Monika and the Owl." [Ploughs] (16:1) Spr-Sum 90, p. 157-158.
"Old Woman, Eskimo." [Kalliope] (12:2) 90, p. 43-44.
"The Recluse." [WestB] (26) 90, p. 26-27.
"Riverwalk." [CrossCur] (9:2) Je 90, p. 69-70.
"Seasons of the War" (for foster mother, Ruth). [Salm] (85/86) Wint-Spr 90, p.
149-151.
"The Trapper and the Arctic Fox." [Caliban] (8) 90, p. 32-33.
3039. INGEBRETSEN, Edward J.
"Unlettered" (Robert Frost's farm, Franconia, New Hampshire). [SoCaR] (23:1)
Fall 90, p. 83.
3040. INGEMANSON, Birgitta
"Morning" (tr. of Fazu G. Alieva, w. Manly Johnson). [Nimrod] (33:2) Spr-Sum
90, p. 44.
"The Thirst for Beauty" (tr. of Fazu G. Alieva, w. Manly Johnson). [Nimrod] (33:2)
Spr-Sum 90, p. 43-44.

233

3041. INGERSON, Martin I.
 "Hello, Diana." [BellArk] (6:1) Ja-F 90, p. 22.
 "On the University Bridge." [BellArk] (6:6) N-D 90, p. 7.
 "Prime Time: Second Person Subjunctive." [BellArk] (6:3) My-Je 90, p. 6.
 "The Sculptor." [BellArk] (6:5) S-O 90, p. 4.
 "Simple Song." [BellArk] (6:3) My-Je 90, p. 5.
 "The Song of Two Snails." [BellArk] (6:2) Mr-Ap 90, p. 1.
 "Three Acts in the Form of a Sonnet." [BellArk] (6:4) Jl-Ag 90, p. 1.
3042. INMAN, Peter
 "Dust Bowl" (Selection: F.). [Verse] (7:1) Spr 90, p. 35-36.
3043. INMAN, Will
 "Beyond Dark Inlet, Savage Sacred Sky." [ChamLR] (4:1, #7) Fall 90, p. 61.
 "Dialogue W/Ms No." [FreeL] (5) Sum 90, p. 24.
 "Will, Workshopping." [Asylum] (6:2) S 90, p. 30.
 "You Have to Know Just When." [ChamLR] (4:1, #7) Fall 90, p. 60.
3044. INNES, Ruth
 "The Daughter of My Daughter." [HolCrit] (27:5) D 90, p. 16.
3045. INVERARITY, Geoffrey
 "Angels of the Air" (Drogheda, Ireland. September 11, 1649). [AntigR] (83) Aut 90,
 p. 29-30.
 "Cromwell's Prayer" (Drogheda, Ireland. September 11, 1649). [AntigR] (83) Aut
 90, p. 28.
 "Spoils of War" (Drogheda, Ireland. September 12, 1649). [AntigR] (83) Aut 90, p.
 31.
IOANNA-VERONIKA
 See WARWICK, Ioanna-Veronika
3046. IOANNOU, Susan
 "Domestic Artistry" (For Merla McMurray). [Dandel] (17:1) Spr-Sum 90, p. 9.
 "Kitchen Territorial." [Descant] (21:4/22:1, #71/72) Wint-Spr 90-91, p. 147-148.
3047. IONESCO, Eugene
 "Country of Cardboard and Cotton Batting" (tr. from the French of Aurelia Roman
 by Bradley R. Strahan and S. G. Sullivan). [Vis] (33) 90, p. 4.
 "Pays de Carton et D'Ouate" (tr. by Aurelia Roman). [Vis] (33) 90, p. 4.
3048. IPELLIE, Alootook
 "The Dancing Sun." [CanLit] (124/125) Spr-Sum 90, p. 272.
 "The Water Moved an Instant Before." [CanLit] (124/125) Spr-Sum 90, p. 272.
3049. IRA
 "Berkeley Beat." [PoetryUSA] ([5:4?]) Wint 90, p. 24.
 "Give Us Barabbas." [PoetryUSA] (5:3) Fall 90, p. 25.
 "No More Cafe." [PoetryUSA] (5:3) Fall 90, p. 24.
3050. IRIE, Kevin
 "Alien Encounters." [Arc] (24) Spr 90, p. 26.
3051. IRION, Mary Jean
 "Complement Returned." [ChrC] (107:7) 28 F 90, p. 206.
 "The Green Gatherers at Sounion." [Poetry] (157:3) D 90, p. 155.
3052. IRWIN, Joe
 "Liar (a Poem)." [CoalC] (2) D 90, p. 12.
3053. IRWIN, Mark
 "As Long As." [Agni] (31/32) 90, p. 271.
 "White." [LaurelR] (24:1) Wint 90, p. 30.
3054. IRWIN, Richard
 "Postmortemanifesto" (Excerpt). [PoetryUSA] (5:2) Sum 90, p. 16.
3055. ISACKSON, Alex D.
 "Fastcar." [EmeraldCR] (1990) c89, p. 46.
ISAMU, Nagase
 See NAGASE, Isamu
3056. ISHII, Michael
 "No Usual Weather to Report." [DogRR] (9:1, #17) Spr 90, p. 6-7.
3057. ISLAS, Maya
 "El Ojo del Camello." [LindLM] (9:4) O-D 90, p. 46.
3058. ISMAILI, Rashidah
 "Onyibo." [LitR] (33:4) Sum 90, p. 476.
3059. ISRAEL, Inge
 "Catherine Palace." [PraF] (11:4) Wint 90-91, p. 51-52.
 "Dealing with the Conundrum." [Dandel] (17:1) Spr-Sum 90, p. 35.

3060. ISTARU, Ana
   "Cannon Time Comes Flying" (tr. by Mark Smith-Soto). [InterPR] (16:1) Spr 90, p.
      31-35.
   "Viene Volando un Tiempo de Cañones." [InterPR] (16:1) Spr 90, p. 30-34.
3061. ITALIA, Paul G.
   "If You Go to the Rodeo." [LitR] (33:3) Spr 90, p. 380.
3062. ITURRALDE, Iraida
   "Discurso de las Infantas." [LindLM] (9:4) O-D 90, p. 12.
3063. IVEREM, Esther
   "Leaving Home." [Obs] (5:3) Wint 90, p. 73-74.
3064. IVERSON, Roderick
   "1965" (Selection: (7), tr. of Ulrich Zieger). [PoetryUSA] (5:3) Fall 90, p. 21.
   "1965" (Selections: 7, 18, tr. of Ulrich Zieger). [Sulfur] (10:2, #27) Fall 90, p.
      92-94.
   "Afterwards" (tr. of Raja Lubinetzki). [Screens] (2) 90, p. 76-77.
   "The Angel of the Situation" (tr. of Andreas Koziol). [Sulfur] (10:2, #27) Fall 90, p.
      105-106.
   "Arianrhod from the Overdoes" (Exceprt, tr. of Bert Papenfuss-Gorek). [Sulfur]
      (10:2, #27) Fall 90, p. 98-100.
   "Between Haste and Deceit" (tr. of Stefan Doring, w. Mitch Cohen). [Sulfur] (10:2,
      #27) Fall 90, p. 101-102.
   "The hours which a brain of sand counts" (tr. of Rainer Schedlinski). [Sulfur] (10:2,
      #27) Fall 90, p. 91.
   "The Knees That Were Ours and the Fruit and the Style" (tr. of Andreas Koziol).
      [Screens] (2) 90, p. 81-82.
   "Mary shelley, i love only you" (tr. of Bert Papenfuss-Gorek). [Sulfur] (10:2, #27)
      Fall 90, p. 96-97.
   "Misforunate am i, a ruffian" (tr. of Bert Papenfuss-Gorek). [Sulfur] (10:2, #27)
      Fall 90, p. 95.
   "Ordinary and unnoticed" (tr. of Rainer Schedlinski). [Sulfur] (10:2, #27) Fall 90, p.
      90.
   "Quietness that in scorn capsizes" (tr. of Bert Papenfuss-Gorek). [Sulfur] (10:2,
      #27) Fall 90, p. 96.
   "Silence the Rest, Awakening" (tr. of Stefan Doring, w. Mitch Cohen). [Sulfur]
      (10:2, #27) Fall 90, p. 102-103.
   "Text and Commentary" (tr. of Elke Erb). [Sulfur] (10:2, #27) Fall 90, p. 107-112.
   "Topless Is Allowed Here" (tr. of Eberhard Haefner). [Screens] (2) 90, p. 78-79.
   "Topless Is Allowed Here" (tr. of Eberhard Hafner). [Sulfur] (10:2, #27) Fall 90, p.
      113-114.
   "Untitled: that which once again befalls the heavens" (tr. of Andreas Koziol).
      [Sulfur] (10:2, #27) Fall 90, p. 104-105.
   "Words" (tr. of Raja Lubinetzki). [Screens] (2) 90, p. 76.
3065. IVERSON, Teresa
   "No Mourning" (tr. of Gottfried Benn). [Agni] (29/30) 90, p. 9.
3066. IVRY, Benjamin
   "Anton Bruckner" (tr. of Adam Zagajewski, w. Renata Gorczynski). [NewYorker]
      (66:5) 19 Mr 90, p. 46.
   "At Midnight" (tr. of Adam Zagajewski, w. Renata Gorczynski). [Antaeus] (64/65)
      Spr-Aut 90, p. 143.
   "Daybreak" (tr. of Adam Zagajewski, w. Renata Gorczynski). [PartR] (57:1) Wint
      90, p. 97.
   "Lava" (tr. of Adam Zagajewski, w. Renata Gorczynski). [PartR] (57:1) Wint 90, p.
      98.
   "Presence" (tr. of Adam Zagajewski, w. Renata Gorczynski). [Antaeus] (64/65)
      Spr-Aut 90, p. 145.
   "R. Says" (tr. of Adam Zagajewski, w. Renata Gorczynski). [Antaeus] (64/65)
      Spr-Aut 90, p. 144.
   "Vacation" (tr. of Adam Zagajewski, w. Renata Gorczynski). [DenQ] (25:1) Sum
      90, p. 54.
3067. IZA, Ana Maria
   "El Costal de las Sombras Vació Todo Su Frío." [InterPR] (16:1) Spr 90, p. 46.
   "The Sack of Shadows Poured Down Cold" (tr. by Mark Smith-Soto). [InterPR]
      (16:1) Spr 90, p. 47.
3068. IZENBERG, Oren
   "Cosmo's Perfect Love Letter" (Honorable Mention). [HarvardA] (124:3) Mr 90, p.
      27.

"Free Diving" (Honorable Mention). [HarvardA] (124:3) Mr 90, p. 18.
3069. IZOARD, Jacques
"Voices, Garments, Plunders" (Excerpts, tr. by Daniel de Bruycker). [Vis] (32) 90, p. 32-33.
3070. J
"Eden" (Selections: 4-9, from "The Book of J," tr. by David Rosenberg). [AmerPoR] (19:6) N-D 90, p. 29-30.
3071. JABES, Edmond
"The Book of Resemblances II: Intimations The Desert" (Selections, tr. by Rosemarie Waldrop). [Epoch] (39:3) 90, p. 304-324.
"Born Viable" (from "Intimations. The Desert. The Book of Resemblances II, tr. by Rosmarie Waldrop). [ManhatR] (5:2) Fall 90, p. 39-40.
"On Blankness, I" (from "Intimations. The Desert. The Book of Resemblances II, tr. by Rosmarie Waldrop). [ManhatR] (5:2) Fall 90, p. 42-44.
"On Blankness, II" (from "Intimations. The Desert. The Book of Resemblances II, tr. by Rosmarie Waldrop). [ManhatR] (5:2) Fall 90, p. 44.
"On Blankness, III" (from "Intimations. The Desert. The Book of Resemblances II, tr. by Rosmarie Waldrop). [ManhatR] (5:2) Fall 90, p. 45.
"On Humor" (from "Intimations. The Desert. The Book of Resemblances II, tr. by Rosmarie Waldrop). [ManhatR] (5:2) Fall 90, p. 37.
"Thought, Death" (from "Intimations. The Desert. The Book of Resemblances II, tr. by Rosmarie Waldrop). [ManhatR] (5:2) Fall 90, p. 41.
"Whose Seal Cannot Be Broken" (from "Intimations. The Desert. The Book of Resemblances II, tr. by Rosmarie Waldrop). [ManhatR] (5:2) Fall 90, p. 38-39.
3072. JABSHEH, Salwa
"In the Autumn of the House" (tr. of Nouri Jarrah, w. John Heath-Stubbs). [Screens] (2) 90, p. 12.
"The Storm" (tr. of Nouri Jarrah, w. John Heath-Stubbs). [Screens] (2) 90, p. 12.
3073. JACCOTTET, Philippe
"Ignorance" (tr. by Derek Mahon). [ManhatR] (5:1) Spr 90, p. 52.
"L'Ignorant." [ManhatR] (5:1) Spr 90, p. 52.
3074. JACKETTI, Maria
"Heaven Stones" (Selections: III, XVII, tr. of Pablo Neruda). [Abraxas] (38/39) 90, p. 65, 67.
3075. JACKSON, Fleda Brown
"Anhinga." [Pembroke] (22) 90, p. 80.
"Coming Home." [MidwQ] (32:1) Aut 90, p. 85.
"Dunes." [WestB] (26) 90, p. 106.
"A Few Lines from Rehoboth Beach." [Pembroke] (22) 90, p. 79.
"Night Swimming." [WestB] (26) 90, p. 107.
"The Sons of the Prophet Are Brave Men and Bold." [ArtfulD] (18/19) 90, p. 61.
"Three-Quarters Moon." [ArtfulD] (18/19) 90, p. 62.
3076. JACKSON, Katherine
"American Landscape Painters in Rome." [SouthwR] (75:4) Aut 90, p. 569.
3077. JACKSON, Laura (Riding)
"In Response to a Manifesto Circulated by the Union of Concerned Scientists." [Chelsea] (49) 90, p. 23-24.
3078. JACKSON, Leslie
"The Reminder." [AntigR] (83) Aut 90, p. 126.
"Used Books." [AntigR] (83) Aut 90, p. 125.
3079. JACKSON, Lorri
"Beat 1990 (the Abbreviated Version)." [ChironR] (9:3) Aut 90, p. 6.
"Brain Garbage." [ChironR] (9:4) Wint 90, p. 4.
"A Character Sketch." [ChironR] (9:1) Spr 90, p. 7.
"Excuse Me, I'm Giving Away Diseases for Free." [ChironR] (9:4) Wint 90, p. 4.
"A Hole & a Pulse." [ChironR] (9:4) Wint 90, p. 5.
"Porch Monkey Eat Me." [ChironR] (9:4) Wint 90, p. 4.
"A Prima Donna Poet Replies." [ChironR] (9:3) Aut 90, p. 6.
"A Prophylactic Rag." [ChironR] (9:1) Spr 90, p. 7.
"Screwage." [ChironR] (9:1) Spr 90, p. 7.
"Still Life (a Triangle of Sorts)." [ChironR] (9:4) Wint 90, p. 4.
3080. JACKSON, Mary Hale
"Open Windows." [ChrC] (107:26) 19-26 S 90, p. 834.
3081. JACKSON, Paula
"Aging." [Obs] (5:3) Wint 90, p. 39-40.

"Evening." [Obs] (5:3) Wint 90, p. 39.
"Laughing Young Man." [Obs] (5:3) Wint 90, p. j39.
3082. JACKSON, Reuben (Reuben M.)
"Driving South." [Gargoyle] (37/38) 90, p. 124.
"For Duke Ellington." [Chelsea] (49) 90, p. 86-87.
"I Didn't Know About You" (for Johnny Hodges). [Chelsea] (49) 90, p. 87.
"My Imaginary Sister Gets Married." [Gargoyle] (37/38) 90, p. 125.
"Paul" (for Paul Gonsalves). [Chelsea] (49) 90, p. 86.
3083. JACKSON, Richard
"About the Dogs of Dachau." [Ploughs] (16:4) Wint 90-91, p. 269-272.
"Benediction." [PraS] (64:3) Fall 90, p. 76-79.
"Circumstances." [Ploughs] (16:4) Wint 90-91, p. 264-265.
"For a Long Time I Have Wanted to Write a Happy Poem" (for Tomaz). [Ploughs]
(16:4) Wint 90-91, p. 266-268.
"Homeric." [PassN] (11:2) Wint 90, p. 18.
"Not Surprised." [TarRP] (29:2) Spr 90, p. 39.
"The Yellow Light of Begunje." [TarRP] (29:2) Spr 90, p. j38.
3084. JACKSON, Spoon
"Not a Poet." [PoetryUSA] (5:3) Fall 90, p. 22.
3085. JACKSON, Steve
"Trailblazer." [FreeL] (6) Aut 90, p. 23.
3086. JACOBIK, Gray
"Astronomy Lesson." [HiramPoR] (47) Wint 90, p. 37.
"The Betrayal." [ManhatPR] (11) [89?], p. 46.
"The Rainy Season." [OxfordM] (6:1) Spr-Sum 90, p. 82-84.
3087. JACOBOWITZ, Judah
"No Bolt from the Blue." [SmPd] (27:2, #79) Spr 90, p. 22.
3088. JACOBSEN, Josephine
"Deplane." [NewL] (57:1) Fall 90, p. 66-67.
"The Mainlanders." [NewL] (57:1) Fall 90, p. 67.
"Motion in One Private Room of the Geriatric Wing." [HampSPR] (Anthology
1975-1990) 90, p. 24.
"The Provider." [HampSPR] (Anthology 1975-1990) 90, p. 25.
3089. JACOBSEN, Rolf
"Dies Illae" (tr. by Robert Hedin). [PoetryE] (30) Fall 90, p. 13.
"In Lands Where Light Has Another Color" (14 poems in Norwegian and English,
tr. by Robert Hedin. Translation Chapbook Series, #14). [MidAR] (10:2) 90,
p. 87-117.
"Knitting Needles, Needle and Thread" (tr. by Robert Hedin). [PoetryE] (30) Fall
90, p. 14.
3090. JACQMIN, Francois
"Autumn" (Excerpt, tr. by David Siefkin). [Vis] (32) 90, p. 29.
"Spring" (Excerpt, tr. by David Siefkin). [Vis] (32) 90, p. 28.
"Summer" (Excerpt, tr. by David Siefkin). [Vis] (32) 90, p. 29.
"Winter" (Excerpt, tr. by David Siefkin). [Vis] (32) 90, p. 30.
3091. JACQUES, Geoffrey
"Coronet Chop Suey." [Screens] (2) 90, p. 202.
"James Baldwin." [Screens] (2) 90, p. 202-203.
3092. JAECH, Linda
"From a Silent Space a Certain Undertone." [BellArk] (6:3) My-Je 90, p. 6.
3093. JAEGER, Lowell
"At 30,000 Feet: Note to My Daughter." [NegC] (10:2/3) 90, p. 91-92.
"Athletics." [PoetryNW] (31:1) Spr 90, p. 29-30.
"Confessions." [CutB] (33) 90, p. 18-20.
"Crossfire." [PoetryNW] (31:1) Spr 90, p. 28-29.
"Door-to-Door Jesus." [PoetryNW] (31:4) Wint 90-91, p. 26-27.
"Passport Photo, 1969." [SlipS] (10) 90, p. 51-52.
"Trading Places." [HighP] (5:2) Fall 90, p. 49.
"Traveling Back." [CutB] (33) 90, p. 21.
"Voices." [SoCoast] (9) Fall 90, p. 36-37.
3094. JAFFE, Louise
"Rebirths." [SoCoast] (8) Spr 90, p. 7.
3095. JAGASICH, Paul
"The Casting of Bells" (Selections, tr. of Jaroslav Seifert, w. Tom O'Grady).
[HampSPR] (Anthology 1975-1990) 90, p. 255-256.
"Dance-Song" (tr. of Jaroslav Seifert, w. Tom O'Grady). [HampSPR] (Anthology

1975-1990) 90, p. 256-257.
3096. JAKIELA, L. (Lori)
"The Lonely." [WestB] (27) 90, p. 66-67.
"Tomato Harvest." [Poem] (63) My 90, p. 32.
"Watching My Father Feed the Birds." [WestB] (27) 90, p. 67-68.
3097. JAMES, Bradley
"Carrousel" (on a photograph by Olivia Parker, to Ted Bundy, who went crazy over
a period of time). [PoetryC] (11:1) Spr 90, p. 11.
3098. JAMES, David
"Body of Knowledge." [Poem] (64) N 90, p. 29.
"The End of the Poetry Line." [ChironR] (9:4) Wint 90, p. 9.
"For the Sake of Yes." [Poem] (63) My 90, p. 52.
"A Future Somewhere." [ChironR] (9:4) Wint 90, p. 9.
"Horoscope of a Dead Man." [Poem] (63) My 90, p. 51.
"In Praise of Age." [Poem] (64) N 90, p. 30-31.
"On Edge." [ChironR] (9:4) Wint 90, p. 9.
3099. JAMES, Milton
"Sneaking Out at Dawn." [OnTheBus] (2:2/3:1, #6/7) Sum-Fall 90 Wint-Spr 91, p.
110.
3100. JAMES, Pat
"Crippled Islands." [FloridaR] (17:2) Fall-Wint 90, p. 76.
"Homage." [FloridaR] (17:2) Fall-Wint 90, p. 72-73.
"Letter to Sally." [SingHM] (18) 90, p. 88.
"Possession." [FloridaR] (17:2) Fall-Wint 90, p. 74-75.
3101. JAMES, Sibyl
"Economies" (1st prize, Black Bear Poetry Competition). [BlackBR] (11) Spr-Sum
90, p. 35.
"Mathematics and Disciples." [AmerV] (21) Wint 90, p. 45.
3102. JAMES, Stewart
"Packing Her Scarves." [DenQ] (25:2) Fall 90, p. 26.
3103. JAMIESON, Robert Alan
"Washboard Apprentice." [Stand] (31:4) Aut 90, p. 56.
3104. JAMISON, Barbara
"Imagine a Clown." [AnotherCM] (21) 90, p. 74-75.
"Stick Horse" (tr. of Jorge Argueta, w. Beatriz Johnston-Hernández). [PoetryUSA]
(5:3) Fall 90, p. 16.
"They Drafted My Son" (tr. of Jorge Argueta, w. Beatriz Johnston-Hernández).
[PoetryUSA] (5:3) Fall 90, p. 16.
3105. JAMMES, Francis
"Old House" (tr. by Antony Oldknow). [WebR] (14:2) Spr 90, p. 106.
"Way Off in the Distance" (tr. by Antony Oldknow). [PoetryE] (30) Fall 90, p.
63-64.
3106. JANECEK, Gerald J.
"And I on the Cosmic" (tr. of Vsevolod Nikolaevich Nekrasov). [Nimrod] (33:2)
Spr-Sum 90, p. 1.
3107. JANEVSKI, Slavko
"Silence" (tr. by Herbert Kuhner, Howard Erksine Hill and Bogomil Gjezel).
[Footwork] 90, p. 106.
3108. JANIK, Phyllis
"My Lord, We Plead Our Bellies." [NewL] (57:1) Fall 90, p. 62-63.
"Nostalgia." [AnotherCM] (21) 90, p. 76-77.
"Overtures: Havana / Chicago / The Four Corners [Arizona-Utah-Colorado-New
Mexico]." [AnotherCM] (21) 90, p. 78-82.
3109. JANKOVIC, Peter
"The Four Corners of the World We Plunge Beyond" (tr. of Dane T. S. Hawk).
[Footwork] 90, p. 49.
3110. JARMAN, Mark
"Gliders." [Shen] (40:2) Sum 90, p. 34-35.
"The NO Collage." [TampaR] (3) 90, p. 67.
"Skin Cancer." [NewYorker] (66:32) 24 S 90, p. 48-49.
"To the Green Man" (for Philip Wilby). [Ploughs] (16:4) Wint 90-91, p. 45.
3111. JARNIEWICZ, Jerzy
"Winter" (tr. of Krzysztof Smoczyk). [TampaR] (3) 90, p. 87.
"XXX. But whom to blame" (tr. of Krzysztof Smoczyk). [TampaR] (3) 90, p. 88.
3112. JARNOT, Lisa
"Liner Notes." [OnTheBus] (2:2/3:1, #6/7) Sum-Fall 90 Wint-Spr 91, p. 111.

3113. JARRAH, Nouri
"In the Autumn of the House" (tr. by Salwa Jabsheh and John Heath-Stubbs).
[Screens] (2) 90, p. 12.
"The Storm" (tr. by Salwa Jabsheh and John Heath-Stubbs). [Screens] (2) 90, p.
12.
3114. JARVIS, Kim
"She's Special." [PoetryUSA] (5:2) Sum 90, p. 8.
3115. JASON, Kathrine
"Ocean." [GreenMR] (NS 4:1) Spr-Sum 90, p. 68.
3116. JASPER, Matt
"Anastasia, Purdy Group Home." [GrandS] (9:4, #36) 90, p. 130-131.
"An Appropriate Song." [Asylum] (5:4) 90, p. 8.
"Evening." [Asylum] (5:4) 90, p. 8.
"Flight." [GrandS] (9:4, #36) 90, p. 131.
"The Mouth I Am Thirsty For." [Asylum] (5:4) 90, p. 8.
3117. JASTRUN, Tomasz
"Alarm" (tr. by Daniel Bourne). [PoetryE] (29) Spr 90, p. 29.
"Coming To" (tr. by Daniel Bourne). [MidAR] (10:2) 90, p. 167.
"Courage" (tr. by Daniel Bourne). [MidAR] (10:2) 90, p. 169.
"Defeat" (tr. by Daniel Bourne). [MidAR] (10:2) 90, p. 166.
"Hands" (tr. by Daniel Bourne). [PoetryE] (29) Spr 90, p. 28.
"In Mourning (1983)" (tr. by Daniel Bourne). [MidAR] (10:2) 90, p. 168.
"In the Exercise Yard" (tr. by Daniel Bourne). [MidAR] (10:2) 90, p. 165.
"Planet" (tr. by Daniel Bourne). [PoetryE] (29) Spr 90, p. 27.
"Rat" (tr. by Daniel Bourne). [PoetryE] (29) Spr 90, p. 26.
"Small Grains" (tr. by Daniel Bourne). [PoetryE] (30) Fall 90, p. 95.
3118. JAUSS, David
"20th Century Disease." [Wind] (20:67) 90, p. 25.
"After Love." [Wind] (20:67) 90, p. 25-26.
"The Anniversary." [LullwaterR] (2:1) Wint 90, p. 24.
"For My Wife, Smiling in Her Sleep." [Wind] (20:67) 90, p. 26.
"Quotations for a Winter Evening." [Poetry] (157:3) D 90, p. 158.
3119. JAYE, Grace A.
"Florida Child." [EmeraldCR] (1990) c89, p. 96-97.
3120. JAYYUSI, Lena
"Absence" (tr. of Walid Khazindar, w. W. S. Merwin). [PaperAir] (4:3) 90, p. 65.
"Another Death" (tr. of Ghassan Zaqtan, w. Jeremy Reed). [Screens] (2) 90, p.
21-22.
"At Least" (tr. of Walid Khazindar, w. W. S. Merwin). [PaperAir] (4:3) 90, p. 64.
"The Cafe Mistress" (tr. of Muhammad Zakariyya, w. Jeremy Reed). [Screens] (2)
90, p. 20.
"Emigration" (tr. of Zakariyya Muhammad, w. Jeremy Reed). [PaperAir] (4:3) 90,
p. 61.
"Everything" (tr. of Zakariyya Muhammad, w. Jeremy Reed). [PaperAir] (4:3) 90,
p. 60.
"The Guards" (tr. of Mureed Barghouthi, w. W. S. Merwin). [PaperAir] (4:3) 90, p.
67.
"Houses" (tr. of Walid Khazindar, w. W. S. Merwin). [PaperAir] (4:3) 90, p. 66.
"An Incident" (tr. of Ghassan Zaqtan, w. Jeremy Reed). [Screens] (2) 90, p. 21.
"A Mirror" (tr. of Chassan Zaqtan, w. Jeremy Reed). [PaperAir] (4:3) 90, p. 62.
"Mulberry Leaves for a Naked Tree" (Excerpt, tr. of Taher Riyadh, w. John
Heath-Stubbs). [Screens] (2) 90, p. 24.
"My Things" (tr. of Zakariyya Muhammad, w. Jeremy Reed). [PaperAir] (4:3) 90,
p. 60.
"Our Country" (tr. of Ahmad Dahbour, w. Jeremy Reed). [PaperAir] (4:3) 90, p.
63.
"Perplexed" (tr. of Walid Khazindar, w. W. S. Merwin). [PaperAir] (4:3) 90, p. 66.
"Profile" (tr. of Walid Khazindar, w. Naomi Shihab Nye). [Screens] (2) 90, p. 19.
"Refuge" (tr. of Mureed Barghouthi, w. W. S. Merwin). [PaperAir] (4:3) 90, p. 68.
"A Tavern" (tr. of Zakariyya Muhammad, w. Jeremy Reed). [PaperAir] (4:3) 90, p.
60.
"To Murder Time" (Excerpt, tr. of Taher Riyadh, w. John Heath-Stubbs). [Screens]
(2) 90, p. 24.
"The Tribes" (tr. of Mureed Barghouthi, w. W. S. Merwin). [PaperAir] (4:3) 90, p.
68.

3121. JAYYUSI, May
"The Earth Also Dies" (Excerpt, tr. of Muhammad al-As'ad, w. Jack Collom).
[Screens] (2) 90, p. 26.
"The Girl Servant" (tr. of Abbas Baydun, w. John Heath-Stubbs). [Screens] (2) 90,
p. 16-18.
"A Non-Personal Account" (tr. of Khairi Mansour, w. Jeremy Reed). [Screens] (2)
90, p. 23.
"Personal Account" (tr. of Muhammad al-As'ad, w. Jack Collom). [Screens] (2) 90,
p. 25-26.
"Suicide" (tr. of Abbas Baydun, w. John Heath-Stubbs). [Screens] (2) 90, p. 13-15.
3122. JEBB, Robert
"The Moon." (tr. of Jaime Sabines). [PoetryE] (30) Fall 90, p. 7.
3123. JECH, Jon
"Family of Roses." [BellArk] (6:2) Mr-Ap 90, p. 12-18.
3124. JEFFREY, Susu
"In South Africa." [SingHM] (17) 90, p. 94-95.
3125. JELLEMA, C. O.
"Reflections on Ruysdael" (tr. by Paul Vincent). [Trans] (24) Fall 90, p. 50-52.
3126. JELLEMA, Rod (Roderick)
"Ash Wednesday" (tr. of Gerben Rypma). [WashR] (16:2) Ag-S 90, p. 13.
"Icy" (tr. of Daniel Daen). [Vis] (34) 90, p. 28.
"Images of a Summer Evening" (tr. of J. B. Schepers). [WashR] (16:2) Ag-S 90, p.
12.
"In the White Field" (tr. of R. P. Sybesma). [WashR] (16:2) Ag-S 90, p. 13.
"Spring 1981" (tr. of Jella Kaspersma). [Vis] (34) 90, p. 28.
"Time and Space" (tr. of Tsjebbe Hettinga). [Vis] (34) 90, p. 29.
"Touching It." [HampSPR] (Anthology 1975-1990) 90, p. 62-63.
"Trakl" (tr. of Jan Wybenga). [WashR] (16:2) Ag-S 90, p. 13.
"A Way to Grow Old" (tr. of Douwe A. Tamminga). [WashR] (16:2) Ag-S 90, p.
13.
"When You Grow Older" (tr. of G. N. Visser). [WashR] (16:2) Ag-S 90, p. 13.
3127. JENKINS, Joyce
"Anthem." [Zyzzyva] (6:1 #21) Spr 90, p. 83.
3128. JENKINS, Louis
"Mr. Watkins." [BostonR] (15:6) D 90, p. 19.
"Out-of-the-Body Travel." [KenR] (NS 12:2) Spr 90, p. 101.
"The Wristwatch." [KenR] (NS 12:2) Spr 90, p. 101.
3129. JENKINS, Lucien
"Emma." [Stand] (31:2) Spr 90, p. 24.
3130. JENKINS, Mike
"The Beach, My Son and the Alltime Batman." [CharR] (16:1) Spr 90, p. 68.
"The Ghost Boy" (For John Davies). [CumbPR] (10:1) Fall 90, p. 23-24.
3131. JENNINGS, Elizabeth
"Springtime for Louise." [BelPoJ] (40:4) Sum 90, p. 34-35.
3132. JENSEN, Bo Green
"I Have Had to Kill You" (from "The Meaning of Places," 1985, tr. by the author
and Monique M. Kennedy). [CimR] (92) Jl 90, p. 23.
"In the Beginning" (from "The Meaning of Places," 1985, tr. by the author and
Monique M. Kennedy). [CimR] (92) Jl 90, p. 22.
3133. JENSEN, Dale
"Letter." [PoetryUSA] ([5:4?]) Wint 90, p. 16.
3134. JENSEN, Laura
"The Piano in Saint Paul." [Field] (43) Fall 90, p. 92-93.
"The Poor Can Be Bled to Death" (scenes from Agnes of God). [Field] (43) Fall 90,
p. 95-96.
"Tack Ska Du Ha" (on Learning Swedish). [Field] (43) Fall 90, p. 94.
3135. JEROME, Judson
"The Bind." [HampSPR] (Anthology 1975-1990) 90, p. 179.
"For Jin Anmei, of Xi'an, Who Asked Would I Please Write Her a Poem." [Amelia]
(6:1, #16) 90, p. 58.
"For Marty, After 15,000 Days and Nights, July 25, 1989." [ManhatR] (5:1) Spr
90, p. 37.
"Job: The Voice Out of the Whirlwind." [ManhatR] (5:1) Spr 90, p. 38-41.
"You Have to Draw a Line Somewhere." [NegC] (10:2/3) 90, p. 9-15.
3136. JEROZAL, Gregory
"Train Halted in Virginia Woods." [HampSPR] (Anthology 1975-1990) 90, p.

233-234.
3137. JESSEN, Claus
"Pain" (tr. from the Danish). [NegC] (10:2/3) 90, p. 145.
"Smerte." [NegC] (10:2/3) 90, p. 144.
JESSEN, Paula Hostrup
See HOSTRUP-JESSEN, Paula
3138. JEVREM, Carol
"Falling Apart at Work." [Pig] (16) 90, p. 100.
"Olde Towne East, Columbus." [Pig] (16) 90, p. 54.
JEW, Shalin Hai
See HAI-JEW, Shalin
3139. JEWELL, Terri L.
"Athlone." [Obs] (5:3) Wint 90, p. 75.
"Basketeer." [Obs] (5:1) Spr 90, p. 52.
"Digestion." [Obs] (5:1) Spr 90, p. 51.
"Family Jewel Heretics." [Cond] (17) 90, p. 118.
"Mister Drummond." [Obs] (5:3) Wint 90, p. 76.
"She Who Bears the Thorn." [SingHM] (17) 90, p. 8d.
"Sleep in Unfamiliar Arms." [Cond] (17) 90, p. 119.
3140. JEWISON, Cathy
"Feminism." [SlipS] (10) 90, p. 43.
"Ticket to the War." [SlipS] (10) 90, p. 42-43.
3141. JI, Tianxiang
"A Narrow Alley" (tr. of Huang Bangjun). [PaintedB] (40/41) 90, p. 48-49.
"Probe" (tr. of Lei Suyan). [PaintedB] (40/41) 90, p. 56-57.
JIA-XIN, Wang
See WANG, Jia-xin
3142. JIANG, He
"You" (tr. by Steven Taylor and Wang Ping). [LitR] (33:4) Sum 90, p. 525.
JIANXIONG, Zhao
See ZHAO, Jianxiong
JIAXIN, Wang
See WANG, Jiaxin
3143. JIMENEZ RAMOS, Gerardo Alfredo
"Accidente." [LindLM] (9:3) Jl-S 90, p. 9.
"Desvio." [LindLM] (9:3) Jl-S 90, p. 9.
"Infancia." [LindLM] (9:3) Jl-S 90, p. 9.
3144. JIN, Zhong
"I Stroke You with All My Years" (tr. of Bei Ling, w. William Slaughter).
[Gargoyle] (37/38) 90, p. 9.
JINGRONG, Chen
See CHEN, Jingrong
JINI, Hwang
See HWANG, Jini
JIPING, Dong
See DONG, Jiping
3145. JOBE, Carey
"Green, White, Red." [KanQ] (22:1/2) Wint-Spr 90, p. 230.
3146. JOE, Rita
"The Dream Was the Answer." [CanLit] (124/125) Spr-Sum 90, p. 123.
"Klu'skap-o'kom." [CanLit] (124/125) Spr-Sum 90, p. 122.
3147. JOHANNESSEN, Matthias
"The Land" (Selections: I-II, IV, tr. by Greg Richter). [CharR] (16:1) Spr 90, p. 50.
"Memory" (Selection: I, tr. by Greg Richter). [CharR] (16:1) Spr 90, p. 49.
3148. JOHLER, Walt
"That Indian Summer Afternoon." [Wind] (20:66) 90, p. 8.
3149. JOHN, Elizabeth Mische
"Advent, Epiphany." [Farm] (7:2) Fall 90, p. 66-68.
"Nursing Home Epiphany." [Farm] (7:2) Fall 90, p. 65.
"Tornado Awareness." [Farm] (7:2) Fall 90, p. 69.
3150. JOHNSON, Dan
"The Bomb Document." [HawaiiR] (14:1, #28) Wint 89-90, p. 31.
"The Camera." [HawaiiR] (14:1, #28) Wint 89-90, p. 30.
"Chanticleer." [HawaiiR] (14:1, #28) Wint 89-90, p. 30.
"The Lorton Anthology." [Gargoyle] (37/38) 90, p. 122.
"Thorns" (for Brian Colella). [HawaiiR] (15:1, #31) Wint 90, p. 13-14.

241

JOHNSON

3151. JOHNSON, David
"Childhood Memory" (tr. of Antonio Machado). [VirQR] (66:3) Sum 90, p. 453-454.
"Flies" (tr. of Antonio Machado). [VirQR] (66:3) Sum 90, p. 452-453.
3152. JOHNSON, Dick
"By the Tomcat's Grave." [GeoR] (44:3) Fall 90, p. 421.
3153. JOHNSON, Don
"Calling" (for Bill Levin). [Iowa] (20:1) Wint 90, p. 97-99.
"No Scripture, Two Hymns." [Iowa] (20:1) Wint 90, p. 90-91.
"Sailin' On to Hawaii." [ChatR] (11:1) Fall 90, p. 41-42.
"Watauga Drawdown." [Iowa] (20:1) Wint 90, p. 92-97.
3154. JOHNSON, Elizabeth Ray
"Crystal Unclear." [OnTheBus] (2:1, #5) Spr 90, p. 77-78.
"What You Want." [OnTheBus] (2:1, #5) Spr 90, p. 77.
3155. JOHNSON, Frank
"Cardiac." [BellR] (13:2, #28) Fall 90, p. 14.
"Gypsy Said." [Asylum] (5:4) 90, p. 4.
"Vigil." [Abraxas] (38/39) 90, p. 130.
3156. JOHNSON, Fred
"Ulysses, My Father." [AntigR] (80) Wint 90, p. 10-11.
3157. JOHNSON, Greg
"Aid and Comfort." [Poetry] (156:2) My 90, p. 72.
"A Death That Dare Not Speak." [OntR] (32) Spr-Sum 90, p. 89-90.
"Sexual Outlaw." [Poetry] (156:2) My 90, p. 73.
"Spinster." [Poetry] (157:1) O 90, p. 15.
3158. JOHNSON, Henry
"The Ball Park." [IndR] (13:2) Spr 90, p. 15-16.
"For My Daughter." [SlipS] (10) 90, p. 49-50.
"A Letter from Prison." [Crazy] (39) Wint 90, p. 27-31.
"The Middle Passage." [IndR] (13:2) Spr 90, p. 12-14.
"To a Woman Standing in a Doorway." [SlipS] (10) 90, p. 50.
3159. JOHNSON, Jacqueline (Jacqueline Joan)
"Déjà Vu." [RiverS] (31) [90?], p. 38.
"Medicine Men" (For John O. Killens). [LitR] (33:4) Sum 90, p. 515.
3160. JOHNSON, Jean Youell
"Divorce." [Bogg] (62) 90, p. 43.
3161. JOHNSON, John
"A Sunday Poem." [Plain] (10:2) Wint 90, p. 11.
3162. JOHNSON, Judith E.
"Before Notre Dame" (For my mother's 80th birthday and my father's 84th: variation one). [Confr] (42/43) Spr-Sum 90, p. 112.
"Before Notre Dame" (variation two). [Confr] (42/43) Spr-Sum 90, p. 113.
3163. JOHNSON, Kenn
"1952." [Wind] (20:66) 90, p. 24.
3164. JOHNSON, Larry
"Death of Caracalla." [Hellas] (1:2) Fall 90, p. 234.
3165. JOHNSON, Linton Kwesi
"John De Crow." [LitR] (34:1) Fall 90, p. 93-98.
3166. JOHNSON, Manly
"I Would Like" (tr. of Tautvyda Marcinkeviciute, w. Julie Kane). [Nimrod] (33:2) Spr-Sum 90, p. 95-96.
"Morning" (tr. of Fazu G. Alieva, w. Birgitta Ingemanson). [Nimrod] (33:2) Spr-Sum 90, p. 44.
"The Thirst for Beauty" (tr. of Fazu G. Alieva, w. Birgitta Ingemanson). [Nimrod] (33:2) Spr-Sum 90, p. 43-44.
"The Wet Nurse" (tr. of Tautvyda Marcinkeviciute, w. Julie Kane). [Nimrod] (33:2) Spr-Sum 90, p. 97.
3167. JOHNSON, Marael
"Ambrosia." [ChironR] (9:1) Spr 90, p. 3.
"Collared and Cuffed." [ChironR] (9:1) Spr 90, p. 3.
"Glass Act." [ChironR] (9:1) Spr 90, p. 3.
"Re-connected." [ChironR] (9:3) Aut 90, p. 40.
"A Sobering Experience." [ChironR] (9:1) Spr 90, p. 3.
"A Sobering Experience." [Pearl] (10) Spr 90, p. 13.
3168. JOHNSON, Marilyn
"A Marilyn by Any Other Name." [Pearl] (12) Fall-Wint 90, p. 57.

3169. JOHNSON, Mark Allan
"After the Blizzard." [BellArk] (6:5) S-O 90, p. 11.
"Books of Common Prayer." [BellArk] (6:2) Mr-Ap 90, p. 28.
"Concepts of Time." [BellArk] (6:4) Jl-Ag 90, p. 22.
"Heirloom." [BellArk] (6:6) N-D 90, p. 6.
"The Orange and Green." [BellArk] (6:5) S-O 90, p. 10.
"Sands of Time." [BellArk] (6:1) Ja-F 90, p. 8.
"Screening Room." [BellArk] (6:1) Ja-F 90, p. 12.
"Wind." [BellArk] (6:3) My-Je 90, p. 21.

3170. JOHNSON, Markham
"Harvest." [Sonora] (19) Spr-Sum 90, p. 5.

3171. JOHNSON, Michael L.
"After the Earthquake in Armenia." [PoetL] (85:4) Wint 90-91, p. 34.
"Bureaucracy." [CoalC] (2) D 90, p. 16.
"During Lunch at Alonzo 'Slick' Smith's Barbecue Restaurant, a Local Holds Forth on the Real Muskogee, Oklahoma." [MidwQ] (31:4) Sum 90, p. 484.
"An Epitaph for Orange Scott Cummins" (for Oscar Scott Cummins). [KanQ] (22:4) Fall 90, p. 132.
"Five Settings." [MidwQ] (31:3) Spr 90, p. 365.
"Five Years After the Treaty Council at Medicine Lodge." [CapeR] (25:2) Fall 90, p. 10.
"J. L. Mahoney Finally Cuts Loose on a California Yuppie Feminist." [Hellas] (1:1) Spr 90, p. 43.
"J. L. Mahoney Makes Love in Autumn." [CoalC] (2) D 90, p. 19.
"John Delorean." [WindO] (53) Fall 90, p. 3.
"A Liberal." [PoetL] (85:4) Wint 90-91, p. 34.
"M.C. Escher's Ascending and Descending." [ManhatPR] (12) [90?], p. 13.
"Miss America Pageant." [ManhatPR] (12) [90?], p. 13.
"My Father's Wisdom" (For Dan and Dave). [MidwQ] (31:3) Spr 90, p. 366.
"Nuda" (tr. of Marcelin Pleynet). [Abraxas] (38/39) 90, p. 74-75.
"On the Line." [Bogg] (62) 90, p. 35.
"Stephen Hawking Oraculates." [WindO] (53) Fall 90, p. 4.
"Tract" (tr. of Marcelin Pleynet). [Abraxas] (38/39) 90, p. 74-75.
"Tucson." [MidwQ] (31:2) Wint 90, p. 220.

3172. JOHNSON, Nancy
"To a White Crow." [WillowS] (25) Wint 90, p. 46.

3173. JOHNSON, Nicholas
"I have not broken the promise" (for Kate Kentish). [Screens] (2) 90, p. 156.
"West Chapple." [Screens] (2) 90, p. 154-155.

JOHNSON, Reetika Vazirani
See JORDAN, Reetika Vazirani

3174. JOHNSON, Robert K.
"An Explanation." [SlipS] (10) 90, p. 44.

3175. JOHNSON, Ronald
"Ark: The Ramparts (Arches I-XVIII)" (for Guy Davenport, Mover & Shaker). [Conjunc] (15) 90, p. 148-189.

3176. JOHNSON, Sheila Golburgh
"Another Myth." [KanQ] (22:1/2) Wint-Spr 90, p. 122-123.
"Ours." [KanQ] (22:1/2) Wint-Spr 90, p. 122.

3177. JOHNSON, Stacey L.
"Pussy." [AnotherCM] (21) 90, p. 83.

3178. JOHNSON, Thomas L.
"A Southern Boy Reflects on Miss Monroe." [Pearl] (12) Fall-Wint 90, p. 33.

3179. JOHNSON, Tom
"Canyon de Chelly." [SouthernR] (26:1) Ja 90, p. 192-193.

3180. JOHNSON, William
"Delivering Milk with Father." [HiramPoR] (48/49) 90-91, p. 41-45.
"Three Musics." [HiramPoR] (48/49) 90-91, p. 40.

3181. JOHNSTON, Fred
"Quixote." [AntigR] (83) Aut 90, p. 67.
"Song for S." [AntigR] (83) Aut 90, p. 68.

3182. JOHNSTON, Mark
"Effigy's Monologue." [SoCoast] (8) Spr 90, p. 48-49.
"Her Blacks." [BlueBldgs] (12) 90, p. 10.
"Pelvis with Moon" (O'Keeffe Upon Her Painting). [PoetL] (85:3) Fall 90, p. 19.
"Sparklers." [OxfordM] (6:1) Spr-Sum 90, p. 63.

243

JOHNSTON HERNANDEZ, Beatriz
  See HERNANDEZ, Beatriz Johnston
3183. JOHNSTONE, Robert
  "Spider." [CutB] (34) Sum-Fall 90, p. 80.
3184. JOLLIFF, William
  "Spring Begins in Williams Grove." [BlackBR] (12) Fall-Wint 90, p. 4.
3185. JONES, Alice
  "The Biopsy." [Zyzzyva] (6:4 #24) Wint 90, p. 59-61.
  "The Lake." [NegC] (10:1) 90, p. 63-66.
  "Persephone." [Poetry] (156:6) S 90, p. 334-335.
3186. JONES, Arlene
  "First Winter of My Sister's Unmarked Grave." [GreenMR] (NS 3:2) Fall-Wint
    89-90, p. 112.
  "The Poet in Late Winter." [Kalliope] (12:1) 90, c89, p. 56.
3187. JONES, Daniel C.
  "Obsessions" (Selections: 12-13, 15-17, 21). [PoetryC] (11:3) Fall 90, p. 6.
3188. JONES, Francis R.
  "Journey of the Magi" (tr. of Wiel Kusters). [Trans] (24) Fall 90, p. 18.
  "Troublesome Gods" (Excerpt, tr. of Hans Faverey). [Trans] (24) Fall 90, p.
    143-149.
3189. JONES, Ina
  "Wedding Picture" (Germany, 1920). [WestB] (27) 90, p. 5-7.
  "White Crocus." [WestB] (27) 90, p. 7-8.
3190. JONES, Jacquie
  "Drugs." [Callaloo] (13:2) Spr 90, p. 299-300.
  "Kisii." [Callaloo] (13:2) Spr 90, p. 298.
3191. JONES, Jamey
  "Scattered Directions." [EmeraldCR] (1990) c89, p. 47-48.
3192. JONES, Jeffrey
  "My Stuffed Bunny." [PoetryUSA] (5:1) Spr 90, p. 17.
3193. JONES, John
  "The Cycle: for Kaya and Cavafy." [HangL] (56) 90, p. 18-19.
3194. JONES, John Chris
  "The Electric Book" (Selection from vol. 5: going south, a series of fictions taking
    place on j-921, a synthetic planet identical to earth: version 2 of chapter 1).
    [Screens] (2) 90, p. 164-167.
3195. JONES, Michael
  "About His Grandchildren." [RagMag] (7:2) Spr 90, p. 26.
  "A Talent for Rivers." [RagMag] (7:2) Spr 90, p. 25.
3196. JONES, Randall Bondurant
  "Sonogram of Padre Island, Texas." [KenR] (NS 12:3) Sum 90, p. 13-15.
3197. JONES, Richard
  "And So I Went Forth" (tr. of Stefan George, w. Ulrike Weber). [PoetryE] (30) Fall
    90, p. 93.
  "Andrew" (1979-1984). [OnTheBus] (2:2/3:1, #6/7) Sum-Fall 90 Wint-Spr 91, p.
    113-114.
  "Ars Poetica." [OnTheBus] (2:1, #5) Spr 90, p. 80.
  "Black-Out." [OnTheBus] (2:1, #5) Spr 90, p. 80.
  "Certain People." [Poetry] (156:3) Je 90, p. 139-140.
  "Devotion" (tr. of Günter Kunert, w. Ulrike Weber). [PoetryE] (29) Spr 90, p. 82.
  "The Examination." [OnTheBus] (2:1, #5) Spr 90, p. 81.
  "The Fence Painter." [OnTheBus] (2:2/3:1, #6/7) Sum-Fall 90 Wint-Spr 91, p. 112.
  "The Flower Box." [OnTheBus] (2:1, #5) Spr 90, p. 81.
  "The Flower I Guard" (tr. of Stefan George, w. Ulrike Weber). [PoetryE] (30) Fall
    90, p. 91.
  "From the Dorotheenstadt Cemetery" (tr. of Günter Kunert, w. Ulrike Weber).
    [PoetryE] (29) Spr 90, p. 81.
  "The Gift." [OnTheBus] (2:1, #5) Spr 90, p. 79.
  "I Am the One" (tr. of Stefan George, w. Ulrike Weber). [PoetryE] (30) Fall 90, p.
    89.
  "In Purple Fire Spoke the Wrath of Heaven" (tr. of Stefan George, w. Ulrike
    Weber). [PoetryE] (30) Fall 90, p. 90.
  "The Mother's Song" (after Georg Trakl). [OnTheBus] (2:2/3:1, #6/7) Sum-Fall 90
    Wint-Spr 91, p. 112-113.
  "My White Parrots" (tr. of Stefan George, w. Ulrike Weber). [Gargoyle] (37/38) 90,
    p. 114.

"Nightwatches Have Glow in the Dark Hands." [WritersF] (16) Fall 90, p. 15-16.
"Niobe" (tr. of Heinz Czechowski, w. Ulrike Weber). [PoetryE] (29) Spr 90, p. 75.
"The Noises of My Country" (tr. of Volker Braun, w. Ulrike Weber). [PoetryE] (29) Spr 90, p. 76.
"The Oysters" (for Alain Lance, tr. of Volker Braun, w. Ulrike Weber). [PoetryE] (29) Spr 90, p. 80.
"Pleasure-Garden, Prussia" (tr. of Volker Braun, w. Ulrike Weber). [PoetryE] (29) Spr 90, p. 78.
"Praise for the Masses" (tr. of Volker Braun, w. Ulrike Weber). [PoetryE] (29) Spr 90, p. 77.
"Song of the Camel." [OnTheBus] (2:1, #5) Spr 90, p. 79.
"Song of the Old Man." [Poetry] (156:3) Je 90, p. 139.
"Was My Question" (tr. of Stefan George, w. Ulrike Weber). [PoetryE] (30) Fall 90, p. 92.
"We Need Language" (tr. of Heinz Czechowski, w. Ulrike Weber). [PoetryE] (29) Spr 90, p. 74.
"Zentrum" (tr. of Volker Braun, w. Ulrike Weber). [PoetryE] (29) Spr 90, p. 79.
3198. JONES, Richard A.
"Harmony." [NewL] (57:1) Fall 90, p. 72.
3199. JONES, Robert
"At the Military Cemetery in San Bruno." [ChrC] (107:21) 11-18 Jl 90, p. 663.
"One Flight from Llao" (to SJ, in memory). [CumbPR] (10:1) Fall 90, p. 25-26.
3200. JONES, Rodney
"Evolving Patois." [GrandS] (9:4, #36) 90, p. 149-150.
3201. JONES, Roger
"Dirt Daubers." [HawaiiR] (15:1, #31) Wint 90, p. 32.
"Original Sin." [HawaiiR] (15:1, #31) Wint 90, p. 33.
"The Standard Oil Company" (tr. of Pablo Neruda). [CrabCR] (6:3) Spr 90, p. 15.
3202. JONES, Tom
"The Mutual Exclusion of Binaries." [Vis] (33) 90, p. 23-24.
3203. JOOLZ
"Nemesis." [Gargoyle] (37/38) 90, p. 112.
3204. JORDAN, Barbara
"Bruegel's Crows." [MissR] (19:1/2, #55/56) 90, p. 255.
"The Discovery Room." [MissR] (19:1/2, #55/56) 90, p. 256.
"Hammond Pond." [Agni] (31/32) 90, p. 199-200.
"A Poem for Orion." [Boulevard] (4:3/5:1, #12/13) Spr 90, p. 222.
"Web." [Boulevard] (4:3/5:1, #12/13) Spr 90, p. 221.
3205. JORDAN, June
"A Song for Soweto" (with music by Adrienne Torf). [SingHM] (17) 90, p. 8a-8c.
3206. JORDAN, Reetika Vazirani
"Biding." [CumbPR] (10:1) Fall 90, p. 29.
"Malik, My First Cousin." [Callaloo] (13:4) Fall 90, p. 737-739.
"On How I Did Not Give Aunt Juni the Right Thing Before She Died." [CumbPR] (10:1) Fall 90, p. 27-28.
3207. JORDAN, Richard
"The Acrobats." [Obs] (5:2) Sum 90, p. 29.
3208. JORIS, Pierre
"December Work" (Excerpts). [Notus] (5:1) Spr 90, p. 20-21.
3209. JORON, Andrew
"Tube Alley / Survival" (with Ivan Argüelles). [Caliban] (8) 90, p. 62-69.
3210. JOSEPH, Allison
"Change Partners and Dance." [Iowa] (20:3) Fall 90, p. 120-121.
3211. JOSEPHS, Laurence
"For a Dead Poet: Not a Friend." [Salm] (85/86) Wint-Spr 90, p. 122.
"June Tony." [Salm] (85/86) Wint-Spr 90, p. 119.
"Sonnet" (For Jacqueline Donnelly). [Salm] (85/86) Wint-Spr 90, p. 123.
"Still Life." [Salm] (85/86) Wint-Spr 90, p. 120-121.
3212. JOUBERT, Jean
"The Tower" (tr. by Denise Levertov). [Trans] (23) Spr 90, p. 23-24.
JOURNOUD, Claude Royet
See ROYET-JOURNOUD, Claude
JOUX, Alicia de
See De JOUX, Alicia
3213. JOVEL, Jinn
"The Sanity of the Insanity of Homelessness" (from "The Andronica"). [PoetryUSA]

(5:3) Fall 90, p. 25.
3214. JOZSEF, Attila
"Corals" (tr. by Len Roberts and Andy Rouse). [ArtfulD] (18/19) 90, p. 26.
JUANA INÉS de la CRUZ, Sor
See CRUZ, Juana Inés de la, Sor
3215. JUDD, Kirk M.
"Tao-Billy." [Bogg] (62) 90, p. 27.
3216. JUDSON, John
"Last Light" (from "Suite for Drury Pond," dedicated to the memory of Felix
Pollak). [Pembroke] (22) 90, p. 20.
"Sift down through dust gone gold" (from "Suite for Drury Pond," dedicated to the
memory of Felix Pollak). [Pembroke] (22) 90, p. 20.
3217. JULES, Jacqueline
"A Careful Man." [CapeR] (25:2) Fall 90, p. 7.
"Unwrapped Gifts." [CapeR] (25:2) Fall 90, p. 6.
3218. JULIET, Charles
"This Country of Silence" (Selections: 1-2, 5, 7-8, tr. by Louis Olivier). [CharR]
(16:2) Fall 90, p. 84-87.
3219. JULIUS, Richard
"Armadillo." [SlipS] (10) 90, p. 90.
JUN, Xiao
See XIAO, Jun
3220. JUNKINS, Donald
"Assisi and Perugia, Late March." [SewanR] (98:2) Spr 90, p. 191-192.
"Driving to School, the English Teacher." [PraS] (64:1) Spr 90, p. 66.
"Easter Monday in Miami: Listening to Eric Satie." [NewL] (57:2) Wint 90-91, p.
48.
"Feverfew, Book-Moth, and Wyrd." [WillowS] (26) Spr 90, p. 56-57.
"Florence: A December Morning Before Solstice, with an Introductory Stanza After
Hardy." [NewL] (57:2) Wint 90-91, p. 49.
"Leaning Over the Wharf in Bimini." [NewL] (57:2) Wint 90-91, p. 47.
"The Lizard of Villa del Corazon." [GreensboroR] (48) Sum 90, p. 76.
"Night Swimming at Las Columnas After the Drive from Ronda." [GreensboroR]
(48) Sum 90, p. 78.
"White Dandelions in Deerfield." [GreensboroR] (48) Sum 90, p. 77.
JUNZABURO, Nishiwaki
See NISHIWAKI, Junzaburo
3221. JUREK, Richard
"Picture of Pre-Arsenal Thoughts." [AntigR] (83) Aut 90, p. 113-114.
3222. JUSKIE-NELLIS, Joan E.
"Climbing Hills with Alice." [Plain] (11:1) Fall 90, p. 25.
3223. JUSTICE, Donald
"Body and Soul." [Antaeus] (64/65) Spr-Aut 90, p. 63-64.
3224. KABES, Petr
"I go straight off to my friends" (tr. by Jaroslav Korán and Daniel Weissbort).
[HampSPR] (Anthology 1975-1990) 90, p. 268.
"I have stopped naming the landscapes of my poems" (tr. by Jaroslav Korán and
Daniel Weissbort). [HampSPR] (Anthology 1975-1990) 90, p. 267.
"Once I lied about it here" (tr. by Jaroslav Korán and Daniel Weissbort).
[HampSPR] (Anthology 1975-1990) 90, p. 267.
3225. KACZMARSKYJ, Vera L.
"Untitled: For some time now I like to kick" (tr. of Taras Mel'nychuk). [Agni]
(31/32) 90, p. 159-160.
"Untitled: Scents, colors, lines and hues fade" (tr. of Natalka Bilotserkivets'). [Agni]
(31/32) 90, p. 119-120.
3226. KAFKA, Paul
"Home." [WashR] (16:4) D 90-Ja 91, p. 10.
"Notes for a visit." [WashR] (16:4) D 90-Ja 91, p. 10.
3227. KAHN, Lisa
"When Emigrating" (tr. of Oskar Kollbrunner). [NoDaQ] (58:4) Fall 90, p. 51.
3228. KAI, Yu
"Found Among Petals Dropping" (tr. by Scott Francis). [Paint] (17:33/34) Spr-Aut
90, p. 37.
"Hidden Light" (tr. by Scott Francis). [Paint] (17:33/34) Spr-Aut 90, p. 38.
3229. KAKINOMOTO no HITOMARO (681-729)
"Kinds of Death" (tr. by Graeme Wilson). [LitR] (33:2) Wint 90, p. 194.

3230. KALAMARAS, George
"Division." [Caliban] (9) 90, p. 85.
"If We Could Go There and Truly Be There." [Caliban] (9) 90, p. 86-87.
"The Lover Comes." [YellowS] (33) Spr 90, p. 5.
"To Be Born We Must Die, to Be Born We Must Be Born." [YellowS] (33) Spr 90, p. 12.
"Waking." [GreenMR] (NS 4:1) Spr-Sum 90, p. 88.
3231. KALINA, Gail
"Landscape Toward a Proper Silence" (After "Eclogues" by Dennis Schmitz). [SpoonRQ] (15:1) Wint 90, p. 20-23.
3232. KALLET, Marilyn
"Bomb Drills: Doug's Story." [SlipS] (10) 90, p. 55.
"Bomb Drills: Eric's Story." [SlipS] (10) 90, p. 55.
3233. KALUZA, Pat
"Doing the Dishes" (for Steve). [LakeSR] (24) 90, p. 6.
3234. KAMERER, Jocelyn
"An Ame." [DustyD] (1:2) O 90, p. 11.
"Clear Flame." [DustyD] (1:2) O 90, p. 10.
"Separation." [DustyD] (1:2) O 90, p. 12.
"Unravelling." [DustyD] (1:2) O 90, p. 11.
KAMP, Alexandra van de
See Van de KAMP, Alexandra
3235. KANDINSKY, Carla
"See Me Dance." [PoetryUSA] (5:3) Fall 90, p. 1.
3236. KANE, Barbara A.
"Initial Shock." [Amelia] (6:1, #16) 90, p. 86.
3237. KANE, George
"Home." [Turnstile] (2:1) 90, p. 20.
"Meditations on White (II)." [Turnstile] (2:1) 90, p. 21.
3238. KANE, Julie
"I Would Like" (tr. of Tautvyda Marcinkeviciute, w. Manly Johnson). [Nimrod] (33:2) Spr-Sum 90, p. 05-96.
"The Wet Nurse" (tr. of Tautvyda Marcinkeviciute, w. Manly Johnson). [Nimrod] (33:2) Spr-Sum 90, p. 97.
3239. KANE, Paul
"Plastic Explosive in Toorak Road." [Hudson] (43:3) Aut 90, p. 515.
KANEKO, Murayama
See MURAYAMA, Kaneko
3240. KANGAS, J. R.
"The Moon As Fat Lady." [WebR] (14:2) Spr 90, p. 62.
"On Being Told I Should Have a Dog." [ChironR] (9:2) Sum 90, p. 7.
3241. KANTARIS, Sylvia
"Before You?" [Stand] (31:1) Wint 89-90, p. 41.
3242. KANTCHEV, Nikolai
"Last Supper" (tr. by B. R. Strahan, w. Pamela Perry). [CrabCR] (6:3) Spr 90, p. 12-13.
"Night Lines" (tr. by B. R. Strahan, w. Pamela Perry). [CrabCR] (6:3) Spr 90, p. 13.
"Transformation" (tr. by B. R. Strahan, w. Pamela Perry). [CrabCR] (6:3) Spr 90, p. 12.
3243. KANYADI, Sándor
"Black-Red" (tr. by Len Roberts). [MidAR] (10:1) 90, p. 65-71.
"Bookmark" (tr. by Len Roberts). [AmerPoR] (19:5) S-O 90, p. 29.
"Fekete-piros." [MidAR] (10:1) 90, p. 64-70.
"In Front of the House All Night Long (A Reminiscence)" (tr. by Len Roberts). [AmerPoR] (19:5) S-O 90, p. 30.
"Jönnek Hozzám." [MidAR] (10:1) 90, p. 60, 62.
"Lithograph" (instead of a greeting in verse for Geua Domokos on his 16th birthday, tr. by Len Roberts). [CrabCR] (6:3) Spr 90, p. 11.
"A Lucky Man" (tr. by Len Roberts). [PoetryE] (30) Fall 90, p. 24.
"There Are Some Countries" (tr. by Len Roberts and Szabó Csabáné). [MidAR] (10:1) 90, p. 59.
"They Come to Me" (tr. by Len Roberts and Mariann Nagy). [MidAR] (10:1) 90, p. 61, 63.
"Towards Noah's Ark" (on the back of the Imre Nagy painting, tr. by Len Roberts and Mariann Nagy). [PoetryE] (30) Fall 90, p. 25.

"Vannak Videkek." [MidAR] (10:1) 90, p. 58.
3244. KAPIKIAN, Albert
"Arshille Gorky: Last Works, Starspray I and II." [GrahamHR] (13) Spr 90, p. 53-54.
3245. KAPLAN, Cheryl
"Breaking the Lawn." [NewYorkQ] (42) Sum 90, p. 70.
"Gets the Barber." [LitR] (33:3) Spr 90, p. 376.
3246. KAPLAN, Saul
"The Machine Maker." [ManhatPR] (11) [89?], p. 25.
3247. KAPLAN, Susan
"The Sciences." [NewOR] (17:1) Spr 90, p. 72.
3248. KAPLOW, Gail
"Eggs." [SingHM] (18) 90, p. 26-27.
3249. KARASICK, Adeena
"In Andean Passes." [WestCL] (24:1) Spr 90, p. 109-114.
3250. KARBE, Beth
"For Joan, in 1967." [SinW] (40) Spr 90, p. 76-77.
3251. KARELL, Miriam
"The Canyon." [PoetryUSA] (5:1) Spr 90, p. 17.
3252. KAREN
"Tinky Tongue." [PoetryUSA] (5:2) Sum 90, p. 8.
3253. KARLBERG, Bryn
"Parks of screaming childhood." [BellR] (13:2, #28) Fall 90, p. 29.
3254. KARLESKI, Karen
"Fire" (tr. of Adam Zagajewski). [PoetryE] (30) Fall 90, p. 50.
"The Grass" (tr. of Tadeusz Rózewicz). [PoetryE] (29) Spr 90, p. 25.
"I Water Flowers." [BlueBldgs] (12) 90, p. 18.
"In May" (tr. of Adam Zagajewski). [PoetryE] (30) Fall 90, p. 49.
"Our Fear" (tr. of Zbigniew Herbert). [PoetryE] (29) Spr 90, p. 15.
"Poems on Poland" (tr. of Adam Zagajewski). [PoetryE] (29) Spr 90, p. 13.
"The Tree" (tr. of Tadeusz Rózewicz). [PoetryE] (29) Spr 90, p. 24.
"The Wanderer" (tr. of Adam Zagajewski). [PoetryE] (29) Spr 90, p. 14.
3255. KAROFF, H. Peter
"Easter Sunday." [Northeast] (5:2) Spr 90, p. 15.
3256. KAROLYI, Amy
"Nature Morte" (in Hungarian). [MidAR] (10:1) 90, p. 56.
"Nature Morte" (tr. by Len Roberts). [MidAR] (10:1) 90, p. 57.
"Poor" (tr. by Len Roberts). [MidAR] (10:1) 90, p. 55.
"Szegények." [MidAR] (10:1) 90, p. 54.
"When the Statues Set Off" (tr. by Len Roberts). [AmerPoR] (19:5) S-O 90, p. 22.
3257. KÄRÖSSY, María (See also KÖRÖSY, Mária)
"The Voice" (tr. of István Vas, w. Daniel Hoffman). [Trans] (24) Fall 90, p. 223.
3258. KARP, Vickie
"Elegy." [NewYorker] (66:33) 1 O 90, p. 38.
"The Red Dress." [NewYorker] (66:40) 19 N 90, p. 58.
3259. KARR, Mary
"Etching of the Plague Years." [Poetry] (156:2) My 90, p. 70-71.
"Final Position." [Poetry] (157:1) O 90, p. 16.
3260. KARR, Muriel
"Bakrulatial." [Screens] (2) 90, p. 195.
"Incomplete." [Screens] (2) 90, p. 195.
"Modified Machismo." [Bogg] (63) 90, p. 41.
3261. KASDORF, Julia
"Along Ocean Parkway in Brooklyn." [WestB] (26) 90, p. 49.
3262. KASHNER, Sam
"This World." [WilliamMR] (28) 90, p. 24.
3263. KASISCHKE, Laura
"Grace." [Parting] (3:1) Sum 90, p. 24.
3264. KASISCHKE, Laura K.
"Massacre of the Innocents" (after Pieter Brueghel). [Journal] (13:2) Fall-Wint 89-90, p. 51-52.
"Radishes." [BellR] (13:2, #28) Fall 90, p. 42-43.
"We Seal Our Daughter in a Tower." [Kalliope] (12:1) 90, c89, p. 23-24.
3265. KASPERSMA, Jella
"Spring 1981" (tr. by Rod Jellema). [Vis] (34) 90, p. 28.

3266. KASZUBA, Sophia
"Bear." [Dandel] (17:2) Fall-Wint 90, p. 25.
"No Time to Go In." [PoetryC] (11:3) Fall 90, p. 17.
"Roadie." [PoetryC] (11:3) Fall 90, p. 17.
"Small History 1990." [PoetryC] (11:3) Fall 90, p. 17.
"The Soup." [Dandel] (17:1) Fall-Wint 90, p. 24.
3267. KATCHADOURIAN, Stina
"It" (Excerpt, tr. of Birgitta Boucht). [Screens] (2) 90, p. 87-90.
3268. KATES, J. (Jim)
"Among Black Trees." (tr. of Olga Popova). [CrabCR] (6:3) Spr 90, p. 8.
"Last Measures." [ConnPR] (9:1) 90, p. 16.
"The Mermaid" (tr. of Tatyana Scherbina). [Gargoyle] (37/38) 90, p. 50.
"What's Left" (tr. of Olga Popova). [CrabCR] (6:3) Spr 90, p. 8.
3269. KATRAK, Ketu H.
"New York City." [Arc] (25) Aut 90, p. 46.
3270. KATROVAS, Richard
"Adam's Wife" (tr. of Pavel Srut). [IndR] (13:3) Fall 90, p. 81.
"And You Don't Ask" (tr. of Pavel Srut). [IndR] (13:3) Fall 90, p. 80.
"Beat Poetry" (tr. of Josef Simon). [IndR] (13:3) Fall 90, p. 77-78.
"English Lesson" (tr. of Jan Rejzek, w. Dominika Winterová). [PoetryE] (29) Spr
90, p. 117.
"Flags" (tr. of Pavel Srut). [IndR] (13:3) Fall 90, p. 82.
"How I Beg Your Pardon, Little Anna" (tr. of Josef Simon). [IndR] (13:3) Fall 90,
p. 75.
"I Want" (tr. of Svetlana Burianová, w. Dominika Winterová). [PoetryE] (29) Spr
90, p. 114.
"Stalin's Monument: Snapshot from 1956" (tr. of Pavel Strut, w. Dominika
Winterová). [PoetryE] (29) Spr 90, p. 113.
"Troja at Eight in the Evening" (tr. of Karel Sys, w. Dominika Winterová).
[PoetryE] (29) Spr 90, p. 116.
"The Trojan Horse" (tr. of Pavel Srut). [IndR] (13:3) Fall 90, p. 79.
"A Walk Around the Brewery" (tr. of Ivan Wernisch, w. Dominika Winterová).
[PoetryE] (29) Spr 90, p. 115.
"You Slowly Undress" (tr. of Josef Simon). [IndR] (13:3) Fall 90, p. 76.
3271. KATZ, David M.
"Pope's Grotto." [NewRep] (203:18) 29 O 90, p. 40.
3272. KATZ, Jeffrey
"The Good Old Days." [SouthernPR] (30:1) Spr 90, p. 17-18.
3273. KATZ-LEVINE, Judy
"Calm Before Birth." [RiverS] (31) [90?], p. 26.
"Can Do." [RiverS] (31) [90?], p. 27.
"Highway Poem After Miro." [Asylum] (5:4) 90, p. 15.
"An Improvisation on 'The Glare of the Sun Wounding the Late Star'" (a painting by
Joan Miro). [Asylum] (6:2) S 90, p. 25.
3274. KAUFFMAN, Elizabeth D.
"Night" (tr. of Luis Rebaza Soraluz). [WashR] (16:2) Ag-S 90, p. 16.
"The Night" (tr. of Luis Rebaza Soraluz). [WashR] (16:2) Ag-S 90, p. 17.
"Not a Window" (tr. of Luis Rebaza Soraluz). [WashR] (16:2) Ag-S 90, p. 17.
"Parade for a Young Girl" (for Claudia, tr. of Luis Rebaza Soraluz). [WashR] (16:2)
Ag-S 90, p. 17.
"Those Who Part Hold Dear" (for Ana Maria Trelancia, tr. of Luis Rebaza Soraluz).
[WashR] (16:2) Ag-S 90, p. 17.
3275. KAUFMAN, Andrew
"Boric Acid." [GreenMR] (NS 4:1) Spr-Sum 90, p. 90-92.
"The Cool Night." [NegC] (10:2/3) 90, p. 77.
"Two Hours After My Brother Called." [BelPoJ] (41:1) Fall 90, p. 18-19.
3276. KAUFMAN, Debra
"Over Coffee." [MinnR] (NS 34/35) Spr-Fall 90, p. 23-24.
"Three Thanksgivings at My Step-Grandmother's." [Pembroke] (22) 90, p. 77-78.
3277. KAUFMAN, Ellen
"On the Road from the Hospital." [PoetryNW] (31:1) Spr 90, p. 22-23.
"The Walker." [PoetryNW] (31:1) Spr 90, p. 21-22.
3278. KAUFMAN, Margaret
"Three Ways to Kill a Goose." [AmerV] (21) Wint 90, p. 49.
3279. KAUFMAN, Merilee
"Trainman." [Confr] (42/43) Spr-Sum 90, p. 249.

249

3280. KAUFMAN, Shirley
"Bread and Water." [Ploughs] (16:4) Wint 90-91, p. 273.
"The Farmer" (On "The Fall of Icarus" by Pieter Breughel, tr. of Judith Herzberg,
w. the author). [Trans] (24) Fall 90, p. 56.
"The Fisherman" (On "The Fall of Icarus" by Pieter Breughel, tr. of Judith
Herzberg, w. the author). [Trans] (24) Fall 90, p. 58.
"Lemon Sponge." [Field] (43) Fall 90, p. 86-87.
"Longing for Prophets." [Field] (43) Fall 90, p. 88.
"Peace March, Jerusalem, 1989." [Field] (43) Fall 90, p. 85.
"The Sailor" (On "The Fall of Icarus" by Pieter Breughel, tr. of Judith Herzberg, w.
the author). [Trans] (24) Fall 90, p. 57.
"Survival Kit." [MassR] (31:3) Aut 90, p. 315-316.
3281. KAVIN, Diana
"Foster Homes." [OnTheBus] (2:2/3:1, #6/7) Sum-Fall 90 Wint-Spr 91, p. 115.
3282. KEAR, Jeff
"Bowling, Nude." [ArtfulD] (18/19) 90, p. 72.
3283. KEARNEY, Adele
"Goodbye." [PoetryUSA] (5:3) Fall 90, p. 8.
"Katharine Hepburn, Quoted." [PoetryUSA] (5:3) Fall 90, p. 9.
"Second Nature." [PoetryUSA] (5:3) Fall 90, p. 8.
3284. KEBE, Mbaye Gana
"On the Straw Fan" (tr. by Jan Pallister). [Vis] (32) 90, p. 14.
"A Smile" (tr. by Jan Pallister). [Vis] (32) 90, p. 15.
3285. KECK, Mary
"Where the Spaces Between the Words Go." [CimR] (93) O 90, p. 40-41.
3286. KEELER, Greg
"How This Motor Works." [SpoonRQ] (15:1) Wint 90, p. 6.
3287. KEELEY, Edmund
"Actaeon" (tr. of Yannis Ritsos). [Trans] (24) Fall 90, p. 212.
"After the Ceremony" (tr. of Yannis Ritsos). [SenR] (20:2) Fall 90, p. 25.
"After the Treaty Between the Athenians and the Lacedaemonians Was Broken" (after
Thucydides, tr. of Yannis Ritsos). [Antaeus] (64/65) Spr-Aut 90, p. 116-117.
"Asclepius" (tr. of Yannis Ritsos). [SenR] (20:2) Fall 90, p. 26.
"The Awakening of Telemachus" (tr. of Yannis Ritsos). [Trans] (24) Fall 90, p.
212.
"Between Ionians and Dorians" (tr. of Yannis Ritsos). [Antaeus] (64/65) Spr-Aut
90, p. 114-115.
"The Disjunctive Conjunction 'Or'" (tr. of Yannis Ritsos). [GrandS] (9:3) Spr 90, p.
24.
"The Diviner" (tr. of Yannis Ritsos). [Antaeus] (64/65) Spr-Aut 90, p. 113.
"First Sensuality" (tr. of Yannis Ritsos). [GrandS] (9:3) Spr 90, p. 22.
"Greek Scene" (tr. of Yannis Ritsos). [TriQ] (79) Fall 90, p. 108.
"Herms I" (tr. of Yannis Ritsos). [SenR] (20:2) Fall 90, p. 24.
"Not Even Mythology" (tr. of Yannis Ritsos). [Antaeus] (64/65) Spr-Aut 90, p. 118.
"The Red Thread" (tr. of Yannis Ritsos). [SenR] (20:2) Fall 90, p. 27.
"Repetitions" (5 selections, tr. of Yannis Ritsos). [Iowa] (20:3) Fall 90, p. 41-44.
"Repetitions" (Selections: 2 poems, tr. of Yannis Ritsos). [ParisR] (32:115) Sum 90,
p. 194-195.
"Return II" (tr. of Yannis Ritsos). [GrandS] (9:3) Spr 90, p. 23.
"Septeria and Daphnephoria" (tr. of Yannis Ritsos). [Trans] (24) Fall 90, p.
208-209.
"Themistocles" (tr. of Yannis Ritsos). [Trans] (24) Fall 90, p. 210-211.
3288. KEEN, Suzanne
"Preface to Elegy." [Chelsea] (49) 90, p. 72.
3289. KEENAN, Deborah
"The Arrangement." [PassN] (11:1) Sum 90, p. 3.
"Nothing to Eat" (for Rebecca Hill). [Shen] (40:4) Wint 90, p. 67.
3290. KEENAN, Gary
"A Mansion." [Stand] (31:4) Aut 90, p. 41.
3291. KEENER, LuAnn
"Kampuchea." [BlackBR] (11) Spr-Sum 90, p. 19.
"The Manatees" (Guy Owen Poetry Prize Winner, Betty Adcock, Judge).
[SouthernPR] (30:2) Fall 90, p. 5.
"Thread." [Nimrod] (34:1) Fall-Wint 90, p. 52.
"Upon the Waters." [Nimrod] (34:1) Fall-Wint 90, p. 53-55.

3292. KEESAN, Cynthia
"The Enlightened Person" (tr. of Jozo T. Boskovski, w. David B. Axelrod).
[Footwork] 90, p. 61.
3293. KEESHIG-TOBIAS, Lenore
"Elm." [PoetryC] (11:1) Spr 90, p. 10.
"I Got Caught." [PoetryC] (11:1) Spr 90, p. 10.
"Trying to Fly." [PoetryC] (11:1) Spr 90, p. 10.
3294. KEINEG, Paol
"Boudica" (Selections: 12-20, tr. by Keith Waldrop). [Sulfur] (10:1, #26) Spr 90, p.
199-203.
"Boudica 21-25" (tr. by Keith Waldrop). [NewAW] (6) Spr 90, p. 59-63.
3295. KEITH, David
"The Little Things." [ContextS] (1:1) 89, p. 17.
KEITH, Roger Kyle
See KYLE-KEITH, Roger
3296. KEITHLEY, George
"Joy." [Manoa] (2:1) Spr 90, p. 25.
"Old Holy Men." [Manoa] (2:1) Spr 90, p. 26.
"The Tempest Sonata." [Manoa] (2:1) Spr 90, p. 24-25.
3297. KELLER, David
"The Dark." [CimR] (91) Ap 90, p. 52.
3298. KELLER, Gene
"Suite Mon Simone." [Gypsy] (15) 90, p. 19.
3299. KELLER, Tsipi Edith
"Ein Leben" (tr. of Dan Pagis). [NowestR] (28:1) 90, p. 98.
"Ein Leben" (tr. of Dan Pagis). [Trans] (23) Spr 90, p. 191.
"Tempt the Devil" (tr. of Dan Pagis). [Trans] (23) Spr 90, p. 190.
"That's father, isn't it?" (tr. of Dan Pagis). [NowestR] (28:1) 90, p. 97.
3300. KELLEY, Karen
"The Boston Poems" (Selections: 10 poems). [PaperAir] (4:3) 90, p. 35-44.
"The Red Snake We Woke." [Sulfur] (10:1, #26) Spr 90, p. 4-16.
3301. KELLEY, Paul
"Only Undo" (for Tom McGauley and Ted Byrne). [WestCL] (24:1) Spr 90, p.
105-108.
3302. KELLEY, Tina
"The Room I Only Spent Summers In." [PraS] (64:1) Spr 90, p. 112-113.
"Slow Approach to a Bright Loud Room." [PraS] (64:1) Spr 90, p. 112.
3303. KELLMAN, Anthony
"Conversation with a Dead Politician (or Chak-Chak)." [Obs] (5:2) Sum 90, p.
48-49.
"Creatures." [Obs] (5:2) Sum 90, p. 46-48.
"Fishing Song." [Chelsea] (49) 90, p. 150-153.
"Somewhere, Somewhere." [Vis] (33) 90, p. 42.
3304. KELLY, Angela (Angi)
"The Good-bye Soup." [SouthernPR] (30:1) Spr 90, p. 50-51.
"Mama in the Medicine Cabinet." [CumbPR] (10:1) Fall 90, p. 30-31.
3305. KELLY, Brigit Pegeen
"Arguments of Everlasting." [GeoR] (44:1/2) Spr-Sum 90, p. 48-49.
"Pipistrelles." [YaleR] (79:2) Wint 90, p. 289-292.
3306. KELLY, Catriona H. M.
"Leviathan" (tr. of Elena Shvarts). [Nimrod] (33:2) Spr-Sum 90, p. 39.
3307. KELLY, James E.
"Scream." [MoodySI] (22/23) Wint 89-90, p. 35.
3308. KELLY, M. T.
"Shoreline, Old Lake Iroquois." [CanLit] (124/125) Spr-Sum 90, p. 91.
3309. KELLY, Robert
"A Baltic Tragedy." [Conjunc] (15) 90, p. 235-242.
"The Meaning of Something." [KenR] (NS 12:2) Spr 90, p. 102-104.
"A Set of Variations Done on Old Music." [Notus] (5:1) Spr 90, p. 4-5.
"Yar." [Notus] (5:1) Spr 90, p. 6.
3310. KELLY-DEWITT, Susan
"Photograph, Port Moresby, New Guinea, 1943." [ClockR] (6:2) 90, p. 76.
KEMING, Wu
See WU, Keming
3311. KEMP, Arnold J.
"Crocodilopilos." [Callaloo] (13:3) Sum 90, p. 381-383.

251

"Elegy" (for Paul Coppola, 1966-1988). [Callaloo] (13:3) Sum 90, p. 386.
"Marketplaces." [Callaloo] (13:3) Sum 90, p. 384-385.
"Self Portrait 'round Midnight." [Callaloo] (13:3) Sum 90, p. 387.
"Through the Heel." [ThRiPo] (35/36) 90, p. 11.
3312. KEMPHER, Ruth Moon
"A Social Gathering." [Bogg] (63) 90, p. 7.
"Unwritten Letter, From the Victim." [DogRR] (9:2, #18) Aut 90, p. 27.
3313. KENDALL, Robert
"August." [Footwork] 90, p. 95.
"The Bridge That Burns for Years." [Footwork] 90, p. 94.
"Empty Boxes" (Prose poem). [Footwork] 90, p. 94.
"Perhaps." [CanLit] (126) Aut 90, p. 64.
"The Prodigal Son." [Footwork] 90, p. 95.
"Returning." [Footwork] 90, p. 94.
3314. KENDRICK, Deborah
"For Mama" (reprinted from #6, 1982). [Kaleid] (20) Wint-Spr 90, p. 109.
"Like opposing lanes of traffic" (reprinted from #6, 1982). [Kaleid] (20) Wint-Spr
90, p. 109.
KENICHI, Nomura
See NOMURA, Kenichi
KENKICHI, Hashimoto
See KITASONO, Katue
3315. KENNEDY, Anne
(Anonymous poem). [FreeL] (4) 90.
3316. KENNEDY, Betsy
"The Linemen." [Pig] (16) 90, p. 16.
"Summer Outing: Olentangy Park." [BellArk] (6:3) My-Je 90, p. 1.
"We Mourn in Various Ways." [BellArk] (6:1) Ja-F 90, p. 12.
3317. KENNEDY, J. H.
"The Crusades" (to Robert Bly). [DustyD] (1:2) O 90, p. 7.
3318. KENNEDY, Monique M.
"Before the Mount of Venus" (from "Rifbjerg Rundt, Gyldendal, 1981, tr. of Klaus
Rifbjerg). [CimR] (92) Jl 90, p. 27.
"Cuckoo" (from "Rifbjerg Rundt, Gyldendal, 1981, tr. of Klaus Rifbjerg). [CimR]
(92) Jl 90, p. 28.
"Fossil" (from "Intetfang," Borgen, 1982, tr. of Pia Tafdrup). [CimR] (92) Jl 90, p.
31.
"Hebride Bay" (tr. of Thorkild Bjørnivig). [CimR] (92) Jl 90, p. 14.
"I Have Had to Kill You" (from "The Meaning of Places," 1985, tr. of Bo Green
Jensen, w. the author). [CimR] (92) Jl 90, p. 23.
"In a Safe-deposit Box" (tr. of Nina Malinovski). [CimR] (92) Jl 90, p. 25.
"In the Beginning" (from "The Meaning of Places," 1985, tr. of Bo Green Jensen,
w. the author). [CimR] (92) Jl 90, p. 22.
"A Mauve Fragrance in the Dark" (tr. of Thorkild Bjørnivig). [CimR] (92) Jl 90, p.
14.
"Yesterday's Tea" (from "When an Angel Is Wounded," Borgen, 1981, tr. of Pia
Tafdrup). [CimR] (92) Jl 90, p. 31-32.
3319. KENNEDY, Patrick
"An Eternal Flame." [ChironR] (9:1) Spr 90, p. 30.
"Report Card." [ChironR] (9:1) Spr 90, p. 30.
3320. KENNEDY, X. J.
"Early April Rattles Severly Professor Oglebock." [HampSPR] (Anthology
1975-1990) 90, p. 165.
"Old Men Pitching Horseshoes." [HampSPR] (Anthology 1975-1990) 90, p. 165.
3321. KENNELLY, Brendan
"Wheels." [Quarry] (39:1) Wint 90, p. 82.
3322. KENNEY, Richard
"Typhoon." [NewEngR] (12:4) Sum 90, p. 443-470.
3323. KENNY, Adele
"Snake Lady." [SingHM] (17) 90, p. 39.
"Stained Glass, the Dream." [SingHM] (17) 90, p. 38.
3324. KENTER, Robert
"Blood -- Ties." [Dandel] (17:1) Spr-Sum 90, p. 14.
"The House Above the River Was the First House." [AntigR] (83) Aut 90, p. 76.
"Pointing the Finger." [PraF] (11:4) Wint 90-91, p. 75.

3325. KENVIN, Natalie
  "Visible Lie." [NewAW] (6) Spr 90, p. 105.
3326. KENWORTHY, Brigham
  "Water." [PoetryUSA] (5:3) Fall 90, p. 27.
3327. KENYON, Jane
  "Catching Frogs." [VirQR] (66:2) Spr 90, p. 270-271.
  "In the Grove." [VirQR] (66:2) Spr 90, p. 269.
  "The Letter." [NewYorker] (66:6) 25 Mr 90, p. 42.
  "Now Where?" [NewYorker] (66:1) 19 F 90, p. 81.
  "Waiting." [VirQR] (66:2) Spr 90, p. 269-270.
3328. KENYON, Michael
  "Artichoke Hearts." [Descant] (21:4/22:1, #71/72) Wint-Spr 90-91, p. 160.
  "Dill Pickles." [Descant] (21:4/22:1, #71/72) Wint-Spr 90-91, p. 157.
  "Girl Guide Cookies." [Descant] (21:4/22:1, #71/72) Wint-Spr 90-91, p. 161.
  "Keepers." [Descant] (21:4/22:1, #71/72) Wint-Spr 90-91, p. 159.
  "Onion." [Descant] (21:4/22:1, #71/72) Wint-Spr 90-91, p. 156.
  "Roast Duck." [Descant] (21:4/22:1, #71/72) Wint-Spr 90-91, p. 155.
  "Spaghetti Bolognese." [Descant] (21:4/22:1, #71/72) Wint-Spr 90-91, p. 158.
3329. KEON, W. (Wayne)
  "xxii. Tell me again what the oppressed look like." [CrossC] (12:1) 90, p. 22.
  "Big Steve." [CanLit] (124/125) Spr-Sum 90, p. 161.
  "Big Steve." [CrossC] (12:1) 90, p. 22.
  "Down on the Yucatan." [CanLit] (124/125) Spr-Sum 90, p. 162-164.
  "Eagle's Work." [CrossC] (12:1) 90, p. 22.
  "Earth Nites." [CanLit] (124/125) Spr-Sum 90, p. 153-154.
  "I'm Not in Charge of This Ritual." [CanLit] (124/125) Spr-Sum 90, p. 154-155.
  "I'm Not in Charge of This Ritual." [Grain] (18:1) Spr 90, p. 11-12.
  "Joseph" (hinmaton yalatkit). [CrossC] (12:1) 90, p. 22.
  "Shaman and the Raven." [CanLit] (124/125) Spr-Sum 90, p. 165-167.
  "South Wheel." [CrossC] (12:1) 90, p. 22.
  "Willow Woman." [Grain] (18:1) Spr 90, p. 12.
3330. KERAN, Shirley
  "White Solitude." [DogRR] (9:2, #18) Aut 90, p. 33.
3331. KERLEY, Gary
  "White Cellars." [LullwaterR] (2:1) Wint 90, p. 10.
3332. KERLINSKY, Nathan
  "I Believe the Pulse." [ColEng] (52:6) O 90, p. 641-642.
  "Nothing Stamps Its Feet." [ColEng] (52:6) O 90, p. 643-644.
3333. KERMANI, Sue
  "Her Hair Exploded." [RagMag] (8:1) 90, p. 16.
3334. KEROUAC, Jack
  "When the girls start puttin Nirvana-No on their lips" (from "Mexico City Blues).
    [PoetryUSA] ([5:4?]) Wint 90, p. 19.
3335. KERR, Debra
  "Deliverance." [Dandel] (17:2) Fall-Wint 90, p. 13-14.
3336. KERR, Luella
  "Easter Sunday, St. Andrew's Cathedral." [Quarry] (39:4) Fall 1990, p. 38.
  "In My Mother's Garden." [PraF] (11:4) Wint 90-91, p. 55.
  "Partner." [Quarry] (39:4) Fall 1990, p. 39.
  "Red Roses." [PraF] (11:4) Wint 90-91, p. 54.
  "Slipper Shuffle." [Quarry] (39:4) Fall 1990, p. 40.
  "Tulips." [PraF] (11:4) Wint 90-91, p. 53.
3337. KERRIGAN, T. S.
  "The Entrance of Souls into Hell." [Hellas] (1:1) Spr 90, p. 58.
3338. KERSHNER, Brandon
  "Responsibilities." [GeoR] (44:4) Wint 90, p. 618.
3339. KESLER, Russell
  "Pileated Woodpecker." [SouthernHR] (24:4) Fall 90, p. 368.
3340. KESSLER, Clyde
  "Colubri's Psalm." [CapeR] (25:1) Spr 90, p. 11.
3341. KESSLER, Jascha
  "At First Hand" (tr. of Otto Orban, w. Mária Körösy). [MidAR] (10:2) 90, p. 178.
  "Capriccio 9" (tr. of Lyubomir Levchev, w. Alexander Shurbanov). [Screens] (2)
    90, p. 60-61.
  "The Golden Fleece" (tr. of Otto Orban, w. Mária Körösy). [MidAR] (10:2) 90, p.
    180.

253

KESSLER

"Intellectuals" (tr. of Otto Orban, w. Mária Körösy). [MidAR] (10:2) 90, p. 179.
"The Old Fortress" (tr. of Elizaveta Bagryana, w. Alexander Shurbanov). [Screens]
    (2) 90, p. 59.
"Our Bearings at Sea" (a novel-in-poems: 2 selections, tr. of Ottó Orbán, w. Maria
    Körösy). [Screens] (2) 90, p. 56-58.
"Poet" (tr. of Luchezar Elenkov, w. Alexander Shurbanov). [Screens] (2) 90, p. 62.
"Roots in the Air" (4 selections, tr. of Milan Richter). [Screens] (2) 90, p. 72-75.
"Secret Love" (Excerpt, tr. of Lyubomir Levchev, w. Alexander Shurbanov).
    [Screens] (2) 90, p. 60.
"Travelling Light" (Selections: 5 poems, tr. of Kirsti Simonsuuri, w. the author).
    [Screens] (2) 90, p. 83-86.
"We Have Bare Hands" (To the Prague students, beaten by police, 17 Nov. 1989, tr.
    of Milan Richter, w. the author). [CityLR] (4) 90, p. 188.
3342. KESSLER, Mary
    "Hope." [Spirit] (10:2) 90, p. 52.
3343. KESSLER, Milton
    "The Grand Concourse" (61 poems. MSS paper book. For Sonia, the best of
        teachers). [MSS] (7:1) 90, 90 p.
    "Zero." [Sulfur] (10:2, #27) Fall 90, p. 4.
3344. KESSLER, Sidney (See also KESSLER, Sydney)
    "Return." [PaintedB] (40/41) 90, p. 182-183.
3345. KESSLER, Stephen
    "Don't Kill Yourself, You're Only 30." [OnTheBus] (2:2/3:1, #6/7) Sum-Fall 90
        Wint-Spr 91, p. 116.
3346. KESSLER, Sydney (See also KESSLER, Sidney)
    "Not One Notched Hour." [LitR] (33:3) Spr 90, p. 366.
3347. KETCHEK, Michael
    "Untitled: For one moment." [ChironR] (9:3) Aut 90, p. 40.
KETHLEY, Fiona Pitt
    See PITT-KETHLEY, Fiona
3348. KETTNER, M.
    "Impressions of the Fatal Voyage of Donald Crowhurst." [CrabCR] (7:1) Wint 90,
        p. 19.
3349. KEVORKIAN, Karen
    "After Puccini." [AntR] (48:2) Spr 90, p. 221.
3350. KEY, Bruce
    "A Drying of 'Shirley Temple' Toes." [Wind] (20:67) 90, p. 8.
    "Untitled: No, we can not see the wind." [Wind] (20:67) 90, p. 29.
3351. KEYES, Claire
    "The Net Swells with That Heavy Fruit" (Greensboro Review Literary Award
        Poem). [GreensboroR] (49) Wint 90-91, p. 43-44.
3352. KEYES, Robert Lord
    "Crossing the Fence." [Wind] (20:67) 90, p. 13.
    "Mt. Lincoln." [Wind] (20:67) 90, p. 2.
KEYES, Rogert Lord
    See KEYES, Robert Lord
3353. KEYS, Kerry Shawn
    "The Aviary of My Liking" (for Saint Francis). [Gargoyle] (37/38) 90, p. 114.
    "Keeping the Song." [Ploughs] (16:4) Wint 90-91, p. 28.
    "A Poem Broken in Parts" (for Mike Jennings). [NewOR] (17:4) Wint 90, p. 88.
3354. KHATIBI, Abdelkebir
    "Dedication to the Coming Year" (Excerpts, tr. by Eric Sellin). [Vis] (32) 90, p. 12.
3355. KHAZINDAR, Walid
    "Absence" (tr. by Lena Jayyusi and W. S. Merwin). [PaperAir] (4:3) 90, p. 65.
    "At Least" (tr. by Lena Jayyusi and W. S. Merwin). [PaperAir] (4:3) 90, p. 64.
    "Houses" (tr. by Lena Jayyusi and W. S. Merwin). [PaperAir] (4:3) 90, p. 66.
    "Perplexed" (tr. by Lena Jayyusi and W. S. Merwin). [PaperAir] (4:3) 90, p. 66.
    "Profile" (tr. by Lena Jayyusi and Naomi Shihab Nye). [Screens] (2) 90, p. 19.
3356. KHOURY-GHATA, Venus
    "He Speaks" (tr. by Jeremy Reed). [Vis] (32) 90, p. 20.
    "His Feet" (tr. by Stephen Scobie). [Vis] (32) 90, p. 20.
3357. KICKNOSWAY, Faye
    "Butcher Scraps" (A Chapbook). [Manoa] (2:1) Spr 90, p. 59-70.
3358. KIDD, David
    "Throne." [KanQ] (22:3) Sum 90, p. 206.

3359. KIKUCHI, Carl
"A Story." [CumbPR] (9:2) Spr 90, p. 18-19.
"There Is No Season Like Summer." [CumbPR] (9:2) Spr 90, p. 17.
3360. KILMARTIN, Eileen Kerin
"Cypress." [PoetryUSA] (5:1) Spr 90, p. 17.
3361. KIM, Chiha
"Inside" (tr. by Kim Uchang). [Manoa] (2:2) Fall 90, p. 50.
"The Mirror in Winter. Does the camellia bloom for me?" (tr. by Kim Uchang).
[Manoa] (2:2) Fall 90, p. 48-49.
"The Mirror in Winter. History is sad" (tr. by Kim Uchang). [Manoa] (2:2) Fall 90,
p. 48.
"The Mirror in Winter. I am not like me" (tr. by Kim Uchang). [Manoa] (2:2) Fall
90, p. 49-50.
"The Mirror in Winter. The sun at zenith" (tr. by Kim Uchang). [Manoa] (2:2) Fall
90, p. 49.
3362. KIM, Sabina
"Miasma." [Grain] (18:4) Wint 90, p. 74.
3363. KIM, Sooyoun
"Animals." [PoetryUSA] (5:3) Fall 90, p. 26.
3364. KIM, Tong-ni
"Pink Flowers" (tr. by Constantine Contogenis and Wolhee Choe). [PoetryE] (30)
Fall 90, p. 103.
3365. KIM, Uchang
"The Crow" (tr. of Paek Musan). [Manoa] (2:2) Fall 90, p. 153.
"I Breathe" (tr. of Choe Sungho). [Manoa] (2:2) Fall 90, p. 150.
"Inside" (tr. of Kim Chiha). [Manoa] (2:2) Fall 90, p. 50.
"The Mirror in Winter. Does the camellia bloom for me?" (tr. of Kim Chiha).
[Manoa] (2:2) Fall 90, p. 48-49.
"The Mirror in Winter. History is sad" (tr. of Kim Chiha). [Manoa] (2:2) Fall 90, p.
48.
"The Mirror in Winter. I am not like me" (tr. of Kim Chiha). [Manoa] (2:2) Fall 90,
p. 49-50.
"The Mirror in Winter. The sun at zenith" (tr. of Kim Chiha). [Manoa] (2:2) Fall 90,
p. 49.
"Snow Falling into a White Night" (tr. of Choe Sungho). [Manoa] (2:2) Fall 90, p.
151.
"That Year" (tr. of Paek Musan). [Manoa] (2:2) Fall 90, p. 152-153.
3366. KIM, Yong U.
"Father's Garden." [CarolQ] (43:1) Fall 90, p. 107-108.
3367. KIM, Yoon Sik
"Born on the 4th of July." [NewYorkQ] (42) Sum 90, p. 38.
3368. KIMBALL, Cynthia A.
"Beachcomer" (for JFC and GW). [PoetryNW] (31:2) Sum 90, p. 24.
3369. KINCAID, Joan Payne
"Aerobics." [Parting] (3:1) Sum 90, p. 15.
"An Appropriate Target" (In memory of Ben Linder, Pablo Rosales, Sergio
Hernandez -- killed while working in Nicaragua, April 28, 1987). [SlipS] (10)
90, p. 101.
"Hijackings." [Gypsy] (15) 90, p. 4.
"Meeting a Falmar." [Gypsy] (15) 90, p. 32.
"Victory" (To the winnah, a Souza March). [Bogg] (63) 90, p. 47.
"X Rated." [Confr] (44/45) Fall 90-Wint 91, p. 193.
3370. KINDEL, Marian
"Transition" (reprinted from #1, 1979). [Kaleid] (20) Wint-Spr 90, p. 73.
3371. KING, Carl
"The Bar" (tr. of Ivan Malinowski). [CimR] (92) Jl 90, p. 24.
3372. KING, Glenngo Allen
"The Age of Anti-Art." [BlackALF] (24:3) Fall 90, p. 548.
"Dancing Demonless." [BlackALF] (24:3) Fall 90, p. 548-549.
3373. KING, Kenneth
"In the Year of Her Daughter's Death My Mother." [PoetryNW] (31:4) Wint 90-91,
p. 19.
"Reprieve." [KanQ] (22:3) Sum 90, p. 180.
"Stereo Poem." [NowestR] (28:3/29:1) 90-91, p. 188.
"Who Killed Her Dog and Put a Snake in Her Mailbox?" [NowestR] (28:3/29:1)
90-91, p. 187.

3374. KING, Larissa
"Oral History." [BellArk] (6:4) Jl-Ag 90, p. 19.
3375. KING, Linda
"Green Jello." [Pearl] (10) Spr 90, p. 12.
"A Stray Kitten." [Pearl] (12) Fall-Wint 90, p. 59.
3376. KING, Lyn
"For My Daughter" (miles away). [MalR] (93) D 90, p. 33.
"Pine Needles." [Arc] (25) Aut 90, p. 10-11.
"Witbank" (old belfast rd., country down, n. ireland). [MalR] (93) D 90, p. 34.
3377. KING, R. D.
"The Lake." [NowestR] (28:2) 90, p. 52-53.
"Waking Up in Barstow." [NowestR] (28:2) 90, p. 50-51.
3378. KING, Robert
"Service." [Interim] (9:2) Fall-Wint 90-91, p. 39.
3379. KING, Thomas
"The City on the Hill." [CanLit] (124/125) Spr-Sum 90, p. 265.
"Coyote Goes to Toronto." [CanLit] (124/125) Spr-Sum 90, p. 252.
"Coyote Learns to Whistle." [CanLit] (124/125) Spr-Sum 90, p. 250-251.
"Coyote Sees the Prime Minister." [CanLit] (124/125) Spr-Sum 90, p. 252.
3380. KINGSTON, Katie
"Hustling Pool." [Plain] (11:1) Fall 90, p. 29.
3381. KINNELL, Galway
"Agapé." [GreenMR] (NS 3:2) Fall-Wint 89-90, p. 12-13.
"The Cat." [BelPoJ] (40:4) Sum 90, p. 36-37.
"The Ceiling." [PartR] (57:4) 90, p. 559.
"Divinity." [BostonR] (15:5) O 90, p. 3.
"Farewell" (fter Haydn's Symphony in F-Sharp Minor, for Paul Zweig,
    1935-1984). [Atlantic] (266:4) O 90, p. 92.
"Flower of Five Blossoms." [AmerPoR] (19:5) S-O 90, p. 8-9.
"Judas-Kiss." [NewYorker] (66:35) 15 O 90, p. 50.
"Kilauea." [NewYorker] (66:23) 23 Jl 90, p. 34-35.
"Last Gods." [Antaeus] (64/65) Spr-Aut 90, p. 65-66.
"The Man on the Hotel Room Bed." [OhioR] (45) 90, p. 21-22.
"The Massage." [GeoR] (44:3) Fall 90, p. 499-500.
"Memories of My Father." [Poetry] (156:6) S 90, p. 341-344.
"The Perch." [NewYorker] (66:30) 10 S 90, p. 42.
"Street of Gold." [MassR] (31:3) Aut 90, p. 338-339.
"The Vow." [BostonR] (15:5) O 90, p. 3.
"The Well-Tempered Clavier." [GreenMR] (NS 3:2) Fall-Wint 89-90, p. 8-9.
"Who, on Earth." [GreenMR] (NS 3:2) Fall-Wint 89-90, p. 10-11.
3382. KINSELLA, Thomas
"Brothers in the Craft." [Quarry] (39:1) Wint 90, p. 83.
3383. KINSLEY, Robert
"Those Mornings." [TarRP] (29:2) Spr 90, p. 12.
3384. KINZIE, Mary
"Canicula." [YaleR] (79:2) Wint 90, p. 287-288.
"Days of Darkness." [Salm] (85/86) Wint-Spr 90, p. 38.
"Down to Quantico." [Salm] (85/86) Wint-Spr 90, p. 36-37.
"Dweller in the Forest." [Salm] (88/89) Fall 90-Wint 91, p. 361.
"Faith." [Salm] (85/86) Wint-Spr 90, p. 41.
"Little Brown Jug." [Salm] (85/86) Wint-Spr 90, p. 39.
"Mannikin." [Salm] (88/89) Fall 90-Wint 91, p. 358-360.
"The Other Children." [Salm] (85/86) Wint-Spr 90, p. 42.
"Taffy." [Salm] (85/86) Wint-Spr 90, p. 40.
"Waltzing Matilda" (For Della and Alan). [Agni] (29/30) 90, p. 96-97.
3385. KIPLING, Rudyard
"The Burden of Jerusalem." [GrandS] (9:3) Spr 90, p. 224-225.
"A Chapter of Proverbs." [GrandS] (9:3) Spr 90, p. 226-229.
"The White Man's Burden." [GrandS] (9:3) Spr 90, p. 204-205.
3386. KIPP, Karen
"April." [GrahamHR] (13) Spr 90, p. 36.
"Bounty" (For my friends from Adamant, 1988). [AntR] (48:1) Wint 90, p. 88-89.
3387. KIRBY, Barney
"Red Patch." [AmerPoR] (19:3) My-Je 90, p. 42.
3388. KIRBY, David
"Be Quiet, Will You." [NegC] (10:2/3) 90, p. 16-17.

"The Cause of the Crash and the Crash Itself." [NegC] (10:2/3) 90, p. 19.
"Dateline, Western Sizzler." [NegC] (10:2/3) 90, p. 18.
"Krafft-Ebing's *Aberrations of Sexual Life*." [SouthernR] (26:2) Ap 90, p. 346.
"Little Stabs of Happiness." [Ploughs] (16:4) Wint 90-91, p. 262.
"Nosebleed, Gold Digger, KGB, Henry James, Handshake." [GettyR] (3:1) Wint
      90, p. 83-84.
"Ode to Languor." [SouthernR] (26:2) Ap 90, p. 347-348.
"Othello." [GettyR] (3:1) Wint 90, p. 81-82.
3389. KIRBY, John T.
"Fragment 543 (Page)" (tr. of Simonides). [SycamoreR] (2:1) Wint 90, p. 567.
3390. KIRBY, Mark
"Baptism." [Comm] (117:14) 10 Ag 90, p. 450.
3391. KIRBY, Martin
"Advice to a Mercenary." [OnTheBus] (2:2/3:1, #6/7) Sum-Fall 90 Wint-Spr 91, p.
      117-118.
3392. KIRCHDORFER, Ulf
"Swedish Dream." [PoetL] (85:2) Sum 90, p. 36.
3393. KIRCHWEY, Karl
"The Diva's First Song (White's Hotel, London)." [PartR] (57:1) Wint 90, p.
      105-106.
"St. Nicholas" (Zürich, 6 December). [NewYorker] (66:42) 3 D 90, p. 46.
"The Transformation of Light." [Antaeus] (64/65) Spr-Aut 90, p. 67-68.
3394. KIRK, Laurie
"The Runaway." [SoCoast] (9) Fall 90, p. 40.
3395. KIRKLAND, Leigh
"Liquor That Will Not Fill an Empty Bottle." [PoetL] (85:4) Wint 90-91, p. 33.
3396. KIRKPATRICK, Kathryn
"Corrida." [Poem] (63) My 90, p. 20.
"The Daughter." [Poem] (63) My 90, p. 21.
"For My Father, Who Never Sang." [Poem] (63) My 90, p. 18-19.
"Nobel Physicist Creates Theory from Geologist Son's Data." [Poem] (63) My 90,
      p. 16.
"Sacrament of Sleep." [Poem] (63) My 90, p. 17.
3397. KIRKUP, James
"On the Birth of a Son Delivered at Home by His Own Father." [Verse] (7:3) Wint
      90, p. 96.
3398. KIRSCHNER, Elizabeth
"Built with the Same Beauty." [GeoR] (44:1/2) Spr-Sum 90, p. 146-147.
"The Essential Universe." [ThRiPo] (35/36) 90, p. 26.
"The Fall of Light." [NoDaQ] (58:1) Wint 90, p. 70.
"Grandmother's Arms." [GettyR] (3:4) Aut 90, p. 776.
"The Life of a Hummingbird." [ThRiPo] (35/36) 90, p. 25.
"On the Night of Falling Comets." [CrabCR] (7:1) Wint 90, p. 11.
"A Person Broken in Two." [NoDaQ] (58:1) Wint 90, p. 69.
"Their Asking." [ThRiPo] (35/36) 90, p. 24.
"Twenty Colors." [NoDaQ] (58:1) Wint 90, p. 71.
"Two Blue Swans." [NoAmR] (275:2) Je 90, p. 27.
3399. KIRSTEN-MARTIN, Diane
"La Vie Intérieure / Yonkers." [HayF] (6) Sum 90, p. 79.
3400. KIRSTIN, Joy
"Montpellier in December." [Grain] (18:1) Spr 90, p. 42.
"Mud Bath." [Grain] (18:1) Spr 90, p. 41.
3401. KISLYCH, Helen
"If I start to write romance" (Poem written in English by high school students from
      the Ukraine, collected by Maureen Hurley). [PoetryUSA] (5:1) Spr 90, p. 18.
3402. KISTLER, William
"The Place of Country." [PoetryUSA] (5:3) Fall 90, p. 15.
"Shostakovich, 2nd Movement, Quartet No. 7." [PoetryUSA] (5:3) Fall 90, p. 17.
3403. KITASONO, Katue
"Blue Background" (tr. by John Solt). [CityLR] (4) 90, p. 174.
"Blue Square" (tr. by John Solt). [CityLR] (4) 90, p. 175.
3404. KIVETTE, Nancy
"Stephanie's Stillness." [ClockR] (6:2) 90, p. 55.
3405. KIYOOKA, Roy
"Notes Toward a Book of Photoglyphs." [CapilR] (2:2) Spr 90, p. 76-94.
"One Signature. Kumo/Cloud/s & Sundry Pieces." [WestCL] (24:3) Wint 90, p.

97-128.
3406. KIYOTOKI, Fumiko
   "The headlights, moving" (tr. by Janet Lewis). [SouthernR] (26:1) Ja 90, p. 203.
3407. KIZER, Carolyn
   "Assembly Line" (tr. of Shu Ting). [Manoa] (2:2) Fall 90, p. 177.
   "Bei Tai-He Beach" (tr. of Shu Ting). [Manoa] (2:2) Fall 90, p. 176.
   "Marriage Song" (with commentary). [Antaeus] (64/65) Spr-Aut 90, p. 69-70.
   "Pro Femina." [CimR] (93) O 90, p. 76-77.
   "Tirade for the Next-to-Last Act" (tr. of Nina Cassian). [AmerPoR] (19:1) Ja-F 90,
      p. 26.
   "Twelve O'Clock." [ParisR] (32:117) Wint 90, p. 62-66.
   "Weekend Evening" (tr. of Shu Ting). [Manoa] (2:2) Fall 90, p. 175.
3408. KLASSEN, Sarah
   "Evidence." [PraF] (11:2) Sum 90, p. 108.
   "In Dreams My Mother." [Quarry] (39:2) Spr 90, p. 48.
   "Interlake Childhood I." [PraF] (11:2) Sum 90, p. 106.
   "Interlake Childhood II." [PraF] (11:2) Sum 90, p. 107.
   "Medication." [PoetryC] (11:3) Fall 90, p. 5.
   "Procedure." [PoetryC] (11:3) Fall 90, p. 5.
   "Summer." [Quarry] (39:2) Spr 90, p. 49.
3409. KLAVAN, Andrew
   "Boston Harbor." [Amelia] (6:1, #16) 90, p. 33.
   "Day of Atonement." [Amelia] (6:1, #16) 90, p. 31-32.
   "Harris Among the Gods." [Salm] (85/86) Wint-Spr 90, p. 136-137.
   "The Lake in the Valley." [Amelia] (6:1, #16) 90, p. 32-33.
   "The Pond." [ParisR] (32:115) Sum 90, p. 261-262.
   "This Morning." [Poetry] (156:3) Je 90, p. 125.
   "Winter Choir." [Amelia] (6:1, #16) 90, p. 32.
KLAVINA, Ilze Mueller
   See MUELLER-KLAVINA, Ilze
3410. KLAWANS, Stuart
   "Junk Shop" (tr. of Enrique Santos Discépolo, w. Amelia Arenas). [Thrpny] (43)
      Fall 90, p. 19.
   "Spinning, Spinning" (tr. of Enrique Santos Discépolo, w. Amelia Arenas).
      [Thrpny] (43) Fall 90, p. 18-19.
   "Tonight I'm Going to Get Drunk" (tr. of Enrique Santos Discépolo, w. Amelia
      Arenas). [Thrpny] (43) Fall 90, p. 18.
3411. KLEBECK, William
   "Ghost." [Grain] (18:4) Wint 90, p. 80.
3412. KLEIN, Evan
   "On a Road." [ChironR] (9:2) Sum 90, p. 20.
3413. KLEIN, James
   "Cleaning Pheasants." [OnTheBus] (2:1, #5) Spr 90, p. 84.
   "The Life Story of Charlie Parker." [OxfordM] (6:1) Spr-Sum 90, p. 70.
   "Nightfishing." [OnTheBus] (2:1, #5) Spr 90, p. 84.
   "Style." [OnTheBus] (2:2/3:1, #6/7) Sum-Fall 90 Wint-Spr 91, p. 119.
3414. KLEIN, Lisa Raquel
   "Carmic Crash." [OnTheBus] (2:1, #5) Spr 90, p. 82-83.
3415. KLEIN, Michael
   "Revealed." [AntR] (48:1) Wint 90, p. 80-81.
   "Whole Lives Missing." [Boulevard] (5:2, #14) Fall 90, p. 130-131.
3416. KLEIN, Rosemary
   "Homing Instincts." [NegC] (10:2/3) 90, p. 89-90.
3417. KLEIN, Stacy A.
   "Song of Betrayal" (6 poems, tr. of Gwido Zlatkes, w. Maya Peretz and the author).
      [Screens] (2) 90, p. 52-55.
3418. KLEINSCHMIDT, Edward
   "About." [LitR] (33:3) Spr 90, p. 308.
   "Artificial Intelligence." [HawaiiR] (14:2, #29) Spr 90, p. 116-117.
   "Atavism." [Witness] (4:1) 90, p. 23.
   "Basically Troubled in the Heat." [HawaiiR] (14:2, #29) Spr 90, p. 114-115.
   "Calling Up." [HawaiiR] (14:3, #30) Fall 90, p. 34-35.
   "Cancerismo." [Witness] (4:1) 90, p. 21.
   "Dinner at Five." [GreenMR] (NS 3:2) Fall-Wint 89-90, p. 81.
   "Doubt." [Witness] (4:1) 90, p. 22.
   "Earshot." [MissouriR] (13:2) 90, p. 151.

"Excitement." [HawaiiR] (14:3, #30) Fall 90, p. 36-37.
"Exploded View." [CalQ] (34) 90, p. 27.
"Hence." [GettyR] (3:4) Aut 90, p. 648-649.
"Like a Wreck." [OnTheBus] (2:2/3:1, #6/7) Sum-Fall 90 Wint-Spr 91, p. 120.
"Mention." [CharR] (16:1) Spr 90, p. 61.
"Page." [GettyR] (3:4) Aut 90, p. 644-645.
"Practice." [GettyR] (3:4) Aut 90, p. 646-647.
"Rapid Fire." [ThRiPo] (35/36) 90, p. 35-36.
"Souvenir." [HighP] (5:2) Fall 90, p. 73-74.
"To Remain." [NewEngR] (13:2) Wint 90, p. 5-7.
"Unpainted Dream" (from Paul Klee's "Diaries"). [ApalQ] (33/34) 90, p. 58.
3419. KLEINZAHLER, August
"At Summer's End." [Zyzzyva] (6:3 #23) Fall 90, p. 100-101.
"Going." [Harp] (281:1685) O 90, p. 40.
"Rubble." [ParisR] (32:116) Fall 90, p. 106-107.
3420. KLESZKA, Marilyn
"Africa Sunrise." [Amelia] (6:1, #16) 90, p. 47.
3421. KLIMASEWISKI, Marshall N.
"Creation of Passion." [Parting] (3:1) Sum 90, p. 38.
3422. KLINE, George L.
"Ninel" (tr. of Evgenii Rein, w. members of the Bryn Mawr Translation Seminar).
    [Nimrod] (33:2) Spr-Sum 90, p. 40-42.
3423. KLINKNER, Marilyn
"Blind Countenance." [Northeast] (5:2) Spr 90, p. 16-17.
3424. KLIPSCHUTZ
"Capitalism Is a Contact Sport." [ChironR] (9:2) Sum 90, p. 12.
"Fragment." [ChironR] (9:2) Sum 90, p. 12.
"MAYBe YOu HAd To Be THERe" [sic]. [ChironR] (9:2) Sum 90, p. 12.
3425. KLOEFKORN, William
"Analgesic Balm." [NoDaQ] (58:4) Fall 90, p. 74-75.
"Fishing with My Two Boys at a Spring-Fed Pond in Kansas." [MidwQ] (31:4)
    Sum 90, p. 480-481.
"Jumping Rope." [GeoR] (44:3) Fall 90, p. 422-423.
"Kicking the Can." [GeoR] (44:4) Wint 90, p. 616-617.
"Kissing Wet." [PoetC] (21:2) Wint 90, p. 31-32.
"On the Kuskokwim River Near Bethel, Alaska." [NoDaQ] (58:4) Fall 90, p. 76-77.
"Outside the Sheldon Gallery, Early June." [MidwQ] (32:1) Aut 90, p. 86.
"Shopping Alone Only for Myself at the Neighborhood Hy-Vee." [PoetC] (21:2)
    Wint 90, p. 33-34.
"Touring the Campus Arboretum, Early Spring." [NoDaQ] (58:4) Fall 90, p. 73-74.
"Wednesday Night Special: Liver & Onions." [LaurelR] (24:2) Sum 90, p. 16-18.
3426. KLOKKER, Jay
"The Accordionist." [Agni] (31/32) 90, p. 232-235.
"For Trakl Under Fire (1914)." [BellR] (13:2, #28) Fall 90, p. 34.
3427. KLUTTS, Randy
"Hocking the Royal." [Bogg] (62) 90, p. 35.
3428. KNIGHT, Arthur Winfield
"Bill Pickett: The Dusky Demon." [ChironR] (9:2) Sum 90, p. 16.
"Billy the Kid: The Baptism." [NewYorkQ] (43) Fall 90, p. 59.
"The Head of Joaquin Murietta." [CapeR] (25:2) Fall 90, p. 18.
"Lawbreakers." [CoalC] (2) D 90, p. 21.
"Sam Bass: Sing to Me." [DogRR] (9:1, #17) Spr 90, p. 48.
"Veronica's Advice." [HangL] (56) 90, p. 20.
"Waiting." [Gypsy] (15) 90, p. 58.
3429. KNIGHT, Elizabeth A.
"Grandparents." [SingHM] (17) 90, p. 78.
3430. KNIGHT, Etheridge
"The car accident." [AmerPoR] (19:1) Ja-F 90, p. 17.
"Haiku for the Homeless." [AmerPoR] (19:1) Ja-F 90, p. 17.
"I watch from afar." [AmerPoR] (19:1) Ja-F 90, p. 17.
"O praying mantis." [AmerPoR] (19:1) Ja-F 90, p. 17.
"Song of the Homeless." [AmerPoR] (19:1) Ja-F 90, p. 17.
3431. KNIGHT, Stephen
"The Answering Machine." [Verse] (7:2) Sum 90, p. 6.
"The Stepfather." [Verse] (7:2) Sum 90, p. 6.

3432. KNIGHTEN, Merrell
    "Sublimation." [TarRP] (29:2) Spr 90, p. 37.
    "Where Only Wolves Were Meant to Be." [TarRP] (29:2) Spr 90, p. 36.
    "The Year the Glaciers Came." [DogRR] (9:2, #18) Aut 90, p. 7.
3433. KNOBLOCH, Marta
    "Lees." [Vis] (33) 90, p. 10.
3434. KNOEPFLE, John
    "Coast Town." [AnotherCM] (22) 90, p. 55.
    "Green Snake Interview #6: Speaking of a Vibrant Woman." [SpoonRQ] (15:2) Spr
       90, p. 47-61.
    "The Man Praying." [NewL] (57:1) Fall 90, p. 65.
    "Memories of Kansas." [KanQ] (22:1/2) Wint-Spr 90, p. 88-103.
    "Once Again the Committee." [NewL] (57:1) Fall 90, p. 64.
    "South of Fort Worth." [NewL] (57:1) Fall 90, p. 65.
    "Variations on an Eskimo Carol." [AnotherCM] (22) 90, p. 56.
3435. KNOTT, Bill
    "Contemporary Outremerican Poetry." [BlackWR] (17:1) Fall-Wint 90, p. 100.
    "Male Menopausal Poem." [MassR] (31:1/2) Spr-Sum 90, p. 289-290.
    "Poemclone #4." [BlackWR] (17:1) Fall-Wint 90, p. 101.
3436. KNOTT, Kip
    "Pictures from El Salvador." [MidAR] (10:2) 90, p. 155.
    "Remembering the Poet Who Died at My Age: George Trakl (1887-1914)." [Os] (30)
       Spr 90, p. 36.
3437. KNOX, Ann B.
    "Amazing Events." [NegC] (10:2/3) 90, p. 98.
    "The Boy Brings His Blind Grandmother a Stone Bird." [Poetry] (157:1) O 90, p.
       30.
    "I Dream Old Dylan Came Back." [NegC] (10:2/3) 90, p. 99.
3438. KNOX, Caroline
    "1989." [WestHR] (44:3) Aut 90, p. 295.
    "Famous Bigshots." [WestHR] (44:3) Aut 90, p. 297.
    "Itasca." [WestHR] (44:3) Aut 90, p. 296.
3439. KNUPFER, Walter
    "Blue Snow." [Turnstile] (2:2) 90, p. 72.
    "A Fine Meal." [Ploughs] (16:4) Wint 90-91, p. 204.
    "Sun Setting, Northport." [AntR] (48:2) Spr 90, p. 230.
3440. KO, Chang Soo
    "A Cat's Landscape." [WebR] (14:2) Spr 90, p. 85.
    "Cricket" (tr. by the author). [Vis] (33) 90, p. 38.
    "Festival in Fishing Village No. 19" (tr. of Park Je-chun). [PoetL] (85:2) Sum 90, p.
       39.
3441. KOBLER, Brian
    "Ode to the Fox." [PoetryUSA] (5:3) Fall 90, p. 26.
3442. KOCH, Claude
    "A Nurse Addresses Her Patron" (for MJK, R.N.). [FourQ] (4:1) Spr 90, p. 36.
3443. KOCH, Kenneth
    "The Life of the City." [KenR] (NS 12:2) Spr 90, p. 106-107.
    "Sea." [KenR] (NS 12:2) Spr 90, p. 105-106.
    "A Time Zone." [ParisR] (32:115) Sum 90, p. 109-120.
3444. KOCHER, Ruth Ellen
    "Blackberry Wine." [WestB] (27) 90, p. 84.
3445. KOCHUYT, Catharina
    "Arranging Space" (tr. of Luuk Gruwez, w. David Siefkin and Bradley R. Strahan).
       [Vis] (34) 90, p. 18.
    "Call This Blindness" (tr. of Erik Spinoy, w. David Siefkin). [Vis] (34) 90, p. 14.
    "Cloaks of Silence" (tr. of Erik Spinoy, w. David Siefkin). [Vis] (34) 90, p. 13.
    "Dawn" (tr. of Charles Ducal, w. David Siefkin). [Vis] (34) 90, p. 9.
    "East of Eden" (tr. of Charles Ducal, w. David Siefkin). [Vis] (34) 90, p. 10.
    "Eden" (tr. of Charles Ducal, w. David Siefkin). [Vis] (34) 90, p. 9.
    "A Glass Falls" (tr. of Guido de Bruyn, w. David Siefkin). [Vis] (34) 90, p. 15.
    "The Hare" (tr. of Charles Ducal, w. David Siefkin). [Vis] (34) 90, p. 10.
    "Home" (for Monique T., died 1987, at 22, in a traffic accident, tr. of Luuk Gruwez,
       w. David Siefkin and Bradley R. Strahan). [Vis] (34) 90, p. 17.
    "Inhospitality" (tr. of Luuk Gruwez, w. David Siefkin). [Vis] (34) 90, p. 16.
    "Mother Tongue" (tr. of Charles Ducal, w. David Siefkin). [Vis] (34) 90, p. 11.
    "Odysseus" (tr. of Charles Ducal, w. David Siefkin). [Vis] (34) 90, p. 12.

"The Streets" (tr. of Erik Spinoy, w. David Siefkin). [Vis] (34) 90, p. 12.
"Tribute" (tr. of Leonard Nolens, w. David Siefkin). [Vis] (34) 90, p. 14.
"The Wall" (tr. of Erik Spinoy, w. David Siefkin). [Vis] (34) 90, p. 13.
"Wife" (tr. of Charles Ducal, w. David Siefkin). [Vis] (34) 90, p. 11.
3446. KOCIK, Robert
    "Xbo" (Excerpts, P.O.L., Paris, 1988, tr. of Dominique Fourcade). [Avec] (3:1) 90,
        p. 87-96.
KOEHN, Lala Heine
    See HEINE-KOEHN, Lala
3447. KOENIG, Michael
    "Poppies." [PoetryUSA] ([5:4?]) Wint 90, p. 16.
3448. KOENINGER, Anthony S.
    "A Supposed Dream from the REM of St. Anthony." [SmPd] (27:3, #80) Fall 90, p.
        24.
    "You Cannot See the Flaming Gasoline." [SmPd] (27:3, #80) Fall 90, p. 18.
3449. KOEPPEL, Mary Sue
    "Sisyphus on Highway 9." [ClockR] (6:2) 90, p. 13.
3450. KOERNER, Edgar
    "Beginning." [ManhatPR] (11) [89?], p. 30.
    "Collector." [ManhatPR] (11) [89?], p. 32.
    "Out There." [ManhatPR] (11) [89?], p. 31.
    "Rich." [ManhatPR] (11) [89?], p. 32-33.
3451. KOERTGE, Ron
    "Beautiful Eyes for a Boy." [OnTheBus] (2:1, #5) Spr 90, p. 85-86.
    "FFA." [OnTheBus] (2:1, #5) Spr 90, p. 85.
    "Ronald the Friendly Ghost." [Pearl] (10) Spr 90, p. 57.
    "With a Million Things to Do The Doctor Muses, Anyway." [OnTheBus] (2:1, #5)
        Spr 90, p. 86.
3452. KOESTENBAUM, Wayne
    "A Professor Young and Old." [Boulevard] (5:2, #14) Fall 90, p. 126-127.
    "Rhapsody." [YaleR] (79:4) Sum 90 c1991, p. 719-728.
3453. KOESTER, Rohn
    "On My Eightieth Nightmare." [CoalC] (1) Ag 90, p. 16-17.
3454. KOETHE, John
    "The Advent of the Ordinary." [AmerPoR] (19:2) Mr-Ap 90, p. 6.
    "Au Train." [DenQ] (24:4) Spr 90, p. 34-35.
    "Un Autre Monde." [TriQ] (80) Wint 90-91, p. 59.
    "Early Morning in Milwaukee." [TriQ] (80) Wint 90-91, p. 62-65.
    "I Heard a Fly Buzz" (for Bruce and Livija Renner). [TriQ] (80) Wint 90-91, p.
        66-67.
    "Morning in America." [AmerPoR] (19:2) Mr-Ap 90, p. 6.
    "A Parking Lot with Trees." [NewAW] (6) Spr 90, p. 21-24.
    "The Saturday Matinee." [TriQ] (80) Wint 90-91, p. 60-61.
3455. KOHLER, Sandra
    "Trying to Talk About Sex -- I." [MassR] (31:3) Aut 90, p. 369-370.
3456. KOLAR, Jiří
    "How Can You Lie So Shamelessly?" (tr. by Bronislava Volková). [PoetryE] (30)
        Fall 90, p. 71.
3457. KOLATKAR, Arun
    "Frog Time" (tr. by Vinay Dharwadker). [Screens] (2) 90, p. 45.
    "Horse" (tr. by Vinay Dharwadker). [Screens] (2) 90, p. 44.
    "Touch" (tr. by Vinay Dharwadker). [Screens] (2) 90, p. 44.
3458. KOLIN, Philip C.
    "Annunciation at the Beach." [CapeR] (25:2) Fall 90, p. 29.
3459. KOLJEVIC, Svetozar
    "Betrothal" (tr. of Rajko Petrov Nogo, w. Andrew Harvey). [Screens] (2) 90, p. 63.
    "Landscape" (tr. of Rajko Petrov Nogo, w. Andrew Harvey). [Screens] (2) 90, p.
        63.
3460. KOLLAR, Mary (Mary E.)
    "For David Lee, Who Left a Day Early." [CrabCR] (7:1) Wint 90, p. 20.
    "On Taking My Thirteen-Year-Old Daughter to the Home of Anne Frank." [Calyx]
        (12:3) Sum 90, p. 13-14.
    "Voyeur." [CrabCR] (7:1) Wint 90, p. 21.
    "Women at Forty" (After Donald Justice's "Men at Forty"). [Calyx] (12:3) Sum 90,
        p. 15.

3461. KOLLBRUNNER, Oskar
"When Emigrating" (tr. by Lisa Kahn). [NoDaQ] (58:4) Fall 90, p. 51.
3462. KOLODINSKY, Alison (Alison Welsh)
"From the Source." [KanQ] (22:3) Sum 90, p. 106.
"In Carroll County, New Hampshire." [Kalliope] (12:1) 90, c89, p. 34-35.
"Midnight." [FreeL] (6) Aut 90, p. 16.
"Natural Selection." [FreeL] (6) Aut 90, p. 17.
"Pre-Op." [FreeL] (6) Aut 90, p. 17.
3463. KOLODNY, Susan
"Neuroanatomy." [BelPoJ] (41:2) Wint 90-91, p. 28-31.
3464. KOLUMBAN, Nicholas
"Bridges" (Budapest, 1945, tr. of Gyula Illyés). [PoetryE] (29) Spr 90, p. 52-53.
"Fleeing Toward Western Europe" (The year 1944, tr. of Gyula Illyés). [PoetryE]
    (29) Spr 90, p. 50-51.
"A Footnote on Small Nations" (tr. of György Gömöri). [PoetryE] (29) Spr 90, p.
    72.
"He and I" (tr. of István Eörsi). [WebR] (14:2) Spr 90, p. 104.
"I Came Home" (tr. of Gyula Illyés). [PoetryE] (29) Spr 90, p. 54-55.
"An Immigrant's Laments." [GrahamHR] (13) Spr 90, p. 71.
"In a Pleading Tone of Voice" (tr. of István Eörsi). [WebR] (14:2) Spr 90, p. 104.
"It Would Be Good to Translate Mallarmé" (tr. of György Petri). [PoetryE] (30) Fall
    90, p. 65.
"Letters to Nowhere" (Selections: VI, VIII-XI, XV, XVII, XXI, tr. of Elemér
    Horváth). [AnotherCM] (21) 90, p. 70-73.
"Mother Always Knows Something New" (tr. of Katalin Mezey). [ArtfulD] (18/19)
    90, p. 33.
"Once:" (tr. of Tibor Zalán). [PoetryE] (30) Fall 90, p. 70.
"Reflections of a Transient." [GrahamHR] (13) Spr 90, p. 72.
"The Small Bicycle" (tr. of Otto Tolnai). [ArtfulD] (18/19) 90, p. 34.
"There Is a Country." [CrabCR] (6:3) Spr 90, p. 3.
"This Is Not Death Yet" (tr. of Otto Tolnai, w. Daniel Bourne and Karen Kovacik).
    [ArtfulD] (18/19) 90, p. 35.
"Two Worlds." [ArtfulD] (18/19) 90, p. 31.
"Utopia" (tr. of István Eörsi). [PoetryE] (30) Fall 90, p. 19.
"The Virile Gold Shimmer of Beaten Eggs." [ArtfulD] (18/19) 90, p. 32.
"Why You Are Sad." [CrabCR] (6:3) Spr 90, p. 3.
"Yes - No" (tr. of György Gömöri). [WebR] (14:2) Spr 90, p. 105.
3465. KOMLOSI, László
"Restless Turning of Fall" (tr. of Miklós Radnóti, w. Len Roberts). [AmerPoR]
    (19:5) S-O 90, p. 22.
"Woods in October" (tr. of Miklós Radnóti, w. Len Roberts). [ArtfulD] (18/19) 90,
    p. 25.
3466. KOMUNYAKAA, Yusef
"2527th Birthday of the Buddha." [Callaloo] (13:2) Spr 90, p. 366.
"Albino." [Callaloo] (13:2) Spr 90, p. 244-245.
"Banking Potatoes." [Callaloo] (13:2) Spr 90, p. 237.
"Between Angels & Monsters." [Callaloo] (13:2) Spr 90, p. 247-248.
"The Breaking." [Callaloo] (13:2) Spr 90, p. 243.
"Changes, or, Reveries at a Window Overlooking a Country Road, with Two
    Women Talking Blues in the Kitchen." [MidAR] (10:2) 90, p. 54-56.
"Death Threat Note." [Callaloo] (13:2) Spr 90, p. 365.
"Gutbucket." [Caliban] (8) 90, p. 38.
"Metho & Plonk." [Caliban] (8) 90, p. 39.
"Millpond." [Callaloo] (13:2) Spr 90, p. 239-240.
"My Father's Loveletters." [Callaloo] (13:2) Spr 90, p. 246.
"The Rebel." [Callaloo] (13:2) Spr 90, p. 235.
"Salomé." [Callaloo] (13:2) Spr 90, p. 251-252.
"The Smokehouse." [Callaloo] (13:2) Spr 90, p. 236.
"The Steel Plate." [Callaloo] (13:2) Spr 90, p. 241-242.
"Venus's-Flytraps." [Callaloo] (13:2) Spr 90, p. 230-231.
"The Whistle." [Callaloo] (13:2) Spr 90, p. 232-234.
"White Port & Lemon Juice." [Callaloo] (13:2) Spr 90, p. 249-250.
"Wild Fruit" (Excerpt). [Callaloo] (13:2) Spr 90, p. 238.
"You and I Are Disappearing." [Callaloo] (13:2) Spr 90, p. 368-369.
3467. KONG, Ann
"Night Poem." [Amelia] (6:2, #17) 90, p. 128.

"Ponies and Spanish Guitars." [Contact] (9:56/57/58) Spr 90, p. 36-37.
"Red Lantern." [Contact] (9:56/57/58) Spr 90, p. 38.
3468. KONO, Juliet S.
"The First Time." [BambooR] (47) Sum 90, p. 50.
3469. KONRAD, Alan
"I'll Always Love You, Kind-of." [NegC] (10:2/3) 90, p. 83-84.
KOON, Woon
   See WOON, Koon
3470. KOONTZ, Tom
"A Charm After Dying." [PaintedB] (40/41) 90, p. 136.
"A Charm to Be Spoken to One with Cancer." [PaintedB] (40/41) 90, p. 136.
"A Charm to Fall Asleep." [PaintedB] (40/41) 90, p. 136.
3471. KOPLAND, Rutger
"Johnson Brothers Ltd." (tr. by James Brockway). [Stand] (31:1) Wint 89-90, p. 24.
"Miss A" (tr. by James Brockway). [Stand] (31:1) Wint 89-90, p. 24.
"The Power of Evangelism" (tr. by James Brockway). [Stand] (31:1) Wint 89-90, p. 23-24.
3472. KOPP, Karl
"Easter in Berkeley 1988." [CharR] (16:1) Spr 90, p. 72.
"Kaimos." [CharR] (16:1) Spr 90, p. 71.
"Sonnet for a Separation." [CharR] (16:1) Spr 90, p. 72.
3473. KORAN, Jaroslav
"I go straight off to my friends" (tr. of Petr Kabes, w. Daniel Weissbort).
   [HampSPR] (Anthology 1975-1990) 90, p. 268.
"I have stopped naming the landscapes of my poems" (tr. of Petr Kabes, w. Daniel
   Weissbort). [HampSPR] (Anthology 1975-1990) 90, p. 267.
"Nightfall" (From "The Hillside Above Radotin," tr. of Jan Zábrava, w. Daniel
   Weissbort). [HampSPR] (Anthology 1975-1990) 90, p. 268-269.
"Once I lied about it here" (tr. of Petr Kabes, w. Daniel Weissbort). [HampSPR]
   (Anthology 1975-1990) 90, p. 267.
3474. KORENYUK, Olga
"A Mysterious Animal Tiger" (Poem written in English by high school students from
   the Ukraine, collected by Maureen Hurley). [PoetryUSA] (5:1) Spr 90, p. 18.
3475. KORN, Eric
"BZ." [Descant] (21:2, #69) Sum 90, p. 143-144.
3476. KÖRÖSY, Mária (*See also* KÁRÖSSY, María)
"At First Hand" (tr. of Otto Orban, w. Jascha Kessler). [MidAR] (10:2) 90, p. 178.
"For Life" (tr. of János Pilinszky, w. Bruce Berlind). [PoetryE] (29) Spr 90, p. 59.
"For Quite Some Time" (tr. of Imre Oravecz, w. Bruce Berlind). [ManhatR] (5:1)
   Spr 90, p. 13.
"The Golden Fleece" (tr. of Otto Orban, w. Jascha Kessler). [MidAR] (10:2) 90, p. 180.
"I No Longer Walk" (tr. of Imre Oravecz, w. Bruce Berlind). [Abraxas] (38/39) 90,
   p. 85.
"I Want Only" (tr. of Imre Oravecz, w. Bruce Berlind). [NewEngR] (13:1) Fall 90,
   p. 41.
"I'd Like to Talk to You Now" (tr. of Imre Oravecz, w. Bruce Berlind). [Abraxas]
   (38/39) 90, p. 81.
"Intellectuals" (tr. of Otto Orban, w. Jascha Kessler). [MidAR] (10:2) 90, p. 179.
"It May Have Begun This Way" (tr. of Imre Oravecz, w. Bruce Berlind).
   [NewEngR] (13:1) Fall 90, p. 40.
"The Last Home" (tr. of Gyula Illyés, w. Bruce Berlind). [Os] (30) Spr 90, p. 9.
"Lorca's New York" (tr. of Ottó Orbán, w. Bruce Berlind). [PoetryE] (29) Spr 90,
   p. 57.
"My Time's Running Out" (tr. of Imre Oravecz, w. Bruce Berlind). [ManhatR] (5:1)
   Spr 90, p. 12.
"On a Private Golgotha" (tr. of Gyula Illyés, w. Bruce Berlind). [Os] (30) Spr 90, p. 7.
"One Sentence on Tyranny" (tr. of Gyula Illyés, w. Bruce Berlind). [PoetryE] (29)
   Spr 90, p. 42-49.
"Our Bearings at Sea" (a novel-in-poems: 2 selections, tr. of Ottó Orbán, w. Jascha
   Kessler). [Screens] (2) 90, p. 56-58.
"Procession in the Fog" (tr. of Gyula Illyés, w. Bruce Berlind). [Os] (30) Spr 90, p. 5.
"Stephen Spender in Mount Vernon" (tr. of Ottó Orbán, w. Bruce Berlind).

[PoetryE] (29) Spr 90, p. 58.
"This Is the City" (tr. of Imre Oravecz, w. Bruce Berlind). [Abraxas] (38/39) 90, p. 83.
"To Be Rich" (tr. of Ottó Orbán, w. Bruce Berlind). [PoetryE] (29) Spr 90, p. 56.
"Veil" (tr. of János Pilinszky, w. Bruce Berlind). [PoetryE] (29) Spr 90, p. 60.
"When It Was Over" (tr. of Imre Oravecz, w. Bruce Berlind). [NewEngR] (13:1) Fall 90, p. 41-42.
"You Had Dressed by Then" (tr. of Imre Oravecz, w. Bruce Berlind). [Abraxas] (38/39) 90, p. 87.
3477. KORZUN, L. June
"Working the Fields." [Wind] (20:66) 90, p. 23.
3478. KOSMANN, Claude
"Visions." [NorthStoneR] (9) 90, p. 65-66.
3479. KOST, Holly Hunt
"In the Kimono Garden." [PraS] (64:4) Wint 90, p. 13.
"On Christina in Her Pink Housedress." [Sequoia] (33:2) Wint 90, p. 37.
"The Onion Lesson." [PraS] (64:4) Wint 90, p. 15.
"Under the Spell of the Yellow Drapes." [PraS] (64:4) Wint 90, p. 13-14.
3480. KOSTELANETZ, Richard
"Epiphanies." [DogRR] (9:1, #17) Spr 90, p. 15, 21, 25, 35, 47.
"Epiphanies (1991)" (Excerpt). [AnotherCM] (22) 90, p. 57-58.
"Minimal Audio Plays" (Selections). [NewYorkQ] (41) Spr 90, p. 76-78.
"One-Word Stories." [HawaiiR] (15:1, #31) Wint 90, p. 43-44.
"Reverberations: A Sequence of Poems" (Excerpt). [HeavenB] (8) Wint 90-91, p. 21.
"Tone Deaf." [Asylum] (6:2) S 90, p. 31.
3481. KOSTENKO, Lina
"An emerald oak grove after the rains" (tr. by Naydan, Michael). [Nimrod] (33:2) Spr-Sum 90, p. 7.
"The rain began to fall, and the day became such a downpour" (tr. by Naydan, Michael). [Nimrod] (33:2) Spr-Sum 90, p. 7.
"A shady spot, twilight, a golden day" (tr. by Naydan, Michael). [Nimrod] (33:2) Spr-Sum 90, p. 4.
"The spring day began with birches" (tr. by Naydan, Michael). [Nimrod] (33:2) Spr-Sum 90, p. 6.
"Watercolors of Childhood" (tr. by Naydan, Michael). [Nimrod] (33:2) Spr-Sum 90, p. 5.
"With your eyes you told me: I love" (tr. by Naydan, Michael). [Nimrod] (33:2) Spr-Sum 90, p. 6.
3482. KOSTOLEFSKY, Joseph
"Aged As You Would." [Pearl] (12) Fall-Wint 90, p. 64.
3483. KOSTOS, Dean
"Cheating Breath." [ChironR] (9:4) Wint 90, p. 17.
3484. KOSTROV, Vladimir
"Urban Irony" (tr. by Paul Graves and Carol Ueland). [Nimrod] (33:2) Spr-Sum 90, p. 3.
3485. KOTTLER, Dorian Brooks
"Music." [NorthStoneR] (9) 90, p. 218-219.
"The Poem and Its Use." [NorthStoneR] (9) 90, p. 217.
"A Woman." [NorthStoneR] (9) 90, p. 216-217.
3486. KOTZIN, Miriam N.
"Astronomy Lesson." [Boulevard] (4:3/5:1, #12/13) Spr 90, p. 160.
3487. KOUROUS, Sharon
"Love." [Writer] (103:12) D 90, p. 24.
3488. KOUZA, Loujaya M.
"I Was There." [Manoa] (2:1) Spr 90, p. 47.
"Roots." [Manoa] (2:1) Spr 90, p. 48.
3489. KOVACIK, Karen
"This Is Not Death Yet" (tr. of Otto Tolnai, w. Nicholas Kolumban and Daniel Bourne). [ArtfulD] (18/19) 90, p. 35.
3490. KOVACS, Edna
"Current Events." [BellArk] (6:3) My-Je 90, p. 24.
3491. KOWIT, Steve
"Crossing the Desert." [Spirit] (10:2) 90, p. 99-100.
"Journey to New York" (tr. of Ernesto Cardenal, w. Cecilia Ubilla-Arenas). [OnTheBus] (2:1, #5) Spr 90, p. 178-183.

3492. KOZAK, Roberta
"Chiaroscuro" (for J.S., 1988). [Crazy] (39) Wint 90, p. 54-56.
"Fallout." [Crazy] (39) Wint 90, p. 52-53.
3493. KOZER, Jose
"Grey." [LindLM] (9:4) O-D 90, p. 33.
"Magnificat" (tr. by Ammiel Alcalay). [LitR] (33:4) Sum 90, p. 446-447.
3494. KOZIOL, Andreas
"The Angel of the Situation" (tr. by Roderick Iverson). [Sulfur] (10:2, #27) Fall 90,
    p. 105-106.
"The Knees That Were Ours and the Fruit and the Style" (tr. by Roderick Iverson).
    [Screens] (2) 90, p. 81-82.
"Untitled: that which once again befalls the heavens" (tr. by Roderick Iverson).
    [Sulfur] (10:2, #27) Fall 90, p. 104-105.
3495. KOZLOWSKI, Gregory
"Lines" (tr. of Ghalib). [PoetryE] (30) Fall 90, p. 73.
3496. KRAFT, Kelley
"Cooling." [RagMag] (7:2) Spr 90, p. 27.
3497. KRAMER, Aaron
"Morning." [CumbPR] (9:2) Spr 90, p. 20.
"Submarines" (tr. of Rajzel Zychlinska). [Vis] (33) 90, p. 26.
"Without a Camera." [CumbPR] (9:2) Spr 90, p. 21.
3498. KRAMER, Joel
"Pelicans." [PoetryUSA] (5:1) Spr 90, p. 11.
3499. KRAMER, Larry
"A View of the Water." [MissouriR] (13:1) 90, p. 155.
3500. KRAMER, Lotte
"Second Thoughts." [Stand] (31:3) Sum 90, p. 49.
3501. KRAPF, Norbert
"Dream of a Cave." [OntR] (33) Fall-Wint 90-91, p. 102-104.
3502. KRASHNER, Sam
"The Kissing Fish." [Talisman] (5) Fall 90, p. 104.
"Pantoum" (to the work and good health of John Yau). [Talisman] (5) Fall 90, p.
    115.
3503. KRATT, Mary
"Eye Level with Brown Pelicans." [Shen] (40:1) Spr 90, p. 80.
"Of Mother and Father." [Shen] (40:1) Spr 90, p. 79.
"Ruby." [NewRena] (8:1, #24) Spr 90, p. 117-118.
"Sweeping the Clay." [NegC] (10:2/3) 90, p. 65.
3504. KRAUS, Sharon
"Rubbing My Father's Back." [MissR] (19:1/2, #55/56) 90, p. 257-258.
3505. KRAUSHAAR, Mark
"At the Greyhound Station." [PoetryNW] (31:3) Aut 90, p. 39-40.
"How Lives Move Forward in the Same Moments." [Shen] (40:3) Fall 90, p. 74-75.
"Mantra." [Shen] (40:3) Fall 90, p. 76.
"On to Something." [PoetryNW] (31:3) Aut 90, p. 38-39.
"Road Kill." [Shen] (40:3) Fall 90, p. 75.
"Wichita 67204." [PoetryNW] (31:3) Aut 90, p. 40-41.
3506. KREGER, Bernice
"The Chosen." [JINJPo] (12:1) Spr 90, p. 37.
"Smoke Screen." [JINJPo] (12:1) Spr 90, p. 36.
3507. KREMER, Pem
"Rumpelstiltskin, Revisited." [AmerV] (19) Sum 90, p. 88-89.
3508. KRESH, KDavid
"Connect the Dots to Make a Picture." [HighP] (5:1) Spr 90, p. 59-61.
3509. KRESS, Leonard
"Boardwalk" (After Hofmannsthal). [WestB] (27) 90, p. 86.
"Night-Shift." [NewL] (57:1) Fall 90, p. 96-97.
3510. KRETZ, T. (Thomas)
"Ballpoint Paper." [HawaiiR] (14:3, #30) Fall 90, p. 91.
"Breath of Darkness." [BellR] (13:1, #27) Spr 90, p. 48.
"Cardiac." [Plain] (11:1) Fall 90, p. 13.
"Coming from School." [HawaiiR] (14:3, #30) Fall 90, p. 90.
"From Matthew to Prime Time." [KanQ] (22:1/2) Wint-Spr 90, p. 115.
"Hagocytosis." [HawaiiR] (15:1, #31) Wint 90, p. 45-46.
"Philly Fever." [CapeR] (25:2) Fall 90, p. 31.
"Pope to Make Lifshin Forget Her Madonnas." [DogRR] (9:1, #17) Spr 90, p. 34.

3511. KRICORIAN, Nancy
"Forgiveness." [RiverS] (32) [90?], p. 14.
"Poem for My Father's Voice." [RiverS] (32) [90?], p. 15-16.
"The Red Armenian Slippers" (incorrectly printed in a previous issue of TLR). [LitR]
(33:2) Wint 90, p. 259.
3512. KRIESER, Michael
"The Dark Rushes" (For Charles Dreher). [Gypsy] (15) 90, p. 4.
3513. KRIM, N. C.
"Olga." [EngJ] (79:6) O 90, p. 94.
3514. KRISLOV, Catherine Harmon
"What Became of My Father." [MissR] (19:1/2, #55/56) 90, p. 259.
3515. KROEKER, G. W.
"Reflections on an Open Reading." [CapeR] (25:2) Fall 90, p. 13.
3516. KROL, Jelle
"As in a Film" (for Joy, tr. of R. R. R. van der Leest). [Vis] (34) 90, p. 26-27.
"Fifteen Years Later" (tr. of R. R. R. van der Leest). [Vis] (34) 90, p. 25.
"Girl" (tr. of R. R. R. van der Leest). [Vis] (34) 90, p. 25.
"Parting" (tr. of R. R. R. van der Leest). [Vis] (34) 90, p. 26.
"Poem: Sometimes when you're standing naked and embarrassed" (tr. of R. R. R.
van der Leest). [Vis] (33) 90, p. 43.
3517. KROL, Sybe
"Hear My Voice" (tr. by the author). [Vis] (34) 90, p. 24.
"Hear My Voice" (tr. by the author). [Vis] (34) 90, p. 24.
3518. KROLL, Ernest
"Ancient Roman Roads." [Sequoia] (33:2) Wint 90, p. 38.
"A Clear Day in January." [MidwQ] (32:1) Aut 90, p. 87.
"Snow Peas." [WindO] (53) Fall 90, p. 42.
KROLL, Jelle
See KROL, Jelle
3519. KRÖLOW, Karl
"Air Conditioning" (tr. by Stuart Friebert). [Chelsea] (49) 90, p. 137.
"All the Same" (tr. by Stuart Friebert). [AmerPoR] (19:5) S-O 90, p. 20.
"At Daybreak" (tr. by Stuart Friebert). [AmerPoR] (19:5) S-O 90, p. 20.
"Family Table" (tr. by Stuart Friebert). [PennR] (4:2) 90, p. 89.
"Let Live" (tr. by Stuart Friebert). [PennR] (4:2) 90, p. 86-87.
"The Park" (tr. by Stuart Friebert). [Chelsea] (49) 90, p. 136.
"Shadow Spots" (tr. by Stuart Friebert). [PennR] (4:2) 90, p. 88.
"Some Things" (tr. by Stuart Friebert). [Chelsea] (49) 90, p. 135.
"Songs Without Names" (tr. by Stuart Friebert). [AmerPoR] (19:5) S-O 90, p. 20.
"Terror" (tr. by Stuart Friebert). [Chelsea] (49) 90, p. 138.
3520. KRONEN, Steve
"Mayflies." [Boulevard] (5:2, #14) Fall 90, p. 105-106.
"The Road-Gang Is Served Supper at a Country Inn." [MissouriR] (13:1) 90, p.
151.
3521. KRONENBERG, Mindy (Mindy H.)
"Magic" (for Randy, who never heard her own name). [ContextS] (1:1) 89, p. 35.
"The Music Lesson." [ChamLR] (3:2, #6) Spr 90, p. 92-93.
"Sundew." [ManhatPR] (12) [90?], p. 27.
3522. KRONENFELD, Judy
"Unwritten." [CrossCur] (9:2) Je 90, p. 21.
3523. KRUK, Laurie
"My Father's Coat." [Grain] (18:4) Wint 90, p. 42.
"Picking Plums." [Event] (19:1) Spr 90, p. 50.
3524. KRYSS, T. L.
"The Fiddler." [SwampR] (5) Wint-Spr 90, p. 64.
3525. KRYUKOVA, Yelena
"The shopping I'll do will be simple and cheap" (tr. by Oleg Atbashian and Maureen
Hurley). [PoetryUSA] (5:2) Sum 90, p. 15.
3526. KUBASAK, Sharon
"Walk Waltz, from the Diner Digressions." [PassN] (11:1) Sum 90, p. 10.
3527. KUBICEK, J. L.
"Perspective." [InterPR] (16:2) Fall 90, p. 110.
"An Unequal Journey." [InterPR] (16:2) Fall 90, p. 111.
3528. KUCHINSKY, Walter
"A Skinny, Little Guy." [Wind] (20:66) 90, p. 3.
"The Whisperer." [Footwork] 90, p. 73.

3529. KUDER, Karin
"The Moon." [EmeraldCR] (1990) c89, p. 17.
3530. KUDERKO, Lynne M.
"Accident Report." [SpoonRQ] (15:2) Spr 90, p. 22-23.
"Restored House" (Victoria, Upper Peninsula, Michigan, Deserted copper mining
town). [AnotherCM] (21) 90, p. 94.
3531. KUHNER, Herbert
"Silence" (tr. of Slavko Janevski, w. Howard Erksine Hill and Bogomil Gjezel).
[Footwork] 90, p. 106.
3532. KULAK, Lorne
"The Silent Brain." [Grain] (18:1) Spr 90, p. 82.
3533. KULIK, William
"Announcement" (tr. of Robert Desnos). [AmerPoR] (19:3) My-Je 90, p. 21.
"The Bottle in the River" (tr. of Robert Desnos). [AmerPoR] (19:3) My-Je 90, p. 24.
"Door to the Second Infinity" (tr. of Robert Desnos). [AmerPoR] (19:3) My-Je 90,
p. 21.
"From the Marble Rose to the Iron Rose" (tr. of Robert Desnos). [AmerPoR] (19:3)
My-Je 90, p. 24.
"Identity of Images" (tr. of Robert Desnos). [AmerPoR] (19:3) My-Je 90, p. 22.
"No, Love Is Not Dead" (tr. of Robert Desnos). [AmerPoR] (19:3) My-Je 90, p. 22.
"Once There Was a Leaf" (tr. of Robert Desnos). [AmerPoR] (19:3) My-Je 90, p.
21.
"The Sun's Despair" (tr. of Robert Desnos). [AmerPoR] (19:3) My-Je 90, p. 23.
"To the Headless" (tr. of Robert Desnos). [AmerPoR] (19:3) My-Je 90, p. 23.
"The Way a Hand at the Moment of Death" (tr. of Robert Desnos). [AmerPoR]
(19:3) My-Je 90, p. 22.
3534. KULIKOV, Cynthia
"April." [OnTheBus] (2:2/3:1, #6/7) Sum-Fall 90 Wint-Spr 91, p. 122-123.
"Cherries." [OnTheBus] (2:2/3:1, #6/7) Sum-Fall 90 Wint-Spr 91, p. 121-122.
3535. KUMBIER, William
"Portato." [PoetryUSA] ([5:4?]) Wint 90, p. 13.
"Vacances." [PoetryUSA] ([5:4?]) Wint 90, p. 13.
3536. KUMBON, Daniel K.
"Everybody's Day (Not Mine)." [Manoa] (2:1) Spr 90, p. 46.
3537. KUMHONG
"Wild Geese Sang" (tr. by Constantine Contogenis and Wolhee Choe). [PoetryE]
(30) Fall 90, p. 104.
3538. KUMIN, Maxine
"Fat Pets On." [KenR] (NS 12:1) Wint 90, p. 109-110.
"Finding the One Brief Note." [Poetry] (157:2) N 90, p. 69.
"The Green Well." [KenR] (NS 12:1) Wint 90, p. 110-111.
"On Visiting a Friend in Southern California." [BelPoJ] (40:4) Sum 90, p. 38.
"The Porch Swing." [BelPoJ] (40:4) Sum 90, p. 39.
"Visiting Flannery O'Connor's Grave" (Milledgeville, Ga., 1988). [GeoR] (44:1/2)
Spr-Sum 90, p. 30-31.
3539. KUMMER, John
"Hunting Stone." [PoetryNW] (31:3) Aut 90, p. 16-17.
"An Instructor, Reading Yeats and Sinking Fast." [PoetryNW] (31:3) Aut 90, p.
15-16.
"The Underground Hum of the Dynamo Works." [PoetryNW] (31:3) Aut 90, p.
17-18.
3540. KUNERT, Guenter (Günter)
"Devotion" (tr. by Ulrike Weber and Richard Jones). [PoetryE] (29) Spr 90, p. 82.
"From the Dorotheenstadt Cemetery" (tr. by Ulrike Weber and Richard Jones).
[PoetryE] (29) Spr 90, p. 81.
"The Jewish Cemetery at Berlin-Weissensee" (tr. by Reinhold Grimm: translation
dedicated to Felix Pollak). [Pembroke] (22) 90, p. 18.
3541. KUNITZ, Stanley
"Greed" (tr. of Nina Cassian). [NewYorker] (65:46) 1 Ja 90, p. 30.
"The Portrait." [EngJ] (79:7) N 90, p. 27.
3542. KUNTZ, Laurie
"Composition." [NegC] (10:1) 90, p. 67.
3543. KUNZ, Don
"Shooting Relatives in Newport." [Confr] (42/43) Spr-Sum 90, p. 185.
3544. KUNZE, Reiner
"The Craftsmen Have Left" (tr. by Thomas Edwards). [PoetryE] (29) Spr 90, p. 84.

"To an Actor, Who Asked That His Role Be Lengthened" (tr. by Thomas Edwards). [PoetryE] (29) Spr 90, p. 84.
KUO, Francois Sengat
   See SENGAT-KUO, Francois
3545. KUPPNER, Frank
   "Eclogue One." [Stand] (31:1) Wint 89-90, p. 56-60.
   "Eclogue Two." [Stand] (31:1) Wint 89-90, p. 61-63.
3546. KUPRIYANOV, Viacheslav
   "Waiting for flaming life" (tr. by Oleg Atbashian and Maureen Hurley). [PoetryUSA] (5:2) Sum 90, p. 15.
3547. KURDI, Mária
   "Above the Things" (tr. of Agnes Nemes Nagy, w. Len Roberts). [MidAR] (10:1) 90, p. 47.
   "Because Our Drowning Is a Sensation" (tr. of Gizella Hervay, w. Len Roberts). [MidAR] (10:1) 90, p. 53.
   "Circle" (tr. of Zsuzsa Takács, w. Len Roberts). [AmerPoR] (19:5) S-O 90, p. 29.
   "For My Mother Again" (tr. of Ida Makay, w. Len Roberts). [AmerPoR] (19:5) S-O 90, p. 27.
   "I Do Not Resemble" (tr. of Ida Makay, w. Len Roberts). [AmerPoR] (19:5) S-O 90, p. 26.
   "Identity" (tr. of Judit Tóth, w. Len Roberts). [AmerPoR] (19:5) S-O 90, p. 28.
   "The Island Dweller" (tr. of Ida Makay, w. Len Roberts). [MidAR] (10:1) 90, p. 49.
   "Magic" (tr. of Ida Makay, w. Len Roberts). [MidAR] (10:1) 90, p. 51.
   "Mrs. Wadsworth's Letter to Emily Dickinson" (tr. of Agnes Gergely, w. Len Roberts). [AmerPoR] (19:5) S-O 90, p. 27.
   "The Night of Ekhnaton" (tr. of Agnes Nemes Nagy, w. Len Roberts). [AmerPoR] (19:5) S-O 90, p. 23-24.
   "Our Creation" (tr. of Judit Pinczési, w. Len Roberts). [AmerPoR] (19:5) S-O 90, p. 29.
   "Rhapsody for My Birthday" (tr. of Agnes Gergely, w. Len Roberts). [AmerPoR] (19:5) S-O 90, p. 27.
   "Such Is the Place, This Unnamable" (tr. of Zsuzsa Takács, w. Len Roberts). [AmerPoR] (19:5) S-O 90, p. 28.
   "They Were Roving" (tr. of Margit Szécsi, w. Len Roberts). [AmerPoR] (19:5) S-O 90, p. 25.
   "The Visible Man" (tr. of Margit Szécsi, w. Len Roberts). [AmerPoR] (19:5) S-O 90, p. 24-25.
   "We Deserve It" (tr. of Ida Makay, w. Len Roberts). [AmerPoR] (19:5) S-O 90, p. 26.
   "Well, I Ask" (tr. of Anna Hajnal, w. Len Roberts). [AmerPoR] (19:5) S-O 90, p. 22.
   "When the New Moon Screamed" (tr. of Margit Szécsi, w. Len Roberts). [AmerPoR] (19:5) S-O 90, p. 24.
3548. KURTZ, Holly
   "Anorexia." [HangL] (56) 90, p. 68.
   "The Best Day of My Life." [HangL] (56) 90, p. 69-70.
3549. KUS, Mira
   "The most acute of all" (tr. by Daniel Bourne). [HawaiiR] (14:3, #30) Fall 90, p. 92.
   "Will There Be Enough Light Years" (tr. by Daniel Bourne). [CrossCur] (9:2) Je 90, p. 157.
3550. KUSCH, Robert
   "Islands." [HawaiiR] (14:1, #28) Wint 89-90, p. 44.
3551. KUSH
   "Condor I Am." [PoetryUSA] (5:3) Fall 90, p. 16.
3552. KUSHNER, Aleksandr
   "Domitian, the last cruel and savage emperor" (tr. by Paul Graves and Carol Ueland). [Nimrod] (33:2) Spr-Sum 90, p. 94.
   "Folded Wings" (tr. by Paul Graves and Carol Ueland). [Nimrod] (33:2) Spr-Sum 90, p. 90-91.
   "O fame, you have passed us by like the rain, vanished" (tr. by Paul Graves and Carol Ueland). [Nimrod] (33:2) Spr-Sum 90, p. 93.
   "Our partings are more difficult, and long" (tr. by Paul Graves and Carol Ueland). [Nimrod] (33:2) Spr-Sum 90, p. 92.
   "This country, huge, wintry and blue" (tr. by Paul Graves and Carol Ueland). [Nimrod] (33:2) Spr-Sum 90, p. 91.

3553. KUSHNER, Dale
"The Dogs." [PraS] (64:1) Spr 90, p. 99-100.
"Luther." [PraS] (64:1) Spr 90, p. 98-99.
"Possession." [PraS] (64:1) Spr 90, p. 97-98.
"Test." [PraS] (64:1) Spr 90, p. 96-97.

3554. KUSNETZ, Ilyse M.
"Danaïde." [SouthernHR] (24:3) Sum 90, p. 254.

3555. KUSTERS, Wiel
"Ballad of the Salamander" (tr. by Scott Rollins). [Trans] (24) Fall 90, p. 16.
"Ballad of the Stoker" (tr. by Peter Nijmeijer). [Trans] (24) Fall 90, p. 17-18.
"Four Poems by a Coal-Miner's Son" (tr. from the Dutch). [Trans] (24) Fall 90, p. 15-18.
"Heads" (tr. by James S Holmes). [Trans] (24) Fall 90, p. 15.
"Journey of the Magi" (tr. by Francis R. Jones). [Trans] (24) Fall 90, p. 18.

3556. KUTCHINS, Laurie
"Alchemy." [SouthernPR] (30:1) Spr 90, p. 27-28.
"Daughter." [Ploughs] (16:4) Wint 90-91, p. 135-136.
"Ohio Nocturne" (for James Wright). [LaurelR] (24:1) Wint 90, p. 53-54.
"Watching Great-Grandma Bean Undress." [GeoR] (44:1/2) Spr-Sum 90, p. 252-253.
"A White Lie." [LaurelR] (24:1) Wint 90, p. 55.

3557. KUUS, Arwo F.
"Birthday." [OnTheBus] (2:2/3:1, #6/7) Sum-Fall 90 Wint-Spr 91, p. 124.

3558. KUUSISTO, Stephen
"Mockingbird." [Sonora] (19) Spr-Sum 90, p. 6.

3559. KUZMA, Greg
"The Day of the Funeral." [KanQ] (22:3) Sum 90, p. 81.
"First Snow." [ConnPR] (9:1) 90, p. 25-26.
"Hearing Sirens." [Poetry] (156:3) Je 90, p. 149.
"Incident with a Car." [HampSPR] (Anthology 1975-1990) 90, p. 68.
"Limits." [KanQ] (22:3) Sum 90, p. 83.
"On a Morning of Birds Singing." [HampSPR] (Anthology 1975-1990) 90, p. 67-68.
"Owl." [HampSPR] (Anthology 1975-1990) 90, p. 66.
"Song." [KanQ] (22:3) Sum 90, p. 82.
"The Squirrel." [HampSPR] (Anthology 1975-1990) 90, p. 68-69.
"Still Life." [HampSPR] (Anthology 1975-1990) 90, p. 66.
"The Stinkbug." [MinnR] (NS 34/35) Spr-Fall 90, p. 29.
"Summer." [MidwQ] (32:1) Aut 90, p. 88.
"The Trout." [HampSPR] (Anthology 1975-1990) 90, p. 67.

3560. KUZMENKO, Vallentina
"A single word -- and I'll know what to do" (tr. by Oleg Atbashian and Maureen Hurley). [PoetryUSA] (5:2) Sum 90, p. 15.

3561. KVASNICKA, Mellanee
"Making Nebraska Home." [Plain] (10:3) Spr 90, p. 27.
"Nebraska West of Kearney." [Plain] (11:1) Fall 90, p. 31.

3562. KWA, Lydia (KWA MAY, Lydia)
"The Difference." [Grain] (18:4) Wint 90, p. 43.
"Subject to Desire." [Descant] (21:4/22:1, #71/72) Wint-Spr 90-91, p. 162-166.
"Two Dreams." [AntigR] (80) Wint 90, p. 12.

3563. KYGER, Joanne
"The Enormous Sigh." [PoetryUSA] (5:1) Spr 90, p. 10.

3564. KYLE, Angela D.
"For Christina and Prince Robert." [EmeraldCR] (1990) c89, p. 12-13.

3565. KYLE-KEITH, Roger
"SR-71." [DogRR] (9:2, #18) Aut 90, p. 39.

KYOKO, Mori
  See MORI, Kyoko
KYUNG-RIM, Shin
  See SHIN, Kyung-rim
La . . .
  See also names beginning with "La" without the following space, filed below in their alphabetic positions, e.g., LaSALLE.
La BRUNO, Michael
  See LaBRUNO, Michael

269

La CHARITY

La CHARITY, Ralph
      See LaCHARITY, Ralph
La CRUZ, Juana Inés de, Sor
      See CRUZ, Juana Inés de la, Sor
La FARGE, Ben
      See LaFARGE, Ben
3566. La FEMINA, Gerry
      "Hunting." [Outbr] (21) 90, p. 43.
La MERS, Joyce
      See LaMERS, Joyce
La ROSE, Raymond Ray
      See LaROSE, Raymond Ray
3567. LAABI, Abdellatif
      "Scheherazade" (tr. by Victor Reinking). [Vis] (32) 90, p. 14.
      "The Torturer" (tr. by Victor Reinking). [Vis] (32) 90, p. 13.
3568. LABINSKI, Marek
      "In my barbaric language" (tr. of Halina Poswiatowska). [InterPR] (16:2) Fall 90, p.
          33.
      "The sliver of my imagination" (tr. of Halina Poswiatowska). [InterPR] (16:2) Fall
          90, p. 33.
3569. LABIS, Nicolae
      "Not Us!" (tr. by Mary Monica Irimescu Grigg). [PoetryE] (29) Spr 90, p. 127.
3570. LaBONTÉ, Karen
      "Seedlings." [TarRP] (30:1) Fall 90, p. 22.
LABRA, Carilda Oliver
      See OLIVER LABRA, Carilda
LABRADA, Emilio Bernal
      See BERNAL LABRADA, Emilio
3571. LaBRUNO, Michael
      "Keeper of the Keys." [Footwork] 90, p. 74-75.
3572. LACEY, Edward
      "Follow Your Destiny" (tr. of Fernando Pessoa). [AntigR] (80) Wint 90, p. 60-61.
      "Freedom in Chains" (tr. of Fernando Pessoa). [AntigR] (80) Wint 90, p. 56-57.
      "Leafstorm" (tr. of Fernando Pessoa). [AntigR] (80) Wint 90, p. 58-59.
      "Ye Shall Be As Gods" (tr. of Fernando Pessoa). [AntigR] (80) Wint 90, p. 62-63.
3573. LaCHARITY, Ralph
      "Hearing the Terrible to Sea." [Contact] (9:56/57/58) Spr 90, p. 25.
3574. LACKEY, Joe
      "Scandinavia." [Bogg] (62) 90, p. 16-18.
3575. LADIN, Jay
      "Aubade." [Plain] (10:2) Wint 90, p. 14.
      "Current Events." [MinnR] (NS 34/35) Spr-Fall 90, p. 18-19.
3576. LADYE, Kosmick
      "Mother Earth is a galactic reform school." [PoetryUSA] (5:1) Spr 90, p. 14.
3577. LaFARGE, Ben
      "Cloudy Issues." [NewRep] (202:16) 16 Ap 90, p. 34.
      "What Bloodcells Understand." [PartR] (57:3) Sum 90, p. 442.
3578. LAGIER, Jennifer
      "Breaking Silence, Broken Faith: The Vietnam Wall" (for Victor). [SlipS] (10) 90, p.
          99-100.
3579. LAGO GONZALEZ, David
      "Autoretrato en Invierno" (a Rogelio Quintana). [LindLM] (9:4) O-D 90, p. 67.
3580. LAGOMARSINO, Nancy
      "Lost Years." [CimR] (91) Ap 90, p. 46.
      "Shadows." [CimR] (91) Ap 90, p. 44.
      "The Tiger." [CimR] (91) Ap 90, p. 45.
      "The Years with Small Children." [CimR] (91) Ap 90, p. 47.
3581. LAHAR, April
      "See this pill it's called Mellaril." [NewYorkQ] (41) Spr 90, p. 91.
3582. LAKE, David
      "Dead Fruit." [OnTheBus] (2:2/3:1, #6/7) Sum-Fall 90 Wint-Spr 91, p. 125.
3583. LAKE, Paul
      "Concord." [Verse] (7:3) Wint 90, p. 54-55.
      "The Gift." [SouthernR] (26:4) O 90, p. 877-879.
      "Inspectors." [SycamoreR] (2:1) Wint 90, p. 28-31.

3584. LAKRITZ, Andrew
"The Machinist." [Pig] (16) 90, p. 43.
3585. LALLY, Margaret
"The Story of Anna Swan" (Selections). [KenR] (NS 12:2) Spr 90, p. 108-119.
3586. LAMANTIA, Philip
"Homage to Simon Rodia." [DenQ] (24:3) Wint 90, p. 83-84.
"Once in a Lifetime Starry Scape." [CityLR] (4) 90, p. 13-14.
3587. LAMB, Jessica
"Madonna without Child." [GreenMR] (NS 4:1) Spr-Sum 90, p. 64.
3588. LAMBERT, Jean-Clarence
"Altair" (tr. of Serge Pey, w. Bradley R. Strahan). [Vis] (32) 90, p. 44.
"Bedroom" (tr. of Jean Pierre Duprey, w. Bradley R. Strahan). [Vis] (32) 90, p. 39.
"Black Smoke" (tr. of Edouard Glissant, w. Bradley R. Strahan). [Vis] (32) 90, p. 25.
"Capella" (tr. of Serge Pey, w. Bradley R. Strahan). [Vis] (32) 90, p. 44.
"Le Cycle de la Parole" (Excerpt, tr. of Christophe Charles, w. Bradley R. Strahan). [Vis] (32) 90, p. 24.
"El Dorado" (tr. of Andre Laude, w. Bradley R. Strahan). [Vis] (32) 90, p. 42.
"Gulf Stream" (tr. of Rene Belance, w. Dennis Egan and Bradley R. Strahan). [Vis] (32) 90, p. 24.
"I Belong to the High Day" (tr. of Paul Dakeyo, w. Dennis Egan and Bradley R. Strahan). [Vis] (32) 90, p. 9.
"The Lovers at Teruel" (tr. by Dennis Egan). [Vis] (32) 90, p. 45.
"Poem: What is it to be face to face?" (tr. of Bernard Noel, w. Dennis Egan and Bradley R. Strahan). [Vis] (32) 90, p. 46.
"Poetique" (tr. of Edouard Glissant, w. Bradley R. Strahan). [Vis] (32) 90, p. 25.
"Poetry Festival" (Paris, 1987, tr. of Jean Baptiste Tiemele, w. Dennis Egan and Bradley R. Strahan). [Vis] (32) 90, p. 11.
"The Prince" (tr. of Andre Laude, w. Bradley R. Strahan). [Vis] (32) 90, p. 42.
"The Queen of Walls" (Excerpt, tr. of Christian Dotremont, w. Bradley R. Strahan). [Vis] (32) 90, p. 35.
"Rose Cross" (Selections: 1-3, tr. by the author and Bradley R. Strahan). [Vis] (32) 90, p. 45.
3589. LAMBERT, N. S.
"Shadowcat Alley." [CentralP] (17/18) Spr-Fall 90, p. 59-61.
3590. LAMBERT, Nancy
"Untitled: I could be white." [ChironR] (9:3) Aut 90, p. 40.
3591. LaMERS, Joyce
"Digital Watch." [SoCoast] (9) Fall 90, p. 53.
"Tinting Tonight" (A Ballade for the Beauty Parlor). [Amelia] (6:2, #17) 90, p. 60.
3592. LAMM, C. Drew
"Teacher Me Sweet." [EngJ] (79:1) Ja 90, p. 101.
3593. LAMMON, Martin
"Like New Gods, Two Japanese Women Guide My Hands." [WestB] (26) 90, p. 25.
3594. LAMON, Laurie
"Prospero." [PoetryNW] (31:3) Aut 90, p. 42-43.
"We Imagine Our New Life." [PoetryNW] (31:3) Aut 90, p. 42.
3595. LAND, Thomas
"Mary As the Fly." [Vis] (33) 90, p. 44.
3596. LANDALE, Zoë
"All I Can Hand You." [PoetryC] (11:2) Sum 90, p. 10.
"Hunger, Answer." [Bogg] (63) 90, p. 28-29.
"Icon." [PoetryC] (11:2) Sum 90, p. 10.
"Operating Instructions: Talisman." [AntigR] (83) Aut 90, p. 129-130.
"Paleolithic." [Dandel] (17:1) Spr-Sum 90, p. 18-21.
"Pressed Flowers." [Dandel] (17:1) Spr-Sum 90, p. 16.
"Reading the Bones." [PoetryC] (11:2) Sum 90, p. 10.
"Rondelay." [Dandel] (17:1) Spr-Sum 90, p. 17.
"Starfished with Microscope." [PoetryC] (11:2) Sum 90, p. 10.
3597. LANDGRAF, Susan
"The Day After." [CrabCR] (6:3) Spr 90, p. 24.
"One Hand." [ChironR] (9:4) Wint 90, p. 15.
"Poetic Affiar." [CrabCR] (6:3) Spr 90, p. 24.
"Puzzles." [ChironR] (9:3) Aut 90, p. 17.

271

3598. LANDOLT, Michael
"Traveling in a Comfortable Car" (tr. of Bertolt Brecht, w. Brent Duffin). [InterPR]
(16:2) Fall 90, p. 21.
3599. LANDOR, Elisabeth Purkis
"Days." [Verse] (7:2) Sum 90, p. 5.
3600. LANDWEHR, A. W.
"The Red-Haired Woman on the Feather River." [SoCoast] (8) Spr 90, p. 22.
3601. LANE, Dixie
"Wisteria." [PoetL] (85:3) Fall 90, p. 29-30.
3602. LANE, Donna M.
"Beggars." [SwampR] (5) Wint-Spr 90, p. 24.
"A Hole in Our Lives." [OnTheBus] (2:2/3:1, #6/7) Sum-Fall 90 Wint-Spr 91, p.
126-127.
"The Inheritance." [SwampR] (5) Wint-Spr 90, p. 21-22.
"Necrophila." [Pearl] (12) Fall-Wint 90, p. 31.
"Pygmalion." [SwampR] (5) Wint-Spr 90, p. 25.
"Water Slide." [SwampR] (5) Wint-Spr 90, p. 23.
3603. LANE, M. Travis
"Not Quite There." [Event] (19:2) Sum 90, p. 72.
"Protext." [CanLit] (127) Wint 90, p. 38-39.
3604. LANE, Patrick
"The Children." [Grain] (18:3) Fall 90, p. 31.
"The Killer." [Grain] (18:3) Fall 90, p. 33.
"The Meadow." [Grain] (18:3) Fall 90, p. 32.
"Winter 20." [Event] (19:3) Fall 90, p. 119.
3605. LANG, Claire
"The Trumpeter Swan." [PoetryUSA] (5:1) Spr 90, p. 17.
3606. LANG, J. Stephen
"Looking for the Department of Daisies." [KanQ] (22:3) Sum 90, p. 179.
"The Window Rattled in the Wind All Night." [KanQ] (22:3) Sum 90, p. 178.
LANG, Meng
See MENG, Lang
3607. LANGAN, Steve
"Solitaire." [Plain] (11:1) Fall 90, p. 12-13.
"Stealing with My Brother" (A Plainsongs Award Poem). [Plain] (10:3) Spr 90, p.
4.
3608. LANGE, Jennifer
"Dirty Word: C." [LaurelR] (24:1) Wint 90, p. 80-81.
3609. LANGEVIN, Donna
"Balloons for a Wake" (for Martin Singleton, 1946-1989. Lines 6, 7, 8 adapted from
a poem by Robert Billings). [AntigR] (83) Aut 90, p. 64.
"Bedtime Ritual." [AntigR] (83) Aut 90, p. 65.
"Bones" (From the desert paintings of Georgia O'Keeffe). [PoetryC] (11:2) Sum 90,
p. 26.
"Canticle" (from a painting by Chagall). [Quarry] (39:4) Fall 1990, p. 33.
"Crucifiction" (After a painting by Francis Bacon). [Quarry] (39:4) Fall 1990, p. 34.
"Elmira." [AntigR] (83) Aut 90, p. 66.
3610. LANGHORNE, Henry
"The Gold Coast." [NegC] (10:2/3) 90, p. 95.
"Reparation for My Home Town." [EmeraldCR] (1990) c89, p. 9-10.
3611. LANGLAND, Joseph
"An Inland Indian Sea" (tr. of Dmitry Bobyshev, w. the author). [Nimrod] (33:2)
Spr-Sum 90, p. 74.
3612. LANGLAS, James (Jim)
"About Words." [SpoonRQ] (15:2) Spr 90, p. 36, also (15:4) Fall 90, p. 33.
"Anxiety." [SwampR] (5) Wint-Spr 90, p. 17.
"August." [SpoonRQ] (15:2) Spr 90, p. 41, also (15:4) Fall 90, p. 38.
"Barbed Wire." [SpoonRQ] (15:2) Spr 90, p. 31-32, also (15:4) Fall 90, p. 28-29.
"Becoming a Miser." [CutB] (33) 90, p. 63.
"Becoming Part of the Night." [SpoonRQ] (15:2) Spr 90, p. 38, also (15:4) Fall 90,
p. 35.
"The Bell" (for Nancy). [SwampR] (5) Wint-Spr 90, p. 16.
"A Boy Waiting." [KanQ] (22:3) Sum 90, p. 227.
"A Broken Branch." [SpoonRQ] (15:2) Spr 90, p. 32, also (15:4) Fall 90, p. 29.
"Coming Home." [SpoonRQ] (15:2) Spr 90, p. 44, also (15:4) Fall 90, p. 42.
"The Difficulty with Maintenance." [SwampR] (5) Wint-Spr 90, p. 12-13.

"First Time." [SpoonRQ] (15:2) Spr 90, p. 35, also (15:4) Fall 90, p. 32.
"Fortieth Anniversary." [SpoonRQ] (15:2) Spr 90, p. 39-40, also (15:4) Fall 90, p. 36-37.
"Infatuation." [SwampR] (5) Wint-Spr 90, p. 15.
"John Frederick Zimmerman" (b. November 6, 1884, d. January 20, 1885). [SpoonRQ] (15:2) Spr 90, p. 40, also (15:4) Fall 90, p. 37.
"Linking the Generations" (for my son). [SpoonRQ] (15:2) Spr 90, p. 33, also (15:4) Fall 90, p. 30.
"Miss Josephine." [CumbPR] (10:1) Fall 90, p. 33.
"Mrs. Oliphant." [KanQ] (22:3) Sum 90, p. 226-227.
"The Nature of Accidents." [SwampR] (5) Wint-Spr 90, p. 14.
"Photo of Seven Traveling Navaho by Edward Curtis, Circa 1904." [SwampR] (5) Wint-Spr 90, p. 19.
"Pitching." [CumbPR] (10:1) Fall 90, p. 32.
"The Secret of Gardening." [SpoonRQ] (15:2) Spr 90, p. 30, also (15:4) Fall 90, p. 27.
"The Smell of Cigars." [SwampR] (5) Wint-Spr 90, p. 10.
"Sparta's Laws." [SpoonRQ] (15:2) Spr 90, p. 37, also (15:4) Fall 90, p. 34.
"Trains" (for Kay and Jim). [SwampR] (5) Wint-Spr 90, p. 18.
"Waiting to Adopt a Child." [Poetry] (156:1) Ap 90, p. 21.
"The Way of Families." [SwampR] (5) Wint-Spr 90, p. 11.
"The Way We Grow Older." [SpoonRQ] (15:2) Spr 90, p. 42-43, also (15:4) Fall 90, p. 39-40.
"What Might Have Been." [CutB] (33) 90, p. 64.
"The Winds Have Everything to do with Memory." [SpoonRQ] (15:2) Spr 90, p. 34, also (15:4) Fall 90, p. 31.
3613. LANGLEY, Glenda Stewart
"Hate Is a White Robe." [Gypsy] (15) 90, p. 41.
3614. LANGLEY, Michael
"Belongings." [NewYorker] (66:9) 16 Ap 90, p. 106.
3615. LANGMAN, Peter
"The Last Days of John Keats" (As recorded by Joseph Severn, . . . nurse and companion). [NegC] (10:2/3) 90, p. 35-44.
3616. LANGNAU, Pat Siegel
"Can I Throw My Gum Out on the Grass So It Won't Stick to the Trash Can?" [EmeraldCR] (1990) c89, p. 39-40.
LANGSTAFF, F. Polito
See POLITO-LANGSTAFF, F.
3617. LANGSTON, Donna
"Welfare Budget Gourmet." [SlipS] (10) 90, p. 44.
3618. LANGTON, Daniel J.
"LAN/707-P." [CreamCR] (14:1) Spr 90, p. 106.
3619. LANSDOWN, Andrew
"Naomi, Nearly Two." [Verse] (7:2) Sum 90, p. 85.
"Wattle." [Verse] (7:2) Sum 90, p. 84.
3620. LANZA, Carmela Delia
"Expectations." [Footwork] 90, p. 80.
"November Day, Fire Island." [Footwork] 90, p. 80.
3621. LAPEYRE, Elisabeth
"Atomic Sun" (tr. of Robert Sabatier, w. Cordell Caudron). [InterPR] (16:2) Fall 90, p. 47.
"The Child Within the Man" (tr. of Robert Sabatier, w. Cordell Caudron). [InterPR] (16:2) Fall 90, p. 39.
"Communication" (tr. of Robert Sabatier, w. Cordell Caudron). [InterPR] (16:2) Fall 90, p. 45.
"The Journey of a Tree" (tr. of Robert Sabatier, w. Cordell Caudron). [InterPR] (16:2) Fall 90, p. 43.
"Summer Earth" (tr. of Robert Sabatier, w. Cordell Caudron). [InterPR] (16:2) Fall 90, p. 41.
3622. LAPINGTON, S. C.
"The Water Candle." [Stand] (31:4) Aut 90, p. 43.
3623. LAPPIN, T. J.
"Along the Japanese Coast." [NorthStoneR] (9) 90, p. 120.
"Glance from a Stairway Fading." [NorthStoneR] (9) 90, p. 120.
"Pittsburgh." [NorthStoneR] (9) 90, p. 121.
"A Throat of a Rose." [NorthStoneR] (9) 90, p. 121.

3624. LAPUZ, P. V.
"First Hit." [PoetryUSA] ([5:4?]) Wint 90, p. 17.
"Point of View." [PoetryUSA] (5:2) Sum 90, p. 5.
3625. LARAQUE, Paul
"Harlem" (tr. by Rosemary Manno). [LitR] (33:4) Sum 90, p. 477.
"Poem for New York" (For Jack Hirschman, tr. by Edouard Roditi). [LitR] (33:4)
    Sum 90, p. 478.
"Sands of Exile" (tr. by Louis Reyes Rivera). [LitR] (33:4) Sum 90, p. 479.
3626. LaRIVIERE, G. M.
"Missionary Thoughts." [ChamLR] (4:1, #7) Fall 90, p. 169.
3627. LARKIN, Joan
"Denis' Photo of Francis." [BrooklynR] (7) 90, p. 15-16.
3628. LARKIN, Peter
"Roots//Feet" (Excerpt). [Screens] (2) 90, p. 161-163.
3629. LARNER, Jeremy
"Take Me Back." [Thrpny] (42) Sum 90, p. 17.
3630. LaROCQUE, Emma
"Nostalgia." [CanLit] (124/125) Spr-Sum 90, p. 132.
"Progress." [CanLit] (124/125) Spr-Sum 90, p. 137.
"The Red in Winter." [CanLit] (124/125) Spr-Sum 90, p. 136.
3631. LaROSE, Raymond Ray
"Ecstasy." [EvergreenC] (6:1) Wint 90-Spr 91, p. 36.
3632. LARS, Krystyna
"Children" (tr. by Daniel Bourne). [LitR] (33:3) Spr 90, p. 294-295.
"A Country Gentleman Stands at the Window, September 24, 1863" (tr. by Daniel
    Bourne). [LitR] (33:3) Spr 90, p. 295.
"Emilia Plater" (tr. by Daniel Bourne). [LitR] (33:3) Spr 90, p. 296.
"The Military Governor Contemplates the Statue of Adam M." (tr. by Daniel
    Bourne). [LitR] (33:3) Spr 90, p. 298.
"Rejtan" (tr. by Daniel Bourne). [LitR] (33:3) Spr 90, p. 296.
"Soiree at the Czar's Plenipotentiary" (tr. by Daniel Bourne). [LitR] (33:3) Spr 90,
    p. 297.
3633. LARSEN, Deborah
"The Feline as Queen Corporeal" (A Negative Conversation after Wallace Stevens).
    [HolCrit] (27:4) O 90, p. 18.
3634. LARSEN, Jeanne
"At Mountain Lake." [HighP] (5:3) Wint 90-91, p. 87-88.
"A Station in Another Place." [GeoR] (44:4) Wint 90, p. 690-691.
3635. LARSEN, Lance
"Dreaming among Hydrangeas." [ApalQ] (33/34) 90, p. 67.
3636. LARSEN, Wendy Wilder
"The Scout." [Confr] (44/45) Fall 90-Wint 91, p. 275.
3637. LARSON, Jean
"Another Crisis." [Amelia] (6:2, #17) 90, p. 138.
"Christina." [Amelia] (6:2, #17) 90, p. 139.
"Respite." [Amelia] (6:2, #17) 90, p. 138.
3638. LARSON, Rustin
"Floaters" (after Roger Weingarten). [PassN] (11:2) Wint 90, p. 5.
"High School." [CimR] (92) Jl 90, p. 111.
"Melons." [CimR] (92) Jl 90, p. 112.
"The Mosquito." [PassN] (11:2) Wint 90, p. 5.
Las CASAS, Walter de
    See CASAS, Walter de las
3639. LASDUN, James
"Edenesque." [Quarry] (39:1) Wint 90, p. 29-30.
3640. LASSELL, M. (Michael)
"Dancing Days." [HangL] (56) 90, p. 21-23.
"Hair Again." [Zyzzyva] (6:1 #21) Spr 90, p. 35-38.
"The Ides of August." [ChironR] (9:1) Spr 90, p. 24.
"Migration." [Amelia] (6:1, #16) 90, p. 10.
"Odd Man Out" (notes on a napkin: Reuben sandwich). [Amelia] (6:2, #17) 90, p.
    56.
"Prism" (For Kenny -- again, two years gone). [OnTheBus] (2:1, #5) Spr 90, p.
    87-88.
"What It Means to Live Alone Again." [CityLR] (4) 90, p. 79.
"White Cat." [CityLR] (4) 90, p. 76-78.

3641. LASSEN, Sandra Lake
"Writers' Workshop." [AnthNEW] 90, p. 20.
3642. LASTRA, Pedro
"Casi Letania." [Inti] (31) Primavera 90, p. 160.
"La Historia Central." [Inti] (31) Primavera 90, p. 159.
"Notas de Viaje." [Inti] (31) Primavera 90, p. 159.
"Paraisos." [Inti] (31) Primavera 90, p. 161.
"Una Sombra." [Inti] (31) Primavera 90, p. 160.
3643. LASZLOFFY, Csaba
"Apocalypse" (tr. by Len Roberts and Erika Urbán). [LitR] (33:3) Spr 90, p. 292.
3644. LATTA, John
"Near Poppit Sands, Wales" (for Alissa Bucher). [SenR] (20:2) Fall 90, p. 34-35.
3645. LAU, Barbara
"Between the Islands." [SpoonRQ] (15:1) Wint 90, p. 57.
"Drought, 1988." [SpoonRQ] (15:1) Wint 90, p. 55.
"Pies Sagradas : At the Feet of the Saints." [SpoonRQ] (15:1) Wint 90, p. 56.
3646. LAU, Carolyn
"A/Typical Marriage." [YellowS] (34) Sum 90, p. 43.
"Fucking Lu Hsun in My Office with William Blake Watching" (for Xu Tao).
[YellowS] (34) Sum 90, p. 43.
"Obituary." [YellowS] (34) Sum 90, p. 43.
3647. LAU, Evelyn
"Conclusion." [CapilR] (2:2) Spr 90, p. 23.
"Freebasing." [CapilR] (2:2) Spr 90, p. 26.
"I Am Sure This Is." [CapilR] (2:2) Spr 90, p. 24-25.
3648. LAUDE, Andre
"El Dorado" (tr. by Jean-Clarence Lambert and Bradley R. Strahan). [Vis] (32) 90,
p. 42.
"The Prince" (tr. by Jean-Clarence Lambert and Bradley R. Strahan). [Vis] (32) 90,
p. 42.
3649. LAUDER, Scott
"Nose?" [Descant] (21:4/22:1, #71/72) Wint-Spr 90-91, p. 169.
3650. LAUE, John
"A Note on the Suspension of Disbelief" (To My Old Friend, Rich). [ChamLR] (4:1,
#7) Fall 90, p. 170.
3651. LAUFER, William
"Assumptions." [NewRena] (8:1, #24) Spr 90, p. 114-115.
"Scission." [NewRena] (8:1, #24) Spr 90, p. 116.
3652. LAUGHLIN, J. (James)
"Ave Atque Vale." [Poetry] (156:3) Je 90, p. 146.
"The Box." [Iowa] (20:2) Spr-Sum 90, p. 44-45.
"A Curious Romance." [Iowa] (20:2) Spr-Sum 90, p. 43.
"Cutting." [YaleR] (79:2) Wint 90, p. 226.
"The Hands." [NewYorkQ] (41) Spr 90, p. 55.
"May Instructions." [ParisR] (32:115) Sum 90, p. 203-204.
"The Sacks." [Poetry] (156:3) Je 90, p. 145.
"Out in the Pasture." [ParisR] (32:115) Sum 90, p. 205.
3653. LAURENCE, Alexander
"A Film Marilyn Monroe Never Made." [Pearl] (12) Fall-Wint 90, p. 37.
3654. LAURENDEAU, Pierre
"The Uranoscopes" (Adapted from the French by Rikki Ducornet). [DenQ] (24:3)
Wint 90, p. 45.
LAURENTIS, Louise Budde de
See DeLAURENTIS, Louise Budde
3655. LAURICELLA, Ellen
"Dada Is God,." [AmerPoR] (19:6) N-D 90, p. 35.
"From Now On." [AmerPoR] (19:6) N-D 90, p. 36.
"Letter from Mt. Pleasant." [AmerPoR] (19:6) N-D 90, p. 36.
3656. LAUTERBACH, Ann
"Blue Iris / Tiananmen Square." [AmerPoR] (19:5) S-O 90, p. 5.
"Broken Skylight." [AmerPoR] (19:5) S-O 90, p. 7.
"Gesture and Flight." [AmerPoR] (19:5) S-O 90, p. 6.
"Not That It Could Be Finished." [LitR] (33:4) Sum 90, p. 467.
"Notes from a Conversation." [AmerPoR] (19:5) S-O 90, p. 7.
"Procedure." [AmerPoR] (19:5) S-O 90, p. 3.
"Prom in Toledo Night." [Conjunc] (15) 90, p. 248-257.

"Revelry in Black-and-White." [AmerPoR] (19:5) S-O 90, p. 3.
"Santa Fe Sky." [AmerPoR] (19:5) S-O 90, p. 5.
"Selective Listening." [AmerPoR] (19:5) S-O 90, p. 3.
"Tuscan Visit (Simone Martini)." [AmerPoR] (19:5) S-O 90, p. 4.
"Untoward." [AmerPoR] (19:5) S-O 90, p. 3.
3657. LAUX, Dorianne
"Rites of Passage." [Pearl] (12) Fall-Wint 90, p. 61.
"The Tooth Fairy." [Pearl] (10) Spr 90, p. 15.
"Two Pictures of My Sister." [Pearl] (12) Fall-Wint 90, p. 62.
3658. LAVANT, Christine
"Auf der elften Fichtenstufe." [Rohwedder] (5) Spr 90, p. 21.
"Drehe die Herzspindel weiter für mich." [Rohwedder] (5) Spr 90, p. 20.
"Ever closer to the Milky Way" (tr. by David Chorlton). [Rohwedder] (5) Spr 90, p. 20.
"Immer näher dem Milchstrassenrand." [Rohwedder] (5) Spr 90, p. 20.
"In a green hollow a horse was grazing" (tr. by David Chorlton). [Rohwedder] (5) Spr 90, p. 20.
"In grüner Mulde graste ein Pferd." [Rohwedder] (5) Spr 90, p. 20.
"On the eleventh step of the fir" (tr. by David Chorlton). [Rohwedder] (5) Spr 90, p. 21.
"Twist the spindle in my heart further" (tr. by David Chorlton). [Rohwedder] (5) Spr 90, p. 20.
3659. LAVIERI, Jon
"Heaven in 5-Gallon Jars." [NewRena] (8:1, #24) Spr 90, p. 125.
3660. LAW, L. Bradley
"Opportunity and the First Words." [Wind] (20:66) 90, p. 25.
3661. LAWDER, Donald
"On Love, Stars, Poetry, and the March Wind" (for a poet who has lost the courage to write, from "The Way the Light's Refracted"). [KanQ] (22:3) Sum 90, p. 49.
"A Passage of Warblers" (for El Salvador, from "The Way the Light's Refracted"). [KanQ] (22:3) Sum 90, p. 47-48.
"To a Man at the Seashore Whose Wife Has Been Staying with Me in the City" (from "The Way the Light's Refracted"). [KanQ] (22:3) Sum 90, p. 48.
3662. LAWLER, Leslie
"An Art Lesson with Aunt Gracie." [LullwaterR] (1:1) Spr 90, p. 82.
3663. LAWRENCE, Anthony
"The Central Bus Station, Beer Sheeba." [RiverC] (10:2) Spr 90, p. 12-13.
3664. LAWRENCE, D. H.
"Piano." [SouthernR] (26:3) Jl 90, p. 486-487.
3665. LAWRY, Mercedes
"At the Borders of the Storm." [RiverC] (10:2) Spr 90, p. 4-5.
"Flight." [RiverC] (10:2) Spr 90, p. 5.
"Restoration." [Caliban] (8) 90, p. 108.
"These Windows." [Caliban] (8) 90, p. 109.
3666. LAWSON, Andrew
"The Embarkation for Cythera." [Screens] (2) 90, p. 157.
"I Listen to the Market." [Screens] (2) 90, p. 159.
"Mensonges." [Screens] (2) 90, p. 158.
3667. LAWSON, D. S.
"Watching Chaplin's A Dog's Life." [JamesWR] (7:2) Wint 90, p. 13.
3668. LAWSON, Paul
"Clinical Games." [CharR] (16:2) Fall 90, p. 95.
3669. LAWTHER, Marcia
"Hear the Chorus." [Caliban] (8) 90, p. 90-91.
"Up Here." [Blueline] (11:1/2) 90, p. 70.
3670. LAX, Robert
"Fast, slow." [NewYorkQ] (42) Sum 90, p. 39-45.
3671. LAY, Kristina
"Inkstains" (tr. of Gizella Hervay, w. Len Roberts). [AmerPoR] (19:5) S-O 90, p. 30.
"Stake-Fire" (tr. of Gizella Hervay, w. Len Roberts). [AmerPoR] (19:5) S-O 90, p. 31.
Le . . .
See also names beginning with "Le" without the following space, filed below in their alphabetic positions, e.g., LeFEVRE.

3672. Le DRESSAY, Anne
"Untitled Poem: There is fire in the bones of my face." [PraF] (11:4) Wint 90-91, p. 50.
3673. Le GUIN, Ursula K.
"Dos Poesías para Mi Diana" ("The Twins," The Dream"). [Imagine] (2:2) Wint 85, c89, p. 143-144.
"For Calyx" (29 September 1989). [Calyx] (12:3) Sum 90, p. 4.
"To Her Masters." [Imagine] (2:2) Wint 85, c89, p. 142.
3674. Le PERA, George
"The Long Drive In." [JINJPo] (12:1) Spr 90, p. 41.
"My Son's Junk Yard." [JINJPo] (12:1) Spr 90, p. 39-40.
"The Party Song." [JINJPo] (12:1) Spr 90, p. 38-39.
3675. LEA, Sydney
"The Hitchhiker." [KenR] (NS 12:2) Spr 90, p. 120-122.
"In the Alley." [Hudson] (43:1) Spr 90, p. 83-84.
"Manifest" (litany: winter walk). [PartR] (57:3) Sum 90, p. 433-435.
"Subjects." [Hudson] (43:1) Spr 90, p. 81-82.
3676. LEAVITT, M. S.
"Mudbones." [Parting] (3:2) Wint 90-91, p. 31.
3677. LEAVITT, Penelope
"Winter Canvas." [ManhatPR] (11) [89?], p. 28.
"Women's Lockeroom" [sic]. [ManhatPR] (11) [89?], p. 28.
3678. LEBLANC, Charles
"Le dépit." [PraF] (11:1) Spr 90, p. 52.
"For the Survivors" (tr. by Jane Brierley). [PraF] (11:1) Spr 90, p. 49, 51.
"Méditation Pas Calme du Tout." [PraF] (11:1) Spr 90, p. 46, 48.
"Pour les Survivantes." [PraF] (11:1) Spr 90, p. 48, 50.
"Uncalm Meditation" (tr. by Jane Brierley). [PraF] (11:1) Spr 90, p. 47, 49.
"Vexation" (tr. by Jane Brierley). [PraF] (11:1) Spr 90, p. 53.
3679. LEBOW, Jeanne
"Field Peas." [Nimrod] (34:1) Fall-Wint 90, p. 104.
"Reticulation." [Nimrod] (34:1) Fall-Wint 90, p. 105.
"Running Feet." [Nimrod] (34:1) Fall-Wint 90, p. 105-106.
"Witnesses: Copeland's Last Tale" (Augusta, Mississippi, Execution Day, October 30, 1857). [CharR] (16:1) Spr 90, p. 76-77.
3680. LECHNER, Michael
"The Dream." [JamesWR] (8:1) Fall 90, p. 11.
3681. LeCLAIR, Linda
"Sarah." [Mildred] (4:1) 90, p. 112.
"Tourists." [Mildred] (4:1) 90, p. 113.
3682. LECLERC, Félix
"A Ses Débuts" (from "Rêves à vendre"). [AntigR] (80) Wint 90, p. 20.
"Autumn Festival" (tr. by John Palander). [AntigR] (83) Aut 90, p. 104.
"Bilan" (from "Dernier calepin"). [AntigR] (80) Wint 90, p. 24.
"Calendrier Rural" (from "Le petit livre bleu de Félix"). [AntigR] (83) Aut 90, p. 103.
"Country Calendar" (tr. by John Palander). [AntigR] (83) Aut 90, p. 103.
"Fête de l'Automne" (from "Dernier calepin"). [AntigR] (83) Aut 90, p. 104.
"The Final Tally" (tr. by John Palander). [AntigR] (80) Wint 90, p. 25.
"In the Beginning" (tr. by John Palander). [AntigR] (80) Wint 90, p. 21.
"My Grandmother's Patron Saint" (tr. by John Palander). [AntigR] (80) Wint 90, p. 23.
"Le Saint-Joseph de Ma Grand'mère." [AntigR] (80) Wint 90, p. 22.
3683. LeCOMPTE, Kendall
"Newton's Ghost Considers the Bicyclist Descending." [ManhatPR] (11) [89?], p. 7.
3684. LECOMTE, Serge
"OTed." [ChironR] (9:3) Aut 90, p. 8.
"Tiananmen Square." [ChironR] (9:3) Aut 90, p. 8.
"When She Was a Child." [ChironR] (9:3) Aut 90, p. 8.
3685. LEDBETTER, J. T.
"How It Is Going to Be." [CrossCur] (9:2) Je 90, p. 64-65.
"On the Ohio River, Golconda, Illinois." [ArtfulD] (18/19) 90, p. 70.
"Winter Farm." [ChironR] (9:4) Wint 90, p. 18.
3686. LEE, Alice
"The Cat at Midnight." [KanQ] (22:1/2) Wint-Spr 90, p. 118.

277

"A Distant Silence." [KanQ] (22:1/2) Wint-Spr 90, p. 118.
3687. LEE, Ann
"After the Flood." [ChrC] (107:33) 14 N 90, p. 1055.
3688. LEE, Betsy
"The Hole." [PoetryUSA] (5:3) Fall 90, p. 22.
3689. LEE, David
"Faith Tittle" (Hebrews 11:1-3). [PoetryE] (29) Spr 90, p. 260-264.
"Feeding." [PoetryE] (29) Spr 90, p. 265-271.
"Machinery." [CrabCR] (7:1) Wint 90, p. 22-25.
"Pain." [PoetryE] (29) Spr 90, p. 272-279.
"Separating Pigs." [CrabCR] (7:1) Wint 90, p. 22.
"The Tree." [PoetryE] (29) Spr 90, p. 248-259.
"Willie and the Water Pipe." [KenR] (NS 12:2) Spr 90, p. 123-126.
3690. LEE, John B.
"Cats." [PraF] (11:4) Wint 90-91, p. 59.
"Contemplating the Salesgirl's Lipstick." [Dandel] (17:1) Spr-Sum 90, p. 34.
"The Music of Tears." [PraF] (11:4) Wint 90-91, p. 58.
"My Mother and I debating Abortion Till Well Past Midnight." [Grain] (18:1) Spr
90, p. 73.
"My Old Dog Died in My Arms." [PraF] (11:4) Wint 90-91, p. 57.
"Somewhere in This Poem I Wanted to Tell You I Am Ashamed of My Own
Nakedness, But I Couldn't Figure Out How." [Grain] (18:1) Spr 90, p. 72.
"The Vet Says My Old Dog Blows Hair." [PraF] (11:4) Wint 90-91, p. 56.
3691. LEE, Li-Young
"The City in Which I Love You." [GrandS] (9:4, #36) 90, p. 103-109.
"The Sacrifice." [Ploughs] (16:4) Wint 90-91, p. 60-61.
"This Hour and What Is Dead." [Ploughs] (16:4) Wint 90-91, p. 62-63.
"This Room and Everything In It." [AmerPoR] (19:3) My-Je 90, p. 38.
3692. LEE, Pete
"Bachelor Album." [SmPd] (27:3, #80) Fall 90, p. 36.
"Bring It On." [CoalC] (2) D 90, p. 20.
"In a Time That Is Now Past." [CoalC] (2) D 90, p. 20.
"Still Life." [SmPd] (27:3, #80) Fall 90, p. 35.
3693. LEE, Richard E.
"Sad Tidings." [Pearl] (10) Spr 90, p. 18.
3694. LEE, Stellasue
"Adding Things Up." [OnTheBus] (2:1, #5) Spr 90, p. 89-90.
"Just Dreaming." [OnTheBus] (2:2/3:1, #6/7) Sum-Fall 90 Wint-Spr 91, p.
129-130.
"Old Woman." [OnTheBus] (2:2/3:1, #6/7) Sum-Fall 90 Wint-Spr 91, p. 128-129.
"Outdoor Men." [OnTheBus] (2:2/3:1, #6/7) Sum-Fall 90 Wint-Spr 91, p. 130.
3695. LEEDAHL, Shelley A.
"Jenny Sleeping with Angels." [Grain] (18:2) Sum 90, p. 16.
3696. LEEST, R. R. R. van der
"As in a Film" (for Joy, tr. by Jelle Krol). [Vis] (34) 90, p. 26-27.
"Fifteen Years Later" (tr. by Jelle Krol). [Vis] (34) 90, p. 25.
"Girl" (tr. by Jelle Krol). [Vis] (34) 90, p. 25.
"Parting" (tr. by Jelle Krol). [Vis] (34) 90, p. 26.
"Poem: Sometimes when you're standing naked and embarrassed" (tr. by Jelle
Kroll). [Vis] (33) 90, p. 43.
3697. LEFCOWITZ, Barbara F.
"The Guide." [LitR] (33:2) Wint 90, p. 241.
3698. LEFKOWITZ, Larry
"From a Dishwasher's Diary." [Pig] (16) 90, p. 65.
3699. LEGGO, Carl
"Antonio." [Grain] (18:2) Sum 90, p. 43.
"Apples." [Grain] (18:2) Sum 90, p. 42.
"Buzz." [AntigR] (80) Wint 90, p. 39.
"A Coffin and a Chevy." [AntigR] (80) Wint 90, p. 40.
"Fathers and Sons." [Grain] (18:2) Sum 90, p. 40.
"A Girl with Bare Feet." [Bogg] (62) 90, p. 33.
"A Girl With Bare Feet." [PottPort] (11) 89, p. 40.
"Maggot." [PottPort] (11) 89, p. 40.
"Molasses." [Grain] (18:2) Sum 90, p. 41.
"The Original Echo." [AntigR] (80) Wint 90, p. 38.
"Potatoes." [AntigR] (80) Wint 90, p. 41.

"Rags." [Grain] (18:2) Sum 90, p. 44.
3700. LEGGOTT, Michele
"Hotel Pearl." [Verse] (7:2) Sum 90, p. 41-42.
LeGUIN, Ursula K.
See Le GUIN, Ursula K.
3701. LEHMAN, David
"The American Religion." [Boulevard] (4:3/5:1, #12/13) Spr 90, p. 90-91.
"The End of the Affair." [NewYorker] (66:15) 28 My 90, p. 42.
"Just Before Sailing" (w. Ron Horning). [Pequod] (31) 90, p. 145-158.
"Salute" (For James Schuyler). [DenQ] (24:4) Spr 90, p. 36-37.
"The Vocalist" (Selections: 1-3, w. Ron Horning). [Shiny] (5) 90, p. 13-15.
3702. LEI, Suyan
"Probe" (in Chinese and English, tr. by Ji Tianxiang). [PaintedB] (40/41) 90, p.
56-57.
3703. LEIPER, Esther M.
"The Wars of Faery" (Selection: Book I [i.e. II?], Canto III, Book II, Canto IV, for
C. S. Lewis). [Amelia] (6:2, #17) 90, p. 83-93.
"The Wars of Faery" (Selection: Book II, Canto I-II, for C. S. Lewis). [Amelia]
(6:1, #16) 90, p. 37-46.
3704. LEITHAUSER, Brad
"First Birthday." [Poetry] (156:3) Je 90, p. 153.
"North of Night" (On the summer solstice). [NewRep] (202:17) 23 Ap 90, p. 34.
"Reykjavík Winter Couplets." [NewYorker] (65:49) 22 Ja 90, p. 38.
"Subarctic." [NewRep] (203:14) 1 O 90, p. 34.
"Through Two Windows." [NewYorker] (66:5) 19 Mr 90, p. 42.
3705. LEIVA, Angel
"Of Visions" (tr. by Carolyne Wright). [HampSPR] (Anthology 1975-1990) 90, p.
258.
3706. LeMASTER, J. R.
"In Pursuit of Chiang Kaishek." [NegC] (10:2/3) 90, p. 85.
3707. LEMM, Richard
"Drill." [Grain] (18:1) Spr 90, p. 71.
"Execution." [Grain] (18:1) Spr 90, p. 70.
"History." [Event] (19:3) Fall 90, p. 44-45.
"O 66." [Event] (19:3) Fall 90, p. 42-43.
"Smart." [MalR] (93) D 90, p. 30-31.
3708. LENHART, Michael
"Cities." [Asylum] (5:4) 90, p. 14.
"Statuette" (Going in Circles Near Venice Beach). [Bogg] (62) 90, p. 27.
3709. LENIHAN, Dan
"All By Herself." [WormR] (30:1, #117) 90, p. 16.
"Honky Tonkin'." [Bogg] (63) 90, p. 20-23.
3710. LENNON, Frank
"The Modern Masters." [FreeL] (5) Sum 90, p. 23.
3711. LENSE, Edward
"Rt. 161 Out of Columbus." [HiramPoR] (48/49) 90-91, p. 46.
3712. LENSON, David
"The Man of Seven Days" (Selections, tr. of André Roy). [MassR] (31:1/2)
Spr-Sum 90, p. 28, 30.
3713. LENT, John
"Chapel in the Residence, Wurzburg." [AntigR] (80) Wint 90, p. 66.
"Roofs of Strasbourg." [Dandel] (17:1) Spr-Sum 90, p. 26.
3714. LEON, Margarita
"Invencion de la Luz." [Abraxas] (38/39) 90, p. 68.
"Invention of Light" (tr. by John Oliver Simon). [Abraxas] (38/39) 90, p. 69.
3715. LEONETTI, Ed
"The Eyes of Athene." [Writer] (103:3) Mr 90, p. 23.
3716. LEOPOLD, Nikia
"Escarpment from Water." [Comm] (117:6) 23 Mr 90, p. 186.
3717. LEPORE, Dominick
"Summer 1983." [Wind] (20:66) 90, p. 6.
3718. LERBERGHE, Charles van
"I Killed Him" (tr. by Carol Poster). [Vis] (32) 90, p. 40.
"Yes the Day Shines Again" (tr. by Carol Poster). [Vis] (32) 90, p. 40.
3719. LERNER, Laurence
"Broken Ornaments." [SouthernHR] (24:2) Spr 90, p. 117.

"In the Alhambra." [SouthernHR] (24:2) Spr 90, p. 118-119.
3720. LesCARBEAU, Mitchell
    "Nightmare Elvis." [SycamoreR] (2:2) Sum 90, p. 18.
    "St. Anselm's Home." [GrahamHR] (13) Spr 90, p. 64-65.
    "The Star of the Sea Hotel." [LitR] (33:2) Wint 90, p. 260.
3721. LESLIE, Naton
    "The Final Terms." [MidAR] (10:2) 90, p. 32-34.
3722. LESSEN, Laurie Suzanne
    "Push-Over." [CapeR] (25:1) Spr 90, p. 10.
3723. LESSER, Rika
    "Black Stones I." [Ploughs] (16:1) Spr-Sum 90, p. 181.
    "Black Stones II." [Ploughs] (16:1) Spr-Sum 90, p. 182.
    "Black Stones III." [Ploughs] (16:1) Spr-Sum 90, p. 183.
    "Breaking up: that large feeling" (tr. of Göran Sonnevi). [PoetryE] (30) Fall 90, p.
       59-60.
    "A Child Is Not a Knife" (tr. of Göran Sonnevi). [PoetryE] (30) Fall 90, p. 61-62.
    "Matthew's Passion" (for Matthew Ward). [Ploughs] (16:1) Spr-Sum 90, p.
       184-185.
    "On Lithium." [WestHR] (44:2) Sum 90, p. 216-220.
    "Other Lives." [NewEngR] (12:3) Spr 90, p. 293-295.
    "The Second Time." [NewEngR] (12:3) Spr 90, p. 291-292.
3724. LESSING, Karin
    "The Lifelong Range." [Sulfur] (10:1, #26) Spr 90, p. 195-198.
3725. LESTER-MASSMAN, Gordon
    "Incriminations." [HampSPR] (Anthology 1975-1990) 90, p. 199.
3726. LeSUEUR, Meridel
    "Arise Ye Prisoners of Starvation." [SingHM] (17) 90, p. 111-112.
3727. LETO, Denise
    "Passion, Danger, Freedom." [SinW] (41) Sum-Fall 90, p. 72-74.
    "We Do the Best I Can: A Series of Portraits." [SinW] (41) Sum-Fall 90, p. 13-18.
3728. LEUNG, Raymond
    "The Bed" (from a Life Magazine photograph). [PoetryUSA] (5:1) Spr 90, p. 17.
3729. LEV, Donald
    "From This Valley." [NewYorkQ] (41) Spr 90, p. 56-59.
    "Spring Again." [NewYorkQ] (43) Fall 90, p. 84.
3730. LEVANT, Jonathan
    "The Dodo's Infertile Daughter." [Caliban] (8) 90, p. 122.
    "A Gathering of Ghettoes." [Caliban] (8) 90, p. 123.
    "The Little Magazines." [Ascent] (15:1) 90, p. 58.
    "Something Has Not Traveled Beyond the Mirror." [ChatR] (10:2) Wint 90, p. 48.
    "Wet Twilight." [Wind] (20:66) 90, p. 26.
    "What the Poem Believes." [Ascent] (15:1) 90, p. 57.
3731. LEVCHEV, Lyubomir
    "Capriccio 9" (tr. by Jascha Kessler and Alexander Shurbanov). [Screens] (2) 90, p.
       60-61.
    "Secret Love" (Excerpt, tr. by Jascha Kessler and Alexander Shurbanov). [Screens]
       (2) 90, p. 60.
3732. LEVCHEV, Vladimir
    "He Is Not In" (tr. by Belin Tonchev). [CityLR] (4) 90, p. 187.
    "Stalin (Saturn -- Satan)" (tr. by the author). [GrahamHR] (13) Spr 90, p. 103.
    "Stalin (Saturn-Satan)" (tr. by the author). [CityLR] (4) 90, p. 186.
    "Theology of Hopelessness" (tr. by the author). [CityLR] (4) 90, p. 186.
    "Theology of Hopelessness" (tr. by the author). [GrahamHR] (13) Spr 90, p. 104.
3733. LÉVEILLÉ, J. R.
    "Histoire de Femmes" (Extrait d'une oeuvre en cours). [PraF] (11:1) Spr 90, p.
       64-70.
    "Women Trouble" (from a work in progress, tr. by David Homel). [PraF] (11:1) Spr
       90, p. 71-77.
3734. LEVENSON, Christopher
    "August." [PraF] (11:4) Wint 90-91, p. 74.
    "Nutrition" (for David Dorken). [PraF] (11:4) Wint 90-91, p. 75.
3735. LEVERING, Donald
    "Blaze" (for Don Lancaster). [Amelia] (6:2, #17) 90, p. 142.
    "New Moon" (after Lisel Mueller). [HiramPoR] (48/49) 90-91, p. 47.
    "Sunchimes." [Contact] (9:56/57/58) Spr 90, p. 39.

3736. LEVERTOV, Denise
  "Batterers." [AmerPoR] (19:6) N-D 90, p. 4.
  "Brother Ivy." [AmerPoR] (19:6) N-D 90, p. 4.
  "Daily Bread." [AmerPoR] (19:6) N-D 90, p. 4.
  "Evening Train." [AmerPoR] (19:6) N-D 90, p. 5.
  "Midnight Gladness." [MassR] (31:1/2) Spr-Sum 90, p. 292.
  "One December Night" (For Yarrow). [AmerPoR] (19:6) N-D 90, p. 4.
  "Stele (I-II c. B.C.)." [AmerPoR] (19:6) N-D 90, p. 4.
  "The Tower" (tr. of Jean Joubert). [Trans] (23) Spr 90, p. 23-24.
  "The Two Magnets." [AmerPoR] (19:6) N-D 90, p. 3.
  "A Young Man Travelling." [HampSPR] (Anthology 1975-1990) 90, p. 84-85.
3737. LEVI, Enrique Jarmillo
  "Oscilaciones." [Sequoia] (33:2) Wint 90, p. 109.
  "Oscillations" (tr. by Leland H. Chambers). [Sequoia] (33:2) Wint 90, p. 110.
3738. LEVI, Jan Heller
  "Sex Is Not Important." [AntR] (48:1) Wint 90, p. 94-95.
3739. LEVI, Primo
  "Decathlon Man" (tr. by Ruth Feldman). [NewYorker] (66:28) 27 Ag 90, p. 36.
3740. LEVI, Toni (Toni Mergentime)
  "The Skin Mites." [NegC] (10:2/3) 90, p. 70-71.
  "Survivor." [Confr] (44/45) Fall 90-Wint 91, p. 316-317.
3741. LEVIN, Dan
  "Vacation on a Latvian River" (tr. of Bella Vernikova). [Confr] (42/43) Spr-Sum 90,
      p. 111.
3742. LEVIN, Gabriel
  "Pelican in the Wilderness." [SouthwR] (75:1) Wint 90, p. 34-40.
3743. LEVIN, Lynn E.
  "Summer." [Northeast] (NS 5:3) Wint 90-91, p. 10.
3744. LEVINE, David
  "Astronomical Phenomena I Have Known." [NewYorkQ] (43) Fall 90, p. 69-70.
  "The Dreamwork That Does Not Sleep." [NewYorkQ] (41) Spr 90, p. 89-90.
LEVINE, Judy Katz
  See KATZ-LEVINE, Judy
3745. LEVINE, Mark
  "Debt." [Ploughs] (16:4) Wint 90-91, p. 84-85.
  "Mourning Song." [Ploughs] (16:4) Wint 90-91, p. 82-83.
  "The Polish Shoemaker." [BlackWR] (17:1) Fall-Wint 90, p. 23-24.
  "Sculpture Garden." [NewYorker] (66:42) 3 D 90, p. 52.
  "Self Portrait." [Ploughs] (16:4) Wint 90-91, p. 86-87.
  "Wild West." [BlackWR] (17:1) Fall-Wint 90, p. 21-22.
  "Work Song." [NewYorker] (66:23) 23 Jl 90, p. 28.
3746. LEVINE, Philip
  "Among Children." [Atlantic] (266:3) S 90, p. 54.
  "Burned." [Poetry] (156:6) S 90, p. 312-328.
  "Coming of Age in Michigan." [NewEngR] (13:2) Wint 90, p. 49-50.
  "Facts." [NewEngR] (13:2) Wint 90, p. 48-49.
  "The Fast." [BelPoJ] (40:4) Sum 90, p. 41-42.
  "The Founding of English Metre." [Agni] (29/30) 90, p. 117-118.
  "The Gift." [BelPoJ] (40:4) Sum 90, p. 40.
  "The History of Human Life." [YaleR] (79:2) Wint 90, p. 222-223.
  "Listen." [YaleR] (79:2) Wint 90, p. 223-225.
  "Roberto." [Antaeus] (64/65) Spr-Aut 90, p. 73-74.
  "The Simple Truth." [NewYorker] (66:36) 22 O 90, p. 48.
  "Soloing." [Antaeus] (64/65) Spr-Aut 90, p. 71-72.
  "Sweetness." [Ploughs] (16:4) Wint 90-91, p. 180.
  "The Sweetness of Bobby Hefka." [NewEngR] (13:2) Wint 90, p. 51-52.
  "Take My Neighbor." [Agni] (29/30) 90, p. 116.
  "Westward Ho!" [Ploughs] (16:4) Wint 90-91, p. 178-179.
  "What Work Is." [NewYorker] (66:4) 12 Mr 90, p. 42.
3747. LEVINE, Suzanne Jill
  "Iridesce" (tr. of Cecilia Vicuña). [LitR] (33:4) Sum 90, p. 496-497.
3748. LEVINSON, James H. (James Heller)
  "The Brake." [OnTheBus] (2:1, #5) Spr 90, p. 91.
  "Gift." [SmPd] (27:1, #78) Wint 90, p. 34.
  "Sales Call." [SmPd] (27:1, #78) Wint 90, p. 35.
  "The Wheel." [OnTheBus] (2:1, #5) Spr 90, p. 91.

3749. LEVIS, Larry
"At the Grave of My Guardian Angel, St.Louis Cemetery, New Orleans" (for Gerald
Stern). [Ploughs] (16:4) Wint 90-91, p. 117-121.
"Coney Island Baby." [KenR] (NS 12:3) Sum 90, p. 19-21.
"Kind of Blue." [KenR] (NS 12:3) Sum 90, p. 18-19.
"Slow Child with a Book of Birds." [IndR] (13:2) Spr 90, p. 30-34.
"The Spell of the Leaves." [KenR] (NS 12:3) Sum 90, p. 16-18.
3750. LEVITIN, Alexis
"Almourol" (tr. of Alexandre O'Neill). [PoetryE] (30) Fall 90, p. 94.
"Another Example: Visconti" (tr. of Eugenio de Andrade). [OnTheBus] (2:2/3:1,
#6/7) Sum-Fall 90 Wint-Spr 91, p. 240.
"Between the First and Last Twilight" (tr. of Eugenio de Andrade). [ApalQ] (33/34)
90, p. 76.
"The Body Does Not Always Seem" (tr. of Eugenio de Andrade). [PoetryE] (30)
Fall 90, p. 68.
"Borges and the Tigers" (tr. of Eugenio de Andrade). [MidAR] (10:1) 90, p. 111.
"Boulevard Delessert" (tr. of Eugenio de Andrade). [HampSPR] (Anthology
1975-1990) 90, p. 273.
"Endless" (tr. of Eugenio de Andrade). [Asylum] (6:2) S 90, p. 16.
"House in the Sun" (tr. of Eugenio de Andrade). [ApalQ] (33/34) 90, p. 78.
"I am faithful to the heat" (tr. of Eugenio de Andrade). [Trans] (24) Fall 90, p. 229.
"I Am Seated in the First Years of My Life" (tr. of Eugenio de Andrade). [NegC]
(10:2/3) 90, p. 147.
"I know of a stone where I can sit" (tr. of Eugenio de Andrade). [Trans] (24) Fall
90, p. 230.
"I saw them in ruins, those houses" (tr. of Eugenio de Andrade). [Trans] (24) Fall
90, p. 229.
"In the Land of Sons-a-Bitches" (tr. of Jorge de Sena). [PoetryE] (30) Fall 90, p.
20.
"Last Example: Carlos de Oliveira" (tr. of Eugenio de Andrade). [OnTheBus]
(2:2/3:1, #6/7) Sum-Fall 90 Wint-Spr 91, p. 241.
"Melusine" (tr. of Eugenio de Andrade). [OnTheBus] (2:2/3:1, #6/7) Sum-Fall 90
Wint-Spr 91, p. 240-214.
"Morandi: An Example" (tr. of Eugenio de Andrade). [OnTheBus] (2:2/3:1, #6/7)
Sum-Fall 90 Wint-Spr 91, p. 240.
"A Name for Earth" (tr. of Eugenio de Andrade). [SenR] (20:2) Fall 90, p. 42.
"Other Days" (tr. of Eugenio de Andrade). [NowestR] (28:1) 90, p. 99.
"Praca da Alegria" (tr. of Eugenio de Andrade). [HampSPR] (Anthology 1975-1990)
90, p. 273.
"The Seagulls" (tr. of Eugenio de Andrade). [SenR] (20:2) Fall 90, p. 41.
"Solar Matter" (Selection: #27, tr. of Eugenio de Andrade). [PoetryE] (30) Fall 90,
p. 69.
"Solar Matter" (Selections: 8-9, 12-13, 19, 32-33, tr. of Eugenio de Andrade).
[InterPR] (16:2) Fall 90, p. 63, 65.
"Sovereignty" (tr. of Eugenio de Andrade). [ApalQ] (33/34) 90, p. 77.
"Stones" (tr. of Eugenio de Andrade). [OnTheBus] (2:2/3:1, #6/7) Sum-Fall 90
Wint-Spr 91, p. 239.
"Terreiro de S. Vicente" (tr. of Eugenio de Andrade). [OnTheBus] (2:2/3:1, #6/7)
Sum-Fall 90 Wint-Spr 91, p. 239.
"That's What Poetry Is Like" (tr. of Eugenio de Andrade). [ApalQ] (33/34) 90, p.
79.
"Two Solar Matters" (tr. of Eugenio de Andrade). [Confr] (44/45) Fall 90-Wint 91,
p. 178.
"Two Time Matters" (tr. of Eugenio de Andrade). [Confr] (44/45) Fall 90-Wint 91,
p. 179.
"With the Eyes" (tr. of Eugenio de Andrade). [Asylum] (6:2) S 90, p. 17.
3751. LEVITT, Peter
"Before he left our village" (tr. of Shuji Terayama, w. Makiko Fujiwara-Skrobak).
[Zyzzyva] (6:3 #23) Fall 90, p. 105.
"Ever since my mother carried me" (tr. of Shuji Terayama, w. Makiko
Fujiwara-Skrobak). [Zyzzyva] (6:3 #23) Fall 90, p. 104.
"I pressed on with the hot teeth" (tr. of Shuji Terayama, w. Makiko
Fujiwara-Skrobak). [Zyzzyva] (6:3 #23) Fall 90, p. 104.
"I stroke the mountain dove" (tr. of Shuji Terayama, w. Makiko Fujiwara-Skrobak).
[Zyzzyva] (6:3 #23) Fall 90, p. 105.
"The rope I haven't used" (tr. of Shuji Terayama, w. Makiko Fujiwara-Skrobak).

[Zyzzyva] (6:3 #23) Fall 90, p. 105.
"Tonight the fingerprint" (tr. of Shuji Terayama, w. Makiko Fujiwara-Skrobak).
[Zyzzyva] (6:3 #23) Fall 90, p. 104.

3752. LEVY, Andrew
"Promise" (Written for a collaborative project with Melanie Neilson, David
Sternbach, Jessica Grim and Fiona Templeton). [CentralP] (17/18) Spr-Fall
90, p. 216-217.

3753. LEVY, Robert J.
"Closed Gentian." [NoAmR] (275:1) Mr 90, p. 42.
"Exiles" (after photographs by Joseph Koudelka). [GeoR] (44:3) Fall 90, p.
483-484.
"Meditation on Virginia Woolf's Final Diary Entry, Written Three Weeks Before her
Suicide." [Poetry] (156:2) My 90, p. 92-93.
"On Making Love After Having Made Love." [Poetry] (155:5) F 90, p. 328-329.
"Painter." [SouthernR] (26:3) Jl 90, p. 644-645.
"Phantom Pain." [SouthernR] (26:3) Jl 90, p. 641-643.
"World of Likenesses." [SouthernR] (26:3) Jl 90, p. 645-646.

3754. LEVY, Ronna J.
"All You Really Wanted to Do." [BrooklynR] (7) 90, p. 47.
"For Phyllis (1933-1983)." [Kalliope] (12:1) 90, c89, p. 10.
"Leave a Message." [BrooklynR] (7) 90, p. 46.

3755. LEVY, William
"Two Coordinates on a Map of Low Revelation" (for John Michell). [CityLR] (4)
90, p. 150.

3756. LEWENZ, S. M. H.
"The Candy Factory." [Amelia] (6:2, #17) 90, p. 112-113.
"Check Number 375." [Amelia] (6:2, #17) 90, p. 113-114.

3757. LEWIS, Graham
"Marjorie Again in Exile." [NewAW] (6) Spr 90, p. 106.

3758. LEWIS, J. Patrick
"The Giraffe." [SenR] (20:2) Fall 90, p. 85.
"Secretary of Defense." [SlipS] (10) 90, p. 57.
"A Sunday to Her Liking." [GettyR] (3:2) Spr 90, p. 375.

3759. LEWIS, Janet
"Amid the green" (tr. of Hideko Furuichi). [SouthernR] (26:1) Ja 90, p. 204.
"The autumn rain" (tr. of Akira Fukuda). [SouthernR] (26:1) Ja 90, p. 206.
"Evening light and shade" (tr. of Tomiko Fukuda). [SouthernR] (26:1) Ja 90, p.
204.
"Having come far on my journey" (tr. of Tamiko Abe). [SouthernR] (26:1) Ja 90, p.
205.
"The headlights, moving" (tr. of Fumiko Kiyotoki). [SouthernR] (26:1) Ja 90, p.
203.
"One cloud is moving" (tr. of Kenichi Nomura). [SouthernR] (26:1) Ja 90, p. 203.
"Rain on the mountain over there!" (tr. of Shigeyo Matsumoto). [SouthernR] (26:1)
Ja 90, p. 205.
"Seagulls are playing" (tr. of Mitsuko Totsugi). [SouthernR] (26:1) Ja 90, p. 204.
"The sun today" (tr. of Isamu Nagase). [SouthernR] (26:1) Ja 90, p. 205.
"Trophy, W.W.I." [Thrpny] (43) Fall 90, p. 14.
"The water brimming" (tr. of Tsutomu Yamaguchi). [SouthernR] (26:1) Ja 90, p.
205.
"When I saw the arrangement" (tr. of Akitaka Uchimura). [SouthernR] (26:1) Ja 90,
p. 203.
"When the camellia blossoms" (tr. of Kaneko Murayama). [SouthernR] (26:1) Ja 90,
p. 204.
"When the garden wood was trimmed" (tr. of Michiko Fu). [SouthernR] (26:1) Ja
90, p. 203.
"Where the clouds rise at Izumo" (tr. of Susano no mikoto). [SouthernR] (26:1) Ja
90, p. 202.

3760. LEWIS, Jim
"My Father's Death." [SpoonRQ] (15:1) Wint 90, p. 62.

3761. LEWIS, Joel
"At the Poetry Stacks of the Engineering College Library." [JINJPo] (12:1) Spr 90,
p. 29.
"Carnival lights fade in the approach." [Abraxas] (38/39) 90, p. 144.
"A Dharma Talk by Johnny Roseboro, Co., March 23, 1983" (for Norman Dubie).
[HangL] (56) 90, p. 24-25.

"The Paterson Going-Away Poem" (with Edward R. Smith). [Abraxas] (38/39) 90, p. 144.
"Report to the Central Committee." [Caliban] (9) 90, p. 136.
"Weehawken Evening." [Talisman] (5) Fall 90, p. 59.
3762. LEWIS, Lisa
"The Accident." [WestHR] (44:2) Sum 90, p. 187-189.
3763. LEWIS, Melvin (Melvin E.)
"Letters" (Selections: 1, 4, 5, 8, 9). [Obs] (5:2) Sum 90, p. 67-71.
"Once I Was a Panther." [BlackALF] (24:3) Fall 90, p. 534-538.
"Windows." [WillowR] Spr 90, p. 18-19.
3764. LEWIS, Reginald S. (Reginald Sinclair)
"For James Baldwin." [PoetryUSA] (5:3) Fall 90, p. 23.
"In the Big Yard." [PoetryUSA] (5:2) Sum 90, p. 10.
"Releasing the Chains" (for Paula Cooper). [PoetryUSA] (5:2) Sum 90, p. 10.
3765. LEWIT, D. W.
"The Triumph of Capitalism." [BlackBR] (11) Spr-Sum 90, p. 17.
3766. LEZON, Dale
"Blue Corn." [OnTheBus] (2:2/3:1, #6/7) Sum-Fall 90 Wint-Spr 91, p. 131-132.
LI, Ma
    See MA, Li
3767. LI, Po
"Seeing a Friend Off" (tr. by Gu Zhen and Harry Thomas). [Agni] (29/30) 90, p. 205.
3768. LI, Xiaoyu
"A Winter Boat" (to my Grandfather, in Chinese and English, tr. by Zhao Qun). [PaintedB] (40/41) 90, p. 54-55.
3769. LI, Xijian
"Burning Books" (tr. of Liu Shahe, w. Gordon Osing). [Abraxas] (38/39) 90, p. 90-91.
"Harvest" (tr. of Gu Cheng, w. Thomas C. Carlson). [AntigR] (81/82) Spr-Sum 90, p. 69.
"Love" (tr. of Xiao Xue, w. Gordon Osing). [Paint] (17:33/34) Spr-Aut 90, p. 33.
"Morning" (tr. of Ruan Zhanjing, w. Gordon Osing). [CarolQ] (42:3) Spr 90, p. 78.
"Multi-Colored Mountains" (tr. of Sha Ou, w. Gordon Osing). [Paint] (17:33/34) Spr-Aut 90, p. 35.
"Oh, You and Me" (tr. of Gu Gong, w. Gordon Osing). [Paint] (17:33/34) Spr-Aut 90, p. 34.
"Outside Our Door" (tr. of Gu Cheng, w. Thomas C. Carlson). [AntigR] (81/82) Spr-Sum 90, p. 68.
"The Pearl Oyster" (tr. of Ai Qing, w. Gordon Osing). [Paint] (17:33/34) Spr-Aut 90, p. 31.
"Sandstorm" (tr. of Ruan Zhanjing, w. Gordon Osing). [CarolQ] (42:3) Spr 90, p. 79-80.
"The Square Shapes and the Round Shapes" (tr. of Yan Yi, w. Gordon Osing). [Paint] (17:33/34) Spr-Aut 90, p. 36.
"To My Sweetheart at Sixty" (tr. of Yu Weiye, w. Gordon Osing). [Paint] (17:33/34) Spr-Aut 90, p. 32.
"Weeping" (tr. of Liu Shahe, w. Gordon Osing). [Abraxas] (38/39) 90, p. 90-91.
3770. LI, Yan
"It Was Difficult to Give a Suitable Title" (tr. by Paulette Roberts). [LitR] (33:4) Sum 90, p. 491.
"Poor People" (tr. by Paulette Roberts). [LitR] (33:4) Sum 90, p. 491.
"Sunshine, Lift Your Foot and Let My Shadow Go" (tr. by John Chow). [LitR] (33:4) Sum 90, p. 492.
3771. LI, Yuansheng
"Listening to a Flute" (tr. by Dong Jiping). [Footwork] 90, p. 40.
"Little Poem" (tr. by Dong Jiping). [Footwork] 90, p. 40.
LI-YOUNG, Lee
    See LEE, Li-Young
3772. LIBBEY, Elizabeth
"Lair." [PraS] (64:1) Spr 90, p. 91.
"Meditation" (for Bette Deane Jones). [PraS] (64:1) Spr 90, p. 89-90.
3773. LIBERTHSON, Daniel
"Soldiers." [ChamLR] (4:1, #7) Fall 90, p. 6.
3774. LIBRO, Antoinette
"Ariadne's Thread." [Footwork] 90, p. 51.

"Baked Goods." [Footwork] 90, p. 50.
"Summer Daydreams of You." [Footwork] 90, p. 50.
"Sunday mornings." [Footwork] 90, p. 51.
"This day I keep seeing what is not there." [Footwork] 90, p. 50.
3775. LICHTENSTEIN, Bernie
"You Blew It Bukowski." [PoetryUSA] ([5:4?]) Wint 90, p. 26.
3776. LIEBERMAN, Laurence
"Dark Songs: Slave House and Synagogue" (St. Eustacious, Summer 1989).
[Pequod] (31) 90, p. 130-137.
"Lifestyles Prince." [KenR] (NS 12:2) Spr 90, p. 127-130.
"Wind Surfer's Revenge at Horseshoe Battery" (In memory of Yvonne Richards
Ochillo). [Boulevard] (4:3/5:1, #12/13) Spr 90, p. 112-131.
3777. LIECHTY, John
"Evening Walk." [CapeR] (25:2) Fall 90, p. 32.
"The Loss." [CapeR] (25:2) Fall 90, p. 33.
"Visit to Mrs. Lewellyn" (For Stephen Handen). [ChamLR] (4:1, #7) Fall 90, p.
118.
3778. LIESKE, Tomas
"Hidden Child" (tr. by Oliver Reynolds). [Verse] (7:2) Sum 90, p. 8-9.
"Lure" (tr. by Oliver Reynolds). [Verse] (7:2) Sum 90, p. 8.
3779. LIETZ, Robert
"The Wednesday before Ascension." [NoDaQ] (58:1) Wint 90, p. 103-104.
3780. LIFSHIN, Lyn
"After I Sent the Poem I Wrote About My Sister to Her Thinking She'd Be High."
[RagMag] (7:2) Spr 90, p. 31.
"Ann Marie." [Footwork] 90, p. 29.
"April Pink Moon." [OnTheBus] (2:2/3:1, #6/7) Sum-Fall 90 Wint-Spr 91, p. 134.
"August First." [PoetryC] (11:1) Spr 90, p. 21.
"Black Rain, Hiroshima." [WormR] (30:1, #117) 90, p. 10.
"Black Rain, Hiroshima (1)." [SlipS] (10) 90, p. 97-98.
"Black Rain, Hiroshima (2)." [SlipS] (10) 90, p. 98.
"Black Rain, Hiroshima: by night fall, Hiroshima was gone." [ChamLR] (4:1, #7)
Fall 90, p. 4.
"Black Rain, Hiroshima: Hiromu Morishiti found her father." [ChamLR] (4:1, #7)
Fall 90, p. 5.
"Black Rose Madonna in the Rain." [PoetryC] (11:1) Spr 90, p. 21.
"Blue Madonna Goes to the Midnight Radio Show." [PoetryC] (11:1) Spr 90, p. 21.
"The Child We Won't Have Is Crowding Us in the Front." [PoetryC] (11:1) Spr 90,
p. 21.
"Cicada." [WormR] (30:1, #117) 90, p. 10.
"Clean Underwear and a Radio." [Footwork] 90, p. 29.
"Dong Ha." [SingHM] (18) 90, p. 72.
"Door Mat Madonna: 1." [WormR] (30:1, #117) 90, p. 9.
"Door Mat Madonna: 2." [WormR] (30:1, #117) 90, p. 9.
"The Dream of Writing." [Bogg] (63) 90, p. 44.
"Even in the Dream." [Footwork] 90, p. 28.
"Even Seven Months Later." [NewYorkQ] (42) Sum 90, p. 85.
"Hard Mattress Madonna." [WormR] (30:1, #117) 90, p. 9.
"He Came In." [NewYorkQ] (41) Spr 90, p. 63.
"He Prefers Paper Women Like Men Who Would Rather Have Porn." [CoalC] (2) D
90, p. 8.
"He Shoves Everyone Away." [ChironR] (9:1) Spr 90, p. 26.
"He Uses All His 'Up' Up On the Radio." [OnTheBus] (2:2/3:1, #6/7) Sum-Fall 90
Wint-Spr 91, p. 133-134.
"Hearing She Said I Told Him Lyn Lifshin Is Going with a Dispatcher." [Parting]
(3:1) Sum 90, p. 7.
"Honey I Shouldn't Have Called." [Footwork] 90, p. 28.
"House of Skin." [HawaiiR] (15:1, #31) Wint 90, p. 56.
"I Looked Young a Long Time, Didn't I." [Caliban] (8) 90, p. 124-125.
"I Shouldn't Have Called." [Footwork] 90, p. 28.
"I Was 17." [NewYorkQ] (42) Sum 90, p. 86.
"Indian Summer." [PoetryC] (11:1) Spr 90, p. 21.
"It Began." [NewYorkQ] (41) Spr 90, p. 64.
"Like a Woman Running into Leaves." [PoetryUSA] (5:3) Fall 90, p. 4.
"Like What Floods Back When." [Footwork] 90, p. 29.
"The Mad Girl Can't Look at Anything Too Near." [OnTheBus] (2:1, #5) Spr 90, p.

97.
"The Mad Girl Doesn't Need Much." [NewYorkQ] (41) Spr 90, p. 65.
"The Mad Girl Feels Betrayal Turn What Was Like Paper She Could." [Plain] (10:3)
   Spr 90, p. 15.
"The Mad Girl Feels So Much Dissolving." [Plain] (10:3) Spr 90, p. 15.
"The Mad Girl Has Two Lovers Come the Same Day." [Plain] (10:3) Spr 90, p. 14.
"The Mad Girl Needs More." [OnTheBus] (2:1, #5) Spr 90, p. 97.
"The Mad Girl Needs More Than Most Others." [DustyD] (1:2) O 90, p. 17.
"The Mad Girl Swears Off Media Men." [Parting] (3:1) Sum 90, p. 33-34.
"The Mad Girl Takes the Radio Out of the Room." [Plain] (10:3) Spr 90, p. 14.
"Madonna of the Obsessions." [WormR] (30:1, #117) 90, p. 9.
"Madonna Who Goes Down on You." [WormR] (30:1, #117) 90, p. 9.
"Madonna Who Hates Change." [Footwork] 90, p. 29.
"Madonna Who Throws So Many Intimate Details Out Fast." [WormR] (30:1, #117)
   90, p. 9.
"My Mother's Visit." [Amelia] (6:1, #16) 90, p. 64.
"Nicolette." [NewYorkQ] (41) Spr 90, p. 66.
"Night of Spoons." [SingHM] (18) 90, p. 71.
"Other Aprils." [WormR] (30:1, #117) 90, p. 10.
"Payola Madonna." [WormR] (30:1, #117) 90, p. 9.
"Poetry Sucks Madonna." [WormR] (30:1, #117) 90, p. 9.
"Prejudice." [WormR] (30:1, #117) 90, p. 10.
"Ramona Weeks." [Footwork] 90, p. 29.
"Rickety Stairs, Serra Negra." [CrabCR] (6:3) Spr 90, p. 20.
"Rose Devorah." [CentR] (34:3) Sum 90, p. 398.
"Santa Claus' Madonna." [WormR] (30:1, #117) 90, p. 9.
"Seeing the Connection." [NewYorkQ] (43) Fall 90, p. 46.
"She Said It Was 41 Years Ago When Japan Surrendered." [Footwork] 90, p. 29.
"Strange Dream Diary Fragments on a Lined Yellow Pad." [HampSPR] (Anthology
   1975-1990) 90, p. 99.
"Tabasco Madonna." [WormR] (30:1, #117) 90, p. 9.
"Taffeta Madonna." [WormR] (30:1, #117) 90, p. 9.
"That July." [Farm] (7:1) Spr 90, p. 36.
"This Long Winter." [HampSPR] (Anthology 1975-1990) 90, p. 99-100.
"Those Julys." [Footwork] 90, p. 28.
"Thought of Faces On." [HawaiiR] (15:1, #31) Wint 90, p. 57-58.
"The Thought of It." [FreeL] (6) Aut 90, p. 9.
"Thru Jade Sea Light." [PoetryUSA] (5:1) Spr 90, p. 4.
"The Thud of Not Seeing You." [Footwork] 90, p. 28.
"Whips at the Ritz." [PoetryC] (11:1) Spr 90, p. 21.
"Whips at the Ritz" (3 poems). [ChironR] (9:3) Aut 90, p. 2.
"With You." [HawaiiR] (15:1, #31) Wint 90, p. 55.
"With You." [PoetryC] (11:1) Spr 90, p. 21.
"With You, Even a Year Later." [Caliban] (8) 90, p. 126.
3781. LIFSHITZ, Leatrice
      "As I Write." [Kalliope] (12:1) 90, c89, p. 36.
      "In Parentheses." [SlipS] (10) 90, p. 72.
3782. LIGHT, Joanne
      "Heavy." [PottPort] (12) 90, p. 48.
      "On the Train From Washington." [PottPort] (11) 89, p. 41.
3783. LIGHTFOOT, Judy
      "Husbandry." [BellR] (13:1, #27) Spr 90, p. 7.
3784. LIHN, Enrique
      "Dawn 1809" (tr. by David Oliphant). [ColR] (NS 17:1) Spr-Sum 90, p. 101-102.
      "Monet's Years at Giverny" (tr. by David Oliphant). [ColR] (NS 17:1) Spr-Sum 90,
         p. 98-100.
3785. LILBURN, Tim
      "All Souls' Day." [Descant] (21:1 #68) Spr 90, p. 69-70.
      "At the Centre, a Woman." [Descant] (21:1 #68) Spr 90, p. 73.
      "Christmas Eve and the Bull." [Descant] (21:1 #68) Spr 90, p. 71-72.
      "The Cow Comes in Heat." [MalR] (90) Spr 90, p. 18-19.
      "Just This." [MalR] (90) Spr 90, p. 16-17.
      "Post Holing." [MalR] (90) Spr 90, p. 20-21.
3786. LILLY, Jeffrey
      "Guernica." [PoetryUSA] (5:3) Fall 90, p. 15.

3787. LIM, Catherine
"Baby Girl." [Vis] (33) 90, p. 10.
3788. LIM, Shirley Geok-Lin
"The Anniversary." [LitR] (33:4) Sum 90, p. 486-487.
3789. LIMA, Robert
"Huecos." [LindLM] (9:4) O-D 90, p. 64.
3790. LIMERICK, Barrie L.
"When Poets Dream of Angels." [EmeraldCR] (1990) c89, p. 108-109.
3791. LIMOGES, Robynne
"Cae Glas." [Stand] (31:2) Spr 90, p. 25.
3792. LINDÉN, Gurli
"Autumn, I Wrote" (tr. by Lennart Bruce and Sonja Bruce). [Spirit] (10:1) 89, p.
105.
"The City Was Emptied" (tr. by Lennart Bruce and Sonja Bruce). [Spirit] (10:1) 89,
p. 109.
"Det Tar Lång Tid." [Spirit] (10:1) 89, p. 94, 96.
"Detta Är en Förvandling." [Spirit] (10:1) 89, p. 104.
"Did You See the Graves" (tr. by Lennart Bruce and Sonja Bruce). [Spirit] (10:1)
89, p. 107.
"Do You Remember" (tr. by Lennart Bruce and Sonja Bruce). [Spirit] (10:1) 89, p.
103.
"Egentligen Vill Jag Älska." [Spirit] (10:1) 89, p. 100.
"Höst Skrev Jag." [Spirit] (10:1) 89, p. 104.
"I Built Small Nests / under Your Heart" (tr. by Lennart Bruce and Sonja Bruce).
[Spirit] (10:1) 89, p. 99.
"I Really Want to Make Love" (tr. by Lennart Bruce and Sonja Bruce). [Spirit]
(10:1) 89, p. 101.
"It Takes a Long Time" (tr. by Lennart Bruce and Sonja Bruce). [Spirit] (10:1) 89,
p. 95-97.
"Minns Du." [Spirit] (10:1) 89, p. 102.
"Såg Du Gravarna." [Spirit] (10:1) 89, p. 106.
"Staden Är Tömd." [Spirit] (10:1) 89, p. 108.
"This Is a Transformation" (tr. by Lennart Bruce and Sonja Bruce). [Spirit] (10:1)
89, p. 105.
"Under Ditt Hjärta / Byggde Jag Små Bon." [Spirit] (10:1) 89, p. 98.
3793. LINDER, Norma West
"The Word Is Out." [Bogg] (63) 90, p. 10.
3794. LINDGREN, John
"The Asymptotic World" (for John Yau). [Chelsea] (49) 90, p. 36.
"Birth of a Stone." [Caliban] (9) 90, p. 78.
"Living by the Sea." [Gypsy] (15) 90, p. 38.
"The Long Approach." [CumbPR] (10:1) Fall 90, p. 36.
"Maple." [CumbPR] (10:1) Fall 90, p. 35.
"Postcard from the Glacier." [BelPoJ] (41:1) Fall 90, p. 5.
"Postcard from the Glacier." [CumbPR] (10:1) Fall 90, p. 34.
3795. LINDNER, Carl
"Cheetah." [FreeL] (6) Aut 90, p. 27.
"Dog on the Track." [Northeast] (NS 5:3) Wint 90-91, p. 9.
"New Sneakers." [FreeL] (6) Aut 90, p. 26.
"Taking Up Fishing at 40." [LitR] (33:2) Wint 90, p. 261.
3796. LINDSAY, Frannie
"Betty's Flowers." [SmPd] (27:2, #79) Spr 90, p. 14.
"The Blue Goodbye." [WindO] (53) Fall 90, p. 7.
"Comfort." [SmPd] (27:1, #78) Wint 90, p. 36.
"Curing Midas." [GrahamHR] (13) Spr 90, p. 84.
"The Hands in the Bowl." [WindO] (53) Fall 90, p. 5.
"Lemmings." [NoDaQ] (58:2) Spr 90, p. 69.
"Lover's Heaven." [Interim] (9:1) Spr-Sum 90, p. 43.
"Magdelene's Communion." [Interim] (9:1) Spr-Sum 90, p. 41.
"The Men in the Lilacs." [CarolQ] (42:2) Wint 90, p. 27.
"My Father's Angel." [NoDaQ] (58:2) Spr 90, p. 67-68.
"Pleasure." [GreenMR] (NS 4:1) Spr-Sum 90, p. 112.
"Remembering Stars." [WindO] (53) Fall 90, p. 8.
"Sleep Hunters." [Interim] (9:1) Spr-Sum 90, p. 42.
"The Snow's Hands." [WindO] (53) Fall 90, p. 6-7.

3797. LINDSTROM, Rena
"Bangkok Liaison." [Crucible] (26) Fall 90, p. 61.
"The Thunderbird." [AmerV] (20) Fall 90, p. 3.
3798. LINEHAN, Don
"Fish 1." [PottPort] (11) 89, p. 3.
"March." [PottPort] (12) 90, p. 9.
"Tribute to Only a Cat." [PottPort] (12) 90, p. 9.
LING, Bei
    See BEI, Ling
LINGBO, Zhu
    See ZHU, Lingbo
3799. LINKER, Richard
"The Lovers." [JamesWR] (7:3) Spr 90, p. 3.
3800. LINTON, David
"The Barman's Quiet Way." [SmPd] (27:1, #78) Wint 90, p. 10-11.
"Dreamtime Song." [GreensboroR] (48) Sum 90, p. 56.
3801. LIOTTA, P. H.
"Epithalamion" (For V. T. and P. J.). [Poetry] (156:3) Je 90, p. 127-128.
3802. LIPKIND, Arnold
"With the Rastafarians." [PoetryUSA] (5:2) Sum 90, p. 4.
3803. LIPMAN, Joel
"November 24, 1963." [OnTheBus] (2:1, #5) Spr 90, p. 98-99.
3804. LIPSITZ, Lou
"Something of Spring" (for Mary Clarke). [SouthernPR] (30:1) Spr 90, p. 68-69.
3805. LIPSKA, Ewa
"At a Border Crossing" (tr. by Reuel K. Wilson). [Trans] (24) Fall 90, p. 193-194.
"When Our Enemies Doze Off" (tr. by William Pitt Root). [PoetryE] (30) Fall 90, p.
        53.
3806. LIPSON, Susan L.
"Insight into Expertise." [Writer] (103:3) Mr 90, p. 24.
3807. LIPSTADT, Helena
"Wax Lips." [SinW] (42) Wint 90-91, p. 68.
3808. LISK, Thomas
"A Dollar Nineteen a Pound." [ApalQ] (33/34) 90, p. 46-47.
"Notre Pierrot Parlant." [ApalQ] (33/34) 90, p. 44-45.
"A Short History of Pens Since the French Revolution." [ApalQ] (33/34) 90, p.
        42-43.
3809. LISOWSKI, Joseph
"The Mission." [NegC] (10:2/3) 90, p. 72.
3810. LITT, Iris
"Some Like It Hot." [Pearl] (12) Fall-Wint 90, p. 58.
3811. LITTAUER, Andrew
"Map." [SewanR] (98:2) Spr 90, p. 193-194.
3812. LITTLE, Carl
"The First Big Hit." [Hudson] (43:1) Spr 90, p. 99.
3813. LITTLE, Geraldine C.
"Caedmon: Antiphon." [LitR] (33:2) Wint 90, p. 256-257.
"Keeping the Word" (Chant Royal for Anna Akhmatova). [Nimrod] (34:1) Fall-Wint
        90, p. 136-137.
"One of Us." [Confr] (44/45) Fall 90-Wint 91, p. 190.
3814. LITTLE, Jeffrey
"Suitcasing at Doldrum." [BlackBR] (12) Fall-Wint 90, p. 9.
3815. LITTWIN, James
"Opera." [WillowR] Spr 90, p. 12-13.
3816. LITWACK, Susan
"Charitable Acts." [SouthernPR] (30:2) Fall 90, p. 28-30.
"Glow." [Outbr] (21) 90, p. 26-27.
"The Hermit Crab." [Outbr] (21) 90, p. 24.
"Insomnia." [Outbr] (21) 90, p. 25.
"The Tunnel." [MalR] (92) S 90, p. 46-47.
3817. LIU, Shahe
"Burning Books" (in Chinese and English, tr. by Li Xijian and Gordon Osing).
        [Abraxas] (38/39) 90, p. 90-91.
"Weeping" (in Chinese and English, tr. by Li Xijian and Gordon Osing). [Abraxas]
        (38/39) 90, p. 90-91.

3818. LIU, Shicong
"Mountain People" (tr. of Han Dong, w. Christine Ferreira). [MichQR] (29:1) Wint
90, p. 94-95.
3819. LIU, Stephen Shu-Ning
"After the Imagists." [EngJ] (79:3) Mr 90, p. 91.
3820. LIU, Timothy
"Awaiting Translation." [NewRep] (202:22) 28 My 90, p. 36.
"Canker." [WestHR] (44:3) Aut 90, p. 298-300.
"Forty Dead, No Survivors." [CimR] (93) O 90, p. 47-48.
"Mama." [NoAmR] (275:3) S 90, p. 23.
"Second Grade Class Photo." [IndR] (14:1) Wint 90, p. 50.
"SFO/HIV/JFK." [IndR] (14:1) Wint 90, p. 49.
"SFO/HIV/JFK." [JamesWR] (7:4) Sum 90, p. 9.
"Two Sonnets from Xian." [QW] (30) Spr 90, p. 118.
"Volunteers at the AIDS Foundation." [CimR] (93) O 90, p. 46.
3821. LIU, Xuemin
"Night: Theme and Variations" (tr. of Bei Dao, w. Tony Barnstone). [CityLR] (4)
90, p. 154.
3822. LIU, Zhan-Qiu
"Bonfire" (tr. by Emily Yau). [PoetryUSA] ([5:4?]) Wint 90, p. 22.
3823. LIZAKOWSKI, Adam
"The Last Surrealistic Dream of Soldier L.Z." [PoetryUSA] (5:1) Spr 90, p. 9.
"The Number 38 Geary Bus." [PoetryUSA] (5:1) Spr 90, p. 9.
"Who Woke Me Up in the Morning." [PoetryUSA] (5:1) Spr 90, p. 9.
3824. LLERENA, Edith
"La Casa Paterna." [LindLM] (9:4) O-D 90, p. 13.
LLOSA, Ricardo Pau
See PAU-LLOSA, Ricardo
3825. LLOYD, D. H.
"Bixby Park." [ChironR] (9:4) Wint 90, p. 6.
"The Christmas Spirit." [ChironR] (9:4) Wint 90, p. 6.
"Don't Drink and Drive." [ChironR] (9:4) Wint 90, p. 6.
"Fan Mail." [ChironR] (9:4) Wint 90, p. 6.
3826. LOCKE, Duane
"A Girl With White Gold Hair at Clearwater Beach." [Wind] (20:67) 90, p. 27.
"Her Husband's Influence Will Send You, Calestrius, into Exile, a Letter Circa 200
A.D." [NegC] (10:2/3) 90, p. 29.
"Speculations upon Angelo Bronzino's 'An Allegory of Time and Love'." [WritersF]
(16) Fall 90, p. 126.
3827. LOCKE, Edward
"Each Name Has a Dream." [CapeR] (25:2) Fall 90, p. 22.
"Rumpelstiltskin." [BelPoJ] (41:1) Fall 90, p. 15.
3828. LOCKE, Mona M.
"Considering the Geometrical Basis of Language and . . ." (Acknowledging excerpts
. . . from [various poets]). [OnTheBus] (2:2/3:1, #6/7) Sum-Fall 90 Wint-Spr
91, p. 135-136.
3829. LOCKLIN, Gerald
"Baked Alaska." [OnTheBus] (2:2/3:1, #6/7) Sum-Fall 90 Wint-Spr 91, p. 137.
"The Bottom Line." [Pearl] (11) Sum 90, p. 11.
"C'Mon, John." [OnTheBus] (2:2/3:1, #6/7) Sum-Fall 90 Wint-Spr 91, p. 137.
"He Need Regret Nothing." [WormR] (30:1, #117) 90, p. 43.
"In Memoriam." [WormR] (30:1, #117) 90, p. 43.
"Marilyn." [Pearl] (12) Fall-Wint 90, p. 46.
"The More Things Change." [ChironR] (9:3) Aut 90, p. 11.
"Morris Meltzer: Bridgetown, 1923, Berlin." [ChironR] (9:3) Aut 90, p. 11.
"Not Quite." [WormR] (30:1, #117) 90, p. 44.
"Public Garden with Weeping Tree." [Gypsy] (15) 90, p. 26.
"Tax Deferred Title." [FreeL] (5) Sum 90, p. 4-5.
"Two from Ellsworth Kelly." [ChironR] (9:3) Aut 90, p. 11.
"Vestigial Organ." [Pearl] (10) Spr 90, p. 31.
"What We Can Do and What We Can't." [WormR] (30:1, #117) 90, p. 44.
3830. LODEIZEN, Hans
"The Awl in the Dark" (tr. by Kees Snoek). [Vis] (34) 90, p. 39.
"Earlier" (tr. by Arie Staal). [Vis] (34) 90, p. 40.
"Evening Ship" (tr. by Sharon Robertson). [Vis] (33) 90, p. 34.
"Everywhere" (tr. by Kees Snoek). [Vis] (34) 90, p. 38.

"The Flexibility of Sorrow" (tr. by Arie Staal). [Vis] (34) 90, p. 41.
"Je Sais Parce Que Je Le Dis" (tr. by Sharon Robertson). [Vis] (34) 90, p. 41.
"Slow" (tr. by Kees Snoek). [Vis] (34) 90, p. 40.
3831. LODEN, Rachel
"After the Shaking Stops." [YellowS] (35) Wint 90-91, p. 8.
"Blood Poisoning." [CumbPR] (9:2) Spr 90, p. 22.
"The Crow on the Cradle." [BelPoJ] (41:1) Fall 90, p. 9.
"A Falling Woman." [CumbPR] (9:2) Spr 90, p. 23.
"Locked Ward, Newtown, Connecticut." [NewYorkQ] (42) Sum 90, p. 69.
"Marrying the Stranger." [YellowS] (33) Spr 90, p. 16.
"Orcas Island." [BelPoJ] (41:1) Fall 90, p. 8-9.
"Saturday, Manoa Valley." [YellowS] (35) Wint 90-91, p. 8.
"Tumbling Dice." [BelPoJ] (41:1) Fall 90, p. 10.
3832. LOGAN, John
"Byron at Shelley's Burning." [PoetryE] (30) Fall 90, p. 127.
"Letter to My Son." [AmerPoR] (19:1) Ja-F 90, p. 36-38.
"Two Preludes for La Push." [PoetryE] (30) Fall 90, p. 128-129.
"Winter Window." [HampSPR] (Anthology 1975-1990) 90, p. 19.
3833. LOGAN, William
"Chamber Music." [PartR] (57:2) Spr 90, p. 272.
"Histoire des Mentalités." [SouthwR] (75:4) Aut 90, p. 470-471.
"The Holy Sea." [Verse] (7:3) Wint 90, p. 55.
"The Long Weekend." [Nat] (250:11) 19 Mr 90, p. 391.
"Nocturne Galant." [DenQ] (25:2) Fall 90, p. 27-28.
"Ode to the Chair" (M. New, Chair of the Department, 1979-1988). [Agni] (31/32) 90, p. 205-206.
"The Plantations of Colonial Jamaica." [SouthwR] (75:4) Aut 90, p. 471.
"Trouble at the Circe Arms." [Verse] (7:3) Wint 90, p. 56.
3834. LOGGHE, Joan (Joan S.)
"And Dream Is Quilt Is Comforter." [SingHM] (17) 90, p. 40-42.
"Becoming Neruda." [SingHM] (18) 90, p. 96-97.
3835. LOGGINS, Vernon Porter
"A Matter of Words." [EngJ] (79:2) F 90, p. 87.
3836. LOGSDON, Lucy
"Girl Not on the Moon." [SouthernPR] (30:2) Fall 90, p. 33-34.
3837. LOGUE, Christopher
"Kings, an Account of Books 1 and 2 of Homer's Iliad" (Excerpts). [ParisR] (32:117) Wint 90, p. 8-21.
3838. LOHN, Rod
"Plus I." [WestCL] (24:3) Wint 90, p. 87-89.
3839. LOMBARDO, Barbara
"The Day Before the Progress Bulletin Reported Alcoholic Genes." [OnTheBus] (2:2/3:1, #6/7) Sum-Fall 90 Wint-Spr 91, p. 138.
"Eating Cauliflower." [OnTheBus] (2:1, #5) Spr 90, p. 101.
"A Mile Up Through Chaparral." [OnTheBus] (2:1, #5) Spr 90, p. 100-101.
3840. LONDON, Jonathan
"Peace Now." [SlipS] (10) 90, p. 73.
LONERGAN, Janet Gill
See GILL-LONERGAN, Janet
3841. LONG, Fred
"Cup of Soup." [EmeraldCR] (1990) c89, p. 52-53.
3842. LONG, John Wingo
"Comeuppance." [HampSPR] (Anthology 1975-1990) 90, p. 220.
"Exorcism." [HampSPR] (Anthology 1975-1990) 90, p. 221.
3843. LONG, Richard
"Rain Miles." [TampaR] (3) 90, p. 44.
"Trace the Scar." [HayF] (7) Fall-Wint 90, p. 101.
"Waterlines." [TampaR] (3) 90, p. 45.
3844. LONG, Robert (Robert Hill)
"Eyes of the Swordfish." [VirQR] (66:1) Wint 90, p. 87-88.
"Fumetti." [CimR] (90) Ja 90, p. 61-62.
"In Country." [NewOR] (17:4) Wint 90, p. 53.
"The Mouse." [Poetry] (156:2) My 90, p. 79-81.
"Parrot in Frostland." [GreenMR] (NS 3:2) Fall-Wint 89-90, p. 74-75.
"Stealing Dirt." [VirQR] (66:1) Wint 90, p. 85-87.
"West Island." [GreenMR] (NS 3:2) Fall-Wint 89-90, p. 72-73.

"The Work of the Bow." [SouthernPR] (30:1) Spr 90, p. 37-39.
3845. LONG-SEVERANCE, Judy (*See also* SEVERENCE, Judith)
"The Elements." [RagMag] (7:2) Spr 90, p. 52-53.
"Environmental Issues." [RagMag] (7:2) Spr 90, p. 54.
"Firstborn, Firstgone." [RagMag] (7:2) Spr 90, p. 45-46.
"Genepool." [RagMag] (7:2) Spr 90, p. 43.
"Gridlock." [RagMag] (7:2) Spr 90, p. 50-51.
"Home of the Brave." [RagMag] (7:2) Spr 90, p. 46.
"Implants, by Cookie Schwarz." [RagMag] (7:2) Spr 90, p. 48.
"Midlife Marriage." [RagMag] (7:2) Spr 90, p. 41.
"Nailbar." [RagMag] (7:2) Spr 90, p. 47-48.
"Second Thoughts." [RagMag] (7:2) Spr 90, p. 45.
"Tips on the Single Life, from Cookie Schwarz." [RagMag] (7:2) Spr 90, p. 49.
"Triangles." [RagMag] (7:2) Spr 90, p. 42.
"Vague Ideas." [RagMag] (7:2) Spr 90, p. 44.
3846. LONGLEY, Judy
"Delta Journal." [Poetry] (156:4) Jl 90, p. 206-207.
"Gauguin and Bonnard." [Poetry] (156:4) Jl 90, p. 205-206.
3847. LONGLEY, Michael
"Font." [NewYorker] (66:44) 17 D 90, p. 50.
"Laertes." [NewYorker] (66:14) 21 My 90, p. 34.
3848. LOOMIS, Jeff
"On Being a Poet (Arcane Minnesota Twin) in October 1987." [CoalC] (1) Ag 90, p.
    12-14.
"A Prayer to Him Who Preyed at Healing" (benedictus -- for Gerald Hubert
    Loomis). [CoalC] (2) D 90, p. 13-14.
3849. LOONEY, George
"Breaking the Surface." [LitR] (33:2) Wint 90, p. 262-263.
"The Persistence of Parakeets." [TarRP] (30:1) Fall 90, p. 18-19.
"Redeeming Value." [PoetL] (85:1) Spr 90, p. 48.
"You Don't Know What to Call This." [SouthernPR] (30:2) Fall 90, p. 36-37.
3850. LOOTS, Barbara
"El Greco: 'The Penitent Magdalen'." [ChrC] (107:12) 11 Ap 90, p. 360.
"In a Dry Season." [ChrC] (107:24) 22-29 Ag 90, p. 759.
"Pelicans at Pawleys Island." [ChrC] (107:35) 5 D 90, p. 1138.
"Seashore Sestina." [NegC] (10:2/3) 90, p. 60-61.
3851. LOPEZ, Leslie
"Across Landscape." [Cond] (17) 90, p. 56.
"Underwater." [Cond] (17) 90, p. 55.
3852. LOPEZ, Matilde Elene
"Something Endures" (tr. by Elizabeth Gamble Miller). [MidAR] (10:1) 90, p. 104.
LOPEZ, Moravia Ochoa
    See OCHOA LOPEZ, Moravia
3853. LOPEZ, Tony
"Hart's Tongue." [Screens] (2) 90, p. 160.
"Ptarmigan." [Screens] (2) 90, p. 160.
3854. LOPEZ ADORNO, Pedro
"17. No necesita legitimarnos la épica" (De "Peregrinajes del reposo," 1980-88,
    inédito). [Inti] (32/33) Otoño 90-Primavera 91, p. 256.
"Desobediencia del Placer." [Inti] (32/33) Otoño 90-Primavera 91, p. 254.
"Estudio para Terminar una Pieza de Juan Morel Campos." [Inti] (32/33) Otoño
    90-Primavera 91, p. 255.
3855. LOPEZ MEJIA, Adelaida
"Bucólico Ajedrez." [Américas] (18:3/4) Fall-Wint 90, p. 98-99.
"La Familia." [Américas] (18:3/4) Fall-Wint 90, p. 100.
LORANT, Laurie Robertson
    See ROBERTSON-LORANT, Laurie
LORCA, Federico García
    See GARCIA LORCA, Federico
3856. LORDE, Audre
"Love Poem." [CimR] (93) O 90, p. 80.
3857. LORENZINI, Jim
"Goddess of Democracy." [EmeraldCR] (1990) c89, p. 90-91.
3858. LORR, Katharine Auchincloss
"They Leave." [PoetL] (85:1) Spr 90, p. 35-36.

291

Los SANTOS, Marisa de
   See SANTOS, Marisa de los
3859. LOTT, Clarinda Harriss
   "Living in the Present." [HampSPR] (Anthology 1975-1990) 90, p. 156.
   "Symbol and Renunciation." [HampSPR] (Anthology 1975-1990) 90, p. 155.
3860. LOURIE, Richard
   "To Robinson Jeffers" (tr. of Czeslaw Milosz, w. the author). [Thrpny] (43) Fall 90, p. 13.
3861. LOVE, Andrew
   "Utterance." [HangL] (57) 90, p. 79.
   "Walking." [HangL] (57) 90, p. 80.
3862. LOVE, B. D.
   "Four Grey Wings of Mercy." [Footwork] 90, p. 65.
   "Newlywed Game." [TarRP] (30:1) Fall 90, p. 22.
   "Pigeons." [ChamLR] (4:1, #7) Fall 90, p. 122-123.
   "Pigeons." [TarRP] (30:1) Fall 90, p. 20-21.
   "Temples, More or Less." [TarRP] (30:1) Fall 90, p. 20.
3863. LOVELOCK, Yann
   "Shore Road" (Excerpts). [Os] (30) Spr 90, p. 16-17.
3864. LoVERDE, Andrew J.
   "Words." [PacificR] (8) 90, p. 66.
LOW, Jackson Mac
   See Mac LOW, Jackson
3865. LOWE, Frederick
   "Papa in the New Age." [YellowS] (33) Spr 90, p. 13.
3866. LOWE, Janet
   "In Dreams." [NewL] (57:1) Fall 90, p. 97.
3867. LOWE, Zachary
   "Disconnection." [ChironR] (9:4) Wint 90, p. 18.
3868. LOWELL, Douglas
   "The Two Cities." [Sulfur] (10:1, #26) Spr 90, p. 165-169.
3869. LOWENSTEIN, Robert
   "Pebble in the Shoe." [DogRR] (9:1, #17) Spr 90, p. 4.
3870. LOWENTHAL, Bennett
   "Variations on a Theme from *Petticoat Junction*." [BelPoJ] (41:1) Fall 90, p. 22-23.
3871. LOWENTHAL, Michael
   "Grading Essay Entitled 'Rejection'." [JamesWR] (7:4) Sum 90, p. 6.
3872. LOWERY, Janet
   "The Crows." [NewMyths] (1:1) 90, p. 138.
3873. LOWERY, Joanne
   "As If Australia." [SpoonRQ] (15:1) Wint 90, p. 30, also (15:4) Fall 90, p. 11.
   "Breathing on Mirrors." [ManhatPR] (11) [89?], p. 4.
   "Buffalo." [SpoonRQ] (15:1) Wint 90, p. 28, also (15:4) Fall 90, p. 9.
   "Cruise." [ManhatPR] (11) [89?], p. 6.
   "Dream's Daughter." [Pembroke] (22) 90, p. 97.
   "God." [ManhatPR] (11) [89?], p. 4.
   "Grandma." [SpoonRQ] (15:1) Wint 90, p. 31, also (15:4) Fall 90, p. 12.
   "Hand Like a Spire, Hand Like a Flag." [SpoonRQ] (15:1) Wint 90, p. 34, also (15:4) Fall 90, p. 15.
   "Hummingbird." [SpoonRQ] (15:1) Wint 90, p. 29, also (15:4) Fall 90, p. 10.
   "Lament." [SpoonRQ] (15:1) Wint 90, p. 32, also (15:4) Fall 90, p. 13.
   "The Pinocchio Poems." [SpoonRQ] (15:1) Wint 90, p. 35-42, also (15:4) Fall 90, p. 16-23.
   "Six Men Find Peace." [SpoonRQ] (15:1) Wint 90, p. 33, also (15:4) Fall 90, p. 14.
   "Sliver." [Pembroke] (22) 90, p. 96.
3874. LOWITZ, Leza
   "What Hoffman Said." [PoetryUSA] (5:3) Fall 90, p. 4.
3875. LOY, Mina
   "Property of Pigeons." [ChiR] (37:1) Wint 90, p. 14-15.
3876. LU, Lu
   "Two Pieces of Birch Bark" (tr. by Ginny MacKenzie and Wei Guo). [PoetryE] (30) Fall 90, p. 11.
3877. LUBENSKI, Andrei
   "The air's full of fumes" (tr. by Oleg Atbashian and Maureen Hurley). [PoetryUSA] (5:2) Sum 90, p. 13.
   "Lik Tvoj" (tr. by Oleg Atbashian and Maureen Hurley). [PoetryUSA] (5:2) Sum 90,

p. 13.
"Talking to the Mirror" (tr. by Oleg Atbashian and Maureen Hurley). [PoetryUSA] (5:2) Sum 90, p. 13.
3878. LUBINETZKI, Raja
"Afterwards" (tr. by Roderick Iverson). [Screens] (2) 90, p. 76-77.
"Words" (tr. by Roderick Iverson). [Screens] (2) 90, p. 76.
3879. LUCAS, Marie B.
"Movement." [Crucible] (26) Fall 90, p. 88.
3880. LUCAS, Tony
"The Last Defenders." [SoCoast] (8) Spr 90, p. 31.
"Making a Space." [SoCoast] (8) Spr 90, p. 32-33.
"The Old Miners' Road." [SoCoast] (8) Spr 90, p. 34-35.
"A Warm House." [SoCoast] (8) Spr 90, p. 36.
3881. LUCIA, Joseph
"Descent." [Outbr] (21) 90, p. 28.
"Of Her Sleeping." [Outbr] (21) 90, p. 29.
3882. LUCIA, Joseph P.
"Physics." [OnTheBus] (2:2/3:1, #6/7) Sum-Fall 90 Wint-Spr 91, p. 139-140.
"Radio." [OnTheBus] (2:2/3:1, #6/7) Sum-Fall 90 Wint-Spr 91, p. 139.
3883. LUCINA, Mary
"Maybe Not." [Nimrod] (34:1) Fall-Wint 90, p. 118.
3884. LUDVIGSON, Susan
"After the Arrest." [SouthernPR] (30:2) Fall 90, p. 22-27.
3885. LUDWIN, Peter
"In the Way." [MidwQ] (31:2) Wint 90, p. 205-206.
3886. LUISI, David
"Zen Garden." [HawaiiR] (14:1, #28) Wint 89-90, p. 45.
3887. LUKASIK, Gail
"Music: Pink & Blue I 1919" (for Georgia O'Keeffe). [Gypsy] (15) 90, p. 68.
"Painting No. 21 (Palo Duro Canyon), 1916" (for Georgia O'Keeffe). [GeoR] (44:1/2) Spr-Sum 90, p. 135.
3888. LUKE
"For Rick, in Honor of His Father." [Callaloo] (13:3) Sum 90, p. 427.
"Outside Subic Bay." [Callaloo] (13:3) Sum 90, p. 426.
3889. LUM, Wing Tek
"Chinese Hot Pot." [BambooR] (47) Sum 90, p. 16.
"This Tree You Told Us Stories Of." [Zyzzyva] (6:1 #21) Spr 90, p. 85-86.
3890. LUMMIS, Suzanne
"A.M./P.M." [OnTheBus] (2:2/3:1, #6/7) Sum-Fall 90 Wint-Spr 91, p. 141-142.
3891. LUNA, Violeta
"Cantos de Temor y de Blasfemia" (Selection: Canto X). [InterPR] (16:1) Spr 90, p. 48, 50.
"Songs of Fear and Blasphemy" (Selection: Song X, tr. by Mark Smith-Soto). [InterPR] (16:1) Spr 90, p. 49, 51.
3892. LUND, Orval
"In the Driver's Seat." [KanQ] (22:3) Sum 90, p. 62.
"January, at Mid-Life." [KanQ] (22:3) Sum 90, p. 60-61.
3893. LUNDAY, Robert
"Maggie" (for McBrearty). [SouthernPR] (30:1) Spr 90, p. 14-16.
3894. LUNDBERG-GRUNKE, Ann
"1966." [MidwQ] (31:4) Sum 90, p. 482-483.
3895. LUNDE, David
"First Will and Testament." [HawaiiR] (14:1, #28) Wint 89-90, p. 64-65.
"The Poem Called Liver" (For Charles Willoughby Smith). [HawaiiR] (14:3, #30) Fall 90, p. 56-57.
3896. LUNDE, Diane
"Annie" (tr. of Guillaume Apollinaire). [SycamoreR] (2:2) Sum 90, p. 53.
"At the Lakebed." [Mildred] (4:1) 90, p. 114.
"Grendalsong." [Mildred] (4:1) 90, p. 115.
"I Had the Courage" (tr. of Guillaume Apollinaire). [SycamoreR] (2:2) Sum 90, p. 51.
3897. LUNDQUIST, Anne
"Small Girl at the Chesapeake" (for lisa). [SinW] (42) Wint 90-91, p. 113.
3898. LUNN, Jean
"Cocoon in the Subway." [ManhatPR] (12) [90?], p. 9.
"Concertos for Wind Instruments." [WebR] (14:2) Spr 90, p. 19-20.

3899. LUSH, Laura
    "Fishing." [AntigR] (83) Aut 90, p. 111.
    "Parting." [AntigR] (83) Aut 90, p. 112.
3900. LUSH, Richard
    "La Compañía de Jesús" (Quito). [Writ] (21) 89 c1990, p. 20.
    "Descent" (Baños). [Writ] (21) 89 c1990, p. 15.
    "The Interior" (Papallacta). [Writ] (21) 89 c1990, p. 16-17.
    "Looking for Cotopaxi" (Latacunga). [Writ] (21) 89 c1990, p. 21.
    "Louise in the Jungle" (Rio Verde). [Writ] (21) 89 c1990, p. 19.
    "Nostrum" (Chichicastenango). [Writ] (21) 89 c1990, p. 22.
    "An Opening to the Amazon" (Puyo). [Writ] (21) 89 c1990, p. 14.
    "Topography" (Guayaquil). [Writ] (21) 89 c1990, p. 18.
3901. LUSK, Dorothy Trujillo
    "This Story." [WestCL] (24:1) Spr 90, p. 122-126.
3902. LUTHER, Susan
    "To a Dour, Dear Friend." [Hellas] (1:1) Spr 90, p. 49.
3903. LUX, Thomas
    "The Swimming Pool." [BlackWR] (17:1) Fall-Wint 90, p. 124.
3904. LUZI, Mario
    "Senior" (tr. by Dana Gioia). [Sequoia] (33:2) Wint 90, p. 4.
3905. LYDEN, Eric
    "Coffee with the Beatniks." [MoodySI] (22/23) Wint 89-90, p. 10.
LYFSHIN, Lyn
    See LIFSHIN, Lyn
3906. LYLE, Joy
    "Desire." [CutB] (34) Sum-Fall 90, p. 63.
    "Ladder Ode." [CutB] (34) Sum-Fall 90, p. 34-35.
    "The Washerwoman Moves Away from Herself." [PoetryNW] (31:3) Aut 90, p. 24.
3907. LYLES, Peggy Willis
    "Haiku" (3 poems). [Northeast] (5:2) Spr 90, p. 33.
    "Haiku" (3 poems). [Northeast] (NS 5:3) Wint 90-91, p. 36.
3908. LYNCH, Alessandra
    "The Fight." [Ploughs] (16:4) Wint 90-91, p. 70.
    "The Fly-Cage." [Ploughs] (16:4) Wint 90-91, p. 72.
    "The Wedding to Black Garter or Trussed." [Ploughs] (16:4) Wint 90-91, p. 71.
3909. LYNCH, Doris
    "Hummingbird." [SwampR] (5) Wint-Spr 90, p. 96.
    "New Year's Eve, New Orleans, 11:55 p.m." [SwampR] (5) Wint-Spr 90, p. 97-98.
    "Praising Invisible Birds." [NegC] (10:1) 90, p. 68-69.
    "Shadows." [SwampR] (5) Wint-Spr 90, p. 95.
3910. LYNCH, Janice
    "Left Behind." [GreenMR] (NS 4:1) Spr-Sum 90, p. 40.
    "Myth of First Lovers." [GreenMR] (NS 4:1) Spr-Sum 90, p. 41.
    "The Past." [HayF] (7) Fall-Wint 90, p. 100.
3911. LYNCH, Mary Ann
    "Dark the Face" (for Max Schwartz). [SlipS] (10) 90, p. 5-6.
    "Let's Talk Rape." [SlipS] (10) 90, p. 6-13.
3912. LYNN, Catherine
    "Coup." [ChironR] (9:4) Wint 90, p. 11.
    "The Criminal Mentality." [WormR] (30:4, #120) 90, p. 98-101.
    "Divorce." [ChironR] (9:4) Wint 90, p. 11.
    "If You Botch It." [ChironR] (9:4) Wint 90, p. 11.
    "Last Act." [Pearl] (12) Fall-Wint 90, p. 32.
    "The Music Lover." [ChironR] (9:4) Wint 90, p. 11.
    "Serpent-Free Garden" (9 poems). [Pearl] (11) Sum 90, p. 15-29.
    "Thanksgiving Day Prayer, 1990." [WormR] (30:4, #120) 90, p. 97-98.
3913. LYNSKEY, Ed C. (Edward C.)
    "All Her Pretty Ones" (Sussex, 1941, a Plainsongs Award Poem). [Plain] (10:3) Spr 90, p. 36.
    "Bartholomew's Cobbler." [NegC] (10:2/3) 90, p. 81.
    "Blue Movies." [OxfordM] (6:1) Spr-Sum 90, p. 67.
    "Honeycutt Goes Iron." [SmPd] (27:1, #78) Wint 90, p. 36.
    "The Hyacinth Girl." [AntigR] (80) Wint 90, p. 9.
    "The Hyacinth Girl." [HolCrit] (27:1) F 90, p. 15.
    "Interview with Mr. Moto, 1939." [Writer] (103:9) S 90, p. 46.
    "Little Haiti." [WilliamMR] (28) 90, p. 89.

"No Idle Boast." [BellR] (13:1, #27) Spr 90, p. 45.
"Portrait of the Outlaw." [KanQ] (22:1/2) Wint-Spr 90, p. 228.
"Shade Tree Mechanics." [HampSPR] (Anthology 1975-1990) 90, p. 229.
"Shade Tree Mechanics." [PoetryUSA] (5:2) Sum 90, p. 9.
"The Tobacco Queen." [ChatR] (11:1) Fall 90, p. 38.
"The Tree Surgeon's Curse." [Amelia] (6:2, #17) 90, p. 12.
"Trout Fishing." [Plain] (11:1) Fall 90, p. 29.
"Vinegar Puss." [Amelia] (6:2, #17) 90, p. 10.
"The War Widow's Pension Runs Out." [Amelia] (6:2, #17) 90, p. 11.

3914. LYON, Arabella
"Extractions." [Kalliope] (12:2) 90, p. 36.

3915. LYON, George Ella
"The Mean Poems." [SingHM] (17) 90, p. 60.
"Silence." [AmerV] (21) Wint 90, p. 61.

3916. LYON, Hillary
"The Urgent, All Consuming." [MidwQ] (32:1) Aut 90, p. 89.

3917. LYONS, Art
"Point of View." [ChangingM] (21) Wint-Spr 90, p. 25.

3918. LYONS, Kimberly
"Poems to the Sea" (after Cy Twombly). [Talisman] (5) Fall 90, p. 135-136.

3919. LYONS, Robert
"Camping Out." [BellArk] (6:3) My-Je 90, p. 3.
"Cold Bay." [BellArk] (6:1) Ja-F 90, p. 20.
"Two Veterans." [BellArk] (6:1) Ja-F 90, p. 12.

3920. LYONS, Stephen
"Song of Steel." [Grain] (18:4) Wint 90, p. 18.
"Swimming with My Daughter." [Grain] (18:1) Spr 90, p. 38.

3921. MA, Li
"Hostages" (tr. by Dong Jiping). [Footwork] 90, p. 35.
"In the Summer Night I and You" (tr. by Tsung Tsung and Richard Terrill).
    [AnotherCM] (21) 90, p. 109-110.
"On That Side" (tr. by Dong Jiping). [Footwork] 90, p. 35.
"A Palm Tree and Two Women" (tr. by Tsung Tsung and Richard Terrill).
    [AnotherCM] (21) 90, p. 107-108.
"Soundless Is Midnight" (tr. by Dong Jiping). [Footwork] 90, p. 35.

MA-CHAY
    See MILLER, D. D.

Mac . . .
    See also names beginning with Mc . . .

3922. MAC, Kathy
"Peru Is Not Far." [PottPort] (12) 90, p. 38.
"Selling My Home." [PottPort] (12) 90, p. 38.

3923. Mac CORMACK, Karen
"Clear Yellow." [Screens] (2) 90, p. 182.
"Export Notwithstanding." [Verse] (7:1) Spr 90, p. 22.
"Hazard." [Verse] (7:1) Spr 90, p. 22.
"Joyance." [Screens] (2) 90, p. 180.
"Shake." [Screens] (2) 90, p. 179.

3924. Mac DOUGALL, Alan
"Fusion." [Pig] (16) 90, p. 80.
"Inland Sailing: New Love's Channels." [Pig] (16) 90, p. 80.
"Maxine." [Vis] (33) 90, p. 35.
"Torquemada Slumbers." [Pig] (16) 90, p. 80.
"Transformations." [Pig] (16) 90, p. 80.
"Truing In." [KanQ] (22:3) Sum 90, p. 192.

3925. Mac DUNCAN, Malcolm
"Anguish." [Nimrod] (34:1) Fall-Wint 90, p. 64.
"The Diary of Anne Frank." [Nimrod] (34:1) Fall-Wint 90, p. 63.
"Janine in Autumn." [Nimrod] (34:1) Fall-Wint 90, p. 65.
"Miscarriage of Her Child." [Nimrod] (34:1) Fall-Wint 90, p. 64.
"Prayer for the Hospice Patient." [Nimrod] (34:1) Fall-Wint 90, p. 64.

3926. Mac LOW, Jackson
"Prose Look Settled." [Sulfur] (10:2, #27) Fall 90, p. 143-151.
"Twenties" (Selections: 1-7). [Avec] (3:1) 90, p. 99-105.
"Twenties: 40" (en route San Diego to New York). [PoetryUSA] (5:3) Fall 90, p.
    12.

3927. MacALPINE, Katherine
"Stranger at the Party." [Hellas] (1:1) Spr 90, p. 52.
3928. MacCAIG, Norman
"Progress." [Verse] (7:2) Sum 90, p. 56.
MacCORMACK, Karen
See Mac CORMACK, Karen
3929. MacDONALD, Alex G.
"Deer-Hunting in Western Pennsylvania." [HiramPoR] (48/49) 90-91, p. 48.
3930. MACDONALD, Cynthia
"The Triborough Bridge a Crown for His Head." [NewYorker] (65:46) 1 Ja 90, p. 36.
3931. MacDONALD, Cyril A.
"Apathy." [PottPort] (11) 89, p. 23.
"Free Trade." [PottPort] (11) 89, p. 23.
3932. MacDONALD, Walter
"River of the Arms of God." [SoDakR] (28:3) Aut 90, p. 133.
MacDOUGALL, Alan
See Mac DOUGALL, Alan
3933. MacDOUGALL, Joan
"There Are Certain Things." [AntigR] (81/82) Spr-Sum 90, p. 64.
MacDUNCAN, Malcolm
See Mac DUNCAN, Malcolm
3934. MACHADO, Antonio
"Childhood Memory" (tr. by David Johnson). [VirQR] (66:3) Sum 90, p. 453-454.
"Flies" (tr. by David Johnson). [VirQR] (66:3) Sum 90, p. 452-453.
3935. MACHADO, Luz
"Elegía por el Alma de las Palabras." [InterPR] (16:1) Spr 90, p. 98-102.
"Elegy for the Soul of Words" (tr. by Mark Smith-Soto). [InterPR] (16:1) Spr 90, p. 99-103.
MACHAN, Kathryn Howd
See AAL, Katharyn Machan
MACHIKO, Okuda
See OKUDA, Machiko
3936. MACHMILLER, Patricia
"Ants." [NowestR] (28:2) 90, p. 19-20.
3937. MACIOCI, R. Nikolas
"Apocryphal Fathers." [CapeR] (25:2) Fall 90, p. 19.
"At the End of Strawberry Season." [Wind] (20:66) 90, p. 27-28.
"Knife." [ArtfulD] (18/19) 90, p. 67.
"Late April Aesthetic." [Wind] (20:66) 90, p. 27.
"Lost Among Old Apples" (for Marcia Preston). [DustyD] (1:2) O 90, p. 4.
"A Young Boy Seeks the Deeply Real Through Astaire and Rogers" (A Plainsongs Award Poem). [Plain] (11:1) Fall 90, p. 38.
3938. MacISAAC, Robert
"One Hand Clapping." [SmPd] (27:3, #80) Fall 90, p. 25-26.
"Walking." [SmPd] (27:3, #80) Fall 90, p. 27.
3939. MACK, Diane
"No Time Beyond." [EmeraldCR] (1990) c89, p. 83.
3940. MACK, Jennifer E.
"Untitled: In the silver-struck silence." [EmeraldCR] (1990) c89, p. 78-79.
3941. MACK, Jon
"Voice or Verse or What." [Verse] (7:1) Spr 90, p. 32.
3942. MacKENZIE, Ginny
"Be Patient, Be Patient" (tr. of Ya Ping Tang, w. Wei Guo). [PoetryE] (30) Fall 90, p. 105.
"An Impression" (tr. of Cheng Gu, w. Wei Guo). [PoetryE] (30) Fall 90, p. 106.
"Today Someone Brought You Flowers" (tr. of Han Dong, w. Wei Guo). [PoetryE] (30) Fall 90, p. 96.
"Two Pieces of Birch Bark" (tr. of Lu Lu, w. Wei Guo). [PoetryE] (30) Fall 90, p. 11.
3943. MacKENZIE, Nancy
"Spring Rain." [PottPort] (11) 89, p. 9.
3944. MACKEY, Mary
"Breaking the Fever." [PoetryUSA] ([5:4?]) Wint 90, p. 17.
"On Turning Forty-Six." [PoetryUSA] ([5:4?]) Wint 90, p. 17.

3945. MACKEY, Nathaniel
    "Aspic Surmise." [Zyzzyva] (6:1 #21) Spr 90, p. 58-67.
3946. MACKLIN, Elizabeth
    "At the Classics Teacher's." [NewYorker] (66:21) 9 Jl 90, p. 40-41.
    "By Daylight." [NewYorker] (66:8) 9 Ap 90, p. 38.
    "A Field Guide to Lesser Desires." [YaleR] (79:3) Spr 90, p. 382.
    "Love Song to the World Leaders." [NewYorker] (66:26) 13 Ag 90, p. 32.
    "More." [NewYorker] (66:14) 21 My 90, p. 42.
    "Now the Heroine Weakens and Speaks." [Verse] (7:3) Wint 90, p. 57.
    "There Is Still Water." [ParisR] (32:115) Sum 90, p. 196-197.
    "We Love It No End." [NewYorker] (66:34) 8 O 90, p. 48.
    "What Now." [ParisR] (32:115) Sum 90, p. 198.
3947. MACKOWSKI, Joanie
    "The Better Vantage for Love." [PoetryNW] (31:4) Wint 90-91, p. 46-47.
    "Deaths and Weather." [PoetryNW] (31:3) Aut 90, p. 45-46.
    "Her Day Speaks for Sleeplessness." [PoetryNW] (31:3) Aut 90, p. 47.
    "Plate 10: Ducks Overhead (As the Sportsman Often Sees Them)." [PoetryNW]
        (31:4) Wint 90-91, p. 43-46.
    "The Woman Who Has Everything." [PoetryNW] (31:3) Aut 90, p. 46.
3948. MacLEOD, Kathryn
    "Mouth-Piece." [Verse] (7:1) Spr 90, p. 52-53.
MacLOW, Jackson
    See Mac LOW, Jackson
3949. MACOUBRIE, John
    "In Memory of W. H. Auden." [NorthStoneR] (9) 90, p. 90.
    "Swift's Ghost Addresses the Reader of Confessional Poetry." [NorthStoneR] (9)
        90, p. 81.
3950. MacSWEEN, R. J.
    "Our Treasures." [AntigR] (81/82) Spr-Sum 90, p. 20.
3951. MacVEAN, Kate
    "Aperture." [HangL] (56) 90, p. 72.
    "One for Burning." [HangL] (56) 90, p. 71.
3952. MADDOCKS, Jim
    "Coming Out." [Bogg] (63) 90, p. 7.
    "Premeditation" (in memoriam W.C.W.). [Bogg] (62) 90, p. 34.
3953. MADDOX, Marjorie
    "Venn Diagrams." [PraS] (64:4) Wint 90, p. 107-108.
    "Winter Mail." [PraS] (64:4) Wint 90, p. 108-109.
3954. MADIGAN, Mark
    "You Never Knew." [AmerS] (59:2) Spr 90, p. 274.
3955. MADIGAN, Rick
    "Third-Shift Waitress at the Coral Reef." [AntR] (48:4) Fall 90, p. 493.
3956. MADISON, Russ
    "The Long Hunt." [SycamoreR] (2:2) Sum 90, p. 33-34.
3957. MADSON, Arthur
    "Clemmie with Hoe." [KanQ] (22:3) Sum 90, p. 205.
    "Hands Like Wings." [SmPd] (27:3, #80) Fall 90, p. 31.
    "Kinder Schadenfreude." [DogRR] (9:1, #17) Spr 90, p. 58.
    "Second Singularity." [KanQ] (22:3) Sum 90, p. 204-205.
    "Taking in the Wash." [PoetC] (21:2) Wint 90, p. 30.
3958. MAERTZ, Susan
    "Opening." [Gypsy] (15) 90, p. 31.
3959. MAGARRELL, Elaine
    "Aspects of Play." [Plain] (10:3) Spr 90, p. 32.
    "Deciduous." [PoetL] (85:1) Spr 90, p. 47.
    "Somehow." [PoetL] (85:1) Spr 90, p. 46.
3960. MAGASIS, Dory
    "Gringa in Paradise." [PoetryUSA] (5:1) Spr 90, p. 4.
3961. MAGER, Don
    "First Riddle" (tr. of Frantisek Halas). [NewOR] (17:3) Fall 90, p. 70.
    "Second Riddle" (tr. of Frantisek Halas). [NewOR] (17:3) Fall 90, p. 70.
    "Third Riddle with Its Solution" (tr. of Frantisek Halas). [NewOR] (17:3) Fall 90, p.
        70.
3962. MAGGI, Maria Theresa
    "Praying for Passion." [FloridaR] (17:2) Fall-Wint 90, p. 137.

3963. MAGGIO, Mike
"Oranges from Palestine." [SoCoast] (9) Fall 90, p. 42-43.
MAGGIOLO, Marcio Veloz
See VELOZ MAGGIOLO, Marcio
3964. MAGGS, Randall
"Berbers." [Dandel] (17:2) Fall-Wint 90, p. 27-28.
3965. MAGINNES, Al
"A Season's Change." [SouthernPR] (30:1) Spr 90, p. 52-53.
3966. MAGORIAN, James
"Interstate." [Bogg] (63) 90, p. 31.
"Shamut Pass." [OxfordM] (6:1) Spr-Sum 90, p. 48.
3967. MAGRELLI, Valerio
"Clecsografie" (Excerpts, tr. by Pasquale Verdicchio). [Screens] (2) 90, p. 104-106.
"Contrapunto May-June 1984" (Excerpts, tr. by Pasquale Verdicchio). [Screens] (2) 90, p. 106.
"I sit, in treatment, at the movies, devoted" (tr. by Dana Gioia). [WilliamMR] (28) 90, p. 8.
"If I must dial a number to call you" (tr. by Dana Gioia). [WilliamMR] (28) 90, p. 7.
"If you melt some lead" (tr. by Dana Gioia). [WilliamMR] (28) 90, p. 63.
3968. MAHA
"Untitled: The little Tibetan." [ChironR] (9:4) Wint 90, p. 17.
3969. MAHAPATRA, Anuradha
"The Hunt" (tr. by Jyotirmoy Datta and Carolyne Wright). [IndR] (13:2) Spr 90, p. 73.
"Mother of the Bud" (tr. by Jyotirmoy Datta and Carolyne Wright). [IndR] (13:2) Spr 90, p. 72.
"To the Mountaintop" (tr. by Jyotirmoy Datta and Carolyne Wright). [IndR] (13:2) Spr 90, p. 74.
"The Year 1984" (tr. by Jyotirmoy Datta and Carolyne Wright). [IndR] (13:2) Spr 90, p. 75.
3970. MAHAPATRA, Jayanta
"In the Autumn Valleys of the Mahanadi." [Arc] (25) Aut 90, p. 51.
"In the Rain." [Arc] (25) Aut 90, p. 52.
"The Photograph." [Arc] (25) Aut 90, p. 53.
3971. MAHON, Derek
"Ignorance" (tr. of Philippe Jaccottet). [ManhatR] (5:1) Spr 90, p. 52.
3972. MAHONEY, Brian
"Drop and Wonder Why." [ChironR] (9:1) Spr 90, p. 25.
3973. MAHONEY, Lisa
"My Name One Morning." [PoetL] (85:2) Sum 90, p. 24.
3974. MAIELLO, Michael J.
"Desert Fathers" ("Theologies of Anger and Doubt," Brooklyn, 1986). [Footwork] 90, p. 68.
3975. MAILMAN, Doug
"Collage." [CimR] (92) Jl 90, p. 120-121.
3976. MAILMAN, Leo
"My Left Finger." [Pearl] (11) Sum 90, p. 5-6.
3977. MAIO, Samuel
"Dark Woman Well." [NowestR] (28:3/29:1) 90-91, p. 82.
"The Dispassionate Shepherd's First Blind Date." [CharR] (16:2) Fall 90, p. 80.
"Domestic Violence." [SoDakR] (28:1) Spr 90, p. 29-30.
"Face Value." [CharR] (16:2) Fall 90, p. 81.
"The Handsome Poet." [CharR] (16:2) Fall 90, p. 82.
"Look." [CharR] (16:2) Fall 90, p. 83.
"Mid-Life Epitaph." [SoDakR] (28:1) Spr 90, p. 31.
"The Real Thing." [CharR] (16:2) Fall 90, p. 79.
MAIPING, Chen
See CHEN, Maiping
3978. MAIRS, Nancy
"For a Child Who Has Lost Her Cat" (reprinted from #10, 1985). [Kaleid] (20) Wint-Spr 90, p. 35.
3979. MAJ, Bronislaw
"Evening, the Krakow train station, three gypsy" (tr. by Daniel Bourne). [ManhatR] (5:1) Spr 90, p. 6.
"A leaf, one of the last, fell away from a maple branch." [PoetryUSA] (5:1) Spr 90, p. 12.

298

MAJ

"Life swells to twice, three times its normal size" (tr. by Daniel Bourne). [ManhatR]
   (5:1) Spr 90, p. 5.
"On her way out this morning, she left" (tr. by Daniel Bourne). [ManhatR] (5:1) Spr
   90, p. 4.
"One of the last leaves to break loose from the maple" (tr. by Daniel Bourne).
   [ManhatR] (5:1) Spr 90, p. 5.
"A September afternoon, I inhale" (tr. by Daniel Bourne). [ManhatR] (5:1) Spr 90,
   p. 4.
"A sudden May downpour, people are hiding." [PoetryUSA] (5:1) Spr 90, p. 12.
"Yes I Am a Stranger." [PoetryUSA] (5:1) Spr 90, p. 12.
3980. MAJOR, Clarence
"Being and Becoming." [Callaloo] (13:2) Spr 90, p. 171.
"Cat Mother." [Callaloo] (13:2) Spr 90, p. 170.
"To Keep Revolving." [Callaloo] (13:2) Spr 90, p. 172.
"Unwanted Memory." [Callaloo] (13:2) Spr 90, p. 169.
3981. MAKAY, Ida
"A Szigetlakó." [MidAR] (10:1) 90, p. 48.
"For My Mother Again" (tr. by Mária Kurdi and Len Roberts). [AmerPoR] (19:5)
   S-O 90, p. 27.
"I Do Not Resemble" (tr. by Mária Kurdi and Len Roberts). [AmerPoR] (19:5) S-O
   90, p. 26.
"The Island Dweller" (tr. by Mária Kurdi and Len Roberts). [MidAR] (10:1) 90, p.
   49.
"Magic" (tr. by Mária Kurdi and Len Roberts). [MidAR] (10:1) 90, p. 51.
"Varázslat." [MidAR] (10:1) 90, p. 50.
"We Deserve It" (tr. by Mária Kurdi and Len Roberts). [AmerPoR] (19:5) S-O 90,
   p. 26.
3982. MAKEEVER, Anne T.
"Anna's Mirror." [RiverS] (32) [90?], p. 60.
"The Grieving Boxes." [RiverS] (32) [90?], p. 62.
"Where All Things Wait." [RiverS] (32) [90?], p. 61.
3983. MAKELA, JoAnne
"Crows." [RagMag] (8:2) 90, p. 25.
"Heron Dance." [RagMag] (8:2) 90, p. 24.
3984. MÄKER, Friedhelm
"Out of Sight" (tr. by Thomas Edwards). [PoetryE] (29) Spr 90, p. 83.
MAKIKO, Fujiwara-Skrobak
   See FUJIWARA-SKROBAK, Makiko
3985. MAKSIMOVIC, Desanka
"Blood-Stained Tale" (tr. by Biljana D. Obradovic). [PoetryE] (29) Spr 90, p.
   95-97.
"Disquietude" (tr. by Biljana D. Obradovic). [PoetryE] (29) Spr 90, p. 101.
"Experience" (tr. by Biljana D. Obradovic). [PoetryE] (29) Spr 90, p. 92.
"I Don't Have Any More Time" (tr. by Biljana D. Obradovic). [PoetryE] (29) Spr
   90, p. 99.
"Man" (tr. by Biljana D. Obradovic). [PoetryE] (29) Spr 90, p. 102.
"The Poet's Blessing" (tr. by Biljana D. Obradovic). [PoetryE] (29) Spr 90, p. 100.
"Remembering the Homeland" (tr. by Biljana D. Obradovic). [PoetryE] (29) Spr 90,
   p. 94.
"Spring" (tr. by Biljana D. Obradovic). [PoetryE] (29) Spr 90, p. 98.
"Winter in the Homeland" (tr. by Biljana D. Obradovic). [PoetryE] (29) Spr 90, p.
   93.
3986. MAKUCK, Peter
"Bluefishing the Bogue Narrows." [PoetC] (21:3) Spr 90, p. 5.
"Brothers of the Double Life" (For Bernard Meredith 1940-1987). [SewanR] (98:2)
   Spr 90, p. 195-197.
"Navajo Land." [SouthernPR] (30:1) Spr 90, p. 56-58.
"Needs." [AmerS] (59:1) Wint 90, p. 116-117.
"Reflections on a Likeness of Luke." [LaurelR] (24:1) Wint 90, p. 8.
"A Sense of the Other Side." [PoetC] (21:3) Spr 90, p. 7.
"Sound Buoy." [PoetC] (21:3) Spr 90, p. 6.
"The Sunken Lightship Off Frying Pan Shoals." [LaurelR] (24:1) Wint 90, p. 5-7.
3987. MALANCIOUI, Ileana
"Antigone" (tr. by Daniela Gioseffi, w. Ivana Spalatin). [PoetryE] (29) Spr 90, p.
   140.

MALE, Belkis Cuza
　　See CUZA MALE, Belkis
3988. MALINOVSKI, Nina
　　"In a Safe-deposit Box" (tr. by Monique M. Kennedy). [CimR] (92) Jl 90, p. 25.
3989. MALINOWITZ, Michael
　　"Equal Time." [Gargoyle] (37/38) 90, p. 48.
3990. MALINOWSKI, Ivan
　　"The Bar" (tr. by Carl King). [CimR] (92) Jl 90, p. 24.
3991. MALKUS, Steven W.
　　"Staying Out of Trouble." [CapeR] (25:2) Fall 90, p. 25.
3992. MALLEY, Kathleen
　　"John Is Dying." [ChironR] (9:4) Wint 90, p. 15.
3993. MALLINSON, Jean
　　"Farewell to My Mother." [PraF] (11:4) Wint 90-91, p. 60.
　　"Glen Gould Playing Bach on Television." [Dandel] (17:2) Fall-Wint 90, p. 10.
　　"Hekla." [PraF] (11:4) Wint 90-91, p. 61.
　　"Intact." [Quarry] (39:2) Spr 90, p. 146.
　　"Matisse." [Dandel] (17:1) Fall-Wint 90, p. 11.
　　"The Quick and the Dead." [PraF] (11:4) Wint 90-91, p. 62.
　　"Terminal Illness." [Quarry] (39:2) Spr 90, p. 47.
3994. MALONE, Hank
　　"Homecoming." [Bogg] (63) 90, p. 33.
　　"My Amazement." [Pearl] (10) Spr 90, p. 44.
3995. MALONE, Jacquelyn
　　"Revival at Diana Church of Christ." [ThRiPo] (35/36) 90, p. 30.
　　"When Samuel Reads the *Daily Times*." [ThRiPo] (35/36) 90, p. 32-34.
　　"Willow." [ThRiPo] (35/36) 90, p. 31.
3996. MALONE, Joe (Joe L., Joseph L.)
　　"Inwood Sketches: III." [Hellas] (1:1) Spr 90, p. 53.
　　"(Seconda Canzone a Cetti)." [JINJPo] (12:2) Aut 90, p. 12.
3997. MALONEY, Tom
　　"Some Nights." [MidwQ] (31:4) Sum 90, p. 472.
3998. MALOY, Angela (Angela M.)
　　"To Father." [EngJ] (79:7) N 90, p. 91.
　　"To Shakespeare, on His Marriage at Eighteen to a Woman Eight Years Older."
　　[EngJ] (79:3) Mr 90, p. 91.
3999. MALTMAN, Kim
　　"The Technology of Industry." [MalR] (90) Spr 90, p. 103.
　　"The Technology of Miracles." [MalR] (90) Spr 90, p. 102.
　　"The Technology of Mortality." [MalR] (90) Spr 90, p. 104-106.
　　"The Technology of Sheep." [MalR] (90) Spr 90, p. 100-101.
　　"The Technology of The Woman in the Dunes." [MalR] (90) Spr 90, p. 98-99.
4000. MALYON, Carol
　　"Buddy Holly Poem." [PoetryC] (11:1) Spr 90, p. 13.
　　"Supper at Grandma's House." [PoetryC] (11:1) Spr 90, p. 13.
　　"Woman Sleeping Alone." [PoetryC] (11:1) Spr 90, p. 12-13.
4001. MAMET, David
　　"The Goshawk." [Boulevard] (5:2, #14) Fall 90, p. 36.
　　"In a Dressingroom." [Bomb] (31) Spr 90, p. 63.
　　"The Joke Code." [Bomb] (31) Spr 90, p. 63.
　　"A Poem." [Bomb] (31) Spr 90, p. 63.
　　"R-." [YellowS] (33) Spr 90, p. 22.
　　"Shannon Estuary. Thirty-Thousand Feet." [Boulevard] (5:2, #14) Fall 90, p. 35.
　　"Two Men." [ParisR] (32:114) Spr 90, p. 43.
　　"Untitled: There is nothing trivial about love." [Bomb] (31) Spr 90, p. 63.
4002. MANCHESTER, Susan A.
　　"Heaven Is Heaven." [Kalliope] (12:2) 90, p. 17.
　　"Under Mud." [Kalliope] (12:2) 90, p. 16.
4003. MANDARA, Emanuele
　　"Flash" (tr. by Nat Scammacca). [Footwork] 90, p. 105.
4004. MANDEL, Charlotte
　　"The Phrenic Nerve at Ninety-Five." [JINJPo] (12:2) Aut 90, p. 6-7.
　　"Rosie to Her Daughter." [Spirit] (10:2) 90, p. 128-129.
　　"Street Photograph, 1930." [JINJPo] (12:2) Aut 90, p. 5.
4005. MANDEL, Tom
　　"Angel Vomit." [Avec] (3:1) 90, p. 131-135.

"Closed letter" (tr. of Mariana Bénézet). [WashR] (16:2) Ag-S 90, p. 18.
"The crêpe of still water's core" (tr. of Mariana Bénézet). [WashR] (16:2) Ag-S 90, p. 18.
"Free Zone" (tr. of Louis Aragon. Translation dedicated to the memory of Thaddeus Poeller). [WashR] (16:2) Ag-S 90, p. 18.
"Gray May Now Buy." [Verse] (7:1) Spr 90, p. 17.
"Poussin." [Verse] (7:1) Spr 90, p. 15-16.
4006. MANDELL, Arlene L.
"Mind Control." [DustyD] (1:2) O 90, p. 12.
4007. MANDEL'SHTAM, Osip
"#3. From the half-dark hall, abruptly" (in transliterated Russian and English, tr. by Paul Hopper). [WashR] (16:2) Ag-S 90, p. 14.
"#286. We live without feeling a country beneath us" (about Stalin, in transliterated Russian and English, tr. by Paul Hopper). [WashR] (16:2) Ag-S 90, p. 14.
"#303. And this, what street is this?" (in transliterated Russian and English, tr. by Paul Hopper). [WashR] (16:2) Ag-S 90, p. 14.
"#367. Armed with the eyesight of the narrow wasps" (in transliterated Russian and English, tr. by Paul Hopper). [WashR] (16:2) Ag-S 90, p. 14.
4008. MANESIOTIS, Joy
"The Artist." [DenQ] (25:2) Fall 90, p. 29.
"Bread & Circus." [NegC] (10:1) 90, p. 70-71.
"The Scar." [PraS] (64:2) Sum 90, p. 28-30.
4009. MANEY, Christy Dowden
"Stump." [EmeraldCR] (1990) c89, p. 11.
4010. MANEY, Jill Marion
"Muse to the Sculptor." [SoCoast] (8) Spr 90, p. 54.
4011. MANFRED, Freya
"My Grandmother's Ass." [PacificR] (8) 90, p. 86.
4012. MANHIRE, Bill
"Milky Way Bar." [Verse] (7:2) Sum 90, p. 35.
"Out West." [Verse] (7:2) Sum 90, p. 35.
"Phar Lap." [Verse] (7:2) Sum 90, p. 33-34.
4013. MANICOM, David
"Aran, Aisling." [Descant] (21:1 #68) Spr 90, p. 99-100.
"Parts for the Marathon." [Quarry] (39:2) Spr 90, p. 57-69.
4014. MANN, Barbara
"Ezekiel's Daughter." [Confr] (44/45) Fall 90-Wint 91, p. 328.
4015. MANN, Charles Edward
"Like a Leash, Trailing Away behind Her." [CumbPR] (9:2) Spr 90, p. 24.
4016. MANN, Jeff
"Crickets." [JamesWR] (8:1) Fall 90, p. 11.
4017. MANNING, Lynn
"Outward Appearances." (reprinted from #13, 1989). [Kaleid] (20) Wint-Spr 90, p. 52.
4018. MANNO, Rosemary
"Harlem" (tr. of Paul Laraque). [LitR] (33:4) Sum 90, p. 477.
4019. MANNO, Yves Di
"Chinatown (Paris, 18th Arrondissement)" (tr. by Barbara Beck). [Trans] (23) Spr 90, p. 158-159.
"Nocturne" (tr. by Julie Fay). [Trans] (23) Spr 90, p. 160.
4020. MANRIQUE, Jaime
"Scarecrow" (For my sister, tr. by Eugene Richie). [LitR] (33:4) Sum 90, p. 438-440.
4021. MANSELL, Chris
"Cicadas." [Arc] (24) Spr 90, p. 18.
4022. MANSK, Izaak
"First Fruit." [Descant] (21:4/22:1, #71/72) Wint-Spr 90-91, p. 176.
4023. MANSOUR, Joyce
"Biography" (tr. by Larry Couch). [Vis] (32) 90, p. 43.
"Cris" (Excerpt, tr. by Jan Pallister). [Paint] (17:33/34) Spr-Aut 90, p. 28.
"I Planted a Hand" (tr. by Larry Couch). [Vis] (32) 90, p. 43.
"Repaces" (Excerpt, tr. by Jan Pallister). [Paint] (17:33/34) Spr-Aut 90, p. 27.
4024. MANSOUR, Khairi
"A Non-Personal Account" (tr. by May Jayyusi and Jeremy Reed). [Screens] (2) 90, p. 23.

301

4025. MANYÉ i MARTI, Lourdes
"After All" (tr. of Miquel Martí i Pol, w. Wayne Cox). [Poetry] (155:6) Mr 90, p. 400.
"If I Talk About Death" (tr. of Miquel Martí i Pol, w. Wayne Cox). [Poetry] (155:6) Mr 90, p. 401.
"Rooms" (tr. of Miquel Martí i Pol, w. Wayne Cox). [Poetry] (155:6) Mr 90, p. 399.
4026. MANZO, David P.
"Untitled: Poor burnt child." [Amelia] (6:2, #17) 90, p. 147.
4027. MAR, Richard Delos
"Wind Rattles." [MidAR] (10:1) 90, p. 138.
4028. MARAULT, Genevieve
"Birthday #26." [OxfordM] (6:1) Spr-Sum 90, p. 89-90.
4029. MARÇAL, Maria Mercè
"Homage to Frida Kahlo" (from "Llengua Abolida," 1989, tr. by Montserrat Abelló). [PoetryC] (11:4) Wint 90, p. 22.
"My Love without a Home" (from "Llengua Abolida," 1989, tr. by Montserrat Abelló). [PoetryC] (11:4) Wint 90, p. 22.
4030. MARCH, Andrew L.
"The Reversal of the Arrow of Time." [KanQ] (22:3) Sum 90, p. 38.
4031. MARCH, Susana
"A un Hombre." [PoetryUSA] (5:3) Fall 90, p. 8.
"To a Man" (tr. by Kate Flores). [PoetryUSA] (5:3) Fall 90, p. 9.
4032. MARCHANT, Fred
"First Song." [ConnPR] (9:1) 90, p. 36.
"Hospital Food." [Agni] (31/32) 90, p. 97.
4033. MARCINKEVICIUTE, Tautvyda
"I Would Like" (tr. by Julie Kane and Manly Johnson). [Nimrod] (33:2) Spr-Sum 90, p. 95-96.
"The Wet Nurse" (tr. by Julie Kane and Manly Johnson). [Nimrod] (33:2) Spr-Sum 90, p. 97.
4034. MARCONI, Catherine
"Seeding the Hill-Pasture Below Prouse Springs." [KanQ] (22:3) Sum 90, p. 198-199.
4035. MARCUS, Mordecai
"MacBlarney's Race." [Hellas] (1:2) Fall 90, p. 229-231.
"Puzzling Out the Signs." [Hellas] (1:2) Fall 90, p. 229.
"Taking What's Good for You." [PoetC] (21:2) Wint 90, p. 13-14.
"Wanting to Make Metaphors about Nothing." [JINJPo] (12:2) Aut 90, p. 4.
4036. MARCUS, Morton
"Rabelais." [Chelsea] (49) 90, p. 67.
"Shortages." [PoetryUSA] (5:3) Fall 90, p. 14.
4037. MARCUS, Peter
"Do You Remember?" [TriQ] (80) Wint 90-91, p. 74.
"On This Bench." [TriQ] (80) Wint 90-91, p. 75.
4038. MARDIS, James
"Heritage." [BlackALF] (24:3) Fall 90, p. 555.
4039. MARGOLIS, Gary
"Behind the Bingham School." [ThRiPo] (35/36) 90, p. 45-46.
"Dinner's End." [AntigR] (81/82) Spr-Sum 90, p. 70-78.
"Names to Faces" (for my twenty-fifth reunion class). [ThRiPo] (35/36) 90, p. 44.
"Still, Before." [PoetryNW] (31:1) Spr 90, p. 35.
"Where No Candle Can Stay Lit." [PoetryNW] (31:1) Spr 90, p. 33-34.
"You Don't Have to Say a Word." [PoetryNW] (31:1) Spr 90, p. 34-35.
4040. MARGOLIS, Karen
"Jewish Jetset" (Selection: "Exhale, End, A," tr. of Sascha Anderson). [Screens] (2) 90, p. 80.
4041. MARGUERITTE
"Untitled: Something about time we cannot grasp." [BlueBldgs] (12) 90, p. 11.
4042. MARIANI, Paul
"Brown Study." [PraS] (64:2) Sum 90, p. 111-113.
"The Conning Towers of My Father's War." [NewEngR] (12:3) Spr 90, p. 281-282.
"Salvage Operations." [NewEngR] (12:3) Spr 90, p. 280-281.
"What Can We Expect of Language!?" (for Bill Matthews & the ghost of E. A. Poe). [GettyR] (3:1) Wint 90, p. 199-200.

4043. MARINELLI, Joanne (Joanne M.)
"Before They Found Him in Neshaminy Creek." [BlackBR] (11) Spr-Sum 90, p. 28-30.
"The Greatest Barbiturate Glitzy Dizz." [Pearl] (12) Fall-Wint 90, p. 55.
4044. MARINELLI, M. L.
"Heart of the formless spring." [Abraxas] (38/39) 90, p. 113.
4045. MARINO, Gigi
"Ceremony of Cows." [PoetL] (85:1) Spr 90, p. 27.
MARIS, Ron de
See De MARIS, Ron
4046. MARKARIAN, Maro
"Altitude" (tr. by Diana Der-Hovanessian). [PoetryE] (30) Fall 90, p. 99.
"It Is Said" (tr. by Diana Der-Hovanessian). [PoetryE] (30) Fall 90, p. 98.
"With Grief and Regret" (tr. by Diana Der-Hovanessian). [PoetryE] (30) Fall 90, p. 100.
4047. MARKHAM, Jacquelyn
"A Brother Born in 1942." [GreensboroR] (49) Wint 90-91, p. 42.
4048. MARKOPOULOS, George
"The Poems, a River, the Poet" (tr. by Despina Efthimiades). [GrahamHR] (13) Spr 90, p. 99.
4049. MARKS, Gigi
"End of the Growing Season." [Farm] (7:2) Fall 90, p. 121.
"In Days." [Farm] (7:2) Fall 90, p. 122.
"Without Skylights." [Pembroke] (22) 90, p. 95.
4050. MARKS, S. J.
"Not for Me." [CimR] (90) Ja 90, p. 75.
"Spain's Forgotten Forest." [DenQ] (25:2) Fall 90, p. 30-31.
4051. MARLATT, Daphne
"Pro-nominally" (for Robert Creeley). [WestCL] (24:3) Wint 90, p. 21-23.
4052. MARLIS, Stefanie
"Ars Poetica." [AntR] (48:4) Fall 90, p. 483.
4053. MARMON, Sharon
"And There Be Monsters." [SoCoast] (8) Spr 90, p. 46-47.
4054. MARN, Theryce
"I told hillary not to step on the ants." [PoetryUSA] (5:1) Spr 90, p. 7.
"Sheryl's Mirrors." [PoetryUSA] (5:1) Spr 90, p. 1.
4055. MARQUART, Deb
"Birthmark." [PoetL] (85:3) Fall 90, p. 31-32.
4056. MARRERO, Melanie
"Her Colors." [SingHM] (18) 90, p. 86-87.
4057. MARRIOTT, Anne
"Living Under Water." [Arc] (25) Aut 90, p. 16-17.
"Two Poems on the Same Subject." [Grain] (18:4) Wint 90, p. 8-9.
4058. MARRIOTT, D. S.
"Leben." [Verse] (7:1) Spr 90, p. 23-24.
4059. MARRIOTT, David
"Mainstay & Vacant." [Avec] (3:1) 90, p. 21.
"Sidereal & Fictus." [Avec] (3:1) 90, p. 19.
"Storm-Rise." [Avec] (3:1) 90, p. 20.
MARRUZ, Fina Garcia
See GARCIA MARRUZ, Fina
MARS, Douglas de
See DeMARS, Douglas
4060. MARSHALL, Ernest
"A Dialogue for Two Landscapes." [Crucible] (26) Fall 90, p. 70-71.
4061. MARSHALL, Gregory
"Memo, to: Search Committee." [LaurelR] (24:2) Sum 90, p. 49.
4062. MARSHALL, Jack
"Autumn in the Fall of Empire." [Caliban] (8) 90, p. 132-133.
"Blue Zones." [AmerPoR] (19:5) S-O 90, p. 43.
"Radio Tehran." [AmerPoR] (19:5) S-O 90, p. 43.
"Sesame." [Zyzzyva] (6:2, #22) Sum 90, p. 59-71.
"Sunset News." [Talisman] (5) Fall 90, p. 8-14.
"Under a Cloud Big as a State." [AmerPoR] (19:5) S-O 90, p. 42-43.
4063. MARSHALL, John
"For Margaret." [PraF] (11:4) Wint 90-91, p. 48.

4064. MARSHALL, Peter
"Teddy Boys." [Bogg] (63) 90, p. 62.
4065. MARSHBURN, Sandra
"Going Home." [TarRP] (29:2) Spr 90, p. 34.
"Three Stories Told on the Same Day." [Wind] (20:67) 90, p. 28.
4066. MARSOCCI, Raymond
"After Failing to End My Celibacy I Mix Metaphors." [OxfordM] (6:1) Spr-Sum 90,
p. 50-51.
4067. MARTEAU, Robert
"Fragments de la France" (Excerpts). [Os] (30) Spr 90, p. 12-15.
4068. MARTENS, Caroline Rowe
"On Sunday." [Amelia] (6:2, #17) 90, p. 122.
4069. MARTENS, Roger
"Learning." [NorthStoneR] (9) 90, p. 51.
MARTHA ELIZABETH
See ELIZABETH, Martha
MARTI, Lourdes Manyé i
See MANYÉ i MARTI, Lourdes
4070. MARTI i POL, Miquel
"After All" (tr. by Wayne Cox and Lourdes Manyé i Martí). [Poetry] (155:6) Mr 90,
p. 400.
"If I Talk About Death" (tr. by Wayne Cox and Lourdes Manyé i Martí). [Poetry]
(155:6) Mr 90, p. 401.
"Rooms" (tr. by Wayne Cox and Lourdes Manyé i Martí). [Poetry] (155:6) Mr 90,
p. 399.
4071. MARTIAL
"Epigrams" (XI:99, Symplegades in Slacks, II:56, Casino Girl, tr. by Richard
O'Connell). [Hellas] (1:1) Spr 90, p. 54.
"Epigrams" (Selections: I,73, IX.41, XII.95, tr. by Joseph S. Salemi). [ArtfulD]
(18/19) 90, p. 100-101.
4072. MARTIN, Carolyn A.
"The Exodus of Two Testaments." [ChrC] (107:17) 16-23 My 90, p. 519.
4073. MARTIN, Charles
"Adolescence." [Verse] (7:3) Wint 90, p. 57-58.
"At Home with Eros & Psyche." [Verse] (7:3) Wint 90, p. 58.
"If any ever deserved such underarm goatodor" (tr. of Catullus). [Hudson] (43:2)
Sum 90, p. 342.
"Lesbia, let us live only for loving" (tr. of Catullus). [Hudson] (43:2) Sum 90, p.
343.
"Out of the Lost and Found." [Thrpny] (41) Spr 90, p. 10.
4074. MARTIN, Charles Casey
"Beds" (for Teri). [HayF] (6) Sum 90, p. 54.
4075. MARTIN, D. Roger
"Poem from a Crisis Center." [SlipS] (10) 90, p. 20.
MARTIN, Diane Kirsten
See KIRSTEN-MARTIN, Diane
4076. MARTIN, Doug
"Nights Like These" (for Christine). [Gypsy] (15) 90, p. 59.
4077. MARTIN, Herbert Woodward
"Final W." (Excerpt). [Poetry] (155:6) Mr 90, p. 402.
4078. MARTIN, Lynn
"Making Contact Near Depoe Bay." [WillowR] Spr 90, p. 27.
4079. MARTIN, Michael
"In the Symposium written by Plato" (For H. A.). [Amelia] (6:2, #17) 90, p. 40.
4080. MARTIN, Paul
"Closing Distances." [SoCoast] (8) Spr 90, p. 38-39.
"Coming Down (After the Latest Tear)." [GreenMR] (NS 4:1) Spr-Sum 90, p. 93.
"October: Harvest and Seeding." [SoCoast] (8) Spr 90, p. 37.
"Slopewatching." [GreenMR] (NS 4:1) Spr-Sum 90, p. 94.
4081. MARTIN, Peter
"Why I Hate Bowling." [Pig] (16) 90, p. 90.
4082. MARTIN, Richard
"How to Produce a Superbaby." [BellR] (13:1, #27) Spr 90, p. 12-13.
4083. MARTIN, Roger D.
"The Shaman." [WritersF] (16) Fall 90, p. 140.

4084. MARTIN, Walter
"Parisian Dream" (for W. T. Bandy, tr. of Charles Baudelaire). [SouthernR] (26:2)
Ap 90, p. 319-323.
4085. MARTINEZ, Demetria
"Turning" (33 poems). [BilingR] (14:1/2) 87-88, c89, p. 101-156.
4086. MARTINEZ, Dionisio (Dionisio D.)
"1929." [Iowa] (20:3) Fall 90, p. 87-88.
"Across These Landscapes of Early Darkness." [Iowa] (20:3) Fall 90, p. 85-86.
"All the Variables." [TampaR] (3) 90, p. 75-76.
"Cole Porter." [Caliban] (9) 90, p. 10.
"East of Trouble Creek." [Caliban] (9) 90, p. 8-9.
"Iberia." [BlackWR] (17:1) Fall-Wint 90, p. 56.
"Lament." [IndR] (13:3) Fall 90, p. 18-19.
"Outtakes." [IndR] (13:3) Fall 90, p. 17.
"The Science of Chaos" (for Rossanne Fajardo). [IndR] (13:3) Fall 90, p. 20-23.
4087. MARTINEZ, Joel
"Pieta" (for Terrence Johnson). [JamesWR] (7:4) Sum 90, p. 9.
4088. MARTONE, John
"Replication, Island." [HeavenB] (8) Wint 90-91, p. 3.
"Shape's Hold" (Selections). [Northeast] (NS 5:3) Wint 90-91, p. 14-17.
4089. MARTSINKEVICH, Ian
"Leaving" (tr. by Oleg Atbashian and Maureen Hurley). [PoetryUSA] (5:3) Fall 90,
p. 19.
"Life As It Is" (tr. by Oleg Atbashian and Maureen Hurley). [PoetryUSA] (5:3) Fall
90, p. 18.
4090. MARTSINKEVICH, Vicktoria
"The Chain" (tr. by Oleg Atbashian and Maureen Hurley). [PoetryUSA] (5:3) Fall
90, p. 18.
MASAMI, Usui
See USUI, Masami
4091. MASARIK, Al
"Telephone Call." [OnTheBus] (2:2/3:1, #6/7) Sum-Fall 90 Wint-Spr 91, p. 143.
4092. MASINI, Donna
"At the Bandshell by the River." [ParisR] (32:114) Spr 90, p. 125-126.
"Hunger." [GeoR] (44:1/2) Spr-Sum 90, p. 242-243.
4093. MASKALERIS, Thanasis
"To Orpheus" (tr. of Yannis Ritsos). [TarRP] (29:2) Spr 90, p. 46-47.
4094. MASLOWSKI, Pat
"A Necklace of Children" (Ula o Tamaiti). [BambooR] (47) Sum 90, p. 51.
4095. MASON, David
"The Catch." [PoetL] (85:2) Sum 90, p. 8.
"Dutch Harbor." [BellR] (13:1, #27) Spr 90, p. 44.
"Explorations" (from a line by Hart Crane). [Boulevard] (4:3/5:1, #12/13) Spr 90, p.
199.
"The Feast of the Rose Garlands" (Rudolf II, 1576-1612). [SewanR] (98:2) Spr 90,
p. 201-202.
"Gusev" (from the story by Anton Chekhov). [NoDaQ] (58:4) Fall 90, p. 78-79.
"In the Physic Garden." [CumbPR] (9:2) Spr 90, p. 25-26.
"Recipe for Jon Griffin." [Hellas] (1:2) Fall 90, p. 233.
"A Scrap of Paper." [PoetL] (85:2) Sum 90, p. 9.
"Spring in the North." [Verse] (7:3) Wint 90, p. 59.
"The Thing Worth Saving" (in memory of Bruce Chatwin). [AmerS] (59:1) Wint 90,
p. 80.
"To a Photojournalist." [CumbPR] (9:2) Spr 90, p. 27.
4096. MASON, Kenneth C.
"The Reprieve." [Plain] (10:3) Spr 90, p. 12-13.
4097. MASSING, Douglas Michael
"American Game: Managua, 1985." [BambooR] (47) Sum 90, p. 52.
"By Now of Course You Will Have Heard." [HawaiiR] (14:2, #29) Spr 90, p. 8.
"Miriam on Unrequited Love." [HawaiiR] (14:2, #29) Spr 90, p. 6.
"When I Think." [HawaiiR] (14:2, #29) Spr 90, p. 7.
MASSMAN, Gordon Lester
See LESTER-MASSMAN, Gordon
MASTER, J. R. le
See LeMASTER, J. R.

4098. MASTERS, Janelle
"Medicine Hole." [Kalliope] (12:1) 90, c89, p. 37.
4099. MASTERSON, Dan
"Bat." [OntR] (32) Spr-Sum 90, p. 67.
"Connemara." [SouthernR] (26:2) Ap 90, p. 344-345.
"Coulter's Road." [SoCaR] (23:1) Fall 90, p. 121.
"Fresh Kill Report" (Predator Count, NYS Conservation Department, Form 627). [NewYorkQ] (42) Sum 90, p. 73.
"Gun Club Smoker for the Prude." [NewYorkQ] (43) Fall 90, p. 77.
"Moutain Swim." [OntR] (32) Spr-Sum 90, p. 65-66.
4100. MATHEWS, Harry
"Safety in Numbers" (with thanks to Jacques Roubaud). [Talisman] (5) Fall 90, p. 15-16.
4101. MATHIAS, Anita
"All Cousins." [HiramPoR] (48/49) 90-91, p. 50-51.
"Art." [HiramPoR] (48/49) 90-91, p. 49.
"At Santa Maria Novella, Florence." [Journal] (13:2) Fall-Wint 89-90, p. 55-56.
"Tryst." [Journal] (13:2) Fall-Wint 89-90, p. 57-58.
4102. MATSAKIS, Cynthia
"Incest." [SouthernPR] (30:2) Fall 90, p. 51-52.
4103. MATSUMOTO, Shigeyo
"Rain on the mountain over there!" (tr. by Janet Lewis). [SouthernR] (26:1) Ja 90, p. 205.
4104. MATTAWA, Khaled
"Pretensions." [GreensboroR] (49) Wint 90-91, p. 30-31.
4105. MATTFIELD, Mary
"The Abandoned Pharmacy" (tr. of Maria Banus). [PoetryE] (30) Fall 90, p. 18.
"The New Notebook" (tr. of Maria Banus). [WebR] (14:2) Spr 90, p. 102.
"On a Glass Icon" (tr. of Maria Banus). [PoetryE] (30) Fall 90, p. 16.
"Die Reichs-Kanzlei" (tr. of Maria Banus). [PoetryE] (30) Fall 90, p. 17.
"Your Name" (tr. of Maria Banus). [WebR] (14:2) Spr 90, p. 100-101.
4106. MATTHEWS, William
"The Dream." [Antaeus] (64/65) Spr-Aut 90, p. 79.
MATTHIAS JOHANNESSEN
See JOHANNESSEN, Matthias
4107. MAURER, Christopher
"Advice to the Poet" (tr. of Federico García Lorca). [NowestR] (28:3/29:1) 90-91, p. 158-159.
4108. MAX, Lin
"On Seeing Alice Neel's Self-Portrait at 80." [Calyx] (13:1) Wint 90-91, p. 47.
"Stone Fruit." [Calyx] (13:1) Wint 90-91, p. 46.
4109. MAXAM, Vernard
"Going to Work in the Morning." [OnTheBus] (2:2/3:1, #6/7) Sum-Fall 90 Wint-Spr 91, p. 145.
"Leo Falling Asleep Next to Me." [OnTheBus] (2:2/3:1, #6/7) Sum-Fall 90 Wint-Spr 91, p. 145.
"Migration of Painted Ladies Through San Diego County." [OnTheBus] (2:2/3:1, #6/7) Sum-Fall 90 Wint-Spr 91, p. 144.
4110. MAXFIELD, Margaret W.
"Father-in-Law." [KanQ] (22:1/2) Wint-Spr 90, p. 115.
4111. MAXWELL, Glyn
"Believe That This." [Verse] (7:3) Wint 90, p. 78.
"Drive to the Seashore." [ManhatR] (5:2) Fall 90, p. 52.
"The Eater." [ManhatR] (5:2) Fall 90, p. 30-31.
"The Judge." [ManhatR] (5:2) Fall 90, p. 31-33.
"Mine." [Stand] (31:4) Aut 90, p. 14-15.
"My Turn." [Agni] (31/32) 90, p. 262.
"Night of the Embersons." [Verse] (7:3) Wint 90, p. 77-78.
"Out of the Rain." [Verse] (7:1) Spr 90, p. 74- 94.
"Quietly Now." [ManhatR] (5:1) Spr 90, p. 14.
"A Whitsun." [Agni] (31/32) 90, p. 260-261.
4112. MAXWELL, Mary
"An Editorial." [Nat] (250:23) 11 Je 90, p. 834.
"Speaks Latin, That Satin Doll." [WestHR] (44:4) Wint 90, p. 348.
"To H. J., the Master." [NewRep] (202:10) 5 Mr 90, p. 35.
"To My Father." [Nat] (250:23) 11 Je 90, p. 834.

"To Robert Lowell, in the Guise of Mentor." [Nat] (250:19) 14 My 90, p. 676.
4113. MAXWELL, Noemie
"Deteriorata" (w. Nico Vassilakis). [ContextS] (1:1) 89, p. 8.
4114. MAY, Eleanor Rodman
"Fever" (First Prize). [Crucible] (26) Fall 90, p. 47.
"Winging South." [Crucible] (26) Fall 90, p. 48.
4115. MAY, Kathy
"After Reading About the Famine." [GreenMR] (NS 3:2) Fall-Wint 89-90, p. 80.
4116. MAY, Kenneth D., Jr.
"Weight." [NegC] (10:1) 90, p. 29.
MAY, Lydia Kwa
See KWA, Lydia (KWA MAY, Lydia)
4117. MAY, Paul
"The Alibi." [Verse] (7:2) Sum 90, p. 70.
"The Stationmaster's Retirement." [Verse] (7:2) Sum 90, p. 70.
4118. MAY, Wong
"Mr. Dobson & the After-Life of Carnations." [PartR] (57:2) Spr 90, p. 267-268.
4119. MAYER, Barbara J.
"Love Is the Only Bond." [Crucible] (26) Fall 90, p. 62.
4120. MAYER, Suzanne
"Flannery O'Connor." [EngJ] (79:3) Mr 90, p. 91.
4121. MAYERS, Florence Cassen
"Artifice." [PoetryNW] (31:2) Sum 90, p. 16.
4122. MAYES, Hubert G.
"Violin's Farewell" (tr. of Emile Nelligan). [AntigR] (81/82) Spr-Sum 90, p. 22.
4123. MAYFIELD, Kimberly
"Iconoclasm." [Verse] (7:3) Wint 90, p. 99.
4124. MAYHALL, Jane
"Ballad of a Circus." [SouthernR] (26:2) Ap 90, p. 334-335.
"More Anti-Matter." [Confr] (42/43) Spr-Sum 90, p. 100.
4125. MAYNE, Seymour
"A King Held Captive in Water Troughs" (tr. of Eytan Eytan). [PoetL] (85:4) Wint
90-91, p. 25.
4126. MAYS, Jeff
"Shampoo and Conditioner." [PacificR] (8) 90, p. 76.
4127. MAZARIK, Al
"Marilyn Monroe." [Pearl] (12) Fall-Wint 90, p. j51.
4128. MAZUR, Gail
"Family Plot, October." [Agni] (29/30) 90, p. 157-158.
"Phonic." [Agni] (29/30) 90, p. 155-156.
"Yahrzeit." [CimR] (91) Ap 90, p. 65.
4129. MAZZARO, Jerome
"Buffalo/Stasis." [CreamCR] (14:1) Spr 90, p. 18-19.
"Library Tapestry." [CreamCR] (14:1) Spr 90, p. 16-17.
"Seal Rocks." [CreamCR] (14:1) Spr 90, p. 20.
"Visions." [CreamCR] (14:1) Spr 90, p. 16.
MAZZIOTTI GILLAN, Maria
See GILLAN, Maria Mazziotti
4130. MAZZOCCO, Robert
"Cities." [NewYorker] (66:20) 2 Jl 90, p. 36.
"World's End." [NewYorker] (66:5) 19 Mr
Mc . . .
See also names beginning with Mac . . .
4131. McADAMS, Janet
"Manifestations." [HighP] (5:1) Spr 90, p. 57-58.
4132. McALEAVEY, David
"Breath of Fire." [GeoR] (44:4) Wint 90, p. 666-667.
"Chris and Bill and His Dog Osley." [FloridaR] (17:1) Spr-Sum 90, p. 102-103.
"Coincidence." [AntR] (48:1) Wint 90, p. 93.
"Construction (II)." [PoetL] (85:2) Sum 90, p. 33.
"Steps." [Farm] (7:1) Spr 90, p. 25.
4133. McALPINE, Katherine
"Then All Smiles Stopped." [Amelia] (6:1, #16) 90, p. 99.
4134. McBRIDE, Mekeel
"Good, I Said." [SenR] (20:2) Fall 90, p. 22-23.
"To the One Lost on the Other Side." [GeoR] (44:1/2) Spr-Sum 90, p. 32.

4135. McBRIDE, Regina
"Stories of Departure." [Pequod] (31) 90, p. 173-77.
"The War Closet." [Sonora] (19) Spr-Sum 90, p. 7-9.
4136. McBRIDE, Susan
"To Someone" (reprinted from #17, 1988). [Kaleid] (20) Wint-Spr 90, p. 27.
4137. McBRIDE, Timothy Patrick
"Grace After Meals." [PoetryNW] (31:3) Aut 90, p. 25.
4138. McCABE, Victoria
"How They Fought the War." [NewYorkQ] (41) Spr 90, p. 75.
"How They Fought the War." [NewYorkQ] (43) Fall 90, p. 49.
"Pound." [NewYorkQ] (42) Sum 90, p. 82.
"Sestina: Families." [HiramPoR] (48/49) 90-91, p. 52-53.
4139. McCAFFERTY, Ed
"Fruits of War, Fruits of Peace." [BlackBR] (12) Fall-Wint 90, p. 44.
"Resurrection." [BellR] (13:1, #27) Spr 90, p. 34.
4140. McCAFFERY, Steve
"A bridge is the passage between two banks." [Verse] (7:1) Spr 90, p. 61.
"Codicil." [Verse] (7:1) Spr 90, p. 62-63.
"The Diameron." [WestCL] (24:2) Fall 90, p. 49.
"Lease on chicken." [WestCL] (24:2) Fall 90, p. 48.
"Some Alpha Amenophes." [WestCL] (24:2) Fall 90, p. 46-47.
"Some Versions of Pastoral" (Selections: Idylls II, V & X). [WestCL] (24:2) Fall
    90, p. 50-51.
4141. McCAFFREY, Phillip
"News." [HampSPR] (Anthology 1975-1990) 90, p. 186.
4142. McCAIN, Gillian
"Postmarked Novia Scotia: a Letter to Clarence Gatemouth Brown (Who Aint No
    Robert Johnson or No Leadbelly But Thats Okay 'Cos They'r Dead)."
    [PottPort] (12) 90, p. 20.
4143. McCALLUM, Victoria
"Mockingbird Love." [OnTheBus] (2:2/3:1, #6/7) Sum-Fall 90 Wint-Spr 91, p.
    154.
4144. McCANN, Janet
"Disorder Poem." [Footwork] 90, p. 81.
"Fiftieth Class Reunion." [BellArk] (6:3) My-Je 90, p. 20.
"Inside the Tear." [DustyD] (1:2) O 90, p. 4.
"Insomnia." [BellR] (13:2, #28) Fall 90, p. 6.
"The Mystical Connections." [BellArk] (6:3) My-Je 90, p. 21.
"New Jersey Notes." [Vis] (33) 90, p. 8-9.
"The Oldish Man in the White Seersucker Suit." [BellArk] (6:3) My-Je 90, p. 12.
"Random Design." [DustyD] (1:2) O 90, p. 4.
4145. McCANN, Kathleen M.
"Cows, Headlines, & the 4th." [BellArk] (6:3) My-Je 90, p. 1.
4146. McCARRISTON, Linda
"Billy." [TriQ] (79) Fall 90, p. 123-124.
"Le Coursier de Jeanne D'Arc." [GeoR] (44:4) Wint 90, p. 651-653.
"In Karlsruhe" (for my son). [GreenMR] (NS 4:1) Spr-Sum 90, p. 50-51.
"My Father's Laughter." [TriQ] (79) Fall 90, p. 127-128.
"My Mother's Chair, 1956." [TriQ] (79) Fall 90, p. 125-126.
"Song of the Scullery." [GreenMR] (NS 4:1) Spr-Sum 90, p. 49.
"Tippet." [TriQ] (79) Fall 90, p. 129-130.
4147. McCARTHY, Colm
"Colorado Buick Mountain Heart" (for Jane). [BellArk] (6:3) My-Je 90, p. 12.
4148. McCARTHY, Gerald
"Flag Burning" (a prayer). [BelPoJ] (41:1) Fall 90, p. 17.
4149. McCARTHY, Maureen
"Christmas Trees." [Event] (19:2) Sum 90, p. 63.
"Driving to Work." [Event] (19:2) Sum 90, p. 61.
"Montreal." [Event] (19:2) Sum 90, p. 65.
"My Head." [Event] (19:2) Sum 90, p. 60.
"There Is No End." [Event] (19:2) Sum 90, p. 62.
"Underworlds." [Event] (19:2) Sum 90, p. 64.
4150. McCARTHY, Penny
"Le Midi." [SoCoast] (9) Fall 90, p. 47.
4151. McCARTHY, Ted
"Judas Gets His Way." [Vis] (33) 90, p. 28.

4152. McCARTHY, Thomas
"October at Coole Park and Ballylee" (for Paul Durcan). [Quarry] (39:1) Wint 90, p. 84.
4153. McCARTNEY, Sharon
"Blanket of Fish." [MalR] (90) Spr 90, p. 28-29.
"She Sleeps in Glasses." [MalR] (90) Spr 90, p. 26-27.
4154. McCARTY, Doug
"Winter Departure." [GreensboroR] (48) Sum 90, p. 119.
4155. McCASLIN, Susan
"Main Street Elegies" (18 poems). [BellArk] (6:6) N-D 90, p. 8-11.
4156. MCCAULEY, Nora
"Letter from a Mermaid" (pencil drawing and poem, with Kristen Ankiewicz). [HarvardA] (125:1) S 90, p. 26.
4157. McCLANAHAN, Cia
"Gift Enclosure." [AmerV] (21) Wint 90, p. 70-71.
4158. McCLATCHY, J. D.
"An Essay on Friendship." [Poetry] (155:5) F 90, p. 315-325.
"The Shield of Herakles." [Raritan] (9:3) Wint 90, p. 24-26.
"The Spanish Hour." [SouthwR] (75:3) Sum 90, p. 344.
"The Window" (after Pavese). [SouthwR] (75:3) Sum 90, p. 343.
"Zion." [Raritan] (9:3) Wint 90, p. 22-23.
4159. McCLELLAN, Jane
"No Drake Is Ever on the Make." [WindO] (53) Fall 90, p. 40.
"The Returning Place of Self." [Parting] (3:1) Sum 90, p. 27.
4160. McCLURE, Keith
"Intercoastal." [Shen] (40:1) Spr 90, p. 19.
4161. McCLURE, Michael
"Song." [Thrpny] (40) Wint 90, p. 32.
"White Boot" (In Golden Gate Park After the Storm, for Sterling Bunnell). [NewYorkQ] (41) Spr 90, p. 50.
4162. McCOMAS, Marilyn
"Cloudburst." [Outbr] (21) 90, p. 14-15.
"Futuristic." [Outbr] (21) 90, p. 13.
"Parrot Talk." [Outbr] (21) 90, p. 12.
4163. McCOMBS, Judith
"Epithet." [Calyx] (12:3) Sum 90, p. 40-41.
"Third Night Home." [PoetL] (85:4) Wint 90-91, p. 35-36.
4164. McCONNEL, Frances (Frances Ruhlen)
"Tanka." [Pearl] (11) Sum 90, p. 48.
"Visiting My Father's House on Orca Street, Anchorage Alaska, Fifteen Years After His Death." [BellArk] (6:1) Ja-F 90, p. 3.
McCONNELL, Nano Pennefather
See PENNEFATHER-McCONNELL, Nano
4165. McCORD, Howard
"Armatures." [WeberS] (7:1) Spr 90, p. 63.
"Emergency." [WeberS] (7:1) Spr 90, p. 63-64.
"Nachtmusik." [WeberS] (7:1) Spr 90, p. 64.
4166. McCORKLE, James
"Eclogue." [Manoa] (2:2) Fall 90, p. 83-84.
"Hours Before Sleep." [PoetC] (21:3) Spr 90, p. 8-9.
"The Seafront." [Manoa] (2:2) Fall 90, p. 85.
4167. McCORKLE, Jennifer Jones
"Shepherds." [Northeast] (NS 5:3) Wint 90-91, p. 3.
4168. McCORMICK, Brian
"Poets Storing Lightning in the Barn" (for M.B.). [Blueline] (11:1/2) 90, p. 26.
4169. McCOY, Jenifer
"Joel's Love." [EmeraldCR] (1990) c89, p. 51.
4170. McCUE, Frances
"According to Neo-Physics." [RiverC] (10:2) Spr 90, p. 8.
"Dead Reckoning." [PoetryNW] (31:4) Wint 90-91, p. 42.
"Doubling Up on Privacy at the Canterbury Juvenile Facility." [PoetryNW] (31:4) Wint 90-91, p. 41-42.
"What's Dangerous About Plumbing." [RiverC] (10:2) Spr 90, p. 6-7.
4171. McCULLOUGH, Ken
"Back Country, Yellowstone." [Nimrod] (34:1) Fall-Wint 90, p. 27.
"Indian Summer." [Nimrod] (34:1) Fall-Wint 90, p. 28.

309

McCULLOUGH

"Instructions" (for Shivani Arjuna). [CrabCR] (6:3) Spr 90, p. 14.
"Love Song." [Nimrod] (34:1) Fall-Wint 90, p. 30-33.
"Peyote Meeting, Late Spring, Lame Deer, Montana." [Spirit] (10:2) 90, p. 69-73.
"Run, Late November." [Nimrod] (34:1) Fall-Wint 90, p. 29.
"The Web." [SlipS] (10) 90, p. 55-56.
4172. McCUNE, Bambi
"Poems for the Horse Latitudes" (a poetic sequence: selections). [RiverS] (32) [90?],
p. 67.
"Three Sisters" (for Pearl, Ida, and Gladys). [RiverS] (32) [90?], p. 66.
4173. McCURDY, Harold
"Inscription for an Outcropping of Rock." [ChrC] (107:35) 5 D 90, p. 1125.
4174. McCURRY, Jim
"Heading for Another Fall." [Farm] (7:1) Spr 90, p. 26.
4175. McDADE, Thomas M. (Thomas Michael)
"Accident." [Gypsy] (15) 90, p. 72.
"Luck." [SmPd] (27:2, #79) Spr 90, p. 19.
"Portraits." [CoalC] (2) D 90, p. 22.
"The Second Son Observes Arbor Day." [Gypsy] (15) 90, p. 53.
"Tires." [SmPd] (27:1, #78) Wint 90, p. 25.
4176. McDANIEL, Wilma Elizabeth
"A Girl from Buttonwillow" (A Wormwood Chapbook). [WormR] (30:2/3,
#118-119) 90, p. 49-96.
4177. McDONALD, Agnes
"The Fact of Windows." [SouthernPR] (30:2) Fall 90, p. 38-39.
4178. McDONALD, Robert
"A Day Like November." [NegC] (10:1) 90, p. 72-73.
"Guilt, the Amorous Octopus." [NegC] (10:1) 90, p. 74-75.
4179. McDONALD, Walter
"After a Week in the Rockies." [Manoa] (2:2) Fall 90, p. 11.
"After the Fall of Saigon." [Confr] (44/45) Fall 90-Wint 91, p. 119.
"After the Flight Home from Saigon." [NowestR] (28:1) 90, p. 93.
"Always, More Light." [ArtfulD] (18/19) 90, p. 69.
"August of the Drinking Well." [WritersF] (16) Fall 90, p. 30.
"Buzzards and Uncle Douglas." [Manoa] (2:2) Fall 90, p. 13.
"The Calendar." [Journal] (13:2) Fall-Wint 89-90, p. 34-35.
"Colonel Mackenzie and the Ghosts of Warriors." [WritersF] (16) Fall 90, p. 31.
"Combinations." [Confr] (44/45) Fall 90-Wint 91, p. 119.
"Dawn of the Bitter Blizzard." [PoetryNW] (31:4) Wint 90-91, p. 40.
"Digging on Hardscrabble." [ParisR] (32:115) Sum 90, p. 51-52.
"The Digs in Escondido Canyon." [CarolQ] (42:2) Wint 90, p. 20.
"The Digs in Escondido Canyon." [KanQ] (22:4) Fall 90, p. 142.
"The Digs in Escondido Canyon." [PoetL] (85:3) Fall 90, p. 35.
"Driving the Hardscrabble." [ArtfulD] (18/19) 90, p. 68.
"Driving the Midnight Bus." [Interim] (9:1) Spr-Sum 90, p. 6-7.
"The Eyes in Grandfather's Oils." [KanQ] (22:4) Fall 90, p. 141.
"Faces We Never Forget." [HampSPR] (Anthology 1975-1990) 90, p. 202-203.
"Farms and the Laws of Harvest." [Manoa] (2:2) Fall 90, p. 12.
"Farms at Auction." [Interim] (9:1) Spr-Sum 90, p. 5.
"Father's Straight Razor." [Poetry] (156:3) Je 90, p. 147.
"Fiddles and Steel Guitars." [SouthernR] (26:4) O 90, p. 896-897.
"Fishing the Brazos." [CutB] (33) 90, p. 31.
"The Gleam of Silver Wings." [Shen] (40:3) Fall 90, p. 22.
"Goat Ranching on Hardscrabble." [ParisR] (32:115) Sum 90, p. 53-54.
"The Goats of Summer." [Atlantic] (265:4) Ap 90, p. 54.
"The Gulls of Padre Island." [SouthwR] (75:2) Spr 90, p. 210.
"Hauling on Hardscrabble." [Gargoyle] (37/38) 90, p. 92.
"Honky-Tonk Blues." [Nimrod] (34:1) Fall-Wint 90, p. 119.
"How Did I Get So Old?" (-- Slaughterhouse-Five). [SouthernPR] (30:1) Spr 90, p.
52.
"Hunting in Escondido." [PoetryC] (11:1) Spr 90, p. 22.
"In the Hibiscus Garden." [ClockR] (6:2) 90, p. 57.
"Living on Hardscrabble." [CalQ] (34) 90, p. 33.
"Loading the Summer Cattle." [ColEng] (52:2) F 90, p. 160.
"The Middle Years." [Nat] (250:2) 8-15 Ja 90, p. 68.
"Nights on the Brazos." [Shen] (40:3) Fall 90, p. 21-22.
"Plains and the Art of Writing." [Journal] (13:2) Fall-Wint 89-90, p. 33.

"The Rainmaker." [WritersF] (16) Fall 90, p. 29.
"Saying the Blessing." [ClockR] (6:2) 90, p. 56.
"Starting a Pasture." [Poetry] (157:3) D 90, p. 151-152.
"Stories We Seem to Remember." [HampSPR] (Anthology 1975-1990) 90, p. 202.
"Sunday Morning Roundup." [ThRiPo] (35/36) 90, p. 77-78.
"Trout in the Clear Calm." [CrossCur] (9:2) Je 90, p. 93.
"West Fork of the San Juan." [WillowS] (26) Spr 90, p. 32.
"With My Father in Winter." [HampSPR] (Anthology 1975-1990) 90, p. 203-204.
4180. McDOUGALL, Bonnie S.
"The Answer" (tr. of Bei Dao). [ManhatR] (5:2) Fall 90, p. 46-47.
"April" (tr. of Bei Dao, w. Chen Maiping). [ManhatR] (5:2) Fall 90, p. 11.
"A Bach Concert" (tr. of Bei Dao, w. Chen Maiping). [ManhatR] (5:2) Fall 90, p. 8.
"Blanks" (tr. of Bei Dao). [ManhatR] (5:2) Fall 90, p. 48-49.
"The Collection" (tr. of Bei Dao, w. Chen Maiping). [ManhatR] (5:2) Fall 90, p. 6.
"Coming Home at Night" (tr. of Bei Dao, w. Chen Maiping). [ManhatR] (5:2) Fall
     90, p. 11.
"Declaration" (for Yu Luoke, tr. of Bei Dao). [PoetryUSA] ([5:4?]) Wint 90, p. 22.
"Discovery" (tr. of Bei Dao, w. Chen Maiping). [ManhatR] (5:2) Fall 90, p. 12.
"The East's Imagination" (tr. of Bei Dao, w. Chen Maiping). [ManhatR] (5:2) Fall
     90, p. 7.
"An End or a Beginning" (for Yu Luoke, tr. of Bei Dao). [PoetryUSA] ([5:4?]) Wint
     90, p. 22.
"Expectation" (tr. of Bei Dao). [PoetryUSA] ([5:4?]) Wint 90, p. 21.
"For Only a Second" (tr. of Bei Dao, w. Chen Maiping). [ManhatR] (5:2) Fall 90, p.
     5.
"Gains" (tr. of Bei Dao, w. Chen Maiping). [ManhatR] (5:2) Fall 90, p. 10.
"Love Story" (tr. of Bei Dao). [PoetryUSA] ([5:4?]) Wint 90, p. 22.
"The Morning's Story" (tr. of Bei Dao, w. Chen Maiping). [ManhatR] (5:2) Fall 90,
     p. 4.
"Notes on Reading" (tr. of Bei Dao, w. Chen Maiping). [ManhatR] (5:2) Fall 90, p.
     9.
"Portrait of a Young Poet" (tr. of Bei Dao). [ManhatR] (5:2) Fall 90, p. 50-51.
"Résumé" (tr. of Bei Dao). [PoetryUSA] ([5:4?]) Wint 90, p. 21.
"Song of Migrating Birds" (tr. of Bei Dao). [PoetryUSA] ([5:4?]) Wint 90, p. 22.
"Untitled: I cannot see" (tr. of Bei Dao). [GrandS] (9:4, #36) 90, p. 174-175.
"Untitled: More unfamiliar than an accident" (tr. of Bei Dao). [GrandS] (9:4, #36)
     90, p. 172-173.
4181. McDOUGALL, Jo
"Vacation, 1943." [MidwQ] (31:2) Wint 90, p. 223.
4182. McDOWELL, Robert
"Sisters." [KenR] (NS 12:2) Spr 90, p. 131-134.
4183. McELHENNEY, John
"Black Ink Days." [ChironR] (9:3) Aut 90, p. 23.
4184. McELHONE, Jeff
"Passing Lane." [HeavenB] (8) Wint 90-91, p. 41.
4185. McELROY, Colleen J.
"Five Black Beauties Romancing Dalmatia" (with Angelita, Rosalind, Geneva, Anita,
     photographed in Dubrovnik one day in May). [RiverS] (32) [90?], p. 50.
"Main Exhibit Hall." [ManhatR] (5:1) Spr 90, p. 26.
"A Skadarlija Walk in Three-Quarter Time." [ManhatR] (5:1) Spr 90, p. 27.
"Way Out Wardell Plays Belgrade." [RiverS] (32) [90?], p. 48-49.
"What the Jackrabbits Know." [ManhatR] (5:1) Spr 90, p. 25.
4186. McFARLAND, John Robert
"Pain." [ChrC] (107:33) 14 N 90, p. 1068.
4187. McFARLAND, Ron
"Deep Sea Fishing." [HampSPR] (Anthology 1975-1990) 90, p. 148-149.
"Herpetologist." [HampSPR] (Anthology 1975-1990) 90, p. 147.
"In the Woods." [HampSPR] (Anthology 1975-1990) 90, p. 149.
"The Return of Tarzan the Apeman." [HampSPR] (Anthology 1975-1990) 90, p.
     147-148.
"Viewing Alcatraz." [Thrpny] (40) Wint 90, p. 15.
"Windfall." [HampSPR] (Anthology 1975-1990) 90, p. 146.
4188. McFEE, Michael
"Letter on Pink Paper." [HampSPR] (Anthology 1975-1990) 90, p. 200.
"Long Story Short." [SouthernHR] (24:1) Wint 90, p. 47.
"Look." [SouthernR] (26:4) O 90, p. 898-890.

"Manuscript from a Delhi Market" (for Skip Johnson). [AmerS] (59:3) Sum 90, p. 427-428.
4189. McFERREN, Martha
"Story Lady." [WillowS] (25) Wint 90, p. 37-38.
4190. McFERRIN, Linda
"Satsuma Plums." [BellR] (13:1, #27) Spr 90, p. 50.
4191. McGAULEY, Tom
"The Sophia Circumstance" (Selection: Book VII: Recarving the Chrysoprase Bowl). [WestCL] (24:1) Spr 90, p. 56-60.
4192. McGEE, Lynn
"Drifting." [OntR] (32) Spr-Sum 90, p. 25-26.
"Past Lives." [LaurelR] (24:1) Wint 90, p. 69.
"Reading Room." [PaintedB] (40/41) 90, p. 137.
4193. McGEEHAN, Charles
"Inside Out" (Excerpt, tr. of Bert Schierbeek). [Trans] (24) Fall 90, p. 83-91.
4194. McGEHEE, Heather
"From the Journal of a 19th Century Aeronaut." [BlackWR] (17:1) Fall-Wint 90, p. 152-153.
4195. McGHEE, Cindy
"Wake." [MidwQ] (31:4) Sum 90, p. 473.
4196. McGINNIS, Mary
"Woman Living Alone in Wagon Mound, New Mexico." [ChironR] (9:4) Wint 90, p. 14.
4197. McGLYNN, John H.
"In Silent Reliefs" (tr. of Linus Suryadi). [TampaR] (3) 90, p. 89.
"Song of a Rebab Player" (tr. of Linus Suryadi). [TampaR] (3) 90, p. 89.
4198. McGLYNN, Paul D.
"Antique Mirror, Detroit Institute of Arts." [BellArk] (6:4) Jl-Ag 90, p. 24.
"Art and Life." [BellArk] (6:5) S-O 90, p. 4.
"My Godless Love." [BellArk] (6:4) Jl-Ag 90, p. 1.
4199. McGOWAN, Whitman
"Chester's on Franklin." [Pig] (16) 90, p. 61.
"Comedians vs. Poets." [PoetryUSA] (5:2) Sum 90, p. 9.
"Mystery Planet Job." [Pig] (16) 90, p. 59.
4200. McGRADY, Nell
"Dehydrated Man." [NegC] (10:2/3) 90, p. 100-101.
4201. McGRATH, Beth
"High Summer." [PoetL] (85:4) Wint 90-91, p. 31-32.
"The Warmth of Blue Glass." [SoCoast] (9) Fall 90, p. 6.
4202. McGRATH, Campbell
"Sunrise and Moonfall, Rosarito Beach." [Antaeus] (64/65) Spr-Aut 90, p. 75.
"Yellowknife." [Antaeus] (64/65) Spr-Aut 90, p. 76-78.
4203. McGRATH, Connell
"Subsonnet on Ethics" (for John Yau). [Talisman] (5) Fall 90, p. 54.
4204. McGRATH, Jill
"Weathering" (Arvika, Sweden 1883). [PoetC] (22:1) Fall 90, p. 14-16.
4205. McGRATH, Kristina
"Child Suppers: Bode." [NewAW] (6) Spr 90, p. 95.
"Walking to the Territory." [Epoch] (39:3) 90, p. 299-302.
4206. McGRATH, Thomas
"The Artist As Cripple." [Spirit] (10:2) 90, p. 101-102.
4207. McGRAW, Kathleen
"My Own Sister." [ManhatPR] (12) [90?], p. 21.
4208. McGUCKIAN, Medbh
"Aviary" (from "Venus and the Rain"). [AntR] (48:3) Sum 90, p. 369.
"Brothers and Uncles." [Quarry] (39:1) Wint 90, p. 85-86.
"Minus 18 Street." [AntR] (48:3) Sum 90, p. 368.
"Whimbrel." [PassN] (11:2) Wint 90, p. 27.
"Zero Eighteen" (In memory of Rudolf Hess, August 1952). [PassN] (11:2) Wint 90, p. 27.
4209. McGUINN, Rex
"After Reading Shu Ting." [PraS] (64:4) Wint 90, p. 115.
"Ashford Station." [HiramPoR] (48/49) 90-91, p. 54.
4210. McGUIRE, Catherine
"Bird Days of Winter." [InterPR] (16:2) Fall 90, p. 109.
"Sunset at the Reservoir." [Wind] (20:67) 90, p. 29.

4211. McHUGH, Heather
   "Amniotic." [Agni] (29/30) 90, p. 109.
   "Garish." [HampSPR] (Anthology 1975-1990) 90, p. 163.
   "Glimpse of Main Event." [Agni] (29/30) 90, p. 110.
   "Missing Person." [HampSPR] (Anthology 1975-1990) 90, p. 163-164.
   "Tornado Survivor." [Gargoyle] (37/38) 90, p. 119.
4212. McINNIS, Nadine
   "Legacy." [PoetryC] (11:3) Fall 90, p. 4.
   "La Petite Mort." [PoetryC] (11:3) Fall 90, p. 4.
   "Purification." [Quarry] (39:2) Spr 90, p. 80-81.
   "Shadow." [Event] (19:3) Fall 90, p. 50-51.
   "Sheep." [Quarry] (39:2) Spr 90, p. 78-79.
4213. McINTOSH, Michael
   "Feeding." [SouthernPR] (30:1) Spr 90, p. 61.
4214. McIRVIN, Michael
   "Bone Cold." [DogRR] (9:1, #17) Spr 90, p. 22.
4215. McKAIN, David
   "Bull Stud." [Thrpny] (41) Spr 90, p. 13.
   "The Hunters." [WestB] (27) 90, p. 64-65.
   "Listening to Stones." [WestB] (27) 90, p. 65-66.
4216. McKANE, Richard
   "Dream of the Firmament" (tr. of Victoria Andreyeva). [LitR] (33:4) Sum 90, p.
      513.
   "Farewell Gentlemen We Are Setting Off" (tr. of Victoria Andreyeva). [LitR] (33:4)
      Sum 90, p. 514.
   "Having Lived an Alien Life" (tr. of Victoria Andreyeva). [LitR] (33:4) Sum 90, p.
      513-514.
   "Oh, Is It Irretrievable or Not?" (tr. of Victoria Andreyeva). [LitR] (33:4) Sum 90, p.
      514.
   "Winter Night" (tr. of Boris Pasternak). [AmerPoR] (19:4) Jl-Ag 90, p. 47.
4217. McKAY, Anne
   "In the Night Subway" (w. Wally Swist). [Os] (31) 90, p. 2-3.
4218. McKAY, Don
   "Choosing the Bow." [MalR] (92) S 90, p. 107-108.
   "The Dumpe." [PoetryC] (11:3) Fall 90, p. 18.
   "Meditation in an Uncut Cornfield, November." [PoetryC] (11:3) Fall 90, p. 18.
   "Meditation on a Geode." [MalR] (92) S 90, p. 111.
   "Meditation on Blue." [PoetryC] (11:3) Fall 90, p. 18.
   "Meditation on Shovels." [MalR] (92) S 90, p. 110.
   "Meditation on Snow Clouds Approaching the University from the North-West."
      [PoetryC] (11:3) Fall 90, p. 18.
   "Night Field." [PoetryC] (11:3) Fall 90, p. 19.
   "Old Ausable River in November." [PoetryC] (11:3) Fall 90, p. 18.
   "Solstice Song for the Snow Blowing Over the Fields." [MalR] (92) S 90, p. 105.
   "Song for the Restless Wind." [MalR] (92) S 90, p. 109.
   "Song for Wild Phlox." [MalR] (92) S 90, p. 112.
   "The Wolf." [MalR] (92) S 90, p. 106.
4219. McKAY, Leo, Jr.
   "It Hides Inside You." [PottPort] (11) 89, p. 24.
4220. McKAY, Linda Back
   "He Wants to Sell You the Blue Lagoon." [SoCoast] (9) Fall 90, p. 44.
4221. McKAY, Robbie
   "I Can't Even Thread a Needle." [LullwaterR] (1:1) Spr 90, p. 88.
   "Pronunciation." [LullwaterR] (1:1) Spr 90, p. 51.
4222. McKEAN, James
   "Silver Thaw." [PraS] (64:3) Fall 90, p. 68-69.
   "A Story after Dinner." [PraS] (64:3) Fall 90, p. 66.
   "Two Magpies." [PraS] (64:3) Fall 90, p. 67.
4223. McKEE, Louis
   "Confession." [Footwork] 90, p. 22.
   "Cool." [Contact] (9:56/57/58) Spr 90, p. 29.
   "Dreaming." [Footwork] 90, p. 22.
   "Dreaming." [NoDaQ] (58:4) Fall 90, p. 109.
   "Every Blue Mile." [FreeL] (5) Sum 90, p. 15.
   "Good Things." [Wind] (20:66) 90, p. 29.
   "Movie Magic." [SwampR] (5) Wint-Spr 90, p. 34.

"On the Other Side." [Pearl] (10) Spr 90, p. 54.
"Remember Me." [Footwork] 90, p. 22.
"The Tattoo." [ChironR] (9:1) Spr 90, p. 21.
"Yard Work." [FreeL] (5) Sum 90, p. 14.
4224. McKEE, Lucie
"Ten Miles North of Danby." [Footwork] 90, p. 67.
4225. McKEE, Michael
"Wilder Brain Collection, Cornell University." [Hudson] (43:1) Spr 90, p. 77-80.
4226. McKENZIE, Lee
"Fiddleback Embalmed." [WeberS] (7:1) Spr 90, p. 39.
"Pas de Deux." [WeberS] (7:1) Spr 90, p. 37-38.
"Texas Jacks." [WeberS] (7:1) Spr 90, p. 38-39.
4227. McKENZIE, Rusty
"Dubious Feast." [RagMag] (8:1) 90, p. 46.
"Journal Entry, March 1990." [RagMag] (8:1) 90, p. 47.
4228. McKERNAN, Llewellyn
"Four Pole Creek." [Amelia] (6:2, #17) 90, p. 140.
4229. McKIERNAN, Ethna
"Dancing the Boys into Bed." [LakeSR] (24) 90, p. 7.
4230. McKIM, Elizabeth
"Onion." [PaintedB] (40/41) 90, p. 144.
4231. McKINNEY, Louise
"Coyotes." [Grain] (18:4) Wint 90, p. 17.
"Wedding Rehearsal." [Grain] (18:4) Wint 90, p. 17.
4232. McKINNON, Pat
"The Pat McKinnon Poem." [Bogg] (62) 90, p. 49-50.
"The Young Alligator." [Bogg] (63) 90, p. 42.
4233. McKINNON, Patrick
"The Glasses Poem." [RagMag] (7:2) Spr 90, p. 28-29.
"Walter & His Children." [ChironR] (9:3) Aut 90, p. 21.
4234. McKINSEY, Martin
"Celestial Symphony." [SlipS] (10) 90, p. 65.
4235. McKOWN, Derek
"Constellation." [PacificR] (8) 90, p. 22-23.
"Sweat House." [PacificR] (8) 90, p. 24-25.
4236. McLAUGHLIN, Catherine
"After Each Collision." [BellR] (13:2, #28) Fall 90, p. 41.
4237. McLAUGHLIN, Dorothy
"Creusa." [JINJPo] (12:2) Aut 90, p. 20-21.
"Squirrels." [JINJPo] (12:2) Aut 90, p. 21.
4238. McLAUGHLIN, John
"The Clearing." [Footwork] 90, p. 67.
"The One-Year-Old" (for my nephew, Devin). [Footwork] 90, p. 67.
4239. McLAUGHLIN, William
"Circumstances Told by a German" (tr. of anonymous Croato-Serbian poem).
   [HampSPR] (Anthology 1975-1990) 90, p. 191.
"Getting Together." [HampSPR] (Anthology 1975-1990) 90, p. 192.
"In the Mind of God" (tr. of anonymous Croato-Serbian poem). [HampSPR]
   (Anthology 1975-1990) 90, p. 190-191.
4240. McLAURIN, Ken
"Blood." [CapeR] (25:1) Spr 90, p. 21.
"Poem Against Geometry." [CapeR] (25:1) Spr 90, p. 22.
4241. McLEAN, Sammy
"Mending Day" (tr. of Helga Novak). [SycamoreR] (2:2) Sum 90, p. 49.
"One of Them Stood Up and Sang" (tr. of Helga Novak). [SycamoreR] (2:2) Sum
   90, p. 47.
"Shame" (tr. of Helga Novak). [SycamoreR] (2:2) Sum 90, p. 45.
4242. McLEISH, Kenneth
"Two personal problems: under-arm goat" (tr. of Catullus, w. Frederic Raphael).
   [Hudson] (43:2) Sum 90, p. 342.
4243. McLEOD, Donald
"Bingo." [WormR] (30:4, #120) 90, p. 110.
"Cavemen." [WormR] (30:4, #120) 90, p. 110.
"Red." [WormR] (30:4, #120) 90, p. 110.
"Starlet reflected." [WormR] (30:4, #120) 90, p. 110.
"Yellow." [WormR] (30:4, #120) 90, p. 110.

4244. McMAHON, Lynne
    "Artifact." [SouthernPR] (30:2) Fall 90, p. 8-9.
    "California." [SouthernPR] (30:2) Fall 90, p. 6-8.
    "Spring Snow." [YaleR] (79:3) Spr 90, p. 439-440.
    "Summons." [YaleR] (79:3) Spr 90, p. 440-441.
4245. McMAHON, Michael B.
    "Song of the Circular Saw." [HiramPoR] (48/49) 90-91, p. 55-56.
    "Turtle Project, Wassaw Island." [HiramPoR] (48/49) 90-91, p. 57.
4246. McMANUS, James
    "Bacon Dance." [AnotherCM] (22) 90, p. 69-71.
4247. McMICHAEL, James
    "Everything was in the way" (from an uncompleted sequence). [Agni] (29/30) 90, p.
        79.
    "It wouldn't be fair to us for her to lie" (from an uncompleted sequence). [Agni]
        (29/30) 90, p. 75.
    "Nothing was more delicious or remote" (from an uncompleted sequence). [Agni]
        (29/30) 90, p. 80.
    "A picture that scares me has gone through my mind" (from an uncompleted
        sequence). [Agni] (29/30) 90, p. 77.
    "She hated loving to be with me, I with her" (from an uncompleted sequence).
        [Agni] (29/30) 90, p. 76.
    "She wrote that yesterday had been very good" (from an uncompleted sequence).
        [Agni] (29/30) 90, p. 78.
    "Surprised at my surprise that I could say" (from an uncompleted sequence). [Agni]
        (29/30) 90, p. 74.
4248. McMILLAN, James A.
    "Fog Off Gaspe." [NegC] (10:2/3) 90, p. 76.
    "Orphic Feast." [NewYorkQ] (43) Fall 90, p. 78.
4249. McMULLEN, Richard E.
    "Quiet Down." [HolCrit] (27:2) Ap 90, p. 18.
    "Quiet Down." [HolCrit] (27:4) O 90, p. 15.
4250. McNAIR, Wesley
    "Trying to Find Her Teeth." [Poetry] (157:1) O 90, p. 19.
4251. McNALLY, John
    "Caligula." [NorthStoneR] (9) 90, p. 84-85.
    "Nine Hundred Miles." [NorthStoneR] (9) 90, p. 87.
    "One Mitten." [NorthStoneR] (9) 90, p. 86.
    "Tiberius to His Sons." [NorthStoneR] (9) 90, p. 82-83.
4252. McNALLY, Stephen
    "Evening of the Trapeze Artist." [CimR] (90) Ja 90, p. 78.
    "Grief for the Living." [CimR] (92) Jl 90, p. 118.
4253. McNAMARA, Eugene
    "At Louis Sullivan's Grave." [Writ] (22) 90 c1991, p. 17-18.
    "Leaving the Rust Belt." [Writ] (22) 90 c1991, p. 14-16.
    "Life at the Beach." [Writ] (22) 90 c1991, p. 12-13.
    "Listening to the Goldberg Variations." [Writ] (22) 90 c1991, p. 23.
    "Nebraska." [Writ] (22) 90 c1991, p. 22.
    "References." [Writ] (22) 90 c1991, p. 19-21.
4254. McNAMARA, Robert
    "Best Coat Company, Roxbury, MA, 1969." [CimR] (93) O 90, p. 49-50.
    "Dust, Port Madison Anchorage" (for Bob Weeks). [NowestR] (28:3/29:1) 90-91,
        p. 191-192.
    "Elephants at Work." [AntR] (48:4) Fall 90, p. 499.
    "In the Cameron Highlands." [NowestR] (28:3/29:1) 90-91, p. 193.
4255. McNAMEE, Gregory
    "Obsession" (tr. of Sappho). [YellowS] (34) Sum 90, p. 38.
4256. McNARIE, Alan Decker
    "Archer's Hope." [ChamLR] (4:1, #7) Fall 90, p. 136-138.
    "Royal Gardens." [ChamLR] (4:1, #7) Fall 90, p. 139.
4257. McNAUGHTON, Duncan
    "The Seagull's Cry Seemed Human." [PoetryUSA] (5:1) Spr 90, p. 10.
4258. McNERNEY, Joan
    "Mysterious." [Kalliope] (12:2) 90, p. 47.
4259. McPHERSON, D. Jayne
    "The Storyteller." [PoetryUSA] (5:1) Spr 90, p. 5.

4260. McPHERSON, Sandra
"Affirmation Against Critics." [Poetry] (157:1) O 90, p. 1-2.
"Center" (Strip and Medallion Quilt, 1890, by Mrs. Longmire, African-American
    Seamstress for Her Town in Maryland). [KenR] (NS 12:4) Fall 90, p. 71-72.
"Eclipse Facsimile." [NewYorker] (66:26) 13 Ag 90, p. 38.
"Finding the Quilter in Her Quilt." [WeberS] (7:2) Fall 90, p. 79.
"Goose-in-the-Pond Improvisations, Southside Estate-Sale Quilt and Ghost."
    [WeberS] (7:2) Fall 90, p. 82.
"I Cannot Teach Hewr Closure." [WeberS] (7:2) Fall 90, p. 80.
"Lowell Fulson, Age 66, Eli's Mile High Club, Oakland, California." [Poetry]
    (156:4) Jl 90, p. 188-189.
"Millionaire Records." [Zyzzyva] (6:2, #22) Sum 90, p. 105-108.
"Mixing the Patches." [Poetry] (157:1) O 90, p. 2-3.
"On the Abundance of Shell Hinges After a Storm." [Thrpny] (41) Spr 90, p. 12.
"One Way She Spoke to Me." [Field] (42) Spr 90, p. 58.
"Persuading My Lover that My Daughter Is Fun to Live with Because We'll Pretend
    She's My Sister." [WeberS] (7:2) Fall 90, p. 81.
"Postcard to the Musician" (For Hip Linkchain). [Poetry] (156:4) Jl 90, p. 187-188.
"Redheart, Greenbark, Blueblossom." [Field] (42) Spr 90, p. 59-60.
"Suit and Tie." [KenR] (NS 12:4) Fall 90, p. 72-73.
"The Thorn-Shaver on Fifth." [ParisR] (32:114) Spr 90, p. 123-124.
"Two Young Trees Bending in the Strong Wind." [NewRep] (202:6) 5 F 90, p. 35.
"Wake-Up Colloquy." [WeberS] (7:2) Fall 90, p. 79-80.
McQUAID, Diana Middleton
    See MIDDLETON-McQUAID, Diana
4261. McQUEEN, Mark
"n + 40, Putting Off Judgement." [ChironR] (9:3) Aut 90, p. 17.
4262. McQUILKIN, Rennie
"Running into Irene Wade in Dense Fog on South Beach." [HampSPR] (Anthology
    1975-1990) 90, p. 196.
"Vision." [BelPoJ] (41:1) Fall 90, p. 19.
"Visit." [Poetry] (156:3) Je 90, p. 148.
4263. McRAY, Paul
"Practice." [PoetL] (85:4) Wint 90-91, p. 7-8.
"What Could Be More Important." [AntR] (48:4) Fall 90, p. 489.
4264. McSWEEN, Harold (Harold B.)
"Beached." [SewanR] (98:2) Spr 90, p. 198.
"Near Cashiers." [PoetC] (21:2) Wint 90, p. 36-37.
"One Night in a Pasture." [SewanR] (98:2) Spr 90, p. 200.
"Parlor." [SewanR] (98:2) Spr 90, p. 199.
"Passing Through." [PoetC] (21:2) Wint 90, p. 35.
"Skepticism." [PoetC] (22:1) Fall 90, p. 27-28.
"Vacations." [PoetC] (22:1) Fall 90, p. 25-26.
4265. McVEIGH, Jane
"Mermaids." [BelPoJ] (41:1) Fall 90, p. 1.
4266. McWHIRTER, George
"Hands, like Asters." [Event] (19:3) Fall 90, p. 56.
4267. MEACHAM, Susan M.
"Admiring Your Sensibility" (For D.L.G.). [LullwaterR] (1:1) Spr 90, p. 57.
4268. MEAD, Jane
"Somewhere I Lost the Quest, Mom." [NoDaQ] (58:4) Fall 90, p. 5-7.
4269. MEADE, Karl
"Walk." [Dandel] (17:2) Fall-Wint 90, p. 21.
4270. MEARS, Alice Monks
"Here" (20 poems). [Sparrow] (57) 90, 24 p.
4271. MEATS, Stephen
"Chief Canassatego Reflects on American Education, 1744" (adaption of remarks by
    Chief Canassatego). [MidwQ] (31:2) Wint 90, p. 198-199.
"Chief Seattle Reflects on the Future of America, 1855" (adaption of remarks by
    Chief Seattle). [MidwQ] (31:2) Wint 90, p. 230-231.
"Chief Speckled Snake Reflects on Patterns in American History, 1829" (adaption of
    remarks by Chief Speckled Snake). [MidwQ] (31:2) Wint 90, p. 207-208.
4272. MECKLAM, Todd
"In the Bar at the Cockatoo Inn" (w. Denise Dumars). [Pearl] (10) Spr 90, p. 11.
4273. MEDINA, Pablo
"Gacela for a Dead Child" (tr. of Federico García Lorca). [ArtfulD] (18/19) 90, p.

29.
"Kassida of the Sleeping Woman" (tr. of Federico García Lorca). [ArtfulD] (18/19)
90, p. 28.
"A Poem for the Epiphany" (for Ellen Jacko). [ArtfulD] (18/19) 90, p. 27.
"Two Words" (tr. of Alfonsina Storni). [ArtfulD] (18/19) 90, p. 30.
4274. MEECE, Terrilynn
"Dying Dreams." [Parting] (3:2) Wint 90-91, p. 5.
4275. MEEHAN, Charlotte
"One of Many Days." [BrooklynR] (7) 90, p. 36.
4276. MEEK, Ed
"Falling." [Poem] (63) My 90, p. 58.
"Flight." [Poem] (63) My 90, p. 57.
"Nothing Lasts." [ConnPR] (9:1) 90, p. 31-32.
4277. MEEK, Jay
"Behind Glass." [ThRiPo] (35/36) 90, p. 48.
"Happy Ending." [ThRiPo] (35/36) 90, p. 49-50.
"Winter House." [ThRiPo] (35/36) 90, p. 51.
4278. MEGHIDDO, Rick
"By the Fork." [OnTheBus] (2:2/3:1, #6/7) Sum-Fall 90 Wint-Spr 91, p. 147-148.
"I Am a Poet Because I Say So." [OnTheBus] (2:1, #5) Spr 90, p. 102-104.
"Sabbath." [OnTheBus] (2:2/3:1, #6/7) Sum-Fall 90 Wint-Spr 91, p. 146-147.
"Three Weeks Later." [OnTheBus] (2:2/3:1, #6/7) Sum-Fall 90 Wint-Spr 91, p.
146.
4279. MEHRHOFF, Charlie
"Background" (for Clarissa P. Estes). [DogRR] (9:1, #17) Spr 90, p. 5.
"I Dream of Dying." [Parting] (3:1) Sum 90, p. 8.
"Phoenix." [Parting] (3:1) Sum 90, p. 8.
"Smell the Death." [Asylum] (5:4) 90, p. 15.
"Somewhere East of Taos." [Parting] (3:1) Sum 90, p. 34.
4280. MEIER, Kay
"Anonymous." [CoalC] (1) Ag 90, p. 15.
"The Falling Day." [CumbPR] (9:2) Spr 90, p. 28.
"Keeping House." [WillowR] Spr 90, p. 23.
"Pictures of the World, October 24, 1983, 6:30 A.M." [EngJ] (79:2) F 90, p. 86.
4281. MEIJINNI
"The March 12th of Stillness." [PoetryUSA] (5:2) Sum 90, p. 18.
4282. MEINHOFF, Michael
"Waikiki Roughwater Swim." [ChamLR] (3:2, #6) Spr 90, p. 38-39.
4283. MEINKE, Peter
"Growing Deaf." [ClockR] (6:2) 90, p. 49.
"Love Poem 1990." [WestB] (27) 90, p. 45.
"The Perch." [GrandS] (9:3) Spr 90, p. 52.
"Steroids." [ChatR] (10:4) Sum 90, p. 30.
4284. MEIRELES, Cecilia
"Alheias e Nossas" (Poemas 60/64, tr. by Aila de Oliveira Gomes). [Interim] (9:1)
Spr-Sum 90, p. 22.
"Miravamos a Jovem Lagartixa" (from "Metal Rosicler," tr. by Aila de Oliveira
Gomes). [Interim] (9:1) Spr-Sum 90, p. 23.
"Por Mais Que Te Celebre" (from "Mar Absoluto, 2o Motivo da Rosa," tr. by Aila de
Oliveira Gomes). [Interim] (9:1) Spr-Sum 90, p. 21.
4285. MEISKEY, Elinor
"After the Poetry Chapbook Was Published." [WritersF] (16) Fall 90, p. 127-128.
4286. MEISSNER, Bill
"1955: James Dean Does a TV Public Service Announcement about Speeding."
[MidAR] (10:2) 90, p. 161-162.
"The Outfielder" (w. Jack Driscoll). [ColEng] (52:8) D 90, p. 884.
"The Trap" (with Jack Driscoll). [KenR] (NS 12:2) Spr 90, p. 65.
"Voices of Ice" (with Jack Driscoll). [KenR] (NS 12:2) Spr 90, p. 65.
MEJIA, Adelaida Lopez
See LOPEZ MEJIA, Adelaida
4287. MEKAS, Jonas
"From Nowhere" (tr. by Vyt Bakaitis). [LitR] (33:4) Sum 90, p. 448-449.
4288. MEKULA, Janice A.
"Overload." [EngJ] (79:3) Mr 90, p. 90.
4289. MELCHER, Michael
"Courage Is a Rafter." [Talisman] (4) Spr 90, p. 4.

317

4290. MELIEH, Sara
"In the Shade of Portola Palace." [HolCrit] (27:4) O 90, p. 17.
4291. MELIEH, Sarah
"Like Van Gogh Transfixed." [PoetryUSA] (5:3) Fall 90, p. 9.
4292. MELIN, C.
"The Gardener's Complaint." [WindO] (53) Fall 90, p. 51.
4293. MELISSEN, Sipko
"Pieter de Hooch" (Painting: Two Women in a Courtyard by Pieter de Hooch, tr. by
Michael O'Loughlin). [Trans] (24) Fall 90, p. 55.
"View of Sloten" (Drawing by Rembrandt, tr. by Michael O'Loughlin). [Trans] (24)
Fall 90, p. 53.
"View of the Amstel" (Drawing by Rembrandt, tr. by Michael O'Loughlin). [Trans]
(24) Fall 90, p. 54.
4294. MELNEECHUK, Joseph
"Tenant." [KanQ] (22:1/2) Wint-Spr 90, p. 150.
4295. MEL'NYCHUK, Taras
"Untitled: For some time now I like to kick" (tr. by Vera L. Kaczmarskyj). [Agni]
(31/32) 90, p. 159-160.
MELNYCZCH, Askold
See MELNYCZUK, Askol
4296. MELNYCZUK, Askold
"The Apocalyptic Horses of the North Shore" (Excerpted from "The Apocryphal
Diaries of Rosinante"). [GrahamHR] (13) Spr 90, p. 29.
"Astronomy Lesson." [HawaiiR] (14:3, #30) Fall 90, p. 116.
"La Boheme." [GrahamHR] (13) Spr 90, p. 26-28.
"The City Rat Returns from the Dead for an Interview." [Boulevard] (4:3/5:1,
#12/13) Spr 90, p. 97-99.
"The Great Blue Heron." [GrahamHR] (13) Spr 90, p. 31-32.
"The Great Feeding." [Caliban] (8) 90, p. 153.
"Lotte." [Chelsea] (49) 90, p. 37-41.
"The Mouth Refuses to Translate." [GrandS] (9:2) Wint 90, p. 128.
"The Odyssey: Revised, Standard." [Boulevard] (4:3/5:1, #12/13) Spr 90, p. 100.
"The Ride Home." [GrahamHR] (13) Spr 90, p. 30.
"The Source of Fear." [Caliban] (8) 90, p. 151-152.
"The Usual Immigrant Uncle Poem." [MassR] (31:1/2) Spr-Sum 90, p. 304.
4297. MENASHE, Samuel
"Demonstration." [Confr] (42/43) Spr-Sum 90, p. 232.
4298. MENDELL, Olga Karman
"Crossing Harvard Yard." [Nat] (251:12) 15 O 90, p. 430.
"Shadow on Stone." [NewRep] (203:1) 2 Jl 90, p. 40.
4299. MENDIVIL, Jose
"Pershing Square Story." [PoetryUSA] ([5:4?]) Wint 90, p. 24.
4300. MENEBROKER, Ann
"After Drinking Chardonnay on a Hot Summer Night." [Pearl] (12) Fall-Wint 90, p.
40.
"Her Lover." [SwampR] (6) Sum-Fall 90, p. 74.
4301. MENEFEE, Sarah
"Over the Hill" (Excerpt). [Conjunc] (15) 90, p. 232-234.
"Unbroken Face: for This American Revolution." [PoetryUSA] (5:2) Sum 90, p. 17.
4302. MENES, Orlando
"A Lover's Leaving." [Poem] (63) My 90, p. 12.
"Saint Augustine Beach." [Poem] (63) My 90, p. 11.
4303. MENG, Chiao
"Cold Creek" (tr. by James A. Wilson). [NewOR] (17:4) Wint 90, p. 66-73.
4304. MENG, Lang
"At the Stern of a Ship" (tr. by Dong Jiping). [Footwork] 90, p. 37.
"Losing" (tr. by Dong Jiping). [Footwork] 90, p. 37.
"Words" (tr. by Dong Jiping). [Footwork] 90, p. 37.
4305. MENGHAM, Rod
"Nomenclature." [Screens] (2) 90, p. 171-172.
MENOZZI, Wallis Wilde
See WILDE-MENOZZI, Wallis
4306. MENSHEK, Emily
"Emily Explains How Life Begins." [Pearl] (11) Sum 90, p. 57.
"Emily's Tribute to Spring." [Pearl] (11) Sum 90, p. 57.
"A Fantasy Poem by Emily." [Pearl] (11) Sum 90, p. 57.

4307. MENZA, Claudia
"Bronx Zoo." [Confr] (44/45) Fall 90-Wint 91, p. 202-204.
4308. MERCHANT, Norris
"Of Demeter's Daughter." [AmerV] (19) Sum 90, p. 60-62.
4309. MERRILL, Christopher
"Magnolia Bluff." [Journal] (13:2) Fall-Wint 89-90, p. 53-54.
"Three Riddles" (adaptions of anonymous poems). [PoetryE] (30) Fall 90, p. 67.
4310. MERRILL, James
"164 East 72nd Street." [NewYorker] (66:1) 19 F 90, p. 40.
"Big Mirror Outdoors." [Antaeus] (64/65) Spr-Aut 90, p. 80-81.
"Home Fires." [NewYRB] (37:5) 29 Mr 90, p. 16.
"Morning Exercise." [SouthwR] (75:2) Spr 90, p. 209-210.
"Nine Lives." [Poetry] (156:5) Ag 90, p. 249-260.
"Pledge." [Pequod] (31) 90, p. 9.
"The 'Ring' Cycle." [NewYorker] (66:12) 7 My 90, p. 46-47.
"To the Reader." [YaleR] (79:3) Spr 90, p. 387-388.
MERS, Joyce la
    See LaMERS, Joyce
4311. MERTON, Vikki
"Birds of Summer." [Grain] (18:2) Sum 90, p. 74.
"Coffin Shortage in Caracas" (Dedicated to the hundreds who were killed in rioting
    against bus fare increases in Venezuela). [Grain] (18:2) Sum 90, p. 75.
"From My Mother's House." [Grain] (18:2) Sum 90, p. 76-77.
4312. MERWIN, W. S. (William S.)
"Absence" (tr. of Walid Khazindar, w. Lena Jayyusi). [PaperAir] (4:3) 90, p. 65.
"Another Place." [NewYorker] (66:27) 20 Ag 90, p. 30-32.
"At Least" (tr. of Walid Khazindar, w. Lena Jayyusi). [PaperAir] (4:3) 90, p. 64.
"The Ceiba" (tr. of Pablo Antonio Cuadra). [Trans] (24) Fall 90, p. 196-198.
"Conqueror." [BambooR] (47) Sum 90, p. 53.
"The Day Itself" (Harvard Phi Beta Kappa Poem, 1989). [Antaeus] (64/65) Spr-Aut
    90, p. 82-85.
"For the Year." [OhioR] (45) 90, p. 7-8.
"The Guards" (tr. of Mureed Barghouthi, w. Lena Jayyusi). [PaperAir] (4:3) 90, p.
    67.
"Houses" (tr. of Walid Khazindar, w. Lena Jayyusi). [PaperAir] (4:3) 90, p. 66.
"Immortelles." [Field] (43) Fall 90, p. 58-59.
"Kites." [GrandS] (9:2) Wint 90, p. 169-170.
"Looking Up." [Nat] (250:7) 19 F 90, p. 244.
"Losing a Language." [BambooR] (47) Sum 90, p. 54-55.
"The Lost Camelia of the Bartrams." [Antaeus] (64/65) Spr-Aut 90, p. 86-88.
"Lunar Landscape." [Antaeus] (64/65) Spr-Aut 90, p. 89.
"One Story." [PoetryUSA] (5:3) Fall 90, p. 13.
"One Tree Less" (tr. of Jaime Sabinas). [Trans] (24) Fall 90, p. 199.
"Perplexed" (tr. of Walid Khazindar, w. Lena Jayyusi). [PaperAir] (4:3) 90, p. 66.
"The Pure Sound Pavilion of the Riverside Temple" (tr. of Muso Soseki, w. Soiku
    Shigematsu). [Hudson] (43:2) Sum 90, p. 339.
"Rain Travel." [NewYorker] (66:8) 9 Ap 90, p. 79.
"Refuge" (tr. of Mureed Barghouthi, w. Lena Jayyusi). [PaperAir] (4:3) 90, p. 68.
"The Sound of the Light." [PoetC] (21:3) Spr 90, p. 38-39.
"The Tribes" (tr. of Mureed Barghouthi, w. Lena Jayyusi). [PaperAir] (4:3) 90, p.
    68.
4313. MESA, Lauren
"Collaborator, Chartres, 1944" (after the photograph by Robert Capa). [LaurelR]
    (24:1) Wint 90, p. 43.
"Hard Wood." [SpoonRQ] (15:2) Spr 90, p. 15.
"Praise." [LaurelR] (24:1) Wint 90, p. 42.
4314. MESQUITA, Henrique de Araujo
"How rapidly, rapidly, rapidly" (from "Punhalada de Poemas," tr. by Aila de
    Oliveira Gomes). [Interim] (9:1) Spr-Sum 90, p. 24.
4315. MESSER, Sarah
"Choose." [MichQR] (29:4) Fall 90, p. 565-566.
4316. MESSERLI, Douglas
"Aller et Retour." [WashR] (15:6) Ap-My 90, p. 30.
"On Edge." [WashR] (15:6) Ap-My 90, p. 31.
4317. MESSINEO, Len, Jr.
"Isleta Paintings." [MidwQ] (31:2) Wint 90, p. 211.

4318. METRAS, Gary
"Northampton Poem" (for David, Barry and Wally). [PoetryE] (29) Spr 90, p. 214-226.
4319. METZ, Robin
"Bearing Gifts" (for Roy and Corine). [InterPR] (16:2) Fall 90, p. 108.
"Buffalo Days." [Farm] (7:2) Fall 90, p. 90.
"December Divorce: A Theorem." [WritersF] (16) Fall 90, p. 169-171.
"Drowning in the Driftless Region -- Near Victory, Wisconsin." [Farm] (7:2) Fall 90, p. 89.
"The Storyteller's Women." [InterPR] (16:2) Fall 90, p. 107.
4320. MEUEL, David
"First Born." [BellArk] (6:6) N-D 90, p. 1.
"The High Country." [BellArk] (6:3) My-Je 90, p. 4.
4321. MEYER, Bruce
"Blackbird on a Balustrade." [PoetryC] (11:3) Fall 90, p. 7.
"Harry's Requiem Picnic." [PoetryC] (11:3) Fall 90, p. 7.
4322. MEYER, William, Jr.
"White Bayou" (for Fred Tramel). [KanQ] (22:3) Sum 90, p. 149.
4323. MEZEY, Katalin
"Mother Always Knows Something New" (tr. by Nicholas Kolumban). [ArtfulD] (18/19) 90, p. 33.
4324. MEZEY, Robert
"Buenos Aires, 1899" (tr. of Jorge Luis Borges, w. R. G. Barnes). [SoCoast] (8) Spr 90, p. 13.
"Emerson" (tr. of Jorge Luis Borges, w. R. G. Barnes). [SoCoast] (8) Spr 90, p. 17.
"Unrecognized Street" (tr. of Jorge Luis Borges, w. R. G. Barnes). [SoCoast] (8) Spr 90, p. 11.
"Written in a Copy of the Geste of Beowulf" (tr. of Jorge Luis Borges, w. R. G. Barnes). [SoCoast] (8) Spr 90, p. 15.
MI OK BRUINING, Anne
See BRUINING, Anne Mi Ok
4325. MICELLE, Jerry, Jr.
"The GM." [DogRR] (9:2, #18) Aut 90, p. 35.
4326. MICHAEL, Naydan,
"An emerald oak grove after the rains" (tr. of Lina Kostenko). [Nimrod] (33:2) Spr-Sum 90, p. 7.
"The rain began to fall, and the day became such a downpour" (tr. of Lina Kostenko). [Nimrod] (33:2) Spr-Sum 90, p. 7.
"A shady spot, twilight, a golden day" (tr. of Lina Kostenko). [Nimrod] (33:2) Spr-Sum 90, p. 4.
"The spring day began with birches" (tr. of Lina Kostenko). [Nimrod] (33:2) Spr-Sum 90, p. 6.
"Watercolors of Childhood" (tr. of Lina Kostenko). [Nimrod] (33:2) Spr-Sum 90, p. 5.
"With your eyes you told me: I love" (tr. of Lina Kostenko). [Nimrod] (33:2) Spr-Sum 90, p. 6.
4327. MICHAELS, Judith
"Final Exams." [PoetryNW] (31:1) Spr 90, p. 36.
4328. MICHAELSON, Liz
"At Sea." [Footwork] 90, p. 58.
"Poem for My Father." [Footwork] 90, p. 58.
4329. MICHAUX, Henri
"Les Ravagés" (Selections: 10, 16, 27, tr. by David Ball). [Notus] (5:1) Spr 90, p. 65-67.
MICHELE, Mary di
See Di MICHELE, Mary
4330. MICHELINE, Jack
"A Face in the City." [PoetryUSA] (5:1) Spr 90, p. 1.
MICHIKO, Fu
See FU, Michiko
4331. MICK, Linda M.
"My Love Is Lost." [EmeraldCR] (1990) c89, p. 38.
4332. MICUS, Edward
"Boy in a Rice Paddy, Head Shot." [IndR] (13:3) Fall 90, p. 107.
"Robertson." [CapeR] (25:2) Fall 90, p. 8.

MICUS

320

"Village Near Landing Zone Dog." [LakeSR] (24) 90, p. 5.
4333. MIDDLETON, Christopher
17 poems (tr. of Hafsa Bint Al-Hajj Ar-Rakuntyya). [PartR] (57:3) Sum 90, p.
386-393.
"Drunken Beauty" (tr. of Ben al-Zaqqaq, w. Leticia Garza Falcón). [Trans] (23) Spr
90, p. 195.
"On the Death of a Friend by Drowning" (tr. of Ar-Rusafi, w. Leticia Garza Falcón).
[Trans] (23) Spr 90, p. 193.
"Seeing Herself Beautiful and Nubile" (tr. of Qazmuna Bint Isma'il Al-Yahudi, w.
Leticia Garza Falcón). [Trans] (23) Spr 90, p. 192.
"The Young Tailor" (tr. of Ben Charuf, w. Leticia Garza Falcón). [Trans] (23) Spr
90, p. 194.
4334. MIDDLETON, David
"The Family Tree" (for my country grandmother, d. 1962). [SewanR] (98:1) Wint
90, p. 28.
"The Journeying Moon." [Hellas] (1:2) Fall 90, p. 247-248.
"Windsor Ruins" (Port Gibson, Mississippi: built, 1860, burned, 1890). [SewanR]
(98:1) Wint 90, p. 26-27.
4335. MIDDLETON-McQUAID, Diana
"This is a really exciting day." [PoetryUSA] (5:1) Spr 90, p. 11.
4336. MIDGETTE, Rocky
"Reading Richard Wilbur." [LullwaterR] (1:1) Spr 90, p. 25.
4337. MIECZKOWSKI, Rondo
"Full Moon." [JamesWR] (7:2) Wint 90, p. 13.
4338. MIEDZYRZECKI, Artur
"Anywhere But Here" (tr. by Reuel K. Wilson). [Trans] (24) Fall 90, p. 191.
"Someone Else" (tr. by Reuel K. Wilson). [Trans] (24) Fall 90, p. 192.
4339. MIELE, Frank
"Angles." [KanQ] (22:3) Sum 90, p. 139.
"The Created World." [PoetC] (21:2) Wint 90, p. 15-16.
"Light on Dark Corners: What Men Love in Women." [HangL] (57) 90, p. 50.
"Light on Dark Corners: What Women Love in Men." [HangL] (57) 90, p. 49.
"The Man in My Memory." [KanQ] (22:1/2) Wint-Spr 90, p. 60.
4340. MIERAU, Maurice
"Settling Up" (for Michael Wiebe, 1961-1985). [PraF] (11:2) Sum 90, p. 134-138.
4341. MIGASH, George
"She Has Always Been Dead to Me." [Pearl] (12) Fall-Wint 90, p. 44.
4342. MIHOPAULOS, Effie
"St. Vitus' Disease: Effie's Story" (for Becky). [Footwork] 90, p. 113.
4343. MIKITA, Nancy
"Crossroads." [DogRR] (9:2, #18) Aut 90, p. 9.
"A Fallacy of Style." [CapeR] (25:1) Spr 90, p. 19.
MIKO, Suzuki
See SUZUKI, Miko
4344. MIKOLOWSKI, Ken
"Derrida & Ladida." [Notus] (5:1) Spr 90, p. 118.
"Imperative." [Notus] (5:1) Spr 90, p. 117.
MIKOTO, Susano no
See SUSANO no MIKOTO
4345. MIKULEC, Patrick B.
"The Aloha Grange." [ChamLR] (4:1, #7) Fall 90, p. 130.
"Chicken Hawk." [WritersF] (16) Fall 90, p. 97-98.
"Honesty" (After reading On Being Yanked from a Favorite Anthology by K.S.).
[NegC] (10:2/3) 90, p. 104.
"Ice Lake." [HawaiiR] (14:1, #28) Wint 89-90, p. 89.
"Lips." [Pearl] (12) Fall-Wint 90, p. 40.
"Looker." [CapeR] (25:1) Spr 90, p. 14.
"Samara." [CapeR] (25:1) Spr 90, p. 13.
"You Know Da Kine." [ChamLR] (4:1, #7) Fall 90, p. 131.
MIKULEC, Patrick K.
See MIKULEC, Patrick B.
4346. MILANKOVA, Ivana
"Commandments" (tr. by Darinka Petkovic and Richard Burns). [Screens] (2) 90, p.
68.
"Visions" (tr. by Darinka Petkovic and Richard Burns). [Screens] (2) 90, p. 69.
"White Angels, As They Crucified Me" (tr. by Darinka Petkovic and Richard Burns).

[Screens] (2) 90, p. 67.
MILER, Errol
    See MILLER, Errol
4347. MILES, Judi Kiefer
    "My Family Quilt." [NegC] (10:1) 90, p. 76.
4348. MILES, Louis
    "Elegy for Sister Mildred" (Who Died at Sabbath-day Lake, January 25, 1990).
        [ChrC] (107:27) 3 O 90, p. 870.
4349. MILES, Ron
    "Boys and Girls Together." [Descant] (21:1 #68) Spr 90, p. 106-107.
    "Dark Lady in White." [Quarry] (39:4) Fall 1990, p. 21.
    "Depot." [Descant] (21:1 #68) Spr 90, p. 104.
    "Harvest." [AntigR] (81/82) Spr-Sum 90, p. 92.
    "Human Voice." [Descant] (21:1 #68) Spr 90, p. 101.
    "Louise." [Dandel] (17:1) Spr-Sum 90, p. 11.
    "The Moon" (for Marie-Louise). [Quarry] (39:4) Fall 1990, p. 18.
    "Only Child." [Quarry] (39:4) Fall 1990, p. 17.
    "Road to Mexico." [Descant] (21:1 #68) Spr 90, p. 105.
    "Wanting the Truth." [Quarry] (39:4) Fall 1990, p. 20.
    "White and Black." [Descant] (21:1 #68) Spr 90, p. 103.
    "Woman Sleeping." [Descant] (21:1 #68) Spr 90, p. 102.
    "Women." [Quarry] (39:4) Fall 1990, p. 19.
4350. MILETIC, Ljubica
    "The Evil Sorcerers" (tr. by Darinka Petkovic). [Screens] (2) 90, p. 64.
4351. MILEY, Jerry David
    "Dim Light." [PoetryUSA] (5:1) Spr 90, p. 14.
    "Feeling Sorry." [PoetryUSA] (5:1) Spr 90, p. 14.
    "Gray Day, Early Afternoon." [PoetryUSA] (5:3) Fall 90, p. 24.
    "It Was Cold." [PoetryUSA] ([5:4?]) Wint 90, p. 23.
    "Memories." [PoetryUSA] (5:2) Sum 90, p. 18.
    "Nazi Cross on an American Tunnel." [PoetryUSA] (5:3) Fall 90, p. 24.
    "Two Poems As One." [PoetryUSA] (5:1) Spr 90, p. 14.
4352. MILIAUSKAITE, Nijole
    "A flowering garden" (tr. by Jonas Zdanys). [CrossCur] (9:2) Je 90, p. 165.
    "You would like to live" (tr. by Jonas Zdanys). [CrossCur] (9:2) Je 90, p. 166.
4353. MILLAY, Edna St. Vincent
    "If I should learn, in some quite casual way." [ChiR] (37:1) Wint 90, p. 30.
4354. MILLER, B. J.
    "The Hook." [EmeraldCR] (1990) c89, p. 6.
4355. MILLER, Carol
    "Hypochondria." [Comm] (117:13) 13 Jl 90, p. 415.
    "Indians." [CapeR] (25:2) Fall 90, p. 49.
    "The Point Is to Get On with It." [Confr] (42/43) Spr-Sum 90, p. 250.
4356. MILLER, Carolyn Reynolds
    "The 100th Princess." [PoetryNW] (31:2) Sum 90, p. 33-34.
    "Bodywork." [PoetryNW] (31:2) Sum 90, p. 36-37.
    "Fairy Tales on Florida Avenue." [PoetryNW] (31:2) Sum 90, p. 35-36.
    "How Things Wind Up." [PoetryNW] (31:2) Sum 90, p. 38-39.
4357. MILLER, Charles
    "Para Mi Calavera." [Os] (31) 90, p. 8.
4358. MILLER, Chuck
    "The Wind." [Spirit] (10:2) 90, p. 103.
4359. MILLER, D. D.
    "Academic Freedom." [Amelia] (6:2, #17) 90, p. 18.
4360. MILLER, David
    "Fire Water" (for Gerhard Richter). [Screens] (2) 90, p. 134-135.
4361. MILLER, Derek
    "Poem: The television sits gray." [HangL] (56) 90, p. 27.
    "When February Follows Close After Christmas Like It Was a Guest Returning
        Home Late from a Party." [HangL] (56) 90, p. 28-29.
4362. MILLER, Elizabeth Gamble
    "At the Moment of Dawn" (tr. of Carlos Ernesto García). [MidAR] (10:1) 90, p.
        107.
    "Brief Love Poem" (tr. of Carlos Ernesto García). [NewOR] (17:4) Wint 90, p. 24.
    "First Kiss" (tr. of Carlos Ernesto García). [NewOR] (17:4) Wint 90, p. 25.
    "I Have No Home" (tr. of Carlos Ernesto García). [NewOR] (17:4) Wint 90, p.

22-23.
"Love with Powder Burns" (tr. of Carlos Ernesto García). [NewOR] (17:4) Wint 90,
p. 28.
"Poor Company" (tr. of Carlos Ernesto García). [NewOR] (17:4) Wint 90, p. 26.
"Something Endures" (tr. of Matilde Elene López). [MidAR] (10:1) 90, p. 104.
"They Are Like the Dew" (tr. of Carlos Ernesto García). [NewOR] (17:4) Wint 90,
p. 27.
"This Immense Oak" (tr. of Miguel Huezo Mixco). [MidAR] (10:1) 90, p. 105.
"Through the Slow Rancor of Water" (to Rigoberto Paredes, tr. of Carlos Ernesto
García). [MidAR] (10:1) 90, p. 106.
"The Warrior's Rest" (tr. of Carlos Ernesto García). [NewOR] (17:4) Wint 90, p.
21.
4363. MILLER, Errol
(Anonymous poem). [FreeL] (4) 90.
"Coming to Pass." [KanQ] (22:1/2) Wint-Spr 90, p. 49.
"From a Crystal Wedding Day." [WestB] (26) 90, p. 105.
"Native Sons." [ChatR] (10:3) Spr 90, p. 34.
"News From Yale." [Plain] (11:1) Fall 90, p. 10-11.
"This Be the Night." [Northeast] (5:2) Spr 90, p. 13.
"Why We Don't Need Asylum." [Plain] (10:2) Wint 90, p. 33.
4364. MILLER, Greg
"Poem: The blue Motel 6 sign through the curtain." [Agni] (29/30) 90, p. 151-153.
"The Ringing." [Agni] (29/30) 90, p. 154.
4365. MILLER, Hugh
"Diptych for Melpone & Thalia" (to Sarah & Kelcey). [AntigR] (83) Aut 90, p.
72-73.
"Portrait of an Academic Parvenu" (for Verna Andersen Miller). [AntigR] (80) Wint
90, p. 17-19.
4366. MILLER, James A.
"Extensions" (In the Cleveland Museum of Art). [HawaiiR] (14:3, #30) Fall 90, p.
38-39.
4367. MILLER, Jane
"Beauty." [RiverS] (32) [90?], p. 3.
"Blanks for New Things." [Ploughs] (16:4) Wint 90-91, p. 13.
"Exposure." [IndR] (13:2) Spr 90, p. 55.
"False Gods." [RiverS] (32) [90?], p. 4.
"Warrior." [Ploughs] (16:4) Wint 90-91, p. 11-12.
4368. MILLER, Jeanette
"Los Ciclos" (Selection: Parte III). [InterPR] (16:1) Spr 90, p. 90.
"The Cycles" (Selection: Part III, tr. by Mark Smith-Soto). [InterPR] (16:1) Spr 90,
p. 91.
"In Situ." [PoetC] (21:4) Sum 90, p. 15-16.
4369. MILLER, Jill C.
"Pickled." [CapeR] (25:2) Fall 90, p. 17.
4370. MILLER, Jim Wayne
"The Faith of Fishermen" (from "Brier, His Book"). [SwampR] (6) Sum-Fall 90, p.
36.
"Land and Language" (from "Brier, His Book"). [SwampR] (6) Sum-Fall 90, p. 37.
"Snafu." [AmerV] (18) Spr 90, p. 4.
4371. MILLER, Judy K.
"A Lesson in Bryology." [GreensboroR] (49) Wint 90-91, p. 84-85.
"The Trees of Monticello." [GreensboroR] (49) Wint 90-91, p. 86.
4372. MILLER, Karl
"Broken-Down Mission." [PoetryUSA] (5:1) Spr 90, p. 1.
4373. MILLER, Leslie A. (Leslie Adrienne)
"Crimes of Passion." [PennR] (4:2) 90, p. 3.
"Indigence." [PennR] (4:2) 90, p. 2.
"Maybe You Were Going to Slink Off into the Sunset." [SouthernPR] (30:1) Spr 90,
p. 47-48.
"On Looking at Photographs of My Grandmother's Old Boyfriends." [PraS] (64:4)
Wint 90, p. 22-23.
"The Police Tent at the County Fair." [IndR] (14:1) Wint 90, p. 53-54.
"Salutation" (for Jonathan Holden). [PennR] (4:2) 90, p. 5.
"Sleepers." [YellowS] (33) Spr 90, p. 29.
"Staying Up for Love." [PennR] (4:2) 90, p. 4.
"Tempting the Universe." [PraS] (64:4) Wint 90, p. 25-26.

"Ungodliness." [KenR] (NS 12:4) Fall 90, p. 157-158.
"Walking around My House in the Dark." [PraS] (64:4) Wint 90, p. 23-24.
"What My Father Doesn't Know." [IndR] (14:1) Wint 90, p. 51-52.
4374. MILLER, Marlene
"The Brain Sandwich." [ChironR] (9:1) Spr 90, p. 27.
4375. MILLER, Pamela
"Mr. Pittney Demonstrates How to Make a Food Hat." [FreeL] (5) Sum 90, p.
30-31.
4376. MILLER, Philip
"The End of October." [FreeL] (5) Sum 90, p. 6-7.
"I Lose Everything." [Boulevard] (5:2, #14) Fall 90, p. 21.
"Imminent Departures." [Plain] (10:2) Wint 90, p. 26.
"In the Middle of March." [Plain] (10:3) Spr 90, p. 9.
"The Long Night Moon." [CapeR] (25:2) Fall 90, p. 9.
"Motel." [NewL] (57:1) Fall 90, p. 78.
"Up Over the Hill." [SwampR] (6) Sum-Fall 90, p. 79-80.
4377. MILLER, Raeburn
"A Curse from Propertius." [Bogg] (62) 90, p. 11.
"For Zeno of Citium." [Parting] (3:2) Wint 90-91, p. 34.
"Listening to Secretaries." [CutB] (34) Sum-Fall 90, p. 61.
"Of Sound Mind." [HiramPoR] (47) Wint 90, p. 38-39.
"Remembering Po Chu-I." [ArtfulD] (18/19) 90, p. 57.
"Sources." [Parting] (3:2) Wint 90-91, p. 33.
4378. MILLER, Richard E.
"De-Exoticizing the Other." [Ploughs] (16:4) Wint 90-91, p. 4-6.
4379. MILLER, Theresa W.
"At Grandfather Mountain." [GreensboroR] (48) Sum 90, p. 57-58.
"Discovering the Continents on Your Grandmother's Antiques." [GreensboroR] (48)
Sum 90, p. 57.
4380. MILLER, Vassar
"Assertion" (reprinted from #7, 1983). [Kaleid] (20) Wint-Spr 90, p. 115.
"Exposition." [HampSPR] (Anthology 1975-1990) 90, p. 107-108.
"Fail." [HampSPR] (Anthology 1975-1990) 90, p. 108-109.
"Foiled." [HampSPR] (Anthology 1975-1990) 90, p. 107.
"I Come to You." [HampSPR] (Anthology 1975-1990) 90, p. 108.
"Mistaken." [HampSPR] (Anthology 1975-1990) 90, p. 109.
"TV Night." [HampSPR] (Anthology 1975-1990) 90, p. 107.
"Without Recourse." [HampSPR] (Anthology 1975-1990) 90, p. 109.
4381. MILLER, Walter James
"A Sequence of Sequins." [HampSPR] (Anthology 1975-1990) 90, p. 219.
4382. MILLER, William
"At the Tomb of Marie Laveau." [WestB] (26) 90, p. 72-73.
"A Circuit Preacher Recalls." [ChironR] (9:1) Spr 90, p. 22.
"Delta, Alabama, 1968." [CumbPR] (9:2) Spr 90, p. 29.
"Divorce, 1969." [CimR] (91) Ap 90, p. 51.
"Divorce, 1969." [SycamoreR] (2:2) Sum 90, p. 14-15.
"Indian Dawn." [MidwQ] (31:2) Wint 90, p. 212-213.
"Zora Hurston in New Orleans." [SouthernR] (26:4) O 90, p. 891-892.
4383. MILLER-DUGGAN, Devon
"Almost." [IndR] (13:3) Fall 90, p. 12-13.
"The Bronze Poet" (from "Trefoil in the Park," #2, tr. of Innokenty Annensky, w.
Nancy Tittler). [Gargoyle] (37/38) 90, p. 87.
"Font" (for Pippa). [IndR] (13:3) Fall 90, p. 14.
"Second Tormenting Sonnet" (tr. of Innokenty Annensky, w. Nancy Tittler).
[Gargoyle] (37/38) 90, p. 87.
"Wake" (for Delia Duggan, d. March 1983). [IndR] (13:3) Fall 90, p. 15-16.
4384. MILLIGAN, Bryce
"Drumsong." [HighP] (5:1) Spr 90, p. 50-51.
4385. MILLIGAN, Paula
"Truth Is Not a Separate Reality (I Like the Word, Raspberry)." [BellArk] (6:4)
Jl-Ag 90, p. 21.
4386. MILLIS, Christopher
"Placebo." [CharR] (16:1) Spr 90, p. 75.
4387. MILLS, David
"Sundance." [HangL] (57) 90, p. 51-52.

4388. MILLS, Jess
"Transition." [BellArk] (6:3) My-Je 90, p. 11.
4389. MILLS, Laurel
"What the Wind Wants." [KanQ] (22:1/2) Wint-Spr 90, p. 228-229.
4390. MILLS, Ralph J., Jr.
"Grey / Layered." [TarRP] (29:2) Spr 90, p. 18.
4391. MILLS, Ron
"The Atlas Lost in the Mails." [HighP] (5:3) Wint 90-91, p. 64-66.
"A Handsel." [CreamCR] (14:1) Spr 90, p. 109.
4392. MILLS, Wilmer Hastings
"An Old Indian's Language." [ChatR] (10:3) Spr 90, p. 16-17.
4393. MILNER, Mark
"Notes From the (Poet's) Nightmare English Class." [Dandel] (17:2) Fall-Wint 90,
   p. 29.
4394. MILNER, Philip
"Mikkleson's Barn" (January 24, 1988). [PottPort] (12) 90, p. 32.
4395. MILOSZ, Czeslaw
"At Yale" (tr. by the author and Robert Hass). [Antaeus] (64/65) Spr-Aut 90, p.
   91-95.
"Creating the World" (tr. by the author and Robert Hass). [NewYorker] (66:2) 26 F
   90, p. 46.
"Gathering Apricots" (tr. by the author and Robert Hass). [NewYorker] (66:37) 29
   O 90, p. 34.
"Meaning" (tr. by the author and Robert Hass). [Antaeus] (64/65) Spr-Aut 90, p. 90.
"To Robinson Jeffers" (tr. by the author and Richard Lourie). [Thrpny] (43) Fall 90,
   p. 13.
4396. MILOVA, Tatiana
"An Attempt at Statistics (Standing in Line for Vodka)" (tr. by Oleg Atbashian and
   Maureen Hurley). [PoetryUSA] (5:2) Sum 90, p. 14.
MIN, Zheng
   See ZHENG, Min
4397. MINCZESKI, John
(Anonymous poem). [FreeL] (4) 90.
"Elvis Impersonator at the World's Largest Office Party: Lacrosse, Wisconsin."
   [PoetC] (21:3) Spr 90, p. 31.
"First Grader." [PoetC] (21:3) Spr 90, p. 32-33.
4398. MINDOCK-DUEHR, Gloria
"Alone." [PoetL] (85:1) Spr 90, p. 44.
"Doppelganger vii." [PoetL] (85:1) Spr 90, p. 45.
"It Has to Be This Way." [Gypsy] (15) 90, p. 7.
4399. MINGWON, Mingwôn (Shirley Bear)
"April 2-3 1985 Aboriginal Rights Conference." [CanLit] (124/125) Spr-Sum 90, p.
   290.
4400. MINH-HA, Trinh T.
"Flying Blind." [CityLR] (4) 90, p. 144.
"For Love of Another." [CityLR] (4) 90, p. 142.
"Refugee." [CityLR] (4) 90, p. 143.
4401. MINHINNICK, Robert
"In the Watchtower." [Quarry] (39:1) Wint 90, p. 31-32.
4402. MIRABAI
"The Clouds" (tr. by Robert Bly). [HampSPR] (Anthology 1975-1990) 90, p. 264.
"Why Mira Can't Go Back to Her Old House" (tr. by Robert Bly). [HampSPR]
   (Anthology 1975-1990) 90, p. 264.
4403. MIRON, Gaston
"The Comrade" (tr. by Dennis Egan). [Vis] (32) 90, p. 50.
"In Outaouais" (tr. by Dennis Egan). [Vis] (32) 90, p. 49.
"Sorrow" (tr. by Dennis Egan). [Vis] (32) 90, p. 50.
4404. MIRRIAM-GOLDBERG, Caryn
"How to Go to Kenya." [CumbPR] (9:2) Spr 90, p. 31-32.
"In the Cab of the Pick-Up Truck." [CumbPR] (9:2) Spr 90, p. 30.
"Pass Through. Separate. Come Back Home" (to a square dance caller). [SpoonRQ]
   (15:3) Sum 90, p. 60-61.
4405. MITCHAM, Judson
"Custom." [LullwaterR] (2:1) Wint 90, p. 14.
"The First Act of Praise." [LullwaterR] (2:1) Wint 90, p. 31.

325

MITCHELL

4406. MITCHELL, Christopher
"The Actress and Her Second-Hand Saxophone." [AntigR] (83) Aut 90, p. 56.
4407. MITCHELL, Felicia
"Necropsy." [OxfordM] (6:1) Spr-Sum 90, p. 32-33.
4408. MITCHELL, John
"Footnote to a Leap of Imagination." [NorthStoneR] (9) 90, p. 17.
"The Last Devotee." [NorthStoneR] (9) 90, p. 18.
"Lying Awake." [NorthStoneR] (9) 90, p. 18.
4409. MITCHELL, Roger
"Borrowing Henry." [PraS] (64:4) Wint 90, p. 48-49.
"First Waking." [Crazy] (38) Spr 90, p. 58.
"Looking Back at the Sky." [Crazy] (38) Spr 90, p. 59.
"Return to a Small Town." [Poetry] (156:4) Jl 90, p. 201.
"Truth Lasts Only a Day, Beauty a Month." [Crazy] (38) Spr 90, p. 60.
4410. MITCHELL, Susan
"The Aviary." [Ploughs] (16:4) Wint 90-91, p. 220-223.
"Children's Ward: New York Hospital." [Ploughs] (16:4) Wint 90-91, p. 216-219.
"The City." [Crazy] (39) Wint 90, p. 7-14.
"Night Music." [Ploughs] (16:4) Wint 90-91, p. 213-215.
4411. MITCHELL-FOUST, Michelle
"Cat-Headed Bast." [BlackWR] (17:1) Fall-Wint 90, p. 53-54.
"Migraine Ghazal." [DenQ] (25:2) Fall 90, p. 34.
"On the Happiest Day of Your Life." [BlackWR] (17:1) Fall-Wint 90, p. 55.
4412. MITCHNER, Gary
"The Secret Not Worth Knowing" (Variations on Lines from Conrad). [WestHR]
    (44:3) Aut 90, p. 253-259.
4413. MITRA, Devarati
"Amnesiac River" (tr. by Paramita Banerjee and Carolyne Wright). [HawaiiR] (14:1,
    #28) Wint 89-90, p. 70.
"Flowers Born Blind" (tr. by Paramita Banerjee and Carolyne Wright). [HawaiiR]
    (14:1, #28) Wint 89-90, p. 69.
"The Green Stigma" (tr. by Paramita Banerjee and Carolyne Wright). [HawaiiR]
    (14:1, #28) Wint 89-90, p. 72.
"No, No, and No" (tr. by Paramita Banerjee and Carolyne Wright). [HawaiiR]
    (14:1, #28) Wint 89-90, p. 71.
4414. MITRE, Eduardo
"Moral de Van Gogh." [Os] (30) Spr 90, p. 19.
MITSUKO, Totsugi
    See TOTSUGI, Mitsuko
MIXCO, Miguel Huezo
    See HUEZO MIXCO, Miguel
4415. MIYA, Shûji
"Grouping Fowl" (tr. by Elizabeth Balestrieri and Machiko Okuda). [PoetryC] (11:2)
    Sum 90, p. 20.
4416. MIZER, Ray
"After the Fall." [BellArk] (6:1) Ja-F 90, p. 1.
"Balancing Act." [BellArk] (6:3) My-Je 90, p. 11.
"Circulars." [BellArk] (6:4) Jl-Ag 90, p. 10.
"Circulars." [BellArk] (6:5) S-O 90, p. 10.
"Dead End Blues." [Plain] (10:3) Spr 90, p. 11.
"Lit 007." [BellArk] (6:3) My-Je 90, p. 20.
"On the Exchange." [BellArk] (6:6) N-D 90, p. 24.
"The Threatened Habit of Perfection." [BellArk] (6:3) My-Je 90, p. 6.
"The Threatened Habit of Perfection." [BellArk] (6:4) Jl-Ag 90, p. 24.
"Time Frame." [Plain] (11:1) Fall 90, p. 8.
4417. MLADINIC, Peter
"Directions to Rutherford." [NorthStoneR] (9) 90, p. 70.
"Little Ritual." [NorthStoneR] (9) 90, p. 71.
"Sea Rations" (Danang 1967). [NorthStoneR] (9) 90, p. 71.
4418. MNOOKIN, Wendy M.
"Rescue." [Kalliope] (12:2) 90, p. 24-25.
4419. MO, Fei
"The Invisible Stone" (tr. by Dong Jiping). [Footwork] 90, p. 35.
4420. MOBILIO, Albert
"Air Show." [Talisman] (5) Fall 90, p. 77.
"Criminal Code." [CentralP] (17/18) Spr-Fall 90, p. 119.

"The Third Kind of Interior Word." [Talisman] (4) Spr 90, p. 56.
4421. MOCK, Jeff
"High Dive." [CharR] (16:2) Fall 90, p. 52-53.
4422. MOE, H. D. (H. David)
"Beginning from a Statue of Diamonds." [AnotherCM] (21) 90, p. 115.
"Coming Home." [NowestR] (28:1) 90, p. 94.
"Ideas." [PoetryUSA] (5:2) Sum 90, p. 6.
"Mt. Diablo." [ContextS] (1:1) 89, p. 23.
"Reluctant Colaboration." [ContextS] (1:1) 89, p. 22.
4423. MOEN, Irvin
"Digging In." [Amelia] (6:1, #16) 90, p. 6.
4424. MOHR, Bill
"The Offering." [OnTheBus] (2:2/3:1, #6/7) Sum-Fall 90 Wint-Spr 91, p. 149.
MOLEN, Robert vander
See VanderMOLEN, Robert
4425. MOLIERE
"The School for Husbands" (Excerpt, tr. by Richard Wilbur). [Trans] (23) Spr 90,
p. 58-61.
4426. MOLLIN, Larry
"The Midnight Bus." [OnTheBus] (2:2/3:1, #6/7) Sum-Fall 90 Wint-Spr 91, p. 150.
"No Names." [OnTheBus] (2:1, #5) Spr 90, p. 105.
4427. MOLLOY, Ruth
"Five Translations from the Tocsik." [TriQ] (79) Fall 90, p. 135-139.
4428. MOLLOY-OLUND, Barbara
"The Virgin." [RiverS] (32) [90?], p. 1-2.
4429. MONACO, Cory
"The Consensus." [WormR] (30:1, #117) 90, p. 8.
"Could It Be." [WormR] (30:1, #117) 90, p. 7.
"The Economy (1989)." [WormR] (30:1, #117) 90, p. 7.
"Karate." [WormR] (30:1, #117) 90, p. 7.
"Status Symbolism." [WormR] (30:1, #117) 90, p. 7.
"Two Black Guys." [WormR] (30:1, #117) 90, p. 8.
4430. MONAGHAN, Patricia
"Home Movies, Home Deaths." [BlackBR] (11) Spr-Sum 90, p. 20.
"Neither Inviting Nor Repelling" (From the letters of Paula Mondersohn-Becker).
[SingHM] (18) 90, p. 18-19.
4431. MONEY, Peter
"The Heart of Bees." [ChironR] (9:3) Aut 90, p. 13.
"Sitting Here Thinking About the Nature of Chaos." [ChironR] (9:3) Aut 90, p. 13.
4432. MONIZ PEREIRA, Luís
"Auto / lisérgico." [Ometeca] (1:2/2:1) 89-90, p. 23-24.
4433. MONK, Aviva
"Rationalizing to a Protagonist." [WillowR] Spr 90, p. 16.
4434. MONROE, Marilyn
"Help Help." [Pearl] (12) Fall-Wint 90, p. 24.
4435. MONROE, Mary
"Poetry -- futile." [Writer] (103:12) D 90, p. 27.
4436. MONROE, Melissa
"Germs of Mind in Plants, by R.H. Francé" (Library of Science for the Workers,
Volume 2, 1905). [Caliban] (9) 90, p. 26-28.
4437. MONSON, Connie Lee
"Sisyphus Comes to the Oxford Bar/Cafe." [BellR] (13:1, #27) Spr 90, p. 16.
4438. MONTAGUE, John
"John Quixote." [NewMyths] (1:1) 90, p. 23.
4439. MONTALE, Eugenio
"The Euphrates" (tr. by William Arrowsmith). [Trans] (23) Spr 90, p. 225.
"Floodwaters" (tr. by William Arrowsmith). [Antaeus] (64/65) Spr-Aut 90, p.
96-97.
"Hoopoe" (tr. by Antony Oldknow). [NoDaQ] (58:1) Wint 90, p. 38.
"House Overlooking the Sea" (tr. by Antony Oldknow). [NoDaQ] (58:1) Wint 90, p.
39-40.
"I Remember Your Smile " (tr. by Antony Oldknow). [NoDaQ] (58:1) Wint 90, p.
38.
"In Silence" (tr. by William Arrowsmith). [Antaeus] (64/65) Spr-Aut 90, p. 98.
"Life, I Do Not Expect" (tr. by Antony Oldknow). [NoDaQ] (58:1) Wint 90, p. 39.
"The Negative" (tr. by William Arrowsmith). [Trans] (23) Spr 90, p. 226.

"On the Beach" (tr. by William Arrowsmith). [Trans] (23) Spr 90, p. 226.
"The Overflowing Brilliance" (tr. by Antony Oldknow). [NoDaQ] (58:1) Wint 90, p.
  40.
"The Triumph of Trash" (tr. by William Arrowsmith). [Trans] (23) Spr 90, p. 227.
MONTELLANO, Ana Ortiz de
  See ORTIZ de MONTELLANO, Ana
4440. MONTOYA, Celina
  "Fat Girl." [PacificR] (8) 90, p. 36-37.
  "Grandmother." [PacificR] (8) 90, p. 38.
4441. MOODY, Rodger
  "Menses." [YellowS] (33) Spr 90, p. 34.
4442. MOODY, Shirley
  "Crawl Space." [Crucible] (26) Fall 90, p. 58-59.
4443. MOOK, Lorne R.
  "Lullaby." [PoetL] (85:3) Fall 90, p. 33-34.
4444. MOOLTEN, David
  "Inevitable." [ThRiPo] (35/36) 90, p. 73-74.
  "Knife Song." [TarRP] (30:1) Fall 90, p. 44-45.
  "Motorcycle Ward." [TarRP] (30:1) Fall 90, p. 43-44.
  "The One." [TarRP] (30:1) Fall 90, p. 45-46.
4445. MOORE, Barbara
  "Ours." [SycamoreR] (2:2) Sum 90, p. 30.
4446. MOORE, Berwyn J.
  "Divorce Dreams." [Shen] (40:1) Spr 90, p. 32-34.
  "From the Porch Swing." [Shen] (40:1) Spr 90, p. 35.
4447. MOORE, Honor
  "Friends." [BrooklynR] (7) 90, p. 48.
4448. MOORE, Jacqueline
  "Chasing the Dog Star." [GreenMR] (NS 4:1) Spr-Sum 90, p. 122.
  "Gert's Place." [GreenMR] (NS 4:1) Spr-Sum 90, p. 124.
  "In the Backwoods Who Visits Dooryards?" [GreenMR] (NS 4:1) Spr-Sum 90, p.
  123.
  "Invader." [GreenMR] (NS 4:1) Spr-Sum 90, p. 125.
  "Picasso's Snake Lady Sings the Blues." [BelPoR] (40:3) Spr 90, p. 20-21.
  "Room in Brooklyn, 1932" (after a painting by Edward Hopper). [Vis] (33) 90, p.
  5.
  "Schubert's Serenade." [SingHM] (17) 90, p. 96-97.
  "Seeing Things Fern." [BellR] (13:2, #28) Fall 90, p. 33.
4449. MOORE, Katrinka
  "Message." [BrooklynR] (7) 90, p. 8.
4450. MOORE, Lenard D.
  "James Brown" (for Quincy Troupe). [BlackALF] (24:3) Fall 90, p. 558-559.
  "Wintry Wind." [CrossCur] (9:2) Je 90, p. 107.
4451. MOORE, Margit
  "Choosing." [BellR] (13:1, #27) Spr 90, p. 41.
4452. MOORE, Mary
  "Cosmology of the Irish Mother" (For Jane and Susan). [Poetry] (156:6) S 90, p.
  331.
4453. MOORE, Mary Jane
  "Salome Surfacing." [GreenMR] (NS 4:1) Spr-Sum 90, p. 69.
4454. MOORE, Mavor
  "Sitting Bull at Standing Rock." [MalR] (91) Je 90, p. 81-82.
  "Sitting Bull's Last Love Song." [MalR] (91) Je 90, p. 83.
4455. MOORE, Melissa
  "The Angel" (tr. of Ernst Herbeck). [Gargoyle] (37/38) 90, p. 27.
  "The Dwarf" (tr. of Ernst Herbeck). [Gargoyle] (37/38) 90, p. 26.
  "I - You" (tr. of Ernst Herbeck). [Gargoyle] (37/38) 90, p. 26.
  "Life" (tr. of Ernst Herbeck). [Gargoyle] (37/38) 90, p. 27.
4456. MOORE, Miles David
  "Keats and the Anchorman." [Bogg] (62) 90, p. 5-6.
4457. MOORE, Richard
  "April Is the Cruelest Month." [Hellas] (1:1) Spr 90, p. 44.
  "Fixed Point Theorem." [NewEngR] (13:1) Fall 90, p. 77.
  "Memories of Marie" (tr. of Bertolt Brecht). [NewEngR] (13:2) Wint 90, p. 148.
  "On High." [Hudson] (43:3) Aut 90, p. 455-456.
  "The Toad." [CrossCur] (9:2) Je 90, p. 46-47.

4458. MOORE, Richard C.
"She Has No Title, But She Has a Home." [Pearl] (10) Spr 90, p. 27.
4459. MOORE, Sally
"Waiting for Poetry." [HolCrit] (27:5) D 90, p. 19.
4460. MOORE, Todd
"Sandy Fished a." [Bogg] (63) 90, p. 14.
4461. MOORE, V. A.
"To an Aids Victim at the Mayo Clinic." [Amelia] (6:1, #16) 90, p. 54.
4462. MOORHEAD, Andrea
"August Is When the Snow Falls." [Os] (31) 90, p. 15.
"Blood Casts a Light." [Os] (31) 90, p. 20.
"Day in Sulfur." [Os] (31) 90, p. 21.
"Death Brings No Light." [Os] (30) Spr 90, p. 30.
"The earth is famished and wears us out" (tr. of Marie Uguay). [AmerPoR] (19:6)
N-D 90, p. 34.
"I have slept where there is no longer room" (tr. of Marie Uguay). [AmerPoR] (19:6)
N-D 90, p. 34.
"Niagara Shines." [Os] (30) Spr 90, p. 31.
"The one I love is sleeping in an open room" (tr. of Marie Uguay). [AmerPoR]
(19:6) N-D 90, p. 34.
"One Light, One Flame." [Os] (30) Spr 90, p. 10.
"Scent of Flowers in Aachen." [Os] (30) Spr 90, p. 11.
"Sometimes when I see you walking I want to be you" (tr. of Marie Uguay).
[AmerPoR] (19:6) N-D 90, p. 34.
"Spring at Eagle Head." [Os] (31) 90, p. 25.
"Spruce in Fire." [LitR] (33:2) Wint 90, p. 239.
"This Sudden Silence" (To the memory of Marie-Claire and Bernard Beaudin, tr. of
Jean Chapdelaine Gagnon). [Rohwedder] (5) Spr 90, p. 3-6.
"Wide necked bays hidden in the territory" (tr. of Marie Uguay). [AmerPoR] (19:6)
N-D 90, p. 34.
"Wilderness." [Paint] (17:33/34) Spr-Aut 90, p. 16.
4463. MOOSE, Ruth
"For My Student Killed in Tiananmen Square" (Second Prize). [Crucible] (26) Fall
90, p. 50.
4464. MORA, Pat
"1910." [EngJ] (79:1) Ja 90, p. 25.
"Mini-*novela: Rosa y Sus Espinas*." [PraS] (64:4) Wint 90, p. 49-54.
4465. MORAGA, Cherrie
"Credo." [Zyzzyva] (6:1 #21) Spr 90, p. 121-122.
4466. MORAMARCO, Fred
"American Madness." [OnTheBus] (2:2/3:1, #6/7) Sum-Fall 90 Wint-Spr 91, p.
151.
"Telling the Pilot." [Bogg] (62) 90, p. 8.
4467. MORAN, Diana
"Es Esa la Imagen." [InterPR] (16:1) Spr 90, p. 68, 70.
"That Is the Image" (tr. by Mark Smith-Soto). [InterPR] (16:1) Spr 90, p. 69, 71.
4468. MORAN, Duncan
"A Man Leaves an Oak Chair in the Rain." [HiramPoR] (47) Wint 90, p. 40.
4469. MORAN, Kevin
"Poetry Business." [Pearl] (10) Spr 90, p. 21.
"Wild Country." [ChironR] (9:1) Spr 90, p. 25.
4470. MORAN, Ronald
"Arnold." [Northeast] (5:2) Spr 90, p. 4-5.
"Dr. Clark and Billy Banks." [Northeast] (5:2) Spr 90, p. 6-7.
4471. MORBEE, Jordaen J., Jr.
"Crosses & Rust." [Pearl] (11) Sum 90, p. 47.
4472. MOREHEAD, Maureen
"The New Stove." [AmerV] (20) Fall 90, p. 37.
4473. MOREJON, Nancy
"Black Woman" (tr. by Mark Smith-Soto). [InterPR] (16:1) Spr 90, p. 41, 43.
"Mujer Negra." [InterPR] (16:1) Spr 90, p. 40, 42.
"The Rope Held Fast" (tr. by Maria Bennett). [CrabCR] (7:1) Wint 90, p. 3.
"Unexpected" (tr. by Maria Bennett). [CrabCR] (7:1) Wint 90, p. 3.
4474. MORENO, Edward
"Tumble." [JamesWR] (7:4) Sum 90, p. 6.

4475. MORENO, Luis
"Cedar Rapids Airport" (for Paul Engle, tr. by Donald Finkel). [SenR] (20:2) Fall
90, p. 19.
"In the South" (tr. by Donald Finkel). [SenR] (20:2) Fall 90, p. 18.
"Poets and Poems" (tr. by Donald Finkel). [SenR] (20:2) Fall 90, p. 20.
"Ratio Rerum" (for José Luis y Angelines, tr. by Donald Finkel). [SenR] (20:2) Fall
90, p. 21.
4476. MORGAN, John
"Jetsam." [ColR] (NS 17:1) Spr-Sum 90, p. 68-69.
"Time Off from Bad Behavior." [ColR] (NS 17:1) Spr-Sum 90, p. 70.
4477. MORGAN, Robert
"Bread." [WilliamMR] (28) 90, p. 69.
"Classic." [WilliamMR] (28) 90, p. 22.
"Polishing the Silver." [Atlantic] (266:6) D 90, p. 94.
"Subduction." [WilliamMR] (28) 90, p. 65.
"We Are the Dream of Jefferson." [KenR] (NS 12:1) Wint 90, p. 150.
4478. MORGAN, Robert C.
"Jack Remembered." [MoodySI] (22/23) Wint 89-90, p. 16.
4479. MORGAN, Robin
"Geography Lesson." [Calyx] (13:1) Wint 90-91, p. 34-35.
4480. MORGAN, Veronica
"A Kansas Story." [SoCoast] (9) Fall 90, p. 13.
"Still Life." [ThRiPo] (35/36) 90, p. 70.
"Within the Greenhouse Effect." [ThRiPo] (35/36) 90, p. 71-72.
4481. MORGENSTERN, Christian
"Der Hecht." [InterPR] (16:2) Fall 90, p. 30.
"The Knee" (tr. by Thomas Dorsett). [InterPR] (16:2) Fall 90, p. 29.
"Das Knie." [InterPR] (16:2) Fall 90, p. 28.
"The Lovely Nasobime" (tr. by Thomas Dorsett). [InterPR] (16:2) Fall 90, p. 31.
"Möwenlied." [InterPR] (16:2) Fall 90, p. 28.
"Das Nasobem." [InterPR] (16:2) Fall 90, p. 30.
"The Pike" (tr. by Thomas Dorsett). [InterPR] (16:2) Fall 90, p. 31.
"Sea Gull Song" (tr. by Thomas Dorsett). [InterPR] (16:2) Fall 90, p. 29.
4482. MORI, Kyoko
"The Arc." [Footwork] 90, p. 27.
"Driving to Milwaukee: for Beth Krom." [Footwork] 90, p. 27.
4483. MORIARTY, Laura
"Normandie." [Talisman] (4) Spr 90, p. 73-78.
"Seven Rondeaux." [Conjunc] (15) 90, p. 216-218.
4484. MORIARTY, Michael
"Hymn X." [NewYorkQ] (42) Sum 90, p. 46-53.
"On the Road with a Special Providence." [NewYorkQ] (43) Fall 90, p. 47.
4485. MORICE, Dave
"Love Po l Rose." [KenR] (NS 12:2) Spr 90, p. 142.
4486. MORIN, Edward
"The Ballad of the Line." [Pig] (16) 90, p. 128.
"Black Marsh" (from "Black Desert," tr. of Tang Yaping, w. Dennis Ding and Dai
Fang). [Screens] (2) 90, p. 42.
"Dark Night on a Southbound Train" (tr. of Wang Xiao-Ni, w. Dennis Ding).
[Screens] (2) 90, p. 41.
"A Language" (tr. of He Xiaozhu, w. Dai Fang). [Screens] (2) 90, p. 43.
"Montages in Twilight" (tr. of Shu Ting, w. Dai Fang). [Screens] (2) 90, p. 38-40.
"Random Thoughts While Skating" (tr. of Gao Fa-Lin, w. Dennis Ding). [Screens]
(2) 90, p. 37.
4487. MORITZ, A. F.
"Christmas Decorations." [YaleR] (79:4) Sum 90 c1991, p. 674.
"The Ducks." [Hudson] (43:1) Spr 90, p. 102.
"Protracted Episode." [SouthwR] (75:1) Wint 90, p. 76.
"The Ruined Cottage." [BelPoJ] (41:2) Wint 90-91, p. 26-27.
"To His Subject Matter." [PartR] (57:1) Wint 90, p. 104-105.
4488. MORITZ, Yunna
"After the War" (tr. by William Jay Smith and Vera Dunham). [AmerPoR] (19:6)
N-D 90, p. 42.
"And Stands Reflected in the Mirror Across the Room" (tr. by William Jay Smith and
Vera Dunham). [AmerPoR] (19:6) N-D 90, p. 42.
"In April" (tr. by William Jay Smith and Vera Dunham). [AmerPoR] (19:6) N-D 90,

p. 42.
4489. MORLEY, David
"A Belfast Kiss." [Stand] (31:1) Wint 89-90, p. 4-8.
4490. MORLEY, Hilda
"Another Geography." [MidAR] (10:2) 90, p. 69-71.
"The Barter." [ParisR] (32:116) Fall 90, p. 141-143.
"Early Morning Music." [MidAR] (10:2) 90, p. 72-73.
"For Elaine de Kooning." [NewAW] (6) Spr 90, p. 3-4.
"The Last Rehearsal." [MidAR] (10:2) 90, p. 74-75.
"Parents." [NewAW] (6) Spr 90, p. 5.
"The Snare." [Pequod] (31) 90, p. 16-17.
4491. MORNER, Stan
"Post-Romantic Striptease in the Style of Richard Strauss." [PoetryUSA] (5:1) Spr
90, p. 7.
4492. MORO, Liliam
"No Tengas Nunca un Hijo." [LindLM] (9:4) O-D 90, p. 24.
4493. MOROMISATO, Doris
"A Este Cuerpo Enamorado." [Cond] (17) 90, p. 40.
"Dwelling Where the Moon Lost Its Pale Glow" (tr. by Mariana Romo-Carmona).
[Cond] (17) 90, p. 43.
"The Immaculate Story of Mnasidika, My Friend" (tr. by Mariana Romo-Carmona).
[Cond] (17) 90, p. 45.
"La Inmaculada Historia de Mnasidika, Mi Amiga." [Cond] (17) 90, p. 44.
"Morada Donde la Luna Perdió Su Palidez." [Cond] (17) 90, p. 42.
"To This Body in Love" (tr. by Mariana Romo-Carmona). [Cond] (17) 90, p. 41.
4494. MORPHEW, Melissa
"At Night." [TarRP] (30:1) Fall 90, p. 7.
"Elegy for Robert Icarius McKee." [NegC] (10:2/3) 90, p. 112.
4495. MORRIEN, Adriaan
"The Pair of Twins" (tr. by Constance Studer). [PoetryE] (30) Fall 90, p. 87.
4496. MORRILL, Donald
"Fairgrounds." [HighP] (5:3) Wint 90-91, p. 62-63.
4497. MORRIS, Bernard E.
"Don't Cross Your Heart." [SmPd] (27:3, #80) Fall 90, p. 8.
"The Earth Is Flat." [DogRR] (9:2, #18) Aut 90, p. 38.
"Liquid Questions." [SmPd] (27:3, #80) Fall 90, p. 7.
"Return to Where It Hurts." [CapeR] (25:1) Spr 90, p. 40-41.
4498. MORRIS, Carol
"Far Rockaway." [ManhatPR] (11) [89?], p. 45.
4499. MORRIS, Herbert
"The George." [DenQ] (25:1) Sum 90, p. 21-26.
4500. MORRIS, Kathryn
"Meal." [AntigR] (83) Aut 90, p. 46.
"Watching." [AntigR] (83) Aut 90, p. 45.
4501. MORRIS, Mike
"Saturday Afternoon." [Bogg] (63) 90, p. 29.
4502. MORRIS, Paul
"Lake Shore" (tr. of Johannes Bobrowski). [BlueBldgs] (12) 90, p. 13.
4503. MORRIS, Peter
"The God of Joy." [ChironR] (9:3) Aut 90, p. 9.
"A Richer Man." [ChironR] (9:3) Aut 90, p. 9.
"The Twin Cities." [ChironR] (9:3) Aut 90, p. 9.
"Twitchin' the Night Away." [ChironR] (9:3) Aut 90, p. 9.
"Yen Up, Dollar Down." [ChironR] (9:3) Aut 90, p. 9.
4504. MORRIS, Sawnie
"How the Woman Becomes the Bear." [SingHM] (18) 90, p. 47-49.
4505. MORRISON, Blake
"Pass It On." [Quarry] (39:1) Wint 90, p. 33.
4506. MORRISON, Carol
"Stag." [WillowR] Spr 90, p. 40.
4507. MORRISON, R. H.,
"The Blue Rose." [Poem] (63) My 90, p. 39.
"The Signet Ring." [Poem] (63) My 90, p. 38.
4508. MORRISSEY, Kim
"Photograph." [Grain] (18:1) Spr 90, p. 85-86.
"These are the photos." [Grain] (18:1) Spr 90, p. 83-84.

4509. MORRISSEY, Stephen
"The Things She Left." [PoetryC] (11:4) Wint 90, p. 27.
4510. MORRO, Henry J.
"Marilyn Monroe Is Dead." [OnTheBus] (2:2/3:1, #6/7) Sum-Fall 90 Wint-Spr 91,
p. 152-153.
"Marilyn Monroe Is Dead." [Pearl] (12) Fall-Wint 90, p. 48.
4511. MORSE, Carl
"Fairy Fuck-In, or, A Call to the States." [JamesWR] (8:1) Fall 90, p. 9.
4512. MORTON, Colin
"Royal Garden Hotel." [CanLit] (126) Aut 90, p. 115.
4513. MORTUS, Cindy
"Bones Dry White." [SpoonRQ] (15:3) Sum 90, p. 51.
"Jack, Setting Places." [SpoonRQ] (15:3) Sum 90, p. 50.
"Open House at the Orphanage." [BlackBR] (11) Spr-Sum 90, p. 26.
4514. MOSER, Johann
"The Bandusian Fountain" (Odes, III, XIII, tr. of Horace). [Hellas] (1:1) Spr 90, p.
90.
"Galileo: A Letter to His Daughter" (Arcetri: March, 1634). [Hellas] (1:2) Fall 90, p.
250-253.
"Roman Fountain" (Borghese, tr. of Rainer Maria Rilke). [Hellas] (1:1) Spr 90, p.
96.
"Terminus: Concedo Nulli" (Device of Erasmus Roterodamus). [Hellas] (1:1) Spr
90, p. 84-86.
4515. MOSES, Daniel (Daniel David)
"Blue Moon." [CanLit] (124/125) Spr-Sum 90, p. 228.
"Breakdown Moon." [CanLit] (124/125) Spr-Sum 90, p. 227-228.
"Inukshuk." [CanLit] (124/125) Spr-Sum 90, p. 241-242.
"The Letter." [PoetryC] (11:1) Spr 90, p. 7.
"Song on Starling Street." [CanLit] (124/125) Spr-Sum 90, p. 226-227.
"Your Parent's Hands." [PoetryC] (11:1) Spr 90, p. 7.
4516. MOSI, Nilda
"In Search of a Poem." [Footwork] 90, p. 91.
4517. MOSIER, Frank
"Will You Miss Me?" (reprinted from #3, 1980). [Kaleid] (20) Wint-Spr 90, p. 108.
4518. MOSLEY, Walter
"Dinner at the End of Time." [Sequoia] (33:2) Wint 90, p. 67.
4519. MOSS, Howard
"Three Dances from the Daily News." [HampSPR] (Anthology 1975-1990) 90, p.
60-61.
4520. MOSS, Stanley
"Lines for a Stammering Turkish Poet." [Poetry] (155:4) Ja 90, p. 257-258.
"New Moon." [Poetry] (157:2) N 90, p. 71.
4521. MOSS, Thylias
"An Anointing." [Epoch] (39:3) 90, p. 296-297.
"Baking the Eucharist" (From *At Redbones*). [AmerPoR] (19:4) Jl-Ag 90, p. 18.
"Birmingham Brown's Turn." [Callaloo] (13:4) Fall 90, p. 731-734.
"Congregations" (for everbody that wanted me to get religion -- I got something
better). [Callaloo] (13:4) Fall 90, p. 727-730.
"Dwarf Tossing." [Field] (42) Spr 90, p. 64.
"Lunchcounter Freedom." [Gargoyle] (37/38) 90, p. 51.
"Poem for My Mothers and Other Makers of Asafetida." [Field] (42) Spr 90, p.
62-63.
"Preferable Truth." [Callaloo] (13:4) Fall 90, p. 735-736.
"Tornadoes." [GrahamHR] (13) Spr 90, p. 43-44.
4522. MOTION, Andrew
"Tamworth." [Quarry] (39:1) Wint 90, p. 34-37.
4523. MOTT, Elaine
"The One Who Disappeared." [GreenMR] (NS 3:2) Fall-Wint 89-90, p. 99.
4524. MOTT, Michael
"Harpsichord in the Rain." [HampSPR] (Anthology 1975-1990) 90, p. 95.
"Wisteria." [HampSPR] (Anthology 1975-1990) 90, p. 95.
4525. MOULDS, Julie
"Billy Martin Speaks to His Team" (Final Game of the World Series. For Rodney
Torreson. With John Rybicki). [NewYorkQ] (41) Spr 90, p. 101.
4526. MOUNTAIN, Marlene
"Haibun: Mad Earths in My Room." [PoetryC] (11:2) Sum 90, p. 12-13.

4527. MOURÉ, Erin
  "6 Notes for a Mazurka." [WestCL] (24:2) Fall 90, p. 61-64.
  "The Cooking." [WestCL] (24:2) Fall 90, p. 58-60.
  "Heat Wave." [PoetryC] (11:2) Sum 90, p. 8.
  "Seams." [MassR] (31:1/2) Spr-Sum 90, p. 48-53.
  "Seems." [MassR] (31:1/2) Spr-Sum 90, p. 54-60.
  "Song of a Murmur." [PoetryC] (11:2) Sum 90, p. 8.
4528. MUEGGE, Richard
  "A Plea for Proper Moderation." [EngJ] (79:4) Ap 90, p. 109.
4529. MUELLER, Jack
  "When Women Ruled." [PoetryUSA] (5:3) Fall 90, p. 4.
4530. MUELLER, John
  "Almost But Not Quite an Academic Breakthrough." [PoetryUSA] (5:2) Sum 90, p.
    5.
  "Humble." [PoetryUSA] (5:3) Fall 90, p. 13.
4531. MUELLER, Lisel
  "Godspeed" (For Felix Pollak). [Pembroke] (22) 90, p. 21.
  "Magnolia." [Hudson] (43:2) Sum 90, p. 336.
  "Missing the Dead." [Hudson] (43:2) Sum 90, p. 335.
4532. MUELLER, Paul Kennedy
  "Reflections at Honneken Castle." [HawaiiR] (14:1, #28) Wint 89-90, p. 46.
  "Tea with Terrorists." [SouthernHR] (24:1) Wint 90, p. 14.
4533. MUELLER-KLAVINA, Ilze
  "Poem: Spring's breath fills the windows" (tr. of Anna Rancane). [Nimrod] (33:2)
    Spr-Sum 90, p. 72.
  "Poem: You are a spray of lilac" (tr. of Mara Zalite). [Nimrod] (33:2) Spr-Sum 90,
    p. 71.
4534. MUHAMMAD, Zakariyya
  "The Cafe Mistress" (tr. by Lena Jayyusi and Jeremy Reed). [Screens] (2) 90, p. 20.
  "Emigration" (tr. by Lena Jayyusi and Jeremy Reed). [PaperAir] (4:3) 90, p. 61.
  "Everything" (tr. by Lena Jayyusi and Jeremy Reed). [PaperAir] (4:3) 90, p. 60.
  "My Things" (tr. by Lena Jayyusi and Jeremy Reed). [PaperAir] (4:3) 90, p. 60.
  "A Tavern" (tr. by Lena Jayyusi and Jeremy Reed). [PaperAir] (4:3) 90, p. 60.
4535. MUKADI, Matala
  "Manzambi" (tr. by Julia Older). [Vis] (32) 90, p. 16-18.
4536. MUKHOPADHYAY, Vijaya
  "Henna" (tr. by Sunil B. Ray and Carolyne Wright with the author). [GrandS] (9:3)
    Spr 90, p. 200.
  "Irrelevant" (tr. by Sunil B. Ray and Carolyne Wright with the author). [GrandS]
    (9:3) Spr 90, p. 202.
  "Which Floor?" (tr. by Sunil B. Ray and Carolyne Wright with the author).
    [GrandS] (9:3) Spr 90, p. 201.
  "The Wrong Place" (tr. by Sunil B. Ray and Carolyne Wright with the author).
    [GrandS] (9:3) Spr 90, p. 199.
4537. MULDOON, Paul
  "The Briefcase" (for Seamus Heaney). [Antaeus] (64/65) Spr-Aut 90, p. 99.
  "Cauliflowers." [Antaeus] (64/65) Spr-Aut 90, p. 100-101.
  "Nude" (tr. of Nuala Ní Dhómhnaill). [Antaeus] (64/65) Spr-Aut 90, p. 17-18.
4538. MULHERN, Maureen
  "In the Outskirts." [IndR] (14:1) Wint 90, p. 67.
  "Narcissus." [IndR] (14:1) Wint 90, p. 65.
  "What the Dead Wear." [IndR] (14:1) Wint 90, p. 66.
4539. MULLEN, Harryette
  "Trimmings" (Selections). [Epoch] (39:1/2) 90, p. 71-88.
4540. MULLEN, Laura
  "Aubade." [Notus] (5:1) Spr 90, p. 78.
  "That Story." [Thrpny] (42) Sum 90, p. 32.
4541. MULLEN, Richard
  "K Mart at the Opera." [NewYorkQ] (42) Sum 90, p. 83-84.
4542. MULLER, Erik
  "Cafe." [DogRR] (9:2, #18) Aut 90, p. 34.
4543. MULLIGAN, J. B.
  "Biko." [SlipS] (10) 90, p. 45.
  "Marilyn Monroe." [Pearl] (12) Fall-Wint 90, p. 49.
4544. MULRANE, Scott
  "Making a Living in Laugharne." [DogRR] (9:1, #17) Spr 90, p. 55.

4545. MULROONEY, C.
  "Boeremusiek." [OnTheBus] (2:1, #5) Spr 90, p. 106.
  "Briskly." [OnTheBus] (2:1, #5) Spr 90, p. 106.
  "Moon-Viewing." [OnTheBus] (2:1, #5) Spr 90, p. 106.
4546. MUNDEN, Susan
  "She Makes a Song for the Delta Girl She Was." [GreensboroR] (48) Sum 90, p. 3.
4547. MUNRO, Donna
  "Siren." [PassN] (11:2) Wint 90, p. 14.
MUNTANER, Frances Negrón
  See NEGRON-MUNTANER, Frances
4548. MURAI, Karen
  "Dictionary." [ParisR] (32:114) Spr 90, p. 188.
  "Postcard from Jupiter, Tennessee." [ParisR] (32:114) Spr 90, p. 190.
  "The Unnecessary." [ParisR] (32:114) Spr 90, p. 189.
4549. MURATORI, Fred
  "Hail on Phobos." [NowestR] (28:2) 90, p. 77.
4550. MURAWSKI, Elisabeth
  "At the Sedona Cafe." [Shen] (40:3) Fall 90, p. 20.
  "Malleable." [LitR] (33:3) Spr 90, p. 345.
  "This Bitter Magic." [PacificR] (8) 90, p. 77.
  "Widower." [Spirit] (10:2) 90, p. 126.
MURAWSKI, Elizabeth
  See MURAWSKI, Elisabeth
4551. MURAYAMA, Kaneko
  "When the camellia blossoms" (tr. by Janet Lewis). [SouthernR] (26:1) Ja 90, p.
      204.
4552. MURDOCK, Rudy
  "Oppression #1." [PoetryUSA] (5:1) Spr 90, p. 15.
4553. MURPHY, Brian
  "The Fox." [Comm] (117:14) 10 Ag 90, p. 455.
4554. MURPHY, Carol
  "Another Saint Lucy." [DenQ] (25:2) Fall 90, p. 35-36.
  "Bite the Hand." [AmerPoR] (19:6) N-D 90, p. 55.
  "Sometimes Beautiful." [AmerPoR] (19:6) N-D 90, p. 55.
4555. MURPHY, Jason
  "Song of Love." [Bogg] (62) 90, p. 51.
4556. MURPHY, Kay
  "Compassion at the World's Cafe." [Outbr] (21) 90, p. 70.
  "County Fairs." [SpoonRQ] (15:1) Wint 90, p. 9.
  "The Day My Grandmother Dies." [Outbr] (21) 90, p. 71-72.
  "The News." [MinnR] (NS 34/35) Spr-Fall 90, p. 21.
  "Should I Get Involved?" (after Ana Mendieta, #4: "Silueta"). [MinnR] (NS 34/35)
      Spr-Fall 90, p. 21-22.
  "The Widows of John F." [SpoonRQ] (15:1) Wint 90, p. 7-8.
4557. MURPHY, Mary-Lynn
  "My Daughter Swimming." [Grain] (18:2) Sum 90, p. 21.
4558. MURPHY, Peter E.
  "The Judgment." [JINJPo] (12:2) Aut 90, p. 22.
  "The Stubborn Child" (after Grimm). [BelPoJ] (41:2) Wint 90-91, p. 1.
4559. MURPHY, Sheila E.
  "I am afraid the face of judgment." [ContextS] (1:1) 89, p. 20.
  "Lucid Temporary Hatches." [Caliban] (9) 90, p. 66.
  "A Monotone." [Talisman] (5) Fall 90, p. 80.
4560. MURRAY, Donald M.
  "At 64, Talking Without Words." [Poetry] (155:6) Mr 90, p. 407.
  "Morning Parade." [RiverC] (10:2) Spr 90, p. 79.
4561. MURRAY, Gloria G.
  "Funeral." [Writer] (103:6) Je 90, p. 24-25.
4562. MURRAY, Les (Les A.)
  "Antarctica." [YaleR] (79:2) Wint 90, p. 286-287.
  "Ariel." [YaleR] (79:2) Wint 90, p. 286.
  "The Gaelic Long Tunes." [Verse] (7:2) Sum 90, p. 72.
  "High River" (for the marriage of Brian and Mary Davis). [GrandS] (9:4, #36) 90,
      p. 43-50.
  "Presence: Translations from the Natural World." [ParisR] (32:117) Wint 90, p.
      208-223.

4563. MURRAY, Virginia
"Jimson weed footpath." [NegC] (10:2/3) 90, p. 118.
4564. MURREY, Matthew
"Cacao, Chicago." [KanQ] (22:3) Sum 90, p. 148.
"Classical Guitar." [FloridaR] (17:1) Spr-Sum 90, p. 53.
"My Father's Gift." [FloridaR] (17:1) Spr-Sum 90, p. 51.
"Remembering Fire." [FloridaR] (17:1) Spr-Sum 90, p. 52.
"Texas Transformation." [KanQ] (22:3) Sum 90, p. 150.
"Under the House, Under the Sun." [KanQ] (22:3) Sum 90, p. 148.
4565. MURRY, Calvin
"Indian Summer in the Ghetto of Reckless Abandon." [PoetryUSA] (5:2) Sum 90,
     p. 10.
"Mid-Life Crisis." [PoetryUSA] (5:2) Sum 90, p. 10.
"Moribund." [PoetryUSA] (5:3) Fall 90, p. 23.
MUSAN, Paek
     See PAEK, Musan
4566. MUSIAL, Grzegorz
"Cavafy's Motif" (tr. by Richard Chetwynd, w. the author). [PoetryE] (29) Spr 90,
     p. 22.
"The Exile" (tr. by Richard Chetwynd, w. the author). [PoetryE] (29) Spr 90, p. 21.
"Poem for Allen Ginsberg" (tr. by Richard Chetwynd). [ArtfulD] (18/19) 90, p.
     98-99.
"Study of a Key" (tr. of Miron Bialoszewski, w. Daniel Weissbort). [PoetryE] (29)
     Spr 90, p. 23.
4567. MUSKAT, Timothy
"First Snow." [KanQ] (22:1/2) Wint-Spr 90, p. 230.
"Susquehanna." [KanQ] (22:1/2) Wint-Spr 90, p. 221.
4568. MUSKE, Carol
"Field Trip." [YaleR] (79:3) Spr 90, p. 441-443.
4569. MUSO, Soseki
"The Pure Sound Pavilion of the Riverside Temple" (tr. by W. S. Merwin and Soiku
     Shigematsu). [Hudson] (43:2) Sum 90, p. 339.
4570. MUTIS, Alvaro
"The Map" (tr. by Alastair Reid). [NewYorker] (65:51) 5 F 90, p. 42.
4571. MUTTON, Paul
"Thirty-Five Dollars." [Gypsy] (15) 90, p. 17.
4572. MYCUE, Edward
"Reward, Boon, Clean, Safe, Easy, Botanic: Sex." [OnTheBus] (2:1, #5) Spr 90, p.
     107.
"See More." [Caliban] (9) 90, p. 117-118.
4573. MYERS, Douglas
"Claimstaking in White Sulfur Springs." [SoDakR] (28:3) Aut 90, p. 134.
"Music My Grandfather Gave Me." [Shen] (40:1) Spr 90, p. 20-21.
4574. MYERS, George, Jr.
"Birds Wild at Night." [Journal] (13:2) Fall-Wint 89-90, p. 59.
4575. MYERS, Jack
"Attack of the Killer Power Tools." [WillowS] (25) Wint 90, p. 30-31.
"The Bambutti: Pygmies of the Congo." [KenR] (NS 12:2) Spr 90, p. 143.
"Blockbuster." [NewMyths] (1:1) 90, p. 134.
"How?" [KenR] (NS 12:3) Sum 90, p. 91.
"The Man of Steel." [NewMyths] (1:1) 90, p. 132-133.
4576. MYERS, Joan Rohr
"Autumn Questions." [ChrC] (107:32) 7 N 90, p. 1028.
4577. MYLES, Eileen
"Things to Do When Your Friend Dies of AIDS." [BrooklynR] (7) 90, p. 38.
4578. MYLES, Naomi
"Dream Mountain." [Pembroke] (22) 90, p. 85.
"Legacy." [Pembroke] (22) 90, p. 86.
"The Mystery of Picasso." [Pembroke] (22) 90, p. 87.
MYOUNG-HO, Sym
     See SYM, Myoung-ho
4579. MYRSIADES, Kostas
"Immobilizing the Boundless" (tr. of Yannis Ritsos). [NewOR] (17:3) Fall 90, p.
     18.
"Morning in Salerno, IV" (tr. of Yannis Ritsos). [NewOR] (17:3) Fall 90, p. 22.
"Sluggishly" (tr. of Yannis Ritsos). [TarRP] (29:2) Spr 90, p. 48.

4580. MYSLIWCZYK, Damian M.
"In Tribute to a Contemporary Poet, Friends." [Writer] (103:6) Je 90, p. 25.
4581. NAAS, Ron
"A Barn Dance in the Level Country." [BellArk] (6:3) My-Je 90, p. 10.
"The Deaf Backpackers." [BellArk] (6:3) My-Je 90, p. 21.
4582. NADEL, Alan
"All Earth Makes Allowance for the Plausible" (for Robert Pinsky). [SycamoreR] (2:2) Sum 90, p. 31-32.
4583. NAGASE, Isamu
"The sun today" (tr. by Janet Lewis). [SouthernR] (26:1) Ja 90, p. 205.
4584. NAGLE, Alice Connelly
"Horizon." [Vis] (33) 90, p. 38.
4585. NAGLER, Robert
"And Counting." [Writ] (22) 90 c1991, p. 32.
"Casserole." [Writ] (22) 90 c1991, p. 34.
"Cold." [Writ] (22) 90 c1991, p. 27.
"Fiori" (Ristorante La Rampa, Rome). [Writ] (22) 90 c1991, p. 26.
"Flying, Her Hand Tries to Escape Her Body." [Writ] (22) 90 c1991, p. 24.
"Girl Urinating" (Variation on a theme by R. Cronshey). [Writ] (22) 90 c1991, p. 25.
"Man Playing Kickball with Demons" (a stone print by Pitseolak, an Eskimo). [ArtfulD] (18/19) 90, p. 73.
"Morocco." [BlackBR] (12) Fall-Wint 90, p. 6.
"My Mother Hints at Rape over the Aperitif" (Grand Cafe, St. Mark's Square, Venice. For EN). [Writ] (22) 90 c1991, p. 35.
"On a Mochica Ceramic, ca. 1200 A.D." [Writ] (22) 90 c1991, p. 28.
"Open and Shut." [BlackBR] (12) Fall-Wint 90, p. 36.
"Remedy." [Writ] (22) 90 c1991, p. 31.
"See, Saw, Blind." [Writ] (22) 90 c1991, p. 33.
"Wall." [Writ] (22) 90 c1991, p. 29-30.
4586. NAGY, Agnes Nemes
"A Tárgy Fölött." [MidAR] (10:1) 90, p. 46.
"Above the Things" (tr. by Mária Kurdi and Len Roberts). [MidAR] (10:1) 90, p. 47.
"Amikor." [MidAR] (10:1) 90, p. 44.
"Defend It" (tr. by Bruce Berlind). [PoetryE] (29) Spr 90, p. 62.
"The Night of Ekhnaton" (tr. by Len Roberts and Mária Kurdi). [AmerPoR] (19:5) S-O 90, p. 23-24.
"To Freedom" (tr. by Bruce Berlind). [PoetryE] (29) Spr 90, p. 63-64.
"Trees" (tr. by Bruce Berlind). [PoetryE] (29) Spr 90, p. 61.
"When" (tr. by Len Roberts and Claudia Zimmerman). [MidAR] (10:1) 90, p. 45.
4587. NAGY, Mariann
"They Come to Me" (tr. of Sándor Kányádi, w. Len Roberts). [MidAR] (10:1) 90, p. 61, 63.
"Towards Noah's Ark" (on the back of the Imre Nagy painting, tr. of Sándor Kányádi, w. Len Roberts). [PoetryE] (30) Fall 90, p. 25.
4588. NAIDEN, James
"Cataclysmic Nippers" (with Michael Tjepkes and Sigrid Bergie). [NorthStoneR] (9) 90, p. 80-81.
4589. NAJLIS, Michele
"Al Comienzo." [InterPR] (16:1) Spr 90, p. 66.
"In the Beginning" (tr. by Mark Smith-Soto). [InterPR] (16:1) Spr 90, p. 67.
4590. NAKAMURA, Charles
"The rains have lowered." [Amelia] (6:1, #16) 90, p. 102.
4591. NAKATOMI, Lady (Early eighth century)
"Pearl Diver" (tr. by Graeme Wilson). [LitR] (33:2) Wint 90, p. 194.
4592. NAMBISAN, Vijay
"Drums at Night." [Arc] (25) Aut 90, p. 62.
4593. NAMEROFF, Rochelle
"Yellow Dog Blues." [MidAR] (10:1) 90, p. 33-34.
4594. NAPIER, Alan
"Breaking." [MidAR] (10:2) 90, p. 9-11.
"Cesare Pavese." [GreenMR] (NS 4:1) Spr-Sum 90, p. 89.
"Farming the Pillow." [NegC] (10:1) 90, p. 77.
"First Cut." [SouthernPR] (30:1) Spr 90, p. 44-46.
"Picasso's-Goat." [BlueBldgs] (12) 90, p. 20.

"Plotting the Stillness." [Spirit] (10:2) 90, p. 44.
"Primal Now." [Pig] (16) 90, p. 60.
4595. NAPORA, Joe
"The Man Learns" (honorable mention, Black Bear Poetry Competition). [BlackBR]
(11) Spr-Sum 90, p. 44-46.
4596. NARBONNE, Andrew
"Nine Days at Anchor" (Leaving the Settlement). [PottPort] (11) 89, p. 50.
4597. NASDOR, Marc
"Words Resound in My Ears to This Day" (tr. of Ina Bliznetsova, w. the author).
[LitR] (33:4) Sum 90, p. 485.
4598. NASH, Ann Walker
"The Barn." [PoetL] (85:2) Sum 90, p. 34.
"Tenth Birthday." [PoetL] (85:2) Sum 90, p. 35.
4599. NASH, Doug
"Hobo Mystic." [PoetryUSA] (5:3) Fall 90, p. 25.
4600. NASH, Roger
"1942." [AntigR] (83) Aut 90, p. 63.
"The Appliances Delivery-Man." [Event] (19:1) Spr 90, p. 84.
"Maxims for Marriages." [AntigR] (81/82) Spr-Sum 90, p. 10.
"Old Man in an Armchair." [MalR] (90) Spr 90, p. 66-67.
4601. NASH, Susan Smith
"156. Portia, what passion, what blind pain" (tr. of Sor Juana Inés de la Cruz).
[WashR] (16:2) Ag-S 90, p. 21.
"164. This evening, my dear, when I was speaking to you" (tr. of Sor Juana Inés de
la Cruz). [WashR] (16:2) Ag-S 90, p. 21.
"Divine rose, you exist in a genteel culture" (tr. of Sor Juana Inés de la Cruz).
[WashR] (16:2) Ag-S 90, p. 20.
"What you see is a painted fraud" (tr. of Sor Juana Inés de la Cruz). [WashR] (16:2)
Ag-S 90, p. 20.
4602. NASH, Valery
"The Evening Hemlocks." [Field] (43) Fall 90, p. 91.
"Light-Struck." [Field] (43) Fall 90, p. 89-90.
4603. NASON, Jim
"Andrew." [JamesWR] (7:4) Sum 90, p. 1.
4604. NATHAN, Leonard
"Hearing Things." [Sequoia] (33:2) Wint 90, p. 20.
"January." [Shen] (40:1) Spr 90, p. 21.
"The Moral of Snow." [Salm] (85/86) Wint-Spr 90, p. 144.
4605. NATHAN, Norman
"Bamboo Shoots Line the Dirt Road." [ChamLR] (4:1, #7) Fall 90, p. 82.
"Love Song in Black." [Poem] (64) N 90, p. 36.
"The Rising Sun." [Poem] (64) N 90, p. 35.
"Slashes of Black Ink." [ChamLR] (4:1, #7) Fall 90, p. 83.
"Tea" (haiku). [Hellas] (1:2) Fall 90, p. 215.
"To Fulke Greville." [KanQ] (22:1/2) Wint-Spr 90, p. 212.
4606. NATHANIEL, Isabel
"Elegy at Mustang Island." [Nat] (250:19) 14 My 90, p. 677.
"Galveston." [Nat] (250:22) 4 Je 90, p. 776.
"Sick at the Gulf." [Poetry] (156:5) Ag 90, p. 286.
4607. NATT, Gregory
"She's Fifteen, She's Got a Great Right Hand" (for K.D.). [Vis] (33) 90, p. 12-13.
4608. NATT, Rochelle
"Marilyn Today." [Pearl] (12) Fall-Wint 90, p. 57.
4609. NAUGHTON, James
"And Today in That Wine Bar on the Corner" (tr. of Silva Fischerová). [Field] (42)
Spr 90, p. 38.
"The Merriest Country on Earth" (tr. of Silva Fischerová). [Field] (42) Spr 90, p.
36-37.
"Without Men" (tr. of Silva Fischerová). [Field] (42) Spr 90, p. 35.
4610. NAUGHTON, John
"The Snow" (tr. of Yves Bonnefoy). [GrahamHR] (13) Spr 90, p. 106.
"The Swiftness of the Clouds" (tr. of Yves Bonnefoy). [GrahamHR] (13) Spr 90, p.
107.
"The Well, the Brambles" (tr. of Yves Bonnefoy). [GrahamHR] (13) Spr 90, p.
105.

337

4611. NAUGLE, Chris
   "My James Dean Poster." [RagMag] (8:1) 90, p. 51.
4612. NAVA, Thelma
   "Mujer Inconveniente." [InterPR] (16:1) Spr 90, p. 64.
   "Unsuitable Woman" (tr. by Mark Smith-Soto). [InterPR] (16:1) Spr 90, p. 65.
4613. NAVARRA, Ignazio
   "An Ancient Diary" (from the Sicilian Antigruppo, tr. by Nat Scammacca and Stanley
      H. Barkan). [Footwork] 90, p. 104.
   "Sichelè" (Selection: 13, in Italian and English). [Footwork] 90, p. 63.
   "Untitled #2: enchantments elegies labyrinths mechanical lights" (tr. by Nat
      Scammacca). [Footwork] 90, p. 105.
4614. NAVARRE, Martinez Porras
   "The Desolated World." [NegC] (10:2/3) 90, p. 68.
4615. NAZARETH, H. O.
   "Lobo and Sylvie" (from "Lobo"). [LitR] (34:1) Fall 90, p. 121-123.
   "One Pair of Eyes" (from "Lobo"). [LitR] (34:1) Fall 90, p. 120-121.
4616. NDEGWA, S. Njuguna
   "Celebration." [ArtfulD] (18/19) 90, p. 135.
   "The Disappeared." [ArtfulD] (18/19) 90, p. 134.
   "Grandmother." [ArtfulD] (18/19) 90, p. 133.
4617. NECAKOV, Lilian
   "Riding the Camel." [WestCL] (24:3) Wint 90, p. 63-64.
   "What's it going to be?" [WestCL] (24:3) Wint 90, p. 63.
4618. NEELD, Judith
   "In the Photograph of a Restored Barn." [TarRP] (29:2) Spr 90, p. 13.
4619. NEELON, Ann
   "Chronicle of the Indies" (tr. of José Emilio Pacheco). [PoetryE] (30) Fall 90, p. 21.
   "Grandfathers" (tr. of Oscar Acosta). [PoetryE] (30) Fall 90, p. 29.
   "If I Could Only Haul in His Heart" (for African guitar, tr. of Léopold Sédar
      Senghor). [PaintedB] (40/41) 90, p. 73.
   "Spring Song" (For a Black Girl with a Pink Heel, tr. of Léopold Sédar Senghor).
      [PaintedB] (40/41) 90, p. 81-85.
   "Teddungal" (Ode to the Accompaniment of African Harp, tr. of Léopold Sédar
      Senghor). [PaintedB] (40/41) 90, p. 77, 79.
   "Tonight Dear" (for African guitar, tr. of Léopold Sédar Senghor). [PaintedB]
      (40/41) 90, p. 75.
4620. NEGRI, Sharon
   "A '57 Chevy in 1969." [RagMag] (8:1) 90, p. 63.
   "Crazy Mary in the Cemetery." [RagMag] (8:1) 90, p. 62.
   "The Kick from Inside." [SlipS] (10) 90, p. 94-95.
4621. NEGRON-MUNTANER, Frances
   "The Body Speaks" (tr. by Kurt Fendeisen and the author). [Cond] (17) 90, p. 65,
      67.
   "Espera" (a l.c.). [SinW] (42) Wint 90-91, p. j83-84.
   "Estampa Puertorriqueña en Filadelfia." [Cond] (17) 90, p. 58.
   "Fixation" (tr. by Kurt Feindeisen). [PaintedB] (40/41) 90, p. 71.
   "Hábito." [PaintedB] (40/41) 90, p. 70.
   "Habla Cuerpo." [Cond] (17) 90, p. 64, 66.
   "Penélope" (in Spanish). [Cond] (17) 90, p. 62.
   "Penelope" (tr. by Kurt Fendeisen). [Cond] (17) 90, p. 63.
   "Puertorican Sketch in Philadelphia" (tr. by the author). [Cond] (17) 90, p. 59.
   "Sorpresa." [Cond] (17) 90, p. 60.
   "Surprise" (tr. by the author). [Cond] (17) 90, p. 61.
   "The Wait" (to l.c.). [SinW] (42) Wint 90-91, p. 82-83.
4622. NEGRONI, Maria
   "Angel in the House" (tr. by Anne Twitty). [LitR] (33:4) Sum 90, p. 437.
   "Badlands" (tr. by Anne Twitty). [LitR] (33:4) Sum 90, p. 436.
   "Goodbyes" (tr. by Anne Twitty). [LitR] (33:4) Sum 90, p. 436.
   "Self-less" (tr. by Anne Twitty). [LitR] (33:4) Sum 90, p. 437.
4623. NEHEMIAH, Marcia
   "Night on Heart Lake." [Blueline] (11:1/2) 90, p. 24.
4624. NEJA, Michael William
   "It's a Battle Li Po." [NewYorkQ] (42) Sum 90, p. 78.
NEJAT, Murat Nemet
   See NEMET-NEJAT, Murat

4625. NEKOLA, Charlotte
"Yes, We're Open." [Footwork] 90, p. 91.
4626. NEKRASOV, Vsevolod Nikolaevich
"And I on the Cosmic" (tr. by Gerald J. Janecek). [Nimrod] (33:2) Spr-Sum 90, p. 1.
4627. NEKRASOVA, Ksenia
"Day" (tr. by Diana L. Burgin). [Boulevard] (4:3/5:1, #12/13) Spr 90, p. 110-111.
"The February Snow Lies at My Feet" (tr. by Diana L. Burgin). [Boulevard] (4:3/5:1, #12/13) Spr 90, p. 107.
"From Childhood" (tr. by Diana L. Burgin). [Boulevard] (4:3/5:1, #12/13) Spr 90, p. 105.
"How Am I to Write My Poems?" (tr. by Diana L. Burgin). [Boulevard] (4:3/5:1, #12/13) Spr 90, p. 106.
"I Know" (tr. by Diana L. Burgin). [Boulevard] (4:3/5:1, #12/13) Spr 90, p. 109.
"My Room" (tr. by Diana L. Burgin). [Boulevard] (4:3/5:1, #12/13) Spr 90, p. 108.
4628. NELLIGAN, Emile
"Violin's Farewell" (tr. by Hubert G. Mayes). [AntigR] (81/82) Spr-Sum 90, p. 22.
"Violon d'Adieu." [AntigR] (81/82) Spr-Sum 90, p. 22-23.
4629. NELMS, Sheryl L.
"He Said Not a Word." [ChironR] (9:4) Wint 90, p. 13.
"Hearts and Doilies." [ChironR] (9:4) Wint 90, p. 13.
"I'll Fly Away." [ChironR] (9:4) Wint 90, p. 13.
"Looking at Your Picture." [ChironR] (9:4) Wint 90, p. 13.
"September in South Dakota." [Kaleid] (21) Sum-Fall 90, p. 33.
4630. NELSON, Eric
"Buttoned Down." [Shen] (40:4) Wint 90, p. 69.
"A Civil Tongue." [Shen] (40:4) Wint 90, p. 68.
"The Interpretation of Waking Life." [MidAR] (10:2) 90, p. 12-14.
"Lovely Until the End." [LaurelR] (24:1) Wint 90, p. 92.
"Pleasures of the Flesh." [Poetry] (156:3) Je 90, p. 151.
4631. NELSON, Gale
"The Concave." [Talisman] (5) Fall 90, p. 83-85.
"The Margin" (reordered words from "The Margin," by Mei-mei Berssenbrugge, Conjunctions 10, 1987). [Avec] (3:1) 90, p. 106-107.
"When Ecstasy Is Inconvenient" (for Paula Vogel, reordered words from "When Ecstasy Is Inconvenient," by Lorine Niedecker, 1985). [Avec] (3:1) 90, p. 107.
"Why I Am Not a Christian" (reordered words from "Why I Am Not a Christian," by Charles Bernstein, The Sophist, 1987). [Avec] (3:1) 90, p. 108.
4632. NELSON, Howard
"The Rattlesnake." [Mildred] (4:1) 90, p. 81-82.
"The Turtle." [Mildred] (4:1) 90, p. 82-83.
4633. NELSON, Jane Baier
"For My Mother, Taveling in Portugal." [BellR] (13:1, #27) Spr 90, p. 51.
4634. NELSON, Nils
"Good for the Soul." [Crazy] (38) Spr 90, p. 35.
"Making Room." [Crazy] (38) Spr 90, p. 36-37.
4635. NELSON, Ralph
"Great Silence" (tr. of Omitsu). [NewL] (57:1) Fall 90, p. 98.
"Nature's Rule" (tr. of Omitsu). [NewL] (57:1) Fall 90, p. 100.
4636. NELSON, Richard
"Mountain in My Head" (from "The Island Within," North Point Press, 1989). [PoetryUSA] (5:3) Fall 90, p. 13.
4637. NELSON, Riki Kólbl
"For Rikilein." [RagMag] (7:2) Spr 90, p. 30.
"Injunction." [RagMag] (7:2) Spr 90, p. 30.
"Smile." [RagMag] (7:2) Spr 90, p. 31.
4638. NELSON, Sandra
"Finally the Rain." [Obs] (5:2) Sum 90, p. 28.
"From the Master Blaster Bator." [Spirit] (10:2) 90, p. 146-147.
"Getting to Be the Lucky One." [PoetC] (22:1) Fall 90, p. 30.
"I Sat for Hours by the Garbage." [SingHM] (17) 90, p. 62-63.
"I Used to Be OK." [Bogg] (63) 90, p. 35.
"I Was Inadequate." [SingHM] (18) 90, p. 44-45.
"In May I Found Some Birds." [Obs] (5:2) Sum 90, p. 27.
"Orange Knot." [Obs] (5:2) Sum 90, p. 27.

"Snow." [Obs] (5:2) Sum 90, p. 28.
"To the Christmas Present Head in Lautrec's 'Le Rat Mort'." [LaurelR] (24:1) Wint
90, p. 71.
"When a Mother in-Law's Tongue Is a Zebra." [CapeR] (25:1) Spr 90, p. 23.
4639. NEMEROV, Howard
"Answering Back." [LullwaterR] (1:1) Spr 90, p. 28.
"August." [BelPoJ] (40:4) Sum 90, p. 43.
"Romantics." [LullwaterR] (1:1) Spr 90, p. 27.
"Waste." [PoetL] (85:3) Fall 90, p. 37-38.
4640. NEMET-NEJAT, Murat
"The Chapel of Santa Maria in Obidos, Portugal." [HangL] (57) 90, p. 56-57.
"Eldorado." [HangL] (57) 90, p. 54.
"The First Moment on the New Land." [HangL] (57) 90, p. 53-54.
"Objects." [HangL] (57) 90, p. 55.
"Rice on the Tray." [HangL] (57) 90, p. 57.
"Toy." [LitR] (33:4) Sum 90, p. 508.
"When My Love Says." [HangL] (57) 90, p. 55.
"Who Are You." [LitR] (33:4) Sum 90, p. 508.
4641. NERUDA, Pablo
"La Deadichada." [NegC] (10:2/3) 90, p. 158, 160.
"The Disavowed" (tr. by James Sallis). [NegC] (10:2/3) 90, p. 159, 161.
"Floods" (tr. by John Felstiner). [AmerPoR] (19:4) Jl-Ag 90, p. 30.
"Heaven Stones" (Selections: III, XVII, tr. by Maria Jacketti). [Abraxas] (38/39) 90,
p. 65, 67.
"How Long?" (tr. by E. Leon Chidester). [InterPR] (16:2) Fall 90, p. 67, 69.
"Ode to Broth of Conger" (tr. by Don Summerhayes). [Descant] (21:4/22:1, #71/72)
Wint-Spr 90-91, p. 247-248.
"Las Piedras del Cielo" (Selections: III, XVII). [Abraxas] (38/39) 90, p. 65-66.
"The Standard Oil Company" (tr. by Roger Jones). [CrabCR] (6:3) Spr 90, p. 15.
"Y Cuanto Vive?" (from "Extravagario," 1958). [InterPR] (16:2) Fall 90, p. 66, 68.
4642. NETHAWAY, Charles D., Jr.
"August funeral." [Amelia] (6:1, #16) 90, p. 104.
4643. NETTELBECK, F. A.
"Like William S. Burroughs Once Told Me." [PoetryUSA] ([5:4?]) Wint 90, p. 8.
"Rise to Civilization." [PoetryUSA] ([5:4?]) Wint 90, p. 8.
4644. NEUFELDT, Leonard
"At the End of the Picking Season." [SycamoreR] (2:1) Wint 90, p. 32.
"Box Factory Girls." [PraF] (11:2) Sum 90, p. 14-16.
"Father Was Known As a Man in Control." [SycamoreR] (2:1) Wint 90, p. 33-34.
"For the Woman Who Remembers Old Songs." [Quarry] (39:4) Fall 1990, p. 58.
"The Immortal." [PraF] (11:4) Wint 90-91, p. 64.
"The Man with the Glass Eye." [PraF] (11:4) Wint 90-91, p. 65-66.
"Mother." [PraF] (11:2) Sum 90, p. 12-13.
"Prayers." [PraF] (11:4) Wint 90-91, p. 63.
"Raspberries Are Not Easily Gotten Rid Of." [CharR] (16:1) Spr 90, p. 37.
"The Tree, with a Hole, in Our Front Yard" (For Di Brandt, and to Those Who Were
Angry). [PraF] (11:2) Sum 90, p. 17.
4645. NEUMANN, Kurt
"Sleeping Figure." [CimR] (92) Jl 90, p. 119.
4646. NEVA, Judith
"Helping My 25-Year-Old Daughter Pack." [SwampR] (5) Wint-Spr 90, p. 20.
"The Musk of Night Flowers: Sheba." [Vis] (33) 90, p. 36.
4647. NEVILL, Sue
"Lindow Man II." [AntigR] (83) Aut 90, p. 18.
"Sisyphus, Asked to Comment." [AntigR] (83) Aut 90, p. 17.
4648. NEVILLE, Michael
"Steven." [JamesWR] (8:1) Fall 90, p. 15.
4649. NEVILLE, Tam Lin
"Prowler by Daylight." [SycamoreR] (2:2) Sum 90, p. 10.
"A Roaming Muse Brings His Silence to My Door." [CimR] (92) Jl 90, p. 124-125.
4650. NEW, Joan
"The Visit." [SpoonRQ] (15:3) Sum 90, p. 52.
4651. NEWALL, Liz
"Preston." [BlackBR] (11) Spr-Sum 90, p. 23.
4652. NEWMAN, Denise J.
"Boxing Match in the Desert." [PoetryUSA] (5:1) Spr 90, p. 3.

4653. NEWMAN, J. H.
"Discipline." [AntigR] (81/82) Spr-Sum 90, p. 102.
4654. NEWMAN, P. B.
"Entrepreneurs' Cottages." [NoDaQ] (58:3) Sum 90, p. 151.
"New Year." [KanQ] (22:1/2) Wint-Spr 90, p. 162.
"Obsession." [HiramPoR] (48/49) 90-91, p. 58.
4655. NEWSON, Charles
"Ambitions of Men." [AntigR] (81/82) Spr-Sum 90, p. 108.
4656. NEWTON, John
"Epithalamium" (Selections: 2, 3). [Verse] (7:2) Sum 90, p. 46-47.
"Mechanism." [Verse] (7:2) Sum 90, p. 45.
4657. NG, Lucy
"China: A Dream of Wild Horses." [Dandel] (17:1) Spr-Sum 90, p. 25.
"Failure." [AntigR] (81/82) Spr-Sum 90, p. 172.
"When They Came." [AntigR] (81/82) Spr-Sum 90, p. 173.
4658. NGWAINMBI, Emmanuel Sim
"Certeris Paribus" (for students studying abroad). [WashR] (16:2) Ag-S 90, p. 23.
"Eddra." [WashR] (16:2) Ag-S 90, p. 23.
"Moments Part II with My Soul." [WashR] (16:2) Ag-S 90, p. 23.
"Umuein." [WashR] (16:2) Ag-S 90, p. 23.
4659. NÍ CHUILLEANAIN, Eileán
"In Rome." [Quarry] (39:1) Wint 90, p. 67.
4660. Ni DHOMHNAILL, Nuala
"Nude" (tr. by Paul Muldoon). [Antaeus] (64/65) Spr-Aut 90, p. 17-18.
4661. NIATUM, Duane
"First Autumn in Ann Arbor." [Contact] (9:56/57/58) Spr 90, p. 43-44.
"Four Mobiles After an Alexander Calder Retrospective" (for my son, Marc).
[Contact] (9:56/57/58) Spr 90, p. 41.
"Poem for the Daughter I Never Had." [Contact] (9:56/57/58) Spr 90, p. 42-43.
"Warrior Artists of the Southern Plains." [MichQR] (29:3) Sum 90, p. 406-409.
4662. NICASTRO, Kathleen
"Dear Rich" (for Richard Perkins). [AntigR] (81/82) Spr-Sum 90, p. 18-19.
"Letter by Firelight" (for JH). [AntigR] (81/82) Spr-Sum 90, p. 19.
4663. NICCUM, Terri
"The Boat." [OnTheBus] (2:1, #5) Spr 90, p. 108-109.
"The Library Poem." [OnTheBus] (2:2/3:1, #6/7) Sum-Fall 90 Wint-Spr 91, p.
157-158.
"Moonlight." [OnTheBus] (2:2/3:1, #6/7) Sum-Fall 90 Wint-Spr 91, p. 156-157.
"One Morning." [OnTheBus] (2:1, #5) Spr 90, p. 109-111.
"What It Takes." [OnTheBus] (2:2/3:1, #6/7) Sum-Fall 90 Wint-Spr 91, p.
155-156.
4664. NICHOL, B. P.
"44 Concrete Poems." [CapilR] (2:4) Wint 90, p. 69-114.
"'IM: mortality play: The Bard Project, The Martyrology: Book (10)10." [WestCL]
(24:2) Fall 90, p. 7-10.
"A Sorted 'Plunkett Papers'" (Selected and Edited by Irene Niechoda). [WestCL]
(24:2) Fall 90, p. 65-82.
4665. NICHOLLS, Sandra
"Bellevue Garden, Kingston" (for Bronwen Wallace). [PoetryC] (11:3) Fall 90, p.
16.
"Mapmaking." [PoetryC] (11:3) Fall 90, p. 16.
4666. NICHOLS, Grace
"The Fat Black Woman's Motto on Her Bedroom Door." [LitR] (34:1) Fall 90, p.
31.
"Sugar Cane." [LitR] (34:1) Fall 90, p. 26-29.
"Thoughts Drifting Through the Fat Black Woman's Head While Having a Full
Bubble Bath." [LitR] (34:1) Fall 90, p. 31.
"Tropical Death." [LitR] (34:1) Fall 90, p. 30.
4667. NICHOLS-ORIANS, Judith
"The Progress of Seasons." [OxfordM] (6:1) Spr-Sum 90, p. 49.
"Washing Dishes." [PoetL] (85:3) Fall 90, p. 36.
4668. NICHOLSON, Wynne
"The Grey Whales." [Grain] (18:3) Fall 90, p. 42.
"Woodworms." [Grain] (18:3) Fall 90, p. 42.
4669. NICKERSON, Sheila
"Hitchhiking the Blossoms of Trees." [DogRR] (9:2, #18) Aut 90, p. 28.

"The Mouse Hunters." [Wind] (20:66) 90, p. 30.
"On Reading the Lives of the Astronomers on a Spring Day, After Rain." [DogRR]
    (9:1, #17) Spr 90, p. 30.
"Still Life: Louise Muillon." [Wind] (20:66) 90, p. 30.
"Waiting for the Kindness of Strangers." [DogRR] (9:2, #18) Aut 90, p. 29.
"Where My Mother Lives, in the Building with a Doorman Named Angel." [DogRR]
    (9:1, #17) Spr 90, p. 31.
"Wishkita: House of the Shark." [SingHM] (17) 90, p. 61.
"A Woman Speaks: Western Alaska." [Wind] (20:66) 90, p. 31.
NICOLA, Deborah de
    See De NICOLA, Deborah
4670. NIDES, John
    "The Edge of Time Is Near!" (tr. of Witold Suder, w. Melanie Heath). [PoetryUSA]
        (5:1) Spr 90, p. 8.
4671. NIDITCH, B. Z.
    "1929" (For Walter Benjamin). [CrabCR] (6:3) Spr 90, p. 6.
    "1989." [CrabCR] (6:3) Spr 90, p. 5.
    "Along the Dead Sea." [CrabCR] (6:3) Spr 90, p. 7.
    "At the Savoy." [Contact] (9:56/57/58) Spr 90, p. 32.
    "At the Vagankovskoye Graveyard" (at the funeral of Yuli M. Daniel, Jan. 2, 1989).
        [CrabCR] (6:3) Spr 90, p. 6.
    "Bucharest, 1986." [Amelia] (6:1, #16) 90, p. 94.
    "A Century Late." [CrabCR] (6:3) Spr 90, p. 7.
    "Compassion Stone." [Contact] (9:56/57/58) Spr 90, p. 32.
    "Day of Robert Lowell's Funeral." [Confr] (44/45) Fall 90-Wint 91, p. 188.
    "Early Advise." [Asylum] (5:4) 90, p. 1.
    "Early Charles." [Gypsy] (15) 90, p. 70.
    "Harvard Square." [MoodySI] (22/23) Wint 89-90, p. 20.
    "Harvard Square." [OxfordM] (6:1) Spr-Sum 90, p. 17-18.
    "Liberation." [Caliban] (9) 90, p. 151.
    "Living Room." [DustyD] (1:2) O 90, p. 3.
    "Martha's Vineyard." [CrabCR] (6:3) Spr 90, p. 7.
    "The Nineties Again." [Abraxas] (38/39) 90, p. 130.
    "On the Arbat." [DenQ] (25:2) Fall 90, p. 37.
    "On the S.S. Pushkin." [CrabCR] (6:3) Spr 90, p. 7.
    "Prague, 1968." [ChamLR] (4:1, #7) Fall 90, p. 7-8.
    "Revolutionary Air." [Caliban] (9) 90, p. 152.
    "Robert Penn Warren" (In Memoriam, 1905-1989). [Interim] (9:1) Spr-Sum 90, p.
        8.
    "Romance About My Motherland" (tr. of Yuli Daniel). [CrabCR] (6:3) Spr 90, p. 4.
    "Siege of Stalingrad." [Confr] (44/45) Fall 90-Wint 91, p. 189.
    "The Somatic Poet." [AnotherCM] (21) 90, p. 125-127.
    "T.V. O.D." [FreeL] (5) Sum 90, p. 18.
4672. NIEDECKER, Lorine
    "Who was Mary Shelley?" [ChiR] (37:1) Wint 90, p. 39-40.
4673. NIELSEN, A. L.
    "Espiral Negra" (Excerpt, tr. of Severo Sarduy). [WashR] (16:2) Ag-S 90, p. 28.
    "Instructions for the Magic Frog." [Gargoyle] (37/38) 90, p. 86.
4674. NIETO, Benigno S.
    "El Escriba Razona Mal Su Destino a Su Paso por España en 1965" (De Osos,
        Poetas y otros Delfines, A Virgilio Piñera, in memoriam). [LindLM] (9:4) O-D
        90, p. 55.
4675. NIGHTINGALE, Eric
    "My Daughter's Sleeping Chest" (For Heather). [RagMag] (8:1) 90, p. 49.
    "Yael Ronen, Flute." [RagMag] (8:1) 90, p. 48.
4676. NIJHOFF, Martinus
    "The Clown" (tr. by Raphael Rudnik). [Trans] (24) Fall 90, p. 164.
    "Con Sordino" (tr. by Raphael Rudnik). [Trans] (24) Fall 90, p. 161.
    "Impasse" (tr. by Raphael Rudnik). [Trans] (24) Fall 90, p. 165.
    "The Ivy" (tr. by Raphael Rudnik). [Trans] (24) Fall 90, p. 162.
    "The Mother, the Woman" (tr. by Raphael Rudnik). [Trans] (24) Fall 90, p. 163.
4677. NIJMEIJER, Peter
    "Ballad of the Stoker" (tr. of Wiel Kusters). [Trans] (24) Fall 90, p. 17-18.
4678. NIMMO, Kurt
    "Chase Game." [ChironR] (9:2) Sum 90, p. 7.

4679. NIMNICHT, Nona
"Aquarium at San Sebastian, Spain." [SingHM] (17) 90, p. 66.
NIORD, Chard de
See DeNIORD, Chard
4680. NISHIKAWA, Lane
"I'm on a Mission from Buddha" (Excerpt: "What happend to all the politically
correct socially conscious community activists"). [Zyzzyva] (6:3 #23) Fall 90,
p. 129-132.
4681. NISHIWAKI, Junzaburo
"A Man Who Reads Homer" (tr. by Masaya Saito). [Trans] (24) Fall 90, p. 228.
"No Traveler Returns" (tr. by Masaya Saito). [Trans] (24) Fall 90, p. 228.
"A Wintry Day" (tr. by Masaya Saito). [Trans] (24) Fall 90, p. 227.
4682. NITINS, Janet
"It Has Happened on Its Own." [Event] (19:1) Spr 90, p. 85.
4683. NIWA, Maureen
"When My Body Knocks." [Grain] (18:4) Wint 90, p. 13.
4684. NIXON, Colin
"City Life." [Bogg] (62) 90, p. 28.
4685. NIXON, John, Jr.
"The Kitchen." [ChrC] (107:4) 31 Ja 90, p. 101.
"Young Tory." [Comm] (117:19) 9 N 90, p. 651.
4686. NOAILLES, Anna, Comtess de
"Pathetique" (tr. by Elinor Briefs). [Vis] (32) 90, p. 36.
4687. NOBEL-CVETAN, Verda
"Out Where the Stillness Is." [BellArk] (6:3) My-Je 90, p. 3.
4688. NOBLES, Edward
"Contention." [WilliamMR] (28) 90, p. 81.
"Fortune." [NewOR] (17:3) Fall 90, p. 12.
"The Phrenologists." [ManhatPR] (12) [90?], p. 23.
"Stonemason." [ManhatPR] (12) [90?], p. 23.
"The Values of Stone." [TarRP] (30:1) Fall 90, p. 3.
4689. NOCK, Judy Ann
"The 20-Year Headache." [EmeraldCR] (1990) c89, p. 110.
4690. NOEL, Bernard
"Poem: What is it to be face to face?" (tr. by Dennis Egan and Jean-Clarence
Lambert, w. Bradley R. Strahan). [Vis] (32) 90, p. 46.
4691. NOETHE, Sheryl
"Embarazada." [CutB] (33) 90, p. 35.
"Who Frankenstein Is to Me & Why I Have the Big Head Dream." [CutB] (33) 90,
p. 37.
4692. NOGO, Rajko Petrov
"Betrothal" (tr. by Svetozar Koljevic and Andrew Harvey). [Screens] (2) 90, p. 63.
"Landscape" (tr. by Svetozar Koljevic and Andrew Harvey). [Screens] (2) 90, p. 63.
4693. NOLAN, James
"Archipelago for a Friend Dying" (for Michael Herthneck). [CityLR] (4) 90, p.
80-81.
"Benares Processional" (for Shurojeet Chaterji). [CityLR] (4) 90, p. 85.
"A Hundred Nails" (in memory, Cruz Luna). [CityLR] (4) 90, p. 83.
"Saturn Devouring His Children." [CityLR] (4) 90, p. 82.
"Walt Whitman Takes the Antibody Test." [CityLR] (4) 90, p. 84.
4694. NOLAN, James E.
"The Decoration of Hindu Pen Dents." [RagMag] (8:1) 90, p. 53.
4695. NOLAN, Patrick
"Et Lux in Tenebris Lucet" (And the light shineth in darkness). [PoetryUSA] ([5:4?])
Wint 90, p. 26.
"Monstrum in Fronte, Monstrum in Animo" (Monster in face, monster in soul).
[PoetryUSA] ([5:4?]) Wint 90, p. 26.
4696. NOLAN, Ruth
"Razor Temptation." [PacificR] (8) 90, p. 91.
4697. NOLAN, Timothy
"Beyond the Sign of the Fish." [Ploughs] (16:1) Spr-Sum 90, p. 10-25.
4698. NOLEN, Robert S.
"How Dear the Payments." [EmeraldCR] (1990) c89, p. 70.
4699. NOLENS, Leonard
"Tribute" (tr. by David Siefkin and Catharina Kochuyt). [Vis] (34) 90, p. 14.

4700. NOLL, Bink
"The Army Corps of Engineers Have Come and Gone, the Cabin Is Gone, the Trees, Acres, Everything" (for A.V.B.). [HampSPR] (Anthology 1975-1990) 90, p. 29-30.
"Of Education: From Ely, Minnesota, Out and Back." [HampSPR] (Anthology 1975-1990) 90, p. 32.

4701. NOLLETTI, Loralee
"My Father's House." [LindLM] (9:1/2) Ja/Mr-Ap/Je 90, p. 10.

4702. NOMURA, Kenichi
"One cloud is moving" (tr. by Janet Lewis). [SouthernR] (26:1) Ja 90, p. 203.

NOORD, Barbara van
See Van NOORD, Barbara

4703. NORD, Gennie
"Descent Through Indian Village -- September, 1967." [CutB] (34) Sum-Fall 90, p. 20.

4704. NORDBRANDT, Henrik
"Gesture" (from "Ode to an Octopus and Other Love Poems," Gyldendal, 1975, tr. by Paula Hostrup-Jessen). [CimR] (92) Jl 90, p. 26.
"Parikia" (from "Glas," Gyldendal, 1976, tr. by Paula Hostrup-Jessen). [CimR] (92) Jl 90, p. 26.

4705. NORDHAUS, Jean
"Quartet with Program Notes by Composer" (after Gunther Schuller's Third String Quartet). [WashR] (16:3) O-N 90, p. 16-17.
"Return." [WestB] (27) 90, p. 78.
"Twenty-Two Windows." [WestB] (27) 90, p. 79.
"Wind in the Hills" (tr. of Moshe Ben Shaul). [PoetL] (85:4) Wint 90-91, p. 21.

4706. NOREAULT, Robert
"Osten Coker" (T.S. Stops Time! Is It No Longer Relative E's Asked). [NegC] (10:2/3) 90, p. 45.
"The Probability of Weeding Out Extremes." [NegC] (10:2/3) 90, p. 46.

4707. NORMAN, Anita
"Family Story." [Plain] (10:2) Wint 90, p. 24.

4708. NORRIS, David
"My Cherry Boy." [PoetryUSA] (5:1) Spr 90, p. 5.

4709. NORRIS, Kathleen
"Ascension." [Poetry] (156:1) Ap 90, p. 13.
"Giveaway." [NewYorker] (66:40) 19 N 90, p. 80.
"The Librarian Confronts Theology" (Lemmon, S.D.). [SoDakR] (28:2) Sum 90, p. 147.
"Mrs. Adam." [Poetry] (156:1) Ap 90, p. 12.
"A Prayer to Eve." [ParisR] (32:115) Sum 90, p. 199.

4710. NORRIS, Ken
"The Eternal and the Infinite." [PoetryC] (11:4) Wint 90, p. 10.
"A Question of Time." [Event] (19:1) Spr 90, p. 83.
"Ravens and Pines" (for John Newlove). [PraF] (11:4) Wint 90-91, p. 67.
"Sonata." [PraF] (11:4) Wint 90-91, p. 67.

4711. NORSE, Harold
"Ready-Made." [CityLR] (4) 90, p. 117-119.

4712. NORTH, Charles
"About Strange Lands & People." [LitR] (33:4) Sum 90, p. 493.
"Albumblatt." [Sulfur] (10:2, #27) Fall 90, p. 152.
"The Dawn." [Sulfur] (10:2, #27) Fall 90, p. 152-155.
"Urban Landscape" (For Ron Padgett). [LitR] (33:4) Sum 90, p. 494.

4713. NORTHUP, Harry
"Times of Love & Loss." [OnTheBus] (2:2/3:1, #6/7) Sum-Fall 90 Wint-Spr 91, p. 159.

4714. NORTON, Sheila
"Shipwrecked" (After Winslow Homer). [WillowR] Spr 90, p. 26.

4715. NOSTRAND, Jennifer
"We Sit by the Fire." [PacificR] (8) 90, p. 78.

4716. NOTLEY, Alice
"Dear Eileen." [BrooklynR] (7) 90, p. 22-24.

4717. NOVAK, Boris A.
"Still Life and Death" (tr. by the author). [MidAR] (10:2) 90, p. 181.

4718. NOVAK, Helga
"Einer Stand und Sang." [SycamoreR] (2:2) Sum 90, p. 46.

"Mending Day" (tr. by Sammy McLean). [SycamoreR] (2:2) Sum 90, p. 49.
"One of Them Stood Up and Sang" (tr. by Sammy McLean). [SycamoreR] (2:2)
    Sum 90, p. 47.
"Reparaturtag." [SycamoreR] (2:2) Sum 90, p. 48.
"Scham." [SycamoreR] (2:2) Sum 90, p. 44.
"Shame" (tr. by Sammy McLean). [SycamoreR] (2:2) Sum 90, p. 45.

4719. NOVAK, Mary
"Night Shift at Goldenbell Chicken." [MissR] (19:1/2, #55/56) 90, p. 260-261.

4720. NOVAK, Michael Paul
"Family Codes" (after Margaret Mead). [KanQ] (22:1/2) Wint-Spr 90, p. 172.
"The Parents of Artists." [Confr] (44/45) Fall 90-Wint 91, p. 264.

4721. NOWAK, Nancy
"Flight." [Sonora] (18) Fall-Wint 90, p. 55-56.

4722. NOWELL, Janie
"Snow Blind." [EmeraldCR] (1990) c89, p. 108.

4723. NOWICKI, Michael E.
"The Cottage on Lake Michigan." [Parting] (3:1) Sum 90, p. 25.

4724. NOYES, H. F.
"In dwindling light." [Amelia] (6:1, #16) 90, p. 9.

4725. NUKADA, Princess (c.645-c.700)
"Wanting" (tr. by Graeme Wilson). [LitR] (33:2) Wint 90, p. 192.

4726. NURKSE, D. (Dennis)
"1956: The Horizon." [ManhatR] (5:1) Spr 90, p. 47-48.
"Bushwick, Latex Flat." [Stand] (31:4) Aut 90, p. 22.
"First Grade Homework." [Poetry] (156:5) Ag 90, p. 281-282.
"The High Gondola." [ManhatR] (5:1) Spr 90, p. 49.
"Introit & Fugue." [Poetry] (156:5) Ag 90, p. 281.
"The Last Incarnation." [CalQ] (34) 90, p. 34.
"Late Spring in a Small City." [ManhatR] (5:1) Spr 90, p. 48.
"Leaving Colombia." [WestB] (27) 90, p. 34.
"Overseas Accounts." [WestB] (27) 90, p. 35.
"Rented Houses." [WestB] (27) 90, p. 99.
"Rope." [HayF] (7) Fall-Wint 90, p. 62.

4727. NURMI, Earl "Pete"
"For a Man Crushed to Death Sleeping in a Dumpster." [LakeSR] (24) 90, p. 3.

NUWAS, Abu
    See ABU NUWAS

4728. NYE, Naomi Shihab
"The House Made of Rain." [CimR] (90) Ja 90, p. 73-74.
"The Light Where Lives Intersect." [PassN] (11:1) Sum 90, p. 23.
"Profile" (tr. of Walid Khazindar, w. Lena Jayyusi). [Screens] (2) 90, p. 19.
"Salt." [PassN] (11:1) Sum 90, p. 23.

4729. NYE, Robert
"Darker Ends." [DenQ] (24:3) Wint 90, p. 125.

4730. NYHART, Nina
"Three Poems After Klee." [Shen] (40:3) Fall 90, p. 88-90.

4731. NYSTROM, Debra
"Cottage Above the Harbor." [TriQ] (79) Fall 90, p. 133.
"January Half-Light." [TriQ] (79) Fall 90, p. 134.
"The Puzzle." [AmerPoR] (19:6) N-D 90, p. 40.

4732. NYSTROM, Karen
"Reasonable Boundaries." [DenQ] (25:2) Fall 90, p. 38-39.

4733. NZUJI, Clementine
"Grief, Don't Leave Me" (tr. by Julia Older). [Vis] (32) 90, p. 15.

4734. O DALAIGH, Gofraidh Fionn
"Reversible" (tr. by Richard O'Connell). [HampSPR] (Anthology 1975-1990) 90, p.
    246.

4735. OAKS, Jeff
"The Crabs." [TarRP] (30:1) Fall 90, p. 28-29.

4736. OANDASAN, William
"Los Angeles / Southern California" (for Lorca's "Paisaje"). [ColR] (NS 17:1)
    Spr-Sum 90, p. 34.

4737. OATES, David
"Apocalypse." [Asylum] (5:4) 90, p. 34.
"Code of Behavior." [EvergreenC] (6:1) Wint 90-Spr 91, p. 51.

4738. OATES, Joyce Carol
"$." [Atlantic] (266:1) Jl 90, p. 74.
"Hands, Prints, Time: A Collage." [WestHR] (44:4) Wint 90, p. 395-397.
"Holiday." [NewMyths] (1:1) 90, p. 127.
"I Stand Before You Naked." [KenR] (NS 12:2) Spr 90, p. 146-147.
"The Maker of Parables." [KenR] (NS 12:2) Spr 90, p. 147.
"Roller Rink, 1954." [MichQR] (29:1) Wint 90, p. 96.
"Such Beauty." [NewMyths] (1:1) 90, p. 129.
"There Was a Shot." [WestHR] (44:4) Wint 90, p. 394.
"What Is Most American Is Most in Motion." [Hudson] (42:4) Wint 90, p. 609-610.
"You Live." [NewMyths] (1:1) 90, p. 128.
4739. OBERMEYER, Jon M.
"Musée Rodin." [InterPR] (16:1) Spr 90, p. 132-133.
"The Reassurance of Ghosts." [InterPR] (16:1) Spr 90, p. 133.
4740. OBERST, Terrance
"Darwin Was Wrong." [Plain] (11:1) Fall 90, p. 34-35.
4741. O'BOYLE, Bill
"Rugmaker." [Crucible] (26) Fall 90, p. 75.
4742. OBRADOVIC, Biljana D.
"Blood-Stained Tale" (tr. of Desanka Maksimovic). [PoetryE] (29) Spr 90, p. 95-97.
"Disquietude" (tr. of Desanka Maksimovic). [PoetryE] (29) Spr 90, p. 101.
"Experience" (tr. of Desanka Maksimovic). [PoetryE] (29) Spr 90, p. 92.
"I Don't Have Any More Time" (tr. of Desanka Maksimovic). [PoetryE] (29) Spr
90, p. 99.
"Man" (tr. of Desanka Maksimovic). [PoetryE] (29) Spr 90, p. 102.
"The Poet's Blessing" (tr. of Desanka Maksimovic). [PoetryE] (29) Spr 90, p. 100.
"Remembering the Homeland" (tr. of Desanka Maksimovic). [PoetryE] (29) Spr 90,
p. 94.
"Spring" (tr. of Desanka Maksimovic). [PoetryE] (29) Spr 90, p. 98.
"Winter in the Homeland" (tr. of Desanka Maksimovic). [PoetryE] (29) Spr 90, p.
93.
4743. O'BRIEN, Geoffrey
"Elements of a Miracle." [HarvardA] (125:2) N 90, p. 32.
"An Expedition." [Pequod] (31) 90, p. 172.
"Haruspex." [ParisR] (32:116) Fall 90, p. 136-138.
"Landscape." [Pequod] (31) 90, p. 169.
"The Prophetic Child." [Talisman] (4) Spr 90, p. 40-42.
"Remnant of Crossroads." [Pequod] (31) 90, p. 170.
"The Streamer Trunk." [Pequod] (31) 90, p. 171.
4744. O'BRIEN, Gregory
"From a Visigothic Prayer to the Mother of Love." [Verse] (7:2) Sum 90, p. 53.
"A Native Wounded While Asleep." [Verse] (7:2) Sum 90, p. 53.
"Portugal." [Verse] (7:2) Sum 90, p. 54.
4745. O'BRIEN, Linda
"Motherhood a Thirty-Seven." [SingHM] (17) 90, p. 108-109.
4746. O'CALLAGHAN, T. Colm
"To Sit and Look for One Still Hour" (. . . murdered by an I.R.A. bomb). [DustyD]
(1:2) O 90, p. 16.
4747. OCHESTER, Ed
"July 4, 1989." [Ploughs] (16:4) Wint 90-91, p. 259.
"Oh, By the Way." [Ploughs] (16:4) Wint 90-91, p. 257-258.
4748. OCHOA, Enriqueta
"Qué Sed Mortal de Dios Se Desamarra en Mí." [InterPR] (16:1) Spr 90, p. 60, 62.
"What a Mortal Thirst for God Shakes Loose inside Me" (tr. by Mark Smith-Soto).
[InterPR] (16:1) Spr 90, p. 61, 63.
4749. OCHOA LOPEZ, Moravia
"Aprendiendo a Cantar." [InterPR] (16:1) Spr 90, p. 72, 74.
"Learning to Sing" (tr. by Mark Smith-Soto). [InterPR] (16:1) Spr 90, p. 73, 75.
4750. O'CONNELL, Richard
"At Finn's" (tr. of Aonghus na n-aor). [HampSPR] (Anthology 1975-1990) 90, p.
245.
"Bardic" (tr. of Flaithri O Maoil Chonaire). [HampSPR] (Anthology 1975-1990) 90,
p. 245.
"Consolation" (tr. of Aonghus na n-aor). [HampSPR] (Anthology 1975-1990) 90,
p. 245.
"Epigrams" (XI:99, Symplegades in Slacks, II:56, Casino Girl, tr. of Martial).

[Hellas] (1:1) Spr 90, p. 54.
"On Killing a Tax Collector" (tr. of Murrough O'Daly). [HampSPR] (Anthology
1975-1990) 90, p. 246.
"Poets Anonymous" (tr. of Aonghus na n-aor). [HampSPR] (Anthology 1975-1990)
90, p. 245.
"Reversible" (tr. of Gofraidh Fionn O Dalaigh). [HampSPR] (Anthology
1975-1990) 90, p. 246.
"Rough House" (tr. of anonymous Irish poem). [HampSPR] (Anthology
1975-1990) 90, p. 246.
4751. O'CONNOR, Deirdre
"Almost Nothing." [Poetry] (157:1) O 90, p. 32.
"My Grandfather's Cronies." [Poetry] (157:1) O 90, p. 31.
O'DALAIGH, Gofraidh Fionn
      See O DALAIGH, Gofraidh Fionn
4752. O'DALY, Murrough
"On Killing a Tax Collector" (tr. by Richard O'Connell). [HampSPR] (Anthology
1975-1990) 90, p. 246.
4753. ODAM, Joyce
"Cosmetic." [Bogg] (62) 90, p. 47.
"The Daughter of the Dreams." [ChamLR] (3:2, #6) Spr 90, p. 113.
"The Dress in the Water." [ChamLR] (3:2, #6) Spr 90, p. 112.
"For All the Tea in Canada." [ChamLR] (3:2, #6) Spr 90, p. 114.
"The Good Son's Mother Dies." [BellR] (13:1, #27) Spr 90, p. 18-19.
"In Your Garden." [ChamLR] (4:1, #7) Fall 90, p. 173.
"Marbles." [NegC] (10:2/3) 90, p. 60.
"Now My Huge Stomach." [ChamLR] (3:2, #6) Spr 90, p. 111.
"The Rain Poem." [Wind] (20:66) 90, p. 32.
"Red Dress." [Bogg] (63) 90, p. 12.
"Satiate." [Bogg] (62) 90, p. 6.
"The White Room." [ChamLR] (4:1, #7) Fall 90, p. 172.
4754. O'DELL, Mary E.
"Clothing of the Dead." [Plain] (10:2) Wint 90, p. 30.
4755. ODIO, Silvia Eugenia
"Fui Pegando Mariposas a Mi Cuerpo." [LindLM] (9:4) O-D 90, p. 28.
4756. ODLIN, Reno
"After the Plague." [AntigR] (83) Aut 90, p. 16.
"The Kid in the Window Seat." [AntigR] (80) Wint 90, p. 54-55.
4757. ODOM, Robert, Jr.
"Secrets." [PoetryUSA] (5:2) Sum 90, p. 5.
4758. O'DRISCOLL, Ciaran
"Great Auks." [Quarry] (39:1) Wint 90, p. 87-88.
4759. O'DRISCOLL, Dennis
"Goodbyes." [LaurelR] (24:1) Wint 90, p. 44.
"Reading Primo Levi on the Train." [Poetry] (157:3) D 90, p. 138.
4760. OERKE, Andrew
"Butterfly." [InterPR] (16:1) Spr 90, p. 114.
"The Great Pyramid." [InterPR] (16:1) Spr 90, p. 113-114.
"The Metaphor of the Body in the Garden of the Mind." [InterPR] (16:1) Spr 90, p.
113.
4761. OERTING, Katherine McKenzie
"Rebounding." [EmeraldCR] (1990) c89, p. 67.
4762. OESTREICHER, Joy
"The Mistaking of Wealth for Plenty." [BlackBR] (12) Fall-Wint 90, p. 16.
"Oatmeal Shirt." [BlackBR] (12) Fall-Wint 90, p. 16.
4763. OFFEN, Ron
"Lyric to Epic Poet re: Poetry" (Fragment of a Letter). [Amelia] (6:2, #17) 90, p.
126.
"Memorial for MMmmm" (After Avedon). [Pearl] (12) Fall-Wint 90, p. 50.
"My soul return'd to me, and answer'd." [PoetC] (21:2) Wint 90, p. 19.
"Winter Incongruities." [CoalC] (1) Ag 90, p. 7.
4764. OGBOWEI, G. 'Ebinyo
"Gani Fawehinmi." [BlackALF] (24:3) Fall 90, p. 542-543.
4765. OGDEN, Hugh
"31 December 1984: The Four Season's Bar [sic]" (for Annette). [Footwork] 90, p.
19.
"Above Salmon Brook, The Darkness" (for Annette). [Footwork] 90, p. 18.

"January: Monte Aventino" (for Annette). [SwampR] (5) Wint-Spr 90, p. 66-67.
"Patterns." [NoDaQ] (58:4) Fall 90, p. 35-36.
"Penn Station, Waiting for the Night Owl to Washington." [NoDaQ] (58:3) Sum 90,
      p. 73-74.
"Waterville: The Mid-Maine Medical Center" (for Annette). [MalR] (92) S 90, p.
      51-52.
"When the Hummingbird" (for Annette). [Footwork] 90, p. 18.
4766. O'GRADY, Desmond
      "Standing Stones" (for Dimitri Hadzi). [Quarry] (39:1) Wint 90, p. 89.
4767. O'GRADY, Tom
      "The Casting of Bells" (Selections, tr. of Jaroslav Seifert, w. Paul Jagasich).
            [HampSPR] (Anthology 1975-1990) 90, p. 255-256.
      "Dance-Song" (tr. of Jaroslav Seifert, w. Paul Jagasich). [HampSPR] (Anthology
            1975-1990) 90, p. 256-257.
      "Deep Mud" (tr. of Pavel Strut, w. the author). [HampSPR] (Anthology 1975-1990)
            90, p. 272.
      "Living in Another Man's House." [HampSPR] (Anthology 1975-1990) 90, p. 22.
      "Not Long Before April" (tr. of Pavel Strut, w. the author). [HampSPR] (Anthology
            1975-1990) 90, p. 272.
      "Sitting on the Porch." [HampSPR] (Anthology 1975-1990) 90, p. 22-23.
4768. O'HALLORAN, Jamie
      "Another Hour." [BellArk] (6:4) Jl-Ag 90, p. 5.
      "A Way to a View." [BellArk] (6:5) S-O 90, p. 24.
4769. O'HARA, Edgar
      "Blanco Y Negro Tiritando Juntos en un Paradero de East Austin." [Americas]
            (18:3/4) Fall-Wint 90, p. 112.
      "Endechas Texanas para un Despechado al Pie de una Wurlitzer en la Frontera."
            [Americas] (18:3/4) Fall-Wint 90, p. 113.
      "Tornado Watch en Saragosa, TX." [Americas] (18:3/4) Fall-Wint 90, p. 111.
4770. O'HARA, Mark
      "Borodin, Dancing." [WindO] (53) Fall 90, p. 17.
      "A Child Composer's Garden." [WindO] (53) Fall 90, p. 18-19.
      "Cicadas." [Farm] (7:1) Spr 90, p. 41.
      "The Last Symphony." [WindO] (53) Fall 90, p. 19-21.
      "Silent Skies: Aaron Copland." [Farm] (7:1) Spr 90, p. 42-43.
4771. O'HARRA, Deborah
      "Arriving at Anchorage International Airport." [Amelia] (6:2, #17) 90, p. 153-154.
      "In the Cup" (Now entering Ridgecrest, California, Home of the China Lake Naval
            Weapons Center). [Amelia] (6:2, #17) 90, p. 152-153.
4772. OHE, Brucette
      "The Morehead Blue Jean Factory." [Pig] (16) 90, p. 34.
4773. OHRBOM, Mary Elizabeth
      "Garden Reveille." [EmeraldCR] (1990) c89, p. 55-56.
4774. OJAIDE, Tanure
      "For Our Own Reasons." [Obs] (5:3) Wint 90, p. 112.
      "I Am Odjelabo, the Invincible" (tr. of Okitiakpe of Ekakpamre). [WashR] (16:2)
            Ag-S 90, p. 24.
      "Isheja" (tr. of anonymous Ujevwe song). [WashR] (16:2) Ag-S 90, p. 25.
      "State Executive." [Obs] (5:3) Wint 90, p. 113-114.
      "Whenever Songs Are to Be Composed" (tr. of anonymous Udu song). [WashR]
            (16:2) Ag-S 90, p. 25.
4775. O'KEEFE, Daniel
      "At This Time." [HarvardA] (124:2) Ja 90, p. 33.
4776. O'KEEFE, Richard R.
      "Funeral Mazurkas." [ThRiPo] (35/36) 90, p. 56-57.
      "Postcard: Voyage to Cythera." [ThRiPo] (35/36) 90, p. 58.
4777. OKITIAKPE of Ekakpamre
      "I Am Odjelabo, the Invincible" (tr. by Tanure Ojaide). [WashR] (16:2) Ag-S 90, p.
            24.
      "Mevwe Odjelabo." [WashR] (16:2) Ag-S 90, p. 24.
4778. OKUDA, Machiko
      "Grouping Fowl" (tr. of Shûji Miya, w. Elizabeth Balestrieri). [PoetryC] (11:2) Sum
            90, p. 20.
4779. OLDER, Julia
      "Grief, Don't Leave Me" (tr. of Clementine Nzuji). [Vis] (32) 90, p. 15.
      "Manzambi" (tr. of Matala Mukadi). [Vis] (32) 90, p. 16-18.

"Words Are Totems" (tr. of Francois Sengat-Kuo). [Vis] (32) 90, p. 8.
4780. OLDKNOW, Antony
"Boat Race." [CreamCR] (14:1) Spr 90, p. 120.
"Hoopoe" (tr. of Eugenio Montale). [NoDaQ] (58:1) Wint 90, p. 38.
"House Overlooking the Sea" (tr. of Eugenio Montale). [NoDaQ] (58:1) Wint 90, p.
39-40.
"I Remember Your Smile " (tr. of Eugenio Montale). [NoDaQ] (58:1) Wint 90, p.
38.
"Life, I Do Not Expect" (tr. of Eugenio Montale). [NoDaQ] (58:1) Wint 90, p. 39.
"The Overflowing Brilliance" (tr. of Eugenio Montale). [NoDaQ] (58:1) Wint 90, p.
40.
"Restaurant Outdoors." [CreamCR] (14:1) Spr 90, p. 121.
"Way Off in the Distance" (tr. of Francis Jammes). [PoetryE] (30) Fall 90, p. 63-64.
4781. OLDS, Jennifer
"Man Letter #1." [Gypsy] (15) 90, p. 36.
4782. OLDS, Sharon
"The Arrival." [Ploughs] (16:4) Wint 90-91, p. 133-134.
"The Connoisseuse of Slugs." [CimR] (93) O 90, p. 83-84.
"The Dead Body Itself." [Agni] (29/30) 90, p. 128-129.
"The Last Day." [Agni] (29/30) 90, p. 125-127.
"The Prepositions." [NewYorker] (66:7) 2 Ap 90, p. 48.
"The Promise." [NewYorker] (66:17) 11 Je 90, p. 80.
4783. OLEART, Maria
"I Am Sure There Are Red Women" (from "Versos a Anais," 1989, tr. by Montserrat
Abelló). [PoetryC] (11:4) Wint 90, p. 23.
"I Will Tell You About" (from "Versos a Anais," 1989, tr. by Montserrat Abelló).
[PoetryC] (11:4) Wint 90, p. 23.
"Moon Born from the Moon" (from "Versos a Anais," 1989, tr. by Montserrat
Abelló). [PoetryC] (11:4) Wint 90, p. 23.
4784. OLES, Carole (Carole Simmons)
"Basil." [PraS] (64:2) Sum 90, p. 40-41.
"Day Ten After Heart Surgery, Signing a Check." [Poetry] (157:1) O 90, p. 17-18.
"February 14th, Driving West." [NewEngR] (13:1) Fall 90, p. 112.
"In My Office, I Think I See." [PraS] (64:2) Sum 90, p. 39-40.
"In This Photo, Taken." [NewEngR] (13:1) Fall 90, p. 111.
"Prayer For What We Are about to Receive." [PraS] (64:2) Sum 90, p. 36-37.
"The Premonition." [PraS] (64:2) Sum 90, p. 38.
"Role Model." [PraS] (64:2) Sum 90, p. 33-34.
"Sleeping Daughter." [PraS] (64:2) Sum 90, p. 31-33.
"Storm, Winter, Walking the Beach After a Separation." [PraS] (64:2) Sum 90, p.
35-36.
"Where Is Everyone Going Who Was Here." [PraS] (64:2) Sum 90, p. 34-35.
4785. OLIENSIS, Jane
"Penelope's First Thoughts During Solitude." [Agni] (31/32) 90, p. 207-208.
4786. OLINKA, Sharon
"The Barriers." [PoetL] (85:4) Wint 90-91, p. 13.
"Bobby's Fall." [Spirit] (10:2) 90, p. 143-145.
4787. OLIPHANT, David
"Dawn 1809" (tr. of Enrique Lihn). [ColR] (NS 17:1) Spr-Sum 90, p. 101-102.
"Monet's Years at Giverny" (tr. of Enrique Lihn). [ColR] (NS 17:1) Spr-Sum 90, p.
98-100.
4788. OLIVE, Harry
"It Is the Small Breaths." [Plain] (10:3) Spr 90, p. 31.
"Listening, to the Bite." [Wind] (20:66) 90, p. 33-34.
"Our Tender Friend Has Come and Gone." [Plain] (10:2) Wint 90, p. 10.
"Walking in the Chills of Winter." [Wind] (20:66) 90, p. 33.
OLIVEIRA GOMES, Aila de
See GOMES, Aila de Oliveira
4789. OLIVER, Judy
"My Walk with Pete" (1990 Seaton Honorable Mention Poem). [KanQ] (22:3) Sum
90, p. 29-31.
4790. OLIVER, Mary
"Everything." [PartR] (57:1) Wint 90, p. 99.
"The Kitten." [Hudson] (43:2) Sum 90, p. 262-263.
"Spring." [Poetry] (156:1) Ap 90, p. 1-2.
"What Is It?" [Poetry] (156:1) Ap 90, p. 2-3.

4791. OLIVER, Raymond
    "To the Lilting Breeze." [Thrpny] (40) Wint 90, p. 22.
4792. OLIVER LABRA, Carilda
    "Declaration of Love" (1963, October Cuban Missile Crisis, tr. by Daniela Gioseffi.
        w. Enildo García). [PoetryE] (30) Fall 90, p. 54.
4793. OLIVIER, Louis
    "This Country of Silence" (Selections: 1-2, 5, 7-8, tr. of Charles Juliet). [CharR]
        (16:2) Fall 90, p. 84-87.
4794. OLLE, Carmen
    "Andrenaline Nights" (Excerpt, tr. by Mark Smith-Soto). [InterPR] (16:1) Spr 90, p.
        81, 83.
    "Noches de Andrenalina" (Excerpt). [InterPR] (16:1) Spr 90, p. 80, 82.
4795. OLMSTED, Marc
    "Gaps in Suffering." [NewYorkQ] (41) Spr 90, p. 105.
4796. O'LOUGHLIN, Michael
    "Dublin." [Quarry] (39:1) Wint 90, p. 90.
    "Pieter de Hooch" (Painting: Two Women in a Courtyard by Pieter de Hooch, tr. of
        Sipko Melissen). [Trans] (24) Fall 90, p. 55.
    "View of Sloten" (Drawing by Rembrandt, tr. of Sipko Melissen). [Trans] (24) Fall
        90, p. 53.
    "View of the Amstel" (Drawing by Rembrandt, tr. of Sipko Melissen). [Trans] (24)
        Fall 90, p. 54.
4797. OLSEN, Curtis
    "Cold Wa(te)r." [SlipS] (10) 90, p. 99.
4798. OLSEN, Lance
    "The Blinding of the Cyclops." [Nimrod] (34:1) Fall-Wint 90, p. 120.
    "Postmodernism Made Simple." [KanQ] (22:1/2) Wint-Spr 90, p. 104.
    "Subtracting the Cat." [KanQ] (22:1/2) Wint-Spr 90, p. 104.
4799. OLSEN, William
    "Sunken Roads." [CimR] (91) Ap 90, p. 57-60.
OLUND, Barbara Molloy
    See MOLLOY-OLUND, Barbara
4800. O'MALLEY, Tom
    "Travelling Shop." [Quarry] (39:1) Wint 90, p. 91.
4801. OMANSON, Bradley
    "August" (from "Clear Lake Journal"). [NorthStoneR] (9) 90, p. 25.
    "Leaves Above a Pool." [NorthStoneR] (9) 90, p. 26.
4802. OMITSU
    "Great Silence" (in Japanese and English, tr. by Ralph Nelson). [NewL] (57:1) Fall
        90, p. 98-99.
    "Nature's Rule" (in Japanese and English, tr. by Ralph Nelson). [NewL] (57:1) Fall
        90, p. 100-101.
4803. O'NEILL, Alexandre
    "Almourol" (tr. by Alexis Levitin). [PoetryE] (30) Fall 90, p. 94.
4804. O'NEILL, John
    "The Caribou Go There." [PoetryC] (11:4) Wint 90, p. 25.
    "Deer Lodge." [PoetryC] (11:4) Wint 90, p. 25.
    "Grizzly." [MalR] (93) D 90, p. 37.
    "Mourning." [PoetryC] (11:4) Wint 90, p. 25.
    "Read About the Bear." [Event] (19:3) Fall 90, p. 48-49.
4805. O'NEILL, Kevin
    "On the cold marble." [WormR] (30:1, #117) 90, p. 6.
    "Poem for Paula." [WormR] (30:1, #117) 90, p. 7.
    "Rope marks." [WormR] (30:1, #117) 90, p. 7.
4806. O'NEILL, Vincent
    "Ark of Triumph." [SoCaR] (23:1) Fall 90, p. 73.
4807. O'NEILL, William
    "Codependency." [LakeSR] (24) 90, p. 13.
4808. ONESS, Chad
    "Family Violence" (after Vallejo). [PoetL] (85:4) Wint 90-91, p. 29.
    "Going to My Brother's" (after Vallejo). [PoetL] (85:4) Wint 90-91, p. 27-28.
    "A Letter Back to You." [CalQ] (34) 90, p. 32.
4809. ONYSHKEVYCH, Larissa
    "Untitled: Keep talking, keep talking" (tr. of Ihor Rymaruk). [Agni] (29/30) 90, p.
        302.

350

OPPENHEIMER

4810. OPPENHEIMER, Paul
"Letter from Aiolia." [LitR] (33:4) Sum 90, p. 468.
4811. ORAVECZ, Imre
"Akkorára Már." [Abraxas] (38/39) 90, p. 86.
"Azokról a Nökröl." [Abraxas] (38/39) 90, p. 80.
"Ez Itt a Város." [Abraxas] (38/39) 90, p. 82.
"For Quite Some Time" (tr. by Bruce Berlind, w. Mária Körösy). [ManhatR] (5:1)
Spr 90, p. 13.
"I No Longer Walk" (tr. by Bruce Berlind, w. Mária Körösy). [Abraxas] (38/39) 90,
p. 85.
"I Want Only" (tr. by Bruce Berlind and Mária Körösy). [NewEngR] (13:1) Fall 90,
p. 41.
"I'd Like to Talk to You Now" (tr. by Bruce Berlind, w. Mária Körösy). [Abraxas]
(38/39) 90, p. 81.
"It May Have Begun This Way" (tr. by Bruce Berlind and Mária Körösy).
[NewEngR] (13:1) Fall 90, p. 40.
"My Time's Running Out" (tr. by Bruce Berlind, w. Mária Körösy). [ManhatR]
(5:1) Spr 90, p. 12.
"Nem Járok Már." [Abraxas] (38/39) 90, p. 84.
"This Is the City" (tr. by Bruce Berlind, w. Mária Körösy). [Abraxas] (38/39) 90, p.
83.
"When It Was Over" (tr. by Bruce Berlind and Mária Körösy). [NewEngR] (13:1)
Fall 90, p. 41-42.
"You Had Dressed by Then" (tr. by Bruce Berlind, w. Mária Körösy). [Abraxas]
(38/39) 90, p. 87.
4812. ORBAN, Ottó
"At First Hand" (tr. by Jascha Kessler and Mária Körösy). [MidAR] (10:2) 90, p.
178.
"The Golden Fleece" (tr. by Jascha Kessler and Mária Körösy). [MidAR] (10:2) 90,
p. 180.
"Intellectuals" (tr. by Jascha Kessler and Mária Körösy). [MidAR] (10:2) 90, p.
179.
"Lorca's New York" (tr. by Bruce Berlind, w. Mária Körösy). [PoetryE] (29) Spr
90, p. 57.
"Our Bearings at Sea" (a novel-in-poems: 2 selections, tr. by Jascha Kessler and
Maria Körösy). [Screens] (2) 90, p. 56-58.
"Stephen Spender in Mount Vernon" (tr. by Bruce Berlind, w. Mária Körösy).
[PoetryE] (29) Spr 90, p. 58.
"To Be Rich" (tr. by Bruce Berlind, w. Mária Körösy). [PoetryE] (29) Spr 90, p.
56.
4813. ORFALEA, Gregory
"My Father Writing Joe Hamrah in a Blackout." [CalQ] (34) 90, p. 28-29.
ORIANS, Judith Nichols
See NICHOLS-ORIANS, Judith
4814. ORLEN, Steve (Steven)
"Acts of God." [NewEngR] (13:1) Fall 90, p. 156.
"Carmen: Not the Opera But the Movie." [AmerPoR] (19:4) Jl-Ag 90, p. 31.
"Celebrity" (Tony Bennett). [Poetry] (157:2) N 90, p. 85.
"A Family of Three." [NewEngR] (13:1) Fall 90, p. 157-158.
"Religious Feeling." [NewEngR] (13:1) Fall 90, p. 158.
"The Short Story." [AmerPoR] (19:4) Jl-Ag 90, p. 31.
4815. ORLOWSKY, Dzvinia
"Visiting Father in Spring." [HayF] (7) Fall-Wint 90, p. 65.
4816. ORMSBY, Eric
"Bullhead Lily." [Blueline] (11:1/2) 90, p. 2.
"Conch Shell." [NewYorker] (65:48) 15 Ja 90, p. 44-45.
"Fingernails." [NewYorker] (66:3) 5 Mr 90, p. 46.
"Pickerelweed." [Blueline] (11:1/2) 90, p. 3.
"Poem in Archaic Meter (Manhukah)" (tr. of Abu Nuwas). [Chelsea] (49) 90, p.
117-120.
"White Waterlilies." [Blueline] (11:1/2) 90, p. 1.
4817. ORMSBY, Frank
"The Sons." [Quarry] (39:1) Wint 90, p. 92.
4818. ORMSHAW, Peter
"First Leave" (Israeli Army). [Dandel] (17:2) Fall-Wint 90, p. 30.
"Making It." [Grain] (18:2) Sum 90, p. 59.

"Prophets." [Grain] (18:2) Sum 90, p. 59.
"You Know Why I'm Mad?" [Grain] (18:2) Sum 90, p. 58.
4819. ORMSHAW, W. P.
"Mail." [Arc] (24) Spr 90, p. 27.
4820. O'ROARK, Frances
"Hit Me One, William." [Shen] (40:3) Fall 90, p. 34-35.
"In Love with the Distance." [NewDeltaR] (7:2) Spr-Sum 90, p. 11-12.
"It Turns Out You Can Make the Earth Absolutely Clean" (-- James Wright).
    [CarolQ] (42:2) Wint 90, p. 30.
"One Whore Town." [CarolQ] (42:2) Wint 90, p. 28-29.
4821. OROZCO, Olga
"Far Away, From My Hill" (tr. by Mary Crow). [AmerPoR] (19:1) Ja-F 90, p. 6.
"It Arrives in Every Storm" (tr. by Mary Crow). [AmerPoR] (19:1) Ja-F 90, p. 6.
4822. ORR, Ed
"Anticlimax." [YellowS] (34) Sum 90, p. 18.
"Summer (After Brandt)." [YellowS] (34) Sum 90, p. 18.
"Vlaminck's Nudes." [YellowS] (34) Sum 90, p. 18.
4823. ORR, Priscilla
"Courage." [Footwork] 90, p. 26.
"In Mourning." [Footwork] 90, p. 26.
4824. ORTALDA, Claire
"I Had a Son and His Name Is John." [PoetryUSA] ([5:4?]) Wint 90, p. 12.
4825. ORTH, Ghita
"Drawing Conclusions." [GreenMR] (NS 3:2) Fall-Wint 89-90, p. 50-51.
"Earthquake Country." [GreenMR] (NS 3:2) Fall-Wint 89-90, p. 49.
"The Hospital, After a Long Enough Time." [GreenMR] (NS 3:2) Fall-Wint 89-90,
    p. 47-48.
"Listening at the Door." [GreenMR] (NS 3:2) Fall-Wint 89-90, p. 46.
ORTIZ COFER, Judith
    See COFER, Judith Ortiz
4826. ORTIZ de MONTELLANO, Ana
"Because I Am a Woman of Color." [SingHM] (17) 90, p. 70-71.
4827. ORTOLANI, Al
"The Heavenbound Canoe." [MidwQ] (31:2) Wint 90, p. 216.
"How Steve Lost His Thumb and the Boy Scouts Became Cannibals." [EngJ] (79:5)
    S 90, p. 103.
"The Junkyard Mechanic Finds His Voice." [MidwQ] (31:4) Sum 90, p. 474.
4828. OSBORN, Andrew
"Largesse" (poem and monotype, with Evelyn Ch'ien). [HarvardA] (125:1) S 90, p.
    4.
"Seven-Minute Storm Song" (poem and monotype, with Evelyn Ch'ien).
    [HarvardA] (125:1) S 90, p. 3.
"Staghorn Sumac" (poem and monotype, with Evelyn Ch'ien). [HarvardA] (125:1)
    S 90, p. 5.
4829. OSBORNE, Alex
"Post Mortem." [Gargoyle] (37/38) 90, p. 82.
"Samhain." [Gargoyle] (37/38) 90, p. 82.
4830. OSHEROW, Jacqueline
"Sonnet, on Magda's Return." [NewRep] (202:7) 12 F 90, p. 38.
4831. O'SIADHAIL, Micheal
"Manhood." [Stand] (31:3) Sum 90, p. 10-11.
"Touchstone." [SouthernHR] (24:3) Sum 90, p. 262.
"Wanderers." [SouthernHR] (24:3) Sum 90, p. 269.
4832. OSING, Gordon
"Burning Books" (tr. of Liu Shahe, w. Li Xijian). [Abraxas] (38/39) 90, p. 90-91.
"Love" (tr. of Xiao Xue, w. Li Xijian). [Paint] (17:33/34) Spr-Aut 90, p. 33.
"Morning" (tr. of Ruan Zhanjing, w. Li Xijian). [CarolQ] (42:3) Spr 90, p. 78.
"Multi-Colored Mountains" (tr. of Sha Ou, w. Li Xijian). [Paint] (17:33/34) Spr-Aut
    90, p. 35.
"Oh, You and Me" (tr. of Gu Gong, w. Li Xijian). [Paint] (17:33/34) Spr-Aut 90, p.
    34.
"The Pearl Oyster" (tr. of Ai Qing, w. Li Xijian). [Paint] (17:33/34) Spr-Aut 90, p.
    31.
"Sandstorm" (tr. of Ruan Zhanjing, w. Li Xijian). [CarolQ] (42:3) Spr 90, p. 79-80.
"The Square Shapes and the Round Shapes" (tr. of Yan Yi, w. Li Xijian). [Paint]
    (17:33/34) Spr-Aut 90, p. 36.

"To My Sweetheart at Sixty" (tr. of Yu Weiye, w. Li Xijian). [Paint] (17:33/34)
Spr-Aut 90, p. 32.
"Weeping" (tr. of Liu Shahe, w. Li Xijian). [Abraxas] (38/39) 90, p. 90-91.
4833. OSMAN, Jena
"Town." [Avec] (3:1) 90, p. 2.
4834. OSMER, James
"Bukowski in a Jar." [DogRR] (9:1, #17) Spr 90, p. 33.
4835. OSTRIKER, Alicia
"Homage to Matisse" (Dedicated to the Memory of Felix Pollak). [Pembroke] (22)
90, p. 16-17.
"A Morning in the Museum." [ClockR] (6:2) 90, p. 25-32.
"The Nakedness of the Fathers" (Selections: "Cain and Abel: A Question in Ethics,
"The Cave"). [OntR] (32) Spr-Sum 90, p. 83-88.
4836. OSTROM, Cheryll K.
"Grandma Julia / Grandma Grace." [SingHM] (17) 90, p. 77.
4837. OSTROM, Hans
"One Feather Shy." [RiverC] (11:1) Fall 90, p. 56.
"The Reinvention of Light in Sweden." [CumbPR] (10:1) Fall 90, p. 37.
4838. O'SULLIVAN, Maggie
"Another Weather System." [PaperAir] (4:3) 90, p. 20-31.
"In the House of the Shaman" (Selections: 2 poems). [Screens] (2) 90, p. 174-178.
"Narcotic Properties." [Avec] (3:1) 90, p. 126-128.
4839. OSWELL, Douglas Evander
"She Is Like Thee, Lute." [YellowS] (33) Spr 90, p. 24.
OTERO, Manuel Ramos
See RAMOS OTERO, Manuel
4840. OTTERY, Jim
"The Moon and the Man in the Hills." [IndR] (13:3) Fall 90, p. 86.
OU, Sha
See SHA, Ou
4841. OUESSANT, Ile d'
"I went away -- alone" (tr. by the author and Elizabeth Eybers). [Trans] (24) Fall 90,
p. 14.
4842. OVERTON, Ron
"The Lost Man" (Ross Macdonald, 1915-1983). [SoDakR] (28:2) Sum 90, p. 168.
"Match Point." [Comm] (117:19) 9 N 90, p. 651.
"On Larkin." [Comm] (117:19) 9 N 90, p. 651.
4843. OVID
"Metamorphosis" (1. 525-539, tr. by James A. Conyer). [Hellas] (1:1) Spr 90, p.
41.
4844. OWEN, Eileen
"Snow White, Waking Up." [Calyx] (13:1) Wint 90-91, p. 42.
4845. OWEN, Sue
"My Doomsday Sampler." [NewOR] (17:3) Fall 90, p. 60-62.
4846. OWENS, Collie
"Variation on a Theme by Leonard Bernstein" (for L.B.: in memoriam, 1918-1990).
[ChatR] (11:1) Fall 90, p. 39.
4847. OWENS, Major
"The S & L Riot." [Harp] (281:1683) Ag 90, p. 21.
4848. OWENS, Scott
"Found Poems." [OnTheBus] (2:2/3:1, #6/7) Sum-Fall 90 Wint-Spr 91, p.
160-161.
"A Simple Binding." [OnTheBus] (2:2/3:1, #6/7) Sum-Fall 90 Wint-Spr 91, p. 160.
4849. OWENS, Suzanne
"Glass Sand." [MissR] (19:1/2, #55/56) 90, p. 262-264.
4850. OWER, John
"January 15" (M.L.K., Jr.'s Birthday). [Wind] (20:67) 90, p. 16.
4851. OXLEY, Kathleen
"Commencement Exercises." [JINJPo] (12:1) Spr 90, p. 16.
"Peeling." [JINJPo] (12:1) Spr 90, p. 15.
"Raspberries." [JINJPo] (12:2) Aut 90, p. 31-32.
"Roosevelt Avenue Express." [JINJPo] (12:2) Aut 90, p. 30.
"Searching for Emilia." [JINJPo] (12:2) Aut 90, p. 33-34.
4852. OZSVATH, Zsuzsanna
"A Vague Ode" (tr. of Miklos Radnoti, w. Frederick Turner). [PartR] (57:2) Spr 90,
p. 269.

4853. PACE, Rosalind
"Letitia Demands the Magic Touch." [Ploughs] (16:4) Wint 90-91, p. 140-141.
4854. PACHECO, José Emilio
"Chronicle of the Indies" (tr. by Ann Neelon). [PoetryE] (30) Fall 90, p. 21.
4855. PACK, Robert
"The Dead King." [Poetry] (156:2) My 90, p. 88-90.
"The Dwarf and Doctor Freud." [KenR] (NS 12:4) Fall 90, p. 42-43.
"Intending Words." [HampSPR] (Anthology 1975-1990) 90, p. 213-214.
"Mozart." [HampSPR] (Anthology 1975-1990) 90, p. 215-216.
"Stepping Out." [AmerS] (59:1) Wint 90, p. 92-94.
"Watchers." [KenR] (NS 12:4) Fall 90, p. 44-45.
4856. PACKARD, Linda McAllister
"Substitutions." [CrabCR] (7:1) Wint 90, p. 7.
4857. PACKARD, William
"Amsterdam Avenue Poem." [NewYorkQ] (43) Fall 90, p. 53-54.
"Chain Poem." [OnTheBus] (2:1, #5) Spr 90, p. 112.
"Have you ever thought." [NewYorkQ] (42) Sum 90, p. 81.
"I Judge the National Scholastic Poetry Contest." [NewYorkQ] (41) Spr 90, p. 103.
"Lincoln Portrait" (Editorial). [NewYorkQ] (41) Spr 90, p. 3-20.
"Pollution Poem." [HampSPR] (Anthology 1975-1990) 90, p. 20-21.
4858. PACOSZ, Christina
"This Time." [BlackBR] (11) Spr-Sum 90, p. 13-14.
4859. PADDOCK, Joe
"The Bullheads." [NorthStoneR] (9) 90, p. 88.
"The Father Flag." [LakeSR] (24) 90, p. 26.
"If a Poet." [NorthStoneR] (9) 90, p. 89.
"Tea with Lemon." [NorthStoneR] (9) 90, p. 89.
4860. PADDOCK, Nancy
"The Haunting." [NorthStoneR] (9) 90, p. 22-23.
"The Machine That Changed Winter." [NorthStoneR] (9) 90, p. 21.
"The Silos." [NorthStoneR] (9) 90, p. 24.
4861. PADGETT, Ron
"Easter in New York" (To Agnès, tr. of Blaise Cendrars). [Shiny] (5) 90, p. 25-32.
"Panama, or the Adventures of My Seven Uncles" (tr. of Blaise Cendrars). [ParisR]
(32:117) Wint 90, p. 43-61.
"Stunned Again." [BrooklynR] (7) 90, p. 4.
4862. PADGETT, Tom
"Galveston." [Amelia] (6:2, #17) 90, p. 76.
4863. PADHI, Bibhu
"Birthplace." [AntigR] (80) Wint 90, p. 64-65.
"Ceasework." [TriQ] (79) Fall 90, p. 117-118.
"Home." [TriQ] (79) Fall 90, p. 115-116.
4864. PADILLA, Heberto
"Entre el Gato y la Casa." [LindLM] (9:4) O-D 90, p. 55.
4865. PADILLA, Martha
"I. Con Tal Que el Avestruz." [LindLM] (9:4) O-D 90, p. 51.
"II. Marinera." [LindLM] (9:4) O-D 90, p. 51.
"Poemas" (6 poems: IIX [sic], XX, XXIII, IV, XIII, XXXVII). [LindLM] (9:1/2)
Ja/Mr-Ap/Je 90, p. 6.
4866. PADMANAB, S.
"Like your cascading hair." [Grain] (18:3) Fall 90, p. 76.
4867. PAEK, Musan
"The Crow" (tr. by Kim Uchang). [Manoa] (2:2) Fall 90, p. 153.
"That Year" (tr. by Kim Uchang). [Manoa] (2:2) Fall 90, p. 152-153.
4868. PAGE, Susan Roxie
"The Bread of Friendship" (for Anne). [Amelia] (6:2, #17) 90, p. 111.
4869. PAGE, Tom
"Dead City" (Excerpts, tr. of Otavio Afonso, from "Cidade Morta"). [MinnR] (NS
34/35) Spr-Fall 90, p. 10-12.
4870. PAGE, William
"Bull." [SouthernR] (26:2) Ap 90, p. 356-357.
"Heart." [SouthernR] (26:2) Ap 90, p. 354-355.
"I." [KanQ] (22:1/2) Wint-Spr 90, p. 180.
"Listening." [SouthernR] (26:2) Ap 90, p. 355.
4871. PAGIS, Dan
"Ein Leben" (tr. by Tsipi Edith Keller). [NowestR] (28:1) 90, p. 98.

"Ein Leben" (tr. by Tsipi Edith Keller). [Trans] (23) Spr 90, p. 191.
"Tempt the Devil" (tr. by Tsipi Edith Keller). [Trans] (23) Spr 90, p. 190.
"That's father, isn't it?" (tr. by Tsipi Edith Keller). [NowestR] (28:1) 90, p. 97.
4872. PAGNOULLE, Christine
"Sap on the Rebound" (tr. of Rose-Marie Francois). [Vis] (32) 90, p. 28.
PAHLITZSCH, Lori Storie
   See STORIE-PAHLITZSCH, Lori
4873. PAINO, Frankie
"The Bard of Diseases." [FreeL] (6) Aut 90, p. 30-31.
"The Cave of Saint Rita." [GreenMR] (NS 3:2) Fall-Wint 89-90, p. 56-57.
"Drowned Girl." [GreenMR] (NS 3:2) Fall-Wint 89-90, p. 52-53.
"Fourth of July." [MidAR] (10:2) 90, p. 17-19.
"The Grace of Conversion." [IndR] (14:1) Wint 90, p. 69-70.
"A Matter of Division." [IndR] (14:1) Wint 90, p. 68.
"Nine of Swords." [SpoonRQ] (15:2) Spr 90, p. 14.
"Nude." [SpoonRQ] (15:2) Spr 90, p. 12-13.
"This Is Not a Sad Poem." [GreenMR] (NS 3:2) Fall-Wint 89-90, p. 54-55.
"Walkingstick." [SpoonRQ] (15:2) Spr 90, p. 10-11.
"The Wisdom of the Body." [SpoonRQ] (15:2) Spr 90, p. 8-9.
4874. PALANDER, John
"Autumn Festival" (tr. of Félix Leclerc). [AntigR] (83) Aut 90, p. 104.
"Country Calendar" (tr. of Félix Leclerc). [AntigR] (83) Aut 90, p. 103.
"The Final Tally" (tr. of Félix Leclerc). [AntigR] (80) Wint 90, p. 25.
"In the Beginning" (tr. of Félix Leclerc). [AntigR] (80) Wint 90, p. 21.
"My Grandmother's Patron Saint" (tr. of Félix Leclerc). [AntigR] (80) Wint 90, p.
   23.
4875. PALCHEVICH, Marta
"V. We have loved each other" (tr. by Todd Burrell). [CrabCR] (6:3) Spr 90, p. 22.
"VIII. I could ask him if it's the sun he wants" (tr. by Todd Burrell). [CrabCR] (6:3)
   Spr 90, p. 22.
"XV. We are they that search for bees in the fold of a curtain" (tr. by Todd Burrell).
   [CrabCR] (6:3) Spr 90, p. 22.
4876. PALCHI, Alfredo de
"Egg laboring in oval light" (tr. by Sonia Raiziss). [HampSPR] (Anthology
   1975-1990) 90, p. 251.
"Over the Delaware River" (tr. by Sonia Raiziss). [HampSPR] (Anthology
   1975-1990) 90, p. 250.
"Total destruction has coherent design" (tr. by Sonia Raiziss). [HampSPR]
   (Anthology 1975-1990) 90, p. 251.
"You subdued me & like a franciscan I pray to your body" (tr. by Sonia Raiziss).
   [HampSPR] (Anthology 1975-1990) 90, p. 252.
4877. PALEN, John
"People at the Beach." [WebR] (14:2) Spr 90, p. 88.
"Teenage Child Blues." [KanQ] (22:1/2) Wint-Spr 90, p. 229.
4878. PALENZUELA, Fernando
"Imagen del Reverso." [LindLM] (9:4) O-D 90, p. 13.
4879. PALLAS, Brent
"Constance Wilde." [Poetry] (157:3) D 90, p. 145-146.
"Winter Flies." [Poetry] (157:3) D 90, p. 144.
4880. PALLEY, Julian
"Vultures." [SoCoast] (9) Fall 90, p. 27.
4881. PALLISTER, Jan
"Cris" (Excerpt, tr. of Joyce Mansour). [Paint] (17:33/34) Spr-Aut 90, p. 28.
"On the Straw Fan" (tr. of Mbaye Gana Kebe). [Vis] (32) 90, p. 14.
"Repaces" (Excerpt, tr. of Joyce Mansour). [Paint] (17:33/34) Spr-Aut 90, p. 27.
"A Smile" (tr. of Mbaye Gana Kebe). [Vis] (32) 90, p. 15.
4882. PALMA, Lisa
"Prenatal Poem." [NewYorkQ] (43) Fall 90, p. 75.
PALMA, Ray di
   See DiPALMA, Ray
4883. PALMER, David
"The Detached Observer." [SlipS] (10) 90, p. 40.
4884. PALMER, Don
"Nicholas" (thoughts on my son three months before birth). [Rohwedder] (5) Spr
   90, p. 40.

355

PALMER

4885. PALMER, Leslie
"Dawn Boat Trip on the White River (Ark.)." [HiramPoR] (48/49) 90-91, p. 59.
4886. PALMER, Michael
"Deck" (Excerpts). [Zyzzyva] (6:3 #23) Fall 90, p. 33-50.
"Letters to Zanzotto" (Letters 4-8). [Conjunc] (15) 90, p. 219-223.
"Letters to Zanzotto" (Selections: Letter 1-3). [Avec] (3:1) 90, p. 24-25.
4887. PAMELA
"The Blue Room." [DenQ] (25:2) Fall 90, p. 32-33.
4888. PANKEY, Eric
"Abstraction." [NewYorker] (65:47) 8 Ja 90, p. 38.
"Clarity." [Poetry] (156:4) Jl 90, p. 204.
"In the Mode of Confession." [Antaeus] (64/65) Spr-Aut 90, p. 102.
"Provision." [DenQ] (25:2) Fall 90, p. 40.
4889. PANOFF, Doris
"You Can Restore Order in Your Universe." [WestB] (27) 90, p. 14.
4890. PANTE, Franco
"Montreal Pool Hall." [Descant] (21:4/22:1, #71/72) Wint-Spr 90-91, p. 205-206.
4891. PAOLA, Suzanne
"Ash Wednesday." [NewEngR] (13:1) Fall 90, p. 76.
"For Lily." [KenR] (NS 12:3) Sum 90, p. 111.
"Nocturne: Insomnia." [Witness] (4:1) 90, p. 81.
"The World Rising As a Mirror" (sunrise through the window, October, 1988).
    [KenR] (NS 12:3) Sum 90, p. 112.
4892. PAPALEO, Joseph
"Accidental Eulogy for the Human Race." [Footwork] 90, p. 25.
"Another House: Wasp Affair." [Footwork] 90, p. 24.
"Art and the Masses." [Footwork] 90, p. 24.
"Local News and a Reflection." [Footwork] 90, p. 25.
"Moguls: L.B. Mayer and My Father." [Footwork] 90, p. 23.
"Waiting for New Students." [Footwork] 90, p. 24.
4893. PAPELL, Helen
"Invisible Friend." [NegC] (10:2/3) 90, p. 107.
4894. PAPENFUSS-GOREK, Bert
"Arianrhod from the Overdoes" (Exceprt, tr. by Roderick Iverson). [Sulfur] (10:2,
    #27) Fall 90, p. 98-100.
"Mary shelley, i love only you" (tr. by Roderick Iverson). [Sulfur] (10:2, #27) Fall
    90, p. 96-97.
"Misforunate am i, a ruffian" (tr. by Roderick Iverson). [Sulfur] (10:2, #27) Fall 90,
    p. 95.
"Quietness that in scorn capsizes" (tr. by Roderick Iverson). [Sulfur] (10:2, #27)
    Fall 90, p. 96.
PAPPAS, Rita Signorelli
    See SIGNORELLI-PAPPAS, Rita
4895. PARADIS, Philip
"Getting Back." [CharR] (16:2) Fall 90, p. 65-66.
"A Semi-Passionate Bookish Commuter to His Love." [SouthernHR] (24:1) Wint
    90, p. 30.
PARADISE, Philip
    See PARADIS, Philip
4896. PAREDES, José
"Huída hacia Adelante." [Americas] (18:3/4) Fall-Wint 90, p. 126.
4897. PARGULSKI, David
"The Falling Children." [BlueBldgs] (12) 90, p. 14.
4898. PARHAM, Robert
"The Butterfly Effect." [Interim] (9:2) Fall-Wint 90-91, p. 36-37.
"Daemonization Towards a Counter-Sublime" (minor apologies to Harold Bloom).
    [CreamCR] (14:1) Spr 90, p. 105.
"Going to the Tent Revival." [ManhatPR] (12) [90?], p. 33.
"Headwaters of Big Creek." [ChatR] (11:1) Fall 90, p. 40.
"A Last Look Back at My Father's Garden." [CumbPR] (10:1) Fall 90, p. 38.
"Ochre and Red on Red" (Rothko, 1954). [CrabCR] (7:1) Wint 90, p. 30.
"Shoreline Mythos." [CrabCR] (7:1) Wint 90, p. 30.
"That Uneasy Creature, Creation." [Gypsy] (15) 90, p. 35.
"Warm Tea Promises." [Plain] (10:2) Wint 90, p. 29.
4899. PARINI, Jay
"Swimming After Thoughts" (In memoriam: Robert Penn Warren). [Poetry] (156:4)

Jl 90, p. 222-223.
4900. PARISH, Barbara Shirk
"Visions of Broken Eye." [Plain] (10:3) Spr 90, p. 22.
4901. PARISI, Philip
"Anniversary" (tr. of Alfonso Gatto). [PartR] (57:3) Sum 90, p. 431.
"An Evening in March" (tr. of Alfonso Gatto). [Chelsea] (49) 90, p. 127.
"Guilt" (tr. of Alfonso Gatto). [ColR] (NS 17:1) Spr-Sum 90, p. 97.
"Hear the Footstep" (tr. of Alfonso Gatto). [Chelsea] (49) 90, p. 126.
"A Mother Who Sleeps" (tr. of Alfonso Gatto). [InterPR] (16:2) Fall 90, p. 57.
"The Tale" (tr. of Alfonso Gatto). [InterPR] (16:2) Fall 90, p. 59, 61.
"They Shot at Midnight" (tr. of Alfonso Gatto). [InterPR] (16:2) Fall 90, p. 57.
4902. PARISOT, Roger
"Le Soleil des Yeux Clos." [Os] (30) Spr 90, p. 32-33.
4903. PARK, Donna M.
"Massacre." [ChironR] (9:4) Wint 90, p. 12.
"The Surgeon's Garden." [ChironR] (9:4) Wint 90, p. 12.
4904. PARK, Je-chun
"Festival in Fishing Village No. 19" (tr. by Chang Soo Ko). [PoetL] (85:2) Sum 90,
p. 39.
4905. PARKER, Alan Michael
"Paying." [NewRep] (202:12) 19 Mr 90, p. 32.
4906. PARKER, Aleksandra
"Garden Party" (tr. of Stanislaw Baranczak, w. Michael Parker). [Verse] (7:2) Sum
90, p. 13.
"Resume" (tr. of Stanislaw Baranczak, w. Michael Parker). [Verse] (7:2) Sum 90, p.
12.
"September" (tr. of Stanislaw Baranczak, w. Michael Parker). [Verse] (7:2) Sum 90,
p. 12.
4907. PARKER, Michael
"Garden Party" (tr. of Stanislaw Baranczak, w. Aleksandra Parker). [Verse] (7:2)
Sum 90, p. 13.
"Resume" (tr. of Stanislaw Baranczak, w. Aleksandra Parker). [Verse] (7:2) Sum
90, p. 12.
"September" (tr. of Stanislaw Baranczak, w. Aleksandra Parker). [Verse] (7:2) Sum
90, p. 12.
4908. PARKERSON, Michelle
"For Cece." [Gargoyle] (37/38) 90, p. 130.
4909. PARKS-SATTERFIELD, Deb
"17 Years Old." [Cond] (17) 90, p. 70.
"More Hair" (from Naps . . . The Politics of Hair, a prose/performance piece in
progress). [SinW] (42) Wint 90-91, p. 57-58.
4910. PARROTT, Kirk
"Make Black the Light." [ChangingM] (21) Wint-Spr 90, p. 25.
4911. PARSONS, Jeff
"Caught in Ice." [WormR] (30:4, #120) 90, p. 102.
"Food." [WormR] (30:4, #120) 90, p. 101.
"Housesitting." [WormR] (30:4, #120) 90, p. 103.
"I Read Poetry Like." [WormR] (30:4, #120) 90, p. 101.
"The Man in the Moon." [WormR] (30:4, #120) 90, p. 101.
"Produce." [WormR] (30:4, #120) 90, p. 103.
"Straightedge Razor." [WormR] (30:4, #120) 90, p. 102.
4912. PARSONS, Peter
"Villanelle." [Interim] (9:1) Spr-Sum 90, p. 46.
4913. PARTAIN, Lee
"How the Son Thanks the Father." [Poetry] (156:3) Je 90, p. 141-142.
4914. PARTRIDGE, Dixie
"After Looking Up Lapwing in the Encyclopedia" (for my mother, reprinted from
#17, 1988). [Kaleid] (20) Wint-Spr 90, p. 109.
"Decoration Day, the '50s." [HiramPoR] (48/49) 90-91, p. 60.
"Dreams Before Sleep." [Kaleid] (21) Sum-Fall 90, p. 44.
"Field Pond." [Comm] (117:16) 28 S 90, p. 537.
4915. PARUN, Vesna
"The Ballad of Deceived Flowers" (tr. by Daniela Gioseffi). [PoetryE] (29) Spr 90,
p. 103-104.
"Return to the Tree of Time" (tr. by Branko Gorjup). [CityLR] (4) 90, p. 196.
"Virginity" (tr. by Branko Gorjup). [CityLR] (4) 90, p. 197.

"The War" (tr. by Daniela Gioseffi). [PoetryE] (29) Spr 90, p. 105-106.
4916. PARVIN, Debbie W.
"The Deaf Couple." [GreensboroR] (49) Wint 90-91, p. 34.
4917. PASCHKE, Mona Toscano
"On the Verge of the August Full Moon." [Footwork] 90, p. 45.
"Prussian Blue Memory." [Footwork] 90, p. 45.
"RE/ Accounting." [Footwork] 90, p. 45.
4918. PASS, John
"Birds." [CanLit] (126) Aut 90, p. 31-32.
"Whose Lineage It Was, Lost." [Event] (19:1) Spr 90, p. 40-41.
4919. PASSER, Jay
"Flow Chart for the Masses." [Caliban] (9) 90, p. 123.
"Fuel for Allergy." [Caliban] (8) 90, p. 138-139.
"Hell Is Somewhere." [Caliban] (9) 90, p. 124.
4920. PASSERA, William (William E.)
"Black and White." [WindO] (53) Fall 90, p. 47.
"Daddy's Old Shoes." [PoetryC] (11:1) Spr 90, p. 26.
"The Trip." [WindO] (53) Fall 90, p. 48.
4921. PASTAN, Linda
"1932- ." [ParisR] (32:116) Fall 90, p. 111.
"Call." [HampSPR] (Anthology 1975-1990) 90, p. 112.
"December 18: For M." [Poetry] (157:3) D 90, p. 142.
"In the Fall." [GettyR] (3:1) Wint 90, p. 71.
"In This Season of Waiting." [NewRep] (203:23) 3 D 90, p. 38.
"Lost Luggage." [GettyR] (3:1) Wint 90, p. 72-73.
"Maria Im Rosenhaag." [GettyR] (3:1) Wint 90, p. 74.
"A New Poet." [GeoR] (44:1/2) Spr-Sum 90, p. 150.
"On the Marginality of Poets." [Atlantic] (266:1) Jl 90, p. 69.
"Orange Street, Kefar Sava" (tr. of Peretz-Dror Banai). [PoetL] (85:4) Wint 90-91,
    p. 23.
"Sculpture Garden." [Antaeus] (64/65) Spr-Aut 90, p. 105-106.
"Sestina at 3 A.M." [Poetry] (157:3) D 90, p. 142-143.
"Under the Resurrection Palm." [Antaeus] (64/65) Spr-Aut 90, p. 103-104.
"Unveiling." [AmerS] (59:3) Sum 90, p. 372.
4922. PASTERNAK, Boris
"Winter Night" (tr. by Richard McKane). [AmerPoR] (19:4) Jl-Ag 90, p. 47.
4923. PASTIOR, Oskar
"Poempoems" (12 poems, tr. by Malcolm Green). [ParisR] (32:115) Sum 90, p.
    46-50.
4924. PASTOR, Ned
"A Curvacious soubrette from St. Paul." [Amelia] (6:2, #17) 90, p. 39.
4925. PATAN, Federico
"Unicorn" (tr. by Rikki Ducornet, w. the author). [DenQ] (24:3) Wint 90, p. 44.
4926. PATCH, Gary
"Algeria." [NorthStoneR] (9) 90, p. 78.
"Lot's Wife." [NorthStoneR] (9) 90, p. 77-78.
"Washed in Salt." [NorthStoneR] (9) 90, p. 78.
4927. PATEL, Gieve
"Giving." [Arc] (25) Aut 90, p. 65.
"Turning Aside." [Arc] (25) Aut 90, p. 63-64.
4928. PATTEN, Karl
"Empathy for Two Poets." [CharR] (16:2) Fall 90, p. 63.
"I Put Down an Anthology of Spanish Poetry and Write." [Journal] (13:2) Fall-Wint
    89-90, p. 30.
"A Pea-Souper." [Journal] (13:2) Fall-Wint 89-90, p. 29.
"Saint Cow." [CharR] (16:2) Fall 90, p. 64.
"Warsaw, 1942: The Photograph, Some Facts." [GreensboroR] (49) Wint 90-91, p.
    54.
"Washing Vegetables." [CharR] (16:2) Fall 90, p. 65.
4929. PATTERSON, Veronica
"The Dream of Our Undoing." [SouthernPR] (30:2) Fall 90, p. 51.
"Tattoos." [ManhatPR] (11) [89?], p. 41.
4930. PATTON, Elizabeth
"For a Student Suicide." [WindO] (53) Fall 90, p. 39.
"Motorcycle Man." [WindO] (53) Fall 90, p. 36.
"Pulling Out the Plot" (A 30-year-old woodcutter charged in bank heist). [WindO]

(53) Fall 90, p. 38-39.
"Reflections on Men: Upstate New York Girl Gets Offers to Travel." [WindO] (53)
Fall 90, p. 37.
4931. PATTON, Laurie
"Mary Contemplating the Second Coming." [WillowR] Spr 90, p. 24.
4932. PATTON, Lee
"When Everything Is Goneril." [Thrpny] (42) Sum 90, p. 11.
4933. PATTON, Sarah
"The Host." [Mildred] (4:1) 90, p. 21-22.
4934. PAU-LLOSA, Ricardo
"Cañaverales." [Iowa] (20:2) Spr-Sum 90, p. 92-93.
"Dart." [MassR] (31:4) Wint 90, p. 548.
"Key Biscayne." [TampaR] (3) 90, p. 20.
"Orchids." [TampaR] (3) 90, p. 21.
"Tabaco de Vuelta Abajo." [Iowa] (20:2) Spr-Sum 90, p. 91.
"Valle de Viñales." [SouthernPR] (30:2) Fall 90, p. 58.
4935. PAUL, Jay
"Her Dream Was of Water" (in memory of Teresa Van Dover). [Shen] (40:4) Wint
90, p. 45.
"Memorial Day." [Shen] (40:4) Wint 90, p. 44.
4936. PAULK, William
"Augustus the Strong to His Keeper of the Green Vault." [Hellas] (1:1) Spr 90, p.
55.
"Butterfly Spring." [Hellas] (1:1) Spr 90, p. 56.
4937. PAVLICH, Walter
"After an Afternoon Showing of Laurel and Hardy's *Brats*." [Shen] (40:2) Sum 90,
p. 37.
"Flying to the Fire with the Doors Off" (for Bruce Latimer). [Pig] (16) 90, p. 81.
"Hardhat Pillow." [Pig] (16) 90, p. 81.
"If You Don't Know It's October." [Shen] (40:2) Sum 90, p. 38.
"Killing the Man Who Wanted to Die." [Manoa] (2:1) Spr 90, p. 20-21.
"A Phobic Describes the Enigma of Bridges." [SoCoast] (9) Fall 90, p. 34-35.
"Snow without Willie." [Manoa] (2:2) Fall 90, p. 132-133.
"To the Physicist Who Named a Type of Pain After Himself." [Manoa] (2:2) Fall 90,
p. 133.
"Visiting Day." [Shen] (40:2) Sum 90, p. 36.
4938. PAVLOPOULOS, Yórges
"Childhood Sketch" (tr. by Robert Head and Darlene Fife). [Bogg] (62) 90, p. 25.
"The Door" (tr. by Darlene Fife). [OnTheBus] (2:2/3:1, #6/7) Sum-Fall 90 Wint-Spr
91, p. 248.
"The Poet and the Moon" (Salute to Jorge Luis Borges, tr. by Darlene Fife).
[OnTheBus] (2:2/3:1, #6/7) Sum-Fall 90 Wint-Spr 91, p. 249.
"Untitled: Hwen the eagle was killed" (tr. by Robert Head). [OnTheBus] (2:2/3:1,
#6/7) Sum-Fall 90 Wint-Spr 91, p. 248.
"The Workman" (tr. by Darlene Fife). [OnTheBus] (2:2/3:1, #6/7) Sum-Fall 90
Wint-Spr 91, p. 249.
4939. PAVLOV, Konstantin
"Capricho for Goya" (tr. by Ludmilla Popova-Wightman). [PoetryE] (29) Spr 90, p.
146.
"The Exquisite in Poetry, or, A Victim of Tropical Fish" (tr. by Ludmilla
Popova-Wightman). [PoetryE] (29) Spr 90, p. 143-145.
"An eye for an eye" (tr. by Ludmilla Popova-Wightman). [PoetryE] (29) Spr 90, p.
153.
"Hector, the Dog" (tr. by Ludmilla Popova-Wightman). [PoetryE] (29) Spr 90, p.
149.
"It Was the 20th Century" (tr. by Ludmilla Popova-Wightman). [PoetryE] (29) Spr
90, p. 152.
"Oedipus Complex" (tr. by Ludmilla Popova-Wightman). [PoetryE] (29) Spr 90, p.
150.
"Paradox" (tr. by Ludmilla Popova-Wightman). [PoetryE] (29) Spr 90, p. 147-148.
"To L. Levchev" (tr. by Ludmilla Popova-Wightman). [PoetryE] (29) Spr 90, p.
151.
4940. PAWELCZACK, Andy
"Deva." [Footwork] 90, p. 100.
"From Each According to His Abilities, to Each According to His Need."
[Footwork] 90, p. 100.

"I Dreamed I Was a Great Painter." [Footwork] 90, p. 100.
"Poem: My wife says." [Footwork] 90, p. 101.
4941. PAWLAK, Mark
"Cambodian Guerrilla Sponsorship Drive Announced." [SlipS] (10) 90, p. 84.
"Never to Forget." [SlipS] (10) 90, p. 83.
"El Salvadorean Army General, Jose Alberto *Chele* Medrano, Speaks." [SlipS] (10) 90, p. 82.
"South Korea's Military Government Complains of 'Misleading Terms Used by the Foreign Press in Reporting Recent Developments'." [SlipS] (10) 90, p. 84-85.
"Turkish Pharmaceuticals Magnate Sees a Sunny Future for His Country" (for Andrzej). [SlipS] (10) 90, p. 81.
4942. PAYNE, Gerrye
"The Dancer." [Mildred] (4:1) 90, p. 19.
"Gerrye, Wound Knower." [Mildred] (4:1) 90, p. 18.
"Ghosts." [Mildred] (4:1) 90, p. 20-21.
"Parc Montsouris." [Mildred] (4:1) 90, p. 17.
4943. PAYTON, Dennis
"Master None." [IndR] (13:3) Fall 90, p. 108.
4944. PEABODY, Richard
"The Death of Smith-Corona." [ChironR] (9:1) Spr 90, p. 23.
"The General Progress." [WashR] (15:5) F-Mr 90, p. 6.
"Secret of the Play." [WashR] (15:5) F-Mr 90, p. 6.
"A Word of Warning." [WashR] (15:5) F-Mr 90, p. 6.
4945. PEACH, LeRoy
"The Descent." [PottPort] (11) 89, p. 48.
"For Langston Hughes." [PottPort] (11) 89, p. 49.
4946. PEACOCK, Molly
"Religious Instruction." [Verse] (7:3) Wint 90, p. 60-61.
"Subway Vespers." [Verse] (7:3) Wint 90, p. 59-60.
4947. PEARCE, Brian Louis
"Head Blowing." [SoCoast] (9) Fall 90, p. 19.
4948. PEARCE, Ellen
"Easter on Lake Erie." [NewL] (57:1) Fall 90, p. 106.
4949. PEARL, Dan
"To Heal a World." [BellArk] (6:1) Ja-F 90, p. 5.
4950. PEARSON, Yvonne
"Bloodroots for April." [SingHM] (18) 90, p. 95.
4951. PEATIKAKIS, Manólis
"Vacations, 1978" (tr. by Despina Efthimiades). [GrahamHR] (13) Spr 90, p. 100-101.
4952. PEATTIE, Noel
"Plumtree." [CapeR] (25:2) Fall 90, p. 21.
4953. PECK, John
"Underworld North of Lugano" (tr. of Rudolf Borchardt). [Salm] (88/89) Fall 90-Wint 91, p. 229-233.
4954. PECKENPAUGH, Angela
"O'Keeffe." [SingHM] (17) 90, p. 110.
4955. PECKHAM, Shannan
"The Root Garden." [Stand] (31:1) Wint 89-90, p. 74.
4956. PECOR, Amanda
"Marian." [MissR] (19:1/2, #55/56) 90, p. 265.
4957. PEDONE, Ann
"The Front" (Excerpt). [Notus] (5:1) Spr 90, p. 98-99.
PEENEN, H. J. Van
See Van PEENEN, H. J.
4958. PEERADINA, Saleem
"Michigan Basement I." [Arc] (25) Aut 90, p. 55.
"Sisters." [Arc] (25) Aut 90, p. 54.
4959. PEIRCE, Kathleen
"Forcing Amaryllis" (After Elizabeth Bishop's "The Gentleman of Shallot"). [Sonora] (19) Spr-Sum 90, p. 10.
"A Portrait." [Sonora] (19) Spr-Sum 90, p. 11.
"This December They Would Speak of Having a Child." [PoetC] (21:4) Sum 90, p. 11-12.
4960. PELIAS, Ronald J.
"An Alternative." [BlackBR] (12) Fall-Wint 90, p. 24.

4961. PEMBER, John
"Distributing The News." [Footwork] 90, p. 66.
"Flint." [Footwork] 90, p. 66.
"Ten in Queens." [Footwork] 90, p. 67.
"Trout Keeper." [Footwork] 90, p. 66.
4962. PENCE, Amy
"The Bowl." [WillowS] (25) Wint 90, p. 60.
"One Shallow in the Body." [WillowS] (25) Wint 90, p. 61.
4963. PENDER, Stephen
"2. Patron forgive us." [Descant] (21:4/22:1, #71/72) Wint-Spr 90-91, p. 211.
"The Artistry of Teeth." [Descant] (21:4/22:1, #71/72) Wint-Spr 90-91, p. 207.
"A Desert Song Unfinished." [CanLit] (127) Wint 90, p. 39.
"A Small Turkish Tableau." [Descant] (21:4/22:1, #71/72) Wint-Spr 90-91, p. 210.
"Tea." [Descant] (21:4/22:1, #71/72) Wint-Spr 90-91, p. 208-209.
4964. PENDOLA, Angelo
"Waiting." [Footwork] 90, p. 103.
4965. PENHA, James W.
"Candles." [Pearl] (12) Fall-Wint 90, p. 45.
4966. PENNANT, Edmund
"Duplicities." [NewYorkQ] (43) Fall 90, p. 52.
"The Museum, Cairo." [LaurelR] (24:1) Wint 90, p. 16-17.
"Newfoundland." [CrossCur] (9:2) Je 90, p. 28-29.
"The Tin Nautilus" (Un mystere d'amour dans le metal repose, de Nerval). [Confr]
(44/45) Fall 90-Wint 91, p. 201.
"Woodcut by Choki." [NegC] (10:2/3) 90, p. 32.
4967. PENNEFATHER-MCCONNELL, Nano
"Madame R." [AntigR] (83) Aut 90, p. 81.
4968. PENNER, Cheryl
"At the Head of North Kimta Basin." [PoetryNW] (31:4) Wint 90-91, p. 38-40.
PENNER, Raylene Hinz
See HINZ-PENNER, Raylene
4969. PENNEY, Scott
"Caracola." [ApalQ] (33/34) 90, p. 41.
4970. PENNISI, Linda Tomol
"Doctor." [SpoonRQ] (15:2) Spr 90, p. 24-25.
"Glass." [SpoonRQ] (15:2) Spr 90, p. 26.
4971. PENNY, Michael
"A Fine Couple, My Muse & I." [Grain] (18:1) Spr 90, p. 50.
"Pellagra, Bone-Tired." [Dandel] (17:1) Spr-Sum 90, p. 23.
"Pellagra, Caterpillar." [Grain] (18:1) Spr 90, p. 51.
"Pellagra's Angel." [Event] (19:1) Spr 90, p. 75-77.
"Pellagra's Eye." [PoetryC] (11:2) Sum 90, p. 27.
"The Physicist Prays." [PoetryC] (11:2) Sum 90, p. 27.
4972. PEPPE, Holly
"Night Reply." [ManhatPR] (12) [90?], p. 34.
"Not That Distance." [ManhatPR] (12) [90?], p. 34.
PERA, George le
See Le PERA, George
4973. PERCHIK, Simon
"115. The spider on this curb." [Rohwedder] (5) Spr 90, p. 39.
"162. Her loom as if some wounds." [PartR] (57:1) Wint 90, p. 100.
"165. You become expert -- the stream." [Rohwedder] (5) Spr 90, p. 39.
"176. These holes limping closer to my arms." [InterPR] (16:1) Spr 90, p. 125.
"207. Motionless, covering what's in back." [Wind] (20:66) 90, p. 35.
"215. This ditch no matter how haggard." [InterPR] (16:1) Spr 90, p. 124.
"219. It has nothing to do with braille." [InterPR] (16:1) Spr 90, p. 123.
"234. What did they see that my cheeks can't bear the weight." [OnTheBus] (2:2/3:1,
#6/7) Sum-Fall 90 Wint-Spr 91, p. 162.
"235. The blood this band-aid vaguely wrings." [OnTheBus] (2:2/3:1, #6/7)
Sum-Fall 90 Wint-Spr 91, p. 163.
"242. The oldest shout is orange." [OnTheBus] (2:2/3:1, #6/7) Sum-Fall 90
Wint-Spr 91, p. 162-163.
"301. This window sweetening the air." [Caliban] (8) 90, p. 131.
"329. With those hefty walls a bank will save forever." [Contact] (9:56/57/58) Spr
90, p. 29.
"335. Again a lull across my cheek." [HolCrit] (27:2) Ap 90, p. 19.

"398. Leave it to the lumber company." [Poem] (64) N 90, p. 37.
"402. Again the sky rubbing against my legs." [Poem] (64) N 90, p. 38.
"Again a brush sealing this boat." [SmPd] (27:1, #78) Wint 90, p. 23.
"And on this table." [HawaiiR] (14:2, #29) Spr 90, p. 121.
"And the dead can't wait, they crouch." [NewYorkQ] (43) Fall 90, p. 50.
"And the sun in ashes." [Os] (31) 90, p. 27.
"The cots, the stove, the crew." [Parting] (3:1) Sum 90, p. 4.
"Each night the longing." [Parting] (3:1) Sum 90, p. 37.
"The final piece tonight." [Northeast] (5:2) Spr 90, p. 14.
"Its branches -- the cold pruned, sap." [Parting] (3:1) Sum 90, p. 3.
"It's Not the Needle, Leaving." [GreenMR] (NS 4:1) Spr-Sum 90, p. 87.
"It's simple. The hole." [Caliban] (9) 90, p. 128-129.
"My fist laid out." [ThRiPo] (35/36) 90, p. 67-68.
"Stone, stone, stone, not a weeping." [Os] (31) 90, p. 26.
"This plaque and over the fireplace." [AnotherCM] (21) 90, p. 148.
"This slab once curled up inside." [Talisman] (5) Fall 90, p. 112.
"Though every evening." [SouthernHR] (24:4) Fall 90, p. 369.
"Until we are hid at last -- Death knows our eyes." [HawaiiR] (14:2, #29) Spr 90, p. 120.
"Untitled: Four in the morning and the dog wants to talk about her dream." [HighP] (5:1) Spr 90, p. 56.
"Untitled: I lift to make it remember, shake." [MidAR] (10:1) 90, p. 136-137.
"Untitled: My eyes close the way the Earth drifts off." [FreeL] (5) Sum 90, p. 16.
"Water Alone Remembers." [SoDakR] (28:1) Spr 90, p. 78-79.
"You See Traces: This Snow." [Farm] (7:1) Spr 90, p. 44-45.
"You send your hands across but the light." [RagMag] (7:2) Spr 90, p. 38.
"Your Shoulders in Overhead Sweeps." [LitR] (33:2) Wint 90, p. 240.
PEREIRA, Luís Moniz
   See MONIZ PEREIRA, Luís
4974. PEREIRA, Sam
   "The Agave Would Know." [CutB] (34) Sum-Fall 90, p. 21.
4975. PERELMAN, Bob
   "Neonew." [Verse] (7:1) Spr 90, p. 41-43.
   "The Net." [Avec] (3:1) 90, p. 141.
4976. PERETZ, Maya
   "Elegy on a Tile Stove" (tr. of Anna Frajlich). [Screens] (2) 90, p. 49.
   "Emigration" (tr. of Anna Frajlich). [Screens] (2) 90, p. 49.
   "I enjoy writing poems" (tr. of Halina Poswiatowska). [Screens] (2) 90, p. 51.
   "In Space and Time" (tr. of Halina Poswiatowska). [Screens] (2) 90, p. 50.
   "Song of Betrayal" (6 poems, tr. of Gwido Zlatkes, w. Stacy A. Klein and the author). [Screens] (2) 90, p. 52-55.
   "This night -- for you" (tr. of Halina Poswiatowska). [Screens] (2) 90, p. 50.
   "Women are valued for their beauty" (tr. of Halina Poswiatowska). [Screens] (2) 90, p. 51.
PEREZ, Matilde Espinosa de
   See ESPINOSA DE PEREZ, Matilde
4977. PEREZ, Nola
   "Ceremonially Drunk." [BlueBldgs] (12) 90, p. 29.
4978. PÉREZ-BUSTILLO, Camilio
   "The Promised Land" (Selection: #18, tr. of Clemente Soto Vélez, w. Martín Espada). [Agni] (29/30) 90, p. 200-201.
   "The Wooden Horse" (Selection: #3, tr. of Clemente Soto Vélez, w. Martín Espada). [Agni] (29/30) 90, p. 199.
4979. PERI ROSSI, Cristina
   "The Age of the Sea" (tr. by Judith Barrington). [Trans] (23) Spr 90, p. 187.
   "General Linguistics" (For Lil, tr. by Frederick H. Fornoff). [NewOR] (17:2) Sum 90, p. 43-52.
   "Infancy" (tr. by Judith Barrington). [Trans] (23) Spr 90, p. 188.
   "Meditation (I)" (tr. by Judith Barrington). [Trans] (23) Spr 90, p. 189.
   "Meditation (II)" (tr. by Judith Barrington). [Trans] (23) Spr 90, p. 189.
   "Quotation from a Poet" (tr. by Judith Barrington). [Trans] (23) Spr 90, p. 188.
4980. PERILLO, Lucia (Lucia Maria)
   "Dangerous Life." [BostonR] (15:1) F 90, p. 20.
   "First Job." [BostonR] (15:1) F 90, p. 20.
   "The News (A Manifesto)." [BostonR] (15:1) F 90, p. 20.
   "The Tone." [Atlantic] (265:3) Mr 90, p. 90.

4981. PERKINS, David
"The Goblins'll Get You." [HighP] (5:3) Wint 90-91, p. 89-90.
4982. PERKINS, Leialoha Apo
"Variations on Inferred War Themes from the *Kumulipo* and *Mo'olelo Hawai'i*" (Second Elegaiac Ode). [ChamLR] (4:1, #7) Fall 90, p. 1-3.
4983. PERLMAN, John
"For Ananda." [Talisman] (5) Fall 90, p. 107.
"The Hierodule's Apologue" (for Ray DiPalma). [Talisman] (4) Spr 90, p. 79.
4984. PERLONGO, Bob
"Cocktail." [WillowR] Spr 90, p. 15.
4985. PERREAULT, Dwayne
"Bones." [Event] (19:1) Spr 90, p. 39.
4986. PERREAULT, George
"This Morning at Tinsley Crossing." [SwampR] (5) Wint-Spr 90, p. 88.
4987. PERRY, Coties J.
"All alone." [PoetryUSA] (5:1) Spr 90, p. 15.
"The Real Rap." [PoetryUSA] (5:1) Spr 90, p. 15.
4988. PERRY, Edgar
"Poet's Epitaph" (ca. 2000). [NegC] (10:2/3) 90, p. 34.
4989. PERRY, Marion
"Sharon's Steady." [HiramPoR] (47) Wint 90, p. 41-42.
4990. PERRY, Pamela
"Last Supper" (tr. of Nikolai Kantchev, w. B. R. Strahan). [CrabCR] (6:3) Spr 90, p. 12-13.
"Night Lines" (tr. of Nikolai Kantchev, w. B. R. Strahan). [CrabCR] (6:3) Spr 90, p. 13.
"Transformation" (tr. of Nikolai Kantchev, w. B. R. Strahan). [CrabCR] (6:3) Spr 90, p. 12.
4991. PERRY, Stephen
"Aquos." [SycamoreR] (2:2) Sum 90, p. 19-20.
"Black-Eyed Susans in the Lemon Tree" (Honorable Mention, 4th Annual Contest). [SoCoast] (8) Spr 90, p. 23.
"A Little Wine, Some Death." [SycamoreR] (2:2) Sum 90, p. 21.
"Napi." [BelPoJ] (41:2) Wint 90-91, p. 23-25.
"Noel." [Nimrod] (34:1) Fall-Wint 90, p. 121.
"Shadows." [Vis] (33) 90, p. 45.
"These Things Are Important." [YellowS] (33) Spr 90, p. 6-8.
4992. PERSINGER, Allan
"Mathematics Was an Invasion from Outer Space." [KanQ] (22:3) Sum 90, p. 228.
4993. PERSUN, Terry L.
"In the Face of Seasons." [Wind] (20:66) 90, p. 36.
"The Worry." [Wind] (20:66) 90, p. 36-37.
4994. PESSOA, Fernando
"The Final Incantation" (tr. by Keith Bosley). [Stand] (31:2) Spr 90, p. 35-36.
"Follow Your Destiny" (in Portuguese and English, tr. by Edward Lacey). [AntigR] (80) Wint 90, p. 60-61.
"Freedom in Chains" (in Portuguese and English, tr. by Edward Lacey). [AntigR] (80) Wint 90, p. 56-57.
"The Keeper of Flocks" (Excerpt, tr. by Keith Bosley). [Stand] (31:2) Spr 90, p. 36.
"Leafstorm" (in Portuguese and English, tr. by Edward Lacey). [AntigR] (80) Wint 90, p. 58-59.
"Martial Ode" (tr. by Keith Bosley). [Stand] (31:2) Spr 90, p. 33-34.
"Ye Shall Be As Gods" (in Portuguese and English, tr. by Edward Lacey). [AntigR] (80) Wint 90, p. 62-63.
4995. PETERS, Nancy (*See also* HASTINGS, Nancy Peters)
"Death Lesson." [Plain] (10:2) Wint 90, p. 19.
"Delphi." [Plain] (10:3) Spr 90, p. 38.
4996. PETERS, Patrick
"Drowned Fisherman's Love Poem." [Farm] (7:2) Fall 90, p. 88.
4997. PETERS, Robert
"B. Davis Dies." [NewYorkQ] (41) Spr 90, p. 82-83.
"Marilyn Monroe Returns." [Pearl] (12) Fall-Wint 90, p. 38-39.
"The Mirror Never Lies." [Spirit] (10:2) 90, p. 152.
"On Visiting T. S. Eliot's Grave, E. Coker, England" (August 1989). [NewYorkQ] (43) Fall 90, p. 51.
"A Rain of Murder." [FreeL] (5) Sum 90, p. 25.

"Screams With Whipped Cream." [OnTheBus] (2:2/3:1, #6/7) Sum-Fall 90 Wint-Spr
        91, p. 164-165.
"Suburbanite Washing His Car." [ChironR] (9:3) Aut 90, p. 3.
"Youth and Car Stalled in Snowy Ravine." [ChironR] (9:3) Aut 90, p. 3.
4998. PETERS, Rosemary A.
        "Heritage." [PoetryUSA] (5:3) Fall 90, p. 8.
4999. PETERSEN, Paulann
        "The Mother Who Became a Tree." [Calyx] (13:1) Wint 90-91, p. 38.
        "Saying Three of the River's Names." [Calyx] (13:1) Wint 90-91, p. 39.
        "Sestina for Two-Eyes." [Calyx] (13:1) Wint 90-91, p. 40-41.
5000. PETERSON, Allan
        "Could have Been Verbs." [EmeraldCR] (1990) c89, p. 74.
        "Granite Is Weightless." [EmeraldCR] (1990) c89, p. 75-76.
        "I Think Rex." [FloridaR] (17:2) Fall-Wint 90, p. 104.
        "Just Cosmetology." [NegC] (10:1) 90, p. 30.
        "X-Ray." [CapeR] (25:1) Spr 90, p. 49.
5001. PETERSON, Jim
        "Daughter." [ClockR] (6:2) 90, p. 46-47.
        "Turtles." [ClockR] (6:2) 90, p. 48.
5002. PETERSON, Nils
        "A Journey." [PaintedB] (40/41) 90, p. 199.
        "Once I Went with a Girl Too Beautiful." [Mildred] (4:1) 90, p. 119.
5003. PETERSON, Phyllis K.
        "Leap, My Soul, in Grateful Joy!" [WorldO] (22:3/4) Spr-Sum 88 c1991, p. 51.
5004. PETERSON, Susan
        "Quick Silver: Ephraim Harbor." [Northeast] (5:2) Spr 90, p. 3.
5005. PETERSON, Walt
        "Marital Aids." [NegC] (10:2/3) 90, p. 56.
5006. PETKOVIC, Darinka
        "Commandments" (tr. of Ivana Milankova, w. Richard Burns). [Screens] (2) 90, p.
        68.
        "The Evil Sorcerers" (tr. of Ljubica Miletic). [Screens] (2) 90, p. 64.
        "Visions" (tr. of Ivana Milankova, w. Richard Burns). [Screens] (2) 90, p. 69.
        "White Angels, As They Crucified Me" (tr. of Ivana Milankova, w. Richard Burns).
        [Screens] (2) 90, p. 67.
5007. PETRI, György
        "It Would Be Good to Translate Mallarmé" (tr. by Nicholas Kolumban). [PoetryE]
        (30) Fall 90, p. 65.
5008. PETRIE, Paul
        "Alzheimers" (Honorable Mention Poem, 1989/1990). [KanQ] (22:1/2) Wint-Spr
        90, p. 18-19.
        "Changing Neighborhood." [KanQ] (22:1/2) Wint-Spr 90, p. 20.
        "The Sunken Cathedral." [HolCrit] (27:4) O 90, p. 16.
        "The Thaw." [ChrC] (107:10) 21-28 Mr 90, p. 302.
5009. PETRINI, Lisa
        "Auletride." [SmPd] (27:2, #79) Spr 90, p. 29.
5010. PETROSKY, Anthony
        "When the Sadness Came." [PraS] (64:1) Spr 90, p. 111.
5011. PETROUSKE, Rosalie Sanara
        "Dark Trees." [AntigR] (80) Wint 90, p. 118-119.
        "Hollyhocks." [AntigR] (80) Wint 90, p. 120-121.
5012. PETTET, Simon
        "The Reassurance." [LitR] (33:4) Sum 90, p. 511.
5013. PETTIT, Michael
        "Watson and the Shark." [ColEng] (52:3) Mr 90, p. 275-276.
5014. PEY, Serge
        "Altair" (tr. by Jean-Clarence Lambert and Bradley R. Strahan). [Vis] (32) 90, p. 44.
        "Capella" (tr. by Jean-Clarence Lambert and Bradley R. Strahan). [Vis] (32) 90, p.
        44.
5015. PFEIFER, Michael
        "Jerdon's Courser" (for Henry Carlile). [LaurelR] (24:1) Wint 90, p. 58.
        "The Obscene Phone Call." [MalR] (92) S 90, p. 98.
        "Snow Angel." [LaurelR] (24:1) Wint 90, p. 59.
        "Water." [MalR] (92) S 90, p. 97.
5016. PFOST, Mia
        "Another Spring." [DenQ] (25:1) Sum 90, p. 27.

"I Never Rode Your Cruel Horses." [DenQ] (25:1) Sum 90, p. 28.
PHILBROOK, Craig Gingrich
    See GINGRICH-PHILBROOK, Craig
5017. PHILIPS, Liz
    "Fields of Care." [Grain] (18:3) Fall 90, p. 21.
    "Solstice." [Grain] (18:3) Fall 90, p. 22.
5018. PHILLIPS, A'Dora
    "Photograph & Story in the *Press*: The Mother Whose Children Burned to Death."
        [ThRiPo] (35/36) 90, p. 8.
    "The Summer My Mother Fell in Love and Wanted to Leave My Father." [ThRiPo]
        (35/36) 90, p. 9-10.
5019. PHILLIPS, Carl
    "Her Hands." [NegC] (10:2/3) 90, p. 57-58.
    "Levitation." [HawaiiR] (14:2, #29) Spr 90, p. 107-108.
    "Undressing for Li Po." [ChamLR] (4:1, #7) Fall 90, p. 78-79.
    "Your Country." [Callaloo] (13:2) Spr 90, p. 305-306.
5020. PHILLIPS, David
    "When building houses the carpenters say" (for Bob Creeley). [WestCL] (24:3) Wint
        90, p. 23-25.
5021. PHILLIPS, Frances
    "Fishing the Light." [Zyzzyva] (6:1 #21) Spr 90, p. 105-110.
5022. PHILLIPS, Frank Lamont
    "Ardella." [Obs] (5:2) Sum 90, p. 101-102.
    "December 12th." [Obs] (5:2) Sum 90, p. 103-1-4.
    "Elegy for the Sea at Night." [Obs] (5:2) Sum 90, p. 100-101.
    "Parade Park." [Obs] (5:2) Sum 90, p. 100.
    "Paula Lorraine." [Obs] (5:2) Sum 90, p. 102-103.
    "Twyla." [Obs] (5:2) Sum 90, p. 102.
5023. PHILLIPS, Glen
    "Dolorous Nightwalker's Song, or Reechy Me a Kiss." [TampaR] (3) 90, p. 57.
5024. PHILLIPS, James L.
    "The Leprechauns of Our Lives." [LaurelR] (24:2) Sum 90, p. 56.
5025. PHILLIPS, Janet
    "Among Struggles Between Life and Death" (reprinted from #5, 1982). [Kaleid] (20)
        Wint-Spr 90, p. 42.
5026. PHILLIPS, Louis
    "30." [Footwork] 90, p. 16.
    "The Deaf Fisherman." [Footwork] 90, p. 17.
    "A Field Guide to the Shells." [KanQ] (22:1/2) Wint-Spr 90, p. 172.
    "Genesis II." [ApalQ] (33/34) 90, p. 75.
    "Johnny Inkslinger Contemplates the Suicide of Marilyn Monroe." [Pearl] (12)
        Fall-Wint 90, p. 29.
    "Just Another Disaster Poem." [DustyD] (1:2) O 90, p. 17.
    "Near La Paz." [Footwork] 90, p. 16.
    "Of Raccoons & Chipmunks." [SoCaR] (23:1) Fall 90, p. 28.
    "Try This Poem Before You Read Any Others." [CapeR] (25:1) Spr 90, p. 1.
5027. PHILLIPS, Michael Lee
    "Following the Map." [KanQ] (22:3) Sum 90, p. 86.
5028. PHILLIPS, Randy (*See also* PHILLIS, Randy)
    "All New! As Sure As the Moon Moves Oceans." [HolCrit] (27:5) D 90, p. 18.
5029. PHILLIPS, Robert
    "Oysters." [Boulevard] (4:3/5:1, #12/13) Spr 90, p. 223.
    "Victory Lunch." [Boulevard] (4:3/5:1, #12/13) Spr 90, p. 224.
5030. PHILLIPS, Walt
    "Common Condition." [Wind] (20:66) 90, p. 35.
    "For Her." [Wind] (20:66) 90, p. 19.
    "The Forbidden." [ChironR] (9:1) Spr 90, p. 2.
    "I Crave a Place in Literary History." [ChironR] (9:1) Spr 90, p. 2.
    "I Think I'm Learning." [ChironR] (9:1) Spr 90, p. 2.
    "Misfit." [FreeL] (5) Sum 90, p. 23.
    "The Panama Hat Couple." [Wind] (20:66) 90, p. 42.
    "Some Think I'm Nuts But It's Just That I'm Artistic As Hell." [ChironR] (9:1) Spr
        90, p. 2.
    "What Karl the Gut Said." [BlackBR] (12) Fall-Wint 90, p. 34.
    "The Wild Man." [BlackBR] (12) Fall-Wint 90, p. 35.

5031. PHILLIS, Randy (*See also* PHILLIPS, Randy)
"Hide and Seek." [SoCaR] (23:1) Fall 90, p. 86.
"The Soon to Be Immortal Talks to Himself." [Iowa] (20:3) Fall 90, p. 122.
5032. PHILPOT, Tracy
"Louisa's Wedding." [AntR] (48:4) Fall 90, p. 498.
"The Lover's City of Art." [MissR] (19:1/2, #55/56) 90, p. 266-267.
"This Faith." [MissouriR] (13:2) 90, p. 153.
"To Live in the Distances." [MissouriR] (13:2) 90, p. 152.
"Why You Close Doors Behind Us." [BlackWR] (17:1) Fall-Wint 90, p. 155-156.
5033. PICIKIN, Zoran
"Beggars' Camp" (tr. by the author). [RagMag] (8:1) 90, p. 22.
"The Heralds" (tr. by the author). [RagMag] (8:1) 90, p. 20.
"Logor Siromaha (Beggars' Camp)." [RagMag] (8:1) 90, p. 23.
"Opazanje (Perception)" (in Croatian). [RagMag] (8:1) 90, p. 21.
"Perception" (tr. by the author). [RagMag] (8:1) 90, p. 21.
"Vjesnici (The Heralds)" (in Croatian). [RagMag] (8:1) 90, p. 20.
5034. PICKER, Daniel
"Moss Hollow." [Sequoia] (33:2) Wint 90, p. 27.
5035. PICKERING, Stephanie
"I Can Remember You." [Kalliope] (12:1) 90, c89, p. 67.
"Saturday Afternoon." [Kalliope] (12:1) 90, c89, p. 66.
5036. PIERCY, Marge
"Detroit Means Strait." [SycamoreR] (2:2) Sum 90, p. 2.
"The Fisherman's Catalogue: A Found Poem." [HampSPR] (Anthology 1975-1990)
90, p. 18.
"Flat on My Back." [HampSPR] (Anthology 1975-1990) 90, p. 15.
"Heel Should Not Be an Insult." [MichQR] (29:4) Fall 90, p. 651-652.
"June 21 at 9:30." [Kalliope] (12:2) 90, p. 15.
"Old Shoes." [ColR] (NS 17:1) Spr-Sum 90, p. 88.
"Spinning My Wheels." [Kalliope] (12:2) 90, p. 14.
"Three Months Exile." [HampSPR] (Anthology 1975-1990) 90, p. 16-17.
"Who Might Have Been Friends." [HampSPR] (Anthology 1975-1990) 90, p.
15-16.
"Yearning to Repossess the Body." [ColR] (NS 17:1) Spr-Sum 90, p. 89.
5037. PIERMAN, Carol J.
"Arson." [Iowa] (20:3) Fall 90, p. 64-65.
"How I Imagine You." [CarolQ] (42:3) Spr 90, p. 10-11.
"Private Lessons." [RiverS] (32) [90?], p. 40-41.
PIERO, W. S. di
See Di PIERO, W. S.
5038. PIJEWSKI, John
"Blind Lesson in History." [Epoch] (39:1/2) 90, p. 55-59.
5039. PILIBOSIAN, Helene
"After Staring at an Owl." [CapeR] (25:1) Spr 90, p. 46.
"The Cinderella Theme." [HawaiiR] (14:2, #29) Spr 90, p. 17.
"My High Heels." [HawaiiR] (14:2, #29) Spr 90, p. 18-19.
5040. PILINSZKY, János
"Definition" (tr. by Emery George). [LitR] (33:2) Wint 90, p. 196.
"For Life" (tr. by Bruce Berlind, w. Mária Körösy). [PoetryE] (29) Spr 90, p. 59.
"From the Henchman's Diary" (For Thomas Tranströmer, tr. by Emery George).
[LitR] (33:2) Wint 90, p. 196.
"Hölderlin" (For György Kurtág, tr. by Emery George). [LitR] (33:2) Wint 90, p.
197.
"The Man Here" (tr. by Len Roberts and Adrienne Fekete). [AmerPoR] (19:5) S-O
90, p. 23.
"Opening" (tr. by Emery George). [LitR] (33:2) Wint 90, p. 196.
"Step by Step" (tr. by Len Roberts and Adrienne Fekete). [AmerPoR] (19:5) S-O 90,
p. 23.
"Two" (tr. by Emery George). [LitR] (33:2) Wint 90, p. 197.
"Veil" (tr. by Bruce Berlind, w. Mária Körösy). [PoetryE] (29) Spr 90, p. 60.
5041. PILKINGTON, Ace G.
"On Being Asked If a Friend Is Happy in Her Marriage." [MidwQ] (32:1) Aut 90, p.
90.
5042. PILKINGTON, Kevin
"Learning to Pray." [Turnstile] (2:2) 90, p. 73-74.

5043. PILLER, John
"Prayer Wheel." [TarRP] (30:1) Fall 90, p. 16-17.

5044. PILTZ, Jennifer
"In the Landscapes of My Heart." [SenR] (20:2) Fall 90, p. 77-78.
"Pastoral." [SenR] (20:2) Fall 90, p. 75-76.

5045. PINCZÉSI, Judit
"Our Creation" (tr. by Mária Kurdi and Len Roberts). [AmerPoR] (19:5) S-O 90, p. 29.

5046. PINDAR
"Fragments and Commentaries" (Friedrich Hölderlin's German translations with commentaries, tr. in English by Michael Hamburger). [Stand] (31:3) Sum 90, p. 36-40.

5047. PINE, Ana
"Freedom." [PoetryUSA] (5:1) Spr 90, p. 7.

PING, Tang Ya
See TANG, Ya Ping

5048. PING, Wang
"Crossing Essex." [LitR] (33:4) Sum 90, p. 456-457.
"Summer Rain." [LitR] (33:4) Sum 90, p. 457.
"You" (tr. of Jiang He, w. Steven Taylor). [LitR] (33:4) Sum 90, p. 525.

5049. PINSKER, Sanford
"In a Funk, the Poet Images His Obit." [KanQ] (22:1/2) Wint-Spr 90, p. 140.

5050. PINSKY, Robert
"Exile." [Salm] (85/86) Wint-Spr 90, p. 35.
"Falling Asleep." [NewYorker] (66:25) 6 Ag 90, p. 42.
"Homecoming" (tr. of Paul Celan). [ParisR] (32:116) Fall 90, p. 186.
"House Hour." [NewYorker] (66:10) 23 Ap 90, p. 46.
"Hut." [Antaeus] (64/65) Spr-Aut 90, p. 107-108.
"In Berkeley." [Ploughs] (16:4) Wint 90-91, p. 96-98.
"Love Crown" (tr. of Paul Celan). [ParisR] (32:116) Fall 90, p. 186.
"Shiva and Parvati Hiding in the Rain." [Salm] (85/86) Wint-Spr 90, p. 33-34.
"Street Music." [NewYorker] (66:46) 31 D 90, p. 70.
"Window." [Agni] (29/30) 90, p. 162.

5051. PINSON, Douglas H.
"An Evening On the Town." [Gargoyle] (37/38) 90, p. 138.

5052. PIOMBINO, Nick
"9/20/88 -- 9/2/89." [Verse] (7:1) Spr 90, p. 30-31.

5053. PIPER, Paul S.
"He sits in the car and stares straight ahead, blankly." [CutB] (34) Sum-Fall 90, p. 22.

5054. PISKOON, Sergey
"I'm not a Pushkin" (Poem written in English by high school students from the Ukraine, collected by Maureen Hurley). [PoetryUSA] (5:1) Spr 90, p. 18.

5055. PITT-KETHLEY, Fiona
"Just Good Friends." [Quarry] (39:1) Wint 90, p. 38-39.

5056. PIUCCI, Joanna A.
"Campagnano, Italy, 1921." [BelPoJ] (41:2) Wint 90-91, p. 17-18.

5057. PIVOVAROVA, Yulia
"The Answering Machine" (tr. by Oleg Atbashian and Maureen Hurley). [PoetryUSA] (5:2) Sum 90, p. 14.

5058. PIZARNIK, Alejandra
"En Esta Noche, En Este Mundo" (A Martha Isabel Moia). [InterPR] (16:1) Spr 90, p. 8, 10.
"In This Night, In This World" (For Martha Isabel Moia, tr. by Mark Smith-Soto). [InterPR] (16:1) Spr 90, p. 9, 11.

5059. PLATH, James
"Before They Closed Down Denny's Billiards." [Amelia] (6:2, #17) 90, p. 118.

5060. PLATIZKY, Roger
"Snapshot." [ChangingM] (21) Wint-Spr 90, p. 25.

5061. PLATT, Donald
"Aria for This Listening Area." [Poetry] (156:1) Ap 90, p. 29-32.
"Kore." [Poetry] (156:1) Ap 90, p. 32-33.
"Short Mass for My Grandfather." [PoetryNW] (31:1) Spr 90, p. 45-47.

5062. PLATT, Teri
"Brothers." [AmerS] (59:2) Spr 90, p. 196-197.

5063. PLAYER, William
"Monster." [DogRR] (9:2, #18) Aut 90, p. 24.
5064. PLEIJEL, Agneta
"Angel Movie" (tr. by Lennart Bruce and Sonja Bruce). [Spirit] (10:1) 89, p. 83-89.
"Änglafilm." [Spirit] (10:1) 89, p. 82-88.
"Är Stilla Nu, Sitter Vid Runda Bordet." [Spirit] (10:1) 89, p. 90.
"Det Finns Djupare Vatten." [Spirit] (10:1) 89, p. 80.
"Det Var i en Främmande Våning." [Spirit] (10:1) 89, p. 78.
"In an Unfamiliar Apartment" (tr. by Lennart Bruce and Sonja Bruce). [Spirit] (10:1) 89, p. 79.
"Min Mormor." [Spirit] (10:1) 89, p. 72.
"My Grandmother" (tr. by Lennart Bruce and Sonja Bruce). [Spirit] (10:1) 89, p. 73.
"När Jag Var Barn / Tanterna." [Spirit] (10:1) 89, p. 72.
"När Jag Var Barn Gick Jag På Ängen." [Spirit] (10:1) 89, p. 74.
"När Jag Var Barn Min Morfar." [Spirit] (10:1) 89, p. 76.
"Quiet Now, by My Round Table" (tr. by Lennart Bruce and Sonja Bruce). [Spirit] (10:1) 89, p. 91.
"There Are Deeper Waters" (tr. by Lennart Bruce and Sonja Bruce). [Spirit] (10:1) 89, p. 81.
"When I Was a Child / the Ladies" (tr. by Lennart Bruce and Sonja Bruce). [Spirit] (10:1) 89, p. 73.
"When I Was a Child I Walked the Meadow" (tr. by Lennart Bruce and Sonja Bruce). [Spirit] (10:1) 89, p. 75.
"When I Was a Child My Grandfather" (tr. by Lennart Bruce and Sonja Bruce). [Spirit] (10:1) 89, p. 77.
PLESSIS, Rachel Blau du
See DuPLESSIS, Rachel Blau
5065. PLEYNET, Marcelin
"Nuda" (in French and English, tr. by Michael L. Johnson). [Abraxas] (38/39) 90, p. 74-75.
"Tract" (in French and English, tr. by Michael L. Johnson). [Abraxas] (38/39) 90, p. 74-75.
5066. PLUMB, Hudson
"Departing from a High School Reunion." [Kaleid] (21) Sum-Fall 90, p. 46.
"Father of a Girl in Memphis." [Kaleid] (21) Sum-Fall 90, p. 46.
5067. PLUMLY, Stanley
"Coming into LaGuardia Late at Night." [Field] (42) Spr 90, p. 97-98.
"Dove." [Iowa] (20:3) Fall 90, p. 90.
"Doves in January." [Iowa] (20:3) Fall 90, p. 91.
"Dwarf with Violin, Government Center Station." [Ploughs] (16:4) Wint 90-91, p. 14-15.
"In Answer to Amy's Question What's a Pickerel." [Atlantic] (266:2) Ag 90, p. 56.
"One-Legged Wooden Red-Wing." [Field] (43) Fall 90, p. 71-72.
"White Bible." [GettyR] (3:2) Spr 90, p. 303-304.
"Woman on Twenty-second Eating Berries." [Antaeus] (64/65) Spr-Aut 90, p. 109.
5068. PLUMPP, Sterling
"10. Hunger/for a sky without a top." [AnotherCM] (22) 90, p. 87-88.
"15. He riffs his soul." [AnotherCM] (22) 90, p. 89-90.
"16. Lil Bro tells us." [AnotherCM] (22) 90, p. 91-92.
"17. My mother's last request is for an other." [AnotherCM] (22) 90, p. 93-94.
"18. Story and tales within tales." [AnotherCM] (22) 90, p. 95-96.
PO, Li
See LI, Po
5069. POBO, Kenneth
"Cicadas." [ChamLR] (4:1, #7) Fall 90, p. 32-33.
"Inauguration." [BlackBR] (11) Spr-Sum 90, p. 12.
"Talking Mica." [ChamLR] (3:2, #6) Spr 90, p. 85.
"Valves." [ChamLR] (3:2, #6) Spr 90, p. 84.
5070. POCH, John E.
"Creators." [ChironR] (9:4) Wint 90, p. 13.
"In My Father's House." [ChironR] (9:4) Wint 90, p. 13.
5071. POENARU, Vasile
"Georgic III" (tr. of Mircea Cartarescu, w. Thomas C. Carlson). [ManhatR] (5:1) Spr 90, p. 8.
"Prophetic Anatomy" (tr. of A. E. Baconsky, w. Thomas C. Carlson). [ManhatR]

(5:1) Spr 90, p. 11.
"So Cold" (tr. of Ana Blandiana, w. Thomas C. Carlson). [ManhatR] (5:1) Spr 90,
    p. 10.
"The Soul" (tr. of Ana Blandiana, w. Thomas C. Carlson). [ManhatR] (5:1) Spr 90,
    p. 10.
"Time" (tr. of Marius Robescu, w. Thomas C. Carlson). [ManhatR] (5:1) Spr 90, p.
    9.
5072. POESINI, Silvino
"Dearest Thrushes" (tr. by Stavros Deligiorgis). [Iowa] (20:1) Wint 90, p. 23-24.
"The Flower of No Smell Is Speaking" (tr. by Stavros Deligiorgis). [Iowa] (20:1)
    Wint 90, p. 24-25.
"From the Earth: Joys and Sorrows" (tr. by Stavros Deligiorgis). [Iowa] (20:1) Wint
    90, p. 25.
"I Call Them the Giants" (tr. by Stavros Deligiorgis). [Iowa] (20:1) Wint 90, p.
    22-23.
5073. POETKER, Audrey
"The Gift." [CanLit] (127) Wint 90, p. 73.
"In careful photos." [PraF] (11:2) Sum 90, p. 118.
"Not with prayers to the dead." [PraF] (11:2) Sum 90, p. 115-116.
"A seer a prophet." [PraF] (11:2) Sum 90, p. 116-117.
5074. POKOJ, Bob
"Four Days in an Unfamiliar Country." [PottPort] (12) 90, p. 40.
POL, Miquel Marti i
    See MARTI i POL, Miquel
5075. POLITO, Robert
"Evidence." [Pequod] (31) 90, p. 32-49.
5076. POLITO-LANGSTAFF, F.
"Sweet and Sour." [Writer] (103:9) S 90, p. 22.
5077. POLIZZI, M. A.
"The Shower." [Pig] (16) 90, p. 41.
5078. POLKINHORN, Christa
"About Dying." [OnTheBus] (2:1, #5) Spr 90, p. 113.
"A Day at Work." [OnTheBus] (2:2/3:1, #6/7) Sum-Fall 90 Wint-Spr 91, p. 166.
"Love." [OnTheBus] (2:1, #5) Spr 90, p. 113-114.
"Memories of Hot Chestnuts or Between Two Worlds" (For Harry). [OnTheBus]
    (2:2/3:1, #6/7) Sum-Fall 90 Wint-Spr 91, p. 166-167.
5079. POLKOWSKI, Jan
"Citizen Jan Polkowski -- Justification for Existence." [PoetryUSA] (5:1) Spr 90, p.
    8.
"The Flow of Eternity." [PoetryUSA] (5:1) Spr 90, p. 8.
"For a moment the hangman will stay his hand." [PoetryUSA] (5:1) Spr 90, p. 12.
5080. POLLACK, Carrie
"Object Lesson." [KanQ] (22:1/2) Wint-Spr 90, p. 189.
5081. POLLAK, Felix
"Visit to the Institute for the Blind" (reprinted from #8, 1984). [Kaleid] (20)
    Wint-Spr 90, p. 108.
5082. POLLET, Sylvester
"At 8 Above." [NewYorkQ] (41) Spr 90, p. 111.
5083. POLLITT, Katha
"From a Notebook." [NewRep] (202:4) 22 Ja 90, p. 34.
"In Memory." [WebR] (14:2) Spr 90, p. 14.
"Near Union Square." [SouthwR] (75:1) Wint 90, p. 73.
"Night Subway." [NewRep] (202:4) 22 Ja 90, p. 34.
"The Old Neighbors." [SouthwR] (75:1) Wint 90, p. 72.
"Playground." [NewYorker] (66:13) 14 My 90, p. 48.
"Signs and Portents." [NewYorker] (66:31) 17 S 90, p. 92.
"Visitors." [GrandS] (9:2) Wint 90, p. 74-75.
5084. POLT, Elizabeth
"Do our wounds make us blood sisters?" [PoetryUSA] (5:1) Spr 90, p. 4.
"Upon waking, I find." [PoetryUSA] (5:1) Spr 90, p. 6.
5085. POMEROY, Maureen
"Leda." [Plain] (10:3) Spr 90, p. 21.
5086. POND, Judith
"Embarking for Cythera." [MalR] (90) Spr 90, p. 41.
"February 15, St. Mary's." [MalR] (90) Spr 90, p. 40.
"Landscape, Pre-School" (for Sarah). [MalR] (90) Spr 90, p. 38.

369

"Pisanello's St. George and the Princess." [MalR] (90) Spr 90, p. 39.
5087. PONSOT, Marie
"Separate Even in the Swim" (Temara Plage, Morocco). [SouthwR] (75:4) Aut 90, p. 506-507.
5088. PONTCHARRA, Nicole de
"In the Café" (tr. by William Jay Smith). [Trans] (23) Spr 90, p. 143.
"The Wells" (tr. by Leland Bardwell). [Trans] (23) Spr 90, p. 142.
5089. POOBAY, Piney
"Help! I'm a Prisoner in the Right Hotel on Exchange Avenue." [PoetryUSA] (5:2) Sum 90, p. 6.
5090. POOLE, Anita
"Dat Boy." [MinnR] (NS 34/35) Spr-Fall 90, p. 4.
5091. POOLE, Joan Lauri
"Rembrandt's 'Jewish Bride'." [MissR] (19:1/2, #55/56) 90, p. 268-269.
5092. POOLE, Richard
"Cameleon." [CharR] (16:1) Spr 90, p. 43.
"Evening on the Beach." [CharR] (16:1) Spr 90, p. 42-43.
5093. POOLOS, James
"To Sleep." [ParisR] (32:116) Fall 90, p. 112.
5094. POPA, Vasko
"Prudent Triangle" (tr. by Charles Simic). [SenR] (20:2) Fall 90, p. 6-7.
5095. POPE.L, William
"The Phone Call." [BlackWR] (16:2) Spr-Sum 90, p. 28.
5096. POPERNIK, Karen E.
"Sestina." [HangL] (57) 90, p. 81-82.
5097. POPOVA, Olga
"Among Black Trees." (tr. by J. Kates). [CrabCR] (6:3) Spr 90, p. 8.
"What's Left" (tr. by J. Kates). [CrabCR] (6:3) Spr 90, p. 8.
5098. POPOVA-WIGHTMAN, Ludmilla
"11. Am I forgetting that until recently" (tr. of Blaga Dimitrova). [PoetryE] (29) Spr 90, p. 155.
"25. Blinded, they march on, the soldiers of Tsar Samuil" (tr. of Blaga Dimitrova). [PoetryE] (29) Spr 90, p. 156-157.
"29. I become more intimate with the dead" (tr. of Blaga Dimitrova). [PoetryE] (29) Spr 90, p. 157-158.
"33. Be prepared, be prepared!" (tr. of Blaga Dimitrova). [PoetryE] (29) Spr 90, p. 158-159.
"42. You set out to measure the world with your step" (tr. of Blaga Dimitrova). [PoetryE] (29) Spr 90, p. 159.
"51. A prisoner in the solitary cell of this body" (tr. of Blaga Dimitrova). [PoetryE] (29) Spr 90, p. 160.
"Bee Lesson" (tr. of Blaga Dimitrova). [PoetryE] (30) Fall 90, p. 57.
"Capricho for Goya" (tr. of Konstantin Pavlov). [PoetryE] (29) Spr 90, p. 146.
"Circle" (tr. of Blaga Dimitrova). [PoetryE] (30) Fall 90, p. 58.
"Dimension or Crucifix" (tr. of Blaga Dimitrova). [PoetryE] (30) Fall 90, p. 55.
"The Exquisite in Poetry, or, A Victim of Tropical Fish" (tr. of Konstantin Pavlov). [PoetryE] (29) Spr 90, p. 143-145.
"An eye for an eye" (tr. of Konstantin Pavlov). [PoetryE] (29) Spr 90, p. 153.
"Frost" (tr. of Blaga Dimitrova). [PoetryE] (29) Spr 90, p. 154.
"Hector, the Dog" (tr. of Konstantin Pavlov). [PoetryE] (29) Spr 90, p. 149.
"It Was the 20th Century" (tr. of Konstantin Pavlov). [PoetryE] (29) Spr 90, p. 152.
"Oedipus Complex" (tr. of Konstantin Pavlov). [PoetryE] (29) Spr 90, p. 150.
"Paradox" (tr. of Konstantin Pavlov). [PoetryE] (29) Spr 90, p. 147-148.
"To L. Levchev" (tr. of Konstantin Pavlov). [PoetryE] (29) Spr 90, p. 151.
"Transformations" (tr. of Blaga Dimitrova). [PoetryE] (30) Fall 90, p. 56.
5099. PORTA, Antonio
"Metrics and Poetry" (tr. by Graziella Sidoli). [Screens] (2) 90, p. 120-121.
"The Spouses" (Selection: 5, tr. by Graziella Sidoli). [Screens] (2) 90, p. 119.
5100. PORTER, Anne
"House-Guests." [Comm] (117:17) 12 O 90, p. 581.
5101. PORTER, Connie
"The Age of Miracles." [Callaloo] (13:4) Fall 90, p. 746.
5102. PORTIA
"Poem for a Lost Uncle." [Vis] (33) 90, p. 7.
5103. PORTWOOD, Pamela
"Books and Dreams." [Mildred] (4:1) 90, p. 116-117.

5104. POSTER, Carol
"I Killed Him" (tr. of Charles van Lerberghe). [Vis] (32) 90, p. 40.
"Yes the Day Shines Again" (tr. of Charles van Lerberghe). [Vis] (32) 90, p. 40.
5105. POSWIATOWSKA, Halina
"Drzazga mojej wyobrazni." [InterPR] (16:2) Fall 90, p. 32.
"I enjoy writing poems" (tr. by Maya Peretz). [Screens] (2) 90, p. 51.
"In my barbaric language" (tr. by Marek Labinski). [InterPR] (16:2) Fall 90, p. 33.
"In Space and Time" (tr. by Maya Peretz). [Screens] (2) 90, p. 50.
"The sliver of my imagination" (tr. by Marek Labinski). [InterPR] (16:2) Fall 90, p. 33.
"This night -- for you" (tr. by Maya Peretz). [Screens] (2) 90, p. 50.
"W moim barbarzynskim jezyku." [InterPR] (16:2) Fall 90, p. 32.
"Women are valued for their beauty" (tr. by Maya Peretz). [Screens] (2) 90, p. 51.
5106. POTTER, Carol
"Because the Egg Was a Door Nailed Shut." [NewL] (57:2) Wint 90-91, p. 10.
"From the Campground in North Truro." [NewL] (57:2) Wint 90-91, p. 11-13.
"Golden Delicious." [NewL] (57:2) Wint 90-91, p. 9.
"The Man at the Pompidou." [Field] (42) Spr 90, p. 54-55.
"A Round of Faces at the Dining Room Window." [NewL] (57:2) Wint 90-91, p. 7.
"They Want Ice Cream the Color of Honeydew Melon." [Field] (42) Spr 90, p. 56-57.
"The Trouble in the Third Floor Window." [NewL] (57:2) Wint 90-91, p. 8-9.
"What the Sign Painter Was Thinking." [NewL] (57:2) Wint 90-91, p. 5-6.
"A Woman Out on the Lake Is Singing." [Blueline] (11:1/2) 90, p. 85.
5107. POTTER, Jacklyn
"Broad Daylight" (tr. of Jean Follain). [WashR] (16:2) Ag-S 90, p. 26.
"The Charge." [Gargoyle] (37/38) 90, p. 137.
"Lamentation" (tr. of Jean Follain). [WashR] (16:2) Ag-S 90, p. 26.
"The Little Towns" (tr. of Anne Hebert). [Vis] (32) 90, p. 50-51.
"The Little Towns" (tr. of Anne Hébert). [WashR] (16:2) Ag-S 90, p. 27.
"The Rag" (tr. of Jean Follain). [WashR] (16:2) Ag-S 90, p. 27.
"Speech Alone" (tr. of Jean Follain). [Vis] (32) 90, p. 39.
"Speech Alone" (tr. of Jean Follain). [WashR] (16:2) Ag-S 90, p. 27.
"There Is Certainly Someone" (tr. of Anne Hébert). [WashR] (16:2) Ag-S 90, p. 27.
5108. POTTINGER, Steve
"Pigeons." [Bogg] (62) 90, p. 45.
5109. POUND, Omar S.
"The Cardinal Dies in Holy Week" (for Bill Chaney). [AntigR] (80) Wint 90, p. 123.
"On One with Magazine Fame." [NewMyths] (1:1) 90, p. 114.
"Politician (Retired)." [AntigR] (80) Wint 90, p. 124.
"Samson." [NewMyths] (1:1) 90, p. 113.
5110. POWELL, Dannye Romine
"Before the News." [PraS] (64:2) Sum 90, p. 16.
5111. POWELL, Douglas A.
"Chins or Criticize." [ChironR] (9:2) Sum 90, p. 10.
"Daily News and Whatever." [ChironR] (9:2) Sum 90, p. 11.
"Flora As Its Apart." [ChironR] (9:2) Sum 90, p. 10.
"Lunch My Accidental." [ChironR] (9:2) Sum 90, p. 10.
5112. POWELL, Jim
"Ars Poetica" (tr. of Jorge Juis Borges). [Agni] (29/30) 90, p. 54-55.
"It Was Fever That Made the World." [Thrpny] (40) Wint 90, p. 23.
"A Victorian Connoisseur of Sunsets." [Thrpny] (41) Spr 90, p. 35.
5113. POWELL, Lynn
"Eye Witness." [WestB] (26) 90, p. 51.
"Hegemonies." [WestB] (26) 90, p. 52-53.
5114. POWER, Marjorie
"The Clay Pot." [HawaiiR] (14:3, #30) Fall 90, p. 86.
"His Sign." [CrabCR] (7:1) Wint 90, p. 29.
"An Invitation." [HawaiiR] (14:2, #29) Spr 90, p. 42.
"May Nineteenth." [HawaiiR] (14:3, #30) Fall 90, p. 85.
"More." [CreamCR] (14:1) Spr 90, p. 115.
"Nightmare: Afterwards." [HawaiiR] (14:1, #28) Wint 89-90, p. 110.
"October in Glimpses." [HawaiiR] (14:3, #30) Fall 90, p. 85.
"Passing Through the Papago Reservation." [HawaiiR] (14:2, #29) Spr 90, p. 43.
"The Rose Garden." [HawaiiR] (14:1, #28) Wint 89-90, p. 111.
"Rowing." [CreamCR] (14:1) Spr 90, p. 116.

"Sand Poem." [HawaiiR] (14:1, #28) Wint 89-90, p. 108.
"Season Tickets." [HawaiiR] (14:1, #28) Wint 89-90, p. 109.
"Tishku Leaves the Party." [ArtfulD] (18/19) 90, p. 60.
"Wirephoto." [HawaiiR] (14:2, #29) Spr 90, p. 42.
"Yielding." [HawaiiR] (14:2, #29) Spr 90, p. 44.
5115. POWERS, Dan W.
"Stains of Onan." [PoetL] (85:4) Wint 90-91, p. 15-16.
5116. POWERS, Emily
"The Women in My Dreams." [PoetryUSA] (5:3) Fall 90, p. 26.
5117. POYNER, Ken
"Confidence." [WestB] (27) 90, p. 81.
"Crying Wolf." [WestB] (27) 90, p. 80.
"Political Disease." [WestB] (26) 90, p. 71.
5118. PRADO, Adélia
"Absence of Poetry" (tr. by Ellen Watson). [AmerPoR] (19:1) Ja-F 90, p. 48.
"Consecration" (tr. by Ellen Watson). [Field] (42) Spr 90, p. 24-25.
"Falsetto" (tr. by Ellen Watson). [Field] (42) Spr 90, p. 27-28.
"Head" (tr. by Ellen Watson). [Field] (42) Spr 90, p. 26.
"Land of the Holy Cross" (tr. by Ellen Watson). [AmerPoR] (19:2) Mr-Ap 90, p. 14.
"Seductive Sadness Winks at Me" (tr. by Ellen Watson). [AmerPoR] (19:2) Mr-Ap 90, p. 14.
5119. PRADO, Holly
"Guidance." [KenR] (NS 12:2) Spr 90, p. 156.
"Requiem" (for Jim Elrod). [KenR] (NS 12:2) Spr 90, p. 157.
5120. PRANGE, Marnie
"Suicide at the 'L' Motel, Flagstaff, AZ." [BlackWR] (16:2) Spr-Sum 90, p. 111.
5121. PRATER, Jane D.
"Grown-Up Tea." [EngJ] (79:1) Ja 90, p. 100.
5122. PRATT, Charles W.
"The Alchemists" (Wilbur and Moana, ca. June 1, 1988-ca. Nov. 1, 1988). [LitR] (33:3) Spr 90, p. 317.
"November: Sparing the Old Apples." [Comm] (117:18) 26 O 90, p. 615.
"On the Road to the Kingston Dump This Morning." [HiramPoR] (47) Wint 90, p. 44.
"Refuting Berkeley." [HiramPoR] (47) Wint 90, p. 43.
"The Verandah." [BelPoR] (40:3) Spr 90, p. 11-13.
5123. PRATT, Jerry Dillon
"Frost Line." [Amelia] (6:2, #17) 90, p. 13.
5124. PRATT, Minnie Bruce
"I Am Ready to Tell All I Know." [AmerV] (18) Spr 90, p. 47-48.
5125. PRECIOUS, Jocelynne
"Song for a Future Age." [Bogg] (63) 90, p. 44.
5126. PRELUTSKY, Jack
"Ballad of a Boneless Chicken." [Writer] (103:11) N 90, p. 8.
"Euphonica Jarre." [Writer] (103:11) N 90, p. 8.
"I Wave Good-bye When Butter Flies." [Writer] (103:11) N 90, p. 9.
5127. PRESNELL, Barbara
"Heredity." [LaurelR] (24:1) Wint 90, p. 32-33.
"He's Packed Up All His Zane Greys." [FloridaR] (17:2) Fall-Wint 90, p. 106.
"We Contemplate Our Second Child." [Kalliope] (12:2) 90, p. 52-53.
5128. PRESSMAN, Stephanie
"Thanksgiving." [ContextS] (1:1) 89, p. 41-43.
5129. PRETTY, Ron
"Shipwreck, Northwest Australia." [SouthernR] (26:3) Jl 90, p. 691-692.
5130. PRICE, Reynolds
"1 January 1990." [PraS] (64:3) Fall 90, p. 10.
"13 February 1984-90." [SouthernHR] (24:2) Spr 90, p. 120.
"15 March 1987." [SouthernR] (26:1) Ja 90, p. 196.
"16 March 1987." [SouthernR] (26:1) Ja 90, p. 196.
"An Afterlife, 1953-1988." [Poetry] (156:4) Jl 90, p. 215-221.
"Antipodes (1969 and on)." [PraS] (64:3) Fall 90, p. 11.
"Easter Sunday." [ChatR] (10:4) Sum 90, p. 26-27.
"First Love, Hayes Barton, 1958." [BlackWR] (17:1) Fall-Wint 90, p. 9.
"Giant." [SouthernR] (26:4) O 90, p. 893-894.
"The Rack." [SouthernR] (26:1) Ja 90, p. 197.

"Safekeeping, 1963-90." [SouthwR] (75:3) Sum 90, p. 376.
"A Single Bed, a Backstreet in Venice. Two Young Men." [ParisR] (32:115) Sum
    90, p. 42-44.
"Spirit Flesh." [PraS] (64:3) Fall 90, p. 11-12.
"Three Dead Voices." [OntR] (32) Spr-Sum 90, p. 16-19.
5131. PRICE, Richard
    "Back." [Verse] (7:2) Sum 90, p. 68.
    "Meat." [Verse] (7:2) Sum 90, p. 68.
    "With Us." [Verse] (7:2) Sum 90, p. 69.
5132. PRICHARD, Dael
    "People Seldom Listen Unless." [Amelia] (6:1, #16) 90, p. 72.-73.
    "Ultra-Violet Light." [Amelia] (6:1, #16) 90, p. 73.
    "What Ladies Wonder About Eminent Writers." [Amelia] (6:1, #16) 90, p. 72.
PRIEST, Travis du
    See DuPRIEST, Travis
PRIMA, Diane di
    See Di PRIMA, Diane
5133. PRIMMER, Mark
    "Drinking Muskies' Brute Look." [AntigR] (83) Aut 90, p. 100.
5134. PRINCE, Mark
    "I Owe You One." [LullwaterR] (1:1) Spr 90, p. 91.
5135. PRINS, Johanna H.
    "Christ As Gardener" (Painting: Christ the Gardener by Rembrandt van Rijn, tr. of
        Ida Gerhardt, w. Johanna W. Prins). [Trans] (24) Fall 90, p. 49.
    "Master Frans" (Painting: Regents of the Old Men's Home by Frans Hals, tr. of
        Bertus Aafjes, w. Johanna W. Prins). [Trans] (24) Fall 90, p. 59-61.
    "The Reviewing" (Painting: River Landscape with Ferry by Salomon van Ruysdael,
        tr. of Ida Gerhardt, w. Johanna W. Prins). [Trans] (24) Fall 90, p. 48.
5136. PRINS, Johanna W.
    "Christ As Gardener" (Painting: Christ the Gardener by Rembrandt van Rijn, tr. of
        Ida Gerhardt, w. Johanna H. Prins). [Trans] (24) Fall 90, p. 49.
    "Master Frans" (Painting: Regents of the Old Men's Home by Frans Hals, tr. of
        Bertus Aafjes, w. Johanna H. Prins). [Trans] (24) Fall 90, p. 59-61.
    "The Reviewing" (Painting: River Landscape with Ferry by Salomon van Ruysdael,
        tr. of Ida Gerhardt, w. Johanna H. Prins). [Trans] (24) Fall 90, p. 48.
5137. PRITZL, Penny
    "Letter to My Son on His Sixteenth Birthday." [SingHM] (18) 90, p. 42-43.
5138. PRIVETT, Katherine
    "Thirsty As Plants, Lonely As Animals." [PoetL] (85:4) Wint 90-91, p. 14.
5139. PROCTOR, Tye
    "Creature." [PoetryUSA] (5:2) Sum 90, p. 8.
5140. PROPER, Stan
    "Just Sit Outside." [BlackBR] (12) Fall-Wint 90, p. 22.
    "Molly." [SmPd] (27:1, #78) Wint 90, p. 9.
    "Pipe Dreams." [SmPd] (27:1, #78) Wint 90, p. 8.
5141. PROSPERE, Susan
    "Frozen Charlottes." [NewYorker] (66:31) 17 S 90, p. 44.
    "Into the Open." [NewYorker] (66:11) 30 Ap 90, p. 48.
    "Peonies." [Antaeus] (64/65) Spr-Aut 90, p. 110-112.
5142. PROUTY, Morton D., Jr.
    "North to Hawaii." [NegC] (10:2/3) 90, p. 94.
5143. PROVOST, Sarah
    "Divers." [SouthernPR] (30:2) Fall 90, p. 44-45.
5144. PRUITT,gladys
    "Cider." [Pearl] (11) Sum 90, p. 10.
5145. PRUNTY, Wyatt
    "Recent History." [Verse] (7:3) Wint 90, p. 62.
5146. PRUZAN, Jeff
    "Now Then." [Gargoyle] (37/38) 90, p. 131.
5147. PUGH, John
    "The Covenant." [PoetryUSA] ([5:4?]) Wint 90, p. 25.
5148. PULTZ, Constance
    "The Son." [NegC] (10:2/3) 90, p. 48.
5149. PURCELL, A. C.
    "Because of the Light." [Bomb] (31) Spr 90, p. 62.
    "Chinese Pornography." [Bomb] (31) Spr 90, p. 62.

"The Herbalist." [Bomb] (31) Spr 90, p. 62.
5150. PURDY, Carol
"Over and Over" (tr. of Rainer Maria Rilke). [NewYorkQ] (42) Sum 90, p. 77.
5151. PURPURA, Lia
"Aida" (tr. of Katarzyna Borun-Jagodzinska, w. the author). [PoetryE] (29) Spr 90,
   p. 16.
"At Dusk" (tr. of Katarzyna Borun-Jagodzinska, w. the author). [PoetryE] (29) Spr
   90, p. 17.
"The Brighter the Veil." [Ploughs] (16:4) Wint 90-91, p. 157-158.
"From the Book of Job" (tr. of Katarzyna Borun-Jagodzinska, w. the author).
   [PoetryE] (29) Spr 90, p. 18.
"Last Photograph of Teresa Martin" (tr. of Katarzyna Borun-Jagodzinska, w. the
   author). [PoetryE] (29) Spr 90, p. 19.
"A Very Bourgeois Lyric" (tr. of Katarzyna Borun-Jagodzinska, w. the author).
   [PoetryE] (29) Spr 90, p. 20.
5152. PURSIFULL, Carmen (Carmen M.)
"The Cage." [CoalC] (2) D 90, p. 18.
"News Item." [WorldO] (22:3/4) Spr-Sum 88 c1991, p. 27.
"Storm Warning." [Amelia] (6:2, #17) 90, p. 96.
"The Ultimate Gift." [CoalC] (1) Ag 90, p. 27-30.
5153. QI, Wei
"Concert" (tr. by Dong Jiping). [Footwork] 90, p. 44.
QING, Ai
   See AI, Qing
5154. QU, Yuan
"Jiu Ge" (Ritual Songs, tr. by Yun Wang). [PoetryC] (11:1) Spr 90, p. 23.
5155. QUAGHEBEUR, Marc
"The Outrage" (Excerpt, tr. by Daniel de Bruycker). [Vis] (32) 90, p. 34.
"The Outrage" (Excerpts, tr. by Mark Hutcheson). [Interim] (9:2) Fall-Wint 90-91,
   p. 44-46.
5156. QUAGLIANO, Tony
"Between a Rock and Mahatma Gandhi." [ChamLR] (3:2, #6) Spr 90, p. 71-72.
"One for William Carlos Williams in Hawaii." [Spirit] (10:2) 90, p. 151.
"Poets in the Schools." [NewYorkQ] (43) Fall 90, p. 76.
"Say Jazz." [MoodySI] (22/23) Wint 89-90, p. 24.
5157. QUALLS, Suzanne
"Au Pair." [Agni] (29/30) 90, p. 81-82.
"Encomium." [Agni] (29/30) 90, p. 83-84.
"The Wrong Son." [Agni] (29/30) 90, p. 85-86.
5158. QUARTO, Alfredo
"Riding the Metro Green Line into Blues." [Pig] (16) 90, p. 55.
5159. QUASIMODO, Salvatore
"Glendalough" (tr. by Will Wells). [PoetryE] (30) Fall 90, p. 52.
"Written, Perhaps, on a Tomb" (tr. by Will Wells). [PoetryE] (30) Fall 90, p. 51.
5160. QUATTLEBAUM, Mary
"The Statue Speaks with Pygmalion." [PoetL] (85:4) Wint 90-91, p. 9-10.
5161. QUEIMADO, Rui
"Song for When I Die" (tr. by Richard Zenith). [LitR] (33:2) Wint 90, p. 187.
"Song of the Death I'm Dying" (tr. by Richard Zenith). [LitR] (33:2) Wint 90, p.
   187.
5162. QUENTIN, Verena
"Cemetery with a View." [PottPort] (12) 90, p. 19.
QUESADA, Isa De
   See De QUESADA, Isa
5163. QUESADA, José Luis
"The Ones Who Died in April" (tr. by Zoë Anglesey). [OnTheBus] (2:1, #5) Spr 90,
   p. 193-194.
5164. QUESENBERRY, Mattie F.
"Shifting Night." [HolCrit] (27:4) O 90, p. 15.
5165. QUETCHENBACH, Bernard
"Moving to Marshland." [SycamoreR] (2:1) Wint 90, p. 35.
5166. QUINLAN, Michael
"Night Shift." [MoodySI] (22/23) Wint 89-90, p. 32.
5167. QUINN, Fran
"Romanesque Vaults" (tr. of Tomas Tranströmer, w. the author). [PaintedB] (40/41)
   90, p. 28.

"Tremor." [PaintedB] (40/41) 90, p. 200.
5168. QUINN, John Robert
"Peonies" (A Reminiscence). [LaurelR] (24:2) Sum 90, p. 53.
5169. QUINTANA, Leroy V.
"Castillo, our scoutmaster claimed." [Zyzzyva] (6:3 #23) Fall 90, p. 63.
"Grandmother's father was killed by some Tejanos." [Zyzzyva] (6:3 #23) Fall 90, p. 65.
"Haircuts at Ramon's were fifty cents." [Zyzzyva] (6:3 #23) Fall 90, p. 64.
"He was a tailor and came to be known as Juan Agujas." [Zyzzyva] (6:3 #23) Fall 90, p. 63.
5170. QUIROGA, José
"Chiaroscuro Defies Clarity." [Caliban] (9) 90, p. 141.
"Escrito en Llamas" (a Joseph). [Americas] (18:3/4) Fall-Wint 90, p. 117-121.
"Laboratorio." [LindLM] (9:1/2) Ja/Mr-Ap/Je 90, p. 10.
QUN, Zhao
    See ZHAO, Qun
5171. RAAB, Lawrence
"Beauty" (to M.D.). [Salm] (88/89) Fall 90-Wint 91, p. 362-363.
"Ghost Stories." [VirQR] (66:4) Aut 90, p. 675-676.
"Happiness." [KenR] (NS 12:4) Fall 90, p. 31-32.
"Learning How to Write." [Salm] (88/89) Fall 90-Wint 91, p. 364-365.
"Lies." [KenR] (NS 12:4) Fall 90, p. 32-33.
"Marriage." [Poetry] (157:2) N 90, p. 87.
"The Other World." [KenR] (NS 12:4) Fall 90, p. 33-39.
"The Shakespeare Lesson" (for John Reichert). [KenR] (NS 12:4) Fall 90, p. 30-31.
"Something Sensible About Desire." [VirQR] (66:4) Aut 90, p. 676-677.
5172. RABBITT, Thomas
"In the Deep End" (for Henry). [OhioR] (45) 90, p. 86-87.
5173. RABINOWITZ, Anna
"The Art of Painting." [CreamCR] (14:1) Spr 90, p. 144.
"Lion, Sand, Moon and You." [Caliban] (8) 90, p. 145-146.
5174. RACHEL, Naomi
"Fields of Vision." [HampSPR] (Anthology 1975-1990) 90, p. 195.
5175. RADAVICH, David
"Grecian Urn." [Farm] (7:2) Fall 90, p. 105.
5176. RADHUBER, Stanley
"Above the Rhône, Fog Coming In." [LitR] (33:2) Wint 90, p. 226-227.
"Monet's Palette: An Aubade." [LitR] (33:2) Wint 90, p. 227-229.
5177. RADISON, Garry
"Notes on a Dying Town" (selections from a poetry sequence). [Grain] (18:2) Sum 90, p. 9-14 and inside front cover.
5178. RADNOTI, Miklós
"Italian Painter" (tr. by Emery George). [HampSPR] (Anthology 1975-1990) 90, p. 259.
"Rain" (tr. by Emery George). [HampSPR] (Anthology 1975-1990) 90, p. 259.
"Restless Turning of Fall" (tr. by László Komlósi and Len Roberts). [AmerPoR] (19:5) S-O 90, p. 22.
"A Vague Ode" (tr. by Zsuzsanna Ozsvath and Frederick Turner). [PartR] (57:2) Spr 90, p. 269.
"Woods in October" (tr. by Len Roberts and László Komlósi). [ArtfulD] (18/19) 90, p. 25.
5179. RADUL, Judy
"Such sullen dust unhappy fate." [WestCL] (24:1) Spr 90, p. 101-104.
5180. RAGAN, Jacie
"Still Life." [MidwQ] (32:1) Aut 90, p. 91.
5181. RAGAN, James
"Happiness Andalusian Style" (tr. of Yevgeny Yevtushenko, w. Albert C. Todd). [Nimrod] (33:2) Spr-Sum 90, p. 122.
"The Heirs of Stalin" (tr. of Yevgeny Yevtushenko, w. Albert C. Todd). [Nimrod] (33:2) Spr-Sum 90, p. 120-121.
"Irpen" (tr. of Yevgeny Yevtushenko, w. Albert C. Todd). [Nimrod] (33:2) Spr-Sum 90, p. 123-124.
"Once the Prehistoric Man." [OhioR] (45) 90, p. 90.
"To the Boily Blind Boy the Sun Spins." [ColR] (NS 17:1) Spr-Sum 90, p. 66-67.
"Waking to Two Moons." [ColR] (NS 17:1) Spr-Sum 90, p. 64-65.

5182. RAIL, DeWayne
"The Door." [AntR] (48:4) Fall 90, p. 496.
5183. RAIMUND, Hans
"E Sopravvivere Alla Morte, Vivere?" (in German and English, tr. by the author,
from "Auf Distanz Gegangen: Gedichte"). [Abraxas] (38/39) 90, p. 76-77.
"Tabula Rasa" (in German and English, tr. by the author, from "Der Lange
Geduldige Blick"). [Abraxas] (38/39) 90, p. 76-77.
5184. RAINE, Craig
"Night Train." [NewRep] (202:24) 11 Je 90, p. 31.
5185. RAISOR, Philip
"Milan vs. Muncie, 1954." [SycamoreR] (2:1) Wint 90, p. 41-44.
5186. RAIZISS, Sonia
"Egg laboring in oval light" (tr. of Alfredo de Palchi). [HampSPR] (Anthology
1975-1990) 90, p. 251.
"Over the Delaware River" (tr. of Alfredo de Palchi). [HampSPR] (Anthology
1975-1990) 90, p. 250.
"Total destruction has coherent design" (tr. of Alfredo de Palchi). [HampSPR]
(Anthology 1975-1990) 90, p. 251.
"You subdued me & like a franciscan I pray to your body" (tr. of Alfredo de Palchi).
[HampSPR] (Anthology 1975-1990) 90, p. 252.
5187. RALEIGH, Robert
"Larry, Curley, and Moe on the Shore of Pine Lake." [TarRP] (29:2) Spr 90, p. 32.
5188. RAMBERG, Bjorn
"Western Love." [PoetryC] (11:2) Sum 90, p. 26.
RAMEY, Debra El
See El RAMEY, Debra
RAMIREZ, Lillian Holden
See HOLDEN-RAMIREZ, Lillian
5189. RAMIREZ, Victoria
"Riding Thru the Rough Side of Town." [Spirit] (10:2) 90, p. 153-154.
RAMIREZ DE HARO, José Elgarresta
See ELGARRESTA, José
5190. RAMKE, Bin
"Arcade: The Search for a Sufficient Landscape." [AmerPoR] (19:1) Ja-F 90, p. 35.
"Artist's Proof." [NewRep] (203:26) 24 D 90, p. 35.
"The Center for Atmospheric Research." [ParisR] (32:114) Spr 90, p. 218-219.
"Elegy as Origin." [ColR] (NS 17:1) Spr-Sum 90, p. 116.
"The Fanciest Forms of Innocence." [OntR] (33) Fall-Wint 90-91, p. 34-36.
"Incandescence." [MissouriR] (13:2) 90, p. 184-185.
"Independence Day." [MissouriR] (13:2) 90, p. 186-187.
"The Poor Miller's Beautiful Daughter." [AmerPoR] (19:1) Ja-F 90, p. 34.
"Summer as a Verb, Nantucket as an Island." [WestHR] (44:2) Sum 90, p. 223.
"Technology As Nostálgia." [MissouriR] (13:2) 90, p. 182-183.
5191. RAMMELKAMP, Charles
"Pregnant with Marilyn." [Pearl] (12) Fall-Wint 90, p. 26.
RAMOS, Gerardo Alfredo Jimenez
See JIMENEZ RAMOS, Gerardo Alfredo
RAMOS, Reinaldo Garcia
See GARCIA RAMOS, Reinaldo
5192. RAMOS OTERO, Manuel
"Dust in Love" (tr. by David Unger). [LitR] (33:4) Sum 90, p. 488-490.
5193. RAMPP, Charles
"Frontier." [Poem] (64) N 90, p. 17.
"Paleoliths." [Poem] (64) N 90, p. 18.
5194. RAMSEY, Paul
"Actions." [LullwaterR] (1:1) Spr 90, p. 11.
"Epitaph for a Mime." [Comm] (117:16) 28 S 90, p. 544.
"Scotland." [LullwaterR] (1:1) Spr 90, p. 61.
5195. RANAN, Wendy
"Summer Break." [Verse] (7:2) Sum 90, p. 91.
"What If." [Agni] (31/32) 90, p. 212-213.
5196. RANCANE, Anna
"Poem: Spring's breath fills the windows" (tr. by Ilze Mueller-Klavina). [Nimrod]
(33:2) Spr-Sum 90, p. 72.
5197. RANCOURT, Jacques
"Gravitation" (tr. by Edric Caldicott). [Trans] (23) Spr 90, p. 138.

"Suddenly You Slipped into Sleep" (tr. by Lindy Henny). [Vis] (32) 90, p. 48.
"Television" (tr. by Sarah Brickwood). [Vis] (32) 90, p. 49.
"This Evening" (tr. by Sarah Brickwood). [Vis] (32) 90, p. 48.
"With a Clear Head" (tr. by Edric Caldicott). [Trans] (23) Spr 90, p. 137.
5198. RANDALL, Belle
"Considering Flowers" (for Marguerite). [LullwaterR] (1:1) Spr 90, p. 33.
"The Severists" (A Manifesto). [Thrpny] (40) Wint 90, p. 25.
"Walking at Dawn." [LullwaterR] (1:1) Spr 90, p. 7.
5199. RANDALL, Julia
"Family Portraits." [HampSPR] (Anthology 1975-1990) 90, p. 139-141.
"Matchman." [HampSPR] (Anthology 1975-1990) 90, p. 139.
5200. RANDALL, Margaret
"Apolitical Intellectuals" (tr. of Otto Rene Castillo). [Quarry] (39:4) Fall 1990, p.
76-78.
"The Earth Is a Satellite of the Moon" (tr. of Leonel Rugama). [Quarry] (39:4) Fall
1990, p. 78-79.
"On Headaches" (tr. of Roque Dalton). [Quarry] (39:4) Fall 1990, p. 95-96.
"Yes, Something Did Happen in My Childhood." [AmerV] (21) Wint 90, p. 94.
5201. RANDALL, Mary Carol
"Commitment." [SinW] (40) Spr 90, p. 10-14.
5202. RANDOLPH, Robert M.
"Hands Like Telephone Wires." [NegC] (10:1) 90, p. 78.
5203. RANKIN, Deneise Deter
"Grandfather." [SouthernR] (26:4) O 90, p. 873-874.
5204. RANKIN, Paula
"Babysitting." [PoetryNW] (31:1) Spr 90, p. 5-6.
"Day by Day." [SenR] (20:2) Fall 90, p. 57.
"Ella, 1950." [PoetryNW] (31:1) Spr 90, p. 7-8.
"The Fathers." [PoetryNW] (31:1) Spr 90, p. 3-5.
"The Mann Children." [TarRP] (29:2) Spr 90, p. 41-42.
"My Mother Advertises for a Boarder." [LaurelR] (24:1) Wint 90, p. 14.
"Sleeping Ghosts." [LaurelR] (24:1) Wint 90, p. 15.
5205. RANKOVIC, Catherine
"Cupid and Psyche." [RiverS] (32) [90?], p. 12.
"Psychography." [RiverS] (32) [90?], p. 13.
5206. RANSFORD, Tessa
"The Willows and the Vines." [Stand] (31:2) Spr 90, p. 60-61.
5207. RANSOM, J. Reavill (Jane Reavill, Jane Reaville)
"About Your Christmas Card Picturing You and Your Husband." [NegC] (10:2/3)
90, p. 67.
"He Looks Like My Father." [Hudson] (43:3) Aut 90, p. 515.
"Sequence." [WebR] (14:2) Spr 90, p. 84-85.
5208. RAO, R. Raj
"Carrying My Father's Ashes by Train to Nasik." [Arc] (25) Aut 90, p. 67-68.
"Karla-Bhaja Caves." [Arc] (25) Aut 90, p. 66.
5209. RAPHAEL, Dan
"Lawrenceville." [Caliban] (8) 90, p. 84.
"Listening What I See." [PoetryUSA] (5:2) Sum 90, p. 6.
5210. RAPHAEL, Frederic
"Two personal problems: under-arm goat" (tr. of Catullus, w. Kenneth McLeish).
[Hudson] (43:2) Sum 90, p. 342.
5211. RAPOPORT, Janis
"Deliverance." [Arc] (24) Spr 90, p. 9.
"The Dreamed." [Arc] (24) Spr 90, p. 10-11.
"The Rebirth of Imagination." [Arc] (24) Spr 90, p. 8.
5212. RASH, Ron
"A Bass Fisherman Adjusts His Vision to a Darker View of the World."
[SycamoreR] (2:2) Sum 90, p. 38.
"A Confederate Sharpshooter Awaits General Forrest." [SouthernHR] (24:2) Spr 90,
p. 144.
"Good Friday, 1989, Driving Westward." [SouthernR] (26:2) Ap 90, p. 353.
"Having Recovered His Sight After Being Struck by Lightning, the Old Farmer
Quiets Those Who Would Question Him." [TarRP] (30:1) Fall 90, p. 32.
"Loss." [Plain] (11:1) Fall 90, p. 28.
"The Professor Visits Winn-Dixie After His Eliot Seminar." [PennR] (4:2) 90, p.
116.

"Respite." [WebR] (14:2) Spr 90, p. 92.
5213. RATCLIFFE, Stephen (Steve)
      "Georgia Minor." [Talisman] (4) Spr 90, p. 58.
      "How Far Is the Water." [Zyzzyva] (6:1 #21) Spr 90, p. 91.
      "Jack be Quick." [PoetryUSA] (5:1) Spr 90, p. 10.
      "Song Instead of *Psycho*." [Caliban] (9) 90, p. 67.
      "Without Thinking." [Caliban] (9) 90, p. 68.
5214. RATH, Sara
      "Horses." [BostonR] (15:2) Ap 90, p. 29.
5215. RATTAN, Walter
      "Hai-Phoo." [Bogg] (62) 90, p. 51.
5216. RATTEE, Michael
      "Spring." [PoetL] (85:4) Wint 90-91, p. 11-12.
5217. RATTRAY, David
      "Anaximander." [Conjunc] (15) 90, p. 144-145.
      "The Mantis." [Conjunc] (15) 90, p. 145-147.
5218. RATUSHINSKAYA, Irina
      "Why is the snow so blue?" (tr. by Oleg Atbashian and Maureen Hurley).
          [PoetryUSA] (5:2) Sum 90, p. 15.
5219. RAWLEY, Donald
      "The Savage Garden." [YellowS] (35) Wint 90-91, p. 15-17.
5220. RAWLINS, Susan
      "After the Spanish Grand Prix Jean-Pierre Jabouille Hangs Up His Helmet."
          [Abraxas] (38/39) 90, p. 134-135.
      "Deposition." [PoetC] (21:3) Spr 90, p. 13.
      "Growing Things." [PoetC] (21:3) Spr 90, p. 14-15.
      "What Is Important." [Calyx] (13:1) Wint 90-91, p. 7-8.
5221. RAWNSLEY, Richard W.
      "Counting Aloud." [PacificR] (8) 90, p. 33.
5222. RAWORTH, Tom
      "An arrangement of prisms and triangles." [Verse] (7:1) Spr 90, p. 49.
      "Maintaining the same distance." [Verse] (7:1) Spr 90, p. 49.
      "More sensitive phonecalls." [Verse] (7:1) Spr 90, p. 49.
      "Ones initial reaction is stunned unbelief." [Verse] (7:1) Spr 90, p. 48.
      "Sharply defined periods of individualism." [Verse] (7:1) Spr 90, p. 48.
      "To improve social behaviour." [Verse] (7:1) Spr 90, p. 48.
5223. RAWSON, Eric
      "Below the Power Plant." [Ploughs] (16:4) Wint 90-91, p. 202-203.
      "Marriage: The Second Year." [Amelia] (6:1, #16) 90, p. 16.
5224. RAY, David
      "The Asylum at Seacliff" (for Janet Frame). [CreamCR] (14:1) Spr 90, p. 122-123.
      "Bill Williams in New Zealand." [Footwork] 90, p. 11.
      "Cathedral." [Footwork] 90, p. 11.
      "Child Sleeping." [HampSPR] (Anthology 1975-1990) 90, p. 72.
      "The Circle of Silence." [Footwork] 90, p. 12.
      "A Dance on the Greek Island." [HampSPR] (Anthology 1975-1990) 90, p. 71.
      "The Dancing Grandmother." [Footwork] 90, p. 12.
      "A Day with Baxter: His Home in New Zealand." [CreamCR] (14:1) Spr 90, p.
          124-125.
      "Demons in the Diner." [MissouriR] (13:2) 90, p. 154.
      "The Early Jobs." [CharR] (16:2) Fall 90, p. 16-19.
      "Easting." [Footwork] 90, p. 10.
      "For Sam." [HampSPR] (Anthology 1975-1990) 90, p. 72.
      "Gathas" (9 poems translated from the Prakrit of the "Gatha-Saptasati"). [PoetryE]
          (30) Fall 90, p. 74-76.
      "Homage to Eugene Witla." [MissouriR] (13:2) 90, p. 155.
      "Legacy" (New Zealand). [WestB] (27) 90, p. 60-61.
      "Like a Dream" (India). [WestB] (27) 90, p. 58-59.
      "Of the Circle." [CharR] (16:2) Fall 90, p. 20.
      "On a Bus in Manhattan." [Confr] (42/43) Spr-Sum 90, p. 98-99.
      "An Outing in New Zealand." [Ploughs] (16:1) Spr-Sum 90, p. 96-97.
      "Pelee" (Second Award Poem, 1989/1990). [KanQ] (22:1/2) Wint-Spr 90, p. 10.
      "The Rendezvous." [Footwork] 90, p. 11.
      "Tipping Wings Over the Grand Canyon." [SouthernPR] (30:1) Spr 90, p. 55-56.
      "Voyage Out: Liverpool to Port Chalmers, N.Z., 1863." [CharR] (16:1) Spr 90, p.
          31-34.

"A Well in India." [HampSPR] (Anthology 1975-1990) 90, p. 72-73.
"The Yogi by the Roadside" (India). [WestB] (27) 90, p. 58.
5225. RAY, Judy
"Gardening" (for Sam). [Farm] (7:2) Fall 90, p. 70.
"Joy's Birthday Party." [Spirit] (10:2) 90, p. 104-105.
"Recipe." [WestB] (27) 90, p. 11.
5226. RAY, LeAnne
"Water Born." [WillowR] Spr 90, p. 26.
5227. RAY, Robert Beverly
"Seven Hundred New Words." [WashR] (16:1) Je-Jl 90, p. 10.
5228. RAY, Sunil B.
"Henna" (tr. of Vijaya Mukhopadhyay, w. Carolyne Wright and the author).
[GrandS] (9:3) Spr 90, p. 200.
"Irrelevant" (tr. of Vijaya Mukhopadhyay, w. Carolyne Wright and the author).
[GrandS] (9:3) Spr 90, p. 202.
"Which Floor?" (tr. of Vijaya Mukhopadhyay, w. Carolyne Wright and the author).
[GrandS] (9:3) Spr 90, p. 201.
"The Wrong Place" (tr. of Vijaya Mukhopadhyay, w. Carolyne Wright and the
author). [GrandS] (9:3) Spr 90, p. 199.
5229. RAZ, Orna
"Back to the Village" (tr. of Naim Araidi, w. Daniel Weissbort). [Trans] (23) Spr 90,
p. 228-229.
"If Only" (tr. of Naim Araidi, w. Daniel Weissbort). [Trans] (23) Spr 90, p. 230.
"Memory" (tr. of Ori Bernstein, w. Daniel Weissbort). [Trans] (24) Fall 90, p. 231.
"Procession" (tr. of Ori Bernstein, w. Daniel Weissbort). [Trans] (24) Fall 90, p.
232.
"What Can You Tell Me?" (tr. of Ori Bernstein, w. Daniel Weissbort). [Trans] (24)
Fall 90, p. 232.
5230. RAZOR, A.
"Against Broken Colors." [Gypsy] (15) 90, p. 67.
"Ode to the Rebellion." [Gypsy] (15) 90, p. 67.
5231. READING, Peter
"Perduta Genta" (Excerpt). [Quarry] (39:1) Wint 90, p. 40-42.
5232. REAGLER, Robin
"Message to the Goldfish." [MissR] (19:1/2, #55/56) 90, p. 270.
5233. REAL, Damienne
"Canoe Maker." [Pembroke] (22) 90, p. 107.
"Potter." [Pembroke] (22) 90, p. 106.
5234. REARDON, Michael
"Edgewater Almanac." [Footwork] 90, p. 108.
"If This Be Not I." [Footwork] 90, p. 108.
"Index to Dawn." [Footwork] 90, p. 108.
5235. REBAZA SORALUZ, Luis
"Corso de la Niña" (para Claudia). [WashR] (16:2) Ag-S 90, p. 17.
"Night" (tr. by Elizabeth D. Kauffman). [WashR] (16:2) Ag-S 90, p. 16.
"The Night" (tr. by Elizabeth D. Kauffman). [WashR] (16:2) Ag-S 90, p. 17.
"La Noche." [WashR] (16:2) Ag-S 90, p. 17.
"Noche." [WashR] (16:2) Ag-S 90, p. 16.
"Not a Window" (tr. by Elizabeth D. Kauffman). [WashR] (16:2) Ag-S 90, p. 17.
"Parade for a Young Girl" (for Claudia, tr. by Elizabeth D. Kauffman). [WashR]
(16:2) Ag-S 90, p. 17.
"Los Que Parten Estiman" (para Ana Maria Trelancia). [WashR] (16:2) Ag-S 90, p.
17.
"Those Who Part Hold Dear" (for Ana Maria Trelancia, tr. by Elizabeth D.
Kauffman). [WashR] (16:2) Ag-S 90, p. 17.
"Ventana Que No Es." [WashR] (16:2) Ag-S 90, p. 17.
RECEPUTI, Natalie
See RECIPUTI, Natalie
5236. RECHNITZ, Emily
"Caterpillars." [NewYorker] (66:16) 4 Je 90, p. 44.
5237. RECIPUTI, Natalie
"A Bit About Nona." [BellArk] (6:6) N-D 90, p. 7.
"In Pondicherry." [BellArk] (6:5) S-O 90, p. 24.
"A Poem for Matthew." [BellArk] (6:6) N-D 90, p. 1.
"Sandro Loves Jackie Forever." [BellArk] (6:5) S-O 90, p. 4.

379

5238. RECTOR, Liam
"My Business Partner." [AmerPoR] (19:6) N-D 90, p. 6.
"The Remarkable Objectivity of Your Old Friends." [NewRep] (202:18) 30 Ap 90, p. 40.
"The Widows." [Boulevard] (5:2, #14) Fall 90, p. 128-129.
5239. RED HAWK
"How the Athabascan Hunts Bear" (for Little Bear). [NewYorkQ] (42) Sum 90, p. 34.
"The Law of Proportion." [NewYorkQ] (42) Sum 90, p. 35.
"The Star-Drillers' Attention" (for Little Moose). [NewYorkQ] (42) Sum 90, p. 33.
"What the Old Cheyenne Women at Sand Creek Knew" (Sand Creek Massacre: November 29, 1864). [Atlantic] (266:5) N 90, p. 122.
"Words Are Not Actions." [NewYorkQ] (42) Sum 90, p. 36.
5240. REDDING, William J.
"Bay Memory." [HighP] (5:2) Fall 90, p. 71-72.
"This Is the Stone." [HighP] (5:2) Fall 90, p. 69-70.
"Where I Could Watch the Sea." [HighP] (5:2) Fall 90, p. 68.
5241. REDGROVE, Peter
"Blackthorn Winter." [ManhatR] (5:1) Spr 90, p. 16.
"Carcass and Balsam." [ManhatR] (5:1) Spr 90, p. 18.
"A Cat." [ManhatR] (5:2) Fall 90, p. 25.
"The Dead." [ManhatR] (5:2) Fall 90, p. 24.
"Illusionist." [ManhatR] (5:2) Fall 90, p. 22.
"Keep Running." [ManhatR] (5:2) Fall 90, p. 27-28.
"Mistress Shivers." [ManhatR] (5:1) Spr 90, p. 19.
"More Than Meets the Eye." [ManhatR] (5:1) Spr 90, p. 16.
"Popular Star." [ManhatR] (5:2) Fall 90, p. 28-29.
"The Secret Examination." [ManhatR] (5:2) Fall 90, p. 23.
"The Small Earthquake." [ManhatR] (5:1) Spr 90, p. 15.
"True Wasp." [ManhatR] (5:1) Spr 90, p. 12.
"Tunes." [ManhatR] (5:2) Fall 90, p. 25-26.
5242. REDHILL, Michael
"The Dream." [Writ] (21) 89 c1990, p. 56.
"Lake Nora Arms" (A regression in four parts). [Writ] (21) 89 c1990, p. 60-64.
"Midnight, I-95, Outside Atlanta." [WestCL] (24:3) Wint 90, p. 80.
"Oscar Wilde Pays a Visit." [WestCL] (24:3) Wint 90, p. 81-82.
"Skin." [Writ] (21) 89 c1990, p. 57.
"Tilted in from the hallway." [Writ] (21) 89 c1990, p. 55.
"You Are the Narcotic." [Writ] (21) 89 c1990, p. 58-59.
5243. REDMAN, Sue
"Mattie Stevens." [ChrC] (107:28) 10 O 90, p. 894.
5244. REDMOND, Mary Anne
"In the Heart of the Philippines." [CimR] (92) Jl 90, p. 126.
5245. REDPOND, Jess
"How to Learn to Break the Lines." [PoetryUSA] (5:3) Fall 90, p. 6.
5246. REDSHAW, Thomas Dillon
"Between Tides" (for L. L. R.). [NorthStoneR] (9) 90, p. 67-68.
"With Dürer's Engraving *The Knight, Death and the Devil*." [NorthStoneR] (9) 90, p. 69.
5247. REECE, Shelley C.
"Ascension" (for Andrew Voznesensky, a Plainsongs Award Poem). [Plain] (10:2) Wint 90, p. 36-37.
"Swan Dive." [Plain] (10:3) Spr 90, p. 26-27.
REED, Alison Touster
See TOUSTER-REED, Alison
5248. REED, Diana
"At the Glove Counter." [HampSPR] (Anthology 1975-1990) 90, p. 207-208.
5249. REED, Jay
"Anatomy Student." [NewRena] (8:1, #24) Spr 90, p. 30.
5250. REED, Jeremy
"Another Death" (tr. of Ghassan Zaqtan, w. Lena Jayyusi). [Screens] (2) 90, p. 21-22.
"The Cafe Mistress" (tr. of Muhammad Zakariyya, w. Lena Jayyusi). [Screens] (2) 90, p. 20.
"Egon Schiele." [Salm] (85/86) Wint-Spr 90, p. 127.
"Emigration" (tr. of Zakariyya Muhammad, w. Lena Jayyusi). [PaperAir] (4:3) 90,

p. 61.
"Everything" (tr. of Zakariyya Muhammad, w. Lena Jayyusi). [PaperAir] (4:3) 90, p. 60.
"Expectation." [Quarry] (39:1) Wint 90, p. 43.
"He Speaks" (tr. of Venus Khoury-Ghata). [Vis] (32) 90, p. 20.
"An Incident" (tr. of Ghassan Zaqtan, w. Lena Jayyusi). [Screens] (2) 90, p. 21.
"Lorca's Death." [Salm] (85/86) Wint-Spr 90, p. 124-126.
"A Mirror" (tr. of Chassan Zaqtan, w. Lena Jayyusi). [PaperAir] (4:3) 90, p. 62.
"My Things" (tr. of Zakariyya Muhammad, w. Lena Jayyusi). [PaperAir] (4:3) 90, p. 60.
"A Non-Personal Account" (tr. of Khairi Mansour, w. May Jayyusi). [Screens] (2) 90, p. 23.
"Our Country" (tr. of Ahmad Dahbour, w. Lena Jayyusi). [PaperAir] (4:3) 90, p. 63.
"Portrait of Flaubert." [Salm] (85/86) Wint-Spr 90, p. 128.
"A Tavern" (tr. of Zakariyya Muhammad, w. Lena Jayyusi). [PaperAir] (4:3) 90, p. 60.
5251. REED, John R.
"Switch." [PartR] (57:1) Wint 90, p. 107.
5252. REED, Walter
"Academic Exercise: Set of Sapphics" (for John Hollander). [LullwaterR] (2:1) Wint 90, p. 68.
5253. REEECE, Shelley
"Hero Lost." [Plain] (11:1) Fall 90, p. 37.
5254. REES, Elizabeth
"Indian Giver." [PoetL] (85:2) Sum 90, p. 7.
5255. REESE, Steve
"From the Road Home." [CapeR] (25:2) Fall 90, p. 3.
"Two Poems for the Guitar." [CapeR] (25:2) Fall 90, p. 4-5.
5256. REEVE, F. D.
"3 Sunsets at Hammonasset." [Poetry] (156:5) Ag 90, p. 293-294.
"January Thaw." [FreeL] (5) Sum 90, p. 8.
"The Toy Soldier." [AmerPoR] (19:6) N-D 90, p. 38.
5257. REEVES, Trish
"Twilight." [PraS] (64:1) Spr 90, p. 93-95.
"When the Farmers Come to Town." [PraS] (64:1) Spr 90, p. 95-96.
5258. REEVES, Troy
"Float." [KanQ] (22:3) Sum 90, p. 63.
"Gordon's Tomb, Jerusalem." [KanQ] (22:3) Sum 90, p. 64.
5259. REFFE, Candice
"Paradise II." [Crazy] (39) Wint 90, p. 15-16.
"Sociales." [Crazy] (39) Wint 90, p. 17-18.
"Spring-Tide." [Agni] (31/32) 90, p. 219-220.
"Tattoo" (for Ed). [Agni] (31/32) 90, p. 221-222.
5260. REGAN, Jennifer
"The Book of Harold" (8 selections). [PraS] (64:1) Spr 90, p. 119-124.
5261. REGENSPAN, David
"In Memory." [SenR] (20:2) Fall 90, p. 74.
5262. REGIER, Gail
"Octopus." [LaurelR] (24:1) Wint 90, p. 52.
5263. REHM, Pat
"A Tiny Disk-toed." [Caliban] (8) 90, p. 106.
"The Underground Ox." [Caliban] (8) 90, p. 105.
"A Wonderfully Rana Macrodactyla." [Caliban] (8) 90, p. 104.
5264. REIBETANZ, John
"The Galley." [AntigR] (80) Wint 90, p. 104-105.
"Herodotus and the Photograph." [Quarry] (39:2) Spr 90, p. 28-30.
5265. REICHARD, William
"For Kay." [BellArk] (6:4) Jl-Ag 90, p. 10.
5266. REID, Alastair
"Babel" (tr. of Louise van Santen). [Trans] (24) Fall 90, p. 12.
"The Map" (tr. of Alvaro Mutis). [NewYorker] (65:51) 5 F 90, p. 42.
"Near-Sighted" (tr. of Louise van Santen). [Trans] (24) Fall 90, p. 13.
5267. REID, Bethany
"Bicycle Villanelle." [BellArk] (6:3) My-Je 90, p. 21.
"Contemplation on the 20th Anniversary of the Moonshot, July 20, 1989." [BellArk]

(6:1) Ja-F 90, p. 9.
"Full Moon Over Dogwood." [BellArk] (6:1) Ja-F 90, p. 22.
"The Sorrel Mare." [BellArk] (6:2) Mr-Ap 90, p. 6-11.
5268. REID, Christopher
"Caretaking" (for Jane and Bernard McCabe). [ParisR] (32:114) Spr 90, p. 121-122.
5269. REID, D. C.
"Trout Fishing in Alberta." [Arc] (24) Spr 90, p. 25.
5270. REID, Randy
"Haiku" (6 poems, reprinted from #1, 1979). [Kaleid] (20) Wint-Spr 90, p. 75.
5271. REIDEL, James
"After Many Years" (tr. of Ingeborg Bachmann). [PaintedB] (40/41) 90, p. 19.
"Autumn Maneuver" (tr. of Ingeborg Bachmann). [PaintedB] (40/41) 90, p. 13.
"Behind the Wall" (tr. of Ingeborg Bachmann). [PaintedB] (40/41) 90, p. 9.
"Estrangement" (tr. of Ingeborg Bachmann). [PaintedB] (40/41) 90, p. 11.
"The Heavy Freight" (tr. of Ingeborg Bachmann). [PaintedB] (40/41) 90, p. 17.
"Invocation to the Great Bear" (tr. of Ingeborg Bachmann). [PaintedB] (40/41) 90,
    p. 15.
5272. REIFF, Sandra
"Vision Quest." [ChironR] (9:4) Wint 90, p. 18.
5273. REILLY, J. L
"The Captor." [SouthernR] (26:1) Ja 90, p. 201.
"In an Empty House." [SouthernR] (26:1) Ja 90, p. 200-201.
5274. REIMER, Dolores
"Chicken Pox." [Grain] (18:3) Fall 90, p. 78.
"This Is How They Left Her." [Grain] (18:3) Fall 90, p. 77.
5275. REIN, Evgenii
"Ninel" (tr. under the supervision of George L. Kline by members of the Bryn Mawr
    Translation Seminar). [Nimrod] (33:2) Spr-Sum 90, p. 40-42.
5276. REINFELD, Linda
"Indulgences." [Talisman] (4) Spr 90, p. 53-55.
5277. REINHOLD, Daniel Gensemer
"Becaue Macaroons without the Sea Air Would Be Nothing: A Love Poem."
    [PaintedB] (40/41) 90, p. 159.
5278. REINISCH, Harold
"Talking with the Wind." [Arc] (24) Spr 90, p. 15-17.
"Thirst." [Arc] (24) Spr 90, p. 14-15.
5279. REINKE, Steve
"How We Dance." [MalR] (90) Spr 90, p. 107.
5280. REINKING, V.
"Moroccan Summer." [InterPR] (16:1) Spr 90, p. 127-128.
"Riddle on the Way to the Bottom." [InterPR] (16:1) Spr 90, p. 126-127.
5281. REINKING, Victor
"Scheherazade" (tr. of Abdellatif Laabi). [Vis] (32) 90, p. 14.
"The Torturer" (tr. of Abdellatif Laabi). [Vis] (32) 90, p. 13.
5282. REIS, Donna
"Same Photo." [HangL] (57) 90, p. 58.
REIS, Ricardo
    See PESSOA, Fernando
REIS, Richardo
    See PESSOA, Fernando
5283. REISCHENBOCK, Faethena
"Sidewalk." [PoetryUSA] (5:2) Sum 90, p. 8.
5284. REISNER, Barbara
"Forty Violins Pursue Mozart." [ManhatPR] (12) [90?], p. 22.
"To Quiet the Earth." [RiverS] (32) [90?], p. 9.
5285. REISS, James
    (Anonymous poem). [FreeL] (4) 90.
5286. REITER, David P.
"Chewing the Pieces." [CanLit] (124/125) Spr-Sum 90, p. 48.
"The Commandant's Ghost." [Dandel] (17:1) Spr-Sum 90, p. 42-43.
"The Faithful Organ." [Bogg] (63) 90, p. 18-19.
"Washing Her Back." [CanLit] (127) Wint 90, p. 58-59.
5287. REITER, Jendi
"Ivy." [SouthernPR] (30:2) Fall 90, p. 60-61.
"A Lack of Monuments." [SouthernPR] (30:2) Fall 90, p. 62-63.
"The Overthrow of the Queen of Grammar." [HangL] (56) 90, p. 75-78.

"The Still Life." [HangL] (56) 90, p. 73-74.
5288. REITER, Lora K.
"Holography in the Mountains." [KanQ] (22:1/2) Wint-Spr 90, p. 190.
5289. REITER, Thomas
"The Gossamer Builder." [CimR] (93) O 90, p. 51-52.
"Stickseeds." [PoetryNW] (31:1) Spr 90, p. 24-25.
5290. REJZEK, Jan
"English Lesson" (tr. by Richard Katrovas and Dominika Winterová). [PoetryE] (29) Spr 90, p. 117.
5291. REMPEL, Ruth
"II. Morning, without Birds." [PraF] (11:2) Sum 90, p. 76.
"IV. In the flash bulb after shock of lightning." [PraF] (11:2) Sum 90, p. 77.
5292. REMY, Philippe
"I Want to See" (tr. by David Siefkin). [Vis] (32) 90, p. 30.
"Liege" (tr. of Marguerite Dessouroux, w. David Siefkin). [Vis] (34) 90, p. 18.
"The 'L's'" (Selections, tr. by Daniel de Bruycker). [Vis] (32) 90, p. 31.
5293. RENBERG, Margareta
"At an Outdoor Cafe" (tr. by Lennart Bruce and Sonja Bruce). [Spirit] (10:1) 89, p. 127.
"Avskedsbrevet." [Spirit] (10:1) 89, p. 124.
"Declaration" (tr. by Lennart Bruce and Sonja Bruce). [Spirit] (10:1) 89, p. 135.
"Deklaration." [Spirit] (10:1) 89, p. 134.
"Det Man Inte Kan Tala Om." [Spirit] (10:1) 89, p. 130.
"Drawing" (tr. by Lennart Bruce and Sonja Bruce). [Spirit] (10:1) 89, p. 123.
"The Farewell Letter" (tr. by Lennart Bruce and Sonja Bruce). [Spirit] (10:1) 89, p. 125.
"Film" (in Swedith). [Spirit] (10:1) 89, p. 128.
"From Home" (tr. by Lennart Bruce and Sonja Bruce). [Spirit] (10:1) 89, p. 121.
"Hemifrån." [Spirit] (10:1) 89, p. 120.
"I en Trädgårdsservering." [Spirit] (10:1) 89, p. 126.
"Isaac Newtons Andra Uppvaknande." [Spirit] (10:1) 89, p. 132.
"Isaac Newton's Second Awakening" (tr. by Lennart Bruce and Sonja Bruce). [Spirit] (10:1) 89, p. 133.
"Movies" (tr. by Lennart Bruce and Sonja Bruce). [Spirit] (10:1) 89, p. 129.
"Teckning." [Spirit] (10:1) 89, p. 122.
"Things You Can't Talk About" (tr. by Lennart Bruce and Sonja Bruce). [Spirit] (10:1) 89, p. 131.
5294. RENDRICK, Bernice
"Shifting Structures." [PoetryUSA] (5:2) Sum 90, p. 9.
5295. RENKL, Margaret
"The Dream Child." [Shen] (40:3) Fall 90, p. 73.
"Hermit Crabs." [Shen] (40:3) Fall 90, p. 72.
"Owl in Afternoon." [SouthernHR] (24:1) Wint 90, p. 34.
5296. RENNERT-CARTER, Roberta
"Damsel in Distress." [OnTheBus] (2:2/3:1, #6/7) Sum-Fall 90 Wint-Spr 91, p. 169-170.
"Eighty Years Young." [OnTheBus] (2:2/3:1, #6/7) Sum-Fall 90 Wint-Spr 91, p. 168-169.
"Messa Road." [OnTheBus] (2:1, #5) Spr 90, p. 115-116.
"No Problem." [OnTheBus] (2:2/3:1, #6/7) Sum-Fall 90 Wint-Spr 91, p. 168.
"Occupational Hazard." [OnTheBus] (2:2/3:1, #6/7) Sum-Fall 90 Wint-Spr 91, p. 169.
"The Woman Inside the Man." [OnTheBus] (2:2/3:1, #6/7) Sum-Fall 90 Wint-Spr 91, p. 168.
5297. RENO, Janet
"The Murderer and His Art." [WebR] (14:2) Spr 90, p. 24-27.
5298. REPP, John
"Dinner at Bud's Beach House." [HiramPoR] (48/49) 90-91, p. 61.
"Elegy for Esposito." [SouthernPR] (30:2) Fall 90, p. 66.
5299. RESS, Lisa
"Laguna Night." [Kalliope] (12:2) 90, p. 7.
"My Third Grade Teacher, Fourth Grade, Fifth." [Kalliope] (12:2) 90, p. 8.
5300. RETSOV, Samuel
"All for Love." [Talisman] (4) Spr 90, p. 87.
"A Fever in the Arm." [Talisman] (5) Fall 90, p. 100.
"The Innocent." [Talisman] (5) Fall 90, p. 100.

"Parcels." [Talisman] (4) Spr 90, p. 87.
"Your Father Wouldn't Let Us In Tonight." [Talisman] (5) Fall 90, p. 100.
5301. RETTBERG, Georgeann Eskievich
"Behind Closed Doors." [Kalliope] (12:1) 90, c89, p. 26.
5302. REVELL, Donald
"1848." [AmerPoR] (19:4) Jl-Ag 90, p. 4.
"1919." [AmerPoR] (19:4) Jl-Ag 90, p. 3.
"The Artists Airlifted, Leningrad 1941." [NewAW] (6) Spr 90, p. 27.
"Drum." [AmerPoR] (19:4) Jl-Ag 90, p. 6.
"Epigone." [Sulfur] (10:1, #26) Spr 90, p. 112-113.
"An Episode of the Great Awakening in New England." [Poetry] (156:1) Ap 90, p.
25-26.
"Europe" (for Richard Howard). [Boulevard] (5:2, #14) Fall 90, p. 140-142.
"Heat Lightning" (for Ralph Angel). [Sulfur] (10:1, #26) Spr 90, p. 111-112.
"How Passion Comes to Matter." [AmerPoR] (19:4) Jl-Ag 90, p. 5.
"Last, 1991." [ParisR] (32:117) Wint 90, p. 154-160.
"Mayakovsky Welcomed to America, 1925." [WillowS] (26) Spr 90, p. 7-8.
"The Next War." [AmerPoR] (19:4) Jl-Ag 90, p. 4.
"Of Africa." [SouthwR] (75:3) Sum 90, p. 377.
"On the Cape." [Agni] (31/32) 90, p. 116-117.
"On the Cards." [Sulfur] (10:1, #26) Spr 90, p. 113.
"Plenitude." [NewL] (57:1) Fall 90, p. 43-49.
"Privacy." [Pequod] (31) 90, p. 187-194.
"Survey." [AmerPoR] (19:4) Jl-Ag 90, p. 4.
"Warm Days in January." [AmerPoR] (19:4) Jl-Ag 90, p. 5.
"The Waters of 1989." [NewAW] (6) Spr 90, p. 28.
"The World." [AmerPoR] (19:4) Jl-Ag 90, p. 3.
5303. REXROTH, Kenneth
"For Eli Jacobson" (December, 1952). [Quarry] (39:4) Fall 1990, p. 83-85.
"The Great Nebula of Andromeda" (from "The Lights in the Sky Are Stars").
[Quarry] (39:4) Fall 1990, p. 85-86.
"Privacy." [HampSPR] (Anthology 1975-1990) 90, p. 26.
5304. REY ROSA, Rodrigo
"The Host" (tr. by Paul Bowles). [Screens] (2) 90, p. 130-131.
5305. REYES, Carlos
"Poem for Sarah Merculief, P.O. Box 978, St. George Island, Alaska 99660."
[WillowS] (26) Spr 90, p. 67.
5306. REYES, Severino Profeta
"Crossing America." [MissR] (19:1/2, #55/56) 90, p. 271-272.
5307. REYES RIVERA, Louis
"Sands of Exile" (tr. of Paul Laraque). [LitR] (33:4) Sum 90, p. 479.
5308. REYNALDO, Andres
"Prebaria del Aprendiz." [LindLM] (9:4) O-D 90, p. 44.
5309. REYNE, John Rosa
"The Guitar" (tr. of Federico Garcia Lorca). [ChatR] (11:1) Fall 90, p. 34.
5310. REYNOLDS, Oliver
"Hidden Child" (tr. of Tomas Lieske). [Verse] (7:2) Sum 90, p. 8-9.
"Lure" (tr. of Tomas Lieske). [Verse] (7:2) Sum 90, p. 8.
"Necropolis." [Quarry] (39:1) Wint 90, p. 44-46.
5311. REYNOLDS, Rebecca
"Testing Perspectives." [Caliban] (8) 90, p. 120-121.
5312. REYNOLDS, Robert P.
"Photographs." [EmeraldCR] (1990) c89, p. 39.
5313. REZMERSKI, John
"Cherry Pop" (from "Growing Down," Westerheim Press, 1982). [NorthStoneR]
(9) 90, p. 141.
"Country Music." [NorthStoneR] (9) 90, p. 134-135.
"Easy Listening." [NorthStoneR] (9) 90, p. 136-137.
"Four Views of Snow at Night." [NorthStoneR] (9) 90, p. 139.
"Poem for Jane Fonda." [NorthStoneR] (9) 90, p. 142.
"The Poetry Beast" (for Franklin Brainard). [NorthStoneR] (9) 90, p. 143.
"A Quiet Party" (from "Growing Down," Westerheim Press, 1982). [NorthStoneR]
(9) 90, p. 140.
"The Solipsist Evaluates His Latest Project." [NorthStoneR] (9) 90, p. 138.
"Walking Home, Half Drunk." [NorthStoneR] (9) 90, p. 142.

5314. RHENISCH, Harold
"The Mint Harvest." [Grain] (18:2) Sum 90, p. 15.
"Visiting Yeats." [CanLit] (127) Wint 90, p. 7-9.
5315. RHETT, K. (Kathryn)
"Blind Man in the Morning." [Ploughs] (16:4) Wint 90-91, p. 29-30.
"Columbus." [RiverC] (11:1) Fall 90, p. 68.
"A Factory by the River." [CutB] (34) Sum-Fall 90, p. 23.
5316. RHODENBAUGH, Suzanne
"The Difference between Me and Bill." [Hudson] (43:3) Aut 90, p. 457-458.
"Gypsy Rose Lee Gets Cancer." [GreenMR] (NS 3:2) Fall-Wint 89-90, p. 94.
5317. RHODES, Martha
"Dreaming of Flight." [BelPoR] (40:3) Spr 90, p. 3.
"Inheriting My Sister." [CapeR] (25:2) Fall 90, p. 38.
"Inside Father's Pockets." [BelPoR] (40:3) Spr 90, p. 3.
"Who Knew." [BelPoR] (40:3) Spr 90, p. 2.
"Without It." [CapeR] (25:2) Fall 90, p. 39.
5318. RHODES, Shane
"Apples on Your Bookshelf." [Bogg] (62) 90, p. 36.
5319. RHYS, Ernest
"In the Train: Portrait of a Navvy." [BelPoJ] (41:1) Fall 90, inside back cover.
5320. RIBELA, Roi Paes de
"Song About a Rich Man's Trout" (tr. by Richard Zenith). [MalR] (93) D 90, p. 32.
5321. RICE, Paul
"Botanical" (for S.T.C.). [SouthernHR] (24:1) Wint 90, p. 31.
"Harris County Grays." [SouthernHR] (24:2) Spr 90, p. 142.
"The King's Gap Stagecoach Road." [KanQ] (22:3) Sum 90, p. 165.
"Reading Light Fiction in the Marine Sentry Box at FDR's Little White House."
[KanQ] (22:3) Sum 90, p. 166.
"Taking Away the L" (The Baker Mine, Pine Mountain, GA). [SouthernHR] (24:2)
Spr 90, p. 143.
"Timber Rattler." [Poetry] (157:3) D 90, p. 149-150.
5322. RICH, Adrienne
"Love in the Museum." [CimR] (93) O 90, p. 68.
"Marghanita." [BelPoJ] (40:4) Sum 90, p. 44-45.
"Prospective Immigrants Please Note." [CimR] (93) O 90, p. 69.
"Sleepwalking Next to Death." [Field] (42) Spr 90, p. 75-79.
"A Valediction Forbidding Mourning." [CimR] (93) O 90, p. 71.
5323. RICHARDS, G. D.
"The Man Who Simplified His Life." [CumbPR] (9:2) Spr 90, p. 33.
5324. RICHARDS, Marilee
"The Brotherhood of Cows." [WestB] (26) 90, p. 89-90.
"Dream." [HolCrit] (27:3) Je 90, p. 19.
"Kneeling Together." [PoetL] (85:1) Spr 90, p. 29-30.
"Surviving." [TarRP] (30:1) Fall 90, p. 27.
"When Cows Fall in Love." [PoetL] (85:1) Spr 90, p. 28.
"When Cows Think." [WestB] (26) 90, p. 88-89.
5325. RICHARDS, Tad
"The Masked Man in Love, II." [LaurelR] (24:1) Wint 90, p. 20.
5326. RICHARDSON, D. Andrew
"When Wolves Lie Down with Lambs." [PottPort] (11) 89, p. 25.
5327. RICHARDSON, Francis L.
"Magic." [HighP] (5:3) Wint 90-91, p. 84-86.
5328. RICHARDSON, Leslie
"I Missed You So Little Today." [CimR] (91) Ap 90, p. 56.
5329. RICHARDSON, Peter
"Caesura." [AntigR] (80) Wint 90, p. 79.
"Ground Equipment Recital." [AntigR] (80) Wint 90, p. 80.
"In the Similkameen." [AntigR] (80) Wint 90, p. 81.
"Notes for a Flight Over Cawston Bench." [AntigR] (80) Wint 90, p. 82.
5330. RICHES, Brenda
"Convergence." [Grain] (18:4) Wint 90, p. 80.
"Convergence." [PraF] (11:4) Wint 90-91, p. 71.
"Damage." [PraF] (11:4) Wint 90-91, p. 70.
"Heigh Ho." [PraF] (11:4) Wint 90-91, p. 69.
5331. RICHEY, Joe
"A Central American Travel Journal" (Chapter Three, in progress: "Welcome to

Buenos Aires"). [HeavenB] (8) Wint 90-91, p. 49-53.
5332. RICHIE, Eugene
"In This Diminishing Hour." [DenQ] (24:4) Spr 90, p. 38-39.
"Not Just Anywhere." [MissouriR] (13:2) 90, p. 180-181.
"Scarecrow" (For my sister, tr. of Jaime Manrique). [LitR] (33:4) Sum 90, p.
438-440.
5333. RICHMAN, Elliot
"The Bombing of the Berlin Zoo, Friday 23 November 1943, 22:48 Hrs." [NegC]
(10:1) 90, p. 31-32.
"A Death Mantra." [BlackBR] (11) Spr-Sum 90, p. 57.
"The Dream Swimmer." [Bogg] (63) 90, p. 39.
"First Snow." [HiramPoR] (47) Wint 90, p. 45.
"The Man with Birds in His Skull." [Caliban] (8) 90, p. 134.
"Marilyn, the First Time I Came Was with You." [Pearl] (12) Fall-Wint 90, p. 54.
"People Like Us." [HiramPoR] (47) Wint 90, p. 46-47.
"Untouched by This World." [ChironR] (9:2) Sum 90, p. 15.
5334. RICHMAN, Robert
"The Evening Snow." [PartR] (57:3) Sum 90, p. 440.
"On Those Nights." [Verse] (7:3) Wint 90, p. 63.
5335. RICHMOND, Steve
"Gagaku." [DogRR] (9:1, #17) Spr 90, p. 20-21.
"Some Gagaku and One Not Gagaku" (25 poems). [WormR] (30:4, #120) 90, p.
111-130.
"Vietnam (a Flexible Title)" (reprinted from *The Earth Rose*, 1966). [Pearl] (10) Spr
90, p. 47.
5336. RICHTER, Greg
"At Evening" (tr. of Einar Bragi). [CharR] (16:1) Spr 90, p. 49.
"Before Sunset" (tr. of Einar Bragi). [CharR] (16:1) Spr 90, p. 49.
"The Land" (Selections: I-II, IV, tr. of Matthias Johannessen). [CharR] (16:1) Spr
90, p. 50.
"Memory" (Selection: I, tr. of Matthias Johannessen). [CharR] (16:1) Spr 90, p. 49.
"Wilderness Landscape" (tr. of Einar Bragi). [CharR] (16:1) Spr 90, p. 48.
5337. RICHTER, Milan
"Roots in the Air" (4 selections, tr. by Jascha Kessler). [Screens] (2) 90, p. 72-75.
"We Have Bare Hands" (To the Prague students, beaten by police, 17 Nov. 1989, tr.
by Jascha Kessler and the author). [CityLR] (4) 90, p. 188.
5338. RICKETTS, Harry
"Prep School Days." [Verse] (7:2) Sum 90, p. 39.
"Under the Radar." [Verse] (7:2) Sum 90, p. 40.
5339. RIDDELL, Amy
"A Word to Her." [ColEng] (52:5) S 90, p. 527.
RIDDICK, Thuong Vuong
See VUONG-RIDDICK, Thuong
5340. RIDL, Jack
"Darker Even Than the Dark Before Dawn." [ChamLR] (4:1, #7) Fall 90, p. 127.
"Somewhere in Town." [FreeL] (5) Sum 90, p. 26.
"Star's Nightmare." [FreeL] (5) Sum 90, p. 27.
"Two Days Before Christmas." [ArtfulD] (18/19) 90, p. 71.
5341. RIEGEL, Katherine
"A Woman and a sparrow." [IndR] (14:1) Wint 90, p. 71-72.
5342. RIEHLE, C. R.
"The Work Ethic." [ChironR] (9:3) Aut 90, p. 17.
5343. RIEMER, Ruby
"The Path through Loantaka." [JINJPo] (12:2) Aut 90, p. 17.
5344. RIFBJERG, Klaus
"Before the Mount of Venus" (from "Rifbjerg Rundt, Gyldendal, 1981, tr. by
Monique M. Kennedy). [CimR] (92) Jl 90, p. 27.
"Cuckoo" (from "Rifbjerg Rundt, Gyldendal, 1981, tr. by Monique M. Kennedy).
[CimR] (92) Jl 90, p. 27.
5345. RIFENBURGH, Daniel
"Postcards of Peru" (For Paola). [SouthernPR] (30:2) Fall 90, p. 67-72.
5346. RIGLIANO, Marisa J.
"Shadow Dance." [EmeraldCR] (1990) c89, p. 103.
5347. RIGSBEE, David
"Bermudas." [SouthernR] (26:1) Ja 90, p. 220-222.
"Heart and Soul." [TarRP] (30:1) Fall 90, p. 12.

"Lumber." [ThRiPo] (35/36) 90, p. 16.
"Mozart." [WillowS] (26) Spr 90, p. 11-12.
"The Rescue." [FloridaR] (17:2) Fall-Wint 90, p. 132.
"Secondary Road." [SouthernHR] (24:4) Fall 90, p. 322.
"Stories Away." [SouthernHR] (24:4) Fall 90, p. 358.
5348. RILEY, Joanne M.
"Fan." [SingHM] (18) 90, p. 17.
5349. RILEY, Mike
"Inheritance." [SwampR] (5) Wint-Spr 90, p. 74.
5350. RILEY, Peter
"Ashlar Facings / Pink Rose." [Screens] (2) 90, p. 144.
"Château Musar." [Screens] (2) 90, p. 145.
"Halifax." [Screens] (2) 90, p. 142.
"Midsummer Common." [Screens] (2) 90, p. 143.
"Parker's Piece." [Screens] (2) 90, p. 145.
"S. Cecilia in Trastevere." [Screens] (2) 90, p. 143.
5351. RILKE, Rainer Maria
"Drafts from Two Winter Evenings" (Excerts from "Entwürfe aus zei
Winterabenden," tr. by Andrew Waterman). [Quarry] (39:1) Wint 90, p.
51-52.
"Herbst" (in German and English, tr. by David Ferry). [Agni] (29/30) 90, p.
166-167.
"Immer Wieder." [NewYorkQ] (42) Sum 90, p. 77.
"Over and Over" (tr. by Carol Purdy). [NewYorkQ] (42) Sum 90, p. 77.
"Portrait of My Father as a Young Man." [GrandS] (9:2) Wint 90, p. 101.
"Roman Fountain" (Borghese, in German and English, tr. by Johann Moser).
[Hellas] (1:1) Spr 90, p. 96.
5352. RINEHART, Robert
"The Large Bathers." [Chelsea] (49) 90, p. 145.
"On Hearing Diane Wakoski Read at California State University, San Bernardino."
[NegC] (10:1) 90, p. 79-80.
5353. RIOS, Alberto
"Dr. Disney's Animation." [BilingR] (14:3) S-D 87-88, c91, p. 75.
"The Good Lunch of Oceans." [AmerPoR] (19:2) Mr-Ap 90, p. 56.
"Indentations in the Sugar." [KenR] (NS 12:3) Sum 90, p. 118.
"The Influenzas." [NewYorker] (66:30) 10 S 90, p. 48.
"Mexico, from the Four Last Letters." [KenR] (NS 12:3) Sum 90, p. 116-118.
"Mr. Luna and History." [ParisR] (32:116) Fall 90, p. 139-140.
"Mr. Luna in the Afternoon." [NewYorker] (66:14) 21 My 90, p. 66.
"Nogales, 1958." [BilingR] (14:3) S-D 87-88, c91, p. 73-74.
"Uncle Maclovio's Secret, Never to Tell." [BilingR] (14:3) S-D 87-88, c91, p. 74.
"Velando." [BilingR] (14:3) S-D 87-88, c91, p. 75-76.
5354. RIOS, Alexandra
"For Argentina on Inauguration Day." [NowestR] (28:1) 90, p. 14-15.
5355. RIOS, Isidro H. (Chilo)
"Voy a cantar estos versos." [Americas] (18:2) Sum 90, p. 76-77.
RIPER, Craig van
See Van RIPER, Craig
5356. RISTAU, Harland
"Dinner Table." [CoalC] (2) D 90, p. 17.
"Senryu: she said : I love you." [Northeast] (5:2) Spr 90, p. 36.
5357. RITCHEY, Jane
"Yesterday." [EmeraldCR] (1990) c89, p. 59-60.
5358. RITCHIE, Elisavietta
"Interlude, Afghanistan." [Amelia] (6:1, #16) 90, p. 12.
"North of the Airbase, at Home." [SwampR] (6) Sum-Fall 90, p. 14-15.
5359. RITCHINGS, Joan Drew
"Knell." [Writer] (103:6) Je 90, p. 25.
5360. RITKES, Daniel
"Gold." [OnTheBus] (2:2/3:1, #6/7) Sum-Fall 90 Wint-Spr 91, p. 171-172.
5361. RITSOS, Yannis
"Actaeon" (tr. by Edmund Keeley). [Trans] (24) Fall 90, p. 212.
"After the Ceremony" (tr. by Edmund Keeley). [SenR] (20:2) Fall 90, p. 25.
"After the Treaty Between the Athenians and the Lacedaemonians Was Broken" (after
Thucydides, tr. by Edmund Keeley). [Antaeus] (64/65) Spr-Aut 90, p.
116-117.

"Asclepius" (tr. by Edmund Keeley). [SenR] (20:2) Fall 90, p. 26.
"The Awakening of Telemachus" (tr. by Edmund Keeley). [Trans] (24) Fall 90, p.
212.
"Between Ionians and Dorians" (tr. by Edmund Keeley). [Antaeus] (64/65) Spr-Aut
90, p. 114-115.
"The Disjunctive Conjunction 'Or'" (tr. by Edmund Keeley). [GrandS] (9:3) Spr 90,
p. 24.
"The Diviner" (tr. by Edmund Keeley). [Antaeus] (64/65) Spr-Aut 90, p. 113.
"First Sensuality" (tr. by Edmund Keeley). [GrandS] (9:3) Spr 90, p. 22.
"Greek Scene" (tr. by Edmund Keeley). [TriQ] (79) Fall 90, p. 108.
"Herms I" (tr. by Edmund Keeley). [SenR] (20:2) Fall 90, p. 24.
"Immobilizing the Boundless" (tr. by Kostas Myrsiades). [NewOR] (17:3) Fall 90,
p. 18.
"Morning in Salerno, IV" (tr. by Kostas Myrsiades). [NewOR] (17:3) Fall 90, p.
22.
"Not Even Mythology" (tr. by Edmund Keeley). [Antaeus] (64/65) Spr-Aut 90, p.
118.
"The Red Thread" (tr. by Edmund Keeley). [SenR] (20:2) Fall 90, p. 27.
"Repetitions" (5 selections, tr. by Edmund Keeley). [Iowa] (20:3) Fall 90, p. 41-44.
"Repetitions" (Selections: 2 poems, tr. by Edmund Keeley). [ParisR] (32:115) Sum
90, p. 194-195.
"Return II" (tr. by Edmund Keeley). [GrandS] (9:3) Spr 90, p. 23.
"Septeria and Daphnephoria" (tr. by Edmund Keeley). [Trans] (24) Fall 90, p.
208-209.
"Sluggishly" (tr. by Kostas Myrsiades). [TarRP] (29:2) Spr 90, p. 48.
"Themistocles" (tr. by Edmund Keeley). [Trans] (24) Fall 90, p. 210-211.
"To Orpheus" (tr. by Thanasis Maskaleris). [TarRP] (29:2) Spr 90, p. 46-47.
5362. RIVARD, David
"C'è un'Altra Possibilità." [Poetry] (156:5) Ag 90, p. 265-266.
"What Kind of Times Are They." [GrahamHR] (13) Spr 90, p. 55.
RIVERA, Louis Reyes
See REYES RIVERA, Louis
5363. RIVERO, Isel
"Cazadora." [LindLM] (9:4) O-D 90, p. 13.
5364. RIVERS, Kinloch
"Snails." [AmerS] (59:3) Sum 90, p. 406.
5365. RIVES, John
"No Applause." [Quarry] (39:4) Fall 1990, p. 60-61.
"Stained Sight." [Quarry] (39:4) Fall 1990, p. 59.
RIVIERE, G. M. La
See LaRIVIERE, G. M.
5366. RIVIERE, William
"Kitayama." [Stand] (31:2) Spr 90, p. 64.
"Quiet Days in Sarawak." [Stand] (31:2) Spr 90, p. 65.
5367. RIYADH, Taher
"Mulberry Leaves for a Naked Tree" (Excerpt, tr. by Lena Jayyusi and John
Heath-Stubbs). [Screens] (2) 90, p. 24.
"To Murder Time" (Excerpt, tr. by Lena Jayyusi and John Heath-Stubbs). [Screens]
(2) 90, p. 24.
5368. ROBBINS, Anthony
"Patriot Without Parole." [PartR] (57:1) Wint 90, p. 104.
5369. ROBBINS, David L.
"Kick." [Amelia] (6:1, #16) 90, p. 77.
5370. ROBBINS, Martin
"Backward Glance / Winter Journey." [InterPR] (16:2) Fall 90, p. 105.
"Crossing the Connecticut at Hartford." [InterPR] (16:2) Fall 90, p. 104.
"Garage Account." [CapeR] (25:1) Spr 90, p. 16.
"Home Pictures." [CapeR] (25:1) Spr 90, p. 15.
"The Language of Bridges." [CrossCur] (9:2) Je 90, p. 45.
"November Vespers." [InterPR] (16:2) Fall 90, p. 105.
"The Old Tea Room Ladies." [InterPR] (16:2) Fall 90, p. 106.
"Whiteout." [Os] (31) 90, p. 30.
5371. ROBBINS, Richard
"Montana Melody: A Farm Wife's Story." [BellArk] (6:6) N-D 90, p. 3-4.
"North by the Line." [LaurelR] (24:1) Wint 90, p. 45.
"Union Hotel, Frankfurt" (from "London Underground," winner of Pearl's 1989

Chapbook Contest). [Pearl] (10) Spr 90, p. 51.
5372. ROBBINS, Tim
"Nostalgia." [HangL] (56) 90, p. 43.
5373. ROBERTS, Andy
"White." [RagMag] (7:2) Spr 90, p. 59.
5374. ROBERTS, Betty
"Polish Tapestries." [Bogg] (62) 90, p. 55.
ROBERTS, Cynthia Day
See DAY-ROBERTS, Cynthia
5375. ROBERTS, George
"After Her First Piano Recital My Daughter with Unusual Grace Takess My Arm and
We Walk Home . . ." (for Juliet, nine years old). [NorthStoneR] (9) 90, p.
119.
"Untitled: What would it mean if a cricket." [NorthStoneR] (9) 90, p. 118.
5376. ROBERTS, Harlan
"Ohio." [OnTheBus] (2:1, #5) Spr 90, p. 117-118.
"Oranges." [OnTheBus] (2:2/3:1, #6/7) Sum-Fall 90 Wint-Spr 91, p. 173-175.
5377. ROBERTS, Kevin
"After John Donne." [MalR] (90) Spr 90, p. 74.
"Caliban Down Under." [CanLit] (127) Wint 90, p. 74-75.
5378. ROBERTS, Kim
"The Bog Man." [Outbr] (21) 90, p. 3.
"How to Imagine Deafness" (for John). [Outbr] (21) 90, p. 4.
"Light Rising from Concrete." [CrossCur] (9:2) Je 90, p. 147.
"Portrait of My Mechanic in Full Sunlight." [MalR] (91) Je 90, p. 80.
"Shenandoah." [HighP] (5:3) Wint 90-91, p. 45.
5379. ROBERTS, Len
"Above the Things" (tr. of Agnes Nemes Nagy, w. Mária Kurdi). [MidAR] (10:1)
90, p. 47.
"Ague" (tr. of Sándor Csoóri). [PoetryE] (30) Fall 90, p. 15.
"Antique Store, Pécs, Hungary." [ArtfulD] (18/19) 90, p. 20-21.
"Apocalypse" (tr. of Csaba Lászlóffy, w. Erika Urbán). [LitR] (33:3) Spr 90, p.
292.
"Barbarous Prayer" (tr. of Sandor Csoóri, w. László Vértes). [AmerPoR] (19:5) S-O
90, p. 26.
"Because Our Drowning Is a Sensation" (tr. of Gizella Hervay, w. Mária Kurdi).
[MidAR] (10:1) 90, p. 53.
"Because There Was a Time" (tr. of Sándor Csoóri, w. Claudia Zimmerman).
[ArtfulD] (18/19) 90, p. 23.
"Because There Was a Time" (tr. of Sandor Csoóri, w. Claudia Zimmerman).
[CrabCR] (6:3) Spr 90, p. 10.
"Black-Red" (tr. of Sándor Kányádi). [MidAR] (10:1) 90, p. 65-71.
"Bookmark" (tr. of Sándor Kányádi). [AmerPoR] (19:5) S-O 90, p. 29.
"Borders" (tr. of Domokos Szilágyi). [AmerPoR] (19:5) S-O 90, p. 31.
"Circle" (tr. of Zsuzsa Takács, w. Mária Kurdi). [AmerPoR] (19:5) S-O 90, p. 29.
"The Coin Trick." [Shen] (40:4) Wint 90, p. 66.
"Cold." [Shen] (40:4) Wint 90, p. 65.
"Corals" (tr. of Attila József, w. Andy Rouse). [ArtfulD] (18/19) 90, p. 26.
"Day by Day" (tr. of Sándor Csoóri, w. Miklós Horváth). [ArtfulD] (18/19) 90, p.
24.
"Day by Day" (tr. of Sándor Csoóri, w. Miklós Horváth). [Chelsea] (49) 90, p. 122.
"Dozing on the Train" (tr. of Sándor Csoóri, w. László Vértes). [MidAR] (10:1) 90,
p. 73, 75.
"Everyday History" (tr. of Sándor Csoóri). [MidAR] (10:1) 90, p. 81.
"For My Mother Again" (tr. of Ida Makay, w. Mária Kurdi). [AmerPoR] (19:5) S-O
90, p. 27.
"Gift Shop in Pécs." [PartR] (57:3) Sum 90, p. 431-432.
"Green Twig in My Hand" (Kezemben Zöld Ag, tr. of Sándor Csoóri, w. Claudia
Zimmerman). [Plain] (10:3) Spr 90, p. 29.
"I Do Not Resemble" (tr. of Ida Makay, w. Mária Kurdi). [AmerPoR] (19:5) S-O
90, p. 26.
"I'd Rather Stay at Home" (tr. of Sandor Csoóri). [CrabCR] (6:3) Spr 90, p. 9-10.
"Identity" (tr. of Judit Tóth, w. Mária Kurdi). [AmerPoR] (19:5) S-O 90, p. 28.
"In Front of the House All Night Long (A Reminiscence)" (tr. of Sándor Kányádi).
[AmerPoR] (19:5) S-O 90, p. 30.
"Indian Words on the Radio" (to the poet, William Least Heat Moon, tr. of Géza

Szőcs). [AmerPoR] (19:5) S-O 90, p. 31.
"Inkstains" (tr. of Gizella Hervay, w. Kristina Lay). [AmerPoR] (19:5) S-O 90, p. 30.
"The Island Dweller" (tr. of Ida Makay, w. Mária Kurdi). [MidAR] (10:1) 90, p. 49.
"Late June, Wassergass" (for Hayden Carruth). [CarolQ] (42:3) Spr 90, p. 67.
"Learning About the Heart." [PoetryNW] (31:4) Wint 90-91, p. 21-22.
"Let the Timbrel Rattle" (Szóljon a csörgódob, tr. of Sándor Csoóri). [Plain] (10:2) Wint 90, p. 32.
"Lithograph" (instead of a greeting in verse for Geua Domokos on his 16th birthday, tr. of Sandor Kányádi). [CrabCR] (6:3) Spr 90, p. 11.
"Looking Up." [Ploughs] (16:4) Wint 90-91, p. 92-93.
"A Lucky Man" (tr. of Sándor Kányádi). [PoetryE] (30) Fall 90, p. 24.
"Magic" (tr. of Ida Makay, w. Mária Kurdi). [MidAR] (10:1) 90, p. 51.
"The Man Here" (tr. of János Pilinszky, w. Adrienne Fekete). [AmerPoR] (19:5) S-O 90, p. 23.
"Memories of November" (tr. of Sandor Csoóri). [CrabCR] (6:3) Spr 90, p. 9.
"Message" (tr. of Sándor Csoóri, w. Miklós Telbisz and Gábor Törő). [NowestR] (28:1) 90, p. 101.
"More Walnuts, Late October." [ParisR] (32:116) Fall 90, p. 104-105.
"Mrs. Wadsworth's Letter to Emily Dickinson" (tr. of Agnes Gergely, w. Mária Kurdi). [AmerPoR] (19:5) S-O 90, p. 27.
"My Father the Mouse." [Ploughs] (16:4) Wint 90-91, p. 91.
"My Mother Wore Fake Pearl Earrings." [WestB] (26) 90, p. 50-51.
"Nature Morte" (tr. of Amy Károlyi). [MidAR] (10:1) 90, p. 57.
"Near the Paulite Church, Pécs, Hungary." [ArtfulD] (18/19) 90, p. 22.
"A Night Journey in Germany" (tr. of Sándor Csoóri, w. Tibor Tengerdi). [MidAR] (10:1) 90, p. 87, 89.
"The Night of Ekhnaton" (tr. of Agnes Nemes Nagy, w. Mária Kurdi). [AmerPoR] (19:5) S-O 90, p. 23-24.
"Nights, Lately, I've Been Going To." [ArtfulD] (18/19) 90, p. 18-19.
"November Riffs." [PoetryNW] (31:4) Wint 90-91, p. 23.
"On the Third Day the Snow Began to Fall" (tr. of Sándor Csoóri, w. Miklós Telbisz and László Vértes). [MidAR] (10:1) 90, p. 83, 85.
"On the Third Day the Snow Began to Fall" (tr. of Sándor Csoóri, w. Miklos Telbisz and László Vértes). [Chelsea] (49) 90, p. 123.
"Our Creation" (tr. of Judit Pinczési, w. Mária Kurdi). [AmerPoR] (19:5) S-O 90, p. 29.
"People, Boughs" (tr. of Sandor Csoóri, w. László Vértes). [AmerPoR] (19:5) S-O 90, p. 25.
"Poor" (tr. of Amy Károlyi). [MidAR] (10:1) 90, p. 55.
"Postponed Nightmare" (tr. of Sándor Csoóri, w. László Vertes). [LitR] (33:3) Spr 90, p. 293.
"Prophesying About Your Time" (tr. of Sandor Csoóri, w. Judit Vértes). [AmerPoR] (19:5) S-O 90, p. 25-26.
"Restless Turning of Fall" (tr. of Miklós Radnóti, w. László Komlósi). [AmerPoR] (19:5) S-O 90, p. 22.
"Rhapsody for My Birthday" (tr. of Agnes Gergely, w. Mária Kurdi). [AmerPoR] (19:5) S-O 90, p. 27.
"Sea Gull-Line" (tr. of Sándor Csoóri, w. László Vértes). [Chelsea] (49) 90, p. 124.
"Stake-Fire" (tr. of Gizella Hervay, w. Kristina Lay). [AmerPoR] (19:5) S-O 90, p. 31.
"Step by Step" (tr. of János Pilinszky, w. Adrienne Fekete). [AmerPoR] (19:5) S-O 90, p. 23.
"Such Is the Place, This Unnamable" (tr. of Zsuzsa Takács, w. Mária Kurdi). [AmerPoR] (19:5) S-O 90, p. 28.
"There Are Some Countries" (tr. of Sándor Kányádi, w. Szabó Csabáné). [MidAR] (10:1) 90, p. 59.
"They Come to Me" (tr. of Sándor Kányádi, w. Mariann Nagy). [MidAR] (10:1) 90, p. 61, 63.
"They Were Roving" (tr. of Margit Szécsi, w. Mária Kurdi). [AmerPoR] (19:5) S-O 90, p. 25.
"A Thin, Black Band" (tr. of Sándor Csoóri, w. Tibor Tengerdi). [MidAR] (10:1) 90, p. 77, 79.
"Tin Ceiling, Pecs, Hungary." [Ploughs] (16:4) Wint 90-91, p. 94-95.
"Towards Noah's Ark" (on the back of the Imre Nagy painting, tr. of Sándor Kányádi, w. Mariann Nagy). [PoetryE] (30) Fall 90, p. 25.

"The Visible Man" (tr. of Margit Szécsi, w. Mária Kurdi). [AmerPoR] (19:5) S-O
90, p. 24-25.
"Walnuts, October, Wassergass." [ArtfulD] (18/19) 90, p. 17.
"We Deserve It" (tr. of Ida Makay, w. Mária Kurdi). [AmerPoR] (19:5) S-O 90, p.
26.
"Well, I Ask" (tr. of Anna Hajnal, w. Mária Kurdi). [AmerPoR] (19:5) S-O 90, p.
22.
"Well, Mom." [ArtfulD] (18/19) 90, p. 16.
"When" (tr. of Agnes Nemes Nagy, w. Claudia Zimmerman). [MidAR] (10:1) 90,
p. 45.
"When the New Moon Screamed" (tr. of Margit Szécsi, w. Mária Kurdi).
[AmerPoR] (19:5) S-O 90, p. 24.
"When the Statues Set Off" (tr. of Amy Károlyi). [AmerPoR] (19:5) S-O 90, p. 22.
"The Wind with Its Nerves" (tr. of Sandor Csoori). [Vis] (33) 90, p. 25-26.
"The Wind with Its Nerves" (tr. of Sándor Csoóri). [Verse] (7:3) Wint 90, p. 100.
"Woods in October" (tr. of Miklós Radnóti, w. László Komlósi). [ArtfulD] (18/19)
90, p. 25.
"The Yellow of Mulberry." [PoetryNW] (31:4) Wint 90-91, p. 22-23.
"You're Rising and Vanishing" (tr. of Sandor Csoóri, w. László Vértes).
[AmerPoR] (19:5) S-O 90, p. 26.
5380. ROBERTS, Michael Symmons
"Between First and Third Worlds." [Verse] (7:2) Sum 90, p. 7.
5381. ROBERTS, Michèle
"The Day the Wall Came Down." [TampaR] (3) 90, p. 23-25.
5382. ROBERTS, Paulette
"It Was Difficult to Give a Suitable Title" (tr. of Yan Li). [LitR] (33:4) Sum 90, p.
491.
"Poor People" (tr. of Yan Li). [LitR] (33:4) Sum 90, p. 491.
5383. ROBERTS, Stephen R.
"The Carpenter's Lament." [TampaR] (3) 90, p. 69.
"Firefinch." [Bogg] (63) 90, p. 5.
5384. ROBERTS, Susan
"Advection." [Talisman] (5) Fall 90, p. 61.
"Fascination." [Talisman] (5) Fall 90, p. 60.
"Innocuous." [Talisman] (5) Fall 90, p. 61.
"Under Sensation" (Excerpts). [CentralP] (17/18) Spr-Fall 90, p. 212-213.
"Voices." [Talisman] (5) Fall 90, p. 60.
5385. ROBERTS, Teresa Noelle
"The Bread Poem" (for Amy). [BellArk] (6:2) Mr-Ap 90, p. 28.
"Lovepoem #67." [BellArk] (6:1) Ja-F 90, p. 22.
ROBERTSON, Charles Stewart
See STEWART-ROBERTSON, Charles
5386. ROBERTSON, Kell
"Another Last Chance Bar" (from "Bear Crossing"). [SwampR] (5) Wint-Spr 90, p.
43.
"The Marr Girls" (from "Bear Crossing"). [SwampR] (5) Wint-Spr 90, p. 42.
"Old Lady Mendoza." [ChironR] (9:4) Wint 90, p. 17.
5387. ROBERTSON, Kirk
"RNO - SFO - LAX." [OnTheBus] (2:1, #5) Spr 90, p. 119.
"Schwitters." [OnTheBus] (2:1, #5) Spr 90, p. 119-120.
5388. ROBERTSON, Michael V.
"Dreamer's Dream." [EmeraldCR] (1990) c89, p. 55.
5389. ROBERTSON, Sharon
"Bombs" (tr. of Paul Rodenko). [Vis] (34) 90, p. 34.
"Do You Love Me Always" (tr. of Jan Hanlo). [Vis] (34) 90, p. 36.
"Evening Ship" (tr. of Hans Lodeizen). [Vis] (33) 90, p. 34.
"Geranium" (tr. of Hans Vlek). [Vis] (34) 90, p. 46.
"Je Sais Parce Que Je Le Dis" (tr. of Hans Lodeizen). [Vis] (34) 90, p. 41.
"Not Unlike" (tr. of Jan Hanlo). [Vis] (34) 90, p. 37.
"Seastone" (tr. of Hans van de Waarsenburg). [Vis] (34) 90, p. 49.
"That Is How I Think of You Too" (tr. of Jan Hanlo). [Vis] (34) 90, p. 36.
"White" (tr. of K. Schippers). [Vis] (34) 90, p. 44.
5390. ROBERTSON, William
"Boys' Annual." [Dandel] (17:2) Fall-Wint 90, p. 33.
"Burning Love Letters." [AntigR] (81/82) Spr-Sum 90, p. 206.
"Charlie Parker Playing Brilliantly 'My Old Flame'." [Grain] (18:3) Fall 90, p. 87.

"Mother Nature." [Grain] (18:3) Fall 90, p. 85.
"The Only Farmer Still Alive in Consul, Saskatchewan." [Grain] (18:1) Spr 90, p. 7-8.
"Quitting Farming." [Grain] (18:3) Fall 90, p. 86.
"Reception Theory." [Event] (19:2) Sum 90, p. 76-77.
"Shooting the Aurora." [Grain] (18:1) Spr 90, p. 10.
"Sieve." [Grain] (18:3) Fall 90, p. 88.
"Wheat Gum." [Grain] (18:1) Spr 90, p. 9.
5391. ROBERTSON-LORANT, Laurie
    "Eve Remembers." [SingHM] (18) 90, p. 24.
5392. ROBESCU, Marius
    "Time" (tr. by Thomas C. Carlson and Vasile Poenaru). [ManhatR] (5:1) Spr 90, p. 9.
5393. ROBIN, Mark
    "The Beetle Eel." [ContextS] (1:1) 89, p. 21.
5394. ROBINSON, Alfred
    "Song of Prophecy, Perjury and Peace" (pour M.). [Abraxas] (38/39) 90, p. 133.
5395. ROBINSON, Diane
    "Visiting Home." [BellR] (13:2, #28) Fall 90, p. 30.
5396. ROBINSON, Elizabeth
    "The Array of Orthodoxy." [Notus] (5:1) Spr 90, p. 8.
    "Kiss." [CentralP] (17/18) Spr-Fall 90, p. 215.
    "Knob." [Notus] (5:1) Spr 90, p. 7.
    "The Sleep." [Notus] (5:1) Spr 90, p. 9-10.
5397. ROBINSON, James Miller
    "Las Cañas." [SwampR] (5) Wint-Spr 90, p. 51-52.
5398. ROBINSON, John
    "Might Meet You Out There." [Epoch] (39:3) 90, p. 298.
5399. ROBINSON, Julia
    "Flood Plain." [CimR] (93) O 90, p. 55-56.
    "Humboldt in Venezuela, 1799." [CimR] (93) O 90, p. 57-58.
5400. ROBINSON, Kit
    "Direct Response." [Shiny] (5) 90, p. 11-12.
    "Lip Service." [Shiny] (5) 90, p. 9-10.
    "A Mental Finding." [Verse] (7:1) Spr 90, p. 54-57.
5401. ROBINSON, Leonard Wallace
    "The Edge Is Always There." [HampSPR] (Anthology 1975-1990) 90, p. 188-189.
5402. ROBINSON, Peter
    "The News." [HawaiiR] (14:1, #28) Wint 89-90, p. 16.
5403. ROBINSON, Ron
    "Endarkenment." [OnTheBus] (2:2/3:1, #6/7) Sum-Fall 90 Wint-Spr 91, p. 176.
5404. ROBSON, Ruthann
    "The Last Three Days of Winter." [NegC] (10:2/3) 90, p. 30-31.
    "Sugar" (in the cane fields of Belle Glade, Florida). [SlipS] (10) 90, p. 88-89.
5405. ROBY, Gayle
    "Zeno's Arrow." [PraS] (64:2) Sum 90, p. 63.
5406. ROCHE, Judith
    "Alternate Insomnia." [WillowS] (25) Wint 90, p. 62.
    "The Flowers." [PoetryUSA] (5:2) Sum 90, p. 12.
    "Thunder After Thunder, Returning Like Rhyme." [PoetryUSA] (5:2) Sum 90, p. 11.
5407. ROCHE, Nancy
    "Pontius Pilate's Dream." [SouthernPR] (30:2) Fall 90, p. 15-16.
5408. ROCHELEAU, Linda
    "Scornavacca, 1965." [Pearl] (12) Fall-Wint 90, p. 63.
5409. ROCHELLE, Belinda
    "From a Distant Place." [Obs] (5:3) Wint 90, p. 72.
5410. ROCKWELL, Tom
    "Let Go, Go Wilding." [NewYorkQ] (43) Fall 90, p. 73-74.
ROCQUE, Emma la
    See LaROCQUE, Emma
5411. RODAS, Ana Maria
    "Poemas de la Izquierda Erótica." [InterPR] (16:1) Spr 90, p. 54-59.
    "Poems of the Erotic Left" (tr. by Mark Smith-Soto). [InterPR] (16:1) Spr 90, p. 55-60.

5412. RODEFER, Stephen
"Desire." [Verse] (7:1) Spr 90, p. 27-28.
5413. RODENKO, Paul
"Bombs" (tr. by Sharon Robertson). [Vis] (34) 90, p. 34.
"February Sun" (tr. by Arie Staal). [Vis] (34) 90, p. 34.
"Night" (tr. by Kees Snoek). [Vis] (34) 90, p. 34.
"Robot Poetry" (tr. from the Dutch). [Vis] (34) 90, p. 33.
5414. RODGRES, Chris
"Tim." [PoetryUSA] (5:2) Sum 90, p. 8.
5415. RODIER, Katharine
"Bears." [PoetryNW] (31:3) Aut 90, p. 26.
5416. RODITI, Edouard
"Poem for New York" (For Jack Hirschman, tr. of Paul Laraque). [LitR] (33:4) Sum
90, p. 478.
"The Railroad Station" (for Arthur Fontaine, tr. of Léon-Paul Fargue). [Trans] (23)
Spr 90, p. 171-173.
5417. RODNEY, Janet
"Echoes from the Spanish Civil War." [Conjunc] (15) 90, p. 190-196.
"The Sacrifice." [Talisman] (4) Spr 90, p. 9-11.
5418. RODNING, Susan
"The Secret Garden." [AntigR] (80) Wint 90, p. 83-85.
5419. RODRIGUEZ, Angela
"Dream Forgetting." [PoetryUSA] (5:3) Fall 90, p. 27.
5420. RODRIGUEZ, Claudio
"Between the Fascinating and the Frightening" (To the artist, José Hernández, tr. by
Louis Bourne). [Stand] (31:3) Sum 90, p. 70-71.
5421. RODRIGUEZ, Luis J.
"Lips." [OnTheBus] (2:2/3:1, #6/7) Sum-Fall 90 Wint-Spr 91, p. 177.
"Piece by Piece." [Contact] (9:56/57/58) Spr 90, p. 28.
"They Come to Dance." [PoetryUSA] ([5:4?]) Wint 90, p. 12.
"The Threshold." [PoetryUSA] ([5:4?]) Wint 90, p. 9.
5422. RODRIGUEZ FLORIDO, Jorge
"Sin Tapas." [LindLM] (9:4) O-D 90, p. 13.
5423. ROESER, Dana
"Black Tulip." [Iowa] (20:3) Fall 90, p. 69.
"The Cow Says, I'm a Hippopotamus." [Iowa] (20:3) Fall 90, p. 68.
5424. ROFFMAN, Rosaly DeMaios
"O Quince." [Blueline] (11:1/2) 90, p. 45-46.
"On Hearing About Your Fall." [NegC] (10:2/3) 90, p. 33.
5425. ROGAL, Stan
"Under Glass" (Francis Bacon). [Grain] (18:1) Spr 90, p. 52.
5426. ROGERS, Bertha
"El Duende." [Nimrod] (34:1) Fall-Wint 90, p. 124-125.
"For the Girl Buried in the Peat Bog, Schleswig, Germany, First Century, A.D."
[Nimrod] (34:1) Fall-Wint 90, p. 122.
"Skating." [NegC] (10:1) 90, p. 81.
"Sleeper, You Wake." [Nimrod] (34:1) Fall-Wint 90, p. 123.
5427. ROGERS, Bruce Holland
"Gwyneth: Chalk." [BellR] (13:1, #27) Spr 90, p. 8.
"Nocturne." [HiramPoR] (48/49) 90-91, p. 62.
"Sophronia: Sand." [BellR] (13:1, #27) Spr 90, p. 9.
5428. ROGERS, Daryl
"I Go." [Bogg] (62) 90, p. 46-47.
"Letter to Ginsberg." [MoodySI] (22/23) Wint 89-90, p. 30.
5429. ROGERS, Garnet
"Body Parts: Love Poem for Sarah." [Writ] (21) 89 c1990, p. 47.
"Passacaglia." [Writ] (21) 89 c1990, p. 48-49.
"Riding Lesson." [Writ] (21) 89 c1990, p. 43.
"Song of the Mystagogue." [Writ] (21) 89 c1990, p. 46.
"Unedited." [Writ] (21) 89 c1990, p. 44-45.
5430. ROGERS, Linda
"Bright in the Harvest." [PoetryC] (11:4) Wint 90, p. 6.
"The Colour Blood." [PoetryC] (11:4) Wint 90, p. 6.
"One Glove to the Other." [PoetryC] (11:4) Wint 90, p. 6.
5431. ROGERS, Pattiann
"An Assumption." [IndR] (13:3) Fall 90, p. 1.

"The Blind Beggar's Dog." [Crazy] (38) Spr 90, p. 16-17.
"Consider the Lily." [Crazy] (38) Spr 90, p. 18-19.
"The Crying of Old Women." [GreenMR] (NS 4:1) Spr-Sum 90, p. 43-44.
"The Mad Linguist." [GettyR] (3:1) Wint 90, p. 51-52.
"A Passing." [GeoR] (44:3) Fall 90, p. 459-460.
"The Process." [GeoR] (44:1/2) Spr-Sum 90, p. 28-29.
"Sea Saviors." [IndR] (13:3) Fall 90, p. 4-7.
"The Shape and Weight of Belief." [IndR] (13:3) Fall 90, p. 2-3.
"To Complete a Thought." [GettyR] (3:1) Wint 90, p. 49-50.
"A Voice Speaks in Earnest, But Nobody Listens." [TriQ] (79) Fall 90, p. 96-97.
"The Warning." [GreenMR] (NS 4:1) Spr-Sum 90, p. 42.
5432. ROGERS, Timothy B.
"Personal Alternative." [BrooklynR] (7) 90, p. 32.
5433. ROGOFF, Jay
"Did the Black-and-White Movies Make My Mother?" [YaleR] (79:4) Sum 90 c1991,
p. 662-663.
"Dirty Linen." [GeoR] (44:4) Wint 90, p. 692.
"The Kindergarten Heart." [PoetryNW] (31:4) Wint 90-91, p. 36-37.
5434. ROITMAN, Judith
"As a child in the tub, thinking the stall shower looked like swans." [Caliban] (9) 90,
p. 143.
"Entire families with leprosy -- the child can't help leaning into the father." [Caliban]
(9) 90, p. 143.
"The false precision of, for example, 188th Street and the Expressway." [Caliban]
(9) 90, p. 142.
"Grief." [Abraxas] (38/39) 90, p. 136-137.
"He Is." [Abraxas] (38/39) 90, p. 137-139.
"You can think of a sonnet as exactly 140 syllables." [Caliban] (9) 90, p. 142.
5435. ROJAS, Gonzalo
"Aquí Cae Mi Pueblo." [Inti] (31) Primavera 90, p. 76.
"Ningunos." [Inti] (31) Primavera 90, p. 76-77.
5436. ROKPELNIS, Janis
"In the springtime you can walk *through* people" (tr. by Gunars Salins). [Nimrod]
(33:2) Spr-Sum 90, p. 73.
"Oh summer summer" (tr. by Gunars Salins). [Nimrod] (33:2) Spr-Sum 90, p. 73.
5437. ROLLINGS, Alane
"The Deep End." [NoDaQ] (58:3) Sum 90, p. 5-7.
"Not What We Used to Be." [NoDaQ] (58:3) Sum 90, p. 7-9.
5438. ROLLINS, Scott
"Ballad of the Salamander" (tr. of Wiel Kusters). [Trans] (24) Fall 90, p. 16.
"Before It Begins" (tr. of J. Bernlef). [Writ] (22) 90 c1991, p. 5.
"An Encounter with Pieter Saenredam" (Painting: St. Bavo Church by Pieter
Saenredam, tr. of J. Bernlef). [Trans] (24) Fall 90, p. 40-41.
"Francis Bacon" (tr. of J. Bernlef). [Writ] (22) 90 c1991, p. 10.
"Grammars" (tr. of J. Bernlef). [Writ] (22) 90 c1991, p. 8.
"On Systems" (tr. of J. Bernlef). [Writ] (22) 90 c1991, p. 7.
"Spirit Grounds" (tr. of J. Bernlef). [Writ] (22) 90 c1991, p. 9.
"Tulle, reed, paper, taffeta" (tr. of J. Bernlef). [Writ] (22) 90 c1991, p. 11.
"Winter Routes" (tr. of J. Bernlef). [Writ] (22) 90 c1991, p. 6.
5439. ROMAINE, E.
"His Daughter." [Confr] (44/45) Fall 90-Wint 91, p. 265.
5440. ROMAN, Aurelia
"Country of Cardboard and Cotton Batting" (tr. of Eugene Ionesco, w. Bradley R.
Strahan and S. G. Sullivan). [Vis] (33) 90, p. 4.
"Pays de Carton et D'Ouate" (tr. of Eugene Ionesco). [Vis] (33) 90, p. 4.
5441. ROMAN, Victor
"And After a Night." [PoetryUSA] ([5:4?]) Wint 90, p. 24.
"Untitled: Making tapes of a musical fast pace." [PoetryUSA] ([5:4?]) Wint 90, p.
24.
5442. ROMANO, Rose
"Italian Bread." [SoCoast] (8) Spr 90, p. 43.
"Puzzling It Out." [Footwork] 90, p. 64.
"Remember." [Footwork] 90, p. 64.
"Surviving." [Footwork] 90, p. 65.
"The Wop Factor." [Footwork] 90, p. 64.

5443. ROMANO, Tom
"The Day School Gives Out." [EngJ] (79:7) N 90, p. 90.
5444. ROMELL, Karen
"Saltspring Sheep." [Event] (19:1) Spr 90, p. 48-49.
5445. ROMER, Stephen
"In the Country." [Quarry] (39:1) Wint 90, p. 47.
5446. ROMERO, Leo
"Diane's Knocking." [Americas] (18:1) Spr 90, p. 50.
"How Did I Land Up in This City." [Americas] (18:1) Spr 90, p. 45.
"I Bring Twins Over to Meet." [Americas] (18:1) Spr 90, p. 41.
"I've Never Known a Dwarf Before." [Americas] (18:1) Spr 90, p. 39-40.
"Pito Had a Dream That." [Americas] (18:1) Spr 90, p. 47-49.
"Pito's Got Time." [Americas] (18:1) Spr 90, p. 46.
"Take My Picture, Says Pito." [Americas] (18:1) Spr 90, p. 38.
"This Is Denise, I Say to Pito." [Americas] (18:1) Spr 90, p. 42-43.
"Welcome, Says Skeleton." [NowestR] (28:2) 90, p. 74.
"Well Look." [NowestR] (28:2) 90, p. 75-76.
"When Pito Tried to Kill." [Americas] (18:1) Spr 90, p. 51-53.
"You Come Back Again." [Americas] (18:1) Spr 90, p. 37.
"You See What Happens." [Americas] (18:1) Spr 90, p. 44.
5447. ROMETS, Dmitry
"Do You Remember?" (Poem written in English by high school students from the
Ukraine, collected by Maureen Hurley). [PoetryUSA] (5:1) Spr 90, p. 18.
5448. ROMO-CARMONA, Mariana
"Dwelling Where the Moon Lost Its Pale Glow" (tr. of Doris Moromisato). [Cond]
(17) 90, p. 43.
"The Immaculate Story of Mnasidika, My Friend" (tr. of Doris Moromisato). [Cond]
(17) 90, p. 45.
"To This Body in Love" (tr. of Doris Moromisato). [Cond] (17) 90, p. 41.
5449. ROMOND, Edwin
"Father Dismas, Gregorian Chant Teacher." [PoetL] (85:3) Fall 90, p. 39-40.
5450. ROMTVEDT, David
"For You Now It Is One Foot in Front of Itself." [HampSPR] (Anthology
1975-1990) 90, p. 162.
"May I Present." [CrabCR] (7:1) Wint 90, p. 28-29.
"Sleeping Under Stars." [CrabCR] (7:1) Wint 90, p. 28.
5451. RONAN, Richard
"Love Among Lepers." [AmerPoR] (19:2) Mr-Ap 90, p. 24.
5452. RONCI, Ray
"Balzac and the Buddha." [GreensboroR] (49) Wint 90-91, p. 75-76.
"The Hands." [Iowa] (20:3) Fall 90, p. 124.
"Homage to Wine." [Plain] (10:3) Spr 90, p. 22.
5453. RONK, Martha (Martha C.)
"Fishes." [Ploughs] (16:4) Wint 90-91, p. 10.
"Habitual." [SouthernR] (26:3) Jl 90, p. 663.
5454. ROOME, Douglas
"Subtext." [JamesWR] (8:1) Fall 90, p. 7.
5455. ROOT, William Pitt
"Dusk Ox" (tr. of Wen I-to). [PoetryE] (30) Fall 90, p. 102.
"The Invader" (tr. of Ilya Ehrenburg). [PoetryE] (30) Fall 90, p. 30.
"Last Words Found in His Pockets" (tr. of Nikola Vaptsarow). [PoetryE] (30) Fall
90, p. 26.
"Nerves of Steel, or The Poet's Prayer" (tr. of Betti Alver). [PoetryE] (30) Fall 90,
p. 12.
"No This Isn't the Time for Poetry" (tr. of Nikola Vaptsarow). [PoetryE] (29) Spr
90, p. 142.
"When Our Enemies Doze Off" (tr. of Ewa Lipska). [PoetryE] (30) Fall 90, p. 53.
5456. ROOTS, Ellen
"Ghostbrother." [DogRR] (9:2, #18) Aut 90, p. 21.
5457. ROQUÉ, Rosa Ma.
"For Our Birth." [Grain] (18:1) Spr 90, p. 24.
"What Steve Says." [Grain] (18:1) Spr 90, p. 23.
ROSA, Rodrigo Rey
See REY ROSA, Rodrigo
5458. ROSARIO SANCHEZ, Elba
"Urge." [Zyzzyva] (6:1 #21) Spr 90, p. 68.

5459. ROSASCO-SOULE, Adelia
"Aloneness (1926)." [EmeraldCR] (1990) c89, p. 69.
"Cobwebs (1919)." [EmeraldCR] (1990) c89, p. 69.
5460. ROSCHER, Marina L.
"The Daughter." [Rohwedder] (5) Spr 90, p. 40.
5461. ROSE, Jennifer
"Gettysburg Postcard." [Verse] (7:3) Wint 90, p. 64.
"Maintenon Postcard." [Nat] (250:5) 5 F 90, p. 178.
"Solstice." [Verse] (7:3) Wint 90, p. 64.
"Southern Postcard." [Verse] (7:3) Wint 90, p. 63.
ROSE, John Richard de
    See DeROSE, John Richard
ROSE, Raymond Ray la
    See LaROSE, Raymond Ray
5462. ROSE, Stephen
"Kongo Power Figure." [PoetryUSA] (5:1) Spr 90, p. 18.
5463. ROSE, Virginia
"As god is my lover." [ChangingM] (21) Wint-Spr 90, p. 29.
5464. ROSE, Wendy
"Lenape" (Baltimore, December 1984). [Contact] (9:56/57/58) Spr 90, p. 34.
"Reminder" (Baltimore, December 1984). [Contact] (9:56/57/58) Spr 90, p. 35.
"What the Mohawk Made the Hopi Say" (Adirondack Mountains, January 1985).
    [Contact] (9:56/57/58) Spr 90, p. 35.
5465. ROSE, Wilga
"Relatively Speaking." [Bogg] (62) 90, p. 24.
"Visionaries" (for Brett Whiteley). [Bogg] (63) 90, p. 24.
5466. ROSEN, Kenneth
"Caribou." [BostonR] (15:6) D 90, p. 8.
"Crying Like a Child." [Journal] (13:2) Fall-Wint 89-90, p. 24-25.
"Fire." [VirQR] (66:4) Aut 90, p. 674.
"Monkey Zero." [MissouriR] (13:1) 90, p. 189-191.
"The Red Pond." [VirQR] (66:4) Aut 90, p. 673.
"A Simple Heart." [MissouriR] (13:1) 90, p. 192-193.
"Soul Flight." [BostonR] (15:6) D 90, p. 8.
"Waiting for You." [BostonR] (15:6) D 90, p. 8.
5467. ROSEN, Michael J.
"Cenotaph." [WestHR] (44:3) Aut 90, p. 324.
"Commission." [NewDeltaR] (7:2) Spr-Sum 90, p. 47-48.
"His Father Phones with an Idea for a Poem." [Salm] (85/86) Wint-Spr 90, p.
    43-46.
"The Measure of Life." [GrandS] (9:3) Spr 90, p. 185-189.
"Penn Concedes His Territories." [Iowa] (20:3) Fall 90, p. 103-110.
"Penn's Findings (However Inconclusive)." [NewDeltaR] (7:2) Spr-Sum 90, p.
    49-50.
"Penn's Spell." [NewDeltaR] (7:2) Spr-Sum 90, p. 51-52.
"Pen's Orchard." [Iowa] (20:2) Spr-Sum 90, p. 122-123.
"Snow Scene with Two Dogs." [WestHR] (44:4) Wint 90, p. 405-406.
"Spelling Bee." [NewDeltaR] (7:2) Spr-Sum 90, p. 45-46.
"Trying to Write You a Poem on Our Anniversary While Downstairs You
    Roughhouse with the Dogs." [NewEngR] (13:1) Fall 90, p. 154-155.
"Videnda." [NewRep] (203:17) 22 O 90, p. 40.
5468. ROSENBERG, Conrad
"Foreplay on MacDougal Street." [NegC] (10:2/3) 90, p. 86.
5469. ROSENBERG, David
"Eden" (Selections: 4-9, from "The Book of J," tr. of J). [AmerPoR] (19:6) N-D 90,
    p. 29-30.
5470. ROSENBERG, Heidi
"Blueberries." [Pearl] (11) Sum 90, p. 59.
5471. ROSENBERG, Liz
"All Those Hours Alone in the Dark." [Poetry] (156:3) Je 90, p. 157.
"The Common Life." [Poetry] (156:3) Je 90, p. 157.
"The Little Red Shoe" (After Perle Hessing). [SenR] (20:2) Fall 90, p. 39.
"The Noble Corpse." [NewYorker] (66:22) 16 Jl 90, p. 72.
"Pentimento." [NewYorker] (66:19) 25 Je 90, p. 32.
"Service." [SenR] (20:2) Fall 90, p. 40.
"A Vanished World" (Based on the work of Roman Vishniac). [HighP] (5:2) Fall

90, p. 65-67.
5472. ROSENBLATT, Joe
"Into the Glow of an Atom" (From "Poetry Hotel"). [DenQ] (24:3) Wint 90, p. 126.
"Rabbit" (from "Poetry Hotel"). [DenQ] (24:3) Wint 90, p. 22.
5473. ROSENFELD, Natania
"Fists: A Poem for the Day of Atonement." [Nimrod] (34:1) Fall-Wint 90, p. 126.
"Hopper Woman." [Nimrod] (34:1) Fall-Wint 90, p. 126.
5474. ROSENFELD, Rhoda
"In the Process of Coming to Be." [WestCL] (24:1) Spr 90, p. 45-46.
5475. ROSENTHAL, Laura
"Dungeon." [NewAW] (6) Spr 90, p. 75.
"Primitive Youth." [NewAW] (6) Spr 90, p. 74.
5476. ROSENTHAL, M. L.
"October Again." [SouthernR] (26:3) Jl 90, p. 664.
"A Place in Time." [SouthernR] (26:3) Jl 90, p. 664-666.
"Wedding Song for Autumn." [SouthernR] (26:3) Jl 90, p. 666-667.
5477. ROSENZWEIG, Don
"Some Days." [PennR] (4:2) 90, p. 49-50.
5478. ROSENZWEIG, Geri
"Home from the Dance." [PoetC] (21:3) Spr 90, p. 19-20.
5479. ROSS, Aden
"Sestina: Waiting Room." [CalQ] (34) 90, p. 26-27.
5480. ROSS, Carolyn B.
"The Cave." [Calyx] (12:3) Sum 90, p. 6-7.
5481. ROSS, Harvey-Ann
"Mother's Day -- 1989." [EngJ] (79:5) S 90, p. 76-77.
5482. ROSS, Joe
"Guards of the Heart" (Selection: Act II). [WashR] (15:6) Ap-My 90, p. 10.
5483. ROSS, Linwood M.
"James Brown." [BlackALF] (24:3) Fall 90, p. 552-553.
"Poverty Deluxe." [BlackALF] (24:3) Fall 90, p. 553-554.
5484. ROSS, Stuart
"And the Road Has Dust in Its Throat." [WestCL] (24:3) Wint 90, p. 62.
"Bundybaby." [WestCL] (24:3) Wint 90, p. 60.
"Nadie." [WestCL] (24:3) Wint 90, p. 61.
5485. ROSSER, J. Allyn
"The City Underneath." [ParisR] (32:115) Sum 90, p. 57.
"A Dream of Ezra Pound." [NewEngR] (13:2) Wint 90, p. 130-131.
"Interview." [OntR] (32) Spr-Sum 90, p. 93.
"Much Later." [Poetry] (157:2) N 90, p. 95.
"The Next Stop Stopping." [OntR] (32) Spr-Sum 90, p. 91-92.
"The Quickness of Things." [Crazy] (38) Spr 90, p. 54-56.
"Renouncing the Tower." [GeoR] (44:1/2) Spr-Sum 90, p. 73-78.
"A Sense of Connection, As In." [ParisR] (32:115) Sum 90, p. 55-56.
"Soundtrack of a Desert Documentary." [Poetry] (155:4) Ja 90, p. 275.
"Suburban Report." [NewEngR] (13:2) Wint 90, p. 131.
"Valerie, Actually." [Verse] (7:2) Sum 90, p. 93.
ROSSI, Cristina Peri
See PERI ROSSI, Cristina
5486. ROSSI, Lee
"Breakfast." [WormR] (30:4, #120) 90, p. 104.
"Chain." [OnTheBus] (2:2/3:1, #6/7) Sum-Fall 90 Wint-Spr 91, p. 178-180.
"Soaps." [WormR] (30:4, #120) 90, p. 104-105.
"Spare Parts." [WormR] (30:4, #120) 90, p. 103-104.
5487. ROSSINI, Clare
"Leave of Absence." [BlackWR] (16:2) Spr-Sum 90, p. 14-15.
"Portrait: The Adolescent Self." [BlackWR] (16:2) Spr-Sum 90, p. 16.
5488. ROTELLA, Alexis
"Dust." [SingHM] (17) 90, p. 26.
"Seashell by God." [CrossC] (12:1) 90, p. 20.
"Unknown Weed." [JINJPo] (12:1) Spr 90, p. 7.
5489. ROTHENBERG, Jerome
"Improvisation No. 4: Reservoir & Rapture." [Ploughs] (16:4) Wint 90-91, p.
64-65.
5490. ROTHMAN, David J.
"Disappearing Barn" (for G. B.). [PoetL] (85:1) Spr 90, p. 25-26.

"The Septic Tank" (for the Mallet family, at Varengeville-sur-Mer." [LitR] (33:3) Spr 90, p. 309-311.
5491. ROUBAUD, Jacques
"Some Thing Black: Three Poems" (tr. by Rosmarie Waldrop). [Trans] (23) Spr 90, p. 107-110.
5492. ROUSE, Andy
"Corals" (tr. of Attila József, w. Len Roberts). [ArtfulD] (18/19) 90, p. 26.
5493. ROUSE, Anne
"Baby Tony at Al's Cafe." [Verse] (7:2) Sum 90, p. 91.
5494. ROWAN, Phyllis
"Bull's-Eye." [PottPort] (11) 89, p. 47.
5495. ROWDER, Jessica
"Why Gravity Doesn't Give Up." [Nimrod] (34:1) Fall-Wint 90, p. 127.
5496. ROWE, Candice
"On Hearing the Pretty Grim News." [ChironR] (9:1) Spr 90, p. 25.
5497. ROWLEY, Mari-Lou
"Boreal Surreal." [Descant] (21:4/22:1, #71/72) Wint-Spr 90-91, p. 236.
5498. ROY, André
"L'Homme des Sept Jours" (Selections). [MassR] (31:1/2) Spr-Sum 90, p. 29, 31.
"The Man of Seven Days" (Selections, tr. by David Lenson). [MassR] (31:1/2) Spr-Sum 90, p. 28, 30.
5499. ROY, Lucinda
"Points of View." [ThRiPo] (35/36) 90, p. 86-87.
"The Votaries." [Callaloo] (13:4) Fall 90, p. 740.
5500. ROYET-JOURNOUD, Claude
"A Descriptive Method" ("Une Méthode descriptive," Le Collet de Buffle, Paris, 1986, tr. by Joseph Simas). [Avec] (3:1) 90, p. 43-55.
5501. ROZEMA, Mark
"The Compost Bin Speaks." [TarRP] (30:1) Fall 90, p. 34.
"The Dam Builder's Dream." [TarRP] (30:1) Fall 90, p. 35.
5502. ROZEWICZ, Tadeusz
"The Grass" (tr. by Karen Karleski). [PoetryE] (29) Spr 90, p. 25.
"The Tree" (tr. by Karen Karleski). [PoetryE] (29) Spr 90, p. 24.
5503. RUAN, Zhanjing
"Morning" (tr. by Li Xijian and Gordon Osing). [CarolQ] (42:3) Spr 90, p. 78.
"Sandstorm" (tr. by Li Xijian and Gordon Osing). [CarolQ] (42:3) Spr 90, p. 79-80.
5504. RUARK, Gibbons
"The Death of Emma Hardy." [HampSPR] (Anthology 1975-1990) 90, p. 183.
"Robert Frost to Ezra Pound's Daughter from His Deathbed." [HampSPR] (Anthology 1975-1990) 90, p. 184.
5505. RUBIN, Diana K.
"The Virgins of Zurbaran." [SmPd] (27:2, #79) Spr 90, p. 30.
5506. RUBIN, Gertrude
"Sciatica." [WillowR] Spr 90, p. 20.
5507. RUBIN, Larry
"Blue Ridge Cemetery" (For My Sister). [NegC] (10:2/3) 90, p. 28.
"Lessons of the Beach: Reaching Infinity." [ManhatPR] (11) [89?], p. 37.
"Lines for a Manic-Depressive Uncle, Divorcing at 71." [JINJPo] (12:2) Aut 90, p. 15.
"Transferring Names into a New Address Book" (For a Loyal Friend). [JINJPo] (12:2) Aut 90, p. 16.
5508. RUBIN, Mark
"Autumn of the Body." [SouthernHR] (24:3) Sum 90, p. 244.
"Beethoven's Fifth in C Minor." [PraS] (64:2) Sum 90, p. 18-19.
"Off Montauk." [SycamoreR] (2:1) Wint 90, p. 20-21.
"The Road Before You Know It." [PraS] (64:2) Sum 90, p. 17.
"With Rex in Montauk." [SycamoreR] (2:1) Wint 90, p. 18-19.
5509. RUBIN, Ronald Simon
"The Exit Sign." [FloridaR] (17:2) Fall-Wint 90, p. 136.
5510. RUCKER, Trish
"Telling the Future on Interstate 75." [TarRP] (30:1) Fall 90, p. 30.
"Variations on a Theme." [SouthernPR] (30:2) Fall 90, p. 41.
"Ways of Seeing Light." [CarolQ] (42:3) Spr 90, p. 40.
"Witching Night." [PoetL] (85:2) Sum 90, p. 41-42.
5511. RUDEL, Jaufre
"Lan Quan Lijorn" (tr. by W. D. Snodgrass). [HampSPR] (Anthology 1975-1990)

90, p. 241-242.
5512. RUDMAN, Mark
"Aftermath, 1956." [NewRep] (203:8/9) 20-27 Ag 90, p. 28.
"Conversation: December, the Night City." [MissouriR] (13:2) 90, p. 45-47.
"The Eclipse." [DenQ] (25:1) Sum 90, p. 29-31.
"Facts of Life." [Pequod] (31) 90, p. 90-111.
"First Asthma." [NewYorker] (66:19) 25 Je 90, p. 36-37.
"The Nowhere Water." [ParisR] (32:114) Spr 90, p. 186-187.
"Shelters and Holes." [Agni] (31/32) 90, p. 145-148.
"Trust." [Ploughs] (16:4) Wint 90-91, p. 112-116.
"Turin: Albergo Roma." [IndR] (13:2) Spr 90, p. 21.
"The World Dies and Is Reborn Again Each Second." [Ploughs] (16:4) Wint 90-91,
p. 110-111.
5513. RUDNIK, Raphael
"The Clown" (tr. of Martinus Nijhoff). [Trans] (24) Fall 90, p. 164.
"Con Sordino" (tr. of Martinus Nijhoff). [Trans] (24) Fall 90, p. 161.
"Impasse" (tr. of Martinus Nijhoff). [Trans] (24) Fall 90, p. 165.
"The Ivy" (tr. of Martinus Nijhoff). [Trans] (24) Fall 90, p. 162.
"The Mother, the Woman" (tr. of Martinus Nijhoff). [Trans] (24) Fall 90, p. 163.
5514. RUEFLE, Mary
"Zorro & the Bats." [BlackWR] (16:2) Spr-Sum 90, p. 95.
5515. RUFFIN, Paul
"Devil's Finger Island." [KanQ] (22:3) Sum 90, p. 32.
"The Rabbit." [MichQR] (29:1) Wint 90, p. 110.
"Redfish." [KanQ] (22:3) Sum 90, p. 32.
"Shrimping." [HawaiiR] (15:1, #31) Wint 90, p. 82-83.
5516. RUFFO, Armand Garnet
"Kebsquasheshing." [Dandel] (17:1) Spr-Sum 90, p. 36.
"Kebsquasheshing." [PoetryC] (11:1) Spr 90, p. 9.
5517. RUGAMA, Leonel
"The Earth Is a Satellite of the Moon" (tr. by Margaret Randall). [Quarry] (39:4) Fall
1990, p. 78-79.
5518. RUGGIERI, Helen
"Great Blue Heron." [RiverC] (10:2) Spr 90, p. 10.
"Roycroft Craftsmen." [Pig] (16) 90, p. 21.
"Salvation by Filing." [Pig] (16) 90, p. 98.
5519. RUGGLES, Eugene
"Homeless." [Manoa] (2:1) Spr 90, p. 94-95.
"Inscription for the Door." [Manoa] (2:1) Spr 90, p. 95.
"An Old Woman Watering Her Plants with Milk." [Manoa] (2:1) Spr 90, p. 93-94.
"The Unemployed Automobile Workers of Detroit Prepare to Share Christmas
Standing in Line." [Manoa] (2:1) Spr 90, p. 93.
"The Winter of 1984." [Manoa] (2:1) Spr 90, p. 92.
RUISSEAUX, Pierre des
See DesRUISSEAUX, Pierre
5520. RUIZ DE ALARCON, Hernando
"Against Unruly Ants" (compilation of original Nahuatl spell, Mexico 1629, in
Nahuatl and English, tr. by Francisco X. Alarcón). [PoetryUSA] (5:3) Fall 90,
p. 14.
5521. RUKEYSER, Muriel
"Along history, forever." [CimR] (93) O 90, p. 62.
"Myth." [CimR] (93) O 90, p. 63-64.
"Rational Man." [CimR] (93) O 90, p. 65.
"To enter that rhythm where the self is lost." [CimR] (93) O 90, p. 61.
5522. RUMBERG, Mayda
"Choices." [Plain] (10:3) Spr 90, p. 33.
"In Defense of Middle Management and Suburban Marriage." [Plain] (10:2) Wint 90,
p. 16-17.
5523. RUMENS, Carol
"Above Cuckmere Haven." [Quarry] (39:1) Wint 90, p. 48-49.
5524. RUNCIMAN, Lex
"Adoption." [MissouriR] (13:1) 90, p. 99.
"Happy." [MissouriR] (13:1) 90, p. 98.
5525. RUNEFELT, Eva
"Augustigräs." [Spirit] (10:1) 89, p. 202, 204.
"Dark Wind" (tr. by Lennart Bruce and Sonja Bruce). [Spirit] (10:1) 89, p. 215.

399

"Flimsy Kitchen Light" (tr. by Lennart Bruce and Sonja Bruce). [Spirit] (10:1) 89,
    p. 209.
"Förortsmorgon." [Spirit] (10:1) 89, p. 212.
"Fransigt Köksljus." [Spirit] (10:1) 89, p. 208.
"Grass in August" (tr. by Lennart Bruce and Sonja Bruce). [Spirit] (10:1) 89, p.
    203, 205.
"Incisions" (tr. by Lennart Bruce and Sonja Bruce). [Spirit] (10:1) 89, p. 211.
"Klyvningar." [Spirit] (10:1) 89, p. 210.
"March, Early Spring" (tr. by Lennart Bruce and Sonja Bruce). [Spirit] (10:1) 89, p.
    201.
"Mars, Förvår." [Spirit] (10:1) 89, p. 200.
"Morgon." [Spirit] (10:1) 89, p. 206.
"Mörk Blåst." [Spirit] (10:1) 89, p. 214.
"Morning" (tr. by Lennart Bruce and Sonja Bruce). [Spirit] (10:1) 89, p. 207.
"Morning in Suburbia" (tr. by Lennart Bruce and Sonja Bruce). [Spirit] (10:1) 89, p.
    213.
"New" (tr. by Lennart Bruce and Sonja Bruce). [Spirit] (10:1) 89, p. 221, 223.
"Ny." [Spirit] (10:1) 89, p. 220, 222.
"Slakthuset." [Spirit] (10:1) 89, p. 216, 218.
"The Slaughterhouse" (tr. by Lennart Bruce and Sonja Bruce). [Spirit] (10:1) 89, p.
    217, 219.
5526. RUNYON, C. D.
    "To a Scorpion Preserved in a Glass Necklace." [FloridaR] (17:2) Fall-Wint 90, p.
        36-37.
5527. RUSEL, Jacob
    "Fish Whose Eyes Are Never Closed in Sleep." [BelPoJ] (41:1) Fall 90, p. 21.
    "Poetry Reading at the Gershman Y." [BelPoJ] (41:1) Fall 90, p. 21.
    "Purim Spiel." [BelPoR] (40:3) Spr 90, p. 18-19.
    "Swimmers." [BelPoJ] (41:1) Fall 90, p. 20.
5528. RUSH, Cherlynn A.
    "Certitude." [WorldO] (23:1/2) Fall 88-Wint 89 c1991, p. 17.
5529. RUSS, Biff
    "Pearl" (Poem for a Mixed-Blood Grandfather). [MidwQ] (31:2) Wint 90, p.
        218-219.
    "To Nicholas and Frieda, in the Voice of Sylvia Plath." [BellR] (13:1, #27) Spr 90,
        p. 20.
5530. RUSS, Don
    "Alcmene, Housewife, Welcomes Her Husband Home from a Hard Day at Work."
        [Poem] (64) N 90, p. 41.
    "The Bachelor Tells a Family Story." [TarRP] (30:1) Fall 90, p. 38.
    "Heads from the Museo Nazionale Romano." [LullwaterR] (1:1) Spr 90, p. 56.
    "Marie's Song" (Marie Dionne, 1934-1970). [LullwaterR] (1:1) Spr 90, p. 81.
    "The Shadow of My Roof." [Poem] (64) N 90, p. 42-44.
    "Vulcan Restored" (Vulcan Park on Red Mountain, Birmingham). [SouthernHR]
        (24:2) Spr 90, p. 158.
5531. RUSSELL, Bruce
    "True North." [MassR] (31:1/2) Spr-Sum 90, p. 81-85.
5532. RUSSELL, Carolann
    "Every Woman's Christmas." [Calyx] (13:1) Wint 90-91, p. 4.
    "A Free Country." [MalR] (92) S 90, p. 72.
    "Kitchen Meditation." [MalR] (92) S 90, p. 70-71.
    "Talking About the Penis." [Calyx] (13:1) Wint 90-91, p. 6.
    "Women in the Sauna." [Calyx] (13:1) Wint 90-91, p. 5.
RUSSELL, Gillian Harding
    See HARDING-RUSSELL, Gillian
5533. RUSSELL, Glenn
    "The Sleepwalker." [Asylum] (6:2) S 90, p. 2.
5534. RUSSELL, Jonathan
    "One Day Before." [SlipS] (10) 90, p. 50.
5535. RUSSELL, Timothy
    "A Veteran hooker in Philly." [Amelia] (6:2, #17) 90, p. 42.
5536. RUSSELL, Valerie
    "Sowing Seed" (to my daughter). [BlackALF] (24:3) Fall 90, p. 539.
5537. RUSSELL, Valerie J.
    "This Poem Is for CJ." [RiverS] (32) [90?], p. 72-73.

5538. RUSSO, A. P.
"The Bay." [Rohwedder] (5) Spr 90, p. 19.
"Blue Shift." [Rohwedder] (5) Spr 90, p. 18.
"Tom's Idea." [Rohwedder] (5) Spr 90, p. 18.
5539. RUTHERFORD, Maurice
"Skulls at Phnom Penh." [Bogg] (63) 90, p. 64.
5540. RUTKOVSKY-RUSKIN, Mary
"Found Poem: Beaufort Scale." [Caliban] (8) 90, p. 135.
5541. RUTSALA, Vern
"The Knocking." [FreeL] (5) Sum 90, p. 19.
"The Moment's Equation." [SycamoreR] (2:2) Sum 90, p. 25-26.
"The Muses of Rooms." [Poetry] (155:4) Ja 90, p. 278-279.
"Portland Hosts the Second Coming." [Agni] (31/32) 90, p. 111-113.
5542. RUVIK, A.
"I wanted to be like Al." [PoetryUSA] (5:1) Spr 90, p. 3.
5543. RUZESKY, Jay
"The Complete Poems of Mr. John Milton." [Bogg] (63) 90, p. 34-35.
"Meeting Diefenbaker." [CanLit] (127) Wint 90, p. 60-61.
5544. RUZICKA, Ed
"The Compass." [InterPR] (16:1) Spr 90, p. 130.
"The Multiplication of Doves." [InterPR] (16:1) Spr 90, p. 129.
5545. RYAN, Gregory
"Rock Concert." [Plain] (10:3) Spr 90, p. 10.
5546. RYAN, Gregory A.
"Terrace View." [HawaiiR] (14:2, #29) Spr 90, p. 40.
"Winter Palace Tour." [HawaiiR] (14:2, #29) Spr 90, p. 40.
5547. RYAN, Kay
"Extraordinary Lengths." [Zyzzyva] (6:3 #23) Fall 90, p. 75.
"Is It Modest?" [PartR] (57:3) Sum 90, p. 435.
"Meniscus." [CalQ] (34) 90, p. 22.
5548. RYAN, Michael
"Boy 'Carrying-in' Bottles in Glass Works" (West Virginia, 1911, Photograph by
Lewis W. Hine). [Nat] (251:13) 22 O 90, p. 462.
"Pedestrian Pastoral." [Nat] (251:13) 22 O 90, p. 462.
"TV Room at the Children's Hospice." [Nat] (251:13) 22 O 90, p. 462.
5549. RYAN, Terry
"Butcher" (For William Packard). [NewYorkQ] (41) Spr 90, p. 102.
"Catholic Girl." [NewYorkQ] (42) Sum 90, p. 63-64.
5550. RYBICKI, John
"Billy Martin Speaks to His Team" (Final Game of the World Series. For Rodney
Torreson. With Julie Moulds). [NewYorkQ] (41) Spr 90, p. 101.
"Cleaning the Auger, Wet Corn Silo" (for Kim Wright). [Sonora] (19) Spr-Sum 90,
p. 12.
"Coal Boys." [Gargoyle] (37/38) 90, p. 48.
5551. RYLANDER, Edith
"Dancing Back the Cranes." [SingHM] (17) 90, p. 93.
5552. RYMARUK, Ihor
"Untitled: Keep talking, keep talking" (tr. by Larissa Onyshkevych). [Agni] (29/30)
90, p. 302.
5553. RYPMA, Gerben
"Ash Wednesday" (tr. by Rod Jellema). [WashR] (16:2) Ag-S 90, p. 13.
"Jiskedei." [WashR] (16:2) Ag-S 90, p. 13.
5554. SABATIER, Robert
"Atomic Sun" (tr. by Elisabeth Lapeyre and Cordell Caudron). [InterPR] (16:2) Fall
90, p. 47.
"The Child Within the Man" (tr. by Elisabeth Lapeyre and Cordell Caudron).
[InterPR] (16:2) Fall 90, p. 39.
"La Communication" (from "Icare et Autres Poèmes"). [InterPR] (16:2) Fall 90, p.
44.
"Communication" (tr. by Elisabeth Lapeyre and Cordell Caudron). [InterPR] (16:2)
Fall 90, p. 45.
"L'Enfant Suit l'Homme." [InterPR] (16:2) Fall 90, p. 38.
"The Feeling of Having Forgotten" (tr. by C. K. Williams). [Trans] (23) Spr 90, p.
71.
"The Journey of a Tree" (tr. by Elisabeth Lapeyre and Cordell Caudron). [InterPR]
(16:2) Fall 90, p. 43.

"Passage de l'Arbre" (from "Les Fêtes Solaires"). [InterPR] (16:2) Fall 90, p. 42.
"Primal Poetry" (tr. by Eric Sellin). [Vis] (32) 90, p. 41.
"Soleil d'Orage" (from "L'Oiseau de Demain"). [InterPR] (16:2) Fall 90, p. 46.
"Summer Earth" (tr. by Elisabeth Lapeyre and Cordell Caudron). [InterPR] (16:2)
    Fall 90, p. 41.
"La Terre de l'Eté." [InterPR] (16:2) Fall 90, p. 40.
"To Each Day" (tr. by C. K. Williams). [Trans] (23) Spr 90, p. 70.
SABINAS, Jaime
    See SABINES, Jaime
5555. SABINES, Jaime
    "The Moon." (tr. by Robert Jebb). [PoetryE] (30) Fall 90, p. 7.
    "One Tree Less" (tr. by W. S. Merwin). [Trans] (24) Fall 90, p. 199.
5556. SACKMANN, Cheryl Karnes
    "Escape Artist." [EngJ] (79:3) Mr 90, p. 91.
    "Stolen North Texas Summer Evening." [EngJ] (79:4) Ap 90, p. 109.
5557. SACKS, Peter
    "Anthem." [Agni] (29/30) 90, p. 87-88.
    "Fort Worth, Texas." [SouthwR] (75:1) Wint 90, p. 91-92.
    "Houw Hoek" (for my mother). [Agni] (29/30) 90, p. 89-90.
    "Safed." [Crazy] (38) Spr 90, p. 13-15.
    "Sea-lion at Santa Cruz" (For Barbara -- on the loss of a favorite earring). [Agni]
        (29/30) 90, p. 91-92.
5558. SACUTA, Norman
    "My Mother's War Story." [Dandel] (17:1) Spr-Sum 90, p. 37.
5559. SADOFF, Ira
    "1848." [Antaeus] (64/65) Spr-Aut 90, p. 119.
    "Against Whitman." [NewRep] (202:9) 26 F 90, p. 37.
    "I Join the Sparrows." [VirQR] (66:4) Aut 90, p. 663.
    "In Switzerland: Father and Daughter." [SouthernR] (26:2) Ap 90, p. 327.
    "In the Bog Behind My House." [SouthernR] (26:2) Ap 90, p. 326.
    "Sparrow Air." [VirQR] (66:4) Aut 90, p. 662.
5560. SADOWAY, Zenovia
    "Impressions of Spain ('89)." [AntigR] (81/82) Spr-Sum 90, p. 183-184.
5561. SAENZ, Benjamin
    "Ring of Life" (for Barbara, who knows about dying). [Sequoia] (33:2) Wint 90, p.
        108.
5562. SAENZ, Benjamín Alire
    "Painting from My Father." [BilingR] (14:3) S-D 87-88, c91, p. 77-78.
5563. SAFDIE, Joe
    "September Song" (Excerpt). [PoetryUSA] (5:1) Spr 90, p. 10.
5564. SAFFIOTI, Carol Lee
    "Lost Shadow Visits." [RagMag] (8:2) 90, p. 55.
    "Public Lands." [AnthNEW] 90, p. 23.
5565. SAFFORD, June Billings
    "The Two Riders." [Kalliope] (12:1) 90, c89, p. 5.
5566. SAGAN, Miriam
    "The Childhood of the Saint." [HeavenB] (8) Wint 90-91, p. 28.
    "Clay." [Bogg] (63) 90, p. 26.
    "Flamenco." [Gargoyle] (37/38) 90, p. 10.
    "Henna." [OnTheBus] (2:1, #5) Spr 90, p. 121.
    "Kaune's Foodtown." [ChironR] (9:3) Aut 90, p. 25.
    "Views of the Pecos." [Gargoyle] (37/38) 90, p. 11.
5567. SAGASER, Elizabeth Harris
    "Coming Round." [SouthernR] (26:2) Ap 90, p. 310.
    "Living Off the Land." [CumbPR] (9:2) Spr 90, p. 35.
    "October." [SouthernR] (26:2) Ap 90, p. 311.
    "Talking about New Hampshire." [CumbPR] (9:2) Spr 90, p. 34.
5568. SAHAY, Raghuvir
    "Solitary" (tr. by Vinay Dharwadker). [Screens] (2) 90, p. 48.
5569. SAINE, Ute Margarete
    "To Ramon and Ana Maria Xirau" (tr. of Verónica Volkow). [OnTheBus] (2:2/3:1,
        #6/7) Sum-Fall 90 Wint-Spr 91, p. 252.
SAINT . . .
    See also ST. . . . (filed as spelled)
5570. SAINT, Assotto
    "Heaven in Hell" (for counsel wright). [BrooklynR] (7) 90, p. 17.

"The Memory of Suffering." [BrooklynR] (7) 90, p. 18.
"Pater Noster." [ChangingM] (21) Wint-Spr 90, p. 12.
5571. SAINT-PIERRE, Raymond
"Aspirations." [Os] (30) Spr 90, p. 37.
5572. SAITO, Masaya
"A Man Who Reads Homer" (tr. of Junzaburo Nishiwaki). [Trans] (24) Fall 90, p. 228.
"No Traveler Returns" (tr. of Junzaburo Nishiwaki). [Trans] (24) Fall 90, p. 228.
"A Wintry Day" (tr. of Junzaburo Nishiwaki). [Trans] (24) Fall 90, p. 227.
5573. SAIZ, Próspero
"And -- there is your you." [Abraxas] (38/39) 90, p. 110-111.
"Malinche." [Abraxas] (38/39) 90, p. 98-101.
"Monotone." [Abraxas] (38/39) 90, p. 107-109.
"Narcisskull." [Abraxas] (38/39) 90, p. 104-105.
"Night." [Abraxas] (38/39) 90, p. 102.
"Surplus." [Abraxas] (38/39) 90, p. 106-107.
"Trilce" (Selections: I-XIII, XXXVI, LXI, LXV, LXXV-LXXVII, tr. of César Abraham Vallejo). [Abraxas] (38/39) 90, p. 5-63.
"Web first rays of dawn." [Abraxas] (38/39) 90, p. 96-97.
"Winslow, Arizona." [Abraxas] (38/39) 90, p. 103.
5574. SAJE, Natasha
"Jamaican Rum." [CumbPR] (10:1) Fall 90, p. 40.
"Suburban Children." [CumbPR] (10:1) Fall 90, p. 39.
5575. SAKNUSSEMM, Kristopher (Kris)
"Dandelion Safari." [Bogg] (62) 90, p. 12-13.
"Don't Get a Gun, Get a Big Dog." [HawaiiR] (14:3, #30) Fall 90, p. 15-16.
"MacArthur Blvd." [PassN] (11:1) Sum 90, p. 14.
"Signal Territory." [Interim] (9:1) Spr-Sum 90, p. 16.
"Sky Class." [HawaiiR] (14:3, #30) Fall 90, p. 17.
"Triage." [SouthwR] (75:1) Wint 90, p. 74-75.
"Wading in the dust." [KanQ] (22:3) Sum 90, p. 103.
"Window Men." [SmPd] (27:1, #78) Wint 90, p. 24.
5576. SALACH, Cindy
"Reasons for Androgyny." [PoetryUSA] (5:3) Fall 90, p. 14.
5577. SALADO, Minerva
"Reportage from Viet Nam, Especially for International Woman's Day" (tr. by Daniela Gioseffi, w. Enildo García). [PoetryE] (30) Fall 90, p. 27.
5578. SALAMONE, Karen
"Highway." [BellArk] (6:6) N-D 90, p. 24.
"Orchid Clouds." [BellArk] (6:4) Jl-Ag 90, p. 20.
"The Silvery Prescription." [BellArk] (6:4) Jl-Ag 90, p. 23.
"Violent Weather." [BellArk] (6:6) N-D 90, p. 6.
5579. SALAMUN, Tomaz
"The Deer" (tr. by Michael Biggins). [Ploughs] (16:4) Wint 90-91, p. 76.
"Epistle to the Angry Ones." [PartR] (57:2) Spr 90, p. 267.
"For David" (tr. by Michael Biggins). [DenQ] (25:1) Sum 90, p. 33.
"Functions" (tr. by Michael Biggins). [Ploughs] (16:4) Wint 90-91, p. 77-79.
"Happiness Is Hot, Splattered Brains" (tr. by Michael Biggins). [Ploughs] (16:4) Wint 90-91, p. 81.
"My Tribe" (tr. by Michael Biggins). [DenQ] (25:1) Sum 90, p. 34-35.
"Nihil Est in Intellectu" (tr. by Michael Biggins). [Ploughs] (16:4) Wint 90-91, p. 80.
"One, My Arm" (tr. by Michael Biggins). [DenQ] (25:1) Sum 90, p. 32.
"Shepherd." [PoetryUSA] (5:3) Fall 90, p. 19.
"To the Deaf Ones" (tr. by Michael Biggins). [DenQ] (25:1) Sum 90, p. 36-37.
5580. SALASIN, Sal
"For some time I was a student of Freud." [AnotherCM] (22) 90, p. 126-127.
"It was almost dark by the time we got back to Manderley." [AnotherCM] (22) 90, p. 122-123.
"It was important at the time." [AnotherCM] (22) 90, p. 131-132.
"New York Sits There." [Spirit] (10:2) 90, p. 45.
"No tongue has soiled it." [AnotherCM] (22) 90, p. 124-125.
"Not only can you be visionary after you're dead." [AnotherCM] (22) 90, p. 129-130.
"Once I courted danger at every subway stop." [Talisman] (5) Fall 90, p. 76.
"So just then this guy with no legs on a skateboard." [AnotherCM] (22) 90, p. 128.

403

5581. SALEH, Dennis
"Antique." [Pearl] (11) Sum 90, p. 52.
"Day of a Cat's Death" (after the Egyptian, "Rites of Bast"). [Turnstile] (2:1) 90, p. 54-56.
"Lady in February." [Pearl] (10) Spr 90, p. 5-6.
5582. SALEMI, Joseph S.
"Epigrams" (Selections: I.73, IX.41, XII.95, tr. of Martial). [ArtfulD] (18/19) 90, p. 100-101.
5583. SALERNO, Joe
"The Bull God." [MidwQ] (31:3) Spr 90, p. 369.
"The Corner." [MidwQ] (31:3) Spr 90, p. 367-368.
"Elegy for William Lebo." [JINJPo] (12:1) Spr 90, p. 1-3.
"The Gift." [WindO] (53) Fall 90, p. 54-55.
"Only Here." [PoetC] (21:3) Spr 90, p. 24-25.
"A River and a Swamp to Ourselves: By Way of an Autobiographical Note." [JINJPo] (12:1) Spr 90, p. 4-6.
"Spring Rain Clears at Evening." [MidwQ] (32:1) Aut 90, p. 92.
5584. SALINAS, Luis Omar
"Courtship of Darkness." [DenQ] (25:2) Fall 90, p. 41.
5585. SALINS, Gunars
"In the springtime you can walk *through* people" (tr. of Janis Rokpelnis). [Nimrod] (33:2) Spr-Sum 90, p. 73.
"Oh summer summer" (tr. of Janis Rokpelnis). [Nimrod] (33:2) Spr-Sum 90, p. 73.
5586. SALLAH, Tijan M.
"Love." [WashR] (16:2) Ag-S 90, p. 29.
"Television as God." [WashR] (16:2) Ag-S 90, p. 29.
5587. SALLI, Donna
"Roadkill." [HawaiiR] (14:2, #29) Spr 90, p. 16.
5588. SALLIS, James
"Another World" (for Kim at six months). [ManhatPR] (11) [89?], p. 29.
"The Art of Poetry" (tr. of Yves Bonnefoy). [NegC] (10:2/3) 90, p. 157.
"The Disavowed" (tr. of Pablo Neruda). [NegC] (10:2/3) 90, p. 159, 161.
"Esenin." [AmerPoR] (19:2) Mr-Ap 90, p. 40.
"The Surrealist Works at His Novel." [NegC] (10:2/3) 90, p. 113.
5589. SALOM, Philip
"A Night in Paris." [TampaR] (3) 90, p. 78-79.
"Traffic-Lights." [TampaR] (3) 90, p. 77.
5590. SALTER, Mary Jo
"Sunday Skaters." [NewYorker] (66:2) 26 F 90, p. 52-53.
5591. SALTMAN, Benjamin
"A Few Days on Ward B." [PoetryNW] (31:4) Wint 90-91, p. 13-14.
"The Greenhouse Effect Reaches the Environmental Agency." [PoetryNW] (31:4) Wint 90-91, p. 14-15.
"The Way to San Onofré." [SouthernPR] (30:2) Fall 90, p. 54-55.
5592. SALZMAN, Jerome
"Sexual geographers." [Bogg] (63) 90, p. 45.
5593. SAMARAS, Nicholas
"Amnesiac." [Poetry] (156:2) My 90, p. 67-68.
"The Nuremberg Executions." [MissouriR] (13:2) 90, p. 128-129.
5594. SAMMONS, Toni
"Almost Home." [CapilR] (2:4) Wint 90, p. 25-26.
"Cakile." [CapilR] (2:4) Wint 90, p. 23-24.
"Laurel." [CapilR] (2:4) Wint 90, p. 29-30.
"Mirror for Time." [CapilR] (2:4) Wint 90, p. 33-35.
"Nagame." [CapilR] (2:4) Wint 90, p. 22.
"Permollis." [MalR] (91) Je 90, p. 58-63.
"Scarce Vapourer." [CapilR] (2:4) Wint 90, p. 27-28.
"Sleep Movements of Leaves." [MalR] (91) Je 90, p. 52-57.
"Thursday Was a Day of Wood." [CapilR] (2:4) Wint 90, p. 31-32.
5595. SAMPSON, Bob
"Echoes." [Bogg] (63) 90, p. 24.
"St. Lazare." [Bogg] (62) 90, p. 40.
5596. SAMPSON, Dennis
".22." [TarRP] (29:2) Spr 90, p. 40.
"Before the Movie Begins." [Hudson] (43:2) Sum 90, p. 257-258.

5597. SAMPSON, Samantha
"Rappin'." [PoetryUSA] (5:1) Spr 90, p. 17.
5598. SAMRANEY, Joanne
"Moon's Child." [PennR] (4:2) 90, p. 55.
5599. SAMSON, Stacie
"Mixed Blood." [SinW] (41) Sum-Fall 90, p. 45-46.
SANCHEZ, Elba Rosario
See ROSARIO SANCHEZ, Elba
5600. SANCHEZ, Ricardo
"Cold Weather" (from "Eagle-Visioned/Feathered Adobes," Cinco Puntos Press, El
Paso, Tx.). [Gypsy] (15) 90, p. 6.
5601. SANDERS, Mark
"Detroit." [KanQ] (22:1/2) Wint-Spr 90, p. 50.
"The Sandhills of Nebraska." [Farm] (7:2) Fall 90, p. 29-32.
"Thesis." [LaurelR] (24:1) Wint 90, p. 72-73.
"The Weather Bureau." [Plain] (10:2) Wint 90, p. 9.
5602. SANDERS, Scott P.
"The Bad Poet." [WeberS] (7:2) Fall 90, p. 95.
"Child's Play." [WeberS] (7:2) Fall 90, p. 94.
"Home Baked Bread." [WeberS] (7:2) Fall 90, p. 94.
"Pastoral." [WeberS] (7:2) Fall 90, p. 95.
5603. SANDERS, Tony
"Birds." [PraS] (64:4) Wint 90, p. 110-111.
"Clearings." [PraS] (64:4) Wint 90, p. 109-110.
"Passengers." [PraS] (64:4) Wint 90, p. 111-112.
5604. SANDFORT, Lolly
"Silent Ordainer." [EmeraldCR] (1990) c89, p. 26.
5605. SANDIFUR, Ann
"Water Shrine" (with musical notation). [Caliban] (8) 90, p. 127.
5606. SANDRINI, Angela
"A Lemon Scent of Clocks." [Amelia] (6:2, #17) 90, p. 114.
5607. SANDSTROEM, Yvonne L.
"Elegy for the Old Mexican Woman and Her Dead Child" (tr. of Lars Gustafsson).
[NewYorker] (66:34) 8 O 90, p. 42.
5608. SANDY, Stephen
"Abandoned Houses South of Stafford." [NewYorker] (66:6) 25 Mr 90, p. 36.
"Mother's Day." [Atlantic] (265:6) Je 90, p. 76.
"Place and Fame." [Salm] (88/89) Fall 90-Wint 91, p. 270-274.
"Walking from Grasmere." [MichQR] (29:3) Sum 90, p. 412.
5609. SANELLI, Mary Lou
"Cultivating a Species" (the northwest coast and southeast Alaska). [CrabCR] (7:1)
Wint 90, p. 25-26.
"My Father's Wing-Tip." [Calyx] (12:3) Sum 90, p. 12-13.
5610. SANER, Reg
"Evening." [Poetry] (156:5) Ag 90, p. 296.
"Keen Edges." [Poetry] (156:5) Ag 90, p. 296.
5611. SANFORD, Christy Sheffield
"Crab Dance." [ArtfulD] (18/19) 90, p. 118.
"Dance of the Five Veils." [NewYorkQ] (42) Sum 90, p. 91-92.
"Hurt Park." [NewYorkQ] (41) Spr 90, p. 73.
5612. SANFORD, Elizabeth
"If I Lay Close." [NorthStoneR] (9) 90, p. 62.
"Your Are Inside of Me." [NorthStoneR] (9) 90, p. 62.
5613. SANGE, Gary
"Elevator." [HampSPR] (Anthology 1975-1990) 90, p. 145.
"Emergency." [HampSPR] (Anthology 1975-1990) 90, p. 144.
5614. SANTE, Luc
"Autobiography." [ParisR] (32:116) Fall 90, p. 108-109.
5615. SANTEN, Louise van
"Babel" (tr. by Alastair Reid). [Trans] (24) Fall 90, p. 12.
"Near-Sighted" (tr. by Alastair Reid). [Trans] (24) Fall 90, p. 13.
SANTO, Grace di
See DiSANTO, Grace
5616. SANTOS, Francisco
"Chevron-Titipapa" (tr. by Eddie Flintoff). [Verse] (7:2) Sum 90, p. 14.

5617. SANTOS, Marisa de los
"Ars Poetica." [Poem] (63) My 90, p. 24.
"Bible Stories." [Poem] (63) My 90, p. 27.
"The Fern" (for my mother). [VirQR] (66:3) Sum 90, p. 457-459.
"Luray, Virginia: The Discovery." [Poem] (63) My 90, p. 26.
"Most of What I Have" (for David Teague). [Poem] (63) My 90, p. 25.
5618. SANTOS, Sherod
"Approaching Middle Age." [KenR] (NS 12:3) Sum 90, p. 9-10.
"The Morning the Doctor." [KenR] (NS 12:3) Sum 90, p. 10-12.
"On the Liberation of Women." [KenR] (NS 12:3) Sum 90, p. 8.
"A Tableau" (Sitges, Spain). [Shen] (40:4) Wint 90, p. 28-29.
"Two Poems." [NewYorker] (66:35) 15 O 90, p. 44.
"The Unsheltering Ground" (Poetry Chapbook: 4 poems). [BlackWR] (16:2)
Spr-Sum 90, p. 73-88.
"Waiting to Be Re-stationed." [KenR] (NS 12:1) Wint 90, p. 221.
SANTOS DISCÉPOLO, Enrique
See DISCÉPOLO, Enrique Santos
5619. SAPIA, Yvonne (Yvonne V.)
"Among the Mermaids." [IndR] (13:2) Spr 90, p. 62.
"La Boba." [TampaR] (3) 90, p. 70.
"Brushing." [SouthernR] (26:4) O 90, p. 895.
"Fire Escape Poem." [IndR] (13:2) Spr 90, p. 63-64.
"La Simpática." [SoCoast] (9) Fall 90, p. 4-5.
5620. SAPINKOPF, Lisa
"Childhood Bolted" (tr. of Georgi Belev, w. the author). [Trans] (23) Spr 90, p.
249.
"Country of the Tree-tops" (tr. of Yves Bonnefoy). [PassN] (11:2) Wint 90, p. 15.
"The Memory" (tr. of Yves Bonnefoy). [PassN] (11:2) Wint 90, p. 16-17.
"Sealed Garden" (tr. of Georgi Belev, w. the author). [AnotherCM] (22) 90, p. 8.
"Spaces" (tr. of Georgi Belev, w. the author). [AnotherCM] (22) 90, p. 9.
"Woman" (tr. of Georgi Belev, w. the author). [Trans] (23) Spr 90, p. 250.
"Women by the Seashore" (tr. of Sophia de Mello Breyner Andresen). [HampSPR]
(Anthology 1975-1990) 90, p. 270.
5621. SAPPHIRE
"American Dreams." [SinW] (42) Wint 90-91, p. 22-28.
"Mickey Mouse Was a Scorpio." [Cond] (17) 90, p. 126-127.
5622. SAPPHO
"Like the succulent apple that blushes" (fragment, tr. by James Stone). [AmerPoR]
(19:6) N-D 90, p. 44.
"Obsession" (tr. by Gregory McNamee). [YellowS] (34) Sum 90, p. 38.
"Selected Fragments" (tr. by James Stone). [AmerPoR] (19:2) Mr-Ap 90, p. 25.
"To die is all I really want" (fragment, tr. by James Stone). [AmerPoR] (19:6) N-D
90, p. 44.
5623. SARAH, Robyn
"The Touchstone." [MalR] (92) S 90, p. 68-69.
5624. SARDIS, Dorrie
"Mom." [OnTheBus] (2:2/3:1, #6/7) Sum-Fall 90 Wint-Spr 91, p. 181-182.
5625. SARDUY, Severo
"Corona de las Frutas" (I-X). [LindLM] (9:4) O-D 90, p. 4.
"Corona de las Frutas" (Selections: II, IV, IX). [LindLM] (9:1/2) Ja/Mr-Ap/Je 90, p.
3.
"Espiral Negra" (Excerpt). [WashR] (16:2) Ag-S 90, p. 28.
"Espiral Negra" (Excerpt, tr. by A. L. Nielsen). [WashR] (16:2) Ag-S 90, p. 28.
5626. SARGENT, Robert
"Sister and Brother." [NegC] (10:2/3) 90, p. 49.
"Tom Ramsey." [Pembroke] (22) 90, p. 130.
5627. SARKIS, Ken
"Not As a Stone But Dancing." [NegC] (10:1) 90, p. 82.
5628. SAROYAN, Aram
"Declaration." [AmerPoR] (19:1) Ja-F 90, p. 27.
"For Paul Blackburn." [AmerPoR] (19:1) Ja-F 90, p. 28.
"Night Flight" (for Robert Bly). [AmerPoR] (19:1) Ja-F 90, p. 17.
5629. SARRACINO, Carmine
"The Elephant Ballroom." [HawaiiR] (15:1, #31) Wint 90, p. 69.
5630. SARTARELLI, Stephen
"(At)tendere" (For Glauco, tr. of Luigi Ballerini). [LitR] (33:4) Sum 90, p. 466.

"Bartered Nights: Three Poems" (tr. of Raphaële George). [Trans] (23) Spr 90, p. 100-101.
"The Stones of Central Park." [LitR] (33:4) Sum 90, p. 480.
5631. SARTON, May
"Contemplation of Poussin." [HampSPR] (Anthology 1975-1990) 90, p. 182.
"December Moon." [BelPoJ] (40:4) Sum 90, p. 46.
5632. SATER, Steven
"An Ode to You." [CapeR] (25:1) Spr 90, p. 6.
"Prayer for My Own Awakening." [CapeR] (25:1) Spr 90, p. 7.
5633. SATHER, Jane
"Death in Mid-winter." [FourQ] (4:1) Spr 90, p. 24.
"A Prayer in Four Seasons" (to be spoken over the bones of the undead). [FourQ] (4:1) Spr 90, p. 23.
SATTERFIELD, Deb Parks
See PARKS-SATTERFIELD, Deb
5634. SATTERFIELD, Jane (Jane M.)
"The Approach." [NoAmR] (275:2) Je 90, p. 33.
"Entropy's Angel." [IndR] (14:1) Wint 90, p. 74.
"Figurative Leaves." [IndR] (14:1) Wint 90, p. 73.
"Still Life." [NegC] (10:2/3) 90, p. 106.
"To the Angel X." [Sonora] (18) Fall-Wint 90, p. 81.
5635. SATTERFIELD, Leon
"Joe's Story." [SoDakR] (28:3) Aut 90, p. 70-71.
"The Weightlifter Takes an Examination in Literature of the Renaissance." [Plain] (10:2) Wint 90, p. 7.
5636. SATTERTHWAITE, J. B.
"Tugging." [BelPoR] (40:3) Spr 90, p. 17.
SAU-LING, Wong
See WONG, Sau-Ling
5637. SAUERS, Frank
"O Huck Finn Adonis." [JamesWR] (8:1) Fall 90, p. 11.
5638. SAUNDERS, Leigh
"Traps." [AnthNEW] 90, p. 28.
5639. SAUSVILLE, Suzanne
"Epitaph for the Twentieth Century" (tr. of Rafael Catala). [Footwork] 90, p. 90-91.
5640. SAVARD, Jeannine
"Celtic Love, a Blood Memory." [HayF] (7) Fall-Wint 90, p. 97.
"The Fall." [NoAmR] (275:4) D 90, p. 39.
"Forced Feeding." [HayF] (7) Fall-Wint 90, p. 69.
"Gauze Landing." [KenR] (NS 12:3) Sum 90, p. 48.
"The Hospital Room." [KenR] (NS 12:3) Sum 90, p. 49.
"On Earth As It Is in This Dream." [HayF] (7) Fall-Wint 90, p. 30.
5641. SAVARD, Michel
"Le Sourire des Chefs" (Selections: 15-17, in French and English, tr. by Neil B. Bishop). [AntigR] (80) Wint 90, p. 96-101.
5642. SAVIN, Judy
"Birthdays." [ContextS] (1:1) 89, p. 19.
5643. SAVITT, Lynne
"High School Sex" (1963). [NewYorkQ] (41) Spr 90, p. 71.
5644. SAWYER, Alex
"October Frost." [CoalC] (1) Ag 90, p. 32.
5645. SAXON, Sonia
"Poking Inside." [PoetryUSA] (5:3) Fall 90, p. 9.
5646. SAXTON, Robert
"Blind Love." [ParisR] (32:115) Sum 90, p. 125-126.
"Stoning Byron's Ghost." [ParisR] (32:115) Sum 90, p. 123-124.
5647. SBARBARO, Camillo
"Even If You Weren't My Father" (tr. by Shirley Hazzard). [NewYorker] (66:25) 6 Ag 90, p. 36.
"I Wake Alone" (tr. by Shirley Hazzard). [NewYorker] (66:40) 19 N 90, p. 52.
5648. SCALAPINO, Leslie
"Essay on the Comic Book." [Conjunc] (15) 90, p. 117-127.
"Orion" (Excerpts). [NewAW] (6) Spr 90, p. 35-46.
5649. SCALF, Sue
"Elemental." [SouthernR] (26:2) Ap 90, p. 328-329.
"Perspective: Powell Valley." [Wind] (20:67) 90, p. 30.

5650. SCAMMACCA, Nat
"Adam Has Finally Understood!" [Footwork] 90, p. 62.
"Adamo Ha Capito!" [Footwork] 90, p. 62.
"An American in Trapani." [Footwork] 90, p. 102.
"An Ancient Diary" (from the Sicilian Antigruppo, tr. of Ignazio Navarra, w. Stanley
    H. Barkan). [Footwork] 90, p. 104.
"And Yet, I'm Ready to Return Again." [Footwork] 90, p. 62.
"Do Not Call Me Queen, Odysseus" (tr. of Enzo Bonventre). [Footwork] 90, p. 63.
"Eppure Sto Per Partire, Dicembre 88." [Footwork] 90, p. 62.
"Fancy." [Footwork] 90, p. 104.
"Flash" (tr. of Emanuele Mandará). [Footwork] 90, p. 105.
"Immaginazione." [Footwork] 90, p. 104.
"Looking West from Mount Eryx" (for Hai Zi). [Footwork] 90, p. 62.
"The Night's One Drifting Petal." [Footwork] 90, p. 62-63.
"Un Petalo Alla Deriva Nella Notte." [Footwork] 90, p. 62.
"The Shadow" (from the Sicilian Antigruppo, tr. of Ignazio Apolloni). [Footwork]
    90, p. 104.
"Sicily, the Peasant Mother" (from the Sicilian Antigruppo, tr. of Gianni Diecidue).
    [Footwork] 90, p. 102.
"Silence" (from the Sicilian Antigruppo, tr. of Pietro Terminelli). [Footwork] 90, p.
    102.
"Untitled #2: enchantments elegies labyrinths mechanical lights" (tr. of Ignazio
    Navarra). [Footwork] 90, p. 105.
5651. SCAMMEL, Michael
"Into Your Eye" (tr. of Veno Taufer). [Vis] (33) 90, p. 39.
5652. SCANLAN, Jill
"Truffle." [Caliban] (8) 90, p. 59.
"The Woman and the Moon." [Caliban] (8) 90, p. 58.
5653. SCANLON, Dennice
"The Golden Years." [PoetryNW] (31:3) Aut 90, p. 31-32.
"Migration." [PoetryNW] (31:3) Aut 90, p. 30-31.
"Words for a Friend" (for Jonni Sorich). [PoetryNW] (31:3) Aut 90, p. 28-30.
5654. SCANLON, Richard
"Bell Makers." [Poem] (63) My 90, p. 5.
5655. SCATES, Maxine
"A Story." [Agni] (31/32) 90, p. 209-211.
5656. SCHAACK, F. J.
"Labyrinthine Passion." [Asylum] (6:2) S 90, p. 5.
5657. SCHACHT, Ulrich
"Attempt at Paradise" (tr. by Thomas Edwards). [PoetryE] (29) Spr 90, p. 86.
"Distant morning" (tr. by Thomas Edwards). [PoetryE] (29) Spr 90, p. 89-90.
"How many dreams" (tr. by Thomas Edwards). [PoetryE] (29) Spr 90, p. 88.
"Lübars" (tr. by Thomas Edwards). [PoetryE] (29) Spr 90, p. 87.
"A man set out" (tr. by Thomas Edwards). [PoetryE] (29) Spr 90, p. 88-89.
"This hardened suspicion" (tr. by Thomas Edwards). [PoetryE] (29) Spr 90, p. 85.
5658. SCHAEFFER, Susan Fromberg
"Harvest." [HampSPR] (Anthology 1975-1990) 90, p. 83.
5659. SCHAFFENBURG, Carlos A.
"XIII. Allá en las Cañas." [LindLM] (9:3) Jl-S 90, p. 17.
"XVI. Detrás de todo muro que amarillo." [LindLM] (9:3) Jl-S 90, p. 17.
5660. SCHAFFNER, Michael A.
"Haze." [Vis] (33) 90, p. 32.
"Lament of the Minor Functionary." [Vis] (33) 90, p. 30-32.
5661. SCHAPIRO, Jane
"Breath." [BlackWR] (17:1) Fall-Wint 90, p. 10.
"Exhibitionist." [BlackWR] (16:2) Spr-Sum 90, p. 11.
"The Final Blast." [BlackWR] (16:2) Spr-Sum 90, p. 9-10.
"Postpartum." [BlackWR] (16:2) Spr-Sum 90, p. 12-13.
5662. SCHAUB, Mark
"Walking Home Again, November." [MidwQ] (31:4) Sum 90, p. 470.
5663. SCHAUER, Dawn
"A Day on the Water." [HolCrit] (27:1) F 90, p. 18.
5664. SCHEDLER, Gilbert
"Matins." [ChrC] (107:32) 7 N 90, p. 1015.
5665. SCHEDLINSKI, Rainer
"The hours which a brain of sand counts" (tr. by Roderick Iverson). [Sulfur] (10:2,

#27) Fall 90, p. 91.
"Ordinary and unnoticed" (tr. by Roderick Iverson). [Sulfur] (10:2, #27) Fall 90, p.
90.
5666. SCHEELE, Roy
"In Minnesota." [Plain] (10:2) Wint 90, p. 29.
"In the Basement." [Plain] (10:3) Spr 90, p. 31.
"The Lookout." [PraS] (64:2) Sum 90, p. 82-88.
5667. SCHEER, Linda
"Incurable" (Selection: Chapter I: "Simulacrum," tr. of David Huerta). [Caliban] (9)
90, p. 111-115.
5668. SCHEIER, Libby
"Poem for My Father." [Descant] (21:2, #69) Sum 90, p. 47-48.
"Sky" (Selections). [MalR] (91) Je 90, p. 84-87.
5669. SCHEINOHA, Gary A.
"Ringing Out." [BlackBR] (12) Fall-Wint 90, p. 14-15.
"Wash N Wear." [BlackBR] (12) Fall-Wint 90, p. 15.
5670. SCHENDEL, Christopher
"Richard." [Pearl] (10) Spr 90, p. 17.
5671. SCHENDLER, Revan
"Key." [NewYorker] (66:3) 5 Mr 90, p. 96.
5672. SCHENKER, Donald
"The Jacob's Ladder" (for Denise Levertov). [PoetryUSA] ([5:4?]) Wint 90, p. 13.
5673. SCHEPERS, J. B.
"Images of a Summer Evening" (tr. by Rod Jellema). [WashR] (16:2) Ag-S 90, p.
12.
"Simmerjunsbyld." [WashR] (16:2) Ag-S 90, p. 12.
5674. SCHERBINA, Tatyana
"The Mermaid" (tr. by Jim Kates). [Gargoyle] (37/38) 90, p. 50.
5675. SCHERTZER, Mike
"The Accident." [PoetryC] (11:2) Sum 90, p. 11.
"The House of Misfortune." [PoetryC] (11:2) Sum 90, p. 11.
"The Man Who Has Not Yet Met His Body." [PoetryC] (11:2) Sum 90, p. 11.
5676. SCHEVILL, James
"Battered Woman in New York." [FreeL] (6) Aut 90, p. 15.
"The Boilerman." [HampSPR] (Anthology 1975-1990) 90, p. 90.
"Dumb Love." [HampSPR] (Anthology 1975-1990) 90, p. 88.
"An Elizabethan Fool Applies for a Corporate Executive Position." [HampSPR]
(Anthology 1975-1990) 90, p. 89.
"Karl Barth's Dream of Mozart." [MichQR] (29:2) Spr 90, p. 273-274.
"Mad Robin in Spring." [FreeL] (6) Aut 90, p. 14.
"Mixed Media." [HampSPR] (Anthology 1975-1990) 90, p. 90-91.
"The New Bicentennial Stamps, 1975." [HampSPR] (Anthology 1975-1990) 90, p.
89.
"Science Fiction: Dizzying Changes in America." [HampSPR] (Anthology
1975-1990) 90, p. 88.
"The Search for a Subject." [HampSPR] (Anthology 1975-1990) 90, p. 91.
5677. SCHIELE, Evelyn
"Affair." [WillowR] Spr 90, p. 68.
5678. SCHIERBEEK, Bert
"Inside Out" (Excerpt, tr. by Charles McGeehan). [Trans] (24) Fall 90, p. 83-91.
SCHIETEKAT, Edmund
See SNOEK, Paul
5679. SCHIFF, Jeff
"Because." [HawaiiR] (14:3, #30) Fall 90, p. 30.
"The Bump." [SpoonRQ] (15:1) Wint 90, p. 13.
"Cash Money." [SouthernHR] (24:4) Fall 90, p. 366-367.
"Croakers." [HawaiiR] (14:2, #29) Spr 90, p. 27.
"Drought." [HawaiiR] (14:2, #29) Spr 90, p. 28.
"Graphing the Arc." [PoetC] (21:2) Wint 90, p. 17-16.
"Great Lakes." [SpoonRQ] (15:1) Wint 90, p. 12.
"The Move." [WillowS] (25) Wint 90, p. 40-41.
"Passing Over." [NewMyths] (1:1) 90, p. 24-25.
"Pigeons." [HawaiiR] (14:3, #30) Fall 90, p. 29.
"Rats." [NewMyths] (1:1) 90, p. 26-27.
"The Student." [InterPR] (16:1) Spr 90, p. 131.

5680. SCHIMMEL, Harold
    "I'm in Uniform" (from "Lowell," tr. by Peter Cole). [PartR] (57:3) Sum 90, p.
       437.
    "The Land" (Selection: VIII, tr. by Peter Cole). [Screens] (2) 90, p. 27-36.
5681. SCHIPPERS, K.
    "In the Park" (tr. by Arie Staal). [Vis] (34) 90, p. 43.
    "Notion of Color in Absence of Skin" (tr. by Kees Snoek). [Vis] (34) 90, p. 45.
    "White" (tr. by Sharon Robertson). [Vis] (34) 90, p. 44.
5682. SCHMEDER, Andrew
    "Untitled: I know a little about the universe." [PoetryUSA] (5:2) Sum 90, p. 7.
5683. SCHMID, Mary
    "The Darkness." [PoetryUSA] (5:3) Fall 90, p. 27.
5684. SCHMIDT, Geoff
    "Platitudes." [CharR] (16:2) Fall 90, p. 59.
5685. SCHMIDT, Lawrence
    "Day Care." [TriQ] (80) Wint 90-91, p. 84.
    "Day Labor" (for Taura). [TriQ] (80) Wint 90-91, p. 81.
    "Drought Summer." [TriQ] (80) Wint 90-91, p. 82.
    "First Fight." [TriQ] (80) Wint 90-91, p. 85.
    "First Home." [TriQ] (80) Wint 90-91, p. 83.
    "In the City." [TriQ] (80) Wint 90-91, p. 86-87.
5686. SCHMIDT, Nancy Carrington
    "Of Night-Tails and Nodding." [Kalliope] (12:1) 90, c89, p. 4.
5687. SCHMIDT, Steven
    "Confessional." [BellR] (13:1, #27) Spr 90, p. 14.
5688. SCHMITTAUER, Jan
    "The Bus Tour of Great Britain." [HolCrit] (27:3) Je 90, p. 18.
5689. SCHMITZ, Dennis
    "Instructions for Fishing the Eel" (for Ray Carver). [Field] (42) Spr 90, p. 87-89.
    "So High" (for my brother, Gerry). [Field] (42) Spr 90, p. 90-91.
5690. SCHMONSEES, Richard Paul
    "'Merica Void Again." [SlipS] (10) 90, p. 91.
5691. SCHNEEMAN, Elio
    "Black Wind." [Shiny] (5) 90, p. 23.
    "Low Planes" (w. Jim Brodey). [Shiny] (5) 90, p. 24.
    "Music." [Shiny] (5) 90, p. 23.
5692. SCHNEIDER, J. L.
    "Blue." [Pig] (16) 90, p. 44.
5693. SCHNEIDER, Pat
    "After They Let You Walk with Me Three Hours in the Rain If We Promised to Stay
      on Hospital Grounds." [MinnR] (NS 34/35) Spr-Fall 90, p. 28.
    "There Is Another Way." [Kalliope] (12:1) 90, c89, p. 68.
5694. SCHNORBUS, Frank
    "The Footnote." [EngJ] (79:4) Ap 90, p. 109.
5695. SCHOENBERGER, Nancy
    "Civilization Comes Out of the Sea." [WilliamMR] (28) 90, p. 51.
    "Common American Crow." [SouthernR] (26:4) O 90, p. 882-883.
    "Deer Heart." [SouthernR] (26:4) O 90, p. 883-884.
5696. SCHOENFELD, Ellie
    "Acapulco Holiday." [Bogg] (63) 90, p. 31.
5697. SCHOERKE, Meg
    "Beyond Mourning." [TriQ] (80) Wint 90-91, p. 76.
5698. SCHOFIELD, Don
    "Callicles Puts a Head on the Argument." [AntR] (48:2) Spr 90, p. 232-233.
    "Fosterling." [BelPoJ] (41:2) Wint 90-91, p. 9-14.
    "Skins." [SycamoreR] (2:1) Wint 90, p. 36-37.
5699. SCHOLL, Sharon
    "Japanese." [Kalliope] (12:1) 90, c89, p. 25.
5700. SCHOLZ-HEERSPINK, Myra
    "Entropy" (tr. of Eva Gerlach). [Trans] (24) Fall 90, p. 132.
    "Letter" (tr. of Eva Gerlach). [Trans] (24) Fall 90, p. 131.
    "Season" (tr. of Eva Gerlach). [Trans] (24) Fall 90, p. 132.
5701. SCHONBRUN, Adam
    "Morning Song for Two Poets." [Interim] (9:1) Spr-Sum 90, p. 7.
    "Shades of Karjala and a Finnish Summer." [Interim] (9:2) Fall-Wint 90-91, p. 38.

5702. SCHÖNMAIER, Eleonore
"Frosted Mirror." [PottPort] (12) 90, p. 25.
5703. SCHOONOVER, Amy Jo
"Light Verse." [HiramPoR] (48/49) 90-91, p. 63.
"Spring Break." [CapeR] (25:2) Fall 90, p. 27.
5704. SCHORB, E. M.
"Elegy for a Late Tornado." [InterPR] (16:2) Fall 90, p. 102-103.
"Ode on Sex." [SouthernR] (26:2) Ap 90, p. 362-364.
"Speculative Ode." [SouthernHR] (24:4) Fall 90, p. 320-321.
5705. SCHORR, Laurie
"Redemption." [PennR] (4:2) 90, p. 117-118.
5706. SCHOTT, John
"August Porch." [HiramPoR] (47) Wint 90, p. 48.
5707. SCHOTT, Penelope Scambly
"Head-on." [BellR] (13:1, #27) Spr 90, p. 43.
"The Reconcilements of Elk Lake." [Blueline] (11:1/2) 90, p. 13-14.
5708. SCHOULTZ, Solveig von
"Dockorna." [Spirit] (10:1) 89, p. 38.
"The Dolls" (tr. by Lennart Bruce and Sonja Bruce). [Spirit] (10:1) 89, p. 39.
"Dream" (tr. by Lennart Bruce and Sonja Bruce). [Spirit] (10:1) 89, p. 35.
"Dröm." [Spirit] (10:1) 89, p. 34.
"Hallonporträtt." [Spirit] (10:1) 89, p. 42.
"Hav I November." [Spirit] (10:1) 89, p. 40.
"Heart" (tr. by Lennart Bruce and Sonja Bruce). [Spirit] (10:1) 89, p. 47.
"Hjärtat." [Spirit] (10:1) 89, p. 46.
"The Instant" (tr. by Lennart Bruce and Sonja Bruce). [Spirit] (10:1) 89, p. 45.
"Look How She Walks!" (tr. by Lennart Bruce and Sonja Bruce). [Spirit] (10:1) 89,
     p. 45.
"November Sea" (tr. by Lennart Bruce and Sonja Bruce). [Spirit] (10:1) 89, p. 41.
"Ögonblicket." [Spirit] (10:1) 89, p. 44.
"Raspberry Portrait" (tr. by Lennart Bruce and Sonja Bruce). [Spirit] (10:1) 89, p.
     43.
"The Room" (tr. by Lennart Bruce and Sonja Bruce). [Spirit] (10:1) 89, p. 33.
"Salen." [Spirit] (10:1) 89, p. 32.
"Som Hon Går." [Spirit] (10:1) 89, p. 44.
"Sommargrav." [Spirit] (10:1) 89, p. 48.
"Summer Grave" (tr. by Lennart Bruce and Sonja Bruce). [Spirit] (10:1) 89, p. 49.
"Vinterstrand." [Spirit] (10:1) 89, p. 36.
"Winter Shore" (tr. by Lennart Bruce and Sonja Bruce). [Spirit] (10:1) 89, p. 37.
5709. SCHRAMM, Darrell G. H.
"Balcony" (for Helmuth Schramm, 1920-1989). [CarolQ] (43:1) Fall 90, p. 81.
5710. SCHRAUFNAGEL, Lynda
"Winter." [WestHR] (44:4) Wint 90, p. 392-393.
5711. SCHREIBER, Ron
"The Long Haul" (5-6-86). [LitR] (33:2) Wint 90, p. 242.
"Memory Exercises." [LitR] (33:2) Wint 90, p. 243.
"Preparing to Visit" (4-30-86). [LitR] (33:2) Wint 90, p. 242.
5712. SCHREIBMAN, Susan
"At Night Alone" (tr. of Jose Augustin Goytisolo). [Confr] (42/43) Spr-Sum 90, p.
     48.
"Choral" (tr. of Joan Brossa). [PaintedB] (40/41) 90, p. 25.
"If It's All Going to Begin Again" (tr. of Jose Augustin Goytisolo). [Confr] (42/43)
     Spr-Sum 90, p. 49.
"It's Like an Echo" (tr. of José Agustín Goytisolo). [PaintedB] (40/41) 90, p. 26.
5713. SCHREIER, Lina
"The Rucksack." [SoCoast] (9) Fall 90, p. 45.
5714. SCHROM, Sara
"For Joe." [PoetryUSA] (5:1) Spr 90, p. 11.
5715. SCHUG, Lawrence
"Art Exhibit -- Minnesota." [SmPd] (27:3, #80) Fall 90, p. 20.
"White Bread." [SmPd] (27:3, #80) Fall 90, p. 20.
5716. SCHULER, Jeanne Leigh
"Clamor." [CoalC] (1) Ag 90, p. 33.
5717. SCHULER, Ruth Wildes
"A Remote Heritage." [CoalC] (2) D 90, p. 14.

5718. SCHULTE, Jane
   "Primer for an Autumn Walk." [WillowR] Spr 90, p. 43.
5719. SCHULTZ, Robert
   "Marriage Fires." [VirQR] (66:3) Sum 90, p. 459-460.
   "Sight & Distance." [VirQR] (66:3) Sum 90, p. 460-461.
   "Snowlight." [Hudson] (42:4) Wint 90, p. 611.
5720. SCHULTZ, Susan
   "Adagios of Islands [Words for Caliban]." [DenQ] (25:1) Sum 90, p. 38-39.
   "Penelope's Letter to Ulysses." [MissouriR] (13:2) 90, p. 126.
   "Proteus in Washington, D.C." [DenQ] (25:1) Sum 90, p. 40-41.
5721. SCHULZ, Joan
   "Final Note." [EngJ] (79:2) F 90, p. 86.
5722. SCHULZ, Lawrence
   "English 101." [Pearl] (12) Fall-Wint 90, p. 53.
5723. SCHUMACHER, Rose
   "The Color of the Trees Is Wet" (For Georgia O'Keefe). [NegC] (10:2/3) 90, p. 53.
5724. SCHUMAN, Joan
   "Friendly Definitions." [SinW] (40) Spr 90, p. 101.
5725. SCHUSTER, Cindy
   "The Virgin of the Panecillo." [NegC] (10:2/3) 90, p. 52.
5726. SCHUTTE, Linda
   "Untitled: Loneliness." [EmeraldCR] (1990) c89, p. 64.
5727. SCHUYLER, James
   "Birds." [DenQ] (24:4) Spr 90, p. 123-124.
   "A Chapel." [DenQ] (24:4) Spr 90, p. 125.
   "Over the Hills." [DenQ] (24:4) Spr 90, p. 126-127.
   "Song." [DenQ] (24:4) Spr 90, p. 94.
5728. SCHWAB, Arnold T.
   "Montgomery Clift: A Portrait" (after reading Patricia Bosworth's biography).
      [Pearl] (12) Fall-Wint 90, p. 41-42.
   "Plain Language from Truthful Chris" (with apologies to Ross Newhan and the Los
      Angeles *Times*). [ChironR] (9:4) Wint 90, p. 10.
   "Touche." [ChironR] (9:4) Wint 90, p. 10.
   "True to Life." [ChironR] (9:4) Wint 90, p. 10.
5729. SCHWARTZ, Delmore
   "Once and For All" (from "Selected Poems: Summer Knowledge," New Directions).
      [PoetryUSA] ([5:4?]) Wint 90, p. 19.
5730. SCHWARTZ, Hillel
   "Cloud Hands." [BelPoJ] (41:1) Fall 90, p. 31.
   "Funny Bones." [HampSPR] (Anthology 1975-1990) 90, p. 150-151.
   "Grandfather Up a Tree." [BelPoJ] (41:1) Fall 90, p. 32-33.
   "Gruidae Americana." [MalR] (90) Spr 90, p. 37.
   "Idiot, Whalewatching from the Deck of the *Galilean*." [GreenMR] (NS 4:1)
      Spr-Sum 90, p. 109-111.
   "Occasional Poem." [HampSPR] (Anthology 1975-1990) 90, p. 150.
   "The Sword Form, First Part." [CapilR] (2:2) Spr 90, p. 27-28.
5731. SCHWARTZ, Jeffrey
   "Emily Dickinson's House, Amherst, Massachusetts." [ConnPR] (9:1) 90, p. 37-38.
5732. SCHWARTZ, Leonard
   "Deep Season Reply." [Talisman] (5) Fall 90, p. 101.
   "Meditation." [LitR] (33:4) Sum 90, p. 526-530.
   "Mtasipol" (tr. of Benjamin Fondane). [Harp] (281:1684) S 90, p. 45-47.
5733. SCHWARTZ, Lloyd
   "Banquet." [SouthwR] (75:1) Wint 90, p. 93.
   "Crossing the Rockies." [Agni] (29/30) 90, p. 101-108.
   "Dead-Battery Blues." [GrandS] (9:3) Spr 90, p. 172-173.
   "Gisela Brüning." [Pequod] (31) 90, p. 138-144.
   "In the Jewish Cemetery in Queens." [GrandS] (9:3) Spr 90, p. 174-181.
   "Leaves." [NewRep] (203:19) 5 N 90, p. 36.
5734. SCHWARTZ, Lynne Sharon
   "At the Border." [Ploughs] (16:4) Wint 90-91, p. 172-177.
5735. SCHWARTZ, Mark
   "Frozen." [PoetryUSA] ([5:4?]) Wint 90, p. 23.
5736. SCHWARTZ, Ruth (Ruth L.)
   "The Burglars" (3rd Prize, 4th Annual Contest). [SoCoast] (8) Spr 90, p. 30.
   "Life in the Forest." [Confr] (44/45) Fall 90-Wint 91, p. 318-319.

5737. SCHWARZ, Ghita
"The Romanian Girl Downstairs" (First Prize). [HarvardA] (124:3) Mr 90, p. 12.
SCHWARZ, Hillel
See SCHWARTZ, Hillel
5738. SCHWEITZER, Leah
"My Wish for You Both" (For Ferdinand and Imelda). [SlipS] (10) 90, p. 104-105.
5739. SCIARRONE, Daria
"Burial." [LullwaterR] (1:1) Spr 90, p. 41.
"Prayer." [LullwaterR] (2:1) Wint 90, p. 76.
5740. SCOBIE, Stephen
"His Feet" (tr. of Venus Khoury-Ghata). [Vis] (32) 90, p. 20.
5741. SCODOVA, Cynthia
"Synapse." [KanQ] (22:3) Sum 90, p. 206.
5742. SCOLLON, Suzie Wong
"Da pig make kaukau from make die dead kanaka" (tr. of Han Shan). [BambooR]
(47) Sum 90, p. 58.
"Dew drops sparkle on da maile curtains" (tr. of Han Shan). [BambooR] (47) Sum
90, p. 59.
"Make me laugh, dis Cold Mountain trail" (tr. of Han Shan). [BambooR] (47) Sum
90, p. 57.
5743. SCOLOW, Elizabeth
"Exile in the Empty Nest." [JINJPo] (12:2) Aut 90, p. 23-24.
"In that House." [JINJPo] (12:2) Aut 90, p. 25-26.
5744. SCOTELLARO, Rocco
"Economics Lesson" (tr. by Ruth Feldman and Brian Swann). [HampSPR]
(Anthology 1975-1990) 90, p. 247.
5745. SCOTT, Gaar
"Burn the Silk Ones." [Gypsy] (15) 90, p. 12.
5746. SCOTT, Georgia
"Three Times Yes." [MinnR] (NS 34/35) Spr-Fall 90, p. 20.
5747. SCOTT, Mark
"Accumulations." [Raritan] (9:4) Spr 90, p. 11-12.
"The China Syndrome." [Raritan] (9:4) Spr 90, p. 13.
5748. SCOTT, Peter Dale
"Listening to the Candle: A Poem on Impulse" (Selection: II.v). [Agni] (31/32) 90,
p. 362-367.
5749. SCOTT, Virginia
"Limoges" (For B.A. and J.S.). [AmerV] (18) Spr 90, p. 24-29.
5750. SCOVILLE, Jane
"Our Marriage: A Puzzle." [BellArk] (6:3) My-Je 90, p. 4.
5751. SCRIVNER, Jay
"The Contortionist." [DenQ] (25:2) Fall 90, p. 42-43.
5752. SCROGGINS, Daryl
"Natural Selection." [NowestR] (28:3/29:1) 90-91, p. 76.
5753. SCRUGGS, Patricia L.
"Black Swans." [OnTheBus] (2:1, #5) Spr 90, p. 122.
"Forecast." [OnTheBus] (2:2/3:1, #6/7) Sum-Fall 90 Wint-Spr 91, p. 184.
"Pink Plastic." [OnTheBus] (2:2/3:1, #6/7) Sum-Fall 90 Wint-Spr 91, p. 183-184.
"Shades." [OnTheBus] (2:1, #5) Spr 90, p. 122-123.
"Weather Report." [OnTheBus] (2:1, #5) Spr 90, p. 123.
5754. SEABURG, Alan
"Down to a Candle." [PoetC] (22:1) Fall 90, p. 34.
"Lying Against Myself, Half Naked." [PoetC] (22:1) Fall 90, p. 35.
"On My Own." [CapeR] (25:2) Fall 90, p. 24.
5755. SEAMAN, Benjamin
"International Mr. Leather Weekend." [AnotherCM] (22) 90, p. 159-164.
5756. SEARS, Peter
"The Brink." [NowestR] (28:2) 90, p. 73.
"The Man Who Lives on Air." [NewL] (57:1) Fall 90, p. 105.
"Oil Spill." [Atlantic] (265:2) F 90, p. 38.
5757. SEATON, Maureen
"The 8:48." [Cond] (17) 90, p. 57.
"The Art of Robbery" (For J. S.). [Confr] (44/45) Fall 90-Wint 91, p. 200.
"Blood." [NewAW] (6) Spr 90, p. 82.
"Harlem." [RiverS] (32) [90?], p. 10.
"Mantras of the Homeless." [RiverS] (32) [90?], p. 11.

"My Daughter Calls from a Halfway House in Houston." [Chelsea] (49) 90, p. 147.
"Photographing Horses." [Chelsea] (49) 90, p. 147.
"Popes" (for Barry Siebelt). [NewAW] (6) Spr 90, p. 80-81.
"Scandals." [SouthwR] (75:2) Spr 90, p. 261-263.
"Stations" (For E.S.). [SouthernPR] (30:1) Spr 90, p. 22-25.
"We Murder Three Sparrows in South Dakota" (for my daughter). [HighP] (5:3)
     Wint 90-91, p. 78-79.
"Witness" (after a sculpture of Aristide Maillol -- MOMA, Manhattan). [WestB] (26)
     90, p. 27.
5758. SEATON, Peter
"An Ethics of Anxiety." [Verse] (7:1) Spr 90, p. 18-19.
5759. SEATTLE, Chief
"Chief Seattle Reflects on the Future of America, 1855" (adapted by Stephen Meats).
     [MidwQ] (31:2) Wint 90, p. 230-231.
5760. SEAY, James
"Audubon Drive, Memphis." [GettyR] (3:3) Sum 90, p. 568-569.
"Cottonmouth, Angus, Redwing" (for James Dickey). [GettyR] (3:3) Sum 90, p.
     570-571.
"Faith As an Arm of Culture, Culture As an Arm of Narration." [SouthernHR] (24:3)
     Sum 90, p. 242.
"An Ideal of Itself." [GeoR] (44:3) Fall 90, p. 448-450.
"Night Fires" (For Beth). [NewEngR] (13:1) Fall 90, p. 54-55.
"Not Something in a Magazine." [GettyR] (3:3) Sum 90, p. 567.
"Tiffany & Co." (for Elizabeth Spencer). [Antaeus] (64/65) Spr-Aut 90, p. 122-123.
"The Weather Wizard's Cloud Book" (to LDR, Jr.). [SouthernHR] (24:3) Sum 90,
     p. 243.
"When Once Friends." [NewEngR] (13:1) Fall 90, p. 52-53.
5761. SEDAKOVA, Olga
"Lines on the Death of a Kitten." [PoetryUSA] (5:3) Fall 90, p. 20.
5762. SEFFINGA, Jeff
"Chicken Little." [Grain] (18:4) Wint 90, p. 81.
5763. SEIBLES, Timothy (Tim)
"Boris By Candlelight." [MissR] (19:1/2, #55/56) 90, p. 273-274.
"Trying for Fire." [CimR] (91) Ap 90, p. 53-55.
5764. SEIBLES, Tom
"Appetite." [SpoonRQ] (15:3) Sum 90, p. 7-8.
"The Good City." [SpoonRQ] (15:3) Sum 90, p. 11-12.
"The Lamps." [SpoonRQ] (15:3) Sum 90, p. 9-10.
5765. SEID, Christopher
"Death of Cezanne." [BelPoJ] (41:1) Fall 90, p. 6-7.
"The End of Summer Vacation." [NoDaQ] (58:3) Sum 90, p. 149.
"Fury" (for Christopher Hewitt). [Kaleid] (21) Sum-Fall 90, p. 45.
5766. SEIDMAN, Hugh
"Current That Cannot Cross the Gap." [HangL] (57) 90, p. 65.
"How Did We Get Here, Said by So Many So Often." [HangL] (57) 90, p. 69-70.
"Mr. Bear." [HangL] (57) 90, p. 68.
"The Senile." [HangL] (57) 90, p. 66.
"Yes, Yes, Like Us." [HangL] (57) 90, p. 67.
5767. SEIFERLE, Rebecca
"Approximate Desires." [IndR] (14:1) Wint 90, p. 75-77.
"At the Edge of the Water." [Calyx] (13:1) Wint 90-91, p. 10-15.
5768. SEIFERT, Jaroslav
"The Casting of Bells" (Selections, tr. by Paul Jagasich and Tom O'Grady).
     [HampSPR] (Anthology 1975-1990) 90, p. 255-256.
"Dance-Song" (tr. by Paul Jagasich and Tom O'Grady). [HampSPR] (Anthology
     1975-1990) 90, p. 256-257.
"Song from an Intermezzo" (tr. by Bronislava Volková). [PoetryE] (30) Fall 90, p.
     10.
5769. SELAWSKY, John T.
"Dowser." [Zyzzyva] (6:1 #21) Spr 90, p. 100.
"Ritual." [CapeR] (25:1) Spr 90, p. 17.
"Walking Towards the Grave of My Grandfather Outside of Benevento, Italy."
     [WestB] (26) 90, p. 109.
5770. SELBY, John
"While Laurel Leaves Grew All Around." [PoetryUSA] (5:1) Spr 90, p. 13.

5771. SELBY, Spencer
"Left to Own Ends." [Caliban] (9) 90, p. 17-18.
"Penult." [Sulfur] (10:2, #27) Fall 90, p. 173-175.
"Pretext Other Side" (for Peter Ganick). [Talisman] (5) Fall 90, p. 78.
"Tractor Feed." [Sulfur] (10:2, #27) Fall 90, p. 176-177.
5772. SELCH, A. H.
"Come Find Winter." [GreensboroR] (48) Sum 90, p. 94.
"Succory." [GreensboroR] (48) Sum 90, p. 93.
5773. SELERIE, Gavin
"Metabasis" (1 of 4 sonnets from an untitled sequence). [Screens] (2) 90, p. 169.
"North Face" (1 of 4 sonnets from an untitled sequence). [Screens] (2) 90, p. 170.
"Roxy" (Excerpt). [Avec] (3:1) 90, p. 118-120.
"Song Space" (1 of 4 sonnets from an untitled sequence). [Screens] (2) 90, p. 170.
"Utility" (1 of 4 sonnets from an untitled sequence). [Screens] (2) 90, p. 169.
5774. SELLERS, Bettie
"Watching Leaves Once Falling." [LullwaterR] (2:1) Wint 90, p. 28.
5775. SELLERS-EPPLER, Vincent
"The Sex Junkie." [Nimrod] (34:1) Fall-Wint 90, p. 56.
5776. SELLIN, Eric
"Dedication to the Coming Year" (Excerpts, tr. of Abdelkebir Khatibi). [Vis] (32) 90, p. 12.
"The Eye that Rejuvenates the Soul" (tr. of Kateb Yacine). [Vis] (32) 90, p. 6.
"Primal Poetry" (tr. of Robert Sabatier). [Vis] (32) 90, p. 41.
5777. SELMAN, Robyn
"Difference Between Us." [Cond] (17) 90, p. 7-10.
5778. SEMANSKY, C. (Chris)
"Baldy." [ContextS] (1:1) 89, p. 39.
"Born Again." [JINJPo] (12:2) Aut 90, p. 38.
"Something." [JINJPo] (12:2) Aut 90, p. 39.
"Swinging." [ContextS] (1:1) 89, p. 40.
5779. SEMONES, Charles
"Bloodtide: A Southern Exposure." [KanQ] (22:4) Fall 90, p. 44.
5780. SENA, Jorge de
"In the Land of Sons-a-Bitches" (tr. by Alexis Levitin). [PoetryE] (30) Fall 90, p. 20.
5781. SENG, Goh Poh
"The Girl from Ermita" (Excerpt). [PoetryUSA] (5:3) Fall 90, p. 20.
5782. SENGAT-KUO, Francois
"Words Are Totems" (tr. by Julia Older). [Vis] (32) 90, p. 8.
5783. SENGHOR, Léopold Sédar
"Ce Soir Sopé" (for Khalam). [PaintedB] (40/41) 90, p. 74.
"Chant de Printemps" (Pour une Jeune Fille Noire au Talon Rose). [PaintedB] (40/41) 90, p. 80-84.
"Elegy for Martin Luther King" (for jazz orchestra, tr. by Melvin Dixon). [Callaloo] (13:1) Wint 90, p. 22-27.
"Elegy of Midnight" (tr. by Melvin Dixon). [Callaloo] (13:1) Wint 90, p. 20-21.
"If I Could Only Haul in His Heart" (for African guitar, tr. by Ann Neelon). [PaintedB] (40/41) 90, p. 73.
"Letter to a Poet" (to Aimé Césaire, tr. by Melvin Dixon). [Callaloo] (13:1) Wint 90, p. 14-15.
"Si Je Pouvais Haler Son Coeur" (pour Khalam). [PaintedB] (40/41) 90, p. 72.
"Spring Song" (For a Black Girl with a Pink Heel, tr. by Ann Neelon). [PaintedB] (40/41) 90, p. 81-85.
"Teddungal" (Ode to the Accompaniment of African Harp, tr. by Ann Neelon). [PaintedB] (40/41) 90, p. 77, 79.
"Teddungal" (woï pour kôra). [PaintedB] (40/41) 90, p. 76, 78.
"To New York" (for jazz orchestra and trumpet solo, tr. by Melvin Dixon). [Callaloo] (13:1) Wint 90, p. 18-19.
"To the Black American Troops" (to Mercer Cook, tr. by Melvin Dixon). [Callaloo] (13:1) Wint 90, p. 16-17.
"Tonight Dear" (for African guitar, tr. by Ann Neelon). [PaintedB] (40/41) 90, p. 75.
5784. SERAFINO, A. (Allan)
"Apprentice." [PoetryC] (11:4) Wint 90, p. 16.
"Fish Gang." [AntigR] (83) Aut 90, p. 47-55.
"Storm Warning." [Dandel] (17:1) Spr-Sum 90, p. 24.

5785. SERCHUK, Peter
"For My Brother: On the Courage of Birds." [ManhatPR] (11) [89?], p. 47.
"Them." [Poetry] (157:2) N 90, p. 86.
5786. SERRANO, Pio E.
"Los Triunfadores." [LindLM] (9:4) O-D 90, p. 62.
5787. SERVICE, Robert
"The Cremation of Sam McGee." [HawaiiR] (15:1, #31) Wint 90, p. 73-74.
5788. SERVIN, Jacques
"Manufacture" (tr. of Michel Deguy, w. Wilson Baldridge and the author).
[NewDeltaR] (7:1) 90, p. 12.
5789. SERVISS, Shirley A.
"Full Circle." [Grain] (18:2) Sum 90, p. 23.
"Like My Father." [Grain] (18:2) Sum 90, p. 22.
5790. SERWATUK, Michele
"Blaine Lake" (In memory of Anna Sapieha 1891-1989 and Michael Sapieha
1890-1975). [AntigR] (80) Wint 90, p. 102-103.
"Prairie Snake." [Dandel] (17:1) Spr-Sum 90, p. 33.
5791. SETH, Vikram
"Soon." [Verse] (7:3) Wint 90, p. 65.
5792. SETHI, Suresh
"Three Cultural Moods." [Event] (19:2) Sum 90, p. 66-67.
5793. SETO, Thelma
"This Shame Is a Carnivore." [SinW] (42) Wint 90-91, p. 44-46.
5794. SEVERENCE, Judith (*See also* LONG-SEVERANCE, Judy)
(Anonymous poem). [FreeL] (4) 90.
5795. SEVERNA, Maia
"Funeral." [Writer] (103:3) Mr 90, p. 23.
5796. SHA, Ou
"Multi-Colored Mountains" (tr. by Li Xijian and Gordon Osing). [Paint] (17:33/34)
Spr-Aut 90, p. 35.
5797. SHADOIAN, Jack
"Instructions, Moving In." [CumbPR] (10:1) Fall 90, p. 41-42.
5798. SHAFARMAN, Gail
"In Florida." [LitR] (33:2) Wint 90, p. 225.
5799. SHAH, Sejal
"Through the Eyes of the Dark-Eyed Americans." [HangL] (57) 90, p. 83.
SHAHID ALI, Agha
See ALI, Agha Shahid
5800. SHAIDLE, Kathy
"Dusting for Fingerprints in Hamilton, Ontario." [WestCL] (24:3) Wint 90, p.
57-59.
"Restoration Conspiracy Notebook." [PoetryC] (11:1) Spr 90, p. 5.
SHALIN, Hai-Jew
See HAI-JEW, Shalin
SHAN, Han
See HAN, Shan
5801. SHANKMAN, Steven
"Ad Hominem." [Hellas] (1:1) Spr 90, p. 48.
5802. SHAPCOTT, Thomas
"Darkness" (tr. of Françoise Han). [Trans] (23) Spr 90, p. 167.
5803. SHAPIRO, Alan
"Home Movie" (for Beth and Russ). [Agni] (29/30) 90, p. 71-72.
"In the Kingdom of Pleasure." [TriQ] (80) Wint 90-91, p. 80.
"Marriage." [Agni] (29/30) 90, p. 73.
"Mud Dancing" (Woodstock, 1969). [TriQ] (80) Wint 90-91, p. 77-78.
"Prayer on the Temple Steps." [TriQ] (80) Wint 90-91, p. 79.
"Separation of the Waters." [Thrpny] (43) Fall 90, p. 8.
"Turkey Vultures." [PartR] (57:1) Wint 90, p. 103.
5804. SHAPIRO, David
"After a Lost Original." [Notus] (5:1) Spr 90, p. 100-106.
"Goofy Plays Second Fiddle in the Family Quartet" (For L. Wieder). [LitR] (33:4)
Sum 90, p. 459.
"Prayer for My Son." [Boulevard] (4:3/5:1, #12/13) Spr 90, p. 242-245.
"The Seasons." [AmerPoR] (19:3) My-Je 90, p. 3-4.
"Smiling in His Sleep." [LitR] (33:4) Sum 90, p. 458.

5805. SHAPIRO, Gregg
"Fowl Play." [HawaiiR] (14:1, #28) Wint 89-90, p. 86.
"From the Air." [HawaiiR] (14:1, #28) Wint 89-90, p. 87.
"Louie Blue." [WillowR] Spr 90, p. 19.
"Miss You Blue." [HawaiiR] (14:1, #28) Wint 89-90, p. 86.
"Money Changing Hands." [ContextS] (1:1) 89, p. 14.
"One of the Boys" (For Linda). [HawaiiR] (14:1, #28) Wint 89-90, p. 88.
"Pat and Joe." [HawaiiR] (14:1, #28) Wint 89-90, p. 85.
"Six Months in the Basement." [EvergreenC] (6:1) Wint 90-Spr 91, p. 34.
5806. SHAPIRO, Harvey
"Amit's Song." [HangL] (57) 90, p. 72.
"Bronx Elegy." [HangL] (57) 90, p. 73.
"From the Arabic." [HangL] (57) 90, p. 72.
"Jerusalem." [HangL] (57) 90, p. 71.
"Tranquility." [HangL] (57) 90, p. 74.
"A Valedictory." [HangL] (57) 90, p. 74.
5807. SHAPIRO, Joel-Peter
"Between You, Me and the Lamp Post." [CharR] (16:2) Fall 90, p. 25.
5808. SHAPIRO, Karl
"Gerard Manley Hopkins Mesmerizes a Duck." [NewYorkQ] (42) Sum 90, p. 54.
"Joyce." [NewYorkQ] (43) Fall 90, p. 42.
"The Smokers." [NewYorkQ] (41) Spr 90, p. 44.
5809. SHAPIRO, Myra
"A Woman Vanishes." [Ploughs] (16:4) Wint 90-91, p. 200-201.
SHARAT CHANDRA, G. S.
  See CHANDRA, G. S. Sharat
5810. SHARE, Don
"After Love" (tr. of Miguel Hernández). [Agni] (29/30) 90, p. 10-12.
"The cemetery lies near" (tr. of Miguel Hernández). [PartR] (57:2) Spr 90, p. 270.
"George Santayana Revisited" (In membory of Jonathan Lieberson, from whose
    essay, "The Sense of Santayana," the first line is quoted). [PartR] (57:3) Sum
    90, p. 439-440.
"The Last Corner" (tr. of Miguel Hernández). [Agni] (29/30) 90, p. 13-14.
"Love rose up between us" (tr. of Miguel Hernández). [PartR] (57:2) Spr 90, p.
    271.
"Song of Sleeplessness" (tr. of Francisco Brines). [PartR] (57:2) Spr 90, p. 270.
"You were like the young" (tr. of Miguel Hernández). [PartR] (57:2) Spr 90, p. 271.
5811. SHATAL, Shmu'el
"Picasso's Woman with Hat" (tr. by Bernhard Frank). [Vis] (33) 90, p. 6.
SHAUL, Moshe Ben
  See BEN SHAUL, Moshe
5812. SHAW, Alan
"Berlin" (To C. S.). [PartR] (57:1) Wint 90, p. 112-113.
5813. SHAW, Catherine
"The Application." [Pig] (16) 90, p. 96.
"Into His Clothes." [SingHM] (18) 90, p. 14-15.
"The Magician of Xerox." [Pig] (16) 90, p. 96.
"Occupational Hazards." [Pig] (16) 90, p. 96.
"Words for a Temp." [Pig] (16) 90, p. 97.
5814. SHAW, Catherine Harnett
"Basic Vocabulary" (tr. of Moshe Dor). [PoetL] (85:4) Wint 90-91, p. 22.
"The Bus." [PoetL] (85:3) Fall 90, p. 45.
"Child Bride." [PoetL] (85:3) Fall 90, p. 44.
"What Women Pray For." [Gargoyle] (37/38) 90, p. 122.
5815. SHAW, Nancy
"Scoptocratic" (Excerpts). [WestCL] (24:1) Spr 90, p. 36-44.
5816. SHAW, Robert B.
"Advanced Research." [PartR] (57:3) Sum 90, p. 444-445.
"The Bookmark." [Poetry] (155:6) Mr 90, p. 395.
"The Leaning Tree." [Verse] (7:3) Wint 90, p. 66.
"A Piece of Rope." [Shen] (40:2) Sum 90, p. 49-51.
"Shut In." [Poetry] (155:6) Mr 90, p. 397-398.
"Still Life: Belt on Bureau." [Poetry] (155:6) Mr 90, p. 396.
5817. SHAW, Stephen I.
"Wired All Wrong." [PoetL] (85:4) Wint 90-91, p. 26.

5818. SHAWGO, Lucy
"At Berry Time." [HolCrit] (27:4) O 90, p. 16.
5819. SHEA, Marilyn
"The Stranger." [BellArk] (6:3) My-Je 90, p. 10.
5820. SHECK, Laurie
"After Melville." [Ploughs] (16:1) Spr-Sum 90, p. 134-136.
"Letter to K." [Ploughs] (16:1) Spr-Sum 90, p. 130-131.
"Living Color." [Ploughs] (16:1) Spr-Sum 90, p. 132-133.
"The Return." [NewYorker] (65:52) 12 F 90, p. 42.
"White Noise." [NewYorker] (66:20) 2 Jl 90, p. 30.
5821. SHEEHAN, Marc (Marc J.)
"Civics Class." [SlipS] (10) 90, p. 87.
"Oban, Scotland, and the Islands." [KanQ] (22:3) Sum 90, p. 138-139.
"A Prayer in Memory of Theodore Roethke." [KanQ] (22:3) Sum 90, p. 138.
"Wild Mushrooms." [OxfordM] (6:1) Spr-Sum 90, p. 36.
5822. SHEEHAN, T. (Tom, Thomas F.)
"Anatomy of a River." [SpoonRQ] (15:3) Sum 90, p. 55.
"High Tension Languages." [SpoonRQ] (15:3) Sum 90, p. 56-57.
"Keys to Friday Sunrise." [Poem] (63) My 90, p. 66.
"Lest the Last Light Flee Also." [SpoonRQ] (15:3) Sum 90, p. 58-59.
"Old Mystic Bridge, Chelsea, 1936." [Parting] (3:2) Wint 90-91, p. 3.
"Second Revisions" (for Seamus Heaney). [CapeR] (25:1) Spr 90, p. 8-9.
"Space for an Interim Dowser." [SpoonRQ] (15:3) Sum 90, p. 53-54.
"This Sudden Silence." [Poem] (63) My 90, p. 67.
5823. SHEERIN, Joe
"Beatitudes." [ParisR] (32:114) Spr 90, p. 80.
"In a Primary School." [ParisR] (32:114) Spr 90, p. 78-79.
"To Interest Your children." [ParisR] (32:114) Spr 90, p. 81.
"Vespers." [ParisR] (32:114) Spr 90, p. 82.
5824. SHEFFER, Thomas A.
"Robert Penn Warren: A Twentieth-Century Tale." [SewanR] (98:2) Spr 90, p.
243-245.
5825. SHEGREN, Gerald E.
"Body Language." [NegC] (10:2/3) 90, p. 105.
5826. SHEINER, Marcy
"A Failure of Imagination." [SlipS] (10) 90, p. 17.
"On the Occasion of the First Official Recognition of Martin Luther King's
Birthday." [SlipS] (10) 90, p. 17-18.
"Politically Correct." [SlipS] (10) 90, p. 18-19.
SHEKERJIAN, Regina deCormier
See DeCORMIER-SHEKERJIAN, Regina
5827. SHELLER, Gayle Hunter
"Brother Bonsai (Daniel)." [BellArk] (6:1) Ja-F 90, p. 5.
"Empathy's Child." [BellArk] (6:3) My-Je 90, p. 5.
"Ivy Weatherwax." [BellArk] (6:5) S-O 90, p. 10.
"Preacher Hands." [BellArk] (6:3) My-Je 90, p. 6.
SHELLNUT, Eve
See SHELNUTT, Eve
5828. SHELNUTT, Eve
"1943." [TarRP] (29:2) Spr 90, p. 33.
"The Adulteress." [SpoonRQ] (15:3) Sum 90, p. 64.
"The Adulteress." [ThRiPo] (35/36) 90, p. 43.
"Alphonse." [ThRiPo] (35/36) 90, p. 40.
"Are the Lives of the Lovers Altered?" [ThRiPo] (35/36) 90, p. 41.
"At the Edge of Dawn." [PraS] (64:4) Wint 90, p. 56.
"Father, His Company." [ThRiPo] (35/36) 90, p. 39.
"Follow Me." [LullwaterR] (2:1) Wint 90, p. 52.
"The Husband." [BlackWR] (16:2) Spr-Sum 90, p. 58.
"Inheritance." [RiverS] (32) [90?], p. 38.
"Many Times." [PraS] (64:4) Wint 90, p. 54-55.
"O Hero." [ChatR] (11:1) Fall 90, p. 35.
"One of the Old Men." [PraS] (64:4) Wint 90, p. 55.
"Outside the Force of Absolute Mourning." [NewDeltaR] (7:2) Spr-Sum 90, p. 21.
"Proper Travel." [ThRiPo] (35/36) 90, p. 42.
"A Selected Story." [RiverS] (32) [90?], p. 39.
"This Is the Hour." [NewDeltaR] (7:2) Spr-Sum 90, p. 20.

"The Triumph of Children." [NoAmR] (275:1) Mr 90, p. 72.
5829. SHELTON, Rick
"Eschatology." [QW] (31) Fall 90, p. 87.
5830. SHEPARD, Neil
"The Bell Bird" (Matari Bay, New Zealand). [AntR] (48:1) Wint 90, p. 92.
"Sailor on Leave Suffocates in Sand." [SpoonRQ] (15:2) Spr 90, p. 45-46.
5831. SHEPARD, Roy
"The American above Avon." [Poem] (63) My 90, p. 14-15.
"Earth to Earth." [Poem] (63) My 90, p. 13.
5832. SHEPHERD, Gail
"Autumnal." [ThRiPo] (35/36) 90, p. 80.
"A Country Auction." [TampaR] (3) 90, p. 61.
"Marillewis." [ThRiPo] (35/36) 90, p. 79.
5833. SHEPHERD, J. Barrie
"Full House November First." [ChrC] (107:31) 31 O 90, p. 995.
"Pentecost Scenario." [ChrC] (107:17) 16-23 My 90, p. 530.
"Reassurance." [ChrC] (107:7) 28 F 90, p. 214.
"Terms in Contradiction." [ChrC] (107:34) 21-28 N 90, p. 1084.
"Through a Glass Darkly" (A Maundy Thursday Tenebrae Meditation). [ChrC]
        (107:11) 4 Ap 90, p. 327-328.
"Trimming." [ChrC] (107:37) 19-26 D 90, p. 1196.
5834. SHEPPARD, Susan
"Dream Ninety-Nine: After Baudelaire." [ChironR] (9:2) Sum 90, p. 4.
"For My Uncle Who Died by His Own Hand." [PennR] (4:2) 90, p. 52-53.
"From Above and Below." [ChironR] (9:2) Sum 90, p. 4.
5835. SHER, Steven
"In Baton Rouge." [Wind] (20:66) 90, p. 38.
"Loretta's Men." [Interim] (9:2) Fall-Wint 90-91, p. 20.
"Separate Peace" (Cave Hill Cemetery). [Wind] (20:66) 90, p. 38-39.
5836. SHERBINA, Tatyana
"Knife knife knife knife knife knife sapper shovel" (tr. by Oleg Atbashian and Maureen
        Hurley). [PoetryUSA] (5:2) Sum 90, p. 14.
5837. SHERIN, Kerry
"Question." [NewEngR] (13:2) Wint 90, p. 192.
5838. SHERLOCK, Karen
"Country." [Grain] (18:4) Wint 90, p. 82.
5839. SHERMAN, Nan
"Grandma Won't Stay Put." [SlipS] (10) 90, p. 71.
"That Kind of Day." [Bogg] (62) 90, p. 7.
5840. SHERMAN, Nancy
"As Change." [SenR] (20:2) Fall 90, p. 60.
5841. SHERRILL, Steven
"The Potter I Am Not." [Crucible] (26) Fall 90, p. 60.
5842. SHERRY, James
"Our Nuclear Heritage" (Selections). [Avec] (3:1) 90, p. 35-39.
5843. SHEVCHENKO, Ruslan
"Wind & Sky." (Poem written in English by high school students from the Ukraine,
        collected by Maureen Hurley). [PoetryUSA] (5:1) Spr 90, p. 18.
SHICONG, Liu
    See LIU, Shicong
5844. SHIELDS, Bill
"The 1st Time." [Pearl] (11) Sum 90, p. 32.
"For My Daughters." [Pearl] (11) Sum 90, p. 34.
"How the Hell Can." [Pearl] (11) Sum 90, p. 34.
"I Didn't Kill 'em" (for Jack Hirschman, a damn good man -- who understands).
        [Pearl] (11) Sum 90, p. 33.
"There Is Something Terribly Wrong with These Lines." [DustyD] (1:2) O 90, p. 7.
"Wife." [Pearl] (11) Sum 90, p. 32.
5845. SHIGEMATSU, Soiku
"The Pure Sound Pavilion of the Riverside Temple" (tr. of Muso Soseki, w. W. S.
        Merwin). [Hudson] (43:2) Sum 90, p. 339-340.
SHIGEYO, Matsumoto
    See MATSUMOTO, Shigeyo
5846. SHIN, Kyung-rim
"The Hongch'on River" (tr. by Lois Cucullu and Sym Myoung-ho). [PoetL] (85:2)
        Sum 90, p. 37-38.

5847. SHINDER, Jason
"The Notebooks of Norman Rockwell." [KenR] (NS 12:2) Spr 90, p. 160-162.
"The Notebooks of Pablo Picasso." [KenR] (NS 12:2) Spr 90, p. 158-160.
5848. SHIPLEY, Vivian
"The Last Wild Horses in Tennessee." [SwampR] (5) Wint-Spr 90, p. 6-7.
5849. SHIPPY, Peter Jay
"Monologue at the Speed of Mercy." [CimR] (91) Ap 90, p. 48-50.
5850. SHIRLEY, Aleda
"Aware." [AmerV] (20) Fall 90, p. 62-63.
"Ellington Indigos." [Crazy] (39) Wint 90, p. 63-64.
"The Natural Angle of Repose." [Crazy] (39) Wint 90, p. 61-62.
"Right As Rain." [Crazy] (39) Wint 90, p. 59-60.
5851. SHIVDASANI, Menka
"Divided Base." [Arc] (25) Aut 90, p. 58.
"Ramayama Revisited." [Arc] (25) Aut 90, p. 56-57.
5852. SHOAF, Diann Blakely
"Adultery." [WestB] (27) 90, p. 26.
"Breakfast." [GreenMR] (NS 3:2) Fall-Wint 89-90, p. 96.
"Christmas Call." [Nat] (251:20) 10 D 90, p. 748.
"The Shuttle Explodes" (1/26/1986). [GreenMR] (NS 3:2) Fall-Wint 89-90, p. 98.
"The Woman in the Mirror" (after a painting by Gustav Klimt). [GreenMR] (NS 3:2) Fall-Wint 89-90, p. 97.
5853. SHOEMAKE, Rebecca
"Suffocation of a Small Southern Town." [LullwaterR] (1:1) Spr 90, p. 42.
5854. SHOEMAKER, Lynn
"The Buddhist Nun's Young Friend" (in remembrance of fire. Runner-up, 1989 John Williams Andrews Contest). [PoetL] (85:1) Spr 90, p. 16-21.
"Interview / Vietnam / 1987, Napalm Woman / Looking at a Photo of Herself / 1967." [MinnR] (NS 34/35) Spr-Fall 90, p. 13-14.
5855. SHOLL, Betsy
"The Feel" (Windham Correctional Center, Poetry Workshop). [WestB] (27) 90, p. 31-33.
"A Girl Named Spring." [CimR] (93) O 90, p. 38-39.
"A Proposition." [GrahamHR] (13) Spr 90, p. 58-59.
"The Red Line." [Ploughs] (16:1) Spr-Sum 90, p. 126-127.
"Something to Say." [GrahamHR] (13) Spr 90, p. 56-57.
"Three Wishes." [Ploughs] (16:1) Spr-Sum 90, p. 128-129.
"You Figure It Out." [GrahamHR] (13) Spr 90, p. 60-61.
5856. SHOMER, Enid
"The Last Father Poem." [Poetry] (156:3) Je 90, p. 138.
"Romantic, at Horseshoe Key." [Poetry] (156:3) Je 90, p. 137-138.
"Saturday in the Dark." [NegC] (10:2/3) 90, p. 55.
5857. SHOPTAW, John
"Six Legs Down and One to Go." [Avec] (3:1) 90, p. 142-146.
5858. SHORT, Gary
"After Reading Thomas James (1946-1973)." [CharR] (16:1) Spr 90, p. 39.
"Arizona." [WritersF] (16) Fall 90, p. 74.
"Driving Nevada / Reprise." [CharR] (16:2) Fall 90, p. 88-89.
"George Pascho Miller." [CharR] (16:1) Spr 90, p. 38-39.
"The Mare Slept Standing." [CharR] (16:1) Spr 90, p. 40.
"Ornament." [CharR] (16:2) Fall 90, p. 88.
"Rains." [WritersF] (16) Fall 90, p. 75.
"Stillwater Marsh." [MidwQ] (31:2) Wint 90, p. 217.
"Toward Morning." [MidwQ] (31:4) Sum 90, p. 470.
"Trajectory." [MidwQ] (31:2) Wint 90, p. 224.
"Yes." [CharR] (16:1) Spr 90, p. 41.
5859. SHOUP, Barbara
"Graceland." [WindO] (53) Fall 90, p. 27.
5860. SHU, Ting
"Assembly Line" (tr. by Carolyn Kizer). [Manoa] (2:2) Fall 90, p. 177.
"Bei Tai-He Beach" (tr. by Carolyn Kizer). [Manoa] (2:2) Fall 90, p. 176.
"Montages in Twilight" (tr. by Edward Morin and Dai Fang). [Screens] (2) 90, p. 38-40.
"Weekend Evening" (tr. by Carolyn Kizer). [Manoa] (2:2) Fall 90, p. 175.
5861. SHUGRUE, Jim
"All the Ingredients for a Poem." [CrabCR] (6:3) Spr 90, p. 28.

SHUJI, Miya
  See MIYA, Shûji
SHUJI, Terayama
  See TERAYAMA, Shuji
5862. SHUMAKER, Peggy
  "Across the Line" (Tucson/Nogales). [HayF] (6) Sum 90, p. 21-22.
  "Bitter Spring." [ColEng] (52:2) F 90, p. 154.
  "Digging a Garden." [CutB] (33) 90, p. 5-6.
  "No Honey in This House." [ColEng] (52:2) F 90, p. 155.
  "Why Ira Pratt Cocked His Head Like That." [CutB] (33) 90, p. 6.
5863. SHUMWALT, Karen Cordelia
  "The New Gray Church." [Vis] (33) 90, p. 24.
SHUNTARO, Tanikawa
  See TANIKAWA, Shuntaro
5864. SHURBANOV, Alexander
  "Capriccio 9" (tr. of Lyubomir Levchev, w. Jascha Kessler). [Screens] (2) 90, p.
    60-61.
  "The Old Fortress" (tr. of Elizaveta Bagryana, w. Jascha Kessler). [Screens] (2) 90,
    p. 59.
  "Poet" (tr. of Luchezar Elenkov, w. Jascha Kessler). [Screens] (2) 90, p. 62.
  "Secret Love" (Excerpt, tr. of Lyubomir Levchev, w. Jascha Kessler). [Screens] (2)
    90, p. 60.
5865. SHURIN, Aaron
  "In the Flesh." [Zyzzyva] (6:3 #23) Fall 90, p. 69-73.
  "The Injuries." [Avec] (3:1) 90, p. 130.
  "This Peculiarity." [Avec] (3:1) 90, p. 129.
5866. SHUTTLE, Penelope
  "After-Life." [ManhatR] (5:1) Spr 90, p. 23.
  "At Once Jesus." [ManhatR] (5:2) Fall 90, p. 17-18.
  "Big Cat." [ManhatR] (5:2) Fall 90, p. 14.
  "Georgette." [ManhatR] (5:2) Fall 90, p. 13.
  "Jesus." [ManhatR] (5:2) Fall 90, p. 15.
  "John." [ManhatR] (5:1) Spr 90, p. 22.
  "Krystallhause, or The End of the Window." [Stand] (31:1) Wint 89-90, p. 43-47.
  "Moon Without End." [ManhatR] (5:1) Spr 90, p. 20.
  "My Table." [ManhatR] (5:2) Fall 90, p. 16.
  "Sieve." [ManhatR] (5:1) Spr 90, p. 21.
5867. SHVARTS, Elena
  "Leviathan" (tr. by Catriona H. M. Kelly). [Nimrod] (33:2) Spr-Sum 90, p. 39.
5868. SHY, Eve Carol
  "Bull's-Eye." [GreensboroR] (49) Wint 90-91, p. 53.
5869. SIBAST, Peer
  "Equinox" (to Fernando Pessoa, from "The Dream of Lucifer," Kimore, 1987, tr. by
    the author). [CimR] (92) Jl 90, p. 29-30.
5870. SICOLI, Dan
  "Head of Shakespeare." [SlipS] (10) 90, p. 62.
5871. SIDNEY, Joan Seliger
  "Poker." [MichQR] (29:4) Fall 90, p. 621-622.
  "Preserves." [MassR] (31:3) Aut 90, p. 383-384.
5872. SIDOLI, Graziella
  "Domus Poetica" (tr. of Adriano Spatola). [Screens] (2) 90, p. 100.
  "In Memoriam Adriani Spatulae" (Excerpts, tr. of Paola Valesio). [Screens] (2) 90,
    p. 98-99.
  "The Lot of Great Waves" (tr. of Giovanni Cecchetti). [Screens] (2) 90, p. 118.
  "Metrics and Poetry" (tr. of Antonio Porta). [Screens] (2) 90, p. 120-121.
  "The Spouses" (Selection: 5, tr. of Antonio Porta). [Screens] (2) 90, p. 119.
5873. SIEBURTH, Richard
  "Allegory" (tr. of Jean-Paul Auxemery). [Sulfur] (10:2, #27) Fall 90, p. 70.
  "Futile Ode to Nobody" (in the manner of Alvaro de Campos, tr. of Jean-Paul
    Auxemery). [Sulfur] (10:2, #27) Fall 90, p. 68.
  "In San Francisco Segalen" (tr. of Jean-Paul Auxemery). [Sulfur] (10:2, #27) Fall
    90, p. 69-70.
  "Nommo" (tr. of Jean-Paul Auxemery). [Sulfur] (10:2, #27) Fall 90, p. 69.
  "Stelae" (tr. of Jean-Paul Auxemery). [Sulfur] (10:2, #27) Fall 90, p. 70-73.
5874. SIEFKIN, David
  "Arranging Space" (tr. of Luuk Gruwez, w. Catharina Kochuyt and Bradley R.

Strahan). [Vis] (34) 90, p. 18.
"Autumn" (Excerpt, tr. of Francois Jacqmin). [Vis] (32) 90, p. 29.
"Call This Blindness" (tr. of Erik Spinoy, w. Catharina Kochuyt). [Vis] (34) 90, p.
   14.
"Cloaks of Silence" (tr. of Erik Spinoy, w. Catharina Kochuyt). [Vis] (34) 90, p.
   13.
"Dawn" (tr. of Charles Ducal, w. Catharina Kochuyt). [Vis] (34) 90, p. 9.
"East of Eden" (tr. of Charles Ducal, w. Catharina Kochuyt). [Vis] (34) 90, p. 10.
"Eden" (tr. of Charles Ducal, w. Catharina Kochuyt). [Vis] (34) 90, p. 9.
"A Glass Falls" (tr. of Guido de Bruyn, w. Catharina Kochuyt). [Vis] (34) 90, p.
   15.
"The Hare" (tr. of Charles Ducal, w. Catharina Kochuyt). [Vis] (34) 90, p. 10.
"Home" (for Monique T., died 1987, at 22, in a traffic accident, tr. of Luuk Gruwez,
   w. Catharina Kochuyt and Bradley R. Strahan). [Vis] (34) 90, p. 17.
"I Want to See" (tr. of Philippe Remy). [Vis] (32) 90, p. 30.
"Inhospitality" (tr. of Luuk Gruwez, w. Catharina Kochuyt). [Vis] (34) 90, p. 16.
"Liege" (tr. of Marguerite Dessouroux, w. Philippe Remy). [Vis] (34) 90, p. 18.
"Mother Tongue" (tr. of Charles Ducal, w. Catharina Kochuyt). [Vis] (34) 90, p.
   11.
"Odysseus" (tr. of Charles Ducal, w. Catharina Kochuyt). [Vis] (34) 90, p. 12.
"Spring" (Excerpt, tr. of Francois Jacqmin). [Vis] (32) 90, p. 28.
"The Streets" (tr. of Erik Spinoy, w. Catharina Kochuyt). [Vis] (34) 90, p. 12.
"Summer" (Excerpt, tr. of Francois Jacqmin). [Vis] (32) 90, p. 29.
"Tribute" (tr. of Leonard Nolens, w. Catharina Kochuyt). [Vis] (34) 90, p. 14.
"The Wall" (tr. of Erik Spinoy, w. Catharina Kochuyt). [Vis] (34) 90, p. 13.
"Wife" (tr. of Charles Ducal, w. Catharina Kochuyt). [Vis] (34) 90, p. 11.
"Winter" (Excerpt, tr. of Francois Jacqmin). [Vis] (32) 90, p. 30.
5875. SIEGEL, Joan I.
   "After Divorcing." [PoetL] (85:1) Spr 90, p. 43.
   "Interim." [Comm] (117:22) 21 D 90, p. 746.
   "Resurrection." [Comm] (117:11) 1 Je 90, p. 352.
   "Resurrection." [Poem] (63) My 90, p. 22.
   "Seasons." [Poem] (63) My 90, p. 23.
5876. SIEGEL, Robert
   "Girl with a Lute." [SewanR] (98:1) Wint 90, p. 29-30.
5877. SIGNORE, R. P.
   "My Father in the Pacific, 1945." [ApalQ] (33/34) 90, p. 54.
5878. SIGNORELLI-PAPPAS, Rita
   "Metamorphosis" (For Benedetta Carlini, 1590-1661, Abbess of the Theatine
      Convent at Pescia). [NegC] (10:2/3) 90, p. 50-51.
5879. SIKÉLIANOS, Eléni
   "O Melena!" [BlackWR] (16:2) Spr-Sum 90, p. 7-8.
5880. SILBER, Cathy
   "On a Picture of Self with Hoe, Cultivating Plum Blossoms in Moonlight" (tr. of Wu
      Tsao). [LitR] (33:2) Wint 90, p. 198.
5881. SILBERSHER, Marvin
   "Ellis Island Feeding on the Stones." [JINJPo] (12:2) Aut 90, p. 35.
5882. SILES, Jaime
   "Abanico." [Inti] (32/33) Otoño 90-Primavera 91, p. 221.
   "Arena." [Inti] (32/33) Otoño 90-Primavera 91, p. 224.
   "Cristal." [Inti] (32/33) Otoño 90-Primavera 91, p. 224.
   "Disoluciones" (A Manuel Alvarez Ortega). [Inti] (32/33) Otoño 90-Primavera 91, p.
      223.
   "Espejo." [Inti] (32/33) Otoño 90-Primavera 91, p. 225.
   "Identidades" (A José Antonio Llardent). [Inti] (32/33) Otoño 90-Primavera 91, p.
      222.
   "Naturaleza" (A José Maria Guelbenzu). [Inti] (32/33) Otoño 90-Primavera 91, p.
      222.
   "Poiesis." [Inti] (32/33) Otoño 90-Primavera 91, p. 223.
   "Propileo." [Inti] (32/33) Otoño 90-Primavera 91, p. 220.
   "Recurrencias." [Inti] (32/33) Otoño 90-Primavera 91, p. 221.
   "Totalidades." [Inti] (32/33) Otoño 90-Primavera 91, p. 220-221.
5883. SILESKY, Barry
   "The Cock of Pomander Walk" (tr. of Pablo Armando Fernandez, w. Neryeda
      Garcia). [AnotherCM] (21) 90, p. 37-47.
   "Jamaica." [NewAW] (6) Spr 90, p. 93.

"Night Game." [OnTheBus] (2:1, #5) Spr 90, p. 124.
"Paradise." [NewAW] (6) Spr 90, p. 94.
"Tourist Attractions: 2 Postcards." [ClockR] (6:1) 90, p. 22-23.
"Woodland Scene, on Loan from Budapest." [Boulevard] (4:3/5:1, #12/13) Spr 90,
    p. 197-198.
5884. SILK, Dennis
    "Eating Out." [Stand] (31:1) Wint 89-90, p. 41.
5885. SILKIN, Jon
    "By the side of the English Office, a black." [Bogg] (63) 90, p. 5.
    "Cherokee." [Bogg] (63) 90, p. 25.
    "Fidelities." [Bogg] (62) 90, p. 22-23.
5886. SILLIMAN, Ron
    "Toner" (Selection: Brucebook). [Avec] (3:1) 90, p. 136-140.
    "Toner (Brucebook)" (Excerpts). [Verse] (7:1) Spr 90, p. 64-65.
5887. SILVA, Jeff
    "The Elect." [NowestR] (28:1) 90, p. 89.
    "Monkey Alone." [NowestR] (28:1) 90, p. 90.
5888. SILVER, Neil
    "Thunder Recedes." [HiramPoR] (48/49) 90-91, p. 64.
5889. SILVER, W.
    "Crossings" (For J.P.S.). [CalQ] (34) 90, p. 25.
    "Soldier" (For My Father). [CalQ] (34) 90, p. 24.
5890. SILVERSTEIN, David
    "Clearing Her, Easing the Obsession: A Flyer's Manual." [YellowS] (34) Sum 90,
    p. 21.
    "A Preference: A Whole Series of Them." [YellowS] (34) Sum 90, p. 20.
5891. SILVERTHORNE, Marty L.
    "In the Shadow of Your Eyes." [Pembroke] (22) 90, p. 114.
    "Thorns and Thistles." [Pembroke] (22) 90, p. 115.
5892. SIMAN, John
    "Lake Alice" (to Richard Eberhart, tr. of Michael Albrecht). [NewYorkQ] (41) Spr
    90, p. 72.
5893. SIMAS, Joseph
    "A Descriptive Method" ("Une Méthode descriptive," Le Collet de Buffle, Paris,
    1986, tr. of Claude Royet-Journoud). [Avec] (3:1) 90, p. 43-55.
    "Vertical Efforts in White" ("Travail vertical et blanc," Spectres Familliers, 1989, tr.
    of Anne-Marie Albiach). [Avec] (3:1) 90, p. 56-58.
5894. SIMIC, Charles
    "Le Beau Monde." [Antaeus] (64/65) Spr-Aut 90, p. 125.
    "The chair was a student of Euclid." [KenR] (NS 12:2) Spr 90, p. 163.
    "Country Fair." [NewYorker] (66:17) 11 Je 90, p. 40.
    "Country Lunch." [NewYorker] (66:24) 30 Jl 90, p. 73.
    "Empires." [NewYorker] (66:11) 30 Ap 90, p. 74.
    "Evening Walk." [Poetry] (156:5) Ag 90, p. 295.
    "Grandmother Logic" (for Jim Tate). [HampSPR] (Anthology 1975-1990) 90, p.
    185.
    "In Pittsfield." [HampSPR] (Anthology 1975-1990) 90, p. 185.
    "In the Library." [SouthwR] (75:3) Sum 90, p. 325.
    "The Infinite." [GettyR] (3:2) Spr 90, p. 265.
    "'Infinite sorrow' I heard someone say that today." [KenR] (NS 12:2) Spr 90, p.
    163.
    "My Secret Identity Is." [Field] (42) Spr 90, p. 79.
    "The Old World." [GettyR] (3:2) Spr 90, p. 268.
    "Paradise." [Antaeus] (64/65) Spr-Aut 90, p. 124.
    "Place at the Outskirts." [GettyR] (3:2) Spr 90, p. 267.
    "Prudent Triangle" (tr. of Vasko Popa). [SenR] (20:2) Fall 90, p. 6-7.
    "Some Nights." [GettyR] (3:2) Spr 90, p. 266.
    "Stub of a Red Pencil." [NewYorker] (66:43) 10 D 90, p. 52.
    "Whistling in the Dark." [GeoR] (44:3) Fall 90, p. 433.
5895. SIMMERMAN, Jim
    "Bumblebee." [CutB] (34) Sum-Fall 90, p. 75.
    "Bushhog." [NegC] (10:2/3) 90, p. 21-23.
    "Dim." [NegC] (10:2/3) 90, p. 20.
    "Fly." [CutB] (34) Sum-Fall 90, p. 36.
    "Tell Them." [WritersF] (16) Fall 90, p. 96-97.

5896. SIMMONS, Brian Lane
"I Was Something." [PaintedB] (40/41) 90, p. 177.
5897. SIMMONS, James
"End of the Affair." [Quarry] (39:1) Wint 90, p. 93.
5898. SIMON, Greg
"Omega" (Poem for the Dead, tr. of Federico García Lorca, w. Steven F. White).
[NowestR] (28:3/29:1) 90-91, p. 178.
"Trip to the Moon" (tr. of Federico García Lorca, w. Steven F. White). [NowestR]
(28:3/29:1) 90-91, p. 170-177.
5899. SIMON, John Oliver
"Bacchantes" (Selections: I, VII, XV, tr. of Elsa Cross). [OnTheBus] (2:1, #5) Spr
90, p. 185-187.
"La Estrellita." [OnTheBus] (2:2/3:1, #6/7) Sum-Fall 90 Wint-Spr 91, p. 185.
"Finally After So Many Years Hernan Cortez Declares" (to Eduardo Langagne, tr. of
Gaspar Aguilera Diaz). [Caliban] (9) 90, p. 144-145.
"Fumador." [OnTheBus] (2:2/3:1, #6/7) Sum-Fall 90 Wint-Spr 91, p. 185-186.
"Imbabura." [Abraxas] (38/39) 90, p. 129.
"In the Waters of Conchan" (tr. of Antonio Cisneros). [Abraxas] (38/39) 90, p. 71,
73.
"Insomniacs." [OnTheBus] (2:1, #5) Spr 90, p. 125.
"Invention of Light" (tr. of Margarita León). [Abraxas] (38/39) 90, p. 69.
"Surfers." [Abraxas] (38/39) 90, p. 128.
5900. SIMON, Josef
"Beat Poetry" (tr. by Richard Katrovas). [IndR] (13:3) Fall 90, p. 77-78.
"How I Beg Your Pardon, Little Anna" (tr. by Richard Katrovas). [IndR] (13:3) Fall
90, p. 75.
"You Slowly Undress" (tr. by Richard Katrovas). [IndR] (13:3) Fall 90, p. 76.
5901. SIMON, Maurya
"Los Angeles, Fin de Siècle." [KenR] (NS 12:4) Fall 90, p. 129-130.
"Conversation / Conversion." [GeoR] (44:1/2) Spr-Sum 90, p. 112.
"Death of a Hummingbird." [Journal] (13:2) Fall-Wint 89-90, p. 11-12.
"Random Silences." [KenR] (NS 12:4) Fall 90, p. 130-131.
"Second Born." [Journal] (13:2) Fall-Wint 89-90, p. 10.
"The Woodpecker." [Journal] (13:2) Fall-Wint 89-90, p. 9.
5902. SIMONIDES
"Fragment 543 (Page)" (in Greek). [SycamoreR] (2:1) Wint 90, p. 56.
"Fragment 543 (Page)" (tr. by John T. Kirby). [SycamoreR] (2:1) Wint 90, p. 567.
5903. SIMONSON, Michael
"Jose Is Twelve and Nicaraguan." [RagMag] (7:2) Spr 90, p. 55.
"Walking In Krakau." [RagMag] (7:2) Spr 90, p. 56.
5904. SIMONSUURI, Kirsti
"Travelling Light" (Selections: 5 poems, tr. by Jascha Kessler and the author).
[Screens] (2) 90, p. 83-86.
5905. SIMPSON, Anne
"Lay Your Head on the Shoulder of Water and the Skin of Air." [MalR] (90) Spr 90,
p. 71.
5906. SIMPSON, Batista
"A Prayer for Healing" (Selections: 2, 5). [PoetC] (21:4) Sum 90, p. 17-19.
5907. SIMPSON, Grace
"Dream Sculpture: Woman Leaving Ocean Liner." [HampSPR] (Anthology
1975-1990) 90, p. 121.
"GWTW." [NegC] (10:1) 90, p. 83.
5908. SIMPSON, Louis
"The Associate." [Hudson] (43:2) Sum 90, p. 213-222.
"Bernie." [HampSPR] (Anthology 1975-1990) 90, p. 5-6.
"A Change of Raiment." [SouthernR] (26:3) Jl 90, p. 647-659.
"The Mysterious Strangers." [KenR] (NS 12:2) Spr 90, p. 164-170.
"Social Comforts." [Witness] (4:1) 90, p. 117-123.
"The Tree Seat." [HampSPR] (Anthology 1975-1990) 90, p. 3-4.
5909. SIMPSON, Nancy
"Tanfastic." [LullwaterR] (2:1) Wint 90, p. 36.
5910. SIMPSON, Richard
"River of Tears." [TarRP] (29:2) Spr 90, p. 9-10.
5911. SIMS, Roberta Laulicht
"Wild Oats." [SwampR] (6) Sum-Fall 90, p. 5.

5912. SIMSER, Guy
"Bushido." [PottPort] (12) 90, p. 23.
5913. SINCLAIR, Bennie Lee
"Al's Poem, As Written by One of His Students." [SoCaR] (22:2) Spr 90, p. 4-6.
5914. SINISGALLI, Leonardo
"I Stand Up" (tr. by Rina Ferrarelli). [InterPR] (16:2) Fall 90, p. 53.
"Mi Difendo." [InterPR] (16:2) Fall 90, p. 52.
"Passiflora." [InterPR] (16:2) Fall 90, p. 52.
"Passionflower" (tr. by Rina Ferrarelli). [InterPR] (16:2) Fall 90, p. 53.
"Quando Torna l'Autunno." [InterPR] (16:2) Fall 90, p. 54.
"When Autumn Returns" (tr. by Rina Ferrarelli). [InterPR] (16:2) Fall 90, p. 55.
5915. SINK, Susan
"Why Carol Ann Stayed." [PoetL] (85:2) Sum 90, p. 43-46.
5916. SINKEVICH, Valentina
"The Trees" (tr. of Aleksandr Tkachenko, w. Robert Bly). [PaintedB] (40/41) 90, p.
27.
5917. SIPLE, James
"Dear Editor." [PoetryUSA] (5:2) Sum 90, p. 2.
"Over a coffee." [PoetryUSA] (5:2) Sum 90, p. 2.
5918. SIRR, Peter
"Swing." [Quarry] (39:1) Wint 90, p. 94.
5919. SISSON, Jonathan
"August New Moon." [NorthStoneR] (9) 90, p. 14-15.
"Eighty-Four Pieces, Eight by Five Inches." [NorthStoneR] (9) 90, p. 16.
"First Taste of Ratcake." [NorthStoneR] (9) 90, p. 11.
"In Search of the Brother-in-Law." [NorthStoneR] (9) 90, p. 12-13.
"Independent Sorts." [NorthStoneR] (9) 90, p. 9.
"So Deep in Snow" (A Pasticcio Minnesotan). [NorthStoneR] (9) 90, p. 16.
"Visiting Filmmaker." [NorthStoneR] (9) 90, p. 10.
5920. SITWELL, Edith
"Aubade." [ChiR] (37:1) Wint 90, p. 28.
5921. SJÖBERG, Leif
"The Dog at Bruges" (tr. of Johannes Edfelt, w. David Ignatow). [OntR] (33)
Fall-Wint 90-91, p. 91.
"Instinct" (tr. of Edith Södergran, w. Daisy Aldan). [PoetryE] (30) Fall 90, p. 97.
"Senex" (tr. of Johannes Edfelt, w. David Ignatow). [OntR] (33) Fall-Wint 90-91,
p. 92.
5922. SKAU, Michael
"The Me and God Poems: Bridge." [NowestR] (28:1) 90, p. 92.
5923. SKEEL, David
"An Adolescent Poet Dreams of Love." [Boulevard] (4:3/5:1, #12/13) Spr 90, p.
200.
5924. SKEEN, Anita
"Blizzard: Western Kansas." [WeberS] (7:1) Spr 90, p. 91.
"Humanities Seminar." [WeberS] (7:1) Spr 90, p. 90-91.
"Underground" (for Nancy Demuth). [WeberS] (7:1) Spr 90, p. 92.
"Where Tornadoes Begin." [WeberS] (7:1) Spr 90, p. 93-94.
5925. SKEEN, Tim
"Scar." [AntR] (48:1) Wint 90, p. 82.
5926. SKELTON, John
"Cloister." [Screens] (2) 90, p. 152.
"Particulars." [Screens] (2) 90, p. 152-153.
5927. SKILLINGS, Roger
"Bird Feeder in the Rain." [VirQR] (66:4) Aut 90, p. 664-665.
"The Way Down." [VirQR] (66:4) Aut 90, p. 665-666.
5928. SKILLMAN, Judith
"The Accident of Water." [GreenMR] (NS 4:1) Spr-Sum 90, p. 66-67.
"Drawing Peonies." [SpoonRQ] (15:3) Sum 90, p. 13-14.
"The Flaws of the World." [WillowS] (26) Spr 90, p. 30-31.
"For a Delirious Child." [NegC] (10:2/3) 90, p. 108-109.
"The Foundation." [SpoonRQ] (15:3) Sum 90, p. 15-16.
"Foxglove." [SwampR] (6) Sum-Fall 90, p. 71-72.
"Gourds." [PoetryNW] (31:4) Wint 90-91, p. 24.
"A Painter's Alphabet." [PoetryNW] (31:1) Spr 90, p. 27.
"The Queen of Fatigue." [PoetryNW] (31:1) Spr 90, p. 26-27.
"A Religion." [NowestR] (28:3/29:1) 90-91, p. 72.

SKILLMAN

"Seepage." [NowestR] (28:3/29:1) 90-91, p. 70-71.
"Sien." [SpoonRQ] (15:3) Sum 90, p. 14.
"The Woman with Fallen Breasts." [YellowS] (33) Spr 90, p. 17.
5929. SKINNER, Jeffrey
"Carver." [Atlantic] (266:5) N 90, p. 124.
"The Delicates." [OhioR] (45) 90, p. 76.
"Girl in a Dogwood Tree." [CumbPR] (9:2) Spr 90, p. 36.
"Late Afternoon, Late in the Twentieth Century." [OhioR] (45) 90, p. 74-75.
"The Ocean All Day, All Night." [SouthernR] (26:4) O 90, p. 902-903.
"Pastoral." [HampSPR] (Anthology 1975-1990) 90, p. 201.
5930. SKINNER, Knute
"The Bears." [HolCrit] (27:3) Je 90, p. 17.
"Warnings." [NewYorkQ] (43) Fall 90, p. 78.
5931. SKLAR, Morty
"Getting Called In" (for Vicki, teaching in Oshamanbe). [Spirit] (10:2) 90, p.
155-156.
5932. SKLAREW, Myra
"Learning to Lead." [LullwaterR] (1:1) Spr 90, p. 12-13.
5933. SKLOOT, Floyd
"1939." [Northeast] (NS 5:3) Wint 90-91, p. 4-5.
"At Home." [WritersF] (16) Fall 90, p. 54.
"Blank Spots." [TarRP] (30:1) Fall 90, p. 33-34.
"Dinnertime." [Paint] (17:33/34) Spr-Aut 90, p. 7.
"Home Security." [GreensboroR] (48) Sum 90, p. 116.
"Max at Table." [NowestR] (28:3/29:1) 90-91, p. 79.
"Morning Shadows" (Brooklyn, NY, 1955). [PoetryNW] (31:3) Aut 90, p. 8-9.
"Paganini and the Powers of Darkness." [GettyR] (3:3) Sum 90, p. 520-521.
"Sonatina for Surf and Sandpiper." [NowestR] (28:3/29:1) 90-91, p. 78.
"The Sunday Chef." [NoDaQ] (58:3) Sum 90, p. 150.
5934. SKOYLES, John
"Bryan, Ohio." [Agni] (29/30) 90, p. 132-133.
"Cousin Barbara." [Agni] (29/30) 90, p. 134.
"December 20, 1963." [NewMyths] (1:1) 90, p. 52-53.
5935. SKRATZ, G. P.
"Far Away / 9 X Kaneka Tota." [BlackBR] (12) Fall-Wint 90, p. 29.
5936. SKRIEF, D. P.
"Opened Views." [ParisR] (32:116) Fall 90, p. 172-173.
5937. SKRUPSKELIS, Viktoria
"Comet" (tr. of Judita Vaiciunaite, w. Stuart Friebert). [PoetryE] (30) Fall 90, p. 83.
"Eurydice" (tr. of Judita Vaiciunaite, w. Stuart Friebert). [Turnstile] (2:2) 90, p. 1.
"Little Gulls" (tr. of Judita Vaiciunaite, w. Stuart Friebert). [SenR] (20:2) Fall 90, p.
46.
"Museum Street" (tr. of Judita Vaiciunaite, w. Stuart Friebert). [Turnstile] (2:2) 90,
p. 2.
"Wild Raspberries" (tr. of Judita Vaiciunaite, w. Stuart Friebert). [SenR] (20:2) Fall
90, p. 48.
"Yellow Summer" (tr. of Judita Vaiciunaite, w. Stuart Friebert). [SenR] (20:2) Fall
90, p. 45.
"Zoological Garden" (tr. of Judita Vaiciunaite, w. Stuart Friebert). [SenR] (20:2)
Fall 90, p. 47.
5938. SLAPIKAS, Carolyn
"Toward the end." [NewYorkQ] (41) Spr 90, p. 107.
5939. SLATTERY, William
"Mitosis." [OnTheBus] (2:1, #5) Spr 90, p. 126.
5940. SLAUGHTER, Lynne Haley
"The Closet, the Clock, and the Thunder." [PoetryNW] (31:3) Aut 90, p. 43-45.
5941. SLAUGHTER, William
"I Stroke You with All My Years" (tr. of Bei Ling, w. Jin Zhong). [Gargoyle]
(37/38) 90, p. 9.
5942. SLAVENS, Kerry (Kerry Ione)
"American Rain." [Descant] (21:1, #68) Spr 90, p. 108-109.
"Have Seen the Silence." [Descant] (21:1, #68) Spr 90, p. 110.
"Poem About a Neighbour." [Descant] (21:1, #68) Spr 90, p. 111.
"Whaling Station Bay." [PoetryC] (11:1) Spr 90, p. 27.
5943. SLAVITT, David R.
"The Wound." [Boulevard] (4:3/5:1, #12/13) Spr 90, p. 164-169.

5944. SLAYMAKER, Bob
"What King George Says." [Contact] (9:56/57/58) Spr 90, p. 23.
5945. SLAYTON, Ann
"Night City." [Pembroke] (22) 90, p. 38.
"The Spell." [Pembroke] (22) 90, p. 39-41.
5946. SLEIGH, Tom
"Dear Customer." [Raritan] (10:2) Fall 90, p. 26.
"Ending." [Agni] (31/32) 90, p. 368-385.
"In June." [Raritan] (10:2) Fall 90, p. 27-29.
"Intelligence." [Pequod] (31) 90, p. 115-117.
"The Physical." [Pequod] (31) 90, p. 112-114.
5947. SLICER, Deborah
"Thinking of Kierkegaard." [CutB] (34) Sum-Fall 90, p. 62.
5948. SLOAN, Margy
"The Argument Needs, and Shall Receive." [Talisman] (4) Spr 90, p. 12-13.
5949. SLOWINSKI, Stephanie
"Death of the Lion Tamer." [GreensboroR] (48) Sum 90, p. 19-20.
"The Flower Artist, Darke County Fair." [GreensboroR] (48) Sum 90, p. 18-19.
"The Lie." [SouthernPR] (30:1) Spr 90, p. 66-67.
"The Romantic Age." [CimR] (93) O 90, p. 42-43.
"The Sea Widow." [SouthernPR] (30:1) Spr 90, p. 48-49.
"Thin Man's Litany." [PoetC] (22:1) Fall 90, p. 29.
5950. SLYMAN, Ernest
"Origin of the Species." [LaurelR] (24:1) Wint 90, p. 11.
5951. SMAILS, William
"Autumn 1963." [BellArk] (6:1) Ja-F 90, p. 11.
"The Pacific Electric Power Plant." [BellArk] (6:1) Ja-F 90, p. 21.
"Socrates." [BellArk] (6:6) N-D 90, p. 12.
5952. SMALLFIELD, Edward
"Blood." [Caliban] (9) 90, p. 62.
5953. SMARR, Janet Levarie
"Two Poems for Kenneth Burke." [Hellas] (1:2) Fall 90, p. 220.
"Untitled: Beware in bloom those fleeting boughs." [Hellas] (1:2) Fall 90, p. 222.
"Untitled: It's the old spring again, flowers as always." [Hellas] (1:2) Fall 90, p. 221.
"Untitled: Who shall sing if I don't sing." [Hellas] (1:2) Fall 90, p. 223.
5954. SMART, Carolyn
"Storms." [Quarry] (39:2) Spr 90, p. 27.
5955. SMELCER, John
"Weeds." [DogRR] (9:1, #17) Spr 90, p. 7.
5956. SMETZER, Michael
"After You Left." [Wind] (20:66) 90, p. 17.
"A Kansas Anthem." [MidwQ] (32:1) Aut 90, p. 93.
5957. SMITH, Alex
"Exploded View." [PoetryUSA] (5:1) Spr 90, p. 13.
5958. SMITH, Anthony
"One Per Cent." [Pearl] (11) Sum 90, p. 39.
5959. SMITH, Arthur
"Beauty." [IndR] (13:2) Spr 90, p. 27-28.
"Bliss." [IndR] (13:2) Spr 90, p. 29.
"Childhood." [GeoR] (44:3) Fall 90, p. 412.
"First Kiss." [Iowa] (20:3) Fall 90, p. 67.
"In the Absence of Love, There Are Engines." [Iowa] (20:3) Fall 90, p. 66.
"Winter Annuals." [Poetry] (155:4) Ja 90, p. 264-265.
5960. SMITH, Bruce
"Amor Fati: Because We Own Nothing." [PartR] (57:3) Sum 90, p. 436-437.
"Blue Letters." [SouthwR] (75:3) Sum 90, p. 355.
"He Was Free." [AmerPoR] (19:5) S-O 90, p. 18.
"In the Absence of War." [Verse] (7:2) Sum 90, p. 90.
"Narcissus in the Maritime Provinces." [AmerPoR] (19:5) S-O 90, p. 18.
"Neruda in Ceylon, 1929." [AmerPoR] (19:5) S-O 90, p. 18.
"Photograph." [AntR] (48:4) Fall 90, p. 495.
"Song of No Account." [AmerPoR] (19:5) S-O 90, p. 18.
5961. SMITH, C. O.
"Birdhouse." [PacificR] (8) 90, p. 90.

5962. SMITH, Charlie
"Amnesia." [SouthernPR] (30:2) Fall 90, p. 64-65.
"Character Part." [Crazy] (38) Spr 90, p. 30-31.
"The Dogwood Tree." [KenR] (NS 12:3) Sum 90, p. 71-72.
"The Exile's Daughter." [Sonora] (18) Fall-Wint 90, p. 42.
"Incident on Canal." [Sonora] (18) Fall-Wint 90, p. 41.
"My Parents' Wedding." [AntR] (48:4) Fall 90, p. 486.
"The Nightmare." [WillowS] (26) Spr 90, p. 77.
"Redneck Riviera." [WillowS] (26) Spr 90, p. 76.
"Segunda Segundo" (Excerpt). [Pequod] (31) 90, p. 178-184.
"Stare." [KenR] (NS 12:3) Sum 90, p. 72.
"The Viewing." [SouthernPR] (30:2) Fall 90, p. 65.
"The Woman As Figure." [NewAW] (6) Spr 90, p. 83.
5963. SMITH, Dave
"Brown Shoes." [SouthernR] (26:3) Jl 90, p. 621-622.
"A Day Off." [SouthernR] (26:3) Jl 90, p. 624-625.
"Duck Pond." [AmerPoR] (19:3) My-Je 90, p. 36.
"Family Ground" (to C. Edward Russell, Jr.). [SouthernR] (26:3) Jl 90, p.
617-620.
"The History of the Queen City Hotel." [SouthernR] (26:3) Jl 90, p. 613-617.
"The Lion's Den." [SouthernR] (26:3) Jl 90, p. 622-623.
"The Matthews County Icehouse." [AmerPoR] (19:3) My-Je 90, p. 36.
"Soda Shop, 1950s." [SouthernR] (26:3) Jl 90, p. 625-627.
SMITH, David Glen
See GLEN-SMITH, David
5964. SMITH, David James
"The Blackcrowned Sparrow." [AntigR] (81/82) Spr-Sum 90, p. 8.
"Endpoint." [KanQ] (22:1/2) Wint-Spr 90, p. 75.
"Home." [TarRP] (30:1) Fall 90, p. 24.
"Moving." [AntigR] (81/82) Spr-Sum 90, p. 7.
"Roses." [Contact] (9:56/57/58) Spr 90, p. 40.
"Wild Chrysanthemums." [TarRP] (30:1) Fall 90, p. 24-26.
5965. SMITH, Edward R.
"The Paterson Going-Away Poem" (with Joel Lewis). [Abraxas] (38/39) 90, p. 144.
5966. SMITH, Grace Haynes
"The Sure Wild Glittering Call." [AnthNEW] 90, p. 18.
5967. SMITH, J. D.
"Angels." [DenQ] (25:2) Fall 90, p. 44-45.
"Coffee." [SenR] (20:2) Fall 90, p. 66-72.
"Nocturne" (reprinted from #18, 1989). [Kaleid] (20) Wint-Spr 90, p. 114.
"Shortness" (reprinted from #18, 1989). [Kaleid] (20) Wint-Spr 90, p. 114.
"The Silence of Trees." [ManhatPR] (11) [89?], p. 18-19.
SMITH, James Sutherland
See SUTHERLAND-SMITH, James
5968. SMITH, Jennifer E.
"Disrespect." [BlackALF] (24:3) Fall 90, p. 550-551.
"Reactionary Deeds." [BlackALF] (24:3) Fall 90, p. 551.
5969. SMITH, Joan Jobe
"Direct Object of the Subjective Case." [WormR] (30:1, #117) 90, p. 20-21.
"Dorothy Lamour and Hedy Lamarr Put Together." [WormR] (30:1, #117) 90, p.
20.
"Female Mud Wrestling." [WormR] (30:1, #117) 90, p. 29.
"Frying Pork Chops Topless." [WormR] (30:1, #117) 90, p. 23-24.
"A Groovy Kind of Love." [WormR] (30:1, #117) 90, p. 24-25.
"Guff." [WormR] (30:1, #117) 90, p. 18-19.
"Heartthrobs." [WormR] (30:1, #117) 90, p. 19-20.
"I Never Went to Bed with Famous Astronaut." [WormR] (30:1, #117) 90, p.
21-22.
"Kafka the Spider." [WormR] (30:1, #117) 90, p. 30-31.
"The Machine Shop." [WormR] (30:1, #117) 90, p. 31.
"Machinist Poet" (for Fred Voss). [ChironR] (9:1) Spr 90, p. 13.
"The Marilyn Monroe Dress." [Pearl] (12) Fall-Wint 90, p. 58.
"Me and My Mother's Morphine." [WormR] (30:1, #117) 90, p. 27-j28.
"Mt. Everest." [WormR] (30:1, #117) 90, p. 25.
"On the Way to Heaven." [WormR] (30:1, #117) 90, p. 26-27.
"Organic Orchard." [WormR] (30:1, #117) 90, p. 29-30.

428

"Spar Sisters." [WormR] (30:1, #117) 90, p. 26.
"Subsequence." [WormR] (30:1, #117) 90, p. 28-29.
"We Drink a Lot When We're ɔgether." [WormR] (30:1, #117) 90, p. 32.
"What You Learn from Getting Burned." [WormR] (30:1, #117) 90, p. 18.
"When It Was Fun, It Was Very Very Fun." [WormR] (30:1, #117) 90, p. 22-23.
"Why Robert Wagner Married Natalie Wood." [WormR] (30:1, #117) 90, p. 16.
5970. SMITH, Jonathan C.
"Goodbye, Ruby Begonia." [Callaloo] (13:2) Spr 90, p. 301.
"MJQ." [Callaloo] (13:2) Spr 90, p. 302.
5971. SMITH, Jordan
"Audiophile." [Poetry] (155:4) Ja 90, p. 274.
"Rexford." [Crazy] (38) Spr 90, p. 47-48.
5972. SMITH, Kevin J.
"Going Fishing." [Parting] (3:1) Sum 90, p. 37.
5973. SMITH, Kirsten M.
"Gaming." [HiramPoR] (48/49) 90-91, p. 65.
5974. SMITH, Larry
"The Mill Gardens -- Dominic Remembers." [Pig] (16) 90, p. 54.
5975. SMITH, Marc
"My Father's Coat." [PoetryUSA] (5:3) Fall 90, p. 14.
SMITH, Martin Corless
See CORLESS-SMITH, Martin
5976. SMITH, Maurine
"Ceremony." [ChiR] (37:1) Wint 90, p. 54.
"Child and Shadows." [ChiR] (37:1) Wint 90, p. 56.
"The Dead." [ChiR] (37:1) Wint 90, p. 58.
"First Comer." [ChiR] (37:1) Wint 90, p. 55.
"I Am As Fair As I Would Be." [ChiR] (37:1) Wint 90, p. 62.
"Joy." [ChiR] (37:1) Wint 90, p. 54.
"The Keen Edge." [ChiR] (37:1) Wint 90, p. 62.
"Lullaby." [ChiR] (37:1) Wint 90, p. 58.
"Muted." [ChiR] (37:1) Wint 90, p. 57.
"October." [ChiR] (37:1) Wint 90, p. 61.
"On the Balustrade." [ChiR] (37:1) Wint 90, p. 60-61.
"Swallows Brush a Pool." [ChiR] (37:1) Wint 90, p. 60.
"They, the Gardeners." [ChiR] (37:1) Wint 90, p. 61.
"This Is Loneliness." [ChiR] (37:1) Wint 90, p. 60.
"Waiting." [ChiR] (37:1) Wint 90, p. 57.
"Wind." [ChiR] (37:1) Wint 90, p. 62.
"You Are Troubled." [ChiR] (37:1) Wint 90, p. 56.
5977. SMITH, Michael
"It a Come." [LitR] (34:1) Fall 90, p. 91-92.
5978. SMITH, Patricia
"The Awakening." [PoetryUSA] (5:3) Fall 90, p. 14.
5979. SMITH, Patrick
"Driving North." [OnTheBus] (2:1, #5) Spr 90, p. 128.
"Home for Christmas." [OnTheBus] (2:1, #5) Spr 90, p. 127-128.
5980. SMITH, R. T.
"Ahab." [InterPR] (16:2) Fall 90, p. 96.
"Bentwood." [EngJ] (79:6) O 90, p. 95.
"Birthstone." [NoDaQ] (58:3) Sum 90, p. 77-78.
"Brieves from *The Book of Kells*." [Poetry] (155:4) Ja 90, p. 259.
"The Chinese Pornographer." [KanQ] (22:1/2) Wint-Spr 90, p. 62.
"Fallen Hawk." [CumbPR] (10:1) Fall 90, p. 43-44.
"From the Second Story" (Second Prize). [Crucible] (26) Fall 90, p. 49.
"Grackles." [InterPR] (16:2) Fall 90, p. 99.
"Ice Pine." [InterPR] (16:2) Fall 90, p. 100.
"Legacy." [SouthernPR] (30:2) Fall 90, p. 55-56.
"Lustre." [FloridaR] (17:2) Fall-Wint 90, p. 102-103.
"Playing the Bones." [InterPR] (16:2) Fall 90, p. 97.
"Poe on Sullivan's Island." [Poem] (63) My 90, p. 1-3.
"Proserpine in Autumn." [PoetC] (21:2) Wint 90, p. 25-26.
"Scribe." [Poem] (63) My 90, p. 4.
"Second Waking." [CumbPR] (10:1) Fall 90, p. 45.
"Sloe Gin." [LullwaterR] (2:1) Wint 90, p. 72-73.
"Susan Gilbert Dickinson, 1887." [PoetC] (21:2) Wint 90, p. 24.

"Widow's Grief." [HiramPoR] (48/49) 90-91, p. 66.
"Woodwork." [InterPR] (16:2) Fall 90, p. 98.
"Words Against Grief." [KanQ] (22:1/2) Wint-Spr 90, p. 60-61.
5981. SMITH, Renée
"More Zen?" [Bogg] (62) 90, p. 28.
5982. SMITH, Ricky K.
"A Coalminer's Last Shift." [EmeraldCR] (1990) c89, p. 29.
5983. SMITH, Robert L.
"When the Pond Was Opened." [Hellas] (1:1) Spr 90, p. 67-68.
5984. SMITH, Rod
"Caution Contains." [WashR] (16:1) Je-Jl 90, p. 14.
"Madison National Bank, Washington, DC Member FDIC." [WashR] (16:1) Je-Jl
90, p. 14.
"The Myth of the Primal Horde." [WashR] (16:1) Je-Jl 90, p. 14.
5985. SMITH, Ron
"Learner's Permit on Skyline Drive." [KenR] (NS 12:3) Sum 90, p. 113-114.
"Repairs." [KenR] (NS 12:3) Sum 90, p. 114-115.
"Washington County, Georgia, 1942." [Verse] (7:2) Sum 90, p. 89.
5986. SMITH, Russell
"Parolles." [AntigR] (83) Aut 90, p. 36.
5987. SMITH, Steven
"Contest Winner. 1912." [Dandel] (17:1) Spr-Sum 90, p. 40.
5988. SMITH, Stevie
"The boat that took my love away." [ChiR] (37:1) Wint 90, p. 38.
"Not Waving But Drowning." [ChiR] (37:1) Wint 90, p. 37.
SMITH, Sybil Woods
    See WOODS-SMITH, Sybil
5989. SMITH, Thomas Michael
"Nameless." [PoetryUSA] (5:1) Spr 90, p. 14.
5990. SMITH, Thomas R.
"The Plowshare" (After a scene in Pagnol's film, "Harvest"). [HighP] (5:2) Fall 90,
p. 104-105.
"Spiral Weeds Under the Water." [HighP] (5:2) Fall 90, p. 106-107.
5991. SMITH, Tom
"Herod Piper." [BelPoJ] (41:2) Wint 90-91, p. 19.
5992. SMITH, William Jay
"After the War" (tr. of Yunna Moritz, w. Vera Dunham). [AmerPoR] (19:6) N-D 90,
p. 42.
"And Stands Reflected in the Mirror Across the Room" (tr. of Yunna Moritz, w.
Vera Dunham). [AmerPoR] (19:6) N-D 90, p. 42.
"A Bad Memory" (tr. of Aleksandr Tkachenko, w. Vera Dunham). [AmerPoR]
(19:6) N-D 90, p. 43.
"Dead Still" (tr. of Nina Cassian). [NewYorker] (65:46) 1 Ja 90, p. 30.
"Enclosed Field" (tr. of Yves Broussard). [Trans] (23) Spr 90, p. 149-151.
"Epitaphs" (4 poems). [HampSPR] (Anthology 1975-1990) 90, p. 178.
"Extraordinary Performance" (tr. of Nina Cassian). [AmerPoR] (19:1) Ja-F 90, p.
25.
"Famine" (tr. of Guy Goffette). [Trans] (23) Spr 90, p. 93.
"The House of Childhood" (tr. of Françoise Han). [Trans] (23) Spr 90, p. 165-166.
"In April" (tr. of Yunna Moritz, w. Vera Dunham). [AmerPoR] (19:6) N-D 90, p.
42.
"In the Café" (tr. of Nicole de Pontcharra). [Trans] (23) Spr 90, p. 143.
"Letters" (tr. of Aleksandr Tkachenko, w. Vera Dunham). [AmerPoR] (19:6) N-D
90, p. 43.
"Life Voyage" (tr. of Andrée Chedid). [Trans] (23) Spr 90, p. 46.
"Man Still Stands" (tr. of Andrée Chedid). [Trans] (23) Spr 90, p. 47.
"The Players." [BelPoJ] (40:4) Sum 90, p. 47-49.
"Ready for Goodbye" (tr. of Nina Cassian). [AmerPoR] (19:1) Ja-F 90, p. 26.
"Sacrilege" (tr. of Nina Cassian, w. Petre Solomon). [AmerPoR] (19:1) Ja-F 90, p.
26.
"Self-Portrait" (tr. of Nina Cassian). [AmerPoR] (19:1) Ja-F 90, p. 25.
"Three Lakes" (tr. of Aleksandr Tkachenko, w. Vera Dunham). [AmerPoR] (19:6)
N-D 90, p. 43.
5993. SMITH, Willie
"The Lyrical Trees." [PoetryUSA] ([5:4?]) Wint 90, p. 11.
"Stuffing It." [PoetryUSA] ([5:4?]) Wint 90, p. 10.

"Wood Stove Complaint." [PoetryUSA] ([5:4?]) Wint 90, p. 10.
5994. SMITH-BOWERS, Cathy
"Tordon." [SouthernPR] (30:1) Spr 90, p. 62.
5995. SMITH-SOTO, Mark
"Andrenaline Nights" (Excerpt, tr. of Carmen Olle). [InterPR] (16:1) Spr 90, p. 81, 83.
"Black Woman" (tr. of Nancy Morejon). [InterPR] (16:1) Spr 90, p. 41, 43.
"Cage of Mirrors, or Man's Conscience" (tr. of Emilia Ayarza de Herrera). [InterPR] (16:1) Spr 90, p. 21-29.
"Cannon Time Comes Flying" (tr. of Ana Istaru). [InterPR] (16:1) Spr 90, p. 31-35.
"The Cycles" (Selection: Part III, tr. of Jeanette Miller). [InterPR] (16:1) Spr 90, p. 91.
"Exile" (tr. of Alaide Fopa). [InterPR] (16:1) Spr 90, p. 53.
"The Great Mammoth" (tr. of Iris Zavala). [InterPR] (16:1) Spr 90, p. 89.
"Here Is the Earth" (Selections, tr. of Cecilia Bustamante). [InterPR] (16:1) Spr 90, p. 77, 79.
"Horse Aflame" (tr. of Delia Dominguez). [InterPR] (16:1) Spr 90, p. 45.
"In the Beginning" (tr. of Michele Najlis). [InterPR] (16:1) Spr 90, p. 67.
"In This Night, In This World" (For Martha Isabel Moia, tr. of Alejandra Pizarnik). [InterPR] (16:1) Spr 90, p. 9, 11.
"The Indians" (tr. of Jean Aristeguieta). [InterPR] (16:1) Spr 90, p. 105, 107.
"Learning to Sing" (tr. of Moravia Ochoa Lopez). [InterPR] (16:1) Spr 90, p. 73, 75.
"The Mad Woman at the Church Door." (tr. of Fina Garcia Marruz). [InterPR] (16:1) Spr 90, p. 37, 39.
"The Mothers" (from "Apocalipsis XX," tr. of Sara de Ibañes). [InterPR] (16:1) Spr 90, p. 93, 95.
"No More" (tr. of Idea Vilarino). [InterPR] (16:1) Spr 90, p. 97.
"Offended Moon" (tr. of Rosario Ferre). [InterPR] (16:1) Spr 90, p. 85, 87.
"Poems of the Erotic Left" (tr. of Ana Maria Rodas). [InterPR] (16:1) Spr 90, p. 55-60.
"The Sack of Shadows Poured Down Cold" (tr. of Ana Maria Iza). [InterPR] (16:1) Spr 90, p. 47.
"The Shadowy Men" (To the natives of Terradentro, tr. of Matilde Espinosa de Perez). [InterPR] (16:1) Spr 90, p. 17, 19.
"Songs of Fear and Blasphemy" (Selection: Song X, tr. of Violeta Luna). [InterPR] (16:1) Spr 90, p. 49, 51.
"That Is the Image" (tr. of Diana Moran). [InterPR] (16:1) Spr 90, p. 69, 71.
"Tin Laughter" (tr. of Alcira Cardona Torrico). [InterPR] (16:1) Spr 90, p. 13, 15.
"Unsuitable Woman" (tr. of Thelma Nava). [InterPR] (16:1) Spr 90, p. 65.
"What a Mortal Thirst for God Shakes Loose inside Me" (tr. of Enriqueta Ochoa). [InterPR] (16:1) Spr 90, p. 61, 63.
5996. SMITHER, Elizabeth
"Effleurage." [Verse] (7:2) Sum 90, p. 28.
"A Small Potato Crop." [Verse] (7:2) Sum 90, p. 28.
"The World of St Francis." [Verse] (7:2) Sum 90, p. 29.
5997. SMITS, Ronald
"The Deer at Dusk." [ThRiPo] (35/36) 90, p. 69.
"The Pennsylvania Turnpike." [LakeSR] (24) 90, p. 4.
"Trajectories." [PoetC] (22:1) Fall 90, p. 32.
5998. SMOCK, Frederick
"At a Bookstore in the Metropolis." [AmerV] (21) Wint 90, p. 105.
"Poem Written at the Algonquin Hotel." [PoetC] (21:3) Spr 90, p. 18.
5999. SMOCZYK, Krzysztof
"XXX. But whom to blame" (tr. by Jerzy Jarniewicz). [TampaR] (3) 90, p. 88.
"Winter" (tr. by Jerzy Jarniewicz). [TampaR] (3) 90, p. 87.
6000. SMYTH, Gerard
"Celtic Landscape." [Quarry] (39:1) Wint 90, p. 95.
6001. SNEFF, Priscilla
"Let a Man." [PartR] (57:3) Sum 90, p. 430.
"The Map and the City" (Thessaloniki, Greece). [SouthwR] (75:3) Sum 90, p. 378.
6002. SNELL, Janet
"A Different Version of Noah's Arc." [Gargoyle] (37/38) 90, p. 75.
6003. SNELLING, Kenneth
"Grandpa." [HolCrit] (27:5) D 90, p. 17.

431

6004. SNIDER, Clifton
"Adam." [OnTheBus] (2:2/3:1, #6/7) Sum-Fall 90 Wint-Spr 91, p. 187.
"Proserpine" (after the painting by D.G. Rossetti). [Bogg] (62) 90, p. 15.
"Scribble Reduction." [ChironR] (9:1) Spr 90, p. 23.
"Sophia" (after a Painting by Leonardo da Vinci). [Pearl] (10) Spr 90, p. 7.
"Two Icons" (for Marilyn Monroe and Virginia Woolf). [Pearl] (12) Fall-Wint 90, p. 28.
6005. SNODGRASS, W. D.
"Adolf Hitler" (16 April 1945). [AmerPoR] (19:4) Jl-Ag 90, p. 34.
"As A Child, Sleepless." [Poetry] (157:2) N 90, p. 67.
"Autumn Variations." [Poetry] (157:2) N 90, p. 63-66.
"Dr. Joseph Goebbels" (20 April 1945). [AmerPoR] (19:4) Jl-Ag 90, p. 36.
"Dr. Joseph Goebbels, Minister for Propaganda" (16 April 1945). [AmerPoR] (19:4) Jl-Ag 90, p. 34-35.
"Dr. Joseph Goebbels, Minister for Propaganda" (23 April 1945). [AmerPoR] (19:4) Jl-Ag 90, p. 36-37.
"Lan Quan Lijorn" (tr. of Jaufre Rudel). [HampSPR] (Anthology 1975-1990) 90, p. 241-242.
"Love Lamp." [Salm] (88/89) Fall 90-Wint 91, p. 367.
"The Midnight Carnival: Tunnel of Romance." [Salm] (88/89) Fall 90-Wint 91, p. 368-370.
"One Wish Left" (tr. of Mihai Eminescu). [NegC] (10:2/3) 90, p. 153, 155.
"Reichsmarschal Hermann Göring" (13 April 1945). [AmerPoR] (19:4) Jl-Ag 90, p. 33.
"Reichsmarschal Hermann Göring" (20 April 1945). [AmerPoR] (19:4) Jl-Ag 90, p. 35.
"Rendezvous" (tr. of Mihai Eminescu). [NegC] (10:2/3) 90, p. 149, 151.
6006. SNOEK, Kees
"The Awl in the Dark" (tr. of Hans Lodeizen). [Vis] (34) 90, p. 39.
"Calamity" (tr. of Gerrit Achterberg). [Vis] (34) 90, p. 33.
"Dream Judgment" (tr. of Gerrit Achterberg). [Vis] (34) 90, p. 31.
"Everywhere" (tr. of Hans Lodeizen). [Vis] (34) 90, p. 38.
"High Time" (tr. of Hans Vlek). [Vis] (34) 90, p. 47.
"In Profundis" (tr. of Gerrit Achterberg). [Vis] (33) 90, p. 47.
"Lying Nights" (tr. of Hans Andreus). [Vis] (34) 90, p. 42.
"Night" (tr. of Paul Rodenko). [Vis] (34) 90, p. 34.
"Notion of Color in Absence of Skin" (tr. of K. Schippers). [Vis] (34) 90, p. 45.
"Our Man in Prague" (tr. of Hans van de Waarsenburg). [Vis] (34) 90, p. 50.
"Slow" (tr. of Hans Lodeizen). [Vis] (34) 90, p. 40.
"Somnambule" (tr. of Gerrit Achterberg). [Vis] (34) 90, p. 31.
"Thebe" (tr. of Gerrit Achterberg). [Vis] (34) 90, p. 32.
"To Winter" (tr. of Jan Hanlo). [Vis] (34) 90, p. 35.
"Verse for 7 June '51" (tr. of Jan Hanlo). [Vis] (34) 90, p. 38.
6007. SNOEK, Paul
"Avonden." [Farm] (7:1) Spr 90, p. 72.
"De Vogelschrik." [Farm] (7:1) Spr 90, p. 68, 70.
"Evenings" (tr. by Kendall Dunkelberg). [Farm] (7:1) Spr 90, p. 73.
"Landscapes" (tr. by Kendall Dunkelberg). [Farm] (7:1) Spr 90, p. 75-79.
"Landschappen." [Farm] (7:1) Spr 90, p. 74-78.
"Park Poem" (tr. by C. J. Stevens). [NewRena] (8:1, #24) Spr 90, p. 17.
"Parkgedlicht." [NewRena] (8:1, #24) Spr 90, p. 16.
"Poem for Beginners" (tr. by Claire Nicolas White). [Trans] (24) Fall 90, p. 34.
"Poem for the Day After Tomorrow" (tr. by Claire Nicolas White). [Trans] (24) Fall 90, p. 33.
"The Scarecrow" (tr. by Kendall Dunkelberg). [Farm] (7:1) Spr 90, p. 69, 71.
"A Secret Better Kept to Yourself" (tr. by Claire Nicolas White). [Trans] (24) Fall 90, p. 35.
"Staande Aan de Lange Leugen." [NewRena] (8:1, #24) Spr 90, p. 18.
"Standing at the Long Lie" (tr. by C. J. Stevens). [NewRena] (8:1, #24) Spr 90, p. 19.
6008. SNOTHERLY, Mary C.
"Starlings: The Dark and Light of It." [SouthernPR] (30:1) Spr 90, p. 60-61.
6009. SNOWDEN, Robert
"Dear Jane." [Arc] (24) Spr 90, p. 22-24.
6010. SNYDAL, James
"After Going Down to His Kitchen at Seven." [DogRR] (9:1, #17) Spr 90, p. 35.

6011. SNYDAL, Laurence
"Torn Ligament." [Hellas] (1:2) Fall 90, p. 248.
6012. SNYDER, J. K
"Ariel Later" (Whitehall. November 1, 1611). [AntigR] (81/82) Spr-Sum 90, p. 186.
6013. SNYDER, Margery
"1999." [OnTheBus] (2:2/3:1, #6/7) Sum-Fall 90 Wint-Spr 91, p. 188-189.
6014. SNYDER, Tom
"The Return." [BellR] (13:2, #28) Fall 90, p. 13.
6015. SOABA, Russell
"Kuburabasu." [Manoa] (2:1) Spr 90, p. 52.
"Pacification Rites" (For the Villager). [Manoa] (2:1) Spr 90, p. 51.
"Third Stanza" (To the memory of Stephen M., the first Anuki martyr). [Manoa]
(2:1) Spr 90, p. 50.
SOBEK, María Herrera
See HERRERA-SOBEK, María
6016. SOBIN, Anthony
"Another Birthday -- Falling the Seventy Stories." [PassN] (11:1) Sum 90, p. 8.
"April Snow." [CimR] (91) Ap 90, p. 69-71.
"Signs of Stress." [CimR] (91) Ap 90, p. 66.
"Sometimes My Brain." [CimR] (91) Ap 90, p. 67-68.
"Waking with Influenza." [PassN] (11:1) Sum 90, p. 8.
6017. SOBIN, Gustaf
"At the Gateways of Aerea" (tr. of Rene Char). [Sulfur] (10:1, #26) Spr 90, p.
76-77.
"Celebrating Giacometti" (tr. of Rene Char). [Sulfur] (10:1, #26) Spr 90, p. 78-79.
"Cherishing Thouzon" (tr. of Rene Char). [Sulfur] (10:1, #26) Spr 90, p. 75.
"Convergence of Multiples" (tr. of Rene Char). [Sulfur] (10:1, #26) Spr 90, p. 78.
"Lied of the Fig Tree" (tr. of Rene Char). [Sulfur] (10:1, #26) Spr 90, p. 80.
"The Merciful Thirst" (tr. of Rene Char). [Sulfur] (10:1, #26) Spr 90, p. 78.
"Mirage of the Needles" (tr. of Rene Char). [Sulfur] (10:1, #26) Spr 90, p. 76.
"October's Judgment" (tr. of Rene Char). [Sulfur] (10:1, #26) Spr 90, p. 80.
"Septentrion" (tr. of Rene Char). [Sulfur] (10:1, #26) Spr 90, p. 79.
"Servant" (tr. of Rene Char). [Sulfur] (10:1, #26) Spr 90, p. 81.
"Slowness of the Future" (tr. of Rene Char). [Sulfur] (10:1, #26) Spr 90, p. 81.
"The Vicinities of Alsace" (tr. of Rene Char). [Sulfur] (10:1, #26) Spr 90, p. 77.
6018. SOCOLOW, Elizabeth Anne
"At the Horizon, Prometheus." [Ometeca] (1:2/2:1) 89-90, p. 35-43.
"Breakthrough." [Nimrod] (34:1) Fall-Wint 90, p. 58.
"Gull." [Nimrod] (34:1) Fall-Wint 90, p. 57.
"Reification: Europe, Spring 1990." [Nimrod] (34:1) Fall-Wint 90, p. 59.
6019. SÖDERGRAN, Edith
"Instinct" (tr. by Leif Sjöberg and Daisy Aldan). [PoetryE] (30) Fall 90, p. 97.
SOIKU, Shigematsu
See SHIGEMATSU, Soiku
SOJUN, Ikkyu
See IKKYU, Sojun
6020. SOKOLOV, Vladimir
"December 14, 1988" (the day of the Armenian earthquake, tr. by Oleg Atbashian
and Maureen Hurley). [PoetryUSA] (5:2) Sum 90, p. 14.
6021. SOLARCZYK, Bart
"In Your Absence." [Bogg] (62) 90, p. 37.
6022. SOLARI, Rose
"The Weather." [MissR] (19:1/2, #55/56) 90, p. 275-276.
6023. SOLDO, John J.
"His Return and Revelation" (after Will Inman's "the latest births of the mother").
[Wind] (20:66) 90, p. 40-41.
"Lizard." [Outbr] (21) 90, p. 73.
6024. SOLDOFSKY, Alan
"Ghazal." [AntR] (48:4) Fall 90, p. 497.
6025. SOLENSTEN, John (John M.)
"Dakota Station." [RagMag] (8:2) 90, p. 62.
"Migrations." [Farm] (7:2) Fall 90, p. 123.
"Reading the 1989 Iowa Trapping Regulations." [RagMag] (8:2) 90, p. 63.
6026. SOLHEIM, James
"Blessed by Meteors and by the Benevolent Men of Space." [Poetry] (156:1) Ap 90,
p. 27-28.

"The Laws of Eddings." [NowestR] (28:1) 90, p. 68-79.
"The Man Who Measures Animals." [Iowa] (20:2) Spr-Sum 90, p. 9-10.
6027. SOLI, Sandra
"Bad Girl Goes Shopping." [NegC] (10:1) 90, p. 84-86.
6028. SOLIKH, Mukhammad
"A Day in the Life" (tr. by Oleg Atbashian and Maureen Hurley). [PoetryUSA] (5:2)
Sum 90, p. 15.
6029. SOLJAK, Katie
"Bodgie Love." [Pearl] (11) Sum 90, p. 42-43.
6030. SOLNICKI, Jill
"Night Rider." [Grain] (18:4) Wint 90, p. 34.
"Tired Blood." [Grain] (18:4) Wint 90, p. 35.
6031. SOLOMON, Arthur
"Leave-Taking." [ChamLR] (3:2, #6) Spr 90, p. 54-55.
6032. SOLOMON, Marvin
"A Dream." [Interim] (9:2) Fall-Wint 90-91, p. 18.
6033. SOLOMON, Petre
"Sacrilege" (tr. of Nina Cassian, w. William Jay Smith). [AmerPoR] (19:1) Ja-F 90,
p. 26.
6034. SOLOMON, Stanley J.
"Post-Modern: To a Literary Critic." [Bogg] (63) 90, p. 9.
"Songs" (From Christina Rossetti's "Song -- When I am dead, my dearest").
[Amelia] (6:2, #17) 90, p. 149.
"To Celia" (From the poem by Ben Jonson). [Amelia] (6:2, #17) 90, p. 149.
6035. SOLONCHE, J. R.
"Love Poem in the Library." [PoetL] (85:3) Fall 90, p. 43.
6036. SOLOTAROFF, Ted
"Male Image." [AmerPoR] (19:4) Jl-Ag 90, p. 32.
6037. SOLT, John
"Blue Background" (tr. of Katue Kitasono). [CityLR] (4) 90, p. 174.
"Blue Square" (tr. of Katue Kitasono). [CityLR] (4) 90, p. 175.
6038. SOLWAY, Arthur
"The Cocktail Hour." [PraS] (64:4) Wint 90, p. 46-48.
"Gone Fishing." [PraS] (64:4) Wint 90, p. 44-45.
6039. SOLWAY, David
"Bedrock" (for Karin). [PoetryC] (11:3) Fall 90, p. 12.
"Birds." [PoetryC] (11:3) Fall 90, p. 12.
"The Earthquake." [PoetryC] (11:3) Fall 90, p. 12.
"Jellyfish." [PartR] (57:1) Wint 90, p. 110-112.
"Mythology." [PoetryC] (11:3) Fall 90, p. 12.
"The Sign." [PoetryC] (11:3) Fall 90, p. 12.
6040. SOMERVILLE, Jane
"All the Pathos, All the Triumph." [GettyR] (3:1) Wint 90, p. 231-232.
"Betrayal." [Shen] (40:2) Sum 90, p. 66.
"Can You Say Hi." [Journal] (13:2) Fall-Wint 89-90, p. 22-23.
"The Garden Before Winter." [Shen] (40:2) Sum 90, p. 65.
"The Scene." [Shen] (40:2) Sum 90, p. 64.
6041. SOMMER, Piotr
"The Provinces" (tr. by Reuel K. Wilson). [Trans] (24) Fall 90, p. 195.
6042. SONDE, Susan
"American Gothic." [Bomb] (33) Fall 90, p. 89.
"Because of the Failure This Experiment Was." [OnTheBus] (2:1, #5) Spr 90, p.
129.
"Go on Vacation Once in a While." [Sonora] (19) Spr-Sum 90, p. 13-14.
"Lone Pine." [Bomb] (33) Fall 90, p. 89.
6043. SONENBERG, Maya
"A Few Things About the Earth." [Chelsea] (49) 90, p. 29-31.
6044. SONG, Cathy
"Birds of Paradise." [Shen] (40:4) Wint 90, p. 89-91.
"The Grammar of Silk." [Poetry] (157:1) O 90, p. 5-6.
"Mother on River Street." [Poetry] (157:1) O 90, p. 7-10.
"Things We Know by Heart." [Shen] (40:4) Wint 90, p. 92-93.
6045. SONGI
"Everything You Do" (tr. by Constantine Contogenis and Wolhee Choe). [PoetryE]
(30) Fall 90, p. 84.
"When Butterfly Sees Flower" (tr. by Constantine Contogenis and Wolhee Choe).

[PoetryE] (30) Fall 90, p. 84.
6046. SONIAT, Katherine
"Fortune." [OhioR] (45) 90, p. 50-51.
"In Spite of Forgetting." [NewEngR] (13:1) Fall 90, p. 151-153.
"Luster's Gate." [KanQ] (22:3) Sum 90, p. 71.
"Myrtle Tree." [PoetC] (21:2) Wint 90, p. 28.
"The Next Day." [NewOR] (17:3) Fall 90, p. 80.
"The Palm Sunday Race." [SouthwR] (75:1) Wint 90, p. 90.
"Rembrandt's Vanities." [SouthernR] (26:2) Ap 90, p. 349-350.
"Rose Cloth Tattering from the Barbed Wire." [Poetry] (155:6) Mr 90, p. 405-406.
"Sawdust." [KanQ] (22:3) Sum 90, p. 72.
"A Shared Life." [OhioR] (45) 90, p. 52-53.
"Strange Music." [Thrpny] (40) Wint 90, p. 29.
"Summer Inversion." [HampSPR] (Anthology 1975-1990) 90, p. 237.
"Toppled Columns, Blue Sky, and Sea." [SouthernR] (26:2) Ap 90, p. 351-352.
"Truck at the Top of the Field." [PennR] (4:2) 90, p. 54.
"What We Keep." [AntR] (48:1) Wint 90, p. 79.
"While We Speak." [LaurelR] (24:2) Sum 90, p. 48.
6047. SONNENBERG, Ben
"Better to Marry, or Better to Burn?" [Raritan] (9:4) Spr 90, p. 9-10.
"Madamina." [Nat] (250:18) 7 My 90, p. 646.
6048. SONNEVI, Göran
"Breaking up: that large feeling" (tr. by Rika Lesser). [PoetryE] (30) Fall 90, p. 59-60.
"A Child Is Not a Knife" (tr. by Rika Lesser). [PoetryE] (30) Fall 90, p. 61-62.
6049. SOOPKIAN, Touba
"Grandpa." [Pearl] (11) Sum 90, p. 56.
6050. SOPPER, F.
"Approaching a Solstice." [OnTheBus] (2:2/3:1, #6/7) Sum-Fall 90 Wint-Spr 91, p. 190.
SORALUZ, Luis Rebaza
See REBAZA SORALUZ, Luis
6051. SORENSEN, Sally Jo
"Beaker Street." [NegC] (10:1) 90, p. 87.
"Mrs. Ledbetter Confesses Events Preceding Her Husband's Demise." [LaurelR] (24:2) Sum 90, p. 15.
"Philadelphia." [SycamoreR] (2:1) Wint 90, p. 17.
6052. SØRENSEN, Villy
"Depression Weather" (from "Weather Days : Vejrdage," 1980, tr. by Paula Hostrup-Jessen). [CimR] (92) Jl 90, p. 43.
6053. SORENSON, Karen D.
"Georges Braque" (tr. of Paul Eluard, w. Malcolm Glass). [CumbPR] (9:2) Spr 90, p. 41.
"To Marc Chagall" (tr. of Paul Eluard, w. Malcolm Glass). [CumbPR] (9:2) Spr 90, p. 39.
6054. SORESCU, Marin
"After the Creation" (tr. by Adriana Varga and Stuart Friebert). [PoetryE] (29) Spr 90, p. 130.
"Alphabet" (tr. by Adriana Varga and Stuart Friebert). [HawaiiR] (14:1, #28) Wint 89-90, p. 41.
"Below the Horizon" (tr. by Adriana Varga and Stuart Friebert). [ArtfulD] (18/19) 90, p. 41.
"Gully" (tr. by Stravros Deligiorgis). [HampSPR] (Anthology 1975-1990) 90, p. 263.
"House Snake" (tr. by Adriana Varga and Stuart Friebert). [HawaiiR] (14:1, #28) Wint 89-90, p. 42.
"How?" (tr. by Adriana Varga and Stuart Friebert). [HawaiiR] (14:1, #28) Wint 89-90, p. 40.
"Let's Help" (tr. by Adriana Varga and Stuart Friebert). [ArtfulD] (18/19) 90, p. 40.
"Looking for Hegel's Portrait" (tr. by Adriana Varga and Stuart Friebert). [PoetryE] (29) Spr 90, p. 131.
"Pure Conversation with a Chinese Character" (tr. by Gabriela Dragnea and Stuart Friebert). [NewYorker] (66:15) 28 My 90, p. 36.
"Rift" (tr. by Adriana Varga and Stuart Friebert). [PoetryE] (29) Spr 90, p. 128-129.
"Signs" (tr. by Adriana Varga and Stuart Friebert). [PoetryE] (29) Spr 90, p. 133.
"Study of Repose" (tr. by Adriana Varga and Stuart Friebert). [HawaiiR] (14:1, #28)

Wint 89-90, p. 43.
"Thoughts" (tr. by Gabriela Dragnea and Stuart Friebert). [PoetryE] (29) Spr 90, p. 132.
6055. SORESTAD, Glen
"Cowboy Christ" (for Tony Clark). [Grain] (18:1) Spr 90, p. 16.
"Missiles for Artesia" (for Peter Christensen). [Grain] (18:1) Spr 90, p. 15.
"Mountain Morels." [Grain] (18:1) Spr 90, p. 17.
"Suitcases of Poetry" (for Earle). [Grain] (18:1) Spr 90, p. 14.
6056. SORNBERGER, Judith
"Judith, the Barren Widow, after Triumph." [PraS] (64:1) Spr 90, p. 51-52.
"Preparations." [PraS] (64:1) Spr 90, p. 52-53.
"Wallpapering to Patsy Cline" (for my mother and sister). [Calyx] (12:3) Sum 90, p. 36-37.
"We Laugh at Our Father's Dreams." [TarRP] (29:2) Spr 90, p. 44.
6057. SORRELL, J. E.
"Emily, Late March." [CanLit] (127) Wint 90, p. 31.
SOSA, Arturo Alvarez
See ALVAREZ-SOSA, Arturo
SOSEKI, Muso
See MUSO, Soseki
6058. SOTO, Gary
"Best Years." [IndR] (13:2) Spr 90, p. 24-26.
"The Gold Cannon." [Nat] (250:4) 29 Ja 90, p. 138.
"In Summer." [IndR] (13:2) Spr 90, p. 22-23.
"The Music at Home." [NewAW] (6) Spr 90, p. 72-73.
SOTO, Mark Smith
See SMITH-SOTO, Mark
6059. SOTO VÉLEZ, Clemente
"The Promised Land" (Selection: #18, tr. by Martín Espada and Camilio Pérez-Bustillo). [Agni] (29/30) 90, p. 200-201.
"The Wooden Horse" (Selection: #3, tr. by Martín Espada and Camilio Pérez-Bustillo). [Agni] (29/30) 90, p. 199.
6060. SOULAR, James
"Night in Ia Drang Valley." [BlackBR] (12) Fall-Wint 90, p. 19-20.
"No More Room." [BlackBR] (12) Fall-Wint 90, p. 18.
6061. SOUTH, Karen
"Hearing." [Abraxas] (38/39) 90, p. 132.
6062. SOUTHWICK, Marcia
"Fear of Angels" (for S. S.). [KenR] (NS 12:4) Fall 90, p. 103-104.
"Notes from the Tower." [KenR] (NS 12:4) Fall 90, p. 104-105.
"Xgtza." [Crazy] (38) Spr 90, p. 52-53.
SOUZA, Charmayne d'
See D'SOUZA, Charmayne
6063. SOWELL, Mary Harper
"From a Train Window." [Wind] (20:67) 90, p. 32.
"Katie Rosa Bradley" (1900-1936). [Wind] (20:67) 90, p. 31.
6064. SPACKS, Barry
"The Other." [OntR] (33) Fall-Wint 90-91, p. 24.
"Reading Rilke." [AntR] (48:1) Wint 90, p. 97.
"Squirrel Cage." [Sequoia] (33:2) Wint 90, p. 68.
6065. SPADY, Susan
"Carrying Eggs." [PoetryNW] (31:1) Spr 90, p. 44.
"Lately." [PoetryNW] (31:1) Spr 90, p. 42-44.
"'Perpetuum Mobile' for Two Pianos, from Bartok's Mikrokosmos" (for John). [NowestR] (28:3/29:1) 90-91, p. 77.
6066. SPALATIN, Ivana
"Antigone" (tr. of Ileana Malancioui, w. Daniela Gioseffi). [PoetryE] (29) Spr 90, p. 140.
6067. SPARA, Walter F.
"The Leavening." [EmeraldCR] (1990) c89, p. 56.
"Trimmer Man." [EmeraldCR] (1990) c89, p. 57.
6068. SPATOLA, Adriano
"Domus Poetica" (tr. by Graziella Sidoli). [Screens] (2) 90, p. 100.
6069. SPEAKES, Richard
"Journeyman." [PassN] (11:1) Sum 90, p. 3.

6070. SPEARS, Heather
"At Chicago Airport." [Event] (19:1) Spr 90, p. 35.
"Earthquake Time." [Arc] (25) Aut 90, p. 22.
"Execution of Pimps and Prostitutes, Busher, Iran, April 1989." [Arc] (25) Aut 90,
p. 24.
"Hind, Eating Fish in Denmark." [Arc] (25) Aut 90, p. 20-21.
"How Animals See." [Event] (19:1) Spr 90, p. 36-37.
"Human Acts." [Arc] (25) Aut 90, p. 25.
"The Human Head." [MalR] (90) Spr 90, p. 53-55.
"Melodi Grand Prix." [Event] (19:1) Spr 90, p. 38.
"Niagara Falls from the Air." [Arc] (25) Aut 90, p. 23.
"Paying Attention at Poetry Readings." [Arc] (25) Aut 90, p. 19.
"The Poem Walked Out." [Arc] (25) Aut 90, p. 26.
6071. SPECKLED SNAKE, Chief
"Chief Speckled Snake Reflects on Patterns in American History, 1829" (adapted by
Stephen Meats). [MidwQ] (31:2) Wint 90, p. 207-208.
6072. SPECTOR, Al
"Gridiron." [BrooklynR] (7) 90, p. 43.
"Moonshining." [ManhatPR] (11) [89?], p. 34.
6073. SPECTOR, Donna
"The Broken Chain." [JINJPo] (12:2) Aut 90, p. 13.
"Sometimes the Lovers." [PoetC] (21:3) Spr 90, p. 16-17.
"White Rose." [JlNJPo] (12:2) Aut 90, p. 14.
6074. SPECTOR, Robert Donald
"Saturday Track Meet." [Confr] (42/43) Spr-Sum 90, p. 128.
6075. SPEER, Laurel
"Colored Glass." [NegC] (10:2/3) 90, p. 59.
"Daddy's Girl." [OnTheBus] (2:2/3:1, #6/7) Sum-Fall 90 Wint-Spr 91, p. 191.
"The Desert O." [Pearl] (10) Spr 90, p. 10.
"Einstein Said." [PoetryC] (11:1) Spr 90, p. 26.
"Hag-Light." [Bogg] (63) 90, p. 66.
"I Never Had a Mother" (-- Emily Dickinson). [Pearl] (11) Sum 90, p. 14.
"Kids." [Paint] (17:33/34) Spr-Aut 90, p. 23.
"The Light, Today, Is Blue." [Bogg] (63) 90, p. 67.
"Our Mother." [PoetC] (21:2) Wint 90, p. 27.
"Reason, My Dear Maria, Brings Us to Proximity." [CoalC] (2) D 90, p. 8.
"Sandwich." [Bogg] (63) 90, p. 66-67.
"Savonarola at 19." [DustyD] (1:2) O 90, p. 12.
"Sin." [Bogg] (62) 90, p. 11.
"Valediction for Señor Lopez." [SlipS] (10) 90, p. 38.
"Zero & Herb." [DogRR] (9:1, #17) Spr 90, p. 47.
6076. SPENCE, Michael
"Beneath the Perseid Meteor Shower" (Bread Loaf, 1987). [SouthernR] (26:2) Ap
90, p. 341-342.
"The Darkest Season" (for Sharon Hashimoto). [SouthernR] (26:2) Ap 90, p. 343.
"The Fig Curtain of Atherton" (Queensland, Australia, 1986). [PoetryUSA] (5:2)
Sum 90, p. 12.
"Trails without Signs" (for my sister, Rosemarie). [PraS] (64:3) Fall 90, p. 85-92.
"Walking the Desert." [SycamoreR] (2:2) Sum 90, p. 35-36.
6077. SPENCER, Patricia
"Gramps." [EngJ] (79:8) D 90, p. 88.
6078. SPERANZA, Anthony
"The Girl in Sandy Hill Park." [Plain] (10:3) Spr 90, p. 25.
"In Chantland Hills." [Plain] (11:1) Fall 90, p. 15.
6079. SPHERES, Duane
"Steer Head." [BellArk] (6:5) S-O 90, p. 23.
6080. SPINELLI, Eileen
"Dreamer." [Footwork] 90, p. 93.
6081. SPINNER, Bettye T.
"Assertion." [EngJ] (79:7) N 90, p. 91.
6082. SPINOY, Erik
"Call This Blindness" (tr. by David Siefkin and Catharina Kochuyt). [Vis] (34) 90,
p. 14.
"Cloaks of Silence" (tr. by David Siefkin and Catharina Kochuyt). [Vis] (34) 90, p.
13.
"The Streets" (tr. by David Siefkin and Catharina Kochuyt). [Vis] (34) 90, p. 12.

437

SPINOY

"The Wall" (tr. by David Siefkin and Catharina Kochuyt). [Vis] (34) 90, p. 13.
6083. SPIRENG, Matthew J.
    "Elementary School." [CapeR] (25:2) Fall 90, p. 1.
6084. SPIRES, Elizabeth
    "The Nap." [KenR] (NS 12:3) Sum 90, p. 33-34.
    "The Wall." [WilliamMR] (28) 90, p. 48-49.
6085. SPIRO, Peter
    "Brian." [ColEng] (52:3) Mr 90, p. 278-279.
    "The Burial Detail." [Parting] (3:2) Wint 90-91, p. 9-10.
    "Lay Off." [ColEng] (52:3) Mr 90, p. 277-278.
    "Tired Stars." [Gypsy] (15) 90, p. 37.
    "Tired Stars." [OxfordM] (6:1) Spr-Sum 90, p. 68-69.
    "We All Need to Get Over the Bridge." [SlipS] (10) 90, p. 93-94.
    "Work." [Pig] (16) 90, p. 124-125.
6086. SPIVACK, Kathleen
    "The Bed." [SoCoast] (9) Fall 90, p. 56-57.
    "The Following Shadow." [BellR] (13:2, #28) Fall 90, p. 7.
    "Hilltop Meadow." [Ploughs] (16:1) Spr-Sum 90, p. 58-59.
    "How Night Falls." [Agni] (31/32) 90, p. 244.
    "Not Waving." [KanQ] (22:1/2) Wint-Spr 90, p. 36.
    "A Path: Monet." [KanQ] (22:1/2) Wint-Spr 90, p. 46.
6087. SPRING, Anne
    "Fire." [LullwaterR] (1:1) Spr 90, p. 74-75.
6088. SPRING, Justin
    "Art." [PassN] (11:2) Wint 90, p. 24.
    "Stolen Poems" (For Dixon Gato). [Turnstile] (2:1) 90, p. 109-112.
6089. SPRINGER, Christina
    "Wishlist" (for my sisters who think process is permanent." [SinW] (42) Wint
        90-91, p. 8-9.
6090. SPRINKLE, Annie
    "Section 4 of Andrea Dwarkin's Anti-Pornography Civil Rights Law Cut Up with a
        Paragraph from *Screw* Magazine." [KenR] (NS 12:2) Spr 90, p. 171.
6091. SPRYSZAK
    "Learning to Speak Spanish Cats Like Martyrs." [Asylum] (5:4) 90, p. 37-38.
6092. SRUBAS, Rachel
    "I Want to Marry You." [AnotherCM] (22) 90, p. 166-167.
6093. SRUT, Pavel
    "Adam's Wife" (tr. by Richard Katrovas). [IndR] (13:3) Fall 90, p. 81.
    "And You Don't Ask" (tr. by Richard Katrovas). [IndR] (13:3) Fall 90, p. 80.
    "Flags" (tr. by Richard Katrovas). [IndR] (13:3) Fall 90, p. 82.
    "The Trojan Horse" (tr. by Richard Katrovas). [IndR] (13:3) Fall 90, p. 79.
ST. . . .
    See also Saint . . .
6094. ST. ANDREWS, B. A.
    "Existential Cocktails." [NegC] (10:2/3) 90, p. 110-111.
    "The Flirt." [HighP] (5:1) Spr 90, p. 54-55.
    "Galahad's Gone." [ClockR] (6:2) 90, p. 75.
    "In the Garden of the Ming Scholar" (Wang Shin Tuan, Master of the Fishing Nets,
        Astor Court, Metropolitan Museum of Art). [PacificR] (8) 90, p. 8.
    "A Meditation on Vermeer." [GettyR] (3:2) Spr 90, p. 415-416.
    "Reading White Sands, 1945." [Confr] (44/45) Fall 90-Wint 91, p. 27.
    "When Your Best Friends Move to L. A." [SpoonRQ] (15:2) Spr 90, p. 21.
6095. ST. CLAIR, Philip
    "Coins." [SpoonRQ] (15:3) Sum 90, p. 25-26.
    "Cysts." [SpoonRQ] (15:3) Sum 90, p. 23-24.
    "Quitting." [SpoonRQ] (15:3) Sum 90, p. 21-22.
6096. ST. GEORGE, E. Y.
    "Bluemoon." [Grain] (18:3) Fall 90, p. 73.
    "Mushroom Woman." [Grain] (18:3) Fall 90, p. 72.
6097. ST. JOHN, David
    "A Fan Sketched with Silver Egrets" (after Mallarmé). [WestHR] (44:3) Aut 90, p.
        305-307.
    "Lonely People in Lonely Places." [HayF] (6) Sum 90, p. 37.
    "Merlin" (Italo Calvino, 1923-1985). [Antaeus] (64/65) Spr-Aut 90, p. 120-121.
    "Uptown Love Poem." [HayF] (6) Sum 90, p. 36.
    "Who Is She" (after Cavalcanti). [PartR] (57:3) Sum 90, p. 433.

6098. STAAL, Arie
"After All" (tr. of Hans Andreus). [Vis] (34) 90, p. 43.
"Billie Holiday" (tr. of Hans Vlek). [Vis] (34) 90, p. 45.
"Earlier" (tr. of Hans Lodeizen). [Vis] (34) 90, p. 40.
"February Sun" (tr. of Paul Rodenko). [Vis] (34) 90, p. 34.
"The Flexibility of Sorrow" (tr. of Hans Lodeizen). [Vis] (34) 90, p. 41.
"In the Park" (tr. of K. Schippers). [Vis] (34) 90, p. 43.
"My Son" (tr. of Hans Andreus). [Vis] (34) 90, p. 42.
"Sonnet" (tr. of Jan Hanlo). [Vis] (34) 90, p. 38.
"Together" (tr. of Leo Vroman, w. the author). [Vis] (34) 90, p. 35.
6099. STABNOW, Clayton M.
"A Killer of Darkness." [DogRR] (9:2, #18) Aut 90, p. 52.
"Question #53." [DogRR] (9:2, #18) Aut 90, p. 52.
6100. STAFFORD, Darrell
"Sacrifice." [SoCoast] (9) Fall 90, p. 39.
6101. STAFFORD, William
"Bad Dreams." [HampSPR] (Anthology 1975-1990) 90, p. 53.
"Birdsongs for the Red Phone." [Paint] (17:33/34) Spr-Aut 90, p. 6.
"Communion." [WeberS] (7:2) Fall 90, p. 47.
"Consolations." [VirQR] (66:3) Sum 90, p. 461.
"Cover Up." [ArtfulD] (18/19) 90, p. 12.
"Evolution." [Field] (42) Spr 90, p. 15.
"An Excursion." [ArtfulD] (18/19) 90, p. 13.
"For a Lost Child." [Field] (42) Spr 90, p. 13.
"Four A.M. on *Crusader*." [Agni] (31/32) 90, p. 185.
"Four Oak Leaves." [HampSPR] (Anthology 1975-1990) 90, p. 52-53.
"Going On." [Nat] (250:18) 7 My 90, p. 644.
"Hi There" (tr. of Shuntaro Tanikawa, w. Yorifumi Yaguchi). [ArtfulD] (18/19) 90,
    p. 15.
"How It Began." [HampSPR] (Anthology 1975-1990) 90, p. 51.
"Identities." [Sequoia] (33:2) Wint 90, p. 1.
"Learned at the Weavers' Barn." [BelPoJ] (40:4) Sum 90, p. 50.
"Looking Out." [WeberS] (7:2) Fall 90, p. 46.
"Not Marble Nor the Gilded Monuments." [WeberS] (7:2) Fall 90, p. 46.
"Our Kind." [HampSPR] (Anthology 1975-1990) 90, p. 52.
"Our Sky." [ChironR] (9:1) Spr 90, p. 22.
"Owning a Pearl." [Paint] (17:33/34) Spr-Aut 90, p. 5.
"Passing Along." [ArtfulD] (18/19) 90, p. 14.
"The Right Time." [Field] (42) Spr 90, p. 17.
"Snow." [BelPoJ] (40:4) Sum 90, p. 51.
"Story Time." [Field] (42) Spr 90, p. 14.
"Thinking for Berky." [CimR] (92) Jl 90, p. 132.
"Visiting." [HampSPR] (Anthology 1975-1990) 90, p. 51.
"Vita." [Agni] (31/32) 90, p. 184.
"Waiting for God." [ArtfulD] (18/19) 90, p. 11.
"Walking the Beach Under the Overcast." [Sequoia] (33:2) Wint 90, p. 2.
"The Way I Write." [VirQR] (66:3) Sum 90, p. 462.
"What They Taught Me in Soledad." [Nat] (251:19) 3 D 90, p. 710.
"What's in My Journal." [Field] (42) Spr 90, p. 16.
"Yes." [Sequoia] (33:2) Wint 90, p. 3.
6102. STAHL, Dick
"Closing Time." [Farm] (7:1) Spr 90, p. 35.
6103. STAHLECKER, Elizabeth
"Night Vision." [AmerPoR] (19:2) Mr-Ap 90, p. 42.
6104. STAINSBY, Martha
"Cinnamon Tea & Olive Liquor." [PoetryC] (11:2) Sum 90, p. 5.
"The Dancing Penguins of the Air." [PoetryC] (11:2) Sum 90, p. 5.
"A Schedule of Events." [PoetryC] (11:2) Sum 90, p. 5.
"Winter, Moving In." [PoetryC] (11:2) Sum 90, p. 5.
6105. STALCUP, Brenda
"Communal Darkroom." [CoalC] (2) D 90, p. 5.
"There Are Bones in the Meadow." [CoalC] (1) Ag 90, p. 35.
6106. STALEY, George
"601 Milford Point Road." [Plain] (10:2) Wint 90, p. 12.
6107. STAMLER, Susan (Susan D.)
"In the Silence of a Stormy Night." [PoetryUSA] ([5:4?]) Wint 90, p. 9.

439

"Perfidious, Ill-Timed Enzymes." [PoetryUSA] (5:3) Fall 90, p. 5.
"To Search Within." [PoetryUSA] (5:3) Fall 90, p. 5.
6108. STANDING, Sue
"Patrilineage." [Agni] (31/32) 90, p. 143-144.
"Wittgenstein's Prayer." [Agni] (31/32) 90, p. 142.
6109. STANDISH, Lorraine
"Beware of the Poet." [EmeraldCR] (1990) c89, p. 78.
6110. STANHOPE, Patrick
"Backwater Street, K.C., MO." [Pig] (16) 90, p. 33.
"Delivery." [KanQ] (22:3) Sum 90, p. 50.
"Self-Employed." [Pig] (16) 90, p. 34.
"Walking the Santa Fe Railhead." [Pig] (16) 90, p. 33.
"Walking the Santa Fe Railhead." [WebR] (14:2) Spr 90, p. 82-83.
6111. STANKARD-GREEN, Linda
"How Such a Thing Could Happen." [ChironR] (9:2) Sum 90, p. 15.
6112. STANKO, Mary Rudbeck
"Blind Faith." [Poem] (64) N 90, p. 46.
"A Foolish Consistency." [Poem] (64) N 90, p. 47.
"One for the Money." [Poem] (64) N 90, p. 45.
"Rite of Passage." [RagMag] (7:2) Spr 90, p. 57.
"Tornado." [Plain] (11:1) Fall 90, p. 36.
6113. STANLEY, George
"Mozart & Cold Cuts" (Flight 513, Vancouver-San Francisco, 1 June 1990). [CapilR] (2:4) Wint 90, p. 64-66.
"Poem: I'll listen to the news the day I die." [CapilR] (2:4) Wint 90, p. 63.
"Raft." [CapilR] (2:4) Wint 90, p. 67-68.
"San Francisco's Gone & Other Poems" (for Gerald, much love & in memory of Edward Dermott 'Ned' Doyle who taught me poetry . . .). [CapilR] (2:4) Wint 90, p. 37-68.
"The World Is the Case." [CapilR] (2:4) Wint 90, p. 62.
6114. STANLEY, Jean W.
"Crystals, Cabochons." [Poem] (63) My 90, p. 69.
"There, Solid." [Poem] (63) My 90, p. 68.
6115. STANNARD, Claire
"Hallowe'en." [WestCL] (24:1) Spr 90, p. 13.
6116. STANNARD, Martin
"A God for Every Occasion." [AnotherCM] (22) 90, p. 168-169.
"One More Brilliant Effect." [AnotherCM] (22) 90, p. 170.
6117. STANTON, Joseph
"Ahead." [ChamLR] (3:2, #6) Spr 90, p. 124.
"Aoi." [Abraxas] (38/39) 90, p. 131.
"Good Night, Moon" (for M.W.B. and C.H.). [HawaiiR] (15:1, #31) Wint 90, p. 1-2.
"Lanikai Sea Burial." [HawaiiR] (15:1, #31) Wint 90, p. 3-4.
"The Loreley." [ChamLR] (4:1, #7) Fall 90, p. 174.
"Thomas Eakins' *William Rush and His Model*." [ChamLR] (4:1, #7) Fall 90, p. 175-176.
"Vermeer's *A Woman Weighing Gold*." [ChamLR] (3:2, #6) Spr 90, p. 122-123.
6118. STANTON, Maura
"Crèche." [Crazy] (39) Wint 90, p. 71-73.
"Driving in Fog in Alaska." [ColR] (NS 17:1) Spr-Sum 90, p. 40-41.
"February 29." [AntR] (48:2) Spr 90, p. 228-229.
"Games." [ColR] (NS 17:1) Spr-Sum 90, p. 42-44.
"Karl Marx's House." [ColR] (NS 17:1) Spr-Sum 90, p. 38-39.
"Ode to Berryman." [Crazy] (39) Wint 90, p. 68-70.
"Otello." [AntR] (48:2) Spr 90, p. 226-227.
"Returning to Arizona." [ColR] (NS 17:1) Spr-Sum 90, p. 48-49.
"Sea Castle." [ColR] (NS 17:1) Spr-Sum 90, p. 45-47.
"Youth Orchestra Playing Mahler's Ninth." [HayF] (6) Sum 90, p. 38-39.
6119. STAPLETON, Laurence
"Valley Forge in the Bicentennial." [ManhatPR] (12) [90?], p. 38.
6120. STARBUCK, George
"Cargo Cult of the Solstice at Hadrian's Wall" (December 1988). [GrandS] (9:4, #36) 90, p. 162.
"Dylan: The Limerick." [LaurelR] (24:1) Wint 90, p. 77.
"Films Trip Comicstrip Column vs.Krazy Kael." [KenR] (NS 12:2) Spr 90, p.

172-173.
"God!" (The Apollo Penthouse Interview). [LaurelR] (24:1) Wint 90, p. 78-79.
"On an Urban Battlefield." [SouthwR] (75:2) Spr 90, p. 280.
"Speedreader Solvesnovel." [GrandS] (9:4, #36) 90, p. 163.
6121. STARK, Andrea
"Traveling to Texas." [WillowR] Spr 90, p. 46.
6122. STARK, Ellen Kreger
"Mother Dreams." [WestB] (27) 90, p. 82.
6123. STARK, Jonathan
"6 Down: Shakespearean King." [Poem] (64) N 90, p. 50.
"Eve of All Saints." [Poem] (64) N 90, p. 49.
"Monet's Water Lilies." [Poem] (64) N 90, p. 51.
6124. STARKEY, David
"Apology." [BelPoJ] (41:1) Fall 90, p. 2-4.
"At the Zoo." [ChatR] (11:1) Fall 90, p. 37.
"The Career of Mungo Park." [HawaiiR] (14:1, #28) Wint 89-90, p. 113.
"Ecce Homo." [WritersF] (16) Fall 90, p. 113.
"Harvest." [CapeR] (25:2) Fall 90, p. 50.
"Joseph of Nazareth." [HawaiiR] (14:1, #28) Wint 89-90, p. 112.
"Mary's Novel." [SoCoast] (9) Fall 90, p. 10-11.
"Mr. Kent's Apartment." [Asylum] (6:2) S 90, p. 16.
6125. STARNES, Sofia M.
"Legacy." [Kalliope] (12:1) 90, c89, p. 7.
6126. STASH
"The Mad Woman" (tr. of Wasyl Barka). [Agni] (31/32) 90, p. 243.
"The Shore of Misgiving." [Agni] (31/32) 90, p. 118.
6127. STATMAN, Mark
"Dust Echo Music." [Notus] (5:1) Spr 90, p. 108-109.
"Time Takes the Woods Forever." [Notus] (5:1) Spr 90, p. 107.
6128. STEARNS, Judy
"For My Father." [OnTheBus] (2:2/3:1, #6/7) Sum-Fall 90 Wint-Spr 91, p. 192.
"New Year's Eve, 1989." [OnTheBus] (2:1, #5) Spr 90, p. 130.
"Pops." [OnTheBus] (2:1, #5) Spr 90, p. 130.
"Primitive." [OnTheBus] (2:1, #5) Spr 90, p. 130.
6129. STEDMAN, Judy
"A Game of Chance." [Bogg] (63) 90, p. 50.
6130. STEDRONSKY, Carole
"It Is November." [CapeR] (25:2) Fall 90, p. 43.
"Which Moment." [CapeR] (25:2) Fall 90, p. 44-45.
6131. STEELE, Charlotte Musial
"Jennifer." [PottPort] (12) 90, p. 48.
6132. STEELE, Janet
"Above Wahiawa." [ChamLR] (4:1, #7) Fall 90, p. 38-39.
"Aloha Shirt." [BambooR] (47) Sum 90, p. 60-61.
"Ohana." [ChamLR] (3:2, #6) Spr 90, p. 35-36.
"Orchard." [ChamLR] (3:2, #6) Spr 90, p. 37.
"The Scent of Rain." [ChamLR] (4:1, #7) Fall 90, p. 36-37.
"Season of Fire." [HawaiiR] (14:3, #30) Fall 90, p. 87-88.
6133. STEELE, Timothy
"On His Cooking." [LullwaterR] (1:1) Spr 90, p. 14.
6134. STEEN, Jennifer
"How can I tell you." [Amelia] (6:2, #17) 90, p. 105.
6135. STEFAN, Marina
"Going to Egypt." [Poetry] (155:4) Ja 90, p. 260-261.
6136. STEFANILE, Felix
"Edie." [SycamoreR] (2:2) Sum 90, p. 11-12.
"Elegy 1942" (Fort Devens, Massachusetts). [SewanR] (98:2) Spr 90, p. 203-204.
"For Lucy, Who Has Alzheimer's Disease." [SycamoreR] (2:2) Sum 90, p. 13.
"The Light-Bringer." [SewanR] (98:2) Spr 90, p. 205.
6137. STEFANILE, Selma
"Variations on a Theme." [KanQ] (22:3) Sum 90, p. 199.
STEFANO, John de
    See De STEFANO, John
STEFANO, John di
    See De STEFANO, John

441

6138. STEFFNEY, John
"Somnambulists." [MissouriR] (13:1) 90, p. 197.
6139. STEIGMAN, Daria H.
"Abbie Hoffman (R.I.P.)." [Parting] (3:2) Wint 90-91, p. 11-13.
"Redefining the Worker's Advocate." [Parting] (3:2) Wint 90-91, p. 25-26.
6140. STEIN, Agnes
"Departure." [CumbPR] (9:2) Spr 90, p. 42.
6141. STEIN, Alice P.
"Déjà Vu While Browsing Woolworths." [Pearl] (12) Fall-Wint 90, p. 56.
6142. STEIN, Charles
"Five Nails." [Conjunc] (15) 90, p. 306-316.
6143. STEIN, Dona Luongo
"Early Snow" (for my mother). [ColEng] (52:4) Ap 90, p. 410.
"Origin of the Romantics." [PennR] (4:2) 90, p. 7-8.
6144. STEIN, Kevin
"Before the Sirens There Was Red." [SpoonRQ] (15:1) Wint 90, p. 43.
"A Chorus." [PoetryNW] (31:1) Spr 90, p. 19.
"Dead Elms." [IndR] (14:1) Wint 90, p. 94-95.
"Goldfinch at the Window Feeder." [MidAR] (10:2) 90, p. 15-16.
"On the Ladder." [SouthernPR] (30:1) Spr 90, p. 31-32.
"Out of Love, the Hideous Comes Unexpected." [IndR] (14:1) Wint 90, p. 92-93.
"Probabilities." [SouthernPR] (30:1) Spr 90, p. 30-31.
"What I Meant to Say." [IndR] (14:1) Wint 90, p. 96-97.
"Whose Tracks Those Are." [Poetry] (155:5) F 90, p. 333-334.
6145. STEIN, M. D.
"Special Needs." [Confr] (42/43) Spr-Sum 90, p. 192.
6146. STEIN, Marion
"Mama." [Footwork] 90, p. 97.
6147. STEINBERGH, Judith W.
"Lighting Tapers in Notre Dame." [Kalliope] (12:1) 90, c89, p. 60-61.
"A Small Thing." [Kalliope] (12:1) 90, c89, p. 6.
6148. STEINGASS, David
"Dinosaur Light." [MidAR] (10:1) 90, p. 14.
"The First Twilight Nail of Spring." [Poetry] (156:1) Ap 90, p. 4.
"The Night Everything Waits for Us." [Poetry] (156:1) Ap 90, p. 5.
"Shadow in the Stump" (Minnesota Pioneer Posters and Photographs). [ClockR]
(6:1) 90, p. 40.
"The Way Children Walk" (for Gordon Clark). [PoetryNW] (31:1) Spr 90, p. 23.
6149. STEINGESSER, Martin
"Wild Geese." [Blueline] (11:1/2) 90, p. 35.
6150. STEINKE, René
"Advice." [CreamCR] (14:1) Spr 90, p. 151.
6151. STEINMAN, Lisa M.
"Biology Lesson." [Zyzzyva] (6:1 #21) Spr 90, p. 41-42.
"The Economics of Foreign Exchange." [Ascent] (15:1) 90, p. 41.
"Theaters of Operation." [Ascent] (15:1) 90, p. 40.
6152. STELMACH, Marjorie
"Dürer for Children." [MalR] (93) D 90, p. 73-103.
"The Hanged Man's Dilemma." [Ascent] (15:1) 90, p. 20.
"A Simple Weather." [SouthernPR] (30:2) Fall 90, p. 40-41.
6153. STENSTROM, Dona
"Writing It Out" (calligraphy by the poet). [EmeraldCR] (1990) c89, p. 77.
6154. STEPANCHEV, Stephen
"Air." [Interim] (9:2) Fall-Wint 90-91, p. 6.
"Anne." [Interim] (9:2) Fall-Wint 90-91, p. 6.
"The Eleventh Day." [Interim] (9:2) Fall-Wint 90-91, p. 5.
"Immigrant." [NewYorker] (65:50) 29 Ja 90, p. 60.
"In Aphrodisias." [NewYorker] (66:4) 12 Mr 90, p. 64.
"Irondale." [Interim] (9:2) Fall-Wint 90-91, p. 3.
"Isadora." [Interim] (9:2) Fall-Wint 90-91, p. 9.
"The Little Theme." [Interim] (9:2) Fall-Wint 90-91, p. 8.
"Opening a Fist." [Interim] (9:2) Fall-Wint 90-91, p. 4.
"Seven Horizons." [Poetry] (156:5) Ag 90, p. 292.
"A Sparrow." [NewYorker] (66:11) 30 Ap 90, p. 42.
"The Spider in My Room." [Interim] (9:2) Fall-Wint 90-91, p. 8.
"Visiting a Grave." [Interim] (9:2) Fall-Wint 90-91, p. 10.

"Waiting for Catastrophe." [NewYorkQ] (41) Spr 90, p. 74.
"Walking." [Interim] (9:2) Fall-Wint 90-91, p. 11.
"Walking in the Snow." [Interim] (9:2) Fall-Wint 90-91, p. 12.
"White Seeds." [Interim] (9:2) Fall-Wint 90-91, p. 7.
"A Wrong Number." [NewYorkQ] (43) Fall 90, p. 55.
6155. STEPHENS, Genevieve
"The Old Woman." [HiramPoR] (48/49) 90-91, p. 67.
"Painting" (I-III). [RagMag] (7:2) Spr 90, p. 60.
6156. STEPHENSON, Birgit
"The Scene" (from "It," tr. of Inger Christensen, w. Gregory Stephenson). [CimR] (92) Jl 90, p. 17.
6157. STEPHENSON, David
"Still Life." [CapeR] (25:2) Fall 90, p. 12.
6158. STEPHENSON, Gregory
"The Scene" (from "It," tr. of Inger Christensen, w. Birgit Stephenson). [CimR] (92) Jl 90, p. 17.
6159. STEPHENSON, Shelby
"Blue Country Rising." [Turnstile] (2:1) 90, p. 53.
"The Green Corn." [Turnstile] (2:1) 90, p. 51-52.
"Minnie Birch and Her Son." [Crucible] (26) Fall 90, p. 76.
6160. STERLING, Phillip
"My Cousin's Scar." [HayF] (7) Fall-Wint 90, p. 79-80.
"The Voice Discovers Betrayal." [HayF] (7) Fall-Wint 90, p. 64.
6161. STERN, Cathy
"Questions." [NewRep] (202:11) 12 Mr 90, p. 32.
6162. STERN, Gerald
"Aspiring to Music." [GettyR] (3:3) Sum 90, p. 493-496.
"Behaving Like a Jew." [AmerPoR] (19:1) Ja-F 90, p. 12.
"Grinnell, Iowa." [Field] (43) Fall 90, p. 69-70.
"The Last Self-Portrait." [HampSPR] (Anthology 1975-1990) 90, p. 111.
"Malagueña." [HampSPR] (Anthology 1975-1990) 90, p. 111.
"The One Thing in Life." [HampSPR] (Anthology 1975-1990) 90, p. 110.
"A Song for Kenneth Burke" (May 7-15, Iowa City, Iowa). [Antaeus] (64/65) Spr-Aut 90, p. 126-128.
"Underground Dancing." [HampSPR] (Anthology 1975-1990) 90, p. 110.
6163. STERN, Joan
"Flirtation." [HiramPoR] (48/49) 90-91, p. 68.
6164. STERN, Robert
"Angels." [AntigR] (81/82) Spr-Sum 90, p. 28.
"The Boats Have Returned." [AntigR] (81/82) Spr-Sum 90, p. 27.
"Icebergs." [AntigR] (81/82) Spr-Sum 90, p. 28.
"Venus." [AntigR] (83) Aut 90, p. 27.
"What if a dragon were discovered alive." [ManhatPR] (11) [89?], p. 21.
"Winter." [AntigR] (81/82) Spr-Sum 90, p. 28.
6165. STERNBERG, Ricardo
"Crooked Sonnets" (Selections: I, IV). [AntigR] (83) Aut 90, p. 74-75.
6166. STERNER, Sandy
"Night Travel." [ThRiPo] (35/36) 90, p. 75-76.
6167. STERNLIEB, Barry
"The Novel." [Confr] (44/45) Fall 90-Wint 91, p. 195.
"Without a Word." [NoDaQ] (58:4) Fall 90, p. 181-182.
6168. STETLER, Charles
"(Just) Pass the Ammunition." [ChironR] (9:3) Aut 90, p. 17.
"Non-Fiction." [ChironR] (9:4) Wint 90, p. 17.
"Passage to England." [Pearl] (10) Spr 90, p. 22.
6169. STEVENS, A. Wilber
"Arlen" (Arlen Collier, 30 January 1933 - 12 October 1990). [Interim] (9:2) Fall-Wint 90-91, p. 2.
6170. STEVENS, Alex
"As We Drove." [NewYorker] (65:52) 12 F 90, p. 36.
6171. STEVENS, C. J.
"Park Poem" (tr. of Paul Snoek). [NewRena] (8:1, #24) Spr 90, p. 17.
"Standing at the Long Lie" (tr. of Paul Snoek). [NewRena] (8:1, #24) Spr 90, p. 19.
6172. STEVENS, Geoff
"Night Tide." [CoalC] (1) Ag 90, p. 34.

6173. STEVENS, J. R.
"Holloween." [AntigR] (81/82) Spr-Sum 90, p. 86-87.
6174. STEVENS, Jim
"Alice, North Dakota." [BlackBR] (11) Spr-Sum 90, p. 31-32.
"Annual Tribute." [PottPort] (12) 90, p. 24.
"Cafes." [NoDaQ] (58:2) Spr 90, p. 118-119.
"Caraquet Coast." [PottPort] (12) 90, p. 24.
"It Is True." [NoDaQ] (58:2) Spr 90, p. 119-120.
"Obvious Things." [Pearl] (12) Fall-Wint 90, p. 47.
6175. STEVENS, Peter
"Before the Storm." [AntigR] (81/82) Spr-Sum 90, p. 197.
"Magnetawan Poems." [AntigR] (83) Aut 90, p. 13-15.
6176. STEVENSON, Anna
"Vacations." [WorldO] (23:1/2) Fall 88-Wint 89 c1991, p. 27.
6177. STEVENSON, Anne
"All Canal Boat Cruises Start Here." [GrahamHR] (13) Spr 90, p. 15-16.
"Elegy." [GrahamHR] (13) Spr 90, p. 19-20.
"Hot Wind, Hard Rain" (For Sylvia Plath, August, 1988). [GrahamHR] (13) Spr
90, p. 17.
"Inverkirkaig" (For Dorothy and Jonathan Brett Young, September 1986). [PartR]
(57:2) Spr 90, p. 266.
"Little Paul and the Sea." [GrahamHR] (13) Spr 90, p. 18.
6178. STEVENSON, Richard
"Making an Angel for Bob." [Grain] (18:1) Spr 90, p. 65-66.
"Shhh, They're Sleeping." [Event] (19:3) Fall 90, p. 52.
6179. STEVER, Edward W.
"Dante's Inferno." [Pearl] (11) Sum 90, p. 40.
"Symmetry." [Pearl] (12) Fall-Wint 90, p. 32.
6180. STEWARD, D. E.
"Decembre." [RiverC] (10:2) Spr 90, p. 36-44.
"July." [Chelsea] (49) 90, p. 49-56.
"Mayo." [Caliban] (9) 90, p. 29-35.
"Septembre." [SouthwR] (75:3) Sum 90, p. 393-397.
6181. STEWART, Caroline
"Without You, Realized." [EmeraldCR] (1990) c89, p. 70-71.
6182. STEWART, Debby
"Orpheus." [AnthNEW] 90, p. 17.
"Your Voices." [AnthNEW] 90, p. 22.
6183. STEWART, Dolores
"January: Wolf Moon." [Mildred] (4:1) 90, p. 15.
"November: Beaver Moon." [Mildred] (4:1) 90, p. 14.
"On the 39th Day of Rain." [Confr] (44/45) Fall 90-Wint 91, p. 196.
6184. STEWART, Isobel Stewart
"A Bowl of Purple Cherries" (a Pantoum). [Amelia] (6:1, #16) 90, p. 75.
6185. STEWART, Jack
"Field Work" (for Mari). [Poem] (64) N 90, p. 20.
"Fishing." [Poem] (64) N 90, p. 21.
"Lost." [Poem] (64) N 90, p. 23.
"The Prodigal." [Poem] (64) N 90, p. 24.
"Sid and Bix" (in memory of my grandfather). [Poem] (64) N 90, p. 22.
"Stepping Stones" (for Karl). [Poem] (64) N 90, p. 19.
6186. STEWART, James
"My Father's Kierkegaard." [NewRep] (202:25) 18 Je 90, p. 42.
"The Women Without Asking." [NewRep] (203:25 [i.e. 24]) 10 D 90, p. 39.
6187. STEWART, Pat
"Banger in the Morning." [Bogg] (63) 90, p. 11.
"Bladed Sky." [Mildred] (4:1) 90, p. 110.
"A Ton of Fleck." [Mildred] (4:1) 90, p. 111.
6188. STEWART, S. E.
"Car Crazy" (tr. of Louise Fiset). [PraF] (11:1) Spr 90, p. 109.
"I Upset Everything" (tr. of Louise Fiset). [PraF] (11:1) Spr 90, p. 115.
"Madrigal" (tr. of Louise Fiset). [PraF] (11:1) Spr 90, p. 117.
"The Ol' Cowboy Saloon" (tr. of Louise Fiset). [PraF] (11:1) Spr 90, p. 111, 113.
6189. STEWART, Susan
"Chopin. May 1988." [AmerPoR] (19:6) N-D 90, p. 36.
"In Questa Reggia. May 1989." [PassN] (11:2) Wint 90, p. 7.

6190. STEWART, W. Gregory
"Advice for Americans." [Amelia] (6:2, #17) 90, p. 70.
6191. STEWART-ROBERTSON, Charles
"A Seep of Morning." [NegC] (10:2/3) 90, p. 54.
6192. STIEBER, Christopher
"October 19, 1987, Dear Kate." [WindO] (53) Fall 90, p. 49.
6193. STINSON, Susan
"Band Class Collaboration." [SinW] (40) Spr 90, p. 78.
6194. STIVER, Mary Weeden
"An Unfulfilled Dream." [NegC] (10:2/3) 90, p. 120.
6195. STOCK, Norman
"Thank You for the Helpful Comments." [NewYorkQ] (43) Fall 90, p. 56.
6196. STOCKWELL, Jeff
"The Blackout." [WillowS] (25) Wint 90, p. 23.
"Moment of Conception." [ThRiPo] (35/36) 90, p. 59-60.
"Pep." [ThRiPo] (35/36) 90, p. 61-62.
"Small Town Fourth." [ThRiPo] (35/36) 90, p. 63-64.
6197. STOKES, Denis
"Pakashgoogan." [CanLit] (124/125) Spr-Sum 90, p. 74-75.
6198. STOKESBURY, Leon
"City Lights." [KenR] (NS 12:1) Wint 90, p. 75-77.
"Glendower Ponders the Vasty Deep." [KenR] (NS 12:1) Wint 90, p. 74-75.
"Jaques Lured by Audrey." [ChatR] (10:4) Sum 90, p. 64.
"The Royal Nonesuch" (Extempore Effusion upon the Death of Everette Maddox,
1944-1989). [KenR] (NS 12:1) Wint 90, p. 78-79.
6199. STONE, Alison (Alison J.)
"December Monday." [KanQ] (22:4) Fall 90, p. 30.
"Self Lullaby." [Ploughs] (16:1) Spr-Sum 90, p. 52.
"What the Spirit Seeks." [Poetry] (156:2) My 90, p. 94-97.
6200. STONE, Ann
"Aging: a Sestina." [WillowR] Spr 90, p. 1-2.
"Creosote Tea." [WillowR] Spr 90, p. 1.
6201. STONE, Arlene
"Disinformation." [Contact] (9:56/57/58) Spr 90, p. 18-19.
"Your Mother's House." [Vis] (33) 90, p. 47.
6202. STONE, Carole
"Bridge" (for Marina Tsvetayeva, 1878-1942). [ManhatPR] (11) [89?], p. 39.
"Church of Atotonilco." [Contact] (9:56/57/58) Spr 90, p. 33.
"Shadow." [Contact] (9:56/57/58) Spr 90, p. 33.
6203. STONE, James
"Like the succulent apple that blushes" (fragment, tr. of Sappho). [AmerPoR] (19:6)
N-D 90, p. 44.
"Selected Fragments" (tr. of Sappho). [AmerPoR] (19:2) Mr-Ap 90, p. 25.
"To die is all I really want" (fragment, tr. of Sappho). [AmerPoR] (19:6) N-D 90, p.
44.
6204. STONE, Jennifer
"End of the Broadcast Day." [PoetryUSA] (5:2) Sum 90, p. 4.
6205. STONE, John
"Elegy and Affirmation" (a meditation written for the Service of Reflection and
Gratitude, Department of Anatomy, Emory University). [LullwaterR] (1:1) Spr
90, p. 35.
"Letter to Philip Larkin on Learning of His Death a Week After the Fact."
[LullwaterR] (1:1) Spr 90, p. 24.
6206. STONE, Ken
"Music Lesson." [CoalC] (1) Ag 90, p. 8.
"Music Lesson II." [CoalC] (1) Ag 90, p. 8.
6207. STONE, Ruth
"For Seven Women." [Boulevard] (4:3/5:1, #12/13) Spr 90, p. 175-176.
"Nuns at Lunch on the Bus." [NewMyths] (1:1) 90, p. 108-109.
"Plumbing." [NewMyths] (1:1) 90, p. 106-107.
"The Widow's Muse" (Selections: 1, 2, 33, 38). [Boulevard] (5:2, #14) Fall 90, p.
87-88.
"The Widow's Muse" (Selections: 20-22, 27, 37-39, 42, 49, 52). [PoetryE] (29)
Spr 90, p. 195-204.
6208. STONEBERGER, W. I.
"How Are You?" [DogRR] (9:2, #18) Aut 90, p. 26.

"The Razor's Edge." [Plain] (10:3) Spr 90, p. 13.
"Reflection." [DogRR] (9:2, #18) Aut 90, p. 26.
"What She Wants." [RagMag] (7:2) Spr 90, p. 58.
6209. STONEHOUSE, Cathy
"The Craft We Journey In." [Grain] (18:1) Spr 90, inside back cover.
"My Brother Is Watching the Stars." [MalR] (90) Spr 90, p. 72.
6210. STOOP, Norma McLain
"Ballad of the Distant Cliff." [ManhatR] (5:1) Spr 90, p. 45-46.
"Harmony." [ManhatR] (5:1) Spr 90, p. 43.
6211. STORACE, Patricia
"Two Portraits of Women Reading." [Verse] (7:3) Wint 90, p. 67-68.
6212. STORIE-PAHLITZSCH, Lori
"Curtains." [PoetL] (85:4) Wint 90-91, p. 17-18.
6213. STORNI, Alfonsina
"Departing" (tr. by Margaret Hanzimanolis and Carlos Garcia-Aranda). [BelPoR]
(40:3) Spr 90, p. 23-25.
"I Am" (tr. by Margaret Hanzimanolis and Carlos García-Aranda). [CarolQ] (43:1)
Fall 90, p. 69.
"I Am Going to Sleep" (tr. by Margaret Hanzimanolis and Carlos García-Aranda).
[CarolQ] (43:1) Fall 90, p. 70.
"I Am Useless" (tr. by Margaret Hanzimanolis and Carlos García-Aranda). [CarolQ]
(43:1) Fall 90, p. 68.
"One More Time" (tr. by Margaret Hanzimanolis and Carlos García-Aranda).
[CarolQ] (43:1) Fall 90, p. 67.
"Tropical" (tr. by Margaret Hanzimanolis and Carlos Garcia-Aranda). [BelPoR]
(40:3) Spr 90, p. 25-26.
"Two Words" (tr. by Pablo Medina). [ArtfulD] (18/19) 90, p. 30.
"You Want Me White" (tr. by Margaret Hanzimanolis and Carlos Garcia-Aranda).
[BelPoR] (40:3) Spr 90, p. 22-23.
6214. STORTONI, Anna
"After March" (tr. of Giuseppe Conte, w. Lowell Bergstedt). [MidwQ] (32:1) Aut
90, p. 94.
6215. STORTONI, Laura
"Tezcatlipoca: The Song of a Human Sacrifice" (tr. of Giuseppe Conte, w. Lowell
Bergstedt). [MidwQ] (31:2) Wint 90, p. 195-196.
6216. STORY, Marshall L.
"The Ocean Calls." [PoetryUSA] (5:3) Fall 90, p. 22.
"That Old Convict Man." [PoetryUSA] ([5:4?]) Wint 90, p. 26.
6217. STOTHART, Rob
"Two Mennonite Graves in a Lutheran Cemetery." [BellArk] (6:4) Jl-Ag 90, p. 4.
6218. STOTTS, Ann
"Self Portrait #4." [WillowR] Spr 90, p. 9.
6219. STOWELL, Phyllis
"#100 and 2." [Epoch] (39:3) 90, p. 293.
"#114, Not Jasper Johns." [Epoch] (39:3) 90, p. 292.
6220. STRAHAN, B. R. (Bradley R.)
"Altair" (tr. of Serge Pey, w. Jean-Clarence Lambert). [Vis] (32) 90, p. 44.
"Arranging Space" (tr. of Luuk Gruwez, w. David Siefkin and Catharina Kochuyt).
[Vis] (34) 90, p. 18.
"Bedroom" (tr. of Jean Pierre Duprey, w. Jean-Clarence Lambert). [Vis] (32) 90, p.
39.
"Black Smoke" (tr. of Edouard Glissant, w. Jean-Clarence Lambert). [Vis] (32) 90,
p. 25.
"Capella" (tr. of Serge Pey, w. Jean-Clarence Lambert). [Vis] (32) 90, p. 44.
"Country of Cardboard and Cotton Batting" (tr. of Eugene Ionesco, w. Aurelia
Roman and S. G. Sullivan). [Vis] (33) 90, p. 4.
"Le Cycle de la Parole" (Excerpt, tr. of Christophe Charles, w. Jean-Clarence
Lambert). [Vis] (32) 90, p. 24.
"El Dorado" (tr. of Andre Laude, w. Jean-Clarence Lambert). [Vis] (32) 90, p. 42.
"Gulf Stream" (tr. of Rene Belance, w. Dennis Egan and Jean-Clarence Lambert).
[Vis] (32) 90, p. 24.
"Home" (for Monique T., died 1987, at 22, in a traffic accident, tr. of Luuk Gruwez,
w. David Siefkin and Catharina Kochuyt). [Vis] (34) 90, p. 17.
"I Belong to the High Day" (tr. of Paul Dakeyo, w. Dennis Egan and Jean-Clarence
Lambert). [Vis] (32) 90, p. 9.
"Last Supper" (tr. of Nikolai Kantchev, w. Pamela Perry). [CrabCR] (6:3) Spr 90,

p. 12-13.
"Liege." [Vis] (32) 90, inside front cover.
"Merlin's Song" (for Jean Clarence Lambert). [HolCrit] (27:3) Je 90, p. 17.
"Night Lines" (tr. of Nikolai Kantchev, w. Pamela Perry). [CrabCR] (6:3) Spr 90,
    p. 13.
"Poem: What is it to be face to face?" (tr. of Bernard Noel, w. Dennis Egan and
    Jean-Clarence Lambert). [Vis] (32) 90, p. 46.
"Poetique" (tr. of Edouard Glissant, w. Jean-Clarence Lambert). [Vis] (32) 90, p.
    25.
"Poetry Festival" (Paris, 1987, tr. of Jean Baptiste Tiemele, w. Dennis Egan and
    Jean-Clarence Lambert). [Vis] (32) 90, p. 11.
"The Prince" (tr. of Andre Laude, w. Jean-Clarence Lambert). [Vis] (32) 90, p. 42.
"The Queen of Walls" (Excerpt, tr. of Christian Dotremont, w. Jean-Clarence
    Lambert). [Vis] (32) 90, p. 35.
"Rose Cross" (Selections: 1-3, tr. of Jean-Clarence Lambert, w. the author). [Vis]
    (32) 90, p. 45.
"Transformation" (tr. of Nikolai Kantchev, w. Pamela Perry). [CrabCR] (6:3) Spr
    90, p. 12.
6221. STRAND, Mark
"The Continental College of Beauty." [Antaeus] (64/65) Spr-Aut 90, p. 129.
"The Couple." [Antaeus] (64/65) Spr-Aut 90, p. 132-135.
"The End." [NewYorker] (66:2) 26 F 90, p. 96.
"Like the Moon Departing." [HampSPR] (Anthology 1975-1990) 90, p. 116.
"No Particular Day." [HampSPR] (Anthology 1975-1990) 90, p. 115.
"Variations on a Theme." [SoCoast] (8) Spr 90, p. 3-5.
"Workshop Miracle" (a short opera). [Antaeus] (64/65) Spr-Aut 90, p. 130-131.
6222. STRANDBERG, Ingela
"Clarity" (tr. by Lennart Bruce and Sonja Bruce). [Spirit] (10:1) 89, p. 163.
"Come Inside" (tr. by Lennart Bruce and Sonja Bruce). [Spirit] (10:1) 89, p. 153.
"Det Är I Maj Och Äppelträden Blommar." [Spirit] (10:1) 89, p. 164, 166.
"Ett Rum För Natten." [Spirit] (10:1) 89, p. 168.
"Förlopp." [Spirit] (10:1) 89, p. 172.
"I Believe in Fresh Starts" (tr. by Lennart Bruce and Sonja Bruce). [Spirit] (10:1)
    89, p. 171.
"I Gräset." [Spirit] (10:1) 89, p. 156, 158.
"I Put My Skis" (tr. by Lennart Bruce and Sonja Bruce). [Spirit] (10:1) 89, p. 161.
"In the Grass" (tr. by Lennart Bruce and Sonja Bruce). [Spirit] (10:1) 89, p. 157,
    159.
"It's May and the Apple Trees Bloom" (tr. by Lennart Bruce and Sonja Bruce).
    [Spirit] (10:1) 89, p. 165, 167.
"Jag Drömmer Ibland." [Spirit] (10:1) 89, p. 154.
"Jag Ställer Skidorna." [Spirit] (10:1) 89, p. 160.
"Jag Tror På Uppbrott." [Spirit] (10:1) 89, p. 170.
"Klarhet." [Spirit] (10:1) 89, p. 162.
"Kom Inom." [Spirit] (10:1) 89, p. 152.
"Room for the Night" (tr. by Lennart Bruce and Sonja Bruce). [Spirit] (10:1) 89, p.
    169.
"Sequence" (tr. by Lennart Bruce and Sonja Bruce). [Spirit] (10:1) 89, p. 173.
"Sometimes I Dream" (tr. by Lennart Bruce and Sonja Bruce). [Spirit] (10:1) 89, p.
    155.
6223. STRANG, Catriona
"From a Translation of the Carmina Burana." [WestCL] (24:1) Spr 90, p. 30-31.
6224. STRANGE, Sharan
"Acts of Power." [Callaloo] (13:3) Sum 90, p. 392.
"The Apprentice Dreams of Promotion." [Callaloo] (13:3) Sum 90, p. 388.
"Matador." [Callaloo] (13:3) Sum 90, p. 393.
"Streetcorner Church." [Callaloo] (13:3) Sum 90, p. 391.
"Transits." [Callaloo] (13:3) Sum 90, p. 389-390.
6225. STRATIDAKIS, Eileen
"Lines." [LullwaterR] (2:1) Wint 90, p. 7.
"Progressions." [LullwaterR] (2:1) Wint 90, p. 91.
6226. STRATTON, R. E.
"Puss in Poots." [Plain] (10:2) Wint 90, p. 10.
6227. STRAW, Silvana R.
"Fede." [Gargoyle] (37/38) 90, p. 126.

6228. STREVER, Linda
"Against My Dreams" (November 1913). [Nimrod] (34:1) Fall-Wint 90, p. 60-62.
6229. STREZOVSKI, Jovan
"Sun and Mist" (tr. by Dusko Tomovski). [Footwork] 90, p. 106.
6230. STRICKER, Meredith
"Gravity" (Excerpt). [PoetC] (21:4) Sum 90, p. 13-14.
6231. STRICKLAND, Larry J.
"Lights Across the Bay." [EmeraldCR] (1990) c89, p. 94-95.
6232. STRICKLAND, Stephanie
"Bench-Hand: 'The Famous "Real Life"'" (from "Resistance: Simone Weil,
       1909-1943"). [PraS] (64:4) Wint 90, p. 82-84.
"Excused for Illness" (from "Resistance: Simone Weil, 1909-1943"). [PraS] (64:4)
       Wint 90, p. 84-85.
"My Dear Albertine" (from "Resistance: Simone Weil, 1909-1943"). [PraS] (64:4)
       Wint 90, p. 85-86.
"Prometheus." [WestB] (26) 90, p. 92-93.
"Simone Weil: Comic Progression, 1939--." [AmerV] (21) Wint 90, p. 112-115.
"Soul Learns Everything from Body" (from "Resistance: Simone Weil,
       1909-1943"). [PraS] (64:4) Wint 90, p. 86-87.
"Ugliness" (from "Resistance: Simone Weil, 1909-1943"). [PraS] (64:4) Wint 90, p.
       81-82.
"War Rations Chosen, London, 1943" (from "Resistance: Simone Weil,
       1909-1943"). [PraS] (64:4) Wint 90, p. 87-88.
6233. STRINGER, A. E.
"Attending *The Tempest*." [KanQ] (22:1/2) Wint-Spr 90, p. 134.
"Monument." [TarRP] (30:1) Fall 90, p. 13.
"Sinkholes." [KanQ] (22:1/2) Wint-Spr 90, p. 133.
6234. STRINGER, David
"Bill in Bed." [Amelia] (6:2, #17) 90, p. 109-110.
6235. STROFFOLINO, Chris
"To Keep Meaning from Emerging from the Mesh." [NewAW] (6) Spr 90, p. 101.
6236. STROUS, Allen
"Dead on Arrival." [OhioR] (45) 90, p. 48.
"Delight." [OhioR] (45) 90, p. 47.
"Drought." [OhioR] (45) 90, p. 49.
6237. STRUT, Pavel
"Deep Mud" (tr. by the author and Tom O'Grady). [HampSPR] (Anthology
       1975-1990) 90, p. 272.
"Not Long Before April" (tr. by the author and Tom O'Grady). [HampSPR]
       (Anthology 1975-1990) 90, p. 272.
"Stalin's Monument: Snapshot from 1956" (tr. by Richard Katrovas and Dominika
       Winterová). [PoetryE] (29) Spr 90, p. 113.
6238. STRUTHERS, Ann
"Alcott's Axe." [Hudson] (43:1) Spr 90, p. 66.
"Dangerous Music." [CumbPR] (10:1) Fall 90, p. 46.
"Kathleen Spivack's Study." [SouthernHR] (24:1) Wint 90, p. 66.
"Nathaniel Hawthorne and Sophia." [Iowa] (20:2) Spr-Sum 90, p. 12.
6239. STRUTHERS, Betsy
"Fifteen Changes All the Rules." [PraF] (11:4) Wint 90-91, p. 72.
"In July, Such Undercurrents." [PraF] (11:4) Wint 90-91, p. 74.
"Opening Up." [PraF] (11:4) Wint 90-91, p. 73.
"Protectivwe Coloration of the Heart." [CapilR] (2:2) Spr 90, p. 32-34.
6240. STRYK, Dan
"Old Shoes." [KanQ] (22:1/2) Wint-Spr 90, p. 87.
6241. STRYK, Lucien
"Fame." [AmerPoR] (19:2) Mr-Ap 90, p. 46.
"Mother and I" (after Shinkichi Takahashi). [HampSPR] (Anthology 1975-1990) 90,
       p. 244.
"Sparrow and Aviary" (after Shinkichi Takahashi). [HampSPR] (Anthology
       1975-1990) 90, p. 243.
"Translating Zen Poems" (In Memory of Takashi Ikemoto). [AmerPoR] (19:2)
       Mr-Ap 90, p. 46.
6242. STUART, Dabney
"Bearings." [PraS] (64:2) Sum 90, p. 20-21.
"A Bird." [Journal] (13:2) Fall-Wint 89-90, p. 20.
"Dressing." [PraS] (64:2) Sum 90, p. 19-20.

"The Executive Discovers Poetry." [GettyR] (3:2) Spr 90, p. 284.
"Fish Magic." [GettyR] (3:2) Spr 90, p. 282-283.
"The Funeral." [NewYorker] (65:50) 29 Ja 90, p. 38.
"How Loss Works." [GettyR] (3:4) Aut 90, p. 685.
"Light Years." [SouthernPR] (30:1) Spr 90, p. 54-55.
"My Children Going." [Journal] (13:2) Fall-Wint 89-90, p. 17-19.
"A Political Fable for Practically Everybody." [HampSPR] (Anthology 1975-1990)
    90, p. 125.
"Sharp Words in the Men's Room." [HampSPR] (Anthology 1975-1990) 90, p.
    124-125.
"Staying in Touch." [GettyR] (3:4) Aut 90, p. 682-684.
STUBBS, John Heath
    See HEATH-STUBBS, John
6243. STUBER, Kendra
"Streetlights." [PoetryUSA] (5:2) Sum 90, p. 7.
6244. STUDER, Constance
"Dear Dr. Williams, Dear Poet." [Kaleid] (21) Sum-Fall 90, p. 49.
"Glass Eye." [Kaleid] (21) Sum-Fall 90, p. 32.
"The Pair of Twins" (tr. of Adriaan Morriën). [PoetryE] (30) Fall 90, p. 87.
"Sirens Rise Like Blood Inside the Heart." [Kaleid] (21) Sum-Fall 90, p. 48.
"Song of Healing, Song of the Sea." [Kaleid] (21) Sum-Fall 90, p. 21.
"The Waiting Room" (reprinted from #14, 1987). [Kaleid] (20) Wint-Spr 90, p. 21.
6245. STULBERG, Sita
"After He Moved Up North." [OnTheBus] (2:2/3:1, #6/7) Sum-Fall 90 Wint-Spr 91,
    p. 193.
"Sogni d'Oro." [OnTheBus] (2:1, #5) Spr 90, p. 131-132.
6246. STURGEON, Rebecca L.
"In the Confessional." [SingHM] (18) 90, p. 25.
6247. STURMANIS, Dona
"Britannia Beach." [AntigR] (81/82) Spr-Sum 90, p. 9.
6248. SU, Adrienne
"Claiming the Find." [Chelsea] (49) 90, p. 96-97.
"The Earthwalker." [Chelsea] (49) 90, p. 98.
"Finishing the Exotic." [Kalliope] (12:2) 90, p. 34-35.
6249. SUBACH, Karen
"Humpen" (tr. of Georges Hausemer). [Vis] (34) 90, p. 21.
"Intruder" (tr. of Georges Hausemer). [Vis] (34) 90, p. 21.
"Marja Glaudl." [CutB] (33) 90, p. 67-68.
"Nightshift" (tr. of Georges Hausemer). [Vis] (34) 90, p. 22.
"The Stones" (tr. of Georges Hausemer). [Vis] (34) 90, p. 20.
"Trees" (tr. of Georges Hausemer). [Vis] (34) 90, p. 21.
"Zoom" (tr. of Georges Hausemer). [Vis] (34) 90, p. 22.
6250. SUBRAMAN, Belinda
"Bar Tale." [DustyD] (1:2) O 90, p. 2.
"Belated Words." [DustyD] (1:2) O 90, p. 3.
"Da Vinci Perplexed." [DustyD] (1:2) O 90, p. 3.
"Everyday." [BlackBR] (11) Spr-Sum 90, p. 15.
"Frankenstein, the Poet." [CoalC] (2) D 90, p. 22.
"Genesis According to Charlie." [DustyD] (1:2) O 90, p. 1.
"Gotmateswara." [CoalC] (1) Ag 90, p. 21.
"Hell." [Asylum] (6:2) S 90, p. 17.
"Holy As Hell." [SlipS] (10) 90, p. 32-33.
"In a Sterile and Elegant Room." [DustyD] (1:2) O 90, p. 1.
"Nowhere People." [Bogg] (63) 90, p. 68.
"Snake Charmer." [BlackBR] (11) Spr-Sum 90, p. 15-16.
6251. SUCOFF, Marjorie
"42nd and Broadway." [NorthStoneR] (9) 90, p. 73.
"Embrace." [NorthStoneR] (9) 90, p. 72.
"Pasar Bogor." [NorthStoneR] (9) 90, p. 73.
"Pinball." [NorthStoneR] (9) 90, p. 72.
6252. SUDER, Witold
"The Edge of Time Is Near!" (tr. by Melanie Heath and John Nides). [PoetryUSA]
    (5:1) Spr 90, p. 8.
6253. SUELTER, Mary Ann
"Thursday" (1990 Seaton Second Award Poem). [KanQ] (22:3) Sum 90, p. 8.

449

6254. SUERMONDT, Tim
"Einstein at Short." [PoetC] (21:2) Wint 90, p. 20-21.
SUEUR, Meridel le
See LeSUEUR, Meridel
6255. SUK, Julie
"From the Stars, Silence." [RiverC] (11:1) Fall 90, p. 67.
"How It Was." [NegC] (10:2/3) 90, p. 26-27.
"In the Garden of Earthly Delights." [GeoR] (44:1/2) Spr-Sum 90, p. 164-165.
"Stories." [NegC] (10:2/3) 90, p. 25.
"Words I Won't Give Up On." [NegC] (10:2/3) 90, p. 24.
6256. SULEIMAN, Robin
"After-Image." [Vis] (33) 90, p. 16-19.
"Capture the Flag." [Vis] (33) 90, p. 15.
6257. SULEIMAN, Susan Rubin
"To a Poet." [MichQR] (29:4) Fall 90, p. 683-684.
6258. SULLIVAN, Anita T.
"In the Hay." [KanQ] (22:3) Sum 90, p. 211.
6259. SULLIVAN, Anne McCrary
"Untimely Bloomings." [EngJ] (79:3) Mr 90, p. 90.
6260. SULLIVAN, Janet
"Matter-of-Fact." [ManhatPR] (11) [89?], p. 24.
6261. SULLIVAN, Jim
"Attempting to Provoke a Set of Decisions" (Selection: 3. "Proposal for a
Photocollage"). [CoalC] (2) D 90, p. 10.
"No Right to Sing the Blues." [CoalC] (1) Ag 90, p. 26.
6262. SULLIVAN, Joan
"If the Universe Could Sing." [PottPort] (11) 89, p. 47.
6263. SULLIVAN, Marva
"Gravity." [SingHM] (17) 90, p. 76.
6264. SULLIVAN, Myra L.
"April 14 and Warner McIntosh Is Dead." [RagMag] (8:1) 90, p. 9.
6265. SULLIVAN, Norma
"Football Practice." [PoetryUSA] (5:2) Sum 90, p. 4.
6266. SULLIVAN, S. G.
"Country of Cardboard and Cotton Batting" (tr. of Eugene Ionesco, w. Aurelia
Roman and Bradley R. Strahan). [Vis] (33) 90, p. 4.
6267. SUMERKIN, Alexander
"Poems to Akhmatova" (June 9 -- July 2, 1916, selections: I, IV-V, IX, tr. of
Marina Tsvetaeva, w. Mary Jane White). [Nimrod] (33:2) Spr-Sum 90, p.
53-55.
6268. SUMMERHAYES, Don
"Invalid Garden." [Descant] (21:4/22:1, #71/72) Wint-Spr 90-91, p. 246.
"Naditas." [Descant] (21:4/22:1, #71/72) Wint-Spr 90-91, p. 244.
"Ode to Broth of Conger" (tr. of Pablo Neruda). [Descant] (21:4/22:1, #71/72)
Wint-Spr 90-91, p. 247-248.
"Reclining Figure." [Event] (19:3) Fall 90, p. 54.
"Spring Upstarts." [Event] (19:3) Fall 90, p. 55.
"The Window 6 A M." [Descant] (21:4/22:1, #71/72) Wint-Spr 90-91, p. 245.
6269. SUMNER, David
"Act 1." [HawaiiR] (14:2, #29) Spr 90, p. 122.
"Healing." [HawaiiR] (14:2, #29) Spr 90, p. 122.
6270. SUMRALL, Amber Coverdale
"First September Rain." [Kaleid] (21) Sum-Fall 90, p. 33.
"Listening to the Language of Birds" (reprinted from #19, 1989). [Kaleid] (20)
Wint-Spr 90, p. 111.
"Tailings" (reprinted from #17, 1988). [Kaleid] (20) Wint-Spr 90, p. 111.
"The Weight of Our Bodies." [SlipS] (10) 90, p. 100-101.
6271. SUN, Wenbo
"At Night, Sleep Leading Me to Another House" (tr. by Dong Jiping). [Footwork]
90, p. 41.
"Organ" (tr. by Dong Jiping). [Footwork] 90, p. 41.
6272. SUNDAHL, Daniel James
"The Apostrophe to Tragedy." [OxfordM] (6:1) Spr-Sum 90, p. 66.
"At Subiaco, the Monks Are Playing Softball." [NegC] (10:2/3) 90, p. 103.
"Bull Whip Days." [PoetL] (85:2) Sum 90, p. 20.
"The Dance of Juba." [MidwQ] (31:4) Sum 90, p. 477-478.

"Five Drunken Manifestations of Zhong Kui (Mid to Late 20th Century)." [HawaiiR] (15:1, #31) Wint 90, p. 40.
"Interjection XIII: An Epitaph for Someone." [MidwQ] (31:3) Spr 90, p. 370.
"Meditation at Baw Beese" (for Megan Forrester, December 10, 1989). [CreamCR] (14:1) Spr 90, p. 110.
"Six Tin-Types" (for Don D. Walker). [WebR] (14:2) Spr 90, p. 28-38.

SUNGHO, Choe
    See CHOE, Sungho

6273. SUPERVIELLE, Jules
"Docilité" (from "La Fable du Monde"). [Sequoia] (33:2) Wint 90, p. 69.
"Docility" (tr. by Geoffrey Gardner). [Sequoia] (33:2) Wint 90, p. 70.
"The House Surrounded" (tr. by Geoffrey Gardner). [WillowS] (26) Spr 90, p. 36.
"I Dream" (tr. by Geoffrey Gardner). [Sequoia] (33:2) Wint 90, p. 72.
"Je Rêve" (from "Oublieuse Mémoire"). [Sequoia] (33:2) Wint 90, p. 71.
"Pines" (tr. by Geoffrey Gardner). [Sequoia] (33:2) Wint 90, p. 74.
"Pins" (in French, from "Poemes, 1939-1945"). [Sequoia] (33:2) Wint 90, p. 73.
"Untitled: Night inside me, night out there" (tr. by Geoffrey Gardner). [WillowS] (26) Spr 90, p. 35.

6274. SUPRANER, Robyn
"Chloe Sings the Blues." [Calyx] (12:3) Sum 90, p. 56.
"Land of the Cyclops." [ConnPR] (9:1) 90, p. 21.
"Oranges." [TarRP] (30:1) Fall 90, p. 42.

6275. SURAN, Justin
"Autobiography." [HarvardA] (125:2) N 90, p. 23.
"Tamar at the Gate of Enaim." [HarvardA] (124:4) My 90, p. 9.

6276. SURAPANENI, Satish
"Rediscovering Paterson" (for Mark Hillringhouse). [Footwork] 90, p. 106.

6277. SURVANT, Joe
"Benediction." [PoetC] (22:1) Fall 90, p. 45.
"Rilke Finds Water." [Hellas] (1:1) Spr 90, p. 117-118.
"A Sisterhood of Labor." [Stand] (31:4) Aut 90, p. 16-17.

6278. SURYADI, Linus
"In Silent Reliefs" (tr. by John H. McGlynn). [TampaR] (3) 90, p. 89.
"Song of a Rebab Player" (tr. by John H. McGlynn). [TampaR] (3) 90, p. 89.

6279. SUSANO no MIKOTO
"Where the clouds rise at Izumo" (tr. by Janet Lewis). [SouthernR] (26:1) Ja 90, p. 202.

6280. SUSSMAN, Dorothy Coffin
"Concerto." [NewEngR] (12:3) Spr 90, p. 228.
"River Stories." [MissR] (19:1/2, #55/56) 90, p. 277-278.
"Woman Holds Forth in Woodruff Park." [ChatR] (10:4) Sum 90, p. 65.

6281. SUTHERLAND, Jenifer
"Eastbound." [PoetryC] (11:2) Sum 90, p. 16.
"Embrace (2)." [PoetryC] (11:2) Sum 90, p. 16.
"Embrace (3)." [PoetryC] (11:2) Sum 90, p. 16.
"Scissors." [PoetryC] (11:2) Sum 90, p. 16.

6282. SUTHERLAND-SMITH, James
"After Rain." [DogRR] (9:1, #17) Spr 90, p. 44.
"Egypt." [CumbPR] (9:2) Spr 90, p. 43.
"Revolt." [LaurelR] (24:1) Wint 90, p. 56-57.
"Searching for My Father." [DogRR] (9:1, #17) Spr 90, p. 32-33.
"Swimming in the Red Sea before a Sandstorm." [CumbPR] (9:2) Spr 90, p. 44-45.
"To Billie Holiday." [WindO] (53) Fall 90, p. 14.

6283. SUTTER, Barton
"Fishing at Forty" (for Louis Jenkins). [CharR] (16:2) Fall 90, p. 70-71.

6284. SUTTON, Dorothy
"When We Got Married." [ChironR] (9:2) Sum 90, p. 7.

6285. SUTTON, Pamela
"The Season of Icarus." [Thrpny] (43) Fall 90, p. 11.

6286. SUTTON, Sheree A.
"Fatherless Fatherhood." [Writer] (103:6) Je 90, p. 24.

6287. SUTZKEVER, Abraham
"Deer at the Red Sea" (in Yiddish and English, tr. by Leonard Fox). [InterPR] (16:2) Fall 90, p. 16-17.
"Here I Am, Then" (in Yiddish and English, tr. by Leonard Fox). [InterPR] (16:2) Fall 90, p. 12-13.

"In the Sack of the Wind" (in Yiddish and English, tr. by Leonard Fox). [InterPR] (16:2) Fall 90, p. 14-15.
"In the Village" (in Yiddish and English, tr. by Leonard Fox). [InterPR] (16:2) Fall 90, p. 6-11.

SUVERO, Victor Di
See Di SUVERO, Victor

SUYAN, Lei
See LEI, Suyan

6288. SUZUKI, M. (Miko)
"Achromatic Sketches." [HawaiiR] (14:3, #30) Fall 90, p. 95.
"Check-Out Counter Vignettes." [HawaiiR] (14:2, #29) Spr 90, p. 119.
"Feh." [HawaiiR] (14:3, #30) Fall 90, p. 95.
"I've Got a Warm Middle Spot." [HawaiiR] (14:3, #30) Fall 90, p. 94.
"Substitute for the Odd Number." [BambooR] (47) Sum 90, p. 64-65.
"Think of Colors." [BambooR] (47) Sum 90, p. 62-63.
"Wishes." [HawaiiR] (14:3, #30) Fall 90, p. 93.

6289. SVENVOLD, Mark
"Erosion." [Atlantic] (266:5) N 90, p. 122.

6290. SVOBODA, Terese
"Permission to Live." [ManhatPR] (11) [89?], p. 38.
"Philomela." [Ploughs] (16:4) Wint 90-91, p. 137-139.
"Picnic." [Nat] (251:1) 2 Jl 90, p. 30.
"The Ranchhand's Daughter." [Boulevard] (5:2, #14) Fall 90, p. 57-65.

6291. SWAN, Alison
"What We Haven't Considered." [BellR] (13:2, #28) Fall 90, p. 10-11.

6292. SWAN, Diane
"Ambush." [CarolQ] (42:2) Wint 90, p. 77.
"Forsythia." [AmerPoR] (19:2) Mr-Ap 90, p. 39.
"Girls from St. Augustine's." [AmerPoR] (19:2) Mr-Ap 90, p. 39.
"Jewelweed." [AmerPoR] (19:2) Mr-Ap 90, p. 39.
"The Need for Birds." [GreenMR] (NS 3:2) Fall-Wint 89-90, p. 70.
"The Other." [GreenMR] (NS 3:2) Fall-Wint 89-90, p. 71.
"Subtraction." [AmerPoR] (19:2) Mr-Ap 90, p. 39.

6293. SWANBERG, Christine
"Tape." [KanQ] (22:1/2) Wint-Spr 90, p. 117.

6294. SWANBERG, Ingrid
"Midnight, hour of the definite silence." [Abraxas] (38/39) 90, p. 126.
"The Night You Were Born." [Abraxas] (38/39) 90, p. 128.
"Psyche." [Abraxas] (38/39) 90, p. 127.
"Why not something small and perfect." [Abraxas] (38/39) 90, p. 127.
"Your shadow disappeared." [Abraxas] (38/39) 90, p. 126.

6295. SWANDER, Mary
"I-80 Lieder." [Iowa] (20:1) Wint 90, p. 47.
"Jackpot." [Iowa] (20:1) Wint 90, p. 46.
"Peelings." [Iowa] (20:1) Wint 90, p. 44-45.

6296. SWANGER, David
"Laundry." [PoetC] (22:1) Fall 90, p. 33.

6297. SWANK, R. T.
(Anonymous poem). [FreeL] (4) 90.

6298. SWANN, Brian
"Basso-Relievo." [PraS] (64:3) Fall 90, p. 12-13.
"Brown Sequence." [HampSPR] (Anthology 1975-1990) 90, p. 106.
"Chimera" (tr. of Bartolo Cattafi, w. Ruth Feldman). [HampSPR] (Anthology 1975-1990) 90, p. 248.
"The Cuckold's Tale." [PraS] (64:3) Fall 90, p. 16-18.
"Economics Lesson" (tr. of Rocco Scotellaro, w. Ruth Feldman). [HampSPR] (Anthology 1975-1990) 90, p. 247.
"Interstellar." [PraS] (64:3) Fall 90, p. 13-14.
"Key Word" (tr. of Bartolo Cattafi, w. Ruth Feldman). [HampSPR] (Anthology 1975-1990) 90, p. 249.
"My Black Socks." [Confr] (44/45) Fall 90-Wint 91, p. 290.
"Retreat." [PraS] (64:3) Fall 90, p. 14-15.
"Uninsured." [CharR] (16:1) Spr 90, p. 48.
"Where I Am." [PraS] (64:3) Fall 90, p. 16.

6299. SWANNELL, Anne
"The Bones of Angels." [PraF] (11:3) Aut 90, p. 29.

"Giralda." [CanLit] (127) Wint 90, p. 75.
"Husband, Flying by Night." [CanLit] (127) Wint 90, p. 93.
"Watching Them." [CanLit] (127) Wint 90, p. 29.
6300. SWARD, Robert
"108,000 Ways of Making Love." [FreeL] (5) Sum 90, p. 12-13.
"Alfa the Dog." [PoetryUSA] ([5:4?]) Wint 90, p. 19.
"Honey Bear." [PoetryUSA] ([5:4?]) Wint 90, p. 17.
6301. SWARTWOUT, Susan
"Folded." [LullwaterR] (2:1) Wint 90, p. 29.
"A Reputation" (Anne Howeson's painting, "Prostitute with Dog and Tulips").
[Farm] (7:2) Fall 90, p. 49.
"Winslow Homer's *Watching the Breakers*." [MissR] (19:1/2, #55/56) 90, p. 279.
"A Year After the Divorce, My Car Gets Wrecked." [Farm] (7:2) Fall 90, p. 48.
6302. SWARTZ, John Roscoe
"Shark Skin Suit." [ArtfulD] (18/19) 90, p. 104-105.
6303. SWEDE, George
"October crumbles in my hand." [CrossC] (12:1) 90, p. 21.
6304. SWEENEY, Matthew
"Calais." [Quarry] (39:1) Wint 90, p. 96.
6305. SWENSEN, Cole
"Bastille Day." [Manoa] (2:1) Spr 90, p. 145.
"Ghazal of a Thousand Years." [Avec] (3:1) 90, p. 18.
"Ghazal of the Secret Mile." [Avec] (3:1) 90, p. 17.
"Ghazal of the Warning." [Avec] (3:1) 90, p. 16.
"Wallace Stevens Waking at Night." [Manoa] (2:1) Spr 90, p. 145-146.
"Wallace Stevens Walks Along the Beach at Night." [Manoa] (2:1) Spr 90, p. 146.
"Wallace Stevens Walks by the Sea." [Manoa] (2:1) Spr 90, p. 146.
"What Is on the Page." [Manoa] (2:1) Spr 90, p. 144.
6306. SWENSON, Karen
"Cold Blood." [SouthernPR] (30:1) Spr 90, p. 40-41.
6307. SWENSON, May
"Last Day." [NewYorker] (66:46) 31 D 90, p. 34.
"Staring at the Sea on the Day of the Death of Another." [NewYorker] (66:39) 12 N
90, p. 66.
"Stripping and Putting On." [NewYorker] (66:36) 22 O 90, p. 52.
"A Tree in Spring." [BelPoJ] (40:4) Sum 90, p. 52.
6308. SWERDLOW, David
"Breathing" (for Donna). [WillowS] (25) Wint 90, p. 44-45.
6309. SWIFT, Joan
"After Surgery: A Friend Sends Bird Sighting from the *Boston Globe*."
[SouthernPR] (30:1) Spr 90, p. 58-59.
"Steelhead." [PoetryNW] (31:3) Aut 90, p. 35.
6310. SWIFT, Michael
"At Marlborough House." [NewYorker] (66:18) 18 Je 90, p. 40.
"Mrs. Jones." [NewRena] (8:1, #24) Spr 90, p. 76-79.
6311. SWIST, Wally
"In the Night Subway" (w. Anne McKay). [Os] (31) 90, p. 2-3.
"Inheritance." [Os] (30) Spr 90, p. 38.
6312. SYBESMA, R. P.
"In the White Field" (tr. by Rod Jellema). [WashR] (16:2) Ag-S 90, p. 13.
"Yn't Wite Fjild." [WashR] (16:2) Ag-S 90, p. 13.
6313. SYLVESTER, Janet
"Love Poem." [Shen] (40:2) Sum 90, p. 27.
"Tsvetayeva, Daily Necessity." [Shen] (40:2) Sum 90, p. 26-27.
6314. SYM, Myoung-ho
"The Hongch'on River" (tr. of Shin Kyung-rim, w. Lois Cucullu). [PoetL] (85:2)
Sum 90, p. 37-38.
6315. SYS, Karel
"Troja at Eight in the Evening" (tr. by Richard Katrovas and Dominika Winterová).
[PoetryE] (29) Spr 90, p. 116.
6316. SZAKSZTYLO, Kathee
"Dialogue." [WillowR] Spr 90, p. 17.
6317. SZE, Arthur
"Configurations." [MidAR] (10:1) 90, p. 15.
"The Silk Road." [Manoa] (2:2) Fall 90, p. 102-105.
"Streamers." [ParisR] (32:116) Fall 90, p. 130-135.

6318. SZÉCSI, Margit
    "They Were Roving" (tr. by Mária Kurdi and Len Roberts). [AmerPoR] (19:5) S-O
        90, p. 25.
    "The Visible Man" (tr. by Mária Kurdi and Len Roberts). [AmerPoR] (19:5) S-O 90,
        p. 24-25.
    "When the New Moon Screamed" (tr. by Mária Kurdi and Len Roberts). [AmerPoR]
        (19:5) S-O 90, p. 24.
6319. SZILAGYI, Domokos
    "Borders" (tr. by Len Roberts). [AmerPoR] (19:5) S-O 90, p. 31.
6320. SZIRTES, George
    "The Comfort of Rooms." [Quarry] (39:1) Wint 90, p. 50.
6321. SZÖCS, Géza
    "Indian Words on the Radio" (to the poet, William Least Heat Moon, tr. by Len
        Roberts). [AmerPoR] (19:5) S-O 90, p. 31.
6322. SZUMOWSKI, Margaret (Margaret C.)
    "Borders." [BilingR] (13:3) S-D 86 c90, p. 65-66.
    "Bringing Home the Tree." [RiverS] (32) [90?], p. 52.
    "Incident on the Gondar Road." [AmerPoR] (19:1) Ja-F 90, p. 17.
    "Memory of Summer: The Rio Grande Valley." [BilingR] (13:3) S-D 86 c90, p.
        62-63.
    "Oranges." [RiverS] (32) [90?], p. 53.
    "Summer Downpour." [RiverS] (32) [90?], p. 54.
    "Sunday at the Paradise Orchards." [RiverS] (32) [90?], p. 51.
    "The Woman Who Loves the Valley." [BilingR] (13:3) S-D 86 c90, p. 64.
6323. TACIUCH, Dean
    "Containment." [Iowa] (20:3) Fall 90, p. 123.
    "Focus." [SouthernHR] (24:2) Spr 90, p. 116.
6324. TAFDRUP, Pia
    "The Beginning" (tr. by Roger Greenwald). [Writ] (21) 89 c1990, p. 29.
    "Darkly Glinting" (tr. by Roger Greenwald). [Writ] (21) 89 c1990, p. 33.
    "Echo" (tr. by Roger Greenwald). [Writ] (21) 89 c1990, p. 25-26.
    "Fossil" (from "Intetfang," Borgen, 1982, tr. by Monique M. Kennedy). [CimR]
        (92) Jl 90, p. 31.
    "Heavenly Geometry" (tr. by Anne Born). [Verse] (7:2) Sum 90, p. 11.
    "New Remembered Places I" (tr. by Roger Greenwald). [Writ] (21) 89 c1990, p.
        31.
    "New Remembered Places II" (tr. by Roger Greenwald). [Writ] (21) 89 c1990, p.
        32.
    "Pause-beat" (tr. by Roger Greenwald). [Writ] (21) 89 c1990, p. 28.
    "Setting Fire" (tr. by Roger Greenwald). [Writ] (21) 89 c1990, p. 23.
    "Sirocco Night" (tr. by Roger Greenwald). [Writ] (21) 89 c1990, p. 27.
    "Surveyor" (tr. by Roger Greenwald). [Writ] (21) 89 c1990, p. 24.
    "Waking Sleep" (tr. by Roger Greenwald). [Writ] (21) 89 c1990, p. 30.
    "Yesterday's Tea" (from "When an Angel Is Wounded," Borgen, 1981, tr. by
        Monique M. Kennedy). [CimR] (92) Jl 90, p. 31-32.
6325. TAGGART, John
    "Like That and Then." [Talisman] (4) Spr 90, p. 59.
    "Prometheos Auomenos" (Fragments, tr. of Aeschylus). [Conjunc] (15) 90, p.
        359-360.
6326. TAGLIABUE, John
    "1. Sentences and Sensibility." [NewYorkQ] (43) Fall 90, p. 57.
    "2. Handy Words." [NewYorkQ] (43) Fall 90, p. 57-58.
    "In 1990 I'm hearing about the different characteristics of rhythms in different
        periods of Chinese Poetry." [CrossCur] (9:2) Je 90, p. 51.
    "Mantras and Meditations." [NewL] (57:1) Fall 90, p. 69.
    "Tra la Perduta Gente." [BostonR] (15:4) Ag 90, p. 23.
6327. TAINTER, B. Bagley
    "On the Ditch." [Ometeca] (1:2/2:1) 89-90, p. 45.
6328. TAKACS, Zsuzsa
á   "Circle" (tr. by Mária Kurdi and Len Roberts). [AmerPoR] (19:5) S-O 90, p. 29.
    "Such Is the Place, This Unnamable" (tr. by Mária Kurdi and Len Roberts).
        [AmerPoR] (19:5) S-O 90, p. 28.
6329. TAKAHARA, Mel
    "From *The Waiting Child*." [ChamLR] (4:1, #7) Fall 90, p. 42-43.
    "The Waiting Child." [ChamLR] (4:1, #7) Fall 90, p. 44-45.

6330. TAKAHASHI, Shinkichi
"Mother and I" (tr. by Lucien Stryk). [HampSPR] (Anthology 1975-1990) 90, p. 244.
"Sparrow and Aviary" (tr. by Lucien Stryk). [HampSPR] (Anthology 1975-1990) 90, p. 243.
6331. TAKARA, Kathryn
"Goat Haikus." [ChamLR] (3:2, #6) Spr 90, p. 61.
6332. TAKIGUCHI, Mimi Nelson
"Compassion." [OnTheBus] (2:1, #5) Spr 90, p. 133-134.
6333. TAKSA, Mark
"Baby Key in the Mechanical Forest." [HawaiiR] (14:1, #28) Wint 89-90, p. 66.
"Living Room in the Park." [HawaiiR] (14:1, #28) Wint 89-90, p. 67.
"Tattoos, Suit Changing." [HawaiiR] (14:2, #29) Spr 90, p. 71-72.
"Words and the Lighted Blanket." [HawaiiR] (14:3, #30) Fall 90, p. 108.
6334. TALBERT, Caroline O.
"Creek Water." [GreensboroR] (49) Wint 90-91, p. 74.
6335. TALCOTT, William
"Earthquake '89." [NewAW] (6) Spr 90, p. 89-90.
"The List." [NewAW] (6) Spr 90, p. 91.
6336. TALENTINO, Arnold
"Distance." [PoetC] (22:1) Fall 90, p. 36.
6337. TALL, Deborah
"Cleaning Smelt." [Ploughs] (16:1) Spr-Sum 90, p. 9.
6338. TALLOSI, Jim
"Belugas." [CanLit] (124/125) Spr-Sum 90, p. 30.
"Four Dancers." [CanLit] (124/125) Spr-Sum 90, p. 31.
"A Prairie Museum." [CanLit] (124/125) Spr-Sum 90, p. 29.
"Spring Day." [AntigR] (80) Wint 90, p. 86.
6339. TAM, Reuben
"Each Step You Take." [Manoa] (2:1) Spr 90, p. 128.
"Makaleha." [Manoa] (2:1) Spr 90, p. 129.
"Stopping Before Olohena." [Manoa] (2:1) Spr 90, p. 127.
6340. TAMBIAH, Yasmin
"The Civil War." [Cond] (17) 90, p. 102.
"May Day, 1985." [Cond] (17) 90, p. 101.
"Sandalwood (For A.)." [Cond] (17) 90, p. 103.
TAMIKO, Abe
See ABE, Tamiko
6341. TAMMINGA, Douwe A.
"Sa Ald Te Wurden." [WashR] (16:2) Ag-S 90, p. 13.
"A Way to Grow Old" (tr. by Rod Jellema). [WashR] (16:2) Ag-S 90, p. 13.
6342. TAM'SI, Tichicaya U
"Bush Fire" (tr. by Dennis Egan). [Vis] (32) 90, p. 9.
"Still Life" (tr. by Dennis Egan). [Vis] (32) 90, p. 10.
6343. TANAKA, A. Y.
"Apples." [SouthernHR] (24:3) Sum 90, p. 218.
6344. TANG, Ya Ping
"Be Patient, Be Patient" (tr. by Ginny MacKenzie and Wei Guo). [PoetryE] (30) Fall 90, p. 105.
"Black Marsh" (from "Black Desert," tr. by Edward Morin, Dennis Ding, and Dai Fang). [Screens] (2) 90, p. 42.
TANG, Yaping
See TANG, Ya Ping
6345. TANGORRA, Joanne
"Morning after Snow." [PraS] (64:1) Spr 90, p. 113-115.
"Visit after Coronary Bypass." [PraS] (64:1) Spr 90, p. 115-116.
6346. TANIKAWA, Shuntaro
"Hi There" (tr. by Yorifumi Yaguchi and William Stafford). [ArtfulD] (18/19) 90, p. 15.
6347. TANNEHILL, Arlene
"Hair Shirt." [ClockR] (6:2) 90, p. 74.
6348. TANNENBAUM, Judith
"Drought." [PoetryUSA] ([5:4?]) Wint 90, p. 17.
"Green Grief" (After Lorca). [Sequoia] (33:2) Wint 90, p. 49.
6349. TANNER, Anita
"Getting the Children to Bed." [Comm] (117:11) 1 Je 90, p. 352.

6350. TANNY, Marlaina
"Aubade." [Vis] (33) 90, p. 33.
6351. TANSEY, John
"Systole." [HeavenB] (8) Wint 90-91, p. 19-20.
6352. TANZY, Mary B.
"Food Shopping." [Kalliope] (12:2) 90, p. 37.
6353. TARANENKO, Liudmila
"And from the suffering you gave me" (tr. by Oleg Atbashian and Maureen Hurley).
[PoetryUSA] (5:2) Sum 90, p. 13.
"If I were grass" (tr. by Oleg Atbashian and Maureen Hurley). [PoetryUSA] (5:2)
Sum 90, p. 13.
"Leaves fall down and down, making circles" (tr. by Oleg Atbashian and Maureen
Hurley). [PoetryUSA] (5:2) Sum 90, p. 13.
6354. TARDIEU, Jean
"Cascade of Genitives" (tr. by Robert Brown). [Vis] (33) 90, p. 23.
6355. TARN, Nathaniel
"And Even the Republic Must Have an End." [Hudson] (43:2) Sum 90, p. 338-339.
"Energetically Singing Against Voracious Earth." [Hudson] (43:2) Sum 90, p. 338.
"Italian Sequence Comma with Italian Words Stop Two Stop (Architextures 15 Dash
21)" (To the wounded spirit of Andrea Mantegna, ad majorem gloriam).
[Notus] (5:1) Spr 90, p. 32-38.
"Italian Sequence Comma with Italian Words Stop, One Stop (Architextures 8 Dash
14)" (ARC8-14). [Conjunc] (15) 90, p. 224-231.
6356. TATE, James
"The Expert." [Iowa] (20:2) Spr-Sum 90, p. 94-95.
"I Am a Finn." [Iowa] (20:2) Spr-Sum 90, p. 96.
"I Am Still a Finn." [Iowa] (20:2) Spr-Sum 90, p. 97-98.
"Vito Takes His Neighbor's Dog for a Drive." [Iowa] (20:2) Spr-Sum 90, p. 95-96.
6357. TAUFER, Veno
"Into Your Eye" (tr. by Michael Scammel). [Vis] (33) 90, p. 39.
6358. TAUS, Roger
"Autumn Night." [OnTheBus] (2:1, #5) Spr 90, p. 136.
"Homage to Vallejo, 12/29/89." [OnTheBus] (2:1, #5) Spr 90, p. 135.
"Poesias." [OnTheBus] (2:1, #5) Spr 90, p. 136.
6359. TAYLOR, Alexander
"It Is the Bird in the Tree" (tr. of Jørgen Gustava Brandt, w. the author). [CimR]
(92) Jl 90, p. 15-16.
6360. TAYLOR, David
"Breasts." [HampSPR] (Anthology 1975-1990) 90, p. 152.
6361. TAYLOR, Eleanor Ross
"The Altar Needlework." [KenR] (NS 12:3) Sum 90, p. 92-93.
"Boiled Peanuts." [SenR] (20:2) Fall 90, p. 17.
"Captive Voices." [NewYorker] (66:46) 31 D 90, p. 40-41.
"The Hostage." [GrandS] (9:2) Wint 90, p. 54.
"How Morning Comes, Out of Sleep." [KenR] (NS 12:3) Sum 90, p. 93-94.
"Next Year." [GrandS] (9:3) Spr 90, p. 261-262.
"A Permanent Dye." [SenR] (20:2) Fall 90, p. 16.
"Rain." [Field] (42) Spr 90, p. 61.
"Short Foray." [TriQ] (79) Fall 90, p. 131-132.
"The Sunny Day." [KenR] (NS 12:3) Sum 90, p. 94-95.
6362. TAYLOR, Henry
"A Field Stoned" (tr. of Ya'akov Besser). [PoetL] (85:4) Wint 90-91, p. 24.
"The House in the Road." [HampSPR] (Anthology 1975-1990) 90, p. 101-102.
6363. TAYLOR, James
"Dream (For Susan)." [HampSPR] (Anthology 1975-1990) 90, p. 57-58.
6364. TAYLOR, Keith
"Lament for the Crested Shelduck" (Tadorna cristata). [Notus] (5:1) Spr 90, p. 86.
6365. TAYLOR, Kent
"Calendar." [SwampR] (5) Wint-Spr 90, p. 79.
"Cleaning the Wound" (in memory of Helen). [SwampR] (5) Wint-Spr 90, p. 80.
"Murmurs." [SwampR] (6) Sum-Fall 90, p. 92.
"Waiting for Morning." [OnTheBus] (2:2/3:1, #6/7) Sum-Fall 90 Wint-Spr 91, p.
194.
6366. TAYLOR, Marcella
"African Child." [Poetry] (156:1) Ap 90, p. 22.

6367. TAYLOR, Reta
"M. M." [Pearl] (12) Fall-Wint 90, p. 27.
6368. TAYLOR, Ron
"A Photograph That Doesn't Yet Exist." [SoCoast] (9) Fall 90, p. 18.
"Year of the Puffball." [SoCoast] (9) Fall 90, p. 51.
6369. TAYLOR, Steven
"You" (tr. of Jiang He, w. Wang Ping). [LitR] (33:4) Sum 90, p. 525.
6370. TAYLOR, Yuval
"Holding Together." [Amelia] (6:2, #17) 90, p. 98-99.
6371. TAYLOR-GRAHAM
"Amos, How We Found You" (paramedic dead at 22). [CoalC] (2) D 90, p. 11.
"Chances." [Confr] (42/43) Spr-Sum 90, p. 176.
"Dreaming You Make Bread." [FreeL] (5) Sum 90, p. 9.
"The River Gathering" (for G.W.D., Oregon Creek). [FreeL] (6) Aut 90, p. 32.
"This Season on the Ridge." [SmPd] (27:3, #80) Fall 90, p. 23.
"Verna." [SmPd] (27:3, #80) Fall 90, p. 19.
6372. TEDLOCK, Dennis
"The Archaeology of Dreams" (Excerpt). [KenR] (NS 12:2) Spr 90, p. 174.
6373. TEICHMANN, Sandra Gail
"Blackeyed Peas Look Like Pussy Willows, But Soft Inside." [CimR] (93) O 90, p.
37.
"How 'Unlikely'." [KanQ] (22:1/2) Wint-Spr 90, p. 73.
"Train Tracks and Trains Forever and Dogs on No Leashes." [HolCrit] (27:4) O 90,
p. 14.
6374. TEIGEN, Sue
"1948: Dr. Williams, Listening to His Own Heart" (for Dr. Harold Segall).
[NowestR] (28:2) 90, p. 17-18.
"While My Mother Was Having Her Stroke." [Sonora] (19) Spr-Sum 90, p. 15-16.
6375. TEILLIER, Jorge
"Afternoon" (tr. by Mary Crow). [CrabCR] (6:3) Spr 90, p. 19.
"Afternoon in Automobile" (for my brother Ivan, tr. by Carolyne Wright). [PartR]
(57:3) Sum 90, p. 445.
"A Day in Madrid" (for Jorge Edwards and Galvarino Plaza, tr. by Carolyne
Wright). [MidAR] (10:1) 90, p. 108-110.
"Golden Age" (tr. by Carolyne Wright). [HampSPR] (Anthology 1975-1990) 90, p.
254.
"Image" (tr. by Carolyne Wright). [NewL] (57:1) Fall 90, p. 11.
"In the Secret House of Night" (tr. by Mary Crow). [CrabCR] (6:3) Spr 90, p. 19.
"One Year, Another Year" (tr. by Carolyne Wright). [NewL] (57:1) Fall 90, p. 9-10.
"The Return of Orpheus" (In memoriam Rosamel del Valle, tr. by Carolyne Wright).
[MissouriR] (13:2) 90, p. 125.
6376. TEITEL, Nathan
"Ave Atque Vale." [NewYorkQ] (42) Sum 90, p. 68.
6377. TELBISZ, Miklós
"Message" (tr. of Sándor Csoóri, w. Len Roberts and Gábor Töró). [NowestR]
(28:1) 90, p. 101.
"On the Third Day the Snow Began to Fall" (tr. of Sándor Csoóri, w. Len Roberts
and László Vértes). [Chelsea] (49) 90, p. 123.
"On the Third Day the Snow Began to Fall" (tr. of Sándor Csoóri, w. Len Roberts
and László Vértes). [MidAR] (10:1) 90, p. 83, 85.
6378. TEMME, Leonard A.
"Dreamscape." [EmeraldCR] (1990) c89, p. 21.
"Father Sonnet." [EmeraldCR] (1990) c89, p. 19.
"A Father's Lament." [EmeraldCR] (1990) c89, p. 19.
"Going to the Post Office." [EmeraldCR] (1990) c89, p. 22-23.
"The Mandelbrot Problem." [Comm] (117:17) 12 O 90, p. 578.
"Night on the Interstate." [EmeraldCR] (1990) c89, p. 25.
"Three Letters to the President of These United States." [EmeraldCR] (1990) c89, p.
20-21.
"Untitled: He folds and leans." [EmeraldCR] (1990) c89, p. 23-25.
6379. TENENBAUM, Molly
"Beach Walk and Bad News." [PoetryNW] (31:4) Wint 90-91, p. 11-12.
"Straw Song." [PoetryNW] (31:4) Wint 90-91, p. 10-11.
"To the Handsome Young Man Who Bought the Old and Wonderful Picture
Dictionary at the Book Sale . . . ." [PoetryNW] (31:4) Wint 90-91, p. 9-10.

457

6380. TENGERDI, Tibor
"A Night Journey in Germany" (tr. of Sándor Csoóri, w. Len Roberts). [MidAR]
(10:1) 90, p. 87, 89.
"A Thin, Black Band" (tr. of Sándor Csoóri, w. Len Roberts). [MidAR] (10:1) 90,
p. 77, 79.
6381. TENNENT, Cheryl E. (Cheryl Ervin)
"Disembarking." [InterPR] (16:1) Spr 90, p. 134.
"Incantations." [InterPR] (16:1) Spr 90, p. 134.
"Old Gentleman Friends Recalled." [SmPd] (27:3, #80) Fall 90, p. 28.
"Old Women Rehearse the End of Time." [SmPd] (27:3, #80) Fall 90, p. 29.
6382. TERASHIMA, R.
"Marriage." [Footwork] 90, p. 91.
6383. TERAYAMA, Shuji
"Before he left our village" (tr. by Peter Levitt, w. Makiko Fujiwara-Skrobak).
[Zyzzyva] (6:3 #23) Fall 90, p. 105.
"Ever since my mother carried me" (tr. by Peter Levitt, w. Makiko
Fujiwara-Skrobak). [Zyzzyva] (6:3 #23) Fall 90, p. 104.
"I pressed on with the hot teeth" (tr. by Peter Levitt, w. Makiko Fujiwara-Skrobak).
[Zyzzyva] (6:3 #23) Fall 90, p. 104.
"I stroke the mountain dove" (tr. by Peter Levitt, w. Makiko Fujiwara-Skrobak).
[Zyzzyva] (6:3 #23) Fall 90, p. 105.
"The rope I haven't used" (tr. by Peter Levitt, w. Makiko Fujiwara-Skrobak).
[Zyzzyva] (6:3 #23) Fall 90, p. 105.
"Tonight the fingerprint" (tr. by Peter Levitt, w. Makiko Fujiwara-Skrobak).
[Zyzzyva] (6:3 #23) Fall 90, p. 104.
6384. TERMAN, Philip
"Somewhere in the Heartland" (for Lois Tyson). [PoetC] (21:3) Spr 90, p. 26.
6385. TERMINELLI, Pietro
"Silence" (from the Sicilian Antigruppo, tr. by Nat Scammacca). [Footwork] 90, p.
102.
6386. TERPSTRA, John
"Physical Mysteries." [PoetryC] (11:2) Sum 90, p. 27.
6387. TERRANOVA, Elaine
"1939." [SpoonRQ] (15:1) Wint 90, p. 10-11.
"Good Girl." [Boulevard] (4:3/5:1, #12/13) Spr 90, p. 170.
"In the New World." [GrahamHR] (13) Spr 90, p. 69-70.
"The Print Skirt." [SpoonRQ] (15:1) Wint 90, p. 11.
6388. TERRILL, Richard
"Elmsford, New York." [AnotherCM] (21) 90, p. 151.
"In the Summer Night I and You" (tr. of Ma Li, w. Tsung Tsung). [AnotherCM]
(21) 90, p. 109-110.
"A Palm Tree and Two Women" (tr. of Ma Li, w. Tsung Tsung). [AnotherCM] (21)
90, p. 107-108.
6389. TERRIS, Virginia (Virginia R.)
"After the Prom." [HampSPR] (Anthology 1975-1990) 90, p. 228.
"Bravado." [HampSPR] (Anthology 1975-1990) 90, p. 228.
"Companions." [HampSPR] (Anthology 1975-1990) 90, p. 142.
"The Poet." [HampSPR] (Anthology 1975-1990) 90, p. 143.
6390. TEST, Becky
"For Release." [CapeR] (25:1) Spr 90, p. 36.
"The Prayer." [CapeR] (25:1) Spr 90, p. 35.
6391. TETI, Zona
"From Nestor to Helen Now of Troy." [MichQR] (29:4) Fall 90, p. 498.
"New Job." [CumbPR] (9:2) Spr 90, p. 46.
"On a Painting Cut with a Knife." [LitR] (33:3) Spr 90, p. 316.
"Perdita Considers Dessert." [Iowa] (20:1) Wint 90, p. 102.
"Perdita in a Large World." [Iowa] (20:1) Wint 90, p. 101.
"Perdita in the Back Room." [Iowa] (20:1) Wint 90, p. 100-101.
"Perdita's Sunday." [Iowa] (20:1) Wint 90, p. 100.
6392. TETTE, Sharan Flynn
"The Vigil." [CumbPR] (10:1) Fall 90, p. 47.
6393. THALMAN, Mark
"Blue Spring Afternoon." [Pearl] (11) Sum 90, p. 51.
6394. THAM, Hilary
"May Means Beautiful in Chinese." [Gargoyle] (37/38) 90, p. 130.

6395. THATCHER, Philip
  "Anywhere." [Event] (19:1) Spr 90, p. 68-69.
  "Poundmaker's Long, Last Walk." [Event] (19:1) Spr 90, p. 70-72.
6396. THÉNON, Susana
  "29. And the hatred" (tr. by Renata Treitel). [Rohwedder] (5) Spr 90, p. 12.
  "29. Y el odio." [Rohwedder] (5) Spr 90, p. 12.
  "30. Cáncer enmarañada primavera." [Rohwedder] (5) Spr 90, p. 12.
  "30. Cancer entangled spring" (tr. by Renata Treitel). [Rohwedder] (5) Spr 90, p.
    12.
  "31. Abortion of a Poem in a Public Office" (tr. by Renata Treitel). [Rohwedder] (5)
    Spr 90, p. 13.
  "31. Aborto de Poema en Oficina Pública." [Rohwedder] (5) Spr 90, p. 13.
  "32. Birth II" (tr. by Renata Treitel). [Rohwedder] (5) Spr 90, p. 13.
  "32. Nacimiento II." [Rohwedder] (5) Spr 90, p. 13.
  "33. Aquella amiga desesperación." [Rohwedder] (5) Spr 90, p. 14.
  "33. That friend -- despair" (tr. by Renata Treitel). [Rohwedder] (5) Spr 90, p. 14.
  "34. Abres sí túnel." [Rohwedder] (5) Spr 90, p. 14.
  "34. You open yes tunnel" (tr. by Renata Treitel). [Rohwedder] (5) Spr 90, p. 14.
  "Distances" (Selections: 28, 36, 37, tr. by Renata Treitel). [Caliban] (8) 90, p.
    60-61.
  "You who read that Dante guy in the comic books" (tr. by Renata Treitel). [PoetryE]
    (30) Fall 90, p. 28.
6397. THEOHARIS, Theoharis C.
  "As Long as You Can" (tr. of Constantine P. Cavafy). [Agni] (31/32) 90, p. 121.
  "Waiting for the Barbarians" (tr. of Constantine P. Cavafy). [Agni] (31/32) 90, p.
    122-123.
6398. THOENNES, Amy
  "Down Like Rain." [PoetryUSA] (5:3) Fall 90, p. 26.
6399. THOMAS, D. M.
  "Transatlantic Greetings" (for Diana Der Hovanessian). [Agni] (31/32) 90, p.
    236-237.
6400. THOMAS, Denise
  "Driving Ohio." [GettyR] (3:4) Aut 90, p. 736.
  "Hardpan." [HighP] (5:1) Spr 90, p. 47.
  "One Sunday We Evaluate Our Marriage." [GettyR] (3:4) Aut 90, p. 737.
  "The Roofer." [Wind] (20:66) 90, p. 11.
  "A Walk with My Son." [SoDakR] (28:3) Aut 90, p. 55.
  "Where I Live Now." [SoDakR] (28:3) Aut 90, p. 54.
6401. THOMAS, Harry
  "Seeing a Friend Off" (tr. of Li Po, w. Gu Zhen). [Agni] (29/30) 90, p. 205.
6402. THOMAS, Jim
  "Breakfast Lovers." [MidwQ] (31:3) Spr 90, p. 371.
  "Feathered." [KanQ] (22:3) Sum 90, p. 104.
  "Morning Windsong." [KanQ] (22:1/2) Wint-Spr 90, p. 47.
  "Stonepath." [KanQ] (22:3) Sum 90, p. 104.
  "Young Owl." [KanQ] (22:1/2) Wint-Spr 90, p. 47.
6403. THOMAS, John
  "Remember Pearl Harbor: Another Historic Day Devoted to the Craft of Poetry."
    [Zyzzyva] (6:3 #23) Fall 90, p. 109-110.
6404. THOMAS, Joyce
  "Waiting for the Ambulance." [NegC] (10:1) 90, p. 88-89.
6405. THOMAS, Julia
  "How Is It." [WindO] (53) Fall 90, p. 24.
  "The Last Poem to My Mother." [WindO] (53) Fall 90, p. 23.
  "Map." [WindO] (53) Fall 90, p. 22.
6406. THOMAS, Kathleen
  "The Parting." [Blueline] (11:1/2) 90, p. 46.
6407. THOMAS, Linda
  "Acacio Araujo's Pig." [Pearl] (11) Sum 90, p. 54.
  "Margarito Thinks of Home." [ContextS] (1:1) 89, p. 37.
  "Las Mujeres of Orange Park Acres Packing House." [SycamoreR] (2:1) Wint 90, p.
    16.
  "Palmyra." [SlipS] (10) 90, p. 96-97.
  "Soledad." [Pearl] (10) Spr 90, p. 14.
6408. THOMAS, Lorenzo
  "Millenarian Joys." [Callaloo] (13:2) Spr 90, p. 197.

"A Mingus Memory." [Callaloo] (13:2) Spr 90, p. 195-196.
6409. THOMAS, Mary Jo
"From a Dictionary of Chinese Ideograms." [CalQ] (34) 90, p. 30-31.
6410. THOMAS, P. L.
"She Could." [CumbPR] (10:1) Fall 90, p. 48.
6411. THOMAS, Stan
"Cinderella: a Sociological Phenomenon." [Bogg] (62) 90, p. 37.
6412. THOMAS, Stanley J.
"Graceland." [Bogg] (63) 90, p. 46.
6413. THOMPKINS, Wayne
"Vanished Faces." [AntigR] (81/82) Spr-Sum 90, p. 90-91.
"Whistlin' with Sweep Pea" (for Margaret Pacsu). [AntigR] (81/82) Spr-Sum 90, p. 88-89.
6414. THOMPSON, Cath
"Recently, It Has Occurred to Me." [SinW] (40) Spr 90, p. 94-95.
6415. THOMPSON, Clive
"Science Fair." [PoetryC] (11:4) Wint 90, p. 17.
"What Little I Have to Say About Living in a Major Urban Centre." [PoetryC] (11:4) Wint 90, p. 17.
6416. THOMPSON, David
"Cypress, Heron: Leaving Camille." [LullwaterR] (1:1) Spr 90, p. 62-63.
6417. THOMPSON, Donna Martin
"For Any Kamikaze Terrorist." [Vis] (33) 90, p. 11-12.
6418. THOMPSON, E. P.
"The First Emperor." [TriQ] (79) Fall 90, p. 140-147.
6419. THOMPSON, Earle
"Wounded Knee Sunrise." [PacificR] (8) 90, p. 35.
6420. THOMPSON, Gary
"Lunch." [HayF] (7) Fall-Wint 90, p. 66-67.
"Words Stay." [HayF] (7) Fall-Wint 90, p. 31.
6421. THOMPSON, Jeanie
"Ceremony on a Summer Night." [RiverS] (32) [90?], p. 74.
"Meditation at the Kitchen Window." [MissouriR] (13:1) 90, p. 152.
"The Mouse." [NoAmR] (275:3) S 90, p. 16.
"Revelation." [PoetryUSA] ([5:4?]) Wint 90, p. 10.
6422. THOMPSON, Marika
"The Dissolving of the Miniature Code" (of Beatrix Potter). [BellArk] (6:3) My-Je 90, p. 1.
6423. THOMPSON, Phil
"Riding Before the Storm" (to Frank Cameron). [PottPort] (11) 89, p. 8.
6424. THOMPSON, Ray
"P.S. to a Christmas Card." [PoetryUSA] (5:2) Sum 90, p. 18.
6425. THOMPSON, Rebecca
"Homage to Samuel Beckett." [NewYorkQ] (42) Sum 90, p. 73.
6426. THOMPSON, Sue Ellen
"The Bride's Story." [NegC] (10:1) 90, p. 90-91.
"Falling Awake." [ManhatPR] (11) [89?], p. 42-43.
"Thaw." [ManhatPR] (11) [89?], p. 43.
6427. THOMPSON, W. B.
"Skate." [SouthernPR] (30:1) Spr 90, p. 71.
6428. THOMSON, David
"Fissure." [NewDeltaR] (7:2) Spr-Sum 90, p. 6-7.
6429. THORBURN, Alexander
"The Beach." [ParisR] (32:116) Fall 90, p. 168-169.
"Wedding." [YaleR] (79:3) Spr 90, p. 443-444.
6430. THORN, David
"Poems Today?" (this little song is dedicated to Maude Meehan who wonders about poetry in this country). [LullwaterR] (2:1) Wint 90, p. 37.
"Sharing the Famine" (for Cheyenne). [LullwaterR] (2:1) Wint 90, p. 74-75.
6431. THORNDIKE, Jonathan L.
"Turtle Poem." [SwampR] (5) Wint-Spr 90, p. 30-31.
"U.A.W." [SwampR] (5) Wint-Spr 90, p. 32.
6432. THORP, Thomas E.
"There Once was a lady from Keele." [Amelia] (6:2, #17) 90, p. 37.
6433. THORTON, Thomas E.
"On Wiesel's *Night*." [EngJ] (79:2) F 90, p. 87.

6434. THORVALDSON, Joanne
"Triumvera." [PraF] (11:4) Wint 90-91, p. 76-77.
TIANXIANG, Ji
See JI, Tianxiang
T'IAO, Hsieh
See HSIEH, T'iao
6435. TIBBETTS, Frederick
"The Academy Prisoners." [BellR] (13:1, #27) Spr 90, p. 21.
"A Day on the *Nautilus*." [NewEngR] (12:4) Sum 90, p. 413-414.
"Fauna of Mirrors." [Sequoia] (33:2) Wint 90, p. 104.
6436. TICHY, Susan
"After a Conversation on Rilke, Darwin, and Rembrandt's Self-Portrait As an Old
Man." [BelPoR] (40:3) Spr 90, p. 8-9.
"Copulation." [BelPoR] (40:3) Spr 90, p. 6-7.
"Night Travel." [BelPoR] (40:3) Spr 90, p. 10.
"On the Place Where the Hospital Tipi Stood." [IndR] (14:1) Wint 90, p. 98-100.
"Weeping: Mimeisthai." [IndR] (14:1) Wint 90, p. 101-103.
6437. TIEBER, Linda
"Monterey." [NewYorkQ] (41) Spr 90, p. 99-100.
6438. TIEMAN, John Samuel
"Passchendaele." [WebR] (14:2) Spr 90, p. 5-7.
"War Story." [CimR] (91) Ap 90, p. 43.
6439. TIEMELE, Jean Baptiste
"Poetry Festival" (Paris, 1987, tr. by Dennis Egan and Jean-Clarence Lambert, w.
Bradley R. Strahan). [Vis] (32) 90, p. 11.
6440. TIERNEY, Karl
"The Blindness of Habit." [JamesWR] (7:2) Wint 90, p. 9.
"Jackie O." [JamesWR] (7:2) Wint 90, p. 9.
"Sot." [JamesWR] (7:2) Wint 90, p. 9.
6441. TIGER, Madeline
"August." [Footwork] 90, p. 111.
"Hallelujah" (for Tom Stainton's 9th Graders). [Footwork] 90, p. 111.
"He Is Not Your Monster." [Footwork] 90, p. 112.
"Her 'Lady of the Depths' Appears at Blue Mountain Center" (for Andrea Budy).
[Blueline] (11:1/2) 90, p. 25-26.
"Opposites." [Blueline] (11:1/2) 90, p. 60.
"Progress Report." [JINJPo] (12:2) Aut 90, p. 28-29.
6442. TILLER, Ruth L.
"Hometown, 1956." [LullwaterR] (1:1) Spr 90, p. 89.
"Midtown Nightfall." [LullwaterR] (1:1) Spr 90, p. 52.
6443. TILLERY, Mary Louise
"Promise." [Writer] (103:3) Mr 90, p. 23.
6444. TILLETT, Jordan
"Insurrection." [AmerV] (20) Fall 90, p. 72.
6445. TIMEWELL, Larry
"Ruck" (Excerpt). [Verse] (7:1) Spr 90, p. 44-45.
TIMEWELL, Lary
See TIMEWELL, Larry
6446. TIMMONS, Susie
"Coo Coo Vision." [BrooklynR] (7) 90, p. 26-27.
"Hexagons in the Hallway." [Shiny] (5) 90, p. 4.
"Horrible Valentine." [BrooklynR] (7) 90, p. 29.
"Rhapsody in Orange." [Shiny] (5) 90, p. 6.
"Russian Folk Songs." [BrooklynR] (7) 90, p. 28.
"A Snowflake and a Ball of Yarn." [Shiny] (5) 90, p. 5.
6447. TIMS, Michael C.
"White Father." [Vis] (33) 90, p. 46.
6448. TINDALL, Robert
"On Ikkyu Sojun Zenji (1394-1481)." [HawaiiR] (15:1, #31) Wint 90, p. 85.
TING, Shu
See SHU, Ting
6449. TINKHAM, Charles
"Recovery Act" (reprinted from #8, 1984). [Kaleid] (20) Wint-Spr 90, p. 41.
6450. TIPTON, Carolyn
"Blue" (tr. of Rafael Alberti). [HawaiiR] (14:3, #30) Fall 90, p. 109-112.
"Yellow" (tr. of Rafael Alberti). [HawaiiR] (14:2, #29) Spr 90, p. 63-66.

6451. TITTLER, Nancy
"The Bronze Poet" (from "Trefoil in the Park," #2, tr. of Innokenty Annensky, w. Devon Miller-Duggan). [Gargoyle] (37/38) 90, p. 87.
"Second Tormenting Sonnet" (tr. of Innokenty Annensky, w. Devon Miller-Duggan). [Gargoyle] (37/38) 90, p. 87.
6452. TJALSMA, H. W.
"Any Excuse" (Venus in a Puddle, tr. of Dmitry Bobyshev). [Nimrod] (33:2) Spr-Sum 90, p. 75.
6453. TJEPKES, Michael
"Cataclysmic Nippers" (with James Naiden and Sigrid Bergie). [NorthStoneR] (9) 90, p. 80-81.
"Sun Cycle." [NorthStoneR] (9) 90, p. 162.
"To Hay Fever Sufferers" (for Sigrid). [NorthStoneR] (9) 90, p. 162.
"Untitled: The downpour struck." [NorthStoneR] (9) 90, p. 161.
6454. TKACHENKO, Aleksandr
"A Bad Memory" (tr. by William Jay Smith and Vera Dunham). [AmerPoR] (19:6) N-D 90, p. 43.
"Letters" (tr. by William Jay Smith and Vera Dunham). [AmerPoR] (19:6) N-D 90, p. 43.
"Three Lakes" (tr. by William Jay Smith and Vera Dunham). [AmerPoR] (19:6) N-D 90, p. 43.
"The Trees" (tr. by Robert Bly and Valentina Sinkevich). [PaintedB] (40/41) 90, p. 27.
TOBIAS, Lenore Keeshig
See KEESHIG-TOBIAS, Lenore
6455. TOBIN, Daniel
"First Memory." [BelPoJ] (41:1) Fall 90, p. 16.
"Wreck." [GreensboroR] (49) Wint 90-91, p. 55-56.
6456. TODD, Albert C.
"Biographical Information" (tr. of Bella Akhmadulina). [Nimrod] (33:2) Spr-Sum 90, p. 51-52.
"Going Up on Stage" (tr. of Bella Akhmadulina). [Nimrod] (33:2) Spr-Sum 90, p. 88.
"Happiness Andalusian Style" (tr. of Yevgeny Yevtushenko, w. James Ragan). [Nimrod] (33:2) Spr-Sum 90, p. 122.
"The Heirs of Stalin" (tr. of Yevgeny Yevtushenko, w. James Ragan). [Nimrod] (33:2) Spr-Sum 90, p. 120-121.
"Insight" (tr. of Andrei Voznesensky). [Nimrod] (33:2) Spr-Sum 90, p. 125.
"Irpen" (tr. of Yevgeny Yevtushenko, w. James Ragan). [Nimrod] (33:2) Spr-Sum 90, p. 123-124.
"Now About Those" (tr. of Bella Akhmadulina). [Nimrod] (33:2) Spr-Sum 90, p. 47-48.
"Remembrances of Yalta" (tr. of Bella Akhmadulina). [Nimrod] (33:2) Spr-Sum 90, p. 45.
"Romance" (tr. of Andrei Voznesensky). [Nimrod] (33:2) Spr-Sum 90, p. 125.
"Snowfall" (tr. of Bella Akhmadulina). [Nimrod] (33:2) Spr-Sum 90, p. 46.
"St. Bartholomew's Night" (tr. of Bella Akhmadulina). [Nimrod] (33:2) Spr-Sum 90, p. 49-50.
TOEWS, David Waltner
See WALTNER-TOEWS, David
6457. TOEWS, Marjorie
"If My Heart." [PraF] (11:2) Sum 90, p. 193.
"Under a Pagan Sun." [PraF] (11:2) Sum 90, p. 192.
6458. TOKUNO, Ken
"Exploring Evanescence." [BellArk] (6:5) S-O 90, p. 10.
"Life Mask." [BellArk] (6:3) My-Je 90, p. 4.
"Twins." [BellArk] (6:3) My-Je 90, p. 5.
6459. TOLLE, Jean
"Easter Sunday" (Lahaina, Maui). [WillowR] Spr 90, p. 44.
6460. TOLLIVER, Lorraine
"The Last Day." [OnTheBus] (2:1, #5) Spr 90, p. 137-138.
"My Cadillac Coffin." [OnTheBus] (2:2/3:1, #6/7) Sum-Fall 90 Wint-Spr 91, p. 195.
6461. TOLLYFIELD, Christine
"Lot's Wife." [Stand] (31:1) Wint 89-90, p. 38.

6462. TOLNAI, Otto
"The Small Bicycle" (tr. by Nicholas Kolumban). [ArtfulD] (18/19) 90, p. 34.
"This Is Not Death Yet" (tr. by Nicholas Kolumban, Daniel Bourne and Karen Kovacik). [ArtfulD] (18/19) 90, p. 35.
TOMIKO, Fukuda
See FUKUDA, Tomiko
6463. TOMKIW, Lydia
"Tender Red Net." [BrooklynR] (7) 90, p. 16.
6464. TOMLINSON, Charles
"At Hanratty's." [Hudson] (43:3) Aut 90, p. 435-436.
"Before the Concert." [Poetry] (155:6) Mr 90, p. 381.
"Eliot at Twelve Years" (from a photograph, tr. of Attilio Bertolucci). [ParisR] (32:116) Fall 90, p. 103.
"Hartland Cliff." [GrahamHR] (13) Spr 90, p. 12-13.
"In a Cambridge Garden" (to the same). [Hudson] (43:3) Aut 90, p. 433-434.
"The Months" (tr. of Attilio Bertolucci). [ParisR] (32:116) Fall 90, p. 98.
"Near Shrine B on an August Day" (tr. of Attilio Bertolucci). [ParisR] (32:116) Fall 90, p. 99-102.
"A Note Left on Finding Two People Asleep." [GrahamHR] (13) Spr 90, p. 14.
"The Operation." [Poetry] (155:6) Mr 90, p. 379-380.
"Paris in Sixty Nine" (for Octavio Paz). [Hudson] (43:3) Aut 90, p. 431-432.
"Siena in Sixty Eight." [Hudson] (43:3) Aut 90, p. 430.
"The Trees." [GrahamHR] (13) Spr 90, p. 11.
6465. TOMLINSON, Rawdon
"Birth" (for my wife and daughters). [HiramPoR] (48/49) 90-91, p. 69-70.
"Closing Time at the Zoo." [HiramPoR] (48/49) 90-91, p. 71-72.
"Evil and Flower." [SoDakR] (28:3) Aut 90, p. 57.
"How They Live." [PoetL] (85:3) Fall 90, p. 41-42.
"Mr. Norwood." [Comm] (117:4) 23 F 90, p. 110.
"With Caitlin After Rain." [SoDakR] (28:3) Aut 90, p. 56.
6466. TOMMARO, Thom
"Isaac's Lament." [SoDakR] (28:3) Aut 90, p. 72-73.
6467. TOMOVSKI, Dusko
"Sun and Mist" (tr. of Jovan Strezovski). [Footwork] 90, p. 106.
6468. TOMPKINS, Leslie C.
"Chiaroscuro." [NewRena] (8:1, #24) Spr 90, p. 15.
6469. TONCHEV, Belin
"He Is Not In" (tr. of Vladimir Levchev). [CityLR] (4) 90, p. 187.
6470. TONEY, Mitchell
"Recreation." [Gargoyle] (37/38) 90, p. 37.
6471. TOPAL, Carine
"El Nino II." [Caliban] (8) 90, p. 154-155.
6472. TOPEROFF, Lily
"Sonnet." [ThRiPo] (35/36) 90, p. 47.
6473. TOPPING, Angela
"Final Examination" (i.m. my father 1911-1978). [SoCoast] (9) Fall 90, p. 23.
6474. TORGERSEN, Eric
"Of What Remains." [LitR] (33:2) Wint 90, p. 217.
"Sons and Fathers: Ashbery." [LitR] (33:2) Wint 90, p. 217.
6475. TORIELLO, Sharon
"3/13/43". [OnTheBus] (2:2/3:1, #6/7) Sum-Fall 90 Wint-Spr 91, p. 196.
6476. TORNEO, Dave
"What I Need." [CrabCR] (7:1) Wint 90, p. 27.
6477. TORNES, Elizabeth
"Summer Solstice." [SouthernR] (26:2) Ap 90, p. 315.
6478. TÖRO, Gábor
"Message" (tr. of Sándor Csoóri, w. Len Roberts and Miklós Telbisz). [NowestR] (28:1) 90, p. 101.
6479. TOROLA, Aileen
"Hurricane." [WillowR] Spr 90, p. 43.
6480. TORRE, Stephan
"Man Living on a Side Creek." [MalR] (93) D 90, p. 16-21.
6481. TORRES, Anabel
"The Tall Grass on the Hill" (tr. by Todd Burrell). [CrabCR] (6:3) Spr 90, p. 23.
"That Second-Rate Film" (tr. by Todd Burrell). [CrabCR] (6:3) Spr 90, p. 22.

6482. TORRESON, Rodney
"Harold Iverson, Teacher." [HiramPoR] (47) Wint 90, p. 49-50.
"Rhyne Duren, Yankee Reliever." [PassN] (11:2) Wint 90, p. 25.
6483. TORREY, Geneva
"Away Goes Jonathan Wheeler!" (A Poem for a Small Boy). [PraS] (64:2) Sum 90,
    p. 114-115.
TORRICO, Alcira Cardona
    See CARDONA TORRICO, Alcira
6484. TORTORICCI, Vince
"Atropos of the Wood." [LullwaterR] (1:1) Spr 90, p. 60.
6485. TOSTEVIN, Lola Lemire
"Cartouches" (hieroglyphs of a visit). [WestCL] (24:2) Fall 90, p. 11-16.
6486. TOTH, Judit
"Identity" (tr. by Mária Kurdi and Len Roberts). [AmerPoR] (19:5) S-O 90, p. 28.
6487. TOTSUGI, Mitsuko
"Seagulls are playing" (tr. by Janet Lewis). [SouthernR] (26:1) Ja 90, p. 204.
6488. TOUSTER-REED, Alison
"An Acre of Grass." [CumbPR] (9:2) Spr 90, p. 47-48.
"Outing." [CumbPR] (9:2) Spr 90, p. 49-50.
6489. TOWLE, Andrew
"Tennyson." [YaleR] (79:4) Sum 90 c1991, p. 661-662.
6490. TOWNSEND, Alison
"Snow Plant." [YellowS] (33) Spr 90, p. 33.
6491. TOWNSEND, Ann
"Getting Up." [TarRP] (30:1) Fall 90, p. 8.
"Guile." [LaurelR] (24:1) Wint 90, p. 76.
"Nude." [IndR] (13:2) Spr 90, p. 65.
6492. TOWNSEND, Cheryl (Cheryl A.)
"Blessed Are the Pro-Choice Children." [ChironR] (9:3) Aut 90, p. 10.
"Connection." [ChironR] (9:3) Aut 90, p. 11.
"Fail Safe." [ChironR] (9:3) Aut 90, p. 10.
"He Tries to Entice." [Bogg] (63) 90, p. 59.
"Issue." [ChironR] (9:3) Aut 90, p. 10.
"Juxtaposition." [ChironR] (9:3) Aut 90, p. 10.
"Pro-Life / Pro-Choice Rally." [ChironR] (9:3) Aut 90, p. 10.
"She Traded In." [Pearl] (12) Fall-Wint 90, p. 44.
"Sometimes She Thinks." [Pearl] (12) Fall-Wint 90, p. 40.
"The Sun Sliding Through." [Amelia] (6:2, #17) 90, p. 48.
"Winning the Battle, Losing the Fight." [ChironR] (9:3) Aut 90, p. 10.
"You Need Say No More!" [ChironR] (9:1) Spr 90, p. 27.
6493. TOWNSEND, Susan
"Stew." [Plain] (10:2) Wint 90, p. 38.
6494. TRACEY, Stephen
"Grief in the Suburbs." [OnTheBus] (2:2/3:1, #6/7) Sum-Fall 90 Wint-Spr 91, p.
    197.
6495. TRACHTENBERG, Paul
"Marilyn." [Pearl] (12) Fall-Wint 90, p. 28.
6496. TRACY, E. C.
"Page 215." [CapeR] (25:2) Fall 90, p. 47.
6497. TRAIL, B. D.
"Great Headlines in History." [NewYorkQ] (43) Fall 90, p. 60.
"The Watch on Hadrian's Wall." [NewYorkQ] (42) Sum 90, p. 71.
6498. TRAINER, Yvonne
"These Days" (For Lanie). [Dandel] (17:1) Spr-Sum 90, p. 10.
6499. TRANBARGER, Ossie E.
"First freezing drizzle." [Amelia] (6:1, #16) 90, p. 26.
6500. TRANSTRÖMER, Tomas
"Epigram" (in Swedish). [WashR] (16:2) Ag-S 90, p. 33.
"Epigram" (tr. by Jim Wine). [WashR] (16:2) Ag-S 90, p. 33.
"The Indoors Is Infinite" (tr. by Jim Wine and Tom Bull). [WashR] (16:2) Ag-S 90,
    p. 33.
"Inomhuset Ar Oandligt." [WashR] (16:2) Ag-S 90, p. 32.
"Näkergalen i Badelunda." [WashR] (16:2) Ag-S 90, p. 33.
"The Nightingale in Badelunda" (tr. by Jim Wine). [WashR] (16:2) Ag-S 90, p. 33.
"Romanesque Vaults" (tr. by the author and Fran Quinn). [PaintedB] (40/41) 90, p.
    28.

6501. TRANTER, John
"Aurora." [Screens] (2) 90, p. 92.
"Burly Girls." [Screens] (2) 90, p. 92.
"Rain." [ParisR] (32:117) Wint 90, p. 106-146.
"Telex Gorilla." [Screens] (2) 90, p. 91.
6502. TRAXLER, Patricia
"House." [Ploughs] (16:4) Wint 90-91, p. 154.
"Spring Lamb." [Ploughs] (16:4) Wint 90-91, p. 152-153.
6503. TREADWELL, Florence
"The Animal and Mineral Orders." [Dandel] (17:2) Fall-Wint 90, p. 40.
"Green Diet." [Grain] (18:4) Wint 90, p. 37.
"Your Photographer's Eye." [Event] (19:3) Fall 90, p. 47.
6504. TREAT, Patricia Ann
"The Circus" (for my sister). [ManhatPR] (11) [89?], p. 36.
6505. TREBY, Ivor C.
"Lois." [PoetryUSA] (5:1) Spr 90, p. 6.
"We Who Burn." [ChangingM] (21) Wint-Spr 90, p. 25.
6506. TREGEBOV, Rhea
"Insomnia." [MalR] (90) Spr 90, p. 68.
"Sleep." [MalR] (90) Spr 90, p. 69-70.
"Stonecrop: Notes Towards an Elegy" (for Brian Shein). [MalR] (91) Je 90, p.
73-75.
6507. TREITEL, Renata
"29. And the hatred" (tr. of Susana Thénon). [Rohwedder] (5) Spr 90, p. 12.
"30. Cancer entangled spring" (tr. of Susana Thénon). [Rohwedder] (5) Spr 90, p.
12.
"31. Abortion of a Poem in a Public Office" (tr. of Susana Thénon). [Rohwedder]
(5) Spr 90, p. 13.
"32. Birth II" (tr. of Susana Thénon). [Rohwedder] (5) Spr 90, p. 13.
"33. That friend -- despair" (tr. of Susana Thénon). [Rohwedder] (5) Spr 90, p. 14.
"34. You open yes tunnel" (tr. of Susana Thénon). [Rohwedder] (5) Spr 90, p.
14.
"Distances" (Selections: 28, 36, 37, tr. of Susana Thénon). [Caliban] (8) 90, p.
60-61.
"You who read that Dante guy in the comic books" (tr. of Susana Thénon).
[PoetryE] (30) Fall 90, p. 28.
6508. TREMBLAY, Bill
"Ode for the Sleepless." [GreenMR] (NS 4:1) Spr-Sum 90, p. 119-120.
"On Blueberry Hill." [HighP] (5:2) Fall 90, p. 50-51.
6509. TRENT, Luke
"The Coming of Fall." [Amelia] (6:2, #17) 90, p. 120.
6510. TRETHEWEY, Eric
"Central Lock-Up." [KenR] (NS 12:3) Sum 90, p. 76-77.
"Civilization and Its Discontents." [HampSPR] (Anthology 1975-1990) 90, p.
235-236.
"Civilization and Its Discontents." [PassN] (11:1) Sum 90, p. 4.
"Encounter." [TarRP] (29:2) Spr 90, p. 30-31.
"Glossary: A Deconstruction." [Ploughs] (16:1) Spr-Sum 90, p. 92-95.
"In the Long Run." [LaurelR] (24:2) Sum 90, p. 54-55.
"Skaters." [HampSPR] (Anthology 1975-1990) 90, p. 235.
"The Tenant Farmer Conducts a Tour." [Outbr] (21) 90, p. 10.
"Waking at the Mount Olive Baptist Church" (Gwendolyn Turnbough, 1944-1985).
[ApalQ] (33/34) 90, p. 71-73.
6511. TRIANA, Jose
"Otro Retrato Olvidado" (Para Lou Lam). [LindLM] (9:4) O-D 90, p. 48.
6512. TRIGG, Lisa
"Breeder Reaction." [EvergreenC] (6:1) Wint 90-Spr 91, p. 18.
"News from a Board." [EvergreenC] (6:1) Wint 90-Spr 91, p. 17.
"Surface Tension." [EvergreenC] (6:1) Wint 90-Spr 91, p. 54.
6513. TRIGILIO, Tony
"Dan Quayle on the Riverboat, August 1988." [LullwaterR] (1:1) Spr 90, p. 22.
6514. TRILLIN, Calvin
"A Bilingual Conversation" (After the Meech Lake Accord Failed to Pass the
Newfoundland and Manitoba Parliaments). [Nat] (251:4) 30 Jl-6 Ag 90, p.
117.
"Change of Seasons." [Nat] (251:8) 17 S 90, p. 261.

"Crisis Queue." [Nat] (251:7) 10 S 90, p. 225.
"Economics, with Power Steering." [Nat] (251:17) 19 N 90, p. 585.
"Fat News." [Nat] (251:13) 22 O 90, p. 441.
"First Lady." [Nat] (251:3) 16-23 Jl 90, p. 77.
"German Reunification: The Downside." [Nat] (251:5) 13-20 Ag 90, p. 153.
"Helping Hand." [Nat] (251:11) 8 O 90, p. 369.
"Historical Perspective." [Nat] (251:10) 1 O 90, p. 333.
"If You Knew What Sununu." [Nat] (251:1) 2 Jl 90, p. 5.
"An Incumbent's Interpretation of the 1990 Congessional Elections." [Nat] (251:19)
    3 D 90, p. 669.
"NC17-Rated Stuff." [Nat] (251:16) 12 N 90, p. 549.
"On Postmodern Buildings." [Nat] (251:14) 29 O 90, p. 477.
"Presidential Words." [Nat] (251:22) 24 D 90, p. 809.
"Questioning David Souter" (Three Tacks Democratic Senators Could Take). [Nat]
    (251:6) 3 S 90, p. 189.
"Remembering Stockman." [Nat] (251:12) 15 O 90, p. 405.
"The Secret of Leadership." [Nat] (251:15) 5 N 90, p. 513.
"Sweet Relief." [Nat] (251:18) 26 N 90, p. 633.
"True Love." [Nat] (251:9) 24 S 90, p. 297.
"Trump Bump." [Nat] (251:2) 9 Jl 90, p. 41.
"Upon Mrs. Thatcher's Withdrawal." [Nat] (251:21) 17 D 90, p. 757.
"Why the Hostages Were Freed." [Nat] (251:23) 31 D 90, p. 829.
"Worth Fighting For." [Nat] (251:20) 10 D 90, p. 721.
6515. TRINIDAD, David
    "Playing with Dolls." [CityLR] (4) 90, p. 90-91.
    "Reruns." [BrooklynR] (7) 90, p. 9-12.
    "Things to Do in *Valley of the Dolls* (The Movie)." [Shiny] (5) 90, p. 7.
6516. TRIPI, Anthony
    "Bone fragments in Argentina." [MinnR] (NS 34/35) Spr-Fall 90, p. 9.
6517. TRIPLETT, Pimone
    "The Aunt." [MissR] (19:1/2, #55/56) 90, p. 280-281.
6518. TRITICA, John
    "Climate Control" (for Bruce Cockburn). [CentralP] (17/18) Spr-Fall 90, p. 144.
    "Ink Pattern." [CentralP] (17/18) Spr-Fall 90, p. 141-143.
6519. TRIVELPIECE, Laurel
    "Caged." [PoetryNW] (31:2) Sum 90, p. 26.
    "Not Much Blows Back." [PoetryNW] (31:2) Sum 90, p. 26.
    "Polonius Revisited." [PartR] (57:1) Wint 90, p. 107-108.
    "White Water." [KanQ] (22:3) Sum 90, p. 191.
6520. TROWBRIDGE, William
    "In My Father's Buick." [NewL] (57:1) Fall 90, p. 70-71.
    "More Surprising Conversions." [NewL] (57:1) Fall 90, p. 71.
    "That'll Be the Day" (February 3, 1959). [Journal] (13:2) Fall-Wint 89-90, p. 21.
6521. TRUSCOTT, Robert Blake
    "The Parliament of Dogs." [HampSPR] (Anthology 1975-1990) 90, p. 78-82.
6522. TRUSSELL, Donna
    "On the Edge of Sleep." [Confr] (42/43) Spr-Sum 90, p. 233.
    "Those Who Roam at Night." [WestB] (26) 90, p. 53.
6523. TRUSZKOWSKA, Teresa
    "Guernica." [PoetryC] (11:1) Spr 90, p. 22.
    "Mother." [PoetryC] (11:1) Spr 90, p. 22.
6524. TSALKA, Dan
    "Arcadian Wall" (tr. by Daniel Weissbort, w. the author). [Stand] (31:4) Aut 90, p.
        44-45.
    "A Lull in the Battle, Exekias the Amphora-Painter Speaks" (tr. by Daniel Weissbort,
        w. the author). [Stand] (31:4) Aut 90, p. 45.
6525. TSAO, Carolyn
    "Fables." [PoetryUSA] (5:3) Fall 90, p. 26.
TSAO, Wu
    See WU, Tsao
6526. TSUJIMOTO, Joe (Joseph)
    "Ghosts." [ChamLR] (3:2, #6) Spr 90, p. 148-152.
    "Gun Smoke." [ChamLR] (4:1, #7) Fall 90, p. 54-56.
    "Mantis (The Horror Show)." [HawaiiR] (14:1, #28) Wint 89-90, p. 60.
    "Paintings" (For Sharon). [HawaiiR] (14:1, #28) Wint 89-90, p. 58-59.
    "Pieta." [ChamLR] (3:2, #6) Spr 90, p. 153-154.

"She Now Serves Out of the D.C. Office of the Peace Corps." [ChamLR] (4:1, #7) Fall 90, p. 57-59.
6527. TSUNG, Tsung
"In the Summer Night I and You" (tr. of Ma Li, w. Richard Terrill). [AnotherCM] (21) 90, p. 109-110.
"A Palm Tree and Two Women" (tr. of Ma Li, w. Richard Terrill). [AnotherCM] (21) 90, p. 107-108.
TSUTOMU, Yamaguchi
See YAMAGUCHI, Tsutomu
6528. TSVETAEVA, Marina
"New Year's" (An Elegy for Rilke, tr. by Mary Jane White). [Nimrod] (33:2) Spr-Sum 90, p. 56-61.
"Poems to Akhmatova" (June 9 -- July 2, 1916, selections: I, IV-V, IX, tr. by Mary Jane White, w. Alexander Sumerkin). [Nimrod] (33:2) Spr-Sum 90, p. 53-55.
TU, Fu
See DU, Fu
6529. TUCKER, Daniel
"The Bengal Tiger." [PoetryUSA] (5:2) Sum 90, p. 8.
6530. TUCKER, Jean
"Ugly Drinkers of Fish Oil" (From a description of Laplanders by a 17th-century French traveler). [Confr] (42/43) Spr-Sum 90, p. 193.
6531. TUCKER, Martin
"In Memoriam: Edythe Cecil (Died 1989), Grand Editor, Grand Lady." [Confr] (42/43) Spr-Sum 90, p. 11.
"Mother: On Dying, Not Death." [Confr] (44/45) Fall 90-Wint 91, p. 307-310.
"On Knowing How Close to Oscar Wilde I Came, or: My Day as a Prospective Juror." [Confr] (42/43) Spr-Sum 90, p. 177.
6532. TUCKER, Memye Curtis
"Bonsai." [LullwaterR] (1:1) Spr 90, p. 23.
"He and the Village." [LullwaterR] (1:1) Spr 90, p. 34.
6533. TUCKERMAN, Frederick Goddard
"And so the day drops by, the horizon draws." [ChiR] (37:1) Wint 90, p. 66.
"But thou, who givest all things, give not me." [ChiR] (37:1) Wint 90, p. 78.
"For Nature daily through her grand design." [ChiR] (37:1) Wint 90, p. 76.
"His heart was in his garden, but his brain." [ChiR] (37:1) Wint 90, p. 72-73.
"Shall I not see her? yes: for one has seen." [ChiR] (37:1) Wint 90, p. 74.
"That boy, the farmer said, with hazel wand." [ChiR] (37:1) Wint 90, p. 66-67.
"An upper chamber in a darkened house." [ChiR] (37:1) Wint 90, p. 68.
6534. TUFTS, Carol
"Waiting for Rain." [MidwQ] (31:2) Wint 90, p. 232.
6535. TULLIS, Rod
"A Fireside Story." [BlackWR] (17:1) Fall-Wint 90, p. 39.
6536. TURCO, Lewis
"Balada of Uncertain Age." [Amelia] (6:1, #16) 90, p. 108-109.
"The Birdsong Blues." [Hellas] (1:1) Spr 90, p. 59.
"The Courthouse" (Maine, 18th century). [HampSPR] (Anthology 1975-1990) 90, p. 10.
"Fading Things" (On lines from Emily Dickinson's letters). [NewYorkQ] (41) Spr 90, p. 70.
"A Family Album" (13 poems, Winner of the 1989 Silverfish Review Chapbook Competition). [SilverFR] (19) 90, 24 p.
"The Fool: Tarot Key O." [HampSPR] (Anthology 1975-1990) 90, p. 8-9.
"The Ice House" (Maine, 19th century). [HampSPR] (Anthology 1975-1990) 90, p. 10.
"The Pharmacy" (New England, 18th century). [HampSPR] (Anthology 1975-1990) 90, p. 11.
"The Poetry Wreck." [HampSPR] (Anthology 1975-1990) 90, p. 11-13.
"Rispetto in Silk and Scarlet." [SouthernR] (26:1) Ja 90, p. 225.
"Sestina in Indian Summer." [SouthernR] (26:1) Ja 90, p. 223-224.
"Terzanelle of the Spider's Web." [SouthernR] (26:1) Ja 90, p. 224-225.
6537. TURNBULL, Becky
"Reconstruction." [PennR] (4:2) 90, p. 113-114.
6538. TURNER, Doug
"The Beasts." [Dandel] (17:1) Spr-Sum 90, p. 38.
6539. TURNER, Frederick
"Early Warning." [SouthwR] (75:1) Wint 90, p. 94.

"A Vague Ode" (tr. of Miklos Radnoti, w. Zsuzsanna Ozsvath). [PartR] (57:2) Spr
90, p. 269.
6540. TURNER, Judy
"All There Was." [SoCoast] (9) Fall 90, p. 54.
"I Knew a Fellow." [SoCoast] (9) Fall 90, p. 55.
6541. TURNER, Keith
"Climbing Down Eggerslack." [Stand] (31:2) Spr 90, p. 12.
6542. TURPIN, Mark
"Downslope." [Agni] (29/30) 90, p. 146-147.
"Everything Under the Sun." [Agni] (29/30) 90, p. 148-150.
6543. TUTHILL, Stacy
"Green Tobacco Worms." [PoetL] (85:1) Spr 90, p. 22-24.
6544. TWARDOWSKI, Jan
"A Confession" (tr. by Iain Higgins and Bogdan Czaykowski). [PoetryE] (29) Spr
90, p. 10-11.
"How many devout books are written" (tr. by Iain Higgins and Bogdan
Czaykowski). [PoetryE] (29) Spr 90, p. 9.
"Intimates and Strangers" (tr. by Iain Higgins and Bogdan Czaykowski). [PoetryE]
(29) Spr 90, p. 12.
"Justice" (tr. by Iain Higgins and Bogdan Czaykowski). [PoetryE] (29) Spr 90, p.
8.
6545. TWICHELL, Chase
"Dream of the Interior." [Iowa] (20:2) Spr-Sum 90, p. 13-14.
"Remember Death." [Iowa] (20:2) Spr-Sum 90, p. 17-18.
"Revenge." [Antaeus] (64/65) Spr-Aut 90, p. 136-137.
"The Shades of Grand Central." [YaleR] (79:3) Spr 90, p. 384-385.
"The Somersault." [Chelsea] (49) 90, p. 58.
"Useless Islands." [Iowa] (20:2) Spr-Sum 90, p. 14-16.
"Why All Good Music Is Sad." [Iowa] (20:2) Spr-Sum 90, p. 16-17.
"Word Silence." [YaleR] (79:3) Spr 90, p. 386.
6546. TWITTY, Anne
"Angel in the House" (tr. of Maria Negroni). [LitR] (33:4) Sum 90, p. 437.
"Badlands" (tr. of Maria Negroni). [LitR] (33:4) Sum 90, p. 436.
"Goodbyes" (tr. of Maria Negroni). [LitR] (33:4) Sum 90, p. 436.
"Self-less" (tr. of Maria Negroni). [LitR] (33:4) Sum 90, p. 437.
6547. TYLER, Robert L.
"The Crisis of Theory." [InterPR] (16:1) Spr 90, p. 122.
"Parent's Day at the College." [ManhatPR] (12) [90?], p. 37.
"Test Cases." [InterPR] (16:1) Spr 90, p. 121.
6548. TYLER, Steve
"Spring 1966." [Gargoyle] (37/38) 90, p. 49.
6549. TYSON, Carla
"Confession." [NegC] (10:1) 90, p. 92-93.
6550. UBILLA-ARENAS, Cecilia
"Journey to New York" (tr. of Ernesto Cardenal, w. Steve Kowit). [OnTheBus]
(2:1, #5) Spr 90, p. 178-183.
UCHANG, Kim
See KIM, Uchang
6551. UCHIMURA, Akitaka
"When I saw the arrangement" (tr. by Janet Lewis). [SouthernR] (26:1) Ja 90, p.
203.
6552. UELAND, Carol
"Domitian, the last cruel and savage emperor" (tr. of Aleksandr Kushner, w. Paul
Graves). [Nimrod] (33:2) Spr-Sum 90, p. 94.
"Folded Wings" (tr. of Aleksandr Kushner, w. Paul Graves). [Nimrod] (33:2)
Spr-Sum 90, p. 90-91.
"O fame, you have passed us by like the rain, vanished" (tr. of Aleksandr Kushner,
w. Paul Graves). [Nimrod] (33:2) Spr-Sum 90, p. 93.
"Our partings are more difficult, and long" (tr. of Aleksandr Kushner, w. Paul
Graves). [Nimrod] (33:2) Spr-Sum 90, p. 92.
"This country, huge, wintry and blue" (tr. of Aleksandr Kushner, w. Paul Graves).
[Nimrod] (33:2) Spr-Sum 90, p. 91.
"Urban Irony" (tr. of Vladimir Kostrov, w. Paul Graves). [Nimrod] (33:2) Spr-Sum
90, p. 3.
UEMA, Marck Beggs (Marck L. Beggs)
See BEGGS-UEMA, Marck (Marck L.)

6553. UGUAY, Marie
"The earth is famished and wears us out" (tr. by Andrea Moorhead). [AmerPoR] (19:6) N-D 90, p. 34.
"I have slept where there is no longer room" (tr. by Andrea Moorhead). [AmerPoR] (19:6) N-D 90, p. 34.
"The one I love is sleeping in an open room" (tr. by Andrea Moorhead). [AmerPoR] (19:6) N-D 90, p. 34.
"Sometimes when I see you walking I want to be you" (tr. by Andrea Moorhead). [AmerPoR] (19:6) N-D 90, p. 34.
"Wide necked bays hidden in the territory" (tr. by Andrea Moorhead). [AmerPoR] (19:6) N-D 90, p. 34.

6554. ULACIA, Manuel
"Ciudad de México Soñada." [Inti] (32/33) Otoño 90-Primavera 91, p. 235-237.
"Concierto de Cítara." [Inti] (32/33) Otoño 90-Primavera 91, p. 237.
"La Piedra en el Fondo." [Inti] (32/33) Otoño 90-Primavera 91, p. 230-235.
"Revelación I." [Inti] (32/33) Otoño 90-Primavera 91, p. 238.
"Revelación II." [Inti] (32/33) Otoño 90-Primavera 91, p. 238.

6555. ULIN, David L.
"Clean Living" (For C.R.D.). [BrooklynR] (7) 90, p. 30.

6556. ULLMAN, Leslie
"Aquamarine." [Poetry] (157:2) N 90, p. 72-73.
"Hair of the Dog." [CimR] (92) Jl 90, p. 127-128.
"Lightning." [Crazy] (38) Spr 90, p. 49-51.
"Rose Quartz." [GreenMR] (NS 4:1) Spr-Sum 90, p. 48.
"Rutilations." [GreenMR] (NS 4:1) Spr-Sum 90, p. 47.

6557. UNDERWOOD, Robert
"Commode Etiquette." [SlipS] (10) 90, p. 102-103.

6558. UNGER, Barbara
"Blue Depression Glass." [NoDaQ] (58:2) Spr 90, p. 108.
"To a Friend Dead of AIDS." [Confr] (44/45) Fall 90-Wint 91, p. 171.

6559. UNGER, David
"Dust in Love" (tr. of Manuel Ramos Otero). [LitR] (33:4) Sum 90, p. 488-490.

6560. UNTERECKER, John
"Catalan Farmer: Figueras, Spain." [HampSPR] (Anthology 1975-1990) 90, p. 38.

6561. UNZUETA, Manuel
"Corrido de Etelvina Menchaca" (w. Armando Vallejo). [Americas] (18:2) Sum 90, p. 74-75.

6562. UPDIKE, John
"Each Summer's Swallows." [Boulevard] (4:3/5:1, #12/13) Spr 90, p. 246-247.
"Fargo." [SycamoreR] (2:2) Sum 90, p. 37.
"Generic College." [OntR] (33) Fall-Wint 90-91, p. 78.
"Granite." [NewYorker] (66:38) 5 N 90, p. 48.
"Indianapolis." [OntR] (33) Fall-Wint 90-91, p. 79.
"Perfection Wasted." [NewYorker] (66:12) 7 My 90, p. 42.
"Seattle Uplift." [Agni] (31/32) 90, p. 268.

6563. UPTON, Lee
"An Almanac" (for Patricia Donahue and Sheila McNamee). [Field] (43) Fall 90, p. 60-61.
"The Architect of Sushi." [Field] (43) Fall 90, p. 64.
"The Autobiographers." [Field] (43) Fall 90, p. 63.
"Bedtime Story." [Field] (42) Spr 90, p. 67.
"The Brontës." [Field] (43) Fall 90, p. 65.
"New Year's Eve." [MissouriR] (13:1) 90, p. 96.
"Orestes in the City." [MissouriR] (13:1) 90, p. 97.
"The Quality of Mercy." [Field] (42) Spr 90, p. 68-69.
"The Stem of August." [Field] (43) Fall 90, p. 62.
"Unsigned Painting." [PassN] (11:1) Sum 90, p. 9.

6564. URBAIN, John
"1930." [NewYorkQ] (41) Spr 90, p. 98.

6565. URBAN, Erika
"Apocalypse" (tr. of Csaba Lászlóffy, w. Len Roberts). [LitR] (33:3) Spr 90, p. 292.

6566. URDANG, Constance
"Hot Days in Early Summer." [HampSPR] (Anthology 1975-1990) 90, p. 130.
"Mourning for Umbrellas." [HampSPR] (Anthology 1975-1990) 90, p. 127.
"Other Countries." [HampSPR] (Anthology 1975-1990) 90, p. 127-130.

6567. URSELL, Geoffrey
"Poison Grain (A Prairie Rap)." [Grain] (18:3) Fall 90, p. 91.
6568. USCHUK, Pamela
"Duck Season." [PennR] (4:2) 90, p. 112.
"Late Winter Storm" (for Victor Jara). [HighP] (5:3) Wint 90-91, p. 80-83.
6569. USUI, Masami
"What He Remembered." [ChamLR] (3:2, #6) Spr 90, p. 70.
6570. UTHE, Deborah
"Where It Comes From." [Amelia] (6:2, #17) 90, p. 137.
6571. VACCA, John
"Andy Warhol's Marilyn." [Pearl] (12) Fall-Wint 90, p. 31.
6572. VAETH, Kim
"The Yes." [AmerV] (18) Spr 90, p. 12.
6573. VAICIUNAITE, Judita
"Comet" (tr. by Viktoria Skrupskelis and Stuart Friebert). [PoetryE] (30) Fall 90, p.
    83.
"Eurydice" (tr. by Viktoria Skrupskelis and Stuart Friebert). [Turnstile] (2:2) 90, p.
    1.
"Little Gulls" (tr. by Viktoria Skrupskelis and Stuart Friebert). [SenR] (20:2) Fall
    90, p. 46.
"Museum Street" (tr. by Viktoria Skrupskelis and Stuart Friebert). [Turnstile] (2:2)
    90, p. 2.
"Wild Raspberries" (tr. by Viktoria Skrupskelis and Stuart Friebert). [SenR] (20:2)
    Fall 90, p. 48.
"Yellow Summer" (tr. by Viktoria Skrupskelis and Stuart Friebert). [SenR] (20:2)
    Fall 90, p. 45.
"Zoological Garden" (tr. by Viktoria Skrupskelis and Stuart Friebert). [SenR] (20:2)
    Fall 90, p. 47.
6574. VAIL, Desire
"Turtle Beach, Tobago, 1988." [Kaleid] (21) Sum-Fall 90, p. 50.
6575. VAISIUS, Andrew
"For Grey." [Grain] (18:1) Spr 90, p. 34-35.
6576. VAJDA, Miklós
"Ulysses' Abandoned Adventure" (tr. of István Vas, w. Daniel Hoffman). [Trans]
    (24) Fall 90, p. 218-222.
6577. VALAVANIDHIS, Christos
"The Porn Collector." [PoetryUSA] (5:2) Sum 90, p. 9.
6578. VALDÉS-GINEBRA, Arminda
"Despliegue de los Bolsillos." [LindLM] (9:4) O-D 90, p. 13.
"Dolor en Geometría." [Ometeca] (1:2/2:1) 89-90, p. 44.
6579. VALENTINE, Jean
"Alfred and the Abortion" (In memory). [AmerPoR] (19:1) Ja-F 90, p. 4.
"The Badlands Said." [NewYorker] (66:7) 2 Ap 90, p. 86.
"Barrie's Dream: The Wild Geese." [NewYorker] (66:15) 28 My 90, p. 104.
"By the Tekapo River, 100 Degrees." [Ploughs] (16:4) Wint 90-91, p. 39.
"The First Station." [AmerPoR] (19:1) Ja-F 90, p. 4.
"Foraging." [AmerPoR] (19:1) Ja-F 90, p. 3.
"Fox Glacier." [Ploughs] (16:4) Wint 90-91, p. 38.
"The Free Abandonment Blues." [AmerPoR] (19:1) Ja-F 90, p. 5.
"Night Lake." [AmerPoR] (19:1) Ja-F 90, p. 5.
"The One You Wanted to Be Is the One You Are." [AmerPoR] (19:1) Ja-F 90, p. 3.
"Redemption." [AmerPoR] (19:1) Ja-F 90, p. 4.
"Rome Dream." [Field] (42) Spr 90, p. 65.
"Seeing You." [AmerPoR] (19:1) Ja-F 90, p. 4.
"Two Dreams." [AmerPoR] (19:1) Ja-F 90, p. 3.
"Willi, Home" (In memory). [WashR] (15:6) Ap-My 90, p. 21.
"The Wisdom Gravy." [NewYorker] (66:37) 29 O 90, p. 102.
"The Year of the Snake." [AmerPoR] (19:1) Ja-F 90, p. 4.
6580. VALENTINE, John
"Auschwitz, 1945." [InterPR] (16:1) Spr 90, p. 119-120.
6581. VALENZUELA, Amy
"For Mary, the Scientist." [Pearl] (10) Spr 90, p. 53.
6582. VALERO, Roberto
"Ante un Viejo Octogenario de Dakota del Sur." [LindLM] (9:4) O-D 90, p. 50.
6583. VALÉRY, Paul
"Pas de Valéry" (for Henry, gone, tr. of "Ebouche d'un serpent" by Gerald Burns).

[WashR] (16:2) Ag-S 90, p. 9.
6584. VALESIO, Paola
"In Memoriam Adriani Spatulae" (Excerpts, tr. by Graziella Sidoli). [Screens] (2)
90, p. 98-99.
6585. VALIS, Noël
"Invitation." [Wind] (20:66) 90, p. 42.
6586. VALLE, Victor
"If You Wish" (tr. of Carlos Illescas). [OnTheBus] (2:2/3:1, #6/7) Sum-Fall 90
Wint-Spr 91, p. 247.
"Invocation" (tr. of Carlos Illescas). [OnTheBus] (2:2/3:1, #6/7) Sum-Fall 90
Wint-Spr 91, p. 246.
"Let's Bite His Hand" (tr. of Carlos Illescas). [OnTheBus] (2:2/3:1, #6/7) Sum-Fall
90 Wint-Spr 91, p. 247.
6587. VALLEJO, Armando
"Corrido de Etelvina Menchaca" (w. Manuel Unzueta). [Americas] (18:2) Sum 90,
p. 74-75.
6588. VALLEJO, César Abraham
"Trilce" (Selections: I-XIII, XXXVI, LXI, LXV, LXXV-LXXVII, in Spanish and
English, tr. by Próspero Saíz). [Abraxas] (38/39) 90, p. 5-63.
6589. VALUENTINE, Jean
"The River at Wolf." [NewYorker] (66:21) 9 Jl 90, p. 72.
Van . . .
See also names beginning with "Van" without the following space, filed below in
their alphabetical positions.
6590. Van ARSDALE, Sarah
"Common Angels." [OxfordM] (6:1) Spr-Sum 90, p. 16.
"Snow Prayer." [Hellas] (1:1) Spr 90, p. 66.
Van BRUNT, H. L.
See Van BRUNT, Lloyd (H. L.)
6591. Van BRUNT, Lloyd (H. L.)
"Distance." [HampSPR] (Anthology 1975-1990) 90, p. 97.
"Meditation on Matthew Arnold" (for Nina). [AmerPoR] (19:6) N-D 90, p. 19.
"Return." [HampSPR] (Anthology 1975-1990) 90, p. 96.
6592. Van de KAMP, Alexandra
"When I Walk on Sidewalks." [GreensboroR] (49) Wint 90-91, p. 102.
Van de WAARSENBURG, Hans
See WAARSENBURG, Hans van de
6593. Van den BROEK, Gonny
"Hard Facts" (tr. of Jan Emmens). [Vis] (34) 90, p. 38.
"A Merl's Farewell" (tr. by the author). [Vis] (34) 90, p. 48.
"Midwinter" (tr. of Ellen Warmond). [Vis] (34) 90, p. 48.
"An Odd Tiger" (tr. of Willem Wilmink). [Vis] (34) 90, p. 51.
Van der LEEST, R. R. R.
See LEEST, R. R. R. van der
6594. Van DUSEN, Kate
"But Blue." [CapilR] (2:2) Spr 90, p. 29-31.
6595. Van DUYN, Mona
"The Burning of Yellowstone." [Poetry] (155:6) Mr 90, p. 378.
"Glad Heart at the Supermarket." [Poetry] (155:5) F 90, p. 326-327.
"The Marriage Sculptor." [NewYorker] (66:24) 30 Jl 90, p. 34.
"Sonnet for Minimalists." [Poetry] (155:6) Mr 90, p. 377.
"Words for the Dumb." [YaleR] (79:4) Sum 90 c1991, p. 647-651.
6596. Van GERVEN, Claudia
"Apotheosis." [Calyx] (13:1) Wint 90-91, p. 16.
"How Can She Rise, Earth-Born." [PraS] (64:3) Fall 90, p. 18-19.
"So These Are the Waters." [PraS] (64:3) Fall 90, p. 21-23.
"They Count Persephone." [PraS] (64:3) Fall 90, p. 20-21.
6597. Van GORDER, Julia
"Letter Home." [PraF] (11:4) Wint 90-91, p. 68.
"Recurrence." [PraF] (11:4) Wint 90-91, p. 68.
6598. Van HOUTEN, Lois
"How I Learned." [Footwork] 90, p. 98.
"Lady in the Lake" (for Dorothy June 10/87). [Footwork] 90, p. 98.
"Snow Ghosts." [Footwork] 90, p. 98.
Van LERBERGHE, Charles
See LERBERGHE, Charles van

6599. Van NOORD, Barbara
"Pears." [OxfordM] (6:1) Spr-Sum 90, p. 21.
6600. Van PEENEN, H. J.
"Tree Houses in Central Park" (from a human interest story in the *New York Times*,
September 27, 1986). [BellArk] (6:3) My-Je 90, p. 12.
6601. Van RIPER, Craig
"Picture This." [SlipS] (10) 90, p. 76.
Van SANTEN, Louise
See SANTEN, Louise van
6602. Van TASSEL, Etta May
"Distance." [EmeraldCR] (1990) c89, p. 71-72.
6603. Van WALLEGHEN, Michael
"Adios Zarathustra." [SouthernR] (26:3) Jl 90, p. 638-640.
"Late." [PassN] (11:1) Sum 90, p. 22.
"Long Division." [PassN] (11:1) Sum 90, p. 22.
"The Other World" (for O.S. --B., tr. of Dmitry Bobyshev). [TriQ] (79) Fall 90, p.
106-107.
"Rush Hour." [CimR] (90) Ja 90, p. 67-68.
"Tall Birds Stalking." [SouthernR] (26:3) Jl 90, p. 633-638.
"The Unbearable Part." [CimR] (90) Ja 90, p. 69-70.
6604. Van WIENEN, Mark
"Written in Near-Darkness." [CoalC] (1) Ag 90, p. 10-11.
6605. Van WINCKEL, Nance
"Cryogenics: Born Again into a Cold Light." [NewEngR] (12:4) Sum 90, p.
385-386.
"Fish Unlimited." [Shen] (40:3) Fall 90, p. 59.
"Going to Krogers." [PraS] (64:1) Spr 90, p. 9-10.
"Madame Tussaud." [Ascent] (15:1) 90, p. 34-35.
"Nothing to Do in Town." [WillowS] (25) Wint 90, p. 10-11.
"Sick Woman in the Fifth Wagon." [PraS] (64:1) Spr 90, p. 11-15.
6606. VANCE, Bob
"In the Sad World." [MinnR] (NS 34/35) Spr-Fall 90, p. 8.
6607. VANCE, Richard
"Awakening." [OxfordM] (6:1) Spr-Sum 90, p. 39.
6608. VANCE, Roger
"The Center of the Beans." [SpoonRQ] (15:3) Sum 90, p. 34-35, also (15:4) Fall
90, p. 49-50.
"Checking on Father, One Saturday Morning in June." [SpoonRQ] (15:3) Sum 90,
p. 44, also (15:4) Fall 90, p. 59.
"China Clipper." [SpoonRQ] (15:3) Sum 90, p. 32, also (15:4) Fall 90, p. 47.
"Dumplings." [SpoonRQ] (15:3) Sum 90, p. 36-37, also (15:4) Fall 90, p. 51-52.
"Father Has Pneumonia." [SpoonRQ] (15:3) Sum 90, p. 45, also (15:4) Fall 90, p.
60.
"A Fever in December." [SpoonRQ] (15:3) Sum 90, p. 40, also (15:4) Fall 90, p.
55.
"John and I, We Tamed the Wildcat." [SpoonRQ] (15:3) Sum 90, p. 41-42, also
(15:4) Fall 90, p. 56-57.
"Laughing in Bed." [SpoonRQ] (15:3) Sum 90, p. 38, also (15:4) Fall 90, p. 53.
"Lucky Ones Are Marching." [SpoonRQ] (15:3) Sum 90, p. 30-31, also (15:4) Fall
90, p. 45-46.
"The Movie at the Edge of Town." [SpoonRQ] (15:3) Sum 90, p. 39, also (15:4)
Fall 90, p. 54.
"My Father's Hands and Mine." [SpoonRQ] (15:3) Sum 90, p. 46-47, also (15:4)
Fall 90, p. 61-62.
"Once More Around the Sun." [SpoonRQ] (15:3) Sum 90, p. 48-49, also (15:4) Fall
90, p. 63-63.
"The Owl." [SpoonRQ] (15:3) Sum 90, p. 33, also (15:4) Fall 90, p. 48.
"The Secret Advertisement of My Sin." [SpoonRQ] (15:3) Sum 90, p. 31, also
(15:4) Fall 90, p. 46.
"Villamoon." [SpoonRQ] (15:3) Sum 90, p. 43, also (15:4) Fall 90, p. 58.
6609. VANDENBERG, Peter
"As the Sun Comes Up in Nebraska." [Plain] (10:2) Wint 90, p. 13.
6610. VanderMOLEN, Robert
"On the Outskirts." [ArtfulD] (18/19) 90, p. 119.
6611. VAPTSAROW, Nikola
"Last Words Found in His Pockets" (tr. by William Pitt Root). [PoetryE] (30) Fall

90, p. 26.
"No This Isn't the Time for Poetry" (tr. by William Pitt Root). [PoetryE] (29) Spr
90, p. 142.
6612. VARGA, Adriana
"After the Creation" (tr. of Marin Sorescu, w. Stuart Friebert). [PoetryE] (29) Spr
90, p. 130.
"Alphabet" (tr. of Marin Sorescu, w. Stuart Friebert). [HawaiiR] (14:1, #28) Wint
89-90, p. 41.
"Below the Horizon" (tr. of Marin Sorescu, w. Stuart Friebert). [ArtfulD] (18/19)
90, p. 41.
"House Snake" (tr. of Marin Sorescu, w. Stuart Friebert). [HawaiiR] (14:1, #28)
Wint 89-90, p. 42.
"How?" (tr. of Marin Sorescu, w. Stuart Friebert). [HawaiiR] (14:1, #28) Wint
89-90, p. 40.
"Let's Help" (tr. of Marin Sorescu, w. Stuart Friebert). [ArtfulD] (18/19) 90, p. 40.
"Looking for Hegel's Portrait" (tr. of Marin Sorescu, w. Stuart Friebert). [PoetryE]
(29) Spr 90, p. 131.
"Rift" (tr. of Marin Sorescu, w. Stuart Friebert). [PoetryE] (29) Spr 90, p. 128-129.
"Signs" (tr. of Marin Sorescu, w. Stuart Friebert). [PoetryE] (29) Spr 90, p. 133.
"Study of Repose" (tr. of Marin Sorescu, w. Stuart Friebert). [HawaiiR] (14:1, #28)
Wint 89-90, p. 43.
6613. VARLEY, Jane
"Mother and Daughter Driving Home." [PoetryNW] (31:2) Sum 90, p. 40-41.
6614. VARNES, Katherine
"The Hook." [Hellas] (1:1) Spr 90, p. 50.
"The Secret." [Hellas] (1:1) Spr 90, p. 51.
6615. VAS, István
"In the Roman Forum" (tr. by Bruce Berlind). [Confr] (42/43) Spr-Sum 90, p. 202.
"Ulysses' Abandoned Adventure" (tr. by Daniel Hoffman, w. Miklós Vajda).
[Trans] (24) Fall 90, p. 218-222.
"The Voice" (tr. by Daniel Hoffman, w. María Kärössy). [Trans] (24) Fall 90, p.
223.
6616. VASCONCELLOS, Cherry Jean
"When Are You Coming Home." [Pearl] (12) Fall-Wint 90, p. 61.
6617. VASSALLO, Philip
"An Intellectually Acceptable Distance." [ChamLR] (3:2, #6) Spr 90, p. 127-128.
"Sonnet: Of Numbered Men and Men of Letters." [Outbr] (21) 90, p. 61.
6618. VASSILAKIS, Nico
"Clearance." [Caliban] (9) 90, p. 121-122.
"Deteriorata" (w. Noemie Maxwell). [ContextS] (1:1) 89, p. 8.
"Gnu Poem." [Caliban] (9) 90, p. 119-120.
6619. VAUGHAN, Will
"Changing Lady." [SoCoast] (9) Fall 90, p. 15.
"Romance." [SoCoast] (9) Fall 90, p. 50.
6620. VECCHIONE, Glen
"Moon on Tower Clock." [SouthernPR] (30:1) Spr 90, p. 26-27.
6621. VEENENDAAL, Cornelia
"The Arborist." [PraS] (64:1) Spr 90, p. 118.
"I Hold the Parasol." [PraS] (64:1) Spr 90, p. 116-117.
"A Scene from Hardy." [PraS] (64:1) Spr 90, p. 117.
6622. VEGIN, Pyotr
"School for the Blind" (Excerpt, tr. by Daniel Weissbort). [CityLR] (4) 90, p.
184-185.
6623. VEGSO, Betsy
"Rehearsals." [Shen] (40:2) Sum 90, p. 25.
"Self-Portrait." [Shen] (40:2) Sum 90, p. 24.
6624. VEITSMAN, Mark
"Spring Waters" (tr. by Oleg Atbashian and Maureen Hurley). [PoetryUSA] (5:2)
Sum 90, p. 13.
VÉLEZ, Clemente Soto
See SOTO VÉLEZ, Clemente
6625. VELOZ MAGGIOLO, Marcio
"La Canción Familiar" (Cuatro Poemas). [CuadP] (7:20) Enero-Abril 90, p. 83-92.
6626. VENEGAS, Sybil
"Shell Shocked." [Pearl] (11) Sum 90, p. 30-31.

473

6627. VENO, Aro
"Baccalà." [SinW] (41) Sum-Fall 90, p. 120.
6628. VENUTI, Lawrence
"The Assassins" (tr. of Milo De Angelis). [WashR] (16:2) Ag-S 90, p. 31.
"Chronology" (tr. of Milo De Angelis). [PaintedB] (40/41) 90, p. 63.
"Continuous Time" (tr. of Milo De Angelis). [PaintedB] (40/41) 90, p. 64.
"The Drop Ready for the Globe" (tr. of Milo De Angelis). [PaintedB] (40/41) 90, p. 69.
"For You Who" (tr. of Milo De Angelis). [WashR] (16:2) Ag-S 90, p. 31.
"Form" (tr. of Milo de Angelis). [PoetryE] (30) Fall 90, p. 86.
"I Recover a Syntax" (tr. of Milo De Angelis). [WashR] (16:2) Ag-S 90, p. 31.
"In History" (tr. of Milo De Angelis). [WashR] (16:2) Ag-S 90, p. 30.
"The Incident" (tr. of Milo De Angelis). [PaintedB] (40/41) 90, p. 65.
"The Legend of Monferrato" (tr. of Milo De Angelis). [WashR] (16:2) Ag-S 90, p. 31.
"The Selection" (tr. of Milo De Angelis). [PaintedB] (40/41) 90, p. 67.
"The Sentries" (tr. of Milo De Angelis). [WashR] (16:2) Ag-S 90, p. 31.
6629. VENZKE, Philip
"The Constellation of Flying Fish." [EngJ] (79:6) O 90, p. 95.
6630. Ver ELLEN, Patricia
"A Dialectic for Spring Quarter." [GeoR] (44:1/2) Spr-Sum 90, p. 182-183.
6631. VERASTEGUI, Enrique
"XII/4." [Inti] (32/33) Otoño 90-Primavera 91, p. 246-247.
"Anotaciones en un Libro de Nietzche." [Inti] (32/33) Otoño 90-Primavera 91, p. 253.
"Apariciones en un Panel de Computador." [Inti] (32/33) Otoño 90-Primavera 91, p. 245-246.
"Marcha de Caballos en la Noche." [Inti] (32/33) Otoño 90-Primavera 91, p. 248-252.
"Vendo al Colegio para Recoger a Mi Hija" (Para Vanessa). [Inti] (32/33) Otoño 90-Primavera 91, p. 247-248.
VERDE, Andrew J. Lo
See LoVERDE, Andrew J.
6632. VERDICCHIO, Pasquale
"5 Short Rehearsals for a Poem (Pagan Nuptials)" (tr. of Gio Ferri). [Screens] (2) 90, p. 114-115.
"And now that moved it cannot" (tr. of Nanni Cagnone). [Screens] (2) 90, p. 109.
"Annual Doorway" (tr. of Milo de Angelis). [Screens] (2) 90, p. 112.
"But dreams that do not lend figures" (tr. of Nanni Cagnone). [Screens] (2) 90, p. 110.
"The Captivity of the Lesser" (tr. of Alessandro Ceni). [Screens] (2) 90, p. 107.
"Clecsografie" (Excerpts, tr. of Valerio Magrelli). [Screens] (2) 90, p. 104-106.
"Contrapunto May-June 1984" (Excerpts, tr. of Valerio Magrelli). [Screens] (2) 90, p. 106.
"The Double" (tr. of Cristina Annino). [Screens] (2) 90, p. 111.
"Double Justice" (for Nadia Campana, tr. of Milo de Angelis). [Screens] (2) 90, p. 113.
"Elegy" (tr. of Milo de Angelis). [Screens] (2) 90, p. 112.
"Envied emptiness" (tr. of Nanni Cagnone). [Screens] (2) 90, p. 110.
"Feuilletons" (Excerpts). [Screens] (2) 90, p. 101-103.
"The Hearts of Eagles" (tr. of Alessandro Ceni). [Screens] (2) 90, p. 108.
"It does not become fond of only one" (tr. of Nanni Cagnone). [Screens] (2) 90, p. 110.
"Not one's own difficult hollowed" (tr. of Nanni Cagnone). [Screens] (2) 90, p. 109.
"Similar Sphynx, which you are not" (tr. of Nanni Cagnone). [Screens] (2) 90, p. 109.
VerELLEN, Patricia
See Ver ELLEN, Patricia
6633. VERNER, Dan
"Notes for a Writing Instructor" (for Mary). [EngJ] (79:4) Ap 90, p. 108.
6634. VERNIER, Tom
"Wind and Whales and Dark Sopranos." [Vis] (33) 90, p. 43.
6635. VERNIKOVA, Bella
"Around the Summer Table." [Confr] (42/43) Spr-Sum 90, p. 110.
"Vacation on a Latvian River" (tr. by Dan Levin). [Confr] (42/43) Spr-Sum 90, p.

111.
6636. VERNON, William J.
"Street People." [Mildred] (4:1) 90, p. 120.
6637. VERONESE, Adrienne
"The Hills Had Caves." [BellR] (13:2, #28) Fall 90, p. 32.
6638. VÉRTES, Judit
"Prophesying About Your Time" (tr. of Sandor Csoóri, w. Len Roberts).
[AmerPoR] (19:5) S-O 90, p. 25-26.
6639. VÉRTES, László
"Barbarous Prayer" (tr. of Sandor Csoóri, w. Len Roberts). [AmerPoR] (19:5) S-O
90, p. 26.
"Dozing on the Train" (tr. of Sándor Csoóri, w. Len Roberts). [MidAR] (10:1) 90,
p. 73, 75.
"On the Third Day the Snow Began to Fall" (tr. of Sándor Csoóri, w. Len Roberts
and Miklos Telbisz). [Chelsea] (49) 90, p. 123.
"On the Third Day the Snow Began to Fall" (tr. of Sándor Csoóri, w. Len Roberts
and Miklós Telbisz). [MidAR] (10:1) 90, p. 83, 85.
"People, Boughs" (tr. of Sandor Csoóri, w. Len Roberts). [AmerPoR] (19:5) S-O
90, p. 25.
"Postponed Nightmare" (tr. of Sándor Csoóri, w. Len Roberts). [LitR] (33:3) Spr
90, p. 293.
"Sea Gull-Line" (tr. of Sándor Csoóri, w. Len Roberts). [Chelsea] (49) 90, p. 124.
"You're Rising and Vanishing" (tr. of Sandor Csoóri, w. Len Roberts). [AmerPoR]
(19:5) S-O 90, p. 26.
6640. VERTREACE, Martha (Martha M.)
"The Celtic Cross." [HawaiiR] (14:3, #30) Fall 90, p. 81-82.
"Driftwood." [ChamLR] (4:1, #7) Fall 90, p. 134-135.
"Jaliscan Sestina." [HawaiiR] (14:3, #30) Fall 90, p. 83-84.
"Scrapbook." [HawaiiR] (14:2, #29) Spr 90, p. 14-15.
"Yarrow." [SpoonRQ] (15:1) Wint 90, p. 63-64.
6641. VESSUP, Aaron
"Believers Are Made in Heaven." [WebR] (14:2) Spr 90, p. 87.
"Cosmic Love on a Disk." [WebR] (14:2) Spr 90, p. 86.
6642. VEST, Jacqueline
"All the Stars" (tr. of Mira Aleckovic, w. Quentin Vest). [HampSPR] (Anthology
1975-1990) 90, p. 260.
"Roll On, River, Weighed Down by the Breath of the Dead" (tr. of Mira Aleckovic,
w. Quentin Vest). [HampSPR] (Anthology 1975-1990) 90, p. 260.
"Sutjeska" (tr. of Mira Aleckovic, w. Quentin Vest). [HampSPR] (Anthology
1975-1990) 90, p. 261.
"Trackless Quest" (tr. of Mira Aleckovic, w. Quentin Vest). [HampSPR] (Anthology
1975-1990) 90, p. 262.
"Wooden Shoes" (tr. of Mira Aleckovic, w. Quentin Vest). [HampSPR] (Anthology
1975-1990) 90, p. 261.
6643. VEST, Quentin
"All the Stars" (tr. of Mira Aleckovic, w. Jacqueline Vest). [HampSPR] (Anthology
1975-1990) 90, p. 260.
"Roll On, River, Weighed Down by the Breath of the Dead" (tr. of Mira Aleckovic,
w. Jacqueline Vest). [HampSPR] (Anthology 1975-1990) 90, p. 260.
"Suiciding the Bats." [HampSPR] (Anthology 1975-1990) 90, p. 39.
"Sutjeska" (tr. of Mira Aleckovic, w. Jacqueline Vest). [HampSPR] (Anthology
1975-1990) 90, p. 261.
"Trackless Quest" (tr. of Mira Aleckovic, w. Jacqueline Vest). [HampSPR]
(Anthology 1975-1990) 90, p. 262.
"When They Found Him He Remembered Nothing." [HampSPR] (Anthology
1975-1990) 90, p. 39-40.
"Wooden Shoes" (tr. of Mira Aleckovic, w. Jacqueline Vest). [HampSPR]
(Anthology 1975-1990) 90, p. 261.
6644. VETERE, Richard
"Global Amnesia." [SlipS] (10) 90, p. 73-75.
6645. VICKERY, Jennifer
"Donna Pressley, 33." [ColEng] (52:1) Ja 90, p. 40-41.
"My Husband, Sergeant Davies, All on Sundays." [ColEng] (52:1) Ja 90, p. 42.
"What Good Is It to Be Blinded." [ColEng] (52:1) Ja 90, p. 43.
6646. VICTOR, Ken
"The Discovery of Mouths." [PaintedB] (40/41) 90, p. 189.

6647. VICUÑA, Cecilia
"Iridesce" (tr. by Suzanne Jill Levine). [LitR] (33:4) Sum 90, p. 496-497.
6648. VIDAL
"Cantiga d'Amor de Refran." [CumbPR] (9:2) Spr 90, p. 54.
"Song to a Lady from Elvas (Cantiga d'Amor)" (tr. by Richard Zenith). [CumbPR]
(9:2) Spr 90, p. 55.
6649. VIERECK, Peter
"Freed from Superstition, Hurrah." [BelPoJ] (40:4) Sum 90, p. 53.
"Hospital Window" (for Joseph Brodsky). [NewL] (57:2) Wint 90-91, p. 74-84.
"Paranoia As Champ." [HampSPR] (Anthology 1975-1990) 90, p. 65.
"White Butterflies of Night, So Often Near Me" (tr. of Georg Heym). [HampSPR]
(Anthology 1975-1990) 90, p. 265.
6650. VILARINO, Idea
"No More" (tr. by Mark Smith-Soto). [InterPR] (16:1) Spr 90, p. 97.
"Ya No." [InterPR] (16:1) Spr 90, p. 96.
6651. VINCENT, Paul
"Flight into Egypt" (Painting: The Massacre of the Innocents by Pieter Breughel, tr.
of Hugo Claus). [Trans] (24) Fall 90, p. 45.
"In the Chicago Museum" (Painting: Saint Jerome by Joachim Patinir, tr. of Hugo
Claus). [Trans] (24) Fall 90, p. 44.
"Reflections on Ruysdael" (tr. of C. O. Jellema). [Trans] (24) Fall 90, p. 50-52.
"Visio Tondalis" (Painting by Hieronymus Bosch, tr. of Hugo Claus). [Trans] (24)
Fall 90, p. 42-43.
6652. VINCIGUERRA, Theresa
"By Scent." [YellowS] (33) Spr 90, p. 4.
VINO, Joanne de
See DeVINO, Joanne
6653. VINOGRAD, Julia
"People Are Living on the Streets" (first published in Bull Horn 2:1, Ja 89).
[PoetryUSA] (5:3) Fall 90, p. 14.
"Street Saxophone." [PoetryUSA] (5:1) Spr 90, p. 3.
6654. VINZ, Mark
"Country Roads." [SoDakR] (28:2) Sum 90, p. 149.
"Keeping the Record Straight." [SoDakR] (28:2) Sum 90, p. 150.
"The Old Hometown." [SoDakR] (28:2) Sum 90, p. 151.
"Trade-In." [SoDakR] (28:2) Sum 90, p. 148.
6655. VIOLI, Paul
"Catalogue of the New Wonderment." [KenR] (NS 12:2) Spr 90, p. 176-177.
"A Movable Snack" (from "Kidstuff Selected Accidents, Pointless Anecdotes,
Unsettling Accounts). [Shiny] (5) 90, p. 3.
6656. VIRGILIO, NIcholas
"Lily." [CrossC] (12:1) 90, p. 21.
6657. VISSER, G. N.
"Mei It Kliuwen Fan de Jierren." [WashR] (16:2) Ag-S 90, p. 13.
"When You Grow Older" (tr. by Rod Jellema). [WashR] (16:2) Ag-S 90, p. 13.
6658. VITIELLO, Christopher
"Exhibitionism." [WilliamMR] (28) 90, p. 67.
"Landscape with Girl." [WilliamMR] (28) 90, p. 77.
"The Trick." [WilliamMR] (28) 90, p. 79.
6659. VITIELLO, Justin
"August, 1977: Arrivederci Roma." [Footwork] 90, p. 76.
"Baby Pictures." [Footwork] 90, p. 76.
"The Missing Link." [Footwork] 90, p. 77.
6660. VITIER, Cintio
"Canto Llano (Plain Song)" (Selection: XXIII, tr. by Maria Bennett). [CrabCR] (6:3)
Spr 90, p. 17.
"Elegy" (tr. by Maria Bennett). [CrabCR] (6:3) Spr 90, p. 17-18.
"Light from the Cay" (tr. by Maria Bennett). [CrabCR] (6:3) Spr 90, p. 18.
"Ofumeyi" (sign given in a divination ceremony among the Yoruba, tr. by Maria
Bennett). [CrabCR] (7:1) Wint 90, p. 4-7.
VITO, Allove de
See DeVITO, Allove
VITO, E. B. de
See De VITO, E. B.
6661. VLASOPOLOS, Anca
"Bridled Lust." [Interim] (9:1) Spr-Sum 90, p. 3.

"Ginger." [Interim] (9:1) Spr-Sum 90, p. 4-5.
6662. VLEK, Hans
"Billie Holiday" (tr. by Arie Staal). [Vis] (34) 90, p. 45.
"Geranium" (tr. by Sharon Robertson). [Vis] (34) 90, p. 46.
"High Time" (tr. by Kees Snoek). [Vis] (34) 90, p. 47.
6663. VOCAT, Laura
"2 + 2 = A Hindu, Not 4." [Grain] (18:3) Fall 90, p. 62.
6664. VOGEL, Constance
"Another State." [WillowR] Spr 90, p. 45.
6665. VOGEL, David
"In the Attic" (tr. by Bernhard Frank). [WebR] (14:2) Spr 90, p. 103.
"When Night Approaches" (tr. by Bernhard Frank). [WebR] (14:2) Spr 90, p. 103.
6666. VOGELSANG, Arthur
"Character." [Ploughs] (16:4) Wint 90-91, p. 8.
"Conversation in Increasing Stanzas." [MissouriR] (13:2) 90, p. 77-79.
"Drifters." [WillowS] (26) Spr 90, p. 13-14.
"The Grass on the Other Side." [DenQ] (25:1) Sum 90, p. 42-46.
"Rue Replique." [Ploughs] (16:4) Wint 90-91, p. 7.
"Secret." [OnTheBus] (2:1, #5) Spr 90, p. 139.
"Swollen Haiku." [Ploughs] (16:4) Wint 90-91, p. 9.
"Tarjetas Postales." [DenQ] (25:1) Sum 90, p. 47-53.
6667. VOIGT, Ellen Bryant
"The Letters." [AntR] (48:2) Spr 90, p. 234.
"The Test." [AntR] (48:2) Spr 90, p. 235.
"Woman Who Weeps." [AntR] (48:2) Spr 90, p. 236.
6668. VOLDSETH, Beverly
"Journal Entry 1989." [RagMag] (7:2) Spr 90, p. 64-65.
"Waiting for Snow." [RagMag] (8:2) 90, p. 26.
"When Dawn Wakes You." [RagMag] (8:1) 90, p. 73.
6669. VOLK, Gregory
"Approaches to Crete." [GrahamHR] (13) Spr 90, p. 23-25.
6670. VOLKMAN, Karen
"Making Won Tons." [Outbr] (21) 90, p. 5-6.
"Mowing after Dark." [PassN] (11:1) Sum 90, p. 4.
"The Vampire's Villanelle." [KanQ] (22:3) Sum 90, p. 225.
6671. VOLKOVA, Bronislava
"How Can You Lie So Shamelessly?" (tr. of Jirí Kolár). [PoetryE] (30) Fall 90, p. 71.
"I Step Over" (tr. by the author). [PoetryE] (29) Spr 90, p. 118.
"Only white walls know the horror" (tr. by the author and Willis Barnstone). [PoetryE] (30) Fall 90, p. 66.
"Song from an Intermezzo" (tr. of Jaroslav Seifert). [PoetryE] (30) Fall 90, p. 10.
6672. VOLKOW, Verónica
"To Ramon and Ana Maria Xirau" (tr. by Ute Margarete Saine). [OnTheBus] (2:2/3:1, #6/7) Sum-Fall 90 Wint-Spr 91, p. 252.
"We Can Choose" (tr. by Iona Wishaw). [Vis] (33) 90, p. 22.
6673. VOLLMER, Judith
"Fabian." [LaurelR] (24:2) Sum 90, p. 61-62.
"The Man in the Gray House." [LaurelR] (24:2) Sum 90, p. 60-61.
"Smoking Cigars with Li Po." [PraS] (64:4) Wint 90, p. 78-79.
"To Hera." [PraS] (64:4) Wint 90, p. 80-81.
6674. VOLO, Alfonso
"Aliens in Southern California." [SlipS] (10) 90, p. 96.
6675. VOLPE, Christopher
"Flower." [LindLM] (9:3) Jl-S 90, p. 15.
"Waves." [LindLM] (9:3) Jl-S 90, p. 15.
"Wildflowers." [LindLM] (9:3) Jl-S 90, p. 15.
Von ALBRECHT, Michael
See ALBRECHT, Michael von
Von BORN, Heidi
See BORN, Heidi von
6676. Von HOLTEN, Dan
"Poncho and the Pig: Dog's Dream." [Farm] (7:1) Spr 90, p. 34.
Von SCHOULTZ, Solveig
See SCHOULTZ, Solveig von

6677. VOROS, Gyorgyi
    "Driving at Midnight." [Sequoia] (33:2) Wint 90, p. 106-107.
    "Redwoods." [Sequoia] (33:2) Wint 90, p. 105.
6678. VOSS, Fred
    "Bad Review." [Pearl] (10) Spr 90, p. 25.
    "Honeymoon." [Pearl] (10) Spr 90, p. 25.
    "Prime" (29 poems). [Pearl] (12) Fall-Wint 90, p. 6-22.
    "The Refugee." [Pearl] (11) Sum 90, p. 37.
    "Sidekick." [Pearl] (11) Sum 90, p. 37.
    "Worship." [Pearl] (12) Fall-Wint 90, p. 50.
6679. VOURVOULIAS, Sabrina
    "Ixquic's Song for Guatemala" (Ixquic: according to Quiché belief, the mother of
        Guatemalans). [GrahamHR] (13) Spr 90, p. 88.
6680. VOZNESENSKY, Andrei
    "Insight" (tr. by Albert C. Todd). [Nimrod] (33:2) Spr-Sum 90, p. 125.
    "Romance" (tr. by Albert C. Todd). [Nimrod] (33:2) Spr-Sum 90, p. 125.
VRIES, Carrow de
    See De VRIES, Carrow
VRIES, Rachel Guido de
    See DeVRIES, Rachel Guido
6681. VROMAN, Leo
    "America" (tr. by the Author). [Trans] (24) Fall 90, p. 104-106.
    "Love Greatly Enlarged" (tr. by the Author). [Trans] (24) Fall 90, p. 107-112.
    "Together" (tr. by Arie Staal and the author). [Vis] (34) 90, p. 35.
    "A Walk After a Late Breakfast" (tr. by the author, w. Claire Nicolas White). [Trans]
        (24) Fall 90, p. 113-114.
6682. VUKAJLOVIC, Dusan
    "Fear" (Excerpt, tr. by Bogdana Gagrica Bobic). [Screens] (2) 90, p. 66.
6683. VUONG-RIDDICK, Thuong
    "Searching." [Event] (19:1) Spr 90, p. 45.
    "Springtime in Victoria." [Event] (19:1) Spr 90, p. 44.
6684. WAARSENBURG, Hans van de
    "Our Man in Prague" (tr. by Kees Snoek). [Vis] (34) 90, p. 50.
    "Seascapes" (tr. by Claire Nicolas White). [Trans] (24) Fall 90, p. 150-154.
    "Seastone" (tr. by Sharon Robertson). [Vis] (34) 90, p. 49.
6685. WADE, Cory
    "Knitting Litany." [Poetry] (157:1) O 90, p. 4.
6686. WADE, Sidney
    "Aquinas on Beauty." [TampaR] (3) 90, p. 54-55.
6687. WADSWORTH, Charles
    "The Sea" (tr. of Karin Boye). [WashR] (16:2) Ag-S 90, p. 34.
    "That Path" (tr. of Karin Boye). [WashR] (16:2) Ag-S 90, p. 34.
    "Those Past Days" (tr. of Karin Boye). [WashR] (16:2) Ag-S 90, p. 34.
6688. WAGNER, Anneliese
    "Birth of Meadows." [PoetL] (85:3) Fall 90, p. 24.
    "The Children of Endingen." [WestB] (26) 90, p. 67-68.
    "God's Scout." [WestB] (26) 90, p. 68-69.
    "Let's Stop Talking" (tr. of Elisabeth Borchers). [PoetryE] (30) Fall 90, p. 22.
    "Salt." [WestB] (26) 90, p. 69-70.
6689. WAGNER, John D.
    "The Starving African Girl." [GreenMR] (NS 4:1) Spr-Sum 90, p. 59-60.
6690. WAGNER, Maryfrances
    "About to Get Up." [HiramPoR] (47) Wint 90, p. 52.
    "The Importance of Kneading." [NewL] (57:1) Fall 90, p. 76-77.
    "Slow Losses." [HiramPoR] (47) Wint 90, p. 51.
    "The Woodworker" (for Lois). [NewL] (57:1) Fall 90, p. 75.
6691. WAGNER, Shelly
    "Passover." [OnTheBus] (2:2/3:1, #6/7) Sum-Fall 90 Wint-Spr 91, p. 199.
    "The Tie." [OnTheBus] (2:2/3:1, #6/7) Sum-Fall 90 Wint-Spr 91, p. 198-199.
    "Voices." [OnTheBus] (2:2/3:1, #6/7) Sum-Fall 90 Wint-Spr 91, p. 198.
6692. WAGONER, David
    "At the Point of No Return." [HampSPR] (Anthology 1975-1990) 90, p. 133-134.
    "Standing in the Middle of a Desert." [HampSPR] (Anthology 1975-1990) 90, p.
        133.
6693. WAH, Fred
    "Artknot 17." [Screens] (2) 90, p. 183.

"Artknot 21." [MassR] (31:1/2) Spr-Sum 90, p. 227.
"Artknot 22." [MassR] (31:1/2) Spr-Sum 90, p. 227.
"Artknot 23." [MassR] (31:1/2) Spr-Sum 90, p. 227.
"Artknot 24." [MassR] (31:1/2) Spr-Sum 90, p. 228.
"Artknot 25." [MassR] (31:1/2) Spr-Sum 90, p. 228.
"Artknot 26." [MassR] (31:1/2) Spr-Sum 90, p. 228.
"Pearagraphs" (On Roy Kiyooka's "Pear Tree Pomes"). [CapilR] (2:2) Spr 90, p.
    95-97.
"Second Question for Hannike Büche." [Screens] (2) 90, p. 183.

6694. WAHL, Gretchen
"Sultry Afternoon in Nowata, Oklahoma" (after a line by Ai). [PennR] (4:2) 90, p.
    119-121.

6695. WAHTO, Diane
"Michael's Kisses." [MidwQ] (31:4) Sum 90, p. 471.

6696. WAIN, John
"Your House." [BelPoJ] (40:4) Sum 90, p. 54-55.

6697. WAINIO
"Greenhouse Effect." [PoetryUSA] (5:3) Fall 90, p. 15.

6698. WAISI, Paschal
"The Changing Social World." [Manoa] (2:1) Spr 90, p. 53.

6699. WAKEFIELD, Kathleen
"Botany." [PennR] (4:2) 90, p. 56.
"The Red Fox." [PoetryNW] (31:3) Aut 90, p. 34-35.
"Waking on the Island." [ThRiPo] (35/36) 90, p. 17.

6700. WAKOSKI, Diane
"Californians." [MichQR] (29:1) Wint 90, p. 59-61.
"Carla Boucher Eats Poppies in Santa Fe" (a meditation on desert images). [Notus]
    (5:1) Spr 90, p. 68.
"Craig's Muse: Wearing the Green" (for Craig Cotter in California). [MichQR]
    (29:1) Wint 90, p. 57-58.
"Dogs" (A Meditation on Gertrude Stein in an Armchair Sitting Under Picasso's
    Portrait of Her in Paris, for Barbara, Wendy & Judith). [Caliban] (9) 90, p.
    11-12.
"He." [Footwork] 90, p. 9-10.
"Hummingbird Light" (for Jackson, Jerry & Diane, Craig, and Carol). [Notus] (5:1)
    Spr 90, p. 70.
"Junk Jewelry." [NegC] (10:1) 90, p. 11-12.
"Light & Destiny: Men Without Hats." [Notus] (5:1) Spr 90, p. 69.
"Media, The New Sorceress" (for Robert Creeley). [Caliban] (9) 90, p. 13-14.
"Mint Flowers" (from "Medea the Sorceress," to be published by Black Sparrow
    Press, Fall 1990). [PoetryUSA] (5:3) Fall 90, p. 11.
"Moneylight" (A meditation on the tarot card, The Hanged Man, . . .). [NegC] (10:1)
    90, p. 9-10.
"Morning Star." [NegC] (10:1) 90, p. 13-14.
"My $15 Lily." [NegC] (10:1) 90, p. 15-16.
"Salt Free Talk" (For Norman Hindley, who sent me some pepper corns called
    "Paradise"). [Footwork] 90, p. 8.
"San Diego." [PoetryC] (11:1) Spr 90, p. 20.
"Snow on Idun's Apples." [SycamoreR] (2:1) Wint 90, p. 54-55.
"Steel Man" (for my husband, Robert). [PoetryC] (11:1) Spr 90, p. 20.

6701. WALCOTT, Derek
"Chapter XXXIX." [Antaeus] (64/65) Spr-Aut 90, p. 138-140.
"From Omeros, Chapter XLVI." [SycamoreR] (2:2) Sum 90, p. 39-42.
"Home." [NewYorker] (66:24) 30 Jl 90, p. 40.
"Omeros" (Selection). [PartR] (57:2) Spr 90, p. 264-266.
"Omeros" (Selection: Chapter XL). [GrahamHR] (13) Spr 90, p. 7-10.
"Omeros" (Selection: Chapter XLIII). [GreenMR] (NS 4:1) Spr-Sum 90, p. 6-10.

6702. WALDEN, Gale Renee
"Everybody's Living Room." [SpoonRQ] (15:1) Wint 90, p. 61.
"From the Porch." [SpoonRQ] (15:1) Wint 90, p. 60.

6703. WALDEN, Michael L.
"Reflections of Icarus." [EmeraldCR] (1990) c89, p. 61.

6704. WALDMAN, Anne
"Ode to Speech." [PoetryUSA] (5:3) Fall 90, p. 1.

6705. WALDNER, Liz
"Assumption." [NowestR] (28:3/29:1) 90-91, p. 81.

479

"Danse Ordinaire" (or, lauren lemme sing it to ya one time honey). [SingHM] (18) 90, p. 76-77.
6706. WALDOR, Peter
"All Night." [Ploughs] (16:4) Wint 90-91, p. 40.
"Ark." [Ploughs] (16:4) Wint 90-91, p. 41.
"Let's Go to the Ruins" (for Cindy Berman). [ManhatPR] (11) [89?], p. 17.
"Ode to the American Cucumber." [NegC] (10:2/3) 90, p. 79-80.
"Ode to the Spine." [Ploughs] (16:4) Wint 90-91, p. 42.
6707. WALDROP, Keith
"Boudica" (Selections: 12-20, tr. of Paol Keineg). [Sulfur] (10:1, #26) Spr 90, p. 199-203.
"Boudica 21-25" (tr. of Paol Keineg). [NewAW] (6) Spr 90, p. 59-63.
"Click-Rose 2" (Selections: X-XIII, XV-XIX, tr. of Dominique Fourcade). [Sulfur] (10:2, #27) Fall 90, p. 74-78.
"Falling in Love Through a Description" (Selections: 4 poems). [Avec] (3:1) 90, p. 3-6.
"MaternA" (Excerpts, Editions Gallimard, Paris, 1954, tr. of Hélène Bessette). [Avec] (3:1) 90, p. 67-70.
"Variations on a Paraphrase." [Conjunc] (15) 90, p. 271-277.
"Wandering Curves." [NewAW] (6) Spr 90, p. 9.
"Will to Will." [NewAW] (6) Spr 90, p. 8.
6708. WALDROP, Rosmarie
"The Attraction of the Ground." [Conjunc] (15) 90, p. 320-323.
"The Book of Resemblances II: Intimations The Desert" (Selections, tr. of Edmond Jabès). [Epoch] (39:3) 90, p. 304-324.
"Born Viable" (from "Intimations. The Desert. The Book of Resemblances II, tr. of Edmond Jabès). [ManhatR] (5:2) Fall 90, p. 39-40.
"Daily Remembered Allowances" (Excerpts). [NewAW] (6) Spr 90, p. 6-7.
"Dawn" (Excerpts, from "Aube," P.O.L., Paris, 1983, tr. of Joseph Guglielmi). [Avec] (3:1) 90, p. 63-66.
"Dawn" (Selections, tr. of Joseph Gugliemi). [Pequod] (31) 90, p. 64-66.
"Landscape Overthrown" (On a Series of Monoprints by Denny Moers). [Avec] (3:1) 90, p. 147-148.
"Lawn of Excluded Middle" (Excerpt). [Chelsea] (49) 90, p. 34-35.
"On Blankness, I" (from "Intimations. The Desert. The Book of Resemblances II, tr. of Edmond Jabès). [ManhatR] (5:2) Fall 90, p. 42-44.
"On Blankness, II" (from "Intimations. The Desert. The Book of Resemblances II, tr. of Edmond Jabès). [ManhatR] (5:2) Fall 90, p. 44.
"On Blankness, III" (from "Intimations. The Desert. The Book of Resemblances II, tr. of Edmond Jabès). [ManhatR] (5:2) Fall 90, p. 45.
"On Humor" (from "Intimations. The Desert. The Book of Resemblances II, tr. of Edmond Jabès). [ManhatR] (5:2) Fall 90, p. 37.
"Slowing Perceptions." [Epoch] (39:1/2) 90, p. 50-52.
"Some Thing Black: Three Poems" (tr. of Jacques Roubaud). [Trans] (23) Spr 90, p. 107-110.
"A Tangent on Lines by Susan Howe." [Talisman] (4) Spr 90, p. 39.
"Thought, Death" (from "Intimations. The Desert. The Book of Resemblances II, tr. of Edmond Jabès). [ManhatR] (5:2) Fall 90, p. 41.
"Whose Seal Cannot Be Broken" (from "Intimations. The Desert. The Book of Resemblances II, tr. of Edmond Jabès). [ManhatR] (5:2) Fall 90, p. 38-39.
6709. WALKER, Alice
"On Stripping Bark from Myself." [CimR] (93) O 90, p. 80.
6710. WALKER, Anne
"Child's" (for D.L.V.). [PoetryC] (11:1) Spr 90, p. 16.
"City and Day" (cobblestones). [PoetryC] (11:1) Spr 90, p. 16.
"Crystal Thin." [PoetryC] (11:1) Spr 90, p. 16.
"Letter of Resignation." [PoetryC] (11:1) Spr 90, p. 16.
"Peach Offering." [PoetryC] (11:1) Spr 90, p. 16.
6711. WALKER, Brian
"1/0 = Infinity." [DustyD] (1:2) O 90, p. 6.
"Courtier of the Core." [DustyD] (1:2) O 90, p. 7.
"Ode to the Independent Claus." [DustyD] (1:2) O 90, p. 6.
"The Outlaw Hitching-Post." [DustyD] (1:2) O 90, p. 5.
"Poet" (for Dylan Thomas). [DustyD] (1:2) O 90, p. 5.
"Poetic Justice." [DustyD] (1:2) O 90, p. 6.
"Silent Revolution." [DustyD] (1:2) O 90, p. 7.

"Stepping Out for Air." [DustyD] (1:2) O 90, p. 6.
6712. WALKER, Christopher
"For Jim Jordan, a Valedictory Pasticcio, with Love." [WindO] (53) Fall 90, p.
52-53.
6713. WALKER, David
"Burning the Leaves" (for F.). [HampSPR] (Anthology 1975-1990) 90, p. 187.
"On Some Poems" (for Charles Wright). [HampSPR] (Anthology 1975-1990) 90, p.
187.
"Street Wise." [Amelia] (6:2, #17) 90, p. 121.
6714. WALKER, Ephraim
"Chariot." [PoetryUSA] (5:2) Sum 90, p. 8.
6715. WALKER, Jeanne (Jeanne Murray)
"Dr. W. F. Schamber and School Board Breaking Ground for the Elementary
School." [PraS] (64:4) Wint 90, p. 91-92.
"How to Turn Garbage into Edible Food." [WestB] (27) 90, p. 16.
"L. J. Sand in His Paint and General Store, 1959." [Poetry] (156:4) Jl 90, p. 203.
"National Enquirer Writer Hospitalized with Nervous Breakdown After Writing His
Thousandth Story." [NegC] (10:2/3) 90, p. 87-88.
"Parker Homesteads, 1867." [PraS] (64:4) Wint 90, p. 89-90.
"Parkers Prairie Celebration on Soo Street, 1920." [PraS] (64:4) Wint 90, p. 90-91.
"Poem for the Missing Beauty Operator." [Poetry] (156:4) Jl 90, p. 202-203.
"Recovering the Commonplace" (For Bob Perkel). [PartR] (57:1) Wint 90, p.
102-103.
"Women Wading in Lake Adley Around 1900." [PraS] (64:4) Wint 90, p. 92-93.
6716. WALKER, John
"Fingernails." [Gypsy] (15) 90, p. 17.
6717. WALKER, K. A.
"Wounded." [EmeraldCR] (1990) c89, p. 72.
6718. WALKER, Kevin
"All It Ever Did Was Lie." [Caliban] (9) 90, p. 76-77.
"For My Mother in Winter." [GreensboroR] (49) Wint 90-91, p. 82.
6719. WALKER, Lynne
"I Love Men." [Spirit] (10:2) 90, p. 28-31.
6720. WALKER, Marylisa
"War." [BlackBR] (11) Spr-Sum 90, p. 21.
6721. WALKER, Shavon K.
"Metamorphosis." [PoetryUSA] (5:3) Fall 90, p. 26.
6722. WALKER, Sue
"The Feet Make Blue Fish Cento." [ChatR] (11:1) Fall 90, p. 23.
"The Football Coach and Mama's Memorial." [Parting] (3:1) Sum 90, p. 17.
"From Marianne Moore to Robert B. Young of the Ford Motor Company in Reply to
His October 19, 1955 Letter Regarding the Name of a Car" (A Sort-of Cento).
[NewYorkQ] (43) Fall 90, p. 66.
6723. WALKER, Vicki
"The Long Blue Coat" (for J.). [CapilR] (2:4) Wint 90, p. 19.
"That Blue" (for Camille). [CapilR] (2:4) Wint 90, p. 20.
"With Red." [CapilR] (2:4) Wint 90, p. 21.
6724. WALL, Alan
"City Stones" (Selection: XV). [Stand] (31:3) Sum 90, p. 69.
6725. WALLACE, Anthony
"Bus Ride in Salt Lake." [HawaiiR] (15:1, #31) Wint 90, p. 15.
"Things." [HawaiiR] (15:1, #31) Wint 90, p. 16.
6726. WALLACE, Nancy (Nancy J.)
"If I Find You." [ArtfulD] (18/19) 90, p. 108.
"In the Yucatan." [RiverC] (11:1) Fall 90, p. 69.
6727. WALLACE, Naomi
"The Devil's Ode." [Nat] (250:19) 14 My 90, p. 677.
"Portrait of a Kentucky Family." [AmerV] (18) Spr 90, p. 55.
6728. WALLACE, Ronald (Ron)
"Bluegills." [PraS] (64:3) Fall 90, p. 83.
"Canzone: Egrets." [LaurelR] (24:2) Sum 90, p. 5-6.
"Early Brass." [LaurelR] (24:2) Sum 90, p. 8.
"Fan Mail." [SouthernR] (26:3) Jl 90, p. 689-690.
"Fresh Oysters and Beer." [Crazy] (38) Spr 90, p. 39-40.
"Headlines." [PraS] (64:3) Fall 90, p. 84.
"Hunger." [PoetC] (21:2) Wint 90, p. 12.

481

WALLACE

"If James Whitmore." [Poem] (63) My 90, p. 49.
"In Doubt." [PoetryNW] (31:1) Spr 90, p. 45.
"In the Amish Bakery." [Crazy] (38) Spr 90, p. 38.
"In the Cards." [TarRP] (29:2) Spr 90, p. 17.
"The Life Next at Hand." [Poetry] (155:6) Mr 90, p. 394.
"The Makings of Happiness" (In Memory of Felix Pollak). [Pembroke] (22) 90, p.
     19.
"Onions." [LaurelR] (24:2) Sum 90, p. 7.
"The Physics of Marriage." [PoetryNW] (31:3) Aut 90, p. 36.
"Plowing." [MidAR] (10:2) 90, p. 35.
"Song of the Butchered Hog." [NewOR] (17:1) Spr 90, p. 60.
"Starling in the Woodstove." [PoetC] (21:2) Wint 90, p. 11.
"The Story." [PoetryNW] (31:2) Sum 90, p. 21-22.
"Tricycling in the Sea." [Poem] (63) My 90, p. 50.
"Vespertilian." [PoetryNW] (31:4) Wint 90-91, p. 30.
6729. WALLACE, T. H. S.
"Blessed." [CumbPR] (10:1) Fall 90, p. 49.
"On First Hearing Ezra Pound at St. Elizabeth's Hospital." [MidwQ] (32:1) Aut 90,
     p. 95-96.
6730. WALLACE-CRABBE, Chris
"The Dead Cartesian." [Poetry] (156:2) My 90, p. 91.
6731. WALLACH, Martin
"Thanks for Your Time." [Plain] (11:1) Fall 90, p. 27.
WALLEGHEN, Michael van
     See Van WALLEGHEN, Michael
6732. WALLENSTEIN, Barry
"Perspective." [Outbr] (21) 90, p. 32.
6733. WALLS, Doyle Wesley
"If You're Hungry, That's a Good Sign." [MinnR] (NS 34/35) Spr-Fall 90, p. 5-6.
6734. WALSH, Chad
"On Building a Cradle for My Grandson, Chad Walsh Hamblin." [HampSPR]
     (Anthology 1975-1990) 90, p. 14.
6735. WALSH, Harry
"On Watch." [AmerS] (59:2) Spr 90, p. 236.
6736. WALSH, Marty
"Branchers." [Poem] (64) N 90, p. 2.
"The Green Widower." [KanQ] (22:3) Sum 90, p. 103.
"If Crow Didn't Exist." [Poem] (64) N 90, p. 1.
"Lingo Anglais." [KanQ] (22:3) Sum 90, p. 102.
"Making Up." [KanQ] (22:1/2) Wint-Spr 90, p. 116.
"Nibblets and Snippets." [Poem] (64) N 90, p. 3.
"The Three Perched Birds." [KanQ] (22:1/2) Wint-Spr 90, p. 116.
6737. WALSH, Michael C.
"The Colors of Indian Corn." [ChamLR] (3:2, #6) Spr 90, p. 88-89.
"Mayan Garden." [ChamLR] (4:1, #7) Fall 90, p. 27-28.
"Silken Kivas." [ChamLR] (3:2, #6) Spr 90, p. 90-91.
"Succession." [ChamLR] (3:2, #6) Spr 90, p. 86-87.
"Turtle of Vision." [ChamLR] (4:1, #7) Fall 90, p. 29-30.
6738. WALSH, Phyllis
"Haiku" (3 poems). [Northeast] (5:2) Spr 90, p. 30.
6739. WALSH, William J.
"Inventory." [AnthNEW] 90, p. 26.
6740. WALTNER-TOEWS, David
"The Ecology of Poetry" (for Bruce Cockburn). [PraF] (11:2) Sum 90, p. 48-49.
"A Moment in Time" (Reflections at the Ny Carlsberg museum in Copenhagen, in a
     room full of 19th-century marble statues). [PraF] (11:2) Sum 90, p. 47-48.
6741. WALTON, Anthony
"In Memory of Robert Hayden." [Chelsea] (49) 90, p. 84-85.
6742. WALZ, JoLynne
"Hiking Above the Monegaw River." [CapeR] (25:1) Spr 90, p. 12.
"I Swear." [ChironR] (9:2) Sum 90, p. 16.
6743. WANG, Jia-xin (Jiaxin)
"At the End of a Street Thinking of Van Gogh" (tr. by Dong Jiping). [Footwork] 90,
     p. 34.
"Autumn" (tr. by Dong Jiping). [Footwork] 90, p. 34.
"Back to My Valley" (tr. by Zhang Ziqing). [PaintedB] (40/41) 90, p. 46.

"I Woke Up to Reality" (tr. by Zhang Ziqing). [PaintedB] (40/41) 90, p. 47.
"Lizard" (tr. by Zhang Ziqing). [PaintedB] (40/41) 90, p. 45.
"Premonition" (tr. by Dong Jiping). [Footwork] 90, p. 34.
"Returning to My Valley" (tr. by Dong Jiping). [Footwork] 90, p. 34.
"Seasons" (tr. by Zhang Ziqing). [PaintedB] (40/41) 90, p. 46.
"Three O'Clock in the Afternoon" (tr. by Dong Jiping). [Footwork] 90, p. 34.
"Touch" (tr. by Zhang Ziqing). [PaintedB] (40/41) 90, p. 47.
WANG, Ping
    See PING, Wang
6744. WANG, Xiao-Ni
"Dark Night on a Southbound Train" (tr. by Edward Morin and Dennis Ding).
    [Screens] (2) 90, p. 41.
6745. WANG, Yun
"Jiu Ge" (Ritual Songs, tr. of Qu Yuan). [PoetryC] (11:1) Spr 90, p. 23.
6746. WANIEK, Marilyn Nelson
"Dusting." [Ploughs] (16:1) Spr-Sum 90, p. 29.
"Enigma Variations" (Elgar: Enigma Variations, Op. 36). [Ploughs] (16:1) Spr-Sum
    90, p. 31.
"Tell Me a Story." [Ploughs] (16:1) Spr-Sum 90, p. 30.
6747. WARD, Diane
"Hold It." [Conjunc] (15) 90, p. 197-198.
6748. WARD, Phil
"Jade." [Bogg] (63) 90, p. 16.
6749. WARD, Robert (Robert R.)
"Day's Harmonies (Unemployment Poem)" (Bend, Oregon, 1983). [CrabCR] (7:1)
    Wint 90, p. 27.
"Sleep." [YellowS] (34) Sum 90, p. 4.
"Some Memories Lie Beyond the Edge of Any Map." [OnTheBus] (2:2/3:1, #6/7)
    Sum-Fall 90 Wint-Spr 91, p. 200.
"Zen of the Empty Page." [PoetryUSA] (5:2) Sum 90, p. 11.
6750. WARD, Scott
"The Bats." [Shen] (40:1) Spr 90, p. 78-79.
6751. WARD-HOGAN, Chris
"In My Father's House." [Dandel] (17:2) Fall-Wint 90, p. 17-18.
WARD-HORGAN, Chris
    See WARD-HOGAN, Chris
6752. WARDEN, Marine Robert
"Freeway 57, Orange County." [NegC] (10:2/3) 90, p. 97.
"Oh Holy Night, Chicago." [NegC] (10:2/3) 90, p. 96.
"Random Phrases From a Critical Review Plus a Poet's Comments." [Asylum] (5:4)
    90, p. 42.
6753. WARING, Belle
"Christmas Eve at Port Authority." [CimR] (93) O 90, p. 36.
"Gringos." [AmerPoR] (19:1) Ja-F 90, p. 5.
"Lucky." [AmerPoR] (19:4) Jl-Ag 90, p. 29.
"Our Lady of the Laundromat." [AmerPoR] (19:4) Jl-Ag 90, p. 29.
"Sick Sex." [CimR] (93) O 90, p. 34.
"So Get Over It, Honey." [CimR] (93) O 90, p. 35.
"Storm Crossing Key Bridge." [GreenMR] (NS 4:1) Spr-Sum 90, p. 63.
"What Dostoevsky Said." [GreenMR] (NS 4:1) Spr-Sum 90, p. 62.
6754. WARLAND, Betsy
"Cutting Re/marks." [SinW] (42) Wint 90-91, p. 94-112.
6755. WARMOND, Ellen
"Midwinter" (tr. by Gonny Van den Broek). [Vis] (34) 90, p. 48.
6756. WARN, Emily
"Border Town" (from "Highway Suite"). [SwampR] (5) Wint-Spr 90, p. 41.
"Johnny's Cafe" (from "Highway Suite"). [SwampR] (5) Wint-Spr 90, p. 40.
"The Rabbi Stumbles." [Calyx] (12:3) Sum 90, p. 46-47.
6757. WARNE, Candice
"Minnesota to Arizona." [Spirit] (10:2) 90, p. 46.
6758. WARNER, Claire
"To the Women-in-the-Moon." [AnthNEW] 90, p. 12.
6759. WARNKE, Dave
"Age." [JINJPo] (12:1) Spr 90, p. 20.
6760. WARREN, Charlotte Gould
"Apple Pie." [HawaiiR] (14:1, #28) Wint 89-90, p. 56-57.

"Spring-Green-Ivory." [BellR] (13:1, #27) Spr 90, p. 17.
6761. WARREN, Chris
"The Weeping Bed." [Dandel] (17:1) Spr-Sum 90, p. 12.
6762. WARREN, Colin
"On a Once Deserted Beach." [CrossCur] (9:2) Je 90, p. 9.
6763. WARREN, Kenneth
"Firebreak." [TriQ] (79) Fall 90, p. 105.
"Johnny Angel." [Gargoyle] (37/38) 90, p. 35.
"Of Death by Drowning." [TriQ] (79) Fall 90, p. 100-101.
"A Spring Heresy." [TriQ] (79) Fall 90, p. 103-104.
"Summer Trains." [TriQ] (79) Fall 90, p. 102.
6764. WARREN, Orlando
"Soliloquy." [NewYorkQ] (41) Spr 90, p. 94.
6765. WARREN, Robert Penn
"Country Burying (1919)." [GettyR] (3:1) Wint 90, p. 212-213.
"Heart of Autumn." [SoCaR] (23:1) Fall 90, p. 67.
"To a Face in the Crowd." [SoCaR] (23:1) Fall 90, p. 61.
6766. WARREN, Rosanna
"Song." [Atlantic] (266:5) N 90, p. 123.
"With You" (for R.P.W.). [Chelsea] (49) 90, p. 102-103.
6767. WARSH, Lewis
"Anyone But You." [Talisman] (5) Fall 90, p. 55-58.
"White Oak." [Notus] (5:1) Spr 90, p. 79-85.
6768. WARSH, Sylvia Maultash
"Love Song." [Bogg] (62) 90, p. 15.
6769. WARWICK, Betsey
"Rain." [OnTheBus] (2:1, #5) Spr 90, p. 141.
"Simple Things." [OnTheBus] (2:1, #5) Spr 90, p. 140-141.
6770. WARWICK, Ioanna-Veronika
"Anna Livia Plurabelle to James Joyce." [BlackWR] (16:2) Spr-Sum 90, p. 101-102.
"An Apple Tree for Osip Mandelstam." [Iowa] (20:3) Fall 90, p. 40.
"Blood Soup" (A Plainsongs Award Poem). [Plain] (10:2) Wint 90, p. 20-21.
"Caterpillar of Smoke." [QW] (31) Fall 90, p. 103-105.
"The Dancer." [OnTheBus] (2:1, #5) Spr 90, p. 75-76.
"Eleanor Marx-Aveling to Her Father, Fifteen Years After His Death." [QW] (31) Fall 90, p. 106-108.
"Elegy for Czesiek" (my classmate in Warsaw, stabbed to death in the park behind the building where I lived). [QW] (31) Fall 90, p. 97-99.
"Exile" (for Robert Pinsky). [Iowa] (20:3) Fall 90, p. 38-39.
"First Snow / Piano Concerti." [QW] (31) Fall 90, p. 109-111.
"Frau Lou." [QW] (31) Fall 90, p. 93-96.
"Frau Lou." [SouthernPR] (30:2) Fall 90, p. 9-12.
"How Horizons Work." [BlackWR] (16:2) Spr-Sum 90, p. 103-104.
"Leda." [Plain] (10:3) Spr 90, p. 20.
"Letter from a School Friend." [QW] (31) Fall 90, p. 100-102.
"Notes Toward Saint Joan." [SouthernPR] (30:2) Fall 90, p. 13-15.
"Scheherezade." [OnTheBus] (2:2/3:1, #6/7) Sum-Fall 90 Wint-Spr 91, p. 108-109.
"Le Temps Perdu." [SoCoast] (8) Spr 90, p. 52-53.
6771. WASHBURN, Laura Lee
"Whelk's Casing." [PoetL] (85:1) Spr 90, p. 41.
6772. WASHBURN, V. Glen
"Jesus of Navarone." [ChironR] (9:2) Sum 90, p. 16.
6773. WASHBUSH, Judy
"Passing On." [Northeast] (5:2) Spr 90, p. 11.
6774. WASSERBURG, Charles
"Below San Simeon." [TriQ] (80) Wint 90-91, p. 72-73.
"The Distances" (Excerpts). [TriQ] (80) Wint 90-91, p. 70-71.
"From Here." [TriQ] (80) Wint 90-91, p. 68-69.
"Geode." [Poetry] (155:6) Mr 90, p. 384-385.
6775. WASSON, Kirsten
"Now and Then." [NoDaQ] (58:4) Fall 90, p. 107-108.
"Stepchild Memory." [NoDaQ] (58:4) Fall 90, p. 108.
"Stepfather's Room" (for Daniel Curley, in memoriam). [NoDaQ] (58:4) Fall 90, p. 106-107.

484

WATERHOUSE

6776. WATERHOUSE, Philip A.
"Haut Goût." [Gypsy] (15) 90, p. 30.
"Takeover." [Amelia] (6:2, #17) 90, p. 81.
6777. WATERMAN, Andrew
"Drafts from Two Winter Evenings" (Excerts from "Entwürfe aus zei
Winterabenden," tr. of Rainer Maria Rilke). [Quarry] (39:1) Wint 90, p.
51-52.
6778. WATERS, Chocolate
"Transformation Is Not a Four-Letter Word" (on the departure of Scruff-o, the
Wonder Cat). [SingHM] (18) 90, p. 21.
6779. WATERS, Michael
"The Art of Tragedy." [CarolQ] (42:2) Wint 90, p. 93.
"Covert Street." [PraS] (64:1) Spr 90, p. 69-70.
"Creation." [CarolQ] (43:1) Fall 90, p. 39-40.
"The Lost Civilization" (Atlantis/Thira, for Robin). [CarolQ] (43:1) Fall 90, p. 41.
"'Night in the Tropics' (1858-59?)." [Poetry] (156:5) Ag 90, p. 283.
"Shhh." [Poetry] (156:5) Ag 90, p. 284.
"Ticks." [Journal] (13:2) Fall-Wint 89-90, p. 6.
"Transmigration." [Journal] (13:2) Fall-Wint 89-90, p. 7-8.
6780. WATERS, Tara
"Adolescence." [ContextS] (1:1) 89, p. 31.
6781. WATKINS, Melanie
"Dancing with Your Devil." [HangL] (57) 90, p. 84.
6782. WATKINS, William John
"Because He Could Not Give Me Wealth." [WindO] (53) Fall 90, p. 11.
"How to Tell If You Have the Makings of a Topnotch New York Literary Agent."
[WritersF] (16) Fall 90, p. 51-52.
"A Jersey Middle Age." [SoCaR] (23:1) Fall 90, p. 135.
"The Persecution of Wilhelm Reich." [KanQ] (22:1/2) Wint-Spr 90, p. 63.
"Polaris." [HawaiiR] (14:2, #29) Spr 90, p. 41.
"Thanatopsis Revisited." [JINJPo] (12:2) Aut 90, p. 9.
"Twenty-Sixth Anniversary Poem." [SpoonRQ] (15:2) Spr 90, p. 7.
"Two Jersey Crows in the Slow Lane of the Parkway." [WindO] (53) Fall 90, p. 12.
"What Scares About the Shark." [PoetC] (22:1) Fall 90, p. 31.
6783. WATLAKAS, Peter
"Speak-Up." [Manoa] (2:1) Spr 90, p. 49.
6784. WATSON, Carl
"Gene Train Suicide." [PaintedB] (40/41) 90, p. 138-139.
6785. WATSON, Elizabeth
"Three Poems for Lisa (1955-1988)." [Crucible] (26) Fall 90, p. 83-85.
6786. WATSON, Ellen
"Consecration" (tr. of Adélia Prado). [Field] (42) Spr 90, p. 24-25.
"Falsetto" (tr. of Adélia Prado). [Field] (42) Spr 90, p. 27-28.
"Head" (tr. of Adélia Prado). [Field] (42) Spr 90, p. 26.
"Land of the Holy Cross" (tr. of Adélia Prado). [AmerPoR] (19:2) Mr-Ap 90, p. 14.
"Seductive Sadness Winks at Me" (tr. of Adélia Prado). [AmerPoR] (19:2) Mr-Ap
90, p. 14.
6787. WATSON, Lawrence
"Grasshoppers." [SoDakR] (28:2) Sum 90, p. 131-132.
"The Population of North Dakota." [SoDakR] (28:2) Sum 90, p. 133-134.
"The Scandinavian-Lutheran Oral Storytelling Tradition Transplanted to the Northern
States of the American Midwest." [SoDakR] (28:2) Sum 90, p. 136.
"Waiting for Snow." [SoDakR] (28:2) Sum 90, p. 135.
6788. WATSON, M. T.
"The Abridged Cat." [NegC] (10:2/3) 90, p. 78.
6789. WATSON, Robert
"Dogs." [TarRP] (29:2) Spr 90, p. 8.
"The Great Wall." [InterPR] (16:2) Fall 90, p. 101.
"Nomads." [LaurelR] (24:2) Sum 90, p. 27.
6790. WATSON, Ron
"American Authors Before 1865." [SoDakR] (28:1) Spr 90, p. 76.
6791. WATTEN, Barrett
"Under Erasure" (Excerpt). [Zyzzyva] (6:4 #24) Wint 90, p. 80-87.
"Under Erasure" (Excerpts). [Verse] (7:1) Spr 90, p. 33-34.
6792. WAUGH, Robert H.
"Crow Moon." [LaurelR] (24:1) Wint 90, p. 29.

"Hunger Moon." [LaurelR] (24:1) Wint 90, p. 28.
6793. WAYBRANT, Linda
"Basalt & Serpentine Rest at Right Angles in the Sun." [PraF] (11:4) Wint 90-91, p. 80.
"Silence." [PraF] (11:4) Wint 90-91, p. 79.
"Sister/poem." [Dandel] (17:2) Fall-Wint 90, p. 26.
"The White Dead." [PraF] (11:4) Wint 90-91, p. 78.
6794. WAYMAN, Tom
"The Chilean Elegies: 4. Larry Tetlock." [Quarry] (39:4) Fall 1990, p. 93-94.
"Did I Miss Anything?" (Questions frequently asked by students after missing a class). [PoetryNW] (31:1) Spr 90, p. 32-33.
"The Dream of the Guerillas." [Quarry] (39:4) Fall 1990, p. 79-80.
"Greed Suite: Attitudes at the Top of a Hierarchy Influence Conduct Below." [Pig] (16) 90, p. 9.
"Greed Suite: Authority." [Pig] (16) 90, p. 8.
"Greed Suite: The False Season." [Pig] (16) 90, p. 10-11.
"Heart Water." [PoetryC] (11:2) Sum 90, p. 9.
"Modifications to the Heart." [Event] (19:2) Sum 90, p. 69-71.
"The Nail." [PraF] (11:4) Wint 90-91, p. 81.
"One World Shutting Out Another." [PoetryC] (11:2) Sum 90, p. 9.
"Sure, I Was Paid Well." [OntR] (32) Spr-Sum 90, p. 68-69.
"Teething." [Quarry] (39:4) Fall 1990, p. 96-97.
6795. WAYNE, Jane O.
"Prone to Worry." [AmerS] (59:3) Sum 90, p. 355-356.
6796. WEATHERFORD, Carole Boston
"Charleston Baskets." [Obs] (5:1) Spr 90, p. 53.
"Leaving Cambridge for Baltimore." [Obs] (5:1) Spr 90, p. 53-54.
"The New South." [SlipS] (10) 90, p. 58-59.
"Yeast Rolls & Water Biscuits." [BlackALF] (24:3) Fall 90, p. 533.
6797. WEAVER, Michael (Michael S.)
"Harlem Society." [Obs] (5:3) Wint 90, p. 34-35.
"Homecoming." [Gargoyle] (37/38) 90, p. 32-33.
"Madame." [Obs] (5:3) Wint 90, p. 37-38.
"Pool Parlor." [Obs] (5:3) Wint 90, p. 35-36.
"Village Quartet." [Obs] (5:3) Wint 90, p. 38.
6798. WEAVER, Roger
"Fragments from a Letter to Herodotus." [DogRR] (9:2, #18) Aut 90, p. 37.
"Homage to Van Gogh." [DogRR] (9:1, #17) Spr 90, p. 52-53.
"What the Azaleas Didn't Say." [DogRR] (9:1, #17) Spr 90, p. 53.
6799. WEBB, Annice
"Men at Sixty." [EmeraldCR] (1990) c89, p. 98.
6800. WEBB, Charles
"Excitable Boy." [Pearl] (11) Sum 90, p. 9.
"Froggie." [OnTheBus] (2:2/3:1, #6/7) Sum-Fall 90 Wint-Spr 91, p. 201.
"Gratitude." [Gypsy] (15) 90, p. 34.
"His Legs Itch." [HiramPoR] (47) Wint 90, p. 54.
"Honorary Spastics." [SlipS] (10) 90, p. 63.
"Interesting Times." [ChironR] (9:1) Spr 90, p. 13.
"The Luminous Time." [HiramPoR] (48/49) 90-91, p. 73.
"Peaches." [SouthernPR] (30:2) Fall 90, p. 20-22.
"Reading the Water." [PoetL] (85:3) Fall 90, p. 25-26.
"Some Day It Will Be Different." [OnTheBus] (2:1, #5) Spr 90, p. 142.
"Surgery." [KanQ] (22:1/2) Wint-Spr 90, p. 179.
"Tinkerbell, the Older Woman, Sorrows for the Loss of Peter Pan." [Pearl] (12) Fall-Wint 90, p. 52.
"To Cure a Broken Heart." [SwampR] (6) Sum-Fall 90, p. 73.
"Wedding." [SoCoast] (8) Spr 90, p. 19-21.
"White Shoulders." [HiramPoR] (47) Wint 90, p. 53.
6801. WEBB, Phyllis
"Anaximander, 610-546? B.C" (for Smaro Kamboureli). [MassR] (31:1/2) Spr-Sum 90, p. 111-112.
"Imprint #2." [MassR] (31:1/2) Spr-Sum 90, p. 113-114.
"Imprint #3." [MassR] (31:1/2) Spr-Sum 90, p. 114.
"Imprint #4." [MassR] (31:1/2) Spr-Sum 90, p. 115-116.
"Self City." [MassR] (31:1/2) Spr-Sum 90, p. 116.

6802. WEBER, Elizabeth
    "The Burning House." [SwampR] (5) Wint-Spr 90, p. 77.
    "Drunk." [SwampR] (5) Wint-Spr 90, p. 75-76.
    "Unemployed Woman Begging: Köln, 1930" (after a photograph by August
        Sander). [Calyx] (13:1) Wint 90-91, p. 9.
6803. WEBER, Maria
    "Bad Birthday." [Footwork] 90, p. 99.
    "Flight 103." [Footwork] 90, p. 99.
6804. WEBER, Mark
    "Bi-Coastal." [ChironR] (9:1) Spr 90, p. 21.
    "Fame." [Pearl] (12) Fall-Wint 90, p. 35.
    "How Do You Say." [WormR] (30:4, #120) 90, p. 135.
    "A New Lid." [WormR] (30:4, #120) 90, p. 135-136.
    "Ode to Being a Poetry Editor." [ChironR] (9:3) Aut 90, p. 25.
    "Rattlesnakes and Guitars." [WormR] (30:4, #120) 90, p. 135.
    "The Way It Goes." [WormR] (30:4, #120) 90, p. 136-137.
    "When the IRS Comes Knocking" (for Scott Preston). [WormR] (30:4, #120) 90, p.
        134-135.
    "When the Wolf Is Biting at the Lace Curtains" (for Tom Albach). [WormR] (30:4,
        #120) 90, p. 137.
6805. WEBER, Ron
    "Leviathan" (for Bill Goodwin). [Sonora] (18) Fall-Wint 90, p. 84-86.
    "On the Death of God, the Incidence of Entropy and the American Novel." [Sonora]
        (18) Fall-Wint 90, p. 82-83.
6806. WEBER, Ulrike
    "And So I Went Forth" (tr. of Stefan George, w. Richard Jones). [PoetryE] (30) Fall
        90, p. 93.
    "Devotion" (tr. of Günter Kunert, w. Richard Jones). [PoetryE] (29) Spr 90, p. 82.
    "The Flower I Guard" (tr. of Stefan George, w. Richard Jones). [PoetryE] (30) Fall
        90, p. 91.
    "From the Dorotheenstadt Cemetery" (tr. of Günter Kunert, w. Richard Jones).
        [PoetryE] (29) Spr 90, p. 81.
    "I Am the One" (tr. of Stefan George, w. Richard Jones). [PoetryE] (30) Fall 90, p.
        89.
    "In Purple Fire Spoke the Wrath of Heaven" (tr. of Stefan George, w. Richard
        Jones). [PoetryE] (30) Fall 90, p. 90.
    "My White Parrots" (tr. of Stefan George, w. Richard Jones). [Gargoyle] (37/38)
        90, p. 114.
    "Niobe" (tr. of Heinz Czechowski, w. Richard Jones). [PoetryE] (29) Spr 90, p. 75.
    "The Noises of My Country" (tr. of Volker Braun, w. Richard Jones). [PoetryE]
        (29) Spr 90, p. 76.
    "The Oysters" (for Alain Lance, tr. of Volker Braun, w. Richard Jones). [PoetryE]
        (29) Spr 90, p. 80.
    "Pleasure-Garden, Prussia" (tr. of Volker Braun, w. Richard Jones). [PoetryE] (29)
        Spr 90, p. 78.
    "Praise for the Masses" (tr. of Volker Braun, w. Richard Jones). [PoetryE] (29) Spr
        90, p. 77.
    "Was My Question" (tr. of Stefan George, w. Richard Jones). [PoetryE] (30) Fall
        90, p. 92.
    "We Need Language" (tr. of Heinz Czechowski, w. Richard Jones). [PoetryE] (29)
        Spr 90, p. 74.
    "Zentrum" (tr. of Volker Braun, w. Richard Jones). [PoetryE] (29) Spr 90, p. 79.
6807. WEDGE, George (George F.)
    "Heinrich 'The Heinie' Holtz." [Amelia] (6:2, #17) 90, p. 146-147.
    "Home Movie" (Shanghai c. 1933). [NegC] (10:2/3) 90, p. 93.
6808. WEDGE, Philip
    "Public Recital." [Wind] (20:67) 90, p. 33.
    "Surfer." [Wind] (20:67) 90, p. 33.
    "Van Gogh's 'Crows Over a Cornfield'" (Nelson Art Gallery, 1963). [KanQ]
        (22:1/2) Wint-Spr 90, p. 132.
6809. WEE, Karen Herseth
    "Changeling." [RagMag] (7:2) Spr 90, p. 66.
    "For My Daughters." [RagMag] (7:2) Spr 90, p. 67.
    "For My Son." [RagMag] (7:2) Spr 90, p. 67.
    "Moon Pause." [RagMag] (7:2) Spr 90, p. 66.

6810. WEE, Rebecca
"After Trakl's 'Autumn Evening': Esther Ponders the Shadows, Denies the Dead."
[RagMag] (8:2) 90, p. 14.
"The Lie." [RagMag] (8:2) 90, p. 10-12.
"Mother." [RagMag] (8:2) 90, p. 12-13.
"Williwaw." [RagMag] (8:2) 90, p. 9.
6811. WEEKS, Ramona
"Hunting Petroglyphs." [SingHM] (17) 90, p. 91.
6812. WEEKS, Robert Lewis
"At the Syria Mosque." [AmerPoR] (19:4) Jl-Ag 90, p. 15.
"Castles and Wolves." [AmerPoR] (19:4) Jl-Ag 90, p. 15.
"Learning to Shoot." [NewYorkQ] (41) Spr 90, p. 92-93.
"The Meaning of Meaning." [AmerPoR] (19:4) Jl-Ag 90, p. 16.
"Theory of Realism." [AmerPoR] (19:4) Jl-Ag 90, p. 16.
WEI, Guo
See GUO, Wei
WEI, Qi
See QI, Wei
6813. WEIDMAN, Phil
"Bouncing on Empty." [WormR] (30:1, #117) 90, p. 12.
"Bouquet." [WormR] (30:1, #117) 90, p. 11.
"Company." [WormR] (30:1, #117) 90, p. 12.
"Dancer." [WormR] (30:1, #117) 90, p. 12.
"Enlightened One." [WormR] (30:1, #117) 90, p. 11.
"In Touch." [WormR] (30:1, #117) 90, p. 12.
"Lotto Player." [WormR] (30:1, #117) 90, p. 11.
"Native Willow." [WormR] (30:1, #117) 90, p. 11.
"A Penchant for Sleep." [WormR] (30:1, #117) 90, p. 11.
"Photo for B. R." [WormR] (30:1, #117) 90, p. 11.
"A Slack Memory." [WormR] (30:1, #117) 90, p. 11.
"Survivor." [WormR] (30:1, #117) 90, p. 12.
"This Moment." [SwampR] (5) Wint-Spr 90, p. 65.
"Truckin'." [WormR] (30:1, #117) 90, p. 12.
"Why the Con?" [WormR] (30:1, #117) 90, p. 11.
6814. WEIGEL, James
"Testament XXVI" (reprinted from #9, 1984). [Kaleid] (20) Wint-Spr 90, p. 113.
"Testament XXVIII" (reprinted from #9, 1984). [Kaleid] (20) Wint-Spr 90, p. 113.
6815. WEIGL, Bruce
"The Impossible." [AmerPoR] (19:4) Jl-Ag 90, p. 48.
"Lullaby." [Manoa] (2:1) Spr 90, p. 23.
"On the Anniversary of Her Grace." [WashR] (15:5) F-Mr 90, p. 9.
"Why Nothing Changes for Miss Ngo Thi Thanh." [Manoa] (2:1) Spr 90, p. 22.
6816. WEIL, James (James L.)
"Kepler." [Northeast] (5:2) Spr 90, p. 10.
"Machu Picchu." [NewYorkQ] (43) Fall 90, p. 33.
"My Teacher, Dying" (for Spencer Brown). [Northeast] (5:2) Spr 90, p. 8.
"The Old Country" (for Felix Stefanile). [Northeast] (5:2) Spr 90, p. 9.
6817. WEIL, Lise
"Matter Harmonious Still Maneuvering" (tr. of Nicole Brossard). [MassR] (31:1/2)
Spr-Sum 90, p. 86-94.
6818. WEIMER, Dana
"Where the Swimming Ends." [OnTheBus] (2:1, #5) Spr 90, p. 143.
"The Widow." [Gargoyle] (37/38) 90, p. 83.
6819. WEINBERGER, Florence
"Earth Shakes Permanently." [OnTheBus] (2:2/3:1, #6/7) Sum-Fall 90 Wint-Spr 91,
p. 202.
"Trendy Is a Six-Letter Word, Which Is Why It Won't Last." [OnTheBus] (2:2/3:1,
#6/7) Sum-Fall 90 Wint-Spr 91, p. 202.
6820. WEINER, Hannah
"Narrative" (with Abigail Child). [Avec] (3:1) 90, p. 121-122.
"Remembered Sequel." [PaperAir] (4:3) 90, p. 47-49.
6821. WEINER, Rebecca
"Bait." [SenR] (20:2) Fall 90, p. 54.
"The Forest." [SenR] (20:2) Fall 90, p. 55-56.
"Lullaby." [AntR] (48:4) Fall 90, p. 485.
"Spring." [SenR] (20:2) Fall 90, p. 53.

6822. WEINGARTEN, Roger
"Children in the Field." [MissouriR] (13:1) 90, p. 92-95.
"Father Hunger and Son." [NoAmR] (275:4) D 90, p. 12-13.
"Goldbarth in Montpelier." [Journal] (13:2) Fall-Wint 89-90, p. 60-61.
"Inferno." [Journal] (13:2) Fall-Wint 89-90, p. 64-65.
"This Poem Is Based on a True Story." [Journal] (13:2) Fall-Wint 89-90, p. 62-63.
6823. WEINMAN, Paul
(Anonymous poem). [FreeL] (4) 90.
"Everyone who wanted to be." [SlipS] (10) 90, p. 105.
6824. WEIR, Mary Ellen
"Danger." [Crucible] (26) Fall 90, p. 73.
6825. WEISERT, Hilde
"Aretha on MTV." [SouthernPR] (30:1) Spr 90, p. 19-20.
6826. WEISS, David
"Living Room." [Crazy] (38) Spr 90, p. 41-42.
"Reconstruction." [PartR] (57:1) Wint 90, p. 101.
"Under Stratton" (In memoriam: Robert Penn Warren). [SouthernR] (26:2) Ap 90,
    p. 338-340.
6827. WEISS, Dora
"2nd Grade Romance." [Pearl] (11) Sum 90, p. 58.
6828. WEISS, Irving
"The Book Closed, the Facing Pages Kiss." [Rohwedder] (5) Spr 90, p. 16.
"Original and Translation." [Rohwedder] (5) Spr 90, p. 17.
"The Poem Speaks in the Poet's Voice." [Rohwedder] (5) Spr 90, p. 17.
6829. WEISS, Theodore
"The Answer." [SouthernR] (26:2) Ap 90, p. 332-333.
"At Once." [HampSPR] (Anthology 1975-1990) 90, p. 54-56.
"Fractions." [AmerPoR] (19:1) Ja-F 90, p. 15.
"The Future of the Past." [TriQ] (79) Fall 90, p. 87-88.
"Haunts." [TriQ] (79) Fall 90, p. 91-95.
"The Key." [OntR] (32) Spr-Sum 90, p. 71-72.
"Later Than Lately." [AmerPoR] (19:1) Ja-F 90, p. 16.
"Odds and Ends." [SouthernR] (26:2) Ap 90, p. 331-332.
"One Not One." [AmerPoR] (19:1) Ja-F 90, p. 15.
"Out of the Cold." [TriQ] (79) Fall 90, p. 85-86.
"A Private Life." [AmerPoR] (19:1) Ja-F 90, p. 16.
"Quartet." [BelPoJ] (40:4) Sum 90, p. 56-63.
"Something New." [OntR] (32) Spr-Sum 90, p. 70-71.
"There." [TriQ] (79) Fall 90, p. 89-90.
"A Troubled Glow." [SouthernR] (26:2) Ap 90, p. 330-331.
6830. WEISSBORT, Daniel
"Again I stare closely at the sea." [Stand] (31:2) Spr 90, p. 59.
"Arcadian Wall" (tr. of Dan Tsalka, w. the author). [Stand] (31:4) Aut 90, p. 44-45.
"As it was before" (tr. of Natalya Gorbanevskaya). [Nimrod] (33:2) Spr-Sum 90, p.
    108.
"Back to the Village" (tr. of Naim Araidi, w. Orna Raz). [Trans] (23) Spr 90, p.
    228-229.
"Do not call me this or anything" (tr. of Natalya Gorbanevskaya). [Nimrod] (33:2)
    Spr-Sum 90, p. 107.
"I go straight off to my friends" (tr. of Petr Kabes, w. Jaroslav Korán). [HampSPR]
    (Anthology 1975-1990) 90, p. 268.
"I have stopped naming the landscapes of my poems" (tr. of Petr Kabes, w. Jaroslav
    Korán). [HampSPR] (Anthology 1975-1990) 90, p. 267.
"I should like to hope that there" (In memory of E.B., tr. of Natalya
    Gorbanevskaya). [PoetryE] (30) Fall 90, p. 79.
"If Only" (tr. of Naim Araidi, w. Orna Raz). [Trans] (23) Spr 90, p. 230.
"Inscription." [Stand] (31:2) Spr 90, p. 59.
"Is this my voice, my voice -- or is it" (tr. of Natalya Gorbanevskaya). [Nimrod]
    (33:2) Spr-Sum 90, p. 107.
"It's time to think" (tr. of Natalya Gorbanevskaya). [PoetryE] (30) Fall 90, p. 80.
"A Lull in the Battle, Exekias the Amphora-Painter Speaks" (tr. of Dan Tsalka, w.
    the author). [Stand] (31:4) Aut 90, p. 45.
"Memory" (tr. of Ori Bernstein, w. Orna Raz). [Trans] (24) Fall 90, p. 231.
"Nightfall" (From "The Hillside Above Radotin," tr. of Jan Zábrava, w. Jaroslav
    Korán). [HampSPR] (Anthology 1975-1990) 90, p. 268-269.
"On Reading Ray Bradbury's *Fahrenheit 451*" (tr. of Natalya Gorbanevskaya).

[PoetryE] (30) Fall 90, p. 81-82.
"Once I lied about it here" (tr. of Petr Kabes, w. Jaroslav Korán). [HampSPR]
(Anthology 1975-1990) 90, p. 267.
"Procession" (tr. of Ori Bernstein, w. Orna Raz). [Trans] (24) Fall 90, p. 232.
"School for the Blind" (Excerpt, tr. of Pyotr Vegin). [CityLR] (4) 90, p. 184-185.
"Study of a Key" (tr. of Miron Bialoszewski, w. Grzegorz Musial). [PoetryE] (29)
Spr 90, p. 23.
"What Can You Tell Me?" (tr. of Ori Bernstein, w. Orna Raz). [Trans] (24) Fall 90,
p. 232.
"When kings fall silent" (tr. of Natalya Gorbanevskaya). [Nimrod] (33:2) Spr-Sum
90, p. 109.
"With our breath we'll warm the shed's cold walls" (tr. of Natalya Gorbanevskaya).
[Nimrod] (33:2) Spr-Sum 90, p. 109.
WEIYE, Yu
See YU, Weiye
6831. WELBURN, Ron
"Crows Among the Hawkweed and Black-Eyed Susans." [PoetryC] (11:1) Spr 90,
p. 9.
6832. WELCH, Don
"For a Girl, Age 12, Who Likes Robert Frost." [EngJ] (79:6) O 90, p. 94.
"Ground Owls." [Plain] (10:2) Wint 90, p. 11.
"A Little Something for an Old English Teacher." [EngJ] (79:4) Ap 90, p. 108.
6833. WELCH, Liliane
"Church." [PottPort] (12) 90, p. 49.
"Deathwatch." [Quarry] (39:4) Fall 1990, p. 5.
"Fifty." [Quarry] (39:4) Fall 1990, p. 5.
"The Witch." [PottPort] (11) 89, p. 25.
6834. WELCH, Philip
"House by Water." [BlackWR] (17:1) Fall-Wint 90, p. 150-151.
6835. WELISH, Marjorie
"Danbury, Connecticut." [Conjunc] (15) 90, p. 267-268.
"Design, with Drawing." [Conjunc] (15) 90, p. 268-269.
"Hymn to Life to Cliff." [DenQ] (24:4) Spr 90, p. 40-41.
"Kiss Tomorrow Goodbye." [Conjunc] (15) 90, p. 269-270.
"Scalpel in Hand." [Sulfur] (10:1, #26) Spr 90, p. 72-74.
6836. WELKER, Holly
"Christian Art." [BlackWR] (17:1) Fall-Wint 90, p. 158-159.
6837. WELLBOURN, Cynthia
"Dead of Night." [NewRena] (8:1, #24) Spr 90, p. 113.
"Saving Grace." [NewRena] (8:1, #24) Spr 90, p. 113.
6838. WELLENDORF, George Carl
"Roadside Photos." [Spirit] (10:2) 90, p. 115.
6839. WELLS, Stan
"The Middle Years." [Bogg] (63) 90, p. 38.
6840. WELLS, Will
"Glendalough" (tr. of Salvatore Quasimodo). [PoetryE] (30) Fall 90, p. 52.
"The New Bed." [LaurelR] (24:1) Wint 90, p. 10.
"Stamping Press / Lackawanna, New York" (for Henry Wells). [Pig] (16) 90, p. 43.
"Written, Perhaps, on a Tomb" (tr. of Salvatore Quasimodo). [PoetryE] (30) Fall 90,
p. 51.
6841. WEN, I-to
"Dusk Ox" (tr. by William Pitt Root). [PoetryE] (30) Fall 90, p. 102.
WENBO, Sun
See SUN, Wenbo
6842. WENDELL, Julia
"Fires at Yellowstone." [HayF] (6) Sum 90, p. 23-24.
"Our Father's Bedroom" (For John). [SouthernPR] (30:1) Spr 90, p. 35-37.
"Prolapse." [Crazy] (38) Spr 90, p. 69-70.
"Witness." [Crazy] (38) Spr 90, p. 67-68.
6843. WENTWORTH, Don
"Dreaming." [ManhatPR] (11) [89?], p. 16.
"Return to the Garden." [ManhatPR] (11) [89?], p. 16.
6844. WERNISCH, Ivan
"A Walk Around the Brewery" (tr. by Richard Katrovas and Dominika Winterová).
[PoetryE] (29) Spr 90, p. 115.

6845. WERRIS, Wendy
"Harvesting." [OnTheBus] (2:2/3:1, #6/7) Sum-Fall 90 Wint-Spr 91, p. 203.
6846. WESCOTT, Glenway
"Autumn." [ChiR] (37:1) Wint 90, p. 118.
"The Bitterns." [ChiR] (37:1) Wint 90, p. 118.
"Black Art." [ChiR] (37:1) Wint 90, p. 116.
"Natives of Rock." [ChiR] (37:1) Wint 90, p. 120.
"The Quiet Land." [ChiR] (37:1) Wint 90, p. 115.
"The Summer Ending." [ChiR] (37:1) Wint 90, p. 125-126.
6847. WESLEY, Marilyn
"The Poppet" (For Graham Duncan). [SingHM] (17) 90, p. 65.
6848. WESLOWSKI, Dieter
"After Walking the Breakwater." [Grain] (18:2) Sum 90, p. 50.
"Cartesianesque." [PoetryC] (11:2) Sum 90, p. 21.
"Cerberus." [Event] (19:1) Spr 90, p. 74.
"Five Stanzas in the Middle of the Night." [PoetryC] (11:2) Sum 90, p. 21.
"The Lost Sainthood." [PoetryC] (11:2) Sum 90, p. 21.
"May Miracle." [Grain] (18:2) Sum 90, p. 50.
"Mid July." [PoetryC] (11:2) Sum 90, p. 21.
"Nessuno." [Caliban] (8) 90, p. 107.
"Pablo." [Event] (19:1) Spr 90, p. 74.
"Paradise Is Not Lost." [WormR] (30:1, #117) 90, p. 3.
"People Keep Telling Me." [WormR] (30:1, #117) 90, p. 2.
"The Sun Is a Brief Incantation." [Caliban] (9) 90, p. 22.
"That Peculiar Hunger for Light." [Event] (19:1) Spr 90, p. 73.
"Three Days, I Waited for My Love." [PoetryC] (11:2) Sum 90, p. 21.
"Transmutation." [Caliban] (9) 90, p. 21.
"The Way They Make a Moon." [PoetryC] (11:2) Sum 90, p. 21.
6849. WEST, Alan
"I Wanted" (tr. of Roque Dalton). [Agni] (29/30) 90, p. 7-8.
"Light Surprised" (for Cristina, tr. by the author). [Agni] (29/30) 90, p. 212-214.
6850. WEST, Jean
"Mother Undressing." [Confr] (44/45) Fall 90-Wint 91, p. 306.
6851. WEST, Richard (Richard M.)
"I Lost It at an Italian Restaurant." [CrabCR] (6:3) Spr 90, p. 27-28.
"Lyn Lifshin Stars in *Modern Times II*." [ChironR] (9:2) Sum 90, p. 19.
6852. WEST, Sandra
"Auction Block." [Obs] (5:1) Spr 90, p. 50.
6853. WEST, Thomas A., Jr.
"The Door Waits." [DustyD] (1:2) O 90, p. 15.
"Need." [DustyD] (1:2) O 90, p. 15.
"Retreat." [OxfordM] (6:1) Spr-Sum 90, p. 85.
6854. WESTBROOK, Matthew W.
"The Exodus." [CapeR] (25:1) Spr 90, p. 38.
"My Myth." [CapeR] (25:1) Spr 90, p. 37.
6855. WESTBURY, Debbie
"Halleys Comet." [BellArk] (6:5) S-O 90, p. 2.
6856. WESTERFIELD, Nancy G.
"Catching the News." [Comm] (117:3) 9 F 90, p. 82.
"Erasing the Angles." [Comm] (117:3) 9 F 90, p. 82.
"Sinking-Heart Moon." [Comm] (117:3) 9 F 90, p. 82.
"The Surveyor." [Comm] (117:3) 9 F 90, p. 82.
"Wet Walking." [Plain] (11:1) Fall 90, p. 30.
6857. WESTON, Mildred
"Begging Your Pardon." [WillowS] (26) Spr 90, p. 29.
"Iris." [WillowS] (26) Spr 90, p. 28.
6858. WESTON, Ruth
"Necessity." [WeberS] (7:2) Fall 90, p. 62.
"Ojibwa Lament." [WeberS] (7:2) Fall 90, p. 63-64.
"Sous la Pluie." [WeberS] (7:2) Fall 90, p. 62.
"Spring Song." [WeberS] (7:2) Fall 90, p. 64.
"Storm in the Osage -- 1989" (for Winston Weathers). [WeberS] (7:2) Fall 90, p. 63.
6859. WEXELBLATT, Robert
"Crossroads." [Poem] (64) N 90, p. 39.
"Empty Field." [CapeR] (25:2) Fall 90, p. 14.

491

"First Dialogue Between the Lone Ranger and Tonto." [MidwQ] (31:2) Wint 90, p. 201.
"Found Inside a Chinese Box." [SouthernHR] (24:2) Spr 90, p. 141.
"Fourth Dialogue Between the Lone Ranger and Tonto." [MidwQ] (31:2) Wint 90, p. 203-204.
"Second Dialogue Between the Lone Ranger and Tonto." [MidwQ] (31:2) Wint 90, p. 201-202.
"Slow Movement." [Poem] (64) N 90, p. 40.
"Third Dialogue Between the Lone Ranger and Tonto." [MidwQ] (31:2) Wint 90, p. 202.
6860. WEXLER, Evelyn
"From the Cocoon." [CapeR] (25:1) Spr 90, p. 39.
6861. WEXLER, Philip
"The Dream of a Thousand Cacti." [KanQ] (22:1/2) Wint-Spr 90, p. 76.
6862. WHALEN, Damian
"On Your Birth" (For Katherine Olivia Sullivan). [SycamoreR] (2:1) Wint 90, p. 53.
6863. WHALEN, John
"Seal Song for Banjo." [SwampR] (6) Sum-Fall 90, p. 38-40.
6864. WHALEN, Tom
"Sestina for Richard Nixon." [SlipS] (10) 90, p. 37-38.
6865. WHALLEY, Karen
"2:00 A.M." [BellArk] (6:3) My-Je 90, p. 21.
"Lantern as a Shelter for Light." [BellArk] (6:3) My-Je 90, p. 4.
"Plowing." [BellArk] (6:3) My-Je 90, p. 10.
6866. WHARTON, Calvin
"Birds, Ledges" (for Tom Egan). [WestCL] (24:1) Spr 90, p. 48-50.
6867. WHATLEY, Wallace
"Three." [Amelia] (6:1, #16) 90, p. 97.
6868. WHEAT, Maxwell Corydon, Jr.
"Leonardo da Vinci Airport, December 27, 1985" (for Natasha Simpson). [SlipS] (10) 90, p. 103.
6869. WHEDON, Tony
"Kunming." [Crazy] (39) Wint 90, p. 19-20.
"Period Piece." [Crazy] (39) Wint 90, p. 21-23.
"The Wilmores." [AntR] (48:1) Wint 90, p. 96.
6870. WHEELER, Barry
"Rejection." [PottPort] (12) 90, p. 47.
"This Poem." [PottPort] (11) 89, p. 8.
6871. WHEELER, Charles B.
"The Creative Writing Class Hears About Submitting Manuscripts." [Outbr] (21) 90, p. 57-58.
6872. WHEELER, L. Ray
"Elegy for Auden." [NorthStoneR] (9) 90, p. 144.
"Prairie Song." [NorthStoneR] (9) 90, p. 145.
6873. WHEELER, Susan
"And a Happy New Year." [BrooklynR] (7) 90, p. 33.
"Lasting Influence." [ParisR] (32:115) Sum 90, p. 121-122.
6874. WHEELER, Sylvia Griffith
"Counting Back: An Oral History of Dakota Territory" (6 selections). [PraS] (64:2) Sum 90, p. 117-122.
6875. WHISNANT, Luke
"Earl." [ChatR] (10:2) Wint 90, p. 11.
6876. WHITAKER, David
"Gardening." [Plain] (11:1) Fall 90, p. 35.
6877. WHITE, Boyd
"1961." [PraS] (64:1) Spr 90, p. 5-7.
"Cullen's Mule." [PraS] (64:1) Spr 90, p. 4.
"Lighthouse." [PraS] (64:1) Spr 90, p. 3.
"Poem After Cesar Vallejo." [CutB] (34) Sum-Fall 90, p. 64.
"The Shotgun Victims of Waldens Ridge." [PraS] (64:1) Spr 90, p. 7-8.
"Today." [PraS] (64:1) Spr 90, p. 5.
6878. WHITE, Claire Nicolas
"Los Alamos" (tr. of Nachoem Wijnberg). [Trans] (24) Fall 90, p. 78.
"The Church Portal" (tr. of Nachoem Wijnberg). [Trans] (24) Fall 90, p. 76.
"Four Swim Sonnets" (tr. of Emma Crebolder). [Trans] (24) Fall 90, p. 127-130.
"The Grand Duke Nicolas Nicolaevitch Sleeps in the Autumn of 1914" (tr. of

Nachoem Wijnberg). [Trans] (24) Fall 90, p. 78.
"Hotel Near Airfield" (tr. of Nachoem Wijnberg). [Trans] (24) Fall 90, p. 75.
"The Idols" (tr. of Nachoem Wijnberg). [Trans] (24) Fall 90, p. 74.
"Inscription on a Tomb" (tr. of Nachoem Wijnberg). [Trans] (24) Fall 90, p. 77.
"Johnny." [Footwork] 90, p. 47.
"Lost Daughter." [Footwork] 90, p. 46.
"On Tape." [Confr] (44/45) Fall 90-Wint 91, p. 183.
"Poem for Beginners" (tr. of Paul Snoek). [Trans] (24) Fall 90, p. 34.
"Poem for the Day After Tomorrow" (tr. of Paul Snoek). [Trans] (24) Fall 90, p. 33.
"Polders." [Confr] (44/45) Fall 90-Wint 91, p. 183.
"Rabbi Nachman the Storyteller" (tr. of Nachoem Wijnberg). [Trans] (24) Fall 90, p. 77.
"Seascapes" (tr. of Hans van de Waarsenburg). [Trans] (24) Fall 90, p. 150-154.
"Second Man" (tr. of Nachoem Wijnberg). [Trans] (24) Fall 90, p. 73.
"A Secret Better Kept to Yourself" (tr. of Paul Snoek). [Trans] (24) Fall 90, p. 35.
"A Walk After a Late Breakfast" (tr. of Leo Vroman, w. the author). [Trans] (24) Fall 90, p. 113-114.
"The Whirligig Beetle" (A Sonnet sequence). [Footwork] 90, p. 46.
6879. WHITE, Gail
"The Embattled Gardener." [ChironR] (9:3) Aut 90, p. 12.
"Fairy Tale." [ChironR] (9:3) Aut 90, p. 12.
"Grafitti on a Roman Wall." [ChironR] (9:3) Aut 90, p. 12.
"Old Woman with 25 Cats." [ChironR] (9:3) Aut 90, p. 12.
"Written on the Head of a Pin." [SoCoast] (9) Fall 90, p. 46.
6880. WHITE, J. P.
"Arapaima" (the world's largest freshwater fish, found in the Amazon basin, nicknamed "water monkey"). [Crazy] (39) Wint 90, p. 57-58.
"The Effigy of John Donne" (St. Paul's Cathedral). [Shen] (40:3) Fall 90, p. 23.
"Federico Talks to His Virgin of the Seven Arrows." [GrahamHR] (13) Spr 90, p. 78-79.
"Lady Franklin Writes to Her Husband 15 Years Gone into the Ice, 1857." [Boulevard] (5:2, #14) Fall 90, p. 108-109.
"Living Among Women" (Skyros, Greece). [Poetry] (155:4) Ja 90, p. 271-272.
"Lorca, Going Home." [GrahamHR] (13) Spr 90, p. 75-77.
"Lorca, Looking for Adam." [GrahamHR] (13) Spr 90, p. 74.
"The Slow End of the Waterfall." [GrahamHR] (13) Spr 90, p. 82-83.
"The Wind from the Sea." [GrahamHR] (13) Spr 90, p. 80-81.
6881. WHITE, James C.
"Love." [NorthStoneR] (9) 90, p. 93.
"Poles Apart." [NorthStoneR] (9) 90, p. 93.
"A Serious Speaker Who Starts with a Quip" (after hearing Allen Tate lecture at the University of Minnesota, 1955). [NorthStoneR] (9) 90, p. 93.
"The Waitress." [NorthStoneR] (9) 90, p. 92.
6882. WHITE, James L.
"Lying in Sadness." [JamesWR] (7:2) Wint 90, p. 1.
"An Ordinary Composure." [JamesWR] (7:2) Wint 90, p. 1.
6883. WHITE, Landeg
"Incident at a Poetry Reading" (for Eduardo White, primo). [Stand] (31:3) Sum 90, p. 64-65.
"Thief." [Stand] (31:3) Sum 90, p. 65.
6884. WHITE, Mary Jane
"New Year's" (An Elegy for Rilke, tr. of Marina Tsvetaeva). [Nimrod] (33:2) Spr-Sum 90, p. 56-61.
"Poems to Akhmatova" (June 9 -- July 2, 1916, selections: I, IV-V, IX, tr. of Marina Tsvetaeva, w. Alexander Sumerkin). [Nimrod] (33:2) Spr-Sum 90, p. 53-55.
6885. WHITE, Michael K.
"Prey." [ContextS] (1:1) 89, p. 18.
"Storms." [ChironR] (9:1) Spr 90, p. 23.
6886. WHITE, Mike
"The Helpless Year" (In memory of Tom McAfee). [MissR] (19:1/2, #55/56) 90, p. 282-285.
6887. WHITE, Nancy
"Going Back, Not Forward, After All." [NewEngR] (13:1) Fall 90, p. 39.
6888. WHITE, Pam
"Song." [NegC] (10:1) 90, p. 94.

6889. WHITE, Steven F.
"Dressed in Dynamite" (tr. of Gioconda Belli). [Calyx] (12:3) Sum 90, p. 55.
"Omega" (Poem for the Dead, tr. of Federico García Lorca, w. Greg Simon).
[NowestR] (28:3/29:1) 90-91, p. 178.
"Trip to the Moon" (tr. of Federico García Lorca, w. Greg Simon). [NowestR]
(28:3/29:1) 90-91, p. 170-177.
6890. WHITE, Sylvia
"Bees." [OnTheBus] (2:1, #5) Spr 90, p. 144.
"Corpses." [OnTheBus] (2:1, #5) Spr 90, p. 145.
6891. WHITE, Vonda
"The Trees of CIW." [PoetryUSA] ([5:4?]) Wint 90, p. 25.
6892. WHITEHEAD, Thomas
"Ornamental." [Interim] (9:2) Fall-Wint 90-91, p. 13-15.
6893. WHITEHILL, Karen
"Dry Cleaners." [VirQR] (66:4) Aut 90, p. 666.
6894. WHITEHOUSE, Sheila
"Concerto for Flute and Strings." [SoCaR] (23:1) Fall 90, p. 157.
6895. WHITEIS-HELM, Mark
"The Rest of Her Life." [QW] (30) Spr 90, p. 117.
6896. WHITEMAN, Roberta Hill
"Waterfall in Como Park." [NoAmR] (275:1) Mr 90, p. 31.
6897. WHITING, Nathan
"Both Long and Disturbing." [Contact] (9:56/57/58) Spr 90, p. 30.
"Clay Birdcall Trombone." [Contact] (9:56/57/58) Spr 90, p. 30.
"Dream Scales." [HawaiiR] (14:1, #28) Wint 89-90, p. 12.
"Goalpost." [ContextS] (1:1) 89, p. 44.
"Living in the Now." [SwampR] (6) Sum-Fall 90, p. 81-82.
"Molecular Lung." [HawaiiR] (14:1, #28) Wint 89-90, p. 13.
"Roped Wires." [Sequoia] (33:2) Wint 90, p. 94.
"White, Gray and Rinse." [HawaiiR] (14:1, #28) Wint 89-90, p. 11.
6898. WHITLEDGE, Jane
"Sleepwalkers." [KanQ] (22:1/2) Wint-Spr 90, p. 227.
6899. WHITMAN, Ruth
"Cruelty." [AmerV] (20) Fall 90, p. 4.
"The Third Wave." [HampSPR] (Anthology 1975-1990) 90, p. 28.
6900. WHITMORE, Susan
"Munchion." [Mildred] (4:1) 90, p. 89.
6901. WHITNEY, Jennifer
"Enough." [CumbPR] (10:1) Fall 90, p. 52.
"The Truth." [CumbPR] (10:1) Fall 90, p. 50-51.
6902. WHITNEY, Ross R.
"All Ye Need to Know" (for Tess). [BelPoJ] (41:2) Wint 90-91, p. 32-34.
"Cautionary Tale." [BelPoJ] (41:2) Wint 90-91, p. 35.
"Death of a Medieval Carpenter." [Amelia] (6:2, #17) 90, p. 103.
"Twins in the Balance." [Amelia] (6:2, #17) 90, p. 6.
6903. WHITT, Laura Anne
"The Eyes of a Dark Horse" (drawn from a painting by Alex Colville, "Horse and
Train"). [HawaiiR] (15:1, #31) Wint 90, p. 86-87.
6904. WHITTAKER, Steven
"Bulletin." [Descant] (21:1, #68) Spr 90, p. 115-116.
"Mother and Son." [Descant] (21:1, #68) Spr 90, p. 113.
"Ontology." [Descant] (21:1, #68) Spr 90, p. 118.
"Opening Act." [Descant] (21:1, #68) Spr 90, p. 114.
"Simply Spring." [Descant] (21:1, #68) Spr 90, p. 117.
"A Werewolf in Yorkshire." [Dandel] (17:1) Spr-Sum 90, p. 31-32.
"Zoology of a Menopause at 28." [Descant] (21:1, #68) Spr 90, p. 112.
6905. WHITTEN, Kathleen
"The Cove of Women." [NegC] (10:1) 90, p. 95.
6906. WHITTINGHAM, Brian
"Heavy Reading." [Bogg] (63) 90, p. 43.
6907. WICKELHAUS, Martha
"Early Shift." [CutB] (33) 90, p. 30.
"Her Lifelist." [ColEng] (52:8) D 90, p. 887-888.
"In the Blue, in the Sky." [ColEng] (52:8) D 90, p. 886.
"Wood Thrush." [ColEng] (52:8) D 90, p. 885.

6908. WIDEBERG, Joy
"Azaleas." [WillowR] Spr 90, p. 22.
6909. WIDERKEHR, Richard
"Islands" (corrected reprint). [CrabCR] (6:3) Spr 90, p. 2.
6910. WIDUP, David
"The Bunkers." [OnTheBus] (2:2/3:1, #6/7) Sum-Fall 90 Wint-Spr 91, p. 204.
"City Snow." [OnTheBus] (2:1, #5) Spr 90, p. 147.
"Combat Boots." [OnTheBus] (2:2/3:1, #6/7) Sum-Fall 90 Wint-Spr 91, p. 204-205.
"Visions of Love." [OnTheBus] (2:1, #5) Spr 90, p. 146.
WIENEN, Mark van
See Van WIENEN, Mark
6911. WIER, Dara
"Again Ernie's Hand on the Hammer." [HampSPR] (Anthology 1975-1990) 90, p. 118-119.
"Ernie and Week's End." [HampSPR] (Anthology 1975-1990) 90, p. 120.
"Ernie, of an Afternoon." [HampSPR] (Anthology 1975-1990) 90, p. 119.
"Ernie Prepares the Trash." [HampSPR] (Anthology 1975-1990) 90, p. 118.
"Ernie's Trip to Mississippi." [HampSPR] (Anthology 1975-1990) 90, p. 120.
"Hypnagogic Adagio." [Shen] (40:4) Wint 90, p. 26-27.
"TVI." [Shen] (40:4) Wint 90, p. 24-25.
6912. WIGGINS, Jean
"The Crown of Flowers." [InterPR] (16:1) Spr 90, p. 115.
6913. WIGGS, Terry
"Post Up, Then Go to the Hoop." [NewYorkQ] (41) Spr 90, p. 95-96.
"Streets of Laredo." [SwampR] (5) Wint-Spr 90, p. 55.
"Where Scholars Fear to Tread." [SwampR] (5) Wint-Spr 90, p. 53-54.
WIGHTMAN, Ludmilla Popova
See POPOVA-WIGHTMAN, Ludmilla
6914. WIGUTOW, Warren
"Men and Women: Ten Phantasies for Robert Browning." [Notus] (5:1) Spr 90, p. 22-31.
6915. WIJNBERG, Nachoem
"Los Alamos" (tr. by Claire Nicolas White). [Trans] (24) Fall 90, p. 78.
"The Church Portal" (tr. by Claire Nicolas White). [Trans] (24) Fall 90, p. 76.
"The Grand Duke Nicolas Nicolaevitch Sleeps in the Autumn of 1914" (tr. by Claire Nicolas White). [Trans] (24) Fall 90, p. 78.
"Hotel Near Airfield" (tr. by Claire Nicolas White). [Trans] (24) Fall 90, p. 75.
"The Idols" (tr. by Claire Nicolas White). [Trans] (24) Fall 90, p. 74.
"Inscription on a Tomb" (tr. by Claire Nicolas White). [Trans] (24) Fall 90, p. 77.
"Rabbi Nachman the Storyteller" (tr. by Claire Nicolas White). [Trans] (24) Fall 90, p. 77.
"Second Man" (tr. by Claire Nicolas White). [Trans] (24) Fall 90, p. 73.
6916. WILBER, Rick
"Dizzy with It." [FreeL] (5) Sum 90, p. 29.
6917. WILBORN, William
"On the Uncompleted Madonna of Michelangelo in the National Gallery." [Poetry] (157:3) D 90, p. 125-126.
"Paysage Demoralisé." [Hellas] (1:2) Fall 90, p. 242-243.
6918. WILBUR, Richard
"Ballad of the Jack of Diamonds" (tr. of Nina Cassian). [NewYorker] (65:46) 1 Ja 90, p. 30.
"The School for Husbands" (Excerpt, tr. of Molière). [Trans] (23) Spr 90, p. 58-61.
6919. WILCOX, Dan
"Barbara Holland." [Contact] (9:56/57/58) Spr 90, p. 24.
6920. WILCOX, Patricia
"Kundry." [MissouriR] (13:2) 90, p. 76.
6921. WILD, Danelia
"Georgia O'Keefe's Bones" [sic, i.e. O'Keeffe?]. [OnTheBus] (2:1, #5) Spr 90, p. 151-152.
"Wolfwalker." [OnTheBus] (2:2/3:1, #6/7) Sum-Fall 90 Wint-Spr 91, p. 206.
6922. WILD, Peter
"The Adulterous Farmwife." [ArtfulD] (18/19) 90, p. 102.
"Butcher." [SycamoreR] (2:2) Sum 90, p. 17.
"Children of Giraffes." [ArtfulD] (18/19) 90, p. 103.
"Faked Orgasms." [FreeL] (5) Sum 90, p. 17.

"Fame." [Gypsy] (15) 90, p. 21.
"First Water." [Confr] (44/45) Fall 90-Wint 91, p. 192.
"Gingerbread Man." [OxfordM] (6:1) Spr-Sum 90, p. 61.
"Happy Man." [ApalQ] (33/34) 90, p. 55-56.
"Local Historical Societies." [Gargoyle] (37/38) 90, p. 35.
"Merchant Marine." [SycamoreR] (2:2) Sum 90, p. 16.
"Musicians." [NewDeltaR] (7:1) 90, p. 26.
"Novelists." [OxfordM] (6:1) Spr-Sum 90, p. 62.
"Real Success." [WillowS] (26) Spr 90, p. 54-55.
"Reporters." [AmerPoR] (19:5) S-O 90, p. 44.
"String Cheese." [ConnPR] (9:1) 90, p. 24.
"Voyageurs." [ApalQ] (33/34) 90, p. 57.
"Women." [AnotherCM] (21) 90, p. 154.
"The Women of Lands' End." [SouthernPR] (30:2) Fall 90, p. 27-28.
6923. WILDE-MENOZZI, Wallis
    "Cottage." [Verse] (7:2) Sum 90, p. 92.
    "In the Towel's Folds." [SouthernR] (26:3) Jl 90, p. 687-688.
6924. WILDER, Jesse Bryant
    "Spaces." [Gypsy] (15) 90, p. 71.
6925. WILHARM, Evelyn S.
    "Mr. History" (In memory of Mr. T.T. Wentworth, Jr., who passed away July 16,
        1989). [EmeraldCR] (1990) c89, p. 111-112.
6926. WILHELM, Kathryn
    "The Persistence of Memory." [CapeR] (25:1) Spr 90, p. 26.
6927. WILJER, Robert
    "An Opening." [HampSPR] (Anthology 1975-1990) 90, p. 193.
    "A Rose for Katie." [HampSPR] (Anthology 1975-1990) 90, p. 193.
    "The Swimming Pool." [HampSPR] (Anthology 1975-1990) 90, p. 194.
6928. WILK, Melvin
    "A Wedding Story." [NewYorker] (66:39) 12 N 90, p. 54-55.
6929. WILKERSON, Thomas E.
    "The Woods of the Watcher." [EmeraldCR] (1990) c89, p. 80-81.
6930. WILKINS, W. R.
    "Due to Injuries." [Pearl] (10) Spr 90, p. 24.
6931. WILKINSON, John
    "Lines on the Pergamon Museum." [Screens] (2) 90, p. 146-151.
6932. WILKINSON, Nicole
    "This Story No One Tells." [LitR] (33:2) Wint 90, p. 263.
6933. WILL, Carl
    "Kill the Buddha." [NewYorkQ] (41) Spr 90, p. 93.
6934. WILLAN, Bill
    "Taste." [NegC] (10:2/3) 90, p. 82.
6935. WILLARD, Carla
    "Grave Poem." [MissR] (19:1/2, #55/56) 90, p. 286.
6936. WILLARD, Nancy
    "An Angel Considers the Naming of Meat." [Field] (42) Spr 90, p. 21.
    "A Conversation Phrase Book for Angels" (Selections). [Caliban] (8) 90, p. 18-19.
    "God Enters the Swept Field." [Field] (42) Spr 90, p. 85.
    "In Praise of the Puffball." [Field] (42) Spr 90, p. 18.
    "Memory Hat." [Field] (42) Spr 90, p. 22-23.
    "Swimming to China." [Field] (42) Spr 90, p. 20.
    "The Wisdom of the Geese." [Field] (42) Spr 90, p. 19.
6937. WILLEY, Edward
    "Senority." [ManhatPR] (12) [90?], p. 30.
6938. WILLEY, Rosemary
    "Dreams in the Seventh Month." [Crazy] (38) Spr 90, p. 45-46.
    "Nightmares and Prayers of Rescue." [Kalliope] (12:2) 90, p. 62.
6939. WILLIAMS, Barbara
    "How to Write a Novel" (for Phyllis Hatfield). [Interim] (9:2) Fall-Wint 90-91, p.
        22.
    "An Interesting Week." [Interim] (9:2) Fall-Wint 90-91, p. 23-24.
6940. WILLIAMS, C. K.
    "The Feeling of Having Forgotten" (tr. of Robert Sabatier). [Trans] (23) Spr 90, p.
        71.
    "Still Life." [AmerPoR] (19:1) Ja-F 90, p. 11.
    "To Each Day" (tr. of Robert Sabatier). [Trans] (23) Spr 90, p. 70.

6941. WILLIAMS, Daniel
"Mark Twain's Cabin." [WritersF] (16) Fall 90, p. 78.
"Windchime Window in Angels Camp." [WritersF] (16) Fall 90, p. 77.
6942. WILLIAMS, Denise
"Carrion." [CutB] (33) 90, p. 74.
"To Maida of Yugoslavia from My Book of Common Flowers: A Letter." [CutB]
(33) 90, p. 73-74.
6943. WILLIAMS, Diane
"Science and Sin or Love and Understanding." [Agni] (29/30) 90, p. 215.
6944. WILLIAMS, Dianne
"Getting the Spirit at the Brass Band Church" (A Radio Interview). [BellArk] (6:6)
N-D 90, p. 1.
"The Maple." [BellArk] (6:6) N-D 90, p. 6.
6945. WILLIAMS, Donna Glee
"What the Matter Is." [NewDeltaR] (7:1) 90, p. 39.
6946. WILLIAMS, Faith
"Drawing an Eggplant." [KanQ] (22:3) Sum 90, p. 189.
"Gretel in Middle Age Hears of Hansel's Death." [Nimrod] (34:1) Fall-Wint 90, p.
128.
"Old Mother Death." [KanQ] (22:3) Sum 90, p. 189.
"Persephone: Another Glance." [Nimrod] (34:1) Fall-Wint 90, p. 129.
"The Relevance of the Humanities to Everyday Life." [Nimrod] (34:1) Fall-Wint 90,
p. 130.
"The Uterus at 47." [Kalliope] (12:1) 90, c89, p. 57.
"The Vale of Soulmaking." [Bogg] (63) 90, p. 9.
6947. WILLIAMS, Hugo
"When I Grow Up." [Quarry] (39:1) Wint 90, p. 53-54.
6948. WILLIAMS, Jack
"Wake." [ChatR] (10:4) Sum 90, p. 170.
6949. WILLIAMS, James Perkins
"Sounds, Silences." [NewEngR] (13:2) Wint 90, p. 201-202.
6950. WILLIAMS, Marcelle
"Phoenix" (Northwest Flight 255). [LakeSR] (24) 90, p. 33.
6951. WILLIAMS, Miller
"Allegory of a Memory and His Man." [HampSPR] (Anthology 1975-1990) 90, p.
64.
"The Curator." [SouthernR] (26:4) O 90, p. 868-871.
"During a Funeral Service the Mind of the Young Preacher Wanders Again."
[SouthernR] (26:4) O 90, p. 871-872.
6952. WILLIAMS, Norman
"A Christmas Song." [NewYorker] (66:45) 24 D 90, p. 58.
"The Conversion Near Jessups on the Big Raccoon." [Verse] (7:3) Wint 90, p. 70.
"Doyle and I: Summer 1969" (On the Occasion of Hugh Hefner's Nuptials Twenty
Years Later). [Verse] (7:3) Wint 90, p. 69.
6953. WILLIAMS, Roger
"Diary of a Lost Man." [Caliban] (9) 90, p. 41-58.
6954. WILLIAMS, Rynn
"Rings of Oil." [SouthernPR] (30:2) Fall 90, p. 19-20.
"The Singer." [SouthernPR] (30:2) Fall 90, p. 17-18.
6955. WILLIAMS, Tami
"Coping with death." [PoetryUSA] ([5:4?]) Wint 90, p. 27.
6956. WILLIAMS, Tyrone
"Real Estate." [Caliban] (9) 90, p. 153.
6957. WILLIAMSON, Alan
"Domestic Architecture." [VirQR] (66:1) Wint 90, p. 91-92.
"Highway Restaurant." [AmerPoR] (19:5) S-O 90, p. 52.
"The Minoan Distance." [Agni] (29/30) 90, p. 67-68.
"November and December." [Agni] (29/30) 90, p. 69-70.
"Wide-Angle Shot: Return to Snowy River." [VirQR] (66:1) Wint 90, p. 90.
6958. WILLIAMSON, Tharin
"And Blind-Man's-Bluff." [CapeR] (25:2) Fall 90, p. 15.
"The Borderland." [HiramPoR] (48/49) 90-91, p. 74.
6959. WILLOUGHBY, Katrina
"Central Otago-Baseline." [Verse] (7:2) Sum 90, p. 36-38.
6960. WILLS, Ora
"Absolution." [EmeraldCR] (1990) c89, p. 4-5.

"Planting Time." [EmeraldCR] (1990) c89, p. 3.
6961. WILLSON, John
"Falling Asleep Hungry." [SycamoreR] (2:1) Wint 90, p. 24-25.
"Narrow Street, Barcelona." [SycamoreR] (2:1) Wint 90, p. 26.
6962. WILMARTH, Richard
"The Diplomat." [ChironR] (9:4) Wint 90, p. 2.
"The End." [ChironR] (9:4) Wint 90, p. 2.
"Tactics." [ChironR] (9:4) Wint 90, p. 2.
6963. WILMINK, Willem
"An Odd Tiger" (tr. by Gonny Van den Broek). [Vis] (34) 90, p. 51.
6964. WILNER, Eleanor
"Atget's Gardens." [TriQ] (80) Wint 90-91, p. 21-22.
"Changing the Imperatives." [TriQ] (80) Wint 90-91, p. 19-20.
"Leda's Handmaiden." [KenR] (NS 12:2) Spr 90, p. 178-180.
"Moonsnails" (a poem for Susan). [Boulevard] (4:3/5:1, #12/13) Spr 90, p.
    219-220.
"Night Fishing in the Sound." [SouthwR] (75:4) Aut 90, p. 468-469.
"Umè: Plum." [TriQ] (80) Wint 90-91, p. 16-18.
6965. WILOCH, Thomas
"The Soldier and the Unicorn." [Asylum] (6:2) S 90, p. 24.
"Torn from the Soil." [OnTheBus] (2:2/3:1, #6/7) Sum-Fall 90 Wint-Spr 91, p.
    207.
6966. WILSON, Barbara H.
"Longing." [PaintedB] (40/41) 90, p. 191.
"Shadows from the Womb." [PaintedB] (40/41) 90, p. 190.
6967. WILSON, David
"After a Party." [Verse] (7:2) Sum 90, p. 14.
6968. WILSON, Fiona
"The Angler." [Amelia] (6:2, #17) 90, p. 69.
6969. WILSON, Frances
"Watching a Cellist Playing Brahms: Sketch with Reference Notes." [Dandel] (17:1)
    Spr-Sum 90, p. 5.
6970. WILSON, Gisela
"Making Light." [OhioR] (45) 90, p. 54.
6971. WILSON, Graeme
"Before the Rebellion" (tr. of Tu Fu). [LitR] (33:2) Wint 90, p. 195.
"Kinds of Death" (tr. of Kakinomoto no Hitomaro, 681-729). [LitR] (33:2) Wint 90,
    p. 194.
"Loneliness" (tr. of anonymous late seventh century Japanese poem). [LitR] (33:2)
    Wint 90, p. 193.
"Modesty" (tr. of anonymous eighth century Japanese poem). [LitR] (33:2) Wint 90,
    p. 192.
"Pearl Diver" (tr. of Lady Nakatomi, early eighth century). [LitR] (33:2) Wint 90, p.
    194.
"Shame" (tr. of Princess Yashiro, 758). [LitR] (33:2) Wint 90, p. 193.
"Sunbear Rapids" (tr. of anonymous seventh century Japanese poem). [LitR] (33:2)
    Wint 90, p. 193.
"This Poem" (tr. of Chao I). [LitR] (33:2) Wint 90, p. 195.
"Upsy Daisy" (tr. of Anonymous). [LitR] (33:2) Wint 90, p. 194.
"Valley of the Hatsuse" (tr. of anonymous eighth century Japanese poem). [LitR]
    (33:2) Wint 90, p. 193.
"Wanting" (tr. of Princess Nukada, c.645-c.700). [LitR] (33:2) Wint 90, p. 192.
6972. WILSON, Harriet
"Cancer Dust." [Calyx] (12:3) Sum 90, p. 48.
"Modified Radical." [Calyx] (12:3) Sum 90, p. 49.
6973. WILSON, James A.
"Cold Creek" (tr. of Meng Chiao). [NewOR] (17:4) Wint 90, p. 66-73.
"Following Thoughts" (tr. of Bei Dao). [CityLR] (4) 90, p. 151-152.
"A Formal Declaration" (tr. of Bei Dao). [CityLR] (4) 90, p. 153.
"Nightmare" (tr. of Bei Dao). [CityLR] (4) 90, p. 152.
6974. WILSON, Leonore
"Little Mother." [SingHM] (18) 90, p. 20.
6975. WILSON, Miles
"Keeping Track." [GeoR] (44:4) Wint 90, p. 654.
6976. WILSON, Randy
"Working." [OnTheBus] (2:2/3:1, #6/7) Sum-Fall 90 Wint-Spr 91, p. 208.

6977. WILSON, Reuel K.
"Anywhere But Here" (tr. of Artur Miedzyrzecki). [Trans] (24) Fall 90, p. 191.
"At a Border Crossing" (tr. of Ewa Lipska). [Trans] (24) Fall 90, p. 193-194.
"Dance" (for Maria Kuncewiczowa, tr. of Jola Barylanka). [Trans] (24) Fall 90, p. 189.
"In Lieu Of" (tr. of Leszek Budrewicz). [Trans] (24) Fall 90, p. 190.
"Music" (tr. of Jola Barylanka). [Trans] (24) Fall 90, p. 188.
"The Provinces" (tr. of Piotr Sommer). [Trans] (24) Fall 90, p. 195.
"Someone Else" (tr. of Artur Miedzyrzecki). [Trans] (24) Fall 90, p. 192.
6978. WILSON, Robert (God) (*See also* GOD (a homeless person, San Francisco))
"Hardening." [PoetryUSA] ([5:4?]) Wint 90, p. 23.
6979. WILSON, Robert N.
"Station Stop." [NegC] (10:2/3) 90, p. 66.
6980. WILSON, Robley
"Vanities." [Poetry] (155:4) Ja 90, p. 273.
6981. WILSON, Steve
"Blue: Steps." [MidwQ] (31:3) Spr 90, p. 372-373.
"The Picture on the Purple Wall" (for Samuel). [LitR] (33:2) Wint 90, p. 264.
6982. WILSON, T. Hunter
"Driving Late at Night." [RiverC] (10:2) Spr 90, p. 1.
"The Effort." [RiverC] (10:2) Spr 90, p. 3.
"Practice." [RiverC] (10:2) Spr 90, p. 2.
6983. WIMAN, Christian
"My Grandfather's Last Summer." [ChatR] (10:4) Sum 90, p. 136.
6984. WIMP, Jet
"Azrael." [Pig] (16) 90, p. 81.
"Touching a Girder." [Pig] (16) 90, p. 44.
6985. WINANS, A. D.
"America." [SlipS] (10) 90, p. 14.
"America" (honorable mention, Black Bear Poetry Competition). [BlackBR] (11) Spr-Sum 90, p. 37-42.
"For Marilyn Monroe." [Pearl] (12) Fall-Wint 90, p. 25.
"Notes from the V.A." [SlipS] (10) 90, p. 16.
"A Poem for John." [SlipS] (10) 90, p. 16.
"Strange Happenings." [PoetryUSA] (5:2) Sum 90, p. 1.
"Strange Happenings." [SlipS] (10) 90, p. 15.
WINCKEL, Nance van
See Van WINCKEL, Nance
6986. WINE, Jim
"Epigram" (tr. of Tomas Tranströmer). [WashR] (16:2) Ag-S 90, p. 33.
"The Indoors Is Infinite" (tr. of Tomas Tranströmer, w. Tom Bull). [WashR] (16:2) Ag-S 90, p. 33.
"The Nightingale in Badelunda" (tr. of Tomas Tranströmer). [WashR] (16:2) Ag-S 90, p. 33.
6987. WINFIELD, William
"November." [Wind] (20:66) 90, p. 37.
6988. WING, Linda
"Rifle." [SingHM] (18) 90, p. 46.
WING, Tek Lum
See LUM, Wing Tek
6989. WINN, Howard
"Burnt Bush." [ApalQ] (33/34) 90, p. 69-70.
"Marilyn Approaches Possible Retirement in 1991." [Pearl] (12) Fall-Wint 90, p. 36.
"Responsibility in Spring." [ApalQ] (33/34) 90, p. 68.
"Sowing." [SmPd] (27:3, #80) Fall 90, p. 9.
6990. WINSLOW, D. Christopher
"The Omniscient Dance." [Gypsy] (15) 90, p. 27.
6991. WINTER, Jonah
"Unrequited Love: A Slide Presentation" (Selections: Slide #3, Slide #5). [NowestR] (28:3/29:1) 90-91, p. 185-186.
6992. WINTEROVA, Dominika
"English Lesson" (tr. of Jan Rejzek, w. Richard Katrovas). [PoetryE] (29) Spr 90, p. 117.
"I Want" (tr. of Svetlana Burianová, w. Richard Katrovas). [PoetryE] (29) Spr 90, p. 114.
"Stalin's Monument: Snapshot from 1956" (tr. of Pavel Strut, w. Richard Katrovas).

[PoetryE] (29) Spr 90, p. 113.
"Troja at Eight in the Evening" (tr. of Karel Sys, w. Richard Katrovas). [PoetryE] (29) Spr 90, p. 116.
"A Walk Around the Brewery" (tr. of Ivan Wernisch, w. Richard Katrovas). [PoetryE] (29) Spr 90, p. 115.
6993. WINTEROWD, Ross
"Code Blue." [Plain] (10:2) Wint 90, p. 30.
"How to Read a Page." [Plain] (10:3) Spr 90, p. 8.
6994. WINTERS, Bayla
"Jell-O on Springs." [Pearl] (12) Fall-Wint 90, p. 35.
"Leather, Steel and Ovaltine." [Pearl] (11) Sum 90, p. 44-45.
"Tiffany's on Fire." [Pearl] (12) Fall-Wint 90, p. 59.
"Yes & No." [Pearl] (10) Spr 90, p. 30.
6995. WISCHNER, Claudia M.
"After Apollo." [NoAmR] (275:4) D 90, p. 19.
6996. WISE, Marie Gray
"Anna." [Footwork] 90, p. 93.
"Gatherings." [Footwork] 90, p. 93.
6997. WISE, Thomas Patrick
"The Prisoner." [EmeraldCR] (1990) c89, p. 95-96.
6998. WISEMAN, Jonathan
"Answering Nietzsche." [PraF] (11:4) Wint 90-91, p. 82.
"The Delivery." [PraF] (11:4) Wint 90-91, p. 83.
6999. WISENBERG, S. L.
"The City: Voting." [AnotherCM] (21) 90, p. 155-157.
7000. WISHAW, Iona
"We Can Choose" (tr. of Veronica Volkow). [Vis] (33) 90, p. 22.
7001. WITT, Harold
"Above Ann Arbor" (from "American Lit"). [LullwaterR] (2:1) Wint 90, p. 51.
"American Lit: Kerouac." [MidwQ] (32:1) Aut 90, p. 97.
"American Lit: No, She Said." [NewYorkQ] (43) Fall 90, p. 58.
"American Lit: She'd Rather Read the Funnies." [WritersF] (16) Fall 90, p. 127.
"American Lit: The Turn of the Screw." [Interim] (9:1) Spr-Sum 90, p. 15.
"American Lit: William Meredith." [Interim] (9:1) Spr-Sum 90, p. 14.
"Auschwitz." [NewYorkQ] (42) Sum 90, p. 80.
"Dreiser" (American Lit). [NewYorkQ] (41) Spr 90, p. 69.
"Gertrude Stein." [InterPR] (16:1) Spr 90, p. 118.
"Hart Crane." [InterPR] (16:1) Spr 90, p. 118.
"Mrs. Black." [BellArk] (6:4) Jl-Ag 90, p. 1.
"Muriel Rukeyser." [BellArk] (6:2) Mr-Ap 90, p. 28.
"Myra." [BellArk] (6:5) S-O 90, p. 3-4.
"Ranch Wife." [BellArk] (6:6) N-D 90, p. 4-5.
"Rappaccini's Daughter." [LullwaterR] (1:1) Spr 90, p. 26.
"Rexroth." [BellArk] (6:1) Ja-F 90, p. 22.
"Robert Penn Warren." [BellArk] (6:3) My-Je 90, p. 20.
7002. WITT, Janice L.
"Neu-ro'sis, N., Pl. -ses." [Pearl] (11) Sum 90, p. 41.
WITT, Jim de
See DeWITT, Jim
7003. WITTE, Francine
"Dawn As a Work in Progress." [FloridaR] (17:2) Fall-Wint 90, p. 158-159.
"Falling." [BellR] (13:1, #27) Spr 90, p. 6.
"Sunset Boulevard." [Outbr] (21) 90, p. 33.
7004. WITTE, George
"Gully." [Poetry] (155:6) Mr 90, p. 386.
"Haptic." [Shen] (40:2) Sum 90, p. 83.
"Narcissus." [Poetry] (155:6) Mr 90, p. 389-390.
"Talus Slope." [Shen] (40:2) Sum 90, p. 82.
"Thaw." [Poetry] (155:6) Mr 90, p. 387.
"Totenwald." [Poetry] (155:6) Mr 90, p. 388.
7005. WITTE, John
"Groundwater." [Zyzzyva] (6:2, #22) Sum 90, p. 47-48.
"Pilgrimage." [KenR] (NS 12:3) Sum 90, p. 50-52.
7006. WOEHRLEN, Sara Heikoff (Sara Heikof)
"The Advertising Man" (tr. of José Elgarresta Ramirez de Haro). [Agni] (29/30) 90, p. 203-204.

"Psalm XVIII" (tr. of José Elgarresta). [LitR] (33:2) Wint 90, p. 190.
"Psalm XXIV" (tr. of José Elgarresta). [LitR] (33:2) Wint 90, p. 191.
"Similarities" (tr. of Marjorie Agosin). [ContextS] (1:1) 89, p. 47.
7007. WOESSNER, Warren
"The Loon." [LakeSR] (24) 90, p. 36.
7008. WOHL, Jane Elkington
"Season's Song." [Plain] (11:1) Fall 90, p. 33.
7009. WOHLFELD, Valerie
"Eloquence." [GreensboroR] (49) Wint 90-91, p. 104.
"Spring's Apprentice." [SouthwR] (75:1) Wint 90, p. 125.
"That Which Is Fugitive, That Which Is Medicinally Sweet or Alterable to Gold, That
Which Is Substantiated by Unscientific Means." [GreensboroR] (49) Wint
90-91, p. 103.
"The Watery Loom." [Chelsea] (49) 90, p. 46-48.
7010. WOJAHN, David
"The Assassination of John Lennon as Depicted by the Madame Tussaud Wax
Museum, Niagara Falls, Ontario, 1987." [PoetryE] (29) Spr 90, p. 246.
"The Assassinations of Robert Goulet as Performed by Elvis Presley: Memphis,
1968." [PoetryE] (29) Spr 90, p. 241.
"Buddy Holly Watching *Rebel Without a Cause*, Lubbock, Texas, 1956." [PoetryE]
(29) Spr 90, p. 236.
"C Train Home: Lou Reed After the Wake of Delmore Schwartz, July, 1966."
[Boulevard] (4:3/5:1, #12/13) Spr 90, p. 67.
"Colorizing: Turner Broadcasting Enterprises, Computer Graphics Division,
Burbank, CA, 1987." [PoetryE] (29) Spr 90, p. 247.
"Delmore Schwartz at the First Performance of the Velvet Underground: New York,
1966." [Boulevard] (4:3/5:1, #12/13) Spr 90, p. 66.
"Elvis Moving a Small Cloud: The Desert Near Las Vegas, 1976" (after the painting
by Susan Baker). [PoetryE] (29) Spr 90, p. 244.
"Extinctions." [NewEngR] (12:4) Sum 90, p. 509-511.
"Fragging, Armed Forces Radio, Credence on the Mekong, 1969." [PoetryE] (29)
Spr 90, p. 242.
"Francis Ford Coppola and Anthropologist Interpreter Teaching Gartewienna
Tribesmen to Sing 'Light My Fire,' Philippine Jungle, 1978." [Boulevard]
(4:3/5:1, #12/13) Spr 90, p. 65.
"'It's Only Rock and Roll But I Like It': The Fall of Saigon, 1975." [KenR] (NS
12:1) Wint 90, p. 160.
"Jerry Lee Lewis' Secret Marriage to Thirteen-Year-Old First Cousin Revealed
During British Isles Tour, 1959. His Manager Speaks." [PoetryE] (29) Spr 90,
p. 237.
"John Berryman Listening to Robert Johnson's *King of the Delta Blues*, January,
1972." [Boulevard] (4:3/5:1, #12/13) Spr 90, p. 63.
"Malcolm McLaren Signs the Sex Pistols, London, 1976." [PoetryE] (29) Spr 90, p.
245.
"Matins: James Brown and His Famous Flames Tour the South, 1958." [KenR] (NS
12:1) Wint 90, p. 169.
"My Father's Pornography." [Agni] (31/32) 90, p. 269-270.
"Necromancy: The Last Days of Brian Jones, 1968." [Boulevard] (4:3/5:1, #12/13)
Spr 90, p. 64.
"Tattoo, *Corazón*: Ritchie Valens, 1959." [PoetryE] (29) Spr 90, p. 238.
"To the Reader" (Ruined Commune, Green Mountains). [NewEngR] (12:3) Spr 90,
p. 229.
"The Trashmen Shaking Hands with Hubert Humphrey at the Opening of Apache
Plaze Shopping Center, Suburban Minneapolis, August 1963." [PoetryE] (29)
Spr 90, p. 240.
"Turbulence: *Exile on Main Street* Tour, 1972." [PoetryE] (29) Spr 90, p. 243.
"WCW Watching Presley's Second Appearance on *The Ed Sullivan Show*: Mercy
Hospital, Newark, 1956." [Boulevard] (4:3/5:1, #12/13) Spr 90, p. 61-62.
"White Lanterns." [Poetry] (157:1) O 90, p. 20-23.
"Woody Guthrie Visited by Bob Dylan: Brooklyn State Hospital, New York, 1961."
[PoetryE] (29) Spr 90, p. 239.
7011. WOLF, Joan
"Miracles." [RagMag] (7:2) Spr 90, p. 68.
"Sister Toad." [RagMag] (7:2) Spr 90, p. 69.
7012. WOLF, Manfred
"The Prince Returned" (Painting: Portrait of William of Orange by Antonie Mor, tr.

of Adriaan Roland Holst). [Trans] (24) Fall 90, p. 46-47.
7013. WOLF, Michele
"Healing Dirt" (El Santuario de Chimayó, Chimayó, New Mexico). [PoetL] (85:3) Fall 90, p. 11-13.
7014. WOLF, Mindy
"Making Our Way." [NewYorkQ] (43) Fall 90, p. 67.
7015. WOLF, Naomi
"Sex Passages." [Verse] (7:2) Sum 90, p. 83-84.
7016. WOLFE, Kathi
"The Woman Talks." [Kaleid] (21) Sum-Fall 90, p. 46.
"The Woman Walks." [ChrC] (107:24) 22-29 Ag 90, p. 771.
7017. WOLFF, Daniel
"The Day They Shot a Wolf in the Ghetto and What It Meant." [Thrpny] (41) Spr 90, p. 14.
"The Thinking Between Two Waves." [PartR] (57:2) Spr 90, p. 275-276.
7018. WOLFF, Susan
"Business Dinner in Bethlehem." [AntigR] (81/82) Spr-Sum 90, p. 104-105.
"Empty Cottages." [AntigR] (81/82) Spr-Sum 90, p. 103.
"Love on Jerusalem's East Side." [AntigR] (81/82) Spr-Sum 90, p. 106-107.
WOLHEE, Choe
See CHOE, Wolhee
7019. WOLIN, Blema
"Night Swim." [BellArk] (6:6) N-D 90, p. 7.
"Teacups." [BellArk] (6:6) N-D 90, p. 6.
7020. WOLKSTEIN, Diane
"The Song of Songs" (An adaptation-translation from the Hebrew). [Confr] (42/43) Spr-Sum 90, p. 74-85.
7021. WOLOCH, Cecilia
"Man as Animal." [OnTheBus] (2:2/3:1, #6/7) Sum-Fall 90 Wint-Spr 91, p. 209.
"Voodoo." [OnTheBus] (2:1, #5) Spr 90, p. 153.
7022. WONDRA, Janet
"Long Division." [SouthernR] (26:4) O 90, p. 900-901.
WONG, May
See MAY, Wong
7023. WONG, Sau-Ling
"The Riverbed of Exile" (tr. of Ye Fei). [PoetryUSA] ([5:4?]) Wint 90, p. 21.
"Singer of the Crimson Century" (tr. of Ye Fei). [PoetryUSA] ([5:4?]) Wint 90, p. 22.
7024. WONG, Sauliey
"The Riverbed of Exile" (tr. of Fei Ye). [Zyzzyva] (6:1 #21) Spr 90, p. 113.
7025. WOO, David
"Salt." [NewYorker] (65:51) 5 F 90, p. 94.
7026. WOOD, Dawn
"Some Women." [OnTheBus] (2:2/3:1, #6/7) Sum-Fall 90 Wint-Spr 91, p. 211.
"Spell." [OnTheBus] (2:2/3:1, #6/7) Sum-Fall 90 Wint-Spr 91, p. 210.
7027. WOOD, Debbie
"Dirty Linen." [PacificR] (8) 90, p. 85.
7028. WOOD, Eve E. M.
"All the Things." [PoetC] (21:2) Wint 90, p. 29.
7029. WOOD, Rodney
"Wrestlers." [Bogg] (63) 90, p. 51.
7030. WOOD, Susan
"Christmas Eve at Rosemound Cemetery." [NewEngR] (13:1) Fall 90, p. 113-114.
7031. WOODARD, Deborah
"Kore" (Excerpt). [SoCoast] (8) Spr 90, p. 9.
7032. WOODCOCK, George
"Dark Angel." [PoetryC] (11:4) Wint 90, p. 12.
"Daydreams and Nightdreams." [PoetryC] (11:4) Wint 90, p. 12.
"Mirror Poem I. Self Portraits" (For Joe Plaskett and Ivan Eyre). [PoetryC] (11:4) Wint 90, p. 12.
"Tolstoy at Yasnaya Polyana" (Epic Fragments). [Event] (19:2) Sum 90, p. 7-23.
7033. WOODFORD, Keisha Lynette
"Sweat." [Footwork] 90, p. 107.
7034. WOODS, Alison
"Eyes." [OnTheBus] (2:1, #5) Spr 90, p. 155-156.
"Last Night." [OnTheBus] (2:1, #5) Spr 90, p. 154-155.

WOODS

"Vertigo" (actual title, "Veritgo," assumed to be a misspelling). [OnTheBus]
    (2:2/3:1, #6/7) Sum-Fall 90 Wint-Spr 91, p. 212-213.
7035. WOODS, Christopher
    (Anonymous poem). [FreeL] (4) 90.
    "Directive." [CoalC] (2) D 90, p. 9.
    "The Moth." [RagMag] (7:2) Spr 90, p. 24.
7036. WOODS, Gregory
    "First of May." [Stand] (31:1) Wint 89-90, p. 28-32.
7037. WOODS, John
    "Bad News from Sears." [NewDeltaR] (7:1) 90, p. 69-70.
7038. WOODS, Macdara
    "Sharing Houseroom." [Quarry] (39:1) Wint 90, p. 97-98.
7039. WOODS-SMITH, Sybil
    "Archaeology." [Hellas] (1:2) Fall 90, p. 218-219.
    "Mixing Metaphors." [Hellas] (1:2) Fall 90, p. 217.
7040. WOODSUM, Douglas
    "Three Answers in Spring." [BelPoR] (40:3) Spr 90, p. 28-29.
7041. WOODWARD, Gerard
    "The Big Cats." [Verse] (7:3) Wint 90, p. 97.
    "Grandfather's Rocking Horse." [Stand] (31:2) Spr 90, p. 5.
    "Mandrax." [Stand] (31:2) Spr 90, p. 5-6.
7042. WOODWARD, Jeffrey
    "April." [Poem] (63) My 90, p. 7.
    "Big Sur." [Poem] (63) My 90, p. 8.
    "The Harpsichord-Maker." [Poem] (63) My 90, p. 6.
7043. WOODWARD, Joe L.
    "To Country." [BrooklynR] (7) 90, p. 52-53.
7044. WOODWARD, Patricia F.
    "Mother" (English Language Poetry Prize). [LindLM] (9:3) Jl-S 90, p. 20.
    "The Pharaoh" (English Language Poetry Prize). [LindLM] (9:3) Jl-S 90, p. 20.
7045. WOODWORTH, Marc
    "Adam's Return." [WestHR] (44:4) Wint 90, p. 345-346.
    "Frieze." [Salm] (88/89) Fall 90-Wint 91, p. 366.
    "An Uncut Scene from Herr Soma's Last Film." [WestHR] (44:4) Wint 90, p. 347.
7046. WOON, Koon
    "1.4, 6.4." [BellArk] (6:3) My-Je 90, p. 5.
    "Autumn." [BellArk] (6:5) S-O 90, p. 1.
    "A Dream." [BellArk] (6:3) My-Je 90, p. 12.
    "Meditating on a Plum and a Banana." [BellArk] (6:2) Mr-Ap 90, p. 1.
    "Perturbations." [BellArk] (6:1) Ja-F 90, p. 8.
    "Water-Skipper." [BellArk] (6:3) My-Je 90, p. 3.
7047. WORDEN, Anne-Marie
    "In Paris." [HangL] (57) 90, p. 75-76.
7048. WORLEY, James
    "'Let Those Who Have eyes to See' Beware." [ChrC] (107:2) 17 Ja 90, p. 36.
    "Listening for a Long-Dead Gardener." [ChrC] (107:10) 21-28 Mr 90, p. 293.
    "Young Cardinal Dead by the Stormdoor." [ChrC] (107:33) 14 N 90, p. 1062.
7049. WORLEY, Jeff
    "After the Last Quarrel." [PraS] (64:3) Fall 90, p. 80-81.
    "Dog." [BlackWR] (16:2) Spr-Sum 90, p. 55.
    "Eunice Winkless's Dive into Pool of Water: Pueblo, Colorado, July 4, 1905"
        (photographer unknown). [PraS] (64:3) Fall 90, p. 82.
    "A Feminist Critique." [NewYorkQ] (41) Spr 90, p. 97.
    "A Few Arguments with the Conspicuous." [PennR] (4:2) 90, p. 75-77.
    "A Happy Death." [TarRP] (30:1) Fall 90, p. 36.
    "Incorrigible in April." [NewYorkQ] (43) Fall 90, p. 68.
    "Main Street." [AntigR] (81/82) Spr-Sum 90, p. 205.
    "The Morning Paper." [HawaiiR] (14:3, #30) Fall 90, p. 40-41.
    "On the Front Lawn After Dinner." [PennR] (4:2) 90, p. 78-79.
    "Phantom Limb." [FloridaR] (17:2) Fall-Wint 90, p. 105.
    "The Pyromaniac's Confession." [PennR] (4:2) 90, p. 80-81.
    "Skunk." [BlackWR] (16:2) Spr-Sum 90, p. 52-54.
    "Toothpaste." [Confr] (42/43) Spr-Sum 90, p. 214.
7050. WORLEY, Stella
    "Skeleton for a Life Drawing Class." [AnthNEW] 90, p. 9.

503

7051. WORMSER, Baron
"The Fall of the Human Empire." [CimR] (92) Jl 90, p. 138.
"Listening to a Baseball Game" (for Charles Baxter). [ParisR] (32:115) Sum 90, p.
200.
"Mark Rothko, 1903-1970." [ManhatR] (5:2) Fall 90, p. 24.
"Myth." [ManhatR] (5:2) Fall 90, p. 35.
"To Happiness." [ParisR] (32:115) Sum 90, p. 201-202.
7052. WOROZBYT, Theodore (Theodore, Jr.)
"Northern Lights." [Poetry] (156:5) Ag 90, p. 274-275.
"A Preparation of Spanish Shrimp." [NowestR] (28:3/29:1) 90-91, p. 72-73.
"Torsos & Horses." [CarolQ] (43:1) Fall 90, p. 18-19.
"A Unified Theory of Light." [Poetry] (156:5) Ag 90, p. 272-273.
7053. WORSHAM, Fabian
"Witchcraft: The Novice." [BellR] (13:2, #28) Fall 90, p. 38-39.
7054. WRAY, Matt
"How to Write a Poem." [PoetryUSA] (5:2) Sum 90, p. 4.
7055. WREGGITT, Andrew
"Moving." [PoetryC] (11:4) Wint 90, p. 18.
"Not Speaking." [PoetryC] (11:4) Wint 90, p. 18.
"Science, a River." [PoetryC] (11:4) Wint 90, p. 18-19.
7056. WRIGHT, C. D.
"The Next Time I Crossed the Line into Oklahoma." [DenQ] (24:3) Wint 90, p.
81-82.
"The Night I Met Little Floyd." [DenQ] (24:3) Wint 90, p. 79-81.
"The Ozark Odes" (this one goes out to Fred). [DenQ] (24:3) Wint 90, p. 75-79.
7057. WRIGHT, Carolyne
"Afternoon in Automobile" (for my brother Ivan, tr. of Jorge Teillier). [PartR] (57:3)
Sum 90, p. 445.
"Amnesiac River" (tr. of Devarati Mitra, w. Paramita Banerjee). [HawaiiR] (14:1,
#28) Wint 89-90, p. 70.
"A Change of Maps." [Poetry] (156:5) Ag 90, p. 270-271.
"A Day in Madrid" (for Jorge Edwards and Galvarino Plaza, tr. of Jorge Teillier).
[MidAR] (10:1) 90, p. 108-110.
"Flowers Born Blind" (tr. of Devarati Mitra, w. Paramita Banerjee). [HawaiiR]
(14:1, #28) Wint 89-90, p. 69.
"Golden Age" (tr. of Jorge Teillier). [HampSPR] (Anthology 1975-1990) 90, p.
254.
"The Green Stigma" (tr. of Devarati Mitra, w. Paramita Banerjee). [HawaiiR] (14:1,
#28) Wint 89-90, p. 72.
"Henna" (tr. of Vijaya Mukhopadhyay, w. Sunil B. Ray and the author). [GrandS]
(9:3) Spr 90, p. with 200.
"The Hunt" (tr. of Anuradha Mahapatra, w. Jyotirmoy Datta). [IndR] (13:2) Spr 90,
p. 73.
"Image" (tr. of Jorge Teillier). [NewL] (57:1) Fall 90, p. 11.
"Irrelevant" (tr. of Vijaya Mukhopadhyay, w. Sunil B. Ray and the author).
[GrandS] (9:3) Spr 90, p. 202.
"The Loveliest Country of Our Lives." [Journal] (13:2) Fall-Wint 89-90, p. 36-37.
"Mother of the Bud" (tr. of Anuradha Mahapatra, w. Jyotirmoy Datta). [IndR] (13:2)
Spr 90, p. 72.
"No, No, and No" (tr. of Devarati Mitra, w. Paramita Banerjee). [HawaiiR] (14:1,
#28) Wint 89-90, p. 71.
"Of Visions" (tr. of Angel Leiva). [HampSPR] (Anthology 1975-1990) 90, p. 258.
"One Year, Another Year" (tr. of Jorge Teillier). [NewL] (57:1) Fall 90, p. 9-10.
"The Retarded Woman on Cooper Street." [Ploughs] (16:1) Spr-Sum 90, p. 90-91.
"The Return of Orpheus" (In memoriam Rosamel del Valle, tr. of Jorge Teillier).
[MissouriR] (13:2) 90, p. 125.
"Sestina After an Etching by William Blake." [HampSPR] (Anthology 1975-1990)
90, p. 180-181.
"Still Life" (tr. of Jorge Guillen). [HampSPR] (Anthology 1975-1990) 90, p. 253.
"To the Mountaintop" (tr. of Anuradha Mahapatra, w. Jyotirmoy Datta). [IndR]
(13:2) Spr 90, p. 74.
"Which Floor?" (tr. of Vijaya Mukhopadhyay, w. Sunil B. Ray and the author).
[GrandS] (9:3) Spr 90, p. 201.
"The Wrong Place" (tr. of Vijaya Mukhopadhyay, w. Sunil B. Ray and the author).
[GrandS] (9:3) Spr 90, p. 199.
"The Year 1984" (tr. of Anuradha Mahapatra, w. Jyotirmoy Datta). [IndR] (13:2)

Spr 90, p. 75.
7058. WRIGHT, Charles
"Bar Giamacia 1959-60." [GrandS] (9:2) Wint 90, p. 105-106.
"Cicada." [WestHR] (44:3) Aut 90, p. 249-250.
"Easter, 1989." [Antaeus] (64/65) Spr-Aut 90, p. 141-142.
"Mid-Winter Snowfall in the Piazza Dante." [Poetry] (155:4) Ja 90, p. 253-254.
"One Morning in Early June." [NewYorker] (66:17) 11 Je 90, p. 46-47.
"Reading Lao Tzu Again in the New Year." [Poetry] (155:4) Ja 90, p. 255-256.
"Tennessee Line." [YaleR] (79:2) Wint 90, p. 246-247.
7059. WRIGHT, Franz
"August Insomnia." [Crazy] (38) Spr 90, p. 64.
"Bild, 1959." [Field] (42) Spr 90, p. 40.
"Certain Tall Buildings" (J.A.). [Field] (42) Spr 90, p. 42.
"Elegy: Breece D'J Pancake." [Field] (42) Spr 90, p. 41.
"Forgotten in an Old Notebook." [ParisR] (32:114) Spr 90, p. 221.
"The Forties." [Crazy] (38) Spr 90, p. 65.
"The Lovers." [Crazy] (38) Spr 90, p. 61.
"Night Said." [Crazy] (38) Spr 90, p. 62-63.
"Thoughts of a Solitary Farmhouse." [Crazy] (38) Spr 90, p. 66.
"Untitled: Whether I grow old, betray my dreams, become a ghost." [ParisR]
     (32:114) Spr 90, p. 220.
"Words." [ParisR] (32:114) Spr 90, p. 222.
7060. WRIGHT, G. T.
"Acknowledgment." [NorthStoneR] (9) 90, p. 32.
"Companions." [NorthStoneR] (9) 90, p. 35.
"Earthquake" (Thessaloniki, June 20, 1978). [NorthStoneR] (9) 90, p. 38-40.
"Images." [NorthStoneR] (9) 90, p. 34.
"Late Letter to My Father." [NorthStoneR] (9) 90, p. 27-30.
"Menage à Trois." [NorthStoneR] (9) 90, p. 36.
"Mortars." [NorthStoneR] (9) 90, p. 32.
"The New Models." [NorthStoneR] (9) 90, p. 31.
"Nightfall Near Louisville." [NorthStoneR] (9) 90, p. 36.
"Old Man in Waiting Room." [NorthStoneR] (9) 90, p. 37.
"Reminiscence of a California Affair." [NorthStoneR] (9) 90, p. 33.
"Scratch Sheet." [NorthStoneR] (9) 90, p. 37.
7061. WRIGHT, Howard
"Terribilita." [Verse] (7:3) Wint 90, p. 96.
7062. WRIGHT, James
"The Angry Mother." [GettyR] (3:1) Wint 90, p. 33-34.
"Contradictory Existence." [GettyR] (3:1) Wint 90, p. 26.
"Lame Apollo." [GettyR] (3:1) Wint 90, p. 28.
"Poem: Back in grammar school ten years ago." [GettyR] (3:1) Wint 90, p. 32.
"Shall We Gather at the River." [Hudson] (43:2) Sum 90, p. 279.
"Sonnet: On My Violent Approval of Robert Service." [GettyR] (3:1) Wint 90, p.
     30.
"Sonnet: Response." [GettyR] (3:1) Wint 90, p. 31.
"To Critics, and to Hell with Them." [GettyR] (3:1) Wint 90, p. 29.
"To Justify My Singing." [GettyR] (3:1) Wint 90, p. 25.
"Untitled: I cannot Write. The words no longer flow." [GettyR] (3:1) Wint 90, p.
     27.
7063. WRIGHT, John
"Sixteen Cents a Pound." [Pig] (16) 90, p. 60.
7064. WRIGHT, Justin
"The Poetry Shop." [MissR] (19:1/2, #55/56) 90, p. 287-289.
7065. WRIGHT, Kirby
"Losing Aphrodite." [PoetryUSA] (5:3) Fall 90, p. 10.
7066. WRIGLEY, Robert
"At the Vietnam Veterans' Memorial -- 1987." [Witness] (4:1) 90, p. 51.
"Invisible Men." [VirQR] (66:4) Aut 90, p. 667-669.
"Light After Light." [Witness] (4:1) 90, p. 49-50.
"Milkflowers." [YellowS] (35) Wint 90-91, p. 38.
"The Model." [GeoR] (44:4) Wint 90, p. 675-677.
"Of Diamonds." [CharR] (16:2) Fall 90, p. 68.
"Ravens at Deer Creek." [GettyR] (3:1) Wint 90, p. 242.
7067. WU, Keming
"Declaration" (to Yu Luoke, martyr, tr. of Bei Dao). [PaintedB] (40/41) 90, p.

50-51.
"Illness" (tr. of Yang Zhi). [PaintedB] (40/41) 90, p. 60.
"A Smiling Flower" (tr. of Yang Zhi). [PaintedB] (40/41) 90, p. 58-59.
"You're Waiting for Me in the Rain" (tr. of Bei Dao). [PaintedB] (40/41) 90, p. 52-53.
7068. WU, Tsao
"On a Picture of Self with Hoe, Cultivating Plum Blossoms in Moonlight" (tr. by Cathy Silber). [LitR] (33:2) Wint 90, p. 198.
7069. WU, Yuancheng
"Celestial Burial" (tr. by Dong Jiping). [Footwork] 90, p. 38.
"A Fresco" (tr. by Dong Jiping). [Footwork] 90, p. 38.
7070. WURSTER, Michael
"A Tall Flame." [PoetryC] (11:1) Spr 90, p. 26.
7071. WYATT, Charles
"Creek Bottom." [Chelsea] (49) 90, p. 28.
"Storm." [CumbPR] (10:1) Fall 90, p. 53-54.
7072. WYBENGA, Jan
"Trakl" (in Frisian). [WashR] (16:2) Ag-S 90, p. 13.
"Trakl" (tr. by Rod Jellema). [WashR] (16:2) Ag-S 90, p. 13.
7073. WYNAND, Derk
"Quinta do Cerrado." [Descant] (21:2, #69) Sum 90, p. 73-77.
7074. WYNN, Pam
"The Doctor Will See You Now." [Writer] (103:9) S 90, p. 20.
7075. WYTTENBERG, Victoria
"For Zoe in Spring." [PoetryNW] (31:2) Sum 90, p. 47.
"Hunger." [PoetryNW] (31:2) Sum 90, p. 44-45.
"Imprecation Against Adultery." [PoetryNW] (31:2) Sum 90, p. 46-47.
"The School Photographer." [PoetryNW] (31:2) Sum 90, p. 45-46.
7076. XI, Chuan
"Dante" (tr. by Dong Jiping). [Footwork] 90, p. 44.
"Night Birds" (tr. by Dong Jiping). [Footwork] 90, p. 44.
7077. XIAO, Jun
"Autumn Afternoon" (tr. by Dong Jiping). [Footwork] 90, p. 44.
"Street Scene" (tr. by Dong Jiping). [Footwork] 90, p. 44.
7078. XIAO, Xue
"Love" (tr. by Li Xijian and Gordon Osing). [Paint] (17:33/34) Spr-Aut 90, p. 33.
XIAO-NI, Wang
    See WANG, Xiao-ni
XIAOYU, Li
    See LI, Xiaoyu
XIAOZHU, He
    See HE, Xiaozhu
XIJIAN, Li
    See LI, Xijian
7079. XIRINACS, Olga
"The Day of the Dead" (from "La pluja sobre els Palaus," 1990, tr. by Montserrat Abelló). [PoetryC] (11:4) Wint 90, p. 23.
"If You Are Not There Anymore" (from "La pluja sobre els Palaus," 1990, tr. by Montserrat Abelló). [PoetryC] (11:4) Wint 90, p. 23.
"Secret" (from "La pluja sobre els Palaus," 1990, tr. by Montserrat Abelló). [PoetryC] (11:4) Wint 90, p. 23.
XUE, Xiao
    See XIAO, Xue
XUEMIN, Liu
    See LIU, Xuemin
7080. YACINE, Kateb
"The Eye that Rejuvenates the Soul" (tr. by Eric Sellin). [Vis] (32) 90, p. 6.
YAFENG, Bao
    See BAO, Yafeng
7081. YAGUCHI, Yorifumi
"Hi There" (tr. of Shuntaro Tanikawa, w. William Stafford). [ArtfulD] (18/19) 90, p. 15.
7082. YAMADA, Leona
"April in the Bay." [HawaiiR] (15:1, #31) Wint 90, p. 42.
"Fifth Grade." [HawaiiR] (14:2, #29) Spr 90, p. 92-93.
"Jack-o'-Lantern." [HawaiiR] (14:2, #29) Spr 90, p. 91.

506

YAMADA

"Letter to NYC" (for John-Mario). [BambooR] (47) Sum 90, p. 66.
"Mrs. O." [HawaiiR] (15:1, #31) Wint 90, p. 41.
"Sushi Bar with Doreen in November." [ChamLR] (3:2, #6) Spr 90, p. 41-42.
7083. YAMAGUCHI, Tsutomu
"The water brimming" (tr. by Janet Lewis). [SouthernR] (26:1) Ja 90, p. 205.
7084. YAMAMOTO, Hisaye
"Seattle Illusion." [PoetryUSA] ([5:4?]) Wint 90, p. 8.
"Something had gone awry." [PoetryUSA] ([5:4?]) Wint 90, p. 5.
7085. YAMANAKA, Lois-Ann
"Kala Gave Me Anykine Advice Especially about Filipinos When I Moved to
Pahala." [MichQR] (29:4) Fall 90, p. 619-620.
"Monday After School." [HawaiiR] (14:3, #30) Fall 90, p. 89.
"Sista: Boss of the Food." [BambooR] (47) Sum 90, p. 67-68.
YAN, Li
See LI, Yan
7086. YAN, Yi
"The Square Shapes and the Round Shapes" (tr. by Li Xijian and Gordon Osing).
[Paint] (17:33/34) Spr-Aut 90, p. 36.
7087. YANG, Zhi
"Illness" (in Chinese and English, tr. by Wu Keming). [PaintedB] (40/41) 90, p. 60.
"A Smiling Flower" (in Chinese and English, tr. by Wu Keming). [PaintedB]
(40/41) 90, p. 58-59.
YAPING, Tang
See TANG, Ya Ping
7088. YARMAL, Ann
"An Unfinished Poem (Interrupted by a Buddhist Scholar)." [BlackBR] (12)
Fall-Wint 90, p. 30.
7089. YARROW, Susan
"Not Not" (Selections). [WestCL] (24:1) Spr 90, p. 76-81.
7090. YASHIRO, Princess (758)
"Shame" (tr. by Graeme Wilson). [LitR] (33:2) Wint 90, p. 193.
7091. YASUTOME, Kay
"January and the Fan." [Kaleid] (21) Sum-Fall 90, p. 35.
"Jay Singh, Incarnate." [Kaleid] (21) Sum-Fall 90, p. 35.
7092. YAU, Emily
"Bonfire" (tr. of Liu Zhan-Qiu). [PoetryUSA] ([5:4?]) Wint 90, p. 22.
"The Forest Is Growing" (tr. of Chen Jingrong). [PoetryUSA] ([5:4?]) Wint 90, p.
22.
"If You Come" (tr. of Chen Jingrong). [PoetryUSA] ([5:4?]) Wint 90, p. 22.
"The Modern Prometheus" (tr. of Chen Jingrong). [PoetryUSA] ([5:4?]) Wint 90, p.
21.
7093. YAU, John
"Genghis Chan: Private Eye VIII." [Talisman] (5) Fall 90, p. 30.
"Mirage." [Talisman] (5) Fall 90, p. 29.
"Proscenium." [Talisman] (5) Fall 90, p. 27-28.
"Western Rectangle." [Talisman] (5) Fall 90, p. 26.
7094. YE, Fei
"Curse" (tr. by Sam Hamill). [PoetryE] (30) Fall 90, p. 32.
"The Riverbed of Exile" (tr. by Sau-Ling Wong). [PoetryUSA] ([5:4?]) Wint 90, p.
21.
"The Riverbed of Exile" (tr. by Sauliey Wong). [Zyzzyva] (6:1 #21) Spr 90, p. 113.
"Singer of the Crimson Century" (tr. by Sau-Ling Wong). [PoetryUSA] ([5:4?])
Wint 90, p. 22.
7095. YENSER, Stephen
"Vertumnal." [YaleR] (79:4) Sum 90 c1991, p. 615-621.
7096. YERPE, Dale G.
"First North American Rights." [CumbPR] (9:2) Spr 90, p. 52.
"Ice Buttons, Wright's Creek." [PoetL] (85:2) Sum 90, p. 40.
"The Storyteller." [CumbPR] (9:2) Spr 90, p. 51.
7097. YEVTUSHENKO, Yevgeny
"Happiness Andalusian Style" (tr. by Albert C. Todd and James Ragan). [Nimrod]
(33:2) Spr-Sum 90, p. 122.
"The Heirs of Stalin" (tr. by Albert C. Todd and James Ragan). [Nimrod] (33:2)
Spr-Sum 90, p. 120-121.
"Irpen" (tr. by Albert C. Todd and James Ragan). [Nimrod] (33:2) Spr-Sum 90, p.
123-124.

YI, Yan
    See YAN, Yi
7098. YILLING, Marjorie Coleman
    "Alley Rats." [EmeraldCR] (1990) c89, p. 106.
7099. YNTEMA, Laurie
    "Between the Buildings of New York." [AnthNEW] 90, p. 27.
YONGMING, Zhai
    See ZHAI, Yongming
YOON, Sik Kim
    See KIM, Yoon Sik
YORIFUMI, Yaguchi
    See YAGUCHI, Yorifumi
7100. YORK, Derrick
    "Hibernation." [PoetryUSA] (5:2) Sum 90, p. 19.
7101. YORK, Gary Page
    "Bellyache for Solo Voice and Clavichord." [Poem] (63) My 90, p. 37.
    "Ectopiac." [Poem] (63) My 90, p. 36.
7102. YOSHINO, Kenji
    "The Invisible Red." [HarvardA] (124:2) Ja 90, p. 17.
    "Notes on Leavetaking." [HarvardA] (124:2) Ja 90, p. 29.
    "To His Good Agnostic -- A Letter." [HarvardA] (124:2) Ja 90, p. 5.
7103. YOTS, Michael
    "Teaching My Sons to Dance." [ChatR] (10:3) Spr 90, p. 35.
7104. YOUMANS, Marlene
    "In a Garden of Wide-Verged Shade" (In memory of Melanie Hook Rice).
        [GreenMR] (NS 4:1) Spr-Sum 90, p. 45.
7105. YOUNG, Al
    "A Poem for Dylan Thomas." [Chelsea] (49) 90, p. 59.
7106. YOUNG, David
    "1751" (tr. of Miroslav Holub, w. Dana Hábová and the author). [AmerPoR] (19:2)
        Mr-Ap 90, p. 4.
    "The Clock" (tr. of Miroslav Holub, w. Dana Hábová). [Field] (42) Spr 90, p. 7.
    "The Fall from the Green Frog" (tr. of Miroslav Holub, w. Dana Hábová). [Field]
        (42) Spr 90, p. 11.
    "Fish" (tr. of Miroslav Holub, w. Dana Hábová). [Field] (42) Spr 90, p. 8-9.
    "Glass" (tr. of Miroslav Holub, w. Dana Hábová). [Field] (42) Spr 90, p. 10.
    "Great Ancestors" (tr. of Miroslav Holub, w. Dana Hábová and the author).
        [AmerPoR] (19:2) Mr-Ap 90, p. 5.
    "Heart Transplant" (tr. of Miroslav Holub, w. Dana Hábová). [Field] (42) Spr 90, p.
        5-6.
    "Mirror Ghazal." [NewEngR] (13:2) Wint 90, p. 143.
    "Night Calamities" (tr. of Miroslav Holub, w. Dana Hábová and the author).
        [AmerPoR] (19:2) Mr-Ap 90, p. 5.
    "Parasite" (tr. of Miroslav Holub, w. Dana Hábová and the author). [AmerPoR]
        (19:2) Mr-Ap 90, p. 3.
    "Skinning" (tr. of Miroslav Holub, w. Dana Hábová and the author). [AmerPoR]
        (19:2) Mr-Ap 90, p. 4.
    "What Else" (tr. of Miroslav Holub, w. Dana Hábová and the author). [AmerPoR]
        (19:2) Mr-Ap 90, p. 3.
    "Worship Ghazal." [NewEngR] (13:2) Wint 90, p. 144.
7107. YOUNG, Dean
    "Aesthetics." [IndR] (14:1) Wint 90, p. 106-107.
    "Biography with Lack of Sleep." [BlackWR] (16:2) Spr-Sum 90, p. 108-109.
    "Drama in Last Acts." [Thrpny] (42) Sum 90, p. 4.
    "The Fine Arts." [GettyR] (3:4) Aut 90, p. 744-745.
    "Like Sadness in Music." [NewAW] (6) Spr 90, p. 84-85.
    "Same Ocean" (to Kirsten). [IndR] (14:1) Wint 90, p. 104-105.
    "Strip / Ruin" (DeKooning Woman). [NewAW] (6) Spr 90, p. 86.
7108. YOUNG, Gary
    "Thinking of the Cold Mountain Poet." [Zyzzyva] (6:1 #21) Spr 90, p. 114.
7109. YOUNG, George
    "Mozart." [CrabCR] (6:3) Spr 90, p. 23.
    "The Prayers of a Nation." [PoetL] (85:4) Wint 90-91, p. 19.
7110. YOUNG, Jim
    "Waiting." [Wind] (20:67) 90, p. 7.

7111. YOUNG, Kevin
"Eddie Priest's Barbershop & Notary: Closed Mondays" (Second Prize). [HarvardA]
(124:3) Mr 90, p. 23.
7112. YOUNG, Patricia
"Abduction." [PoetryC] (11:2) Sum 90, p. 18.
"Adoption." [PoetryC] (11:2) Sum 90, p. 18.
"For My Father" (1st Prize for Poetry, Aya Press / The Mercury Press 10th
Anniversary Literary Competition). [CrossC] (12:1) 90, p. 32.
"Hit and Run." [Event] (19:3) Fall 90, p. 41.
"Hothouse." [PoetryC] (11:2) Sum 90, p. 19.
"Mermaid Days." [PoetryC] (11:2) Sum 90, p. 19.
"Nameless Poem." [PraF] (11:4) Wint 90-91, p. 84.
"The Neighbours Are Tossing a Salad." [PraF] (11:4) Wint 90-91, p. 85.
"Peculiar Habit." [Event] (19:3) Fall 90, p. 40.
"Phone Call." [PraF] (11:4) Wint 90-91, p. 86.
"Runaway." [PoetryC] (11:2) Sum 90, p. 18.
"Somewhere on This Earth I Am Sleeping." [PraF] (11:4) Wint 90-91, p. 87.
"When We Were Birds" (for Mary). [PoetryC] (11:2) Sum 90, p. 19.
7113. YOUNG, Reggie
"Praise in Bluesville" (Rev. Red Clay Jones). [BlackALF] (24:3) Fall 90, p.
560-563.
YOUNG, Robert de
See DeYOUNG, Robert
7114. YOUNG, Ruth Hubbard
"After Supper." [Crucible] (26) Fall 90, p. 66-67.
"Bridle Path." [Crucible] (26) Fall 90, p. 68-69.
7115. YOUNG, Tom
"For Herman Melville." [PoetryUSA] (5:1) Spr 90, p. 13.
7116. YOUNG, William
"Recent and Forthcoming." [Shen] (40:3) Fall 90, p. 87-88.
7117. YOUNG, William J.
"The Hawk." [WindO] (53) Fall 90, p. 43.
7118. YOUNGBERG, Gail A. McConnell
"Otherwise." [Grain] (18:3) Fall 90, p. 60-61.
"Riel in Saskatchewan." [Grain] (18:3) Fall 90, p. 61.
7119. YOUNT, Lisa
"Badger." [Asylum] (6:2) S 90, p. 15.
7120. YSKAMP, Amanda
"The Sister Cure." [Caliban] (9) 90, p. 59-61.
YU, Kai
See KAI, Yu
7121. YU, Weiye
"To My Sweetheart at Sixty" (tr. by Li Xijian and Gordon Osing). [Paint] (17:33/34)
Spr-Aut 90, p. 32.
YUAN, Qu
See QU, Yuan
YUANCHENG, Wu
See WU, Yuancheng
YUANSHENG, Li
See LI, Yuansheng
7122. YUEN, D. Leilehua
"As How Come." [BambooR] (47) Sum 90, p. 69.
YUN, Wang
See WANG, Yun
7123. YUNGKANS, Jonathan
"Sleep." [OnTheBus] (2:2/3:1, #6/7) Sum-Fall 90 Wint-Spr 91, p. 214.
"The Unhappy Life of a Sex Goddess" (inspired by Salvador Dali). [Pearl] (12)
Fall-Wint 90, p. 24.
7124. YURKIEVICH, Saúl
"Snare" (tr. by Cola Franzen). [NewOR] (17:2) Sum 90, p. 16.
"El Trasver" (Selections: 2 poems, tr. by Cola Franzen). [Screens] (2) 90, p.
122-129.
7125. YURMAN, R.
"The Exquisite Art." [Bogg] (62) 90, p. 20.
7126. ZABIELSKI, Laverne
"No Credit." [AmerV] (20) Fall 90, p. 7-8.

7127. ZABLE, Jeffrey
"A Bedtime Story." [Caliban] (8) 90, p. 142.
"The Burden." [Caliban] (8) 90, p. 140.
"This Is It." [Caliban] (8) 90, p. 141.
"Today." [Gypsy] (15) 90, p. 12.
7128. ZABRAVÁ, Jan
"Nightfall" (From "The Hillside Above Radotin," tr. by Jaroslav Korán and Daniel Weissbort). [HampSPR] (Anthology 1975-1990) 90, p. 268-269.
7129. ZAGAJEWSKI, Adam
"Anton Bruckner" (tr. by Renata Gorczynski and Benjamin Ivry). [NewYorker] (66:5) 19 Mr 90, p. 46.
"At Midnight" (tr. by Renata Gorczynski and Benjamin Ivry). [Antaeus] (64/65) Spr-Aut 90, p. 143.
"Daybreak" (tr. by Renata Gorczynski and Benjamin Ivry). [PartR] (57:1) Wint 90, p. 97.
"Fire" (tr. by Karen Karleski). [PoetryE] (30) Fall 90, p. 50.
"In May" (tr. by Karen Karleski). [PoetryE] (30) Fall 90, p. 49.
"Lava" (tr. by Renata Gorczynski and Benjamin Ivry). [PartR] (57:1) Wint 90, p. 98.
"Poems on Poland" (tr. by Karen Karleski). [PoetryE] (29) Spr 90, p. 13.
"Presence" (tr. by Renata Gorczynski and Benjamin Ivry). [Antaeus] (64/65) Spr-Aut 90, p. 145.
"R. Says" (tr. by Renata Gorczynski and Benjamin Ivry). [Antaeus] (64/65) Spr-Aut 90, p. 144.
"Vacation" (tr. by Renata Gorczynski and Benjamin Ivry). [DenQ] (25:1) Sum 90, p. 54.
"The Wanderer" (tr. by Karen Karleski). [PoetryE] (29) Spr 90, p. 14.
7130. ZAHORSKY, Jean
"Bone Simple." [OnTheBus] (2:1, #5) Spr 90, p. 157.
"Widower." [OnTheBus] (2:1, #5) Spr 90, p. 157.
7131. ZAHRAD
"Etchmiadzin" (tr. by Diana Der-Hovanessian). [Trans] (23) Spr 90, p. 251.
"Florence" (tr. by Diana Der-Hovanessian). [Trans] (23) Spr 90, p. 252.
"Mykonos" (tr. by Diana Der-Hovanessian). [Trans] (23) Spr 90, p. 252.
"Shiraz" (tr. by Diana Der-Hovanessian). [Trans] (23) Spr 90, p. 253.
ZAKARIYYA MUHAMMAD
    See MUHAMMAD, Zakariyya
7132. ZALAN, Tibor
"Once:" (tr. by Nicholas Kolumban). [PoetryE] (30) Fall 90, p. 70.
7133. ZALDIVAR, Gladys
"Heliotropo." [LindLM] (9:4) O-D 90, p. 12.
7134. ZALITE, Mara
"Poem: You are a spray of lilac" (tr. by Ilze Mueller-Klavina). [Nimrod] (33:2) Spr-Sum 90, p. 71.
7135. ZAMASTIL, Carmen
"Can't You See." [PoetryUSA] ([5:4?]) Wint 90, p. 25.
"Feathered Warrior." [PoetryUSA] (5:3) Fall 90, p. 23.
7136. ZANA
"Wrap Me in Violets" (reprinted from #16, 1988). [Kaleid] (20) Wint-Spr 90, p. 112.
7137. ZAPATA, Miguel Angel
"8 Invenciones: Paul Klee, Dibujos Verbales" (A Zunilda Gertel, De "Poemas para violín y orquesta"). [Inti] (32/33) Otoño 90-Primavera 91, p. 243.
"Morada de la Voz" (A Pepe Durand). [Inti] (31) Primavera 90, p. 170-171.
"Morada de la Voz" (A Pepe Durand, De "Poemas para violín y orquesta"). [Inti] (32/33) Otoño 90-Primavera 91, p. 241-242.
"Paul Celan" (De "Poemas para violín y orquesta"). [Inti] (32/33) Otoño 90-Primavera 91, p. 244.
"Saint-Saens Caminando en el Muelle" (De "Poemas para violín y orquesta"). [Inti] (32/33) Otoño 90-Primavera 91, p. 240-241.
"Sincronia de Mujer" (De "Poemas para violín y orquesta"). [Inti] (32/33) Otoño 90-Primavera 91, p. 244.
"Taberna" (De "Imágenes los juegos"). [Inti] (32/33) Otoño 90-Primavera 91, p. 240.
"Tragaluz" (De "Imágenes los juegos"). [Inti] (32/33) Otoño 90-Primavera 91, p. 240.

7138. ZAQTAN, Chassan (Ghassan)
"Another Death" (tr. by Lena Jayyusi and Jeremy Reed). [Screens] (2) 90, p. 21-22.
"An Incident" (tr. by Lena Jayyusi and Jeremy Reed). [Screens] (2) 90, p. 21.
"A Mirror" (tr. by Lena Jayyusi and Jeremy Reed). [PaperAir] (4:3) 90, p. 62.
7139. ZARANKA, William
"Examination in Literature." [HampSPR] (Anthology 1975-1990) 90, p. 137-138.
"Glass." [HampSPR] (Anthology 1975-1990) 90, p. 138.
7140. ZARIN, Cynthia
"The Hare." [NewYorker] (66:9) 16 Ap 90, p. 46.
7141. ZARZYSKI, Paul
"Angelina, My Noni's Name, Means Messenger." [Poetry] (157:1) O 90, p. 28-29.
"Las Ballenas de Bahia Magdalena." [CreamCR] (14:1) Spr 90, p. 111.
"Living in Snake Country." [PraS] (64:4) Wint 90, p. 112-113.
"Tsankawi" (for Elizabeth). [PraS] (64:4) Wint 90, p. 113-114.
7142. ZAVALA, Iris
"El Gran Mamut." [InterPR] (16:1) Spr 90, p. 88.
"The Great Mammoth" (tr. by Mark Smith-Soto). [InterPR] (16:1) Spr 90, p. 89.
7143. ZAVATSKY, Bill
(Anonymous poem). [FreeL] (4) 90.
7144. ZDANYS, Jonas
"A flowering garden" (tr. of Nijole Miliauskaite). [CrossCur] (9:2) Je 90, p. 165.
"Inheritance." [YaleR] (79:2) Wint 90, p. 225-226.
"You would like to live" (tr. of Nijole Miliauskaite). [CrossCur] (9:2) Je 90, p. 166.
7145. ZEGERS, Kip
"Far Out in the Pond, Lazing." [SycamoreR] (2:2) Sum 90, p. 27.
7146. ZEIGER, Gene
"Could We." [ClockR] (6:2) 90, p. 10.
"Double." [GreenMR] (NS 3:2) Fall-Wint 89-90, p. 76.
"From Nothing." [ClockR] (6:2) 90, p. 11-12.
"From the Second Story." [Crazy] (39) Wint 90, p. 50-51.
"Night Blooming Cereus." [Crazy] (39) Wint 90, p. 49.
"The Photographer's Model." [GreenMR] (NS 3:2) Fall-Wint 89-90, p. 77.
7147. ZEIGER, Lila
(Anonymous poem). [FreeL] (4) 90.
"A Concert at the Phillips" (Washington, D.C.). [Bogg] (62) 90, p. 39.
"Duped Pests Find Death in Mating." [SouthernPR] (30:1) Spr 90, p. 63-65.
"Watching Pina Bausch's 'Kontakthof'." [FreeL] (6) Aut 90, p. 8.
7148. ZEILER, Gina
"Warming the Toes" (above the register in January). [Gypsy] (15) 90, p. 30.
7149. ZELTZER, Joel
"A Reminder" (tr. of Federico García Lorca). [ChironR] (9:3) Aut 90, p. 5.
"Romance of the Moon" (tr. of Federico García Lorca). [ChironR] (9:3) Aut 90, p. 5.
"Song of the Tiny Death" (tr. of Federico García Lorca). [ChironR] (9:3) Aut 90, p. 5.
7150. ZENITH, Richard
"The Chicken" (tr. of Ferreira Gullar). [Chelsea] (49) 90, p. 131.
"Life Pulses" (tr. of Ferreira Gullar). [Chelsea] (49) 90, p. 132-133.
"Memory" (tr. of Ferreira Gullar). [Chelsea] (49) 90, p. 134.
"Rooster Rooster" (tr. of Ferreira Gullar). [Chelsea] (49) 90, p. 129-130.
"Song for a Lover Who Would die" (tr. of Joam Garcia de Guilhade). [LitR] (33:2) Wint 90, p. 189.
"Song for a Troubadour Who Dies and Dies" (tr. of Pero Garcia Burgalês). [LitR] (33:2) Wint 90, p. 188.
"Song for When I Die" (tr. of Rui Queimado). [LitR] (33:2) Wint 90, p. 187.
"Song of the Death I'm Dying" (tr. of Rui Queimado). [LitR] (33:2) Wint 90, p. 187.
"Song to a Lady from Elvas (Cantiga d'Amor)" (tr. of Vidal). [CumbPR] (9:2) Spr 90, p. 55.
"Sugar" (tr. of Ferreira Gullar). [NewOR] (17:2) Sum 90, p. 64.
7151. ZEPPER, Kevin
"Dark Star." [SlipS] (10) 90, p. 40-41.
"Wires." [SlipS] (10) 90, p. 41.
7152. ZERDEN, D. L.
"Riverside Drive." [Poetry] (157:3) D 90, p. 156-157.

7153. ZETZEL, Geraldine
"Gift." [CumbPR] (9:2) Spr 90, p. 53.
7154. ZHAI, Yongming
"After Being Toothless" (tr. by Dong Jiping). [Footwork] 90, p. 38.
"Premonition" (tr. by Dong Jiping). [Footwork] 90, p. 37.
"There Is Something Drawing Me" (tr. by Dong Jiping). [Footwork] 90, p. 38.
7155. ZHANG, Ziqing
"Back to My Valley" (tr. of Wang Jia-xin). [PaintedB] (40/41) 90, p. 46.
"A Blind Black Singer in Washington Street." [PaintedB] (40/41) 90, p. 61.
"I Woke Up to Reality" (tr. of Wang Jia-xin). [PaintedB] (40/41) 90, p. 47.
"Lizard" (tr. of Wang Jia-xin). [PaintedB] (40/41) 90, p. 45.
"Seasons" (tr. of Wang Jia-xin). [PaintedB] (40/41) 90, p. 46.
"Touch" (tr. of Wang Jia-xin). [PaintedB] (40/41) 90, p. 47.
ZHANJING, Ruan
        See RUAN, Zhanjing
7156. ZHAO, Jianxiong
"Black Horse and Fish" (tr. by Dong Jiping). [Footwork] 90, p. 40.
"The Day Without Wind" (tr. by Dong Jiping). [Footwork] 90, p. 40.
7157. ZHAO, Qun
"A Winter Boat" (to my Grandfather, tr. of Li Xiaoyu). [PaintedB] (40/41) 90, p.
        54-55.
ZHEN, Gu
        See GU, Zhen
7158. ZHENG, Min
"Letter" (tr. by Elizabeth Balestrieri and Yafeng Bao). [PoetryC] (11:1) Spr 90, p.
        22.
ZHI, Yang
        See YANG, Zhi
ZHONG, Jin
        See JIN, Zhong
7159. ZHU, Lingbo
"Empty Seat" (tr. by Dong Jiping). [Footwork] 90, p. 41.
"White Night" (tr. by Dong Jiping). [Footwork] 90, p. 41.
ZI, Hai
        See HAI, Zi
7160. ZIEGER, Ulrich
"1965" (Selection: (7), tr. by Roderick Iverson). [PoetryUSA] (5:3) Fall 90, p. 21.
"1965" (Selections: 7, 18, tr. by Roderick Iverson). [Sulfur] (10:2, #27) Fall 90, p.
        92-94.
7161. ZIEROTH, Dale
"Accident." [MalR] (90) Spr 90, p. 24.
"Here on the Coast." [MalR] (90) Spr 90, p. 25.
"Meditation on Separation." [MalR] (90) Spr 90, p. 23.
"Phone Call." [MalR] (90) Spr 90, p. 22.
7162. ZIMMER, Paul
"A Light Riff for MSH" (with love from Zimmer). [Chelsea] (49) 90, p. 93-95.
"Thirteen Ways of Looking at the National Endowment for the Arts." [GettyR] (3:3)
        Sum 90, p. 447-451.
"Zimmer's Existential Year." [GettyR] (3:2) Spr 90, p. 407.
7163. ZIMMERMAN, Alois
"And So Forth." [Nimrod] (34:1) Fall-Wint 90, p. 132-133.
"Gulls." [Nimrod] (34:1) Fall-Wint 90, p. 131-132.
"Hunter's Moon." [Nimrod] (34:1) Fall-Wint 90, p. 134-135.
7164. ZIMMERMAN, Claudia
"Because There Was a Time" (tr. of Sándor Csoóri, w. Len Roberts). [ArtfulD]
        (18/19) 90, p. 23.
"Because There Was a Time" (tr. of Sandor Csoóri, w. Len Roberts). [CrabCR]
        (6:3) Spr 90, p. 10.
"Green Twig in My Hand" (Kezemben Zöld Ag, tr. of Sándor Csoóri, w. Len
        Roberts). [Plain] (10:3) Spr 90, p. 29.
"When" (tr. of Agnes Nemes Nagy, w. Len Roberts). [MidAR] (10:1) 90, p. 45.
7165. ZIMMERMAN, Irene
"Apple Picking: Eden Revisited." [ChrC] (107:31) 31 O 90, p. 989.
7166. ZIMMERMAN, Ken
"Bones." [TarRP] (30:1) Fall 90, p. 17.

7167. ZIMMERMAN, Lisa Horton
"The Day My Daughter Smeared the Car with Lipstick." [ChironR] (9:2) Sum 90, p. 20.
"How I See It" (for my sister). [FloridaR] (17:2) Fall-Wint 90, p. 61.
"Persian Gulf, January 25, 1991." [FloridaR] (17:2) Fall-Wint 90, p. 60.
7168. ZIMMERMAN, Ruth
"Inventory." [JINJPo] (12:1) Spr 90, p. 27-28.
7169. ZINKEL, Brian
"The Oxygen Fish." [KanQ] (22:1/2) Wint-Spr 90, p. 162.
7170. ZINNES, Harriet
"Light and Darkness." [Chelsea] (49) 90, p. 148-149.
"A Moment a Line Brecht and the Void." [Confr] (44/45) Fall 90-Wint 91, p. 187.
7171. ZIOLKOWSKI, Heidi
"Hey, Lady, We Don't Serve No Froufrou Coffee Here." [ChironR] (9:1) Spr 90, p. 21.
ZIQING, Zhang
See ZHANG, Ziqing
7172. ZIRLIN, Larry
"Anniversary." [HangL] (56) 90, p. 56.
"Press Check." [HangL] (56) 90, p. 58.
"Under the Tongue." [HangL] (56) 90, p. 57.
7173. ZISQUIT, Linda
"Choose." [Ploughs] (16:1) Spr-Sum 90, p. 7.
"Ethics of the Fathers." [Ploughs] (16:1) Spr-Sum 90, p. 8.
"A Modern Midrash." [Ploughs] (16:1) Spr-Sum 90, p. 6.
"Morning Exercise." [Ploughs] (16:1) Spr-Sum 90, p. 5.
7174. ZIVANCEVIC, Nina
"February." [LitR] (33:4) Sum 90, p. 421.
"March." [LitR] (33:4) Sum 90, p. 422.
7175. ZIZIK, Joel
"Hypoglycemia and the Need to Practice It." [JamesWR] (8:1) Fall 90, p. 8.
"Swallowing." [JamesWR] (8:1) Fall 90, p. 8.
7176. ZLATKES, Gwido
"Song of Betrayal" (6 poems, tr. by Maya Peretz, Stacy A. Klein and the author). [Screens] (2) 90, p. 52-55.
7177. ZOEGER, Kate
"Convalescence." [OnTheBus] (2:1, #5) Spr 90, p. 158.
"Feed." [OnTheBus] (2:1, #5) Spr 90, p. 159.
"The Man on the Pillow." [OnTheBus] (2:2/3:1, #6/7) Sum-Fall 90 Wint-Spr 91, p. 227-228.
7178. ZOLA, Jim
"Breaking & Entering." [Parting] (3:1) Sum 90, p. 31.
"Breaking & Entering." [Parting] (3:2) Wint 90-91, p. 7.
"Columbine Pass, August, 1983." [Parting] (3:1) Sum 90, p. 32.
"Columbine Pass, August, 1983." [Parting] (3:2) Wint 90-91, p. 8.
"Fish Stories." [Parting] (3:2) Wint 90-91, p. 28.
"Forecasting." [NegC] (10:2/3) 90, p. 74-75.
"Hotel Chipinique, August, 1984." [PassN] (11:2) Wint 90, p. 26.
"The Way We Travel." [HiramPoR] (47) Wint 90, p. 55.
7179. ZOLOTOW, Steve
"Why She Lost Interest in Men." [NewYorkQ] (42) Sum 90, p. 79.
7180. ZOLYNAS, A.
"Trompe d'Oeil." [OnTheBus] (2:1, #5) Spr 90, p. 160.
7181. ZONTELLI, Patricia
"Could This Be True?" (From a series of poems titled "Edith Jacobson Begins to Fly"). [KanQ] (22:1/2) Wint-Spr 90, p. 222.
"The Distant Flickering." [CumbPR] (10:1) Fall 90, p. 55-57.
"Reconciliation Viewed from Great Distance." [HiramPoR] (48/49) 90-91, p. 75.
"Salt." [Calyx] (12:3) Sum 90, p. 38-39.
7182. ZORACH, Rebecca
"Before the Fault Lines" (poem, monotypes and collographs, with Deborah Fass). [HarvardA] (125:1) S 90, p. 22-23.
"A Reconstruction." [HarvardA] (125:1) S 90, p. 24-25.
7183. ZORDANI, Bob
"Cover Letter." [Farm] (7:1) Spr 90, p. 33.
"My Strongest Man." [Farm] (7:1) Spr 90, p. 32.

513

"My Strongest Man." [NewEngR] (13:2) Wint 90, p. 203.
7184. ZORN, Marilyn
"St. Melania's Gift" (Based on Helen Waddell's translation of the 4th Century Desert
Fathers). [KanQ] (22:3) Sum 90, p. 124.
7185. ZUBER, Isabel
"Croning." [Poetry] (157:1) O 90, p. 25.
7186. ZUCKER, David
"Album." [Chelsea] (49) 90, p. 42-45.
7187. ZUKOFSHY, Louis
"Securer a bo? no sacred armpits lair hops as that he-goat's" (tr. of Catullus).
[Hudson] (43:2) Sum 90, p. 342.
7188. ZULAUF, Sander
"As Far as Einstein Goes." [Ometeca] (1:2/2:1) 89-90, p. 25.
7189. ZURITA, Raul
"A las Inmaculadas Llanuras." [Inti] (32/33) Otoño 90-Primavera 91, p. 214-215.
"/CIII/." [Inti] (32/33) Otoño 90-Primavera 91, p. 214.
"Las Espejeantes Playas." [Inti] (32/33) Otoño 90-Primavera 91, p. 215-216.
"Nieves del Aconcagua -- La Muerte --." [Inti] (32/33) Otoño 90-Primavera 91, p.
216-217.
"Las Playas de Chile X." [Inti] (32/33) Otoño 90-Primavera 91, p. 217-218.
"La Vida Nueva." [Inti] (32/33) Otoño 90-Primavera 91, p. 213-214.
7190. ZURLO, Tony
"Mallam Ibrahim." [Plain] (11:1) Fall 90, p. 26-27.
7191. ZWICKY, Jan
"Empty Houses." [Descant] (21:1, #68) Spr 90, p. 121-122.
"Grey Whales in Migration." [Descant] (21:1, #68) Spr 90, p. 123-124.
"Language Is Hands." [Descant] (21:1, #68) Spr 90, p. 119-120.
7192. ZYCHLINSKA, Rajzel
"Submarines" (tr. by Aaron Kramer). [Vis] (33) 90, p. 26.
7193. ZYDEK, Fredrick
"Black Gospel." [CrossCur] (9:2) Je 90, p. 121-122.
"Letter to the Young Poet Who Stole My Lines." [AntigR] (81/82) Spr-Sum 90, p.
215.
"Taking Highway 80 to Lincoln." [CharR] (16:1) Spr 90, p. 75.

Title Index

Titles are arranged alphanumerically, with numerals filed in numerical order before letters. Each title is followed by one or more author entry numbers, which refer to the numbered entries in the first part of the volume. Entry numbers are preceded by a space colon space (:). Any numeral which preceeds the space colon space (:) is part of the title, not an entry number. Poems with "Untitled" in the title position are entered under "Untitled" followed by the first line of the poem and also directly under the first line. Numbered titles are entered under the number and also under the part following the number.

$: 4738
.22 : 5596
I : 4870
I. Con Tal Que el Avestruz : 4865
I. Humanismo : 400
1 January 1990 : 5130
1. Sentences and Sensibility : 6326
1/ There Are No Others : 1286
I. Yeats was right: the old patterns can't hold : 2275
The 1st Time : 5844
1/0 = Infinity : 6711
1.4, 6.4 : 7046
1:25 a.m : 462
2:00 A.M : 6865
2 + 2 = A Hindu, Not 4 : 6663
2. Handy Words : 6326
2 Henry Miller Paintings and Etc : 841
II. Justicia Social : 400
II. Marinera : 4865
II. Morning, without Birds : 5291
2. Patron forgive us : 4963
II. The closure of an end-rhyme line stops : 2275
2/ The Four-Letter Word : 1286
2 Victims : 68
2nd Grade Romance : 6827
3/13/43 : 6475
#3. From the half-dark hall, abruptly : 2936, 4007
III. Metanoia : 400
3 Odes to Crones : 490
3 Sunsets at Hammonasset : 5256
3/ The Shuffle : 1286
3 Untitled: I wish you would cum back with your black hose. Bach seems to have been a rather happy man. It took a lot of courage of Xenophanes : 2741
4 A.M. : 2866
IV. Credo : 400
IV. In the flash bulb after shock of lightning : 5291
V : 2215
5 Short Rehearsals for a Poem (Pagan Nuptials) : 1944, 6632

V. We have loved each other : 883, 4875
6:00 a.m. in Tegucigalpa : 179
6 A.M. : 807
VI. Cuando la calma vuelva : 2167
6 Down: Shakespearean King : 6123
6 Notes for a Mazurka : 4527
VI Variations : 14, 325
VII Canto de la Piedra : 1936
The 8:48 : 5757
VIII. I could ask him if it's the sun he wants : 883, 4875
8 Invenciones: Paul Klee, Dibujos Verbales : 7137
9/9/88 : 2524
9/20/88 — 9/2/89 : 5052
9 of Cups, Motherpeace Tarot : 2053
10. Hunger/for a sky without a top : 5068
10 Years on Acid, 20 Years on King Street : 2809
11. Am I forgetting that until recently : 1582, 5098
11:42 p.m., May 07, 1989 : 1335
XII/4 : 6631
XIII. Allá en las Cañas : 5659
13 February 1984-90 : 5130
13 Ways of Looking at an Unidentified Flying Woman : 2398
13th & Aloha : 2566
13/16 : 96
15. He riffs his soul : 5068
15 March 1987 : 5130
XV. We are they that search for bees in the fold of a curtain : 883, 4875
XVI. Detrás de todo muro que amarillo : 5659
16 Dolomite appletree icons people the hill : 1464
16. Lil Bro tells us : 5068
16 March 1987 : 5130
17. My mother's last request is for an other : 5068
17. No necesita legitimarnos la épica : 3854
17 poems : 2544, 4333
17 Years Old : 4909
17th Sunday in Ordinary Time : 1975
18. Story and tales within tales : 5068

The 20-Year Headache : 4689
20th Century Disease : 3118
21 Feb '65, San Francisco : 2656
XXII. De una isla : 2167
xxii. Tell me again what the oppressed look like
    : 3329
25. Blinded, they march on, the soldiers of Tsar
    Samuil : 1582, 5098
26. The only loves they've known longer : 1774
27. For a moment she does not feel : 1774
28. I looked in her mirror : 1774
29. And the hatred : 6396, 6507
29. I become more intimate with the dead :
    1582, 5098
29. The flies that had been driven mad : 1774
29. Y el odio : 6396
30 : 5026
XXX. But whom to blame : 3111, 5999
30. Cáncer enmarañada primavera : 6396
30. Cancer entangled spring : 6396, 6507
30 Day Evaluation : 1456
31. Abortion of a Poem in a Public Office :
    6396, 6507
31. Aborto de Poema en Oficina Pública : 6396
31 December 1984: The Four Season's Bar [sic]
    : 4765
31 October : 322
32. Birth II : 6396, 6507
32. Nacimiento II : 6396
33. Aquella amiga desesperación : 6396
33. Be prepared, be prepared! : 1582, 5098
33. That friend — despair : 6396, 6507
34. Abres sí túnel : 6396
34. You open yes tunnel : 6396, 6507
40 : 1844
42. You set out to measure the world with your
    step : 1582, 5098
42nd and Broadway : 6251
44 Concrete Poems : 4664
48 Hours with a Loaded Gun That Never Went
    Off in My Hands : 307
51. A prisoner in the solitary cell of this body :
    1582, 5098
A '57 Chevy in 1969 : 4620
#100 and 2 : 6219
100 Flowers : 2428
The 100th Princess : 4356
/CIII/ : 7189
108 1/2 ° : 2009
#114, Not Jasper Johns : 6219
115. The spider on this curb : 4973
125. Oh, it was a cold day : 67, 2778
145. Este, que ves, engaño colorido : 1358
147. Rosa divina que en gentil cultura : 1358
156. Portia, what passion, what blind pain :
    1358, 4601
156. Que pasión, Porcia, qué dolor tan ciego :
    1358
162. Her loom as if some wounds : 4973
164 East 72nd Street : 4310
164. This evening, my dear, when I was
    speaking to you : 1358, 4601
165. You become expert — the stream : 4973
176. These holes limping closer to my arms :
    4973
207. Motionless, covering what's in back : 4973
208. To wake at dawn : 67, 2778
212. And now you are depressed and despon-
    dent : 67, 2778
215. This ditch no matter how haggard : 4973
219. It has nothing to do with braille : 4973
234. What did they see that my cheeks can't
    bear the weight : 4973
235. The blood this band-aid vaguely wrings :
    4973
242. The oldest shout is orange : 4973
#286. We live without feeling a country beneath
    us : 2936, 4007
289. Betrayal : 67, 2778
301. This window sweetening the air : 4973
#303. And this, what street is this? : 2936, 4007
329. With those hefty walls a bank will save
    forever : 4973
335. Again a lull across my cheek : 4973
#367. Armed with the eyesight of the narrow
    wasps : 2936, 4007
398. Leave it to the lumber company : 4973
402. Again the sky rubbing against my legs :
    4973
541. This is how I am. I wish you another : 67,
    2778
601 Milford Point Road : 6106
*856 : 2179
1751 : 2532, 2922, 7106
1832, Kona Wind, Honolulu : 120
1845, Parnelly Pierce Draws the Night-
    Blooming Cereus : 120
1848 : 5302, 5559
1910 : 4464
1919 : 5302
1929 : 4086, 4671
The 1929 Tuscaloosa Shout : 2435
1930 : 6564
1932-   : 4921
1939 : 5933, 6387
1942 : 4600
1943 : 5828
1948: Dr. Williams, Listening to His Own Heart
    : 6374
1952 : 3163
1955: James Dean Does a TV Public Service
    Announcement about Speeding : 4286
1956: The Horizon : 4726
1961 : 6877
1965 : 3064, 7160, 7160
1966 : 1513, 3894
1969 : 1497
1970 : 3009
1989 : 3438, 4671
1990 : 1190
1990's Fantasy, or, Song for One's Self : 2401
1999 : 6013
2527th Birthday of the Buddha : 3466
108,000 Ways of Making Love : 6300
A Este Cuerpo Enamorado : 4493
A las Inmaculadas Llanuras : 7189
A Marc Chagall : 1794
A.M./P.M. : 3890

A Ses Débuts : 3682
A/Typical Marriage : 3646
A un Hombre : 4031
Ab:Prophetics : 508
Ab:Prophetics #9 : 508
Abandoned & Etc! : 2595
Abandoned Houses South of Stafford : 5608
The Abandoned Pharmacy : 333, 4105
Abandoned Sailboat : 157
The Abandonment of Poetry : 1514
Abanico : 5882
Abbie Hoffman (R.I.P.) : 6139
Abduction : 7112
Les abeilles seules remuent : 1691
An Abidance : 879
Abishag the Shunammite : 871
Aboard the *Friendship Rose*, Bequia Channel :
    1548
Aborted Fetus : 1458
Abortion of a Poem in a Public Office : 6396,
    6507
Aborto de Poema en Oficina Pública : 6396
About : 3418
About Dying : 5078
About Fathers : 245
About His Grandchildren : 3195
About Myself and Time : 244
About Strange Lands & People : 4712
About Summer : 1824
About the 95 Minutes Spent at Studio 'C' :
    2894
About the Dogs of Dachau : 3083
About to Get Up : 6690
About Words : 3612
About Your Christmas Card Picturing You and
    Your Husband : 5207
Above Ann Arbor : 7001
Above Cuckmere Haven : 5523
Above Salmon Brook, The Darkness : 4765
Above the Rhône, Fog Coming In : 5176
Above the Things : 3547, 4586, 5379
Above Wahiawa : 6132
Ab:Prophetics : 508
Ab:Prophetics #9 : 508
Abres sí túnel : 6396
The Abridged Cat : 6788
Absence : 3120, 3355, 4312
Absence of Poetry : 5118
Absentee Landlord : 2265
Absolutely : 446
Absolution : 6960
Abstract : 1332
Abstraction : 4888
Absurd, Idaho : 2104
Abundant Paradigm : 467
Acacio Araujo's Pig : 6407
Academia : 2992
Academic Exercise: Set of Sapphics : 5252
Academic Freedom : 4359
An Academic Reading : 588
The Academy Prisoners : 6435
Acapulco Holiday : 5696
Accepted : 841
Accepting the Body : 2607

Accident : 2706, 4175, 7161
The Accident : 1323, 1401, 1436, 3762, 5675
Accident of Inheritance : 203
The Accident of Water : 5928
The Accident on Peakskill Mountain : 2681
Accident Report : 3530
Accidental Eulogy for the Human Race : 4892
An Accidental Is a Migrant : 2372
Accidentals : 2706
Accidente : 3143
According to Neo-Physics : 4170
The Accordionist : 3426
Accumulations : 5747
The Achill Woman : 616
Achromatic Sketches : 6288
Acid Trip : 490
Acknowledgement : 1787
Acknowledgment : 7060
An Acre of Grass : 6488
The Acrobats : 3207
Across Landscape : 3851
Across the Bay the Saxony Is Burning : 994
Across the Line : 5862
Across These Landscapes of Early Darkness :
    4086
Act 1 : 6269
Actaeon : 3287, 5361
Actions : 5194
The Actress and Her Second-Hand Saxophone :
    4406
Acts of God : 4814
Acts of Power : 6224
Acts of Vanishing : 2540
Acupuncture : 2494
Ad Hominem : 5801
Adagios of Islands [Words for Caliban] : 5720
Adam : 1808, 2388, 6004
Adam Has Finally Understood! : 5650
Adamo Ha Capito! : 5650
Adam's Return : 7045
Adam's Song, and Mine : 863
Adam's Wife : 3270, 6093
Adan : 2388
Adaptation : 285
Adapting to Land : 2133
Addiction : 88
Adding Things Up : 3694
Additional Evidence of the Onset of Aging :
    1613
Address : 1594
Adidas : 837
Adios Zarathustra : 6603
Adjustments : 427
Admiring Your Sensibility : 4267
Adolescence : 465, 4073, 6780
An Adolescent Poet Dreams of Love : 5923
Adolf Hitler : 6005
The Adopted Child : 813, 814, 2526
Adoption : 5524, 7112
Adoptivbarnet : 2526
The Adulteress : 5828
The Adulterous Farmwife : 6922
Adultery : 126, 3032, 5852
Advanced Research : 5816

Advection : 5384
Advent, Epiphany : 3149
The Advent of the Ordinary : 3454
The Adventure into Someone Else's Life : 106
The Advertising Man : 1780, 7006
Advice : 6150
Advice for a Mother Looking for her Child after
    a Day of Unrest : 243
Advice for Americans : 6190
Advice Given Freely from a Dream : 2029
Advice to a Mercenary : 3391
Advice to the Lovelorn : 2468
Advice to the Poet : 2191, 4107
Advocate & Enthusiast : 2867
Aeolian : 999
Aerobics : 3369
Aéroplane : 1867
Aesthetics : 3032, 7107
The Aesthetics of a Chicago Winter : 2928
Affair : 5677
The Affect of Elms : 2256
Affirmation Against Critics : 4260
Afflatus : 1735
Afraid of Myself : 1764
Africa Sunrise : 3420
African Child : 6366
African Jack Benny : 1490
After a Conversation on Rilke, Darwin, and
    Rembrandt's Self-Portrait As an Old Man
    : 6436
After a Lost Original : 5804
After a Party : 6967
After a Week in the Rockies : 4179
After All : 161, 1319, 4025, 4070, 6098
After an Adoration : 419
After an Afternoon Showing of Laurel and
    Hardy's Brats : 4937
After Apollo : 6995
After Being Toothless : 1625, 7154
After Being Wanted : 1417
After Christoph Hein's The Distant Lover :
    1770
After Divorcing : 5875
After Drinking Chardonnay on a Hot Summer
    Night : 4300
After Each Collision : 4236
After Emergency Surgery : 1142
After Failing to End My Celibacy I Mix
    Metaphors : 4066
After Gethsemane : 1991
After Going Down to His Kitchen at Seven :
    6010
After He Moved Up North : 6245
After Her First Piano Recital My Daughter with
    Unusual Grace Takess My Arm and We
    Walk Home . . . : 5375
After I Sent the Poem I Wrote About My Sister
    to Her Thinking She'd Be High : 3780
After-Image : 6256
After January 2 : 2258
After John Donne : 5377
After Leafing Through a Book of Classical
    Sculpture : 680
After-Life : 5866

After-Lives : 880
After Looking Up Lapwing in the Encyclopedia
    : 4914
After Love : 2806, 3118, 5810
After Many Years : 284, 5271
After March : 484, 1250, 6214
After Melville : 5820
After Ontario : 1218
After Puccini : 3349
After Rain : 6282
After Reading About the Famine : 4115
After Reading Marguerite Duras, We Celebrate
    Electricity : 2665
After Reading Shu Ting : 4209
After Reading That Joanna Burden Has Grown
    Too Old : 192
After Reading Thomas James (1946-1973) :
    5858
After Scattering My Mother's Ashes : 2436
After Staring at an Owl : 5039
After Supper : 7114
After Surgery: A Friend Sends Bird Sighting
    from the Boston Globe : 6309
After the Arrest : 3884
After the Blizzard : 3169
After the Blues : 2345
After the Canoe Trip: How We Leave the
    Boundary Waters : 245
After the Ceremony : 3287, 5361
After the Chiropractor : 2643
After the Creation : 2104, 6054, 6612
After the Earthquake in Armenia : 3171
After the Eyes Have It : 179
After the Fall : 4416
After the Fall Equinox : 2653
After the Fall of Saigon : 4179
After the Flight Home from Saigon : 4179
After the Flood : 732, 3687
After the Fog Lifted : 2483
After the Funeral : 233, 1782
After the Glacier: Lascaux : 1593
After the Imagists : 3819
After the Last Practice : 2866
After the Last Quarrel : 7049
After the Plague : 4756
After the Poetry Chapbook Was Published :
    4285
After the Prom : 6389
After the Rain : 1309
After the Shaking Stops : 3831
After the Spanish Grand Prix Jean-Pierre
    Jabouille Hangs Up His Helmet : 5220
After the Storm : 1289, 1314
After the Treaty Between the Athenians and the
    Lacedaemonians Was Broken : 3287, 5361
After the War : 1712, 4488, 5992
After They Let You Walk with Me Three Hours
    in the Rain If We Promised to Stay on
    Hospital Grounds : 5693
After Trakl's 'Autumn Evening': Esther
    Ponders the Shadows, Denies the Dead :
    6810
After Walking the Breakwater : 6848
After You Left : 5956

Afterbirth : 2702
Afterlife : 579, 592, 1393
The Afterlife : 1213, 2457
An Afterlife, 1953-1988 : 5130
Aftermath : 417
Aftermath, 1956 : 5512
Afternoon : 1350, 6375
Afternoon in Automobile : 6375, 7057
The Afternoon, the Neighborhood : 1834
Afterwards : 2642, 3064, 3878
Again a brush sealing this boat : 4973
Again a lull across my cheek : 4973
Again Consider the Wind : 2725
Again Ernie's Hand on the Hammer : 6911
Again I stare closely at the sea : 6830
Again the sky rubbing against my legs : 4973
Against Broken Colors : 5230
Against Fate : 2860
Against My Dreams : 6228
Against the Impenetrable Blue Light : 1238
Against the Stars : 2426
Against the Text 'Art Is Immortal' : 1701
Against the Urban Night : 2928
Against Unruly Ants : 72, 5520
Against Whitman : 5559
Agapé : 3381
The Agave Would Know : 4974
Age : 6759
The Age of Anti-Art : 3372
The Age of Miracles : 5101
The Age of Reason : 2007
The Age of the Sea : 376, 4979
Aged As You Would : 3482
Aging : 3081
Aging: a Sestina : 6200
Agnes Smedley with Mao Zedong in China,
    1934 : 1269
Agostinho Neto : 20
Ague : 1363, 5379
Ahab : 5980
Ahead : 6117
Aid and Comfort : 3157
Aida : 651, 5151
Air : 6154
The Air : 232
Air Conditioning : 2104, 3519
Air Mail : 1643
Air Show : 4420
Airplane : 748, 1867
Airports : 270
The air's full of fumes : 244, 3011, 3877
Aisling : 1488
Akkorára Már : 4811
Al Comienzo : 4589
Los Alamos : 6878, 6915
Alarm : 666, 3117
Alban Berg : 623
Albania & the Death of Enver Hoxha : 95
Albert : 2467
Albino : 3466
Albright : 599
Album : 7186
Albumblatt : 4712
Alchemist : 2713

The Alchemists : 5122
Alchemy : 3556
Alcmene, Housewife, Welcomes Her Husband
    Home from a Hard Day at Work : 5530
Alcott's Axe : 6238
Ålderdomshem : 645
Aldrig Trodde Jag : 206
The Aleph & Anselm Kiefer: Pieces Toward a
    Parable : 1921
Alexander Isaevich Solzhenitsyn : 2616
Alexander the Conqueror : 1243
Alfa the Dog : 6300
Alferd Packard : 2482
Alfred and the Abortion : 6579
Algeria : 4926
Algún Día : 639
Alheias e Nossas : 2356, 4284
The Alibi : 4117
Alice, North Dakota : 6174
Alien : 1966
Alien Encounters : 3050
Aliens in Southern California : 6674
All alone : 4987
All By Herself : 3709
All Canal Boat Cruises Start Here : 6177
All Cousins : 4101
All Earth Makes Allowance for the Plausible :
    4582
All for Love : 5300
All for My Baby : 462
All Giving Is Not Kindness : 321
All God! : 2595
All Her Pretty Ones : 3913
All I Can Hand You : 3596
All Is Not Lost at Sea : 1123
All It Ever Did Was Lie : 6718
All New! As Sure As the Moon Moves Oceans :
    5028
All Night : 6706
All of It : 1831
All Rivers Flow South : 1639
All Saints' Day : 1914, 2335
All Souls' Day : 1258, 1307
All Soul's Day : 1346
All Souls' Day : 3785
All Souls' Day, Blessing the Graves : 2727
All Souls' Morning : 1279
All That Jazz : 375, 2769
All That Surrounds Me Here This Night : 1608
All That You Can Be : 232
All the Breaths : 193
All the Good Women Have Been : 1613
All the Ingredients for a Poem : 5861
All the King's Men : 2639
All the Odors : 1200
All the Pathos, All the Triumph : 6040
All the Same : 2104, 3519
All the Stars : 84, 6642, 6643
All the Things : 7028
All the Variables : 4086
All the Walls in Gubbio Will One Day Con-
    verge : 540
All There Was : 6540
All Things Being Equal : 1594

All Those Hours Alone in the Dark : 5471
All Through March : 1377
All Through Winter : 1377
All Ye Need to Know : 6902
All You Do to Call : 2893
All You Really Wanted to Do : 3754
All Yours or Nothing Doing : 1286
Allá en las Cañas : 5659
Allegory : 264, 5873
Allegory of a Memory and His Man : 6951
Aller et Retour : 4316
Alley Rats : 7098
Alligator : 500
Alma Mater : 2953
An Almanac : 6563
Almost : 4383
Almost Always : 2445
Almost But Not Quite an Academic Break-
     through : 4530
Almost Home : 5594
Almost Nothing : 4751
Almourol : 3750, 4803
The Aloha Grange : 4345
Aloha Shirt : 6132
Alone : 4398
Aloneness (1926) : 5459
Along history, forever : 5521
Along Ocean Parkway in Brooklyn : 3261
Along the Common Road One Cattail : 742
Along the Dead Sea : 4671
Along the Japanese Coast : 3623
Along the Platte : 2711
Along the Route of the Donner Party : 1058
Alphabet : 2104, 6054, 6612
Alphonse : 5828
Already in 1927 : 2577
Al's Poem, As Written by One of His Students :
     5913
Also Frankenstein : 611
Altair : 3588, 5014, 6220
The Altar Needlework : 6361
Altar of the Visible : 593
Altered States: The Lilies : 1596
Alternate Insomnia : 5406
Alternate Island II : 1624
An Alternative : 4960
Although : 2291
Altitude : 1526, 4046
Always, More Light : 4179
Alzheimer's : 2236
Alzheimers : 5008
Am : 1450
Am I forgetting that until recently : 1582, 5098
A.M./P.M. : 3890
Amarillo : 1556
Amaya : 1240
Amazing Events : 3437
Ambitions of Men : 4655
Ambrosia : 3167
Ambush : 142, 6292
An Ame : 3234
Amelia Earhart : 228
America : 946, 3032, 6681, 6985, 6985
America Enters the 1990's : 1764

America Farts at Commercials : 1151
The American above Avon : 5831
American Authors Before 1865 : 6790
American Dreams : 5621
American Game: Managua, 1985 : 4097
American Gothic : 2211, 6042
American Hero : 1835
An American in Paris, 1984 : 1965
An American in Trapani : 5650
American Landscape Painters in Rome : 3076
American Lit: Kerouac : 7001
American Lit: No, She Said : 7001
American Lit: She'd Rather Read the Funnies :
     7001
American Lit: The Turn of the Screw : 7001
American Lit: William Meredith : 7001
American Literature in Context : 193
American Madness : 4466
American Mystic : 660
American Rain : 5942
The American Religion : 3701
American Scene : 1296
Amid the green : 2151, 3759
Amidst Stones : 453, 926
Amikor : 4586
Amit's Song : 5806
Amnesia : 5962
Amnesiac : 5593
Amnesiac River : 329, 4413, 7057
Amnesty Orange : 839
Amniotic : 4211
Among Black Trees : 3268, 5097
Among Children : 3746
Among Fields of Shocked Corn : 173
Among Struggles Between Life and Death :
     5025
Among the Mermaids : 5619
Amor Fati: Because We Own Nothing : 5960
Amos, How We Found You : 6371
Amsterdam Avenue Poem : 4857
Amtrak : 2966
Anahola Store : 915
Analgesic Balm : 3425
Analogue : 2688
The Analysis of Beauty : 944
Anastasia, Purdy Group Home : 3116
Anatomy : 3025
Anatomy of a River : 5822
Anatomy Student : 5249
Anaximander : 5217
Anaximander, 610-546? B.C. : 6801
The Ancestor Tree : 31
Ancestors : 542
Anchorage : 2453
An Ancient Alphabet : 954
Ancient Beliefs : 1947
An Ancient Diary : 348, 4613, 5650
Ancient Eskimo Masks : 2770
Ancient Hawaiian Village : 1001
Ancient Roman Roads : 3518
Ancient Songs : 110
And : 1813
And a Happy New Year : 6873
And a Thousand Miles Behind : 1162

And After a Night : 5441
And another one is gone : 725
And Blind-Man's-Bluff : 6958
And Counting : 4585
And Dream Is Quilt Is Comforter : 3834
And Even the Republic Must Have an End :
    6355
And from the suffering you gave me : 244,
    3011, 6353
And I on the Cosmic : 3106, 4626
And Inside Me a Voice Tells Me : 14
And Me in My First Suit : 1611
And now that moved it cannot : 924, 6632
And now you are depressed and despondent :
    67, 2778
And on this table : 4973
And Over It Was : 1442
And So Forth : 7163
And So I Went Forth : 2233, 3197, 6806
And so the day drops by, the horizon draws :
    6533
And Stands Reflected in the Mirror Across the
    Room : 1712, 4488, 5992
And Tell Sad Stories : 2964
And the dead can't wait, they crouch : 4973
And the hatred : 6396, 6507
And the Road Has Dust in Its Throat : 5484
And the Ship Sails On : 529
And the sun in ashes : 4973
And Then, Her Mother's Dresses Torn Out of
    the Closet : 500
And There Be Monsters : 4053
And — there is your you : 5573
And These Beds : 2677
And this, what street is this? : 2936, 4007
And to See the City Again : 407, 1037
And Today in That Wine Bar on the Corner :
    1982, 4609
And we'll head for the horror of loveless beds :
    748, 1275
And Yet, I'm Ready to Return Again : 5650
And You Don't Ask : 3270, 6093
Andares del Subsuelo : 2263
Andre Chenier Writes His Last Poem, 1794 :
    1269
Andrenaline Nights : 4794, 5995
Andrew : 3197, 4603
Andy Warhol : 2451
Andy Warhol's Marilyn : 6571
Angel : 383, 744, 1393
The Angel : 2798, 4455
An Angel Considers the Naming of Meat : 6936
Angel in the House : 4622, 6546
Angel Movie : 813, 814, 5064
Angel of Bees : 1352
Angel of Mercy : 1352
Angel of Slapstick : 1552
The Angel of the Situation : 3064, 3494
Angel Vomit : 4005
Los Angeles: 12th and Olive : 1457
Los Angeles, Fin de Siècle : 5901
Los Angeles / Southern California : 4736
Angelina, My Noni's Name, Means Messenger
    : 7141

Angels : 5967, 6164
Angels of the Air : 3045
Änglafilm : 5064
The Angler : 6968
Angles : 4339
An Anglo-Saxon Garden : 1962
Angola (Louisiana) : 2656
The Angry Mother : 7062
The Angry Poem : 1339
Anguish : 3925
Anhinga : 3075
Anima : 1726, 2470
The Animal and Mineral Orders : 6503
Animal Bodies in Virginia : 3038
Animals : 2341, 3363
The Animals : 2
Animals — Especially a Squirrel on
    Grandfather's Far Hill : 416
Animate Road : 3022
Anita, a New Hire on the Line : 1429
Ann Marie : 3780
Anna : 6996
Anna Livia Plurabelle to James Joyce : 6770
Anna's Hummingbird : 1304
Anna's Mirror : 3982
Anne : 6154
Anne Frank Huis : 417
Annie : 195, 3896
Annie's Doll : 1161
Anniversary : 1300, 2216, 2454, 4901, 7172
The Anniversary : 3118, 3788
Anniversary Poem : 1221
Announcement : 1536, 3533
Annual Doorway : 1473, 6632
Annual Tribute : 6174
Annunciation at the Beach : 3458
An Anointing : 4521
Anonymous : 4280
(Anonymous poem) : 77, 214, 437, 467, 675,
    711, 1407, 1411, 2050, 2307, 2416, 3315,
    4363, 4397, 5285, 5794, 6297, 6823,
    7035, 7143, 7147
Anorexia : 3548
Anotaciones en un Libro de Nietzsche : 6631
Another Autumn : 263
Another Birthday — Falling the Seventy Stories
    : 6016
Another Crisis : 3637
Another Death : 3120, 5250, 7138
Another Example: Visconti : 158, 3750
Another for My Father : 271
Another Geography : 4490
Another Gift From the Sea : 943
Another Hour : 4768
Another House: Wasp Affair : 4892
Another Hunger : 2579
Another Kimono : 1768
Another Kind of a Rhinoceros : 2592
Another Last Chance Bar : 5386
Another Man : 2577
Another Mexico : 184
Another Myth : 3176
Another One That Won't Tell : 2305
Another Place : 4312

Another Saint Lucy : 4554
Another Spring : 5016
Another State : 6664
Another Weather System : 4838
Another World : 5588
Anrufung des Grossen Bären : 284
The Answer : 435, 4180, 6829
An Answer for My Mother : 691
Answer to 'The Suicide' : 2289
Answering Back : 4639
The Answering Machine : 244, 3011, 3431, 5057
Answering Nietzsche : 6998
Antarctica : 4562
Antarctica Considers Her Explorers : 24
Ante un Viejo Octogenario de Dakota del Sur : 6582
Anthem : 2688, 3127, 5557
Anthem: Love and the Antipodes : 839
Anthony (1946-1966) : 1460
The Anthropic Cosmological Principle : 1521
Anti-Clockwise 1 : 18
Anti-Clockwise 2 : 18
Anticlimax : 4822
Antigone : 2289, 3987, 6066
Antipodes (1969 and on) : 5130
Antique : 5581
Antique Mirror, Detroit Institute of Arts : 4198
Antique Shop : 368
Antique Store, Pécs, Hungary : 5379
Antithesis : 132
The Antithetical Movement of Post-Production : 1146
Anton Bruckner : 2380, 3066, 7129
Antonio : 3699
Ants : 3936
Anxiety : 3612
Anxious About the Streak : 15
Any Excuse : 597, 6452
Anyone But You : 6767
Anyone's Life : 1975
Anyone's Relation : 2628
Anywhere : 829, 6395
Anywhere But Here : 4338, 6977
Aoi : 6117
Apariciones en un Panel de Computador : 6631
The Apartment : 266
Apathy : 3931
Aperture : 3951
Aphasia: The Breakdown of Language : 2096
Aplomb : 232
Apocalypse : 3643, 4737, 5379, 6565
The Apocalyptic Horses of the North Shore : 4296
The Apocrypha of Liana : 1145
Apocryphal Fathers : 3937
Apolitical Intellectuals : 1022, 5200
Apologia : 2147
Apologia to the Back of Our Necks : 1765
Apology : 2149, 6124
The Apostrophe to Tragedy : 6272
Apotheosis : 6596
An Appalachian Town: Points of Definition : 2581

Appetite : 1105, 5764
The Application : 5813
Apple Blossoms : 68
Apple Picking: Eden Revisited : 7165
Apple Pie : 6760
An Apple Tree for Osip Mandelstam : 6770
Apples : 3699, 6343
Apples on Your Bookshelf : 5318
The Appliances Delivery-Man : 4600
The Appointment : 2130
Apprentice : 5784
The Apprentice Dreams of Promotion : 6224
The Approach : 5634
The Approach of Winter : 1260
An Approach to the Sea — Illumination : 1058
Approaches to Crete : 6669
Approaching a Significant Birthday, He Peruses The Norton Anthology of Poetry : 2529
Approaching a Solstice : 6050
Approaching Antarctica : 1121
Approaching Middle Age : 5618
An Appropriate Song : 3116
An Appropriate Target : 3369
Approximate Desires : 5767
Aprendiendo a Cantar : 4749
L'Apres-Midi : 3011
April : 435, 529, 1085, 3386, 3534, 4180, 7042
April 2-3 1985 Aboriginal Rights Conference : 4399
April 14 and Warner McIntosh Is Dead : 6264
April Fools' Day, New York State : 767
April in the Bay : 7082
April Is the Cruelest Month : 4457
April Pink Moon : 3780
April Snow : 6016
Aquamarine : 1425, 6556
Aquarium at San Sebastian, Spain : 4679
Aquarius Pouring It On : 1146
Aquella amiga desesperación : 6396
Aquí Cae Mi Pueblo : 5435
Aquí Es la Tierra : 899
Aquinas on Beauty : 6686
Aquos : 4991
Är Stilla Nu, Sitter Vid Runda Bordet : 5064
Arahova : 1113
Aran, Aisling : 4013
Arapaima : 6880
An Arbor : 2459
Arbor Vitae : 2712
The Arborist : 6621
The Arc : 4482
Arcade: The Search for a Sufficient Landscape : 5190
Arcadian Wall : 6524, 6830
Arcanum : 53
Archaeology : 7039
The Archaeology of Dreams : 6372
Archangel : 56
Archeology : 734
Archeology Professor, Emeritus : 783
Archer's Hope : 4256
Archery Lesson : 2120
Archetypes of the Collective Unconscious : 2909

Archilochos : 1246
Archipelago for a Friend Dying : 4693
The Architect of Sushi : 6563
Ardella : 5022
Are the Lives of the Lovers Altered? : 5828
Arena : 5882
Aretha on MTV : 6825
The Argument : 1145, 2123
An Argument Against Jumping Off a Balcony :
     2586
The Argument Needs, and Shall Receive : 5948
Arguments of Everlasting : 3305
Aria for This Listening Area : 5061
Ariadne's Thread : 3774
Arianrhod from the Overdoes : 3064, 4894
Ariel : 4562
Ariel Later : 6012
Arise Ye Prisoners of Starvation : 3726
Arising from the Sea : 2644
Aristocracy : 371, 2808
Arizona : 5858
Ark : 6706
Ark of Triumph : 4806
Ark: The Ramparts (Arches I-XVIII) : 3175
Arlen : 6169
The Arm : 260
Armadillo : 3219
Armagnac : 537
Armatures : 4165
Armed with the eyesight of the narrow wasps :
     2936, 4007
Armistice Day, Reading Aeschylus : 2756
The Army Corps of Engineers Have Come and
     Gone, the Cabin Is Gone, the Trees, Acres,
     Everything : 4700
Arnold : 4470
Around the Summer Table : 6635
The Arrangement : 3289
An arrangement of prisms and triangles : 5222
Arranging Space : 2498, 3445, 5874, 6220
The Array of Orthodoxy : 5396
Arrested Motion : 2505
The Arrival : 4782
Arriving at Anchorage International Airport :
     4771
Ars Poetica : 640, 1536, 2023, 2623, 3197,
     4052, 5112, 5617
Arshile Gorky Avoids the War : 1951
Arshille Gorky: Last Works, Starspray I and II :
     3244
Arson : 5037
Art : 4101, 6088
Art & Imagination in the New World : 1169
Art and Life : 4198
Art and the Masses : 4892
Art Catalogue #4 : 1143
Art de la Poesie : 628
Art Exhibit — Minnesota : 5715
Art Is Doing: A Bowl : 741
An Art Lesson with Aunt Gracie : 3662
The Art of Amateur Photography : 2784
The Art of Painting : 5173
The Art of Poetry : 628, 5588
The Art of Robbery : 5757

The Art of Seeing : 970
The Art of Talking Indian Art Shows : 182
The Art of Tragedy : 6779
The Art of Translation : 1308
Art Reflecting Life? : 490
Artichoke Hearts : 3328
Articulation of a Still Life : 2168
Artifact : 4244
Artifacts : 1234
Artifice : 2625, 4121
Artificial Intelligence : 3418
Artificial Light : 864
The Artist : 4008
The Artist As Cripple : 4206
Artist Loft Party : 2684
The Artistry of Teeth : 4963
The Artists Airlifted, Leningrad 1941 : 5302
The Artists' and Models' Ball : 777
The Artist's Lady : 2412
Artist's Proof : 5190
Artknot 17 : 6693
Artknot 21 : 6693
Artknot 22 : 6693
Artknot 23 : 6693
Artknot 24 : 6693
Artknot 25 : 6693
Artknot 26 : 6693
As a child in the tub, thinking the stall shower
     looked like swans : 5434
As A Child, Sleepless : 6005
As Always : 2781
As Change : 5840
As Columbus Would Have It, the Earth Like a
     Pear : 2027
As Far as Einstein Goes : 7188
As god is my lover : 5463
As How Come : 7122
As I Write : 3781
As If Australia : 3873
As if hinted by distant mountains : 435, 1625
As If in Child's Play : 1300, 2454
As in a Film : 3516, 3696
As it was before : 2379, 6830
As Long As : 3053
As Long as You Can : 1035, 6397
As Promise Is Related to Fulfillment : 1565
As the Crow Flies : 163
As the Sun Comes Up in Nebraska : 6609
As We Drove : 6170
Ascension : 4709, 5247
Asclepius : 3287, 5361
Ash Tuesday : 2281
Ash Wednesday : 3126, 4891, 5553
Ashford Station : 4209
Ashlar Facings / Pink Rose : 5350
Ashtray : 2164
Ashtrays : 1192
Asking to Be Useful Somewhere Near the End :
     1458
Asleep in the Forest : 836
Aspects of Play : 3959
Asphalt Cigar : 1243
Asphodel : 2928
Aspic Surmise : 3945

Aspirations : 5571
Aspiring to Music : 6162
The Assassination of John Lennon as Depicted
    by the Madame Tussaud Wax Museum,
    Niagara Falls, Ontario, 1987 : 7010
The Assassinations of Robert Goulet as
    Performed by Elvis Presley: Memphis,
    1968 : 7010
The Assassins : 1473, 6628
Assembly Line : 3407, 5860
Assertion : 4380, 6081
Assignment : 2083
Assisi and Perugia, Late March : 3220
The Associate : 5908
Assumption : 6705
An Assumption : 5431
Assumptions : 3651
Assurance : 2295, 2947
Astarte : 214
Asthma : 1704
The Asthma Revenge : 1966
Astounded Souls : 723
Astronomical Phenomena I Have Known : 3744
Astronomy : 736
Astronomy Lesson : 3086, 3486, 4296
Asylum : 2979
The Asylum at Seacliff : 5224
The Asymptotic World : 3794
At 8 Above : 5082
At 64, Talking Without Words : 4560
At 81 : 2957
At 30,000 Feet: Note to My Daughter : 3093
At a Bookstore in the Metropolis : 5998
At a Border Crossing : 3805, 6977
At a Crossing, Somewhere in Ulster : 354
At a Crosswalk : 1680
At a Motel in Summer : 1577
At a time when I was without love : 271, 653
At an Outdoor Cafe : 813, 814, 5293
At an Unknown Altitude : 579
At Aqua Aqaba : 2837
At Bay : 1709
At Berry Time : 5818
At Chicago Airport : 6070
At Dawn : 1536, 2023
At Daybreak : 2104, 3519
At Donkey Butte : 249
At Dusk : 651, 1298, 5151
At Eighty-Five : 765
At Evening : 705, 5336
At Finn's : 194, 4750
At First Hand : 3341, 3476, 4812
At Forty : 764
At Grandfather Mountain : 4379
At Hann's Cliff : 53
At Hanratty's : 6464
At Haying Time : 2787
At Home : 2113, 2202, 5933
At Home with Eros & Psyche : 4073
At Last, at a Gas Station in Ohio : 2084
At Least : 3120, 3355, 4312
At Lipp's : 1181, 2503
At Louis Sullivan's Grave : 4253
At Marlborough House : 6310

At Mendenhall Glacier : 1142
At Midnight : 2380, 3066, 7129
At Mountain Lake : 3634
At Muker, Upper Swaledale : 1132
At My Garage Sale : 511
At My Loom : 1016
At Neptune's Locker : 3009
At Night : 1577, 4494
At Night Alone : 2402, 5712
At Night on the Ranch : 2447
At Night, Sleep Leading Me to Another House :
    1625, 6271
At Nightfall : 2870
At Once : 6829
At Once Jesus : 5866
At Paramount in 1945 They Used to Send Out
    My Picture with Wendell Corey's Name
    Under It and Wendell's Picture With My
    Name Under It : 970
At Parting : 3007
At Santa Maria Novella, Florence : 4101
At Sea : 4328
At Shag and Rosie's : 1561
At Subiaco, the Monks Are Playing Softball :
    6272
At Summer's End : 3419
At Sundown : 2825
At That Very Instant : 1597
At the Astronomy Lecture : 1215
At the Bandshell by the River : 4092
At the Bar : 1304
At the Border : 5734
At the Borders of the Storm : 3665
At the Centre, a Woman : 3785
At the Classics Teacher's : 3946
At the Club : 1401
At the Corner of the Eye : 2931
At the Drive-In : 2307
At the Edge of Dawn : 5828
At the Edge of the Water : 5767
At the End of a Street Thinking of Van Gogh :
    1625, 6743
At the End of Strawberry Season : 3937
At the End of the Picking Season : 4644
At the Fireplace : 2026
At the Gateways of Aerea : 1071, 6017
At the Glove Counter : 5248
At the Grave of My Guardian Angel, St. Louis
    Cemetery, New Orleans : 3749
At the Grave of the Fourth Man : 1308
At the Greyhound Station : 3505
At the Head of North Kimta Basin : 4968
At the Horizon, Prometheus : 6018
At the Krystal : 2706
At the Lake : 1521
At the Lakebed : 3896
At the Military Cemetery in San Bruno : 3199
At the Moment of Dawn : 2184, 4362
At the Moon-Lit Drive-In : 987
At the Museum : 99
At the Poetry Stacks of the Engineering College
    Library : 3761
At the Point of No Return : 6692
At the Roosevelt Baths : 2870

At the Ruins of the Aztec Goddess Ix-Chel : 891
At the Savoy : 4671
At the Seams : 173
At the Sedona Cafe : 4550
At the Sorbonne, 1925 : 1080
At the Stern of a Ship : 1625, 4304
At the Syria Mosque : 6812
At the Terminal : 2878
At the Tomb of Marie Laveau : 4382
At the Vagankovskoye Graveyard : 4671
At the Vietnam Veterans' Memorial — 1987 : 7066
At the Zoo : 6124
At Thirteen: Kneeling Beside My Father : 2613
At Thirty : 2715
At This Time : 4775
At Vicksburg : 1577
At Yale : 2707, 4395
Atavism : 3418
Atget's Gardens : 6964
Athletics : 3093
Athlone : 3139
Atlantic City : 588
Atlas and Mary, If Thy Son Lives, Where? : 1458
The Atlas Lost in the Mails : 4391
Atmospheric Burn : 1293
Atomic Sun : 1033, 3621, 5554
The Atonement : 2752
Atropos of the Wood : 6484
Attack of the Killer Power Tools : 4575
Attempt at Paradise : 1754, 5657
An Attempt at Statistics (Standing in Line for Vodka) : 244, 3011, 4396
An Attempted Portrait of the North in Short Trousers : 457
Attempting to Provoke a Set of Decisions : 6261
(At)tendere : 324, 5630
Attending *The Tempest* : 6233
Attention Miniature Lovers : 465
The Attic : 2620
Attitude : 2271
The Attitude : 1571
The Attraction of the Ground : 6708
Attractive Possibility : 189
A/Typical Marriage : 3646
Au Pair : 5157
Au Train : 3454
Aubade : 184, 433, 619, 786, 1258, 1838, 3575, 4540, 5920, 6350
Aubade: Cardboard Fan from a Baptist Church : 1142
Aubade (Light) : 1972
Aube : 1867
Auction Block : 6852
Audiophile : 5971
Audubon Drive, Memphis : 5760
Auf der elften Fichtenstufe : 3658
Augury : 2986
August : 2282, 3313, 3612, 3734, 4639, 4801, 6441
August, 1977: Arrivederci Roma : 6659

August First : 3780
August funeral : 4642
August Insomnia : 7059
August Is When the Snow Falls : 4462
August Moonlight : 828
August New Moon : 5919
August of the Drinking Well : 4179
August Porch : 5706
An August White : 3000
Augustan Elegies : 2961
Augustigräs : 5525
Augustus Purchases His New Teeth : 623
Augustus the Strong to His Keeper of the Green Vault : 4936
Auletride : 5009
The Aunt : 6517
Aunt Esther : 2755
Aunt I : 2142
Aurora : 1202, 6501
L'Aurore blonde fond sur la chose endormie : 1275
Auschwitz : 7001
Auschwitz, 1945 : 6580
Author in Search of a Sonnet : 1728
Auto / lisérgico : 4432
Auto Wreck : 2733
Autobiographer : 1467
The Autobiographers : 6563
Autobiography : 5614, 6275
Autobiography #1 : 1821
Automata : 2654
Autopsy : 2470
The Autopsy : 1240
Autoretrato en Invierno : 3579
Un Autre Monde : 3454
Autumn : 243, 551, 1625, 1625, 2554, 3090, 5874, 6743, 6846, 7046
Autumn 1963 : 5951
Autumn Afternoon : 1625, 7077
Autumn Ends : 2471
Autumn Festival : 3682, 4874
Autumn Fog : 458
Autumn Garden : 872
Autumn, I Wrote : 813, 814, 3792
Autumn in the Fall of Empire : 4062
Autumn Jumps : 1300, 2454
Autumn Leaves : 1101
Autumn Maneuver : 284, 5271
Autumn Moon : 2854
Autumn Night : 6358
Autumn of the Body : 5508
The Autumn of the Body : 530
Autumn Questions : 4576
The autumn rain : 2136, 3759
Autumn Sunrise : 1087
Autumn Variations : 6005
Autumnal : 5832
Aux Arbres : 2994
Avant de Quitter Ces Lieux : 236
Ave Atque Vale : 3652, 6376
Aviary : 1606, 4208
The Aviary : 4410
The Aviary of My Liking : 3353
Avonden : 6007

Avskedsbrevet : 5293
Awaiting Translation : 3820
Awakening : 6607
The Awakening : 5978
The Awakening of Telemachus : 3287, 5361
Awards : 345
Aware : 5850
Away : 824
Away Goes Jonathan Wheeler! : 6483
The Awl in the Dark : 3830, 6006
Axioms : 2283
Ayme walkynge on aire : 392
Azaleas : 80, 6908
Azimuth : 2225
Azokról a Nökröl : 4811
Azrael : 6984
B. Davis Dies : 4997
Babel : 5266, 5615
Baby Blue : 747
Baby Boomer : 1091
The Baby Dreams : 2740
Baby Girl : 3787
Baby Key in the Mechanical Forest : 6333
Baby Pictures : 6659
Baby Tony at Al's Cafe : 5493
Baby's Awake Now : 489
Babysitting : 5204
Baccalà : 6627
Bacchante : 2565
Bacchantes : 1348, 5899
A Bach Concert : 435, 1085, 4180
Bachelor Album : 3692
The Bachelor Tells a Family Story : 5530
Bach's Idiot Son : 623
Back : 5131
Back Country, Yellowstone : 4171
Back in grammar school ten years ago : 7062
Back to My Valley : 6743, 7155
Back to the Village : 208, 5229, 6830
Back Trouble : 2486
Background : 4279
Background/Information : 1218
Backgrounds : 1082, 1625
Backstreets : 110
Backstroke : 2148
Backward Glance / Winter Journey : 5370
Backwater Street, K.C., MO : 6110
Bacon Dance : 4246
Bad : 244, 1054, 3011
Bad Animals : 686
Bad Birthday : 6803
Bad Blood Blues : 298
Bad Boy : 2296
Bad Conscience : 341
Bad Dogs : 2405
Bad Dreams : 6101
Bad for You : 267
Bad Girl Goes Shopping : 6027
Bad Habits : 871
A Bad Memory : 1712, 5992, 6454
Bad News from Sears : 7037
The Bad Poet : 5602
Bad Review : 6678
A Badge : 2875

Badger : 7119
Badlands : 4622, 6546
The Badlands Said : 6579
Bag Lady on My Street : 2205
Bait : 6821
Baja Journal : 2518
Baked Alaska : 3829
Baked Goods : 3774
The Baker : 1352
The Baker's Apprentice : 1526
Baking the Eucharist : 4521
Bakrulatial : 3260
Balada of Uncertain Age : 6536
Balancing : 2658
Balancing Act : 4416
Balcony : 5709
Baldy : 5778
The Ball Park : 3158
Ball-peen : 957
Ballad of a Boneless Chicken : 5126
Ballad of a Circus : 4124
Ballad of Captain Jack Macfadden : 26
The Ballad of Deceived Flowers : 2289, 4915
The Ballad of Othello Clemence : 1145
Ballad of the Distant Cliff : 6210
Ballad of the Jack of Diamonds : 1018, 6918
The Ballad of the Line : 4486
Ballad of the Salamander : 3555, 5438
Ballad of the Stoker : 3555, 4677
Ballast : 190
Las Ballenas de Bahia Magdalena : 7141
Ballet Studio at Noon : 98
Ballista and Bassoon in March : 172
Balloons for a Wake : 3609
Ballpoint Paper : 3510
A Baltic Tragedy : 3309
Balzac and the Buddha : 5452
Bamboo Bridge : 142
Bamboo Shoots Line the Dirt Road : 4605
The Bambutti: Pygmies of the Congo : 4575
Band Class Collaboration : 6193
Bandages : 1934
The Bandusian Fountain : 2937, 4514
Banger in the Morning : 6187
Bangkok Liaison : 3797
Bangladesh-II : 99, 1883
Bangladesh Poems : 1062
Banished : 783
Bank : 595
Banking Potatoes : 3466
A Banner : 1629
Banquet : 5733
Baptism : 319, 3390
The Baptism : 1286
The Baptistry : 837
The Bar : 3371, 3990
Bar Giamacia 1959-60 : 7058
Bar Tale : 6250
Bar Xanadu : 2998
Barabello : 2394
Barbara Holland : 6919
The Barbarians Are Coming : 1101
Barbarous Prayer : 1363, 5379, 6639
Barbed Wire : 3612

Barbeque Sauce : 1268
Barber : 1519
The Barber : 1212
The Bard of Diseases : 4873
The Bard, or Hanging the Moon : 893
Bardic : 1111, 4750
Bareback : 2111
The Barefoot Widow : 2027
The Bargain : 1792
Barking Up the Wrong Tree : 3011
Barlaban: a Mandinka Epic : 184, 1674
The Barman's Quiet Way : 3800
Barn : 2418
The Barn : 189, 4598
A Barn Dance in the Level Country : 4581
Barred Owl : 227
The Barriers : 4786
Barrie's Dream: The Wild Geese : 6579
Bartelby : 364
The Barter : 4490
Bartered Nights: Three Poems : 2232, 5630
Bartholomew's Cobbler : 3913
Basalt & Serpentine Rest at Right Angles in the
    Sun : 6793
Basic Vocabulary : 1638, 5814
Basically Troubled in the Heat : 3418
Basil : 4784
Basilico : 126
Basketball Legs : 1950
Basketeer : 3139
Basking in Blue : 2945
A Bass Fisherman Adjusts His Vision to a
    Darker View of the World : 5212
Basso-Relievo : 6298
Bastille Day : 6305
Bat : 4099
The Bat : 1991, 2346
Bat Mother : 1090
Bath Mirror : 1594
Bath Time : 2324
The Bathers: A Triptych : 443
The Bats : 6750
The Bats' Rebellion : 1113
Battered Woman in New York : 5676
Batterers : 3736
Battle-Piece : 443
Baudelaire's Letter to Ancelle : 2131
The Bay : 5538
Bay Memory : 5240
Bayou Morning : 2698
Be- : 914
Be Brave : 402
Be Patient, Be Patient : 2522, 3942, 6344
Be prepared, be prepared! : 1582, 5098
Be Quiet, Will You : 3388
The Beach : 820, 1078, 1546, 6429
The Beach, My Son and the Alltime Batman :
    3130
Beach Walk and Bad News : 6379
Beachcomer : 3368
Beached : 4264
Beaker Street : 6051
Beans in the Attic : 1858
The Beanstalk : 2566

Bear : 3266
The Bear : 2623
Bear Bell : 387
Bearing Gifts : 4319
Bearing the Body Back to Philadelphia : 2395
Bearings : 6242
Bears : 5415
The Bears : 5930
The Beasts : 6538
The Beasts of the Field : 921
Beat 1990 (the Abbreviated Version) : 3079
The Beat of the Wind : 131
Beat Poetry : 3270, 5900
A Beatification : 2964
Beatitudes : 5823
Le Beau Monde : 5894
Beauties : 83
Beautiful Eyes for a Boy : 3451
Beautiful Women : 1715
Beauty : 2, 2279, 4367, 5171, 5959
Beauty Is Nothing But the Beginning of Terror :
    590
Beauty Sleep : 2340
Beaver Run : 2874
Becaue Macaroons without the Sea Air Would
    Be Nothing: A Love Poem : 5277
Because : 5679
Because Everything Is Passed On : 1371
Because He Could Not Give Me Wealth : 6782
Because I Am a Woman of Color : 4826
Because in Space : 550
Because Nothing Stands Still : 1380
Because of Local Flooding : 1225
Because of the Failure This Experiment Was :
    6042
Because of the Light : 5149
Because Our Drowning Is a Sensation : 2816,
    3547, 5379
Because the Egg Was a Door Nailed Shut :
    5106
Because the Fish Did Not Seem Real : 1823
Because There Was a Time : 1363, 5379, 5379,
    7164, 7164
Because They're Happy : 1269
Because You Are Weak You Must Be Strong :
    2875
Beckett Remembered : 330
Becoming a Miser : 3612
Becoming Neruda : 3834
Becoming Part of the Night : 3612
The Bed : 1744, 1976, 2145, 3728, 6086
Bedouin Tent : 2854
Bedrock : 6039
Bedroom : 1722, 3588, 6220
Bedroom Walks : 2881
Beds : 4074
Bedtime Ritual : 3609
Bedtime Stories : 1380
Bedtime Story : 6563
A Bedtime Story : 7127
Bee Lesson : 1582, 5098
Beeper : 1975
Beer : 1810
The Beer Drinkers : 236

Bees : 6890
Bees at Termes : 2821
Beethoven : 684
Beethoven's Fifth in C Minor : 5508
The Beetle Eel : 5393
Before : 2256
Before Goodbye : 413
Before he left our village : 2135, 3751, 6383
Before It Begins : 499, 5438
Before Notre Dame : 3162
Before Poetry There Is Truth : 588
Before She Sleeps : 290
Before Sunset : 705, 5336
Before the Autumn Equinox : 434
Before the Concert : 6464
Before the Fault Lines : 1909, 7182
Before the Mount of Venus : 3318, 5344
Before the Movie Begins : 5596
Before the News : 5110
Before the Rebellion : 1686, 6971
Before the Sirens There Was Red : 6144
Before the Storm : 6175
Before They Closed Down Denny's Billiards : 5059
Before They Found Him in Neshaminy Creek : 4043
Before You? : 3241
Beggar on the Córdoba Bridge : 73
Beggars : 3602
Beggars' Camp : 5033
Begging Your Pardon : 6857
Begin in the Middle : 2048
Beginning : 3450
The Beginning : 7, 2454, 6324
Beginning from a Statue of Diamonds : 4422
Beginning Love : 122
Beginning with Lines Torn from Irby : 501
Beginnings : 110
Behaving Like a Jew : 6162
The Beheading : 104
Behind Closed Doors : 5301
Behind Glass : 4277
Behind the Beaux-Arts : 2907
Behind the Bingham School : 4039
Behind the Wall : 284, 5271
Beholden : 824
Bei Tai-He Beach : 3407, 5860
Beijing Voices : 2020
Being a little kid and trying to masturbate is rough : 1327
Being and Becoming : 3980
Belated Words : 6250
A Belfast Kiss : 4489
Beliefs from the Gulf: A Southern Upbringing : 2612
Believe That This : 4111
Believers Are Made in Heaven : 6641
The Bell : 3612
The Bell Bird : 5830
Bell Makers : 5654
Bella Roma : 1750
Les Belles Dames Sans Merci : 1042
Bellevue Garden, Kingston : 4665
The Belly : 1605

Belly of the Flames : 1206
Bellyache for Solo Voice and Clavichord : 7101
Belongings : 3614
Below San Simeon : 6774
Below the Dam Site: The Caribou : 1299
Below the Horizon : 2104, 6054, 6612
Below the Power Plant : 5223
Belugas : 6338
Benares Processional : 4693
Bench-Hand: 'The Famous Real Life' : 6232
Bending the Light : 2100
Beneath a City-light : 1029
Beneath a Full Summer Moon : 533
Beneath the Perseid Meteor Shower : 6076
Benediction : 3083, 6277
The Bengal Tiger : 6529
Benina : 2116
Bent After Dinner : 1611
Bent July Landscape : 2098
Bentwood : 5980
Berate, Berattle : 1789
Berbers : 3964
Berkeley Beat : 3049
The Berkeley Dusk : 1985
Berlin : 5812
Berlin: An Epithalamion : 1090
Bermudas : 5347
Bernie : 5908
The Berry House — Route 555 in Northern Kentucky : 1577
Beside the arroyo : 1304
Best Coat Company, Roxbury, MA, 1969 : 4254
The Best Day of My Life : 3548
Best Friend : 1667
Best Years : 6058
Betrayal : 67, 2778, 6040
The Betrayal : 3086
Betrothal : 2696, 3459, 4692
Better to Marry, or Better to Burn? : 6047
The Better Vantage for Love : 3947
Betty's Flowers : 3796
Between : 2245
Between a Rock and Mahatma Gandhi : 5156
Between Angels & Monsters : 3466
Between First and Third Worlds : 5380
Between Forests : 2454, 2716
Between Friends : 2621
Between Haste and Deceit : 1193, 1641, 3064
Between Heaven and Hell : 2449
Between Ionians and Dorians : 3287, 5361
Between the Buildings of New York : 7099
Between the Fascinating and the Frightening : 668, 5420
Between the First and Last Twilight : 158, 3750
Between the Islands : 3645
Between the Shadow and Its Object : 1377
Between Tides : 5246
Between Us : 3032
Between You, Me and the Lamp Post : 5807
Beware in bloom those fleeting boughs : 5953
Beware of Accidents in the Home : 1265
Beware of the Poet : 6109
Beyond : 2029

Beyond Dark Inlet, Savage Sacred Sky : 3043
Beyond India : 2959
Beyond Mourning : 5697
Beyond the Ash Rains : 99
Beyond the Sign of the Fish : 4697
Beyond Words : 2711
Bi-Coastal : 6804
Bible Stories : 5617
Bicycle Villanelle : 5267
Bicycles and Other Machines — 1986 : 1645
Biding : 3206
The Big Apple : 1564
Big Brother : 1961
Big Cat : 5866
The Big Cats : 7041
The Big Fish of the Mind : 1566
Big Mirror Outdoors : 4310
The Big Move : 426
Big Sister : 151
Big Steve : 3329
Big Sur : 7042
The Big Things : 473
The Biggest Species of Hylid Frog in the World
    Joins Us for Dinner : 1238
Biko : 4543
Bilan : 3682
Bild, 1959 : 7059
A Bilingual Conversation : 6514
Bill : 2251
Bill in Bed : 6234
Bill Pickett: The Dusky Demon : 3428
Bill Williams in New Zealand : 5224
Billie Holiday : 6098, 6662
Billy : 4146
Billy Martin Speaks to His Team : 4525, 5550
Billy the Kid: The Baptism : 3428
The Bind : 3135
Bingo : 4243
Biographical Information : 66, 6456
Biography : 1306, 4023
Biography with Lack of Sleep : 7107
Biology Lesson : 6151
Bioluminescence : 2148
The Biopsy : 3185
A Bird : 6242
Bird Days of Winter : 4210
Bird Feeder in the Rain : 5927
Bird in Space: First Study : 529
Bird Love : 2970
The Bird of Life : 1269
The Bird Show at Aubagne : 1199
Bird That Flies : 2875
Bird — Watching : 2686
Birdbrain : 971
Birdcage : 834
Birdhouse : 2828, 5961
Birds : 2600, 4918, 5603, 5727, 6039
The Birds : 2979
Birds and the Reader : 1150
Bird's Eye, Turning From Side to Side : 2694
Birds in August : 3000
Birds, Ledges : 6866
Birds of Paradise : 6044
Birds of Summer : 4311

Birds Sing All the Words for Yes : 1957
Birds Wild at Night : 4574
The Birdsong Blues : 6536
Birdsongs for the Red Phone : 6101
Birmingham Brown's Turn : 4521
Birth : 6465
Birth II : 6396, 6507
Birth of a Stone : 3794
Birth of Meadows : 6688
The Birth of Tally's Blues : 704
Birthday : 3557
Birthday #26 : 4028
Birthday Boy : 2656
Birthday in Autumn : 2120
A Birthday in the Dust : 301
Birthday Poem at 67 : 841
A Birthday R.S.V.P., or, 2 out of 3 Women Do
    Not Recommend Sleeping with the
    Kennedys : 1611
Birthday Song : 252
Birthdays : 5642
Birthmark : 4055
Birthplace : 4863
Birthstone : 5980
A Bit About Nona : 5237
Bite the Hand : 4554
Bitter Bread : 1820
Bitter Resins : 1161
Bitter Spring : 5862
The Bitterns : 6846
Bixby Park : 3825
Black and White : 4920
Black Art : 6846
The Black Bells from Gina's House : 1121
Black-Eyed Susans in the Lemon Tree : 4991
Black Girl Vanishing: Detroit, 1970 : 1605
Black Gospel : 7193
Black Horse and Fish : 1625, 7156
Black Humor : 1422
Black Ink Days : 4183
The Black Lace Fan My Mother Gave Me : 616
Black Landscape : 1242
Black Marsh : 1584, 1889, 4486, 6344
Black Mutes : 2441
Black-Out : 3197
Black Rain, Hiroshima : 3780
Black Rain, Hiroshima (1) : 3780
Black Rain, Hiroshima (2) : 3780
Black Rain, Hiroshima: by night fall, Hiroshima
    was gone : 3780
Black Rain, Hiroshima: Hiromu Morishiti
    found her father : 3780
Black-Red : 3243, 5379
Black Rose Madonna in the Rain : 3780
The Black Skirt : 1048
Black Smoke : 2323, 3588, 6220
Black Stones I : 3723
Black Stones II : 3723
Black Stones III : 3723
The Black Swan : 1125
Black Swans : 5753
Black Tulip : 5423
A Black Wedding Song : 777
Black Wednesday with Ashes : 419

Black Wind : 5691
Black Woman : 4473, 5995
Blackberry Wine : 3444
Blackbird : 1617, 2164
Blackbird on a Balustrade : 4321
The Blackcrowned Sparrow : 5964
Blackeyed Peas Look Like Pussy Willows, But
    Soft Inside : 6373
The Blackout : 6196
Blackthorn Winter : 5241
Bladed Sky : 6187
Blaine Lake : 5790
Blanco Y Negro Tiritando Juntos en un
    Paradero de East Austin : 4769
Blank Spots : 5933
Blanket of Fish : 4153
Blanks : 435, 4180
Blanks for New Things : 4367
Blaze : 3735
Blessed : 6729
Blessed Are the Pro-Choice Children : 6492
Blessed by Meteors and by the Benevolent Men
    of Space : 6026
Blessing : 1161
A Blessing for Midgets and Dwarves : 1307
The Blessings of Liberty : 2752
Blessings Sonnet : 1703
The Blind Beggar's Dog : 5431
A Blind Black Singer in Washington Street :
    7155
The Blind Cavefish : 2506
Blind Countenance : 3423
A Blind Elephant Man in the Underground :
    1249
Blind Faith : 6112
Blind Lesson in History : 5038
Blind Love : 5646
Blind Man in the Morning : 5315
Blinded, they march on, the soldiers of Tsar
    Samuil : 1582, 5098
The Blinding of the Cyclops : 4798
Blindly. Because you, my two real friends, are
    strangers to me tonight : 1148
The Blindness of Habit : 6440
The Blinds : 2909
Blips : 2838
Bliss : 2771, 5959
The Blizzard : 1401
The Blizzard Moans My Name : 1324
Blizzard: Western Kansas : 5924
Block Island: After *The Tempest* : 443
Blockbuster : 4575
Blonde As a Bat : 230
Blood : 1183, 4240, 5757, 5952
Blood Casts a Light : 4462
Blood Line : 92
Blood Poisoning : 3831
Blood Sisters : 511
Blood Soup : 6770
Blood-Stained Tale : 3985, 4742
The blood this band-aid vaguely wrings : 4973
Blood — Ties : 3324
Bloodroot : 1264
Bloodroots for April : 4950

Bloodtide: A Southern Exposure : 5779
Bloodwork : 1055
Blossom : 1955
Blue : 75, 1464, 5692, 6450
The Blue : 2107
Blue and Green : 2598
Blue Background : 3403, 6037
Blue-Black : 579
Blue Blood's Bard : 2156
Blue Collar Goodbyes : 1645
Blue Corn : 3766
Blue Country Rising : 6159
Blue Cowboy Sky Behind Him : 2436
Blue Coyote : 815
Blue Dancers : 1735
Blue Depression Glass : 6558
Blue for You : 296
The Blue Goodbye : 3796
Blue Iris / Tiananmen Square : 3656
Blue Letters : 5960
Blue Madonna Goes to the Midnight Radio
    Show : 3780
Blue Marriage : 772
Blue Monody : 2591
Blue Moon : 4515
The blue Motel 6 sign through the curtain :
    4364
Blue Movies : 3913
The Blue Oranda : 2120
Blue Ridge Cemetery : 5507
The Blue Room : 4887
The Blue Rose : 4507
Blue Shift : 5538
Blue Shoes : 2118
Blue Snow : 3439
Blue Spring Afternoon : 6393
Blue Square : 3403, 6037
Blue: Steps : 6981
Blue Vault : 1976
Blue Zones : 4062
Bluebeard's Bungalow : 2856
Bluebells : 349
Blueberries : 5470
Blueberry Pie : 2389
Bluebirds : 2973
Bluefishing the Bogue Narrows : 3986
Bluegill Silhouette : 794
Bluegills : 6728
Bluemoon : 6096
Blues for a Dancer : 783
Blues for Lowell : 1410
Blues for the Nightowl : 2305
Blurting : 467
Boardwalk : 3509
The Boat : 4663
Boat Race : 4780
The boat that took my love away : 5988
The Boats Have Returned : 6164
La Boba : 5619
Bobby's Fall : 4786
Boca do Inferno : 290
Bodgie Love : 6029
Body : 1332
Body and Soul : 3223

Body Count 1952 : 1726
The Body Does Not Always Seem : 158, 3750
Body Language : 2682, 5825
Body of Knowledge : 3098
Body Parts : 2470
Body Parts: Love Poem for Sarah : 5429
The Body Speaks : 1930, 4621
The Body's Curse : 1605
The Body's Hope : 1605
The Body's Journey : 1605
The Body's Joy : 1605
The Body's Repose and Discontent : 1605
The Body's Weight : 1605
Bodywork : 4356
Boeremusiek : 4545
Bog Man : 1465
The Bog Man : 5378
Bogotá Declaration : 1808, 2388
La Boheme : 4296
Bohemians, Bohemians : 2431
Boiled Peanuts : 6361
The Boilerman : 5676
The Bomb Document : 3150
Bomb Drills: Doug's Story : 3232
Bomb Drills: Eric's Story : 3232
Bombers : 2208
The Bombing of the Berlin Zoo, Friday 23
    November 1943, 22:48 Hrs : 5333
The Bombing of Tripoli : 1639
Bombs : 5389, 5413
Bone Cold : 4214
Bone fragments in Argentina : 6516
Bone Simple : 7130
Bones : 2724, 3609, 4985, 7166
The Bones Die and Go on Living : 1465
Bones Dry White : 4513
The Bones of Angels : 6299
The Bones of Montgomert Clift : 2470
Bonfire : 3822, 7092
Bonnard : 871
Bonsai : 6532
The Book Closed, the Facing Pages Kiss : 6828
The Book of Harold : 5260
The Book of Resemblances II: Intimations The
    Desert : 3071, 6708
Book to Close : 2319
Bookmaking : 122
Bookmark : 3243, 5379
The Bookmark : 5816
Books and Dreams : 5103
Books of Common Prayer : 3169
The Bootleg Coal Hole : 3000
A Border : 431
Border Town : 6756
The Borderland : 6958
Borderline : 368
Borders : 5379, 6319, 6322
Boreal Surreal : 5497
Boredom : 1213
Borges and the Tigers : 158, 3750
Boric Acid : 3275
Boris By Candlelight : 5763
Born Again : 5778
Born on the 4th of July : 3367

Born Viable : 3071, 6708
Borodin, Dancing : 4770
The Borrower : 1048
Borrowing Henry : 4409
Boston Harbor : 3409
The Boston Poems : 3300
Botanical : 5321
Botany : 6699
Both Long and Disturbing : 6897
Botticelli : 2366
Botticelli: The Cestello Annunciation : 2981
The Bottle in the River : 1536, 3533
The Bottom Line : 3829
Boudica : 3294, 6707
Boudica 21-25 : 3294, 6707
Boulders : 2009
Boulevard Delessert : 158, 3750
Bouncing on Empty : 6813
Bound : 2550
Bounty : 3386
Bounty Hunting for Snappers : 1679
Bouquet : 6813
The Bourgeois Life : 2373
Le Bourreau Chinois : 1181
The Bow : 445
The Bowl : 4962
Bowl of Dreams : 2361
A Bowl of Purple Cherries : 6184
Bowling, Nude : 3282
The Box : 3652
Box Factory Girls : 4644
Boxing Match in the Desert : 4652
Boy : 1704
The Boy Brings His Blind Grandmother a Stone
    Bird : 3437
Boy 'Carrying-in' Bottles in Glass Works :
    5548
A Boy Dives from a Rock : 368
Boy in a Rice Paddy, Head Shot : 4332
The Boy Juliet : 2457
A Boy to His Girl (Just Inside Her Front Door) :
    450
Boy Travelling : 2217
A Boy Waiting : 3612
The Boy Who Dimmed Light Bulbs : 1704
Boys and Girls Together : 4349
Boys' Annual : 5390
Brackish Water : 3000
Brahms Pours Into : 1613
The Brain : 1838
Brain Garbage : 3079
The Brain Sandwich : 4374
The Brake : 3748
Branchers : 6736
Brands : 1142
Bravado : 6389
Bread : 871, 2482, 4477
Bread & Circus : 4008
Bread and Water : 3280
The Bread Itself : 3032
Bread Loaf : 588
Bread Makes Stone : 1589
The Bread of Friendship : 4868
The Bread Poem : 5385

Breakdown : 1607, 1748
Breakdown Moon : 4515
Breakfast : 2103, 2369, 5486, 5852
Breakfast Lovers : 6402
Breaking : 4594
The Breaking : 3466
Breaking & Entering : 7178
Breaking Faith : 1598
Breaking in the New Boss : 1611
Breaking Rhythm : 173
Breaking Silence, Broken Faith: The Vietnam
    Wall : 3578
Breaking the Fever : 3944
Breaking the Lawn : 3245
Breaking the Surface : 3849
Breaking Up : 1981
Breaking up: that large feeling : 3723, 6048
Breakout : 2292
Breakthrough : 6018
Breasts : 6360
Breath : 1369, 5661
Breath in the Mouth of Sorrow : 1862
Breath of Darkness : 3510
Breath of Fire : 4132
Breath Poem : 1055
Breathing : 6308
Breathing on Mirrors : 3873
Breeder Reaction : 6512
Brethren : 2592
Brian : 1748, 6085
The Brides : 1666
The Bride's Story : 6426
Bridge : 6202
The Bridge : 2378
Bridge at Giverny : 2248
A bridge is the passage between two banks :
    4140
The Bridge That Burns for Years : 3313
Bridges : 3035, 3464
Bridges We Know : 2884
Bridle Path : 7114
Bridled Lust : 6661
Brief Love Poem : 2184, 4362
A Brief Note on Principles : 345
A Brief Secular History : 1072
Briefcase : 2262, 2553
The Briefcase : 4537
Brieves from The Book of Kells : 5980
Bright in the Harvest : 5430
Bright Wings : 2909
The Brighter the Veil : 5151
Bring It On : 3692
Bring Them All Back : 2382
Bringing Home the Tree : 6322
The Brink : 5756
Briskly : 4545
Britannia Beach : 6247
Bro : 2250
Broad Daylight : 2013, 5107
Broken : 168
A Broken Branch : 3612
The Broken Chain : 6073
A Broken Contract: 110 : 1032, 1255
Broken-Down Mission : 4372

A Broken Egg at Breakfast : 856
Broken Ornaments : 3719
Broken Skylight : 3656
The Broker : 3006
Bronko Nagurski : 261
The Brontës : 6563
Bronx Elegy : 5806
Bronx Zoo : 4307
The Bronze Poet : 181, 4383, 6451
Brook or Rill : 2469
Brother Ass : 1185
Brother Bat : 903
Brother Bonsai (Daniel) : 5827
A Brother Born in 1942 : 4047
Brother Ivy : 3736
The Brotherhood of Cows : 5324
Brothers : 5062
Brothers and Bootleggers : 163
Brothers and Uncles : 4208
Brothers in the Craft : 3382
Brother's Keeper : 1009, 2157
Brothers of the Double Life : 3986
Brown Sequence : 6298
Brown Shoes : 5963
Brown Study : 4042
Bruegel's Crows : 3204
Brushing : 5619
Brute Image : 236
Bryan, Ohio : 5934
The Bubble : 2862
Bubble Hubbub : 193
Bucharest, 1986 : 4671
Bucólico Ajedrez : 3855
The Buddhist Nun's Young Friend : 5854
The Budding of Sand : 2477
Buddy Holly Poem : 4000
Buddy Holly Watching Rebel Without a Cause,
    Lubbock, Texas, 1956 : 7010
Buenos Aires, 1899 : 356, 640, 640, 4324
Buffalo : 3873
Buffalo Days : 4319
The Buffalo Soldier's Wife : 563
Buffalo/Stasis : 4129
Bugged to New York City! : 2595
The Builder : 2691
Building, Naming, Flying : 2872
Building the Beach Fire : 2895
A Building We Perceive As Standing Still :
    2304
Built with the Same Beauty : 3398
Bukowski in a Jar : 4834
Bulbs : 1452
Bull : 4870
Bull Eating Pears : 2228
The Bull God : 5583
Bull Stud : 4215
Bull Thistle : 391
Bull Whip Days : 6272
Bulletin : 6904
Bullhead Lily : 4816
The Bullheads : 4859
Bull's-Eye : 5494, 5868
Bumblebee : 5895
Bumblebee Duck : 2104

The Bump : 5679
Bunch-Ups : 1439
Bundybaby : 5484
The Bunkers : 6910
The Burden : 7127
The Burden of Jerusalem : 3385
Bureaucracy : 3171
Bureaucrat with Portraits : 2723
The Burglars : 5736
Burial : 5739
Burial and Blaze of Pablo Neruda : 49, 2076
The Burial Detail : 6085
Burial Grounds : 567
The Buried Son, 1907 : 757
Buried Tooth : 1307
Burly Girls : 6501
Burn the Silk Ones : 5745
Burned : 3746
Burning : 415
The Burning : 1208
Burning Books : 3769, 3817, 4832
Burning Flower : 1064
The Burning House : 6802
Burning Love Letters : 5390
The Burning of Yellowstone : 6595
Burning the Flags : 1684
Burning the Leaves : 6713
Burning to Return : 2310
Burnt Bush : 6989
The Burnt Pages : 235
Burrowing Owls : 2307
A Burst of Iris : 1964
The Bus : 5814
Bus Ride : 481
Bus Ride in Salt Lake : 6725
Bus Stop : 1030
The Bus Tour of Great Britain : 5688
Bush Fire : 1757, 6342
Bushbody : 1891
Bushhog : 5895
Bushido : 5912
Bushwick, Latex Flat : 4726
Business Dinner in Bethlehem : 7018
The Business of Fancydancing : 96
But Beautiful : 859
But Blue : 6594
But Do You Remember August : 813, 814,
     2031
But dreams that do not lend figures : 924, 6632
But Incessantly : 813, 814, 2031
But Marriage, God : 1525
But That's What You Are : 2595
But thou, who givest all things, give not me :
     6533
But What About the Stepsisters : 2299
But whom to blame : 3111, 5999
Butcher : 5549, 6922
The Butcher : 868
Butcher Scraps : 3357
Butterflies on Ice : 326
Butterfly : 20, 4760
The Butterfly Effect : 4898
Butterfly Spring : 4936
Buttoned Down : 4630

Buttonwood : 368
Buzz : 3699
Buzzards and Uncle Douglas : 4179
By Daylight : 3946
By Inference : 1454
By Now of Course You Will Have Heard : 4097
By Scent : 6652
By Scottish Roads : 1696
By the Fork : 4278
By the Iowa : 445
By the side of the English Office, a black : 5885
By the Tekapo River, 100 Degrees : 6579
By the Time You Get to Phoenix It May All Be
     Over : 1019
By the Tomcat's Grave : 3152
By Word of Mouth : 2458
Byron at Shelley's Burning : 3832
BZ : 3475
C-Squared Vision : 1426
C Train Home: Lou Reed After the Wake of
     Delmore Schwartz, July, 1966 : 7010
Caballo de Palo : 215
Caballo en Llamaradas : 1620
Cacao, Chicago : 4564
Cactus : 940
Cactus Salad : 2945
Cadence : 2565
Cae Glas : 3791
Caedmon: Antiphon : 3813
Caelian : 1367
Caesura : 5329
Cafe : 4542
A Cafe in New Mexico : 3016
The Cafe Mistress : 3120, 4534, 5250
Cafes : 6174
Caffe Lena, November 25, 1989 : 1144
Cage : 1622
The Cage : 5152
Cage of Mirrors, or Man's Conscience : 273,
     5995
Caged : 6519
Cages : 991, 2082
Cairns : 2021
Cakile : 5594
Calais : 6304
Calamity : 22, 6006
Calculating Pi : 1966
Calculating the Evening : 1012
Calendar : 6365
The Calendar : 4179
A Calendar of Women : 155
Calendrier Rural : 3682
Calf Creek Falls : 1753
Caliban Down Under : 5377
California : 492, 4244
California Forest : 1526
Californians : 6700
Caligula : 4251
Call : 4921
Call This Blindness : 3445, 5874, 6082
Calle Bolivar : 2178
Calle Desconocida : 640
Called Back : 1429
Caller by the Constant Sea : 2879

Callicles Puts a Head on the Argument : 5698
Calling : 3153
Calling All Bards : 782
Calling All Epic Seers : 1336
Calling Down the Geese : 2988
The Calling of the Apostles Peter and Andrew : 2906
Calling Up : 3418
The Calling Woods : 31
Calm Before Birth : 3273
Cambodian Guerrilla Sponsorship Drive Announced : 4941
The Cambrian Dusk Should Evoke Some : 1337
Cameleon : 5092
The Camera : 3150
Camera Obscura : 870
Camerography of Death : 2803
Camisado : 446
Campagnano, Italy, 1921 : 5056
Camping Near Teton Mountain : 730
Camping Out : 3919
Can Do : 3273
Can I Throw My Gum Out on the Grass So It Won't Stick to the Trash Can? : 3616
Can You Say Hi : 6040
Can You Tell Us Something About Him? : 681
Canada Day Parade : 1352
The Canadian Legion : 2783
Las Cañas : 5397
Cañaverales : 4934
Cancer Dust : 6972
Cáncer enmarañada primavera : 6396
Cancer entangled spring : 6396, 6507
Cancerismo : 3418
La Cancion de Silvia Plath : 1394
Cancion del Naranjo Seco : 2191
La Cancion Familiar : 6625
Candlemas : 184
Candles : 4965
The Candy Factory : 3756
The Cane of a Duck : 2660
Cangrejos de la Playa de Ma'Bwá : 1028
Canicula : 3384
Canker : 3820
Cannon Time Comes Flying : 3060, 5995
Cannot Be a Tourist : 1287
Canoe Maker : 5233
Cant : 216
Can't You See : 7135
Canterbury Cathedral : 910
Canticle : 3609
Cantiga d'Amor de Refran : 6648
Canto 12: Canto for a Grotesque Dance : 2852
Canto 14 : 2852
Canto Cuántico : 966
Canto de la Piedra : 1936
Canto Hondo : 1605
Canto Llano (Plain Song) : 468, 6660
Cantos de Temor y de Blasfemia : 3891
Canvas Eagles : 2431
The Canyon : 3251
Canyon de Chelly : 3179
Canyon Venture : 2183
Canzone: Egrets : 6728

Cape Cod Evening : 1528
A Cape Mendocino Rose : 1592
The Cape Vulture : 2059
Capella : 3588, 5014, 6220
Capitalism Is a Contact Sport : 3424
Capitalism on the Moon : 588
Capitoline : 1367
Cappuccino at the Marconi Hotel in Venice : 2199
Capriccio 9 : 3341, 3731, 5864
Capricho for Goya : 4939, 5098
Capsule : 2774
Captive Audience : 2322
Captive Voices : 6361
The Captivity of the Lesser : 1046, 6632
The Captor : 5273
Capture the Flag : 6256
The Car : 1200
The car accident : 3430
Car Crazy : 1984, 6188
Caracola : 4969
Caraquet Coast : 6174
Carcajada de Estaño : 967
Carcass and Balsam : 5241
Card Trick : 2300
Cardiac : 907, 3155, 3510
The Cardinal Dies in Holy Week : 5109
The Career of Mungo Park : 6124
Careers : 1605
A Careful Man : 3217
Cares : 1593
Caretaking : 5268
Cargo Cult of the Solstice at Hadrian's Wall : 6120
Caribou : 5466
The Caribou Go There : 4804
The Caribs : 578
Carl Among the Heathen : 712
Carla Boucher Eats Poppies in Santa Fe : 6700
Carmen: Not the Opera But the Movie : 4814
Carmic Crash : 3414
Carnival '89 : 626
Carnival lights fade in the approach : 3761
Carol : 2278
A Carolina Wren : 2170
Carousel : 1258
Carpe Diem : 1783
The Carpenter's Lament : 5383
The Carpet : 500
Carreras : 642
Carrion : 6942
(Carrion Comfort) : 2934
Carrousel : 3097
Carrying Eggs : 6065
Carrying My Father's Ashes by Train to Nasik : 5208
Carsick Children : 2010
Carta a : 1841
Carta a un Compatriota : 480
Carta de Una Aclla a Su Amante : 1034
Cartesianesque : 6848
The Cartographer's Vacation : 1188
Cartouches : 6485
Carver : 5929

La Casa Paterna : 3824
Casablanca : 703
Cascade of Genitives : 800, 6354
Case History : 863
Case History of a Terrorist : 2700
Cash Money : 5679
Casi Letania : 3642
Casserole : 4585
Castidad Maya : 1034
Castillo, our scoutmaster claimed : 5169
The Casting of Bells : 3095, 4767, 5768
Castle in Spain : 1129
Castles and Wolves : 6812
Casualty : 1411
The Casualty : 2040
Cat : 670
A Cat : 5241
The Cat : 3381
Cat and Flowers : 1386
The Cat at Midnight : 3686
Cat-Headed Bast : 4411
Cat in Window, Late Winter : 3003
Cat Mother : 3980
Cataclysmic Nippers : 481, 4588, 6453
Catalan Farmer: Figueras, Spain : 6560
Catalogue of the New Wonderment : 6655
Catalpa : 3006
The Catch : 4095
Catching Frogs : 3327
Catching the News : 6856
Caterpillar of Smoke : 6770
Caterpillars : 5236
Catfish : 921
Catfish, Like Me : 2241
Cathedral : 5224
Catherine Palace : 3059
Catholic Girl : 5549
A Catholic Shredding in Beverly Hills : 970
Cats : 2644, 3690
The Cat's Face : 1652
A Cat's Landscape : 3440
Cattle Shooting : 2165
Caught : 500
Caught in Ice : 4911
Cauliflowers : 4537
Causation : 2842
The Cause of the Crash and the Crash Itself :
      3388
Caution Contains : 5984
Cautionary Tale : 6902
Cavafy's Motif : 1093, 4566
The Cave : 5480
The Cave of Saint Rita : 4873
Cavemen : 4243
Caves : 2656
Cazadora : 5363
Ce Silence Soudain : 2160
Ce soir j'ai vu une rose : 1270
Ce Soir Sopé : 5783
C'è un'Altra Possibilità : 5362
Cease Fire : 2431
Ceasework : 4863
Cebolla Church : 2750
Cedar Rapids Airport : 1969, 4475

The Ceiba : 1364, 4312
The Ceiling : 3381
Celadon : 469
Celebrating Giacometti : 1071, 6017
Celebration : 4616
Celebration Oberman : 214
Celebrity : 4814
Celestial Burial : 1625, 7069
Celestial Symphony : 4234
Cellar Door : 1968
The Celtic Cross : 6640
Celtic Landscape : 6000
Celtic Love, a Blood Memory : 5640
Cement Town : 1709
The Cemetery at Bark River : 434
The cemetery lies near : 2806, 5810
Cemetery of Acatitlan : 1157
Cemetery Wings : 660
Cemetery with a View : 5162
Cenotaph : 5467
The Centaur Comes Down Main Street in
      March : 1228
A Centenary Observation : 1592
Centennial : 2720
Center : 4260
The Center for Atmospheric Research : 5190
The Center of the Beans : 6608
The Centerfold : 2084
A Central American Travel Journal : 5331
The Central Bus Station, Beer Sheeba : 3663
Central Lock-Up : 6510
Central Otago-Baseline : 6959
A Century Late : 4671
Cerberus : 6848
Ceremonially Drunk : 4977
Ceremonies for Boys and Girls : 184
Ceremony : 5976
Ceremony for Morning : 918
Ceremony of Cows : 4045
Ceremony on a Summer Night : 6421
Ceres Bakery : 1997
Certain Assumptions Concerning the Curricu-
      lum Vitae : 316
A Certain Geography : 2304
Certain People : 3197
A Certain Song to Palestine : 464, 1441
Certain Tall Buildings : 7059
Certeris Paribus : 4658
Certitude : 2662, 5528
The Certitude of Laundromats : 2986
Ces Poèmes Obscurs : 2504
Cesare Pavese : 4594
Cézanne and the Love of Color : 1605
Cézanne's A Modern Olympia — 1872 : 1605
Chain : 1332, 5486
The Chain : 244, 3011, 4090
Chain Mail : 2105
Chain Poem : 4857
Chain Reaction : 797
Chains, My Own : 627
The chair was a student of Euclid : 5894
Chalk the Rabbit : 2104
The Chamber : 2127
Chamber Music : 3833

The Chameleon : 641
The Chameleon Changes His Colors : 1611
Chances : 6371
Change of Clothes : 2369
A Change of Maps : 7057
A Change of Raiment : 5908
Change of Seasons : 6514
Change Partners and Dance : 3210
Changeling : 6809
Changes in My Father : 383
Changes, or, Reveries at a Window Overlook-
    ing a Country Road, with Two Women
    Talking Blues in the Kitchen : 3466
Changing Lady : 6619
Changing Neighborhood : 5008
Changing Order : 297
Changing Seasons : 2872
The Changing Social World : 6698
Changing States : 969
Changing the Imperatives : 6964
Changing the Oil : 2742
Chant de Printemps : 5783
Chanteuse : 1650
Chanteuse — 1955 : 2331
Chanticleer : 3150
A Chapel : 5727
Chapel in the Residence, Wurzburg : 3713
Chapel of Forgiveness : 929
The Chapel of Santa Maria in Obidos, Portugal
    : 4640
Chapels at Dauchau, 1971 : 1678
Chapter XXXIX : 6701
A Chapter of Proverbs : 3385
Character : 6666
Character Part : 5962
A Character Sketch : 3079
The Charge : 5107
Chariot : 6714
Charitable Acts : 3816
Charleston Baskets : 6796
Charlie Parker Playing Brilliantly 'My Old
    Flame' : 5390
A Charm After Dying : 3470
Charm for an Imagined Girl : 2983
A Charm to Be Spoken to One with Cancer :
    3470
A Charm to Fall Asleep : 3470
Charting What to Say : 1981
Chase Game : 4678
Chasing a Black Dog : 664
Chasing Amelia : 1864
Chasing the Dog Star : 4448
Chateau Cliche : 457
Château Musar : 5350
The Chattel Element : 641
Cheating Breath : 3483
Check Number 375 : 3756
Check-Out Counter Vignettes : 6288
Checking on Father, One Saturday Morning in
    June : 6608
Cheetah : 3795
Cheetah Is Gone : 2427
Chekhov's Visit : 159
Chemo : 1632

Cherishing Thouzon : 1071, 6017
Cherokee : 5885
Cherries : 3534
Cherry Pop : 5313
Chert Quarry : 1006
Chester's on Franklin : 4199
Chevron-Titipapa : 1999, 5616
Chewing the Pieces : 5286
Cheyne Row, Chelsea : 2008
Chez Lipp : 1181
Chez Pierre, 1961 : 579
Chiaroscuro : 1401, 3492, 6468
Chiaroscuro Defies Clarity : 5170
Chicago, 1983 : 2471
Chichen Itza : 1808
The Chicken : 2515, 7150
Chicken Hawk : 4345
Chicken Little : 5762
Chicken Pox : 5274
Chickens on the Top : 1292
Chief Canassatego Reflects on American
    Education, 1744 : 953, 4271
Chief Never Wearying : 886
Chief Seattle Reflects on the Future of America,
    1855 : 4271, 5759
Chief Speckled Snake Reflects on Patterns in
    American History, 1829 : 4271, 6071
Child and Shadows : 5976
Child at Play : 1258
Child Bride : 5814
A Child Composer's Garden : 4770
Child Eyes : 791
A Child Is Not a Knife : 3723, 6048
The Child of Chess : 1008
Child Sleeping : 5224
Child Suppers: Bode : 4205
The Child We Won't Have Is Crowding Us in
    the Front : 3780
The Child Within the Man : 1033, 3621, 5554
Childhood : 5959
Childhood Bolted : 441, 5620
Childhood Memory : 3151, 3934
The Childhood of the Saint : 5566
Childhood Sketch : 1953, 2741, 4938
Children : 666, 813, 814, 2418, 3632
The Children : 3604
The Children Help Me Die : 1142
Children in Autumn Memory : 973
Children in the Field : 6822
The Children of Elmer : 2337
The Children of Endingen : 6688
Children of Giraffes : 6922
The Children of Paradise : 858
Children Threatened by a Nightingale : 313
Children's Games : 1853
Children's Ward: New York Hospital : 4410
Child's : 6710
Child's Play : 5602
The Chilean Elegies: 4. Larry Tetlock : 6794
Chimera : 1031, 1925, 6298
China: A Dream of Wild Horses : 4657
The China Cabinet : 2228
China Clipper : 6608
China in the News : 3027

The China Syndrome : 5747
Chinatown (Paris, 18th Arrondissement) : 424, 4019
Chinese Dragons : 660
The Chinese Executioner : 1181, 2503
Chinese Hot Pot : 3889
The Chinese Pornographer : 5980
Chinese Pornography : 5149
Chins or Criticize : 5111
Chloe Sings the Blues : 6274
Chocolate Ice Cream : 1285
The Chocolate Lambs : 578
Choices : 5522
Choose : 4315, 7173
Choosing : 4451
Choosing a Pomegranate : 870
Choosing the Bow : 4218
Chop Suey : 265
Chopin : 463, 2552
Chopin. May 1988 : 6189
Choral : 780, 5712
A Chorus : 6144
The Chosen : 3506
Chris and Bill and His Dog Osley : 4132
Christ As Gardener : 2238, 5135, 5136
Christ Enters Manhattan : 1624
Christ in Abeyance : 1666
Christ of Lonely Beach : 1957
Christening in Coimbra : 290
Christian Art : 6836
The Christian Science Minotaur : 2970
Christina : 3637
Christina, Queen of the Swedes : 1495
Christmas 1988, Each Breath a Tennis Court Oath : 1146
Christmas Call : 5852
Christmas Card for Norman : 1914
Christmas Decorations : 4487
Christmas Eve and the Bull : 3785
Christmas Eve at Port Authority : 6753
Christmas Eve at Rosemound Cemetery : 7030
Christmas in Carthage : 1199
Christmas Morning : 1356
Christmas (Portland, Oregon, 1969) : 896
A Christmas Song : 6952
Christmas Spell : 2693
The Christmas Spirit : 3825
Christmas Trees : 2681, 4149
Christmas Vacation : 1829
Chronicle of the Indies : 4619, 4854
Chronology : 1473, 6628
Church : 6833
Church of Atotonilco : 6202
The Church Portal : 6878, 6915
Churchyard in Umanaq : 2913, 2956
Cicada : 3780, 7058
Cicadas : 2308, 4021, 4770, 5069
Los Ciclos : 4368
Cider : 5144
The Cigarette Box : 2722
The Cinder Garden : 1983
Cinderella: a Sociological Phenomenon : 6411
Cinderella and Lazarus, Part II : 372
Cinderella Rediviva : 2740

The Cinderella Theme : 5039
Cinnamon Tea & Olive Liquor : 6104
Ciphering : 675
Circe : 1007
Circle : 1582, 3547, 5098, 5379, 6328
Circle of Chalk : 2643
The Circle of Silence : 5224
Circles, Always Circles : 1265
Circling : 1772
A Circuit Preacher Recalls : 4382
Circuit Rider : 912
Circularity : 2606
Circulars : 4416
Circumcision : 2553
Circumstances : 3083
Circumstances Told by a German : 184, 4239
The Circus : 6504
Cities : 3708, 4130
Citizen Jan Polkowski — Justification for Existence : 5079
Citizens : 2194
Citrus Workers : 1528
City : 2312
The City : 4410
City and Day : 6710
City Fog : 373
The City in Which I Love You : 3691
City Life : 4684
City Lights : 6198
The City on the Hill : 3379
The City Rat Returns from the Dead for an Interview : 4296
City Snow : 6910
City Stones : 6724
The City Underneath : 5485
The City: Voting : 6999
The City Was Emptied : 813, 814, 3792
City Winterscape : 918
City Without Walls : 786
Cityscape : 1350
Ciudad de México Soñada : 6554
Civic Duties: My Neighbor, Marn, Volunteer Fireman : 2665
Civics Class : 5821
Civil Defense : 747
A Civil Tongue : 4630
The Civil War : 6340
Civilization and Its Discontents : 6510
Civilization Comes Out of the Sea : 5695
Civilized : 2139
Claiming the Find : 6248
Claimstaking in White Sulfur Springs : 4573
Clamor : 5716
The clanking : 1237
Clarity : 813, 814, 4888, 6222
The Clarity of Programs : 134
Class Notes on Painting and the Arts : 1574
Classic : 2410, 4477
Classical Guitar : 4564
Clay : 5566
Clay Birdcall Trombone : 6897
The Clay Pot : 5114
Clay's Birthday : 2236
Clean Living : 6555

Clean Sweep : 1908
Clean Underwear and a Radio : 3780
Cleaning Pheasants : 3413
Cleaning Smelt : 6337
Cleaning the Auger, Wet Corn Silo : 5550
Cleaning the Wound : 6365
A Clear Day in January : 3518
Clear Flame : 3234
Clear Purple, Two Stars, Moon : 2673
Clear White Stream : 1101
Clear Yellow : 3923
Clearance : 6618
Cleared Away : 2288
Clearing : 1739
The Clearing : 4238
Clearing Her, Easing the Obsession: A Flyer's
    Manual : 5890
Clearing the Table : 921
Clearings : 5603
Clecsografie : 3967, 6632
Clemente's Bullets : 1830
Clemmie with Hoe : 3957
Cleopatra in the Afterworld : 2457
Clepsydra : 2874
Click-Rose 2 : 2047, 6707
Clifford Brown : 3036
Climacteric Sonnet : 2740
Climate Control : 6518
Climbers : 1908
Climbing Down Eggerslack : 6541
Climbing Hills with Alice : 3222
Climbing to Ngorongoro : 1366
Clinical Games : 3668
Cloaks of Silence : 3445, 5874, 6082
The Clock : 2532, 2922, 7106
Clock Mania : 184
Clocks of the Sea : 234
Cloister : 5926
Cloisters : 184
A Close Call : 2714
Close Calling : 1746
Close to Home : 2648
Close-UP : 271, 653
Close-Up of Death : 74, 2028
Closed Gentian : 3753
Closed letter : 461, 4005
Closer to the Warning of Age : 256
Closet : 467
The Closet : 2949
The Closet, the Clock, and the Thunder : 5940
Closing Distances : 4080
Closing Time : 6102
Closing Time at the Zoo : 6465
The closure of an end-rhyme line stops : 2275
Clothes : 674
Clothing of the Dead : 4754
Cloud Hands : 5730
A Cloud No Bigger than a Man's Hand : 940
The Cloud of Unknowing : 1976
A Cloud of White Linen : 2663
Cloudburst : 4162
The Clouds : 591, 4402
Cloudy Issues : 3577
The Clown : 4676, 5513

The Clown in the Closet : 1735
The Club House : 839
C'Mon, John : 3829
Coal Boys : 5550
A Coalminer's Last Shift : 5982
Coast : 1218
Coast to Coast : 992
Coast Town : 3434
The Coastal Access Stairway : 1267
Cobra : 885
Cobwebs (1919) : 5459
Cocaine : 2776
A Cock and Fox Story : 2682
The Cock of Pomander Walk : 1938, 2188,
    5883
Cock of the August Berm, or, Rise and Fall :
    796
Cocktail : 4984
The Cocktail Hour : 6038
Cocoon in the Subway : 3898
Coda : 241
Code Blue : 6993
Code of Behavior : 4737
Codependency : 4807
Codicil : 4140
Coffee : 5967
The Coffee Cup : 2567
Coffee with the Beatniks : 3905
A Coffin and a Chevy : 3699
Coffin Shortage in Caracas : 4311
The Coin : 2168
The Coin Trick : 5379
Coincidence : 4132
Coins : 6095
Coke : 1214
Cold : 4585, 5379
Cold Bay : 3919
Cold Blood : 6306
Cold Creek : 4303, 6973
Cold Ones : 2567
Cold Springs : 2492
Cold Wa(te)r : 4797
Cold Weather : 5600
Cole Porter : 4086
Colibrí : 1830
Collaborator, Chartres, 1944 : 4313
Collage : 3975
Collage with Paint : 274
Collared and Cuffed : 3167
Collect for Women : 370
Collected Works : 1449
The Collecting Bug : 1795
The Collection : 435, 1085, 4180
Collector : 77, 3450
The Collector : 1374
The Collectors : 345
Colonel Mackenzie and the Ghosts of Warriors
    : 4179
The Color of Grief : 2390
The Color of Money : 2754
The Color of the Trees Is Wet : 5723
Colorado Buick Mountain Heart : 4147
Colored Glass : 6075
Coloring the Tree of Night : 691

Colorizing: Turner Broadcasting Enterprises, Computer Graphics Division, Burbank, CA, 1987 : 7010
Colorless Green Ideas Sleep Furiously : 546
The Colors of Indian Corn : 6737
The Colors of Passion : 2898
The Colors of Saint Josephs : 2604
The Colour Blood : 5430
Colour Codes : 1403
Colubri's Psalm : 3340
Columbine Pass, August, 1983 : 7178
Columbus : 5315
Columbus's Children : 230
Columnar : 1266
Combat Boots : 6910
Combinations : 4179
Combine : 2898
Come Back Safely : 1526, 2155
Come Find Winter : 5772
Come Inside : 813, 814, 6222
Come One Step Closer : 2782
Comedians vs. Poets : 4199
Comedy with Gulkis: A Craft Interview : 2345
Comet : 2104, 5937, 6573
Comeuppance : 3842
Comfort : 3796
The Comfort of Rooms : 6320
The Coming Disaster : 171
Coming Down : 515
Coming Down (After the Latest Tear) : 4080
Coming from School : 3510
Coming Home : 3075, 3612, 4422
Coming Home at Night : 435, 1085, 4180
Coming Home in a Window Seat : 107
Coming into LaGuardia Late at Night : 5067
Coming of Age in Michigan : 3746
The Coming of Fall : 6509
The Coming of the King : 590
The Coming of Winter in North Dakota : 1577
The Coming On : 1684
Coming Out : 3952
Coming Round : 5567
Coming Through Winter : 940
Coming To : 666, 3117
Coming to Mind : 1927
Coming to Pass : 4363
Coming to Terms : 1308
Comma : 312
The Commandant's Ghost : 5286
Commandments : 878, 4346, 5006
Commencement Exercises : 4851
Commission : 5467
The Commissioner of Salt : 131
Commitment : 5201
Commode Etiquette : 6557
Common American Crow : 5695
Common Angels : 6590
Common Condition : 5030
Common Knowledge : 1821
The Common Life : 5471
Common Rock : 2677
Communal Darkroom : 6105
The Communal Pleasures of the Intermezzi : 1840

Communicant : 2749
Communication : 1033, 3621, 5554
La Communication : 5554
Communion : 6101
Communion Meditation : 1179
Communist : 2236
Commutation : 2425
La Compañía de Jesús : 3900
Companion Studies : 2588
Companions : 6389, 7060
Company : 6813
Compass : 90
The Compass : 5544
Compassion : 6332
Compassion at the World's Cafe : 4556
Compassion Stone : 4671
Complement Returned : 3051
The Complete Angler : 588
The Complete Poems of Mr. John Milton : 5543
The Composer's Daughter : 630
Composición Escrita en un Ejemplar de la Gesta de Beowulf : 640
Composition : 3542
Composition #12 : 2480
The Compost Bin Speaks : 5501
The Compromise : 1848
Compulsories : 2574
The Comrade : 1757, 4403
Con Sordino : 4676, 5513
Con Tal Que el Avestruz : 4865
Con Text : 52
The Concave : 4631
The Concepts of Integrity and Closure in Poetry As I Believe They Relate to Sappho : 2742
Concepts of Time : 3169
Concert : 1625, 5153
A Concert at the Phillips : 7147
Concerto : 6280
Concerto for Flute and Strings : 6894
Concertos for Wind Instruments : 3898
Conch Shell : 4816
Concierto de Cítara : 6554
Conclusion : 3647
Concord : 3583
Concrete Poem : 1175
Concurrence : 2476
Condor I Am : 3551
Coney Island Baby : 3749
A Confederate Sharpshooter Awaits General Forrest : 5212
Confession : 4223, 6549
A Confession : 1397, 2839, 6544
Confessional : 5687
Confessions : 3093
Confessions and Conclusions : 2244
Confidence : 5117
Configurations : 6317
Congères : 1867
Congregations : 4521
Connect the Dots to Make a Picture : 3508
Connection : 6492
Connections : 2277
Connectives in the Night : 326
Connemara : 4099

The Conning Towers of My Father's War : 4042
The Connoisseuse of Slugs : 4782
Conqueror : 4312
A Conquistador's Testament : 1113
Consecration : 5118, 6786
The Consensus : 4429
Consider the House : 1343
Consider the Lily : 5431
Considering Flowers : 5198
Considering the Geometrical Basis of Language and . . . : 3828
Consolation : 194, 4750
Consolation at Ground Zero : 2949
The Consolation of Boethius : 2440
Consolations : 6101
The Consort to the King of Naples : 1749
Constance Wilde : 4879
Constellation : 4235
The Constellation of Flying Fish : 6629
Constellations : 2594
Construction (II) : 4132
El Consul del Mar del Norte : 1028
Consummation : 2563
Containment : 6323
Contemplating the Salesgirl's Lipstick : 3690
Contemplation of Poussin : 5631
Contemplation on the 20th Anniversary of the Moonshot, July 20, 1989 : 5267
Contemporary Culture and the Letter 'K' : 1287
Contemporary Outremerican Poetry : 3435
Contention : 4688
Contentment: December Twenty-Ninth : 2303
Contest Winner. 1912 : 5987
Contexts : 258
The Continental College of Beauty : 6221
Continental Drift : 643
Continuing Education : 666
Continuous Time : 1473, 6628
The Contortionist : 5751
Contract : 298
Contradictory Existence : 7062
Contrappunto : 2687
Contrapunto May-June 1984 : 3967, 6632
Contrived : 1331
Convalescence : 7177
Convalescents : 535
Convection : 1050
Convergence : 5330
Convergence of Multiples : 1071, 6017
Conversation / Conversion : 5901
Conversation: December, the Night City : 5512
Conversation in Increasing Stanzas : 6666
A Conversation Phrase Book for Angels : 6936
Conversation with a Dead Politician (or Chak-Chak) : 3303
Conversation with a Zuni Indian : 478
Conversation with Isadora Duncan : 455
The Conversion Near Jessups on the Big Raccoon : 6952
Convert : 397
Convict : 150
Coo Coo Vision : 6446
The Cookie Jar : 1609

The Cooking : 4527
Cool : 4223
Cool for April : 1635
The Cool Night : 3275
Cooling : 3496
Copenhagen Interpretation : 1094
Coping with death : 6955
Copper, Khetri, Rajasthan : 1550
Copulation : 6436
Coral : 780
Corals : 3214, 5379, 5492
The Corner : 5583
A Corner of the Garden with Dahlias : 989
Corona de las Frutas : 5625
Coronet Chop Suey : 3091
Corpse Cradle : 2164
Corpses : 6890
Correspondence : 1308
The Correspondence : 2005
Corrida : 3396
Corrido de Etelvina Menchaca : 6561, 6587
Corsage : 1412
Corso de la Niña : 5235
Corvus : 2470
Cosmetic : 4753
Cosmic Love on a Disk : 6641
Cosmic Pleasure : 2854
Cosmology of the Irish Mother : 4452
Cosmo's Perfect Love Letter : 3068
El Costal de las Sombras Vació Todo Su Frío : 3067
The Costs : 1429
The cots, the stove, the crew : 4973
Cottage : 6923
Cottage Above the Harbor : 4731
The Cottage on Lake Michigan : 4723
Cottonmouth : 1735
Cottonmouth, Angus, Redwing : 5760
Could have Been Verbs : 5000
Could It Be : 4429
Could This Be True? : 7181
Could We : 7146
Coulter's Road : 4099
Countdown : 1258
Countershading : 2258
Counting Aloud : 5221
Counting Back: An Oral History of Dakota Territory : 6874
Counting By Rote : 326
Counting the Children : 2288
Country : 5838
A Country Auction : 5832
Country Burying (1919) : 6765
Country Calendar : 3682, 4874
Country Fair : 5894
A Country Gentleman Stands at the Window, September 24, 1863 : 666, 3632
Country Is Photos : 1520
Country Lunch : 5894
Country Music : 5313
Country of Cardboard and Cotton Batting : 3047, 5440, 6220, 6266
Country of the Tree-tops : 628, 5620
Country Radio : 2566

Country Roads : 6654
Country Singer : 1854
Country Wash : 1610
County Fairs : 4556
Coup : 3912
The Coup : 2706
Coup de Grâce : 794
The Couple : 1018, 2826, 6221
A Couple in the Café de la Gare : 989
Courage : 666, 3117, 4823
Courage, 1983 : 396
Courage Is a Rafter : 4289
Le Coursier de Jeanne D'Arc : 4146
Court Documents: Infidelity : 271
Court of the Lions, Alhambra : 1161
The Courthouse : 6536
Courtier of the Core : 6711
Courtly Love : 3002
Courtship of Darkness : 5584
Cousin : 2042
Cousin Barbara : 5934
Cove Neighbor : 2796
The Cove of Women : 6905
Covenant : 666
The Covenant : 5147
Cover Letter : 7183
Cover Up : 6101
Covering the Earth: I, an Ant : 1108, 1112,
    1252
Covers : 219
Covert Street : 6779
The Cow and Her Uterus : 444
The Cow Comes in Heat : 3785
The Cow Says, I'm a Hippopotamus : 5423
Cowboy-Boot Sale : 1227
Cowboy Christ : 6055
Cowboy I fell for : 1482
Cowboys : 1265
Cows : 2465
Cows, Headlines, & the 4th : 4145
Coyote Goes to Toronto : 3379
Coyote Learns to Whistle : 3379
Coyote Sees the Prime Minister : 3379
Coyotes : 4231
Coyotismo : 2396
Crab Dance : 5611
Crabdance : 2212
The Crabs : 4735
Cracking a Few Hundred Million Years : 132
Cracking the Whip : 2086
Craft : 1625
The Craft We Journey In : 6209
The Craftsmen Have Left : 1754, 3544
Craig's Muse: Wearing the Green : 6700
Crane : 1526, 1657
The Crank : 1735
Crawl Space : 4442
Crazy Blue : 1570
Crazy Horse Speaks : 96
Crazy Mary in the Cemetery : 4620
Crazy Ralphie's : 1456
Crazy Woman Creek : 2677
The Created World : 4339
Creating the World : 2707, 4395

Creation : 2654, 6779
The Creation : 2297
Creation Myths : 2131
The Creation of Birds : 74, 2028
Creation of Passion : 3421
Creative Process : 1385
The Creative Writing Class Hears About
    Submitting Manuscripts : 6871
Creators : 5070
Creature : 5139
Creatures : 3303
Crèche : 6118
Credo : 400, 841, 4465
Creek Bottom : 7071
Creek Water : 6334
Creeks : 2447
Creeley In : 672
The Cremation of Sam McGee : 5787
Creosote Tea : 6200
The crêpe of still water's core : 461, 4005
Crepuscule : 774
Le crépuscule d'eau où le ciel blanc s'éclaircit
    encore : 461
Creusa : 4237
Cricket : 3440
Crickets : 4016
Crickets Crush Woman : 1821
Cries : 791
Cries and Shispers : 485
Crimes of Passion : 4373
Criminal Code : 4420
The Criminal Mentality : 3912
Crimson Quest : 1174
Crippled Islands : 3100
Cris : 4023, 4881
The Crisis : 832
The Crisis of Theory : 6547
Crisis Queue : 6514
Cristal : 5882
Critique at a Local Show : 374
Croakers : 5679
Crochet : 2222
Crocodilopilos : 3311
Cromwell's Prayer : 3045
Croning : 7185
Cronologia : 1473
Crooked Sonnets : 6165
Cross Words : 1933
Crosses & Rust : 4471
Crossfire : 3093
Crossing America : 5306
Crossing Essex : 5048
Crossing Harvard Yard : 4298
The Crossing of Legs : 1666
Crossing Over : 203, 2863
Crossing the Connecticut at Hartford : 5370
Crossing the Desert : 3491
Crossing the Fence : 3352
Crossing the River : 212
Crossing the Rockies : 5733
Crossings : 1113, 5889
Crossroads : 4343, 6859
The Crow : 3365, 4867
Crow Moon : 6792

The Crow on the Cradle : 3831
A Crow, the First One We've Seen This Spring
    : 1040
The Crown Conch Shell : 2092
A Crown for Fox Point at Ives & William : 175
The Crown of Flowers : 6912
Crown Vetch : 2200
Crows : 3983
The Crows : 3872
Crows Among the Hawkweed and Black-Eyed
    Susans : 6831
Crucifiction : 3609
Crucifixion: Montgomery, Alabama : 2981
Cruelty : 6899
Cruise : 3873
The Crusades : 3317
Crutches : 2290
Crying Like a Child : 5466
The Crying of Old Women : 5431
Crying Wolf : 5117
Cryogenics: Born Again into a Cold Light :
    6605
Crypto Erotica #3 : 1143
Crystal Thin : 6710
Crystal Unclear : 3154
Crystals, Cabochons : 6114
Cuando la calma vuelva : 2167
El Cuarto Viaje de Colon : 2054
The Cuckold's Tale : 6298
Cuckoo : 3318, 5344
Cuervos : 1011
Cullen's Mule : 6877
Cultivating a Species : 5609
Cultural Literacy : 232
Cumulative Erasure : 501
Cup of Soup : 3841
Cupid and Psyche : 5205
The Curator : 6951
Curing Midas : 3796
The Curious Night Before Elizabeth : 1438
A Curious Romance : 3652
Current Events : 3490, 3575
Current That Cannot Cross the Gap : 5766
Curse : 53, 2591, 7094
The Curse : 2161
A Curse from Propertius : 4377
The Cursing of the Fig Tree : 419
Curtains : 6212
A Curvacious soubrette from St. Paul : 4924
The Curve of Forgetting : 937
Custom : 4405
The Customer : 337
Cutaway : 368
Cutting : 3652
Cutting a Firebreak : 1142
Cutting Re/marks : 6754
Cycle : 939
Le Cycle de la Parole : 1073, 3588, 6220
The Cycle: for Kaya and Cavafy : 3193
The Cycles : 4368, 5995
Cypress : 3360
Cypress, Heron: Leaving Camille : 6416
Cysts : 6095
D-Day : 2506

D. W. Griffith's Dreamgirl : 1136
Da History of Pigeon : 311
Da pig make kaukau from make die dead
    kanaka : 2611, 5742
Da Vinci Perplexed : 6250
Dad : 2960
Dada Is God, : 3655
Daddy : 1649
Daddy-O : 1973
Daddy's Girl : 6075
Daddy's Old Shoes : 4920
Daemonization Towards a Counter-Sublime :
    4898
Dahlias : 2431
Daily Bread : 3736
The Daily Life of the Poem : 143
Daily News and Whatever : 5111
Daily Remembered Allowances : 6708
Dakota Station : 6025
The Dam Builder's Dream : 5501
Damage : 5330
Damage Control : 501
Damned : 813, 814, 2418
D'Amour et D'Eau Fraîche : 1661
Damsel in Distress : 5296
Dan Quayle on the Riverboat, August 1988 :
    6513
Danaïde : 3554
Danbury, Connecticut : 6835
Dance : 393, 6977
The Dance : 103, 2107
The Dance of Juba : 6272
Dance of the Five Veils : 5611
A Dance on the Greek Island : 5224
Dance-Song : 3095, 4767, 5768
Dance the Night Away : 1535
Dancer : 6813
The Dancer : 4942, 6770
Dancer in an All Day, All Night Festival for the
    Revolution, Paris 1794 : 485
Dancer in the Window : 1209
Dancer, PS 122, 10/14/89 : 1173
Dancers of the Night : 1881
Dancing Back the Cranes : 5551
Dancing Days : 3640
Dancing Demonless : 3372
The Dancing Grandmother : 5224
Dancing on the Glacier : 1113
The Dancing Penguins of the Air : 6104
The Dancing Sun : 3048
Dancing the Boys into Bed : 4229
Dancing with Your Devil : 6781
Dandelion : 2332, 2705
The Dandelion : 887, 1200
Dandelion Safari : 5575
Danger : 6824
Danger in the Ocean : 1222
The Danger of Shelter : 252
Dangerous Life : 4980
Dangerous Music : 6238
Dangerous Words : 1618
Dans la Chaleur Vacante (In the Vacant Heat) :
    1286, 1687
Danse Macabre : 2732

Danse Ordinaire : 6705
Dante : 1625, 7076
Dante's Inferno : 6179
Daphne Heard with Horror the Addresses of the
    God : 616
The Dare : 675, 2494
The Dark : 172, 3297
Dark Angel : 7032
Dark Angels : 2900
Dark Lady in White : 4349
Dark Matter : 833, 2854
Dark Night on a Southbound Train : 1584,
    4486, 6744
The Dark Rushes : 3512
Dark, Small-Town Streets : 2928
Dark Songs: Slave House and Synagogue :
    3776
Dark Star : 7151
Dark the Face : 3911
Dark Trees : 5011
Dark Wind : 813, 814, 5525
Dark Woman Well : 3977
Darker Ends : 4729
Darker Even Than the Dark Before Dawn :
    5340
The Darkest Season : 6076
Darkly Glinting : 2454, 6324
Darkness : 2610, 5802
The Darkness : 5683
The Darlings : 841
Dart : 4934
Darwin Was Wrong : 4740
Dat Boy : 5090
Dateline, Western Sizzler : 3388
Dating the Dick Heads : 1170
Daughter : 1362, 3556, 5001
The Daughter : 3396, 5460
Daughter, My Daughter : 1532
The Daughter of My Daughter : 3044
The Daughter of the Dreams : 4753
The Daughter's Runes for the Stepmother : 120
David : 670
Davida and I Check Out Saks : 1974
Dawn : 1638, 1690, 2339, 2508, 2508, 2508,
    3445, 5874, 6708, 6708
The Dawn : 4712
Dawn 1809 : 3784, 4787
Dawn As a Work in Progress : 7003
Dawn Boat Trip on the White River (Ark.) :
    4885
Dawn of the Bitter Blizzard : 4179
Day : 854, 4627
The Day After : 1601, 3597
The Day After Labor Day : 2170
Day and Night Baroque : 2693
A Day at Work : 5078
The Day Before the Progress Bulletin Reported
    Alcoholic Genes : 3839
Day Break : 2713
Day by Day : 1363, 2952, 2952, 5204, 5379,
    5379
Day Care : 5685
A Day for Fishing : 1138
The Day I Became Golden : 710

A Day in Madrid : 6375, 7057
Day in Sulfur : 4462
A Day in the Life : 244, 3011, 6028
The Day Itself : 4312
The Day Joy Discomeboomulated, Disappeared
    : 938
Day Labor : 5685
A Day Like November : 4178
Day Lilies : 234, 1735
Day Lily : 547
The Day My Daughter Smeared the Car with
    Lipstick : 7167
The Day My Grandmother Dies : 4556
Day of a Cat's Death : 5581
Day of Atonement : 3409
Day of Atonements : 891
Day of Robert Lowell's Funeral : 4671
The Day of the Big Wind : 82
The Day of the Dead : 14, 7079
The Day of the Funeral : 3559
Day of the Soft Mouth : 2470
A Day Off : 5963
A Day on the Nautilus : 6435
A Day on the Water : 5663
The Day School Gives Out : 5443
Day Ten After Heart Surgery, Signing a Check :
    4784
The Day the Wall Came Down : 5381
The Day There Was Only Michael Friedman :
    2114
The Day They Shot a Wolf in the Ghetto and
    What It Meant : 7017
Day Up London : 1099
The Day We Bombed Utah : 1030
The Day Willie Missed the Bus : 1917
A Day with Baxter: His Home in New Zealand :
    5224
The Day Without Wind : 1625, 7156
Daybreak : 748, 1867, 2380, 3066, 7129
Daydreams and Nightdreams : 7032
Days : 3599
Day's Harmonies (Unemployment Poem) :
    6749
Days of Darkness : 3384
The Dazzled One : 403, 822
De Enda Krig : 206
De-Exoticizing the Other : 4378
The de facto Territory : 1469
De Gangna Dagarna : 685
De Lacu Aliciae : 78
De los Nombres : 2514
De Tocqueville Revisited : 1613
De una isla : 2167
De Vogelschrik : 6007
Dead : 184
The Dead : 2828, 5241, 5976
Dead-Battery Blues : 5733
The Dead Body Itself : 4782
Dead Boys : 340
Dead Butterfly : 363
The Dead Cartesian : 6730
Dead City : 47, 4869
Dead Classmates : 281
Dead Drive-In : 1975

Dead Elms : 6144
Dead End Blues : 4416
Dead Fruit : 3582
The Dead King : 4855
Dead of Night : 6837
Dead on Arrival : 6236
The Dead Poets : 1753
Dead Reckoning : 2492, 4170
Dead Sea Nursery Rimes : 1207
Dead Set : 1903
Dead Still : 1018, 5992
La Deadichada : 4641
Deaf and Blind : 1527
The Deaf Backpackers : 4581
The Deaf Couple : 4916
Deaf Enough : 2655
The Deaf Fisherman : 5026
A Deaf Woman Describes a Concert : 2792
The Dealer : 535
Dealing with the Conundrum : 3059
Dear Absence : 406
Dear Ann Landers : 2614
Dear be still! Time's start of us lengthens
    slowly : 847
Dear Customer : 5946
Dear Dr. Williams, Dear Poet : 6244
Dear Editor : 5917
Dear Eileen : 4716
Dear Friend : 112
Dear Jane : 6009
Dear Nominalist : 792
Dear Rich : 4662
Dear Robert: I Dreamed Last Night That You
    Were Dead : 1128
Dear Sam, Taken by the Adoption Agency :
    2194
Dear Sinking Ship : 2361
Dear World, *fuck off* advice ingredients, empty
    swing : 162
Dearest Thrushes : 1511, 5072
Death : 2072, 2933
Death Anniversary : 53
Death Became a Habit : 1613
Death Brings No Light : 4462
Death Fugue : 1043, 1647
Death in Mid-winter : 5633
Death Is Not for Duffers : 588
Death Lesson : 4995
A Death Mantra : 5333
The Death of a Child in Winter : 2027
Death of a Hummingbird : 5901
Death of a Medieval Carpenter : 6902
The Death of Allegory : 1213
Death of an Irishwoman : 2692
The Death of Antinoüs : 1650
The Death of Birds : 2098
Death of Caracalla : 3164
Death of Cezanne : 5765
The Death of Emma Hardy : 5504
The Death of God : 298
The Death of Harry S. Truman : 2946
The Death of Hector : 1874, 2923
The Death of Smith-Corona : 4944
Death of the Inshore : 1634

Death of the Lion Tamer : 5949
Death Row : 99
Death Speaks of a Man Who Started the Day
    Reading Rubber Trees : 472
A Death That Dare Not Speak : 3157
Death Threat Note : 3466
Deaths and Weather : 3947
Deathwatch : 6833
Debbie Louise in Odessa TX : 2407
Debris of Shock/Shock of Debris : 501
Debt : 3745
Debt Is Survival's Ringing Phone : 1458
Decathlon Man : 1925, 3739
December : 348, 803, 2364
December 1st : 487
December 12th : 5022
December 14, 1988 : 244, 3011, 6020
December 18: For M : 4921
December 20, 1963 : 5934
December 24th : 1670
December 27, 1988 : 1750
December Divorce: A Theorem : 4319
December Monday : 6199
December Moon : 5631
December Work : 3208
Decembre : 6180
Deciduous : 3959
Decision : 960
The Decision : 2109
Decisioning Sky : 792
Deck : 4886
Deckertown Falls : 569
Declaración de Bogotá : 2388
Declaration : 435, 813, 814, 4180, 5293, 5628,
    7067
Declaration of Love : 2185, 2289, 4792
Declension : 467
Deconstruction : 2493
Deconstructions : 588
Decoration Day, the '50s : 4914
The Decoration of Hindu Pen Dents : 4694
Dedication to the Coming Year : 3354, 5776
The Deep End : 5437
Deep Listening : 2944
Deep Mud : 4767, 6237
Deep Sea Fishing : 4187
Deep Season Reply : 5732
Deep under water where every bit of my surface
    is pressed : 1148
The Deeper : 2520
The Deer : 532, 5579
The Deer at Dusk : 5997
Deer at the Red Sea : 2052, 6287
Deer Heart : 5695
Deer-Hunting in Western Pennsylvania : 3929
Deer Lodge : 4804
The Deer Man : 1248
Deer Park at Sarnath : 92
Deer Xing : 367
Defeat : 666, 3117
Defend It : 491, 4586
Defensive Rapture : 2507
Defining Time : 1521
Definitely No Marilyn Monroe : 3031

Definition : 162, 1226, 2231, 2420, 5040
Dehydrated Man : 4200
Déjà Vu : 3159
Déjà Vu While Browsing Woolworths : 6141
Deklaration : 5293
The Delay : 2875
Delft : 2337
The Delicates : 5929
Delight : 6236
Deliverance : 3335, 5211
Delivering Milk with Father : 3180
Delivery : 6110
The Delivery : 6998
Delmore Schwartz at the First Performance of
    the Velvet Underground: New York, 1966
    : 7010
Delphi : 4995
Delta : 234, 1735
Delta, Alabama, 1968 : 4382
Delta Journal : 3846
La Demente en la Puerta de la Iglesia : 2192
Democracy in the Corporate States of America :
    166
Demolition Night at the Speedway : 298
Demonic Metamorphoses : 437
Demons in the Diner : 5224
Demonstration : 4297
Den Vägen Ar Smal : 685
Denis' Photo of Francis : 3627
Denmother Volunteers at the School Carnival :
    2728
Deora Dé : 1506
Departing : 2190, 2629, 6213
Departing from a High School Reunion : 5066
Departure : 1462, 6140
The Departure : 1462
Dependence Day : 1427
Le dépit : 3678
Deplane : 3088
Deportees : 2482
Deposition : 5220
Depot : 4349
Depot of Dreams : 440
Depression Weather : 2956, 6052
Derrida & Ladida : 4344
Des Éclairs de Chaleur : 732
Descent : 3881, 3900
The Descent : 4945
Descent Through Indian Village — September,
    1967 : 4703
Description of a Friend: His Peace, Made of
    Terror : 43
A Descriptive Method : 5500, 5893
The Desert as My Cradle : 1016
Desert Fathers : 3974
The Desert O : 6075
A Desert Song Unfinished : 4963
Desert Town : 450
Design for a Menu : 1182
Design, with Drawing : 6835
Desirable Residence : 2463
Desire : 99, 1605, 1743, 1883, 3906, 5412
Desobediencia del Placer : 3854
The Desolated World : 4614

Despedidas Desperdician la Sobremesa : 1937
Despliegue de los Bolsillos : 6578
Destierro : 2019
Destinations : 1821
Desvio : 3143
Det Är I Maj Och Äppelträden Blommar : 6222
Det Finns Djupare Vatten : 5064
Det Kommer Ändå Tillbaka : 2031
Det Man Inte Kan Tala Om : 5293
Det Tar Lång Tid : 3792
Det Var i en Främmande Våning : 5064
The Detached Observer : 4883
Detail from the Creation of Man : 2406
Details : 2929
Detainee Cuban Refugee Camp : 1030
Detections have shown that the sky : 2593
The Detective's Valentine : 184
Deteriorata : 4113, 6618
Detrás de todo muro que amarillo : 5659
Detroit : 5601
Detroit Means Strait : 5036
Detta Är en Förvandling : 3792
Deva : 4940
Devil Captured, See Page 3 : 1456
Devil's Finger Island : 5515
The Devil's Ode : 6727
Devotion : 3197, 3540, 6806
Devotion Street : 1323
Devotional #1 : 2387
Devotions : 410, 2784
Dew drops sparkle on da maile curtains : 2611,
    5742
Dexter Leaps In : 2656
A Dharma Talk by Johnny Roseboro, Co.,
    March 23, 1983 : 3761
El Día Que Yo Muera : 480
A Dialectic for Spring Quarter : 6630
Dialects : 345
Dialogue : 1471, 6316
A Dialogue for Two Landscapes : 4060
Dialogue W/Ms No : 3043
The Diameron : 4140
Diamond Transform : 467
Diane's Knocking : 5446
Diary of a Lost Man : 6953
The Diary of Anne Frank : 3925
A Diatribe : 1592
Dictionary : 4548
A Dictionary of Angels : 2909
Did I Miss Anything? : 6794
Did the Black-and-White Movies Make My
    Mother? : 5433
Did you ever drift like smoke : 2125
Did You See the Graves : 813, 814, 3792
Did You Tell It Like It Is, Robert Frost? : 1446
Dies Illae : 2751, 3089
Dietrich : 1950
The Difference : 3562
The Difference Between Art and Science. II :
    2887
The Difference between Me and Bill : 5316
Difference Between Us : 5777
The Difference the Sky Makes : 744
A Different Disposition : 275, 2704

Different Shoes : 678
A Different Version of Noah's Arc : 6002
The Difficulty with Maintenance : 3612
The Dig : 1796
Digestion : 3139
Digging a Garden : 5862
Digging at Babylon : 1643
Digging In : 4423
Digging on Hardscrabble : 4179
Digital Watch : 3591
The Digs in Escondido Canyon : 4179
Dilemmas of Fatherhood : 2395
Dill Pickles : 3328
Dim : 5895
Dim Light : 4351
Dime Western : 535
Dimension or Crucifix : 1582, 5098
Dinner at Bud's Beach House : 5298
Dinner at Five : 3418
Dinner at Seven : 2226
Dinner at the End of Time : 4518
A Dinner in Plano, Texas : 1058
Dinner in the Garden District : 2425
Dinner Table : 5356
Dinner's End : 4039
Dinnertime : 5933
Dinosaur Light : 6148
The Dioxin Blues : 409
The Diplomat : 6962
Diptych for Melpone & Thalia : 4365
Direct Object of the Subjective Case : 5969
Direct Response : 5400
Directing a LOVE STORY : 1284
Directions to Rutherford : 4417
Directive : 7035
Dirt : 2470
Dirt Daubers : 3201
Dirty Linen : 5433, 7027
Dirty Word: C : 3608
Disappearances : 623
The Disappeared : 4616
Disappearing Barn : 5490
Disastrous Love : 1684
The Disavowed : 4641, 5588
Disbelieving Anti-Veal Propaganda, White Boy
    Gets in Calf Costume : 184
Discipline : 4653
Disconnection : 3867
Discovering the Continents on Your
    Grandmother's Antiques : 4379
Discovery : 435, 1085, 4180
The Discovery of Mouths : 6646
The Discovery Room : 3204
Discurso de las Infantas : 3062
Disembarking : 6381
Disguised : 2307
Disinformation : 6201
The Disjunctive Conjunction 'Or' : 3287, 5361
The Dismorphia Butterfly: Protective Mimicry
    in a Single Species : 1725
Disoluciones : 5882
Disorder Poem : 4144
Disordering : 1274
Disorderly Images : 141

The Dispassionate Shepherd's First Blind Date :
    3977
Dispatch Window Dressing : 2073
Displaced : 1569
A Display of Birds : 989
Disquietude : 3985, 4742
Disrespect : 5968
Dissatisfaction : 1079
Dissecting Drosophila with Marcie: Tucson,
    Arizona : 1632
Dissection at Nine Years : 1048
Dissections : 53
Dissembler : 368
The Dissolving of the Miniature Code : 6422
Distance : 6336, 6591, 6602
The Distance : 2409
Distances : 96, 616, 6396, 6507
The Distances : 6774
Distances across the Sink : 1072
The Distant Flickering : 7181
Distant morning : 1754, 5657
A Distant Silence : 3686
Distant Voices in My Heart : 532, 1491
Distinction : 1162
Distracted by Sirens : 1135
Distraction : 2986
Distributing The News : 4961
The Diva's First Song (White's Hotel, London)
    : 3393
Diver : 2209
Divers : 5143
Divided Base : 5851
Dividing by Zero : 2812
Divine rose, you exist in a genteel culture :
    1358, 4601
The Diviner : 3287, 5361
Divinity : 3381
Division : 3230
Divorce : 974, 3160, 3912
Divorce, 1969 : 4382
Divorce Dreams : 4446
Dizzy with It : 6916
Do Flies Sleep? : 977
Do Not Call Me Queen, Odysseus : 629, 5650
Do not call me this or anything : 2379, 6830
Do Not Come : 1828
Do our wounds make us blood sisters? : 5084
Do You Love Me Always : 2619, 5389
Do You Remember : 813, 814, 3792
Do You Remember? : 4037, 5447
Docilité : 6273
Docility : 2197, 6273
Dock of the Bay : 2715
Dockorna : 5708
Doctor : 1628, 4970
The Doctor Will See You Now : 7074
Document : 1437
The Document : 1113
Documentary : 305
Dodo : 2828
The Dodo's Infertile Daughter : 3730
Does the government have the power to take
    our lives? : 1486
Dog : 1748, 7049

The Dog at Bruges : 1744, 3032, 5921
A dog digs like a madman : 2125
Dog on the Track : 3795
Dogs : 6700, 6789
The Dogs : 3553
Dogs Could Forgive Me : 37
Dog's Life — Rejoice! : 2595
The Dogwood Tree : 5962
Doing Mazes : 106
Doing the Dishes : 3233
Doing Well in the Restaurant : 1072
A Dollar Nineteen a Pound : 3808
The Dolls : 813, 814, 5708
Dolor en Geometría : 6578
Dolores Street : 2147
Dolorous Nightwalker's Song, or Reechy Me a
    Kiss : 5023
Dolphins at the Aquarium : 2429
Domestic Architecture : 6957
Domestic Artistry : 3046
Domestic Violence : 1796, 3977
Domitian, the last cruel and savage emperor :
    2422, 3552, 6552
Domus Poetica : 5872, 6068
Donde Estuvieron Sentadas la Dama y Su
    Piedra : 1841
Dong Ha : 3780
Donna Pressley, 33 : 6645
Don't! Stop! : 184
Don't Call Me, I'll Call You : 841
Don't Cross Your Heart : 4497
Don't Distrust Me : 813, 814, 2031
Don't Drink and Drive : 3825
Don't Get a Gun, Get a Big Dog : 5575
Don't Kill Yourself, You're Only 30 : 3345
Don't Knock It : 489
Door : 1807
The Door : 1953, 4938, 5182
Door Mat Madonna: 1 : 3780
Door Mat Madonna: 2 : 3780
Door-to-Door Jesus : 3093
Door to the Second Infinity : 1536, 3533
The Door Waits : 6853
The door Was Left Open : 2559
The Doorgunner : 1530
Doppelganger vii : 4398
Dopplering Central Deeming Melanogensis :
    1146
El Dorado : 3588, 3648, 6220
Dorothy Dandridge : 2025
Dorothy Lamour and Hedy Lamarr Put To-
    gether : 5969
Dos Poesías para Mi Diana : 3673
A Dot Against the Moon : 2919
Double : 2131, 7146
The Double : 183, 6632
Double Justice : 1473, 6632
The Double Negatives of the Living : 1966
Doubles : 1113
Doubling Up on Privacy at the Canterbury
    Juvenile Facility : 4170
Doubt : 3418
Doug & Marilyn : 747
The Doughnut Pantry : 2766

Dove : 2507, 5067
Dover : 1320
Doves in January : 5067
Dovetail of the Day : 1437
Down by the Foam-Washed Shore : 184, 1246
Down Like Rain : 6398
Down on the Yucatan : 3329
Down the Coastal Highway : 2502
Down to a Candle : 5754
Down to Quantico : 3384
Down to the Park : 2431
The downpour struck : 6453
Downslope : 6542
Downtown L.A. : 282
Dowser : 5769
Dowsing for the Mole at Age Eight : 879
Doyle and I: Summer 1969 : 6952
Dozing on the Train : 1363, 5379, 6639
Dr. Clark and Billy Banks : 4470
Dr. Disney's Animation : 5353
Dr. Joseph Goebbels : 6005
Dr. Joseph Goebbels, Minister for Propaganda :
    6005
Dr. W. F. Schamber and School Board Break-
    ing Ground for the Elementary School :
    6715
Dr. Williams' Desk : 650
Drafts from Two Winter Evenings : 5351, 6777
Drama in Last Acts : 7107
Drawing : 813, 814, 5293
Drawing an Eggplant : 6946
Drawing Conclusions : 4825
Drawing Peonies : 5928
Drawing Room Drama : 2932
Dreadlocks : 1821
Dream : 813, 814, 3032, 5324, 5708
A Dream : 6032, 7046
The Dream : 167, 3680, 4106, 5242
Dream and Ambition : 588
The Dream Child : 5295
Dream (For Susan) : 6363
Dream Forgetting : 5419
Dream in the Hospital : 213
Dream Judgment : 22, 6006
The Dream Machine : 2540
Dream Mountain : 4578
Dream Ninety-Nine: After Baudelaire : 5834
A Dream of 1300 : 1577
Dream of a Cave : 3501
The Dream of a Thousand Cacti : 6861
Dream of an Indian : 1792
The Dream of Being Just Like Everyone Else :
    2436
The Dream of Birth : 1183
A Dream of Ezra Pound : 5485
Dream of Grand Teton : 1074
The Dream of Our Undoing : 4929
A Dream of Permanence : 1693
Dream of the Firmament : 170, 4216
The Dream of the Guerillas : 6794
Dream of the Interior : 6545
A Dream of Venice : 1577
A Dream of Water : 2589
The Dream of Writing : 3780

Dream People : 3006
Dream Pictures : 648, 779
Dream Poem #7 : 1753
Dream Poem #8 : 1753
Dream Scales : 6897
Dream Sculpture: Woman Leaving Ocean Liner
    : 5907
The Dream Swimmer : 5333
The Dream Was the Answer : 3146
Dream With a Bad Reputation : 2218
Dreamboy: Laser Fantabulast : 2578
The Dreamed : 5211
Dreamer : 6080
Dreamer's Dream : 5388
Dreamers Twist : 2893
Dreaming : 4223, 6843
Dreaming among Hydrangeas : 3635
Dreaming of Flight : 5317
Dreaming of Madrid : 297
Dreaming You Make Bread : 6371
Dreams : 921
Dreams Before Sleep : 4914
Dream's Daughter : 3873
Dreams in the Seventh Month : 6938
Dreams, or, On the Occasion of My Sister's
    Wedding : 1023
Dreamscape : 6378
Dreamtime Song : 3800
The Dreamwork That Does Not Sleep : 3744
Drehe die Herzspindel weiter für mich : 3658
Dreiser : 7001
The Dress in the Water : 4753
Dressed in Dynamite : 447, 6889
Dresses : 2763
Dressing : 6242
Dressing the Stage : 456
Dried Flowers, the Chance of Fire : 2453
The Drift of It : 2720
Drifter : 1527
Drifters : 6666
Drifting : 584, 4192
Driftwood : 6640
Drill : 3707
Drinking Muskies' Brute Look : 5133
A Drinking Song : 1470
Drinking to Forget : 2416
Drive : 319
Drive to the Seashore : 4111
Driving at Midnight : 6677
Driving Father Down a Mountain Road in
    Farmington, Connecticut, 1983 : 2032
Driving in Fog in Alaska : 6118
Driving Late at Night : 6982
Driving Nevada / Reprise : 5858
Driving North : 5979
Driving North, Early Spring : 2465
Driving Ohio : 6400
Driving South : 3082
Driving the Hardscrabble : 4179
Driving the Midnight Bus : 4179
Driving Through Fog : 2465
Driving Through Kansas : 1457
Driving to Milwaukee: for Beth Krom : 4482
Driving to School, the English Teacher : 3220

Driving to Work : 4149
Dröm : 5708
Drop and Wonder Why : 3972
The Drop Ready for the Globe : 1473, 6628
Droplets of Milk : 474
Dropparna : 2031
The Drops : 813, 814, 2031
Drought : 649, 1539, 1843, 5679, 6236, 6348
Drought, 1988 : 3645
A Drought Is a Kind of Winter : 921
Drought Summer : 5685
Drowned Fisherman's Love Poem : 4996
Drowned Girl : 4873
The Drowned Woman Waits : 2810
The Drowning : 645, 813, 814
Drowning in the Driftless Region — Near
    Victory, Wisconsin : 4319
Drugs : 3190
Drum : 5302
Drums at Night : 4592
Drumsong : 4384
Drunk : 6802
Drunken Beauty : 451, 1885, 4333
Drunkningen : 645
Dry Cleaners : 6893
Dry Winter : 971
A Drying of 'Shirley Temple' Toes : 3350
Drzazga mojej wyobrazni : 5105
Dubious Feast : 4227
Dublin : 4796
Duck Pond : 5963
Duck Season : 6568
Duckert the Effeminate, Zephyr-Like Surgeon :
    1890
The Ducks : 4487
Due to Injuries : 6930
Duende : 2482
El Duende : 5426
Duet : 1459
Duet with My Five Year Old Son : 739
The Dulcimer in the Basement : 2025
Dumb Love : 5676
The Dumpe : 4218
Dumplings : 6608
Dunes : 3075
The Dungeness Spit Apocalypses : 471
Dungeon : 5475
Duped Pests Find Death in Mating : 7147
Duplicities : 4966
Durable Rustproof Saturday Night : 1733
Dürer for Children : 6152
During a Funeral Service the Mind of the
    Young Preacher Wanders Again : 6951
During Early Snow : 2791
During Lunch at Alonzo 'Slick' Smith's
    Barbecue Restaurant, a Local Holds Forth
    on the Real Muskogee, Oklahoma : 3171
During the 'Dirty Little War' : 2824
Dusk Comes All the Time Now : 206, 813, 814
Dusk Ox : 5455, 6841
Dust : 1120, 1884, 5488
Dust Bowl : 3042
Dust Echo Music : 6127
Dust in Love : 5192, 6559

The Dust Jacket at Waldenbooks : 588
Dust, Port Madison Anchorage : 4254
Dust Settling Before Sleep : 800
Dusting : 6746
Dusting for Fingerprints in Hamilton, Ontario :
     5800
Dutch : 2546
Dutch Harbor : 4095
The Dutchess County Fair : 2413
Duty : 2661
The Dwarf : 2798, 4455
The Dwarf and Doctor Freud : 4855
Dwarf Tossing : 4521
Dwarf with Violin, Government Center Station
     : 5067
Dweller in the Forest : 3384
Dwelling On/In : 2954
Dwelling Where the Moon Lost Its Pale Glow :
     4493, 5448
Dying : 2
Dying Dreams : 4274
Dylan: The Limerick : 6120
The Dynamizer and the Oscilloclast : 1307
EECummings : 881
E-li, E-li, La-ma Sa-bach-tha-ni? : 26
EP : 421
E Qui Che Dio : 1031
E Sopravvivere Alla Morte, Vivere? : 5183
Each Name Has a Dream : 3827
Each night the longing : 4973
Each November : 1456
Each Step You Take : 6339
Each Summer's Swallows : 6562
Eagles Are Whirling : 1300, 2454
Eagles Caught Salmon : 1092
Eagle's Work : 3329
Eala! : 607, 2311
Earl : 6875
Earl Reconsiders His Views on Israel : 402
Earlier : 3830, 6098
Early : 3010
Early Advise : 4671
Early April Rattles Severly Professor Oglebock
     : 3320
Early Brass : 6728
Early Charles : 4671
Early Incense : 2791
The Early Jobs : 5224
Early Morning in Milwaukee : 3454
Early Morning Music : 4490
The Early Part of the Day : 1553
Early Shift : 6907
Early Snow : 6143
Early Warning : 6539
The Ears : 1876
Earshot : 3418
The Earth Also Dies : 69, 1224, 3121
The Earth Is a Satellite of the Moon : 5200,
     5517
The earth is famished and wears us out : 4462,
     6553
The Earth Is Flat : 4497
Earth Is Their Memorial : 1113
The Earth Movers : 1196

Earth Nites : 3329
Earth Shakes Permanently : 6819
Earth to Earth : 5831
Earthly House : 2279
Earthquake : 7060
The Earthquake : 6039
Earthquake '89 : 6335
Earthquake Country : 4825
Earthquake Time : 6070
The Earthwalker : 6248
Earthworm and Narcissus: Pas de Deux : 2728
Easily Recognized : 2466
East and West : 309
East of Eden : 1690, 3445, 5874
East of Trouble Creek : 4086
Eastbound : 6281
Easter : 1047, 2497
Easter, 1989 : 7058
Easter Bunny Poem : 2104
Easter Eggs : 148
Easter Flood : 434
Easter in Berkeley 1988 : 3472
Easter in New York : 1045, 4861
Easter Monday in Miami: Listening to Eric
     Satie : 3220
Easter on Lake Erie : 4948
Easter Season: Turtle Pond : 1122
Easter Sunday : 3255, 5130, 6459
Easter Sunday, St. Andrew's Cathedral : 3336
Easting : 5224
The East's Imagination : 435, 1085, 4180
Easy Listening : 5313
Easy Passage : 1730
The Eater : 4111
Eating Cauliflower : 3839
Eating Houses : 1072
Eating Out : 5884
Ebb Tide : 1881
Ebbtide : 773
Ebony : 2164
Ecce Homo : 6124
Ecclesiastes : 795
Eche Rori Ile : 184
Echo : 1695, 2454, 2786, 6324
Echoes : 29, 5595
Echoes Blossom with Remembered Prayer :
     1025
Echoes from the Spanish Civil War : 5417
The Echoing Lake : 1427
The Eclipse : 5512
Eclipse Facsimile : 4260
Eclipse Over Kiev, 8/17/89 : 3011
Eclogue : 4166
Eclogue One : 3545
Eclogue Two : 3545
The Ecology of Poetry : 6740
Economics Lesson : 1925, 5744, 6298
The Economics of Foreign Exchange : 6151
Economics, with Power Steering : 6514
Economics : 3101
The Economy (1989) : 4429
Ecstasy : 3631
The Ecstasy : 2340
Ectopiac : 7101

Ectopic Pregnancy : 1746
Eddie Priest's Barbershop & Notary: Closed
    Mondays : 7111
Eddra : 4658
Eddy Johnson's American Dream : 612
Eden : 1690, 3070, 3445, 5469, 5874
Edenesque : 3639
The Edge Is Always There : 5401
The Edge of Time Is Near! : 2746, 4670, 6252
Edgewater Almanac : 5234
The Edible Woman : 1291
Edie : 6136
Edison Films an Execution : 535
Editio Princeps : 2856
An Editorial : 4112
An Education : 2104
An Edward Hopper Painting : 382
Edward's Anecdote : 2567
EECummings : 881
The Effigy of John Donne : 6880
Effigy's Monologue : 3182
Effleurage : 5996
The Effort : 6982
Egentligen Vill Jag Älska : 3792
The Egg Boiler : 777
Egg laboring in oval light : 4876, 5186
Egg Lake : 916
Eggplants and Lotus Root : 2177
Eggs : 3248
Egon Schiele : 5250
Egret's Alley : 2261
Egypt : 6282
Eh, You Like Poetry or Wat? : 311
Eidetic Images : 1418
The Eightfold Way : 1591
Eighty-Four Pieces, Eight by Five Inches : 5919
Eighty Years Young : 5296
Ein Leben : 3299, 4871, 4871
Eine Kleine Light Music : 1198
Einer Stand und Sang : 4718
Einstein at Short : 6254
Einstein Said : 6075
Éjszakai Utazás Némethonban : 1363
El Greco: 'The Penitent Magdalen' : 3850
Elaboration of a Line from *The Tale of Genji* :
    2694
Eldorado : 4640
Eleanor Marx-Aveling to Her Father, Fifteen
    Years After His Death : 6770
Eleatic Electric : 2588
The Elect : 5887
Election Mutter : 378
Election Results : 2992
The Electric Book : 3194
Electric Chair : 99
Electrophorus Electricus : 1238
Elegía por el Alma de las Palabras : 3935
The Elegist : 2577
Elegy : 468, 1473, 1606, 3258, 3311, 6177,
    6632, 6660
Elegy 1942 : 6136
Elegy and Affirmation : 6205
Elegy as Origin : 5190
Elegy at Mustang Island : 4606

Elegy: Breece D'J Pancake : 7059
Elegy for a Late Tornado : 5704
Elegy for a Young Man Dying of AIDS : 2664
Elegy for Auden : 6872
Elegy for Czesiek : 6770
Elegy for Esposito : 5298
Elegy for Martin Luther King : 1599, 5783
Elegy for My Corpse : 1838
Elegy for My Innocence : 1715
Elegy for My Virginity : 2677
Elegy for Robert Icarius McKee : 4494
Elegy for Sister Mildred : 4348
Elegy for the Departure of Pen, Ink and Lamp :
    984, 986, 2800
Elegy for the Girls of Jiangxi Province : 708
Elegy for the Old Mexican Woman and Her
    Dead Child : 2525, 5607
Elegy for the Sea at Night : 5022
Elegy for the Soul of Words : 3935
Elegy for the Woman across the Street : 666
Elegy for William Lebo : 5583
Elegy of Midnight : 1599, 5783
Elegy on a Tile Stove : 2061, 4976
The Elegy Writer's Blues : 358
Elemental : 5649
Elemental, This Roundness : 2390
Elementary School : 6083
The Elements : 3845
Elements of a Miracle : 4743
The Elephant Ballroom : 5629
The Elephants : 888, 1528
Elephants at Work : 4254
Elevator : 5613
Eleven for Paul Klee : 1633
Elevens : 1393
The Eleventh Day : 6154
Eliot at Twelve Years : 514, 6464
Eliza Westbrook, After the Suicide of Her
    Sister, Harriet Westbrook Shelley, 1816 :
    1269
An Elizabethan Fool Applies for a Corporate
    Executive Position : 5676
Ella, 1950 : 5204
Ella's Son Brings Her Gifts from Riverview
    Cemetery : 267
Ellington Indigos : 5850
Ellis Island Feeding on the Stones : 5881
Elm : 3293
Elmer Hunter Does His Time : 2667
Elmira : 3609
Elms and Tudor Cottages : 316
Elmsford, New York : 6388
Elmwood : 2828
Eloquence : 7009
Elusive Presence : 2507
Elvis Impersonator at the World's Largest
    Office Party: Lacrosse, Wisconsin : 4397
Elvis Is Dead, Bubba : 1456
Elvis Moving a Small Cloud: The Desert Near
    Las Vegas, 1976 : 7010
Ely Cathedral: Toward Evensong : 7
Embarazada : 4691
The Embarkation for Cythera : 3666
Embarking for Cythera : 5086

The Embattled Gardener : 6879
Embers : 1083
Emblem : 2774
Embrace : 6251
Embrace (2) : 6281
Embrace (3) : 6281
Embraced by Stalin : 214
Emellanåt Går Vi Upp : 206
An emerald oak grove after the rains : 3481,
    4326
Emergency : 1205, 4165, 5613
Emergency Haying : 999
Emerson : 356, 640, 640, 4324
Emigration : 2061, 3120, 4534, 4976, 5250
Emilia Plater : 666, 3632
Emily Dickinson: In Retrospect : 522
Emily Dickinson's House, Amherst, Massachu-
    setts : 5731
Emily Explains How Life Begins : 4306
Emily, Late March : 6057
Emily's Tribute to Spring : 4306
Emma : 3129
Emma's Crochet : 2434
Empathy for Two Poets : 4928
Empathy's Child : 5827
The Emperor, Kao Tsung : 1113
The Emperor, Shun : 1113
The Empire of Meat : 131
Empires : 5894
The Empress's Fan : 2384
Empty Boxes : 3313
Empty Cottages : 7018
Empty Field : 6859
The Empty Fireplace : 442
The Empty House : 2826
Empty Houses : 7191
Empty Seat : 1625, 7159
The Empty Set of Instructions : 717
Empty Space : 362
En Esta Noche, En Este Mundo : 5058
Encanto Park, 1961 : 1212
The Enchantment : 1751
Enchantments elegies labyrinths mechanical
    lights : 4613, 5650
Enclosed Field : 784, 5992
Encomium : 5157
Enconado : 1950
Encounter : 53, 348, 1113, 6510
Encounter with a Cooper's Hawk : 918
An Encounter with Pieter Saenredam : 499,
    5438
The End : 2642, 6221, 6962
End in Sight : 719
End of March : 2133
The End of October : 4376
The End of Summer : 2471
End of Summer, Below the Fall-line, Central
    Georgia : 959
The End of Summer Vacation : 5765
The End of the Absolute : 586
End of the Affair : 5897
The End of the Affair : 3701
End of the Broadcast Day : 6204
End of the Growing Season : 4049

The End of the Poetry Line : 3098
The End of the Road : 2038
End of the Weekend : 1577
The End of Undressing Is the End of Flesh :
    1345
An End or a Beginning : 435, 4180
Endarkenment : 5403
Endechas Texanas para un Despechado al Pie
    de una Wurlitzer en la Frontera : 4769
Ending : 5946
Ending with a Line from Lear : 445
Endless : 158, 3750
Endlessly Rocking : 1458
Endpoint : 5964
Energetically Singing Against Voracious Earth :
    6355
L'Enfant Suit l'Homme : 5554
Der Engel : 2798
English 101 : 5722
English Class : 1110
English Lesson : 3270, 5290, 6992
Enigma Variations : 6746
Enjambements : 2266
Enlightened One : 6813
The Enlightened Person : 271, 653, 3292
The Enormous Sigh : 3563
Enough : 2659, 6901
Ensam Igen, Jag Också : 2526
Entfremdung : 284
Entire families with leprosy — the child can't
    help leaning into the father : 5434
The Entomologist's Notebooks : 2564
Entonces Algo Vuelve a Suceder : 1841
Entonces en las Aguas de Conchán : 1127
The Entrance of Souls into Hell : 3337
Entre el Gato y la Casa : 4864
The Entrepreneur : 716
Entrepreneurs' Cottages : 4654
Entropy : 2239, 5700
Entropy of Everyday Things : 2096
The Entropy of Pleasure : 1242
Entropy's Angel : 5634
The Entry of James Ensor into My Memories of
    Brussels : 3038
Envied emptiness : 924, 6632
Environmental Issues : 3845
Envoi : 1186
L'Envoy : 786
Envy : 1518
Envy 5 : 1518
EP : 421
Epigone : 5302
Epigram : 6500, 6986
Epigrams : 4071, 4750, 5582
Epilogue : 1808, 2388
Epiphanies : 3480
Epiphanies (1991) : 3480
Epiphany on the Crooked River : 1123
An Episode of the Great Awakening in New
    England : 5302
Epistemology : 2451
Epistle : 2745
Epistle to the Angry Ones : 5579
Epitaph : 1791

Epitaph for a Mime : 5194
An Epitaph for Orange Scott Cummins : 3171
Epitaph for the Twentieth Century : 1027, 5639
Epitaphs : 5992
Epithalamion : 1715, 2934, 3801
Epithalamium : 2653, 4656
Epithet : 4163
Epodo : 2388
Eppure Sto Per Partire, Dicembre 88 : 5650
Equal Time : 3989
Equinox : 5869
Erasing the Angles : 6856
Erg : 1893
Erinnerung an die Marie A : 724
Ernie and Week's End : 6911
Ernie, of an Afternoon : 6911
Ernie Prepares the Trash : 6911
Ernie's Trip to Mississippi : 6911
Erosion : 2493, 6289
Erosion Factor : 677
An Erotics for Browsing in a Museum : 1715
Es Como el Eco : 2402
Es Esa la Imagen : 4467
Es War Erde in Ihnen, Und Sie Gruben : 1043
Escape : 465
Escape Artist : 5556
The Escape of the Birdwomen : 165
Escarpment from Water : 3716
Eschatology : 5829
El Escriba Razona Mal Su Destino a Su Paso
    por España en 1965 : 4674
Escrito en Llamas : 5170
Esenin : 5588
Esmiss Esmoor : 443
Las Espejeantes Playas : 7189
Espejo : 5882
Espejo No : 2388
Espera : 4621
Espiral Negra : 4673, 5625, 5625
An Essay on Friendship : 4158
Essay on the Comic Book : 5648
Essays in Divinity : 846
The Essential Universe : 3398
Esta tarde, mi bien, cuando te hablaba : 1358
Estampa Puertorriqueña en Filadelfia : 4621
Este, que ves, engaño colorido : 1358
Estéban in Cibola : 1113
Estou Sentado Nos Primeiros Anos de Minha
    Vida : 158
Estrangement : 284, 5271
La Estrellita : 5899
Estudio para Terminar una Pieza de Juan Morel
    Campos : 3854
Et Lux in Tenebris Lucet : 4695
Et nous irons vers l'horreur des lits sans amour :
    1275
Etching of the Plague Years : 3259
Etchmiadzin : 1526, 7131
The Eternal and the Infinite : 4710
An Eternal Flame : 3319
Eternal Lights : 1349
The Ether Dome (An Entertainment) : 2490
The Ethical Hunter : 621
An Ethics of Anxiety : 5758

Ethics of the Fathers : 7173
Ett Långt Farväl : 2031
Ett Rum För Natten : 6222
Etymology of Love : 271
Eunice Winkless's Dive into Pool of Water:
    Pueblo, Colorado, July 4, 1905 : 7049
Euphonica Jarre : 5126
The Euphrates : 229, 4439
Europe : 5302
Europe in 1914 : 1169
Eurydice : 99, 2104, 5937, 6573
The Eurydice Chorus : 1954
Eurydice in Hades : 419
Eve : 202
Eve of All Saints : 6123
Eve Recollecting the Garden : 406
Eve Remembers : 5391
Even If You Weren't My Father : 2737, 5647
Even in the Dream : 3780
Even on Sunday : 566
Even Seven Months Later : 3780
Even the Blues : 110
Evening : 3081, 3116, 5610
The Evening Hemlocks : 4602
Evening in Bath : 203
An Evening in March : 2216, 4901
Evening light and shade : 2137, 3759
Evening News in February : 1430
Evening of the Trapeze Artist : 4252
Evening on the Beach : 5092
An Evening On the Town : 5051
Evening Raga : 2454
Evening Ship : 3830, 5389
The Evening Snow : 5334
Evening, the Krakow train station, three gypsy :
    666, 3979
Evening Train : 3736
Evening Walk : 3777, 5894
Evenings : 1713, 6007
The Event : 2932
Ever closer to the Milky Way : 1113, 3658
Ever since my mother carried me : 2135, 3751,
    6383
Every Blue Mile : 4223
Every Day : 3032
Every Night in Our Sleeping : 184
Every Night She Dreams : 2
Every Reachable Feather : 1966
Every Woman's Christmas : 5532
Everybody Knows! : 2595
Everybody's Day (Not Mine) : 3536
Everybody's Living Room : 6702
Everyday : 6250
Everyday History : 1363, 5379
Everyone who wanted to be : 6823
Everything : 3120, 4534, 4790, 5250
Everything About Winter : 1294
Everything in This City Is Afraid : 1958
Everything Is Its Opposite : 796
Everything Under the Sun : 6542
Everything was in the way : 4247
Everything You Do : 1108, 1252, 6045
Everything's Funny (Till the Tiny Seed
    Surrenders) : 1072

Everywhere : 3830, 6006
Eve's Story : 56
Evidence : 3408, 5075
Evidence: From a Reporter's Notebook : 56
Evil and Flower : 6465
The evil shadows of Orcius : 1032, 1255
The Evil Sorcerers : 4350, 5006
Evolution : 1913, 6101
Evolution, an Unfinished Sestina : 583
Evolving Patois : 3200
Ex-Roommate : 2300
The Examination : 3197
Examination in Literature : 7139
Excavation : 2117
Excavation of a Burial Mound : 2331
Excerpt from the History of Navigation : 1784
Exchange Student : 1513
Excitable Boy : 6800
Excitement : 3418
An Excursion : 6101
Excuse Me, I'm Giving Away Diseases for Free
     : 3079
Excused for Illness : 6232
Execution : 3707
Execution of Pimps and Prostitutes, Busher,
     Iran, April 1989 : 6070
The Executive Discovers Poetry : 6242
Exhibitionism : 6658
Exhibitionist : 5661
Exile : 1971, 2019, 5050, 5995, 6770
The Exile : 1093, 4566
Exile in the Empty Nest : 5743
Exiles : 3753
The Exile's Daughter : 5962
Exile's Letter: After the Failed Revolution :
     1101
Existence : 371, 2808
Existential Cocktails : 6094
Exit, Pursued by a Bear : 2941
The Exit Sign : 5509
Exit to Calcutta : 99
Exits : 1068
The Exodus : 6854
The Exodus of Two Testaments : 4072
Exorcism : 3842
Expansion Slots : 1605
Expectation : 435, 1625, 1708, 4180, 5250
Expectations : 3620
An Expedition : 4743
Experience : 3985, 4742
The Expert : 6356
An Explanation : 3174
Explanations : 1269
Exploded View : 3418, 5957
Explorations : 4095
Exploring : 1429
Exploring Evanescence : 6458
Export Notwithstanding : 3923
Exposition : 4380
Exposure : 1238, 4367
The Exquisite Art : 7125
The Exquisite in Poetry, or, A Victim of
     Tropical Fish : 4939, 5098
Extensions : 4366

Extinction Ode: For Pansies : 1143
Extinctions : 7010
Extractions : 3914
Extraordinary Instruments : 2688
Extraordinary Lengths : 5547
Extraordinary Performance : 1018, 5992
The Extrapolation Dreams : 1966
The Extravagance of Dirt and the Comparable
     Merits of Root Systems : 971
An eye for an eye : 4939, 5098
Eye Level with Brown Pelicans : 3503
The Eye that Rejuvenates the Soul : 5776, 7080
Eye Witness : 5113
The Eyebrows of Penmanship : 2433
Eyes : 649, 7034
(The Eyes Do Not See Objectively) : 2124
The Eyes in Grandfather's Oils : 4179
The Eyes of a Dark Horse : 6903
The Eyes of Athene : 3715
Eyes of the Swordfish : 3844
Ez Itt a Város : 4811
Ezekiel's Daughter : 4014
FFA : 3451
F Train: Beards Going to Work : 2815
F Train: The Cloak of Respectability : 2815
Fabian : 6673
Fables : 6525
The Face about the Face : 139, 140
The Face Given : 1975
A Face in the City : 4330
The Face of Madness : 199
Face Value : 3977
The Faceless : 1755
Faces That We Mean to Leave Behind : 2667
Faces We Never Forget : 4179
The Fact of Windows : 4177
A Factory by the River : 5315
Facts : 233, 3746
Facts Are Stupid Things : 162
Facts of Life : 5512
Faculty X : 1966
Fading Things : 6536
Fady Frem Takes It Back : 2078
Fahrend in einem Bequemen Wagen : 724
Fail : 4380
Fail Safe : 6492
Failure : 2577, 4657
A Failure of Imagination : 5826
Fairgrounds : 4496
Fairy Fuck-In, or, A Call to the States : 4511
Fairy Tale : 836, 6879
Fairy Tales on Florida Avenue : 4356
Faith : 298, 1484, 3384
Faith As an Arm of Culture, Culture As an Arm
     of Narration : 5760
The Faith of Fishermen : 4370
The Faith of Forty : 2305
Faith Tittle : 3689
The Faithful Organ : 5286
Fake Oracle : 2195
Faked Orgasms : 6922
Fall : 2186
The Fall : 623, 1850, 5640
The Fall from the Green Frog : 2532, 2922,

7106
The Fall of Light : 3398
The Fall of the Human Empire : 7051
A Fallacy of Style : 4343
A Fallen Candle at the Center of Our Picnic :
    1458
Fallen Hawk : 5980
The Fallen Thing : 341
Falling : 4276, 7003
Falling Apart at Work : 3138
Falling Asleep : 5050
Falling Asleep Hungry : 6961
Falling Awake : 6426
The Falling Children : 4897
The Falling Day : 4280
Falling in Love Through a Description : 6707
A Falling Woman : 3831
Fallout : 3492
Fallow : 1598
The Falls Revisited : 1710
False Gods : 4367
The false precision of, for example, 188th Street
    and the Expressway : 5434
False Spring : 2623
A False Spring : 616
Falsetto : 5118, 6786
Fame : 6241, 6804, 6922
La Familia : 3855
Families : 1195
The Family : 2827
Family Album : 535, 1436
A Family Album : 6536
Family Codes : 4720
Family Ground : 5963
Family History: Final Examination : 2284
Family Jewel Heretics : 3139
Family of Roses : 3123
A Family of Three : 4814
Family Photo in Black and White : 1597
Family Plot, October : 4128
Family Portraits : 5199
Family Reunion : 1113
Family Story : 4707
Family Table : 2104, 3519
The Family Tree : 4334
Family Violence : 4808
Famine : 2335, 5992
Famous Bigshots : 3438
The Famous Book of Russian Poems : 1614
Fan : 5348
Fan Mail : 3825, 6728
A Fan Sketched with Silver Egrets : 6097
The Fanciest Forms of Innocence : 5190
Fancy : 5650
The Fans : 2231
A Fantasy Poem by Emily : 4306
Far Away / 9 X Kaneka Tota : 5935
Far Away, From My Hill : 1350, 4821
Far from Kingdoms : 407, 1037
Far Out in the Pond, Lazing : 7145
Far Rockaway : 4498
Far West : 1553
Farewell : 3381
Farewell Gentlemen We Are Setting Off : 170,

4216
The Farewell Letter : 813, 814, 5293
Farewell to My Mother : 3993
Fargo : 6562
Farm : 523
The Farm : 1332
Farm Cornerstone : 2407
The Farm Hand : 2400
The Farmer : 2817, 3280
Farmers : 323
The Farmer's Daughter and the Travelling
    Salesman : 1244
A Farmer's Son Gives Up and Moves to the
    City, or The Implications of Liquidating a
    Farm Operation : 2240
Farming the Pillow : 4594
Farms and the Laws of Harvest : 4179
Farms at Auction : 4179
Farther On : 1865
Farting with James Joyce : 171
Fascination : 5384
Fast : 1886
The Fast : 3746
Fast Is : 1627
Fast, slow : 3670
Fastcar : 3055
The Fat Black Woman's Motto on Her Bed-
    room Door : 4666
Fat Chance : 166
Fat Girl : 4440
The Fat Laugh : 2904
The Fat Life : 1579
Fat News : 6514
Fat Pets On : 3538
Fatal Response : 2116
Fate : 56
Father? : 1990
The Father : 2818
Father and Children : 1258
A Father and Son : 203
Father Chant : 952
Father Dismas, Gregorian Chant Teacher : 5449
The Father Flag : 4859
Father Has Pneumonia : 6608
Father, His Company : 5828
Father Hunger and Son : 6822
Father, I Wade : 1797
Father-in-Law : 4110
Father of a Girl in Memphis : 5066
Father Remember Me : 2852
Father Sonnet : 6378
Father Was Known As a Man in Control : 4644
Fatherless Fatherhood : 6286
The Fathers : 5204
Fathers and Sons : 3699
Father's Fish : 350
Father's Garden : 3366
A Father's Lament : 6378
Father's Straight Razor : 4179
Fatigue, This Afternoon, Weariness: A Conceit
    : 312
Fauna of Mirrors : 6435
Fear : 594, 6682
The Fear : 2001

Fear of Angels : 6062
Fearful Flyers, Inc : 1531
The Feast of St. Lawrence : 257
The Feast of the Rose Garlands : 4095
Feathered : 6402
Feathered Warrior : 7135
February : 1431, 7174
February 11, 1990 : 1167
February 14th, Driving West : 4784
February 15, St. Mary's : 5086
February 29 : 6118
February Arroyo : 223
February Days : 2171
February Faultline : 1707
February Ice Years : 2371
The February Snow Lies at My Feet : 854, 4627
February Sun : 5413, 6098
February Twenty-Second : 1213
Fede : 6227
Federico Talks to His Virgin of the Seven
    Arrows : 6880
Fedoras : 2199
Feed : 7177
Feeding : 3689, 4213
The Feel : 5855
Feeling Defensive? : 352
The Feeling of Having Forgotten : 5554, 6940
Feeling Sorry : 4351
Feeling the Trees' Breath : 998
Feels Like a Real Fight (Ted and Steve) : 1878
Feet : 1605
The Feet Make Blue Fish Cento : 6722
Feh : 6288
Fekete-piros : 3243
The Feline as Queen Corporeal : 3633
Felix Randal : 2934
Felling : 2369
Female Mud Wrestling : 5969
Femininity : 242
Feminism : 3140
A Feminist Critique : 7049
Fence : 2728
The Fence : 727
The Fence Painter : 3197
The Fern : 5617
Ferry : 410
Festival in Fishing Village No. 19 : 3440, 4904
Festive Isolation : 881
Festology : 2941
Fête de l'Automne : 3682
Fetish : 1080
Feuilletons : 6632
Fever : 4114
A Fever in December : 6608
A Fever in the Arm : 5300
Feverfew, Book-Moth, and Wyrd : 3220
A Few Arguments with the Conspicuous : 7049
A Few Days Left : 1343
A Few Days on Ward B : 5591
A Few Lines from Rehoboth Beach : 3075
A Few Riffs for Hayden, Sitting in With His
    Horn : 632
A Few Things About the Earth : 6043
FFA : 3451

Fibel : 1442
Fiction : 1853
Fiddleback Embalmed : 4226
The Fiddler : 3524
Fiddles and Steel Guitars : 4179
Fidelities : 5885
Fidelity : 2577
The Field : 2093
A Field Guide to Lesser Desires : 3946
A Field Guide to the Shells : 5026
A Field of Rape : 2457
Field Peas : 3679
Field Pond : 4914
A Field Stoned : 516, 6362
Field Tone : 1371
Field Trip : 4568
Field Work : 6185
Fields of Care : 5017
Fields of Vision : 5174
Fieldwork, Devil's Lake, Wisconsin : 1705
Fifteen : 1304, 2127
Fifteen Changes All the Rules : 6239
Fifteen Years Ago : 1042
Fifteen Years Later : 3516, 3696
Fifth Grade : 7082
Fiftieth Class Reunion : 4144
The Fiftieth Element Makes Soft Soldiers :
    1267
Fifty : 6833
The Fig Curtain of Atherton : 6076
The Fight : 3908
The Fighting Cocks : 2840
Figural Study : 2337
Figurative Leaves : 5634
Figure of Fun : 1332
Filled with Cheer : 1616
Filling in the Blanks : 1438
Film : 5293
A Film Marilyn Monroe Never Made : 3653
Film Noir : 236
Films Trip Comicstrip Column vs. Krazy Kael :
    6120
The Final Blast : 5661
Final Examination : 6473
Final Exams : 4327
The Final Incantation : 655, 4994
Final Note : 5721
The final piece tonight : 4973
Final Position : 3259
The Final Tally : 3682, 4874
The Final Terms : 3721
Final W : 4077
Finale : 675
Finally After So Many Years Hernan Cortez
    Declares : 54, 5899
Finally the Rain : 4638
Finding Home : 2953
Finding the One Brief Note : 3538
Finding the Quilter in Her Quilt : 4260
Finding Your Job : 3006
Findings : 1218
The Fine Arts : 7107
A Fine Couple, My Muse & I : 4971
A Fine Meal : 3439

Finger Reading : 1076
Finger-Stories in the Blue Room : 15
Fingernails : 4816, 6716
Finishing the Exotic : 6248
Finnish Tango: In Memory of Felix Pollak :
    1817, 2478
Fiori : 4585
Fire : 836, 2875, 3254, 5466, 6087, 7129
The Fire : 500
Fire and Water : 1238
Fire Dance : 295
Fire Escape Poem : 5619
The Fire Next Time : 764
Fire Road : 1519
Fire Water : 4360
Firebreak : 6763
Firefinch : 5383
Fireflies : 961, 2285
Firefly : 267
Fireman's Auction : 2074
Fires at Yellowstone : 6842
A Fireside Story : 6535
Fireweed : 1132
Fireworks : 2889
Firmly Married : 836
The First Act of Praise : 4405
The First and Last Date : 1611
First Assembly of God : 3002
First Asthma : 5512
First Autumn in Ann Arbor : 4661
The First Big Hit : 3812
First Birthday : 3704
First Born : 4320
First Comer : 5976
First Cut : 4594
The First Day of Desire : 1145
The First Death was Seismic : 2813
First Desire / First Time : 1545
First Dialogue Between the Lone Ranger and
    Tonto : 6859
First Earth : 2305
The First Emperor : 6418
The First Few Lines: A Synopsis : 875
First Fight : 5685
First freezing drizzle : 6499
First Fruit : 4022
The First Gods : 2367
First Grade Homework : 4726
First Grader : 4397
First Hand-Plant: Skating the Petaluma Ramp :
    2392
First Hit : 3624
First Home : 5685
First Impression : 177
First Job : 4980
First Kiss : 2184, 4362, 5959
First Ladies' Room : 618
First Lady : 6514
First Leave : 4818
First Lent : 1539
The First Long-Range Artillery Fire on Lenin-
    grad : 67, 911, 2289
First Love : 199, 275, 2704
First Love, Hayes Barton, 1958 : 5130

First Memory : 6455
The First Moment on the New Land : 4640
First North American Rights : 7096
First of May : 7036
First Riddle : 2558, 3961
First Sensuality : 3287, 5361
First September Rain : 6270
First Shall Be, and Last Shall Be : 2146
First Snow : 547, 1468, 1526, 3559, 4567, 5333
First Snow / Piano Concerti : 6770
First Snowfall: Intimations : 2866
First Son : 1452
First Song : 4032
The First Station : 6579
First Swim : 312
First Taste of Ratcake : 5919
The first that I have seen : 1432
First Time : 3612
The First Time : 3468
The First Twilight Nail of Spring : 6148
The First Visit : 1577
First Waking : 4409
First Water : 6922
First Will and Testament : 3895
First Winter : 2885
First Winter of My Sister's Unmarked Grave :
    3186
First Words : 131
Firstborn, Firstgone : 3845
Fiscal Year : 2250
Fish : 2532, 2922, 7106
Fish 1 : 3798
Fish Eagles : 2675
Fish Gang : 5784
Fish Magic : 6242
Fish Stories : 7178
Fish Story : 2676
The fish that lives at the bottom : 3032
Fish Unlimited : 6605
Fish Whose Eyes Are Never Closed in Sleep :
    5527
The Fisherman : 2817, 3280
The Fisherman and His Wife : 921
The Fisherman's Catalogue: A Found Poem :
    5036
Fishes : 5453
Fishing : 3899, 6185
Fishing at Forty : 6283
Fishing Song : 3303
Fishing the Brazos : 4179
Fishing the Light : 5021
Fishing with My Two Boys at a Spring-Fed
    Pond in Kansas : 3425
Fishing, Wyoming : 1577
The Fishway at Holyoke : 1632
Fissure : 6428
Fists: A Poem for the Day of Atonement : 5473
Fitful Sleep : 1219
The Five-and-Ten : 1200
Five Black Beauties Romancing Dalmatia :
    4185
Five Drunken Manifestations of Zhong Kui
    (Mid to Late 20th Century) : 6272
Five Nails : 6142

Five Rumi Quatrains : 2696
Five Settings : 3171
Five Stanzas in the Middle of the Night : 6848
Five Thousand Acre Paddock : 2882
Five Translations from the Tocsik : 4427
Five Women in a Bed : 1884
Five Years After the Treaty Council at Medi-
    cine Lodge : 3171
Fixation : 1918, 4621
Fixed Point Theorem : 4457
Flag Burning : 4148
Flagellation : 2361
Flagman, Northeast Montana : 2958
Flags : 3270, 6093
Flamenco : 5566
Flamingos : 619
Flannelette : 2853
Flannery O'Connor : 4120
Flash : 4003, 5650
Flashes : 910
Flat on My Back : 5036
Flat Tire : 841
Flatbush Avenue : 2506
Flaws : 1735, 2221
The Flaws of the World : 5928
Fleeing Toward Western Europe : 3035, 3464
The Fleet's In : 477
The Flexibility of Sorrow : 3830, 6098
Flickan : 206
Flies : 3151, 3934
Flies, Bumblebees, and God : 576
The flies had been driven mad : 1774
Flight : 3116, 3665, 4276, 4721
Flight 103 : 6803
Flight into Egypt : 1149, 6651
The Flight of Frogs : 391
Flight of the Gulls : 2689
Flimsy Kitchen Light : 813, 814, 5525
Flint : 4961
The Flirt : 6094
Flirtation : 6163
Float : 5258
Floaters : 3638
Flood : 2833
Flood Plain : 5399
Floods : 1928, 4641
Floodwaters : 229, 4439
Floorscrapers : 1505
Flora As Its Apart : 5111
The Floral Apron : 1101
Florence : 1526, 7131
Florence: A December Morning Before
    Solstice, with an Introductory Stanza After
    Hardy : 3220
A Florid Story : 2337
Florida : 583, 1824, 2706
Florida Child : 3119
Florida — So Sam Said : 1824
Flour Angels : 929
Flow Chart for the Masses : 4919
The Flow of Eternity : 5079
Flower : 6675
A Flower and a Stem on the Twelfth Day : 2658
The Flower Artist, Darke County Fair : 5949

The Flower Box : 3197
The Flower I Guard : 2233, 3197, 6806
Flower of Five Blossoms : 3381
The Flower of No Smell Is Speaking : 1511,
    5072
Flower Street West : 1065
A flowering garden : 4352, 7144
Flowers : 2201
The Flowers : 5406
Flowers Born Blind : 329, 4413, 7057
Flute on the Mountain : 1142
Fly : 5895
The Fly-Cage : 3908
Flying : 20, 1727
Flying Blind : 4400
Flying, Her Hand Tries to Escape Her Body :
    4585
Flying Home on Sunday Morning : 1723
Flying to the Fire with the Doors Off : 4937
Flying West Into Light : 2429
Flypaper Poem : 1198
Focus : 6323
Fog : 420, 848
The Fog Casts Its Spell : 494
Fog Covering the Pier : 341
Fog Light : 1047
Fog Off Gaspe : 4248
A Foghorn : 2854
Foiled : 4380
Folate di Primavera : 1031
Folded : 6301
Folded Rose : 2314
Folded Wings : 2422, 3552, 6552
Folk Dance : 1821
Follow Me : 5828
Follow Your Destiny : 3572, 4994
The Following Shadow : 6086
Following the Map : 5027
Following Thoughts : 435, 6973
Font : 3847, 4383
Food : 4911
Food Shopping : 6352
Food Stamps : 1561
The Fool: Tarot Key O : 6536
A Foolish Consistency : 6112
Foolscap : 1217
The Football Coach and Mama's Memorial :
    6722
Football Practice : 6265
Footlights : 1739
The Footnote : 5694
A Footnote on Small Nations : 2359, 3464
Footnote to a Leap of Imagination : 4408
Footnoted : 1626
Footnotes to the Soul in Anticipation : 214
Footprints of Whales : 718
For a Child Who Has Lost Her Cat : 3978
For a Daughter Gone Away : 2170
For a Dead Poet: Not a Friend : 3211
For a Delirious Child : 5928
For a Girl, Age 12, Who Likes Robert Frost :
    6832
For a Liar : 2583
For a Long Time I Have Wanted to Write a

Happy Poem : 3083
For a Lost Child : 6101
For a Man Crushed to Death Sleeping in a
  Dumpster : 4727
For a moment she does not feel : 1774
For a moment the hangman will stay his hand :
  5079
For a Spell : 1336
For a Stranger : 119
For a Student Suicide : 4930
For Alison, My Niece, Recovering from a
  Gunshot Wound to the Head : 1338
For All the Tea in Canada : 4753
For an Anniversary : 1102
For an Encore We Trace the Spark : 2433
For an Old Flame : 1006
For Ananda : 4983
For Any Kamikaze Terrorist : 6417
For Argentina on Inauguration Day : 5354
For As Long As We've Worn Our Bodies :
  1726
For Billy, at 19 : 2081
For Calyx : 3673
For Cece : 4908
For Christina and Prince Robert : 3564
For Christ's Sake : 534
For David : 532, 5579
For David Lee, Who Left a Day Early : 3460
For Duke Ellington : 3082
For Elaine de Kooning : 4490
For Eli Jacobson : 5303
For Emily Dickinson : 650
For Grey : 6575
For Groucho Marx : 2831
For Haiti : 1523, 1757
For Her : 5030
For Herman Melville : 7115
For I-90 — in South Dakota : 1577
For in Them the Void Becomes Eloquent : 2142
For James Baldwin : 3764
For Jean Migrenne : 2534
For Jim Jordan, a Valedictory Pasticcio, with
  Love : 6712
For Jin Anmei, of Xi'an, Who Asked Would I
  Please Write Her a Poem : 3135
For Joan, in 1967 : 3250
For Joe : 5714
For John Berryman : 1320
For Kay : 5265
For Kimi : 1423
For Langston Hughes : 4945
For Leonora : 1304
For Life : 491, 3476, 5040
For Lily : 4891
For Love of Another : 4400
For Lucy, Who Has Alzheimer's Disease : 6136
For Lynn MacGillivray : 1130
For Mama : 3314
For Margaret : 4063
For Marilyn M : 841
For Marilyn Monroe : 6985
For Martin Luther King's Birthday : 976
For Marty, After 15,000 Days and Nights, July
  25, 1989 : 3135

For Mary, the Scientist : 6581
For Me When I Am Myself : 1209
For Mothers : 1604
For My Autistic Brother, Chutta : 131
For My Brother: On the Courage of Birds :
  5785
For My Daughter : 184, 3158, 3376
For My Daughter, Age 8 : 1849
For My Daughters : 5844, 6809
For My Father : 6128, 7112
For My Father, Belatedly : 1795
For My Father on the Occasion of Carrie's
  Wedding : 121
For My Father, Who Never Sang : 3396
For My Future Biographer : 2760
For My Mother Again : 3547, 3981, 5379
For My Mother in Winter : 6718
For My Mother, Traveling in Portugal : 4633
For My Mother (Yes, You Are Happy) : 2980
For My Sister Elizabeth, Bookkeeper and
  Mother of Four : 55
For My Son : 6809
For My Son Gone to College : 903
For My Student Killed in Tiananmen Square :
  4463
For My Uncle Who Died by His Own Hand :
  5834
For My Wife, Smiling in Her Sleep : 3118
For Nature daily through her grand design :
  6533
For Nelson Mandela, a Rejoicing : 2354
For one moment : 3347
For Only a Second : 435, 1085, 4180
For Our Birth : 5457
For Our Fifth Anniversary, Seven Days Late :
  1427
For Our Own Reasons : 4774
For Paul Blackburn : 5628
For Phyllis (1933-1983) : 3754
For Quite Some Time : 491, 3476, 4811
For Release : 6390
For Rick, in Honor of His Father : 3888
For Rikilein : 4637
For Roland, Presumed Taken : 354
For Sam : 5224
For Sara M. at Twelve : 1233
For Seven Women : 6207
For Sherry : 2086
For some time I was a student of Freud : 5580
For some time now I like to kick : 3225, 4295
For Sterling Brown : 1144
For the Dirty Thirties : 2846
For the Fans : 233
For the Farm : 2404
For the First Time in Twenty-Three Years Your
  Family Has Dinner Together : 2665
For the Girl Buried in the Peat Bog, Schleswig,
  Germany, First Century, A.D. : 5426
For the God Poseidon : 1401
For the Landlord's Repairman, Since He Asked
  : 1830
For the Long Distance Rider : 165
For the Missing in Action : 308
For the Old Gang : 79

For the raindrop, joy is in entering the river :
       2253, 2870
For the Sake of Yes : 3098
For the Survivors : 748, 3678
For the Time Being : 2969
For the Woman Who Remembers Old Songs :
       4644
For the Women I Slept with Years Ago : 2365
For the Year : 4312
For Their Wellbeing : 776
For Those Days of Mr. and Mrs. Carmen : 1827
For Three Weeks in May : 1550
For Trakl Under Fire (1914) : 3426
For Wiley, Age Six Months : 2332
For Wilfred Owen : 1236
For Xen, Because You Asked Me and Because I
       Wanted to Tell You : 602
For You at Five : 2706
For You Now It Is One Foot in Front of Itself :
       5450
For You Who : 1473, 6628
For Zeno of Citium : 4377
For Zoe in Spring : 7075
Foraging : 6579
Förbannad : 2418
The Forbidden : 5030
Forced Feeding : 5640
Forcing Amaryllis : 4959
The Ford Plant at River Rouge — 1930 : 1824
Forecast : 5753
Forecasting : 7178
Foreign : 558, 1699
Forensics : 2337
Foreplay : 2324
Foreplay on MacDougal Street : 5468
The Forest : 6821
The Forest Is Growing : 1084, 7092
Forestation : 184
Forever like this : 435, 1625
Forgetfulness : 1213
Forgetting : 786
Forgetting Is Remembering Intensely : 813,
       814, 2031
Forgive Me If I'm Confused : 2813
Forgiveness : 945, 3511
Forgotten in an Old Notebook : 7059
Förlopp : 6222
Form : 1473, 6628
A Formal Declaration : 435, 6973
The Forms of Love : 532, 1491
Förortsmorgon : 5525
Forsythia : 6292
Fort Worth, Texas : 5557
The Forties : 7059
Fortieth Anniversary : 3612
Fortuna : 2361
Fortune : 4688, 6046
Forty : 2730
Forty Dead, No Survivors : 3820
Forty Violins Pursue Mozart : 5284
Fossil : 3318, 6324
The Fossil Route : 1966
Foster Homes : 3281
Fosterling : 5698

Found Among Petals Dropping : 2065, 3228
Found Inside a Chinese Box : 6859
Found Poem: Beaufort Scale : 5540
Found Poems : 4848
The Foundation : 5928
The Founding of English Metre : 3746
The Fountains : 2201
Four A.M. on *Crusader* : 6101
Four and Five : 1526
The Four Corners of the World We Plunge
       Beyond : 2721, 3109
Four Dancers : 6338
Four Days in an Unfamiliar Country : 5074
Four Grey Wings of Mercy : 3862
Four Impromptus : 1971
Four in the morning and the dog wants to talk
       about her dream : 4973
The Four-Letter Word : 1286
Four Men in a Car : 1401
Four Mobiles After an Alexander Calder Retro-
       spective : 4661
Four Oak Leaves : 6101
Four Poems About Poetry : 1607
Four Poems by a Coal-Miner's Son : 3555
Four Poems From a Sequence : 1143
Four Pole Creek : 4228
Four Speeds of an Overhead Fan : 2331
Four Swim Sonnets : 1328, 6878
Four Views of Snow at Night : 5313
Four Weeks Unemployed: I Fail the Water
       Department's Lift and Carry Exam : 2705
Fourteen Constituents of Happiness : 949
Fourteen Lines a Sonnet Makes : 988
Fourth Dialogue Between the Lone Ranger and
       Tonto : 6859
Fourth of July : 4873
Fowl Play : 5805
The Fox : 2988, 4553
The Fox and the Wolf : 2271
Fox Glacier : 6579
Foxglove : 5928
The Fractal Lanes : 2142
Fractions : 381, 1526, 6829
Fragen eines Lesenden Arbeiters : 724
Fragging, Armed Forces Radio, Credence on
       the Mekong, 1969 : 7010
Fragility Is My Goal : 1231
Fragment : 1550, 1551, 1793, 3424
Fragment 543 (Page) : 3389, 5902, 5902
Fragments : 1445, 2797
Fragments and Commentaries : 2589, 5046
Fragments de la France : 4067
Fragments from a Letter to Herodotus : 6798
Fragments from Fort Worth, 1959 : 2150
Fragrant Hands : 99, 1883
Francis Bacon : 499, 5438
Francis Ford Coppola and Anthropologist
       Interpreter Teaching Gartewienna Tribes-
       men to Sing 'Light My Fire,' Philippine
       Jungle, 1978 : 7010
Frank : 676
Frankenstein, the Poet : 6250
Fransigt Köksljus : 5525
Frau Lou : 6770

Freak : 2464
Freckle Remover : 2773
Fred : 885
The Free Abandonment Blues : 6579
A Free Country : 5532
Free Diving : 3068
Free Trade : 3931
Free Verse : 2466
Free (Your Father) : 1651
Free Zone : 207, 4005
Freebasing : 3647
Freed from Superstition, Hurrah : 6649
Freedom : 841, 5047
Freedom in Chains : 3572, 4994
Freeway 57, Orange County : 6752
Freezing Cigarettes : 2855
French Tickler he says proudly : 1327
A Fresco : 1625, 7069
Fresh Kill Report : 4099
Fresh Oysters and Beer : 6728
Fretwork : 500
Freud Says My Dreams About Losing Teeth
    Are Sexual : 2731
Frida Digresses on Red : 406
Friday Nights : 3029
A Friend Gets Divorced : 876
Friendly Definitions : 5724
Friends : 4447
Frieze : 7045
Frog : 1890
The Frog Princess : 397
Frog Time : 1550, 3457
Froggie : 6800
Frogless : 253
From a Crystal Wedding Day : 4363
From a Dictionary of Chinese Ideograms : 6409
From a Dishwasher's Diary : 3698
From a Distant Place : 5409
From a Notebook : 5083
From a Photograph : 1123
From a Silent Space a Certain Undertone : 3092
From a Train Window : 6063
From a Translation of the *Carmina Burana* :
    6223
From a Visigothic Prayer to the Mother of Love
    : 4744
From Above and Below : 5834
From Attu, 1943 : 1976
From *Best-Loved Lives of the Bards* : 1991
From Childhood : 854, 4627
From Each According to His Abilities, to Each
    According to His Need : 4940
From Far Away : 304, 2283
From Here : 6774
From Home : 813, 814, 5293
From Marianne Moore to Robert B. Young of
    the Ford Motor Company in Reply to His
    October 19, 1955 Letter Regarding the
    Name of a Car : 6722
From Matthew to Prime Time : 3510
From My Mother's House : 4311
From My Window : 3032
From Nestor to Helen Now of Troy : 6391
From Nothing : 7146

From Now On : 3655
From Nowhere : 296, 4287
From Omeros, Chapter XLVI : 6701
From One Pair of Hands : 2101
From the Air : 5805
From the Arabic : 5806
From the Archives : 1971
From the Attic at Thornfield : 350
From the Book of Job : 651, 5151
From the Campground in North Truro : 5106
From the Cocoon : 6860
From the Corner of His Eye : 1323
From the Danube, 1829 : 529
From the Desert Inn / Out : 2025
From the Diary of D. Burnam : 53
From the Dorotheenstadt Cemetery : 3197,
    3540, 6806
From the Earth: Joys and Sorrows : 1511, 5072
From the Front Door to the Mailbox and Back :
    117
From the half-dark hall, abruptly : 2936, 4007
From the Henchman's Diary : 2231, 5040
From the Journal of a 19th Century Aeronaut :
    4194
From the Lady Fleur : 1786
From the Marble Rose to the Iron Rose : 1536,
    3533
From the Master Blaster Bator : 4638
From the Porch : 6702
From the Porch Swing : 4446
From the Road Home : 5255
From the Second Story : 5980, 7146
From the Source : 3462
From the Stars, Silence : 6255
From *The Waiting Child* : 6329
From the Worm's Eye : 467
From This Valley : 3729
The Front : 4957
Front Porch Glider : 1735
Frontier : 5193
Frost : 1582, 5098
Frost Line : 5123
Frosted Mirror : 5702
Frozen : 5735
Frozen Charlottes : 5141
Frozen Harvest : 971
Frozen Shut : 1634
A Fruit Fell Down : 897
Fruit of Fruit : 2051
Fruits of War, Fruits of Peace : 4139
Frying Pork Chops Topless : 5969
Fucking Lu Hsun in My Office with William
    Blake Watching : 3646
Fuel for Allergy : 4919
Fui Pegando Mariposas a Mi Cuerpo : 4755
Fulcrum : 1266
Fulfill Desire : 1762
Full Circle : 5789
Full House November First : 5833
Full Moon : 4337
Full Moon Over Dogwood : 5267
Full Moon This Night in January : 2638
Full of Desire, Dreaming : 1545
Fulton Valley Washout : 1230

Fumador : 5899
A Fumbling Poem : 1087
Fumetti : 3844
Functional Poetry : 1241
Functions : 532, 5579
Funeral : 4561, 5795
The Funeral : 6242
Funeral Mazurkas : 4776
Funny Bones : 5730
A Furniture Maker : 2361
Fury : 5765
Fusion : 3924
Futile Ode to Nobody : 264, 5873
The Future : 1605
Future Language : 1681
The Future of the Past : 6829
A Future Somewhere : 3098
Futuristic : 4162
G-9 : 1602
Gacela for a Dead Child : 2191, 4273
The Gaelic Long Tunes : 4562
Gagaku : 5335
Gains : 435, 1085, 4180
Galahad's Gone : 6094
Galapagos Islands, Guillotine Eyelids : 1890
Galileo: A Letter to His Daughter : 4514
Gall, Wormwood : 2210
Galleries of Angels : 1504
The Galley : 5264
Gallup : 813, 814, 2031, 2031
Galveston : 4606, 4862
The Game : 624, 826
Game Mistress : 1018
A Game of Chance : 6129
Games : 6118
Games People Play : 1764
Gaming : 5973
Gamma : 2337
La Gamme d'Amour : 2740
Gani Fawehinmi : 4764
Gaps in Suffering : 4795
Garage Account : 5370
Garbo : 1950
Garden : 2257, 2725
The Garden : 1539
The Garden Before Winter : 6040
The Garden of Paradise : 1307
Garden Party : 338, 4906, 4907
Garden Reprieve: The Paradox of Fortunate
    Forgetfulness : 2252
Garden Reveille : 4773
The Gardener's Complaint : 4292
Gardenias : 108
Gardening : 5225, 6876
The Gardens Wtihin Us : 1352
Garibaldi Leaves Rome : 1158
Garish : 4211
A Garvey Man : 1290
A gas station explodes : 37
The Gatekeeper : 1415
Gathas : 184, 5224
A Gatherer's Love : 268
Gathering Apricots : 2707, 4395
Gathering Constellations : 2369

A Gathering of Ghettoes : 3730
A Gathering of Men : 1935
Gathering the Sparks : 2718
Gatherings : 6996
Gatsby : 829
Gauguin and Bonnard : 3846
Gauguin: The Yellow Christ : 2981
Gauze Landing : 5640
Gazebo : 2935
Geese : 252, 945
Geisha Mime : 2037
Geishas : 2247
Gelsey Kirkland in 'The Nutcracker' : 1824
Gemini's Portrait : 2819
Gender Fuck Gender : 936
Gene Train Suicide : 6784
Genealogy : 2540
Genepool : 3845
General Linguistics : 2028, 4979
The General Progress : 4944
A Generation : 2499, 2591
Generic : 1821
Generic College : 6562
The Generous Past : 783
Genesis : 588, 1458
Genesis II : 5026
Genesis According to Charlie : 6250
Genghis Chan: Private Eye VIII : 7093
The Genius of Sleep : 239
Gentle Hands: An Art Preview : 2140
Geode : 6774
Geography Lesson : 4479
The Geography of Desire : 950
The George : 4499
George Pascho Miller : 5858
George Santayana Revisited : 5810
George Segal: *Girl Putting on Scarab Necklace*
    : 2260
Georges Braque : 1794, 2307, 6053
Georgette : 5866
Georgia Minor : 5213
Georgia O'Keefe's Bones [sic] : 6921
Georgic III : 980, 1003, 5071
A Georgic for Doug Crase : 697
Geranium : 5389, 6662
Gerard Manley Hopkins Mesmerizes a Duck :
    5808
German Reunification: The Downside : 6514
Germs of Mind in Plants, by R.H. Francé : 4436
Gerrye, Wound Knower : 4942
Gershwin : 2012
Gertrude Stein : 7001
Gert's Place : 4448
Gesture : 2956, 4704
Gesture and Flight : 3656
Get Flat : 726
Get Rid of Unsightly : 493
Gethsemane : 1553
Geting Beyond Unity : 2249
Gets the Barber : 3245
Getting an Electric Shock : 435, 1625
Getting Back : 4895
Getting Called In : 5931
Getting Clean : 688

Getting Honest : 173
Getting Old : 841
Getting the Children to Bed : 6349
Getting the Spirit at the Brass Band Church :
6944
Getting to Be the Lucky One : 4638
Getting Together : 4239
Getting Up : 6491
Gettysburg Postcard : 5461
Ghazal : 99, 1883, 6024
Ghazal of a Thousand Years : 6305
Ghazal of the Secret Mile : 6305
Ghazal of the Warning : 6305
Ghost : 3411
The Ghost Boy : 3130
Ghost Marriage : 1931
Ghost Pain : 2884
Ghost Stories : 5171
Ghost Story : 1313
Ghost Town : 2443
Ghostbrother : 5456
Ghosts : 2196, 2997, 4942, 6526
Giant : 5130
Gift : 3748, 7153
The Gift : 389, 710, 1597, 2124, 2527, 3197,
3583, 3746, 5073, 5583
Gift Enclosure : 4157
The Gift of a Wallet : 271
The Gift of Fury : 472
Gift Shop in Pécs : 5379
Gifts : 147, 2299
The GIGANTIC Thirst : 841
Ginger : 6661
Gingerbread Man : 6922
The Gingerbread Man : 921
The Gingham Dog : 2101
Gingko : 1777
The Giraffe : 3758
Giralda : 6299
Girl : 3516, 3696
The Girl : 206, 813, 814
A Girl from Buttonwillow : 4176
The Girl from Ermita : 5781
The Girl from Morbisch : 1078
Girl Guide Cookies : 3328
Girl in a Dogwood Tree : 5929
The Girl in Sandy Hill Park : 6078
A Girl Named Spring : 5855
Girl Not on the Moon : 3836
The Girl Servant : 412, 2747, 3121
Girl Urinating : 4585
Girl with a Lute : 5876
A Girl With Bare Feet : 3699
A Girl With White Gold Hair at Clearwater
Beach : 3826
Girls from St. Augustine's : 6292
Girls in the Museum : 1923
Gisela Brüning : 5733
Giulio Agricola : 2992
Give Me Only Silence : 1086
Give Us Barabbas : 3049
Giveaway : 4709
Giving : 4927
Giving the Glitter to Some Body Else and Not

Wanting It Back : 566
The Glacier on Crystal Lake : 2709
Glad Heart at the Supermarket : 6595
Gladioli : 1810
Glance from a Stairway Fading : 3623
Glanmore Revisited : 2743
Glass : 2532, 2922, 4970, 7106, 7139
Glass Act : 3167
Glass Eye : 6244
A Glass Falls : 823, 3445, 5874
Glass Opera : 234
Glass Sand : 4849
The Glasses Poem : 4233
Glassworks : 2584
The Gleam of Silver Wings : 4179
Glen Gould Playing Bach on Television : 3993
Glendalough : 5159, 6840
Glendower Ponders the Vasty Deep : 6198
Glenn's Bird : 1466
Gliders : 3110
Glimpse : 2255
Glimpse of Main Event : 4211
Glint of Gold Tooth in a Poorly Lit Kitchen :
1890
Global Amnesia : 6644
The Global Economy : 2828
Global Inequalities : 1293
Glömska Är Att Minnas Häftigt : 2031
Gloom : 1162
Gloomy Sunday with Orange Quangaroos : 107
Glory : 2340
Glory Pig : 2319
Gloss : 2726
Glossary: A Deconstruction : 6510
Glow : 1476, 3816
The GM : 4325
Gnu Poem : 6618
Go on Vacation Once in a While : 6042
Goa Lawah, Bali : 64
Goalpost : 6897
Goat : 1279
Goat Haikus : 6331
Goat Ranching on Hardscrabble : 4179
Goats : 1105
Goat's Horn with Red : 698
The Goats of Summer : 4179
Goatsucker : 2074
The Goblins'll Get You : 4981
La Goccia Pronta per il Mappamondo : 1473
God : 1625, 2521, 3873
God! : 6120
God Enters the Swept Field : 6936
A God for Every Occasion : 6116
God forgives volcanic eruptions : 2393
The God Hole : 433
The God of Joy : 4503
God-the-Father Crafty in His Bathtub : 2108
Goddess of Democracy : 3857
Goddess of Hunting : 1526
Gods : 999
God's Grandeur : 2934
God's Moustache : 2852
God's One-eyed Horse : 1142
God's Precis : 1420

God's Scout : 6688
God's Torment : 6, 656
God's Will? : 1685
Godspeed : 345, 4531
Goethe at Naples : 1698
Gogol's Madman : 1188
Goin Home : 2363
Going : 1063, 3419
Going Ahead : 1382
Going Away from the River : 2534
Going Back, Not Forward, After All : 6887
Going Back to the River : 2534
Going Fishing : 5972
Going Home : 2785, 4065
Going Into Moonlight : 306
Going On : 6101
The Going On : 1726
Going Out : 841
Going Out for Cigarettes : 1213
Going the Distance : 1269
Going to Egypt : 6135
Going to Hsüan-ch'eng Past Hsin-lin Beach
    toward Pan-ch'iao : 1992, 2976
Going to Krogers : 6605
Going to My Brother's : 4808
Going to My Child : 1457
Going to Oklahoma : 2445
Going to the Butcher's with Daddy : 1343
Going to the Post Office : 6378
Going to the Tent Revival : 4898
Going to Work in the Morning : 4109
Going Up on Stage : 66, 6456
Gold : 5360
The Gold Cannon : 6058
The Gold Coast : 3610
Gold Rail : 1266
Goldbarth in Montpelier : 6822
Golden Age : 6375, 7057
Golden Delicious : 5106
Golden Dragon : 623
The Golden Fleece : 3341, 3476, 4812
The Golden Years : 5653
Goldfinch at the Window Feeder : 6144
Gonaives : 798
Gone : 445
Gone Fishing : 6038
The Good-bye Soup : 3304
The Good City : 5764
Good for the Soul : 4634
Good Friday : 1218, 1458
Good Friday, 1989, Driving Westward : 5212
Good Girl : 6387
A Good Hag's Advice : 2312
Good, I Said : 4134
The Good Job : 2970
The Good Lunch of Oceans : 5353
Good News : 1307, 2459
Good Night, Moon : 6117
Good Night, Sleep Tight : 808
The Good Old Days : 3272
The Good Son's Mother Dies : 4753
Good Things : 4223
Good Waters : 1359
A Good Year : 2189

Goodbye : 3283
Goodbye Big Ed : 353
Goodbye, Ruby Begonia : 5970
Goodbyes : 4622, 4759, 6546
Goodwill : 2206
Goofy Plays Second Fiddle in the Family
    Quartet : 5804
Goose-in-the-Pond Improvisations, Southside
    Estate-Sale Quilt and Ghost : 4260
Gordon's Tomb, Jerusalem : 5258
Gorgon : 2398
Gorgon Song for Patient Zero : 1068
The gorilla dressed as a bellhop : 932
The Goshawk : 4001
Gospel of Eve with Adam : 361
Gospel of the Moon : 361
The Gossamer Builder : 5289
Gotmateswara : 6250
Gouldsboro : 1078
Gourds : 5928
Government of Rhapsody : 2037
The Governor Powell Building : 1644
Grace : 1090, 2983, 3263
A Grace : 2567
Grace After Meals : 4137
The Grace of Conversion : 4873
Graceland : 5859, 6412
Grackles : 5980
Grading Essay Entitled 'Rejection' : 3871
The Graduate : 1587
Graduation Present : 902
Graffiti : 443
Grafitti on a Roman Wall : 6879
Gramma Inie and the Bear : 2085
The Grammar of Hope : 1585
The Grammar of Silk : 6044
Grammars : 499, 5438
Grammie's Rescue of Me with Pillsbury Rolls :
    1621
Gramps : 6077
El Gran Mamut : 7142
The Grand Concourse : 3343
The Grand Duke Nicolas Nicolaevitch Sleeps in
    the Autumn of 1914 : 6878, 6915
Grandfather : 5203
Grandfather Up a Tree : 5730
Grandfathers : 25, 4619
Grandfather's Rocking Horse : 7041
Grandma : 3873
Grandma Budde : 1508
Grandma Came to America : 604
Grandma Julia / Grandma Grace : 4836
Grandma Won't Stay Put : 5839
Grandmother : 951, 4440, 4616
Grandmother Logic : 5894
Grandmother Was a Doctor : 2101
Grandmothers : 2171
Grandmother's Arms : 3398
Grandmother's father was killed by some
    Tejanos : 5169
Grandpa : 6003, 6049
Grandparents : 3429
Granite : 6562
Granite Is Weightless : 5000

Grant Wood's People : 413
Graphing the Arc : 5679
The Grass : 3254, 5502
Grass in August : 813, 814, 5525
The Grass on the Other Side : 6666
Grasshoppers : 6787
Gratitude : 6800
Grave : 431
Grave Goods : 2925
Grave Poem : 6935
The Gravel of Sunlight : 841
The Graves in October : 769
Graveyard Shift : 974
Gravitation : 931, 5197
Gravity : 1258, 6230, 6263
Gray Day, Early Afternoon : 4351
Gray May Now Buy : 4005
Great Ancestors : 2532, 2922, 7106
Great Auks : 4758
Great Aunt Laura : 1205
Great Blue Heron : 5518
The Great Blue Heron : 4296
The Great Feeding : 4296
Great Grandmother's Bridesmaid : 719
Great Headlines in History : 6497
Great Lakes : 5679
The Great Mammoth : 5995, 7142
The Great Nebula of Andromeda : 5303
Great Owl : 2886
The Great Pyramid : 4760
Great Silence : 4635, 4802
Great Stone Face : 697
The Great Test : 2568
The Great Wall : 6789
The Greatest Barbiturate Glitzy Dizz : 4043
The Greatest Western of All Time : 232
Grecian Urn : 5175
El Greco: 'The Penitent Magdalen' : 3850
Greed : 1018, 3541
Greed Suite: Attitudes at the Top of a Hierarchy
     Influence Conduct Below : 6794
Greed Suite: Authority : 6794
Greed Suite: The False Season : 6794
Greek Scene : 3287, 5361
Green : 1695
The Green and the Brown : 2902
The Green at Midnight : 3018
The Green Corn : 6159
Green Diet : 6503
Green Field : 1707
The Green Gatherers at Sounion : 3051
Green Grief : 6348
Green Haloes : 711
Green Jello : 3375
Green Moths : 368
Green Mountain Fever : 3002
Green on a Black and White Planet : 244
Green Religions : 993
Green Snake Interview #6: Speaking of a
     Vibrant Woman : 3434
The Green Stigma : 329, 4413, 7057
Green Street : 189
Green That Inspires Longings for Joy : 1090
Green Tobacco Worms : 6543

Green Twig in My Hand : 1363, 5379, 7164
The Green Well : 3538
Green, White, Red : 3145
The Green Widower : 6736
Greenhouse Effect : 6697
The Greenhouse Effect Reaches the Environ-
     mental Agency : 5591
Greenland on the Map : 1808
The Greenlanders' Problem : 2913, 2956
Greenland's History : 2913, 2956
A Greeting to All Who Still Care : 1168
Greetings, Friends : 176
Greg : 1946
Grendalsong : 3896
Gretel in Middle Age Hears of Hansel's Death :
     6946
Grey : 3493
Grey / Layered : 4390
The Grey Whales : 4668
Grey Whales in Migration : 7191
Gridiron : 6072
Gridlock : 3845
Grief : 126, 2506, 5434
Grief, Don't Leave Me : 4733, 4779
Grief for the Living : 4252
Grief in the Suburbs : 6494
The Grieving Boxes : 3982
Gringa in Paradise : 3960
Gringos : 6753
Grinnell, Iowa : 6162
Grizzly : 4804
A Groovy Kind of Love : 5969
Die Grosse Fracht : 284
Grotesques : 2693
Ground Breaking : 2869
Ground Equipment Recital : 5329
Ground Owls : 6832
Groundhog Days : 2255
Groundwater : 7005
Grouping Fowl : 318, 4415, 4778
Growing Deaf : 4283
Growing Old in Arizona : 237
Growing Old with Frank and Joe : 1433
Growing Things : 5220
Grown-Up Tea : 5121
Gruidae Americana : 5730
Grunion Run with My Imaginary Children :
     2734
Guard Tower : 1802
Guardian : 368
A Guardian Tanya : 989
The Guards : 346, 3120, 4312
Guards National Stadium, Santiago, Chile 1973
     : 1030
Guards of the Heart : 5482
Guatemala : 2399
La Guenille : 2013
Guernica : 3786, 6523
A Guest in a Strange House : 921
Guff : 5969
Guidance : 5119
The Guide : 813, 814, 2526, 3697
Guide to the Other Gallery : 2288
Guile : 6491

Guillotine : 2714
Guilt : 2216, 4901
Guilt, the Amorous Octopus : 4178
The Guitar : 2191, 5309
La Guitarra : 2191
The Gulf : 2850, 2884
Gulf Stream : 438, 1757, 3588, 6220
Gull : 6018
Gulls : 7163
The Gulls of Padre Island : 4179
Gully : 1511, 6054, 7004
Gun Club Smoker for the Prude : 4099
Gun Smoke : 6526
Gusev : 4095
A Gust inside a God : 2852
Gusts of Spring Air : 1031, 1939
Gutbucket : 3466
A Guy I Know : 402
The Guys : 1116
GWTW : 5907
Gwyneth: Chalk : 5427
Gypsy Rose Lee Gets Cancer : 5316
Gypsy Said : 3155
Habito : 4621
The Habits of Eating : 1966
Habitual : 5453
Habla Cuerpo : 4621
Hag-Light : 6075
Hagocytosis : 3510
Hai-Phoo : 5215
Haibun: Mad Earths in My Room : 4526
Haiku : 1482, 1625, 2491, 3907, 3907, 5270,
    6738
Haiku Collection : 357
Haiku for the Homeless : 3430
Hail on Phobos : 4549
Hair : 820
Hair Again : 3640
Hair of the Dog : 6556
Hair Shirt : 6347
Hairbrain : 582
Haircuts at Ramon's were fifty cents : 5169
Hais and Lows : 50
Haiti Painting: Alabama Women at a Bedside :
    2637
The Half-life of Sorrow : 2454
Half-willed absence. Neckband, cosmetology,
    it's o.k. : 162
Halfway Home : 1055
Halifax : 5350
Hall of Souls : 1572
Hallelujah : 6441
Hallelujah Pancake Syrup : 1520
Halleys Comet : 6855
Hallonporträtt : 5708
Hallowe'en : 6115
Halloween Kimonos : 2035
Halloweening : 1702
Hamlet Exits the Castle : 829
Hammond Pond : 3204
Han Haiku : 1625, 2554
Hand Like a Spire, Hand Like a Flag : 3873
Handiwork : 1139
Handless Maiden and Child : 55

Handling the Dead : 1656
Hands : 155, 666, 865, 3038, 3117
The Hands : 3652, 5452
The Hands in the Bowl : 3796
Hands, like Asters : 4266
Hands Like Telephone Wires : 5202
Hands Like Wings : 3957
Hands, Prints, Time: A Collage : 4738
A Handsel : 4391
The Handsome Poet : 3977
Handy Words : 6326
The Hang-Glider : 2681
The Hanged Man's Dilemma : 6152
Hangover : 490
Hannah at the Creek : 1142
Hanno Sparato a Mezzanotte : 2216
Hansel in Recovery : 1980
Hansel's Version : 2606
Happiness : 2707, 5171
Happiness Andalusian Style : 5181, 6456, 7097
Happiness Is Hot, Splattered Brains : 532, 5579
Happy : 5524
A Happy Death : 7049
Happy Ending : 4277
Happy Hunting Ground : 191
Happy Man : 6922
Happy Mouth : 2853
Haptic : 7004
Här, Jag Har Skalat en Apelsin : 2031
Harbour House : 380
Hard Facts : 1801, 6593
Hard Jaws : 1847
Hard Mattress Madonna : 3780
Hard Things : 1350
Hard Wood : 4313
Hardening : 6978
Hardhat Pillow : 4937
Hardpan : 6400
The Hare : 1690, 3445, 5874, 7140
Harlem : 3625, 4018, 5757
Harlem Society : 6797
A Harmadik Nap Esni Kezdett a Hó : 1363
Harmony : 3198, 6210
Harold Bloom : 1519
Harold Iverson, Teacher : 6482
Harpoon : 2828
Harpsichord in the Rain : 4524
The Harpsichord-Maker : 7042
Harris Among the Gods : 3409
Harris County Grays : 5321
Harrowed Minds : 699
Harry's Requiem Picnic : 4321
Hart Crane : 925, 2888, 7001
Hartland Cliff : 6464
Hart's Tongue : 3853
Haruspex : 4743
Harvard Square : 4671
Harvest : 575, 980, 2499, 3170, 3769, 4349,
    5658, 6124
Harvest Letter : 1494
Harvesting : 6845
Hate Is a White Robe : 3613
Hates : 1593
Hatfield Apts : 1371

Hauling Manure, Late October : 1105
Hauling on Hardscrabble : 4179
A Haunt of Echoes : 1576
Haunted, As If. Haunted with a Fear : 1337
Haunted Landscape : 236
The Haunting : 4860
Haunts : 6829
Haut Goût : 6776
Hav I November : 5708
Have a Good Time : 2595
Have a Heart : 1332
Have Seen the Silence : 5942
Have you ever thought : 4857
Havet : 685
Having come far on my journey : 11, 3759
Having Lived an Alien Life : 170, 4216
Having Lunch at Brasenose : 1132
Having Recovered His Sight After Being Struck
    by Lightning, the Old Farmer Quiets
    Those Who Would Question Him : 5212
The Hawaiian Shirt : 2551
Hawaiian Time : 1483
The Hawk : 7117
Hawkedon : 3008
Hazard : 3923
Haze : 5660
He : 6700
He and I : 1818, 3464
He and the Village : 6532
He Came In : 3780
He Didn't Get Leda : 1726
He Died at Dawn : 2191, 2779
He Enjoins Her to Be Quiet : 2677
He folds and leans : 6378
He Had a Good Year : 445
He Is : 5434
He Is Not In : 3732, 6469
He Is Not Your Monster : 6441
He Looks Like My Father : 5207
He Need Regret Nothing : 3829
He Prefers Paper Women Like Men Who
    Would Rather Have Porn : 3780
He riffs his soul : 5068
He Said Not a Word : 4629
He Shoves Everyone Away : 3780
He sits in the car and stares straight ahead,
    blankly : 5053
He Sits There and Suddenly : 2577
He Speaks : 3356, 5250
He Tries to Entice : 6492
He Uses All His 'Up' Up On the Radio : 3780
He Wants to Sell You the Blue Lagoon : 4220
He was a tailor and came to be known as Juan
    Agujas : 5169
He Was Free : 5960
He Whom Ye Seek : 1019
Head : 5118, 6786
Head Blowing : 4947
The Head of Joaquin Murietta : 3428
Head of Shakespeare : 5870
Head of the God of the Number Zero : 1006
Head-on : 5707
Heading for Another Fall : 4174
Headless is Delos : 2945

The headlights, moving : 3406, 3759
Headlines : 6728
Heads : 2916, 3555
Heads from the Museo Nazionale Romano :
    5530
Headwaters of Big Creek : 4898
Healing : 6269
Healing Dirt : 7013
Healing Powers : 1396
Healing Properties : 2905
Healing Thyself : 423
Heap Yourself Free : 1146
Hear My Voice : 3517
Hear the Chorus : 3669
Hear the Footstep : 2216, 4901
Hearing : 6061
Hearing a Poem the First Time : 2345
Hearing She Said I Told Him Lyn Lifshin Is
    Going with a Dispatcher : 3780
Hearing Sirens : 3559
Hearing the Terrible to Sea : 3573
Hearing Things : 4604
Hearing through Light : 148
Hearings (the Effects of Light) : 1406
Heart : 813, 814, 4870, 5708
Heart Ache : 2438
Heart and Soul : 5347
Heart Labor : 147
Heart Lake August : 31
Heart Land : 2332
Heart of Autumn : 6765
The Heart of Bees : 4431
Heart of the formless spring : 4044
Heart Transplant : 2532, 2922, 7106
Heart Water : 6794
Hearts : 1813
Hearts and Doilies : 4629
Hearts and Flowers : 184
The Hearts of Eagles : 1046, 6632
Heartthrobs : 5969
The Heat : 2551
Heat at the Center : 445
Heat, Letting Go : 350
Heat Lightning : 5302
Heat Wave : 4527
Heather's Vision : 2202
Heatwave : 9
Heaven : 961
Heaven in 5-Gallon Jars : 3659
Heaven in Hell : 5570
Heaven Is Heaven : 4002
Heaven Stones : 3074, 4641
The Heavenbound Canoe : 4827
Heavenly Geometry : 644, 6324
Heavenly Host : 345
Heavy : 3782
The Heavy Freight : 284, 5271
Heavy Reading : 6906
Hebride Bay : 554, 3318
Der Hecht : 4481
Hecksher Park : 233
Hector, the Dog : 4939, 5098
A Hedge of Rubber Trees : 1132
Heel Should Not Be an Insult : 5036

Heere i aym : 392
Hegemonies : 875, 5113
Heigh Ho : 5330
Heine in Paris : 1455
Heinrich 'The Heinie' Holtz : 6807
Heirloom : 1717, 3169
The Heirs of Stalin : 5181, 6456, 7097
Hekla : 3993
Helen : 2
Heliotropo : 7133
Hell : 1498, 6250
The Hell Crowds : 1966
Hell Is Somewhere : 4919
Hello, Diana : 3041
Help Help : 4434
Help! I'm a Prisoner in the Right Hotel on
    Exchange Avenue : 5089
The Help She Can Get : 1892
Helping Hand : 6514
Helping My 25-Year-Old Daughter Pack : 4646
The Helpless Year : 6886
Hemifrån : 5293
The Hemlock Prince : 2074
Hence : 3418
Henceforth, from the mind : 608
Henna : 4536, 5228, 5566, 7057
Henry Miller and Burroughs : 841
Her Blacks : 3182
Her Colors : 4056
Her Day Speaks for Sleeplessness : 3947
Her Diamond Ring : 989
Her Dream Was of Water : 4935
Her Face : 601
Her Great Escape : 406
Her Hair Exploded : 3333
Her Hands : 5019
Her Husband's Influence Will Send You,
    Calestrius, into Exile, a Letter Circa 200
    A.D. : 3826
Her 'Lady of the Depths' Appears at Blue
    Mountain Center : 6441
Her Lifelist : 6907
Her loom as if some wounds : 4973
Her Lover : 4300
Her Mother Explains : 108
Her Name Is Laughter : 2189
Her two brothers came : 1855
Her Word : 2381
The Heralds : 5033
The Herbalist : 5149
Herbs: Our Catalog : 298
Herbst : 1945, 5351
Herbstmanöver : 284
Here : 1031, 1427, 1939, 2365, 4270
Here Comes Debbie : 1378
Here I am again letting my thoughts : 156
Here I Am, Then : 2052, 6287
Here Is the Earth : 899, 5995
Here Is the House That Has Folded : 1343
Here, I've Peeled an Orange : 813, 814, 2031
Here on the Coast : 7161
Heredity : 5127
Here's an Example : 2914
Here's What Thistles Can Do : 2887

Heritage : 331, 4038, 4998
The Hermit Crab : 3816
Hermit Crabs : 5295
The Hermit Poem : 2326
Hermosa Nightmare : 2269
Hermosillo : 711
Herms I : 3287, 5361
Hero and Leander : 1269
Hero Lost : 5253
Herod Piper : 5991
Herodotus and the Photograph : 5264
Heron Dance : 3983
Heron, Muskrat, Hobo, Spider : 267
Herpetologist : 4187
Herself Com Passionate : 1815
He's Packed Up All His Zane Greys : 5127
The Hex : 1759
Hexagons in the Hallway : 6446
Hey, Bro : 632
Hey, Lady, We Don't Serve No Froufrou
    Coffee Here : 7171
Hey Mister, You Want to Look at My Junk Just
    for the Hell of It? : 2495
$HI (Sunday Want Ads) : 2603
Hi There : 6101, 6346, 7081
Hibernation : 7100
Hidden Child : 3778, 5310
Hidden Light : 2065, 3228
Hide and Seek : 5031
Hide from Time : 2256
Hiding the Knives : 666
Hiding the Skeleton : 1128
The Hierodule's Apologue : 4983
The High Country : 4320
High Dive : 4421
The High Gondola : 4726
High River : 4562
High School : 3638
The High School of O : 1667
High School Sex : 5643
High Summer : 4201
High Tension Languages : 5822
High Time : 6006, 6662
High Utterance : 1745
Higher Ground : 958
Highway : 5578
Highway Poem After Miro : 3273
Highway Restaurant : 6957
Highway Safety : 2328
Hijackings : 3369
Hiking Above the Monegaw River : 6742
Hill Estate Auction — Stella, Missouri : 2957
The Hills Had Caves : 6637
Hilltop Meadow : 6086
Him : 2587
Hind, Eating Fish in Denmark : 6070
The Hint of Rain : 2254
Hinter der Wand : 284
Hired : 1191
Hiros' Rock Garden in Bloom : 1598
Der Hirt Auf Dem Felsen (The Shepherd on the
    Rock) after F. Schubert : 1370
His Conversion : 1752
His Daughter : 5439

His Daughters : 2941
His Father Phones with an Idea for a Poem : 5467
His Feet : 3356, 5740
His Hands : 1498
His heart was in his garden, but his brain : 6533
His Legs Itch : 6800
His Name Was Steve : 402
His Return and Revelation : 6023
His Shadow : 2854
His Sign : 5114
Histoire de Femmes : 3733
Histoire des Mentalités : 3833
La Historia Central : 3642
Historic Houses in Virginia : 1577
Historical Perspective : 6514
Historicity : 1901
History : 496, 1090, 1440, 3707
History as the Painter Bonnard : 2870
History: But in the myth, at the beginning of our world : 2406
History Lesson : 1782
The History of Death : 1145
The History of Human Life : 3746
The History of the Queen City Hotel : 5963
History: So that I had to look up just now to see them : 2406
A History Through Dreams : 1266
Hit and Run : 7112
Hit Me One, William : 4820
The Hitchhiker : 3675
Hitchhiking the Blossoms of Trees : 4669
HIV : 1253
Hjärtat : 5708
Hobo : 319
Hobo Mystic : 4599
Hobos on Long Trains : 2699
Hocking the Royal : 3427
The Hoe : 2011
The Hoe Makes a Hushed Sound : 1214
Hold It : 6747
Hölderlin : 2231, 5040
The Holding : 1539
Holding Pattern : 588
Holding Patterns : 413
Holding Together : 6370
The Hole : 3688
A Hole & a Pulse : 3079
A Hole in Our Lives : 3602
The Hole in the Moon : 2652
Holiday : 4738
Holland, May 1940 : 2946
Holloween : 6173
Holloween Morning Before the Mergansers and Others : 2791
Hollyhocks : 5011
Hologram : 413
Holograph : 2458
Holography : 2672
Holography in the Mountains : 5288
Holy As Hell : 6250
The Holy Ghost Attends Vacation Bible School : 2728
The Holy Ghost Goes Out for Little League : 2728
The Holy Ghost Moves to Kilgore : 2728
Holy Night : 1614
Holy Orders : 2116
The Holy Sea : 3833
The Holy Trinity : 1485
Holy Wars (1944) : 2445
Homage : 3100
Homage to Cocteau : 2375
Homage to Eugene Witla : 5224
Homage to Frida Kahlo : 14, 4029
Homage to Kenny Poff : 1985
Homage to Kleist : 1181, 2503
Homage to Matisse : 4835
Homage to Mondrian : 430
Homage to Samuel Beckett : 6425
Homage to Senator J. Helms : 395
Homage to Simon Rodia : 3586
Homage to Vallejo, 12/29/89 : 6358
Homage to Van Gogh : 6798
Homage to White Bread, Circa 1956 : 2199
Homage to Wine : 5452
El Hombre de Montevideo : 1028
Los Hombres Penumbrosos : 1833
Home : 110, 649, 2498, 3226, 3237, 3445, 4863, 5874, 5964, 6220, 6701
Home Baked Bread : 5602
Home Care : 2740
The Home Family : 860
Home Fires : 4310
Home for Christmas : 5979
Home from the Dance : 5478
Home Movie : 481, 5803, 6807
Home Movies, Home Deaths : 4430
Home of the Brave : 3845
Home Pictures : 5370
Home Security : 5933
The Home Team : 2846
Home Thoughts from Abroad : 1735
Homecoming : 148, 1043, 3994, 5050, 6797
The Homecoming : 588
Homeless : 5519
Homeless on the Range : 2063
Homeric : 3083
The Homesick River : 913
Hometown, 1956 : 6442
Homework : 2303
Homing Instincts : 3416
Hommage a Kleist : 1181
Hommage to Adriano Spatola in the Shape of a Sonnet : 52
L'Homme des Sept Jours : 5498
Homo Sapiens : 1987
Honesty : 4345
Honey Bear : 6300
Honey Carcass : 2677
Honey I Shouldn't Have Called : 3780
Honey Man : 2171
Honey, Would You Kill for Me? : 734
Honeycutt Goes Iron : 3913
Honeymoon : 6678
Honeymoon Cottage : 423
The Hongch'on River : 1365, 5846, 6314
Honky-Tonk Blues : 4179

Honky Tonkin' : 3709
Honorary Spastics : 6800
Hood and Leathers : 612
The Hook : 4354, 6614
Hook and Bloodline : 1424
Hoopoe : 4439, 4780
Hop-A-Long Hunter : 943
Hop-Along Hunter : 943
Hope : 3342
Hopper Woman : 5473
Horace, IV, 1 : 1308
Hörendesjön, Augusti : 2526
Horizon : 4584
The Hornet's House : 443
Horoscope of a Dead Man : 3098
Horrible Valentine : 6446
Horror and Passion : 2778
Horse : 1550, 3457
The Horse : 2365
Horse Aflame : 1620, 5995
Horse-and-Buggy Heart : 129
Horse on a Fence : 1850
Horses : 1945, 5214
Horses Drinking : 1307
Horseshoe Canyon : 885
Hospital : 1044
The Hospital, After a Long Enough Time : 4825
Hospital Food : 4032
Hospital Poems : 2573
The Hospital Room : 5640
Hospital Sidewalk : 1890
Hospital Window : 6649
The Hospitality : 1286
Host : 3020
The Host : 679, 4933, 5304
Höst Skrev Jag : 3792
The Hostage : 6361
Hostages : 1625, 3921
Hot Days in Early Summer : 6566
Hot Wind, Hard Rain : 6177
The Hotel Arawak : 1548
Hotel Chipinique, August, 1984 : 7178
Hotel de Dream : 1264
Hotel Lautréamont : 236
Hotel Near Airfield : 6878, 6915
Hotel Pearl : 3700
Hothouse : 7112
Houdini : 1053
The Hours : 1666
Hours Before Sleep : 4166
The hours which a brain of sand counts : 3064, 5665
House : 2066, 2995, 6502
The House Above the River Was the First House : 3324
House by the Sea : 859
House by Water : 6834
House Fires : 96
The House Frog : 1751
The House Grants Favor : 853
House-Guests : 5100
House Hour : 5050
The House in the Road : 6362
House in the Sun : 158, 3750

House Inside This One : 2466
The House Made of Rain : 4728
The House Next Door : 1138
The House of Childhood : 2610, 5992
The House of I, the House of You : 2361
The House of Misfortune : 5675
House of Skin : 3780
House on Water : 1897
House Overlooking the Sea : 4439, 4780
House-Sitting : 545
House Snake : 2104, 6054, 6612
House Spider : 1549
The House Surrounded : 2197, 6273
The House without Us : 805
Household Gods : 1593
Houses : 3120, 3355, 4312
Houses in a Landscape, Saint George's Cove, Forillon, Quebec : 1355
Housesitting : 4911
Housewife : 388
Housework : 2043
Houw Hoek : 5557
How? : 2104, 4575, 6054, 6612
How Am I to Write My Poems? : 854, 4627
How Animals See : 6070
How Are You? : 6208
How can I tell you : 6134
How Can It Be That My Sexual Imagery : 1337
How Can She Rise, Earth-Born : 6596
How Can We Not? : 2685
How Can You Lie So Shamelessly? : 3456, 6671
How Creation Occurs on Old 61 : 769
How Dear the Payments : 4698
How Did I Get So Old? : 4179
How Did I Land Up in This City : 5446
How Did We Get Here, Said by So Many So Often : 5766
How Do You Know : 2989
How Do You Say : 6804
How Far Is the Water : 5213
How Horizons Work : 6770
How I Beg Your Pardon, Little Anna : 3270, 5900
How I Got That Name : 1101
How I Got to the Desert : 2875
How I Imagine You : 5037
How I Learned : 6598
How I See It : 7167
How I Spent My Vietnam : 2903
How I Was Advised by an Elderly Woman to Restrain My Sensual Heat : 3038
How I'm Doing. What It's Like : 406
How Is It : 6405
How It Began : 6101
How It Is Going to Be : 3685
How It Was : 6255
How It Was at the End : 1605
How Lives Move Forward in the Same Moments : 3505
How Long? : 1095, 4641
How Long Can Love Go Wrong? : 1145
How Loss Works : 6242
How many devout books are written : 1397,

2839, 6544
How many dreams : 1754, 5657
How Morning Comes, Out of Sleep : 6361
How Name Was Invaded : 1853
How Night Falls : 6086
How Passion Comes to Matter : 5302
How Pluperfect Our Past Lives : 1704
How rapidly, rapidly, rapidly : 2356, 4314
How She Got Thin : 2677
How Steve Lost His Thumb and the Boy Scouts
      Became Cannibals : 4827
How Such a Thing Could Happen : 6111
How the Athabascan Hunts Bear : 5239
How the Hell Can : 5844
How the Solar : 2036
How the Son Thanks the Father : 4913
How the Woman Becomes the Bear : 4504
How They Fought the War : 4138
How They Live : 6465
How Things Wind Up : 4356
How This Motor Works : 3286
How to Beat Dr. Feel Good : 507
How to Eat in the House of Death : 2
How to Everything : 445
How to Fall : 2285
How to Fall Asleep : 1526
How to Go to Kenya : 4404
How to Imagine Deafness : 5378
How to Learn to Break the Lines : 5245
How to Produce a Superbaby : 4082
How to Read a Page : 6993
How to Tell If You Have the Makings of a
      Topnotch New York Literary Agent : 6782
How to Turn Garbage into Edible Food : 6715
How to Write a Novel : 6939
How to Write a Poem : 7054
How to Write Poetry : 521
How 'Unlikely' : 6373
How We Dance : 5279
How We Imagine the Famous, As Our Mother :
      2940
How You Are Linked : 1605
However I Miss You : 1481
Hsan the Monk : 1020
Huancayo, February 1984 : 252
Huecos : 3789
Huehueteotl : 2769
The Huge High Engines Unheard : 306
Huída hacia Adelante : 4896
Human : 1177
Human Abstract : 898
Human Acts : 6070
The Human Head : 6070
Human Voice : 4349
Humanismo : 400
Humanities Seminar : 5924
Humble : 4530
Humboldt in Venezuela, 1799 : 5399
Hummingbird : 900, 3873, 3909
Hummingbird Light : 6700
Humors Off My Coast : 2766
Humpen : 2719, 6249
A Hundred Flowers : 2428
The Hundred Flowers : 1814

A Hundred Nails : 4693
Hunger : 1266, 2084, 4092, 6728, 7075
Hunger, Answer : 3596
Hunger/for a sky without a top : 5068
Hunger Moon : 6792
The Hunt : 1443, 3969, 7057
Hunt of Color : 665
Hunters : 1050
The Hunters : 4215
Hunter's Moon : 1525, 7163
Hunting : 3566
Hunting Ducks at Dawn : 690
Hunting in Escondido : 4179
Hunting Petroglyphs : 6811
Hunting Season : 2777
Hunting Stone : 3539
Hunting with My Brother : 2981
Hurricane : 1279, 6479
Hurt Park : 5611
The Husband : 5828
Husband and Wife : 1258
Husband, Flying by Night : 6299
Husbanding España : 2873
Husbandry : 433, 3783
Hush Yo Mouf : 1788
Hustlers : 1263
Hustling Pool : 3380
Hut : 5050
Hwen the eagle was killed : 2741, 4938
The Hyacinth Girl : 3913
Hybrid Song : 3038
Hymn to Life to Cliff : 6835
A Hymn to the 21st Century : 2768
Hymn X : 4484
Hypnagogic Adagio : 6911
Hypochondria : 4355
Hypoglycemia and the Need to Practice It :
      7175
Hyrcania : 214
I : 4870
I-80 Lieder : 6295
I Am : 758, 2190, 2629, 6213
I Am a Finn : 6356
I Am a Poet Because I Say So : 4278
I am afraid the face of judgment : 4559
I Am As Fair As I Would Be : 5976
I Am Chastised : 841
I am faithful to the heat : 158, 3750
I Am Going to Sleep : 2190, 2629, 6213
I Am Mama Bear : 1463
I Am Odjelabo, the Invincible : 4774, 4777
I Am Ready to Tell All I Know : 5124
I Am Seated in the First Years of My Life : 158,
      3750
I Am Sick : 1625, 2554
I Am Still a Finn : 6356
I Am Sure There Are Red Women : 14, 4783
I Am Sure This Is : 3647
I Am the One : 2233, 3197, 6806
I Am Useless : 2190, 2629, 6213
I become more intimate with the dead : 1582,
      5098
I Beg to Disagree : 193
I Believe in Fresh Starts : 813, 814, 6222

I Believe the Pulse : 3332
I Belong to the High Day : 1409, 1757, 3588, 6220
I bowl to avoid silence : 652
I Breathe : 1107, 3365
I Bring Twins Over to Meet : 5446
I Built Small Nests / under Your Heart : 813, 814, 3792
I Call Them the Giants : 1511, 5072
I Came Home : 3035, 3464
I came home late : 1235
I can remember : 1771
I Can Remember You : 5035
I Can See Why : 1847
I cannot see : 435, 4180
I Cannot Teach Hewr Closure : 4260
I cannot Write. The words no longer flow: 7062
I Can't Even Thread a Needle : 4221
I carry my thoughts in an ocular bucket : 2764
I carry on a debate between the living : 3032
I Come to You : 4380
I could ask him if it's the sun he wants : 883, 4875
I could be white : 3590
I Crave a Place in Literary History : 5030
I Dare to Be True to Myself : 933
I Didn't Kill 'em : 5844
I Didn't Know About You : 3082
I Do Belive Her : 2425
I Do Not Resemble : 3547, 3981, 5379
I do not want to do the intelligent thing : 3032
I Don't Have Any More Time : 3985, 4742
I don't think I'll ever make it home : 492
I Dream : 2197, 6273
I Dream I Return to Tucson in the Monsoons : 99
I Dream of Dying : 4279
I Dream Old Dylan Came Back : 3437
I Dreamed About You Last Night : 2455
I Dreamed I Was a Great Painter : 4940
I Dreamt One Night in Autumn : 1194
I en Trädgårdsservering : 5293
I enjoy writing poems : 4976, 5105
I gave them life : 240
I Get Sick : 2753
I Go : 5428
I go straight off to my friends : 3224, 3473, 6830
I got big poems : 2153
I Got Caught : 3293
I Gräset : 6222
I Guess I'm Too Dumb to Give Up : 702
I Had a Son and His Name Is John : 4824
I Had the Courage : 195, 3896
I had wondered what color were the trees at night : 2811
I Have Forgotten the Word I Wanted to Say : 1244
I Have Had to Kill You : 3132, 3318
I Have Met Persons Who : 463, 2353
I Have No Home : 2184, 4362
I have not broken the promise : 3173
I have played in the optics of human perspectives : 748, 1275

I have saw something : 810
I have slept where there is no longer room : 4462, 6553
I have stopped naming the landscapes of my poems : 3224, 3473, 6830
I Have Trouble with the Endings : 1291
I Hear You Breathing : 1561
I Heard a Fly Buzz : 3454
I Hold the Parasol : 6621
I Join the Sparrows : 5559
I Judge the National Scholastic Poetry Contest : 4857
I Killed Him : 3718, 5104
I Knew a Fellow : 6540
I knew a man once : 2695
I Know : 854, 4627
I know a little about the universe : 5682
I know of a stone where I can sit : 158, 3750
I lift to make it remember, shake: 4973
I Listen : 3032
I Listen to the Market : 3666
I Look Like Ogden Nash : 2436
I looked in her mirror : 1774
I Looked Young a Long Time, Didn't I : 3780
I Lose Everything : 4376
I Lost It at an Italian Restaurant : 6851
I Love a Broad Margin to My Life : 1123
I Love Butches : 936
I Love Men : 6719
'IM: mortality play: The Bard Project, The Martyrology: Book (10)10 : 4664
I Might Get Traded : 841
I Missed You So Little Today : 5328
I Need a Hearing Aid : 1479
I Never Believed : 206, 813, 814
I Never Had a Mother : 6075
I Never Rode Your Cruel Horses : 5016
I Never Went to Bed with Famous Astronaut : 5969
I No Longer Walk : 491, 3476, 4811
I Owe You One : 5134
I Paint Twelve Hours a Day : 1858
I Planted a Hand : 1306, 4023
I pressed on with the hot teeth : 2135, 3751, 6383
I Put Down an Anthology of Spanish Poetry and Write : 4928
I Put My Skis : 813, 814, 6222
I Read Poetry Like : 4911
I Really Want to Make Love : 813, 814, 3792
I Recover a Syntax : 1473, 6628
I Remember Peter : 941
I Remember Your Smile : 4439, 4780
I Sat for Hours by the Garbage : 4638
I Saw a Possum in the Road : 2062
I saw them in ruins, those houses : 158, 3750
I see high old trees : 184
I See You, Standing at a Sticky Table : 754
I Send My Birds Out : 2213
I Sent Roses to My Mother : 94
I should like to hope that there : 2379, 6830
I Shouldn't Have Called : 3780
I Sicari : 1473
I sit, in treatment, at the movies, devoted : 2288,

3967

I Snapped the End of My Screaming Hunger :
3038

I spent the night with a man who loves me :
1906

I Stand Before You Naked : 4738

I Stand Up : 1939, 5914

I Step Over : 6671

I stroke the mountain dove : 2135, 3751, 6383

I Stroke You with All My Years : 436, 3144,
5941

I Swallowed You : 2779

I Swear : 1269, 6742

I Think I'm Learning : 5030

I Think Rex : 5000

I Thought I Was a Mailbox : 2165

I told hillary not to step on the ants : 4054

I Too Am Alone Again : 813, 814, 2526

I touch a woman who is not mine : 2880

I Upset Everything : 1984, 6188

I Used to Be OK : 4638

I Wake Alone : 2737, 5647

I Want : 857, 3270, 6992

I Want Only : 491, 3476, 4811

I Want Silence : 2755

I want to go home : 1767

I Want to Marry You : 6092

I Want to See : 5292, 5874

I Wanted : 1419, 6849

I wanted to be like Al : 5542

I Was 17 : 3780

I Was Five and She Was Eleven : 2431

I Was Inadequate : 4638

I Was Small and You Were Dying : 1539

I Was Something : 5896

I Was There : 3488

I watch from afar : 3430

I Watch the People : 206, 813, 814

I Water Flowers : 3254

I Wave Good-bye When Butter Flies : 5126

I went away — alone : 1866, 4841

I Will Not Be Claimed : 445

I Will Tell You About : 14, 4783

I wish you would cum back with your black
hose. Bach seems to have been a rather
happy man. It took a lot of courage of
Xenophanes : 2741

I Woke Up to Reality : 6743, 7155

I Wonder Who : 1176

I Would Like : 3166, 3238, 4033

I Would Like to Have a Movie Cowboy for a
Husband : 1685

I - You : 2798, 4455

Iberia : 4086

Icarus Thought : 445

Ice : 1452, 2395

Ice Buttons, Wright's Creek : 7096

Ice Fishing at Night : 434

The Ice House : 6536

Ice Lake : 4345

Ice Music : 1987

Ice Patches on Parquet : 326

Ice Pine : 5980

Icebergs : 6164

Ich - Du : 2798

The Ichor of Chthonios : 1146

Icon : 3596

Iconoclasm : 4123

Icy : 1402, 3126

I'd Like a Little Love in the Wine-Red After-
noon : 1244

I'd Like to Talk to You Now : 491, 3476, 4811

I'd Rather Stay at Home : 1363, 5379

The Idea of Rexroth, the Idea of Looking Up :
2365

Ideal : 510

An Ideal of Itself : 5760

Ideas : 4422

Identidades : 5882

Identification : 2149

Identities : 6101

Identity : 3547, 5379, 6486

Identity of Images : 1536, 3533

The Ides of August : 3640

Idiot, Whalewatching from the Deck of the
Galilean : 5730

The Idols : 6878, 6915

'Idz Spac' Means 'Go to Bed' : 2327

If a Poet : 4859

If any ever deserved such underarm goatodor :
1032, 4073

If Crow Didn't Exist : 6736

If I Could Only Haul in His Heart : 4619, 5783

If I could watch the calliopied prance of the
orange-maned poinies : 1716

If I Don't Love You : 1526, 2155

If I Find You : 6726

If I Knew the Names of Everything : 387

If I Lay Close : 5612

If I must dial a number to call you : 2288, 3967

If I should learn, in some quite casual way :
4353

If I start to write romance : 3401

If I Talk About Death : 1319, 4025, 4070

If I Were a Bell : 1389

If I were grass : 244, 3011, 6353

If It's All Going to Begin Again : 2402, 5712

If it's not bugs, it's the weather : 492

If James Whitmore : 6728

If, Like the Winds Drawn on the Compass Face
: 1536, 2023

If Memory Comes to the Tongue : 2170

If My Heart : 6457

If Only : 208, 5229, 6830

If Pleasure Were Happiness : 1626

If She Could Talk, You Couldn't Explain : 1532

If the Universe Could Sing : 6262

If This Be Not I : 5234

If We Can't Be Instructed by Grief : 1835

If We Could Go There and Truly Be There :
3230

If we could home : 1623

If you and I were to turn the world inside out . .
. : 2721

If You Are a Poet : 1526, 1799

If You Are Not There Anymore : 14, 7079

If You Are Suicidal, Marry a Writer : 1178

If You Botch It : 3912

If You Come : 1084, 7092
If You Don't Know It's October : 4937
If You Go to the Rodeo : 3061
If You Knew What Sununu : 6514
If You Meet a White Horse at Sunrise : 1597
If you melt some lead : 2288, 3967
If you really want to see yourself : 2759
If You Think It's Hot Now : 1269
If You Were You I'd Write About : 2321
If You Wish : 3034, 6586
If Your Hair : 474
If You're Hungry, That's a Good Sign : 6733
Ignorance : 3073, 3971
L'Ignorant : 3073
Ikinokoru : 1726
Il Cristo Velato : 1920
Il Faut Faire la Fête : 1034
Il Racconto : 2216
Il Tuo Rilievo : 1031
Il y a Certainement Quelqu'un : 2748
The *Iliad* : 1963
I'll Always Love You, Kind-of : 3469
I'll Be Home for Christmas : 588
I'll Fly Away : 4629
I'll listen to the news the day I die : 6113
An Illegal Photograph in *American Poetry
    Review* : 666
Illinois Quakers : 2670
Illness : 7067, 7087
The Illusion of Necessity : 2982
Illusionist : 5241
Illustration : 1213
I'm in Uniform : 1203, 5680
I'm Just : 2815
'IM: mortality play: The Bard Project, The
    Martyrology: Book (10)10 : 4664
I'm not a Pushkin : 5054
I'm Not in Charge of This Ritual : 3329
I'm on a Mission from Buddha : 4680
I'm Scared of Shampoo : 1078
I'm Shrinking : 942
I'm Still Alive! : 1381
I'm thinking of you : 648, 779
Image : 6375, 7057
An Image from Howard Coughlin : 1239
Imagen del Reverso : 4878
Images : 7060
Images of a Summer Evening : 3126, 5673
Images Through a Cracked Mirror : 243
Imagine : 3032
Imagine a Clown : 3104
Imagining the Soul : 1916
Imbabura : 5899
Imitations of Mortality : 824
The Immaculate Story of Mnasidika, My Friend
    : 4493, 5448
Immaginazione : 5650
Immer näher dem Milchstrassenrand : 3658
Immer Wieder : 5351
Immigrant : 6154
The Immigrant : 369, 748
L'Immigrant/e : 369
An Immigrant's Laments : 3464
Imminent Departures : 4376

Immobilism : 2406
Immobilizing the Boundless : 4579, 5361
The Immortal : 4644
Immortelles : 4312
Imp : 2656
Impasse : 496, 4676, 5513
Imperative : 4344
Imperial Gown : 2384
Implants, by Cookie Schwarz : 3845
The Importance of Kneading : 6690
The Impossible : 6815
Impotence : 2152, 2700
Imprecation Against Adultery : 7075
An Impression : 2499, 2522, 3942
Impressions of Spain ('89) : 5560
Impressions of the Fatal Voyage of Donald
    Crowhurst : 3348
Imprint #2 : 6801
Imprint #3 : 6801
Imprint #4 : 6801
Improbable Proverbs : 2310
The Impropriety of Trees : 2245
Improvisation No. 4: Reservoir & Rapture :
    5489
An Improvisation on 'The Glare of the Sun
    Wounding the Late Star' : 3273
In 1990 I'm hearing about the different charac-
    teristics of rhythms in different periods of
    Chinese Poetry : 6326
In a Beijing Studio : 255
In a Cafe near Tuba City, Arizona, Beating My
    Head Against a Cigarette Machine : 1879
In a Cambridge Garden : 6464
In a Dark Age : 2909
In a Dressingroom : 4001
In a Dry Season : 3850
In a Funk, the Poet Images *His* Obit : 5049
In a Garden of Wide-Verged Shade : 7104
In a green hollow a horse was grazing : 1113,
    3658
In a Hurry : 1017
In a Letter Unsent : 1080
In a Place Where the Wood Is Rough : 2110
In a Pleading Tone of Voice : 1818, 3464
In a Previous Manner of Dunkan MkNaughton :
    2109
In a Primary School : 5823
In a Russian Garden : 1106
In a Safe-deposit Box : 3318, 3988
In a Sterile and Elegant Room : 6250
In a Time Out of Joint : 1688
In a Time That Is Now Past : 3692
In Alligator Country : 2060
In Amsterdam : 2334
In an Empty House : 5273
In an Unfamiliar Apartment : 813, 814, 5064
In Andean Passes : 3249
In Answer to Amy's Question What's a
    Pickerel : 5067
In Answer to Their Questions : 962
In Aphrodisias : 6154
In April : 650, 1712, 4488, 5992
In Awe of My Mother's Insanity : 1827
In Baton Rouge : 5835

In Bed, Having Just Fallen Asleep : 2104
In Berkeley : 5050
In Black and White : 1218
In Black Gloves : 1429
In careful photos : 5073
In Carlyle, Illinois : 1577
In Carroll County, New Hampshire : 3462
In Chantland Hills : 6078
In Concert : 2313
In Consideration of Your Heart : 2370
In Country : 3844
In Days : 4049
In Defense of Allen Ginsberg : 2834
In Defense of Middle Management and Subur-
    ban Marriage : 5522
In Doubt : 6728
In Dream : 1259
In Dreams : 3866
In Dreams I Am Always Smoking : 2348
In Dreams My Mother : 3408
In dwindling light : 4724
In Ellipsis : 486
In every color and circumstance, may the eyes
    be open for what comes : 2253, 2870
In Exile : 616
In Florida : 5798
In Freefall Over Florida : 1904
In Front of the House All Night Long (A Remi-
    niscence) : 3243, 5379
In Granada : 625
In grüner Mulde graste ein Pferd : 3658
In Harrisonville Missouri : 478
In Her Heaven of Sorts : 769
In Her Image : 8
In Her *Selected Poems* : 872
In Heraclitus' City : 2756
In His Requiem Mozart Said : 1625, 2554
In History : 1473, 6628
In-House Sonnet : 1577
In July, Such Undercurrents : 6239
In June : 5946
In Karlsruhe : 4146
In L.A. You Don't Walk : 184
In Lands Where Light Has Another Color :
    2751, 3089
In Lapland, Kansas : 2548
In Leningrad : 1113
In Lieu Of : 835, 6977
In Love : 254
In Love with the Distance : 4820
In May : 3254, 7129
In May I Found Some Birds : 4638
In Memoriam : 3829
In Memoriam Adriani Spatulae : 5872, 6584
In Memoriam: Edythe Cecil (Died 1989), Grand
    Editor, Grand Lady : 6531
In Memoriam: William C. Velásquez : 2974
In Memory : 5083, 5261
In Memory of My Father: Australia : 768
In Memory of Robert Hayden : 6741
In Memory of W. H. Auden : 3949
In Minnesota : 5666
In Missouri : 478
In Mourning : 4823

In Mourning (1983) : 666, 3117
In My 49th Summer : 1798
In my barbaric language : 3568, 5105
In My Best Recurrent Dream : 1258
In My Father's Buick : 6520
In My Father's House : 5070, 6751
In my mind : 1869
In My Mother's Garden : 3336
In My Office, I Think I See : 4784
In Outaouais : 1757, 4403
In Parentheses : 3781
In Paris : 7047
In Passing : 2018
In P'ing-Hsi : 2878
In Pittsfield : 5894
In Pondicherry : 5237
In Praise of Age : 3098
In Praise of Skimmerhorn : 2482
In Praise of the Puffball : 6936
In Praise of the Urban : 874
In Profundis : 22, 6006
In Purple Fire Spoke the Wrath of Heaven :
    2233, 3197, 6806
In Pursuit of Chiang Kaishek : 3706
In Questa Reggia. May 1989 : 6189
In Response to a Manifesto Circulated by the
    Union of Concerned Scientists : 3077
In Retrospective Prospect : 863
In Rome : 4659
In San Francisco Segalen : 264, 5873
In Search of a Foremother : 861
In Search of a Poem : 4516
In Search of Mom's Cafe : 943
In Search of the Brother-in-Law : 5919
In Siberia : 478
In Silence : 229, 1640, 4439
In Silent Reliefs : 4197, 6278
In Situ : 4368
In Sky Lakes Wilderness : 1427
In South Africa : 2596, 3124
In Space and Time : 4976, 5105
In Spite of Forgetting : 6046
In Stinsford Churchyard, Dorset : 2058
In Summer : 546, 6058
In Switzerland: Father and Daughter : 5559
In Thanks for Feeling Happier : 1427
In that House : 5743
In the Absence of Love, There Are Engines :
    5959
In the Absence of War : 5960
In the Alhambra : 3719
In the Alley : 3675
In the Amish Bakery : 6728
In the Asian Section of the Cleveland Art
    Museum : 2411
In the Attic : 2069, 6665
In the Autumn of the House : 2747, 3072, 3113
In the Autumn Valleys of the Mahanadi : 3970
In the Backwoods Who Visits Dooryards? :
    4448
In the Backyard : 1597
In the Bar at the Cockatoo Inn : 1706, 4272
In the Basement : 5666
In the Beginning : 2540, 3132, 3318, 3682,

4589, 4874, 5995
In the Big Yard : 3764
In the Blue, in the Sky : 6907
In the Bog Behind My House : 5559
In the Botanical Park : 312
In the Cab of the Pick-Up Truck : 4404
In the Café : 5088, 5992
In the Cameron Highlands : 4254
In the Cards : 6728
In the Careful Night : 252
In the Chicago Museum : 1149, 6651
In the Chronicles of Paradise : 2120
In the City : 5685
In the Company of Hawks : 542
In the Confessional : 6246
In the Country : 5445
In the Crazy Mountains : 867
In the Cup : 4771
In the Deep End : 5172
In the Dream of My Father Running : 2436
In the Driver's Seat : 3892
In the Exercise Yard : 666, 3117
In the Face of Seasons : 4993
In the Fall : 4921
In the Field : 1090
In the flash bulb after shock of lightning : 5291
In the Flesh : 5865
In the Flowers of Your Leaving : 1109
In the Foggy Mirror, Beneath Ockham's Razor :
    800
In the Garden : 1945
In the Garden After the Rain : 1457
In the Garden of Earthly Delights : 6255
In the Garden of the Ming Scholar : 6094
In the Grass : 813, 814, 6222
In the Grove : 3327
In the Hay : 6258
In the Heart of the Philippines : 5244
In the Hibiscus Garden : 4179
In the House of the Deafman : 234
In the House of the Shaman : 4838
In the Icebox : 1614
In the Islands : 1431
In the Jewish Cemetery in Queens : 5733
In the Kimono Garden : 3479
In the Kingdom of Pleasure : 5803
In the Land of Sons-a-Bitches : 3750, 5780
In the Land of the Body : 579
In the Landscapes of My Heart : 5044
In the Library : 5894
In the Long Run : 6510
In the Middle : 55
In the Middle of March : 4376
In the Middle of Things, Begin : 2340
In the Mind of God : 184, 4239
In the Mode of Confession : 4888
In the morning, smoke from the garbage of
    Soller caught in the blinds : 1148
In the Museum : 2908
In the Museum of Man : 165
In the New World : 6387
In the Night Subway : 4217, 6311
In the Ninth Month : 1232
In the Outskirts : 4538

In the Park : 5681, 6098
In the Photograph of a Restored Barn : 4618
In the Physic Garden : 4095
In the Playground : 2540
In the Process of Coming to Be : 5474
In the Rain : 3970
In the Rain Today : 2045
In the Roman Forum : 491, 6615
In the Sack of the Wind : 2052, 6287
In the Sad World : 6606
In the Secret House of Night : 1350, 6375
In the Shade of Portola Palace : 4290
In the Shadow of the Holy Heights : 893
In the Shadow of Your Eyes : 5891
In the Shoe and Garment District : 1652
In the Silence of a Stormy Night : 6107
In the silver-struck silence : 3940
In the Similkameen : 5329
In the South : 1969, 4475
In the springtime you can walk *through* people :
    5436, 5585
In the Storm : 1040
In the Summer Night I and You : 3921, 6388,
    6527
In the Sweat Lodge the Women Are Singing :
    815
In the *Symposium* written by Plato : 4079
In the Towel's Folds : 6923
In the Train: Portrait of a Navvy : 5319
In the Twilight Lounge : 811
In the Village : 2052, 6287
In the Watchtower : 4401
In the Water That Comes Before Dawn : 1415
In the Waters of Conchan : 1127, 5899
In the Way : 3885
In the Weave Room : 1105
In the White Field : 3126, 6312
In the Woods : 4187
In the Year Eight Hundred : 2870
In the Year of Her Daughter's Death My
    Mother : 3373
In the Yucatan : 6726
In Their City, the Desert : 1371
In This Diminishing Hour : 5332
In This Flickering : 2332
In this globe of numbers : 2559
In This Night, In This World : 5058, 5995
In This Photo, Taken : 4784
In This Season of Waiting : 4921
In Tiananmen Square : 2963
In Time, for Margaret Mee : 1316
In Touch : 6813
In Tribute to a Contemporary Poet, Friends :
    4580
In University Gardens : 2756
In Vikki's Photograph : 2204
In Vino Veritas : 1727
In Vitro : 1375
In/vocation : 3036
In Western Kansas: Boswell's First Wife : 2484
In Which I Forgive My Mother Her Intentions :
    2728
In Your Absence : 6021
In Your Garden : 4753

Inauguration : 5069
Incandescence : 5190
Incantations : 6381
Incest : 4102
An Incident : 3120, 5250, 7138
The Incident : 1473, 6628
Incident at a Poetry Reading : 6883
Incident on Canal : 5962
Incident on the Gondar Road : 6322
Incident on the Night Watch in the Pacific High
    : 2795
Incident with a Car : 3559
L'Incidente : 1473
Incisions : 813, 814, 5525
Incomplete : 3260
Incorrigible in April : 7049
Incriminations : 3725
An Incumbent's Interpretation of the 1990
    Congensional Elections : 6514
Incurable : 2984, 5667
Indentations in the Sugar : 5353
Independence Day : 921, 5190
Independent Sorts : 5919
Index to Dawn : 5234
Indian Agent : 1058
Indian Dawn : 4382
An Indian Girl from Iowa : 2426
Indian Giver : 5254
Indian Movie, New Jersey : 1597
Indian Sandstone : 92
Indian Sonnets : 1719
Indian Summer : 3780, 4171
Indian Summer in the Ghetto of Reckless
    Abandon : 4565
Indian Woman : 225
Indian Words on the Radio : 5379, 6321
Indiana : 300
Indianapolis : 6562
Indians : 4355
The Indians : 217, 5995
Indifference : 398
Indigence : 4373
Los Indios : 217
The Indoors Is Infinite : 842, 6500, 6986
Indulgences : 5276
Industry Leader : 1420
Inevitable : 4444
Infancia : 3143
Infancy : 376, 4979
Infantry Assault : 142
Infatuation : 3612
Infernal Regions and the Invisible Girl : 1287
Inferno : 6822
Infidel : 1521
The Infinite : 5894
'Infinite sorrow' I heard someone say that today
    : 5894
Inflation : 1189, 1850
The Influenzas : 5353
Inheritance : 490, 1856, 2757, 5349, 5828,
    6311, 7144
The Inheritance : 1907, 3602.
Inheriting My Sister : 5317
Inheriting the Farm : 921

Inhibitions : 2951
Inhospitality : 2498, 3445, 5874
The Inishdhugan Clay : 2170
Initial Conditions : 445
Initial Shock : 3236
Initiation : 1539
Initiation, 1965 : 2199
Injunction : 4637
The Injuries : 5865
Ink Pattern : 6518
Inkstains : 2816, 3671, 5379
An Inland Indian Sea : 597, 3611
Inland Sailing: New Love's Channels : 3924
La Inmaculada Historia de Mnasidika, Mi
    Amiga : 4493
The Inmate of This Forest : 2119
The Innocent : 5300
Innocent Action : 2975
Innocuous : 5384
Inomhuset Ar Oandligt : 6500
Inquiries into the Technology of Hell and
    Certain Rumors Recently Circulating :
    2519
Inquiry into the Nurturing and Elimination of
    Life Forms within Marginally Controlled
    Ecosystems on the Fifteenth Anniversary
    of My Wedding : 2519
Inquiry on Resistance, or Snow on Martin
    Luther King, Jr., Day : 2519
Insanity : 1580
Inscribing : 1562
Inscription : 6830
Inscription for a Sundial : 1437
Inscription for an Outcropping of Rock : 4173
Inscription for the Door : 5519
Inscription on a Tomb : 6878, 6915
Inseminating the Cows : 2071
Inside : 758, 3361, 3365
Inside a Painting : 1985
Inside a World the World Fits Into : 173
Inside Father's Pockets : 5317
Inside Out : 4193, 5678
Inside the Heart : 4144
Insight : 6456, 6680
Insight into Expertise : 3806
Insomnia : 3816, 4144, 6506
Insomniacs : 5899
Inspectors : 3583
Inspiration : 2870
The Instant : 813, 814, 5708
Instinct : 81, 5921, 6019
Instructions : 4171
Instructions for a Somnambulist : 2258
Instructions for Fishing the Eel : 5689
Instructions for the Magic Frog : 4673
Instructions for the Onset of Winter : 2942
Instructions, Moving In : 5797
Instructions to Friends Who Have Lost Touch :
    448
An Instructor, Reading Yeats and Sinking Fast :
    3539
Insurance Policy : 299
Insurrection : 6444
Intact : 3993

Integers : 3018
Integrations : 675
An Intellectually Acceptable Distance : 6617
Intellectuals : 3341, 3476, 4812
Intelligence : 5946
Intending Words : 4855
Intercoastal : 4160
Interesting Times : 6800
An Interesting Week : 6939
Interim : 5875
The Interior : 3900
Interjection XIII: An Epitaph for Someone :
     6272
Interlake Childhood I : 3408
Interlake Childhood II : 3408
Interlude, Afghanistan : 5358
International Mr. Leather Weekend : 5755
The Interpretation of Waking Life : 4630
Interstate : 2361, 3966
Interstellar : 6298
Interview : 5485
The Interview : 2608
Interview / Vietnam / 1987, Napalm Woman /
     Looking at a Photo of Herself / 1967 :
     5854
Interview with an Alchemist in the New Age :
     802
Interview with Mr. Moto, 1939 : 3913
Intimacy : 2686
Intimates and Strangers : 1397, 2839, 6544
Into His Clothes : 5813
Into Its Cold : 1031, 1939
Into the Gathering Dark : 1238
Into the Glow of an Atom : 5472
Into the Open : 5141
Into the Stadium : 2887
Into Your Eye : 5651, 6357
Intone : 328
Introduction to the Phenomena, Circa 1959 :
     2199
Introit & Fugue : 4726
Intruder : 2719, 6249
Inukshuk : 4515
Invader : 4448
The Invader : 1763, 5455
Invalid Garden : 6268
Invasions : 1605
Invencion de la Luz : 3714
Inventing the Universe : 712
Invention of Light : 3714, 5899
Inventory : 6739, 7168
Inverkirkaig : 6177
Inversnaid : 2934
Investigation and Lament : 1606
Invisible : 2231
Invisible Friend : 4893
Invisible Men : 7066
The Invisible Red : 7102
The Invisible Stone : 1625, 4419
Invitation : 6585
An Invitation : 5114
The Invitations : 609, 1124
Invocation : 2074, 3034, 6586
Invocation to the Great Bear : 284, 5271

Invoking the Goddess : 1440
Inwood Sketches: III : 3996
Iowa Cow : 666
Ipiutak Burial Site, Point Hope, Alaska : 2223
Iridesce : 3747, 6647
Iris : 6857
The Iris Work in the Year's Rhythm : 1346
Irish Monk, Near the Year 1000 : 1002
Iron : 2582
Iron Events : 2616
Iron, or Ion : 2441
Iron Rails : 2016
Irondale : 6154
Ironing after Midnight : 1267
Irons at Her Feet : 1978
Ironwood : 2788
Irpen : 5181, 6456, 7097
Irrelevant : 4536, 5228, 7057
Irrésolu le matin : 1691
Is a Small Red Bird Like a Heart : 1414
Is for the use of th peopul : 548
Is It Modest? : 5547
Is the Title a Headstone or the Manifest on a
     Bus? : 553
Is There a Hiss of Love As Snakes Get To-
     gether? : 1337
Is this my voice, my voice — or is it : 2379,
     6830
Is This Snow : 940
Isaac Newtons Andra Uppvaknande : 5293
Isaac Newton's Second Awakening : 813, 814,
     5293
Isaac's Lament : 6466
Isadora : 6154
Isheja : 184, 4774
Ishmael in the White Again : 918
Island : 2415
The Island Dweller : 3547, 3981, 5379
Islands : 3550, 6909
The Isle of Lepers : 1976
Isleta Paintings : 4317
Issue : 6492
It : 662, 3267
It a Come : 5977
It All Started Very Early : 1706
It Arrives in Every Storm : 1350, 4821
It Began : 3780
It Could Have Been More : 173
It does not become fond of only one : 924,
     6632
It Gets That I Hate Words for Their Echoes,
     Dumb Repetitions in My Head : 2109
It Happened Again : 362
It Has Happened on Its Own : 4682
It has nothing to do with braille : 4973
It Has to Be This Way : 4398
It Hides Inside You : 4219
It Is Enough : 1407
It Is Near Toussaints : 2523
It Is November : 6130
It Is Said : 1526, 4046
It Is Spring Again : 99, 1883
It Is the Bird in the Tree : 715, 6359
It Is the Small Breaths : 4788

It Is True : 6174
It is wonderful to die amidst the pleasures I
    have known : 3032
It May Have Begun This Way : 491, 3476, 4811
It Seems That Everything : 14
It Takes a Long Time : 813, 814, 3792
It Turns Out You Can Make the Earth Abso-
    lutely Clean : 4820
It was almost dark by the time we got back to
    Manderley : 5580
It Was Cold : 4351
It Was Difficult to Give a Suitable Title : 3770,
    5382
It Was Fever That Made the World : 5112
It was important at the time : 5580
It was in the plains : 49, 2938
It was taken from us : 932
It Was the 20th Century : 4939, 5098
It Would Be Good to Translate Mallarmé :
    3464, 5007
It Would Have Taken So Little : 338
It wouldn't be fair to us for her to lie : 4247
Italian Bread : 5442
Italian Painter : 2231, 5178
Italian Sequence Comma with Italian Words
    Stop, One Stop (Architextures 8 Dash 14)
    : 6355
Italian Sequence Comma with Italian Words
    Stop Two Stop (Architextures 15 Dash 21)
    : 6355
Itasca : 3438
Itch : 1411
It's a Battle Li Po : 4624
It's All Over Now But the Drinking : 923
Its branches — the cold pruned, sap : 4973
It's Here That God : 1031, 1939
It's Like an Echo : 2402, 5712
It's March. We're Out on the Porch with
    Cabernet Sauvignon : 1004
It's May and the Apple Trees Bloom : 813, 814,
    6222
It's Not How You Look, But How They Look
    At You : 1613
It's Not the Needle, Leaving : 4973
'It's Only Rock and Roll But I Like It': The
    Fall of Saigon, 1975 : 7010
It's Raining : 649
It's simple. The hole : 4973
It's the old spring again, flowers as always :
    5953
It's These Bodies : 171
It's time to think : 2379, 6830
Ivan of a Urals Village : 1547
I've Decided to Tell You Anyway : 811
I've Got a Warm Middle Spot : 6288
I've Got to Write : 1304
I've Never Known a Dwarf Before : 5446
I've Tried So Many Times : 190
Ivory Bracelets : 1155
Ivy : 423, 5287
The Ivy : 4676, 5513
Ivy bears yellow blossoms : 1201
Ivy Weatherwax : 5827
Ixquic's Song for Guatemala : 6679

J. L. Mahoney Finally Cuts Loose on a Califor-
    nia Yuppie Feminist : 3171
J. L. Mahoney Makes Love in Autumn : 3171
Jack be Quick : 5213
Jack-o'-Lantern : 7082
Jack Remembered : 4478
Jack, Setting Places : 4513
Jack Talks about Politics in Lee County : 2987
Jackals : 653, 1825
The Jackdaw : 2990
Jackie O : 6440
Jackpot : 6295
The Jacob's Ladder : 5672
Jade : 6748
Jag Betraktar Människorna : 206
Jag Drömmer Ibland : 6222
Jag Ställer Skidorna : 6222
Jag Tror På Uppbrott : 6222
J'Ai Eu le Courage : 195
J'ai joué dans l'optique des perspectives
    humaines : 1275
Jake's Garden : 686
Jaleh Talking : 3026
Jaliscan Sestina : 6640
Jalousies : 756
Jamaica : 319, 5883
Jamaican Rum : 5574
James A. Garfield and All the Shot People : 492
James Baldwin : 3091
James Brown : 4450, 5483
James Dickey : 790
James Koyle Became Paralyzed : 2286
James River in March : 2646
James Wharton Is an Honest Man : 1952
Jane Addams : 777
Janine in Autumn : 3925
January : 4604
January 15 : 4850
January 21 : 2524
January: A Woman Chases Her Horse : 30
January and the Fan : 7091
January, at Mid-Life : 3892
January Half-Light : 4731
January: Monte Aventino : 4765
January Thaw : 419, 5256
January: Wolf Moon : 6183
Japanese : 5699
Jaques Lured by Audrey : 6198
A Jar : 2828
Jarman Said, 'Our Whole Universe Is Gener-
    ated by a Rhythm' : 337
Jason : 1898
Jaula de Espejos o la Conciencia del Hombre :
    273
The Jaunt : 1287
The Javelin : 1735
Jay Singh, Incarnate : 7091
Je Dérange Tout : 1984
Je Rêve : 6273
Je Sais Parce Que Je Le Dis : 3830, 5389
Je t'appelle du fond de l'hiver : 1297
Jell-O on Springs : 6994
Jellyfish : 6039
Jennifer : 6131

Jenny Sleeping with Angels : 3695
Jerdon's Courser : 5015
Jeremy : 410
Jerry Lee Lewis' Secret Marriage to Thirteen-
    Year-Old First Cousin Revealed During
    British Isles Tour, 1959. His Manager
    Speaks : 7010
A Jersey Middle Age : 6782
Jerusalem : 5806
Jesus : 2852, 5866
Jesus of Navarone : 6772
Jetsam : 4476
The Jeweler : 1633
Jewelweed : 6292
The Jewish Cemetery at Berlin-Weissensee :
    2478, 3540
Jewish Jetset : 152, 4040
Jimmy Keenan : 1078
Jimmy Told Me : 1837
Jimson weed footpath : 4563
Jiskedei : 5553
Jiu Ge : 5154, 6745
Joanie: Moncton, 1946 : 1388
The Job : 2730
Job: The Voice Out of the Whirlwind : 3135
Joe Liar : 133
Joel's Love : 4169
Joe's Story : 5635
Joey Nee : 1415
John : 5866
John and I, We Tamed the Wildcat : 6608
John Berryman Listening to Robert Johnson's
    King of the Delta Blues, January, 1972 :
    7010
John De Crow : 3165
John Delorean : 3171
John Frederick Zimmerman : 3612
John Is Dying : 3992
John Keats, King of Bohemia : 224
John Moody, 1888 : 2
John Quixote : 4438
John the Fisherman : 1997
John Xantus: The Tidal Station at Cabo San
    Lucas : 1058
Johnny : 6878
Johnny Angel : 6763
Johnny Inkslinger Contemplates the Suicide of
    Marilyn Monroe : 5026
Johnny's Cafe : 6756
Johnson Brothers Ltd : 761, 3471
Joining In : 2948
The Joke Code : 4001
Jokes and Their Relation to Art History : 2361
Jonah : 2198
Jönnek Hozzám : 3243
The Joplin Nightingale : 2340
Jorge Louis Borges: 'The Secret Miracle' :
    1625, 2521
Jorge the Church Janitor Finally Quits : 1830
Jose Is Twelve and Nicaraguan : 5903
Joseph : 16, 3329
Joseph of Nazareth : 6124
The Joshua Tree : 1258
Journal Entry 1989 : 6668

Journal Entry, March 1990 : 4227
Journey : 546, 1006
A Journey : 5002
The Journey of a Tree : 1033, 3621, 5554
Journey of the Fat Man and His Barren Wife :
    1142
Journey of the Magi : 3188, 3555
Journey to Calabria : 1128
Journey to New York : 966, 3491, 6550
Journeying from Canyon de Chelly : 778
The Journeying Moon : 4334
Journeyman : 6069
Joy : 3296, 5976
Joyance : 3923
Joyce : 465, 5808
Joyful Sacrifice : 1018, 1390, 2972
Joy's Birthday Party : 5225
Juana: An Old Story : 1183
Juarez : 1614
Juarez, 1978 : 1604
Juba : 110
Judas : 2157
Judas Gets His Way : 4151
Judas-Kiss : 3381
Judge : 2739
The Judge : 4111
The Judgment : 4558
Judith, the Barren Widow, after Triumph : 6056
The Juice : 2365
The Jukebox War of '67 : 224
Jules Dubrin, Continuous Cat : 1974
Julio Es un Mes Oscuro : 1841
Julius II : 1676
July : 2607, 6180
July 4, 1989 : 4747
July 4, 1989: The Tyranny of Flags : 2807
Jumping Rope : 3425
June : 348, 990
June 21 at 9:30 : 5036
June 22 : 1736
June Night, 1953 : 174
June Tony : 3211
Junk Calls : 1042
Junk Jewelry : 6700
Junk Male : 1243
Junk Shop : 211, 1590, 3410
The Junked Cars : 650
The Junkyard Mechanic Finds His voice : 4827
Jury Duty : 595
Just a Junkyard Dog : 1504
Just a Moment — I Am Busy Being a Man :
    445
Just Another Disaster Poem : 5026
Just Before Sailing : 2943, 3701
Just Cosmetology : 5000
Just Dreaming : 3694
Just Good Friends : 5055
Just on the Thirty-first : 1739
(Just) Pass the Ammunition : 6168
Just Right : 2134
Just Sit Outside : 5140
Just This : 3785
Just Wednesday : 236
Justice : 1397, 2839, 6544

Justicia Social : 400
(Justification) : 1013
Juxtaposition : 6492
The 'K.M.' File (3) : 1814
K Mart at the Opera : 4541
Kafka Nodded, Boarding a Train : 1823
Kafka the Spider : 5969
Kafka's Angels : 234
Kafka's Janitor : 957
Kaikoura : 1077
Kaimos : 3472
Kala Gave Me Anykine Advice Especially
    about Filipinos When I Moved to Pahala :
    7085
Kalahari : 1236
Kalawao, Molokai : 1421
Kampuchea : 3291
A Kansas Anthem : 5956
A Kansas Story : 4480
Kära : 2031
Karate : 4429
Karl Barth's Dream of Mozart : 5676
Karl Marx's House : 6118
Karla-Bhaja Caves : 5208
Karloff and the Rock : 1553
Karmic Revolution : 73
Kassida of the Sleeping Woman : 2191, 4273
Katharine Hepburn, Quoted : 3283
Katherine Mansfield Contemplates a Painting of
    Elizabeth I (1533-1603) : 1814
The Katherine Mansfield Signature As Zen
    Painting : 1814
Kathleen Spivack's Study : 6238
Kathy I Love You Jerry 1-4-83 : 2815
Katie Rosa Bradley : 6063
Kaune's Foodtown : 5566
Keats and the Anchorman : 4456
Keats's House, Rome : 2618
Kebsquasheshing : 5516
The Keen Edge : 5976
Keen Edges : 5610
Keep Running : 5241
Keep talking, keep talking : 4809, 5552
The Keeper of Flocks : 655, 4994
Keeper of the Keys : 3571
Keepers : 3328
Keeping House : 4280
Keeping in Touch : 406
Keeping Secrets : 1935
Keeping the Record Straight : 6654
Keeping the Song : 3353
Keeping the Word : 3813
Keeping Track : 6975
Kemmel Hill : 2620
Kepler : 6816
Key : 696, 5671
The Key : 6829
Key Biscayne : 4934
Key Word : 1031, 1925, 6298
Keys : 2416
The Keys : 1759
Keys to Friday Sunrise : 5822
Kick : 5369
The Kick from Inside : 4620

Kick the Can : 828
Kicking the Can : 3425
The Kid Believes in Management : 402
The Kid in the Window Seat : 4756
The Kidnapping : 2124
Kids : 6075
Kilauea : 3381
Kilhope : 1541
Kill the Buddha : 6933
Killdeer : 1854
The Killer : 3604
A Killer of Darkness : 6099
The Killing of the Cobra : 1366
Killing the Man Who Wanted to Die : 4937
Kilty Sue : 431
Kimono : 2856
Kind of Blue : 448, 3749
A Kind of Ink against the Twilight : 859
Kinder Schadenfreude : 3957
The Kindergarten Heart : 5433
Kindly Refrain from Sneezing on the Exhibits :
    1627
Kindly Stopped : 615
Kinds of Death : 3229, 6971
A King Held Captive in Water Troughs : 1868,
    4125
King Joey : 1194
The King of Books : 1830
King of Spring : 2050
Kingbird : 2924
Kingdom Come : 2676
Kings, an Account of Books 1 and 2 of
    Homer's Iliad : 3837
King's Choir Cambridge: Christmas Eve 1989 :
    2246
The King's Dwarf : 1991
The King's Gap Stagecoach Road : 5321
Kingston, Friday Afternoon : 1353
Kisii : 3190
Kiss : 5396
A Kiss in Church : 2981
The Kiss of Death : 1637
Kiss Tomorrow Goodbye : 6835
Kisses of Blake : 231
The Kissing Fish : 3502
Kissing in the Carwash : 387
Kissing the Lips of Orphanage Girls : 3038
Kissing Wet : 3425
Kitayama : 5366
The Kitchen : 4685
Kitchen Meditation : 5532
Kitchen Territorial : 3046
Kitchen Work : 92
The Kite Flyer : 2122
Kites : 4312
The Kitten : 4790
Klarhet : 6222
Klee at Bauhaus: Parallel Bodies : 2079
Klu'skap-o'kom : 3146
Klyvningar : 5525
The 'K.M.' File (3) : 1814
The Knee : 1647, 4481
Kneeling Together : 5324
The Knees That Were Ours and the Fruit and

the Style : 3064, 3494
Knell : 5359
Das Knie : 4481
Knife : 3937
Knife knife knife knife knife sapper shovel :
244, 3011, 5836
Knife Song : 4444
Knitting Litany : 6685
Knitting Needles, Needle and Thread : 2751,
3089
Knob : 5396
The Knocking : 5541
Knots : 2104, 2800
Know Thyself : 1701
Knowing Robs Us : 20
Knowing the Time Is Nothing : 1442
Knowledge : 1088
Kol Nidre : 2109
Kom Inom : 6222
Kongo Power Figure : 5462
Kore : 5061, 7031
Korean Soap Opera : 236
Krafft-Ebing's Aberrations of Sexual Life :
3388
Kreuzberg : 2009
Krystallhause, or The End of the Window :
5866
Kuburabasu : 6015
Kundry : 6920
Kunming : 6869
Ku'u Momi Makamae : 311
L.A. : 2362
LBJ Ranch Barbecue : 681
L. J. Sand in His Paint and General Store, 1959
: 6715
L.K. XXV : S.B. I (Lucy Strikes Back) : 518
La Push Apocalypse : 471
Laager : 2431
Labor Day : 1578
Laboratorio : 5170
Laboring the Obvious : 193
Labyrinthine Passion : 5656
Lace Huts : 2502
A Lack of Monuments : 5287
Ladder : 2425
Ladder Ode : 3906
The Ladies Auxiliary : 1145
Ladies' Night at the Disco : 788
Ladies of the Farthest Province : 2740
Lady Caroline Lamb Remembers Lord Byron :
1269
Lady Chatterly's Younger Lover : 2466
Lady Franklin Writes to Her Husband 15 Years
Gone into the Ice, 1857 : 6880
Lady in a Wood : 623
Lady in February : 5581
Lady in the Lake : 6598
The Lady Oboeist Uses a Razor Blade to Make
Her Reeds : 3000
Lady on the Bus : 490
Lady Shelley Replies to Her Son's Accusations
of Adultery : 1269
Laertes : 3847
Laguna Night : 5299

Lair : 3772
Lajo : 1802
The Lake : 3185, 3377
Lake Alice : 78, 5892
Lake Douglas, September 11, 1988 : 2865
Lake Hörende, August : 813, 814, 2526
The Lake in the Valley : 3409
Lake Nora Arms : 5242
(Lake Ohrid, Late Summer) : 2454, 2716
Lake Shore : 596, 4502
Lakeview : 985
Lame Apollo : 7062
Lament : 2946, 3873, 4086
Lament for a Stranger, Alone Among Savages :
184
Lament for the Crested Shelduck : 6364
Lament for the Holy Places : 2961
Lament-Heaven : 1650
Lament of the Minor Functionary : 5660
Lamentation : 2013, 5107
The Lamps : 5764
LAN/707-P : 3618
Lan Quan Lijorn : 5511, 6005
The Land : 1203, 3147, 5336, 5680
Land and Language : 4370
Land of Mutational Artists : 2555
Land of the Cyclops : 6274
Land of the Dead : 2339
Land of the Holy Cross : 5118, 6786
Landlocked : 44
Landlords, We Don't Just Disappear into Those
Homes : 789
Landscape : 2696, 3459, 4692, 4743
Landscape at the End of the Century : 1715
Landscape Overthrown : 6708
Landscape, Pre-School : 5086
Landscape Toward a Proper Silence : 3231
Landscape with Door : 92
Landscape with Girl : 6658
Landscape with Ponytrack : 1649
Landscape with Sheep : 2819
Landscape with Snow : 126
Landscapes : 1713, 6007
Landschappen : 6007
Längtan Är Sveket Mot Dig Själv : 206
A Language : 1889, 2738, 4486
Language Drill : 2272
Language Envying Geometry : 1561
Language Is Hands : 7191
The Language of Bridges : 5370
The Language of the Making : 1561
The Language of Trains : 134
Language Without Miracles : 445
Lanikai Sea Burial : 6117
Lantern as a Shelter for Light : 6865
Lara in It : 377
Larchmont, Winter 1986 : 439
The Large Bathers : 5352
Largesse : 1096, 4828
Larry, Curley, and Moe on the Shore of Pine
Lake : 5187
Las vegas no neon red goddess cafe : 1940
Last, 1991 : 5302
Last Act : 3912

The Last Class in Rhetoric : 2928
The Last Corner : 2806, 5810
Last Day : 6307
The Last Day : 4782, 6460
Last Days : 1343
The Last Days : 1879
Last Days of Jerry Bill Smith : 1515
The Last Days of John Keats : 3615
The Last Defenders : 3880
The Last Devotee : 4408
Last Example: Carlos de Oliveira : 158, 3750
The Last Father Poem : 5856
Last Gods : 3381
The Last Home : 491, 3035, 3476
The Last Incarnation : 4726
Last Light : 3216
A Last Look Back at My Father's Garden :
     4898
A Last Lullaby : 2580
Last Measures : 3268
Last Night : 2348, 7034
Last Night I Slept Under a Dying Tree : 2779
The Last Nun : 2590
The Last of the Medici : 5
Last Photograph of My Days as an Idealist :
     1994
Last Photograph of Teresa Martin : 651, 5151
The Last Poem to My Mother : 6405
Last Protrusion : 1547
The Last Rehearsal : 4490
Last Request : 2384
Last Seder: the Four Cups : 2452
Last Seen : 56
The Last Self-Portrait : 6162
The Last Sermon of Gnarley Never : 782
Last Supper : 2104, 3242, 4990, 6220
The Last Surrealistic Dream of Soldier L.Z. :
     3823
The Last Symphony : 4770
The Last Three Days of Winter : 5404
The Last Wild Horses in Tennessee : 5848
A Last Will and Testament Poem : 1030
Last Words : 1967
Last Words Found in His Pockets : 5455, 6611
Lasting Influence : 6873
Late : 6603
Late Afternoon, Late in the Twentieth Century :
     5929
Late April Aesthetic : 3937
Late at Night, the Lightning : 620
Late Evening : 792
Late Irises: A Goodbye Sonnet : 2430
Late June, Wassergass : 5379
Late Letter to My Father : 7060
Late One Afternoon : 1597
Late Spring in a Small City : 4726
Late Summer Golf : 2183
Late Summer Sunset, West Coast of Florida :
     1660
Late Winter Storm : 6568
Lately : 6065
Lately I have given up on birthdays : 1963
Lately She Can't Stand : 930
Later : 1102

Later Than Lately : 6829
The Latest from a Little World Gently Abuzz
     with Itself : 755
The Latin Lesson : 616
Lauds, or, L'Allegro, or, Khan of the High
     Light : 2654
Laughing in Bed : 6608
Laughing Matter : 782
Laughing Young Man : 3081
Laughter : 1605
Laundry : 6296
Laura : 693
Laurel : 5594
Lava : 2380, 3066, 7129
The Law of Proportion : 5239
Lawbreakers : 3428
The Lawn : 2224
Lawn of Excluded Middle : 6708
Lawrenceville : 5209
The Laws of Eddings : 6026
Laws of Nature : 675
Lay Off : 6085
Lay Your Head on the Shoulder of Water and
     the Skin of Air : 5905
Lazarus : 1559
LBJ Ranch Barbecue : 681
Lead Letters : 1056
The Leaf : 2939
Leaf Machines : 3
A leaf, one of the last, fell away from a maple
     branch : 3979
Leaf Shadows on a Door : 2166
Leafstorm : 3572, 4994
(Lean In) : 2454, 2716
Leaning Over the Wharf in Bimini : 3220
The Leaning Tree : 5816
Leap, My Soul, in Grateful Joy! : 5003
Leap Year : 2905
Learned at the Weavers' Barn : 6101
Learner's Permit on Skyline Drive : 5985
Learning : 4069
Learning a New Language : 1155
Learning About Him : 1877
Learning About the Heart : 5379
Learning Balance : 354
Learning How to Sing : 1518
Learning How to Write : 5171
Learning the Words : 1362
Learning to Dance : 971
Learning to Drive : 306
Learning to Drown : 96
Learning to Lead : 5932
Learning to Love By Hand : 2708
Learning to Pray : 5042
Learning to Read : 959
Learning to Sail : 1583
Learning to Shoot : 6812
Learning to Sing : 4749, 5995
Learning to Speak Neurosurgery : 1346
Learning to Speak Spanish Cats Like Martyrs :
     6091
Learning to Tango : 903
Lease on chicken : 4140
Leather, Steel and Ovaltine : 6994

Leave a Message : 3754
Leave it to the lumber company : 4973
Leave of Absence : 5487
Leave-Taking : 6031
The Leavening : 6067
Leaves : 5733
Leaves Above a Pool : 4801
Leaves fall down and down, making circles :
    244, 3011, 6353
Leaving : 244, 3011, 4089
Leaving Cambridge for Baltimore : 6796
Leaving Colombia : 4726
Leaving for the Trees : 2735
Leaving Home : 3063
Leaving the Rust Belt : 4253
Leaving the Valley : 2255
Leben : 4058
Das Leben : 2798
Leccion de Ojos : 2388
Leccion en Los Compos : 2890
Lecture : 2587
The Lecturer : 1680
Leda : 2340, 5085, 6770
Leda's Handmaiden : 6964
Lees : 3433
Left : 2711
Left Behind : 3910
Left to Own Ends : 5771
Legacy : 1760, 4212, 4578, 5224, 5980, 6125
The Legal Killing of Elephants : 1325
Legend : 53
The Legend of Monferrato : 1473, 6628
Legend with Sea Breeze : 2164
Leggenda del Monferrato : 1473
The Legitimate Smart-Ass : 50
Leland : 1776
Lemmings : 3796
Lemon Doorknob in the Rain : 36
A Lemon Scent of Clocks : 5606
Lemon Sponge : 3280
Lemonade and Lobsters : 2690
Lenape : 5464
The Length of These Generations : 918
The Lensman : 2481
Leo Falling Asleep Next to Me : 4109
Leonardo da Vinci Airport, December 27, 1985
    : 6868
Leopardi's *La sera del dì di festa* : 1553
The Leprechauns of Our Lives : 5024
Lesbia, let us live only for loving : 1032, 4073
Lesbian Poem, Age 15 : 226
Less Pleasant Music : 1571
Lesson : 1015
The Lesson in 'A Waltz for Debby' : 1026
A Lesson in Bryology : 4371
A Lesson in What Romance Is : 1704
Lesson, Lesson : 56
Lessons in Zen Pessimism : 1579
Lessons of the Beach: Reaching Infinity : 5507
Lessons Taught by the Eyes : 1808, 2388
Lest the Last Light Flee Also : 5822
Let a Man : 6001
Let Go, Go Wilding : 5410
Let Live : 2104, 3519

Let Me Think : 99, 1883
Let me try to explain this rather cryptic state-
    ment : 162
Let the Timbrel Rattle : 1363, 5379
Let This Be a Lesson : 2296
Let This Cup Pass From Me : 887
'Let Those Who Have eyes to See' Beware :
    7048
Let Us Pledge : 509
Letitia Demands the Magic Touch : 4853
Let's Bite His Hand : 3034, 6586
Let's Count the Bodies Over Again : 591
Let's Enact the Santa 'Claus' : 2310
Let's Go : 435, 2591
Let's Go to the Ruins : 6706
Let's Help : 2104, 6054, 6612
Let's Stop Talking : 635, 6688
Let's Talk Rape : 3911
Letter : 318, 334, 2239, 2961, 3133, 5700, 7158
The Letter : 3327, 4515
A Letter Back to You : 4808
Letter by Firelight : 4662
Letter from a Connecticut Country House : 106
Letter from a Mermaid : 180, 4156
Letter from a School Friend : 6770
Letter from Aiolia : 4810
Letter from Diotima : 2283, 2901
Letter from Mt. Pleasant : 3655
A Letter from Prison : 3158
Letter from the Shaman: The Contrary Tribe :
    1128
Letter Home : 6597
Letter Home from the Tropic of Cancer : 1453
Letter Home to Ann : 700
Letter of Resignation : 6710
Letter on Pink Paper : 4188
Letter to a Poet : 1599, 5783
Letter to Cape Cod from Minnesota : 1795
Letter to Ginsberg : 5428
Letter to His Daughter : 1401
Letter to Jon : 1457
Letter to K : 5820
Letter to My Great, Great, Great Aunt Olive
    Strong Tenney : 2957
Letter to My Son : 3832
Letter to My Son on His Sixteenth Birthday :
    5137
Letter to My Twin : 686
Letter to NYC : 7082
Letter to Peter : 928
Letter to Philip Larkin on Learning of His
    Death a Week After the Fact : 6205
Letter to Sally : 3100
Letter to the Young Poet Who Stole My Lines :
    7193
A Letter to Those Who Stayed : 617
Letter to Youki : 1536, 2023
Letters : 1712, 3763, 5992, 6454
The Letters : 6667
Letters form Kansas : 573
Letters From My Father : 683
Letters I Did Not Get : 288
Letters to Nowhere : 2950, 3464
Letters to Zanzotto : 4886

Letting the Gowns Blow and Open : 2312
Lettre close : 461
Level 2, Room 20 : 1628
Leviathan : 3306, 5867, 6805
Levitation : 5019
Liar (a Poem) : 3052
A Liberal : 3171
Liberal Learning : 2465
Liberation : 4671
Libido : 913
The Librarian Confronts Theology : 4709
The Library : 1654
The Library Poem : 4663
Library Tapestry : 4129
Licking the Fun Up : 562
The Lie : 5949, 6810
Liebe / Querida : 71
Lied of the Fig Tree : 1071, 6017
Liege : 1538, 5292, 5874, 6220
Lies : 2244, 5171
Lies About Magnolias : 184
Life : 2798, 4455
Life After Wuthering Heights : 2760
Life As It Is : 244, 3011, 4089
Life at the Beach : 4253
A Life: Exploded View : 686
Life, I Do Not Expect : 4439, 4780
Life in the Forest : 5736
Life Mask : 6458
The Life Next at Hand : 6728
The Life of a Hummingbird : 3398
The Life of Desire : 1079
The Life of the City : 3443
Life on the Mississippi Queen : 202
Life Pulses : 2515, 7150
Life Sentence : 2778
The Life Story of Charlie Parker : 3413
Life swells to twice, three times its normal size
    : 666, 3979
Life Voyage : 1081, 5992
The Life We Learn With : 3030
Lifelines : 567
The Lifelong Range : 3724
Life's Waitress : 2330
Lifestyles Prince : 3776
Light After Light : 7066
Light and Darkness : 7170
Light & Destiny: Men Without Hats : 6700
The Light-Bringer : 6136
Light from the Cay : 468, 6660
Light in the Open Air : 1574
The Light of the Living : 2752
Light on Dark Corners: What Men Love in
    Women : 4339
Light on Dark Corners: What Women Love in
    Men : 4339
Light on the Sound : 2720
A Light Riff for MSH : 7162
Light Rising from Concrete : 5378
Light-Struck : 4602
Light Surprised : 6849
The Light, Today, Is Blue : 6075
Light Verse : 5703
The Light Where Lives Intersect : 4728

Light Years : 614, 1192, 6242
Lighthouse : 6877
Lighting Tapers in Notre Dame : 6147
Lightning : 6556
Lightning's Attraction to Solitary Objects : 570
Lights Across the Bay : 6231
Lights at One O'Clock : 1854
Lik Tvoj : 244, 3011, 3877
Like a Dead Man's Life : 478
Like a Dream : 5224
Like a Fourteenth Century Love Poem : 214
Like a knifeblade the moon will be full then less
    : 476, 3033
Like a Leash, Trailing Away behind Her : 4015
Like a Woman : 2457
Like a Woman Running into Leaves : 3780
Like a Wreck : 3418
Like Always : 1785
Like Manna : 2235
Like My Father : 5789
Like New Gods, Two Japanese Women Guide
    My Hands : 3593
Like opposing lanes of traffic : 3314
Like Sadness in Music : 7107
Like That and Then : 6325
Like the Moon Departing : 6221
Like the Spaniards : 989
Like the succulent apple that blushes : 5622,
    6203
Like Ulysses : 2775
Like Van Gogh Transfixed : 4291
Like What Floods Back When : 3780
Like William S. Burroughs Once Told Me :
    4643
Like your cascading hair : 4866
Lil Bro tells us : 5068
Lily : 6656
Lily Briscoe: A Failed Painting : 443
Lily Fiero : 2933
Limbo Dancer & the Press : 48
Limbo Dancer's Reading Habits : 48
Lime Harbor : 15
Limits : 1878, 3559
Limits II : 1878
Limoges : 5749
Lincoln Portrait : 4857
Lindow Man II : 4647
The Line : 1128
Lineage : 1177
Linear Arrangement : 1340
Linear Time : 2928
The Linemen : 3316
Liner Notes : 3112
Lines : 2253, 3495, 6225
Lines for a Blue Lady : 1308
Lines for a Manic-Depressive Uncle, Divorcing
    at 71 : 5507
Lines for a Stammering Turkish Poet : 4520
Lines for Anne Pasternak, 1957-1985 : 1910
Lines for Eastern Bluebirds : 3038
Lines on the Death of a Kitten : 5761
Lines on the Pergamon Museum : 6931
Lines to Restore Van Gogh's Ear : 513
Lines Written Near an Elegant and Romantic

Garden Adjacent to Passaick River, in Essex County, July, 1820 : 2099
Lingo Anglais : 6736
Linking the Generations : 3612
The Lion : 1247
Lion, Sand, Moon and You : 5173
Lion's Bay: Death by Drowning : 305
The Lion's Den : 5963
Lip : 3019
Lip Service : 5400
Lips : 4345, 5421
Liquid Questions : 4497
Liquor That Will Not Fill an Empty Bottle : 3395
The List : 6335
List Poem for the Birds in My Backyard : 1159
Listen : 611, 2583, 3746
Listen whose face is it a piece : 476, 3033
Listening : 4870
Listening at the Door : 4825
Listening for a Long-Dead Gardener : 7048
Listening to a Baseball Game : 7051
Listening to a Flute : 1625, 3771
Listening to a White Man Play the Blues : 1380
Listening to Advice : 222
Listening to Secretaries : 4377
Listening to Stones : 4215
Listening, to the Bite : 4788
Listening to the Candle: A Poem on Impulse : 5748
Listening to the Fifth : 1948
Listening to the Goldberg Variations : 4253
Listening to the Language of Birds : 6270
Listening to the Radio (FM) : 1611
Listening to the Radio Late at Night : 2804
Listening What I See : 5209
Liszts : 841
Lit 007 : 4416
Litanies of Satan : 2012
Litany (1) : 286
Litany (II) : 286
Litany on the Equinox : 1545
Literature, so boyish : 1454
Lithograph : 3243, 5379
Little Anarchies : 1872
A Little Background: The Sisters : 2079
Little Brother at Six : 2601
Little Brown Jug : 3384
Little Disgestion Ode : 2426
Little Essay on Communication : 1715
Little Fires : 1545
The Little Grey Man : 1567
Little Gulls : 2104, 5937, 6573
Little Haiti : 3913
Little Love Poem : 579
The Little Magazines : 3730
Little Mother : 6974
A Little Movie : 2044
Little or Nothing : 2568
Little Paul and the Sea : 6177
Little Poem : 1625, 3771
The Little Poem : 706
The Little Red Shoe : 5471
Little Ritual : 4417

Little Saint Anthony and the Supreme Temptation : 515
The Little Shop Around the Corner : 2592
A Little Something for an Old English Teacher : 6832
Little Spanish Poems : 831
Little Stabs of Happiness : 3388
A Little Suite for Rochester or a City Similar : 1824
A Little Tent History : 755
The Little Theme : 6154
The Little Things : 3295
The little Tibetan : 3968
The Little Towns : 2748, 5107, 5107
A Little Twist of the Lips : 1746
A Little Wine, Some Death : 4991
Live from the Met : 2000
Live from the Rust Belt : 2831
Live Girls : 2801
Livelong Days : 236
Living Among Women : 6880
Living by the Sea : 3794
Living Color : 5820
Living in Another Man's House : 4767
Living in Snake Country : 7141
Living in the Now : 6897
Living in the Present : 3859
Living Nowhere : 1240
Living Off the Land : 5567
Living on Hardscrabble : 4179
Living Room : 4671, 6826
The Living Room : 2321
Living Room in the Park : 6333
Living Under Water : 4057
Living Underground: Nicaragua, 1988 : 1597
Living Without John Rose : 2855
Lizard : 6023, 6743, 7155
The Lizard of Villa del Corazon : 3220
The Lizards of Ios : 1341
Llego en Sueños : 218
Lo Que Le Dijo la Mama : 642
Loading the Summer Cattle : 4179
The Loaner : 675
Lobo and Sylvie : 4615
Local Aesthetic : 2154
Local Historical Societies : 6922
Local Knowledge : 1879
Local News and a Reflection : 4892
Location Shot : 2799
Locked in the Stone : 745
Locked Ward, Newtown, Connecticut : 3831
Locution, Locomotive Case : 839
La Loge : 1735
The Logjam : 1744, 2145
Logor Siromaha (Beggars' Camp) : 5033
Lois : 6505
Lola Somebody Dreams : 2342
London Kid : 2193
London Zoo : 1572
Lone Dog's Winter Count : 2303
Lone Pine : 6042
Loneliness : 105, 186, 271, 653, 5726, 6971
The Loneliness of the Military Historian : 253
The Lonely : 3096

Lonely People in Lonely Places : 6097
Long After Chamfort : 428, 1059
Long ago we were swiftly flowing water : 653, 1581
The Long Approach : 3794
The Long Blue Coat : 6723
Long Cool Silhouette : 221
The long day's journey : 822
Long, Disconsolate Lines : 1264
Long Division : 6603, 7022
The Long Drive In : 3674
A Long Farewell : 813, 814, 2031
The Long Grief : 1619
The Long Haul : 2784, 5711
The Long Hunt : 3956
Long in the Tooth : 2305
Long Island Night : 2457
Long Island Sounds : 1024
A Long Line : 1337
The Long Night Moon : 4376
Long Story Short : 4188
Long Term : 1715
The Long Weekend : 3833
Long-Winged Bird : 1625
The Longest Sidewalk in the Western World : 1810
Longing : 6966
The Longing : 2881
Longing for Prophets : 3280
Longing Is Betrayal of Oneself : 206, 813, 814
Look : 3977, 4188
Look How She Walks! : 813, 814, 5708
Look Park: Florence, Massachusetts, 1958 : 1679
Look Up : 2406
Looked like a flip visor, a 'technical mother lode,' one loser called it : 162
Looker : 4345
Looking Ahead : 1563
Looking at Family Slides with His Children : 475
Looking at Love-Making: I : 2708
Looking at the X-Rays : 579
Looking at Your Picture : 4629
Looking Away : 2828
Looking Back at the Sky : 4409
Looking for Cotopaxi : 3900
Looking for Hegel's Portrait : 2104, 6054, 6612
Looking for Loons : 1346
Looking for the Department of Daisies : 3606
Looking for the Joads : 1862
Looking Glass : 92
Looking Out : 2523, 6101
Looking Up : 4312, 5379
Looking West from Mount Eryx : 5650
The Lookout : 5666
The Loon : 7007
Loose Change : 2981
The Loose Garment : 1401
Looser Talk : 2714
Loplop Twines : 1259
Lorca, Going Home : 6880
Lorca, Looking for Adam : 6880
Lorca's Death : 5250

Lorca's New York : 491, 3476, 4812
Loreen : 1451
The Loreley : 6117
Loretta's Men : 5835
Lorna Sue Cantrell, Singing in the Choir : 291
The Lorton Anthology : 3150
Los Angeles: 12th and Olive : 1457
Los Angeles, Fin de Siècle : 5901
Los Angeles / Southern California : 4736
Losers, Keepers: The Opus of Wilhelmina Scrowd : 2539
Losing : 1625, 4304
Losing a Breast: Prayer Before Surgery : 853
Losing a Language : 4312
Losing Aphrodite : 7065
Losing Grace : 2045
Loss : 5212
The Loss : 3777
Losses : 1087
Lost : 2332, 6185
The Lost : 894
Lost Among Old Apples : 3937
Lost Art : 2387
The Lost Camelia of the Bartrams : 4312
The Lost Civilization : 6779
Lost Daughter : 6878
Lost Imagoes : 2390
Lost in the Fire : 1163
Lost in the Lens : 934
Lost Language : 92
Lost Library of Bucharest : 734
Lost Little Lost : 246
Lost Luggage : 4921
The Lost Man : 4842
The Lost Sainthood : 6848
Lost Shadow Visits : 5564
Lost Souls : 2693
Lost Years : 3580
The Lot of Great Waves : 1041, 5872
Lot's Wife : 4926, 6461
Lot's Wife, Amzar by Name : 1766
Lotte : 4296
Lotto Player : 6813
Louie : 1318
Louie Blue : 5805
Louisa's Wedding : 5032
Louise : 4349
Louise in the Jungle : 3900
Love : 649, 2075, 3487, 3769, 4832, 5078, 5586, 6881, 7078
Love Affair : 2009
Love After a Long Absence (of Love) : 2702
Love Among Lepers : 5451
Love Caught : 1141
Love Crown : 1043, 5050
Love, Do You Remember : 2664
Love Greatly Enlarged : 6681
Love, Hate: The Life We Learn : 839
Love in the Museum : 5322
Love Is the Only Bond : 4119
Love, Itself : 164
Love Lamp : 6005
Love Letter : 363, 884
Love Letters : 2965

Love Made : 2242
The Love of Small Cold Towns : 587
Love on Jerusalem's East Side : 7018
Love Po I Rose : 4485
Love Poem : 420, 760, 1793, 2234, 2395, 3856,
    6313
Love Poem #3 : 1464
Love Poem #4 : 1464
Love Poem 1990 : 4283
Love Poem for the Nuclear Age: Utah, 1950-[
    ] : 1211
Love Poem in the Library : 6035
Love Poems : 287, 598
Love Relics : 791
Love rose up between us : 2806, 5810
Love Song : 531, 1131, 4171, 6768
Love Song in Black : 4605
Love Song in the Humidity : 107
Love Song to the World Leaders : 3946
Love Songs for My People : 110
Love Story : 435, 4180
Love substantiates comedy : 2764
Love, the Word : 1732
A Love Triangle: Howard and Pearl and John :
    918
Love with Powder Burns : 2184, 4362
The Loveliest Country of Our Lives : 7057
The Lovely Chthonic Roots : 1143
The Lovely Nasobime : 1647, 4481
Lovely Until the End : 4630
Lovepoem #67 : 5385
The Lover Comes : 3230
The Lover Rejects Himself : 2970
The Lover Snake : 2841
A Lover Spurned : 2574
The Lovers : 3799, 7059
The Lovers at Teruel : 1757, 3588
The Lover's City of Art : 5032
Lover's Heaven : 3796
Lover's Leap : 1177
A Lover's Leaving : 4302
Loves : 1715
Love's Fugitive on the Run : 2970
Low Planes : 766, 5691
Low Tide : 885
Lowell Fulson, Age 66, Eli's Mile High Club,
    Oakland, California : 4260
The 'L's' : 822, 5292
Lübars : 1754, 5657
Lucerne : 852
Lucia di Lammermore, More More : 1789
Lucid Temporary Hatches : 4559
Lucille : 524
Luck : 4175
Lucky : 6753
Lucky 7 : 2643
A Lucky Man : 3243, 5379
Lucky Ones Are Marching : 6608
Lucky Pierre : 1019
Lucretius Addresses the Academic Senate : 184
Lucy in the Sky : 943
Lucy Kent XXIV (Poem for the Sucks) : 518
A Luddite Lullaby : 610
Un Lugar de Nombres Cariñosos : 2192

A Lull in the Battle, Exekias the Amphora-
    Painter Speaks : 6524, 6830
Lullaby : 340, 2960, 4443, 5976, 6815, 6821
Lullaby for My Unborn Child : 813, 814, 2418
Lumber : 5347
The Luminous Time : 6800
La Luna Asoma : 2191
La Luna Ofendida : 1941
Lunar Eclipse : 2329
Lunar Landscape : 4312
Lunatick Bawling : 804
The Lunatic's Prayer : 2631
Lunch : 6420
Lunch My Accidental : 5111
Lunchcounter Freedom : 4521
Luray, Virginia: The Discovery : 5617
Lure : 3778, 5310
Lust : 1876, 2482
Luster's Gate : 6046
Lustre : 5980
Luther : 3553
Luz I : 1368
Luz II : 1368
Luz III : 1368
Lydia : 1242
Lying Against Myself, Half Naked : 5754
Lying Awake : 4408
Lying Awake, I Hear the Wind and Think
    About James Wright : 905
Lying Back Like Proust : 1966
Lying Beside That Woman : 1550, 1551
Lying in Sadness : 6882
Lying Nights : 161, 6006
Lying with Susan : 2115
Lyn Lifshin Stars in *Modern Times II* : 6851
Lyra Graeca : 214
Lyric Lyric : 1278
Lyric to Epic Poet re: Poetry : 4763
The Lyrical Trees : 5993
M-80s : 1429
M.C. Escher's Ascending and Descending :
    3171
(MD) : 2454, 2716
MJQ : 5970
M. M. : 6367
MacArthur Blvd : 5575
MacBlarney's Race : 4035
The Machine Gunner : 2756
The Machine Maker : 3246
The Machine Shop : 5969
The Machine That Changed Winter : 4860
Machinery : 3689
The Machinist : 3584
Machinist Poet : 5969
Machu Picchu : 6816
Mackerel : 652
The Mad Girl Can't Look at Anything Too
    Near : 3780
The Mad Girl Doesn't Need Much : 3780
The Mad Girl Feels Betrayal Turn What Was
    Like Paper She Could : 3780
The Mad Girl Feels So Much Dissolving : 3780
The Mad Girl Has Two Lovers Come the Same
    Day : 3780

The Mad Girl Needs More : 3780
The Mad Girl Needs More Than Most Others :
3780
The Mad Girl Swears Off Media Men : 3780
The Mad Girl Takes the Radio Out of the Room
: 3780
The Mad Linguist : 5431
The Mad Message : 2540
Mad People : 262
A Mad Poet's Estate : 588
Mad Robin in Spring : 5676
Mad Sonnet : 858
The Mad Woman : 347, 6126
The Mad Woman at the Church Door : 2192,
5995
A Madam at the Funeral of One of Her Girls,
Galveston, Texas, 1891 : 1269
Madame : 6797
Madame Butterfly, some Met travelling
company : 2050
Madame R : 4967
Madame Tussaud : 6605
Madamina : 6047
Made in the Shade : 1976
Madeline : 1517
Madison National Bank, Washington, DC
Member FDIC : 5984
Madonna : 214
Madonna of the Obsessions : 3780
Madonna Who Goes Down on You : 3780
Madonna Who Hates Change : 3780
Madonna Who Throws So Many Intimate
Details Out Fast : 3780
Madonna without Child : 3587
Una Madre Che Dorme : 2216
Las Madres : 3028
Madrigal : 1984, 6188
Madstone : 1006
Magalhães' Last Testament : 1312
Magán-Golgotán : 3035
Magazine Dream, Video Queens : 1542
Magdelene's Communion : 3796
Maggie : 3893
Maggot : 3699
Magic : 3521, 3547, 3981, 5327, 5379
Magic Hour : 1047
Magic Stones : 903
The Magician of Xerox : 5813
Magnetawan Poems : 6175
Magnificat : 79, 3493
Magnolia : 4531
Magnolia Bluff : 4309
Mai Am un Singur Dor : 1800
Mail : 4819
The Mail from Tunis : 2204
Main Exhibit Hall : 4185
Main Street : 7049
Main Street Elegies : 4155
The Mainlanders : 3088
Mainstay & Vacant : 4059
Maintaining the same distance : 5222
Maintenance : 163
Maintenon Postcard : 5461
Makaleha : 6339

Make Black the Light : 4910
Make me laugh, dis Cold Mountain trail : 2611,
5742
The Maker of Parables : 4738
Making a Living in Laugharne : 4544
Making a Poem : 1798
Making a Space : 3880
Making an Angel for Bob : 6178
Making Art : 918
Making Breakfast : 2607
Making Contact Near Depoe Bay : 4078
Making It : 4818
Making It Up : 219
Making Light : 6970
Making Love to a New Woman : 2365
Making Nebraska Home : 3561
The Making of an Irish Goddess : 616
Making Our Way : 7014
Making Room : 4634
Making Sandbags : 1267
Making tapes of a musical fast pace : 5441
Making the Broomstick Poem : 1857
Making the Choice : 2706
Making the Mouth : 1282
Making Up : 6736
Making Won Tons : 6670
The Makings of Happiness : 6728
Mala Memoria : 1557
Malagueña : 6162
The Malaysian Students Play Badminton : 1269
Malcolm McLaren Signs the Sex Pistols,
London, 1976 : 7010
Male Image : 6036
Male Menopausal Poem : 3435
Malik, My First Cousin : 3206
Malinche : 5573
Mallam Ibrahim : 7190
Malleable : 4550
Maluku in Cornish : 989
Mamá : 954
Mama : 3820, 6146
Mama in the Medicine Cabinet : 3304
Mama's Boy : 923
Mama's Dream : 1388
Mama's Shadow : 928
Mami and Gauguin : 122
Mammography : 923
Man : 964, 3985, 4742
A Man : 1018, 2289
Man and Woman on a Balcony in Indian
Summer : 3016
Man as Animal : 7021
The Man at the Pompidou : 5106
The Man Here : 1922, 5040, 5379
The Man in My Memory : 4339
A man in the fur trade named Jeeve : 1643
The Man in the Gray House : 6673
The Man in the Moon : 4911
The Man Learns : 4595
A Man Leaves an Oak Chair in the Rain : 4468
Man Letter #1 : 4781
Man Living on a Side Creek : 6480
A Man May Change : 445
The Man of Seven Days : 3712, 5498

The Man of Steel : 4575
The Man on the Hotel Room Bed : 3381
The Man on the Pillow : 7177
Man Playing Kickball with Demons : 4585
The Man Praying : 3434
A man set out : 1754, 5657
Man Still Stands : 1081, 5992
The Man, the Woman and the Other Man : 961
The Man Who Disappeared : 981
The Man Who Discovered Entropy While on
    Vacation : 570
The Man Who Found a Poem in Everything :
    1128
The Man Who Has Not Yet Met His Body :
    5675
The Man Who Lives on Air : 5756
The Man Who Measures Animals : 6026
A Man Who Reads Homer : 4681, 5572
The Man Who Simplified His Life : 5323
The Man Who Won't Pay Dues : 2177
The Man with Birds in His Skull : 5333
The Man with the Chair : 1847
The Man with the Glass Eye : 4644
The Manacled Youth : 3032
The Manatees : 3291
The Mandarin House : 801
The Mandelbrot Problem : 6378
The Mandelbrot Set : 216
Mandelstam in Armenia, 1930 : 309
Mandrax : 7041
Maneuvers : 2545
Manhattan : 1496
Manhood : 4831
Manifest : 3675
Manifestations : 4131
Manifesto : 666, 979
Manissean Burial Ground : 314
The Mann Children : 5204
Manna : 2394
Mannikin : 3384
Manon Senses the Presence of an Approaching
    Storm : 1781
Manon Wonders About Her Lover After
    Meeting One of His Former Lovers : 1781
A Mansion : 3290
Mansions : 2843
Manter Creek : 2210
The Mantis : 5217
Mantis (The Horror Show) : 6526
Mantra : 3505
Mantras and Meditations : 6326
Mantras of the Homeless : 5757
Manuela Saenz Baila con Giuseppe Garibaldi el
    Rigodon Final de la Existencia : 336
Manufacture : 315, 1503, 5788
Manuscript from a Delhi Market : 4188
The Many Nostrils of Prana : 1851
Many of Our Fathers : 2506
Many Times : 5828
Manzambi : 4535, 4779
Map : 1995, 3811, 6405
The Map : 4570, 5266
The Map and the City : 6001
The Map-Maker's Daughter : 1804

The Map of the Heart : 564
Maple : 3794
The Maple : 6944
Maple Tree and Bench : 189
Maples Yellow as the Centre of My Cat's Eye :
    2929
Mapmaking : 4665
Mappamundi : 1213
Mappemonde : 783
Marbles : 4753
March : 3798, 7174
The March 12th of Stillness : 4281
March, Early Spring : 813, 814, 5525
March Hill Road : 807
Marcha de Caballos en la Noche : 6631
The Mare Slept Standing : 5858
Margaret Fuller in the Abruzzi Mountains, June
    1848 : 2761
Margarito Thinks of Home : 6407
Marghanita : 5322
The Margin : 4631
Marguerite's Book : 2819
Maria Im Rosenhaag : 4921
Marian : 4956
Marie's Song : 5530
Marillewis : 5832
Marilyn : 2381, 3829, 6495
Marilyn Approaches Possible Retirement in
    1991 : 6989
A Marilyn by Any Other Name : 3168
Marilyn Lives (in Japan with James Dean) :
    2859
The Marilyn Moment : 713
Marilyn Monroe : 1985, 4127, 4543
The Marilyn Monroe Dress : 5969
Marilyn Monroe Is Dead : 4510
The Marilyn Monroe Poll : 2717
Marilyn Monroe Returns : 4997
The Marilyn Poem : 2844
Marilyn Reading Rilke : 1706
Marilyn, the First Time I Came Was with You :
    5333
Marilyn Today : 4608
Marilyn's Mouth : 2436
The Marine Observer's Handbook : 2097
Marinera : 4865
Marital Aids : 5005
Marja Glaudl : 6249
Marjorie Again in Exile : 3757
Mark Bowden : 769
Mark Rothko, 1903-1970 : 7051
Mark Twain's Cabin : 6941
Market Day in Jiangxi : 1897
Marketplaces : 3311
Marking the Blue : 1057
Marley's Ghost : 798
The Marr Girls : 5386
Marriage : 5171, 5803, 6382
The Marriage : 298
Marriage Fires : 5719
The Marriage Sculptor : 6595
Marriage Song : 1743, 3407
Marriage: The Second Year : 5223
Marrianne Reynolds Writes to Keats About Her

Ex-Suitor, Benjamin Bailey : 1269
Married To It : 2852
Married Under Water : 2450
Marrying the Stranger : 3831
Mars and Venus : 2540
Mars, Förvår : 5525
Martha's Vineyard : 4671
Martial Ode : 655, 4994
The Martian Landscape : 921
Martyrdom of the Onions : 1105
The Martyrs' Memorial : 2681
Marvel Mystery Oil : 2105
Mary As the Fly : 3595
Mary Contemplating the Second Coming : 4931
Mary Elizabeth : 2403
Mary shelley, i love only you : 3064, 4894
Mary Shelley Receives Her Dead Husband's
    Heart from Captain Trelawny : 1269
Mary Snorak the Cook, Skermo the Gardener,
    and Jack the Parts Man Provide Dinner for
    a Wandering Stranger : 2490
Mary's Novel : 6124
Mas Felices Que en Vietnam : 1832
Mask : 2623
The Masked Man in Love, II : 5325
Masks : 271, 653, 1825
Massacre : 4903
Massacre of the Innocents : 3264
The Massage : 3381
Master Frans : 1, 5135, 5136
Master None : 4943
Mata Hari in Saint-Lazare Prison, 1917 : 485
Matador : 6224
The Match : 890
Match Point : 4842
Matchman : 5199
Mater Diminuendo : 1385
Mater Dolorosa : 2346
Materia Solar : 158
Materials : 319
MaternA : 517, 6707
Maternal Grandmother : 2009
Mathematics and Disciples : 3101
Mathematics Was an Invasion from Outer
    Space : 4992
La Matière Harmonieuse Manoeuvre encore :
    781
Matinee : 1684
Matins : 1258, 5664
Matins: James Brown and His Famous Flames
    Tour the South, 1958 : 7010
Matisse : 2832, 3993
Matter Harmonious Still Maneuvering : 781,
    6817
A Matter of Division : 4873
Matter-of-Fact : 6260
A Matter of Pride : 1429
A Matter of Words : 3835
Matthew 6:9-13 : 1585
The Matthews County Icehouse : 5963
Matthew's Passion : 3723
Mattie Stevens : 5243
Maundy Thursday's Candles : 2567
A Mauve Fragrance in the Dark : 554, 3318

Mavericks do not become great leaders : 162
Max at Table : 5933
Maxims for Marriages : 4600
Maxine : 3924
May : 348
May 19__ : 1145
May Day, 1985 : 6340
May I Present : 5450
May Instructions : 3652
May Lightning Strike Me Dead : 1966
May Means Beautiful in Chinese : 6394
May Miracle : 6848
May Nineteenth : 5114
Mayakovsky Welcomed to America, 1925 :
    5302
Mayan Garden : 6737
Maybe Not : 3883
MAYBe YOu HAd To Be THERe : 3424
Maybe You Were Going to Slink Off into the
    Sunset : 4373
Mayflies : 3520
Mayo : 6180
El Mayordomo de Moctezuma : 2054
McPherson, Kansas : 1577
(MD) : 2454, 2716
Me aguardan celosías : 2538
The Me and God Poems: Bridge : 5922
Me and My Mother's Morphine : 5969
Me Reclutaron a Mi Hijo : 215
The Meadow : 3604
Meadow in a Can : 193
Meal : 4500
The Meal : 1284
The Mean Poems : 3915
Meaning : 2707, 4395
The Meaning of Meaning : 6812
The Meaning of Something : 3309
The Measure of Life : 5467
Measuring : 1089
Meat : 5131
Mechanism : 4656
Medea : 1178
Media, The New Sorceress : 6700
Median with Weeds : 2527
Medical Center : 2214
Medication : 3408
Medicine Hole : 4098
Medicine Men : 3159
Meditating on a Plum and a Banana : 7046
Meditation : 106, 3772, 5732
Meditation at Baw Beese : 6272
Meditation at the Kitchen Window : 6421
Meditation (I) : 376, 4979
Meditation (II) : 376, 4979
Meditation in an Uncut Cornfield, November :
    4218
Meditation on a Geode : 4218
Meditation on Blue : 4218
Meditation on Gödel's Second Incompleteness
    Theorem : 1128
Meditation on Matthew Arnold : 6591
Meditation on My Son's Sixth Birthday : 1104
Meditation on Separation : 7161
Meditation on Shovels : 4218

Meditation on Silence : 2349
Meditation on Snow Clouds Approaching the
    University from the North-West : 4218
Meditation on the *Meditations* : 737
A Meditation on Vermeer : 6094
Meditation on Virginia Woolf's Final Diary
    Entry, Written Three Weeks Before her
    Suicide : 3753
Méditation Pas Calme du Tout : 3678
Meditations: 4 : 2421
Meditations on Grass : 1346
Meditations on the Serene Blue Shirt : 723
Meditations on White (II) : 3237
The Medium : 470
Meeting a Falmar : 3369
Meeting Diefenbaker : 5543
Meeting Gogol's Akaky Akakiyevich on
    Kalinkin Bridge : 1106
Meeting the Man on the Road : 1036
Meeting the Occasion : 2249
Meeting You in Me : 1694
Mei It Kliuwen Fan de Jierren : 6657
Mein Holocaust — Gedicht : 839
Mellow Yellow : 862
Melodi Grand Prix : 6070
Melodia en lo Mio : 2358
Melodía Imposible para Seguir a un Caballo :
    1841
Melons : 3638
The Melons : 1808
Melusine : 158, 3750
Melville's Old Men : 734
Mêm' Rain : 1834
Memento Mori : 1854
Memento - Oval Office : 2250
Memo, to: Search Committee : 4061
Memoir : 1308
Memorial : 1042
Memorial Day : 4935
Memorial for MMmmm : 4763
Memories : 4351
Memories of Hot Chestnuts or Between Two
    Worlds : 5078
Memories of Kansas : 3434
Memories of Marie : 724, 4457
Memories of My Father : 3381
Memories of November : 1363, 5379
Memorizing Chaucer : 113
Memory : 88, 503, 877, 2515, 2823, 3147,
    5229, 5336, 6830, 7150
The Memory : 628, 5620
Memory Exercises : 5711
Memory Forgets : 1916
Memory Hat : 6936
The Memory of Suffering : 5570
Memory of Summer: The Rio Grande Valley :
    6322
The Memory of Water : 543, 922
Memory Unsettled : 2520
Memory XXIII : 77
Men and Women: Ten Phantasies for Robert
    Browning : 6914
Men at Sixty : 6799
The Men in the Lilacs : 3796

Men Minns Du Angusti : 2031
Men Oavbrutet : 2031
Men on Motorcycles : 1087
Men Who Carry Women Like Lanterns : 1816
Menage à Trois : 7060
Menage-a-Trois Beginning : 1547
Mending Day : 4241, 4718
Menet a Ködben : 3035
Meniscus : 5547
Mens : 110
Men's Middles : 1861
Menses : 4441
Mensonges : 3666
A Mental Finding : 5400
Mental Health : 184
Mental Illness Has No Manners : 2129
La Mentalité d'un Char : 1984
Menthol Eucalyptus Cough Drops : 1500
Mention : 3418
Merchant Marine : 6922
The Merciful Thirst : 1071, 6017
A Mere Freak, They Said : 2009
'Merica Void Again : 5690
Meridians : 184
Merlin : 6097
Merlin's Song : 6220
A Merl's Farewell : 6593
The Mermaid : 3268, 5674
Mermaid Days : 7112
Mermaids : 4265
The Merriest Country on Earth : 1982, 4609
Mert Fuldoklásunk Szenzáció : 2816
Merville Findley, 1988 : 2
Merwin's Inlet : 3011
Messa Road : 5296
Message : 284, 1363, 1959, 4449, 5379, 6377,
    6478
Message to the Goldfish : 5232
Messenger : 2714
Metabasis : 5773
Metamorphosis : 26, 860, 1254, 2917, 4843,
    5878, 6721
Metamorphosis and Marriage : 974
Metanoia : 400
The Metaphor of the Body in the Garden of the
    Mind : 4760
Metaphors : 2266
The Metaphysician's Weekend : 2316
Metho & Plonk : 3466
Metrics and Poetry : 5099, 5872
Metro Forecast I : 423
Mevwe Odjelabo : 4777
Mexican Vacation : 1208
Mexico, from the Four Last Letters : 5353
The Mezzo-Soprano : 212
Mi avvicino alla pagina in ombra : 965
Mi Difendo : 5914
Mi Poema : 209
Mi Venganza Personal : 639
Mi vida? : 639
Miami Mimesis : 2953
Miasma : 3362
Michael's Kisses : 6695
Michigan Basement I : 4958

Michoacan : 40
Mickey Mouse Was a Scorpio : 5621
Mid July : 6848
Mid-Life Crisis : 4565
Mid-Life Epitaph : 3977
Mid-Winter Snowfall in the Piazza Dante :
    7058
Middle-aged : 1577
Middle Class Poem : 1715
The Middle Passage : 3158
The Middle Years : 4179, 6839
Le Midi : 4150
Midlife : 2, 833
Midlife Marriage : 3845
Midnight : 3462
The Midnight Bus : 4426
The Midnight Carnival: Tunnel of Romance :
    6005
Midnight Gladness : 3736
Midnight, hour of the definite silence : 6294
Midnight, I-95, Outside Atlanta : 5242
Midnight, Listening to the Spotted Hound Seen
    Wandering Through the Kobashi's Farm :
    2705
The Midnight Shark : 588
Midnight Water Song : 72
Midsummer Common : 5350
Midsummer Day : 2445
Midtown Nightfall : 6442
Midwest Haiku : 572
Midwestern Villanelle : 433
Midwinter : 6593, 6755
Might Meet You Out There : 5398
Mighty Forms : 2854
Migraine Ghazal : 4411
Migration : 617, 1867, 3640, 5653
Migration of Painted Ladies Through San
    Diego County : 4109
Migrations : 748, 1867, 6025
Mikkleson's Barn : 4394
Milan vs. Muncie, 1954 : 5185
Mild Instructions for Travel : 1188
A Mile Up Through Chaparral : 3839
The Military Governor Contemplates the Statue
    of Adam M : 666, 3632
Milkers Broken Up : 2567
The Milkfish Gatherers : 1932
Milkflowers : 7066
Milky Way Bar : 4012
Milky Way Exposé from Gogebic Peak : 193
The Mill Gardens — Dominic Remembers :
    5974
Mill of the Fates : 165
Mille Lacs Ice : 2085
Millenarian Joys : 6408
Millionaire Records : 4260
Millpond : 3466
Mime : 106
The Mimic : 2425
Min Mormor : 5064
Mind Control : 4006
Mindennapi Történelem : 1363
Minding Our Business : 2595
Mine : 4111

Mine Settlement : 3000
Miners' Heaven : 1401
A Mingus Memory : 6408
Minimal Audio Plays : 3480
Mini- novela: Rosa y Sus Espinas : 4464
The Minister's Wife : 1974
The Ministry of G : 908
Minneapolis, for Joel O : 2454
Minnesota to Arizona : 6757
Minnie Birch and Her Son : 6159
Minns Du : 3792
The Minoan Distance : 6957
The Minor Poets: An Afterlife : 2961
Minor Traveler : 236
Mint Flowers : 6700
The Mint Harvest : 5314
Minton : 550
Minus 18 Street : 4208
A Miracle : 2857
Miracles : 1095, 7011
Mirage : 7093
Mirage of the Needles : 1071, 6017
Miravamos a Jovem Lagartixa : 2356, 4284
Miriam on Unrequited Love : 4097
A Mirror : 3120, 5250, 7138
Mirror for Time : 5594
Mirror Ghazal : 7106
The Mirror in Winter. Does the camellia bloom
    for me? : 3361, 3365
The Mirror in Winter. History is sad : 3361,
    3365
The Mirror in Winter. I am not like me : 3361,
    3365
The Mirror in Winter. The sun at zenith : 3361,
    3365
The Mirror Never Lies : 4997
Mirror No! : 1808, 2388
The Mirror of Matsuyama : 2705
Mirror Poem I. Self Portraits : 7032
Miscarriage of Her Child : 3925
Misconception of Richness : 235
Misconceptions of Childhood : 564
Mise en Scène : 2297
Misfit : 184, 5030
Misforunate am i, a ruffian : 3064, 4894
Miss A : 761, 3471
Miss America : 2407
Miss America Pageant : 3171
Miss Johnson Poems : 2927
Miss Josephine : 3612
Miss Pamela's Mercy : 1347
Miss Sunbeam : 2361
Miss You Blue : 5805
Missiles for Artesia : 6055
Missing : 2307
The Missing Link : 6659
Missing Person : 4211
Missing the Dead : 4531
Missing You from Illinois : 1842
The Mission : 3809
Missionary Thoughts : 3626
Misstro Mig Inte : 2031
The Mist : 2969
Mistaken : 4380

The Mistaking of Wealth for Plenty : 4762
Mister : 1529
Mister Drummond : 3139
Mister Moonlight : 1420
Misterioso : 1047
Mistress : 1900
Mistress Shivers : 5241
Misty : 1389
The Misunderstanding of Nature : 557
Mit Wechselndem Schlüssel : 1043
Mitosis : 5939
Mixed Blood : 5599
Mixed Feelings : 236
Mixed Marriages, Broken Homes : 1269
Mixed Media : 5676
Mixing Metaphors : 7039
Mixing the Patches : 4260
MJQ : 5970
Mobile, January 1989 : 2528
Mock Fandango : 1588
Mockingbird : 3558
Mockingbird Love : 4143
The Model : 7066
The Modern Masters : 3710
A Modern Midrash : 7173
The Modern Prometheus : 1084, 7092
Modesty : 187, 6971
Modifications to the Heart : 6794
Modified Machismo : 3260
Modified Radical : 6972
Modified Rapture : 2560
Modulations on a Theme: For Josephus Long :
    2656
Moguls: L.B. Mayer and My Father : 4892
Moisture : 429
Molasses : 3699
Molecular Lung : 6897
Molly : 5140
Mom : 5624
A Moment a Line Brecht and the Void : 7170
A Moment in Time : 6740
Moment of Conception : 6196
El Momento Que Más Amo : 2192
Moments : 2523
The Moment's Equation : 5541
Moments Part II with My Soul : 4658
Momma Mia : 719
Momma Was Dead : 1827
Mona Richards, R.F.D. : 894
Monday After School : 7085
Monday Wash in Winter : 2653
Monet's Palette: An Aubade : 5176
Monet's Water Lilies : 6123
Monet's Years at Giverny : 3784, 4787
Money Changing Hands : 5805
Moneylight : 6700
Monica : 2986
Monika and the Owl : 3038
Monkey Alone : 5887
Monkey Zero : 5466
The Monks at Large : 2752
Monologue at the Speed of Mercy : 5849
Monotone : 5573
A Monotone : 4559

Monsoon : 2223, 2340
Monster : 5063
Monsters of the Deep : 1075
Monstrum in Fronte, Monstrum in Animo :
    4695
Montages in Twilight : 1889, 4486, 5860
Montagne des Singes : 113
Montana Melody: A Farm Wife's Story : 5371
Monterey : 6437
Monterey Pine Cone, Fallen from an Aged Tree
    : 2302
Montgomery Clift: A Portrait : 5728
Month with the Word May : 2308
The Months : 514, 6464
The Months: Twelve Vignettes : 1229
Montpellier in December : 3400
Montreal : 4149
Montreal Pool Hall : 4890
Monument : 6233
Moolack Apocalypse : 471
The Moon : 3122, 3529, 4349, 5555
The Moon and the Man in the Hills : 4840
The Moon and the Tides Are Not in Simple
    Relation : 394
The Moon As Fat Lady : 3240
A Moon at Maximum Eclipse : 319
Moon Born from the Moon : 14, 4783
Moon in Adolescence : 2340
Moon in Cancer : 836
Moon / Mirror : 1294
Moon on Tower Clock : 6620
Moon Over Midland : 2890
Moon Pause : 6809
The Moon Rising : 2191, 2779
Moon-Viewing : 4545
Moon Without End : 5866
Moondance : 2021
Moonglow : 1334
Moonlight : 4663
Moonlight Marine : 716
Moon's Child : 5598
Moons Dancing in Stillness : 2244
Moonshining : 6072
Moonsnails : 6964
Morada de la Voz : 7137
Morada Donde la Luna Perdio Su Palidez :
    4493
Moral de Van Gogh : 4414
Moral Fabric : 661
The Moral of Snow : 4604
Morality Play : 2317
Morandi: An Example : 158, 3750
More : 3946, 5114
More and More : 615
More Anti-Matter : 4124
More Bones and Some Thank You's for
    Porridge and Soup : 1266
More Hair : 4909
More sensitive phonecalls : 5222
More Surprising Conversions : 6520
More Than Meets the Eye : 5241
The More Things Change : 3829
More unfamiliar than an accident : 435, 4180
More Walnuts, Late October : 5379

More With Than On : 1471
More Zen? : 5981
The Morehead Blue Jean Factory : 4772
Morgon : 5525
Moribund : 4565
Mörk Blåst : 5525
Morley Callaghan, 1903-1990 : 1634
Morning : 32, 100, 813, 814, 1884, 3040, 3166, 3497, 3769, 4832, 5503, 5525
Morning after Snow : 6345
Morning at Kamari : 2187
Morning Bath : 167
Morning Beside the Sea : 227
Morning Exercise : 4310, 7173
Morning in America : 3454
Morning in Salerno, IV : 4579, 5361
Morning in Suburbia : 813, 814, 5525
A Morning in the Museum : 4835
Morning of the Bears : 1171
The Morning Paper : 7049
Morning Parade : 4560
Morning Sea : 977, 1035
Morning Shadows : 5933
Morning Song for Two Poets : 5701
Morning Star : 2909, 6700
Morning Surprise : 201
The Morning the Doctor : 5618
Morning Trilogy : 2162
Morning Windsong : 6402
Morning, without Birds : 5291
The Morning's Story : 435, 1085, 4180
Moroccan Summer : 5280
Morocco : 4585
Morris Meltzer: *Bridgetown*, 1923, Berlin : 3829
Mortality : 2947
Mortars : 7060
Moskva Hotel : 1113
The Mosquito : 3638
Moss Hollow : 5034
Moss-hung trees : 305
The most acute of all : 666, 3549
The Most Hated Man in Mexico : 2495
Most Men : 166
Most of What I Have : 5617
The Most You Least Expect : 2736
Motel : 4376
Motel Room : 2656
Motels in the Night : 2087
Motet : 623
The Moth : 7035
Mother : 2823, 4644, 6523, 6810, 7044
The Mother : 777
Mother Always Knows Something New : 3464, 4323
Mother and Child : 1597
Mother and Daughter : 1577
Mother and Daughter Driving Home : 6613
Mother and I : 6241, 6330
Mother and Son : 1258, 6904
Mother Dreams : 6122
Mother Earth is a galactic reform school : 3576
A Mother in a Refugee Camp : 20
Mother Nature : 5390

Mother of the Bud : 1443, 3969, 7057
Mother: On Dying, Not Death : 6531
Mother on River Street : 6044
Mother Superior's Deathbed : 701
The Mother, the Woman : 4676, 5513
Mother Tongue : 1690, 2780, 3445, 5874
Mother Undressing : 6850
Mother Waken : 2089
The Mother Who Became a Tree : 4999
A Mother Who Sleeps : 2216, 4901
Motherhood a Thirty-Seven : 4745
The Mothers : 3028, 5995
Mother's Day : 5608
A Mother's Day : 265
Mother's Day — 1989 : 5481
A Mother's Odyssey : 2585
The Mother's Song : 3197
A Mother's Tale : 128
Mother's Visit No. 29 : 2644
Moths : 1062
Motion : 146
Motion in One Private Room of the Geriatric Wing : 3088
The Motionless Angel : 1352
Motionless, covering what's in back : 4973
Motivational Tape Pantoum : 606
Motorcycle Man : 4930
Motorcycle Ward : 4444
Motto : 2991
Mounds : 1006
Mountain in My Head : 4636
Mountain Morels : 6055
Mountain People : 1943, 2609, 3818
Mountains : 734
Mountains Behind Her : 2968
Mountie Knife : 2783
Mourning : 4804
The Mourning Dove : 1344
Mourning for Umbrellas : 6566
Mourning Song : 3745
The Mouse : 3844, 6421
The Mouse Hunters : 4669
Moutain Swim : 4099
A Mouth Full of Hair : 2600
The Mouth I Am Thirsty For : 3116
Mouth-Piece : 3948
The Mouth Refuses to Translate : 4296
A Movable Snack : 6655
The Move : 5679
Move Me : 2340
Movement : 3879
Movie : 961
The Movie at the Edge of Town : 6608
Movie Magic : 4223
Movies : 813, 814, 5293
Moving : 2365, 5964, 7055
Moving to Marshland : 5165
Möwenlied : 4481
Mowing after Dark : 6670
Mozart : 2802, 4855, 5347, 7109
Mozart & Cold Cuts : 6113
Mr. and Mrs. McClusky : 2039
Mr. Bear : 5766
Mr. Cogito and Pure Thought : 2104, 2800

Mr. Dobson & the After-Life of Carnations : 4118
Mr. Donut : 1704
Mr. Fuchs : 2877
Mr. History : 6925
Mr. Kent's Apartment : 6124
Mr. Lopez : 1209
Mr. Luna and History : 5353
Mr. Luna in the Afternoon : 5353
Mr. Norwood : 6465
Mr. Pittney Demonstrates How to Make a Food Hat : 4375
Mr. Poetry : 1636
Mr. Softee : 233
Mr. Watkins : 3128
Mrs. Adam : 4709
Mrs. Bach : 1495
Mrs. Black : 7001
Mrs. Jones : 6310
Mrs. Ledbetter Confesses Events Preceding Her Husband's Demise : 6051
Mrs. O : 7082
Mrs. O'Leary's Cat : 2490
Mrs. Oliphant : 3612
Mrs. Richards Plays a Starlight Waltz : 819
Mrs. Wadsworth's Letter to Emily Dickinson : 2237, 3547, 5379
Mt. Diablo : 4422
Mt. Everest : 5969
Mt. Lincoln : 3352
Mt. Tajumulco Climb : 59
Mtasipol : 2014, 5732
Much Later : 5485
Mud : 2130
Mud Bath : 3400
The Mud Boat : 2395
Mud Dancing : 5803
Mudbones : 3676
Muddy Waters & The Chicago Blues : 1734
Mugged : 841
Mujer : 494
Mujer Inconveniente : 4612
Mujer Negra : 4473
Las Mujeres of Orange Park Acres Packing House : 6407
Mulberry Leaves for a Naked Tree : 2747, 3120, 5367
Mulier Cantat : 2250
Multi-Colored Mountains : 3769, 4832, 5796
The Multiplication of Doves : 5544
The Mummers : 1553
Munchion : 6900
Munda the Italian Witch, Rome, New York : 2095
Mural : 2341
Murder : 1422
Murder at the Library : 990
The Murdered Idealist : 1647
The Murderer and His Art : 5297
Muriel Rukeyser : 7001
Murió al Almancer : 2191
Murmurs : 6365
Muscle and Prayer : 1016
Muse Away : 1795

The Muse Is Angry : 7
The Muse Is Gone : 7
The Muse Is Silent : 7
The Muse Is Sullen : 7
Muse to the Sculptor : 4010
Musée Rodin : 4739
The Muses : 1142
The Muses of Rooms : 5541
The Museum, Cairo : 4966
Museum of the Moving Image : 850
Museum Street : 2104, 5937, 6573
Mushroom Woman : 6096
Mushrooms : 1427
Music : 393, 3485, 5691, 6977
Music at Dawn : 908
The Music at Home : 6058
Music Box : 368
Music from Bavaria : 1603
Music in the Night : 1775
Music Lesson : 6206
The Music Lesson : 3521
Music Lesson II : 6206
The Music Lover : 3912
Music My Grandfather Gave Me : 4573
The Music of Tears : 3690
Music: Pink & Blue I 1919 : 3887
Musical Moments : 18
Musical Notes : 2487
The Musician Talks About 'Process' : 1659
Musicians : 6922
Musings in a Hospital Room : 2277
The Musk of Night Flowers: Sheba : 4646
Muted : 5976
The Mutual Exclusion of Binaries : 3202
My $15 Lily : 6700
My Amaryllis : 1572
My Amazement : 3994
My Aunt Gives Me a Clarinet Lesson : 1600
My Bird Book : 1202
My Black Socks : 6298
My Brother Is Watching the Stars : 6209
My Business Partner : 5238
My Cadillac Coffin : 6460
My Cherry Boy : 4708
My Children Going : 6242
My Cousin Told Me This : 359
My Cousin's Children : 1914
My Cousin's Scar : 6160
My Daddy Wrote Rock 'n' Roll : 328
My Daughter Calls from a Halfway House in Houston : 5757
My Daughter Swimming : 4557
My Daughters : 271
My Daughter's Sleeping Chest : 4675
My Dear Albertine : 6232
My Doomsday Sampler : 4845
My eyes close the way the Earth drifts off : 4973
My Family Has Arshile Gorky for Dinner : 1951
My Family Quilt : 4347
My Father : 841
My Father After Work : 2268
My Father at 75 : 2656

My father had never eaten a banana : 1812
My Father-in-Law's Contract : 2669
My Father in the Pacific, 1945 : 5877
My Father Spoke with Swans : 2172
My Father Steps Clear Into the Future : 838
My Father Teaches Me to Fly : 600
My Father the Mouse : 5379
My father was an inspector of weights and
    measures : 2826
My Father Writing Joe Hamrah in a Blackout :
    4813
My Father's Angel : 3796
My Father's Coat : 3523, 5975
My Father's Corpse : 2981
My Father's Death : 3760
My Father's Gift : 4564
My Father's Hands and Mine : 6608
My Father's House : 4701
My Father's Kierkegaard : 6186
My Father's Laughter : 4146
My Father's Loveletters : 3466
My Father's Pornography : 7010
My Father's Promise : 216
My Father's Wing-Tip : 5609
My Father's Wisdom : 3171
My Feathered Friend : 2909
My fist laid out : 4973
My Foot Is On My Tongue : 156
My Girl : 2949
My Godless Love : 4198
My Grandfather's Cronies : 4751
My Grandfather's Last Summer : 6983
My Grandmother : 813, 814, 5064
My Grandmother Started Dying : 406
My Grandmother's Ass : 4011
My Grandmother's Heart : 564
My Grandmother's Patron Saint : 3682, 4874
My Gratitude : 1734
My Hair Talks : 710
My Head : 4149
My Heart : 230
My High Heels : 5039
My Howl : 691
My Husband, Sergeant Davies, All on Sundays
    : 6645
My Imaginary Sister Gets Married : 3082
My James Dean Poster : 4611
My Last Executive : 787
My Left Finger : 3976
My Life, I Lose You : 483
My Lord, We Plead Our Bellies : 3108
My Lord's Little Volta : 89
My Love Is Lost : 4331
My Love without a Home : 14, 4029
My Mama Done Told Me : 2974
My Mom : 820
My Mother Advertises for a Boarder : 5204
My Mother and I debating Abortion Till Well
    Past Midnight : 3690
My Mother Combs My Hair : 1597
My mother dancing in the kitchen : 2812
My Mother Dreams: If Her Husband Dies, Who
    Will Cut the Lawn? : 1704
My Mother Hints at Rape over the Aperitif :
    4585
My Mother Phoned Tonight : 3027
My Mother Wore Fake Pearl Earrings : 5379
My Mother's Chair, 1956 : 4146
My Mother's Drippings : 1426
My mother's last request is for an other : 5068
My Mother's Mouth : 1890
My Mother's Visit : 3780
My Mother's War Story : 5558
My Myth : 6854
My Name : 2513
My Name One Morning : 3973
My Neighbor, the Distinguished Count : 1287
My Old Dog Died in My Arms : 3690
My Own Sister : 4207
My Parabolic Muse : 2632
My Parents' Wedding : 5962
My Poetry Teacher Sells Used Cars : 1307
My Precious Pearl : 311
My Room : 854, 4627
My Secret Identity Is : 5894
My Sister's Hair : 1914
My Sister's Hair, the Sequel : 1914
My Son : 161, 6098
My Son Thinks : 2001
My Son's Junk Yard : 3674
My soul return'd to me, and answer'd : 4763
My Story : 2398
My Strongest Man : 7183
My Stuffed Bunny : 3192
My Table : 5866
My Teacher, Dying : 6816
My telling is numb, the listeners are people I've
    invented : 1148
My Things : 3120, 4534, 5250
My Third Grade Teacher, Fourth Grade, Fifth :
    5299
My Time's Running Out : 491, 3476, 4811
My Tribe : 532, 5579
My Turn : 841, 4111
My Uncle : 1720
My Uncle's Chair : 2729
My Walk with Pete : 4789
My White Parrots : 2233, 3197, 6806
My Wife Believes in Reincarnation : 1204
My wife says : 4940
My Wish for You Both : 5738
My Words : 1543
My Year of Death : 2580
My Young People : 2174
Mykonos : 1526, 7131
Myra : 7001
Myrtle Tree : 6046
Mysterious : 4258
A Mysterious Animal Tiger : 3474
Mysterious Shoes : 1307
The Mysterious Strangers : 5908
Mystery : 2630
The Mystery of Picasso : 4578
Mystery Planet Job : 4199
The Mystical Connections : 4144
The Mystified Staring Babies : 1325
Myth : 5521, 7051
Myth of First Lovers : 3910

The Myth of the Primal Horde : 5984
Mythology : 6039
Myths Before Breakfast : 343
n + 40, Putting Off Judgement : 4261
NC17-Rated Stuff : 6514
'N' Street Mobile : 1187
Nach Vielen Jahren : 284
Nachtmusik : 4165
Nacimiento II : 6396
La Nada : 1183
Nada or the Golden Egg of Poetry : 2638
Nadie : 5484
Naditas : 6268
Nagame : 5594
The Nail : 6794
Nailbar : 3845
Naked Moon / Luna Desnuda : 2808
The Naked Spiral : 1265
The Nakedness of the Fathers : 4835
Näkergalen i Badelunda : 6500
A Name : 1295
The Name : 1090
A Name for Earth : 158, 3750
The Name of God : 433
Nameless : 5989
Nameless Poem : 7112
Names and Sorrows : 2435
Names to Faces : 4039
Naming the Snow : 1245
Naming the Twins : 3006
Naomi, Nearly Two : 3619
The Nap : 6084
Napi : 4991
Naples, Florida, March 5, 1990 : 1159
När Jag Var Barn Gick Jag På Ängen : 5064
När Jag Var Barn Min Morfar : 5064
När Jag Var Barn / Tanterna : 5064
NarcisoLASER : 124
Narcisskull : 5573
Narcissus : 673, 1384, 4538, 7004
Narcissus in the Maritime Provinces : 5960
A Narcoleptic in Los Angeles : 623
Narcotic Properties : 4838
Nargis' Toilette : 1597
Narration d'Equilibre 5-America Domino : 43,
    1408
Narrative : 298, 1097, 6820
A Narrow Alley : 2978, 3141
Narrow Street, Barcelona : 6961
Das Nasobem : 4481
Nathaniel Hawthorne and Sophia : 6238
The National Endowment for the Farts : 841
National Enquirer Writer Hospitalized with
    Nervous Breakdown After Writing His
    Thousandth Story : 6715
Native Grace : 1244
Native Sons : 4363
Native Willow : 6813
A Native Wounded While Asleep : 4744
Natives of Rock : 6846
The Natural Angle of Repose : 5850
Natural Disaster : 1118
Natural History : 63
Natural Selection : 3462, 5752

Natural Things : 3008
Naturaleza : 5882
Nature : 445
Nature Morte : 3256, 5379
The Nature of Accidents : 3612
Nature Walk : 1975
Nature's Rule : 4635, 4802
Navajo Land : 3986
Nazi Cross on an American Tunnel : 4351
NC17-Rated Stuff : 6514
Near and Far : 2499, 2591
Near Arivaca, Arizona : 1230
Near Cashiers : 4264
Near Damascus : 1553
Near Folsom, New Mexico : 1058
Near La Paz : 5026
Near Poppit Sands, Wales : 3644
Near Shrine B on an August Day : 514, 6464
Near-Sighted : 5266, 5615
Near the Paulite Church, Pécs, Hungary : 5379
Near the Sundial : 1854
Near Union Square : 5083
Nebraska : 2447, 4253
Nebraska West of Kearney : 3561
Necessity : 6858
The Necessity of an Inner Nativity : 1345
A Necklace of Children : 4094
Necromancy: The Last Days of Brian Jones,
    1968 : 7010
Necrophila : 3602
Necropolis : 5310
Necropsy : 4407
Need : 6853
The Need for Birds : 6292
Needs : 1593, 3986
The Negative : 229, 4439
Negative of You : 1324
Negociando : 1808
Negotiations : 1808
Neighborhood : 3032
Neighbors : 747, 1880
The Neighbor's Child : 2948
The Neighbours Are Tossing a Salad : 7112
Neither Inviting Nor Repelling : 4430
Nej, Tätt Skall Det Vara : 2031
Nel Suo Gelo : 1031
Nella Storia : 1473
Nem Járok Már : 4811
Nemesis : 588, 3203
The Neon Cross : 37
Neonew : 4975
Neruda in Ceylon, 1929 : 5960
Nerves of Steel, or The Poet's Prayer : 125,
    5455
Nessuno : 6848
Nesting : 1882
The Net : 4975
The Net Swells with That Heavy Fruit : 3351
Net Words : 1017
Nether John and John Harbinger : 2967
Nettle : 1155
Neu-ro'sis, N., Pl. -ses : 7002
Neuroanatomy : 3463
Never go to bed : 184

Never Listening : 2438
Never to Forget : 4941
New : 813, 814, 5525
New Alphabet : 1638, 2339
The New Bed : 6840
The New Bicentennial Stamps, 1975 : 5676
The New Gray Church : 5863
New Headstones at the Shelby Springs Confed-
    erate Cemetery : 2981
New Jersey Notes : 4144
New Job : 6391
New Landscape : 2466
A New Lid : 6804
The New Math : 130
The New Models : 7060
The New Money : 1089
New Moon : 3735, 4520
The New Notebook : 333, 4105
New Poem for a Late Spring : 1894
A New Poet : 4921
New Remembered Places I : 2454, 6324
New Remembered Places II : 2454, 6324
New Season : 996
The New Sentience : 1454
New Sneakers : 3795
The New South : 6796
The New Stove : 4472
New Uncle : 2144
New Year : 4654
A New Year in Vermont : 2560
New Year's : 6528, 6884
New Year's Day, 1990 : 2890
New Year's Eve : 1300, 2454, 6563
New Year's Eve, 1989 : 6128
New Year's Eve, New Orleans, 11:55 p.m. :
    3909
New York City : 3269
New York Sits There : 5580
New York's Bullfighter Gums : 1293
The Newer Testament : 2595
Newfoundland : 4966
Newlywed Game : 3862
News : 1540, 1607, 4141
The News : 4556, 5402
The News (A Manifesto) : 4980
News Flash from the Fashion Magazines : 1352
News from a Board : 6512
The News from Mars : 401
News from the North : 1393
News From Yale : 4363
News Item : 5152
News of a Death : 849
Newsreel : 2815
Newton's Ghost Considers the Bicyclist
    Descending : 3683
The Next Day : 6046
The Next Room : 1553
The Next Stop Stopping : 5485
The Next Time I Crossed the Line into Okla-
    homa : 7056
The Next War : 5302
Next Year : 6361
Niagara Falls from the Air : 6070
Niagara Shines : 4462

Nibblets and Snippets : 6736
Nicholas : 4884
Nicolette : 3780
Niebla Encantada : 494
Nieves del Aconcagua — La Muerte — : 7189
Nigger Island : 1966
Night : 3274, 5235, 5413, 5573, 6006
The Night : 3274, 5235
Night Birds : 1625, 7076
Night Blooming Cereus : 7146
Night Calamities : 2532, 2922, 7106
Night City : 5945
The Night Everything Waits for Us : 6148
Night-Fall in Cachipe : 1086
Night Field : 4218
Night Fires : 5760
Night Fishing for Catfish : 2148
Night Fishing in the Sound : 6964
Night Flight : 5628
Night Flight from England : 2828
Night Gallery : 1761
Night Game : 1210, 5883
Night Hunting : 2682
The Night I Met Little Floyd : 7056
Night in a Greek Village : 280
Night in Ia Drang Valley : 6060
A Night in Paris : 5589
'Night in the Tropics' (1858-59?) : 6779
Night inside me, night out there : 2197, 6273
Night Janitor, McMahon Oil : 1429
A Night Journey in Germany : 1363, 5379,
    6380
Night Lake : 6579
Night Lines : 3242, 4990, 6220
Night Music : 4410
The Night of Ekhnaton : 3547, 4586, 5379
The Night of His Life : 772
A Night of Lovers : 2779
Night of Repercussions : 2904
Night of Spoons : 3780
Night of the Embersons : 4111
Night on Heart Lake : 4623
Night on the Interstate : 6378
Night Poem : 3467
Night Reply : 4972
Night Rider : 6030
Night Said : 7059
Night Sail to Mallorca : 1808
Night Shift : 2324, 5166
Night-Shift : 3509
Night Shift at Goldenbell Chicken : 4719
Night Song : 1974
Night Subway : 5083
Night Sweats : 2740
Night Swim : 7019
Night Swimming : 3075
Night Swimming at Las Columnas After the
    Drive from Ronda : 3220
Night Terror : 2702
The Night the V-2's Hit London : 1444
Night: Theme and Variations : 360, 435, 3821
Night Tide : 6172
Night Train : 5184
Night Travel : 6166, 6436

Night Vision : 6103
The Night Watchman of Pont-au-Change :
    1536, 2023
The Night You Were Born : 6294
Nightfall : 3473, 6830, 7128
Nightfall Near Louisville : 7060
Nightfishing : 3413
The Nightingale in Badelunda : 6500, 6986
Nightmare : 435, 2369, 6973
The Nightmare : 5962
Nightmare: Afterwards : 5114
Nightmare Comfort : 12
Nightmare Elvis : 3720
Nightmares : 1746
Nightmares and Prayers of Rescue : 6938
Nights, Lately, I've Been Going To : 5379
Nights Like These : 4076
Nights on the Brazos : 4179
The Night's One Drifting Petal : 5650
Nightshift : 2719, 6249
Nightwatches Have Glow in the Dark Hands :
    3197
Nihil Est in Intellectu : 532, 5579
Nine Days at Anchor : 4596
The Nine Decades : 2446
Nine Hundred Miles : 4251
Nine Lives : 4310
Nine of Swords : 4873
Ninel : 827, 3422, 5275
Nineteen Poems : 1655
The Nineties : 2577
The Nineties Again : 4671
Ningunos : 5435
El Nino II : 6471
Niobe : 1398, 3197, 6806
No : 99, 385
No Applause : 5365
No Bird : 1300, 2454
No Bolt from the Blue : 3087
The NO Collage : 3110
No Credit : 7126
No Drake Is Ever on the Make : 4159
No Expectations : 2678
No Fingertips : 2164
No Flowers on Magnolia Street : 3009
No Friends of the Heart : 1768
No God But God : 2623
No Grand Answers : 2951
No Honey in This House : 5862
No Idle Boast : 3913
No, It Has to Fit Tightly : 813, 814, 2031
No Love : 2344
No Love in This Poem : 1291
No, Love Is Not Dead : 1536, 3533
No Man's Land : 92
No More : 5995, 6650
No More Back of the Bus : 2169
No More Cafe : 3049
No More Room : 6060
No Mourning : 463, 3065
No Names : 4426
No necesita legitimarnos la épica : 3854
No Need to Rush Into Print : 1137
No, No, and No : 329, 4413, 7057

No Not, Say the Words, As If : 1607
No One Listens to Poetry : 2643
No One Wants to Be the Witch : 836
No One Will Report You : 2896
No Particular Day : 6221
No Pilikia, or, Piece of Cake : 1483
No Problem : 5296
No Right to Sing the Blues : 6261
No Scripture, Two Hymns : 3153
No See 'Ums : 1954
No Sostener Nada Jamás : 1028
No Strangers : 2722
No Subject But a Matter 1 : 437
No Subject But a Matter 2 : 437
No Tengas Nunca un Hijo : 4492
No This Isn't the Time for Poetry : 5455, 6611
No Time Beyond : 3939
No Time to Go In : 3266
No tongue has soiled it : 5580
No Trace of Blood : 99, 1883
No Traveler Returns : 4681, 5572
No Turkeys Allowed : 1718
No Usual Weather to Report : 3056
No, we can not see the wind : 3350
No Word for Now — Dreamscape : 949
Nobel Physicist Creates Theory from Geologist
    Son's Data : 3396
The Noble Corpse : 5471
Noche : 5235
La Noche : 5235
Noches de Andrenalina : 4794
Nocturne : 786, 1025, 1838, 1914, 2425, 2830,
    2832, 4019, 5427, 5967
Nocturne Galant : 3833
Nocturne in an Oriental Garden : 374
Nocturne: Insomnia : 4891
Nocturne, Late Spring : 800
Nocturne (No Parking) : 2830
Noel : 4991
Nogales, 1958 : 5353
The Noise : 1360
Noises in the House : 1859
The Noises of My Country : 720, 3197, 6806
Noli Me Tangere : 1028
The Nomad : 1129
Nomads : 6789
Nomenclature : 2458, 4305
Nommo : 264, 5873
Non Chiamarmi Regina Ulisse : 629
Non-Fiction : 6168
A Non-Personal Account : 3121, 4024, 5250
The Noncomformist's Memorial : 2967
Nonresistance or, Love Mennonite Style : 714
The Noonan Variations : 675
Nor Am I Who I Was Then : 2968
Normal Life : 2225
Normandie : 4483
North : 2453
North by the Line : 5371
North Face : 5773
North of Night : 3704
North of the Airbase, at Home : 5358
North Pownal: Pulling in the Moon : 2606
The North Road : 1548

North to Hawaii : 5142
Northampton Poem : 4318
The Northeast Field : 2705
Northern Lights : 7052
Northwest Flight #1173 : 2120
Northwesterly : 184
Nos Dar : 678
Nose? : 3649
Nosebleed, Gold Digger, KGB, Henry James, Handshake : 3388
Nostalgia : 893, 1269, 3108, 3630, 5372
Nostrum : 3900
Not a Boy : 2355
Not a Poet : 3084
Not a Window : 3274, 5235
Not As a Stone But Dancing : 5627
Not by Bread Alone : 1134
Not Catching Whitefish : 2583
Not Death : 707
Not Even Mythology : 3287, 5361
Not for Me : 4050
Not Jasper Johns : 6219
Not Joining the Wars : 445
Not Just Anywhere : 5332
Not Long Before April : 4767, 6237
Not Marble Nor the Gilded Monuments : 6101
Not Much Blows Back : 6519
Not Not : 7089
Not One Notched Hour : 3346
Not one's own difficult hollowed : 924, 6632
Not only can you be visionary after you're dead : 5580
Not Quite : 3829
Not Quite There : 3603
Not Responsible : 1970
Not Satisfied : 2055
Not Something in a Magazine : 5760
Not Speaking : 7055
Not Standing Still : 2465
Not Surprised : 3083
Not That Distance : 4972
Not That It Could Be Finished : 3656
Not the Dance : 1533
Not the Occult : 1715
Not Thinking About Gardenias : 420
Not Unlike : 2619, 5389
Not Us! : 2473, 3569
Not Waving : 6086
Not Waving But Drowning : 5988
Not What We Used to Be : 5437
Not with prayers to the dead : 5073
Notas de Viaje : 3642
The Note : 1689
A Note Left on Finding Two People Asleep : 6464
A Note on the Suspension of Disbelief : 3650
Note to Tomaz Salamun While Flying Through a Thunderstorm en Route to a Writers' Conference : 833
Notebooks 1956-78 : 1202, 1223
The Notebooks of Norman Rockwell : 5847
The Notebooks of Pablo Picasso : 5847
Notes for a Flight Over Cawston Bench : 5329
Notes for a Mural : 1089

Notes for a visit : 3226
Notes for a Writing Instructor : 6633
Notes for an Epigram : 697
Notes for Nobody : 2567
Notes from a Conversation : 3656
Notes from a Greek Mother : 200
Notes From the (Poet's) Nightmare English Class : 4393
Notes from the Tower : 6062
Notes from the V.A. : 6985
Notes on a Dying Town : 5177
Notes on Leavetaking : 7102
Notes on Reading : 435, 1085, 4180
Notes on the Creation : 2405
Notes on 'The Nature of Poetry' : 1554
Notes to an Epileptic : 1792
Notes Toward a Book of Photoglyphs : 3405
Notes Toward Saint Joan : 6770
Nothing : 2405
Nothing Can Be Rushed : 2677
A Nothing Generation : 2651
Nothing Happened : 2355
Nothing Is Ever Mutual : 85
Nothing Lasts : 4276
Nothing Stamps Its Feet : 3332
Nothing substance utters : 847
Nothing to Do in Town : 6605
Nothing to Eat : 840, 3289
Nothing was more delicious or remote : 4247
Notion of Color in Absence of Skin : 5681, 6006
Notre Dame de Paris : 2346
Notre Dame des Tourists : 2457
Notre Pierrot Parlant : 3808
The Novel : 6167
Novelists : 6922
November : 206, 807, 813, 814, 2189, 2961, 6987
November 24, 1963 : 3803
November and December : 6957
November: Beaver Moon : 6183
November Day, Fire Island : 3620
November Morning: Augsburg : 1604
November on Her Way : 2207
November Riffs : 5379
November Salmon Run : 901
November Sea : 813, 814, 5708
November Snow, Bristol, Virginia : 919
November: Sparing the Old Apples : 5122
November, Stay Calm : 2815
November Vespers : 5370
Novena for Grace Kelly : 1143
La Novia de Hitler : 1832
Now : 841, 1317, 1384, 2341, 3032
Now About Those : 66, 6456
Now and Then : 727, 6775
Now and Then We Get Up : 206, 813, 814
Now I Know : 1300, 2454
Now in Your Hand : 528
Now My Huge Stomach : 4753
Now Rejoice! : 2595
Now That Dad Is Gone : 2104
Now That I Am Never Alone : 2164
Now That It's June : 4

Now the Heroine Weakens and Speaks : 3946
Now Then : 5146
Now What? : 1000
Now Where? : 3327
Nowhere People : 6250
The Nowhere Water : 5512
Nuclear Winter and Bicycle Dust : 2530
Nuda : 3171, 5065
Nude : 4537, 4660, 4873, 6491
The Number 38 Geary Bus : 3823
Nuns at Lunch on the Bus : 6207
The Nuremberg Executions : 5593
A Nurse Addresses Her Patron : 3442
Nursing Home Epiphany : 3149
Nurturer-Torturer : 2871
Nutrition : 3734
Ny : 5525
O : 492
O 66 : 3707
O-Bon : 2279
O fame, you have passed us by like the rain,
    vanished : 2422, 3552, 6552
O Hero : 5828
O Huck Finn Adonis : 5637
O Melena! : 5879
O My Soul : 2714
O praying mantis : 3430
O Quince : 5424
O.R. 1964 : 2789
Oakley, Kansas : 1577
Oatmeal Shirt : 4762
Oban, Scotland, and the Islands : 5821
Obemannade Telefonlurar : 2418
Obituary : 3646
Object Lesson : 5080
Objects : 4640
Oblivion : 476, 2764
The Oboist : 433
The Obscene Phone Call : 5015
Observation in a War Zone : 1835
Observations and Experiments : 1574
Observations and Experiments in Natural
    History : 1574
Observed : 3032
Obsession : 4255, 4654, 5622
Obsessions : 3187
Obvious Things : 6174
Occasional Poem : 5730
Occupational Hazard : 5296
Occupational Hazards : 5813
Ocean : 3115
The Ocean All Day, All Night : 5929
The Ocean Calls : 6216
The Ocean from the Cliffs at Sopelana : 1240
Oceanic Kisses : 2875
Ochre and Red on Red : 4898
October : 2624, 5567, 5976
October 19, 1987, Dear Kate : 6192
October 1989 : 691
October Again : 5476
October at Coole Park and Ballylee : 4152
October Chill : 478
October Clear : 2676
October crumbles in my hand : 6303

October Frost : 5644
October: Harvest and Seeding : 4080
October in Glimpses : 5114
October Nocturne : 2305
October: November : 2566
October Snow : 1452
October's Judgment : 1071, 6017
Octopus : 5262
Odd Man Out : 3640
An Odd Tiger : 6593, 6963
Odds and Ends : 6829
Ode for the Sleepless : 6508
Ode on Sex : 5704
Ode to a Drunk Fly : 23
Ode to a Vermilion Flycatcher Seen in February
    in Redmond, Washington : 885
Ode to Being a Poetry Editor : 6804
Ode to Berryman : 6118
Ode to Broth of Conger : 4641, 6268
Ode to Languor : 3388
Ode to Prized Koi and Baby Finches : 1101
Ode to Salvador Dali : 405, 2191
Ode to Speech : 6704
Ode to the American Cucumber : 6706
Ode to the Chair : 3833
Ode to the Fox : 3441
Ode to the Independent Claus : 6711
Ode to the Rebellion : 5230
Ode to the Spine : 6706
An Ode to You : 5632
Odie's Story : 1429
Odin Marz : 395
L'Odore di Resina e C'era : 837
Odysseus : 1690, 3445, 5874
Odysseus on the Côte d'Azur : 1585
The Odyssey: An Epic for Minimalists : 298
The Odyssey: Revised, Standard : 4296
Oedipus Complex : 4939, 5098
Oedipus the King : 1521
Of a Sudden : 1159
Of Africa : 5302
Of Death by Drowning : 6763
Of Demeter's Daughter : 4308
Of Diamonds : 7066
Of Dreams and Dreaming : 236
Of Education: From Ely, Minnesota, Out and
    Back : 4700
Of Her Sleeping : 3881
Of Light and Silence : 669
Of Linnets and Dull Time : 236
Of Mere Being in Autumn : 2351
Of Mother and Father : 3503
Of Night-Tails and Nodding : 5686
The of of explanation : 1202
Of Raccoons & Chipmunks : 5026
Of Scatological Interest : 2887
Of Sound Mind : 4377
Of the Circle : 5224
Of the Land of Culture : 566
Of Visions : 3705, 7057
Of What Remains : 6474
Of You and the Scotch : 1534
Of Your Love : 1683
Off Montauk : 5508

Off Watch : 1431
Offended Moon : 1941, 5995
The Offering : 4424
The Offerings : 1286
Ofumeyi : 468, 6660
Ögonblicket : 5708
Oh Bawd : 314
Oh, By the Way : 4747
Oh Dear : 813, 814, 2031
Oh Holy Night, Chicago : 6752
Oh, Is It Irretrievable or Not? : 170, 4216
Oh, it was a cold day : 67, 2778
Oh summer summer : 5436, 5585
Oh, You and Me : 2500, 3769, 4832
Ohana : 6132
Ohio : 2455, 5376
Ohio Nocturne : 3556
Oil Spill : 5756
Ojibwa Lament : 6858
El Ojo del Camello : 3057
O'Keeffe : 4954
O'Keeffe and Stieglitz : 1635
O'Keeffe Left to Herself : 445
The Ol' Cowboy Saloon : 1984, 6188
Old : 1332
Old and Young : 1525
Old Ausable River in November : 4218
The Old Chief and the Census : 20
The Old Country : 6816
Old crumbling wall : 91
The Old Days : 1332
Old Dog : 1658
Old Eight-by-Ten Glossy : 485
Old Enough to Know : 695
Old Folks Home : 645, 813, 814
The Old Fortress : 292, 3341, 5864
Old Gentleman Friends Recalled : 6381
Old Holy Men : 3296
The Old Hometown : 6654
Old House : 3105
An Old Indian's Language : 4392
Old Ladies Banking : 490
Old Lady Mendoza : 5386
The Old Liberators : 2751
Old Man at the Municipal Pool : 675
Old Man Dead in a Room : 841
Old Man in an Armchair : 4600
Old Man in Waiting Room : 7060
Old Mazart! : 2595
Old Men Pitching Horseshoes : 3320
The Old Miners' Road : 3880
Old Mister Moonlight : 1332
Old Mother Death : 6946
Old Mountain : 1108, 1252, 3021
Old Mystic Bridge, Chelsea, 1936 : 5822
The Old Neighbors : 5083
The Old Ones — a Journey : 542
The Old Order : 2953
Old Photos: 2 : 1845
The Old Portraits of the Indians : 669
An Old Riddle : 783
Old Shoes : 5036, 6240
An Old Steel Engraving : 616
Old Stories : 2210

The Old Tea Room Ladies : 5370
Old Woman : 722, 3694
The Old Woman : 6155
Old Woman, Eskimo : 3038
An Old Woman Watering Her Plants with Milk : 5519
Old Woman with 25 Cats : 6879
Old Women Rehearse the End of Time : 6381
Old Words : 1332
The Old World : 5894
Olde Towne East, Columbus : 3138
The oldest shout is orange : 4973
The Oldish Man in the White Seersucker Suit : 4144
Olé, Manuel Báez 'Litri', Olé! : 480
Olga : 3513
The Olive Branch : 2289
Omega : 2191, 5898, 6889
Omens : 2329
Omeros : 6701
Omertà : 276
The Omniscient Dance : 6990
On a Bus in Manhattan : 5224
On a Dark Night : 1487
On a Given Day : 2006
On a Glass Icon : 333, 4105
On a Gray Street : 1103
On a Japanese Beach : 1018, 2289
On a Line by Whitman : 2868
On a Mochica Ceramic, ca. 1200 A.D. : 4585
On a Morning of Birds Singing : 3559
On a Once Deserted Beach : 6762
On a Painting by David Hockney : 328
On a Painting Cut with a Knife : 6391
On a Picture of Self with Hoe, Cultivating Plum Blossoms in Moonlight : 5880, 7068
On a Private Golgotha : 491, 3035, 3476
On a Road : 3412
On a Winter's Night : 1618
On an Urban Battlefield : 6120
On Audubon's *Passenger Pigeon* : 2988
On Being a Poet (Arcane Minnesota Twin) in October 1987 : 3848
On Being Asked If a Friend Is Happy in Her Marriage : 5041
On Being Introspective : 2851
On Being Told I Should Have a Dog : 3240
On Blankness, I : 3071, 6708
On Blankness, II : 3071, 6708
On Blankness, III : 3071, 6708
On Blueberry Hill : 6508
On Board Their Boat *Tigress* : 3022
On Broadcastinbg : 3032
On Building a Cradle for My Grandson, Chad Walsh Hamblin : 6734
On Christina in Her Pink Housedress : 3479
On Contemplating My Wife's Bed : 588
On Dante, Scorpions, Love, the Grazing Light : 2860
On Display : 1788
On Driving Into Town : 843
On Earth As It Is in This Dream : 5640
On Edge : 3098, 4316
On Election Day Morning : 2791

On Finding Your Letter in My Notebook : 2778
On First Hearing Ezra Pound at St. Elizabeth's
    Hospital : 6729
On Forgetting to Cry : 1227
On Headaches : 1419, 5200
On Hearing About Your Fall : 5424
On Hearing Diane Wakoski Read at California
    State University, San Bernardino : 5352
On Hearing of the Death of My Father : 2221
On Hearing Our Plans for Homesteading My
    Grandmother Said, 'It Will Ruin Your
    Hands' : 2442
On Hearing the News That Hitler Was Dead :
    354
On Hearing the Pretty Grim News : 5496
On her way out this morning, she left : 666,
    3979
On High : 4457
On His Cooking : 6133
On How I Did Not Give Aunt Juni the Right
    Thing Before She Died : 3206
On Humor : 3071, 6708
On Ikkyu Sojun Zenji (1394-1481) : 6448
On Killing a Tax Collector : 4750, 4752
On Knowing How Close to Oscar Wilde I
    Came, or: My Day as a Prospective Juror :
    6531
On Larkin : 4842
On Learning I'm to Be a Father Again : 769
On Learning of the Suspension of the Caboose :
    1065
On Lithium : 3723
On Looking at a Yellow Wagon : 1090
On Looking at Photographs of My
    Grandmother's Old Boyfriends : 4373
On Love, Stars, Poetry, and the March Wind :
    3661
On Making Love After Having Made Love :
    3753
On Margins : 2493
On My Eightieth Nightmare : 3453
On My Own : 5754
On My Return from Dhaka (Bangladesh-III) :
    99, 1883
On One with Magazine Fame : 5109
On Origins : 2536
On Perfection : 2120
On Postmodern Buildings : 6514
On Professing Henry James to an Empty Seat :
    89
On Quaking Bog : 443
On Quantitative Analysis : 3032
On Reading an X-ray : 1480
On Reading Ray Bradbury's Fahrenheit 451 :
    2379, 6830
On Reading the Lives of the Astronomers on a
    Spring Day, After Rain : 4669
On Route to Nong Khai : 382
On Seeing Alice Neel's Self-Portrait at 80 :
    4108
On Smoking Things Out : 2104, 2800
On Some Poems : 6713
On Stripping Bark from Myself : 6709
On Studying the Fragments of Heraclitus : 2187

On Sunday : 4068
On Systems : 499, 5438
On Taking My Thirteen-Year-Old Daughter to
    the Home of Anne Frank : 3460
On Tape : 6878
On That Side : 1625, 3921
On the 8th Anniversary of James Wright's
    Death, March 25th, Death by Cancer of
    the Tongue : 2365
On the 39th Day of Rain : 6183
On the Abundance of Shell Hinges After a
    Storm : 4260
On the Anniversary of Her Grace : 6815
On the Arbat : 4671
On the Arm of Gravity : 1512
On the Balustrade : 5976
On the Bars : 1376
On the Beach : 229, 490, 4439
On the Beginning of Wisdom : 1615
On the Birth of a Son Delivered at Home by His
    Own Father : 3397
On the Cape : 5302
On the Cards : 5302
On the Chihuahua-Pacifico Railway : 546
On the cold marble : 4805
On the Curvature of Space : 2796
On the Death of a Friend by Drowning : 205,
    1885, 4333
On the Death of Francis Bacon, 1626 : 1229
On the Death of God, the Incidence of Entropy
    and the American Novel : 6805
On the Ditch : 6327
On the Edge of Sleep : 6522
On the eleventh step of the fir : 1113, 3658
On the Empress's Mind : 236
On the Eve of Hallow's Eve : 2
On the Exchange : 4416
On the Far Bank : 223
On the Fear of Going Down : 1049
On the Ferry to Waterford : 1098
On the First Day of Class : 794
On the Front Lawn After Dinner : 7049
On the Gift of The Birds of America by John
    James Audubon : 616
On the Happiest Day of Your Life : 4411
On the Highway to the Temple of the Sun :
    3006
On the Importance of Prickles : 223
On the Kuskokwim River Near Bethel, Alaska :
    3425
On the Ladder : 6144
On the Liberation of Women : 5618
On the Line : 3171
On the Marginality of Poets : 4921
On the New Haven Line : 106
On the Night of Falling Comets : 3398
On the Occasion of the First Official Recogni-
    tion of Martin Luther King's Birthday :
    5826
On the Ohio River, Golconda, Illinois : 3685
On the Other Side : 4223
On the Outskirts : 6610
On the Page : 1607
On the Place Where the Hospital Tipi Stood :

6436
On the Ritual Courtship of Poets : 3011
On the Road from the Hospital : 3277
On the Road to the Kingston Dump This
   Morning : 5122
On the Road with a Special Providence : 4484
On the S.S. Pushkin : 4671
On the Sabbath : 464
On the Steps of Temple Shalom : 2583
On the Straw Fan : 3284, 4881
On the Third Day the Snow Began to Fall :
   1363, 5379, 5379, 6377, 6377, 6639, 6639
On the Train From Washington : 3782
On the Uncompleted Madonna of Michelangelo
   in the National Gallery : 6917
On the University Bridge : 3041
On the Verge of the August Full Moon : 4917
On the Way to Heaven : 5969
On This Bench : 4037
On Those Nights : 5334
On Throwing Away a Bottle of Tranquilizers :
   1628
On to Something : 3505
On Turning Forty-Six : 3944
On Veronica : 1659
On Visiting a Friend in Southern California :
   3538
On Visiting T. S. Eliot's Grave, E. Coker,
   England : 4997
On Watch : 6735
On Wiesel's *Night* : 6433
On Woodward : 263
On Writing Poetry : 2850
On Your Birth : 6862
Once: : 3464, 7132
Once a Week : 2625
Once Again the Committee : 3434
Once and For All : 5729
Once I courted danger at every subway stop :
   5580
Once I lied about it here : 3224, 3473, 6830
Once I Thought I Saw You : 2779
Once I wanted to Real Bad : 1547
Once I Was a Panther : 3763
Once I Went with a Girl Too Beautiful : 5002
Once in a Lifetime Starry Scape : 3586
Once More Around the Sun : 6608
Once the Prehistoric Man : 5181
Once There Was a Leaf : 1536, 3533
Once There Were Great Birds in the World:
   The Auk : 2988
Once Upon a Suburb : 233
Once You've Collected Your Selves Like
   Books About You : 1371
One : 401
The One : 4444
One Art : 541
One cloud is moving : 3759, 4702
One Continuous Substance : 2337
One Day : 1276
One Day at a Time : 2623
One Day Before : 5534
One December Night : 3736
One Feather Shy : 4837

One Flight from Llao : 3199
One for Burning : 3951
One for the Money : 6112
One for William Carlos Williams in Hawaii :
   5156
One Glove to the Other : 5430
One Hand : 3597
One Hand Clapping : 3938
One Hopes For a Monster : 2905
The one I love is sleeping in an open room :
   4462, 6553
One legge on th'grounde : 392
One-Legged Wooden Red-Wing : 5067
One Light, One Flame : 4462
The One Longed For Is Never Enjoyed in the
   Anticipated Way : 2929
One Man Band : 2189
One Mitten : 4251
One More Anti Ghazal Ghazal : 2213
One More Brilliant Effect : 6116
One More Time : 2190, 2629, 6213
One Morning : 916, 4663
One Morning in Early June : 7058
One, My Arm : 532, 5579
One Night in a Pasture : 4264
One-Night Stand : 1156
One Not One : 6829
One of Many Days : 4275
One of the Boys : 5805
One of the last leaves to break loose from the
   maple : 666, 3979
One of the Old Men : 5828
One of Them Stood Up and Sang : 4241, 4718
One of Those Things, Detroit : 1429
One of Us : 3813
One on the Shore : 1142
One Pair of Eyes : 4615
One Per Cent : 5958
One Sentence on Tyranny : 491, 3035, 3476
One Shallow in the Body : 4962
One Signature. Kumo/Cloud/s & Sundry Pieces
   : 3405
One Story : 4312
One Summer : 226
One Sunday in Velvet : 1964
One Sunday We Evaluate Our Marriage : 6400
The One That Got Away : 2241
The One Thing in Life : 6162
One to Bet: A Jerusalem Pamphlet : 1203
One Tree Less : 4312, 5555
One Way of Dying : 2307
One Way She Spoke to Me : 4260
The One Who Disappeared : 4523
One Who Is Praised : 1461
One Whore Town : 4820
One Whose Child Dies at Birth : 168
One Wish Left : 1800, 6005
One-Word Stories : 3480
One World Shutting Out Another : 6794
One Year, Another Year : 6375, 7057
The One-Year-Old : 4238
The One You Wanted to Be Is the One You Are
   : 6579
Ones initial reaction is stunned unbelief : 5222

The Ones Who Died in April : 179, 5163
Onion : 3328, 4230
The Onion Lesson : 3479
Onions : 6728
Only Child : 4349
Only Connect : 946
The Only Farmer Still Alive in Consul, Sas-
    katchewan : 5390
Only Forest : 1343
Only Here : 5583
Only Human : 1976
The Only Life : 841
The only loves they've known longer : 1774
Only Undo : 3301
The Only Wars : 206, 813, 814
Only white walls know the horror : 361, 6671
The Onset of Literacy : 1639
Ontology : 6904
Onyibo : 3058
Opal Creek : 1427
Opals Receive Their Coloration : 937
Opazanje (Perception) : 5033
Open and Shut : 4585
The Open-Ended Bill for Sacrifice : 1103
Open Hearted : 2836
Open House at the Orphanage : 4513
Open Windows : 3080
Opened Views : 5936
Opening : 2231, 2474, 3958, 5040
An Opening : 6927
Opening a Fist : 6154
Opening Act : 6904
Opening Gates : 2360
An Opening to the Amazon : 3900
Opening Up : 6239
Opera : 3815
Operating Instructions: Talisman : 3596
Operation : 1519
The Operation : 6464
Opportunity and the First Words : 3660
Opposites : 6441
Oppression #1 : 4552
Optica : 366
Opusthirteen : 999
Oral Extracourse : 2426
Oral History : 3374
The Orange and Green : 3169
Orange Juice : 155
Orange Knot : 4638
Orange Poem : 2556
Orange Street, Kefar Sava : 327, 4921
Oranges : 5376, 6274, 6322
Oranges from Palestine : 3963
Orcas Island : 3831
Orchard : 1743, 6132
An Orchard Oriole : 2725
Orchestra : 1018, 2288
Orchid Clouds : 5578
Orchids : 1269, 4934
Order of Battle : 2256
Ordering : 1966
Ordinary and unnoticed : 3064, 5665
An Ordinary Composure : 6882
Ordinary Mawning : 726

Oresteia : 885
Orestes in the City : 6563
Organ : 1625, 6271
Organic Orchard : 5969
Organize the Heart : 2868
The Origin of the Milky Way : 1666
Origin of the Romantics : 6143
Origin of the Species : 5950
Original and Translation : 6828
The Original Echo : 3699
Original Sin : 3201
La Orilla : 1841
Orion : 151, 5648
Ornament : 2199, 5858
Ornamental : 6892
Oroborus : 2623
Orpheus : 6182
Orphic Feast : 4248
Oscar Wilde Pays a Visit : 5242
Oscilaciones : 3737
Oscillations : 3737
Osten Coker : 4706
Osun : 110
OTed : 3684
Otello : 6118
Othello : 3388
The Other : 1875, 2332, 6064, 6292
Other Aprils : 3780
The Other Children : 3384
Other Countries : 6566
Other Days : 158, 3750
The Other Eye : 2337
Other Lives : 3723
The Other Window : 1300, 2454
The Other World : 597, 5171, 6603
Other Worlds : 1369
Otherwise : 7118
Otra Vez Otoño en New England : 2219
Otro Retrato Olvidado : 6511
Où au commencement est la cicatrice sur la
    pierre : 1537
Our Bearings at Sea : 3341, 3476, 4812
Our Calling : 2142
Our Country : 1405, 3120, 5250
Our Creation : 3547, 5045, 5379
Our Father's Bedroom : 6842
Our Fear : 2800, 3254
Our first haiku, koans, and other nonsense : 603
Our Guardians : 1521
Our Hands Our Coffee Cups : 60
Our Heaven's Words : 2966
Our Kind : 6101
Our Lady of Guadalupe : 751
Our Lady of the Laundromat : 6753
Our Lady of the Snows : 2707
Our Last Night in Italy : 478
Our Man in Prague : 6006, 6684
Our Marriage: A Puzzle : 5750
Our Men : 386
Our Mother : 6075
Our Neighbour : 114
Our New Apartment : 478
Our Nuclear Heritage : 5842
Our partings are more difficult, and long : 2422,

3552, 6552
Our Secret Garden : 3004
Our Sky : 6101
Our Tender Friend Has Come and Gone : 4788
Our Treasures : 3950
Ouroboros : 559
Ours : 3176, 4445
Out in the Pasture : 3652
Out of Body Travel : 1853
Out of Darkness He Comes : 904
Out of Hibernation : 2921
Out of Love, the Hideous Comes Unexpected :
    6144
Out of Sight : 1754, 3984
Out of Step : 2951
Out-of-the-Body Travel : 3128
Out of the Cold : 6829
Out of the Lost and Found : 4073
Out of the Rain : 4111
Out There : 148, 2465, 3450
Out West : 4012
Out Where the Stillness Is : 4687
Outdoor Concert : 2198
Outdoor Men : 3694
Outer Lives : 2090
The Outfielder : 1679, 4286
Outing : 6488
An Outing in New Zealand : 5224
The Outlaw Hitching-Post : 6711
Outline of History 7 : 532, 1491
(Outlying Areas) : 2293
The Outrage : 822, 3015, 5155, 5155
Outside History : 616
Outside In : 783
Outside Our Door : 980, 2499, 3769
Outside Perpignan in Heavy Rain : 1121
Outside Pisa : 1597
Outside Room Six : 1796
Outside Subic Bay : 3888
Outside the Force of Absolute Mourning : 5828
Outside the Library the Woman in the Safari
    Dress : 2706
Outside the Sheldon Gallery, Early June : 3425
Outtakes : 4086
Outward Appearances : 4017
Over a coffee : 5917
Over and Over : 5150, 5351
Over Coffee : 3276
Over the Delaware River : 4876, 5186
Over the Hill : 4301
Over the Hills : 5727
The Overflowing Brilliance : 4439, 4780
Overheard : 2098
An Overheard Conversation : 841
Overheard on the Soul Train : 2243
Overload : 4288
Overseas Accounts : 4726
The Overthrow of the Queen of Grammar :
    5287
Overtime : 1244
Overtures: Havana / Chicago / The Four
    Corners [Arizona-Utah-Colorado-New
    Mexico] : 3108
Ovid in Exile : 1269

Owed to Betty Hodges : 38
Owl : 3559
The Owl : 6608
Owl in Afternoon : 5295
Owls : 126
Owning a Pearl : 6101
Oxherding : 2993
Oxota: A Short Russian Novel : 2764
The Oxygen Fish : 7169
Oysters : 5029
The Oysters : 720, 3197, 6806
Ozark Halley's : 2744
The Ozark Odes : 7056
Ozy's Mandate : 1675
O Rilke! : 2159
The P.R. Person's Story: Debbie and I : 2373
P.S. to a Christmas Card : 6424
Pablo : 6848
The Pacific Electric Power Plant : 5951
Pacification Rites : 6015
Packing : 2175
Packing Her Scarves : 3102
Packing the Car : 2760
Pagan Love Song : 131
Paganini and the Powers of Darkness : 5933
Page : 1721, 3418
Page 215 : 6496
A Page Falls Open : 1014
Paging Through an Old Anthology : 1539
Pain : 3137, 3689, 4186
Paint Island Nursery : 1399
Painter : 24, 3753
The Painter Discusses 'Apples' : 1089
A Painter of Destinies : 455
The Painters : 1200
A Painter's Alphabet : 5928
Painting : 6155
Painting Ferns a Mile from the Stadium : 650
Painting from My Father : 5562
Painting No. 21 (Palo Duro Canyon), 1916 :
    3887
Painting the Statues : 1539
Painting with My Daughter : 2955
Paintings : 6526
The Pair of Twins : 4495, 6244
Pakashgoogan : 6197
Palatine : 1367
Pale dawn melts over the sleeping thing : 748,
    1275
Pale Yellow : 1821
Paleolithic : 3596
Paleoliths : 5193
A Palestinian Dream : 893
The Palimpsest : 609, 1124
The Palm Sunday Race : 6046
Palm to Palm : 2793
A Palm Tree and Two Women : 3921, 6388,
    6527
Palm Tree King : 48
Palm Tropic : 223
Palmy Days : 1735
Palmyra : 6407
La Pampa : 1808
Pan and Syrinx : 2547

Panama : 2150
The Panama Hat Couple : 5030
Panama, or the Adventures of My Seven Uncles
    : 1045, 4861
Panteon : 71
The Pantheist Who Loved His Wife : 3013
The Panther : 2059
Pantograph : 214
Pantoum : 3502
A Pantoum for Anselm Kiefer : 353
Pantoun for the New Year, New Year's Eve
    1989 : 1274
Papa in the New Age : 3865
Paper Art : 1805
Paper Route, Northwest Montana : 660
Para Mi Calavera : 4357
Parable in Wolves' Clothing : 2177
Parables : 2254
The Parade, 1968 : 1323
Parade for a Young Girl : 3274, 5235
Parade Park : 5022
Paradise : 5883, 5894
Paradise II : 5259
Paradise Carnival : 623
Paradise Is Not Lost : 6848
Paradise Retained : 1813
Paradox : 4939, 5098
The Paradox of Chinese Pots on Exhibition :
    979
Paragraph from a Letter to Suzanne : 1652
Paraisos : 3642
Parallel Universe : 588
Paranoia As Champ : 6649
Parasite : 2532, 2922, 7106
Parc Montsouris : 4942
Parcels : 5300
The Pardon : 2251
Pardons (from A. Lincoln) : 2656
Parenting : 1693
Parents : 4490
Parent's Day at the College : 6547
The Parents of Artists : 4720
Parikia : 2956, 4704
Paris : 748, 1270, 1270
Paris in Sixty Nine : 6464
Parisian Dream : 404, 4084
The Park : 2104, 3519
Park Poem : 6007, 6171
Parked : 1852
Parker Homesteads, 1867 : 6715
Parker's Piece : 5350
Parkers Prairie Celebration on Soo Street, 1920
    : 6715
Parkgedlicht : 6007
A Parking Lot with Trees : 3454
Parks of screaming childhood : 3253
Parler Seul : 2013
The Parliament of Dogs : 6521
Parlor : 4264
Parolles : 5986
Parrot in Frostland : 3844
Parrot Talk : 4162
Part of Speech : 1213
A Part of the Thousand Ways to Say Goodbye :

1554
Parthenogenesis : 2337
Particulars : 5926
Parting : 3516, 3696, 3899
The Parting : 6406
Partner : 3336
Parts for the Marathon : 4013
The Party : 2091
Party Pieces : 1205
The Party Song : 3674
Pas de Deux : 4226
Pas de Valéry : 872, 6583
Pasar Bogor : 6251
Pass It On : 4505
Pass Through. Separate. Come Back Home :
    4404
Passacaglia : 5429
Passage de l'Arbre : 5554
A Passage of Warblers : 3661
Passage to England : 6168
Passagework : 1624
Passchendaele : 6438
Passengers : 406, 5603
Passerby : 2454
A Passerby and His Companions Visit the
    Widow After the Mad Avenger's Dreadful
    Accident : 2752
Passiflora : 5914
A Passing : 5431
Passing Along : 6101
Passing Lane : 4184
Passing On : 6773
Passing Over : 5679
Passing the Outer Light : 1894
Passing Through : 4264
Passing Through the Papago Reservation : 5114
Passing Zone : 2465
Passion, Danger, Freedom : 3727
Passionflower : 1939, 5914
Passive Today : 423
Passover : 2944, 6691
Passport Photo, 1969 : 3093
The Past : 1796, 3910
Past Lives : 4192
Past Tension : 1681
Pastoral : 1810, 2325, 5044, 5602, 5929
Pastorals : 479, 2512
Pat and Joe : 5805
The Pat McKinnon Poem : 4232
Pater Noster : 1815, 5570
Paterson : 719
The Paterson Going-Away Poem : 3761, 5965
A Path: Monet : 6086
The Path through Loantaka : 5343
Path to the River: Bangkok : 2331
Pathetic Fallacy: A Field Guide for the Biolo-
    gist : 658
Pathetique : 746, 4686
Patio : 1283
La Patria : 49
The Patriarchs : 702
Patrilineage : 6108
Patrimony : 2617
The Patriot : 1458

Patriot Without Parole : 5368
Patriotics : 298
Patron forgive us : 4963
Patterns : 390, 4765
Paul : 3082
Paul Celan : 7137
Paul Robeson : 777
Paula Lorraine : 5022
Paulownia : 2507
Pause-beat : 2454, 6324
Paving Stones : 1655
Pavlova: Elements of Evening : 455
Pawn Shop : 1808
Pawnee Buttes : 35
Paying : 4905
Paying Attention at Poetry Readings : 6070
Paying the Anesthesiologist : 2008
Payola Madonna : 3780
Pays de Carton et D'Ouate : 3047, 5440
Paysage Demoralisé : 6917
A Pea-Souper : 4928
Peace Day (1919) : 457
Peace March, Jerusalem, 1989 : 3280
Peace Now : 3840
Peacekeeper : 1241
Peach Offering : 6710
Peaches : 6800
Peanuts : 126
Pearagraphs : 6693
Pearl : 5529
Pearl Diver : 4591, 6971
Pearl Divers : 1350
The Pearl Oyster : 57, 3769, 4832
Pears : 6599
Pebble in the Shoe : 3869
Peculiar Habit : 7112
Pedestrian Pastoral : 5548
Peeling : 4851
Peelings : 6295
Pelee : 5224
Pelican in the Wilderness : 3742
Pelicans : 3498
Pelicans at Pawleys Island : 3850
The Pelicans of San Felipe : 1427
Pellagra, Bone-Tired : 4971
Pellagra, Caterpillar : 4971
Pellagra's Angel : 4971
Pellagra's Eye : 4971
Pelvis with Moon : 3182
A Penchant for Sleep : 6813
El Péndulo de Foucault : 124
Pendulum : 8
Penelope : 1930, 2787, 4621, 4621
Penelope's First Thoughts During Solitude : 4785
Penelope's Letter to Ulysses : 5720
Penn Concedes His Territories : 5467
Penn Station, Waiting for the Night Owl to Washington : 4765
Penn's Findings (However Inconclusive) : 5467
Penn's Spell : 5467
The Pennsylvania Turnpike : 5997
Pen's Orchard : 5467
Pentecost : 2980

Pentecost Scenario : 5833
Pentimento : 2488, 2885, 5471
Penult : 5771
Peonies : 5141, 5168
People Are Living on the Streets : 6653
People at the Beach : 4877
People, Boughs : 1363, 5379, 6639
People Keep Telling Me : 6848
People Like Us : 5333
People Seldom Listen Unless : 5132
People Under Water : 2762
Pep : 6196
Per Missions : 2180
Per Voi Che : 1473
La Pera : 2538
Perception : 5033
The Perch : 3381, 4283
Percolation : 2870
Percy Bysshe Shelley aboard the Don Juan : 1269
Percy Bysshe Shelley Is Shown, by Lord Byron, the Fifth Canto of Don Juan, Ravenna, 1821 : 1269
Perdita Considers Dessert : 6391
Perdita in a Large World : 6391
Perdita in the Back Room : 6391
Perdita's Sunday : 6391
Perduta Genta : 5231
A Perfect Example of Luck Is Choked with No One Thing : 2433
A Perfect Forehead : 1618
The Perfect Garden : 723
Perfect Pitch : 1123
A perfect purple opening, within : 2633
The Perfect Woman : 540
Perfection Wasted : 6562
Perfidious, Ill-Timed Enzymes : 6107
Perhaps : 3313
Perichoresis: Letter of Gregory of Nazianzus to Gregory of Nyssa, 362 : 2650
Period Piece : 1308, 6869
Peripheral Vision : 2884
The Periscope of the Eye : 2332
Permanent Disability : 233
A Permanent Dye : 6361
Permanent Ink : 567
Permission : 836
Permission to Live : 6290
Permollis : 5594
Perpetual Motion : 2875
'Perpetuum Mobile' for Two Pianos, from Bartok's Mikrokosmos : 6065
Perplexed : 3120, 3355, 4312
Perry Como Sings : 2386
The Persecution of Wilhelm Reich : 6782
Persephone : 2338, 3185
Persephone: A Letter Home : 1180
Persephone: Another Glance : 6946
Persephone at the Festival : 1516
Persephone in Suburbia : 1197
Pershing Square Story : 4299
Persian Gulf, January 25, 1991 : 7167
Persistance of Time : 2879
Persistence of 1937 : 2567

The Persistence of Memory : 6926
The Persistence of Parakeets : 3849
A Person Broken in Two : 3398
Personal Account : 69, 1224, 3121
Personal Ad : 2287
Personal Alternative : 5432
Personal History : 567
Perspective : 534, 1354, 1773, 3527, 6732
Perspective: Powell Valley : 5649
Persuading My Lover that My Daughter Is Fun
    to Live with Because We'll Pretend She's
    My Sister : 4260
Persuasion : 1521
Perturbations : 7046
Peru Is Not Far : 3922
Pestilence : 2369
Un Petalo Alla Deriva Nella Notte : 5650
Peter Calls Again : 941
Petit Derangement : 2386
La Petite Mort : 4212
Les Petites Villes : 2748
Petition to Common Sense : 2897
Petros : 1836
Peyote : 2030
Peyote Meeting, Late Spring, Lame Deer,
    Montana : 4171
Phantom Limb : 7049
Phantom Pain : 3753
Phar Lap : 4012
The Pharaoh : 7044
The Pharmacy : 6536
The Phenomenology of Roundness : 698
Philadelphia : 6051
Philly Fever : 3510
Philomela : 6290
The Philosophy of Frijoles : 73
A Phobic Describes the Enigma of Bridges :
    4937
Phoenicia : 1437
Phoenix : 2490, 2570, 4279, 6950
Phoenix to Photons : 1647
Phone Call : 7112, 7161
The Phone Call : 5095
Phonic : 4128
Phorkyads : 747
Photo for B. R. : 6813
Photo of a Hobo Camp, 1931 : 2416
Photo of Seven Traveling Navaho by Edward
    Curtis, Circa 1904 : 3612
Photograph : 4508, 5960
A Photograph : 1614
The Photograph : 3970
Photograph & Story in the *Press*: The Mother
    Whose Children Burned to Death : 5018
Photograph from Berlin : 1380
Photograph of a Writer : 338
Photograph of You in Late Evening : 2424
The Photograph on My Father's Desk : 616
Photograph, Port Moresby, New Guinea, 1943 :
    3310
A Photograph That Doesn't Yet Exist : 6368
The Photographer : 1653
The Photographers : 1989
The Photographer's Model : 7146

Photographing Horses : 5757
Photographs : 5312
Photographs of Mountains : 2756
The Phrenic Nerve at Ninety-Five : 4004
The Phrenologists : 4688
The Physical : 5946
Physical Mysteries : 6386
The Physicist Prays : 4971
The Physicist's Wife : 1478
Physics : 3882
The Physics of Marriage : 6728
Physics One : 2668
The Pianist Who Keeps a Loaded Gun on Her
    Piano When She Practices : 2706
Piano : 623, 3664
The Piano in Saint Paul : 3134
Picasso in Shorts : 2735
Picasso's-Goat : 4594
Picasso's Snake Lady Sings the Blues : 4448
Picasso's Woman with Hat : 5811
Pickerelweed : 4816
Picking Lettuce for Magdalena : 2110
Picking Over the Bones : 126
Picking Plums : 3523
Picking Raspberries : 2280
Pickled : 4369
Pickups : 1595
Picnic : 6290
The Picture : 1202, 1404
Picture of Pre-Arsenal Thoughts : 3221
The Picture on the Purple Wall : 6981
A picture that scares me has gone through my
    mind : 4247
Picture This : 6601
Picture This Cove : 145
Pictures from El Salvador : 3436
Pictures of the World, October 24, 1983, 6:30
    A.M. : 4280
Piece by Piece : 5421
A Piece of Rope : 5816
La Piedra en el Fondo : 6554
Las Piedras del Cielo : 4641
Las Piedras del Momentaneo : 1832
Pies Sagradas : At the Feet of the Saints : 3645
Pieta : 198, 4087, 6526
Pieter de Hooch : 4293, 4796
Pigeon Amazement : 2595
Pigeons : 3862, 5108, 5679
The Pike : 1647, 4481
Pileated Woodpecker : 3339
The Pilgrim : 68
Pilgrimage : 2653, 2866, 7005
Pilgrimage '88 : 1303
Pilgrimage to Medugorje : 1401
Pilgrims : 1806
Pillow Mints : 1509
Pilot Entries, Ohio River, Sistersville to Belpre :
    2680
Pilot's Dream : 272
Pinball : 6251
Pine Needles : 3376
Pine Tree in Spring : 20
Pines : 2197, 6273
Piney Point : 1373

Pingst, Trettio År Senare : 2526
The Pink Bathroom : 335
Pink Flowers : 1108, 1252, 3364
The pink in the morning sky : 2741
The Pink Letters of Grade School : 1510
Pink Panties : 1917
Pink Plastic : 5753
The Pinocchio Poems : 3873
Pins : 6273
Pioneers : 916
Pipe Dreams : 5140
Pipistrelles : 3305
Pisanello's St. George and the Princess : 5086
Pitching : 3612
Pito Had a Dream That : 5446
Pito's Got Time : 5446
Pittsburgh : 3623
The Pivotal Kingdom : 2142
Place and Fame : 5608
Place at the Outskirts : 5894
The Place Called There : 2096
A Place in the Past : 203
A Place in Time : 5476
The Place of Beautiful Trees : 3009
The Place of Country : 3402
A Place to Be : 2022
A Place to Come Back To : 472
Placebo : 4386
The Placebo Poem : 2974
Places Everyone : 1429
Plain Geometry : 1281
Plain Language from Truthful Chris : 5728
Plain Voices : 2861
Plaines : 1867
Plains : 748, 1867
Plains and the Art of Writing : 4179
Plainsong : 1887
Plainte : 2013
Plane Choice : 1961
Plane Expressions : 1639
Planet : 666, 3117
The Planet Krypton : 1796
Planetarium : 623
A Planetary Directory : 1060
Planets, Cars, Observers, Living Under Siege,
    Reading Schuyler's Selected : 173
Plantation Road : 2121
The Plantations of Colonial Jamaica : 3833
Planting Time : 6960
Planting Trees : 2890
Plastic Explosive in Toorak Road : 3239
Plate 10: Ducks Overhead (As the Sportsman
    Often Sees Them) : 3947
Plate Tectonics : 2445
Plath's Hair : 2854
Platitudes : 5684
Plato's Angel : 1352
Las Playas de Chile X : 7189
The Players : 5992
Playground : 5083
Playing Ball : 523
Playing the Bones : 5980
Playing the Lounge : 689
Playing with Dolls : 6515

A Plea for Proper Moderation : 4528
Please Tell Me Lies : 1782
Pleasure : 3796
Pleasure-Garden, Prussia : 720, 3197, 6806
Pleasures of the Flesh : 4630
Pledge : 4310
Plein Jour : 2013
Plenitude : 5302
A Plenitude : 2870
Pliers : 1735
Plotting the Stillness : 4594
Plowing : 6728, 6865
The Plowshare : 5990
Plum Blossom : 1803
The Plum Tree: Self-Portrait : 1294
Plumbing : 6207
Plumeria, Sunset (Kauai) : 1061
Plumosa : 1047
Plumpes Denken : 2905
Plums (1989) : 266
Plumtree : 4952
Plus I : 3838
La Pobre, Encantadora Melodía : 2192
Pocket Knife : 2890
Poe on Sullivan's Island : 5980
A Poem : 4001
The Poem : 574
Poem About a Neighbour : 5942
Poem After Cesar Vallejo : 6877
Poem After Fixing the Fence : 1144
Poem Against Geometry : 4240
The Poem and Its Use : 3485
Poem: Back in grammar school ten years ago :
    7062
Poem Based on a Chinese Character Meaning
    'A Fire to Notify Heaven' : 2970
Poem Beginning in No and Ending in Yes :
    1167
A Poem Broken in Parts : 3353
Poem by Dino : 1586
The Poem Called Liver : 3895
Poem: Cowboy I fell for : 1482
Poem for a Lost Uncle : 5102
Poem for Allen Ginsberg : 1093, 4566
A Poem for Barbara : 2245
Poem for Beginners : 6007, 6878
A Poem for Dylan Thomas : 7105
Poem for Jade : 1388
Poem for Jane Fonda : 5313
Poem for Joe Beam : 2962
A Poem for John : 6985
A Poem for Matthew : 5237
Poem for My Father : 4328, 5668
Poem for My Father at 85 After Cross-Country
    Skiing with My Nephew, Marlon, Age 7 :
    589
Poem for My Father's Voice : 3511
Poem for My Mothers and Other Makers of
    Asafetida : 4521
Poem for New York : 3625, 5416
A Poem for Orion : 3204
Poem for Paula : 4805
Poem for Sarah Merculief, P.O. Box 978, St.
    George Island, Alaska 99660 : 5305

Poem for the Daughter I Never Had : 4661
Poem for the Day After Tomorrow : 6007, 6878
A Poem for the Epiphany : 4273
Poem for the Fall Equinox : 259
Poem for the Last Day of March : 2767
Poem for the Missing Beauty Operator : 6715
A Poem for Tourists : 2415
Poem for Two Voices : 2138
Poem from a Crisis Center : 4075
The Poem I Couldn't Write : 1847
Poem: I'll listen to the news the day I die : 6113
Poem in Archaic Meter (Manhukah) : 19, 4816
Poem in Praise of Menstruation : 1167
Poem in the Stanza of the 'Rubaiyat' : 528
Poem in the Tradition of the Poet Maudit : 23
A Poem Is Not a Poem : 2796
Poem Lost in Mind Tibet : 1143
Poem: My mother dancing in the kitchen : 2812
Poem: My wife says : 4940
Poem of Mercy : 2860
Poem of the Beginning : 949
Poem: Reason and felicity dissolves : 501, 1588
Poem: Sometimes when you're standing naked
    and embarrassed : 3516, 3696
The Poem Speaks in the Poet's Voice : 6828
Poem: Spring's breath fills the windows : 4533,
    5196
Poem: The blue Motel 6 sign through the
    curtain : 4364
Poem: The long day's journey : 822
Poem: The right hand : 2690
Poem: The television sits gray : 4361
Poem to a Lady Movie (Falling) Star : 2025
Poem to Be Sung to No One : 153
Poem to the Child Never to Be Born : 1651
The Poem Walked Out : 6070
Poem: What is it to be face to face? : 1757,
    3588, 4690, 6220
A Poem with Two Endings : 457
Poem Written at the Algonquin Hotel : 5998
Poem Written from Memory : 921
Poem: You are a spray of lilac : 4533, 7134
Poema para Nicolas Perez Diez-Arguelles,
    Largo Nombre de Tan Buen Hombre, Que
    No Lo Necesita . . . : 123
Poema para Paul Klee : 1841
Poemas : 4865
Poemas de la Izquierda Erótica : 5411
Poemclone #4 : 3435
Poèmes : 1642
Poempoems : 2439, 4923
The Poems, a River, the Poet : 1756, 4048
Poems for Central America : 2435
Poems for the Horse Latitudes : 4172
Poems of the Erotic Left : 5411, 5995
Poems on Poland : 3254, 7129
Poems to Akhmatova : 6267, 6528, 6884
Poems to the Sea : 3918
Poems Today? : 6430
Poems Written During a Period of Sickness :
    2336
Poesi Är Farligt : 2418
Poesias : 6358
Poésie Mode d'Emploi : 1537

Poet : 1779, 3341, 5864, 6711
The Poet : 6389
The Poet and the Moon : 1953, 4938
The Poet as the Letter P: Stevens Requests
    More Prunes : 1061
The Poet in Late Winter : 3186
The Poet, the Lovers and the Nuns : 7
Poetic Affiar : 3597
Poetic Justice : 6711
Poetique : 2323, 3588, 6220
Poetry : 1618, 2551
The Poetry Beast : 5313
Poetry Business : 4469
Poetry Contest : 841
Poetry Festival : 1757, 3588, 6220, 6439
Poetry — futile : 4435
Poetry Is Dangerous : 813, 814, 2418
The Poetry Reading : 2666
Poetry Reading at the Gershman Y : 5527
The Poetry Shop : 7064
Poetry Sucks Madonna : 3780
The Poetry Wreck : 6536
Poets and Poems : 1969, 4475
Poets Anonymous : 194, 4750
The Poet's Blessing : 3985, 4742
Poet's Epitaph : 4988
The Poet's Husband : 2270
Poets in the Schools : 5156
Poets Storing Lightning in the Barn : 4168
Poiesis : 5882
The Poinsettia : 1142
Point Arena, CA : 2186
Point Defiance : 821
The Point Is to Get On with It : 4355
Point of View : 3624, 3917
Point Road : 6106
Le Pointe D'Appui IV : 864
Pointing the Finger : 3324
Points : 731
Points of View : 5499
Poison Grain (A Prairie Rap) : 6567
Poker : 5871
The Poker Bar (Sitges) : 1129
Poking Inside : 5645
Polaris : 6782
Polders : 6878
Poles Apart : 6881
The Police Tent at the County Fair : 4373
The Polish Shoemaker : 3745
Polish Tapestries : 5374
Polishing the Hardware : 1743
Polishing the Silver : 4477
Political Disease : 5117
A Political Fable for Practically Everybody :
    6242
Politically Correct : 5826
Politician (Retired) : 5109
Pollen : 1257
Pollution Poem : 4857
Pollywog : 1452
Polonius Revisited : 6519
Poncho and the Pig: Dog's Dream : 6676
The Pond : 1126, 3409
Pond, by Dürer : 1639

Ponies and Spanish Guitars : 3467
Pontius Pilate's Dream : 5407
The Poodle in Offit's Bayou: Galveston, Texas, 1964 : 1269
The Pool : 2107
Pool-Boy : 1233
Pool Parlor : 6797
The Pool Player : 747
The Pool Shark, an American Fairytale : 2893
Poor : 3256, 5379
Poor burnt child : 4026
The Poor Can Be Bled to Death : 3134
Poor Company : 2184, 4362
The Poor Miller's Beautiful Daughter : 5190
Poor People : 3770, 5382
Pope to Make Lifshin Forget Her Madonnas : 3510
Popes : 5757
Pope's Grotto : 3271
Poplar : 261
The Popol Vuh : 268
The Poppet : 6847
Poppies : 3447
Poppies in Rain : 1913
Poppies Twisted to Peaks by Evening Light : 1850
The Poppy : 2395
Pops : 6128
Popular Classics : 2021
Popular Star : 5241
The Population of North Dakota : 6787
Por Mais Que Te Celebre : 2356, 4284
Porch Monkey Eat Me : 3079
The Porch Swing : 3538
The Porn Collector : 6577
Pornographer X Musing on Hiroshima : 214
Portato : 3535
Portents : 1413
Portia, what passion, what blind pain : 1358, 4601
Portland Hosts the Second Coming : 5541
A Portrait : 2722, 4959
The Portrait : 3541
Portrait for My Mother : 928
Portrait in 'P' of Eye and Piano : 2113
Portrait of a Kentucky Family : 6727
A Portrait of a Marriage: 'The Red Roofs' of Camille Pissarro : 588
Portrait of a Real Hijo de Puta : 1830
Portrait of a Young Poet : 435, 4180
Portrait of an Academic Parvenu : 4365
Portrait of Flaubert : 5250
Portrait of Lynn : 2656
A Portrait of Marriage: 'The Red Roofs' of Camille Pissarro : 588
Portrait of My Father as a Young Man : 5351
Portrait of My Mechanic in Full Sunlight : 5378
Portrait of the Outlaw : 3913
Portrait: The Adolescent Self : 5487
Portraits : 2274, 4175
Portugal : 4744
The Position : 1751
Possession : 3100, 3553
Possessions : 443

The Possibilities : 2340
Post-Copernican : 1585
Post-Feminist Ode : 2140
Post Holing : 3785
Post Masturbation : 1950
Post-Metaphysical Man at Home : 1357
Post-Modern: To a Literary Critic : 6034
Post Mortem : 4829
Post-Operative Video Therapy : 490
Post-Romantic Striptease in the Style of Richard Strauss : 4491
Post Time (Belmont Park) : 1790
Post Up, Then Go to the Hoop : 6913
The Postal Confessions : 2199
Postcard from Jupiter, Tennessee : 4548
A Postcard from Kanawha City : 892
Postcard from the Glacier : 3794
Postcard from Weeping Water, Nebraska : 1778
Postcard to the Musician : 4260
Postcard: Voyage to Cythera : 4776
Postcards of Peru : 5345
A Posteriori : 2677
Posthumous Orpheus : 2866
Postmarked Novia Scotia: a Letter to Clarence Gatemouth Brown (Who Aint No Robert Johnson or No Leadbelly But Thats Okay 'Cos They'r Dead) : 4142
Postmodernism Made Simple : 4798
Postortemanifesto : 3054
Postpartum : 5661
Postponed Nightmare : 1363, 5379, 6639
Postscript : 1308
Pot of Gold : 1055
Potatoes : 1991, 3699
Potter : 5233
The Potter I Am Not : 5841
Pound : 4138
Poundmaker's Long, Last Walk : 6395
Pour les Survivantes : 3678
Poussin : 4005
Poverty Deluxe : 5483
The Power of Evangelism : 761, 3471
Powerless : 1602
Praca da Alegria : 158, 3750
Practice : 3418, 4263, 6982
The Practiced Distance : 2051
Prague, 1968 : 4671
The Prairie : 1132
Prairie Interview : 2832
A Prairie Museum : 6338
Prairie Snake : 5790
Prairie Song : 6872
Praise : 4313
Praise for the Masses : 720, 3197, 6806
Praise in Bluesville : 7113
Praising Invisible Birds : 3909
Prana Yama : 1416
Pray You Young Woman : 999
Prayer : 623, 5739
The Prayer : 6390
Prayer Before Killing a Doe : 3006
Prayer-Box on the Road from Delphi : 189
A Prayer for Healing : 5906
Prayer for My Own Awakening : 5632

Prayer for My Son : 5804
Prayer for Simplicity : 490
Prayer for the Hospice Patient : 3925
Prayer For What We Are about to Receive :
    4784
A Prayer in Four Seasons : 5633
A Prayer in Memory of Theodore Roethke :
    5821
Prayer on the Temple Steps : 5803
A Prayer to Eve : 4709
A Prayer to Him Who Preyed at Healing : 3848
Prayer Wheel : 5043
Prayers : 4644
The Prayers of a Nation : 7109
Praying for Father : 3013
Praying for Passion : 3962
Pre-Op : 3462
Preacher Hands : 5827
Prebaria del Aprendiz : 5308
Precision : 1448
Predictions : 1238
Preface to Elegy : 3288
Preferable Truth : 4521
A Preference: A Whole Series of Them : 5890
Pregnant Cow : 2882
Pregnant with Marilyn : 5191
Prejudice : 3780
Preliminary Sketch : 1155
Prelude : 1808, 2388
Prelude on Milk River : 2876
Preludio : 2388
Premeditation : 3952
Prèmiere Pédicurie : 387
Premonition : 1625, 6743, 7154
The Premonition : 4784
Prenatal Poem : 4882
Prep School Days : 5338
A Preparation of Spanish Shrimp : 7052
Preparations : 6056
Preparing to Visit : 5711
The Prepositions : 4782
Presence : 2380, 3066, 7129
Presence and Fugue : 1808, 2388
Presence: Translations from the Natural World :
    4562
Presencia y Fuga : 2388
Present Perfected : 1681
Preserves : 5871
The President : 1372
Presidential Words : 6514
Press Check : 7172
Pressed Flowers : 3596
Preston : 4651
Pretending : 2307
Pretending You Were Joseph : 1839
Pretensions : 4104
Pretext Other Side : 5771
Preview of America : 110
Prey : 6885
A Prima Donna Poet Replies : 3079
Primal Now : 4594
Primal Poetry : 5554, 5776
Primapara : 2264
Primary Process : 2176

Prime : 6678
Prime Time: Second Person Subjunctive : 3041
Primer for an Autumn Walk : 5718
Primer for Blacks : 777
Primitive : 1607, 6128
Primitive Youth : 5475
Primitives : 1813
The Prince : 3588, 3648, 6220
The Prince Returned : 2918, 7012
The Print Skirt : 6387
Prism : 3640
The Prisoner : 6997
A prisoner in the solitary cell of this body :
    1582, 5098
Privacy : 5302, 5303
Private Lessons : 5037
A Private Life : 6829
Pro Femina : 3407
Pro-Life / Pro-Choice Rally : 6492
Pro-nominally : 4051
Probabilities : 6144
The Probability of Weeding Out Extremes :
    4706
Probe : 3141, 3702
Problem Thinkers : 2310
Procedure : 3408, 3656
The Process : 5431
Procession : 503, 5229, 6830
Procession in the Fog : 491, 3035, 3476
Processionals : 623
The Prodigal : 6185
The Prodigal Son : 3313
Produce : 4911
The Professor Visits Winn-Dixie After His
    Eliot Seminar : 5212
A Professor Young and Old : 3452
Profile : 3120, 3355, 4728
Progress : 3630, 3928
The Progress of Seasons : 4667
Progress Report : 6441
Progressions : 6225
Prolapse : 6842
Prólogo a la Lengua : 1028
Prologue to an Explanation : 1465
Prologue to the Happy Poem You Asked For :
    1047
Prom in Toledo Night : 3656
Prometheos Auomenos : 46, 6325
Prometheus : 6232
Promise : 3752, 6443
The Promise : 148, 1090, 4782
The Promise of Flight : 2601
The Promised Land : 1830, 4978, 6059
Prone to Worry : 6795
Pronouns : 2243
Pronunciation : 4221
The Proof : 1605
Proofreading : 1925
Proofreading with My Mother : 657
A Proper Introduction : 1726
Proper Travel : 5828
Property of Pigeons : 3875
Prophecy in July : 721
Prophecy in May : 721

Prophesying About Your Time : 1363, 5379, 6638
Prophetic Anatomy : 289, 980, 5071
The Prophetic Child : 4743
Prophets : 4818
A Prophylactic Rag : 3079
Propileo : 5882
A Proposition : 5855
Proscenium : 7093
Prose Look Settled : 3926
The prose poem the perfect incubator for the imagination : 2774
Proserpine : 6004
Proserpine in Autumn : 5980
Prospect of a Village in Devon : 2256
Prospective Immigrants Please Note : 5322
Prospero : 3594
The Prostitutes of Nairobi : 2814
The Protective Waves of the Ordinary : 1632
Protectivwe Coloration of the Heart : 6239
Proteus : 1483
Proteus in Washington, D.C. : 5720
Protext : 3603
Protocol : 1595
Protracted Episode : 4487
The Provider : 3088
The Provinces : 6041, 6977
Provision : 4888
Prowler by Daylight : 4649
Proximal Desire : 2339
Prudent Triangle : 5094, 5894
Prussian Blue Memory : 4917
Psalm #1 : 51
Psalm XVIII : 1780, 7006
Psalm XXIV : 1780, 7006
Psalm Four : 464, 1441
Psalm of the Canal-Dweller : 495
Psalm of the City-Dweller Gone Home : 495
Psalm of the Spit-Dweller : 495
Psalm of the Surprised : 495
Psych Ward Queen : 809
Psyche : 6294
Psyche's First Task : 382
Psychography : 5205
Ptarmigan : 3853
Pub Crawl : 305
Public Education : 1846
Public Garden with Weeping Tree : 3829
Public Lands : 5564
Public Recital : 6808
Public School No. 18: Paterson, New Jersey : 2277
The Public Well in Mathraki : 216
Puertorican Sketch in Philadelphia : 4621
The Puffin's Song : 1558
Pulitzer Prize Action Photo 1989 : 507
Pull Over : 13
Pulling Out the Plot : 4930
Pumpkin Seeds : 1369
Pumpkins : 223
Punk Girl, Wedding : 1768
Pure Conversation with a Chinese Character : 1671, 2104, 6054
The Pure Sound Pavilion of the Riverside

Temple : 4312, 4569, 5845
Purgatory : 502
Purge : 1266
Purification : 4212
Purim Spiel : 5527
The Puritan Commander of the Firing Squad During the English Civil War : 1269
The Pursuit of Daphne : 2735
La Push Apocalypse : 471
Push-Over : 3722
Puss in Poots : 6226
Pussy : 3177
Put This Gown On : 1966
Putting It in Perspective : 1165
Putting Out the Fires : 2735
Puukohola : 1060
The Puzzle : 1286, 4731
Puzzle of Foreclosure : 1387
Puzzles : 3597
Puzzling It Out : 5442
Puzzling Out the Signs : 4035
Pygmalion : 3602
Pyracantha : 1031, 1939
Pyro : 2772
The Pyromaniac's Confession : 7049
Pythia : 363
Quadriplegic : 2860
Quality / Control : 1429
The Quality of Mercy : 6563
Quandary : 1663
Quando Torna l'Autunno : 5914
Los Quarks Saben Contar : 124
Quarry : 2492
Quartet : 6829
Quartet with Program Notes by Composer : 4705
Quasimodo of the Singing Tower : 1019
Quatrains of Doubt and Death : 2907
Que C'Est Drole, l'Amour Qui Marche dans les Rues : 1950
Que no se nos enquiste el absurdo : 414
Los Que Parten Estiman : 5235
Que pasión, Porcia, qué dolor tan ciego : 1358
Qué Sed Mortal de Dios Se Desamarra en Mí : 4748
Quebec North of Englishtown, Cape Breton : 1634
The Queen Bee under the Waterfall : 1976
The Queen of Fatigue : 5928
The Queen of Walls : 1648, 3588, 6220
Quel oiseau étonné : 1297
Quelqu'un rit : 1691
Question : 5837
Question #53 : 6099
Question of a Shovel : 1989
A Question of Time : 4710
Questioning David Souter : 6514
Questioning the Source : 2100
Questions : 1300, 2454, 6161
Questions for the Kingfisher : 918
Questions of a Literate Worker : 724
Questions of Healing : 2396
Questions of Love : 189
Qui : 1031

The Quick and the Dead : 3993
Quick Silver: Ephraim Harbor : 5004
The Quickness of Things : 5485
Quiet Days in Sarawak : 5366
Quiet Down : 4249
The Quiet Land : 6846
Quiet Now, by My Round Table : 813, 814,
    5064
The Quiet of Night : 1068
A Quiet Party : 5313
Quiet Time : 1475
Quietly Now : 4111
Quietness that in scorn capsizes : 3064, 4894
The Quilt : 915
Quinta do Cerrado : 7073
Quintana Roo Beach, 6 A.M. : 1224
Quintius: 82 : 1032, 1255
The Quitter : 555
Quitting : 6095
Quitting Farming : 5390
Quixote : 3181
Quo Vadis? : 2476
Quotation from a Poet : 376, 4979
Quotations for a Winter Evening : 3118
R- : 4001
R and R : 2210
R.E.M. : 1288
The REM Sleep of Birds : 1966
RSVP : 675
R. Says : 2380, 3066, 7129
Rabbi Nachman the Storyteller : 6878, 6915
The Rabbi Stumbles : 6756
Rabbit : 5472
The Rabbit : 5515
Rabelais : 4036
The Race : 2255
Races : 642, 2076
Racial Memory : 3011
Racing with the Hare : 590
The Rack : 5130
Racquet Ball : 2585
Radio : 3882
The Radio : 623
Radio Tehran : 4062
Radishes : 3264
Raffles Hotel : 2999
Raft : 6113
The Rag : 2013, 5107
Rag Time : 28
Rage : 1876
The Ragman : 228
Rags : 3699
Rahsaan Roland Kirk : 790
The Railroad Station : 1895, 5416
Rain : 895, 2231, 2858, 5178, 6361, 6501, 6769
Rain and Pain : 2015
Rain at Midnight — Insomnia I : 968
The rain began to fall, and the day became such
    a downpour : 3481, 4326
Rain Crow : 379
Rain, I Recon : 812
Rain Miles : 3843
A Rain of Murder : 4997
Rain on the mountain over there! : 3759, 4103

The Rain Poem : 4753
Rain Stanzas : 750
Rain Travel : 4312
Rain Upon the Snow in the Spring : 803, 2364
Rainbow Man : 1501
The Rainflies : 1597
The Rainmaker : 4179
Rains : 5858
The rains have lowered : 4590
Rainy Day : 228
The Rainy Season : 3086
Ramayama Revisited : 5851
Ramillete para Elena Poniatowska : 2974
Ramona Weeks : 3780
Ranch Wife : 7001
The Ranch, Wild Horse Canyon, 1943 : 354
The Ranchhand's Daughter : 6290
Random Design : 4144
Random Phrases From a Critical Review Plus a
    Poet's Comments : 6752
Random Silences : 5901
Random Thoughts While Skating : 1584, 2181,
    4486
Range : 132
Rapid Fire : 3418
Rappaccini's Daughter : 7001
Rappin' : 5597
Rapture : 1458
Rare Old Violins : 650
Raspberries : 2222, 4851
Raspberries Are Not Easily Gotten Rid Of :
    4644
Raspberry Portrait : 813, 814, 5708
Rat : 666, 3117
A Rat in the Room : 173
The Rat Trap : 1597
Rather Than Stories : 62
Ratio Rerum : 1969, 4475
Rational Man : 5521
Rationalizing to a Protagonist : 4433
Rats : 5679
Ratting : 3018
The Rattlesnake : 4632
Rattlesnakes and Guitars : 6804
Ratushinskaya : 2148
Les Ravagés : 320, 4329
Raven : 1610, 2074
Ravens and Pines : 4710
Ravens at Deer Creek : 7066
Raw October : 1429
Razor Stubble : 2977
Razor Temptation : 4696
The Razor's Edge : 6208
RE/ Accounting : 4917
Re-connected : 3167
Reactionary Deeds : 5968
Read About the Bear : 4804
The Reading : 305
Reading a Biography : 1968
Reading Jeremiah to the Rats : 1991
Reading Lao Tzu Again in the New Year : 7058
Reading Light Fiction in the Marine Sentry Box
    at FDR's Little White House : 5321
Reading Myself to Sleep : 1213

Reading Primo Levi on the Train : 4759
Reading Richard Wilbur : 4336
Reading Rilke : 6064
Reading Room : 4192
Reading the 1989 Iowa Trapping Regulations :
    6025
Reading the Bones : 3596
Reading the Landscape Again : 108
Reading the Water : 6800
Reading the Waterfall : 2164
Reading White Sands, 1945 : 6094
Ready for Goodbye : 1018, 5992
Ready-Made : 4711
Ready to Set Out : 1300, 2454
A Real Comedian: The True Genius of Bob
    Hope : 1429
Real Estate : 6956
Real Eyes : 2944
Real Jazz : 1105
The Real News : 2828
The Real Rap : 4987
Real Success : 6922
The Real Thing : 3977
The Real Wed Pharoah : 2845
Reality Organization : 2337
Really Driving America : 1577
Reason and felicity dissolves : 501, 1588
The Reason for Poetry : 971
Reason, My Dear Maria, Brings Us to Proxim-
    ity : 6075
Reasonable Boundaries : 4732
Reasons for Androgyny : 5576
Reasons for Winter : 2527
Reassurance : 5833
The Reassurance : 5012
The Reassurance of Ghosts : 4739
Reba Talks of the August Strike : 1505
The Rebel : 3466
Rebellion Is the Circle of a Lover's Hands
    (Pellín and Nina : 1830
The Rebirth of Imagination : 5211
Rebirths : 3094
Rebounding : 4761
Rebus Brag : 1588
Receivers of the World's Attention : 1605
Recent and Forthcoming : 7116
Recent History : 5145
Recently, It Has Occurred to Me : 6414
Reception Theory : 5390
Recipe : 5225
Recipe for Jon Griffin : 4095
Reclining Figure : 6268
The Recluse : 3038
Recognizing a Salvadoran in Safeway, Yakima,
    1984 : 1415
Recollection & Misunderstanding : 830
Recommended Planting Depth When My Time
    Comes : 2158
The Reconcilements of Elk Lake : 5707
Reconciliation : 1300, 2454
Reconciliation Viewed from Great Distance :
    7181
Reconstituting : 339
Reconstruction : 2041, 6537, 6826

A Reconstruction : 7182
Record Album Eulogy : 498
The Recording Angel : 2023
Recovering the Commonplace : 6715
Recovery : 2120
Recovery Act : 6449
Recreation : 6470
Recurrence : 6597
Recurrencias : 5882
Recursion : 2765
Recycling a Memory : 1280
Recycling Center : 2854
Red : 836, 4243
The Red Armenian Slippers : 3511
Red Cats : 1417
Red Clay : 2198
Red Dress : 4753
The Red Dress : 3258
The Red Fox : 6699
Red, Green & Black : 501, 920
The Red-Haired Woman on the Feather River :
    3600
Red Haze : 2275
Red in Houses : 2403
The Red in Winter : 3630
Red Lantern : 3467
Red Letters : 1023
The Red Line : 5855
Red Patch : 3387
The Red Pond : 5466
The Red Poppy : 1426
Red Red Wine : 1500
The Red Room of Happiness : 2077
Red Roses : 3336
The Red Scare : 728
Red Shift : 2255
The Red Snake We Woke : 3300
The Red Stove : 2714
Red Sweater : 686
The Red Thread : 3287, 5361
Red White Blue : 1259
Red-winged Sea Gull : 2603
Redeeming Value : 3849
Redefining the Worker's Advocate : 6139
Redemption : 5705, 6579
Redfish : 5515
Redheart, Greenbark, Blueblossom : 4260
Rediscovering Paterson : 6276
Rediscovering Wonder: Santa Cruz Mts,
    California, 1989 : 2346
Redland IV : 2594
Redneck Riviera : 5962
Redwoods : 6677
Reed : 719
References : 4253
Reflection : 6208
Reflections : 880, 1051, 2533
Reflections at Honneken Castle : 4532
Reflections of a Transient : 3464
Reflections of Icarus : 6703
Reflections on a Likeness of Luke : 3986
Reflections on a Yardbird : 1209
Reflections on an Open Reading : 3515
Reflections on Men: Upstate New York Girl

Gets Offers to Travel : 4930
Reflections on Ruysdael : 3125, 6651
Reflex : 2410
The Reformation of Rhetoric on the Occasion
        of the Dead : 658
Refuge : 346, 3120, 4312
Refugee : 4400
The Refugee : 6678
Refugees : 1965
A Refusal, Like Hers : 106
Refuting Berkeley : 5122
Regrets Only : 1735
Rehearsals : 6623
Die Reichs-Kanzlei : 333, 4105
Reichsmarschal Hermann Göring : 6005
Reification: Europe, Spring 1990 : 6018
Reincarnation and the Holy Commonwealth :
        50
The Reinvention of Light in Sweden : 4837
Rejection : 6870
Rejtan : 666, 3632
Relatively Speaking : 5465
Relativity : 345
Relativity, Babycakes : 1437
Released Persona : 2932
Releasing the Chains : 3764
The Relevance of the Humanities to Everyday
        Life : 6946
Relic : 1052, 2070
Relics : 256
A Religion : 5928
Religious Feeling : 4814
Religious Instruction : 4946
Reluctant Colaboration : 4422
The REM Sleep of Birds : 1966
The Remainder : 2109
Remaining Inward : 2704
Remains : 1668
The Remarkable Objectivity of Your Old
        Friends : 5238
Rembrandt's 'Jewish Bride' : 5091
Rembrandt's Vanities : 6046
Remedy : 4585
Remember : 5442
Remember Death : 6545
Remember Me : 4223
Remember me as you go along the street : 3037
Remember Pearl Harbor: Another Historic Day
        Devoted to the Craft of Poetry : 6403
Remembered Sequel : 6820
Remembering August in February : 2227
Remembering Butchering : 2682
Remembering Fire : 4564
Remembering Po Chu-I : 4377
Remembering Skye : 2752
Remembering Stars : 3796
Remembering Stockman : 6514
Remembering the Homeland : 3985, 4742
Remembering the Poet Who Died at My Age:
        George Trakl (1887-1914) : 3436
Remembering the Waves on the Rocks : 1480
Remembering the Wind : 2017
Remembering William Blackburn in a Leaf :
        203

A Remembrance of Class : 2203
Remembrances of Yalta : 66, 6456
Reminder : 5464
A Reminder : 2191, 7149
The Reminder : 3078
Reminiscence of a California Affair : 7060
Reminiscences of Planet Crabby : 2064
Remnant of Crossroads : 4743
A Remote Heritage : 5717
The Renaissance in England : 1308
Rendezvous : 1800, 6005
The Rendezvous : 5224
Renewal : 267
Renoir's Last Painting : 459
Renouncing the Tower : 5485
Rented Houses : 4726
A Renunciation of the Desert Primrose : 1688
Repaces : 4023, 4881
Repairs : 5985
Reparation for My Home Town : 3610
Reparaturtag : 4718
The Repellant : 443
Repentance : 2595
Repetitions : 3287, 5361, 5361
Replication, Island : 4088
Reply : 1838
Reply to Robert Bly : 252
The Report : 106
Report Card : 3319
The Report of the Corrosion Committee : 2457
Report on the Discovery of the City into Which
        the Saints Have Been Said to Go, March-
        ing : 2519
Report to the Central Committee : 3761
Reportage from Viet Nam, Especially for Inter-
        national Woman's Day : 2185, 2289, 5577
Reporter Covering an Auto Wreck : 422
Reporters : 6922
Reprieve : 3373
The Reprieve : 4096
A Reputation : 6301
Requiem : 2255, 5119
Reruns : 6515
Rescue : 4418
The Rescue : 2201, 5347
Residencia Plural : 2167
Resident Aliens : 2465
The residue or fall-out flaking my : 1337
Resistance : 223
Resolutions : 371, 1287, 2808
Resort : 1205
Respite : 3637, 5212
Responsibilities : 3338
Responsibility in Spring : 6989
Rest : 2346
The Rest of Her Life : 6895
Restaurant Outdoors : 4780
Resting Place : 1834
Restless Turning of Fall : 3465, 5178, 5379
Restoration : 3665
Restoration Conspiracy Notebook : 5800
Restored House : 3530
Résumé : 338, 435, 1329, 4180, 4906, 4907
Resurrection : 4139, 5875, 5875

The Resurrection of the Body : 2230
The Resurrection of the Bones : 1465
The Retarded Woman on Cooper Street : 7057
Reticulation : 3679
Retornos : 49
Retraction : 219
Retreat : 6298, 6853
Return : 3344, 4705, 6591
The Return : 2635, 5820, 6014
Return II : 3287, 5361
Return Flight : 2617
The Return of Orpheus : 6375, 7057
The Return of Robinson Jeffers : 2707
The Return of Tarzan the Apeman : 4187
The Return of the Native : 798
Return to a Small Town : 4409
Return to the Garden : 6843
Return to the Tree of Time : 2385, 4915
Return to Where It Hurts : 4497
Return Visit : 44
The Returner : 485
Returning : 3313
The Returning Place of Self : 4159
Returning to Arizona : 6118
Returning to My Valley : 1625, 6743
Reunion : 2663
The Rev. Jocelyn Walker, Fellow of New
    College, Oxford, Explains the Expulsion
    of Percy Bysshe Shelley : 1269
Rêve Parisien : 404
Reveal Codes : 501
Revealed : 3415
Revedere : 1800
Revelación I : 6554
Revelación II : 6554
Revelation : 92, 504, 2322, 6421
Revelry in Black-and-White : 3656
The Revenant : 2540
Revenge : 6545
Reverberations: A Sequence of Poems : 3480
The Reverend George Whitefield, on His
    Orphanage, Savannah, Ga., 1735 : 1269
Reverie for a Seventy-Seventh Birthday : 560
The Reversal of the Arrow of Time : 4030
Reverse : 2592
Reversible : 4734, 4750
The Reviewer : 465
The Reviewing : 2238, 5135, 5136
Reviewing Options : 734
Revising the Atlas : 235
Revision : 2469
Revival at Diana Church of Christ : 3995
Revolt : 6282
Revolution : 2393, 2432
Revolutionary Air : 4671
Revolutionary Epoch : 1145
Revolutionary Spanish Lesson : 1830
Reward, Boon, Clean, Safe, Easy, Botanic: Sex
    : 4572
Rexford : 5971
Rexroth : 7001
Reykjavík Winter Couplets : 3704
Rezar en Roma : 71
Rhapsody : 3452

Rhapsody for My Birthday : 2237, 3547, 5379
Rhapsody in Orange : 6446
Rhetoric Lesson : 1917
A Rhyme : 3032
Rhyme-time Crime-time But who Care : 48
Rhyne Duren, Yankee Reliever : 6482
Rice on the Tray : 4640
Rich : 3450
The Rich January of the Duke of Berry : 2309
The Rich Man Eats a Cracker : 1656
Richard : 5670
A Richer Man : 4503
Rickety Stairs, Serra Negra : 3780
Riddle : 1592, 1688
Riddle on the Way to the Bottom : 5280
The Ride Home : 4296
The Ride of the Pale Horse : 1683
Riding Before the Storm : 6423
Riding Lesson : 5429
Riding the Camel : 4617
Riding the Conservancy Trail : 2895
Riding the Eye : 41
Riding the Metro Green Line into Blues : 5158
Riding Thru the Rough Side of Town : 5189
Riel in Saskatchewan : 7118
Rifle : 6988
Rift : 2104, 6054, 6612
Right As Rain : 5850
The right hand : 2690
The Right Question : 2104
The Right Time : 6101
Rights : 2465
Rilke Finds Water : 6277
Rimbaud, a Self-Elegy : 1639
The 'Ring' Cycle : 4310
Ring of Life : 5561
The Ringing : 4364
Ringing Out : 5669
Rings of Oil : 6954
Los Rios : 220
Rip : 1429
Rip Tide : 214
Rise to Civilization : 4643
Rising Before Dawn on a Winter Morning to
    Make Coffee : 1256
Rising Sun : 2714
The Rising Sun : 4605
Rising Tide : 2241
Rising to Meet It : 579
The Rising Wind : 1427
Rispetto in Silk and Scarlet : 6536
Rite of Passage : 6112
The Rite of Passage : 1120
Rites of Passage : 3657
Ritrovo una Sintassi : 1473
Ritual : 5769
Ritual for a White Rabbit : 2565
Ritual for Hairwashing : 918
Riva Looking Towards Sirmione : 1585
The River : 449, 2482
A River and a Swamp to Ourselves: By Way of
    an Autobiographical Note : 5583
The River at Wolf : 6589
The River Gathering : 6371

The River Has No Hair to Hold Onto : 173
The River of No Return : 2025
River of Tears : 5910
River of the Arms of God : 3932
River Remembered : 2907
River Stories : 6280
The Riverbed of Exile : 7023, 7024, 7094, 7094
Riverside Drive : 7152
Riverwalk : 3038
RNO - SFO - LAX : 5387
Road : 520
The Road Before You Know It : 5508
The Road-Gang Is Served Supper at a Country
    Inn : 3520
Road Kill : 1177, 3505
Road Signs : 96
Road to Mexico : 4349
Road Work Ahead : 1140
Roadblock : 2540
Roadie : 3266
Roadkill : 5587
Roadside Photos : 6838
Roadskating : 2549
The Roadsweeper of Rochester High Street :
    1099
The Roadwraithes : 1489
A Roaming Muse Brings His Silence to My
    Door : 4649
Roast Duck : 3328
Roast hot red pepper : 1276
Robert Frost to Ezra Pound's Daughter from
    His Deathbed : 5504
Robert Penn Warren : 4671, 7001
Robert Penn Warren: A Twentieth-Century Tale
    : 5824
Robert Wilson : 1212
Roberto : 3746
Robertson : 4332
Robot Poetry : 5413
Rock Concert : 5545
Rock of Ages : 1307
Rodework : 2475
Role Model : 4784
Roll On, River, Weighed Down by the Breath
    of the Dead : 84, 6642, 6643
Roller Rink, 1954 : 4738
Roman Fall: In Memoriam : 2866
Roman Fountain : 4514, 5351
Romance : 670, 6456, 6619, 6680
Romance About My Motherland : 1428, 4671
The Romance of the Bees : 686
Romance of the Moon : 2191, 7149
Romanesque Vaults : 5167, 6500
The Romanian Girl Downstairs : 5737
The Romantic Age : 5949
Romantic, at Horseshoe Key : 5856
Romantic Traces : 771
Romantics : 4639
Rome Dream : 6579
Ronald the Friendly Ghost : 3451
Rondelay : 3596
The Roofer : 6400
Roofs of Strasbourg : 3713
Rooftop : 1121

The Room : 813, 814, 2551, 5708
Room at Nine : 1644
Room for the Night : 813, 814, 6222
The Room I Only Spent Summers In : 3302
Room in Brooklyn, 1932 : 4448
Room Without Walls : 92
Roomer : 2224
Rooms : 1319, 4025, 4070
Roosevelt Avenue Express : 4851
Rooster Rooster : 2515, 7150
The Root Garden : 4955
Roots : 3488
Roots/ /Feet : 3628
Roots in the Air : 3341, 5337
Rope : 4726
The Rope Held Fast : 468, 4473
The rope I haven't used : 2135, 3751, 6383
Rope marks : 4805
Roped Wires : 6897
Rosa divina que en gentil cultura : 1358
La Rosa Mordida : 213
Rose Cloth Tattering from the Barbed Wire :
    6046
Rose Cross : 3588, 6220
Rose Devorah : 3780
A Rose for Katie : 6927
The Rose Garden : 5114
Rose Quartz : 6556
Rose Window : 102
Roses : 5964
Roses, You Say, Roses : 744
Rosie to Her Daughter : 4004
Rote of Forgetfulness : 1667
Rouge, Vert & Noir : 920
Rough Country : 2288
Rough House : 184, 4750
A Round of Faces at the Dining Room Window
    : 5106
Round Trip : 2516
Routine : 1539
The Routine Things Around the House : 1715
Row 23 : 671
Rowing : 5114
Roxy : 5773
Royal Garden Hotel : 4512
Royal Gardens : 4256
The Royal Nonesuch : 6198
Roycroft Craftsmen : 5518
RSVP : 675
Rt. 161 Out of Columbus : 3711
Rubber Rats : 476
Rubber Roses : 1810
Rubbing Along the Chimes with 3 Brass Bells :
    2433
Rubbing My Father's Back : 3504
Rubble : 3419
Ruby : 3503
Ruck : 6445
The Rucksack : 5713
Rue des Martyrs : 2059
Rue Replique : 6666
Rugmaker : 4741
The Ruined Cottage : 4487
Ruined Secret : 525

Ruins of Sabratha : 713
Ruler : 348
Ruminations of a Single Father : 2004
Rumpelstiltskin : 3827
Rumpelstiltskin, Revisited : 3507
Run Away? : 813, 814, 2526
Run, Late November : 4171
Runaway : 7112
The Runaway : 3394
Running : 1429
Running Feet : 3679
Running from Selinsgrove : 2904
Running in the Sun : 86
Running into Irene Wade in Dense Fog on
    South Beach : 4262
Running the Film Backwards : 448
Rural Electrification : 1631
Rural Free Delivery, 1952 : 2941
Rush Hour : 6603
Russian Folk Songs : 6446
Rust Belt : 2455
Rutilations : 6556
The S & L Riot : 4847
S. Cecilia in Trastevere : 5350
Sa Ald Te Wurden : 6341
Sabbath : 2281, 4278
Sabbatical : 112
The Sack of Shadows Poured Down Cold :
    3067, 5995
The Sacks : 3652
Sacrament of Sleep : 3396
Sacrifice : 6100
The Sacrifice : 3691, 5417
Sacrilege : 1018, 5992, 6033
Sad black mole on hip : 37
Sad Tidings : 3693
The Sadness Within Us All : 138
Safe : 2459
Safe Conduct : 1688
Safed : 5557
Safekeeping, 1963-90 : 5130
Safer Shadow : 2652
Safety in Numbers : 4100
Såg Du Gravarna : 3792
Sailin' On to Hawaii : 3153
Sailing : 1142
The Sailor : 2817, 3280
Sailor on Leave Suffocates in Sand : 5830
Saint . . . : See also St. . . ., filed below under
    'St.'
Saint Augustine Beach : 4302
Saint Cow : 4928
Saint Dolores : 2656
Saint Erkenwald : 188, 1963
Saint Femina's Liquefaction : 872
Le Saint-Joseph de Ma Grand'mère : 3682
Saint-Rémy : 2900
Saint Rose of Lima (Isabel de Flores) : 1183
Saint-Saens Caminando en el Muelle : 7137
Saint Sassy Divine : 2656
Saints in Their Ox-Hide Boat : 2170
The Sale Barn : 2627
Salen : 5708
Sales Call : 3748

The Salmon : 586, 1939
Salomé : 3466
Salome Surfacing : 4453
Salsa di Pomodoro : 1949
Salt : 238, 4728, 6688, 7025, 7181
Salt Flats : 2971
Salt Free Talk : 6700
Salt of the Earth : 248
Salt? Scrape : 804
Saltspring Sheep : 5444
Salutation : 4373
Salute : 682, 3701
El Salvadorean Army General, Jose Alberto
    Chele Medrano, Speaks : 4941
Salvage Operations : 4042
Salvation by Filing : 5518
Salz : 2009
Sam Bass: Sing to Me : 3428
Samara : 4345
Same Bench, Same Bronze : 2318
Same Ocean : 7107
Same Photo : 5282
Same Title As Before : 2815
Samhain : 4829
Samson : 5109
San Carlos Speaks : 809
San Diego : 6700
San Francisco's Gone & Other Poems : 6113
San Salvador : 215, 2805
The Sanctity of the Unwritten : 2656
Sanctuary : 917
Sanctuary of the Newborn : 165
Sand Baby Grand : 1957
Sand Girls : 2171
Sand Poem : 5114
Sandalwood (For A.) : 6340
Sandhill Crane : 546
The Sandhills of Nebraska : 5601
Sandro Loves Jackie Forever : 5237
Sands of Exile : 3625, 5307
Sands of Time : 3169
Sands Poured : 735
Sandstorm : 3769, 4832, 5503
Sandwich : 6075
Sandy Fished a : 4460
The Sanity of the Insanity of Homelessness :
    3213
Sans 11 (The Whitney Museum) : 266
Santa Claus' Madonna : 3780
Santa Claus Memorial : 799
Santa Fe : 1808
Santa Fe Sky : 3656
Santa Lucia : 887
Santiago and the Insane Asylum in Juarez :
    1182
Sap on the Rebound : 2068, 4872
Sarah : 3681
Sarah's Story : 1914
Sarasota Vespers : 725
Sardis Reservoir, Mississippi : 619
Sasha at Three and a Half : 498
Satiate : 4753
Satisfaction : 179, 1022
Satsuma Plums : 4190

Saturday Afternoon : 4501, 5035
Saturday Bath : 1810
Saturday Blues : 110
Saturday in the Dark : 5856
Saturday, Manoa Valley : 3831
Saturday Matinee : 2101
The Saturday Matinee : 3454
Saturday Morning : 1470
Saturday Story : 1216
Saturday Track Meet : 6074
Saturn Devouring His Children : 4693
The Savage Garden : 5219
Save for Their Likeness : 556
Saving Grace : 6837
Saving the Dead : 2467
Savonarola at 19 : 6075
Sawdust : 6046
Say It : 1268
Say Jazz : 5156
Say the Toughest Thing : 2890
Saying It : 632
Saying the Blessing : 4179
Saying Three of the River's Names : 4999
Saying Yes to a Drink : 2207
Says the Morning Voyeur : 2811
Scales and Clocks : 2223
Scalpel in Hand : 6835
Scandals : 5757
Scandanavia : 1465
Scandinavia : 3574
The Scandinavian-Lutheran Oral Storytelling
    Tradition Transplanted to the Northern
    States of the American Midwest : 6787
Scapegoat : 714
Scar : 5925
The Scar : 4008
Scarce Vapourer : 5594
Scarecrow : 4020, 5332
The Scarecrow : 1713, 6007
Scarlet Lake : 1121
Scars and Apologies : 2305
Scattered Directions : 3191
Scavenger : 1142
The Scene : 1119, 6040, 6156, 6158
A Scene from Hardy : 6621
Scene Remembered : 1899
Scenes From a Romance : 2893
Scenes from a Suite of Rooms : 2423
Scenes from a Western Movie : 3009
Scenes From Schumann : 235
The Scenic Side : 1711
Scent of Flowers in Aachen : 4462
The Scent of Rain : 6132
Scent of Snow : 2605
Scents, colors, lines and hues fade : 536, 3225
Scham : 4718
A Schedule of Events : 6104
Scheherazade : 3567, 5281
Scheherezade : 6770
The Schizophrenia Projects : 2106
Schizophrenic Baby : 478
School Bus : 2471
School, by the Nose : 1393
The School for Husbands : 4425, 6918

School for the Blind : 6622, 6830
School Lunch Work Program : 2563
The School Photographer : 7075
Schooling Fish : 1001
School's Ugliest Girl Dies : 2183
Schubert's Serenade : 4448
Schwitters : 5387
Sciatica : 5506
Science, a River : 7055
Science and Sin or Love and Understanding :
    6943
Science Fair : 6415
Science Fiction: Dizzying Changes in America :
    5676
The Science of Chaos : 4086
The Sciences : 3247
Scission : 3651
Scissors : 6281
Scoff Scoff : 1547
Scoptocratic : 5815
Scoring : 1006
Scornavacca, 1965 : 5408
Scotland : 5194
The Scout : 1595, 3636
A Scrap of Paper : 4095
Scrapbook : 6640
Scrape memory from my brain : 110
Scratch : 785
Scratch Sheet : 7060
Scream : 3307
The Screaming Eagle Papers : 2657
Screams With Whipped Cream : 4997
Screen for the Still Hours of Memory : 783
Screening Room : 3169
Screwage : 3079
Scribble Reduction : 6004
Scribe : 5980
Sculptor : 2832
The Sculptor : 3041
The Sculpture : 1666
Sculpture Garden : 3745, 4921
Se Me Acaba España : 2357
Sea : 3443
The Sea : 685, 734, 6687
Sea Castle : 6118
Sea Full : 1522
Sea Gull-Line : 1363, 5379, 6639
Sea Gull Song : 1647, 4481
Sea-lion at Santa Cruz : 5557
Sea Rations : 4417
Sea Saviors : 5431
The Sea Widow : 5949
Seaforth Remembered : 1117
The Seafront : 4166
The Seagulls : 158, 3750
Seagulls are playing : 3759, 6487
The Seagull's Cry Seemed Human : 4257
Seal Island : 1544
Seal Rocks : 4129
Seal Song for Banjo : 6863
Sealed Garden : 441, 5620
Sealink : 1154
Seals : 1607
Seams : 4527

The Search for a Subject : 5676
The Search Party : 2506
Searching : 6683
Searching for Emilia : 4851
Searching for My Father : 6282
Seascapes : 6684, 6878
Seashell by God : 5488
Seashore Sestina : 3850
Season : 2239, 5700
Season Drink : 493
Season of Fire : 6132
The Season of Icarus : 6285
Season Tickets : 5114
Seasonal Changes : 1465
Seasons : 5875, 6743, 7155
The Seasons : 5804
A Season's Change : 3965
Seasons of the War : 3038
Season's Song : 7008
Seastone : 5389, 6684
Seated Alone : 294
Seattle Illusion : 7084
Seattle Uplift : 6562
Second Born : 5901
Second Dialogue Between the Lone Ranger and
    Tonto : 6859
Second Flight : 2307
Second Grade Class Photo : 3820
Second Lining at My Own Jazz Funeral : 406
Second Man : 6878, 6915
Second Nature : 2875, 2943, 3283
Second Question for Hannike Büche : 6693
Second Revisions : 5822
Second Riddle : 2558, 3961
Second Sight : 1594
Second Singularity : 3957
The Second Son Observes Arbor Day : 4175
Second Thoughts : 3500, 3845
The Second Time : 3723
Second Tormenting Sonnet : 181, 4383, 6451
Second Waking : 5980
(Seconda Canzone a Cetti) : 3996
Secondary Road : 5347
Secret : 14, 6666, 7079
The Secret : 6614
The Secret Advertisement of My Sin : 6608
A Secret Better Kept to Yourself : 6007, 6878
The Secret Dream of Space : 1664
The Secret Examination : 5241
A Secret: Four Images : 1322
The Secret Garden : 5418
The Secret Language : 53
A Secret Life : 1715
Secret Love : 3341, 3731, 5864
The Secret Not Worth Knowing : 4412
The Secret of Gardening : 3612
The Secret of Leadership : 6514
The secret of life : 277
Secret of the Play : 4944
The Secret Truth : 2921
Secretary of Defense : 3758
Secrets : 2920, 4757
Secrets for the Wind : 1543
Section 4 of Andrea Dwarkin's Anti-Pornogra-
phy Civil Rights Law Cut Up with a
    Paragraph from *Screw* Magazine : 6090
The Section Called O : 1721
Securer a bo? no sacred armpits lair hops as that
    he-goat's : 1032, 7187
Seductive Sadness Winks at Me : 5118, 6786
See Me Dance : 3235
See More : 4572
The See-Saw : 2907
See, Saw, Blind : 4585
See this pill it's called Mellaril : 3581
Seed Storm : 1006
Seeding the Hill-Pasture Below Prouse Springs
    : 4034
Seedlings : 3570
Seeds : 348
Seeing a Friend Off : 2501, 3767, 6401
Seeing Eye to Eye with My Father : 55
Seeing Herself Beautiful and Nubile : 70, 1885,
    4333
Seeing Plain : 2941
Seeing the Connection : 3780
Seeing Their Shoes : 184
Seeing Things : 2743
Seeing Things Fern : 4448
Seeing Through Dark Eyes : 326
Seeing You : 6579
Seekers : 1564
Seeking Red As Green : 2112
Seems : 4527
A Seep of Morning : 6191
Seepage : 5928
A seer a prophet : 5073
Seeufer : 596
Segesta : 1393
Segunda Segundo : 5962
Seis Poemas : 505
Seis Sacerdotes Jesuitas Estuvieron Torturado y
    Matado en el Salvador : 1808
Selected Fragments : 5622, 6203
A Selected Story : 5828
The Selection : 1473, 6628
Selective Listening : 3656
La Selezione : 1473
Self : 1651
Self City : 6801
Self-Deception : 2257
Self-Employed : 6110
Self-Knowledge : 2623
Self-less : 4622, 6546
Self Lullaby : 6199
Self-Portrait : 1018
Self Portrait : 2123, 3745
Self-Portrait : 5992, 6623
Self Portrait #4 : 6218
Self Portrait in Water : 759
Self Portrait 'round Midnight : 3311
Self-Portrait with Wisecracks : 2405
Self-Portraits : 518
Self-Storage : 1975
The Self Talks to the Self : 63
Self-Taught : 1269
Selifke : 118
Selling My Home : 3922

Selling the Car : 2850
Semejanzas : 49
A Semi-Passionate Bookish Commuter to His
     Love : 4895
Seminole Finery : 2594
Senda de Agua : 636
Senex : 1744, 3032, 5921
The Senile : 5766
Senior : 2288, 3904
Senority : 6937
Senryu: she said : I love you : 5356
A Sense of Connection, As In : 5485
A Sense of the Other Side : 3986
Sensors : 723
The Sensual Laboratory Assistant : 2887
Sentences and Sensibility : 6326
Sentences for a New Year : 298
/Sentencing/ : 2033
Sentimental : 2337
Le Sentinelle : 1473
The Sentries : 1473, 6628
Separate Even in the Swim : 5087
Separate Peace : 5835
Separating Pigs : 3689
Separation : 3234
Separation of the Waters : 5803
Separation Ritual : 3
September : 338, 4906, 4907
September, 1988 : 1539
A September afternoon, I inhale : 666, 3979
September in South Dakota : 4629
September Song : 5563
Septembre : 6180
Septentrion : 1071, 6017
Septeria and Daphnephoria : 3287, 5361
The Septic Tank : 5490
The Sequel as Prelude to an Emotion : 588
Sequence : 813, 814, 5207, 6222
A Sequence of Sequins : 4381
Sequence of Thought : 1058
Sera, Sera : 728
Serenade : 489
Serenade for Winds : 783
Serenade in Blue : 833
A Serious Speaker Who Starts with a Quip :
     6881
Serious Thinking : 783
Serpent : 497
Serpent-Free Garden : 3912
Servant : 1071, 6017
The Servants' Song : 1400
Service : 3378, 5471
Sesame : 4062
Sestina : 5096
Sestina After an Etching by William Blake :
     7057
Sestina at 3 A.M. : 4921
Sestina: Families : 4138
Sestina for Richard Nixon : 6864
Sestina for Tea : 605
Sestina for the Dancing Smile : 1504
Sestina for the Twin : 2163
Sestina for Two-Eyes : 4999
Sestina in Indian Summer : 6536

Sestina: Waiting Room : 5479
Sestina Written While Baking Easter Dragons :
     2728
A Set of Variations Done on Old Music : 3309
The Set-Up : 465
Setting Fire : 2454, 6324
Settling Up : 4340
A Seven Day Diary : 1100
Seven Horizons : 6154
Seven Hundred New Words : 5227
Seven-Minute Storm Song : 1096, 4828
Seven Pieces for Unaccompanied Voice : 136
Seven Rondeaux : 4483
Sevens (Version 3): In the Closed Iris of
     Creation : 445
The Seventh : 1630
Several Errands : 2854
Several Heavens : 1942
The Severists : 5198
Sex Dies : 466
Sex Is Not Important : 3738
The Sex Junkie : 5775
The Sex of Hamlet : 1916
Sex Passages : 7015
Sexual geographers : 5592
Sexual Outlaw : 3157
SFO/HIV/JFK : 3820
Shade Tree Mechanics : 3913
Shades : 5753
The Shades of Grand Central : 6545
Shades of Karjala and a Finnish Summer : 5701
Shadow : 506, 1332, 4212, 6202
The Shadow : 196, 5650
Shadow and Light : 1355
The Shadow Behind the Watercress : 2561
Shadow Dance : 5346
Shadow in the Stump : 6148
The Shadow Knows : 2962
Shadow Man : 1362
The Shadow of My Roof : 5530
Shadow on Stone : 4298
Shadow Optics : 394
Shadow Sister : 2419
Shadow Spots : 2104, 3519
Shadowcat Alley : 3589
Shadowing the Ground : 3032
Shadows : 1369, 3580, 3909, 4991
Shadows at Yellowstone : 730
Shadows from the Womb : 6966
The Shadowy Men : 1833, 5995
A shady spot, twilight, a golden day : 3481,
     4326
Shake : 3923
The Shakespeare Lesson : 5171
Shaking Hands with Mongo : 1830
Shall I not see her? yes: for one has seen : 6533
Shall We Gather at the River : 7062
The Shaman : 4083
Shaman and the Raven : 3329
Shaman Fable : 1753
Shame : 4241, 4718, 6971, 7090
Shamisen Duel : 1964
Shampoo and Conditioner : 4126
Shamut Pass : 3966

Shannon Estuary. Thirty-Thousand Feet : 4001
Shanty : 1576
Shanty-Town Shankton Lee : 365
The Shape and Weight of Belief : 5431
The Shape of All Things : 2479
Shape's Hold : 4088
A Shared Life : 6046
Sharing Houseroom : 7038
Sharing the Famine : 6430
Shark Skin Suit : 6302
Sharon's Steady : 4989
Sharp Words in the Men's Room : 6242
Sharpening the Craft : 1579
Sharply defined periods of individualism : 5222
The Shaw Memorial : 1875
Shawls : 2674
Shawnandithit (Last of the Beothuks) : 1324
She : 2381
She Asked : 1030
She Attempts to Create : 564
She Becomes the Body : 564
She Conquers the Heart : 564
She Could : 6410
She Had Been Born : 2541
She has 2 minds : 1274
She Has Always Been Dead to Me : 4341
She Has No Title, But She Has a Home : 4458
She hated loving to be with me, I with her :
    4247
She Is Like Thee, Lute : 4839
She Laid a Lot of Eggs, Blew Them : 1337
She Looks Outside : 564
She Makes a Song for the Delta Girl She Was :
    4546
She Never Expected : 1837
She Now Serves Out of the D.C. Office of the
    Peace Corps : 6526
She Pours : 1896
She Said : 841
She Said It Was 41 Years Ago When Japan Sur-
    rendered : 3780
She Sleeps in Glasses : 4153
She Still Loves My After-Shave : 1493
She Teaches Him to Reach Out : 1781
She Traded In : 6492
She Was Waiting to Be Told : 2207
She Who Bears the Thorn : 3139
She wrote that yesterday had been very good :
    4247
Sheep : 4212
Sheep Camp : 1726
Sheep Sacrifice : 1005
The Shell Game : 2296
Shell Shocked : 6626
Shelley Sees Spirits, Casa Magni, Bay of
    Spezia, June, 1822 : 1269
Shelters and Holes : 5512
Shelton's Moon : 2147
Shenandoah : 5378
Shepherd : 5579
Shepherding (Transporting Sheep) : 1669
Shepherds : 4167
The Sheriff's Last Pronouncement : 927
Sheryl's Mirrors : 4054

She's Fifteen, She's Got a Great Right Hand :
    4607
She's Special : 3114
She's Thinking About : 486
Shhh : 6779
Shhh, They're Sleeping : 6178
Shied Witnesses : 1259
The Shield of Herakles : 4158
Shifting Night : 5164
Shifting Structures : 5294
Ships : 2143
Shipwreck, Northwest Australia : 5129
Shipwrecked : 4714
The Shipyard : 743
Shiraz : 1526, 7131
Shirley's Place : 946
Shiva and Parvati Hiding in the Rain : 5050
Shiver : 893
Shoes : 21
Shooting Relatives in Newport : 3543
Shooting Star : 1167
Shooting the Aurora : 5390
Shopping Alone Only for Myself at the Neigh-
    borhood Hy-Vee : 3425
The shopping I'll do will be simple and cheap :
    244, 3011, 3525
The Shore of Misgiving : 6126
Shore Road : 3863
Shoreline Mythos : 4898
Shoreline, Old Lake Iroquois : 3308
A Short Discourse on Snow : 1824
Short Foray : 6361
A Short History of Pens Since the French
    Revolution : 3808
A Short History of Sarasota : 2640
Short History of the Bourgeoisie : 1817
Short Mass for My Grandfather : 5061
Short Note : 321
A Short Note to Marilyn Monroe Twenty-Six
    Years After Her Death : 753
The Short Story : 4814
A Short Timer's Bed : 166
Shortages : 4036
Shortly after the Death of Huey Newton : 561
Shortness : 5967
Shostakovich, 2nd Movement, Quartet No. 7 :
    3402
Shot Through the Head by Zeno's Arrow : 184
The Shotgun Victims of Waldens Ridge : 6877
Should I Get Involved? : 4556
Show Us the Sea : 1560
The Shower : 5077
Shred of Dignity : 2568
Shrimping : 5515
The Shuffle : 1286
Shut In : 5816
The Shuttle Explodes : 5852
Si Je Pouvais Haler Son Coeur : 5783
Sibelius : 2592
Sichelè : 4613
Sicily, the Peasant Mother : 1568, 5650
Sick at the Gulf : 4606
Sick Sex : 6753
Sick Woman in the Fifth Wagon : 6605

Snowlight : 5719
The Snowman : 588
The Snow's Hands : 3796
So : 2837
So Cold : 565, 980, 5071
So Deep in Snow : 5919
So Get Over It, Honey : 6753
So High : 5689
So just then this guy with no legs on a skate-
    board : 5580
So many social laws — why? : 1502
So Much! So Much! : 2837
So, Rexroth : 1337
So These Are the Waters : 6596
So What? : 2595
Soap : 894
Soaps : 5486
The Sob of the Body : 2702
A Sobering Experience : 3167
Social Comforts : 5908
A Social Gathering : 3312
Social Rising : 1919
Sociales : 5259
Society : 426
Socrates : 5951
Soda Shop, 1950s : 5963
Sogni d'Oro : 6245
Soil Sampling : 2471
Soiree at the Czar's Plenipotentiary : 666, 3632
Solace : 1529
Solar Matter : 158, 3750, 3750
Sold Girl : 954
Soldier : 5889
The Soldier and the Unicorn : 6965
Soldiers : 3773
Soledad : 6407
Le Soleil des Yeux Clos : 4902
Soleil d'Orage : 5554
Soliloquy : 1854, 6764
The Solipsist Evaluates His Latest Project :
    5313
Solitaire : 134, 3607
Solitary : 1550, 5568
The Solitary : 1744, 2145
Soloing : 3746
Solstice : 341, 5017, 5461
Solstice Song for the Snow Blowing Over the
    Fields : 4218
Som Hon Går : 5708
The Somatic Poet : 4671
Una Sombra : 3642
Some Alpha Amenophes : 4140
Some Body : 2456
Some Day It Will Be Different : 6800
Some Days : 5477
Some Enchanted Evening : 1389
Some First Line : 1607
Some Gagaku and One Not Gagaku : 5335
Some Incidental Figures : 2009
Some Laundry : 2337
Some Like It Hot : 3810
Some Memories Lie Beyond the Edge of Any
    Map : 6749
Some Nights : 3997, 5894

Some Nights You Crank Up the Car Radio and
    Just Drive : 1380
Some Note I Can Not Hold : 144
Some of us would like to save the world and
    some of us : 1626
Some Thing Black: Three Poems : 5491, 6708
Some Things : 2104, 3519
Some Things Chava Meyer Says : 1731
Some Things Your Mother Didn't Tell You :
    2574
Some Think I'm Nuts But It's Just That I'm
    Artistic As Hell : 5030
Some Tuesday at Two O'Clock : 637
Some Versions of Pastoral : 4140
Some Women : 7026
Somehow : 3959
Someone Else : 4338, 6977
Someone My Father Knew : 1700
Someone Says So : 1888
Someone Tells You : 2638
The Somersault : 6545
Something : 1539, 5778
Something about time we cannot grasp : 4041
Something Endures : 3852, 4362
Something had gone awry : 7084
Something Harder : 1056
Something Has Happened in This World : 244,
    909, 3011
Something Has Not Traveled Beyond the
    Mirror : 3730
Something is stolen or disappears : 2125
Something New : 6829
Something of Spring : 3804
Something Sensible About Desire : 5171
Something Spoken : 1601
Something to Do : 2714
Something to Say : 5855
Sometimes All at Once : 1726
Sometimes at Night : 1146
Sometimes Beautiful : 4554
Sometimes I Dream : 813, 814, 6222
Sometimes Mr. Cogito Receives Strange Letters
    Written with Irony, and an Even Larger
    Dose of Compassion : 2104, 2800
Sometimes My Brain : 6016
Sometimes My Words Are Right : 2852
Sometimes She Thinks : 6492
Sometimes the First Boys Don't Count : 1704
Sometimes the Lovers : 6073
Sometimes the Sun : 1477
Sometimes when I see you walking I want to be
    you : 4462, 6553
Sometimes when you're standing naked and
    embarrassed : 3516, 3696
Somewhere East of Taos : 4279
Somewhere I Lost the Quest, Mom : 4268
Somewhere in the Heartland : 6384
Somewhere in This Poem I Wanted to Tell You
    I Am Ashamed of My Own Nakedness,
    But I Couldn't Figure Out How : 3690
Somewhere in Town : 5340
Somewhere on Route 15 : 825
Somewhere on This Earth I Am Sleeping : 7112
Somewhere Someone Is Saying Goodbye :

2652

Somewhere, Somewhere : 3303
Sommargrav : 5708
Somnambule : 22, 6006
Somnambulists : 6138
The Son : 5148
Son, When I Hold You Tightly : 877
Sonata : 4710
Sonata for Tuba and Piccolo : 2819
Sonatina for Surf and Sandpiper : 5933
Song : 1607, 2523, 2680, 3559, 4161, 5727,
	6766, 6888
Song About a Rich Man's Trout : 5320
A Song at Season's End : 815
Song for a Future Age : 5125
Song for a Lover Who Would die : 2510, 7150
Song for a Troubadour Who Dies and Dies :
	851, 7150
A Song for Kenneth Burke : 6162
Song for S : 3181
A Song for Soweto : 3205
Song for the Red-Haired Widow : 2089
Song for the Restless Wind : 4218
A Song for TWU : 2529
Song for When I Die : 5161, 7150
Song for Wild Phlox : 4218
Song from an Intermezzo : 5768, 6671
Song in Praise of Thunder : 1112
Song Instead of *Psycho* : 5213
Song: Newborn : 2860
The Song, Not the Singer : 2623
The Song of a Bird on a Gravel Shore : 2694
Song of a Murmur : 4527
Song of a Rebab Player : 4197, 6278
Song of Betrayal : 3417, 4976, 7176
Song of Healing, Song of the Sea : 6244
Song of Love : 4555
Song of Migrating Birds : 435, 4180
Song of No Account : 5960
Song of Prophecy, Perjury and Peace : 5394
Song of Racquetball : 1847
Song of Sleeplessness : 752, 5810
The Song of Songs : 527, 7020
Song of Steel : 3920
A Song of Summer : 1782
Song of Taboo : 1536, 2023
Song of the Barren Orange Tree : 2191, 2779
Song of the Butchered Hog : 6728
Song of the Camel : 3197
Song of the Circular Saw : 4245
Song of the Death I'm Dying : 5161, 7150
Song of the Homeless : 3430
Song of the Lost Self : 2517
Song of the Mystagogue : 5429
Song of the Old Man : 3197
Song of the Potato : 815
Song of the Scullery : 4146
Song of the Tiny Death : 2191, 7149
The Song of Two Snails : 3041
Song on Starling Street : 4515
Song Space : 5773
Song to a Lady from Elvas (Cantiga d'Amor) :
	6648, 7150
Song to Sing a Song : 803, 2364

Songs : 6034
Songs of Fear and Blasphemy : 3891, 5995
Songs of the Dead : 2496
Songs Without Names : 2104, 3519
Sonnet : 2619, 3211, 6098, 6472
Sonnet 67 : 2701
Sonnet for a Separation : 3472
Sonnet for Minimalists : 6595
Sonnet: News from the World, Tompkins
	Square Park & the Metropolitan Transpor-
	tation Authority : 51
Sonnet: Of Numbered Men and Men of Letters :
	6617
Sonnet, on Magda's Return : 4830
Sonnet: On My Violent Approval of Robert
	Service : 7062
Sonnet: Response : 7062
Sonnet to My Father: After His Stroke : 2437
Sonnets : 999
The Sonnets : 1665
Sonogram of Padre Island, Texas : 3196
Sons : 2259
The Sons : 4817
Sons and Fathers: Ashbery : 6474
The Sons of the Prophet Are Brave Men and
	Bold : 3075
Soon : 5791
The Soon to Be Immortal Talks to Himself :
	5031
Sophia : 6004
The Sophia Circumstance : 4191
Sophia Starling Attends the Episcopal Church
	in Denver, 1874 : 1269
Sophia Starling Considers the Sinclairs,
	Colorado Territory, 1873 : 1269
Sophia Starling Writes to Her Sister in England:
	Denver, September, 1873 : 1269
Sophronia: Sand : 5427
Sorpresa : 4621
The Sorrel Mare : 5267
Sorrow : 1757, 4403
The Sorrow of the World : 1307
A Sort of Love Poem from a Bathtub in Winter
	: 425
A Sorted 'Plunkett Papers' : 4664
Sorting Out the Garbage : 307
Sot : 6440
Sotto Voce Over a Shopping Cart : 126
The Soul : 565, 980, 5071
Soul Flight : 5466
The Soul in the Bowl : 1970
Soul Learns Everything from Body : 6232
Soul Making : 1258
Souls : 2105
Sound : 2374
Sound Buoy : 3986
The Sound of the Light : 4312
Sound Stage : 588
Soundless Is Midnight : 1625, 3921
Sounds of Gurgling Water : 437
Sounds, Silences : 6949
Soundtrack of a Desert Documentary : 5485
Sounion : 2892
The Soup : 3266

Soup Song : 1751
Sour Wine : 27
The Source of Fear : 4296
Sources : 137, 4377
Le Sourire des Chefs : 544, 5641
Sous la Pluie : 6858
South Korea's Military Government Complains
      of 'Misleading Terms Used by the Foreign
      Press in Reporting Recent Developments'
      : 4941
South of Fort Worth : 3434
South Wheel : 3329
A Southern Boy Reflects on Miss Monroe :
      3178
Southern Postcard : 5461
Southpaws Are As Rare : 2268
Souvenir : 3418
Sovereignty : 158, 3750
The Sow : 1142
Sowing : 6989
Sowing Seed : 5536
The Space Between Stars : 2241
Space for an Interim Dowser : 5822
Spaces : 441, 5620, 6924
Spaghetti Bolognese : 3328
Spain's Forgotten Forest : 4050
The Spanish Hour : 4158
Spar Sisters : 5969
Spare Parts : 5486
Sparklers : 3182
Sparks Flying : 791
Sparrow : 507
A Sparrow : 6154
Sparrow Air : 5559
Sparrow and Aviary : 6241, 6330
The Sparrow Drawer : 723
Sparrow Hawk Season : 1725
Sparrows : 3029
Sparta's Laws : 3612
Speak to Me : 206, 813, 814
Speak-Up : 6783
Speaks Latin, That Satin Doll : 4112
Special Needs : 6145
Speculations upon Angelo Bronzino's 'An
      Allegory of Time and Love' : 3826
Speculative Ode : 5704
Speech : 2886
Speech Alone : 2013, 5107, 5107
Speech for a Possible Ending : 2245
Speedreader Solvesnovel : 6120
Spell : 7026
The Spell : 2854, 5945
Spell Against Love : 2960
Spell for Not Entering into the Shambles of the
      Gods : 2299
The Spell of the Leaves : 3749
Spelling Bee : 5467
Spelt from Sibyl's Leaves : 2934
Spelunking : 1160
Spider : 3183
The Spider in My Room : 6154
The spider on this curb : 4973
Spider Tumor : 1212
Spiders : 932

The Spiders Are But Sirens : 391
Spies (Spies? *Spies*) : 2337
The Spill : 841
Spill and Scape : 539, 1909
Spinning My Wheels : 5036
Spinning, Spinning : 211, 1590, 3410
Spinster : 3157
The Spiral of Archimedes : 432
Spiral Weeds Under the Water : 5990
Spirit Flesh : 5130
Spirit Grounds : 499, 5438
The Spirit Of : 2846
Spirits in the Suburbs : 108
A Spiritual Note to NEA Flock Within Context
      of Stoma : 437
Spiro Mounds : 2303
Spitting Like the Treed Lynx : 1269
Spleen : 1605
The Split of Wood : 1466
Spoils of War : 3045
Spot Six Differences : 445
A Spotted Cat in Indonesia : 1998
The Spouses : 5099, 5872
Spray Nozzle : 1243
Spring : 2540, 3090, 3985, 4742, 4790, 5216,
      5874, 6821
Spring 1966 : 6548
Spring 1981 : 3126, 3265
Spring Again : 3729
Spring at Eagle Head : 4462
Spring Begins in Williams Grove : 3184
Spring Break : 5703
Spring Day : 6338
The spring day began with birches : 3481, 4326
Spring-Green-Ivory : 6760
A Spring Heresy : 6763
Spring in the North : 4095
Spring Lamb : 6502
Spring Night in Montenegro : 1113
Spring Rain : 2707, 3943
Spring Rain Clears at Evening : 5583
Spring Snow : 4244
Spring Song : 4619, 5783, 6858
Spring-Tide : 5259
Spring Training : 2643
Spring Upstarts : 6268
Spring Waters : 244, 3011, 6624
Spring Wind : 61
Springa Undan? : 2526
Spring's Apprentice : 7009
Spring's breath fills the windows : 4533, 5196
Springtime : 2877
Springtime for Louise : 3131
Springtime in Victoria : 6683
Sprouting Legs : 928
Spruce in Fire : 4462
Spry Declensions : 2305
Spyder Rockett : 1588
Spying on My Father as Gardener : 861
The Square Root of Tyranny : 2333
The Square Shapes and the Round Shapes :
      3769, 4832, 7086
Squarings : 2743
Squashes : 1735

Squeegee : 1735
The Squirrel : 3559
Squirrel Cage : 6064
Squirrels : 4237
SR-71 : 3565
St. . . . : *See also* Saint . . ., filed above under
    'Saint'
St. Anselm's Home : 3720
St. Bartholomew's Night : 66, 6456
St. Croix June : 2919
St. Joseph : 2271
St. Lazare : 5595
St. Louis Art Museum, a Blue Harem: Portraits
    of Three Women : 2303
St. Melania's Gift : 7184
St. Misbehavin' : 1714
St. Nicholas : 3393
St. Valentine's Day : 2
St. Vitus' Disease: Effie's Story : 4342
Staande Aan de Lange Leugen : 6007
Staden Är Tömd : 3792
Stag : 4506
Stagenotes for the History of the World : 2297
Stages of Family Life : 1499
Staghorn Sumac : 1096, 4828
Stained Glass, the Dream : 3323
Stained Sight : 5365
Stains of Onan : 5115
The stairs are in a certain relationship : 2764
Stake-Fire : 2816, 3671, 5379
Stalactite : 1735
Stalin (Saturn — Satan) : 3732
Stalin (Saturn-Satan) : 3732
Stalin's Monument: Snapshot from 1956 : 3270,
    6237, 6992
Stamping Press / Lackawanna, New York :
    6840
Standard Hay Bales : 2882
The Standard Oil Company : 3201, 4641
Standing at the Long Lie : 6007, 6171
Standing in November : 1271
Standing in the Middle of a Desert : 6692
Standing Stones : 4766
Standing Up : 638
Standing Up There : 2104
(Standing, Upright) Bass : 2282
Stanley Smith Is Dead : 2470
Stanley's Confectionery : 1220
Star : 900
The Star-Diver : 2454, 2636
The Star-Drillers' Attention : 5239
The Star of the Sea Hotel : 3720
Starburst : 2148
Stardom : 345
Stare : 5962
Starfished with Microscope : 3596
Staring at the Sea on the Day of the Death of
    Another : 6307
Staring Out a Window : 2634
Starlet reflected : 4243
Starling in the Woodstove : 6728
Starlings : 1262, 1279
Starlings: The Dark and Light of It : 6008
Stars : 2256

The stars are a pale pox on the sky's dark
    chicken : 392
Star's Nightmare : 5340
Starting a Pasture : 4179
Starting as Weather-Lore : 2912
Starting the Tape : 649
The Starving African Girl : 6689
State Executive : 4774
The State House in Columbia, South Carolina :
    1916
Station : 2465
A Station in Another Place : 3634
Station Stop : 6979
The Stationmaster's Retirement : 4117
Stations : 5757
The Statue Speaks with Pygmalion : 5160
Statues of Kings Can Be Categorized As
    Follows : 1915
Statuette : 3708
Status Symbolism : 4429
Stay Away from Me (Bangladesh-I) : 99, 1883
Staying Home from Work : 1852
Staying in Touch : 6242
Staying Out of Trouble : 3991
Staying Up : 873
Staying Up for Love : 4373
Stealing Dirt : 3844
Stealing with My Brother : 3607
Steel Man : 6700
The Steel Plate : 3466
Steelhead : 6309
Steer Head : 6079
Stelae : 264, 5873
Stele (I-II c. B.C.) : 3736
Stella : 332
The Stem of August : 6563
Step Between : 2667
Step by Step : 1922, 5040, 5379
Step Out : 2318
Stepchild Memory : 6775
The Stepfather : 3431
Stepfather's Room : 6775
Stephanie's Stillness : 3404
Stephen Hawking Oraculates : 3171
Stephen Spender in Mount Vernon : 491, 3476,
    4812
Stepping In : 1258
Stepping Out : 4855
Stepping Out for Air : 6711
Stepping Stones : 6185
Steps : 4132
Stereo Poem : 3373
Sterilitism : 244, 1956, 3011
Steroids : 4283
Steven : 4648
Stew : 6493
Stick Horse : 215, 2805, 3104
Stickseeds : 5289
Still : 423
Still at War : 1726
Still, Before : 4039
The Still-Bound : 446
Still It Returns : 813, 814, 2031
Still Life : 955, 1175, 1310, 1757, 2511, 3211,

3559, 3692, 4480, 5180, 5634, 6157,
    6342, 6940, 7057
The Still Life : 5287
Still Life (a Triangle of Sorts) : 3079
Still Life and Death : 4717
Still Life: Belt on Bureau : 5816
Still Life: Louise Muillon : 4669
Still Life with Brioche 1880, Edouard Manet :
    2919
Still Life with Orange : 1860
Stillness : 1062, 1267
Stillwater Marsh : 5858
The Sting : 2870
The Stinkbug : 3559
Stolen Kisses Are the Sweetest, Louveciennes,
    1932 : 1034
Stolen North Texas Summer Evening : 5556
Stolen Poems : 6088
Stoma 1903 : 184
Stoma 1932 : 437
Stoma 1934 : 437
Stoma 1935 : 437
Stoma 1936 : 437
The Stone : 2217
Stone Cross : 371, 2808
Stone Fruit : 4108
Stone Speech : 1873
Stone, stone, stone, not a weeping : 4973
Stonecrop: Notes Towards an Elegy : 6506
Stonemason : 4688
Stonepath : 6402
Stones : 158, 973, 3750
The Stones : 2719, 6249
Stones in Somerville : 817
The Stones of Central Park : 5630
Stoning Byron's Ghost : 5646
Stopover in Martigny : 2472
Stopping Before Olohena : 6339
Stories : 6255
Stories Away : 5347
Stories of Departure : 4135
Stories of Women : 2101
Stories We Seem to Remember : 4179
Storm : 7071
The Storm : 1715, 2747, 3072, 3113
Storm Belt : 2115
Storm Crossing Key Bridge : 6753
Storm in the Osage — 1989 : 6858
Storm-Rise : 4059
Storm Warning : 5152, 5784
Storm, Winter, Walking the Beach After a
    Separation : 4784
Storms : 5954, 6885
Story : 1890
A Story : 3359, 5655
The Story : 2120, 6728
A Story after Dinner : 4222
Story and tales within tales : 5068
Story Heard through a Wall : 3009
Story Lady : 4189
The Story of Anna Swan : 3585
The Story of Our Lives : 971
The Story of Pears : 667
The Story of This Place : 793

Story Time : 6101
The Story Told: Blues Had a Baby : 110
The Storyteller : 4259, 7096
The Storyteller's Women : 4319
Storyville : 2305
Straight : 1295
Straightedge Razor : 4911
Strange Bedfellows : 2330
Strange Dream Diary Fragments on a Lined
    Yellow Pad : 3780
Strange Happenings : 6985
Strange Music : 6046
Strange Thanksgiving : 2164
The Stranger : 2096, 5819
Stranger at the Party : 3927
A Stranger Takes Photos on a Boat : 2454
Strangers Buried Him : 633
Straw into Gold : 372
Straw on Canvas : 1371
Straw Song : 6379
Strawberries : 1479
A Stray Kitten : 3375
The Streamer Trunk : 4743
Streamers : 6317
Street Dance, 1959 : 3009
Street Music : 5050
Street of Gold : 3381
The Street of the Lost Child : 21
Street People : 6636
Street Photograph, 1930 : 4004
Street Saxophone : 6653
Street Scene : 1625, 7077
Street Wise : 6713
Streetcorner Church : 6224
Streetlights : 6243
The Streets : 3445, 5874, 6082
Streets of Laredo : 6913
Stretched out, I'm a carrier, open and empty :
    1148
String Cheese : 6922
Strip / Ruin : 7107
Stripping and Putting On : 6307
Structural Texture : 52
Stub of a Red Pencil : 5894
The Stubborn Child : 4558
Stubborn Woman : 398
Studebaker : 2196
The Student : 5679
A Student of Forsythia : 1766
Studies : 1113
Studies from Life : 2998
Study of a Key : 526, 4566, 6830
Study of Repose : 2104, 6054, 6612
Stuffing It : 5993
Stum of Love : 2917
Stump : 4009
Stunned Again : 4861
Style : 3413
Stylebook : 1735
Subarctic : 3704
Subdivision : 2467
Subduction : 4477
Subject to Desire : 3562
Subjects : 3675

Subjunctive : 1607
Sublimation : 3432
Submarine : 1431
Submarines : 3497, 7192
Subsequence : 5969
Subsonnet on Ethics : 4203
Substantial : 154
Substitute for the Odd Number : 6288
Substitutions : 4856
The Subterranean Battle : 991
Subtext : 5454
Subtracting the Cat : 4798
Subtraction : 6292
Suburban Children : 5574
Suburban Drought : 1261
Suburban Report : 5485
Suburbanite Washing His Car : 4997
Subway Pocket Poems : 2324
Subway Vespers : 4946
Succession : 6737
Succory : 5772
Succubus : 2369
Such Beauty : 4738
Such Is the Place, This Unnamable : 3547,
    5379, 6328
Such Luck : 841
Such sullen dust unhappy fate : 5179
The Sudden Light and the Trees : 1715
A sudden May downpour, people are hiding :
    3979
Suddenly You Slipped into Sleep : 2794, 5197
Suffering Writer : 2284
Suffocation of a Small Southern Town : 5853
Suffrage : 2607
Sugar : 2515, 5404, 7150
Sugar and Spice : 1114
Sugar Cane : 4666
Suicide : 412, 2191, 2747, 2779, 3121
Suicide at the 'L' Motel, Flagstaff, AZ : 5120
Suicide Bridge : 1684
Suiciding the Bats : 6643
Suicidio : 2191
Suit and Tie : 4260
Suitcases of Poetry : 6055
Suitcasing at Doldrum : 3814
Suite Mon Simone : 3298
Sultry Afternoon in Nowata, Oklahoma : 6694
Sumac : 443
Summary : 3032
Summation : 2986
Summer : 3090, 3408, 3559, 3743, 5874
Summer 1983 : 3717
Summer (After Brandt) : 4822
Summer as a Verb, Nantucket as an Island :
    5190
Summer Break : 5195
Summer Daydreams of You : 3774
Summer Downpour : 6322
Summer Earth : 1033, 3621, 5554
The Summer Ending : 6846
Summer Grave : 813, 814, 5708
Summer in a Very Small Town : 1425
Summer in Beirut : 1269
Summer in Full Bloom : 2663

Summer in Pennsylvania : 2904
Summer in the Saddle : 1899
Summer Inversion : 6046
The Summer My Mother Fell in Love and
    Wanted to Leave My Father : 5018
Summer Nights : 1301
The Summer of the Yellow Bikini : 1302
Summer on the Boat : 2401
Summer Outing: Olentangy Park : 3316
A Summer Poem : 321
Summer Rain : 5048
Summer Rain Haiku : 1979
Summer Rites : 706
Summer Solstice : 6477
Summer Storm : 1380
Summer Threnody : 1808
Summer Trains : 6763
Summertime Brochure : 1662
Summons : 4244
Sun and Mist : 6229, 6467
Sun Cycle : 6453
The Sun Is a Brief Incantation : 6848
Sun Setting, Northport : 3439
The Sun Sliding Through : 6492
Sun Spots : 833
The sun today : 3759, 4583
Sunbear Rapids : 185, 6971
Sunchimes : 3735
Sundance : 4387
Sunday : 2715
Sunday Afternoon : 659
Sunday at the Paradise Orchards : 6322
The Sunday Chef : 5933
Sunday Morning : 699
Sunday Morning Roundup : 4179
Sunday mornings : 3774
Sunday Night Rapids : 1743
Sunday Picnic : 2248
A Sunday Poem : 3161
Sunday Skaters : 5590
A Sunday to Her Liking : 3758
Sundew : 3521
Sunfall and Waterrise : 1533
The Sunflower : 2704
The Sunken Cathedral : 5008
The Sunken Lightship Off Frying Pan Shoals :
    3986
Sunken Roads : 4799
Sunlight : 251, 1908
The Sunny Day : 6361
Sunny Side Up : 2305
Sunoco Kid : 2080
Sunrise and Moonfall, Rosarito Beach : 4202
Sunrise in St. Louis : 2911
The Sun's Despair : 1536, 3533
Sunset at Ocean Beach : 65
Sunset at the Reservoir : 4210
Sunset Beach : 567
Sunset Boulevard : 7003
Sunset News : 4062
Sunset on My Son : 293
Sunshine, Lift Your Foot and Let My Shadow
    Go : 1115, 3770
A Supermarket in California : 2287

Supper at Grandma's House : 4000
Suppose : 2456
A Supposed Dream from the REM of St.
    Anthony : 3448
The Supremes : 1734
Sure, I Was Paid Well : 6794
A Sure Thing : 1730
The Sure Wild Glittering Call : 5966
Surely everyone is born unfinished : 173
Surface Tension : 6512
Surfer : 6808
Surfers : 5899
A surgeon from far Indonesia : 1067
The Surgeon's Garden : 4903
Surgery : 382, 574, 6800
Surplus : 5573
Surprise : 1605, 4621
Surprised at my surprise that I could say : 4247
Surprising Event : 1870
The Surrealist Works at His Novel : 5588
The Surrender of the Senses : 590
Survey : 5302
The Surveying Class : 650
Surveyor : 2454, 6324
The Surveyor : 6856
Survival Kit : 3280
Surviving : 5324, 5442
Surviving Like Dummies : 2436
Survivor : 3740, 6813
The Survivor : 2996
Susan Gilbert Dickinson, 1887 : 5980
Sushi Bar with Doreen in November : 7082
Susquehanna : 4567
Sutjeska : 84, 6642, 6643
Suzuki Lullaby : 1426
Swallow It : 972
Swallowing : 7175
Swallows Brush a Pool : 5976
Swan Dive : 5247
Swan Lake : 443
Swans of Sligo : 1161
Sweat : 7033
Sweat House : 4235
Swedish Dream : 3392
Sweeney: A Man for All Seasons : 1126
Sweeney Descends the Stairs : 1126
Sweeping the Clay : 3503
Sweet and Sour : 5076
Sweet Paradise : 214
Sweet Potato Pie : 913
Sweet Relief : 6514
Sweet-Talk : 193
Sweetened Change : 132
The Sweetest Word on Sunday : 2787
Sweetness : 3746
The Sweetness of Bobby Hefka : 3746
The Swiftness of the Clouds : 628, 4610
Swift's Ghost Addresses the Reader of Confes-
    sional Poetry : 3949
The Swim : 2779
Swimmers : 5527
Swimming After Thoughts : 4899
Swimming in the Red Sea before a Sandstorm :
    6282

Swimming in the Trees : 2909
Swimming in Yugoslavia : 2114
Swimming Laps and Mozart : 2946
Swimming Lesson : 1960, 2414
The Swimming Pool : 3903, 6927
Swimming to China : 6936
Swimming with My Children : 2173
Swimming with My Daughter : 3920
Swing : 2036, 5918
Swinging : 5778
Swinging London Poem : 1911
Swiss Thoughts : 2778
Switch : 5251
Switching Shadows : 1300, 2454
Swollen Haiku : 6666
The Sword Form, First Part : 5730
Sybil Is Doing the Dishes : 3009
Sycamores : 3006
Symbol and Renunciation : 3859
Symbolon : 500
Symmetry : 6179
Synapse : 1453, 5741
Syndrome : 345
Syracuse to Albany : 1527
Systematic : 1177
Systole : 6351
Syzygy : 1859
Szegények : 3256
Szendergés Vonaton : 1363
A Szigetlakó : 3981
TV Dinner : 2250
TV Night : 4380
T.V. O.D. : 4671
TV Room at the Children's Hospice : 5548
TVI : 6911
Tabaco de Vuelta Abajo : 4934
Tabasco Madonna : 3780
Taberna : 7137
Table Sugar : 1652
Table Talk : 2588
Tableau : 610
A Tableau : 5618
Tabula Rasa : 833
Tabula Rasa? : 2856
Tabula Rasa : 5183
Tack Ska Du Ha : 3134
Tactics : 6962
Taffeta Madonna : 3780
Taffy : 3384
Tag : 900
Tahafut al-Falasifah : 2651
Tailings : 6270
Tait : 546
Take a Listen : 179
Take Five : 2694
Take Me Back : 3629
Take My Neighbor : 3746
Take My Picture, Says Pito : 5446
Take the Kid Out : 935
Takeover : 6776
Taking Along the Dust : 338
Taking Apart the Porch : 342
Taking Away the L : 5321
Taking Chances : 440

Taking Chances: Windward in a Time of
    Butterflies : 328
Taking Highway 80 to Lincoln : 7193
Taking in the Wash : 3957
Taking It Back : 2556
Taking Pictures : 921
Taking the Blame : 184
Taking Up Fishing at 40 : 3795
Taking What's Good for You : 4035
Tala till Mig : 206
The Tale : 2216, 4901
The Tale of the Man Who Loves Too Much :
    568
A Talent for Rivers : 3195
Tales from Daddima : 243
Talk with the Moon : 2970
Talking about New Hampshire : 5567
Talking About the Penis : 5532
Talking Mica : 5069
Talking of the Flying Rollers with Gary Snyder
    : 1082, 1625
Talking to the Mirror : 244, 3011, 3877
Talking with Poets : 106
Talking with the Wind : 5278
Tall Birds Stalking : 6603
A Tall Flame : 7070
The Tall Grass on the Hill : 883, 6481
Talus Slope : 7004
Tamar at the Gate of Enaim : 6275
Tamarack : 306
Tamworth : 4522
The Tandem : 2864
Tanfastic : 5909
A Tangent on Lines by Susan Howe : 6708
Tank Hill : 1251
Tanka : 4164
Tansy Ragwort : 1673
Tantalus : 2166
Tante Lottie Suffers Concussion : 87
Tao-Billy : 3215
Tape : 6293
Tapestries of Song : 1269
Taps : 2315
Tarantula : 1311
Tarascon : 1113
A Tárgy Fölött : 4586
Tarjetas Postales : 6666
Tartarchos : 1572
Taste : 6934
Tattoo : 623, 5259
The Tattoo : 4223
Tattoo, Corazón: Ritchie Valens, 1959 : 7010
Tattoos : 4929
Tattoos, Suit Changing : 6333
Taurus Glares Down the Giant Hunter : 1464
A Tavern : 3120, 4534, 5250
Tax Deferred Title : 3829
Tea : 1106, 4605, 4963
Tea in Heliopolis : 2533
Tea Party : 1312
Tea with Lemon : 4859
Tea with Terrorists : 4532
Teacher Me Sweet : 3592
The teacher scrawls cold calculations : 1724

Teachers : 923
The Teacher's Story : 2702
Teaching : 1434
Teaching Institutes : 2656
Teaching Literature : 2682
Teaching My Sons to Dance : 7103
Teachings : 1842
Teacups : 7019
Technology As Nostálgia : 5190
The Technology of Industry : 3999
The Technology of Miracles : 3999
The Technology of Mortality : 3999
The Technology of Sheep : 3999
The Technology of The Woman in the Dunes :
    3999
Teckning : 5293
Tectonics : 2339
Teddungal : 4619, 5783, 5783
Teddy Boys : 4064
Teddy's Purples : 2667
Teenage Child Blues : 4877
Teenagers at the Mall : 1498
Teething : 6794
Teevee With Grandmomma : 2981
Telephone Call : 1525, 4091
Telescoped : 2594
Television : 116, 738, 5197
Television as God : 5586
The television sits gray : 4361
Telex Gorilla : 6501
Tell Me a Story : 6746
Tell Me About the Soul: Leonardo at Cloux,
    1916-19 : 1676
Tell me again what the oppressed look like :
    3329
Tell Me If: Leonardo in the Belvedere, 1513-16
    : 1676
Tell Them : 5895
Telling : 1986
Telling the Future on Interstate 75 : 5510
Telling the Missing Days : 2839
Telling the Pilot : 4466
A Tempest : 2689
The Tempest Sonata : 3296
Temples, More or Less : 3862
Templos Extranjeros : 2193
Tempo Continuato : 1473
Temporary Limitations : 338
Le Temps Perdu : 6770
Tempt the Devil : 3299, 4871
Tempting the Universe : 4373
Ten Approaches to Her : 457
Ten in Queens : 4961
Ten Miles North of Danby : 4224
Ten of St. Helens : 1492
Ten Qualities As a Cosmo Girl I Really Want in
    My Man : 1704
Ten Years After Your Deliberate Drowning :
    433
Tenant : 4294
The Tenant Farmer Conducts a Tour : 6510
Tender Red Net : 6463
Tenement Night : 581
Tennessee Line : 7058

Tennyson : 6489
A Tent Pitched Among White Birches : 885
The Tentative Steps of the Obese : 1966
Tenth Birthday : 4598
Tenth-Year Elegy : 675
Terminal : 1336
Terminal Illness : 3993
The Terminology of Winter (How the Past Exists) : 1294
Terminus: Concedo Nulli : 4514
Terms in Contradiction : 5833
Terra Cotta : 216
Terrace View : 5546
La Terre de l'Ete : 5554
Terreiro de S. Vicente : 158, 3750
Terribilita : 7061
Territory : 2466
The Territory : 271
Terror : 2104, 2368, 3519
The Terror of Travel : 2182
Terrors from Beyond the Grave : 1143
Terzanelle of the Spider's Web : 6536
Test : 3553
The Test : 6667
Test Cases : 6547
Testament : 1425, 2860
Testament XXVI : 6814
Testament XXVIII : 6814
Testaments : 2204
Testimony : 1960
Testing : 1727
Testing Perspectives : 5311
Tete-a-tete : 2542
Texas : 492
Texas Jacks : 4226
The Texas Prophet : 90
Texas Skyline : 1258
Texas Transformation : 4564
Text and Commentary : 1822, 3064
Tezcatlipoca: The Song of a Human Sacrifice : 484, 1250, 6215
Than I Have Ever Been : 2285
Thanatopsis Revisited : 6782
Thanh Mai's Letter : 1996
Thank You for the Helpful Comments : 6195
Thanks for Your Time : 6731
Thanksgiving : 2537, 2599, 5128
Thanksgiving Day Prayer, 1990 : 3912
That Blue : 6723
That boy, the farmer said, with hazel wand : 6533
That Diet Cock, Lite, That Never Cums Off : 1337
That friend — despair : 6396, 6507
That House : 2706
That Humans Could Be Numb : 918
That Indian Summer Afternoon : 3148
That Is How I Think of You Too : 2619, 5389
That Is the Image : 4467, 5995
That July : 3780
That Kind of Day : 5839
That Little : 2595
That Local Knowledge : 2462
That Old Convict Man : 6216

That Old Garden and Etcetera : 2481
That Old Tune : 1183
That Past : 2220
That Path : 685, 6687
That Peculiar Hunger for Light : 6848
That Second-Rate Film : 883, 6481
That Story : 4540
That Uneasy Creature, Creation : 4898
That Which Impedes : 2597
That Which Is Fugitive, That Which Is Medicinally Sweet or Alterable to Gold, That Which Is Substantiated by Unscientific Means : 7009
That which once again befalls the heavens : 3064, 3494
That Year : 3365, 4867
That You Tell : 236
That'll Be the Day : 6520
That's Enough for Me : 803, 2364
That's father, isn't it? : 3299, 4871
That's What Poetry Is Like : 158, 3750
Thaw : 184, 675, 839, 6426, 7004
The Thaw : 5008
The Thaw on Slack's Pond : 148
Thawing the Vultures : 2255
The : 1858
Theaters of Operation : 6151
The Theatre Party : 1546
Thebe : 22, 6006
Thebes Revisited : 2127
Thee : 164
Their Asking : 3398
Them : 5785
Theme: The Freudian Eve-&-Adam : 1391
Themistocles : 3287, 5361
Then All Smiles Stopped : 4133
Then She Says : 734
Then the Sickness : 707
Theology of Hopelessness : 3732
Theorem : 2879
Theory of Flight, 1908 : 2964
Theory of Realism : 6812
There : 6829
There Are Bones in the Meadow : 6105
There Are Certain Things : 3933
There Are Deeper Waters : 813, 814, 5064
There Are No Others : 1286
There Are People Who Cannot Cross Bridges Without Wanting to Jump : 1155
There Are Some Countries : 1361, 3243, 5379
There at the Circle : 1884
There Is a Cheapness to the Statues : 2466
There Is a Country : 3464
There Is Another Way : 5693
There Is Certainly Someone : 2748, 5107
There is fire in the bones of my face : 3672
There Is No End : 4149
There Is No Season Like Summer : 3359
There is nothing trivial about love : 4001
There Is Something Drawing Me : 1625, 7154
There Is Something Terribly Wrong with These Lines : 5844
There Is Still Water : 3946
There Once was a lady from Keele : 6432

There, Solid : 6114
There Was a Shot : 4738
There Was Earth Inside Them : 1043, 1928
There Was Earth Inside Them, and They Dug :
     1043, 1928
These are the photos : 4508
These Days : 6498
These holes limping closer to my arms : 4973
These Things Are Important : 4991
These Windows : 3665
Thesis : 5601
They Are Like the Dew : 2184, 4362
They Are the Seagulls, My Love : 803, 2364
They Come to Dance : 5421
They Come to Me : 3243, 4587, 5379
They Count Persephone : 6596
They Drafted My Son : 215, 2805, 3104
They Leave : 3858
They Never Grew Old : 1183
They Remain Hatless : 1243
They Shot at Midnight : 2216, 4901
They, the Gardeners : 5976
They Want Ice Cream the Color of Honeydew
     Melon : 5106
They Were Roving : 3547, 5379, 6318
They're waiting for me to entertain them : 1902
Thief : 6883
A Thin, Black Band : 1363, 5379, 6380
The Thin Country : 318
Thin Ice : 2021
Thin Man's Litany : 5949
A Thin Moon : 670
The Thing Which in the Waking World Comes
     Nearest to a Dream Is a Night Alone in a
     Big Town : 2929
The Thing Worth Saving : 4095
Things : 6725
Things and Their Absence : 184
Things Are Only Things : 2164
Things Past : 2915
The Things She Left : 4509
Things That Break : 166
Things to Do in *Valley of the Dolls* (The Movie)
     : 6515
Things to Do When Your Friend Dies of AIDS :
     4577
Things We Know by Heart : 6044
Things You Can't Talk About : 813, 814, 5293
Think Like a Weightlifter, Think Like a
     Woman : 706
Think of Colors : 6288
Thinking About My Father : 2979
Thinking About the Weather : 727
The Thinking Between Two Waves : 7017
Thinking for Berky : 6101
Thinking Like a Mountain : 1626
Thinking of Kierkegaard : 5947
Thinking of the Cold Mountain Poet : 7108
Thinks the Peeping Toms : 1490
Thinning Peach Trees : 2171
Third Dialogue Between the Lone Ranger and
     Tonto : 6859
The Third Kind of Interior Word : 4420
Third Night Home : 4163

Third Riddle with Its Solution : 2558, 3961
Third-Shift Waitress at the Coral Reef : 3955
Third Stanza : 6015
The Third Wave : 6899
Thirst : 5278
The Thirst for Beauty : 100, 3040, 3166
Thirsty As Plants, Lonely As Animals : 5138
Thirteen Shapes of Desire : 2460
Thirteen Ways of Looking at the National En-
     dowment for the Arts : 7162
Thirty, Feeling Like Seventeen Again : 2094
Thirty-Five Dollars : 4571
Thirty-Gallon Heater : 2105
Thirty-three Girls Are Taken to See Ninety-
     eight Paintings by a Dead Artist of Their
     Own Sex : 2647
This Ain't Plutonic, Baby, or, She Knows She
     Has the Divine Gift : 1504
This Be the Night : 4363
This Bitter Magic : 4550
This country, huge, wintry and blue : 2422,
     3552, 6552
This Country of Silence : 3218, 4793
This day I keep seeing what is not there : 3774
This December They Would Speak of Having a
     Child : 4959
This ditch no matter how haggard : 4973
This Evening : 738, 5197
This evening, my dear, when I was speaking to
     you : 1358, 4601
This Faith : 5032
This Far From Town : 1269
This hardened suspicion : 1754, 5657
This Heart That Hated War : 1536, 2023
This Hour and What Is Dead : 3691
This Immense Oak : 2985, 4362
This is a really exciting day : 4335
This Is a Transformation : 813, 814, 3792
This Is an Answer : 836
This Is Denise, I Say to Pito : 5446
This is how I am. I wish you another : 67, 2778
This Is How They Left Her : 5274
This Is It : 7127
This is just to say : 399
This Is Loneliness : 5976
This Is Not a Sad Poem : 4873
This Is Not an American Planet : 1435
This Is Not Death Yet : 666, 3464, 3489, 6462
This is salamander country : 1746
This Is the City : 491, 3476, 4811
This Is the Hour : 5828
This Is the Stone : 5240
This leaf is death : 1454
This Long Winter : 3780
This Love : 2870
This Magazine Is Full of Poems : 1393
This Moment : 6813
This Morning : 3409
This Morning at Tinsley Crossing : 4986
This Morning I Woke into the Body : 1651
This night — for you : 4976, 5105
This Peculiarity : 5865
This plaque and over the fireplace : 4973
This Poem : 1066, 2567, 6870, 6971

This Poem Is Based on a True Story : 6822
This Poem Is for CJ : 5537
This Poem Speaks for Itself : 1737
This Rain : 473
This Room and Everything In It : 3691
This Scribe, My Hand : 443
This Season on the Ridge : 6371
This Shame Is a Carnivore : 5793
This slab once curled up inside : 4973
This Story : 3901
This Story No One Tells : 6932
This Stranger : 411
This Sudden Silence : 2160, 4462, 5822
This Thing We All Have to Get Through : 994
This Time : 2393, 4858
This Tree You Told Us Stories Of : 3889
This Unborn Child : 2090
This Will Be My Only : 836
This window sweetening the air : 4973
This World : 3262
Thistlebloom : 868
Thistles : 2656
Thomas Eakins' *William Rush and His Model* :
    6117
Thoreau on Paran Creek : 443
The Thorn-Shaver on Fifth : 4260
Thorns : 3150
Thorns and Thistles : 5891
Those Julys : 3780
Those Mornings : 3383
Those Old Faces : 1824
Those old koans meaningless just ways of
    faking virtue : 476, 3033
Those Past Days : 685, 6687
Those Who Cannot Be Together : 1472
Those Who Part Hold Dear : 3274, 5235
Those Who Roam at Night : 6522
Thou Art Indeed Just, Lord : 2934
Though every evening : 4973
Thought, Death : 3071, 6708
Thought of Faces On : 3780
The Thought of It : 3780
Thoughts : 33, 1671, 2104, 6054
Thoughts Drifting Through the Fat Black
    Woman's Head While Having a Full
    Bubble Bath : 4666
Thoughts of a Solitary Farmhouse : 7059
Thoughts on a Jet Flight to New York City :
    2595
Thrall : 723
Thread : 3291
The Thread : 1735
Threads : 2489
The Threatened Habit of Perfection : 4416
Three : 6867
Three Acts in the Form of a Sonnet : 3041
Three Answers in Spring : 7040
Three Chairs in Creel, Mexico : 1383
Three Cultural Moods : 5792
Three Dances from the Daily News : 4519
Three Days, I Waited for My Love : 6848
Three Dead Voices : 5130
Three Entertainments : 2343
The Three Faces of Eve : 485

Three Finger Bones : 943
Three Fish Stories : 606
Three Lakes : 1712, 5992, 6454
Three Letters Not Written, 1926 : 1442
Three Letters to the President of These United
    States : 6378
Three Masses of Light : 1644
Three Mile Island : 687
Three Months Exile : 5036
Three Musics : 3180
Three O'Clock in the Afternoon : 1625, 6743
The Three Perched Birds : 6736
Three Poems about Audubon : 93
Three Poems After Klee : 4730
Three Poems for Lisa (1955-1988) : 6785
Three Poems on Larrieu's *Le Lit Défait* (The
    Bed Unmade) : 1391
Three Purgatory Poems : 169
Three-Quarters Moon : 3075
Three Riddles : 184, 4309
Three Scenes : 235
Three Sisters : 4172
Three Song Bird : 848
Three Stories Told on the Same Day : 4065
Three Thanksgivings at My Step-
    Grandmother's : 3276
Three Times Yes : 5746
Three Variations on an Absent Theme : 304
Three Versions Culminating in the Minimal :
    1128
Three Ways to Kill a Goose : 3278
Three Weeks Later : 4278
Three Wishes : 646, 2017, 5855
Three Years Ago : 2429
The Threshold : 5421
Thrift Shop, Ypsilanti : 2352
A Throat of a Rose : 3623
Throne : 3358
Through a Glass Darkly : 5833
Through a Window : 418
Through and Through : 58, 1070
Through the Eyes of the Dark-Eyed Americans
    : 5799
Through the Heel : 3311
Through the Red Sea (After the Paintings of
    Anselm Kiefer) : 3005
Through the Slow Rancor of Water : 2184,
    4362
Through Two Windows : 3704
Throwaway : 1342
Throwbacks : 595
Thru Jade Sea Light : 3780
The Thud of Not Seeing You : 3780
Thunder After Thunder, Returning Like Rhyme
    : 5406
The Thunder Chair : 1598
Thunder Recedes : 5888
The Thunderbird : 3797
Thunderhead : 973
Thursday : 6253
Thursday Night : 2482
Thursday Was a Day of Wood : 5594
Tiananmen Square : 3684
Tiara : 1650

Tiberius to His Sons : 4251
Ticket to the War : 3140
Ticks : 6779
The Tie : 6691
Tie-Down of A Bonsai : 445
Tiffany & Co : 5760
Tiffany's on Fire : 6994
The Tiger : 3580
Tiger Grease : 1044
Tiger Lily : 1887
Tilapia : 252
Tilted in from the hallway : 5242
Tim : 5414
Timber Rattler : 5321
Timbre : 615
Time : 980, 5071, 5392
Time and Space : 2822, 3126
Time Crawls into Our Pores : 2367
Time Flies at 22 : 756
Time Frame : 4416
The Time I Was Very Quiet and Just Listened : 1725
Time in His Aging Overtakes All Things Alike : 2796
The Time It Takes to See : 2736
Time Off from Bad Behavior : 4476
Time Takes the Woods Forever : 6127
Time Was, She Declares : 622
A Time Zone : 3443
The Times and Trials of Moses Austin : 1969
Times My Father Almost Died : 2760
Times of Love & Loss : 4713
Timidity : 1477
Tin Ceiling, Pecs, Hungary : 5379
Tin Laughter : 967, 5995
The Tin Nautilus : 4966
Tinkerbell, the Older Woman, Sorrows for the Loss of Peter Pan : 6800
Tinky Tongue : 3252
Tinting Tonight : 3591
A Tiny Disk-toed : 5263
Tipped over : 2491
Tippet : 4146
Tipping Wings Over the Grand Canyon : 5224
Tips on the Single Life, from Cookie Schwarz : 3845
Tirade for the Next-to-Last Act : 1018, 3407
Tired Blood : 6030
Tired Light : 2198
Tired Stars : 6085
Tires : 4175
Tirza in the Land of Numbers : 21
Tishku Leaves the Party : 5114
Tithes : 1481
Titian Makes Preliminary Studies for a Picture of Saint Sebastian : 989
To a Child : 767
To a Dour, Dear Friend : 3902
To a Face in the Crowd : 6765
To a Friend : 2377
To a Friend Dead of AIDS : 6558
To a Friend Who Mailed Me His Latest Epic : 1643
To a Girl Writing Her Father's Death : 2340

To a Hummingbird Moth : 1991
To a Man : 2002, 4031
To a Man at the Seashore Whose Wife Has Been Staying with Me in the City : 3661
To a Man Who Said He Would Live Forever : 384
To a Photojournalist : 4095
To a Poet : 6257
To a Posthumous Hyena : 2832
To a Satanic Friend : 734
To a Scorpion Preserved in a Glass Necklace : 5526
To a Small Lizard : 916
To a White Crow : 3172
To a Woman Standing in a Doorway : 3158
To All Those Poets One Reads in Childhood : 650
To an Actor, Who Asked That His Role Be Lengthened : 1754, 3544
To an Aids Victim at the Mayo Clinic : 4461
To an Ex-Lover and D. H. Lawrence : 2731
To Be Born We Must Die, to Be Born We Must Be Born : 3230
To Be Rich : 491, 3476, 4812
To Bill Stafford : 1577
To Billie Holiday : 6282
To Build On : 2395
To Celia : 6034
To Chekhov and Konchalovski : 1601
To Complete a Thought : 5431
To Country : 7043
To Critics, and to Hell with Them : 7062
To Cross : 1295
To Cross Barbed Wire : 298
To Cure a Broken Heart : 6800
To die is all I really want : 5622, 6203
To Each Day : 5554, 6940
To Each His Own : 2790
To Earthward : 2128
To Emerson — and Jeanette : 882
To enter that rhythm where the self is lost : 5521
To Father : 3998
To Freedom : 491, 4586
To Fulke Greville : 4605
To Grandmother's Bed : 1742
To H. J., the Master : 4112
To Happiness : 7051
To Have and Have Not : 184, 321
To Hay Fever Sufferers : 6453
To Heal a World : 4949
To Her Gigolo : 571
To Her Masters : 3673
To Hera : 6673
To His Good Agnostic — A Letter : 7102
To His Mistress : 19, 464
To His Subject Matter : 4487
To improve social behaviour : 5222
To Interest Your children : 5823
To James Wright 1 : 2293
To James Wright 2 : 2293
To Jimmy, Found in His Room at 28 : 1375
To John : 1907
To Johns Hopkins University : 2306

To Justify My Singing : 7062
To Keep Meaning from Emerging from the
   Mesh : 6235
To Keep Revolving : 3980
To L. Levchev : 4939, 5098
To Leonora : 1304
To Live in the Distances : 5032
To Maida of Yugoslavia from My Book of
   Common Flowers: A Letter : 6942
To Marc Chagall : 1794, 2307, 6053
To Murder Time : 2747, 3120, 5367
To My Brother in His Casket : 2967
To My Daughter at Her Window : 621
To My Father : 4112
To My Friend Jerina : 1167
To My Lover : 691
To My Mother, Remembering How We Bought
   Candles : 756
To My Sweetheart at Sixty : 3769, 4832, 7121
To New York : 1599, 5783
To Nicholas and Frieda, in the Voice of Sylvia
   Plath : 5529
To Orpheus : 4093, 5361
To Paul of Saint Victor : 872
To Peggy Gabson in Boston from New York
   City, the 22nd of December : 460
To Quiet the Earth : 5284
To Ramon and Ana Maria Xirau : 5569, 6672
To Remain : 3418
To Robert Lowell, in the Guise of Mentor :
   4112
To Robinson Jeffers : 3860, 4395
To Search Within : 6107
To Shakespeare, on His Marriage at Eighteen to
   a Woman Eight Years Older : 3998
To Sit and Look for One Still Hour : 4746
To Sleep : 5093
To Sleep and Back : 2711
To Someone : 4136
To the Angel X : 5634
To the Black American Troops : 1599, 5783
To the Boily Blind Boy the Sun Spins : 5181
To the Christmas Present Head in Lautrec's 'Le
   Rat Mort' : 4638
To the Deaf Ones : 532, 5579
To the Edge : 2690
To the Green Man : 3110
To the Handsome Young Man Who Bought the
   Old and Wonderful Picture Dictionary at
   the Book Sale . . . : 6379
To the Harpy : 2084
To the Headless : 1536, 3533
To the Lilting Breeze : 4791
To the Lord or to Me : 1504
To the Mountaintop : 1443, 3969, 7057
To the One Lost on the Other Side : 4134
To the Person Who Stole My Camera : 1893
To the Photographer of the Egg Woman in
   Juarez : 1182
To the Physicist Who Named a Type of Pain
   After Himself : 4937
To the Protestors Who Violated St. Patrick's
   Cathedral for the Love of A.I.D.S. Victims
   : 50

To the Reader : 1963, 4310, 7010
To the Trees : 2911, 2994
To the Women-in-the-Moon : 6758
To This Body in Love : 4493, 5448
To Those Who Ask : 215, 2805
To wake at dawn : 67, 2778
To Winter : 2619, 6006
The Toad : 4457
The Tobacco Queen : 3913
Tobogganing : 762
Today : 1743, 6877, 7127
Today at the Start : 10
Today for Breakfast We Had : 354, 1164
Today Someone Brought You Flowers : 2522,
   2609, 3942
Today the Poetry Reading Review : 10
Todesfuge : 1043
Together : 6098, 6681
Token : 1289, 1314
Tokens : 1271
Tolstoy at Yasnaya Polyana : 7032
Tom : 2680
Tom Ramsey : 5626
Tomato Harvest : 3096
Tombstones : 1782
Tom's Idea : 5538
A Ton of Fleck : 6187
The Tone : 4980
Tone Deaf : 3480
Toner : 5886
Toner (Brucebook) : 5886
Tongue : 1605
Tonight : 775
Tonight Dear : 4619, 5783
Tonight, He Is Travelling in the Past : 769
Tonight I saw a rose : 748, 1270
Tonight I'm Going to Get Drunk : 211, 1590,
   3410
Tonight the fingerprint : 2135, 3751, 6383
Tony : 1858
Too Early for Questions : 1611
Too Much : 2577
Too Much Exquisite Petrarch : 2697
Too Palm Tree, Too Pool : 2229
Too Soon : 943
The Tools of Ignorance : 523
The Tooth Fairy : 3657
Toothpaste : 7049
Topless Is Allowed Here : 2543, 3064, 3064
The Topless Lunch : 423
Topography : 3900
Toppled Columns, Blue Sky, and Sea : 6046
Tops Off : 654
Tordon : 5994
Torino : 599
Torn from the Soil : 6965
Torn Ligament : 6011
Tornado : 6112
Tornado Awareness : 3149
Tornado Survivor : 4211
Tornado Watch en Saragosa, TX : 4769
Tornadoes : 4521
Torquemada Slumbers : 3924
Torrigiano : 1676

Torsos & Horses : 7052
The Torturer : 3567, 5281
Total destruction has coherent design : 4876, 5186
Totalidades : 5882
Totenwald : 7004
Toting It Up : 1605
Touch : 1550, 3457, 6743, 7155
Touch and Go : 1735
Touche : 5728
Touched : 110
Touching a Girder : 6984
Touching It : 3126
Touchstone : 4831
The Touchstone : 5623
Tough Enough : 1626
Tour of Duty : 2979
Tour of the Tomb : 1536, 2023
Touring the Campus Arboretum, Early Spring : 3425
Tourist Attractions: 2 Postcards : 5883
Tourists : 3681
Toward Light : 783
Toward Morning : 5858
Toward the end : 5938
Towards Noah's Ark : 3243, 4587, 5379
The Tower : 3212, 3736
Town : 4833
Toxic Petals : 92
Toy : 4640
The Toy Soldier : 5256
Tra la Perduta Gente : 6326
Trace : 234
Trace, in Unison : 2164
Trace the Scar : 3843
Trackless Quest : 84, 6642, 6643
Tracks : 17
Tract : 3171, 5065
Tractor Accident : 163
Tractor Feed : 5771
Trade-In : 6654
Trade Routes, With Silk : 2079
Tradición : 1359
Trading Places : 3093
Traffic : 1605
Traffic-Lights : 5589
Tragaluz : 7137
La Tragedia de No Llamarse Rosa Luxemburgo : 2358
The Tragedy of Open Spaces : 2602
The Tragedy of Snappen-Sara : 645, 813, 814
The Trail That Turns on Itself : 2332
Trailblazer : 3085
Trails without Signs : 6076
The Train Cure : 1966
Train Halted in Virginia Woods : 3136
The Train into the Mountainside, the Miracle of the Bus : 1128
Train to Munich : 2110
Train Tracks and Trains Forever and Dogs on No Leashes : 6373
Trainman : 3279
Trains : 3612
Trajectories : 5997

Trajectory : 5858
Trakl : 3126, 7072, 7072
Tranquility : 5806
Transatlantic Greetings : 6399
Transference : 39
Transferring Names into a New Address Book : 5507
Transformation : 3242, 4990, 6220
Transformation Is Not a Four-Letter Word : 6778
The Transformation of Light : 3393
Transformations : 1582, 3924, 5098
Transit Confessional : 641
Transition : 666, 3370, 4388
Transits : 6224
Translated from the American : 96
Translating Zen Poems : 6241
The Translation of Marangat into Morongo : 2182
Transmigration : 6779
Transmutation : 6848
The Trap : 1099, 1679, 4286
Trapo, trapos : 414
The Trapper and the Arctic Fox : 3038
Traps : 5638
Trash : 2909
The Trashmen Shaking Hands with Hubert Humphrey at the Opening of Apache Plaze Shopping Center, Suburban Minneapolis, August 1963 : 7010
El Trasver : 2076, 7124
Travel : 774
Travel Back in Time Not So Far Out : 103
Travelers : 1157
Travelers Three : 2466
Traveling : 1914
Traveling Back : 3093
Traveling in a Comfortable Car : 724, 1697, 3598
Traveling Small Distances : 269
Traveling to Texas : 6121
Travellers : 2875
Travelling Light : 3341, 5904
Travelling Shop : 4800
Travelogue : 666
Treadle : 2056
Treatise : 1963
The Tree : 3254, 3689, 5502
Tree Cutting : 2997
Tree Houses in Central Park : 6600
A Tree in Spring : 6307
Tree, Mend Us : 2383
The Tree of Rubber Tires : 1810
The Tree Seat : 5908
The Tree Surgeon's Curse : 3913
The Tree, with a Hole, in Our Front Yard : 4644
Treefishing : 1256
Trees : 491, 2474, 2719, 4586, 6249
The Trees : 591, 5916, 6454, 6464
The Trees, All Their Green : 2531, 2910
Trees and Mirrors : 109
Trees Come to the River : 1640
Trees in the Night : 298
The Trees of CIW : 6891

The Trees of Monticello : 4371
Treestains : 2296
Trek : 2819
Tremor : 5167
Trendy Is a Six-Letter Word, Which Is Why It
    Won't Last : 6819
Trenton High : 1036
Trespass : 4
Trestle : 1257
Triage : 2360, 5575
The Triangle : 974
Triangles : 3845
The Tribes : 346, 3120, 4312
The Triborough Bridge a Crown for His Head :
    3930
Tribute : 3445, 4699, 5874
Tribute to Only a Cat : 3798
A Tribute to the 'Unknown Hero' : 956
The Trick : 6658
Tricycling in the Sea : 6728
Trident II: 720,000 Hiroshimas : 2828
Trigger Housings : 2470
Trilce : 5573, 6588
Trimmer Man : 6067
Trimming : 5833
Trimmings : 4539
The Trip : 4920
The Trip to Auschwitz : 2268
Trip to the Moon : 2191, 5898, 6889
Tripping Out As Narcissus : 490
Triptych : 2410
The Triumph of Capitalism : 3765
The Triumph of Children : 5828
Triumph of Measure : 3012
Triumph of the Holy Cross : 1326
The Triumph of Trash : 229, 4439
Triumvera : 6434
Los Triunfadores : 5786
Troja at Eight in the Evening : 3270, 6315,
    6992
The Trojan Horse : 3270, 6093
Trompe d'Oeil : 7180
Troop 603 : 1228
Trophies : 2142
Trophy, W.W.I : 3759
The Tropic Gardens of St. Gallen : 2248
Tropical : 2190, 2629, 6213
Tropical Death : 4666
Tropical Watercolor: Sarasota : 619
Trouble at the Circe Arms : 3833
Trouble in a Minnesota Town : 675
Trouble in Summer : 250
The Trouble in the Third Floor Window : 5106
The Trouble We've Always Had with April :
    998
A Troubled Glow : 6829
Troublesome Gods : 1912, 3188
The Trout : 3559
Trout Fishing : 3913
Trout Fishing in Alberta : 5269
Trout in the Clear Calm : 4179
Trout Keeper : 4961
Troy : 1401
Truce : 1496

A Truce in January : 14, 178
Truck at the Top of the Field : 6046
Truckin' : 6813
True Confessions : 2101
True Love : 6514
True North : 5531
True Places : 1315
True Religion : 2929
True Stories : 1277
A True Story : 941
True to Life : 5728
True Wasp : 5241
Truffle : 5652
Truing In : 3924
Trump Bump : 6514
The Trumpeter Swan : 3605
Trust : 5512
Trusted Remedies : 27
The Truth : 464, 6901
Truth Is Not a Separate Reality (I Like the
    Word, Raspberry) : 4385
Truth Lasts Only a Day, Beauty a Month : 4409
Try and Run : 173
Try This Poem Before You Read Any Others :
    5026
Trying for Fire : 5763
Trying Not to Tease Him : 1458
Trying Not to Think of Politics, May Day,
    Belgrade 1989 : 833
Trying to Catch Up : 2268
Trying to Crow : 2303
Trying to Find Her Teeth : 4250
Trying to Flee a Dark Bedroom : 1458
Trying to Fly : 3293
Trying to Get Across the Line : 1330
Trying to Stop, Trying to Keep Him : 2121
Trying to Talk About Sex — I : 3455
Trying to Write You a Poem on Our Anniver-
    sary While Downstairs You Roughhouse
    with the Dogs : 5467
Tryst : 34, 4101
Tsankawi : 7141
Tsvetayeva, Daily Necessity : 6313
Tu m'as ravie : 2159
Tube Alley / Survival : 214, 3209
Tubes : 2567
Tuck : 964
Tucson : 3171
Tugging : 5636
Tulips : 1153, 3336
Tulle, reed, paper, taffeta : 499, 5438
La Tumba de Buenaventura Roig : 1830
Tumble : 4474
Tumbling Dice : 3831
Tunes : 5241
The Tunnel : 3816
The Tunnel Men : 749
Turbulence: *Exile on Main Street* Tour, 1972 :
    7010
Turin: Albergo Roma : 5512
Turkey Vultures : 5803
Turkish Pharmaceuticals Magnate Sees a Sunny
    Future for His Country : 4941
Turning : 4085

Turning Aside : 4927
Turning the Breech Baby (Around) : 2638
Turnips : 135
The Turtle : 4632
Turtle Beach, Tobago, 1988 : 6574
Turtle of Vision : 6737
Turtle Poem : 6431
Turtle Project, Wassaw Island : 4245
Turtles : 5001
Tuscan Visit (Simone Martini) : 3656
TV Dinner : 2250
TV Night : 4380
T.V. O.D. : 4671
TV Room at the Children's Hospice : 5548
TVI : 6911
Twelve Arrests, No Convictions : 1243
Twelve O'Clock : 3407
Twenties : 3926
Twenties: 40 : 3926
Twenty Colors : 3398
Twenty-One : 56, 1451
Twenty-Sixth Anniversary Poem : 6782
Twenty-Two Windows : 4705
Twilight : 5257
The Twin Cities : 4503
Twined Dream : 1276
Twinkle Little Star : 1507
Twins : 6458
Twins in the Balance : 6902
Twist the spindle in my heart further : 1113,
    3658
Twisting : 1192
Twitchin' the Night Away : 4503
Two : 1259, 2231, 5040
Two Black Guys : 4429
Two Blue Swans : 3398
Two Boys : 2194
The Two Cities : 3868
Two Coordinates on a Map of Low Revelation :
    3755
Two Days Before Christmas : 5340
Two Dead Marriages : 1458
Two Dreams : 3562, 6579
Two from Ellsworth Kelly : 3829
Two Holiday Meals : 2629
Two Hours After My Brother Called : 3275
Two Icons : 6004
Two Jersey Crows in the Slow Lane of the
    Parkway : 6782
Two Journeys Across the Lake : 368
The Two Magnets : 3736
Two Magpies : 4222
Two Men : 4001
Two Mennonite Graves in a Lutheran Cemetery
    : 6217
Two Nights in 1956 : 769
Two personal problems: under-arm goat : 1032,
    4242, 5210
Two Photographs : 2465
Two Pictures of My Sister : 3657
Two Pieces of Birch Bark : 2522, 3876, 3942
Two Pints and a Prayer : 1975
Two Poems : 5618
Two Poems As One : 4351

Two Poems for Kenneth Burke : 5953
Two Poems for the Guitar : 5255
Two Poems / Matins : 1480
Two Poems on Exile : 1460
Two Poems on the Same Subject : 4057
Two Portraits of Women Reading : 6211
Two Preludes for La Push : 3832
The Two Riders : 5565
Two (Separate) Extracts from a Collaborative
    Renga (1989) Odd-Numbered Stanzas:
    Harry Gilonis, Even-Numbered Stanzas:
    Tony Baker : 304, 2283
Two Simple Words : 210
Two Solar Matters : 158, 3750
Two Sonnets from Xian : 3820
Two Time Matters : 158, 3750
Two Veterans : 3919
Two Wars : 1729
The Two Who Jumped : 747
Two Women on the Potomac Parkway : 1688
Two Words : 4273, 6213
Two Worlds : 1758, 3464
Two Young Trees Bending in the Strong Wind :
    4260
Twos : 709
Twyla : 5022
Typhoon : 3322
U.A.W. : 6431
U.S. Out of El Salvador, or, Amy & Bill 4-Ever
    : 947
U-Turn : 2104
Ubi Caritas : 2961
Ugliness : 6232
Ugly Drinkers of Fish Oil : 6530
Ultimate Death : 2580
The Ultimate Gift : 5152
Ultra-Violet Light : 5132
Ulysses' Abandoned Adventure : 2886, 6576,
    6615
Ulysses, My Father : 3156
Umbilical Cord : 2790
Umè: Plum : 6964
The Umpteenth Wonder : 2067
Umuein : 4658
An Unaccountable Meshing of Gears : 1337
Unaccustomed Mercies : 1764
Unanswered Letters : 1393
The Unbearable Part : 6603
Unborn : 1155
Unbrainwash Work-Ethic : 193
Unbroken Face: for This American Revolution :
    4301
Uncalm Meditation : 748, 3678
Unchained Melody : 1244
Unchanged : 2284
The Unclaimed Corpse : 2482
Uncle Ace : 894
'Uncle Billy' Goodwin : 2431
Uncle Maclovio's Secret, Never to Tell : 5353
Uncle Patrick Roots for the Fuzzy-Wuzzies :
    2170
Uncolicited : 1172
Uncommon Parents : 2017
An Uncut Scene from Herr Soma's Last Film :

7045
Under a Cloud Big as a State : 4062
Under a Crown of Thorns, Some Questions
    Arise about Genesis I:27 : 202
Under a Pagan Sun : 6457
Under August : 592
Under Ditt Hjärta / Byggde Jag Små Bon : 3792
Under Erasure : 6791
Under Glass : 5425
Under Late Capitalism : 1351
Under Mud : 4002
Under Sensation : 5384
Under Stratton : 6826
Under the Ambassador Bridge : 2212
Under the Fourth Watch of the Night : 1909
Under the House, Under the Sun : 4564
Under the Locust Tree : 740
Under the Mountain : 770
Under the Radar : 5338
Under the Resurrection Palm : 4921
Under the Spell of the Yellow Drapes : 3479
Under the Stars : 2820
Under the Sun : 2401
Under the Tent : 354
Under the Tongue : 7172
Underground : 5924
Underground at the Marmottan : 1954
Underground Dancing : 6162
The Underground Hum of the Dynamo Works :
    3539
The Underground Ox : 5263
The Undertaker's Comfort : 2752
Underwater : 368, 3851
Underwater House : 732
Underworld North of Lugano : 634, 4953
Underworlds : 4149
Undressing for Li Po : 5019
Unedited : 5429
The Unemployed Automobile Workers of
    Detroit Prepare to Share Christmas
    Standing in Line : 5519
Unemployed Woman Begging: Köln : 6802
Unemployment Office : 1988
An Unending Dream : 1837
An Unequal Journey : 3527
Unexpected : 468, 4473
The Unfaithful : 538
Unfinished Buddha, Samed Island : 2756
An Unfinished Poem (Interrupted by a Buddhist
    Scholar) : 7088
An Unfulfilled Dream : 6194
Ungodliness : 4373
The Unhappy Life of a Sex Goddess : 7123
Unicorn : 1692, 4925
A Unified Theory of Light : 7052
Uninsured : 6298
An Uninvited Guest's Description of a Parisian
    Cafe : 641
Union Hotel, Frankfurt : 5371
Union Men : 1740
The Unitarian Minister in Oak Ridge, Tennes-
    see : 1069
The Universe : 2703
The Unknown Angel : 1352

Unknown Veteran : 1644
Unknown Weed : 5488
The Unkown Pain: Matos : 476
Unlettered : 3039
The Unlikely Bluff of Sight : 1966
Unlucky for Some : 1205
Unmanned Telephone Receivers : 813, 814,
    2418
Unmoving : 786
The Unnaming of the World : 2062
Unnatural Disaster : 1145
The Unnecessary : 4548
Unpainted Dream : 3418
Unplanned Obsolescence : 2575
Unplugging the Drain : 2050
Unpublished Number : 2177
Unravelling : 3234
Unrecognized Street : 356, 640, 4324
Unrequited Love: A Slide Presentation : 6991
The Unsheltering Ground : 5618
Unsigned Painting : 6563
Unsliced Bread : 1123
Unstructured Time: Wir Haben Nur Einmal,
    Einmal, Gewesen zu Sein / We Have Only
    One Time, One Time to Be : 2050
Unsuitable Woman : 4612, 5995
Until the Parodist Arrives, We'll Have to Settle
    for These Prophets : 1356
Until v. Universal : 2433
Until we are hid at last — Death knows our
    eyes : 4973
Untimely Bloomings : 6259
Untitled #2: enchantments elegies labyrinths
    mechanical lights : 4613, 5650
Untitled: A gas station explodes : 37
Untitled: As if hinted by distant mountains :
    435, 1625
Untitled: At a time when I was without love :
    271, 653
Untitled: Being a little kid and trying to
    masturbate is rough : 1327
Untitled: Beware in bloom those fleeting
    boughs : 5953
Untitled: For one moment : 3347
Untitled: For some time now I like to kick :
    3225, 4295
Untitled: Forever like this : 435, 1625
Untitled: Four in the morning and the dog wants
    to talk about her dream : 4973
Untitled: French Tickler he says proudly : 1327
Untitled: He folds and leans : 6378
Untitled: Hwen the eagle was killed : 2741,
    4938
Untitled: I cannot see : 435, 4180
Untitled: I cannot Write. The words no longer
    flow : 7062
Untitled: I could be white : 3590
Untitled: I don't think I'll ever make it home :
    492
Untitled: I had wondered what color were the
    trees at night : 2811
Untitled: I knew a man once : 2695
Untitled: I know a little about the universe :
    5682

Untitled: I lift to make it remember : 4973
Untitled: If it's not bugs, it's the weather : 492
Untitled: If we could home : 1623
Untitled: If you and I were to turn the world inside out . . . : 2721
Untitled: I'm thinking of you : 648, 779
Untitled: In the silver-struck silence : 3940
Untitled: In this globe of numbers : 2559
Untitled: It was in the plains : 49, 2938
Untitled: It's the old spring again, flowers as always : 5953
Untitled: Keep talking, keep talking : 4809, 5552
Untitled: Loneliness : 5726
Untitled: Long ago we were swiftly flowing water : 653, 1581
Untitled: Making tapes of a musical fast pace : 5441
Untitled: More unfamiliar than an accident : 435, 4180
Untitled: My eyes close the way the Earth drifts off : 4973
Untitled: Night inside me, night out there : 2197, 6273
Untitled: No, we can not see the wind : 3350
Untitled Poem: There is fire in the bones of my face : 3672
Untitled: Poor burnt child : 4026
Untitled: Sad black mole on hip : 37
Untitled: Scents, colors, lines and hues fade : 536, 3225
Untitled: Scrape memory from my brain : 110
Untitled: Something about time we cannot grasp : 4041
Untitled: Surely everyone is born unfinished : 173
Untitled: that which once again befalls the heavens : 3064, 3494
Untitled: The door Was Left Open : 2559
Untitled: The downpour struck : 6453
Untitled: The little Tibetan : 3968
Untitled: The wind makes the cats crazy, blowin up their kazoos : 1575
Untitled: There is nothing trivial about love : 4001
Untitled: What would it mean if a cricket : 5375
Untitled: Whether I grow old, betray my dreams, become a ghost : 7059
Untitled: Who shall sing if I don't sing : 5953
Untouched by This World : 5333
Untoward : 3656
Unveiling : 4921
The Unveiling : 585
The Unveiling of the Paris Collections, 1926 : 1080
Unwanted Memory : 3980
Unwrapped Gifts : 3217
Unwritten : 3522
Unwritten Letter, From the Victim : 3312
Up Here : 3669
Up Over the Hill : 4376
Upbraid : 182
Upon Mrs. Thatcher's Withdrawal : 6514
Upon the Waters : 3291

Upon waking, I find : 5084
An upper chamber in a darkened house : 6533
The Upstairs Tenant : 271
Upsy Daisy : 184, 6971
Uptown Love Poem : 6097
The Uranoscopes : 1692, 3654
Urban Irony : 2422, 3484, 6552
Urban Landscape : 4712
Urbano Corazon : 2358
Urge : 5458
The Urge to Be Polish : 2669
The Urgent, All Consuming : 3916
Urtext : 214
U.S. Out of El Salvador, or, Amy & Bill 4-Ever : 947
Usahn : 2194
Used Books : 3078
Useless Islands : 6545
The Uses of Philosophy : 2796
The Usual Immigrant Uncle Poem : 4296
The Usual Time : 811
The Uterus at 47 : 6946
Utility : 1626, 5773
Utolsó Otthon : 3035
Utopia : 1818, 3464
Utterance : 3861
V : 2215
Vacances : 3535
The Vacant Chair : 1845
Vacating the Premises : 2932
Vacation : 2380, 3066, 7129
Vacation, 1943 : 4181
Vacation on a Latvian River : 3741, 6635
Vacations : 4264, 6176
Vacations, 1978 : 1756, 4951
Vaggvisa för Mitt Ofödda Barn : 2418
Vague Ideas : 3845
A Vague Ode : 4852, 5178, 6539
Vägvisaren : 2526
Valdez : 2649
The Vale of Soulmaking : 6946
Valediction for Señor Lopez : 6075
A Valediction Forbidding Mourning : 5322
A Valedictory : 5806
Valentine : 1272, 1561
Valerie, Actually : 5485
The Valet : 841
Valle de Viñales : 4934
Valley Forge in the Bicentennial : 6119
The Valley of Morning : 2567
Valley of the Hatsuse : 187, 6971
The Value of Art : 2924
The Values of Stone : 4688
Valves : 5069
The Vampire's Villanelle : 6670
Van Gogh Among the Poor on the Subject of His Art (Deferred) : 372
Van Gogh's 'Crows Over a Cornfield' : 6808
Van Gogh's Cyclist : 2104
Van Gogh's Man with a Straw Hat : 1939
Vanessa : 719
Vanished Faces : 6413
A Vanished World : 5471
Vanities : 6980

Vanity : 1147
Vannak Vidékek : 3243
Varázslat : 3981
Variation on a Theme by Leonard Bernstein :
    4846
Variation on a Theme from Stevens : 1465
Variations on a Paraphrase : 6707
Variations on a Theme : 5510, 6137, 6221
Variations on a Theme from *Petticoat Junction*
    : 3870
Variations on an Eskimo Carol : 3434
Variations on Inferred War Themes from the
    Kumulipo and *Mo'olelo Hawai'i* : 4982
Veil : 491, 3476, 5040
Vékony, Fekete Csík : 1363
Velando : 5353
Vendo al Colegio para Recoger a Mi Hija :
    6631
Veni Creator Spiritus : 1815
Venice Beach: Brief Song : 372
Venn Diagrams : 3953
Venom, Thorn : 876
Ventana Que No Es : 5235
Venus : 6164
Venus's-Flytraps : 3466
The Verandah : 5122
Los Verdados & After & Long After : 2337
The Verdict : 2332
Die Vergangenheit : 214
Vermeer : 1824, 2457
Vermeer's *A Woman Weighing Gold* : 6117
Vermin : 1927
Verna : 6371
Vernal Tea : 423
Veronica's Advice : 3428
Verse for 7 June '51 : 2619, 6006
Versions of Corot : 989
Vertical Efforts in White : 76, 5893
Vertigo : 7034
Vertumnal : 7095
A Very Bourgeois Lyric : 651, 5151
Vespers : 5823
Vespers, or, Il Penseroso, or, Bualand : 2654
Vespertilian : 6728
The Vestibule : 3009
Vestigial Organ : 3829
The Vet Says My Old Dog Blows Hair : 3690
A Veteran hooker in Philly : 5535
Vexation : 748, 3678
Vi Hade Alla Möjligheter i Hela Världen : 206
Viaje por la Noche a Mallorca : 1808
The Vicinities of Alsace : 1071, 6017
The Victor Vanquished : 2964
The Victoria and Albert Museum on a Rainy
    Morning : 459
A Victorian Connoisseur of Sunsets : 5112
Victorian Ladies : 2175
Victory : 3369
Victory Lunch : 5029
La Vida Nueva : 7189
Videnda : 5467
Video : 1427
La Vie Intérieure / Yonkers : 3399
Viene Volando un Tiempo de Cañones : 3060

Vietnam : 2736
Vietnam (a Flexible Title) : 5335
View From My Window : 2273
A View of Advent from High Street: Hollowell,
    ME : 30
View of Sloten : 4293, 4796
View of the Amstel : 4293, 4796
A View of the Desert : 1639
A View of the Water : 3499
The Viewing : 5962
Viewing Alcatraz : 4187
Viewing Sweet Peas and Their Absence
    Acutely : 1974
Views of the Pecos : 5566
Vigil : 3155
The Vigil : 6392
Vigil Strange : 1401
Vignettes : 1113
Vignettes: The Senator Visits Georgia Out-
    Counties : 272
The Village : 1666
Village Near Landing Zone Dog : 4332
Village Quartet : 6797
Villamoon : 6608
Villanelle : 4912
Vinegar Puss : 3913
Vinterstrand : 5708
Violence : 486
Violent Weather : 5578
The Violinist to His Love : 1646
Violin's Farewell : 4122, 4628
Violon d'Adieu : 4628
The Virgin : 4428
Virgin in a Rainstorm : 1534
The Virgin of the Panecillo : 5725
Virginia Woolf at Giggleswick : 1677
Virginity : 2385, 4915
The Virgins of Zurbaran : 5505
The Virile Gold Shimmer of Beaten Eggs :
    3464
Virtual Reality : 501
Visible Lie : 3325
The Visible Man : 3547, 5379, 6318
The Visible World : 216
Visio Tondalis : 1149, 6651
Vision : 2279, 4262
Vision & Providence : 175
Vision Near Ice : 433
A Vision of Love : 431
Vision of the World Instantly White : 1196
Vision Quest : 5272
Visionaries : 5465
Visions : 878, 3478, 4129, 4346, 5006
Visions of Broken Eye : 4900
Visions of Love : 6910
Visit : 4262
The Visit : 948, 2930, 4650
A Visit (1959) : 733
Visit after Coronary Bypass : 6345
A Visit to Amherst : 1768
Visit to Bainbridge Island : 261
Visit to Mrs. Lewellyn : 3777
Visit to the Institute for the Blind : 5081
A Visit to West New York : 2953

Visitation : 1573, 1662, 2041
Visiting : 6101
Visiting a Grave : 6154
Visiting Day : 4937
Visiting Father in Spring : 4815
Visiting Filmmaker : 5919
Visiting Flannery O'Connor's Grave : 3538
Visiting Home : 5395
Visiting Hours : 1835
Visiting My Father a Few Days Before His
    Operation : 420
Visiting My Father's House on Orca Street, An-
    chorage Alaska, Fifteen Years After His
    Death : 4164
The Visiting Paleontologist Feels Her Thigh :
    406
Visiting the Relatives : 2417
Visiting Yeats : 5314
Visiting Your Sister in the Psychiatric Ward :
    1738
A Visitor : 101
Visitors : 5083
Vita : 6101
Vita Brevis : 2998
Vita Nuova : 2426
Vital : 175
Vito Takes His Neighbor's Dog for a Drive :
    6356
Vjesnici (The Heralds) : 5033
Vlaminck's Nudes : 4822
The Vocalist : 2943, 3701
Las Voces II : 2003
Vogelsang 5 : 2470
The Voice : 2886, 3257, 6615
Voice Against Christ from Inside a Clock Mask
    : 1458
The Voice Discovers Betrayal : 6160
The Voice from Paxos : 5
The Voice of One Raging in the Suburbs : 1184
Voice of the Bodhi Tree : 1020
Voice or Verse or What : 3941
A Voice Speaks in Earnest, But Nobody Listens
    : 5431
Voices : 2769, 3093, 5384, 6691
Voices, Garments, Plunders : 822, 3069
Voices Inside and Out : 2267
Voices of Ice : 1679, 4286
Voices on the Air : 757
Volunteer Corps : 2279
Volunteers at the AIDS Foundation : 3820
The Voluntry Red Cross Stroke-Patient Reha-
    bilitation Scheme : 559
Voodoo : 7021
Vortex : 2114
The Votaries : 5499
Vous observez : 1537
The Vow : 3381
Vowels and Single Vase : 2314
Voy a cantar estos versos : 5355
Voyage Out: Liverpool to Port Chalmers, N.Z.,
    1863 : 5224
Voyager : 2710
Voyageurs : 6922
Voyeur : 1477, 3460

The Voyeur : 168
The Voyeuress of Mintrop Strasse : 1305
Vulcan Restored : 5530
Vultures : 4880
WCW Watching Presley's Second Appearance
    on The Ed Sullivan Show: Mercy Hospital,
    Newark, 1956 : 7010
W moim barbarzynskim jezyku : 5105
WWI (Writing While Under the Influence) :
    1924
Wade : 1626
Wading in the dust : 5575
Waikiki Roughwater Swim : 4282
The Wait : 4621
Waiting : 2849, 3327, 3428, 4964, 5976, 7110
The Waiting Child : 6329
Waiting for Catastrophe : 6154
Waiting for Fillings : 2312
Waiting for flaming life : 244, 3011, 3546
Waiting for God : 6101
Waiting for Morning : 6365
Waiting for New Students : 4892
Waiting for Poetry : 4459
Waiting for Rain : 6534
Waiting for Snow : 6668, 6787
Waiting for the Ambulance : 6404
Waiting for the Barbarians : 1035, 6397
Waiting for the Bus with the Ghost on It, in
    Back : 2462
Waiting for the Kindness of Strangers : 4669
Waiting for the Silkworms : 2088
Waiting for the Test Results : 1352
Waiting for the Word : 900
Waiting for You : 5466
Waiting Is Forever : 2535
The Waiting Room : 6244
Waiting Shelter : 647
Waiting Tables : 807
Waiting Thaw : 2337
Waiting to Adopt a Child : 3612
Waiting to Be Re-stationed : 5618
Waiting with the Rug : 1858
The Waitress : 6881
The Waitress at the Yogurt Shop : 841
Wake : 4195, 4383, 6948
Wake-Up Colloquy : 4260
Waking : 999, 3230
Waking at Fifty : 1062
Waking at the Mount Olive Baptist Church :
    6510
Waking on the Island : 6699
Waking Sleep : 2454, 6324
Waking to Two Moons : 5181
Waking Up in Barstow : 3377
Waking Vision for Franklin Brainard : 918
Waking with Influenza : 6016
Waldoboro Eve : 1332
Walk : 4269
The Walk : 1038
A Walk After a Late Breakfast : 6681, 6878
A Walk Around the Brewery : 3270, 6844,
    6992
A Walk in the Alfama : 1783
Walk, Night Falling, Memory of My Father :

2465
The Walk, Paris, 1960 : 485
Walk softly & carry a wept stream : 1333
Walk Waltz, from the Diner Digressions : 3526
A Walk with My Son : 6400
The Walker : 3277
Walking : 3861, 3938, 6154
Walking around My House in the Dark : 4373
Walking at Dawn : 5198
Walking Away from Things That Are Impor-
    tand : 1725
Walking Behind the Window Glass : 2562
Walking Canlit in India : 1447
Walking from Grasmere : 5608
Walking Home Again, November : 5662
Walking Home, Half Drunk : 5313
Walking In Krakau : 5903
Walking in the Chills of Winter : 4788
Walking in the Snow : 6154
Walking in Traffic : 1190
Walking July 13 Down Columbia Street in
    Boston Way Down : 2919
Walking on Water : 184
Walking Past Construction : 1652
Walking the Beach Under the Overcast : 6101
Walking the Desert : 6076
Walking the Santa Fe Railhead : 6110
Walking the Schnauzer : 1200
Walking to the Territory : 4205
Walking Towards the Grave of My Grandfather
    Outside of Benevento, Italy : 5769
Walkingstick : 4873
Wall : 4585
The Wall : 142, 1395, 3445, 5874, 6082, 6084
Wallace Stevens Waking at Night : 6305
Wallace Stevens Walks Along the Beach at
    Night : 6305
Wallace Stevens Walks by the Sea : 6305
Wallpapering to Patsy Cline : 6056
Walls : 2147
The Walls : 723
Walls to Put Up, Walls to Take Down : 1605
Walnuts, October, Wassergass : 5379
Walt Whitman Takes the Antibody Test : 4693
Walt Whitman Was Always Out There : 694
Walter & His Children : 4233
Waltz : 118
The Waltz : 2037
Waltzing Matilda : 3384
Wanda : 163
The Wanderer : 1819, 3254, 7129
Wanderers : 4831
Wandering Curves : 6707
The Wandering Linguist : 866
Wanting : 4725, 6971
Wanting a Child at Forty : 2726
Wanting the Truth : 4349
Wanting to Know the End : 2348
Wanting to Make Metaphors about Nothing :
    4035
War : 2034, 6720
The War : 2289, 4915
The War Closet : 4135
War Ich Wie Du. Warst Du Wie Ich (Si Yo

Fuera Como Tu, Si Tu Feueras Como Yo)
    : 1034
War Rations Chosen, London, 1943 : 6232
War Story : 6438
War: trading real estate for men : 162
The War Widow's Pension Runs Out : 3913
The Ware Collection of Glass Flowers and
    Fruit, Harvard Museum : 1650
Warm Days in January : 5302
A Warm House : 3880
Warm in Winter : 2373
A Warm Spell in November : 880
Warm Tea Promises : 4898
Warming the Toes : 7148
The Warmth of Blue Glass : 4201
The Warning : 5431
Warning: War Toys : 488
Warnings : 5930
Warrior : 4367
Warrior Artists of the Southern Plains : 4661
The Warrior's Rest : 2184, 4362
Wars I Have Known : 2276
The Wars of Faery : 3703
Warsaw, 1942: The Photograph, Some Facts :
    4928
Was My Question : 2233, 3197, 6806
Wash N Wear : 5669
Wash the Blood Off Your Feet : 99, 1883
Washboard Apprentice : 3103
Washed in Salt : 4926
The Washerwoman Moves Away from Herself :
    3906
Washing Dishes : 4667
Washing Her Back : 5286
Washing My Old Yellow Car : 1639
Washing Vegetables : 4928
Washington County, Georgia, 1942 : 5985
Waste : 4639
Watauga Drawdown : 3153
The Watch on Hadrian's Wall : 6497
The Watcher : 164, 2423
Watchers : 4855
Watching : 4500
Watching a Cellist Playing Brahms: Sketch
    with Reference Notes : 6969
Watching a Fat Woman on the Beach : 2920
Watching Chaplin's *A Dog's Life* : 3667
Watching for the Next Poem : 2255
Watching Great-Grandma Bean Undress : 3556
Watching Her Sleep : 2885
Watching Leaves Once Falling : 5774
Watching My Father Feed the Birds : 3096
Watching My Mother Dress : 2929
Watching My Neighbor Work on His Car, I Fall
    Asleep in My Lawn Chair : 2471
Watching Pina Bausch's 'Kontakthof' : 7147
Watching Spiders : 2666
Watching the Gibbons : 261
Watching Them : 6299
Water : 3326, 5015
Water Alone Remembers : 4973
The Water Bed : 367
Water Born : 5226
The water brimming : 3759, 7083

The Water Candle : 3622
The Water Moved an Instant Before : 3048
Water Shrine : 5605
Water-Skipper : 7046
Water Slide : 3602
Water Web : 2347
Waterbed Dreams : 399
Watercolors of Childhood : 3481, 4326
Waterfall : 328
Waterfall in Como Park : 6896
Waterlines : 3843
The Watermelon Season : 1562
Watermill : 707
The Waters of 1989 : 5302
Waterville: The Mid-Maine Medical Center : 4765
The Watery Loom : 7009
Watson and the Shark : 5013
Wattle : 3619
The Watusi : 2059
Waves : 6675
Wax Lips : 3807
The Wax Problem : 1379
The Way a Hand at the Moment of Death : 1536, 3533
The Way Children Walk : 6148
The Way Down : 5927
The Way I Write : 6101
The Way It Goes : 6804
The Way It Is Now : 2214
The Way of Families : 3612
Way of Life : 236
The Way of the Conventicle of the Trees : 999
Way Off in the Distance : 3105, 4780
The Way Out of the Fly Bottle : 2545
Way Out Wardell Plays Belgrade : 4185
The Way They Come Ashore : 3000
The Way They Make a Moon : 6848
A Way to a View : 4768
A Way to Grow Old : 3126, 6341
The Way to San Onofré : 5591
The Way We Grow Older : 3612
The Way We Travel : 237, 7178
Ways of Seeing Light : 5510
WCW Watching Presley's Second Appearance on The Ed Sullivan Show: Mercy Hospital, Newark, 1956 : 7010
We All Need to Get Over the Bridge : 6085
We Are Always Too Late : 616
We Are Human History. We Are Not Natural History : 616
We Are the Dream of Jefferson : 4477
We Are the Junction : 2267
We are they that search for bees in the fold of a curtain : 883, 4875
We Can Choose : 6672, 7000
We Cannot Keep It : 408
We can't afford to write or not to : 1274
We Contemplate Our Second Child : 5127
We Deserve It : 3547, 3981, 5379
We Did What Was Expected of Us : 101, 127
We Do the Best I Can: A Series of Portraits : 3727
We Drink a Lot When We're Together : 5969

We Had All the Possibilities in the World : 206, 813, 814
We Have Bare Hands : 3341, 5337
We have loved each other : 883, 4875
We Imagine Our New Life : 3594
We Laugh at Our Father's Dreams : 6056
We live without feeling a country beneath us : 2936, 4007
We Lived in Eugene : 2126
We Love It No End : 3946
We Mourn in Various Ways : 3316
We Murder Three Sparrows in South Dakota : 5757
We Need Language : 1398, 3197, 6806
We Plan Our Days : 111
We Return at Last to the Place We Dreamed of : 921
We Seal Our Daughter in a Tower : 3264
We Sing a Bit Less Often : 793
We Sit by the Fire : 4715
We Sweat : 142
We Walk : 14, 993, 1871
We Were All Hungry : 806
We Were Just Tired of Their Monopoly of Power : 1905
We Who Burn : 6505
We will speak when we'll feel : 2391
The Weather : 1353, 6022
The Weather Bureau : 5601
Weather Report : 2397, 5753
The Weather Wizard's Cloud Book : 5760
Weathering : 4204
Web : 3204
The Web : 4171
Web first rays of dawn : 5573
Wedding : 6429, 6800
The Wedding : 3032
Wedding Figures : 805
Wedding Picture : 3189
Wedding Portrait of My Father : 692
Wedding Rehearsal : 4231
Wedding Song for Autumn : 5476
A Wedding Story : 6928
The Wedding to Black Garter or Trussed : 3908
The Wednesday before Ascension : 3779
Wednesday Night Special: Liver & Onions : 3425
Wednesday's Poetry Reader : 3023
Weeds : 5955
Weedy Lullaby : 844
Weehawken Evening : 3761
The Week : 1091
Week as an Example of Years : 2572
Weekdays in Wilmette : 1977
Weekend Evening : 3407, 5860
Weeping : 3769, 3817, 4832
The Weeping Bed : 6761
Weeping: Mimeisthai : 6436
The Weeping Sharks : 1577
Weight : 2470, 4116
The Weight of Our Bodies : 6270
The Weight of This Night : 1614
The Weightlifter Takes an Examination in Literature of the Renaissance : 5635

Weir Fisherman : 2783
Welcome : 2683
The Welcome : 2048
Welcome, Says Skeleton : 5446
The Welcoming : 2866
Welfare Budget Gourmet : 3617
Well, I Ask : 2557, 3547, 5379
A Well in India : 5224
Well Look : 5446
Well Met by Moonlight : 1911
Well, Mom : 5379
The Well-Tempered Clavier : 3381
The Well, the Brambles : 628, 4610
Wellfleet : 2615
The Wells : 344, 5088
A Werewolf in Yorkshire : 6904
West Branch : 1524
West Chapple : 3173
West Fork of the San Juan : 4179
West Island : 3844
West Palm Beach : 300
Western Love : 5188
Western Rectangle : 7093
Westward Ho! : 3746
The Wet : 1092
Wet Fire Dream : 818
The Wet Nurse : 3166, 3238, 4033
Wet Pavement : 2470
Wet Twilight : 3730
Wet Walking : 6856
The Wetback : 1735
The Whale : 732
The Whaler : 418
The Whales of *Mare Serenitatis* : 2320
Whaling Station Bay : 5942
What a Girl : 841
What a Mortal Thirst for God Shakes Loose
    inside Me : 4748, 5995
What about dying? : 3032
What an O'Brien Is : 1002
What Are We Doing Here? : 1808
What Became of My Father : 3514
What Becomes Clear : 259
What Bloodcells Understand : 3577
What Can We Expect of Language!? : 4042
What Can You Tell Me? : 503, 5229, 6830
What Could Be More Important : 4263
What did they see that my cheeks can't bear the
    weight : 4973
What Do You Say at a Communist Funeral?
    (Everyone Gets Buried Sometime, Mr.
    Krushchev) : 50
What Dostoevsky Said : 6753
What Else : 2532, 2922, 7106
What Falls : 2870
What Goes Down Must Come Up : 2310
What Good Is It to Be Blinded : 6645
What Happened Was : 2369
What He Remembered : 6569
What Her Mother Told Her : 642, 2076
What Hoffman Said : 3874
What Hurt So Much : 994
What I Do for a Living : 204
What I Have Learned : 1809

What I Meant to Say : 448, 6144
What I Meant Was This : 1850
What I Need : 6476
What I Remember of What They Told Me :
    1810
What I Think My Brother Saw : 1702
What If : 5195
What if a dragon were discovered alive : 6164
What I'm Doing at This Very Moment in 12
    Parallel Universes : 2944
What I'm Wild For : 1109
What Is America? : 1294
What Is Called Thinking: After Trakl : 2406
What Is Her Vulva Really Like — a Tiger :
    1337
What Is Important : 5220
What Is It? : 4790
What Is It Makes My Eyes So Weary : 889
What is it to be face to face? : 1757, 3588,
    4690, 6220
What Is Most American Is Most in Motion :
    4738
What Is on the Page : 6305
What Is the Word : 428
What Is There to Say : 148
What It Means to Live Alone Again : 3640
What It Takes : 4663
What Karl the Gut Said : 5030
What Kind of Love Was That? : 943
What Kind of Mistress He Wants : 384
What Kind of Times Are They : 5362
What King George Says : 5944
What Ladies Wonder About Eminent Writers :
    5132
What Little I Have to Say About Living in a
    Major Urban Centre : 6415
What Might Have Been : 3612
What Mr. Cogito Thinks About Hell : 2104,
    2800
What My Father Doesn't Know : 4373
What Never Comes Back: Huidobro : 476
What Now : 3946
What Scares About the Shark : 6782
What Shall We Tell Li Po : 1814
What She Could Do : 2407
What She Is : 1036
What She Wants : 6208
What Steve Says : 5457
What the Azaleas Didn't Say : 6798
What the Dead Wear : 4538
What the Jackrabbits Know : 4185
What the Matter Is : 6945
What the Minstrel Thinks : 935
What the Mohawk Made the Hopi Say : 5464
What the Old Cheyenne Women at Sand Creek
    Knew : 5239
What the Poem Believes : 3730
What the Poets Are : 1655
What the Sign Painter Was Thinking : 5106
What the Skin Knows : 2332
What the Spirit Seeks : 6199
What the War Was About : 2466
What the Wind Wants : 4389
What They Taught Me in Soledad : 6101

What They Wanted : 1715
What To Do During the First Rain After Ten
    Weeks of Drought : 2519
What We Can Count On : 420
What We Can Do and What We Can't : 3829
What We Did with the Bodies : 1682
What We Haven't Considered : 6291
What We Keep : 6046
What We Knew : 2049
What We Lost : 616
What We Saw : 2890
What Women Pray For : 5814
What Word Did the Greeks Have for It? : 2964
What Work Is : 3746
What Would Emma Goldman Do? : 2057
What Would it mean if a cricket : 5375
What You Learn from Getting Burned : 5969
What You Read : 2690
What you see is a painted fraud : 1358, 4601
What You Want : 3154
What Your Body Holds Against You : 570
Whatever Happened to Leda, Mother? : 1863
What's Dangerous About Plumbing : 4170
What's in My Journal : 6101
What's it going to be? : 4617
What's Left : 3268, 5097
What's Really Going On : 2595
Wheat Gum : 5390
Wheel : 1266
The Wheel : 3748
Wheels : 3321
Whelk's Casing : 6771
The Whelping Box : 1267
When : 4586, 5379, 7164
When a Mother in-Law's Tongue Is a Zebra :
    4638
When Are You Coming Home : 6616
When Autumn Returns : 1939, 5914
When building houses the carpenters say : 5020
When Butterfly Sees Flower : 1108, 1252, 6045
When Caroline Visits Her Sister Susan : 2367
When Conventional Methods Fail : 2974
When Cows Fall in Love : 5324
When Cows Think : 5324
When Dawn Wakes You : 6668
When Ecstasy Is Inconvenient : 4631
When Emigrating : 3227, 3461
When Everything Is Goneril : 4932
When February Follows Close After Christmas
    Like It Was a Guest Returning Home Late
    from a Party : 4361
When grandmother on my father's side died :
    3032
When Handling *Desolata* : 24
When I Am Old I will Be Very Nasty : 2826
When I Die : 552
When I Feel Your Soul, I Reach for You with
    These Arms : 839
When I Grow Up : 6947
When I lived in Bay City Michigan : 1993
When I saw the arrangement : 3759, 6551
When I Think : 4097
When I Think of You : 214
When I Walk on Sidewalks : 6592

When I Was a Child I Walked the Meadow :
    813, 814, 5064
When I Was a Child My Grandfather : 813,
    814, 5064
When I Was a Child / the Ladies: 813,814, 5064
When in Doubt : 406
When It Rains Bubble Gum : 1087
When It Was Fun, It Was Very Very Fun : 5969
When It Was Good : 898
When It Was Over : 491, 3476, 4811
When kings fall silent : 2379, 6830
When Meret Oppenheim Was Thirty-Six : 580
When Mother Receives Gentlemen Visitors :
    267
When My Body Knocks : 4683
When my hand refuses to hold the pen : 3032
When My Love Says : 4640
When Night Approaches : 2069, 6665
When Once Friends : 5760
When Our Enemies Doze Off : 3805, 5455
When Pito Tried to Kill : 5446
When Poets Dream of Angels : 3790
When Samuel Reads the *Daily Times* : 3995
When She Hears the Wolves : 800
When She Named Fire : 836
When She Steps Out : 279
When She Was a Child : 3684
When the camellia blossoms : 3759, 4551
When the End Comes : 1854
When the Farmers Come to Town : 5257
When the garden wood was trimmed : 2132,
    3759
When the girls start puttin Nirvana-No on their
    lips : 3334
When the Hummingbird : 4765
When the IRS Comes Knocking : 6804
When the New Moon Screamed : 3547, 5379,
    6318
When the Orange Sun Burns : 2485
When the Pond Was Opened : 5983
When the Sadness Came : 5010
When the Statues Set Off : 3256, 5379
When the Universe Halts Its Infinite Spinning
    and Light Breaks : 2277
When the Wild Geese Move Past the Mercantile
    in a Long Body, Dancing : 267
When the Wolf Is Biting at the Lace Curtains :
    6804
When They Came : 4657
When They Found Him He Remembered
    Nothing : 6643
When we become like two drunken suns : 982,
    2926
When We Got Married : 6284
When We Were Birds : 7112
When Wolves Lie Down with Lambs : 5326
When Women Ruled : 4529
When You Grow Older : 3126, 6657
When You Left : 930
When Your Best Friends Move to L. A. : 6094
When You're Away : 149
Whenever I Hear a Siren : 2755
Whenever Songs Are to Be Composed : 184,
    4774

Where All the Streets Lead to the Sea : 173
Where All Things Wait : 3982
Where Did She Go? : 1636
Where Do You Sleep? : 2210
Where Everyone Walked : 2141
Where I Am : 6298
Where I Could Watch the Sea : 5240
Where I Live Now : 6400
Where If I Dared I Would Put My Small Hand :
    2571
Where Is Everyone Going Who Was Here :
    4784
Where Is the Moralizer, Your Mother? : 1101
Where It Comes From : 6570
Where Little Pond Meets the Ocean : 113
Where My Mother Lives, in the Building with a
    Doorman Named Angel : 4669
Where No Candle Can Stay Lit : 4039
Where No One Spoke the Language : 666
Where Only Wolves Were Meant to Be : 3432
Where Scholars Fear to Tread : 6913
Where the clouds rise at Izumo : 3759, 6279
Where the Deer Were : 355
Where the Music Comes From : 1726
Where the Poetry Comes From : 1221
Where the Spaces Between the Words Go :
    3285
Where the Swimming Ends : 6818
Where Tornadoes Begin : 5924
Whether I grow old, betray my dreams, become
    a ghost : 7059
Which Floor? : 4536, 5228, 7057
Which Moment : 6130
The While Awaying : 1751
While Canoeing the Red Lake River Near
    Goodridge, Minnesota, We Speak of
    Direction : 2085
While Dancing with Fred Astaire, She Reflects
    : 1109
While Laurel Leaves Grew All Around : 5770
While My Mother Was Having Her Stroke :
    6374
While Reading Virginia Woolf at a Campsite :
    2230
While the Ground Is Still Warm : 666
While There's Still Time : 1269
While We Speak : 6046
While Women Were Washing Corpses : 711
Whimbrel : 4208
A Whippoorwill in the Woods : 1132
Whips at the Ritz : 3780
The Whirligig Beetle : 6878
The Whisperer : 3528
The Whistle : 3466
The Whistle in the Field : 1273
Whistler: The White Girl : 623
Whistlin' with Sweep Pea : 6413
Whistling in the Dark : 5894
White : 3053, 5373, 5389, 5681
White and Black : 4349
White Angels, As They Crucified Me : 878,
    4346, 5006
White Bayou : 4322
White Bears: Tolstoy at Astapovo : 529

White Bible : 5067
The White Birch : 623
White-Blind : 2369
White-Bone Demon : 1897
White Boot : 4161
The White Brass Bed : 2533
White Bread : 5715
White Butterflies of Night, So Often Near Me :
    2829, 6649
White Cat : 3640
White Cellars : 3331
White Crocus : 3189
White Dandelions in Deerfield : 3220
The White Dead : 6793
White Doors : 2248
White Egg Shells : 2622
White Father : 6447
A White Friend Flies in from the Coast : 2656
White, Gray and Rinse : 6897
White Hawthorn in the West of Ireland : 616
White Histories : 1709
White Lady : 1167
White Lanterns : 7010
A White Lie : 3556
The White Lily : 1350
White Limousine : 2461
The White Loft : 234
The White Man's Burden : 3385
White Night : 1625, 7159
White Noise : 5820
White Oak : 6767
White Out : 345
White Petticoats : 579
White Pigeons : 2401
White Plane in a March Sky : 2899
White Port & Lemon Juice : 3466
The White Room : 4753
White Rose : 6073
White Seeds : 6154
White Shoulders : 6800
White Slippers : 797
White Solitude : 3330
White Stone : 1976
White Water : 6519
White Waterlilies : 4816
Whiteout : 5370
Whitetail Omen : 2645
Whitewater Camp at Black Rock : 1392
Whitman, Come Again to the Cities : 1531
A Whitsun : 4111
Whitsun, Thirty Years Later : 813, 814, 2526
Whittling : 1269
Who Are the People : 2294
Who Are You : 4640
Who Art You? : 1756, 2046
Who Frankenstein Is to Me & Why I Have the
    Big Head Dream : 4691
Who Is She : 6097
Who Killed Her Dog and Put a Snake in Her
    Mailbox? : 3373
Who Knew : 5317
Who Knows What There Is Under This Mask :
    14, 1871
Who Might Have Been Friends : 5036

Who, on Earth : 3381
Who shall sing if I don't sing : 5953
Who was Mary Shelley? : 4672
Who Was That Masked Man : 1929
Who Watches from the Dark Porch : 2406
Who We Are : 2886
Who We Are Now : 816
Who Woke Me Up in the Morning : 3823
The (W)Hole : 512
A Whole Lake to Yourself : 193
Whole Life in Suitcases : 338
Whole Lives Missing : 3415
The Whole Point Is Freedom : 2182
The Whole Point of Apples : 2369
The Whole World of History and You : 707
Whom Will I Love When You Are Here? :
    2758
Whores : 943
Who's the Worst? : 841
Whose Lineage It Was, Lost : 4918
Whose Seal Cannot Be Broken : 3071, 6708
Whose Son, Whose Daughter : 313
Whose Tracks Those Are : 6144
Why All Good Music Is Sad : 6545
Why Carol Ann Stayed : 5915
Why Do So Few Blacks Study Creative
    Writing? : 1734
Why Do They Talk Sex to Me : 2164
Why Does Reality Pretend Itself Alive? : 1025
Why Gravity Doesn't Give Up : 5495
Why I Am Not a Christian : 4631
Why I Hate Bowling : 4081
Why I Like My Father : 1426
Why I Would Think I Am Leaving : 2408
Why Ira Pratt Cocked His Head Like That :
    5862
Why Is It the Road : 969
Why is the snow so blue? : 244, 3011, 5218
Why It Is Necessary to Love : 1090
Why LeRoi Wanted Himself As Dance : 301
Why Mira Can't Go Back to Her Old House :
    591, 4402
Why My Father Beat Us (When We Were
    Little) : 714
Why not something small and perfect : 6294
Why Nothing Changes for Miss Ngo Thi Thanh
    : 6815
Why Robert Wagner Married Natalie Wood :
    5969
Why She Lost Interest in Men : 7179
Why She Will Not Sleep : 836
Why the Con? : 6813
Why the Hostages Were Freed : 6514
Why We Don't Need Asylum : 4363
Why You Are Sad : 3464
Why You Close Doors Behind Us : 5032
Whylah Falls : 1145
Whys : 2045
Wichita 67204 : 3505
Wide-Angle Shot: Return to Snowy River :
    6957
Wide necked bays hidden in the territory : 4462,
    6553
The Widener Bird : 1628

Widow : 312
The Widow : 6818
The Widow at 'Roadstead's End' : 2170
Widow in Red Shoes : 2164
The Widow Map : 2340
Widower : 4550, 7130
The Widows : 5238
Widow's Grief : 5980
The Widow's Muse : 6207
The Widows of John F : 4556
Wielder of Men : 2509
Wife : 1690, 3445, 5844, 5874
The Wife in the Mural at Pompeii : 1824
Wilbur Wright Remembers His First Landing :
    1269
Wild : 1545
Wild Chrysanthemums : 5964
Wild Country : 4469
Wild Fruit : 3466
Wild Geese : 6149
Wild Geese Sang : 1108, 1252, 3537
Wild Greek Chickens : 328
Wild Horses : 1080
The Wild Man : 5030
Wild Mushrooms : 5821
Wild Oats : 5911
Wild Places Such As Eyes : 1087
Wild Raspberries : 2104, 5937, 6573
The Wild Streak in My Stallion : 1547
Wild West : 3745
Wilder Brain Collection, Cornell University :
    4225
Wilderness : 4462
Wilderness Landscape : 705, 5336
Wildflowers : 2802, 6675
Will : 234
Will Berkeley, CA., Become Just Another Sick
    American City? : 1708
Will There Be Enough Light Years : 666, 3549
Will to Will : 6707
Will, Workshopping : 3043
Will You Miss Me? : 4517
Willard : 2482
Willi, Home : 6579
Williams : 1116
Williamsburg : 869
Willie and the Water Pipe : 3689
Williwaw : 6810
Willow : 3995
Willow Woman : 3329
The Willows and the Vines : 5206
The Wilmores : 6869
Winces : 2448
Wind : 2431, 3169, 5976
The Wind : 4358
Wind & Sky : 5843
Wind and Whales and Dark Sopranos : 6634
Wind From the Sea : 1477
The Wind from the Sea : 6880
Wind in the Hills : 454, 4705
The Wind Last Night : 2919
The wind makes the cats crazy, blowin up their
    kazoos : 1575
Wind Rattles : 4027

Wind Surfer's Revenge at Horseshoe Battery : 3776
The Wind Tunnel : 529
The Wind with Its Nerves : 1363, 5379, 5379
Windchime Window in Angels Camp : 6941
Windfall : 4187
Window : 5050
The Window : 1521, 4158
The Window 6 A M : 6268
Window Garden : 2471
Window Men : 5575
The Window on the Cliff : 435, 1625
The Window Rattled in the Wind All Night : 3606
Window Zen : 2337
Windows : 3763
Windows and Mirrors : 2350
The Winds Have Everything to do with Memory : 3612
Windshield : 3014
Windsor Ruins : 4334
Winging South : 4114
The Wings : 1650
Wings Between the Sun and Me : 2257
Wings Come in Pairs : 278
Winning the Battle, Losing the Fight : 6492
Winslow, Arizona : 5573
Winslow Homer's *Two Birds Shot in Flight* : 2677
Winslow Homer's *Watching the Breakers* : 6301
Winter : 1357, 3090, 3111, 5710, 5874, 5999, 6164
Winter 20 : 3604
Winter Among the Blackfeet : 1658
Winter and Summer : 880
Winter Annuals : 5959
Winter Beacon : 1317
A Winter Boat : 3768, 7157
Winter Canvas : 3677
Winter Choir : 3409
Winter Departure : 4154
The Winter Drowse : 1321
Winter Farm : 3685
Winter Flies : 4879
Winter Garden : 1811, 1914
Winter House : 4277
Winter in Glenmacnass : 1166
Winter in the Homeland : 3985, 4742
Winter in the House : 678
Winter Incongruities : 4763
Winter Journal : 1650
Winter Mail : 3953
Winter, Moving In : 6104
Winter Night : 4216, 4922
The Winter of 1984 : 5519
Winter Palace Tour : 5546
Winter Prayer : 2799
Winter Pruning : 2183
Winter Roses : 234
Winter Routes : 499, 5438
Winter Shore : 813, 814, 5708
Winter Solstice : 2909
Winter Sparrow : 1525

Winter Window : 3832
Winterset : 1465
A Wintry Day : 4681, 5572
Wintry Wind : 4450
Wired All Wrong : 5817
Wirephoto : 5114
Wires : 7151
Wiscasset : 2622
The Wisdom Gravy : 6579
The Wisdom of the Body : 4873
The Wisdom of the Geese : 6936
Wish for the New Year : 1069
Wish You Were Here : 1836
Wishbone : 845
Wishes : 6288
Wishes for My Niece : 963
Wishkita: House of the Shark : 4669
Wishlist : 6089
Wisteria : 3601, 4524
Witbank : 3376
The Witch : 6833
Witch Children of Samhain : 1456
Witchcraft Made with Marmalade : 988
Witchcraft: The Novice : 7053
Witching Night : 5510
With a Changing Key : 1043, 1647
With a Clear Head : 931, 5197
With a Knowing Smile : 1683
With a Million Things to Do The Doctor Muses, Anyway : 3451
With a tact, with a tact that renders them almost subliminal : 162
With All That Beauty, Raving : 2332
With Caitlin After Rain : 6465
With Dürer's Engraving *The Knight, Death and the Devil* : 5246
With Each Other : 1555
With Grief and Regret : 1526, 4046
With My Father in Winter : 4179
With our breath we'll warm the shed's cold walls : 2379, 6830
With Red : 6723
With Rex in Montauk : 5508
With the Conchero Dancers, Mission Espada, July : 1026
With the Eyes : 158, 3750
With the Koi : 1725
With the Rastafarians : 3802
With those hefty walls a bank will save forever : 4973
With Us : 5131
With You : 3780, 6766
With You, Even a Year Later : 3780
With your eyes you told me: I love : 3481, 4326
Withdrawal : 1271
Within Doves Within : 1058
Within the Greenhouse Effect : 4480
Within Without : 2883
Without a Camera : 3497
Without a Word : 6167
Without Anaesthetic : 532, 1491
Without It : 5317
Without Men : 1982, 4609
Without Recourse : 4380

Without Skylights : 4049
Without Thinking : 5213
Without You, Realized : 6181
Witness : 298, 5757, 6842
The Witness : 2331
Witnesses: Copeland's Last Tale : 3679
Witnessing Wind : 1707
Wittgenstein's Prayer : 6108
Wivestales : 247
The Wolf : 2626, 4218
Wolfwalker : 6921
Wolsey's Death : 2223
Woman : 441, 494, 5620
A Woman : 3485
The Woman : 1826
A Woman and a sparrow : 5341
The Woman and the Moon : 5652
The Woman As Figure : 5962
A Woman from Jamaica : 2118
Woman Holding a Balance : 2465
Woman Holds Forth in Woodruff Park : 6280
Woman in a Windshield : 2960
The Woman in the Brown Coat : 2
The Woman in the Mirror : 5852
Woman in the Well : 45
Woman in Yellow Bathrobe, Montmartre : 1161
The Woman Inside the Man : 5296
Woman Living Alone in Wagon Mound, New
    Mexico : 4196
Woman of the Sand : 997
The Woman on the Homecoming Float : 1244
The Woman on the Road from Kamari : 2199
Woman on Twenty-second Eating Berries :
    5067
A Woman Out on the Lake Is Singing : 5106
Woman Sleeping : 4349
Woman Sleeping Alone : 4000
A Woman Speaks: Western Alaska : 4669
Woman Statement : 613
The Woman Talks : 7016
The Woman Tribe : 943
The Woman Unchanged : 2466
A Woman Vanishes : 5809
Woman, Waking : 317
The Woman Walks : 7016
The Woman Who Has Everything : 3947
The Woman Who Held Waterfalls : 1248
The Woman Who Lost Her Breast to Cancer
    and Said She Didn't Mind : 1459
The Woman Who Loves the Valley : 6322
The Woman Who Sits in the Sun : 321
Woman Who Walks : 1161
Woman Who Weeps : 6667
Woman with a Red Wall : 995
The Woman with Fallen Breasts : 5928
Womb Envy : 978
Women : 1099, 4349, 6922
The Women : 1607
Women are valued for their beauty : 4976, 5105
Women at Forty : 3460
Women by the Seashore : 160, 5620
The Women Fell Like Beautiful Horses : 538
The Women in My Dreams : 5116
Women in the Sauna : 5532

The Women of Lands' End : 6922
Women Trouble : 3733
Women Wading in Lake Adley Around 1900 :
    6715
The Women Who Drink at the Sea : 2331
Women Who Love Angels : 1183
The Women Without Asking : 6186
Women's Lockerroom : 3677
The Women's Room in Pennsylvania Station :
    1430
The Wonder of the Actual : 2671
A Wonderfully Rana Macrodactyla : 5263
Wood Nymph : 2376
Wood-Split : 431
Wood Stove Complaint : 5993
Wood Thrush : 6907
Woodchucks : 895
Woodcut by Choki : 4966
Woodcuts: Au Bois Dormant : 2856
The Wooden Horse : 1830, 4978, 6059
Wooden Shoes : 84, 6642, 6643
Woodland Scene, on Loan from Budapest :
    5883
The Woodpecker : 5901
Woods in October : 3465, 5178, 5379
The Woods of the Watcher : 6929
Woodwind and Thunderbird : 1016
Woodwork : 902, 5980
The Woodworker : 6690
Woodworms : 4668
Woody Guthrie Visited by Bob Dylan:
    Brooklyn State Hospital, New York, 1961
    : 7010
The Wop Factor : 5442
Word Hoard : 2405
The Word Is Out : 1981, 3793
A Word of Warning : 4944
Word Silence : 6545
A Word to Her : 5339
Words : 1577, 1625, 3064, 3864, 3878, 4304,
    7059
The Words : 2679
Words Against Grief : 5980
Words and the Lighted Blanket : 6333
Words Are Not Actions : 5239
Words Are Totems : 4779, 5782
Words for a Friend : 5653
Words for a Temp : 5813
Words for the Dumb : 6595
Words I Won't Give Up On : 6255
Words in July : 721
Words in July (2) : 721
The Words of the Mute Are Like Silver Dollars
    : 1830
Words Out of Reach : 1989
Words Resound in My Ears to This Day : 577,
    4597
Words Stay : 6420
Work : 650, 6085
The Work Ethic : 5342
The Work of the Bow : 3844
Work Song : 3745
Working : 6976
Working on Titles : 1092

Working the Fields : 3477
Working Yourself Sick : 2104
The Workman : 1953, 4938
Workshop Miracle : 6221
World : 1082, 1625
The World : 2870, 3032, 5302
World As Will : 2740
World Class Vixen : 42
The World Dies and Is Reborn Again Each
    Second : 5512
The World Is the Case : 6113
World of Likenesses : 3753
The World of St Francis : 5996
The World Rising As a Mirror : 4891
World War : 1018, 2289
World Without End : 407
World's End : 4130
Worldy Beauty : 3002
The Worry : 4993
The Worry Dolls : 2494
The Worry Prayer : 1789
Worship : 6678
Worship Ghazal : 7106
Worth Avenue : 1747
Worth Fighting For : 6514
Would You Like That Giftwrapped? : 1611
Wouldn't You Know It! : 684
The Wound : 2463, 5943
Wounded : 6717
Wounded Knee Sunrise : 6419
Woven Hands : 2301
Wrap Me in Violets : 7136
Wreck : 6455
Wreckage : 2279
Wrestlers : 7029
Wrestling : 2096
The Wristwatch : 3128
The Writer at Home : 402
Writers' Workshop : 3641
Writing Again, In Maine : 2946
Writing Alone : 1039
Writing As Cunt or Eat Me Just You Try It :
    1327
Writing It Out : 6153
Writing on the Wall : 1639, 1748
Writing Poems at the Slaughterhouse : 1612
Writing the Coherent Poem : 2426
Writing the Novel : 115
Written in a Copy of the Geste of Beowulf :
    356, 640, 4324
Written in Near-Darkness : 6604
Written on the Head of a Pin : 6879
Written, Perhaps, on a Tomb : 5159, 6840
The Wrong Boy : 631
A Wrong Number : 6154
The Wrong Place : 4536, 5228, 7057
The Wrong Son : 5157
Wrote after Reading Some Poems Composed
    by Phillis Wheatley, an African Girl : 97
Wuot Woth (Mad Po(e)t : 131
WWI (Writing While Under the Influence) :
    1924
X Rated : 3369
X-Ray : 5000

X-Ray of Vermeer's 'Woman in Blue Reading
    a Letter' : 921
X-Rays : 2624
X-Rays II : 2624
Xbo : 2047, 3446
Xenia : 310, 1672, 1672, 2764, 2764
Xerox : 443
Xgtza : 6062
Xochitl-Poem for Paul Perry, Joseph Booker,
    and the Palo Alto Writer's Guild : 2974
Y Cuanto Vive? : 4641
Y el odio : 6396
Ya No : 6650
Ya No Me Acuerdo, No : 2167
Yacimientos del Verano : 1021
Yael Ronen, Flute : 4675
Yahrzeit : 4128
Yar : 3309
Yard Man : 3003
Yard Work : 2569, 4223
Yarrow : 6640
Yasmin : 1155
Ye Shall Be As Gods : 3572, 4994
The Year 1984 : 1443, 3969, 7057
A Year After : 1589
A Year After the Divorce, My Car Gets
    Wrecked : 6301
The Year Began in Crystalline : 902
Year of the Puffball : 6368
The Year of the Snake : 6579
The Year the Glaciers Came : 3432
Yearly Visits : 2625
Yearning to Repossess the Body : 5036
Years Like Leaves : 644, 983
The Years with Small Children : 3580
Yeast Rolls & Water Biscuits : 6796
Yeats was right: the old patterns can't hold :
    2275
Yedi Koule : 184, 1246
Yellow : 75, 2909, 4243, 6450
Yellow Chambers : 529
Yellow Dog Blues : 4593
Yellow Jacket : 1516
Yellow Jackets : 2981
The Yellow Light of Begunje : 3083
The Yellow of Mulberry : 5379
Yellow Primrose : 2569
Yellow-Starred : 1474
Yellow Summer : 2104, 5937, 6573
Yellowknife : 4202
Yellowthroat in October : 2465
Yen Up, Dollar Down : 4503
Yes : 1142, 2164, 5858, 6101
The Yes : 6572
Yes & No : 6994
Yes I Am a Stranger : 3979
Yes - No : 2359, 3464
Yes, overre theire : 392
Yes, Something Did Happen in My Childhood :
    5200
Yes the Day Shines Again : 3718, 5104
Yes, We're Open : 4625
Yes, Yes, Like Us : 5766
Yesterday : 5357

Yesterday's Tea : 3318, 6324
Yielding : 5114
Yin and Yang : 589
Yn't Wite Fjild : 6312
Yo Te Habia Visto : 1741
The Yogi by the Roadside : 5224
Yom Kippur Again : 2583
You : 1139, 3142, 5048, 6369
You and I Are Disappearing : 3466
You are a spray of lilac : 4533, 7134
You Are of More Value : 1525
You Are the Narcotic : 5242
You Are Troubled : 5976
You Ask How to Know a Good Man : 2249
You become expert — the stream : 4973
You Bet : 2126
You Better Enjoy This, It's Costing a Fortune :
    2728
You Blew It Bukowski : 3775
You Can Restore Order in Your Universe :
    4889
You can think of a sonnet as exactly 140
    syllables : 5434
You Cannot See the Flaming Gasoline : 3448
You can't help but : 2891
You Come Back Again : 5446
You Conjure a Mother and Father : 248
You Don't Have to Say a Word : 4039
You Don't Know What to Call This : 3849
You Drove Out from Drogheda : 2170
You Figure It Out : 5855
You Find the Poets Among the Men : 519
You Firmly Built Alps! : 2589, 2901
You Go Out : 2584
You Had Dressed by Then : 491, 3476, 4811
You Have to Draw a Line Somewhere : 3135
You Have to Know Just When : 3043
You Know Da Kine : 4345
You Know Why I'm Mad? : 4818
You Live : 4738
You Need Say No More! : 6492
You Never Knew : 3954
You open yes tunnel : 6396, 6507
You Remain : 528
You remember : 1304
You See Traces: This Snow : 4973
You See What Happens : 5446
You send your hands across but the light : 4973
You set out to measure the world with your step
    : 1582, 5098
You Slowly Undress : 3270, 5900
You subdued me & like a franciscan I pray to
    your body : 4876, 5186
You Visit Me by the Sea : 2576
You Want Me White : 2190, 2629, 6213
You were like the young : 2806, 5810
You, Who Have Left : 1300, 2454
You who read that Dante guy in the comic
    books : 6396, 6507
You wish you could bring her back from so far
    away : 1716
You would like to live : 4352, 7144
The Young Alligator : 4232
A Young Boy Seeks the Deeply Real Through

Astaire and Rogers : 3937
Young Cardinal Dead by the Stormdoor : 7048
The Young Girl: Miss : 2448
A Young Man Travelling : 3736
A Young Newspaperboy Mistaken for the
    Messiah : 549
Young Owl : 6402
The Young Tailor : 452, 1885, 4333
Young Tory : 4685
Your Are Inside of Me : 5612
Your Country : 5019
Your Face : 1703
Your Father Wouldn't Let Us In Tonight : 5300
Your Frame, or Mine? : 302
Your Full-Cupboard Strength : 2929
Your House : 6696
Your Mother's House : 6201
Your Name : 333, 4105
Your Own Hour : 1258
Your Parent's Hands : 4515
Your Photographer's Eye : 6503
Your Relief : 1031, 1939
Your shadow disappeared : 6294
Your Shoulders in Overhead Sweeps : 4973
Your Sisters' Proximity : 2404
Your Voices : 6182
Your Words : 197
You're In It Now : 2680
You're Rising and Vanishing : 1363, 5379,
    6639
You're Waiting for Me in the Rain : 435, 7067
Youth and Car Stalled in Snowy Ravine : 4997
Youth Orchestra Playing Mahler's Ninth : 6118
Z Particles & Summer Morning Rain : 171
Zelda : 303
Zen Garden : 3886
Zen of the Empty Page : 6749
Zeno's Arrow : 5405
Zeno's Paradox : 1069
Zentrum : 720, 3197, 6806
Zero : 1776, 2842, 3343
Zero & Herb : 6075
Zero Eighteen : 4208
Zimmer's Existential Year : 7162
Zion : 4158
Zippy Mitchell : 1060
Ziu Piu : 906
Zoccoli, Esos Zapatos Tan Altos, Tan Altos :
    1034
Zone Libre : 207
Zoological Garden : 2104, 5937, 6573
Zoology of a Menopause at 28 : 6904
Zoom : 2719, 6249
Zora Hurston in New Orleans : 4382
Zorro & the Bats : 5514